McDougal Littell

CLASSZONE

Visit **classzone.com** and get connected.

ClassZone resources provide instruction, practice and learning support for students and parents.

Literature and Reading Center

- Selection-specific content includes vocabulary practice, research links, and extension activities for writing and critical thinking

- Author Online provides information about each author, as well as in-depth author studies on selected writers

- English Learner support for a variety of languages includes audio summaries of selections and a Multi-Language Academic Glossary

Vocabulary Center

- Vocabulary practice and games reinforce skills

Writing and Grammar Center

- Quick-Fix Editing Machine provides grammar help in a student-friendly format

- Writing Templates and graphic organizers promote clear, orderly communication

Media Center

- Media Analysis Guides encourage critical thinking skills

- Project Ideas, Storyboards, and Production Templates inspire creative media projects

Access the online version of your textbook at classzone.com

Your complete text is available for immediate use!

McDougal Littell
Where Great Lessons Begin

McDougal Littell

LITERATURE

AMERICAN LITERATURE

Life is full of questions.
LITERATURE *helps you answer them.*

What is the price
of **FREEDOM**?

Is **SAFETY**
an illusion?

What is an
AMERICAN?

Do all
CAGES
have bars?

Does
EVERYONE
have a dark side?

When is
SILENCE
louder than words?

ACKNOWLEDGMENTS

INTRODUCTORY UNIT

Scribner: From *The Great Gatsby* by F. Scott Fitzgerald. Copyright 1925 by Charles Scribner's Sons. Copyright renewed 1953 by Frances Scott Fitzgerald Lanahan. Reprinted with permission of Scribner, an imprint of Simon & Schuster Adult Publishing Group.

Continued on page R168

ART CREDITS

COVER, TITLE PAGE

La Maison noire, East Hampton, New York, 1965, Jeanloup Sieff. © The Estate of Jeanloup Sieff.

Continued on page R172

ISBN 13: 978-0-618-56866-6   ISBN 10: 0-618-56866-2

Printed in the United States of America.

6 7 8 9   0868   12 11 10   4500245726

McDougal Littell
LITERATURE

Janet Allen

Arthur N. Applebee

Jim Burke

Douglas Carnine

Yvette Jackson

Robert T. Jiménez

Judith A. Langer

Robert J. Marzano

Mary Lou McCloskey

Donna M. Ogle

Carol Booth Olson

Lydia Stack

Carol Ann Tomlinson

McDougal Littell

EVANSTON, ILLINOIS • BOSTON • DALLAS

SENIOR PROGRAM CONSULTANTS

JANET ALLEN Reading and Literacy Specialist; creator of the popular "It's Never Too Late"/"Reading for Life" Institutes. Dr. Allen is an internationally known consultant who specializes in literacy work with at-risk students. Her publications include *Tools for Content Literacy; It's Never Too Late: Leading Adolescents to Lifelong Learning; Yellow Brick Roads: Shared and Guided Paths to Independent Reading; Words, Words, Words: Teaching Vocabulary in Grades 4–12;* and *Testing 1, 2, 3 . . . Bridging Best Practice and High-Stakes Assessments.* Dr. Allen was a high school reading and English teacher for more than 20 years and has taught courses in both subjects at the University of Central Florida. She directed the Central Florida Writing Project and received the Milken Foundation National Educator Award.

ARTHUR N. APPLEBEE Leading Professor, School of Education at the University at Albany, State University of New York; Director of the Center on English Learning and Achievement. During his varied career, Dr. Applebee has been both a researcher and a teacher, working in institutional settings with children with severe learning problems, in public schools, as a staff member of the National Council of Teachers of English, and in professional education. Among his many books are *Curriculum as Conversation: Transforming Traditions of Teaching and Learning; Literature in the Secondary School: Studies of Curriculum and Instruction in the United States;* and *Tradition and Reform in the Teaching of English: A History.* He was elected to the International Reading Hall of Fame and has received, among other honors, the David H. Russell Award for Distinguished Research in the Teaching of English.

JIM BURKE Lecturer and Author; Teacher of English at Burlingame High School, Burlingame, California. Mr. Burke is a popular presenter at educational conferences across the country and is the author of numerous books for teachers, including *School Smarts: The Four Cs of Academic Success; The English Teacher's Companion; Reading Reminders; Writing Reminders;* and *ACCESSing School: Teaching Struggling Readers to Achieve Academic and Personal Success.* He is the recipient of NCTE's Exemplary English Leadership Award and was inducted into the California Reading Association's Hall of Fame.

DOUGLAS CARNINE Professor of Education at the University of Oregon; Director of the Western Region Reading First Technical Assistance Center. Dr. Carnine is nationally known for his focus on research-based practices in education, especially curriculum designs that prepare instructors of K-12 students. He has received the Lifetime Achievement Award from the Council for Exceptional Children and the Ersted Award for outstanding teaching at the University of Oregon. Dr. Carnine frequently consults on educational policy with government groups, businesses, communities, and teacher unions.

YVETTE JACKSON Executive Director of the National Urban Alliance for Effective Education. Nationally recognized for her work in assessing the learning potential of underachieving urban students, Dr. Jackson is also a presenter for the Harvard Principal Center and is a member of the Differentiation Faculty of the Association for Supervision and Curriculum Development. Dr. Jackson's research focuses on literacy, gifted education, and cognitive mediation theory. She designed the Comprehensive Education Plan for the New York City Public Schools and has served as their Director of Gifted Programs and Executive Director of Instruction and Professional Development.

ROBERT T. JIMÉNEZ Professor of Language, Literacy, and Culture at Vanderbilt University. Dr. Jiménez's research focuses on the language and literacy practices of Latino students. A former bilingual education teacher, he is now conducting research on how written language is thought about and used in contemporary Mexico. Dr. Jiménez has received several research and teaching honors, including two Fulbright awards from the Council for the International Exchange of Scholars and the Albert J. Harris Award from the International Reading Association. His published work has appeared in the *American Educational Research Journal, Reading Research Quarterly, The Reading Teacher, Journal of Adolescent and Adult Literacy,* and *Lectura y Vida.*

JUDITH A. LANGER Distinguished Professor at the University at Albany, State University of New York; Director of the Center on English Learning and Achievement; Director of the Albany Institute for Research in Education. An internationally known scholar in English language arts education, Dr. Langer specializes in developing teaching approaches that can enrich and improve what gets done on a daily basis in classrooms. Her publications include *Getting to Excellent: How to Create Better Schools* and *Effective Literacy Instruction: Building Successful Reading and Writing Programs.* She was inducted into the International Reading Hall of Fame and has received many other notable awards, including an honorary doctorate from the University of Uppsala, Sweden, for her research on literacy education.

ROBERT J. MARZANO Senior Scholar at Mid-Continent Research for Education and Learning (McREL); Associate Professor at Cardinal Stritch University in Milwaukee, Wisconsin; President of Marzano & Associates. An internationally known researcher, trainer, and speaker, Dr. Marzano has developed programs that translate research and theory into practical tools for K-12 teachers and administrators. He has written extensively on such topics as reading and writing instruction, thinking skills, school effectiveness, assessment, and standards implementation. His books include *Building Background Knowledge for Academic Achievement; Classroom Management That Works: Research-Based Strategies for Every Teacher;* and *What Works in Schools: Translating Research Into Action.*

DONNA M. OGLE Professor of Reading and Language at National-Louis University in Chicago, Illinois; Past President of the International Reading Association. Creator of the well-known KWL strategy, Dr. Ogle has directed many staff development projects translating theory and research into school practice in middle and secondary schools throughout the United States and has served as a consultant on literacy projects worldwide. Her extensive international experience includes coordinating the Reading and Writing for Critical Thinking Project in Eastern Europe, developing integrated curriculum for a USAID Afghan Education Project, and speaking and consulting on projects in several Latin American countries and in Asia. Her books include *Coming Together as Readers; Reading Comprehension: Strategies for Independent Learners; All Children Read;* and *Literacy for a Democratic Society.*

CAROL BOOTH OLSON Senior Lecturer in the Department of Education at the University of California, Irvine; Director of the UCI site of the National Writing Project. Dr. Olson writes and lectures extensively on the reading/writing connection, critical thinking through writing, interactive strategies for teaching writing, and the use of multicultural literature with students of culturally diverse backgrounds. She has received many awards, including the California Association of Teachers of English Award of Merit, the Outstanding California Education Research Award, and the UC Irvine Excellence in Teaching Award. Dr. Olson's books include *Reading, Thinking, and Writing About Multicultural Literature* and *The Reading/Writing Connection: Strategies for Teaching and Learning in the Secondary Classroom.*

CAROL ANN TOMLINSON Professor of Educational Research, Foundations, and Policy at the University of Virginia; Co-Director of the University's Institutes on Academic Diversity. An internationally known expert on differentiated instruction, Dr. Tomlinson helps teachers and administrators develop effective methods of teaching academically diverse learners. She was a teacher of middle and high school English for 22 years prior to teaching at the University of Virginia. Her books on differentiated instruction have been translated into eight languages. Among her many publications are *How to Differentiate Instruction in Mixed-Ability Classrooms* and *The Differentiated Classroom: Responding to the Needs of All Learners.*

ENGLISH LEARNER SPECIALISTS

MARY LOU MCCLOSKEY Past President of Teachers of English to Speakers of Other Languages (TESOL); Director of Teacher Development and Curriculum Design for Educo in Atlanta, Georgia. Dr. McCloskey is a former teacher in multilingual and multicultural classrooms. She has worked with teachers, teacher educators, and departments of education around the world on teaching English as a second and foreign language. She is author of *On Our Way to English, Voices in Literature, Integrating English,* and *Visions: Language, Literature, Content.* Her awards include the Le Moyne College Ignatian Award for Professional Achievement and the TESOL D. Scott Enright Service Award.

LYDIA STACK International ESL consultant. Her areas of expertise are English language teaching strategies, ESL standards for students and teachers, and curriculum writing. Her teaching experience includes 25 years as an elementary and high school ESL teacher. She is a past president of TESOL. Her awards include the James E. Alatis Award for Service to TESOL (2003) and the San Francisco STAR Teacher Award (1989). Her publications include *On Our Way to English; Wordways: Games for Language Learning;* and *Visions: Language, Literature, Content.*

CURRICULUM SPECIALIST

WILLIAM L. MCBRIDE Curriculum Specialist. Dr. McBride is a nationally known speaker, educator, and author who now trains teachers in instructional methodologies. A former reading specialist, English teacher, and social studies teacher, he holds a Masters in Reading and a Ph.D. in Curriculum and Instruction from the University of North Carolina at Chapel Hill. Dr. McBride has contributed to the development of textbook series in language arts, social studies, science, and vocabulary. He is also known for his novel *Entertaining an Elephant,* which tells the story of a burned-out teacher who becomes re-inspired with both his profession and his life.

MEDIA SPECIALISTS

DAVID M. CONSIDINE Professor of Instructional Technology and Media Studies at Appalachian State University in North Carolina. Dr. Considine has served as a media literacy consultant to the U.S. government and to the media industry, including Discovery Communications and Cable in the Classroom. He has also conducted media literacy workshops and training for county and state health departments across the United States. Among his many publications are *Visual Messages: Integrating Imagery into Instruction,* and *Imagine That: Developing Critical Viewing and Thinking Through Children's Literature.*

LARKIN PAULUZZI Teacher and Media Specialist; trainer for the New Jersey Writing Project. Ms. Pauluzzi puts her extensive classroom experience to use in developing teacher-friendly curriculum materials and workshops in many different areas, including media literacy. She has led media literacy training workshops in several districts throughout Texas, guiding teachers in the meaningful and practical uses of media in the classroom. Ms. Pauluzzi has taught students at all levels, from Title I Reading to AP English IV. She also spearheads a technology club at her school, working with students to produce media and technology to serve both the school and the community.

LISA K. SCHEFFLER Teacher and Media Specialist. Ms. Scheffler has designed and taught media literacy and video production curriculum, in addition to teaching language arts and speech. Using her knowledge of mass communication theory, coupled with real classroom experience, she has developed ready-to-use materials that help teachers incorporate media literacy into their curricula. She has taught film and television studies at the University of North Texas and has served as a contributing writer for the Texas Education Agency's statewide viewing and representing curriculum.

TEACHER ADVISORS

These are some of the many educators from across the country who played a crucial role in the development of the tables of contents, the lesson design, and other key components of this program:

Virginia L. Alford, MacArthur High School, San Antonio, Texas

Yvonne L. Allen, Shaker Heights High School, Shaker Heights, Ohio

Dave T. Anderson, Hinsdale South High School, Darien, Illinois

Kacy Colleen Anglim, Portland Public Schools District, Portland, Oregon

Beverly Scott Bass, Arlington Heights High School, Fort Worth, Texas

Jordana Benone, North High School, Torrance, California

Patricia Blood, Howell High School, Farmingdale, New Jersey

Marjorie Bloom, Eau Gallie High School, Melbourne, Florida

Edward J. Blotzer, Wilkinsburg Junior/Senior High School, Wilkinsburg, Pennsylvania

Stephen D. Bournes, Evanston Township High School, Evanston, Illinois

Barbara M. Bowling, Mt. Tabor High School, Winston-Salem, North Carolina

Kiala Boykin-Givehand, Duval County Public Schools, Jacksonville, Florida

Laura L. Brown, Adlai Stevenson High School, Lincolnshire, Illinois

Cynthia Burke, Yavneh Academy, Dallas, Texas

Hoppy Chandler, San Diego City Schools, San Diego, California

Gary Chmielewski, St. Benedict High School, Chicago, Illinois

Delorse Cole-Stewart, Milwaukee Public Schools, Milwaukee, Wisconsin

L. Calvin Dillon, Gaither High School, Tampa, Florida

Dori Dolata, Rufus King High School, Milwaukee, Wisconsin

Jon Epstein, Marietta High School, Marietta, Georgia

Helen Ervin, Fort Bend Independent School District, Sugarland, Texas

Sue Friedman, Buffalo Grove High School, Buffalo Grove, Illinois

Chris Gee, Bel Air High School, El Paso, Texas

Paula Grasel, The Horizon Center, Gainesville, Georgia

Christopher Guarraia, Centreville High School, Clifton, Virginia

Rochelle L. Greene-Brady, Kenwood Academy, Chicago, Illinois

Michele M. Hettinger, Niles West High School, Skokie, Illinois

Elizabeth Holcomb, Forest Hill High School, Jackson, Mississippi

Jim Horan, Hinsdale Central High School, Hinsdale, Illinois

James Paul Hunter, Oak Park-River Forest High School, Oak Park, Illinois

Susan P. Kelly, Director of Curriculum, Island Trees School District, Levittown, New York

Beverley A. Lanier, Varina High School, Richmond, Virginia

Pat Laws, Charlotte-Mecklenburg Schools, Charlotte, North Carolina

Diana R. Martinez, Treviño School of Communications & Fine Arts, Laredo, Texas

Natalie Martinez, Stephen F. Austin High School, Houston, Texas

Elizabeth Matarazzo, Ysleta High School, El Paso, Texas

Carol M. McDonald, J. Frank Dobie High School, Houston, Texas

Amy Millikan, Consultant, Chicago, Illinois

Terri Morgan, Caprock High School, Amarillo, Texas

Eileen Murphy, Walter Payton Preparatory High School, Chicago, Illinois

Lisa Omark, New Haven Public Schools, New Haven, Connecticut

Kaine Osburn, Wheeling High School, Wheeling, Illinois

Andrea J. Phillips, Terry Sanford High School, Fayetteville, North Carolina

Cathy Reilly, Sayreville Public Schools, Sayreville, New Jersey

Mark D. Simon, Neuqua Valley High School, Naperville, Illinois

Nancy Sjostrom, Fenwick High School, Oak Park, Illinois

Scott Snow, Sequin High School, Arlington, Texas

Jane W. Speidel, Brevard County Schools, Viera, Florida

Cheryl E. Sullivan, Lisle Community School District, Lisle, Illinois

Anita Usmiani, Hamilton Township Public Schools, Hamilton Square, New Jersey

Linda Valdez, Oxnard Union High School District, Oxnard, California

Nancy Walker, Longview High School, Longview, Texas

Kurt Weiler, New Trier High School, Winnetka, Illinois

Elizabeth Whittaker, Larkin High School, Elgin, Illinois

Linda S. Williams, Woodlawn High School, Baltimore, Maryland

John R. Williamson, Fort Thomas Independent Schools, Fort Thomas, Kentucky

Anna N. Winters, Simeon High School, Chicago, Illinois

Tonora D. Wyckoff, North Shore Senior High School, Houston, Texas

Karen Zajac, Glenbard South High School, Glen Ellyn, Illinois

Cynthia Zimmerman, Mose Vines Preparatory High School, Chicago, Illinois

Lynda Zimmerman, El Camino High School, South San Francisco, California

Ruth E. Zurich, Brown Deer High School, Brown Deer, Wisconsin

CONTENTS IN BRIEF

Online LITERATURE
CLASSZONE.COM

LITERATURE AND READING CENTER
- Author Biographies
- Additional Selection Background
- Literary Analysis Frames
- Power Thinking Activities

WRITING AND GRAMMAR CENTER
- Writing Templates and Graphic Organizers
- Publishing Options
- Grammar Arcade

MEDIA CENTER
- Production Templates
- Analysis Guides

VOCABULARY CENTER
- Vocabulary Strategies and Practice
- Vocabulary Flip Cards
- Multi-Language Glossary of Academic Vocabulary

RESEARCH CENTER
- Web Research Guide
- Citation Guide

ASSESSMENT CENTER
- Assessment Practice and Test-Taking Tips
- SAT/ACT Practice and Tips

MORE TECHNOLOGY

eEdition
- Interactive Selections
- Audio Summaries

WriteSmart
- Writing Prompts and Templates
- Interactive Student Models
- Interactive Graphic Organizers
- Interactive Revision Lessons
- Rubric Generator

MediaSmart
- Media Lessons
- Interactive Media Studies

EssaySmart
- Online Essay Analyzer

UNIT 1

An Emerging Nation
EARLY AMERICAN WRITING
1600–1800

VOCABULARY STRATEGIES

Specialized vocabulary, *p. 60*   Connotation, *p. 127*
Etymologies, *p. 76*   Context clues, *p. 210*
Latin roots: *nom, p. 86*   Words from gods and mythology, *p. 232*
Multiple meanings, *p. 97*   Political words, *p. 242*
Words from French, *p. 108*   Words from Middle English, *p. 253*
Synonyms, *p. 119*   Latin roots: *fic, p. 273*

UNIT

2

Celebrating the Individual
AMERICAN ROMANTICISM

1800–1855

UNIT 2 INTRODUCTION
- QUESTIONS OF THE TIMES • HISTORICAL ESSAY • TIMELINE
- THE LEGACY OF THE ERA

The Early Romantics

VOCABULARY STRATEGIES

Latin roots: *spec, p. 326*
Words with multiple affixes, *p. 368*
Prefixes: *ab-* and *per-, p. 390*

Greek roots: *path, p. 425*
Affixes and spelling changes, *p. 436*
Latin roots: *ambi, p. 472*

An Age of Transition
FROM ROMANTICISM TO REALISM

1855–1870

Literature of the Civil War

VOCABULARY STRATEGY
Latin roots: *lud, p. 594*

UNIT 4

Capturing the American Landscape
REGIONALISM AND NATURALISM

1870–1910

The Rise of Naturalism

A New Role for Women

VOCABULARY STRATEGIES

Words pronounced differently, *p. 648*   Greek prefixes: *epi, p. 736*
Words with misleading prefixes, *p. 668*   Denotation and connotation, *p. 754*
Latin roots: *equ, p. 686*   Temperament words, *p. 786*
Music terminology, *p. 704*   Latin roots: *rog, p. 802*

UNIT 5

A Changing Awareness
THE HARLEM RENAISSANCE AND MODERNISM

1910–1940

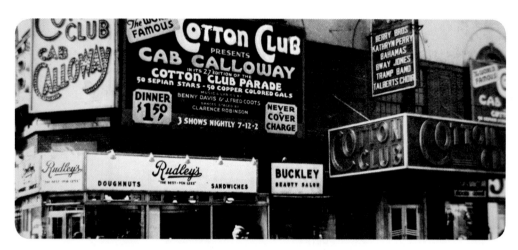

UNIT 5 CONTINUED

The New Poetry

VOCABULARY STRATEGIES

Greek roots: *cosm* or *cosmo, p. 866*
Words from the Jazz Age, *p. 960*
Words from Italian, *p. 976*

Nouns and figurative verbs, *p. 1000*
Latin roots: *med* and its meanings, *p. 1016*
Etymologies, *p. 1030*

UNIT 6

New Perspectives
CONTEMPORARY LITERATURE
1940–PRESENT

Civil Rights and Protest Literature

VOCABULARY STRATEGIES

Analogies, *p. 1158*   Idioms, *p. 1200*
Greek prefixes: *syn-, p. 1171*

UNIT 7

Investigation and Discovery
THE POWER OF RESEARCH

Student Resource Bank

Selections by Genre

(continued)

Selections by Genre

DRAMA

Features

 LITERATURE CENTER at ClassZone.com

VOCABULARY STRATEGIES

pages 60, 76, 86, 97, 108, 127, 210, 232, 242, 253, 273, 326, 368, 390, 425, 436, 472, 594, 648, 668, 686, 704, 736, 754, 786, 802, 866, 960, 976, 1000, 1016, 1030, 1158, 1171, 1200

GRAMMAR AND STYLE

pages 77, 87, 211, 233, 243, 327, 369, 391, 426, 444, 549, 559, 569, 669, 687, 737, 765, 787, 867, 911, 919, 961, 977, 1001, 1017, 1031, 1057, 1065, 1121, 1159, 1191, 1213

 WriteSmart

 MEDIA CENTER at ClassZone.com

MediaSmart DVD

Exploring American Literature

INTRODUCING THE ESSENTIALS

- Literary Essentials Workshop
- Writing Essentials Workshop

In CONGRESS, July 4,

A DECLARAT

By the REPRESENTATIVES of

UNITED STATES OF AM

In GENERAL CONGRESS ASSEM

WHEN in the Courſe of human Events, it becomes neceſſary for one People to diſſolve the Political B
with another, and to aſſume among the Powers of the Earth, the ſeparate and equal Station to wh
Nature's God entitle them, a decent Reſpect to the Opinions of Mankind requires that they ſhould decla
to the Separation.

We hold theſe Truths to be ſelf-evident, that all Men are created equal, that they are endow
unalienable Rights, that among theſe are Life, Liberty, and the Purſuit of Happineſs—That to ſecu
inſtituted among Men, deriving their juſt Powers from the Conſent of the Governed, that whenever any Form of Governm
Ends, it is the Right of the People to alter or to aboliſh it, and to inſtitute new Government, laying its Foundation on
its Powers in ſuch Form, as to them ſhall ſeem moſt likely to effect their Safety and Happineſs. Prudence, indeed, will d
eſtabliſhed ſhould not be changed for light and tranſient Cauſes; and accordingly all Experience hath ſhewn, that Mankind
Evils are ſufferable, than to right themſelves by aboliſhing the Forms to which they are accuſtomed. But when a long Train o
ing invariably the ſame Object, evinces a Deſign to reduce them under abſolute Deſpotiſm, it is their Right, it is their Duty,
and to provide new Guards for their future Security. Such has been the patient Sufferance of theſe Colonies; and ſuch is no
them to alter their former Syſtems of Government. The Hiſtory of the preſent King of Great-Britain is a Hiſtory of repea
having in direct Object the Eſtabliſhment of an abſolute Tyranny over theſe States. To prove this, let Facts be ſubmitted to a c

Insights and Perspectives

America's literature comes from all of us and belongs to everyone. It began with the lore of the Native Americans, then appeared in the journals of settlers, the letters of Civil War soldiers, and the tales of Mark Twain. Fast forward another century, and it lives in the books of John Steinbeck and shines from the poems of Gwendolyn Brooks.

Why does American literature matter? Not only does it keep us connected to the past, but it also gives us insights into the events and issues that challenge the nation today. The literature in this book can help you . . .

Explore BIG IDEAS

Why do we explore new horizons? What is the American dream? Today's generations aren't the first to grapple with questions about freedom, progress, exploration, and injustice. Some ideas and issues are timeless, as you'll discover when you read the dramatic accounts of early explorers and F. Scott Fitzgerald's fiction.

Build CULTURAL LITERACY

There are some questions that all Americans should be able to answer. In the area of American literature, such questions include: Who is Mark Twain? Why was *The Crucible* a work of great courage? By reading American literature, you become aware of the pioneering authors and literary milestones that are a part of the American heritage.

Connect *HISTORY* and *Literature*

Whether it's the Gettysburg Address or the poetry of the Harlem Renaissance, all works of American literature are products of the events and ideas that inspired their authors. By examining history and literature together, you can gain a deeper understanding of how the country changed over the centuries, and what makes its people unique.

Appreciate a LEGACY

Trailblazers in their times, Margaret Fuller and Martin Luther King Jr. fought for equal rights—a fight that still continues. Learning about the great writers, thinkers, and ideas of the past helps you better appreciate how we all continue to build on what we learned from them.

Literature in Context

The growth of the Internet, the discovery of a new medical treatment, a declaration of war, a decision of the Supreme Court—consider how events like these affect your attitudes, your outlook, your politics. They shape the attitudes of writers, as well, who then express their ideas in stories, poems, speeches, blogs, and public documents. In the same way, the writing of every time period reflects its unique historical context. By reading it, you can transport yourself back through time and gain perspective on people and events you could never otherwise experience.

LITERARY MOVEMENTS IN CONTEXT

NATIVE AMERICAN EXPERIENCE 1200 B.C.–1600	PURITAN AGE/ COLONIAL PERIOD 1600–1700	REVOLUTIONARY PERIOD/AGE OF REASON 1750–1800	ROMANTICISM/ AMERICAN GOTHIC 1800–1855	TRANSCENDENTALISM 1840–1860
• Sioux • Okanogan • Iroquois • Kiowa	• William Bradford • Anne Bradstreet • Edward Taylor	• Ben Franklin • Thomas Jefferson • Thomas Paine	• Henry Wadsworth Longfellow • Edgar Allan Poe	• Ralph Waldo Emerson • Henry David Thoreau • Margaret Fuller

1200 B.C.–1600 Native American cultures flourish. **1492** Christopher Columbus lands in the Bahamas.	**1607** British settlers establish colony in Jamestown, Virginia. **1692** Witch trials take place in Salem, Massachussetts.	**1776** American colonies declare independence. **1788** U.S. Constitution is ratified.	**1803** Louisiana Purchase doubles the country's size. **1808** United States bans slave trade. **1812** War of 1812 spurs Industrial Revolution.	**1846** Mexican-American War begins. **1848** Gold discoveries in California lead to first gold rush. **1857** Supreme Court's Dred Scott decision denies slaves basic rights.

Literary Movements

Think about how certain types of music reflect the times in which they were written. Some folk songs, for example, can remind listeners of an earlier time of protest. Similarly, the literature of each historical period has a unique flavor. Subject matter, style, form, and attitude all combine to create a **literary movement,** such as **realism** or **regionalism.** While not all writers fit neatly into specific categories, it is still helpful to know the major movements that have defined the nation's literature. By studying these movements in context, you can see not only the overlap between them, but also better appreciate the writers and works from particular time periods.

REALISM 1855–1900	REGIONALISM/ NATURALISM 1870–1910	MODERNISM 1910–1945	HARLEM RENAISSANCE 1920–1930	CONTEMPORARY LITERATURE 1940–PRESENT
• Stephen Crane • Ambrose Bierce	• Mark Twain • Willa Cather • Jack London	• T. S. Eliot • Ernest Hemingway • Ezra Pound	• Langston Hughes • Zora Neale Hurston • Countee Cullen	• Kurt Vonnegut Jr. • John Steinbeck • Rita Dove • Amy Tan

1861–1865 North and South fight in Civil War. **1865** 13th Amendment abolishes slavery. **1879** Thomas Edison invents the light bulb.	**1889** Oklahoma is opened for settlement, triggering a land rush. **1903** Wright brothers achieve first airplane flight.	**1917** United States enters World War I. **1920** 19th Amendment is passed, giving women the right to vote.	**1919** Race riots erupt in 25 American cities. **1929** The Wall Street stock market crashes and the Great Depression begins.	**1941** Japanese bomb Pearl Harbor, bringing United States into World War II. **1965** U.S. combat troops enter Vietnam War. **2001** Terrorists attack World Trade Center and Pentagon.

Using Critical Lenses

Have you ever looked through a prism or camera lens and seen the world in an entirely new way? Critical lenses, or lenses of the mind, can affect your perception—and your reading—in a similar manner. They allow you to notice details you might otherwise have missed, and can lead you to unexpected insights about a writer and his or her work. Use the following lenses, as well as others you might develop, to see beyond your own personal perspective.

THE LENSES	QUESTIONS TO ASK	
LITERARY LENS The literary lens is the one you're used to using with literature. It focuses your attention on the author's style and on such elements as plot, setting, character, and theme.	• What is unique about this author's style? • How do the plot, characters, and setting help to communicate the author's message? • How are language and imagery used to support the theme?	
HISTORICAL AND CULTURAL LENSES Historical and cultural lenses force you to consider how elements of history and culture may have influenced the author and the writing.	• What was going on in the country at the time this work was written? • What attitudes, trends, and priorities characterized the times? • How are those events and attitudes, and the author's reactions to them, reflected in the writing?	
BIOGRAPHICAL LENS The biographical lens draws you into the arena of an author's personal life. By considering a writer's heritage, experiences, and economic circumstances, you are able to "read into" a piece of literature with far more insight.	• What were some key events and people in the author's life? • What were his or her social and economic circumstances? • Did culture and heritage play a strong role in shaping the author's attitudes?	
OTHER LENSES • psychological • social • political • philosophical/moral	• What motivations might be influencing a character's behavior? (psychological) • Are the characters' choices, behavior, and actions ethical and honest? (philosophical/moral)	

MODEL: CRITICAL LENSES

The Great Gatsby is a novel set in the 1920s. World War I had just ended, and the country was embarking on a time of great self-indulgence, eager to forget what it had just experienced. In this scene, the narrator describes an outing with his friendly but mysterious neighbor, Jay Gatsby. Read the passage twice—with and without lenses.

from
The Great Gatsby

Novel by **F. Scott Fitzgerald**

At nine o'clock, one morning late in July, Gatsby's gorgeous car lurched up the rocky drive to my door and gave out a burst of melody from its three-noted horn. It was the first time he had called on me, though I had gone to two of his parties, mounted in his hydroplane, and, at his urgent invitation, made
5   frequent use of his beach.

"Good morning, old sport. You're having lunch with me today and I thought we'd ride up together."

He was balancing himself on the running board of his car with that resourcefulness of movement that is so peculiarly American—that comes,
10 I suppose, with the absence of lifting work or rigid sitting in youth and, even more, with the formless grace of our nervous, sporadic games. This quality was continually breaking through his punctilious manner in the shape of restlessness. He was never quite still; there was always a tapping foot somewhere or the impatient opening and closing of a hand.

15 He saw me looking with admiration at his car.

"It's pretty, isn't it, old sport!" He jumped off to give me a better view. "Haven't you ever seen it before?"

I'd seen it. Everybody had seen it. It was a rich cream color, bright with nickel, swollen here and there in its monstrous length with triumphant hat-
20 boxes and supper-boxes and tool-boxes, and terraced with a labyrinth of wind-shields that mirrored a dozen suns. Sitting down behind many layers of glass in a sort of green leather conservatory, we started to town.

I had talked with him perhaps half a dozen times in the past month and found, to my disappointment, that he had little to say. So my first impression,
25 that he was a person of some undefined consequence, had gradually faded and he had become simply the proprietor of an elaborate road-house next door.

And then came that disconcerting ride. We hadn't reached West Egg Village before Gatsby began leaving his elegant sentences unfinished and slapping himself indecisively on the knee of his caramel-colored suit.
30 "Look here, old sport," he broke out surprisingly, "what's your opinion of me, anyhow?"

Close Read

1. **Literary Lens** What do the details in lines 1–5 tell you about Gatsby and his relationship with the narrator?

2. **Cultural Lens** Reread the boxed text. What is the narrator's attitude toward Americans of this time period? What reality might this attitude be reflecting?

3. **Psychological Lens** Private cars were not common in the 1920s. Why might Gatsby not only want to own a car, but also insist on such a luxurious one?

A little overwhelmed, I began the generalized evasions which that question deserves.

"Well, I'm going to tell you something about my life," he interrupted.
35 "I don't want you to get a wrong idea of me from all these stories you hear."

So he was aware of the bizarre accusations that flavored conversation in his halls.

"I'll tell you God's truth." His right hand suddenly ordered divine retribution to stand by. "I am the son of some wealthy people in the
40 Middle West—all dead now. I was brought up in America but educated at Oxford, because all my ancestors have been educated there for many years. It is a family tradition."

He looked at me sideways—and I knew why Jordan Baker had believed he was lying. He hurried the phrase "educated at Oxford," or swallowed it, or
45 choked on it, as though it had bothered him before. And with this doubt, his whole statement fell to pieces, and I wondered if there wasn't something a little sinister about him, after all.

"What part of the Middle West?" I inquired casually.

"San Francisco."
50 "I see."

Close Read

4. **Cultural Lens** What "facts" about himself and his background does Gatsby provide? What does this tell you about the cultural values of the time?

5. **Literary Lens** What techniques has Fitzgerald used in this excerpt to create the intriguing character of Jay Gatsby?

Now read the biographical information about F. Scott Fitzgerald and answer the questions. Refer back to the excerpt from *The Great Gatsby* as needed.

F. Scott Fitzgerald

Born in 1896 of southern and Irish heritage, Francis Scott Key Fitzgerald began writing in his early teens. Encouraged by a mentor at school, Fitzgerald pursued
5 his dream of becoming a writer, quickly neglecting his studies in the process. He served in the army during World War I, and convinced he was going to die, dashed off an autobiographical novel. A few years—and
10 several revisions—later, he sold his novel, titled *Tender Is the Night,* and became an overnight success. One week after the novel's publication, Fitzgerald married a southern belle, Zelda Sayre. He and his wife embarked on a flamboyant, high-spending life, although their extravagance and
15 Zelda's illnesses kept Fitzgerald constantly in debt. Fitzgerald died in 1940, impoverished, after spending his lifetime in pursuit of wealth and privilege.

Close Read

1. **Biographical Lens** How might Fitzgerald's own experiences have influenced his characterization of Gatsby?

2. **Biographical Lens** What similarities do you see between Fitzgerald's and Gatsby's values? What was Fitzgerald's attitude toward these values? Why do you think so?

Reading American Literature

The varied formats and distinctive language that make American literature unique can also make it a challenge. In addition to applying the reading strategies you've always used, you will need to develop more advanced strategies.

CONSIDER THE CONTEXT

American literature includes not only short stories, novels, essays, and poems, but also a vast array of **primary sources**—historical documents, letters, and journals, for example. To gain the most from all these reading experiences, ask the following questions as you read:

• What is the format? How might this affect the content and language?

• What was the writer's purpose? In what ways might the purpose have affected the writer's choice of details or presentation of ideas?

• Who was the writer's audience? How might it have impacted what was written?

• What was the writer's perspective? Does the work reflect his or her biases or viewpoint?

SOURCE AND FORMAT	WRITER'S PURPOSE	POSSIBLE PURPOSES FOR READING
Chronicle "Of Plymouth Plantation" (William Bradford)	To record the experiences of Plymouth's first settlers	• To gain a sense of how the settlers lived • To understand the settlers' attitudes toward the Native Americans as well as their biases and beliefs
Speech "To the American Equal Rights Association" (Sojourner Truth)	To make a case for women's rights	• To understand the cultural and social influences affecting African Americans and women • To gain insight into one woman's perspective

LEARN THE LANGUAGE

The literature in this book is presented in the language of its time and place. This language may include words we no longer use; words that have different meanings today; dialect; and unfamiliar sentence constructions, conventions, and style. Use these reminders and strategies to help you break the time barrier:

• Remember that language that sounds dauntingly formal may not always be complicated or serious. These works were written by people just like you, and often express straightforward ideas, and even humor.

• Dialects have their own rules of grammar and pronunciation, which you can figure out from context clues. Read passages aloud until you become more familiar with the words and structure.

• Complex sentence structures are made up of simple parts. Break down difficult sentences, then restate them more simply, rearranging them, if necessary.

Writing Essentials Workshop

Critical Thinking and Writing

Good writing is much more than a process of gathering and organizing information. It is also a powerful tool—a way of clarifying concepts, exploring opinions, and adding something new to the world of ideas. That is what every writer represented in this book knew, and it's what you can discover as well. It's time to begin seriously analyzing and honing your thinking, then challenging yourself to express your thoughts in increasingly sophisticated ways.

Focus on Thinking Skills

Author Ambrose Bierce once said, "Good writing is clear thinking made visible." In other words, before you can write well, you have to think well. By challenging yourself to higher levels of thinking, you can give your writing increased depth and sophistication.

THINKING SKILL	HOW TO APPLY IT	
COMPARISON Juxtaposing ideas and weighing their similarities and differences	• How does realism differ from romanticism? • How did Martin Luther King Jr.'s protest strategies differ from Malcolm X's?	
ANALYSIS Breaking down subjects and examining their component parts	• What makes E.E. Cummings's style unique? • What characteristics make Nathaniel Hawthorne's *The Scarlet Letter* an American Gothic novel?	**anyone lived in a pretty how town** E. E. Cummings
SYNTHESIS Drawing from ideas in multiple sources to answer a question or arrive at a conclusion	• What messages do an Iroquois myth and Okanogan folk tale have for teenagers in the 21st century? • How do the unique cultural experiences of authors like César Chávez and Amy Tan contribute to American literature?	
EVALUATION Using established criteria to make judgments about subjects or ideas	• Does Stephen Crane create a realistic portrayal of war in *The Red Badge of Courage*? • How effective is the movie *The Crucible* at recreating Arthur Miller's drama?	

The Writing Process

As you complete the **Writing Workshops** in this book, you'll follow the process that suits your own working style. Use this model as a starting point.

What To Do	What It Looks Like
1. Analyze the prompt. <u>Underline</u> key words that indicate the content, format, audience, and purpose of your writing. If you are developing your own topic, make sure your goals are both clear and challenging.	**WRITING PROMPT** Society has viewed and treated women differently from men throughout history. Write <u>an essay analyzing how two women from different centuries or cultures have responded to these biased social attitudes</u> in their works. *I will be writing an essay analyzing works of two women. Since the audience isn't specified, I assume I'm writing for my teacher and classmates.*
2. Choose your subjects. Decide which authors and literary works you want to examine. Consider whether they will provide you with enough material for a rich analysis.	*It would be interesting to explore how Sojourner Truth and Sandra Cisneros responded to social biases. Both women explore issues of equality in "Speech to the American Equal Rights Association" and "Straw into Gold: The Metamorphosis of the Everyday."*
3. Explore what you know. Use a chart or other graphic organizer to explore your key ideas and make sure your subject choices are sound.	**Sojourner Truth** • 18th-century black slave • abused by white owners • not given same freedoms as black men **Both** • social minorities • defy society's expectations • describe their own lives **Sandra Cisneros** • 20th-century Latina • left home as an unmarried woman • treated differently from brothers
4. Develop a thesis. In a sentence or two, state the main point you want to make about the works and their authors. You can use this statement to guide your writing and revise it as you draft so it is clear, specific, and able to be supported.	*Born centuries apart, Sojourner Truth and Sandra Cisneros suffered social discrimination. Sojourner Truth's "Speech to the American Equal Rights Association" and Cisneros's "Straw into Gold" reflect both society's attitudes toward women of their times and the authors' strength in defying those attitudes.*

What To Do	What It Looks Like

5. Gather evidence.
Find evidence from the works to support your statements. Choose strong quotations and details and clearly explain how they illustrate your ideas.

▶

Sojourner Truth's speech	"Straw into Gold"
"I have been forty years a slave and forty years free, and would be here forty years more to have equal rights for all."	"I've managed to do a lot of things . . . which many others didn't think I was capable of either. Especially because I am a woman, a Latina . . ."

6. Plan your structure.
Make an informal outline to help you organize your ideas. Consider beginning—or ending—with your most important point, and make sure there is a logical progression in your presentation. You might want to try several structures and decide which works best.

▶

Introduction

Historical background (Sojourner Truth, Sandra Cisneros)

Message (Sojourner Truth, Sandra Cisneros)

Style of communication (Sojourner Truth, Sandra Cisneros)

Conclusion (changing attitudes toward women)

7. Create a draft.
Get your ideas down on paper, following the structure you have outlined. As you draft, **cite evidence** that supports your ideas. Feel free to alter your approach as your ideas develop. You'll eventually want to hook readers with a strong beginning, but don't worry about getting it perfect at this point.

▶

Sojourner Truth was a slave born at the end of the 18th century; Sandra Cisneros is a mid-20th-century Latina. Although worlds apart, both women defied discrimination and documented their struggles in their works.

8. Revise your writing.
Read your draft critically, and enlist the help of a peer reader. Consider these questions:
- How clearly have I expressed my ideas?
- Is my structure logical?
- Do my examples support my points?
- Have I added new insights and drawn conclusions?
- Do I have an engaging introduction and a solid conclusion?

Make necessary changes and proofread the final product.

▶

Sojourner Truth dealt with ongoing oppression as a black woman, as reflected in her statement, "so much good luck to have slavery partly destroyed; not entirely."

How does the quote show her oppression?

Good question. I'll substitute this quote instead: "I have done a great deal of work; as much as a man, but did not get so much pay."

Analyze a Student Model

Read the beginning of one student's essay, noting the comments in the margins.

Sruba Desai
Randolph High School

Similar Struggles, Different Worlds

What could Sojourner Truth, a slave born at the end of the 18th century, and Sandra Cisneros, a mid-20th-century Latina, have in common? Although their heritage and times were strikingly different, both women faced discrimination and described their experiences in their works. Comparing
5 their lives and messages shows both the social inequality women have had to face throughout history and the way strong individuals can rise above it.

Sojourner Truth was born in New York more than 60 years before the Emancipation Proclamation freed the slaves. Although she ran away to freedom decades earlier, she still suffered under the unequal treatment afforded
10 American blacks, especially black women. She summarized this history in her 1867 "Speech to the American Equal Rights Association": "I have been forty years a slave and forty years free, and would be here forty years more to have equal rights for all. I suppose I am kept here because something remains for me to do; I suppose I am yet to help to break the chain."

15 Sojourner Truth did help break that chain of inequality; and a century and a half later, Sandra Cisneros was born into an America in which women had continued struggling for and finally earned the right to vote. Like Sojourner Truth, Cisneros grew up in poverty, but she also straddled two cultures—Mexican and American—moving back and forth between
20 the two and not belonging fully to either. Despite social advances for women, she experienced biased attitudes similar to those Sojourner Truth faced. She explains these in her essay "Straw into Gold: The Metamorphosis of the Everyday": "In our culture men and women don't leave their father's house except by way of marriage. I crossed my father's threshold with
25 nothing carrying me but my own two feet. . . . To make matters worse, I left before any of my six brothers had ventured away from home. I broke a terrible taboo."

KEY TRAITS IN ACTION

Hooks readers with an intriguing question and states the **thesis** clearly and concisely.

Supports the main idea about the time in which Sojourner Truth lived with a strong **quotation** from her speech.

Includes cultural and biographical information about Cisneros that clearly shows the influences on her as a writer.

A quotation from Cisneros's work provides **evidence** to illustrate the biographical information.

Exhibits a logical **structure,** discussing one writer's life and times and then the other's.

Preview Unit Goals

LITERARY ANALYSIS
- Analyze the influence of historical context
- Identify and analyze cultural characteristics
- Analyze figurative language and descriptive details
- Identify characteristics of creation myth, folk tale, memoir, historical narrative, drama, and autobiography
- Analyze diction and tone

READING
- Develop strategies for reading older texts
- Analyze and evaluate elements of an argument
- Analyze persuasive techniques and rhetorical devices
- Analyze and evaluate primary sources

WRITING AND GRAMMAR
- Write a persuasive speech
- Use prepositional phrases and adverb clauses as modifiers
- Understand and use compound and compound-complex sentences

SPEAKING, LISTENING, AND VIEWING
- Deliver a persuasive speech
- Analyze how media influence cultural values and stereotypes
- Evaluate film techniques
- Compare a film and a play

VOCABULARY
- Determine the meaning of multiple-meaning words
- Understand and use specialized vocabulary

ACADEMIC VOCABULARY
- argument
- persuasion
- rhetorical devices
- primary source
- historical context
- cultural characteristics

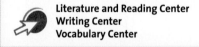

Literature and Reading Center
Writing Center
Vocabulary Center

Early American Writing

Mourning Dove

1600–1800

AN EMERGING NATION

- The Native American Experience
- Exploration and the Early Settlers
- The Puritan Tradition
- Writers of the Revolution

Questions of the Times

DISCUSS With your whole class or in small groups, discuss these questions. Keep them in mind as you read the selections in this unit and consider how **Early American Writers** tried to answer them.

Who owns the LAND?

For thousands of years, Native Americans regarded themselves as caretakers, not owners, of the land. The Europeans who began arriving in North America, however, saw things differently. They laid claim to the land and aggressively defended it from Native Americans—and from one another. In the end, the British claim overpowered all others. Yet the question remains: What entitles people to claim land as their own?

What makes an EXPLORER?

America's early explorers traveled for many reasons: to gain glory for themselves or for their countries, to find gold or other riches, to discover new routes for travel and trade. Yet none of these motivators alone seems enough to make the uncertainties of exploration—unknown destinations, unknown rewards, unknown dangers—worth the risk. What is it that causes people to seek out the unknown?

Are people basically GOOD?

Puritan settlers believed that human beings were sinful creatures doomed to a fiery eternity unless saved by the grace of God. Yet others who came to North America celebrated the powers of reason and proclaimed the goodness and intrinsic worth of humans. Are people destined always to struggle against their basest instincts? Or are they fundamentally good—and capable of becoming even better?

Who has the right to RULE?

For centuries, European kings and queens had ruled because it was believed that they had a God-given right to do so. But in the Age of Enlightenment, people began to question basic assumptions about government. In America, a popular uprising put a new kind of government to the test: democracy. With this experiment, the young American nation was asking: Who really has the right to rule?

IN CONGRESS, JULY 4, 1776.

A DECLARATION

BY THE REPRESENTATIVES OF THE

UNITED STATES OF AMERICA,

IN GENERAL CONGRESS ASSEMBLED.

Early American Writing
1600–1800

An Emerging Nation

For many people, early America was an experiment in hope. Explorers seeking adventure, settlers searching for religious freedom, colonists building communities, revolutionaries designing a new government—all embraced their challenges with a sense of faith and purpose. Writers of the day recorded and interpreted the extraordinary experiences of these ordinary people. They and their fellow colonists imagined and created an entirely new country and unique way of life.

Early American Writing: Historical Context

KEY IDEAS Early American literature captures a nation in its infancy. From the first interactions between Native Americans and Europeans to the stirring cries of the Revolutionary War, writers chronicled the tensions and the triumphs of the day.

The Meeting of Two Worlds

Explorers and early settlers forged a life for themselves in America that was completely foreign to what they had known in their home countries. In fact, so extraordinary were their experiences that the earliest American writers concentrated mainly on describing and trying to make sense out of their challenging new environment and the unfamiliar people with whom they shared it. In diaries, letters, and reports back home, they recorded a historical turning point: when the world of the Europeans first intersected with that of the Native Americans.

Unknown to Europeans, people had been living in the Americas for at least tens of thousands of years, adapting to its diverse environments, forming communities, establishing trading networks, and building working cities. Millions of people lived in the Americas on the eve of the arrival of the Europeans—as many as lived in Europe at the time.

The earliest writers chronicled how the Europeans and Native Americans viewed one another and the North American land. In 1634, for example, **William Wood** of Massachusetts Bay Colony noted that the Native Americans "took the first ship they saw for a walking island, the mast to be a tree, the sail white clouds." **William Bradford,** governor of Plymouth Plantation, in turn described North America as "a hideous and desolate wilderness, full of wild beasts and wild men." The land, however, was neither desolate nor hideous, and the Native Americans were usually cooperative—at least until they began to be forced off their land by European colonists.

From Colony to Country

The first permanent colony was established at **Jamestown** in 1607. By 1733, English colonies stretched all along the Atlantic coast. Once rooted in North American soil, the colonies became increasingly self-reliant and practiced local self-rule.

LOYALTY TO ENGLAND The first colonists thought of themselves as English subjects, even though they did not have representatives in the British parliament. They supported England economically by exporting raw materials to the homeland and importing Britain's manufactured goods.

Britain, in turn, protected its territory. It sent soldiers to fight during the **French and Indian War** (1759–1763), when France allied with a

► **TAKING NOTES**

Outlining As you read this introduction, use an outline to record the main ideas about the characteristics and the literature of the period. You can use article headings, boldfaced terms, and the information in these boxes as starting points. (See page R49 in the **Handbook** for more help with outlining.)

Early American Writing
I. Historical Context
  A. The Meeting of Two Worlds
    1. Early writers described land and people.
    2. Native Americans had well-established communities when Europeans arrived.
    3. Writers chronicled Native American and European views of one another.
  B. From Colony to Country

ADDITIONAL BACKGROUND
For more on Early American Writing, visit **The Literature Center** at ClassZone.com.

The Mayflower in Plymouth Harbor, (1882), William Formby Halsall. © Pilgrim Hall Museum, Plymouth, Massachusetts.

number of Native American groups to drive the British out of North America. After many defeats, England brought in new military leaders and made its own alliance with Native Americans—the powerful Iroquois. After a long and costly war, the victorious Great Britain claimed all of North America east of the Mississippi River.

A BREAK WITH ENGLAND When Great Britain tried to tax the colonists to recover some of the money spent on the war, however, it ended up losing far more than its war costs. Fired by cries of "No taxation without representation," the colonists protested British control—in both fiery words and bold actions. With each new act of British "tyranny," writers for colonial newspapers and pamphlets stirred the hearts and minds of the colonists to support independence.

The colonies declared themselves to be "free and independent" in 1776 and fought and defeated one of the greatest military powers on earth to turn their declaration into a reality. The remarkable minds of **Benjamin Franklin, Thomas Jefferson,** and other colonial thinkers put timeless words to this experiment in the form of the **Declaration of Independence** and the **Constitution of the United States.** When the Constitution was approved in 1788, the United States of America was born.

British parliament imposed the Stamp Act and the Tea Act to gain revenue from the colonies. Instead, these acts incited revolt. The Boston Tea Party was but one of many skirmishes leading to the Revolutionary War.

Cultural Influences

KEY IDEAS Religion was the most influential cultural force on writers of this period. Puritan values and beliefs directed people's everyday lives as well as the formation of an American society.

Puritan Beliefs

Many of the settlers in the 1600s were Puritans. **Puritans** were a group of English Protestants who had sought to "purify" the Church of England and return to simpler ways of worshiping. Their efforts had been most unwelcome in England, however, and many left the country for America to escape persecution.

Puritan settlers believed themselves chosen by God to create a new order in America. **John Winthrop,** for example, wrote in 1630 that "we must consider that we shall be as a City upon a hill. The eyes of all people are upon us." Puritans' values directed every aspect of their lives. They saw human struggle with sin as a daily mission and believed, above all else, that the Bible would help them through the torments of human weakness. Although they felt that humans were essentially sinful, they believed that some, the "elect," would be spared from eternal punishment by God's grace.

Hard work, thrift, and responsibility were therefore seen as morally good, a sign that God was working within. The thriving settlements and financial success that grew from these qualities were thought to be a mark of God's approval. However, Puritanism had a dark side as well. Puritans tended to be inflexible in their religious faith and intolerant of viewpoints other than their own. In one famous case, the Salem witchcraft trials, a whole community fell victim to the hysteria of the witch-hunt, ending with more than 20 people dead by execution.

Ideas of the Age

KEY IDEAS In the 1700s, both Enlightenment ideals and Puritan values contributed to the country's thirst for independence.

The Enlightenment

In the 1700s, there was a burst of intellectual energy taking place in Europe that came to be known as the **Enlightenment**. Enlightenment thinkers had begun to question previously accepted truths about who should hold the power in government. Their thinking pointed the way to a government by the people—one in which people consent to government limitations in exchange for the government's protection of their basic rights and liberties.

American colonists adapted these Enlightenment ideals to their own environment. The political writings of **Benjamin Franklin, Thomas Paine,** and **Thomas Jefferson** shaped the **American Enlightenment** and began to eclipse even the most brilliant European thought. Enlightenment ideals prompted action and gave colonists a philosophical footing for their revolution. "I know not what course others may take," **Patrick Henry** thundered to the delegates at the second Virginia Convention in 1775, "but as for me, give me liberty, or give me death!"

> **A Voice from the Times**
>
> *We hold these truths to be self-evident, that all men are created equal, that they are endowed by their Creator with certain unalienable Rights, that among these are Life, Liberty, and the pursuit of Happiness.*
>
> —Thomas Jefferson
> from the Declaration
> of Independence

The Great Awakening

At the same time, many people began to worry that Puritan values were being lost. Preachers such as **Jonathan Edwards** called for people to rededicate themselves to the original Puritan vision, and a new wave of religious enthusiasm began to rise. This movement, called the **First Great Awakening,** united colonists who were in other ways diverse. Across the colonies, people began to feel joined in the belief that a higher power was helping Americans set a new standard for an ethical life.

While the Enlightenment and the Great Awakening emphasized opposing aspects of human experience—reason and emotionalism, respectively—they had similar consequences. Both caused people to question traditional authority, eventually leading colonists to break from Britain's control and embrace democracy.

Early American Literature

Early American writing is as varied as early Americans themselves. Native Americans, explorers, settlers, and revolutionaries all contributed their own perspectives to our knowledge of this literary period.

The Native American Experience

When the Europeans arrived, there were more than 300 different Native American cultures in North America with strongly differing customs and about 200 different languages spoken. Yet wherever they lived—in the smoky longhouses of the Northeastern woodlands, the well-defended cliff dwellings of the desert Southwest, the cedar-scented lodges of the Pacific Northwest—one activity was common to all: storytelling.

The Native North American cultures did not have a written language. Instead, a group's history, legends, and myths were entrusted to memory and faithfully passed from generation to generation through **oral tradition.** In the words of one Native American holy woman, "When you write things down you don't have to remember them. But for us it is different. . . . [A]ll that we are, all that we have ever been, all the great names of our heroes and their songs and deeds are alive within each of us. . . living in our blood."

> **► For Your Notes**
>
> **NATIVE AMERICANS**
>
> • were culturally diverse
>
> • had an oral tradition
>
> • had many different genres of spoken literature
>
> • explored common themes, such as a reverence for nature and the worship of many gods

ANALYZE VISUALS
This modern depiction of a Haida creation story shows the Raven (a popular cultural hero in many Native American myths and legends) opening a shell to release the first humans into the world. What relationship between humans and the natural world does this sculpture suggest?

Raven and the First Men (1980), Bill Reid. Yellow cedar. University of British Columbia Museum of Anthropology, Vancouver, Canada.

LITERARY STYLE The forms of Native American oral literature are rich and varied. Creation stories, ways to explain how the universe and humans came into being, can be found in every Native American culture. Other forms include legendary histories tracing the migration of peoples or the deeds of great leaders, fairy tales, lyrics, chants, children's songs, healing songs, and dream visions.

Tragically, much of this literature did not survive after so many Native Americans fell to European diseases. Some groups lost as many as 90 percent of their people, all of whom had a share in preserving the traditional stories. The surviving works, however, show that diverse Native American groups explored common themes in their spoken literature, including a reverence for nature and the worship of many gods.

Exploration and the Early Settlers

While Native American literature offers us a glimpse into the ways and values of America's indigenous peoples, much of our understanding of pre-colonial America comes from the first-person accounts of its early explorers, settlers, and colonists. The journals, diaries, letters, logs, and historical narratives of those first Europeans to view the American landscape describe in vivid detail its many sights and wonders, as well as its dangers and challenges.

THE EXPLORERS The first of these writings were the journals and letters of **Christopher Columbus,** which recounted his four voyages to the Americas begun in 1492. Columbus's adventures opened the door to a century of Spanish expeditions in the Americas. Incapable of visualizing the historical significance of his travels, however, he died disappointed, convinced that he had barely missed the cities of gold described by Marco Polo. His fascinating journals provide a vivid record of the most significant journeys of his time.

Just over 50 years later came *La Relación.* This report by **Álvar Núñez Cabeza de Vaca,** one of the four survivors of the 600-man Narváez expedition, chronicled his eight years of wandering through Florida, Texas, and Mexico. In it he describes the landscape and people he encountered, as well as animals that were new to Europeans. The French and Dutch also sent explorers such as **Samuel de Champlain,** the "Father of New France," who in the early 1600s wrote vivid accounts of New England and the Iroquois.

EARLY SETTLERS The early English settlers described their difficult and amazing new lives in letters, reports, and chronicles to friends and family back home. Their writings helped people in England imagine what life might be like in America. One of the most influential writings was *A Brief and True Report of the New Found Land of Virginia,* by **Thomas Harriot,** which faithfully captured the area's natural resources, the ways of life of the Native Americans, and the potential for building a successful colony. It was published in 1588 and was accompanied by illustrations that helped thousands upon thousands of English readers form their first clear picture of North America.

▶ *For Your Notes*

EXPLORERS

- Columbus's journals chronicle his four voyages to the Americas.
- Cabeza de Vaca's *La Relación* tells of his failed expedition.
- Samuel de Champlain wrote accounts of New England and the Iroquois.

EARLY SETTLERS

- Settlers described the new land for those still in Europe.
- Accounts helped English readers visualize North America.

COLONISTS

- Writers focused on the story of the new settlements and their larger purpose.
- Equiano, an enslaved African, described his unjust treatment.

A modern reconstruction of the original Jamestown, Virginia, settlement

COLONIAL HISTORIES As the colonies took root, writing began to focus less on pure description and more on the story of the growth of the colonies. In contrast to the carefully accurate Harriot, for example, **Captain John Smith** wrote sometimes-embroidered accounts of the history of Virginia and New England. By force of his vivid and engaging writing, he created an enduring record of life in the early colonies and an intriguing self-portrait of a man proud of his great deeds and eager to gain recognition. His accounts were also instrumental in attracting settlers to Virginia, thus ensuring the eventual success of that colony.

Other writers who documented the history of the New England settlements wrote in a plainer style and with a more serious purpose. **William Bradford,** longtime governor of Plymouth, and **John Winthrop Sr.,** who served as governor of Massachusetts, reflected upon what they saw as their role in God's plan for a better society. But not all who wrote narrative histories saw the colonists' efforts as following God's plan. **Olaudah Equiano** described his harsh capture from his African home and the brutal and "un-Christian" treatment he received as a slave in the West Indies.

The Puritan Tradition

Puritan writers had their own purposes for recording history. They believed writing should be useful, a tool to help readers understand the Bible and guide them in their daily lives. For this reason, logic, clarity, and order were more prized in writing than beauty or adornment. One Puritan compared adorned writing to stained-glass windows. "The paint upon the glass may feed the fancy, but the room is not well lighted by it." Using a familiar, down-to-earth metaphor such as this to make a deeper point is a common feature of Puritan writing. The direct, powerful, plain language of much of American literature owes a debt to the Puritans.

▶ *For Your Notes*

PURITAN WRITERS

- believed writing should be useful and clear
- wrote histories, sermons, scientific works, and essays
- delivered sermons contrasting good and evil
- wrote poems with religious themes

SERMONS AND OTHER WRITINGS The works of Puritan writers, such as **Cotton Mather** and **Jonathan Edwards,** include histories of the colonies and fiery sermons on the dangers of sinful ways. Along with histories and sermons, Cotton Mather chronicled the disturbing Salem witch trials, where 20 people were condemned to death in an atmosphere of mass hysteria. He also wrote about scientific matters, including inoculation for smallpox.

Like Mather, Jonathan Edwards wrote on a variety of subjects, including the flying (or ballooning) spiders he had observed as a boy. His account of these spiders is considered the first natural history essay on that subject. A spider makes another, very different kind of appearance in Edwards's best-known work, his sermon "Sinners in the Hands of an Angry God." In that sermon he warns his listeners that God "holds you over the pit of hell, much as one holds a spider, or some loathsome insect over the fire."

Imagine the scene when Edwards first delivered this sermon: the congregation quaking in fear from Edwards's vivid descriptions of hellfire and a vengeful god. "Sinners in the Hands of an Angry God," while perhaps more fiery than most, is typical of the Puritan sermon. Melodramatic contrasts between good and evil, vivid imagery, powerful language, and strong moral lessons characterized this form of literature.

PURITAN POETRY Most Puritan writers composed "plain" sermons, histories, and treatises, but poetry was the means of expression for others. In fact, the first book issued in the North American colonies was the the *Bay Psalm Book* in 1640, in which the Bible's psalms were rewritten to fit the rhythms of familiar Puritan hymns.

Puritan poets such as **Anne Bradstreet** and **Edward Taylor** viewed poetry primarily as a means of exploring the relationship between the individual and God. Bradstreet's poems reflect her wide learning, deep faith, and love for her husband and children. They also provide insight into the position of women in the male-dominated Puritan society. Her book of poetry, *The Tenth Muse Lately Sprung Up in America* (1650), was the first work by a North American woman to be published. Minister Edward Taylor, possibly considered the best-known Puritan poet, wrote most of his poems as aids for his meditations. His poetry, like much Puritan writing, uses vivid images from nature and from everyday life as a way to help readers grasp the spiritual world beyond.

Evangelical preacher George Whitefield was a key figure in the revival movement of America's "Great Awakening."

Writers of the Revolution

It is curious to consider now, but some of the most famous figures of the American Revolution lived at the same time as Puritans such as Jonathan Edwards. As products of the Enlightenment, however, revolutionary writers focused their energies on matters of government rather than religion.

PAMPHLETS AND PROPAGANDA Many of the gifted minds of this period were drawn to political writing as the effort to launch a grand experiment in government took shape in North America. The most important outlet for the spread of these political writings was the pamphlet. Between 1763 and 1783, about two thousand pamphlets were published. These inexpensive "little books" became the fuel of the revolution, reaching thousands of people quickly and stirring debate and action in response to growing discontent with British rule.

Through these pamphlets the words that would define the American cause against Great Britain became the currency of the day, and the debate about independence grew louder and louder. One such pamphlet, *Common Sense,* by **Thomas Paine,** helped propel the colonists to revolution. Though

Soldier of the Revolution (1876), George Willoughby Maynard. Oil on canvas, 51″ × 39″. Photo © Christie's Images Ltd.

A Voice from the Times

These are the times that try men's souls: The summer soldier and the sunshine patriot will, in this crisis, shrink from the service of his country; but he that stands it NOW, *deserves the love and thanks of man and woman.*

—Thomas Paine
from *The Crisis*

expressing the views of the rational Enlightenment, Paine also agreed with the Puritan belief that America had a special destiny to be a model to the rest of the world. At the end of his stirring essay, he says that freedom had been hunted down around the globe and calls on America to "receive the fugitive," to give freedom a home, and to welcome people from around the world to its free society.

WRITING THAT LAUNCHED A NATION Thomas Jefferson also wrote pamphlets, but his great contribution to American government, literature, and the cause of freedom throughout the world is the **Declaration of Independence,** in which he eloquently articulated the **natural law** that would govern America. This natural law is the idea that people are born with rights and freedoms and that it is the function of government to protect those freedoms.

Eleven years later, after the Revolutionary War had ended, delegates from all but one state gathered at the Philadelphia State House—in the same room in which the Declaration of Independence had been signed—in order to discuss forming a new government. The delegates included many outstanding leaders of the time, such as **Benjamin Franklin, Alexander Hamilton,** and **George Washington.** Four months later, they emerged with perhaps the country's most important piece of writing: the **Constitution of the United States of America.** Although Washington said at the time, "I do not expect the Constitution to last for more than 20 years," it was indeed flexible enough to last through the centuries to come.

VOICES OF THE PEOPLE Statesmen were not the only ones to contribute to the discussion of the day, however. In that age of political writing, even poetry sometimes examined political and social themes. Among the finest is the work of former slave **Phillis Wheatley.** In her poems and letters, Wheatley wrote of the "natural rights" of African-Americans and pointed out the discrepancy between the colonists' "cry for freedom" and their enslavement of fellow human beings.

Another voice calling for the rights of all citizens was **Abigail Adams,** whose husband John became the nation's second president. In letters written while the couple was apart, Adams encouraged her husband to include the rights of women in the nation's founding documents.

Wheatley, Adams, and other women writers join the Native Americans, colonists, Puritans, and patriots who came before them to give us an understanding of the dreams and values that shaped our nation. All contributed their voices and ideals to building this "city upon a hill."

THE ARTISTS' GALLERY

The "Father of American Portraiture"

Many colonial artists earned their livings with portraits, which were in high demand. Gilbert Stuart was among the best of colonial portrait painters. Because he painted the likenesses of virtually all the notable men and women of the period (including the first five American presidents), he earned himself the moniker "The Father of American Portraiture" by his contemporaries.

Painting the President One of Stuart's favorite subjects was the first president of the United States, George Washington. His 104 likenesses of Washington inform the image most of us have of our first president. In fact, one of his paintings became the basis for the one-dollar bill.

Stuart was known to chat with his subjects as they sat for his paintings. By entertaining them during the long hours of posing, he hoped to capture an unguarded, fresh expression on their faces. The serious George Washington, however, found Stuart's chat annoying. The artist says of Washington, "An apathy seemed to seize him, and a vacuity spread over his countenance, most appalling to paint." Nevertheless, in *George Washington (Vaughan portrait)*, 1795, shown here, Stuart was able to capture Washington's imposing presence by placing his head high in the design and adding a crimson glow around it.

Connecting Literature, History, and Culture

Early American writing reflects the growing pains of a new nation but also reveals much about trends occurring elsewhere in the world. Use this timeline and the questions on page 29 to find connections between literature, history, and culture.

AMERICAN LITERARY MILESTONES

1600

1624 John Smith publishes *The General History of Virginia.*

1630 William Bradford describes his journey across the Atlantic and pilgrims' settlement in *Of Plymouth Plantation.*

1640 *Bay Psalm Book* is the first book to be printed in America. ▶

1650

1650 Anne Bradstreet's poems, collected as *The Tenth Muse Lately Sprung Up in America,* are published in London.

1682 Mary Rowlandson publishes *The Sovereignty and Goodness of God,* an account of her captivity at the hands of Algonquian Indians.

1693 Cotton Mather publishes *The Wonders of the Invisible World* in defense of the Salem witch trials.

HISTORICAL CONTEXT

1600

1607 The first permanent English settlement is founded in Jamestown, Virginia.

1619 The first enslaved Africans arrive in North America at Jamestown.

1620 The *Mayflower* pilgrims establish the Massachusetts Bay Colony at Plymouth. ▶

1635 North America's first public school is founded in Boston.

1650

1676 The Puritans' victory in King Philip's War ends Native American resistance in New England colonies.

1682 William Penn founds the colony of Pennsylvania.

1688 Quakers voice opposition to slavery.

1692 Salem witch trials show atmosphere of mass hysteria. ▶

WORLD CULTURE AND EVENTS

1600

1615 Inquisition condemns Italian scientist Galileo Galilei for supporting Copernicus's theory.

1616 Shakespeare dies.

1632 Indian emperor Shah Jahan begins construction of Taj Mahal. ▶

1650

1652 Dutch found Cape Town on the southern tip of South Africa.

1687 Isaac Newton publishes *Philosophiae naturalis principia mathematica,* considered to be the most important work of the Scientific Revolution.

1694 Japanese poet Matsuo Bashō, known for revitalizing the haiku form, dies.

MAKING CONNECTIONS

- Religion played a central role in America during this period. What works written at this time might support this observation?
- While American writers of this period worked mostly in nonfiction and poetry, groundbreaking novels were being written elsewhere in the world. Name one.
- The Revolutionary War was a defining event in American history. What other country held a bloody revolution during this period?

1700

1704 The *Boston Newsletter,* the first American newspaper, is established. ▶

1722 Benjamin Franklin uses humor to criticize the Puritan establishment in his first published work, *The Dogood Papers.*

1741 Jonathan Edwards delivers a sermon called "Sinners in the Hands of an Angry God." The sermon typifies the religious movement known as the Great Awakening.

1750

1774 Abigail Adams writes first entry in what is published as *Familiar Letters of John Adams and His Wife, Abigail.*

1776 Thomas Paine's widely read pamphlet *Common Sense* passionately argues the case for independence.

1776 George Washington invites Phillis Wheatley to visit after receiving from her a poem and letter.

1789 Olaudah Equiano's *Interesting Narrative of ... Olaudah Equiano* details harsh treatment of captive Africans. ▶

1700

1720 The colonial population reaches about a half million; Boston's population is about 12,000.

1739 The religious revival known as the Great Awakening (1739–1742) begins.

1744 The six nations of the Iroquois Confederation (whose tribe-mark is shown here) cede Ohio Valley territory north of the Ohio River to Britain. ▶

1750

1773 The Boston Tea Party marks a violent rejection of Britain's taxation policies. The Revolutionary War begins two years later. ▶

1776 July 4: Second Continental Congress adopts the Declaration of Independence.

1781 British defeat at Yorktown ends the American Revolution.

1787 U.S. Constitution is approved.

1700

1721 Johann Sebastian Bach composes the *Brandenburg Concertos.*

1725 Peter the Great, czar of Russia, dies.

1726 Jonathan Swift publishes *Gulliver's Travels.* ▶

1750

1752 Calcutta's population reaches 120,000.

1762 Catherine the Great, an "enlightened despot," becomes empress of Russia.

1784 The Indian sacred text the *Bhagavad-Gita* is translated into English for the first time.

1789 Storming of the Bastille incites the French Revolution.

1791 The classic Chinese novel *Dream of the Red Chamber* is published.

The Legacy of Early America

An American Work Ethic

Shunning frivolous pleasures that would distract them from thoughts of God, Puritans instead trained their energy on hard, useful work. That hard work often led to material success, which was in turn seen as a sign of God's favor. Many Americans today also believe in the intrinsic value of hard work—as well as the idea that hard work leads to financial success.

DISCUSS With your class, discuss whether work in and of itself is something to value. What does work provide? In your opinion, does work indeed lead to success? What other factors might be involved?

Government by the People

Democracy is surely the most significant legacy of the early American period. Reacting against the monarchy they had left behind and embracing Enlightenment ideals, the framers of the Constitution ensured that governmental power would be shared by the people. The people would elect representatives to carry out their will, and a system of checks and balances would ensure that no one person could rule over all. More than two centuries later, the system still stands.

TAKE ACTION Contact your local representative or senator and ask for support on a current issue that affects you. For example, you may wish to discuss the condition of your local parks or the lack of an after-school center in your area. Contact information can be found at www.congress.org.

The Power of Political Writing

During the early American period, political writing served as an agent for change. Thomas Paine's *Common Sense,* for example, furthered the case for American independence. Later, when the army suffered several brutal defeats and many soldiers were deserting, Paine wrote a series of articles called *The Crisis.* These articles inspired greater public support for the war and convinced many soldiers to reenlist. Today, political writers of all stripes are working in nearly every form—hardcover, softcover, editorial, blog, newsmagazine—to influence our current political landscape.

WRITE AND DISCUSS Catalog the political writing you encounter over the course of one week. Make a list that includes the formats, the topics covered, and your response to each. Then, with a small group, discuss the issues that are motivating today's political writers. Are these writers changing the public debate, or merely recording it?

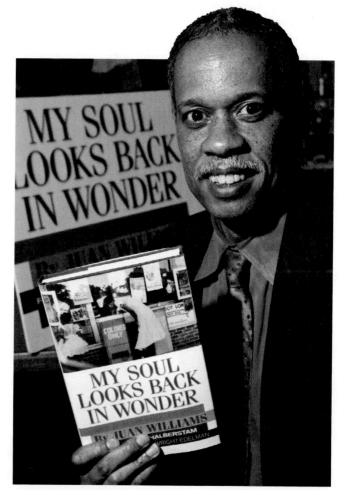

Journalist Juan Williams

The World on the Turtle's Back

Iroquois Creation Myth

**BUILDING
BACKGROUND**
To learn more about
the Iroquois, visit the
Literature Center at
ClassZone.com.

The totem, or tribal symbol, of the Iroquois

"The World on the Turtle's Back" is an Iroquois (ĭr′ə-kwoi′) creation story filled with conflict and compelling characters. The Iroquois passed down this story from one generation to the next by telling it in elaborate performances. In the 1800s, David Cusick, an Iroquois author, recorded one version of the story in print. Today, more than 25 written versions of the story exist.

The Power of Unity The term *Iroquois* refers to six separate Native American groups—the Seneca, Cayuga, Oneida, Onondaga, Mohawk, and Tuscarora. Five of these groups—all but the Tuscarora—once resided in what is now New York State. They continually waged war with one another, putting themselves at risk of attack from neighboring Algonquin tribes. Troubled by the bloodshed, a Huron named Deganawidah (də-gä′nə-wē′-də) joined forces with an Onondaga chief

named Hiawatha (hī′ə-wŏth′ə) to end the fighting. Sometime between 1570 and 1600, they formed the Iroquois League, a confederacy empowered to negotiate treaties with foreign nations and to resolve conflicts among the five nations. In 1722, the Tuscarora, from North Carolina, joined the league. For the next 175 to 200 years, the Iroquois managed to dominate other Native American groups and to remain free of both British and French rule.

The Iroquois Way of Life The league's effectiveness stemmed in part from the nations' shared culture. The groups spoke similar languages, held similar beliefs, and followed similar ways of life. They lived in longhouses made of pole frames covered with elm bark, and they built fences around their villages for protection. Up to 50 people occupied each longhouse, and 300 to 600 people lived in each village. Villages were governed by a chief or chiefs, who received advice from a council of adult males. Groups of women gathered wild fruits and nuts and cultivated corn, beans, and squash. In addition to waging war, the men traded, hunted, fished, and built the longhouses.

The Iroquois Through Time During the American Revolution, the Iroquois nations disagreed about whether to support the rebelling colonists or Great Britain. This dispute severely weakened the Iroquois League. Today, the league shows renewed vigor as it fights for environmental protection and increased recognition by the U.S. government.

● LITERARY ANALYSIS: CREATION MYTHS

A **myth** is a traditional story, usually involving supernatural beings or events, that explains how some aspect of human nature or the natural world came to be. **Creation myths** are a specific kind of myth that typically

- describes how the universe, the earth, and life began
- explains the workings of the natural world
- supports and validates social customs and values
- guides people through the trials of living

As you read "The World on the Turtle's Back," note the supernatural explanation it offers of the world's origin. Think about how this myth serves the functions listed here.

● READING STRATEGY: READING FOLK LITERATURE

You're probably already familiar with different types of **folk literature**, which includes folk tales, myths, fables, and legends passed orally from one generation to the next. The creation myth you are about to read is another example of folk literature. Using the following strategies as you read will help you not only understand and appreciate the myth's message but also glean information about the culture it comes from:

- Read the myth aloud, or imagine a storyteller's voice as you read silently.
- Note mysteries of nature and details about creation that the myth explains.
- Make inferences about the social values or customs taught through the characters and situations.
- Look for details that reveal other aspects of Iroquois culture.

As you read, use a chart like the one shown to record your notes and observations about the three kinds of information you find in this myth.

Details About Creation/Nature	Social Values or Customs	Other Cultural Details
Before the earth was created, humans and animals "of the kind that are around us now" did not exist.		

How do we make SENSE of our world?

KEY IDEA Since the beginning of time, people of all cultures have gathered to discuss one of life's biggest questions: how was the world created? The Iroquois creation myth you're about to read offers one answer to this question about the **origin** of the world.

DISCUSS What different accounts of creation—biblical narratives, scientific theories, or stories from other cultures, for example—have you heard or read? With a small group of classmates, summarize as many of these accounts as you know.

The *World* on the Turtle's Back

IROQUOIS

In the beginning there was no world, no land, no creatures of the kind that are around us now, and there were no men. But there was a great ocean which occupied space as far as anyone could see. Above the ocean was a great void of air. And in the air there lived the birds of the sea; in the ocean lived the fish and the creatures of the deep. Far above this unpeopled world, there was a Sky-World. Here lived gods who were like people—like Iroquois.

In the Sky-World there was a man who had a wife, and the wife was expecting a child. The woman became hungry for all kinds of strange delicacies, as women do when they are with child. She kept her husband busy almost to distraction finding
10 delicious things for her to eat.

In the middle of the Sky-World there grew a Great Tree which was not like any of the trees that we know. It was tremendous; it had grown there forever. It had enormous roots that spread out from the floor of the Sky-World. And on its branches there were many different kinds of leaves and different kinds of fruits and flowers. The tree was not supposed to be marked or mutilated by any of the beings who dwelt in the Sky-World. It was a sacred tree that stood at the center of the universe. **A**

The woman decided that she wanted some bark from one of the roots of the Great Tree—perhaps as a food or as a medicine, we don't know. She told her husband this.
20 He didn't like the idea. He knew it was wrong. But she insisted, and he gave in. So he dug a hole among the roots of this great sky tree, and he bared some of its roots. But the floor of the Sky-World wasn't very thick, and he broke a hole through it. He was terrified, for he had never expected to find empty space underneath the world.

ANALYZE VISUALS
Examine the painting on page 35. How does the artist use light and color to emphasize the division between the Sky-World and the void below it?

A CREATION MYTHS
So far, how is this myth similar to and different from other accounts of creation you've heard or read? Explain your answer, citing details.

Sky Woman (1936), Ernest Smith. Courtesy of the Rochester Museum and Science Center, Rochester, New York.

But his wife was filled with curiosity. He wouldn't get any of the roots for her, so she set out to do it herself. She bent over and she looked down, and she saw the ocean far below. She leaned down and stuck her head through the hole and looked all around. No one knows just what happened next. Some say she slipped. Some say that her husband, fed up with all the demands she had made on him, pushed her.

So she fell through the hole. As she fell, she frantically grabbed at its edges, but
30 her hands slipped. However, between her fingers there clung bits of things that were growing on the floor of the Sky-World and bits of the root tips of the Great Tree. And so she began to fall toward the great ocean far below.

The birds of the sea saw the woman falling, and they immediately consulted with each other as to what they could do to help her. Flying wingtip to wingtip they made a great feathery raft in the sky to support her, and thus they broke her fall. But of course it was not possible for them to carry the woman very long. Some of the other birds of the sky flew down to the surface of the ocean and called up the ocean creatures to see what they could do to help. The great sea turtle came and agreed to receive her on his back. The birds placed her gently
40 on the shell of the turtle, and now the turtle floated about on the huge ocean with the woman safely on his back.

The beings up in the Sky-World paid no attention to this. They knew what was happening, but they chose to ignore it.

When the woman recovered from her shock and terror, she looked around her. All that she could see were the birds and the sea creatures and the sky and the ocean.

And the woman said to herself that she would die. But the creatures of the sea came to her and said that they would try to help her and asked her what they could do. She told them that if they could find some soil, she could plant the roots stuck between her fingers, and from them plants would grow. The sea
50 animals said perhaps there was dirt at the bottom of the ocean, but no one had ever been down there so they could not be sure.

If there was dirt at the bottom of the ocean, it was far, far below the surface in the cold deeps. But the animals said they would try to get some. One by one the diving birds and animals tried and failed. They went to the limits of their endurance, but they could not get to the bottom of the ocean. Finally, the muskrat said he would try. He dived and disappeared. All the creatures waited, holding their breath, but he did not return. After a long time, his little body floated up to the surface of the ocean, a tiny crumb of earth clutched in his paw. He seemed to be dead. They pulled him up on the turtle's back and they sang and prayed
60 over him and breathed air into his mouth, and finally, he stirred. Thus it was the muskrat, the Earth-Diver, who brought from the bottom of the ocean the soil from which the earth was to grow. **B**

The woman took the tiny clod of dirt and placed it on the middle of the great sea turtle's back. Then the woman began to walk in a circle around it, moving in the direction that the sun goes. The earth began to grow. When the earth was big

B FOLK LITERATURE
Reread lines 46–62 and consider the role that "all the creatures" play in this myth. What does this suggest about the Iroquois' attitude toward animals?

enough, she planted the roots she had clutched between her fingers when she fell from the Sky-World. Thus the plants grew on the earth.

To keep the earth growing, the woman walked as the sun goes, moving in the direction that the people still move in the dance rituals. She gathered roots and plants to eat and built herself a little hut. After a while, the woman's time came, and she was delivered of a daughter. The woman and her daughter kept walking in a circle around the earth, so that the earth and plants would continue to grow. They lived on the plants and roots they gathered. The girl grew up with her mother, cut off forever from the Sky-World above, knowing only the birds and the creatures of the sea, seeing no other beings like herself.

One day, when the girl had grown to womanhood, a man appeared. No one knows for sure who this man was. He had something to do with the gods above. Perhaps he was the West Wind. As the girl looked at him, she was filled with terror, and amazement, and warmth, and she fainted dead away. As she lay on the ground, the man reached into his quiver, and he took out two arrows, one sharp and one blunt, and he laid them across the body of the girl, and quietly went away.

When the girl awoke from her faint, she and her mother continued to walk around the earth. After a while, they knew that the girl was to bear a child. They did not know it, but the girl was to bear twins.

Within the girl's body, the twins began to argue and quarrel with one another. There could be no peace between them. As the time approached for them to be born, the twins fought about their birth. The right-handed twin wanted to be born in the normal way, as all children are born. But the left-handed twin said no. He said he saw light in another direction, and said he would be born that way. The right-handed twin beseeched him not to, saying that he would kill their mother. But the left-handed twin was stubborn. He went in the direction where he saw light. But he could not be born through his mother's mouth or her nose. He was born through her left armpit, and killed her. And meanwhile, the right-handed twin was born in the normal way, as all children are born.

The twins met in the world outside, and the right-handed twin accused his brother of murdering their mother. But the grandmother told them to stop their quarreling. They buried their mother. And from her grave grew the plants which the people still use. From her head grew the corn, the beans, and the squash—"our supporters, the three sisters."[1] And from her heart grew the sacred tobacco, which the people still use in the ceremonies and by whose upward-floating smoke they send thanks. The women call her "our mother," and they dance and sing in the rituals so that the corn, the beans, and the squash may grow to feed the people. **C**

But the conflict of the twins did not end at the grave of their mother. And, strangely enough, the grandmother favored the left-handed twin.

The right-handed twin was angry, and he grew more angry as he thought how his brother had killed their mother. The right-handed twin was the one who did everything just as he should. He said what he meant, and he meant what he said.

C CREATION MYTHS
Creation myths often contain **symbols**—people, places, and things that stand for something beyond themselves. Reread lines 97–102. What might the twins' mother symbolize?

---

1. **the three sisters:** Corn, beans, and squash—the Iroquois' staple food crops—were grown together. The bean vines climbed and were supported by the corn stalks; squash, which spread across the ground and kept weeds from growing, was planted around the bean plants.

He always told the truth, and he always tried to accomplish what seemed to be right and reasonable. The left-handed twin never said what he meant or meant
110 what he said. He always lied, and he always did things backward. You could never tell what he was trying to do because he always made it look as if he were doing the opposite. He was the devious one. **D**

These two brothers, as they grew up, represented two ways of the world which are in all people. The Indians did not call these the right and the wrong. They called them the straight mind and the crooked mind, the upright man and the devious man, the right and the left.

The twins had creative powers. They took clay and modeled it into animals, and they gave these animals life. And in this they contended with one another. The right-handed twin made the deer, and the left-handed twin made the
120 mountain lion which kills the deer. But the right-handed twin knew there would always be more deer than mountain lions. And he made another animal. He made the ground squirrel. The left-handed twin saw that the mountain lion could not get to the ground squirrel, who digs a hole, so he made the weasel. And although the weasel can go into the ground squirrel's hole and kill him, there are lots of ground squirrels and not so many weasels. Next the right-handed twin decided he would make an animal that the weasel could not kill, so he made the porcupine. But the left-handed twin made the bear, who flips the porcupine over on his back and tears out his belly.

And the right-handed twin made berries and fruits of other kinds for his
130 creatures to live on. The left-handed twin made briars and poison ivy, and the poisonous plants like the baneberry and the dogberry, and the suicide root with which people kill themselves when they go out of their minds. And the left-handed twin made medicines, for good and for evil, for doctoring and for witchcraft.

And finally, the right-handed twin made man. The people do not know just how much the left-handed twin had to do with making man. Man was made of clay, like pottery, and baked in the fire. . . .

The world the twins made was a balanced and orderly world, and this was good. The plant-eating animals created by the right-handed twin would eat up all the vegetation if their number was not kept down by the meat-eating animals,
140 which the left-handed twin created. But if these carnivorous animals ate too many other animals, then they would starve, for they would run out of meat. So the right- and the left-handed twins built balance into the world.

As the twins became men full grown, they still contested with one another. No one had won, and no one had lost. And they knew that the conflict was becoming sharper and sharper, and one of them would have to vanquish the other.

And so they came to the duel. They started with gambling. They took a wooden bowl, and in it they put wild plum pits. One side of the pits was burned black, and by tossing the pits in the bowl and betting on how these would fall, they gambled against one another, as the people still do in the New Year's

D FOLK LITERATURE
Reread lines 95–112. Which twin is characterized as being more admirable? What does this characterization tell you about Iroquois values?

Detail of *Sky Woman* (1936), Ernest Smith. Courtesy of the Rochester Museum and Science Center, Rochester, New York.

150 rites.[2] All through the morning they gambled at this game, and all through the afternoon, and the sun went down. And when the sun went down, the game was done, and neither one had won.

So they went on to battle one another at the lacrosse[3] game. And they contested all day, and the sun went down, and the game was done. And neither had won.

And now they battled with clubs, and they fought all day, and the sun went down, and the fight was done. But neither had won. **E**

And they went from one duel to another to see which one would succumb. Each one knew in his deepest mind that there was something, somewhere, that would vanquish the other. But what was it? Where to find it?

160 Each knew somewhere in his mind what it was that was his own weak point. They talked about this as they contested in these duels, day after day, and somehow the deep mind of each entered into the other. And the deep mind of the right-handed twin lied to his brother, and the deep mind of the left-handed twin told the truth.

On the last day of the duel, as they stood, they at last knew how the right-handed twin was to kill his brother. Each selected his weapon. The left-handed twin chose a mere stick that would do him no good. But the right-handed twin

E FOLK LITERATURE
Reread lines 146–156. Note in your chart the information about Iroquois customs and rituals you learn from these lines.

---

2. **New Year's rites:** various ceremonies to get ready for the New Year. They often included community confession of sins, the replenishing of hearths in the homes, and sacred dances, as well as the gambling ritual.

3. **lacrosse:** a game of Native American origin wherein participants on two teams use long-handled sticks with webbed pouches to maneuver a ball into the opposing team's goal.

picked out the deer antler, and with one touch he destroyed his brother. And the left-handed twin died, but he died and he didn't die. The right-handed twin
170 picked up the body and cast it off the edge of the earth. And some place below the world, the left-handed twin still lives and reigns.

When the sun rises from the east and travels in a huge arc along the sky dome, which rests like a great upside-down cup on the saucer of the earth, the people are in the daylight realm of the right-handed twin. But when the sun slips down in the west at nightfall and the dome lifts to let it escape at the western rim, the people are again in the domain of the left-handed twin—the fearful realm of night.

Having killed his brother, the right-handed twin returned home to his grandmother. And she met him in anger. She threw the food out of the cabin onto the ground and said that he was a murderer, for he had killed his brother. He grew
180 angry and told her she had always helped his brother, who had killed their mother. In his anger, he grabbed her by the throat and cut her head off. Her body he threw into the ocean, and her head, into the sky. There, "Our Grandmother, the Moon" still keeps watch at night over the realm of her favorite grandson. **F**

The right-handed twin has many names. One of them is Sapling. It means smooth, young, green and fresh and innocent, straightforward, straight-growing, soft and pliable, teachable and trainable. These are the old ways of describing him. But since he has gone away, he has other names. He is called "He Holds Up the Skies," "Master of Life," and "Great Creator."

The left-handed twin also has many names. One of them is Flint. He is called
190 the devious one, the one covered with boils. Old Warty. He is stubborn. He is thought of as being dark in color.

These two beings rule the world and keep an eye on the affairs of men. The right-handed twin, the Master of Life, lives in the Sky-World. He is content with the world he helped to create and with his favorite creatures, the humans. The scent of sacred tobacco rising from the earth comes gloriously to his nostrils.

In the world below lives the left-handed twin. He knows the world of men, and he finds contentment in it. He hears the sounds of warfare and torture, and he finds them good.

In the daytime, the people have rituals which honor the right-handed twin.
200 Through the daytime rituals, they thank the Master of Life. In the nighttime, the people dance and sing for the left-handed twin. ❧

F **CREATION MYTHS**
The transformation of a character is a common element of mythology, often used to explain natural phenomena. Consider the natural feature explained in lines 172–183. How does this myth explain the fact that the moon is visible mainly at night?

Comprehension

1. **Recall** How do the animals help the woman who fell from the sky?

2. **Recall** What roles do the grandmother and her daughter play in the earth's creation?

3. **Summarize** What is the outcome of the battles between the twins?

Literary Analysis

4. **Compare and Contrast** How does this myth compare with the accounts of the world's origin you summarized before you read? Use a Venn diagram to record the differences and similarities between "The World on the Turtle's Back" and one of the accounts you discussed.

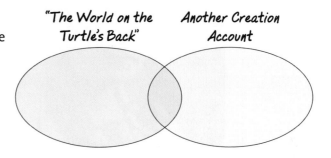

"The World on the Turtle's Back"   Another Creation Account

5. **Analyze a Creation Myth** Reread lines 105–112. Summarize the differences between the right-handed twin and the left-handed twin. Why do you think the Iroquois honor both twins? What elements of human nature are explained by "The World on the Turtle's Back"?

6. **Draw Conclusions from Folk Literature** Folk literature often transmits information about a people's culture and way of life. Review the details you noted in your chart as you read. From this myth, what did you learn about the Iroquois'

   • attitude toward nature?
   • view of their gods?
   • important food, games, and rituals?
   • beliefs about good and evil?

7. **Synthesize Cultural Ideas** How would you relate the Iroquois reverence for both the right-handed and left-handed twins to your own concept of good and evil? Explain your response, citing details and description from the text.

Literary Criticism

8. **Critical Interpretations** Creation stories often serve many purposes. According to Larry Evers and Paul Pavich, scholars of Native American literature, such stories "remind the people of who and what they are, why they are in this particular place, and how they should continue to live here." Do you think that "The World on the Turtle's Back" fulfills these functions? Explain, citing evidence from the text to support your interpretation.

Coyote and the Buffalo

Folk Tale Retold by Mourning Dove

Mourning Dove
c. 1885–1936

Mourning Dove is the pen name of Christine Quintasket (kwən-tăs′kət), who triumphed over adversity to become one of the first female Native American novelists. As a child, Quintasket was enthralled by the traditional stories told by her elders. As an adult, she worked to preserve these tales. By publishing stories that recount the history of her people, she carried on the work of the storytellers she so admired.

Determined to Write Quintasket grew up on the Colville Reservation in Washington State with her mother, the daughter of a Colville chief, and her father, an Okanogan. When Quintasket was 14, her mother died, leaving her to run the household and help raise her younger siblings. Despite her many responsibilities, Quintasket pushed herself to learn to write in English. She later attended secretarial school to learn how to type and business school to hone her grammar and writing skills. She drafted a novel in 1912 but put it away for several years until she met Lucullus McWhorter, a Native American–rights activist, who offered to edit it.

Battling Stereotypes Published in 1927, Mourning Dove's novel, *Cogewea, the Half-Blood,* is credited with breaking down the stereotype of Native Americans as stoic, or unfeeling. "It is all wrong, this saying that Indians do not feel as deeply as whites," the author asserted. "We do feel, and by and by some of us are going to make our feelings appreciated, and then will the true Indian character be revealed."

Chronicling Her Culture After *Cogewea* was published, Mourning Dove began to record traditional stories of the Okanogan and other Colville tribes. A migrant worker, she picked fruit ten hours a day but managed to do her writing at night. *Coyote Stories,* from which "Coyote and the Buffalo" is taken, was published in 1933. "Coyote and the Buffalo" is a folk tale once told by Okanogan storytellers in Salish, their native language. Mourning Dove's retelling includes Salish words and place names. This story and others like it help keep the Okanogan culture alive today.

Mourning Dove's Legacy In addition to preserving her people's culture, Mourning Dove worked hard to promote their welfare. She fought for their rights in court, started organizations supporting Native American crafts, and paved the way for female participation on tribal councils. Worn down by chronic illness and fatigue, the writer and activist died in 1936.

● LITERARY ANALYSIS: TRICKSTER TALES

You already know that a folk tale is a simple story passed orally from one generation to the next. **Trickster tales** are a type of folk tale that features an animal or human character who typically engages in deceit, violence, and magic. Often, trickster tales are mythic, explaining how some aspect of human nature or the natural world came to be. The opening lines of "Coyote and the Buffalo" announce what this trickster tale will explain.

No buffalo ever lived in the Swah-netk'-qhu *country. That was Coyote's fault.*

Tricksters are **archetypal characters**—character types that can be found in literary works from different cultures throughout the ages. As you read this tale, notice how the coyote demonstrates the trickster's contradictory qualities: he is foolish yet clever, greedy yet helpful, immoral yet moral.

● READING STRATEGY: PREDICT

Tricksters are often schemers or scoundrels—they don't usually act as other characters do. Using your background knowledge of this character's contradictory qualities, as well as text clues, can help you **predict** upcoming story events. As you read, use a chart like the one shown to record Coyote's key traits and unusual behavior. Pause occasionally to predict what will happen next.

Coyote's Traits and Behavior	My Predictions
Coyote is "foolish and greedy"; it is his fault there are no buffalo in Swah-netk̓-qhu country.	This story will reveal that Coyote did something reckless or unwise to scare away the buffalo.

Explore the Key Idea

Why do we root for the "BAD GUY"?

KEY IDEA Wherever they go, they ignore the rules. They stir up trouble. And yet we admire and love them despite—or maybe because of—their bad behavior. Many societies have famous **villains** or trickster figures, who both infuriate and inspire the people around them.

QUICKWRITE Think about movies or books in which the villain is more compelling than the hero. What qualities does such a villain typically display? Which of these traits contribute most to his or her appeal? Record your responses in a short paragraph.

COYOTE
and the
BUFFALO

Retold by Mourning Dove

BACKGROUND "Coyote and the Buffalo" is one of many traditional stories featuring the Animal People, a race of supernatural beings believed by the Okanogan to have been the first inhabitants of the world. The Animal People had magical powers and could alter their shapes. When human beings appeared on the earth, the Animal People were changed into different animal species. Coyote, one of the most important Animal People, is thought to have made the world habitable for humans by killing monsters and bringing fire and salmon.

ANALYZE VISUALS
Describe the artwork on page 45. How is the use of color significant? Does the color treatment cause this coyote to reflect the **traits** of a trickster? Explain your answer.

No buffalo ever lived in the *Swah-netk'-qhu*[1] country. That was Coyote's fault. If he had not been so foolish and greedy, the people beside the *Swah-netk'-qhu* would not have had to cross the Rockies to hunt the *quas-peet-za*[2] (curled-hairs).

This is the way it happened:

Coyote was traveling over the plains beyond the big mountains. He came to a flat. There he found an old buffalo skull. It was the skull of Buffalo Bull. Coyote always had been afraid of Buffalo Bull. He remembered the many times Bull Buffalo had scared him, and he laughed upon seeing the old skull there on the flat.

"Now I will have some fun," Coyote remarked. "I will have revenge for the
10 times Buffalo made me run."

He picked up the skull and threw it into the air; he kicked it and spat on it; he threw dust in the eye sockets. He did these things many times, until he grew tired. Then he went his way. Soon he heard a rumbling behind him. He thought it ⒶAnalysis was thunder, and he looked at the sky. The sky was clear. Thinking he must have imagined the sound, he walked on, singing. He heard the rumbling again, only

Ⓐ TRICKSTER TALES
In the first paragraph, the tale's narrator pronounces Coyote "foolish and greedy." Based on lines 5–13, what other **character traits** would you attribute to this trickster?

---

1. *Swah-netk'-qhu* (shwə-nĭt'kwə): the Salish name for the Columbia River and its waterfall.
2. *quas-peet-za* (kwəs-pēt'zä): a Salish word for buffalo.

Coyote Survivor, John Nieto.
Serigraph, 29″ × 22″.

much closer and louder. Turning around, he saw Buffalo Bull pounding along after him, chasing him. His old enemy had come to life!

Coyote ran, faster than he thought he could run, but Buffalo gained steadily. Soon Buffalo was right at his heels. Coyote felt his hot breath.

20 "Oh, *Squas-tenk',*[3] help me!" Coyote begged, and his power answered by putting three trees in front of him. They were there in the wink of an eye. Coyote jumped and caught a branch of the first tree and swung out of Buffalo's way. Buffalo rammed the tree hard, and it shook as if in a strong wind. Then Buffalo chopped at the trunk with his horns, first with one horn and then the other. He chopped fast, and in a little while over went the tree, and with it went Coyote. But he was up and into the second tree before Buffalo Bull could reach him. Buffalo soon laid that tree low, but he was not quick enough to catch Coyote, who scrambled into the third and last tree.

"Buffalo, my friend, let me talk with you," said Coyote, as his enemy hacked
30 away at the tree's trunk. "Let me smoke my pipe. I like the *kinnikinnick.*[4] Let me smoke. Then I can die more content."

"You may have time for one smoke," grunted Bull Buffalo, resting from his chopping.

Coyote spoke to his medicine-power, and a pipe, loaded and lighted, was given to him. He puffed on it once and held out the pipe to Buffalo Bull.

"No, I will not smoke with you," said that one. "You made fun of my bones. I have enough enemies without you. Young Buffalo is one of them. He killed me and stole all my fine herd."

"My uncle,"[5] said Coyote, "you need new horns. Let me make new horns for
40 you. Then you can kill Young Buffalo. Those old horns are dull and worn."

Bull Buffalo was pleased with that talk. He decided he did not want to kill Coyote. He told Coyote to get down out of the tree and make the new horns. Coyote jumped down and called to his power. It scolded him for getting into trouble, but it gave him a flint knife and a stump of pitchwood.[6] From this stump Coyote carved a pair of fine heavy horns with sharp points. He gave them to Buffalo Bull. All buffalo bulls have worn the same kind of horns since. **B**

Buffalo Bull was very proud of his new horns. He liked their sharpness and weight and their pitch-black color. He tried them out on what was left of the pitchwood stump. He made one toss and the stump flew high in the air, and he
50 forgave Coyote for his mischief. They became good friends right there. Coyote said he would go along with Buffalo Bull to find Young Buffalo.

They soon came upon Young Buffalo and the big herd he had won from Buffalo Bull. Young Buffalo laughed when he saw his old enemy, and he walked out to meet him. He did not know, of course, about the new horns. It was not much of a fight,

B TRICKSTER TALES
This trickster tale is **mythic** in that it explains how something came to be—in this case, the lack of buffalo in a certain geographic area. What second mythic explanation is offered in lines 39–46?

---

3. ***Squas-tenk'*** (skwəs-tĭnk'): a Salish word referring to Coyote's spirit helper.

4. ***kinnikinnick*** (kĭn'ĭ-kĭ-nĭk'): the Salish word for the bearberry shrub. The Okanogan toasted bearberry leaves and then crumbled them and mixed them with tobacco for pipe smoking.

5. **my uncle:** Terms like *uncle, brother, sister,* and *cousin* were sometimes used as a sign of respect. Here, Coyote is using the term to flatter Buffalo Bull.

6. **pitchwood:** the sap-filled wood of a pine or fir tree.

that fight between Young Buffalo and Buffalo Bull. With the fine new horns, Buffalo Bull killed the other easily, and then he took back his herd, all his former wives and their children. He gave Coyote a young cow, the youngest cow, and he said:

"Never kill her, *Sin-ka-lip'*![7] Take good care of her and she will supply you with meat forever. When you get hungry, just slice off some choice fat with a flint
60 knife. Then rub ashes on the wound and the cut will heal at once." **C**

Coyote promised to remember that, and they parted. Coyote started back to his own country, and the cow followed. For a few suns he ate only the fat when he was hungry. But after awhile he became tired of eating fat, and he began to long for the sweet marrow-bones and the other good parts of the buffalo. He smacked his lips at the thought of having some warm liver.

C PREDICT
Consider what you know about the **archetypal** trickster character and think about Coyote's behavior thus far. How do you think Coyote will respond to Buffalo Bull's instructions? Give reasons for your prediction.

---

7. ***Sin-ka-lip'*** (sĭng′kə-lĭp′): the Salish name for Coyote; it means "imitator."

Buffalo, John Nieto. Acrylic, 30″ × 40″.

"Buffalo Bull will never know," Coyote told himself, and he took his young cow down beside a creek and killed her.

As he peeled off the hide, crows and magpies came from all directions. They settled on the carcass and picked at the meat. Coyote tried to chase them away, 70 but there were too many of them. While he was chasing some, others returned and ate the meat. It was not long until they had devoured every bit of the meat.

"Well, I can get some good from the bones and marrow-fat," Coyote remarked, and he built a fire to cook the bones. Then he saw an old woman walking toward him. She came up to the fire.

"*Sin-ka-lip'*," she said, "you are a brave warrior, a great chief. Why should you do woman's work? Let me cook the bones while you rest."

Vain Coyote! He was flattered. He believed she spoke her true mind. He stretched out to rest and he fell asleep. In his sleep he had a bad dream. It awoke him, and he saw the old woman running away with the marrow-fat and the boiled 80 grease. He looked into the cooking-basket. There was not a drop of soup left in it. He chased the old woman. He would punish her! But she could run, too, and she easily kept ahead of him. Every once in awhile she stopped and held up the marrow-fat and shouted: "*Sin-ka-lip'*, do you want this?" **D**

Finally Coyote gave up trying to catch her. He went back to get the bones. He thought he would boil them again. He found the bones scattered all around, so he gathered them up and put them into the cooking-basket. Needing some more water to boil them in, he went to the creek for it, and when he got back, there were no bones in the basket! In place of the bones was a little pile of tree limbs!

Coyote thought he might be able to get another cow from Buffalo Bull, so he 90 set out to find him. When he came to the herd, he was astonished to see the cow he had killed. She was there with the others! She refused to go with Coyote again, and Buffalo Bull would not give him another cow. Coyote had to return to his own country without a buffalo.

That is why there never have been any buffalo along the *Swah-netk'-qhu*. 〰

D TRICKSTER TALES
Who else, besides Coyote, plays the role of a trickster in this tale? Explain which of the trickster's qualities this character exhibits.

Comprehension

1. **Recall** Why is Buffalo Bull so enraged at Coyote at the beginning of the story?

2. **Recall** How does Coyote convince Buffalo Bull to spare his life?

3. **Summarize** According to the story, why don't buffalo live in the *Swah-netk'-qhu* country?

Literary Analysis

4. **Analyze Predictions** Review the chart you completed as you read. How accurate were your predictions? Did the fact that the trickster is a somewhat familiar **archetypal character** make it easier to predict Coyote's actions, or did his behavior surprise you? Explain your answer, referring to both your chart and the selection.

5. **Interpret Trickster Tales** Trickster tales endure, in part, simply because they are fun to read. But they also often serve to teach a lesson or moral. What does "Coyote and the Buffalo" teach or explain? Support your answer with specific lines from the story.

6. **Draw Conclusions** Trickster tales, like other forms of folk literature, offer readers insight into a society's way of life. What information about the following aspects of Okanogan culture did you glean from this tale?

   - traits or qualities the Okanogan admired as well as those they disapproved of
   - the traditional role of women in Okanogan society
   - Okanogan rituals and religious beliefs

7. **Make Judgments** Review the paragraph you wrote earlier about famous or compelling villains and tricksters. What qualities does Coyote have in common with these characters? In your opinion, is Coyote an admirable character? Explain, citing evidence from the text to support your opinion.

Literary Criticism

8. **Critical Interpretations** Critic Paul Rodin has argued that a trickster "is at one and the same time creator and destroyer, giver and negator, he who dupes others and who is always duped himself. . . . He possesses no values, moral or social, is at the mercy of his passions and appetites." Identify the ways in which Coyote fits this definition of a trickster. Cite evidence from the selection to support your answer.

from **The Way to Rainy Mountain**

Memoir by N. Scott Momaday

N. Scott Momaday

born 1934

"The most important question one can ask is 'Who am I?'" N. Scott Momaday (mŏm′ə-dā′) has asserted. "People tend to define you. As a child, you can't help that, but as you grow older, the goal is to garner enough strength to insist on your own definition of yourself." In his writing, Momaday focuses on the search for identity, and he locates the key to self-understanding in awareness of the past.

Native American Roots Momaday developed a deep sense of his own roots early on. His father, a successful artist and a member of the Kiowa (kī′ə-wô′) tribe, routinely told him Kiowa folk tales. His mother, an accomplished writer of French, English, and Cherokee ancestry, instructed him in traditional ways. Momaday grew up on reservations in the Southwest and often spent his summers with his grandparents and other Kiowa relatives in Oklahoma.

The Making of a Writer Growing up on reservations, Momaday developed a reverence for the land and a strong Native American identity. "I saw people," he recalls, "who were deeply involved in their traditional life, in the memories of their blood. They had, as far as I could see, a certain strength and beauty that I find missing in the modern world at large." The lives of these people, together with the Southwestern landscape, inspired Momaday to begin writing at an early age. With the encouragement of his parents, Momaday began composing poetry. Years of hard work and determination paid off when he was awarded a poetry fellowship by Stanford University in 1959.

Voice of the Kiowa In both his poetry and prose, Momaday pays tribute to Native American storytelling traditions and culture. His first novel, *House Made of Dawn,* tells the story of one man's struggle to recover his identity after a stint in the U.S. Army. Original in both theme and structure, the novel was awarded the Pulitzer Prize in 1969. In one of his most popular works, *The Way to Rainy Mountain,* Momaday mixes Kiowa myths, legends, and history with autobiographical details. In addition to his poetry and fiction, Momaday has published essays and articles on preserving the environment. He says, "Writing is a way of expressing your spirit. So there's much more to it than the question of material success. You are out to save your soul after all, and be the best thing that you can be."

● LITERARY ANALYSIS: MEMOIR

A **memoir** is a form of autobiographical writing in which a person shares personal experiences along with observations of significant events or people. Memoirs give readers insight into the impact of historical events on people's lives. They can also be elegantly written texts containing elements such as a distinctive tone, rich sensory details, and symbols.

As you read M. Scott Momaday's memoir, note passages in which he shares strictly personal experiences as well as sections in which he comments on larger historical events.

● READING SKILL: ANALYZE STRUCTURE

Writers usually arrange their information using a **structure** that helps the reader see how the ideas are related. Momaday interweaves three distinct strands throughout his memoir:

- geographical details about the landscape
- historical details about the rise and fall of the Kiowa
- personal details about his grandmother, Aho

As you read, use a chart like the one shown to record details about each topic. Jot down what you learn about each topic, and consider how the three separate strands are related.

The Landscape	The Kiowa	Momaday's Grandmother

▲ VOCABULARY IN CONTEXT

Momaday used the following words in this exploration of his heritage. To test your knowledge, substitute one vocabulary word for the boldfaced word or phrase in each sentence.

WORD LIST		
enmity	opaque	solstice
inherently	pillage	tenuous
luxuriant	preeminently	
nocturnal	profusion	

1. My mother's garden yields an **abundance** of flowers.
2. The feuding brothers eyed each other with **hostility**.
3. There is something **intrinsically** funny about seeing pictures of my father as a teenager.
4. The summer reunion is held on the **longest day of the year.**

What is your HERITAGE?

KEY IDEA What makes you who you are? Part of the answer lies in your **heritage,** or the beliefs, traditions, and culture passed down to you from preceding generations. Think of the things you have gained or learned from older relatives—the recipe for your favorite meal, perhaps, or a sense of humor, or an attitude toward hardship. How have the things you've learned helped shape who you are today? In the selection that follows, N. Scott Momaday offers his own perspective on the importance of heritage.

INTERVIEW Interview one of your classmates about his or her heritage. Ask your subject about a family tradition, an important belief or value, or a story about his or her family's roots. Find out if your classmate thinks heritage has affected his or her identity.

THE WAY TO
Rainy Mountain

N. Scott Momaday

BACKGROUND In the 1600s, after a bitter dispute between two chiefs, a band of Kiowa moved from what is now Montana to South Dakota's Black Hills. In around 1785, the Kiowa migrated farther south to escape attacks by neighboring tribes, settling in what is now western Kansas and Oklahoma. With their Comanche allies, the Kiowa ruled the southern Great Plains for a century. One of the last tribes to be defeated by the U.S. government, the Kiowa surrendered in 1875 and were forced onto a reservation in Oklahoma, where members of the tribe still live today.

A single knoll[1] rises out of the plain in Oklahoma, north and west of the Wichita Range. For my people, the Kiowas, it is an old landmark, and they gave it the name Rainy Mountain. The hardest weather in the world is there. Winter brings blizzards, hot tornadic winds arise in the spring, and in summer the prairie is an anvil's edge. The grass turns brittle and brown, and it cracks beneath your feet. There are green belts along the rivers and creeks, linear groves of hickory and pecan, willow and witch hazel. At a distance in July or August the steaming foliage seems almost to writhe in fire. Great green and yellow grasshoppers are everywhere in the tall grass, popping up like corn to sting the flesh, and tortoises crawl about
10 on the red earth, going nowhere in the plenty of time. Loneliness is an aspect of the land. All things in the plain are isolate; there is no confusion of objects in the eye, but one hill or one tree or one man. To look upon that landscape in the early morning, with the sun at your back, is to lose the sense of proportion. Your imagination comes to life, and this, you think, is where Creation was begun. **A**

   I returned to Rainy Mountain in July. My grandmother had died in the spring, and I wanted to be at her grave. She had lived to be very old and at last infirm.

ANALYZE VISUALS
Examine the portrait on page 53, and consider the photographer's use of high-contrast lighting. What **traits** are suggested by this emphasis of light and shadow? Do you think the subject might look stronger or more vulnerable in a different kind of light? Explain your answer.

A **MEMOIR**
Note the **descriptive language** in the opening paragraph. How might a reader respond differently to this type of writing than to a more scientific description of the Oklahoma plains?

---

   1. **knoll** (nōl): a small round hill.

Her only living daughter was with her when she died, and I was told that in death her face was that of a child.

I like to think of her as a child. When she was born, the Kiowas were living
20 the last great moment of their history. For more than a hundred years they had controlled the open range from the Smoky Hill River to the Red, from the headwaters of the Canadian to the fork of the Arkansas and Cimarron. In alliance with the Comanches, they had ruled the whole of the southern Plains. War was their sacred business, and they were among the finest horsemen the world has ever known. But warfare for the Kiowas was **preeminently** a matter of disposition rather than of survival, and they never understood the grim, unrelenting advance of the U.S. Cavalry. When at last, divided and ill-provisioned, they were driven onto the Staked Plains in the cold rains of autumn, they fell into panic. In Palo Duro Canyon they abandoned their crucial stores to **pillage** and had nothing then
30 but their lives. In order to save themselves, they surrendered to the soldiers at Fort Sill[2] and were imprisoned in the old stone corral that now stands as a military museum. My grandmother was spared the humiliation of those high gray walls by eight or ten years, but she must have known from birth the affliction of defeat, the dark brooding of old warriors.

Her name was Aho, and she belonged to the last culture to evolve in North America. Her forebears came down from the high country in western Montana nearly three centuries ago. They were a mountain people, a mysterious tribe of hunters whose language has never been positively classified in any major group. In the late seventeenth century they began a long migration to the south and east.
40 It was a journey toward the dawn, and it led to a golden age. Along the way the Kiowas were befriended by the Crows,[3] who gave them the culture and religion of the Plains. They acquired horses, and their ancient nomadic spirit was suddenly free of the ground. They acquired Tai-me, the sacred Sun Dance doll, from that moment the object and symbol of their worship, and so shared in the divinity of the sun. Not least, they acquired the sense of destiny, therefore courage and pride. When they entered upon the southern Plains they had been transformed. No longer were they slaves to the simple necessity of survival; they were a lordly and dangerous society of fighters and thieves, hunters and priests of the sun. According to their origin myth, they entered the world through a hollow log. From one point
50 of view, their migration was the fruit of an old prophecy, for indeed they emerged from a sunless world.

Although my grandmother lived out her long life in the shadow of Rainy Mountain, the immense landscape of the continental interior lay like memory in her blood. She could tell of the Crows, whom she had never seen, and of the Black Hills, where she had never been. I wanted to see in reality what she had seen more perfectly in the mind's eye, and traveled fifteen hundred miles to begin my pilgrimage. **B**

---

2. **Fort Sill:** a U.S. army post established in 1869 in the Indian Territory (now Oklahoma).

3. **Crows:** a group of Native Americans who once inhabited the region between the Platte and Yellowstone rivers in the northern Great Plains. The Crows are now settled in Montana.

preeminently
(prē-ĕm′ə-nnənt-lē)
adv. above all; most importantly

pillage (pĭl′ĭj) *n.* the act of looting or plundering by force

B ANALYZE STRUCTURE
Reread lines 35–57. Which lines convey historical information? Which offer more personal details? Identify the key words or phrases that allowed you to distinguish between the two types of information.

Yellowstone, it seemed to me, was the top of the world, a region of deep lakes and dark timber, canyons and waterfalls. But, beautiful as it is, one might have the sense of confinement there. The skyline in all directions is close at hand, the high wall of the woods and deep cleavages of shade. There is a perfect freedom in the mountains, but it belongs to the eagle and the elk, the badger and the bear. The Kiowas reckoned their stature by the distance they could see, and they were bent and blind in the wilderness.

Descending eastward, the highland meadows are a stairway to the plain. In July the inland slope of the Rockies is **luxuriant** with flax and buckwheat, stonecrop and larkspur. The earth unfolds and the limit of the land recedes. Clusters of trees, and animals grazing far in the distance, cause the vision to reach away and wonder to build upon the mind. The sun follows a longer course in the day, and the sky is immense beyond all comparison. The great billowing clouds that sail upon it are shadows that move upon the grain like water, dividing light. Farther down, in the land of the Crows and Blackfeet,[4] the plain is yellow. Sweet clover takes hold of the hills and bends upon itself to cover and seal the soil. There the Kiowas paused on their way; they had come to the place where they must change their lives. The sun is at home on the plains. Precisely there does it have the certain character of a god. When the Kiowas came to the land of the Crows, they could see the dark lees of the hills at dawn across the Bighorn River, the **profusion** of light on the grain shelves, the oldest deity ranging after the **solstices.** Not yet would they veer southward to the caldron of the land that lay below; they must wean their blood from the northern winter and hold the mountains a while longer in their view. They bore Tai-me in procession to the east.

A dark mist lay over the Black Hills, and the land was like iron. At the top of a ridge I caught sight of Devil's Tower upthrust against the gray sky as if in the birth of time the core of the earth had broken through its crust and the motion of the world was begun. There are things in nature that engender an awful quiet in the heart of man; Devil's Tower is one of them. Two centuries ago, because they could not do otherwise, the Kiowas made a legend at the base of the rock. My grandmother said:

Eight children were there at play, seven sisters and their brother. Suddenly the boy was struck dumb; he trembled and began to run upon his hands and feet. His fingers became claws, and his body was covered with fur. Directly there was a bear where the boy had been. The sisters were terrified; they ran, and the bear after them. They came to the stump of a great tree, and the tree spoke to them. It bade them climb upon it, and as they did so it began to rise into the air. The bear came to kill them, but they were just beyond its reach. It reared against the tree and scored the bark all around with its claws. The seven sisters were borne into the sky, and they became the stars of the Big Dipper.

luxuriant (lŭg-zhōŏr′ē-ənt) *adj.* characterized by abundant growth

profusion (prə-fyōō′zhən) *n.* abundance; lavishness

solstice (sŏl′stĭs) *n.* either of two days of the year when the sun is farthest from the celestial equator; the summer solstice is the longest day of the year, and the winter solstice is the shortest.

---

4. **Blackfeet:** a group of Native Americans who once inhabited a region now occupied by parts of Montana and the Canadian provinces of Alberta and Saskatchewan.

From that moment, and so long as the legend lives, the Kiowas have kinsmen in the night sky. Whatever they were in the mountains, they could be no more. However **tenuous** their well-being, however much they had suffered and would suffer again, they had found a way out of the wilderness. **C**

My grandmother had a reverence for the sun, a holy regard that now is all but gone out of mankind. There was a wariness in her, and an ancient awe. She was a Christian in her later years, but she had come a long way about, and she never forgot her birthright. As a child she had been to the Sun Dances; she had taken part in those annual rites, and by them she had learned the restoration of her people in the presence of Tai-me. She was about seven when the last Kiowa Sun Dance was held in 1887 on the Washita River above Rainy Mountain Creek. The buffalo were gone. In order to consummate the ancient sacrifice—to impale the head of a buffalo bull upon the medicine tree—a delegation of old men journeyed into Texas, there to beg and barter for an animal from the Goodnight herd.[5] She was ten when the Kiowas came together for the last time as a living Sun Dance culture. They could find no buffalo; they had to hang an old hide from the sacred tree. Before the dance could begin, a company of soldiers rode out from Fort Sill under orders to disperse the tribe. Forbidden without cause the essential act of their faith, having seen the wild herds slaughtered and left to rot upon the ground, the Kiowas backed away forever from the medicine tree. That was July 20, 1890, at the great bend of the Washita. My grandmother was there. Without bitterness, and for as long as she lived, she bore a vision of deicide.[6]

Now that I can have her only in memory, I see my grandmother in the several postures that were peculiar to her: standing at the wood stove on a winter morning and turning meat in a great iron skillet; sitting at the south window, bent above her beadwork, and afterwards, when her vision failed, looking down for a long time into the fold of her hands; going out upon a cane, very slowly as she did when the weight of age came upon her; praying. I remember her most often at prayer. She made long, rambling prayers out of suffering and hope, having seen many things. I was never sure that I had the right to hear, so exclusive were they of all mere custom and company. The last time I saw her she prayed standing by the side of her bed at night, naked to the waist, the light of a kerosene lamp moving upon her dark skin. Her long, black hair, always drawn and braided in the day, lay upon her shoulders and against her breasts like a shawl. I do not speak Kiowa, and I never understood her prayers, but there was something **inherently** sad in the sound, some merest hesitation upon the syllables of sorrow. She began in a high and descending pitch, exhausting her breath to silence; then again and again—and always the same intensity of effort, of something that is, and is not, like urgency in the human voice. Transported so in the dancing light among the shadows of her room, she seemed beyond the reach of time. But that was illusion; I think I knew then that I should not see her again.

---

5. **Goodnight herd:** a herd of Southern Plains bison established in the 1870s by Charles and Molly Goodnight for the purpose of preserving the animals from extinction.

6. **a vision of deicide** (dē′ə-sīd′): a picture in her mind of the killing of a god.

tenuous (tĕn′yo̅o̅-əs) *adj.* having little substance or strength; flimsy

C ANALYZE STRUCTURE
Reread lines 98–101. What does Momaday mean when he says that "the Kiowas have kinsmen in the night sky"? How does the inclusion of this legend add depth to the personal elements of this memoir?

inherently (ĭn-hîr′ənt-lē′) *adv.* related to part of something's inmost nature

ANALYZE VISUALS
In your opinion, does this photograph convey the same **mood** that Momaday evokes in his autobiography? Explain your answer, citing details from both the photograph and the text.

Mandan Offering the Buffalo Skull, Edward S. Curtis, photographer. McCormick Library of Special Collections, Northwestern University Library.

Houses are like sentinels in the plain, old keepers of the weather watch. There,
140 in a very little while, wood takes on the appearance of great age. All colors wear soon away in the wind and rain, and then the wood is burned gray and the grain appears and the nails turn red with rust. The windowpanes are black and **opaque;** you imagine there is nothing within, and indeed there are many ghosts, bones given up to the land. They stand here and there against the sky, and you approach them for a longer time than you expect. They belong in the distance; it is their domain. **D**

Once there was a lot of sound in my grandmother's house, a lot of coming and going, feasting and talk. The summers there were full of excitement and reunion. The Kiowas are a summer people; they abide the cold and keep to themselves, but when the season turns and the land becomes warm and vital they cannot
150 hold still; an old love of going returns upon them. The aged visitors who came to my grandmother's house when I was a child were made of lean and leather, and they bore themselves upright. They wore great black hats and bright ample shirts

opaque (ō-pāk') *adj.* not allowing light to pass through

D MEMOIR
Reread lines 120–145. What words and phrases give you an indication of Momaday's **tone**, or attitude toward his subject matter?

that shook in the wind. They rubbed fat upon their hair and wound their braids with strips of colored cloth. Some of them painted their faces and carried the scars of old and cherished **enmities.** They were an old council of warlords, come to remind and be reminded of who they were. Their wives and daughters served them well. The women might indulge themselves; gossip was at once the mark and compensation of their servitude. They made loud and elaborate talk among themselves, full of jest and gesture, fright and false alarm. They went abroad in

160 fringed and flowered shawls, bright beadwork and German silver. They were at home in the kitchen, and they prepared meals that were banquets.

There were frequent prayer meetings, and great **nocturnal** feasts. When I was a child I played with my cousins outside, where the lamplight fell upon the ground and the singing of the old people rose up around us and carried away into the darkness. There were a lot of good things to eat, a lot of laughter and surprise. And afterwards, when the quiet returned, I lay down with my grandmother and could hear the frogs away by the river and feel the motion of the air.

Now there is a funeral silence in the rooms, the endless wake of some final word. The walls have closed in upon my grandmother's house. When I returned

170 to it in mourning, I saw for the first time in my life how small it was. It was late at night, and there was a white moon, nearly full. I sat for a long time on the stone steps by the kitchen door. From there I could see out across the land; I could see the long row of trees by the creek, the low light upon the rolling plains, and the stars of the Big Dipper. Once I looked at the moon and caught sight of a strange thing. A cricket had perched upon the handrail, only a few inches away from me. My line of vision was such that the creature filled the moon like a fossil. It had gone there, I thought, to live and die, for there, of all places, was its small definition made whole and eternal. A warm wind rose up and purled like the longing within me. **E**

180 The next morning I awoke at dawn and went out on the dirt road to Rainy Mountain. It was already hot, and the grasshoppers began to fill the air. Still, it was early in the morning, and the birds sang out of the shadows. The long yellow grass on the mountain shone in the bright light, and a scissortail hied[7] above the land. There, where it ought to be, at the end of a long and legendary way, was my grandmother's grave. Here and there on the dark stones were ancestral names. Looking back once, I saw the mountain and came away. ◖◗

enmity (ĕn′mĭ-tē) *n.* hostility; hatred

nocturnal (nŏk-tûr′nəl) *adj.* occurring at night

E MEMOIR
Think about how Momaday contrasts his grandmother's house as it was during his childhood visits with how it is now. What might this house **symbolize?**

---

7. **a scissortail hied:** a fork-tailed bird of the Southwest hied, or hurried.

Comprehension

1. **Recall** Where is Rainy Mountain, and why does Momaday return there?

2. **Clarify** What two natural phenomena are explained by the Kiowa legend about the seven sisters and their brother?

3. **Summarize** What important events in Kiowa history does Momaday recount?

Literary Analysis

4. **Draw Conclusions** In your opinion, what is the most important insight Momaday gains about his **heritage** during his pilgrimage from Yellowstone to his grandmother's grave at Rainy Mountain? Support your opinion with evidence from the text.

5. **Understand Memoirs** Reread lines 52–101. What does Momaday's account of the Kiowa's migration offer you that a description in a history book might not? Explain, citing specific lines of the selection that support your answer.

6. **Analyze Structure** Review the chart you created as you read, and summarize the geographical, historical, and personal details that Momaday includes in each of the three strands. How are they related? Describe the impact of Momaday's technique of weaving the three strands together.

7. **Examine Author's Style** Although best known as a novelist, Momaday is also an accomplished poet. In what way might this selection be described as poetic? In a chart like the one shown, record examples of the poetic elements Momaday uses in his memoir. Use your completed chart to explain what you think these stylistic choices add to the selection. (Refer to the **Glossary of Literary Terms** on page R104 if needed.)

Poetic Elements		
Alliteration	Consonance	Imagery
"The grass turns brittle and brown ..."		

Literary Criticism

8. **Critical Interpretations** Teacher and scholar Kenneth M. Roemer has argued that "in *The Way to Rainy Mountain,* M. Scott Momaday links the survival of his people to their ability to remember, preserve and pass on stories." Do you agree that a culture's survival rests on this ability? Explain, using evidence from this selection to support your opinion.

Vocabulary in Context

WORD LIST

enmity

inherently

luxuriant

nocturnal

opaque

pillage

preeminently

profusion

solstice

tenuous

VOCABULARY PRACTICE

Choose the vocabulary word that answers each riddle.

1. I refer to things that do not happen in daylight.
2. I represent extremes of time, both shortest and longest.
3. I am the opposite of friendship.
4. I describe something uncertain or insubstantial.
5. I mean the same thing as *chiefly*.
6. I am the act of looting by force.
7. I am an adjective that could describe a field filled with wildflowers.
8. I am a noun indicating an abundance of wildflowers.
9. Air filled with dense fog is one example of what I am.
10. One of my meanings is "essentially."

VOCABULARY IN WRITING

Which location, event, or person in this account do you find most memorable? Using three or more vocabulary words, write a brief description of the person, place, or event, including your own response to it. You might start this way.

> **EXAMPLE SENTENCE**
> *The final Sun Dance of the Kiowa had only a **tenuous** connection with earlier rituals.*

VOCABULARY STRATEGY: SPECIALIZED VOCABULARY

The Kiowa recognize the importance of seasonal events such as the solstices. There are a number of terms that describe other natural phenomena relating Earth to the sun and the moon. Some of these terms have only technical meanings, but others are also used in more general ways.

PRACTICE Match each term with its definition. Use a dictionary if you need help. Then choose the term that also has a nontechnical meaning, and write a definition for it.

1. apogee
2. equinox
3. diurnal
4. perigee
5. eccentric

a. two dates each year when day and night are of equal length
b. having a noncircular planetary orbits such as Earth's
c. point when the moon is farthest from Earth
d. relating to the daily rotation of Earth
e. point when the moon is closest to Earth

VOCABULARY PRACTICE
For more practice, go to the **Vocabulary Center** at **ClassZone.com.**

Native American Values

Stereotypes have long characterized the portrayal of Native Americans in our culture. Early explorers' and settlers' lack of knowledge about Native American ways colored their written accounts, while later writers indulged in blatant "cowboys and Indians" stereotyping. Yet by reading the literature written by Native American groups, both past and present, one can move past the stereotypes to gain a clearer understanding of the Native American experience.

Writing to Synthesize

Make a list of the things you have in common with the Native Americans you've read about in this section—the things that connect us all as people. Then write one paragraph describing something that Native Americans valued in the past that many people still value today and one paragraph describing something they found objectionable with which you might also agree.

Consider

- the theme of each selection
- passages that shed light on traditional Native American values
- characters who are portrayed as "good" or "bad" and what they reveal about the culture

Extension Online

RESEARCH Historically, many university and professional sports teams have employed Native American mascots. In recent years, this practice has come under attack. With a partner, go online to **research** images of three such mascots and print them to share with the class. Also find out what routines or traditions each mascot has performed. Then, as a class, discuss why people might find such mascots offensive. As you discuss, be sure to take into account what you learned from your reading.

The Buffalo Chase with Bow (1832), George Catlin. The Granger Collection, New York.

Changing Views of Native Americans

Film Clips on ◉ **MediaSmart** DVD

How do media shape PERCEPTIONS?

KEY IDEA In this unit, Native American voices from the past and present reveal their way of life and worldview. In contrast, many 20th-century films about the Old West lacked this Native American perspective, often reinforcing inaccurate **stereotypes** and creating new ones. In this lesson, you will watch three film clips that present images of Native Americans from three different time periods.

Background

How the Western Won America's fascination with the Old West began with late 19th-century dime-novel westerns. These low-priced, fast-paced stories were typically set in the frontier between the mid-1800s and the turn of the century. Alongside dime novels arose Wild West shows. These colorful, outdoor spectacles featured frontier figures, such as Buffalo Bill, Sitting Bull, and Annie Oakley, and staged reenactments of battles. Both dime novels and Wild West shows presented simplistic morality tales. To establish order and perhaps justify the taking of Native American lands and lives, the so-called good guys—cowboys and settlers—had to overcome the alleged bad guys—rampaging Indians or marauding outlaws. Thus was born a source for stereotyping that would endure in other forms.

At the start of the 20th century, as the motion picture industry evolved, the western film genre burst onto the screen. While Hollywood filmmakers glorified the frontier by shooting in spectacular locations, they recycled the simple formulas of the earlier western forms and perpetuated some of the inaccurate images.

By the mid-1900s, as TV became commonplace, westerns dominated both big and small screens. At the peak of the western's golden age, over 20 westerns were televised each week, exposing viewers to themes and images that went unquestioned. It didn't seem to matter if an Indian's costume wasn't historically accurate or if his or her language wasn't realistic. Little was said about the effects of western expansion on Native American life and culture. The Hollywood images took hold in the minds of viewers. Aware of this, filmmakers of more recent times have made deliberate efforts to bring more authentic portrayals to the screen.

Media Literacy: Images in Mass Media

The **western** is a film and TV genre that portrays the early days of the American frontier. In many TV shows and movies, particularly classic westerns, the film and TV industry depended on **stereotypes,** oversimplified or inaccurate representations of people. Stereotypes can create misconceptions, especially when there are no alternative portrayals to displace them. Use your knowledge of characterization and film techniques to help you spot these stereotypes.

STRATEGIES FOR ANALYZING FILM AND TELEVISION STEREOTYPES

A Character's Appearance	Look for how actors are costumed and how make-up is applied. Keep in mind that most often, little historical research was done to present Native Americans accurately. Costumes and language were often a mix of different tribes.	
A Character's Dialogue	Focus on how characters speak. Which characters speak dialogue in complete sentences? Which speak in simple words or phrases? Stereotypical characters are usually depicted as being somehow outside of the mainstream culture and as holding a different set of values.	
A Character's Actions	Ask yourself: Do characters behave according to a stereotype? Are the actions more negative than positive? Notice how **lighting** and **music** reinforce these impressions. How does the director film the actions? Be aware of camera placement. • **Low-angle shots** position the camera to look up at an object or a person. Such shots convey an imposing or powerful presence. • **High-angle shots** position the camera to look down, often conveying helplessness.	
Other Characters' Responses to the Character	Notice how other characters react to the individual. Do **close-up shots** reveal expressions of tolerance, condescension, or superiority? In what ways do the dialogue and the acting convey how the character is regarded?	

MediaSmart DVD

- **Film 1:** *Stagecoach*
- **Director:** John Ford
- **Genre:** Movie Western
- **Running Time:** 2 minutes

- **Film 2:** *The Lone Ranger*
- **Genre:** TV Western
- **Running Time:** 2 minutes

- **Film 3:** *Smoke Signals*
- **Director:** Chris Eyre
- **Rating:** PG-13
- **Genre:** Drama
- **Running Time:** 2.5 minutes

Viewing Guide for

Changing Views of Native Americans

Watch the first two clips to explore how Native Americans were portrayed during the glory days of the western. The scene from *Stagecoach* (1939) brings two groups into direct contact. In the clip from *The Lone Ranger* TV series (1949–1957), the two main characters prepare to take action. Watch the third clip to see a more recent Native American portrayal—one that challenges the old Hollywood images. In *Smoke Signals* (1998), friends Victor and Thomas engage in lively conversation during a road trip.

To critically analyze the clips, view them more than once. Examine the portrayals, and answer these questions.

NOW VIEW

FIRST VIEWING: Comprehension

1. **Recall** In *Stagecoach*, what do the travelers do as soon as they spot the Native Americans?

2. **Summarize** Think about Victor in *Smoke Signals*. Summarize his view of the acceptable look and behavior for "Indian" males.

CLOSE VIEWING: Media Literacy

3. **Identify Film Techniques** Consider how the use of music and the **high-** and **low-angle** shots contribute to characterization in the beginning of the *Stagecoach* clip. How might the effect reinforce **stereotypes?**

4. **Analyze Stereotypes** In *The Lone Ranger* clip, the character Tonto might be considered an improvement over past portrayals of Native Americans. However, what might still be **stereotypical** about this character?

5. **Analyze Characters** Recall how Victor in *Smoke Signals* describes "real Indian" behavior. Might their portrayal be perceived as a step forward? Why or why not?

6. **Evaluate Characterization** *Smoke Signals* director Chris Eyre has said, "I'm interested in telling stories about Indians who are normal, everyday people." How effectively do the character portrayals in the scene from his film counter the stereotypes in *Stagecoach* and *The Lone Ranger*? Base your opinion on the modern-day setting in *Smoke Signals* and on the characterizations of Thomas and Victor.

Write or Discuss

Compare Portrayals What impressions of Native Americans do you get from each clip? At the time each portrayal was first presented, how might it have affected perceptions of Native Americans? Write a comparison of the three clips you've viewed. Consider:

- the portrayals of individuals or groups
- the techniques of camera position, lighting, and music
- the fact that *Smoke Signals* was written and directed by Native Americans

Produce Your Own Media

Create an Image Award Consider any films or TV shows that you think rise above the simplistic techniques of stereotyping. What character portrayals or story lines strike you as complex and true to life? How sensitively are different social groups portrayed? As a class, create a name for the award and devise basic criteria for judging the pieces. After brainstorming choices with a partner, present your nominees to the class and choose one award winner.

HERE'S HOW Follow these guidelines as you plan your presentation:

- As you brainstorm choices, ask yourself: In what aspects has this work succeeded while others have missed the mark? What impact might the choice have on viewers' perceptions over time?
- As you present each of your films or shows, explain the reasons it was nominated. The choice that meets (or exceeds) most of the criteria wins the image award.

MEDIA TOOLS

For help with devising the image award criteria, visit the **Media Center** at **ClassZone.com.**

Tech Tip

Use presentational software to show the title and attributes of each nominee.

Further Exploration

Hold a Native American Film Festival According to Native American filmmaker Bird Runningwater, "Filmmaking provides a new way to merge a strong oral tradition of storytelling with technology and, in the process, revitalize ourselves." Research Native American films and reviews. If possible, rent movies to view as a group, and then critique them in a panel discussion.

Conduct a Native American Film Study Savage warrior. Noble savage. Sage protector of the earth. One hundred years of moviemaking hasn't begun to cover the complexity and diversity of Native American cultural groups. Research westerns ranging from the 1950s to the present. What historical inaccuracies are evident? In contemporary works, have attempts to present more positive depictions fully succeeded?

Historical Narratives

If you wanted to know what life was like for someone 400 years ago, where could you get the information? History books could give you a general account, but what if you wanted to know the details of someone's daily life or what it was like to actually be at an important historical event? In American literature, there are many personal accounts that have been published and passed down through the centuries that give unique perspectives on the events of the past.

Recording the American Experience

Europeans began voyages by ship to the Americas in the late 15th century and reported news of their explorations and settlement. These historical narratives of the survivors told gripping adventure stories, written down in journals and letters, of the the first Europeans' experiences of coming to America. **Historical narratives** are accounts of real-life historical experiences, written by either a person who experienced those events or someone

Indian Summer, Regis François Gignoux. © Christie's Images/Corbis.

who studied or observed them. In many cases, the narratives became important historical documents that now exist as our principal record of events. Historical narratives can be divided into two categories:

- **Primary sources** are materials written by people who were either participants in or observers of the events written about. Letters, diaries, journals, speeches, autobiographies, and interviews are all primary sources.

- **Secondary sources** are records of events written by people who were not directly involved in the events. Two typical examples of secondary sources are biographies and histories.

Bringing the Past to Life

Primary sources offer valuable insights into the thinking and culture of a given time period. Use these strategies to bring the information to life:

- Determine a document's origin.

- Try to understand the **perspective** and **motives** of the writer.

- Note **sensory details** that depict people, places, and events.

- Identify customs, values, or conditions of the **culture** or **time period.**

Álvar Núñez Cabeza de Vaca was one of many explorers who sailed to the New World after Christopher Columbus. The historical narrative *La Relación* (page 70) was Cabeza de Vaca's report to the king of Spain. Note the personal **perspective** he provides in this excerpt about one night in his crossing of the Atlantic Ocean.

> When night fell, only the navigator and I remained able to tend the barge. Two hours after dark he told me I must take over; he believed he was going to die that night.
>
> —**Álvar Núñez Cabeza de Vaca,** *La Relación*

In 1620, the Puritans survived a journey across the Atlantic in the *Mayflower* and landed at Cape Cod. In 1630, William Bradford, Plymouth Colony's second governor, began writing *Of Plymouth Plantation* (page 100), a chronicle of his colony's experiences. Notice the use of **sensory details** in Bradford's description of the colony's first winter.

> The weather was very cold and it froze so hard as the spray of the sea lighting on their coats, they were as if they had been glazed.
>
> —**William Bradford,** *Of Plymouth Plantation*

As the American colonies expanded from the 16th through the 18th centuries, the slave trade expanded as well. Olaudah Equiano was one of the millions of Africans captured and transported to the Americas. He survived this ordeal and published his autobiography in 1789. These lines from his autobiography describe the conditions below the decks of a slave ship and his first reaction to what he saw.

> When I looked round the ship too, and saw a large furnace of copper boiling, and a multitude of black people of every description chained together, every one of their countenances expressing dejection and sorrow, I no longer doubted of my fate.
>
> —**Olaudah Equiano,** *The Interesting Narrative of the Life of Olaudah Equiano*

THE SLAVE NARRATIVE

The **slave narrative** is an American literary genre that portrays the daily life of slaves as written by the slaves themselves after gaining their freedom. Some 6,000 slave narratives are known to exist. The Reverend Ephraim Peabody wrote in 1849 about three recently published slave narratives:

> *We place these volumes without hesitation among the most remarkable productions of the age—remarkable as being pictures of slavery by the slave, remarkable as disclosing under a new light the mixed elements of American civilization, and not less remarkable as a vivid exhibition of the force and working of the native love of freedom in the individual mind.*
>
> –**The Reverend Ephraim Peabody**

Probably the most influential example of the genre is the autobiography of Frederick Douglass, *Narrative of the Life of Frederick Douglass, an American Slave,* published in 1845.

Close Read

Describe what you think were the writer's motives for recording the events in the first two **primary source** examples on this page.

Close Read

Point out details that are particularly vivid. Describe how you would visualize the scene.

from La Relación

Report by Álvar Núñez Cabeza de Vaca

FYI

Did you know that Cabeza de Vaca . . .

- recorded the only accounts of some now-extinct Native American groups?
- was the first European to cross North and South America?
- was accompanied by an enslaved African named Esteban?

Álvar Núñez Cabeza de Vaca

c. 1490–1557

In 1536, Spanish slave hunters raiding in northern Mexico were startled by a strange sight: a Spaniard "strangely dressed and in company with Indians." Long given up for dead, Álvar Núñez Cabeza de Vaca had survived one of the most disastrous expeditions in the history of the Spanish conquest to become the first European to cross North America.

Conquering Hero Cabeza de Vaca came from a family of Spanish *conquistadors,* or conquerors. He had been a soldier for nearly 20 years when, in 1527, he joined an expedition to Spanish North America. Appointed by the king of Spain, he became treasurer and second in command, assigned the task of colonizing the territory north and east of the Gulf of Mexico.

Disaster Strikes Led by Pánfilo de Narváez, the expedition sailed with five ships and 600 men. Two ships were lost in a hurricane; 200 men drowned or deserted. After landing in Tampa Bay, Narváez sent his ships north and ordered 300 men to march to New Spain (present-day Mexico), which he guessed to be a few weeks away. Months later, the ships were gone and the desperate landing party was eating its horses to survive. Using horsehide and nails made from melted armor, they built five barges and sailed along the Gulf Coast from Florida to Texas, hoping to reach Spanish settlements in northern Mexico. Two barges and 80 men washed up on or near Galveston Island. Ultimately, only Cabeza de Vaca and three other men survived.

Cabeza de Vaca survived by adapting to his new surroundings. For six years, he lived with dozens of Native American groups in various roles—as a captive, a trader, and a well-known healer. In 1534, the four survivors escaped, setting out across the desert in search of New Spain. In 1536, they finally reached their goal. A year later, Cabeza de Vaca returned to Spain, where he wrote his account of the expedition, *La Relación* (The Account), as a report to the king.

Conqueror No More The king rewarded Cabeza de Vaca by appointing him governor of a South American colony, where his humane treatment of Native Americans may have cost him his job. By 1545, he had been ousted from his position and convicted on a corruption charge in Spain. Exiled to Africa, Cabeza de Vaca was eventually pardoned. In 1552, he returned to Spain to end his days as a judge.

LITERARY ANALYSIS: HISTORICAL CONTEXT

When you read historical works, you may notice statements that seem strange or even offensive. These remarks might be a reflection of the work's **historical context**—the ideas and details from the author's time that influence the written work.

It was amazing to see these wild, untaught savages howling like brutes in compassion for us.

The author's statement reflects views about Indians that most people of his time shared. To familiarize yourself with the historical context of *La Relación*, read the author biography on page 68 and the background information on page 70. Then, as you read the work, note details that reflect this context.

READING STRATEGY: READING A PRIMARY SOURCE

Unlike a history book, *La Relación* is an eyewitness report of events. Such **primary sources** give us special insight into historical events. When using these sources, consider

- the intended audience
- the author's role in events
- where and when the document was written

As you read, complete a chart like the one shown. Consult the author biography and background information as needed.

Questions	Answers
What do I know about the author and his times?	
What details tell me about life in 16th-century North America?	
What is the relationship between the author and his audience?	
What is the author's role in the events he describes?	

VOCABULARY IN CONTEXT

The following words help bring this explorer's account to life. Choose a synonym for each word from the numbered terms.

WORD LIST	cauterize	ingratiate	locomotion
	embody	inundate	tarry

1. movement
2. personify
3. burn
4. seek favor
5. flood
6. delay

What's the STORY behind the GLORY?

KEY IDEA Dreams of wealth, glory, and conquest lured adventurers to the Americas, but few were prepared for the harsh reality that awaited them. For every hero who claimed a fortune, there were hundreds of others who died trying. Often, the greatest prize of all was living to tell the tale. What enabled some to **survive** while others failed?

DISCUSS In a small group, share stories you've read or heard that describe a person's struggle to survive in desperate circumstances, such as a shipwreck, war, or a natural disaster. Then make a list of traits that those people or characters exhibit. Decide what qualities seem essential in a survivor.

La Relación

Álvar Núñez Cabeza de Vaca

> **BACKGROUND** In the 1500s, Spanish conquistadors took to the seas to claim new land for Spain. Seeking gold and silver, they explored unfamiliar territory and encountered Native American cultures they did not understand. By the time Cabeza de Vaca sailed, Spaniards had conquered the Aztecs of Mexico and the Inca of Peru, two of the most advanced civilizations in the Americas. Millions of Native Americans would die in this often brutal cultural encounter. In *La Relación,* Cabeza de Vaca finds himself unexpectedly at the mercy of the people he came to conquer.

At this point in the account, Narváez's barge has abandoned the rest, and Cabeza de Vaca's barge has joined one commanded by two other officers. The next three chapters describe the shipwreck of Cabeza de Vaca's barge on Galveston Island and the crew's encounter with the Karankawa Indians who lived there.

ANALYZE VISUALS
What **details** in the image convey the desperate situation of the shipwrecked men?

A Sinking and a Landing

Our two barges continued in company for four days, each man eating a ration of half a handful of raw corn a day. Then the other barge was lost in a storm. Nothing but God's great mercy kept us from going down, too.

It was winter and bitterly cold, and we had suffered hunger and the heavy beating of the waves for many days. Next day, the men began to collapse. By sunset, all in my barge had fallen over on one another, close to death. Few were any longer conscious. Not five could stand. When night fell, only the navigator and I remained able to tend the barge. Two hours after dark he told me I must take over; he believed he was going to die that night. **A**

10   So I took the tiller. After midnight I moved over to see if he were dead. He said no, in fact was better, and would steer till daylight. In that hour I would have welcomed death rather than see so many around me in such a condition. When I had returned the helm to the navigator, I lay down to rest—but without much rest, for nothing was farther from my mind than sleep.

Near dawn I seemed to hear breakers resounding; the coast lying low, they roared louder. Surprised at this, I called to the navigator, who said he thought we

A **PRIMARY SOURCE**
Describe the **tone** of lines 4–9. In what ways might the author's choice of tone be influenced by his intended **audience**?

Illustration by Tom McNeely.

were coming close to land. We sounded and found ourselves in seven fathoms.[1]
The navigator felt we should stay clear of the shore till daylight; so I took an oar
and pulled it on the shore side, wheeling the stern to seaward about a league[2] out.

20   As we drifted into shore, a wave caught us and heaved the barge a horseshoe-
throw [about 42 feet] out of the water. The jolt when it hit brought the dead-
looking men to. Seeing land at hand, they crawled through the surf to some rocks.
Here we made a fire and parched some of our corn. We also found rain water. The
men began to regain their senses, their **locomotion,** and their hope.

This day of our landing was November 6.

What Befell Oviedo with the Indians

After we ate, I ordered Lope de Oviedo, our strongest man, to climb one of the
trees not far off and ascertain the lay of the land. He complied and found out
from the treetop that we were on an island. [This was Galveston Island.] He also
said that the ground looked as if cattle had trampled it and therefore that this
30   must be a country of Christians. **B**

I sent him back for a closer look, to see if he could find any worn trails, but
warned him not to risk going too far. He went and came upon a path which he
followed for half a league to some empty huts. The Indians were gone to shoal-
flats[3] [to dig roots]. He took an earthen pot, a little dog, and a few mullets[4] and
started back.

We had begun to worry what might have happened to him, so I detailed
another two men to check. They met him shortly and saw three Indians with
bows and arrows following him. The Indians were calling to him and he was
gesturing them to keep coming. When he reached us, the Indians held back
40   and sat down on the shore.

Half an hour later a hundred bowmen reinforced the first three individuals.
Whatever their stature, they looked like giants to us in our fright. We could not
hope to defend ourselves; not half a dozen of us could even stand up.

The Inspector [Solís] and I walked out and greeted them. They advanced, and
we did our best to placate and **ingratiate.** We gave them beads and bells, and each
one of them gave us an arrow in pledge of friendship. They told us by signs that
they would return at sunrise and bring food, having none then.

The Indians' Hospitality Before and After a New Calamity

As the sun rose next morning, the Indians appeared as they promised, bringing
an abundance of fish and of certain roots which taste like nuts, some bigger than
50   walnuts, some smaller, mostly grubbed from the water with great labor.

That evening they came again with more fish and roots and brought their
women and children to look at us. They thought themselves rich with the little
bells and beads we gave them, and they repeated their visits on other days.

---

1. **We sounded . . . fathoms:** We measured the depth of the water and found it to be about 42 feet.
   (A fathom is equal to 6 feet, or 1.83 meters.)
2. **league:** a unit of distance; Cabeza de Vaca probably used the Spanish league, equal to 3.1 miles (5 kilometers).
3. **shoal-flats:** stretches of level ground under shallow water.
4. **mullets:** certain edible fish.

locomotion
(lō′kə-mō′shən) *n.* the
power to move from place
to place

B **HISTORICAL CONTEXT**
In the 1500s, "Christians"
was used as a synonym for
Europeans. What does this
suggest about how the
Spaniards saw the world?

ingratiate (ĭn-grā′shē-āt′)
v. to gain another's favor
by deliberate effort

Being provided with what we needed, we thought to embark again. It was a struggle to dig our barge out of the sand it had sunk in, and another struggle to launch her. For the work in the water while launching, we stripped and stowed our clothes in the craft.

Quickly clambering in and grabbing our oars, we had rowed two crossbow shots from shore when a wave **inundated** us. Being naked and the cold intense,
60   we let our oars go. The next big wave capsized the barge. The Inspector and two others held fast, but that only carried them more certainly underneath, where they drowned.

A single roll of the sea tossed the rest of the men into the rushing surf and back onto shore half-drowned.

We lost only those the barge took down; but the survivors escaped as naked as they were born, with the loss of everything we had. That was not much, but valuable to us in that bitter November cold, our bodies so emaciated we could easily count every bone and looked the very picture of death. I can say for myself that from the month of May I had eaten nothing but corn, and that sometimes
70   raw. I never could bring myself to eat any of the horse-meat at the time our beasts were slaughtered; and fish I did not taste ten times. On top of everything else, a cruel north wind commenced to complete our killing. **C**

The Lord willed that we should find embers while searching the remnants of our former fire. We found more wood and soon had big fires raging. Before them, with flowing tears, we prayed for mercy and pardon, each filled with pity not only for himself but for all his wretched fellows.

At sunset the Indians, not knowing we had gone, came again with food. When they saw us looking so strangely different, they turned back in alarm. I went after them calling, and they returned, though frightened. I explained to them by signs
80   that our barge had sunk and three of our number drowned. They could see at their feet two of the dead men who had washed ashore. They could also see that the rest of us were not far from joining these two.

The Indians, understanding our full plight, sat down and lamented for half an hour so loudly they could have been heard a long way off. It was amazing to see these wild, untaught savages howling like brutes in compassion for us. It intensified my own grief at our calamity and had the same effect on the other victims.

When the cries died down, I conferred with the Christians about asking the Indians to take us to their homes. Some of our number who had been to New Spain warned that the Indians would sacrifice us to their idols.[5] But death being
90   surer and nearer if we stayed where we were, I went ahead and beseeched the Indians. They were delighted. They told us to **tarry** a little while, then they would do as we wished.

Presently thirty of them gathered loads of wood and disappeared to their huts, which were a long walk away; while we waited with the remainder until near nightfall. Then, supporting us under our arms, they hurried us from one

inundate (ĭn′ŭn-dāt′) *v.* to cover with water; to overwhelm

C PRIMARY SOURCE
Reread lines 68–71. What does the author's reponse to his current situation tell you about his usual diet?

tarry (tăr′ē) *v.* to delay

---

5. **New Spain ... their idols:** New Spain included what is now the southwest United States, Mexico, Central America north of Panama, and some West Indian islands. In Mexico, conquistadors had encountered Aztecs who practiced human sacrifice.

to another of the four big fires they had built along the path. At each fire, when we regained a little warmth and strength, they took us on so swiftly our feet hardly touched ground. **D**

Thus we made their village, where we saw they had erected a hut for us with 100 many fires inside. An hour later they began a dance celebration that lasted all night. For us there was no joy, feasting, or sleep, as we waited the hour they should make us victims.

In the morning, when they brought us fish and roots and acted in every way hospitably, we felt reassured and somewhat lost our anxiety of the sacrificial knife.

Cabeza de Vaca learned that men from one of the other barges had also landed on the island, bringing the number of Europeans there to about 90. In a matter of weeks, all but 16 of them died of disease, which spread to the Karankawas and killed half of them as well. Some of the Karankawas wanted to put the remaining Europeans to death but were dissuaded by Cabeza de Vaca's host. Cabeza de Vaca and his men were later forced to act as healers.

How We Became Medicine-Men

The islanders wanted to make physicians of us without examination or a review of diplomas. Their method of cure is to blow on the sick, the breath and the laying-on of hands supposedly casting out the infirmity. They insisted we should do this too and be of some use to them. We scoffed at their cures and at the idea we knew how to heal. But they withheld food from us until we complied. An Indian told 110 me I knew not whereof I spoke in saying their methods had no effect. Stones and other things growing about in the fields, he said, had a virtue whereby passing a pebble along the stomach could take away pain and heal; surely extraordinary men like us **embodied** such powers over nature. Hunger forced us to obey, but disclaiming any responsibility for our failure or success.

An Indian, falling sick, would send for a medicine-man, who would apply his cure. The patient would then give the medicine-man all he had and seek more from his relatives to give. The medicine-man makes incisions over the point of the pain, sucks the wound, and **cauterizes** it. This remedy enjoys high repute among the Indians. I have, as a matter of fact, tried it on myself with good results. The 120 medicine-men blow on the spot they have treated, as a finishing touch, and the patient regards himself relieved.

Our method, however, was to bless the sick, breathe upon them, recite a *Pater noster* and *Ave Maria,*[6] and pray earnestly to God our Lord for their recovery. When we concluded with the sign of the cross, He willed that our patients should directly spread the news that they had been restored to health. **E**

In consequence, the Indians treated us kindly. They deprived themselves of food to give to us, and presented us skins and other tokens of gratitude. ❧

Translated by Cyclone Covey

---

6. *Pater noster* (pā′tər nŏs′tər) **and** *Ave Maria* (ä′vä mə-rē′ə): the Lord's Prayer ("Our Father") and the Hail Mary, named for the prayers' opening words in Latin.

74   UNIT 1: EARLY AMERICAN WRITING

D GRAMMAR AND STYLE
Reread lines 93–98. Note how the author uses **prepositional phrases,** such as "until near nightfall" and "along the path," to add important details about where and when events are happening.

embody (ĕm-bŏd′ē) *v.* to represent in human form

cauterize (kô′tə-rīz′) *v.* to burn or sear to destroy diseased tissue

E HISTORICAL CONTEXT
In Cabeza de Vaca's time, no one had good knowledge of what caused disease. Reread lines 105–125. In what ways did the Spanish and the Karankawas have similiar ideas about healing?

Comprehension

1. **Summarize** What was life like for the Spaniards on the barges?

2. **Recall** What happened to Cabeza de Vaca's men when they tried to leave Galveston Island?

3. **Clarify** Why did the Karankawas enlist the Spaniards as healers?

Literary Analysis

4. **Make Inferences** Based on the events and reactions Cabeza de Vaca describes, what appears to be the Karankawas' view of the Spaniards? Cite details to support your answer.

5. **Examine Character Traits** What qualities of a **survivor** does Cabeza de Vaca demonstrate in each situation?

   • approaching Galveston Island (lines 10–17)

   • meeting the Karankawas (lines 41–46)

   • asking the Karankawas for help (lines 89–91)

   • adopting a new healing practice (lines 118–119)

6. **Evaluate a Primary Source** Review the information you collected about *La Relación* as you read. In what ways would you consider this account a valuable and reliable source of information? What are its shortcomings? Explain your conclusions.

7. **Make Generalizations About Historical Context** To understand the historical context of a work, you need to consult sources outside of the work for information. Identify three passages from *La Relación* that reflect ideas, values, or events from the author's time. Then, using the footnotes to the text and the background information on page 70 as sources, explain the historical context of each example. Based on your results, what generalizations can you make about 16th-century Spanish perspectives? Create a chart to organize your notes.

Examples from Text	Information from Other Sources
•	
•	•
•	•
	•
Generalizations About Historical Context	
•	
•	
•	

Literary Criticism

8. **Biographical Context** Later in life, Cabeza de Vaca spoke out against the enslavement of Native Americans. How might his experiences as a captive, trader, and healer among the Karankawas and other groups have influenced his position? Explain your answer, citing evidence from the text.

Vocabulary in Context

WORD LIST
cauterize
embody
ingratiate
inundate
locomotion
tarry

VOCABULARY PRACTICE

Choose the word that is not related in meaning to the other words.

1. (a) transit, (b) locomotion, (c) movement, (d) connection
2. (a) inane, (b) incompetent, (c) ingratiate, (d) inept
3. (a) deluge, (b) inundate, (c) wind, (d) overwhelm
4. (a) cauterize, (b) sear, (c) singe, (d) weep
5. (a) obtain, (b) dawdle, (c) tarry, (d) linger
6. (a) embody, (b) personify, (c) actualize, (d) construct

VOCABULARY IN WRITING

How do you suppose Cabeza de Vaca's men looked to the Karankawas when they first met? Write a brief description of the crew from the Karankawas' point of view. Include two or more vocabulary words. You could start like this.

> **EXAMPLE SENTENCE**
> The strangers on shore seemed to **embody** pure misery.

VOCABULARY STRATEGY: ETYMOLOGIES

The **etymology** of a word, or its origin and history, can provide insight into the word's meaning. Information about a word's etymology will often appear near the beginning or end of a dictionary entry, as in the following example:

cau•ter•ize (kô′tə-rīz′) *tr.v.* **-ized, -iz•ing, -iz•es 1.** To burn or sear with a cautery. **2.** To deaden, as to feelings or moral scruples. [Middle English *cauterizen,* from Late Latin *cautērizāre,* to cauterize, brand, from Latin *cautērium,* cautery.] **—cau•ter•i•za•tion** (-tər-ĭ-zā′shən) *n.*

PRACTICE Use a dictionary to answer these questions.

1. From what language did *oratorio* enter English?
2. From which Greek word is *cynosure* derived? What is the word's current meaning?
3. What is the origin of the word *malaprop?*
4. Through which languages can the history of *querulous* be traced?

VOCABULARY PRACTICE
For more practice, go to the **Vocabulary Center** at **ClassZone.com.**

Reading-Writing Connection

EXPLORER'S ACCOUNT Explorers often keep journals to record their experiences. These accounts—from the historical writings of Lewis and Clark to the reports of a modern astronaut—describe what the explorers see, when events on their journey occur, and how the writers are changed by their experiences.

Write a **two-to-four-paragraph journal entry** to describe an interesting moment in an exploration. Your journey can be real or fictional, physical or mental—a trip to a new town or a new galaxy, a trek across the desert or the race to a new invention. Be sure to share your reactions to it.

A successful journal entry will . . .

• be written in the first person, using the pronouns *I* and *me*

• clearly recount a specific event or moment in the writer's exploration

• vividly describe the surroundings, people, or events influencing the moment

• reveal the writer's reactions to the experience or event

GRAMMAR AND STYLE

ADD NECESSARY DETAILS Review the **Grammar and Style** note on page 74. Cabeza de Vaca uses numerous details throughout his account to help readers visualize his amazing journey. **Prepositional phrases** include details about what happens, as well as where, when, and how. Read this example from *La Relación*:

> *A single roll of the sea tossed the rest of the men into the rushing surf and back onto shore half-drowned.* (lines 63–64)

PRACTICE Rewrite each sentence, adding prepositional phrases that modify the boldfaced words. Follow the directions in parentheses. An example has been done for you.

EXAMPLE

The barges, filled with half-starved men, **drifted** for days. (Tell where they drifted.)

The barges, filled with half-starved men, drifted on the stormy seas for days.

---

1. They told us they **would return** and bring us food. (Tell when they will return.)

2. We **traveled** through the woods to the **village.** (Add two phrases. Tell how long they traveled and where the village was located.)

3. We waited anxiously for **news.** (Tell what kind of news was expected.)

WRITING TOOLS
For prewriting, revision, and editing tools, visit the **Writing Center** at ClassZone.com.

from The Interesting Narrative of the Life of Olaudah Equiano

Slave Narrative by Olaudah Equiano

Diagram of the cargo hold of a fully loaded slave ship

Olaudah Equiano

c. 1745–1797

Soldier, sailor, North Pole explorer—Olaudah Equiano led a remarkable life by the standards of any age. Writing as a former slave in the 1700s, Equiano left powerful testimony on the brutality of enslavement that became the model for a new genre, the slave narrative.

Ocean Crossings According to his autobiography, Equiano was born a chief's son in the Ibo (or Igbo) culture of present-day Nigeria. When he was 11, he was captured and sold as a slave to a series of African masters before making the miserable journey to the Americas known as the Middle Passage. Sold in the West Indies to British navy officer Michael Pascal, Equiano returned to sea with his new owner, who renamed him Gustavus Vassa.

Equiano spent years fighting for Britain, hoping to be freed for good service.

Instead, in 1762 he was sold again, to Quaker merchant Robert King, who trained him in business. In 1766, after 21 years as a slave, Equiano bought back his freedom, moved to London, and promptly launched his business career. But by 1773, he was at sea again, first on an expedition to find a northwest passage, and later traveling to Central America and Turkey.

Turning Points In the late 1770s, Equiano returned to London where he got involved in antislavery efforts and converted to Christianity. In 1789, as public debate over abolishing the slave trade began in Britain, Equiano wrote, self-published, and promoted his narrative. Equiano's life story exposed the cruelty of the slave trade and made him an important public figure. He died in 1797, just ten years before Britain abolished the slave trade.

Historians Look More Closely Equiano's narrative includes a wealth of specific details, most of which check out against other sources. But, in 1999, English professor Vincent Carretta uncovered two documents that suggested Equiano was not born in Africa: his baptismal record from England and a ship's passenger list, both of which identify Equiano's birthplace as South Carolina. Historians continue to debate the evidence and how, if at all, it changes the value of *The Interesting Narrative.* Carretta himself points out that even if the narrative is based on the oral accounts of other slaves, its descriptions still provide a valuable portrait of early African life and the Middle Passage.

● LITERARY ANALYSIS: SLAVE NARRATIVE

Few of us can imagine what slavery was really like. **Slave narratives,** the life stories of people who survived slavery, help us understand the grim realities of this experience.

Olaudah Equiano wrote *The Interesting Narrative* at a time when many Africans remembered their lives before enslavement. Like other 18th-century slave narratives, his work

- portrays the culture shock of a newly captured African
- focuses criticism on slave traders, not slave owners
- includes religious and moral appeals against slavery

As you read, note how the author develops these topics.

● READING SKILL: ANALYZE DETAILS

Equiano's readers had little contact with slavery. He chose powerful **descriptive details** to bring the experience to life.

The closeness of the place, and the heat of the climate, added to the number in the ship, which was so crowded that each had scarcely room to turn himself, almost suffocated us.

To reach his readers, Equiano uses

- **sensory details,** ones that appeal to the five senses
- descriptions of his own reactions
- **anecdotes,** brief stories that support his points

As you read, use a chart like the one shown to record effective examples of each kind of detail.

Sensory Details	Reactions	Anecdotes

▲ VOCABULARY IN CONTEXT

Equiano used the following words in his argument against slavery. Restate each phrase, using a different word or words for the boldfaced term.

1. **copious** amounts of rain, causing a flood
2. the **nominal** boss, but with no real authority
3. her **countenance** betraying her fear
4. cruel rulers acting without worry or **scruple**
5. to our **consternation,** revealed all our plans
6. deadly effects of **pestilential** beetles

Explore the Key Idea

What does it mean to be a SLAVE?

KEY IDEA From the 1500s to the 1800s, millions of Africans were enslaved to work in the Americas. Their experiences have been documented in books and portrayed in films. What do you know about the realities of **slavery?**

TEST YOURSELF Decide whether each statement is true or false. Think about the facts or impressions that helped you choose your answer.

SLAVERY: *Fact or Fiction*

1. Slavery was a common practice in Africa.
   ☐ TRUE   ○ FALSE

2. No Africans participated willingly in the slave trade.
   ☐ TRUE   ○ FALSE

3. Most enslaved Africans were brought to North America.
   ☐ TRUE   ○ FALSE

4. Captured Africans were packed like cargo into slave ships.
   ☐ TRUE   ○ FALSE

5. Slave traders typically sold families as a single group.
   ☐ TRUE   ○ FALSE

THE INTERESTING NARRATIVE
of the Life of Olaudah Equiano

OLAUDAH EQUIANO

> **BACKGROUND** As European colonies in the Americas expanded, so did the slave trade. Slaves were captured in Africa, then taken by ship to the West Indies—a journey called the Middle Passage. For two months, Africans lay tightly chained in storage compartments with hardly enough air to breathe. Millions died from bad food, harsh treatment, disease, and despair. Olaudah Equiano is one of the few to describe this horrific journey.

When Olaudah Equiano was 11 years old, he and his sister were kidnapped while the adults in his village were working in the fields. After being forced to travel for several days, Equiano and his sister were separated. For the next six or seven months, Equiano was sold several times to African masters in different countries. He was eventually taken to the west coast of Africa and carried aboard a slave ship bound for the West Indies.

The first object which saluted my eyes when I arrived on the coast, was the sea, and a slave ship, which was then riding at anchor, and waiting for its cargo. These filled me with astonishment, which was soon converted into terror, when I was carried on board. I was immediately handled, and tossed up to see if I were sound, by some of the crew; and I was now persuaded that I had gotten into a world of bad spirits, and that they were going to kill me. Their complexions, too, differing so much from ours, their long hair, and the language they spoke (which was very different from any I had ever heard), united to confirm me in this belief. **A**
Indeed, such were the horrors of my views and fears at the moment, that, if ten
10 thousand worlds had been my own, I would have freely parted with them all to

ANALYZE VISUALS
Describe the mood of this painting. What does the image reveal about the conditions on board a slave ship?

A **SLAVE NARRATIVE**
Note Equiano's use of **first-person point of view** in lines 1–8. In what ways might this description be startling to Equiano's mostly European audience?

Detail of *The Slave Ship* (1956), Robert Riggs. N.A. Courtesy of Les Mansfield, Cincinnati, Ohio.

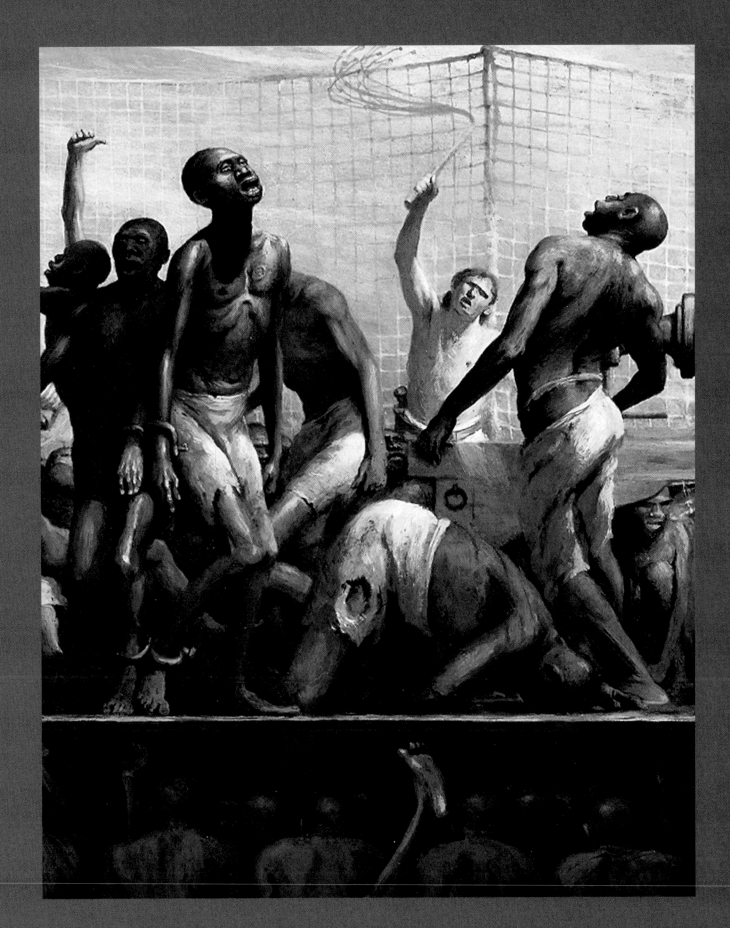

have exchanged my condition with that of the meanest slave[1] in my own country. When I looked round the ship too, and saw a large furnace of copper boiling, and a multitude of black people of every description chained together, every one of their **countenances** expressing dejection and sorrow, I no longer doubted of my fate; and, quite overpowered with horror and anguish, I fell motionless on the deck and fainted. When I recovered a little, I found some black people about me, who I believed were some of those who had brought me on board, and had been receiving their pay; they talked to me in order to cheer me, but all in vain. I asked them if we were not to be eaten by those white men with horrible looks, red faces, and long hair. They told me I was not, and one of the crew brought me a small portion of spirituous liquor in a wine glass; but, being afraid of him, I would not take it out of his hand. One of the blacks, therefore, took it from him and gave it to me, and I took a little down my palate, which, instead of reviving me, as they thought it would, threw me into the greatest **consternation** at the strange feeling it produced, having never tasted any such liquor before. Soon after this, the blacks who brought me on board went off, and left me abandoned to despair. **B**

I now saw myself deprived of all chance of returning to my native country, or even the least glimpse of hope of gaining the shore, which I now considered as friendly; and I even wished for my former slavery in preference to my present situation, which was filled with horrors of every kind, still heightened by my ignorance of what I was to undergo. I was not long suffered to indulge my grief; I was soon put down under the decks, and there I received such a salutation in my nostrils as I had never experienced in my life; so that, with the loathsomeness of the stench, and crying together, I became so sick and low that I was not able to eat, nor had I the least desire to taste anything. I now wished for the last friend, death, to relieve me; but soon, to my grief, two of the white men offered me eatables; and, on my refusing to eat, one of them held me fast by the hands, and laid me across, I think, the windlass,[2] and tied my feet, while the other flogged[3] me severely. I had never experienced anything of this kind before, and, although not being used to the water, I naturally feared that element the first time I saw it, yet, nevertheless, could I have got over the nettings,[4] I would have jumped over the side, but I could not; and besides, the crew used to watch us very closely who were not chained down to the decks, lest we should leap into the water; and I have seen some of these poor African prisoners most severely cut, for attempting to do so, and hourly whipped for not eating. This indeed was often the case with myself. In a little time after, amongst the poor chained men, I found some of my own nation, which in a small degree gave ease to my mind. I inquired of these what was to be done with us? They gave me to understand, we were to be carried to these white people's country to work for them. I then was a little revived, and thought, if it were no worse than working, my situation was not so desperate; but still I feared

countenance
(koun'tə-nəns) *n.*
appearance, especially the expression of the face

consternation
(kŏn'stər-nā'shən) *n.*
a state of paralyzing dismay; fear

B ANALYZE DETAILS
Reread lines 1–26. What details reinforce Equiano's impression that he has been captured by bad spirits?

---

1. **the meanest slave:** the poorest or most wretched slave.
2. **windlass** (wĭnd'ləs): a device for raising and lowering a ship's anchor.
3. **flogged:** beat with a whip or rod.
4. **nettings:** networks of small ropes on the sides of a ship that were used for various purposes, such as stowing sails. On slave ships, the nettings helped keep the slaves from jumping overboard.

I should be put to death, the white people looked and acted, as I thought, in so savage a manner; for I had never seen among any people such instances of brutal cruelty; and this not only shown towards us blacks, but also to some of the whites themselves. One white man in particular I saw, when we were permitted to be on deck, flogged so unmercifully with a large rope near the foremast,[5] that he died in consequence of it; and they tossed him over the side as they would have done a brute. This made me fear these people the more; and I expected nothing less ⓒ than to be treated in the same manner. I could not help expressing my fears and apprehensions to some of my countrymen; I asked them if these people had no coun-
60 try, but lived in this hollow place (the ship)? They told me they did not, but came from a distant one. "Then," said I, "how comes it in all our country we never heard of them?" They told me because they lived so very far off. I then asked where were their women? had they any like themselves? I was told they had. "And why," said I, "do we not see them?" They answered, because they were left behind. I asked how the vessel could go? They told me they could not tell; but that there was cloth put upon the masts by the help of the ropes I saw, and then the vessel went on; and the white men had some spell or magic they put in the water when they liked, in order to stop the vessel. I was exceedingly amazed at this account, and really thought they were spirits. I therefore wished much to be from amongst them, for I expected they
70 would sacrifice me; but my wishes were vain—for we were so quartered that it was impossible for any of us to make our escape. . . . ⓓ

At last, when the ship we were in, had got in all her cargo, they made ready with many fearful noises, and we were all put under deck, so that we could not see how they managed the vessel. But this disappointment was the least of my sorrow. The stench of the hold while we were on the coast was so intolerably loathsome, that it was dangerous to remain there for any time, and some of us had been permitted to stay on the deck for the fresh air; but now that the whole ship's cargo were confined together, it became absolutely **pestilential.** The closeness of the place, and the heat of the climate, added to the number in the ship, which
80 was so crowded that each had scarcely room to turn himself, almost suffocated us. This produced **copious** perspirations, so that the air soon became unfit for respiration, from a variety of loathsome smells, and brought on a sickness among the slaves, of which many died. . . . This wretched situation was again aggravated by the galling[6] of the chains. . . . The shrieks of the women, and the groans of the dying, rendered the whole a scene of horror almost inconceivable. Happily perhaps, for myself, I was soon reduced so low here that it was thought necessary to keep me almost always on deck; and from my extreme youth I was not put in fetters. In this situation I expected every hour to share the fate of my companions, some of whom were almost daily brought upon deck at the point of death, which I began
90 to hope would soon put an end to my miseries. . . . ⓔ

One day they had taken a number of fishes; and when they had killed and satisfied themselves with as many as they thought fit, to our astonishment who

ⓒ **GRAMMAR AND STYLE**
Reread lines 54–57. Note how Equiano uses **adverb clauses,** such as "when we were permitted to be on deck," to modify verbs and adverbs in the sentence.

ⓓ **SLAVE NARRATIVE**
Look back at lines 48–52. What does Equiano's reaction reveal about the way he regards slavery?

pestilential (pĕs′tə-lĕn′shəl) adj. deadly; poisonous

copious (kō′pē-əs) adj. in large amounts; abundant

ⓔ **ANALYZE DETAILS**
What details in lines 75–85 does Equiano use to describe conditions below decks?

5. **foremast** (fôr′məst): the mast (tall pole that supports sails and rigging) nearest the forward end of a sailing ship.

6. **galling:** rubbing or chafing, enough to produce sores.

were on deck, rather than give any of them to us to eat, as we expected, they tossed the remaining fish into the sea again, although we begged and prayed for some as well as we could, but in vain; and some of my countrymen, being pressed by hunger, took an opportunity, when they thought no one saw them, of trying to get a little privately; but they were discovered, and the attempt procured them some very severe floggings. One day, when we had a smooth sea and moderate wind, two of my wearied countrymen who were chained together (I was near

100 them at the time), preferring death to such a life of misery, somehow made through the nettings and jumped into the sea; immediately, another quite dejected fellow, who, on account of his illness, was suffered to be out of irons, also followed their example; and I believe many more would very soon have done the same, if they had not been prevented by the ship's crew, who were instantly alarmed. . . .

During the rest of his voyage to the West Indies, Equiano continued to endure hardships. After the ship anchored on the coast of Barbados, Equiano and the other slaves were brought ashore and herded together in a slave merchant's yard to be sold.

We were not many days in the merchant's custody, before we were sold after their usual manner, which is this: On a signal given (as the beat of a drum), the buyers rush at once into the yard where the slaves are confined, and make choice of that parcel[7] they like best. The noise and clamor with which this is attended, and the eagerness visible in the countenances of the buyers, serve not a little to

110 increase the apprehension of terrified Africans, who may well be supposed to consider them as the ministers of that destruction to which they think themselves devoted. In this manner, without **scruple,** are relations and friends separated, most of them never to see each other again. I remember, in the vessel in which I was brought over, in the men's apartment, there were several brothers, who, in the sale, were sold in different lots; and it was very moving on this occasion, to see and hear their cries at parting. O, ye **nominal** Christians! might not an African ask you—Learned you this from your God, who says unto you, Do unto all men as you would men should do unto you? Is it not enough that we are torn from our country and friends, to toil for your luxury and lust of gain? Must every tender

120 feeling be likewise sacrificed to your avarice? Are the dearest friends and relations now rendered more dear by their separation from their kindred, still to be parted from each other, and thus prevented from cheering the gloom of slavery, with the small comfort of being together, and mingling their sufferings and sorrows? Why are parents to lose their children, brothers their sisters, or husbands their wives? Surely, this is a new refinement in cruelty, which . . . thus aggravates distress, and adds fresh horrors even to the wretchedness of slavery. ❧ **F**

scruple (skrōō′pəl) *n.* feeling of uneasiness or guilt that keeps a person from doing something

nominal (nŏm′ə-nəl) *adj.* in name but not in reality

F **SLAVE NARRATIVE**
What point is Equiano making in lines 116–118? To what emotions is he appealing?

---

7. **parcel:** a group of slaves offered for sale as one "package."

Comprehension

1. **Recall** Who has brought Equiano to the slave ship?

2. **Recall** What does Equiano think will happen to him when he is brought on board ship?

3. **Clarify** What does Equiano mean when he refers to "nominal Christians"?

Literary Analysis

4. **Analyze Descriptive Details** Review the chart you made while reading. Identify the details that had the strongest impact on you as a reader. Why were those details so effective?

5. **Make Inferences About Cultural Context** Equiano portrays himself as an African encountering Europeans for the very first time. By describing his shocked and confused responses to the men of this different culture, Equiano reveals clues about African beliefs and customs. In each example, what inferences can you make about the narrator's cultural context?

   - his fears of white men (lines 18–20)
   - how he responds to fellow Africans (lines 20–23)
   - his questions about the ship (lines 59–68)
   - his reactions to cruelty around him (lines 50–57 and 91–95)

6. **Compare and Contrast** Like Cabeza de Vaca, Equiano describes a journey to the Americas. In what ways does his narrative resemble *La Relación?* Identify at least two similarities and two differences.

7. **Synthesize Information** Review your answers to the quiz about **slavery** that you took before reading Equiano's narrative. What facts or details in his account most surprised you? Correct your quiz answers to reflect what you learned.

8. **Evaluate a Slave Narrative** Some historians have questioned whether Equiano's narrative is authentic. Read the information on this debate in the author's biography on page 78. Based on the issues raised, what you have learned about slave narratives, and your own reading, make an argument for or against the historical value of Equiano's account. Support your answer with details.

Literary Criticism

9. **Biographical Context** In 1775, just 14 years before writing his life story, Equiano bought slaves to work on his Central American plantation. He explained his actions by saying he did what he could "to comfort the poor creatures, and render their condition easy." Do you find this explanation consistent with the views of slavery put forth in *The Interesting Narrative?* Cite evidence from the text to support your answer.

Vocabulary in Context

VOCABULARY PRACTICE

Choose the letter of the phrase that defines or is related to the boldfaced word.

1. **countenance:** (a) a sad expression, (b) a well-toned body, (c) a cash register
2. **consternation:** (a) a freight ship, (b) a serious accident, (c) a peace treaty
3. **copious:** (a) a nest of baby birds, (b) a xerographic machine, (c) a 20-inch snowfall
4. **pestilential**: (a) a contagious disease, (b) a cooking implement, (c) a vegetarian meal
5. **scruple:** (a) an attack of conscience, (b) a two-handed card game, (c) a ruffle on a skirt
6. **nominal:** (a) a stretch limousine, (b) a word derived from a foreign language, (c) a leader with no real power

WORD LIST
consternation
copious
countenance
nominal
pestilential
scruple

VOCABULARY IN WRITING

Imagine yourself as an observer at a slave auction in early America. Using three or more vocabulary words, write a brief description of what you might have observed. Here is a sample beginning.

> **EXAMPLE SENTENCE**
>
> On the **countenance** of every prisoner to be sold at the auction was an expression of terror and panic.

VOCABULARY STRATEGY: THE LATIN ROOT *nom*

The vocabulary word *nominal* contains the Latin root *nom*, which means "name." This root is found in a number of English words. To understand words with *nom*, use context clues as well as your knowledge of the root.

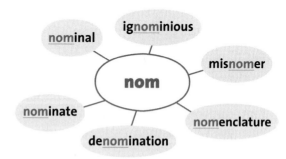

PRACTICE Choose the word from the word web that best completes each sentence. Consider what you know about the Latin root *nom* and other word parts shown. If necessary, consult a dictionary.

1. The president decided to _____ a young woman to fill the job.
2. It is a real_____ to call this stringy meat "tenderloin."
3. Scientific _____ often makes use of Latin words.
4. The 20-dollar bill is a _____ that is frequently counterfeited.
5. After that _____ defeat, he was ashamed to show his face.

VOCABULARY PRACTICE
For more practice, go to the **Vocabulary Center** at ClassZone.com.

Reading-Writing Connection

WRITING PROMPT

WRITE A PERSONAL LETTER Equiano writes about his experiences for readers who did not know him personally. By contrast, in a personal letter, the relationship between the writer and the audience influences the language and details chosen by the writer to convey his or her message.

Choose an experience or a scene you want to describe. Write a **one-page personal letter** to communicate your observations to someone close to you. Include details that are especially meaningful to your audience.

SELF-CHECK

A successful letter will . . .

- be written in the first person, using the pronouns *I* or *me*
- address a familiar audience
- include language appropriate to the audience
- conform to standard letter-writing formats

GRAMMAR AND STYLE

ADD DESCRIPTIVE DETAILS Review the **Grammar and Style** note on page 83. Equiano uses elaborate and richly detailed sentences to describe his experiences. Some of the details are contained in **adverb clauses,** as in this example:

> *These filled me with astonishment, which was soon converted into terror, when I was carried on board.* (lines 2–4)

In this sentence, the adverb clause modifies *filled,* describing when the action occurred. Adverb clauses also help answer the questions *where, why, how,* or *to what degree.* Like other **subordinate clauses,** adverb clauses include a subject and a predicate, but they cannot stand alone as independent sentences. They are often introduced with words such as *as if, because, since, so that, until, while, when,* or *where.*

PRACTICE Add adverb clauses to the following sentences to modify the boldfaced words, as instructed in parentheses. A sample answer has been done for you.

EXAMPLE

He **saw** the ship for the first time. (Tell when he saw it.)

He saw the ship for the first time when he arrived at the harbor.

---

1. The men on the ship **had been captured.** (Tell why they were captured.)

2. The prisoners **were kept** in the ship's hold. (Tell how long they were kept there.)

3. Many slaves **became** ill. (Add two details. Tell why and when the slaves became ill.)

WRITING TOOLS
For prewriting, revision, and editing tools, visit the **Writing Center** at ClassZone.com.

from The General History of Virginia

Historical Narrative by John Smith

John Smith
c. 1580–1631

Replicas of Jamestown ships

The author of one of the earliest works of American literature continues to inspire widely varied reactions among historians. Called a boastful bully by some and an early American hero by others, John Smith created a legend around himself that lasts to this day.

Great Adventures At age 16, Smith left England to become a soldier for hire and occasional pirate. In 1605, after traveling to Austria, Turkey, and North Africa, he returned to England. Smith's military experience made him a good leader in the eyes of the Virginia Company, the group of investors hoping for huge profits from their New World venture. They hired him to help run the Jamestown colony, where he arrived in 1607.

Struggles for Control Conflicts broke out in Jamestown almost immediately. The first president died and the next two were deposed; colonists mutinied and deserted the colony, living in the nearby woods. Smith took control of the colony in 1608. As he tells it, he focused on survival—safety, shelter, and food—and led forcefully, pushing settlers of all social levels to work as hard as he did. History tells us a slightly different story: Smith was nearly executed for the deaths of two colonists on an expedition he led. It also tells us, however, that Jamestown thrived under his command and fell into greed, chaos, and starvation after his departure in 1610.

Fact or Fiction? Shortly after arriving in Virginia, John Smith was captured by the Powhatan Indians. Smith writes several times of his 1607 capture and of being brought before the tribe's leader, Powhatan. Only in the final version, the 1624 *General History of Virginia,* does Smith mention his rescue by Powhatan's daughter Pocahontas, who would have been ten years old at the time. The story may have been an attempt by Smith to cash in on Pocahontas's later fame: she had visited England in 1616 and become a celebrity.

In the meantime, Smith had fallen on hard times. After one early success, his attempts to colonize New England were dismal failures. Smith wanted to prove that hard work was the smartest way to develop a colony, but he never got his chance. He made his living from tales of his adventurous life and died unemployed in London in 1631.

● LITERARY ANALYSIS: NARRATOR

A **narrator** is the voice that tells a story. The voice an author chooses shapes the way readers perceive the events described. Most nonfiction authors write about themselves in the **first person.** John Smith writes about himself mostly in the **third person,** using a voice that sounds like an objective observer.

As you read, notice how Smith uses the narrator to portray himself and his role in events. Consider how the third-person point of view affects your perceptions of the account.

● READING STRATEGY: READING OLDER TEXTS

Reading centuries-old texts can be like reading a foreign language. Here are some strategies you can use to confront common difficulties in reading older texts:

- Replace unclear pronouns with names.
- Simplify difficult **syntax** (word order) by paraphrasing. For a difficult sentence, first establish who is doing what. Then sort out the meaning in the phrases and clauses.
- Use footnotes or side notes to translate **archaic expressions,** words and phrases no longer in use.
- Focus on key details by setting a purpose for reading.

In this case, your purpose for reading is to make sense of the conflicts among the Jamestown colonists. Use a chart like the one shown to take notes about these key individuals.

Individuals	Connection to Smith	Actions
President Wingfield		
Captain Kendall		
Robinson and Emry		
George Cassen		

▲ VOCABULARY IN CONTEXT

Choose words from the list to complete the phrases below.

WORD LIST	depose	industry	mollify
	entreaty	interim	

1. a corrupt leader whom they voted to _____
2. a peacemaker trying to _____ the unruly crowd
3. a desperate _____ for our assistance
4. admired by co-workers for her _____

Explore the Key Idea

What makes a LEADER?

KEY IDEA In some societies, like 17th-century Britain, leaders were chosen on the basis of their social status. But men used to luxury and privilege didn't thrive in the Jamestown colony, where hard work and scarce supplies were facts of daily life. In this context, where leaders needed common sense and determination to succeed, a new standard of **leadership** emerged.

DISCUSS Working with a small group, brainstorm examples of strong leaders who demonstrate different leadership styles. Use your examples to debate the pros and cons of each style. Is any one style best in all situations?

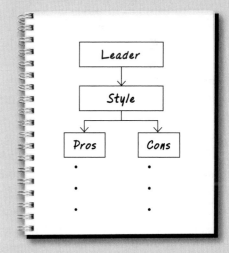

THE GENERAL HISTORY OF VIRGINIA

John Smith

BACKGROUND The Jamestown colony was modeled after a military expedition, transplanting about 100 hardy men into the Virginia wilderness in May 1607. Five members of Jamestown's ruling council—Edward Wingfield, Bartholomew Gosnold, John Ratcliffe, George Kendall, and John Smith—soon found themselves wrestling for control of the colony. As Smith's account opens, the colonists' ships have returned to England for supplies, leaving the men to survive on their own.

ANALYZE VISUALS
Which details of this map do not seem realistic? Explain what helps you distinguish accurate details from fictitious ones.

The Struggle for Jamestown

Being thus left to our fortunes, it fortuned that within ten days, scarce ten amongst us could either go or well stand, such extreme weakness and sickness oppressed us. And thereat none need marvel if they consider the cause and reason which was this: While the ships stayed, our allowance was somewhat bettered by a daily proportion of biscuit which the sailors would pilfer to sell, give, or exchange with us for money, sassafras, furs, or love. But when they departed, there remained neither tavern, beer-house, nor place of relief but the common kettle. Had we been as free from all sins as [we were free from] gluttony and drunkenness we might have been canonized 10 for saints, but our President [Edward Wingfield] would never have been admitted for engrossing to his private, oatmeal, sack, oil, aqua vitae, beef, eggs, or what not but the kettle; that indeed he allowed equally to be distributed, and that was half a pint of wheat and as much barley boiled with water for a man a day, and this, having fried some twenty-six weeks in the ship's hold, contained as many worms as grains so that we might truly call it rather so much bran than corn; our drink was water, our lodgings castles in the air. **A**

6 **sassafras:** A kind of tree believed to have medical properties.

8 **common kettle:** food that was available to everyone.

11 **engrossing to his private:** taking for his private use; **sack:** wine; **aqua vitae:** brandy.

A OLDER TEXTS
Using the side notes, restate lines 8–12 in modern English. What joke is Smith making?

Arrival of the English in Virginia (1585–1588), Theodore de Bry. Engraving © Giraudon/Art Resource, New York.

With this lodging and diet, our extreme toil in bearing and planting palisades so strained and bruised us and our continual labor in the extremity
20 of the heat had so weakened us, as were cause sufficient to have made us as miserable in our native country or any other place in the world.

From May to September, those that escaped lived upon sturgeon and sea crabs. Fifty in this time we buried; the rest seeing the President's projects to escape these miseries in our pinnace by flight (who all this time had neither felt want nor sickness) so moved our dead spirits as we **deposed** him and established Ratcliffe in his place (Gosnold being dead), Kendall deposed. Smith newly recovered, Martin and Ratcliffe were by his care preserved and relieved, and the most of the soldiers recovered with the skillful diligence of Master Thomas Wotton our surgeon general. **B**

30 But now was all our provision spent, the sturgeon gone, all helps abandoned, each hour expecting the fury of the savages, when God, the patron of all good endeavors, in that desperate extremity so changed the hearts of the savages that they brought such plenty of their fruits and provision as no man wanted.

The new President [Ratcliffe] and Martin, being little beloved, of weak judgment in dangers, and less **industry** in peace, committed the managing of all things abroad to Captain Smith, who, by his own example, good words, and fair promises, set some to mow, others to bind thatch, some to build houses, others to thatch them, himself always bearing the greatest task
40 for his own share, so that in short time he provided most of them lodgings, neglecting any for himself. . . . **C**

A Surprise Attack

Smith, perceiving (notwithstanding their late misery) not any regarded but from hand to mouth, (the company being well recovered) caused the pinnace to be provided with things fitting to get provision for the year following, but in the **interim** he made three or four journeys and discovered the people of Chickahominy, yet what he carefully provided the rest carelessly spent.

Wingfield and Kendall, living in disgrace strengthened themselves with the sailors and other confederates to regain their former credit and authority,
50 or at least such means aboard the pinnace (being fitted to sail as Smith had appointed for trade), to alter her course and to go for England.

Smith, unexpectedly returning, had the plot discovered to him, much trouble he had to prevent it, till with the store of saker and musket shot he forced them [to] stay or sink in the river: which action cost the life of Captain Kendall.

These brawls are so disgustful, as some will say they are better forgotten, yet all men of good judgment will conclude it were better their baseness should be manifest to the world, than the business bear the scorn and shame of their excused disorders.

19 **palisades:** walls made of tall, pointed wooden stakes.

24 **pinnace:** a small sailing ship.

depose (dǐ-pōz′) v. to remove from rule

B OLDER TEXTS
Reread lines 27–28. **Clarify** the pronoun referent for the word *his* in line 27. Who is responsible for healing Martin and Ratcliffe?

industry (ǐn′də-strē) n. hard work; diligence

37 **abroad:** outside the palisades.

C NARRATOR
Reread lines 35–41. Do Smith's claims sound more or less credible than they would if stated by a **first-person narrator**? Give reasons for your answer.

interim (ǐn′tər-ǐm) n. period in between; interval

46 **Chickahominy** (chǐ′kə-hä′mə-nē): a river in Virginia.

52 **discovered:** revealed.
53 **saker:** cannon shot.

55 **Captain Kendall:** Kendall was executed for mutiny in 1607.

57–59 **it were . . . disorders:** It is better to reveal the troublemakers than to have the "business" of the colony get a bad name.

Illustration of Jamestown Fort, Virginia, about 1608. Getty Images.

60   The President and Captain Archer not long after intended also to have abandoned the country, which project also was curbed and suppressed by Smith.

    The Spaniard never more greedily desired gold than he [Smith] victual, nor his soldiers more to abandon the country than he to keep it. But [he found] plenty of corn in the river of Chickahominy, where hundreds of savages in divers places stood with baskets expecting his coming.

    And now the winter approaching, the rivers became so covered with swans, geese, ducks, and cranes that we daily feasted with good bread, Virginia peas, pumpkins, and putchamins, fish, fowl, and divers sort of wild
70 beasts as fast as we could eat them, so that none of our tuftaffety humorists desired to go for England.

    But our comedies never endured long without a tragedy, some idle exceptions being muttered against Captain Smith for not discovering the head of Chickahominy river and [he being] taxed by the Council to be too slow in so worthy an attempt. The next voyage he proceeded so far that with much labor by cutting of trees asunder he made his passage, but when his barge could pass no farther, he left her in a broad bay of danger of shot, commanding none should go ashore till his return, himself with two English and two savages went up higher in a canoe, but he was not long absent but
80 his men went ashore, whose want of government gave both occasion and opportunity to the savages to surprise one George Cassen whom they slew and much failed not to have cut off the boat and all the rest.

60 Captain Archer: Gabriel Archer had abandoned the colony and then returned. He did not support Smith.

63 victual: food.

69 putchamins: persimmons.
70 tuftaffety humorists: unreliable lace-wearers

73 exceptions: objections.

80–82 whose want . . . the rest: the men's lack of discipline in going ashore led to the surprise attack on Cassen; only by some failure on the attackers' side did the others survive.

Smith little dreaming of that accident, being got to the marshes at the river's head twenty miles in the desert, had his two men [Robinson and Emry] slain (as is supposed) sleeping by the canoe, while himself by fowling sought them victual, who finding he was beset with 200 savages, two of them he slew, still defending himself with the aid of the savage his guide, whom he bound to his arms with his garters and used him as a buckler, yet he was shot in his thigh a little, and had many arrows that stuck in his
90 clothes but no great hurt, till at last they took him prisoner. . . . **D**

At Powhatan's Court

At last they brought him to Werowocomoco, where was Powhatan, their Emperor. Here more than two hundred of those grim courtiers stood wondering at him, as [if] he had been a monster, till Powhatan and his train had put themselves in their greatest braveries. Before a fire upon a seat like a bedstead, he sat covered with a great robe made of raccoon skins and all the tails hanging by. On either hand did sit a young wench of sixteen or eighteen years and along on each side [of] the house, two rows of men and behind them as many women, with all their heads and shoulders painted red, many of their heads bedecked with the white down of birds, but every
100 one with something, and a great chain of white beads around their necks.

At his entrance before the King, all the people gave a great shout. The Queen of Appomattoc was appointed to bring him water to wash his hands, and another brought him a bunch of feathers, instead of a towel, to dry them; having feasted him after their best barbarous manner they could, a long consultation was held, but the conclusion was, two great stones were brought before Powhatan; then as many as could, laid hands on him, dragged him to them, and thereon laid his head and being ready with their clubs to beat out his brains, Pocahontas, the King's dearest daughter, when no **entreaty** could prevail, got his head in her arms and laid her own upon
110 his to save him from death, whereat the Emperor was contended he should live to make him hatchets, and her bells, beads, and copper, for they thought him as well of all occupations as themselves. For the King himself will make his own robes, shoes, bows, arrows, pots; plant, hunt, or do anything so well as the rest.

Two days after, Powhatan, having disguised himself in the most fearfulest manner he could, caused Captain Smith to be brought forth to a great house in the woods and there upon a mat by the fire to be left alone. Not long after, from behind a mat that divided the house, was made the most dolefulest noise he ever heard; then Powhatan more like a devil than a man,
120 with some two hundred more as black as himself, came unto him and told him now that they were friends, and presently he should go to Jamestown to send him two great guns and a grindstone for which he would give him the country of Capahowasic and forever esteem him as his son Nantaquoud.

So to Jamestown with twelve guides Powhatan sent him. That night they quartered in the woods, he still expecting (as he had done all this long time of his imprisonment) every hour to be put to one death or other, for all

84 **desert:** wilderness; **85–86 by fowling . . . victual:** hunted birds to find them food.

88 **garters:** shirtlaces; **buckler:** shield.

D NARRATOR
Reread lines 83–90. What details does the narrator include that suggest Smith is not responsible for the deaths of the two men?

94 **greatest braveries:** fanciest clothes.

102 **the Queen of Appomattoc** (ăp′ə-măt′ək): the leader of the nearby village of Appomattoc.

entreaty (ĕn-trē′tē) *n.* plea

112 **as well . . . themselves:** The Indians thought Smith had varied skills as they did.

122–123 **the country of Capahowasic** (căp′ə-hou′ə-sĭk′) . . . **Nantaquoud** (nŏn′tə-kwōōd′): Powhatan would give Smith control of a nearby village and also promised to think as highly of him as he did of his own son.

their feasting. But almighty God (by His divine providence) had **mollified** the hearts of those stern barbarians with compassion. The next morning betimes they came to the fort, where Smith having used the savages with
130 what kindness he could, he showed Rawhunt, Powhatan's trusty servant, two demi-culverins and a millstone to carry [to] Powhatan; they found them somewhat too heavy, but when they did see him discharge them, being loaded with stones, among the boughs of a great tree loaded with icicles, the ice and branches came so tumbling down that the poor savages ran away half dead with fear. But at last we regained some conference with them and gave them such toys and sent to Powhatan, his women, and children such presents as gave them in general full content. **E**

Now in Jamestown they were all combustion, the strongest preparing once more to run away with the pinnace; which, with the hazard of his life,
140 with saker falcon and musket shot, Smith forced now the third time to stay or sink.

Some, no better than they should be, had plotted with the President the next day to have him put to death by the Levitical law, for the lives of Robinson and Emry; pretending the fault was his that had led them to their ends; but he quickly took such order with such lawyers that he laid them by the heels till he sent some of them prisoners for England.

Now every once in four or five days, Pocahontas with her attendants brought him so much provision that saved many of their lives, that else for all this had starved with hunger.

150 His relation of the plenty he had seen, especially at Werowocomoco, and of the state and bounty of Powhatan (which till that time was unknown), so revived their dead spirits (especially the love of Pocahontas) as all men's fear was abandoned.

Thus you may see what difficulties still crossed any good endeavor; and the good success of the business being thus oft brought to the very period of destruction; yet you see by what strange means God hath still delivered it. ❧

mollify (mŏl′ə-fī′) *v.* to soothe; to reduce in intensity

131 **demi-culverins** (dĕm′ē-kŭl′vər-ĭnz): large cannons.

E **OLDER TEXTS**
Reread lines 128–137. **Paraphrase this passage to clarify its meaning. What does Smith do to keep his promise to Powhatan?**

143 **Levitical law:** According to the Book of Leviticus in the Bible, "He that killeth any man shall surely be put to death."

Comprehension

1. **Recall** Why does Ratcliffe become the leader of Jamestown?

2. **Recall** What leads to the killing of Captain Kendall?

3. **Clarify** How does Smith become Powhatan's captive?

4. **Summarize** What happens to Smith during his stay with Powhatan?

Literary Analysis

5. **Draw Conclusions About Attitudes** In each example, what conclusions can you draw about each man's idea of **leadership?**

   - Wingfield's distribution of supplies (lines 10–14)
   - Smith's criticism of the colonists (lines 42–47)
   - Smith's determination in dire circumstances (lines 63–64)
   - Powhatan's assumption about Smith's abilities (lines 111–114)

6. **Interpret Older Texts** Review the character chart you made. Consider Smith's connection to each character. What motives might have influenced Smith's portrayal of his fellow colonists? Cite details to support your answer.

7. **Make Inferences About Historical Context** Reread lines 91–102. Notice that Smith uses the terms *Emperor, King, Queen,* and *courtiers* to describe Native American tribal structures. What does this tell you about the time and place in which he lived?

8. **Examine a Historical Narrative** Smith's account of his explorations along the Chickahominy River is filled with details that suggest he is a hero. But if you read closely, he reveals that he was severely criticized for the way he performed. Reread lines 72–90, and record the coflicting information in a chart like the one shown. What accusations is Smith defending himself against?

Smith's Version	Accusations Against Him

9. **Evaluate Narrator** Consider Smith's use of **third-person point of view** as well as the **motives** that influenced his writing. Given these factors, is Smith a credible narrator? Evaluate the reliability of Smith's narrative as a source on the following topics. Give reasons for your answers.

   - daily life in Jamestown
   - Native American culture
   - Smith's own actions
   - conflicts in Jamestown

Literary Criticism

10. **Different Perspectives** If Wingfield had written a report, how might it have differed from Smith's description of these events? Cite details to support your answer.

Vocabulary in Context

VOCABULARY PRACTICE

Decide whether the words in each pair are synonyms or antonyms.

1. depose/appoint
2. interim/gap
3. mollify/anger
4. industry/diligence
5. entreaty/plea

WORD LIST

depose
entreaty
industry
interim
mollify

VOCABULARY IN WRITING

Write a brief explanation of the animosity and hard feelings that sprang up among members of Smith's expedition. Use two or more vocabulary words in your explanation. You might begin like this.

> **EXAMPLE SENTENCE**
>
> *Within Smith's expedition it was not uncommon to **depose** a leader or blame others for one's problems.*

VOCABULARY STRATEGY: MULTIPLE MEANINGS

Many words have more than one meaning. To make sense of what you read, you need to make sure you understand which meaning a writer intends. This is particularly true with words that are used as more than one part of speech, or with words that occur in older texts. For example, the noun *industry* usually refers to a specific branch of manufacture or trade. Smith uses it to mean "dedication to a task."

PRACTICE Determine the meaning of each boldfaced word as it is used in the sentence. Refer to a dictionary if you need to.

1. Was John Smith a **contemporary** of Olaudah Equiano?
2. The **gravity** of the situation required the presence of several police officers.
3. What **accommodations** have the two leaders managed to reach?
4. The governor intends to **commute** several prisoners' sentences.
5. At this point we cannot **countenance** any more delays.
6. The hotel employees **agitated** for better working conditions.

> **VOCABULARY PRACTICE**
> For more practice, go to the **Vocabulary Center** at ClassZone.com.

from **Of Plymouth Plantation**

Chronicle by William Bradford

NOTABLE QUOTE

"The difficulties were many, but not invincible."

FYI

Did you know that William Bradford . . .

- lost his first wife to drowning shortly after the *Mayflower* landed?
- sold one of his farms to help pay Plymouth Colony's debts?
- was elected governor of Plymouth 30 times?

Author Online

For more on William Bradford, visit the **Literature Center** at ClassZone.com.

Plymouth Plantation today

William Bradford

c. 1590–1657

Long before there were holiday legends of Pilgrims and Indians, a group of English Puritans set off to create a new, pure society in the North American wilderness. Their leader was William Bradford.

Early Rebel Born into a time of religious upheaval in England, Bradford joined the crusade for religious reform at age 12. He was inspired by the ideals of the Puritans, a Protestant religious group that wanted to purify the Church of England and create simpler, more democratic ways to worship. By 17, Bradford had joined the radical Puritans known as Separatists, who called for a total break with the official church.

Not surprisingly, the Separatists clashed with the king of England, who also headed the church. Emigration to North America offered the hope of freedom, and Bradford helped plan and finance the voyage across the Atlantic. In 1620, Bradford and his wife, Dorothy, left behind their four-year-old son to join nearly 40 other Separatists on the ship *Mayflower.* Facing the journey with typical resolve, Bradford described the group as "pilgrims," or religious wanderers, the name we use for them today.

A Natural Leader Although the Pilgrims initiated the voyage, they made up fewer than half of the ship's 102 passengers. During the long, difficult journey, disagreements broke out among the group, and Bradford took decisive action. He helped craft the Mayflower Compact, often called the first U.S. Constitution. Signed by the 41 men on board, the compact was an agreement to work together for the good of the entire group. And they kept their promise. In April 1621, when the *Mayflower* returned to England, not one colonist left Plymouth Colony—a tribute to Bradford's sound leadership.

Bradford was also effective in forging alliances with local Native American tribes such as the Wampanoag (wäm′pə-nō′ăg), a union of tribes led by Massasoit (măs′ə-soit′). The Wampanoag, who had lost 80 percent of their people to smallpox shortly before the Pilgrims' arrival, faced their own struggle to survive. Out of mutual need, Bradford and Massasoit created a strong alliance that lasted throughout their lifetimes.

Historian in the Making With a historian's instinct, Bradford saved many documents from the trip's planning phase. During his 30 years as governor, he continued to document the challenges of the growing colony, which owed its survival to his energy, vision, and expert diplomacy. His chronicle, *Of Plymouth Plantation,* is our best history of these adventurous times.

● LITERARY ANALYSIS: CULTURAL CHARACTERISTICS

Many texts, especially those about community life, reflect the **cultural characteristics** of the communities they describe, such as their shared beliefs, values, and goals. *Of Plymouth Plantation* is a record of the Pilgrims' efforts to create a model Puritan society. In it, William Bradford describes the outcome of an Indian attack.

Thus it pleased God to vanquish their enemies and give them deliverance; and by His special providence so to dispose that not any one of them were either hurt or hit....

Bradford's description makes it clear that the Pilgrims see the victory as a gift from God. As you read, consider what else Bradford's descriptions and sometimes subtle word choice reveal about Puritan ideals.

● READING STRATEGY: SUMMARIZE

When you **summarize,** you restate the **main ideas** and the most important **details** of what you read. This process will help you sift through Bradford's long, complex sentences for key information.

This excerpt from *Of Plymouth Plantation* has five sections. As you read each section, record

- the date or time of year events occur
- a one- or two-sentence summary of the section

> *Section*: *Their Safe Arrival at Cape Cod*
> *Time of Year:*
> *Summary:*

▲ VOCABULARY IN CONTEXT

The following boldfaced words help tell the story of the founding of Plymouth Colony. Use context clues to guess the meaning of each word, then write a brief definition.

1. found **solace** in the peaceful woodland setting
2. her survival was an act of **providence**
3. will **tender** her resignation in a letter
4. chose a **rendezvous** convenient for everyone
5. tried to **procure** enough food for the family
6. an illness **feigned** in order to avoid work

Explore the Key Idea

When does HARDSHIP unite us?

KEY IDEA Hard times can bring people together or tear them apart. For example, in a blackout after a serious storm, people could respond by sharing supplies or by stealing what they need from unprotected homes. When does facing **hardship** become a source of strength and unity rather than one of distrust and division?

DISCUSS Working with a small group, list events you know from history or from the news that imposed great hardships on a community. Compare situations that had a unifying effect with those that divided the community. Identify factors that may account for the different responses.

99

Of *Plymouth Plantation*

William Bradford

BACKGROUND By the time the Pilgrims landed at Cape Cod, the local Native American tribes had had 100 years of contact and conflict with European explorers. Squanto, who became the Pilgrims' interpreter, had learned English when he was kidnapped by an English expedition in 1605. The Nauset Indians, who attacked the Pilgrims shortly after their arrival, had survived years of skirmishes with English explorers, including a 1609 battle with John Smith of Jamestown fame. Keep these events in mind as you read Bradford's account.

Their Safe Arrival at Cape Cod

But to omit other things (that I may be brief) after long beating at sea they[1] fell with that land which is called Cape Cod; the which being made and certainly known to be it, they were not a little joyful. . . .

Being thus arrived in a good harbor, and brought safe to land, they fell upon their knees and blessed the God of Heaven who had brought them over the vast and furious ocean, and delivered them from all the perils and miseries thereof, again to set their feet on the firm and stable earth, their proper element. . . . **A**

But here I cannot but stay and make a pause, and stand half amazed at this poor people's present condition; and so I think will the reader, too, when he

10 well considers the same. Being thus passed the vast ocean, and a sea of troubles before in their preparation (as may be remembered by that which went before), they had now no friends to welcome them nor inns to entertain or refresh their weatherbeaten bodies; no houses or much less towns to repair to, to seek for

ANALYZE VISUALS
Describe the landscape that awaits the travellers. What emotional response might they have had to this sight?

A CULTURAL CHARACTERISTICS
Reread lines 4–7. What does this paragraph reveal about the way Puritans viewed God?

---

1. **they:** Bradford refers to the Pilgrims in the third person, even though he is one of them.

The Landing of the Pilgrims (1803–1806), Michael Felice Corne. Tempera on canvas. Pilgrim Hall Museum. Plymouth, Massachusetts.

succor.[2] It is recorded in Scripture as a mercy to the Apostle and his shipwrecked company, that the barbarians showed them no small kindness in refreshing them,[3] but these savage barbarians, when they met with them (as after will appear) were readier to fill their sides full of arrows than otherwise. And for the season it was winter, and they that know the winters of that country know them to be sharp and violent, and subject to cruel and fierce storms, dangerous to travel to known
20 places, much more to search an unknown coast. Besides, what could they see but a hideous and desolate wilderness, full of wild beasts and wild men—and what multitudes there might be of them they knew not. Neither could they, as it were, go up to the top of Pisgah[4] to view from this wilderness a more goodly country to feed their hopes; for which way soever they turned their eyes (save upward to the heavens) they could have little **solace** or content in respect of any outward objects. For summer being done, all things stand upon them with a weatherbeaten face, and the whole country, full of woods and thickets, represented a wild and savage hue. If they looked behind them, there was the mighty ocean which they had passed and was now as a main bar and gulf to separate them from all the civil
30 parts of the world. . . . **B**

solace (sŏl'ĭs) *n.* comfort in sorrow or distress

B **SUMMARIZE**
Reread lines 16–30. What challenges confronted the colonists when they arrived at Cape Cod?

---

2. **to seek for succor:** to look for help or relief.

3. **It is . . . refreshing them:** a reference to the Biblical account of the courteous reception given to Paul ("the Apostle") and his companions by the inhabitants of Malta (Acts 27:41–28:2).

4. **Pisgah:** the mountain from whose peak Moses saw the Promised Land (Deuteronomy 34:1–4).

The First Winter of the Pilgrims in Massachusetts, 1620 (1800s). Colored engraving. The Granger Collection, New York.

The First Encounter

Being thus arrived at Cape Cod the 11th of November, and necessity calling them to look out a place for habitation (as well as the master's and mariners' importunity); they having brought a large shallop[5] with them out of England, stowed in quarters in the ship, they now got her out and set their carpenters to work to trim her up; but being much bruised and shattered in the ship with foul weather, they saw she would be long in mending. Whereupon a few of them **tendered** themselves to go by land and discover those nearest places, whilst the shallop was in mending; . . .

After this, the shallop being got ready, they set out again for the better discovery
40 of this place, and the master of the ship desired to go himself. So there went some thirty men but found it to be no harbor for ships but only for boats. There was also found two of their [the Indians'] houses covered with mats, and sundry of their implements in them, but the people were run away and could not be seen. Also there was found more of their corn and of their beans of various colors; the corn and beans they [the English] brought away, purposing to give them [the Indians] full satisfaction when they should meet with any of them as, about some six months afterward they did, to their good content.[6]

And here is to be noted a special **providence** of God, and a great mercy to this poor people, that here they got seed to plant them corn the next year, or else they
50 might have starved, for they had none nor any likelihood to get any till the season had been past, as the sequel did manifest.[7] Neither is it likely they had had this, if the first voyage had not been made, for the ground was now all covered with snow and hard frozen; but the Lord is never wanting unto His in their greatest needs; let His holy name have all the praise. **C**

The month of November being spent in these affairs, and much foul weather falling in, the 6th of December they sent out their shallop again with ten of their principal men and some seamen, upon further discovery, intending to circulate that deep bay of Cape Cod. The weather was very cold and it froze so hard as the spray of the sea lighting on their coats, they were as if they had been
60 glazed. . . . [The next night they landed and] made them a barricado[8] as usually they did every night, with logs, stakes, and thick pine boughs, the height of a man, leaving it open to leeward,[9] partly to shelter them from the cold and wind (making their fire in the middle and lying round about it) and partly to defend them from any sudden assaults of the savages, if they should surround them; so being very weary, they betook them to rest. But about midnight they heard a hideous and great cry, and their sentinel called "Arm! arm!" So they bestirred them and stood to their arms and shot off a couple of muskets, and then the noise

---

tender (tĕn'dər) v. to offer formally

providence (prŏv'ĭ-dəns) n. an instance of divine care

C CULTURAL CHARACTERISTICS
Reread lines 48–54. What belief helps Bradford justify taking the corn?

---

5. **shallop** (shăl'əp): an open boat usually used in shallow waters.

6. **purposing ... content:** intending to repay the Nauset Indians for the corn and beans they took, as they in fact did, to the Indians' satisfaction, six months later.

7. **as the sequel did manifest:** as the events that followed proved to be the case.

8. **barricado** (băr'ĭ-kä'dō): a barrier for defense.

9. **to leeward:** on the side sheltered from the wind.

ceased. They concluded it was a company of wolves or such like wild beasts, for one of the seamen told them he had often heard such a noise in Newfoundland.

70 So they rested till about five of the clock in the morning; for the tide, and their purpose to go from thence, made them be stirring betimes. So after prayer they prepared for breakfast, and it being day dawning it was thought best to be carrying things down to the boat. But some said it was not best to carry the arms down, others said they would be the readier, for they had lapped them up in their coats from the dew; but some three or four would not carry theirs till they went themselves. Yet as it fell out, the water being not high enough, they laid them down on the bank side and came up to breakfast.

But presently, all on the sudden, they heard a great and strange cry, which they knew to be the same voices they heard in the night, though they varied
80 their notes; and one of their company being abroad came running in and cried, "Men, Indians! Indians!" And withal, their arrows came flying amongst them. Their men ran with all speed to recover their arms, as by the good providence of God they did. In the meantime, of those that were there ready, two muskets were discharged at them, and two more stood ready in the entrance of their **rendezvous** but were commanded not to shoot till they could take full aim at them. And the other two charged again with all speed, for there were only four had arms there, and defended the barricado, which was first assaulted. The cry of the Indians was dreadful, especially when they [the Indians] saw their men [the English] run out of the rendezvous toward the shallop to recover their arms, the Indians wheeling
90 about upon them. But some running out with coats of mail on, and cutlasses in their hands, they [the English] soon got their arms and let fly amongst them [the Indians] and quickly stopped their violence. . . .

rendezvous (rän′dä-vōō) *n.* a gathering place

Thus it pleased God to vanquish their enemies and give them deliverance; and by His special providence so to dispose that not any one of them were either hurt or hit, though their arrows came close by them and on every side [of] them; and sundry of their coats, which hung up in the barricado, were shot through and through. Afterwards they gave God solemn thanks and praise for their deliverance, and gathered up a bundle of their arrows and sent them into England afterward by the master of the ship, and called that place the First Encounter. . . .

The Starving Time

100 But that which was most sad and lamentable was, that in two or three months' time half of their company died, especially in January and February, being the depth of winter, and wanting houses and other comforts; being infected with the scurvy[10] and other diseases which this long voyage and their inaccommodate condition had brought upon them. So as there died some times two or three of a day in the foresaid time, that of 100 and odd persons, scarce fifty remained. And of these, in the time of most distress, there was but six or seven sound persons who to their great commendations, be it spoken, spared no pains night nor day, but with abundance of toil and hazard of their own health fetched them wood, made them fires, dressed them meat, made their beds, washed their loathsome clothes,

---

10. **scurvy** (skûr′vē): a disease caused by lack of vitamin C.

The First Thanksgiving (1914), Jennie Augusta Brownscombe. © Burstein Collection/Corbis.

110 clothed and unclothed them. . . . In a word, did all the homely and necessary
offices for them which dainty and queasy stomachs cannot endure to hear named;
and all this willingly and cheerfully, without any grudging in the least, showing
herein their true love unto their friends and brethren; a rare example and worthy
to be remembered. Two of these seven were Mr. William Brewster, their reverend
Elder, and Myles Standish, their Captain and military commander, unto whom
myself and many others were much beholden in our low and sick condition. And
yet the Lord so upheld these persons as in this general calamity they were not at all
infected either with sickness or lameness. . . . **D**

Indian Relations

All this while the Indians came skulking about them, and would sometimes show
120 themselves aloof off, but when any approached near them, they would run away;
and once they [the Indians] stole away their [the colonists'] tools where they had
been at work and were gone to dinner. But about the 16th of March, a certain
Indian came boldly amongst them and spoke to them in broken English, which
they could well understand but marveled at it. At length they understood by
discourse with him, that he was not of these parts, but belonged to the eastern
parts where some English ships came to fish, with whom he was acquainted
and could name sundry of them by their names, amongst whom he had got his
language. He became profitable to them in acquainting them with many things
concerning the state of the country in the east parts where he lived, which was
130 afterwards profitable unto them; as also of the people here, of their names,
number and strength, of their situation and distance from this place, and who was
chief amongst them. His name was Samoset. He told them also of another Indian
whose name was Squanto, a native of this place, who had been in England and
could speak better English than himself.

ANALYZE VISUALS
Contrast the scenery
in this image with the
landscape on page 102.
How has the view of
nature changed?

D **CULTURAL
CHARACTERISTICS**
Reread lines 106–114.
What values are
demonstrated by
the seven colonists'
responses to their ailing
companions?

Being, after some time of entertainment and gifts dismissed, a while after he came again, and five more with him, and they brought again all the tools that were stolen away before, and made way for the coming of their great Sachem,[11] called Massasoit. Who, about four or five days after, came with the chief of his friends and other attendance, with the aforesaid Squanto. With whom, after friendly
140 entertainment and some gifts given him, they made a peace with him (which hath now continued this 24 years) in these terms: **E**

E SUMMARIZE
Reread lines 122–141. What events led to the treaty with Massasoit?

    1. That neither he nor any of his should injure or do hurt to any of their people.

    2. That if any of his did hurt to any of theirs, he should send the offender, that they might punish him.

    3. That if anything were taken away from any of theirs, he should cause it to be restored; and they should do the like to his.

    4. If any did unjustly war against him, they would aid him; if any did war against them, he should aid them.

150 **5.** He should send to his neighbors confederates to certify them of this, that they might not wrong them, but might be likewise comprised in the conditions of peace.[12]

    6. That when their men came to them, they should leave their bows and arrows behind them.

After these things he returned to his place called Sowams,[13] some 40 miles from this place, but Squanto continued with them and was their interpreter and was a special instrument sent of God for their good beyond their expectation. He directed them how to set their corn, where to take fish, and to **procure** other commodities, and was also their pilot to bring them to unknown places for their
160 profit, and never left them till he died.

procure (prō-kyŏŏr′) *v.* to get by special effort; to obtain

First Thanksgiving

They began now to gather in the small harvest they had, and to fit up their houses and dwellings against winter, being all well recovered in health and strength and had all things in good plenty. For as some were thus employed in affairs abroad, others were exercised in fishing, about cod and bass and other fish, of which they took good store, of which every family had their portion. All the summer there was no want; and now began to come in store of fowl, as winter approached, of which this place did abound when they came first (but afterward decreased by degrees). And besides waterfowl there was great store of wild turkeys, of which they took many, besides venison, etc. Besides they had about a peck a meal a week
170 to a person, or now since harvest, Indian corn to that proportion. Which made many afterwards write so largely of their plenty here to their friends in England, which were not **feigned** but true reports. ❧

feigned (fānd) *adj.* not real; pretended **feign** *v.*

---

11. **Sachem** (sā′chəm): chief.

12. **He should send . . . peace:** Massasoit was to send representatives to other tribes to let them know about the treaty with the Pilgrims.

13. **Sowams** (sō′əmz): near the site of present-day Barrington, Rhode Island.

Comprehension

1. **Recall** What happens to the colonists during "the starving time"?

2. **Recall** Who is Squanto?

3. **Clarify** In what ways did the Wampanoag help the colonists survive?

Literary Analysis

4. **Make Inferences About Cultural Characteristics** Bradford's **word choice** and his choice of details provide subtle clues to Puritan beliefs. Reread Bradford's account of the arrival at Cape Cod (lines 4–30). What does his description reveal about Puritan attitudes toward nature? Use a chart like the one shown to gather evidence and make inferences.

5. **Analyze Outcomes** Using the **summary** chart you created as you read, review the events of the first year at Plymouth. How did events change the colonists'

   - prospects for survival?
   - impressions of Native Americans?
   - attitude toward the region?
   - sense of providence?

6. **Analyze Form** A **chronicle** is a chronological, objective account of historical events. What features of Bradford's narrative might have changed had he written a personal account of his experiences?

7. **Make Judgments** Review the terms of the treaty between the Plymouth colonists and the Wampanoag (lines 142–154). Notice which terms apply to both parties equally and which do not. In your opinion, is the treaty fair? Explain your answer.

8. **Evaluate Motivations** Which of the following most contributed to the colonists' willingness to face **hardships** together? Support your answer with details from Bradford's account and from the historical background provided.

   - Puritan values
   - fears of Indian attack
   - landscape and climate
   - the events of "the starving time"

Literary Criticism

9. **Different Perspectives** How might a Wampanoag historian's version of events differ from Bradford's? Choose an episode from *Of Plymouth Plantation* and cite specific details that might change to reflect this different perspective.

Vocabulary in Context

WORD LIST

feigned

procure

providence

rendezvous

solace

tender

VOCABULARY PRACTICE

Show you understand the vocabulary words by answering these questions.

1. If you wanted to **procure** something, would you go to a store or go swimming?
2. If someone's sorrow is **feigned,** is it genuine or bogus?
3. Is a **rendezvous** a good place to be alone?
4. What would be a sign of **providence**—an unexpected victory or a deadly accident?
5. Who would be in more need of **solace**—a person who has just won a race or someone whose grandmother has just died?
6. To **tender** yourself as a mayoral candidate, would you write a letter to the election board or tell a friend about your idea?

VOCABULARY IN WRITING

What experiences might have convinced the Pilgrims that their struggle was worthwhile? Using two or more vocabulary words, write a brief paragraph identifying a few positive things that happened. Here is a sample beginning.

> **EXAMPLE SENTENCE**
>
> *Despite many hardships, several events did provide **solace** for the Pilgrims.*

VOCABULARY STRATEGY: WORDS FROM FRENCH

Rendezvous is one of a number of words in English that comes directly from French. The meaning of some French words and terms may change slightly in English; *rendezvous,* for example, means "present yourself" in French. Other terms keep the same meaning. If you are not sure of the meaning of a French term when you hear or read it, it is a good idea to check a dictionary.

PRACTICE Create a three-column chart with these headings: *Term, Original Meaning,* and *Meaning in English.* Then, using a dictionary that contains etymologies, fill in the chart for each of the following terms.

1. laissez faire
2. vis-à-vis
3. hors d'oeuvre
4. noblesse oblige
5. faux pas
6. coup de grâce
7. esprit de corps
8. savoir-faire

VOCABULARY PRACTICE
For more practice, go to the **Vocabulary Center** at ClassZone.com.

Personal Accounts of Exploration and Settlement

The selections in this section not only provide information about life in early America but are also sources of insight into the personal challenges and moral conflicts that shaped so much of our colonial culture. Because they are all firsthand accounts, the reader's understanding of the events, places, and people described is colored by the very personal feelings of each writer. Their fears, opinions, and doubts help bring this long-past world to life, as shown here.

Pocahontas rescues John Smith.

"In that hour, I would have welcomed death rather than see so many around me in such a condition."
—**Álvar Núñez Cabeza de Vaca**

"I was soon put down under the decks, and there I received a salutation in my nostrils as I had never experienced in my life; so that, with the loathsomeness of the stench, and crying together, I became so sick and low that I was not able to eat.
—**Olaudah Equiano**

"That night they quartered in the woods, he still expecting (as he had done all this long time of his imprisonment) every hour to be put to one death or other, for all their feasting."
—**Captain John Smith**

"Besides, what could they see but a hideous and desolate wilderness, full of wild beasts and wild men—and what multitudes there might be of them they knew not."
—**William Bradford**

Extension

SPEAKING & LISTENING In a group of four students **debate** the following statement:

The narrators of the selections in this section are unreliable because of their personal and emotional involvement in the events and experiences they relate.

Writing to Evaluate

Review the selections beginning on page 68 and choose the one that gives you the most complete picture of an event, experience, or person. In a brief essay, describe the elements that help bring that selection to life.

Consider

- which selection had the greatest impact on you
- descriptive details, images, and dialogue that enhance meaning and aid visualization
- what the writer's personal feelings and opinions add to your understanding and interest in the work

Anne Bradstreet
1612–1672

To My Dear and Loving Husband *and* Upon the Burning of Our House, July 10th, 1666

Poetry by Anne Bradstreet

Anne Bradstreet was essentially the first notable American poet, man or woman. Considering that Puritan women were not encouraged to improve their minds—let alone express their ideas—this achievement is remarkable.

Coming to America Anne Dudley Bradstreet was born in England and raised on an estate, which her father managed for the Earl of Lincoln. With access to the earl's library, she received a good education. In 1628, 16-year-old Anne married Simon Bradstreet. Two years later, the young couple sailed for Massachusetts.

After her privileged upbringing, Anne Bradstreet was not prepared for the harsh living conditions of colonial America. Her religious faith helped her endure these hardships—as did writing poetry.

Personal Poetry Bradstreet focused primarily on the realities of her life—her husband, her eight children, and her house. In 1650, without her knowledge, Bradstreet's brother-in-law had some of her verses published in London in a volume titled *The Tenth Muse Lately Sprung Up in America.* It was the first book of poetry ever published by an American colonist.

Edward Taylor
1642?–1729

Huswifery

Poetry by Edward Taylor

For over 200 years, the work of Edward Taylor, one of colonial America's most inventive poets, remained unread. His poetry did not come to light until the 1930s when his long-forgotten manuscripts were discovered in the Yale University Library.

Frontier Parson and Poet Born in England, Taylor came to America in 1668 to escape religious persecution in his homeland. In 1671, after graduating from Harvard University, Taylor became the minister of a church in Westfield, Massachusetts. He held that position until his death 58 years later.

The wilderness town of Westfield presented many challenges to the highly intellectual Taylor. But he undertook his roles as farmer, physician, and minister with energy. He even called his flock to worship by beating a drum.

Like Anne Bradstreet—a volume of whose work he owned—Taylor wrote his poetry to glorify God. He found his subjects in human life, nature, and everyday activities. His poems on these topics served as a form of worship.

Author Online

For more on Anne Bradstreet and Edward Taylor, visit the **Literature Center** at ClassZone.com.

● LITERARY ANALYSIS: FIGURATIVE LANGUAGE

Like all poets, Puritan poets used **figurative language** to communicate ideas beyond the literal meaning of words. Figurative language helped the Puritan poets convey ideas about their religious faith and their personal lives. As you read, look for the following types of figurative language, also called **figures of speech,** in the poems by Anne Bradstreet and Edward Taylor:

- A **metaphor** is a figure of speech that directly compares two unlike things without using *like* or *as*. (*Our house is our nest.*)

- An **extended metaphor** is one that draws the comparison out and compares the two things at length and in many ways. (*Our house is our nest; we fly away only to return to its snug protection.*)

- **Personification** is a figure of speech in which an object, animal, or idea is given human characteristics. (*Our house wraps our family in a warm embrace.*)

- **Hyperbole** is a figure of speech in which the truth is exaggerated for emphasis. (*Our house means more to us than all the money in the world.*)

● READING STRATEGY: CLARIFY MEANING IN OLDER POETRY

When reading works from the Puritan era, it is important to stop and **clarify meaning** by rereading and restating difficult passages as needed in order to fully appreciate the literature. Be aware of the following as you read the Puritan poets:

- **Archaic language**—words that were once in common use but that are now considered old-fashioned or out-of-date

- **Inverted syntax**—sentence structure in which the expected order of words is reversed

As you read each poem, use a chart like the one shown to record and restate examples of archaic language and inverted syntax.

"Upon the Burning of Our House"	
Archaic Language	Inverted Syntax
"blest" (blessed)	"when rest I took" (when I took rest)

What do you VALUE *most?*

KEY IDEA The things that we **value** in life may be actual objects or they may be less tangible. For instance, a person might prize a favorite CD or jacket. On the other hand, the gift of family may outweigh more material possessions. The Puritan poets you are about to read valued family life and their religious faith above all things. What do you prize most in your life?

QUICKWRITE Imagine that a reality show has offered you the chance to win a million dollars. The catch is that you will have to give up an object, a person, or a belief that you truly value. Assume that you are not willing to make the sacrifice. Write a brief letter to explain why you must turn down the money.

To My Dear and Loving Husband

Anne Bradstreet

If ever two were one, then surely we.
If ever man were loved by wife, then thee;
If ever wife was happy in a man,
Compare with me, ye women, if you can.
5 I prize thy love more than whole mines of gold
Or all the riches that the East doth hold.
My love is such that rivers cannot quench, **A**
Nor ought but love from thee, give recompense.[1]
Thy love is such I can no way repay,
10 The heavens reward thee manifold, I pray.
Then while we live, in love let's so persevere[2]
That when we live no more, we may live ever. **B**

A FIGURATIVE LANGUAGE
Reread lines 5–7. How does the poet use **hyperbole** in these lines to emphasize her feelings for her husband?

B CLARIFY MEANING
Use conventional word order to restate the **inverted syntax** in lines 11–12. What relationship do the lines suggest between earthly love and eternal life?

ANALYZE VISUALS
Many Puritan women stitched samplers like the one shown here. The samplers often depicted nature scenes or stories from the Bible. What values are suggested by the subject matter of the sampler?

1. **recompense** (rĕk′əm-pĕns′): payment in return for something, such as a service.

2. **persevere**: In Bradstreet's time, *persevere* would have been pronounced pûr-səv′ər, which rhymes with *ever*.

Upon the Burning of Our House,
July 10th, 1666

Anne Bradstreet

In silent night when rest I took
For sorrow near I did not look
I wakened was with thund'ring noise
And piteous shrieks of dreadful voice.
5 That fearful sound of "Fire!" and "Fire!"
Let no man know is my desire. **C**

I, starting up, the light did spy,
And to my God my heart did cry
To strengthen me in my distress
10 And not to leave me succorless.[1]
Then, coming out, beheld a space
The flame consume my dwelling place.

And when I could no longer look,
I blest His name that gave and took,[2]
15 That laid my goods now in the dust:
Yea, so it was, and so 'twas just.
It was His own, it was not mine,
Far be it that I should repine;[3]

C CLARIFY MEANING
Paraphrase lines 1–6 to clarify their meaning. How does the poet use contrast to convey a sense of fear?

---

1. **succorless** (sŭk'ər-lĭs): without help or relief.
2. **I . . . took:** an allusion to Job 1:21 in the Bible—"The Lord gave, and the Lord hath taken away; blessed be the name of the Lord."
3. **repine:** to complain or fret; to long for something.

He might of all justly bereft,
20 But yet sufficient for us left.
When by the ruins oft I past,
My sorrowing eyes aside did cast,
And here and there the places spy
Where oft I sat and long did lie:

25 Here stood that trunk and there that chest,
There lay that store I counted best.
My pleasant things in ashes lie,
And them behold no more shall I.
Under thy roof no guest shall sit,
30 Nor at thy table eat a bit.

No pleasant tale shall e'er be told,
Nor things recounted done of old.
No candle e'er shall shine in thee,
Nor bridegroom's voice e'er heard shall be.
35 In silence ever shalt thou lie;
Adieu, Adieu, all's vanity.[4] **D**

Then straight I 'gin my heart to chide,[5]
And did thy wealth on earth abide?
Didst fix thy hope on mold'ring dust?
40 The arm of flesh didst make thy trust?
Raise up thy thoughts above the sky
That dunghill mists away may fly. **E**

Thou hast an house on high erect,
Framed by that mighty Architect,
45 With glory richly furnishéd,
Stands permanent though this be fled.
It's purchaséd and paid for too
By Him who hath enough to do. **F**

A price so vast as is unknown
50 Yet by His gift is made thine own;
There's wealth enough, I need no more,
Farewell, my pelf,[6] farewell my store.
The world no longer let me love,
My hope and treasure lies above.

D FIGURATIVE LANGUAGE
What does the use of **personification** in lines 29–36 reveal about the speaker's feelings for her house?

E CLARIFY MEANING
Use contemporary vocabulary to restate the **archaic language** in lines 37–40. What does the speaker chide, or scold, herself for?

F FIGURATIVE LANGUAGE
Reread lines 43–48. What two things does Bradstreet compare in the **metaphor** in these lines?

---

4. **all's vanity:** an allusion to Ecclesiastes 1:2 in the Bible—"All is vanity," meaning that all is temporary and meaningless.

5. **chide:** to scold mildly so as to correct or improve.

6. **pelf:** wealth or riches, especially when dishonestly acquired.

Huswifery   Edward Taylor

Make me, O Lord, Thy spinning wheel complete.
Thy holy word my distaff[1] make for me.
Make mine affections Thy swift flyers[2] neat,
And make my soul Thy holy spool to be.
5   My conversation make to be Thy reel,
And reel the yarn thereon spun of Thy wheel. **G**

Make me Thy loom then, knit therein this twine:
And make Thy holy spirit, Lord, wind quills:[3]
Then weave the web Thyself. The yarn is fine.
10 Thine ordinances make my fulling mills.[4]
Then dye the same in heavenly colors choice,
All pinked[5] with varnished flowers of paradise.

Then clothe therewith mine understanding, will,
Affections, judgment, conscience, memory;
15 My words and actions, that their shine may fill
My ways with glory and Thee glorify.
Then mine apparel shall display before Ye
That I am clothed in holy robes for glory. **H**

G CLARIFY MEANING
Huswifery means "housekeeping." What housekeeping activity is being described in lines 1–6?

H FIGURATIVE LANGUAGE
What **extended metaphor** does Taylor use throughout the poem to express his relationship to God?

---

1. **distaff:** staff on a spinning wheel for holding the wool or flax to be spun.
2. **flyers:** parts of spinning wheels that twist fibers into yarn.
3. **quills:** rods or spindles used to wind and hold yarn.
4. **fulling mills:** machines that beat and process woven cloth to make it denser and more compact.
5. **pinked:** decorated.

Comprehension

1. **Recall** In "To My Dear and Loving Husband," what does the speaker value more than gold?

2. **Recall** When the speaker in "Upon the Burning of Our House" wakes up to find her house on fire, what is her initial reaction?

3. **Clarify** The speaker in Taylor's "Huswifery" compares himself to a loom. Who or what is compared to the weaver?

Literary Analysis

4. **Clarify Meaning** Review the examples of **archaic language** and **inverted syntax** you recorded as you read the poems. How would you restate lines 19–20 of "Upon the Burning of Our House": "He might of all justly bereft, / But yet sufficient for us left"?

5. **Draw Conclusions** Use details from the two poems by Anne Bradstreet to explain what she reveals about her

   • marriage   • religious beliefs   • daily life

6. **Make Inferences** What did Bradstreet **value** more than her house? How did this help her accept the loss of her house by fire?

7. **Analyze Figurative Language** How do the "holy robes for glory" mentioned in line 18 of "Huswifery" complete the poem's **extended metaphor**?

8. **Evaluate Description** Why do you think Taylor used a typical Puritan housekeeping activity to express his religious faith?

9. **Compare Literary Works** What do the poems by Bradstreet and Taylor have in common? What distinguishes one poet's work from the other's? In a chart like the one shown, compare and contrast the poets' work, noting the religious views expressed, the formality of each poet's **style**, and the personality revealed. Use specific details from the poems to complete the chart.

	Bradstreet	Taylor
Religious Views		
Style		
Personality		

Literary Criticism

10. **Examine Social Context** The Puritans strongly disapproved of women writers. A Puritan minister even wrote a letter to his sister in England saying, "Your printing of a book, beyond the custom of your sex, doth rankly smell." In spite of this disapproval, do you think the Puritan community would have considered any aspects of Anne Bradstreet's poetry praiseworthy? Explain your answer.

from **Sinners in the Hands of an Angry God**

Sermon by Jonathan Edwards

Jonathan Edwards
1703–1758

When Jonathan Edwards delivered a sermon, with its fiery descriptions of hell and eternal damnation, people listened. Edwards believed that religion should be rooted in emotion rather than reason. Although 19th-century editors tried to tone down his style, Edwards is recognized today as a masterful preacher. In fact, he is considered by many to be America's greatest religious thinker.

A Spiritual Calling Born in East Windsor, Connecticut, Edwards was a child prodigy and entered what is now Yale University at the age of 12. While a graduate student there, Edwards experienced a spiritual crisis that led to what he later described as "religious joy." He came to believe that such an intense religious experience was an important step toward salvation.

In 1722, after finishing his education, Edwards followed the path of his father and grandfather and became a Puritan minister. In 1726, Edwards began assisting his grandfather, who was the minister at the parish church in Northampton, Massachusetts. When his grandfather died three years later, Edwards became the church's pastor.

Religious Revivalist Edwards soon became an effective preacher. In 1734 and 1735, he delivered a series of sermons that resulted in a great number of conversions. The converts believed they had felt God's grace and were "born again" when they accepted Jesus Christ.

Edwards's sermons helped trigger the Great Awakening, a religious revival that swept through New England from 1734 to 1750. The movement grew out of a sense among some Puritan ministers that their congregations had grown too self-satisfied. Delivered at the height of the Great Awakening, "Sinners in the Hands of an Angry God" is the most famous of Edwards's nearly 1,200 sermons.

Last Years Although Edwards inspired thousands, his church dismissed him in 1750 because he wanted to limit membership to those who had undergone conversion. A year later, Edwards went to Stockbridge, Massachusetts, where he became a missionary in a Native American settlement. In 1757, he accepted an appointment as president of what is now Princeton University.

By the time of Edwards's death the following year, the extremism of the Great Awakening had been rejected. However, his vision of humanity suspended, like a spider, over the burning pit of hell still maintains its emotional impact.

● LITERARY ANALYSIS: SERMON

A **sermon** is a form of religious persuasion in which a speaker exhorts listeners to behave in a more spiritual and moral fashion. Like all sermons, Jonathan Edwards's is shaped by

- **purpose**—why Edwards delivers the sermon
- **audience**—whom Edwards is addressing
- **context**—when and where Edwards delivers the sermon

As you read Edwards's sermon, look for passages that reveal his purpose, his audience, and the context for his delivery.

● READING SKILL: ANALYZE EMOTIONAL APPEALS

Emotional appeals are messages designed to persuade an audience by creating strong feelings rather than by providing facts and evidence. Writers often use **tone, imagery,** and **figurative language** to make these types of emotional appeals:

- **appeal to fear,** which taps into people's fear of losing their safety or security
- **appeal to pity,** which takes advantage of people's sympathy and compassion for others
- **appeal to vanity,** which relies on people's desire to feel good about themselves

As you read, use a chart like the one shown to record examples of language used to appeal to the audience's emotions.

Examples	Emotional Appeals
"arrows of death fly unseen"	appeals to fear by creating anxiety, unease

▲ VOCABULARY IN CONTEXT

Jonathan Edwards uses the listed words to help convey his spiritual message. Choose a word from the list that is a synonym for each of the numbered words.

WORD LIST	abhor	deliverance	mitigation
	abominable	discern	whet
	appease	incense	
	ascribe	induce	

1. detest   3. sharpened   5. attribute

2. easing   4. anger greatly

Explore the Key Idea

What keeps you IN LINE?

KEY IDEA A sense of **morality** probably keeps you from cheating on a test. In other words, you know cheating is wrong. But there are other reasons for behaving morally. Some people are anxious to please. Others fear the consequences of breaking the rules. Jonathan Edwards uses fear to get his point across in the sermon you're about to read. Is fear the best motivator?

ROLE-PLAY With a partner, take turns role-playing a conversation with a child who has been stealing. Your mission is to persuade him or her to stop. Before you begin, consider how best to keep the child in line. For example, you might frighten or shame the child or appeal to his or her pride.

Sinners in the Hands
of an
Angry God

Jonathan Edwards

BACKGROUND Jonathan Edwards delivered his sermon "Sinners in the Hands of an Angry God" in 1741 to a congregation in Enfield, Connecticut. Edwards read the sermon, as he always did, in a composed style, with few gestures or movements. However, the sermon had a dramatic effect on his parishioners, many of whom wept and moaned. Some even considered suicide.

ANALYZE VISUALS
This painting by Italian artist Giuseppe Arcimboldo presents an **allegory** of fire. What lesson or message does the painting seem to suggest about the meaning of fire?

We find it easy to tread on and crush a worm that we see crawling on the earth; so it is easy for us to cut or singe a slender thread that any thing hangs by; thus easy is it for God when he pleases to cast his enemies down to hell. . . .

They[1] are now the objects of that very same *anger* and wrath of God, that is expressed in the torments of hell. And the reason why they do not go down to hell at each moment, is not because God, in whose power they are, is not then very angry with them; as angry as he is with many miserable creatures now tormented in hell, who there feel and bear the fierceness of his wrath. Yea, God is a great deal more angry with great numbers that are now on earth; yea, doubtless, with many
10 that are now in this congregation, who it may be are at ease, than he is with many of those who are now in the flames of hell. Ⓐ

Ⓐ SERMON
Reread lines 8–11. Notice that Edwards directly addresses his **audience** in these lines. How do you imagine the audience responded to these words?

---

1. **they:** Earlier in the sermon, Edwards refers to all "unconverted men," whom he considers God's enemies. Unconverted men are people who have not been "born again," meaning that they have not accepted Jesus Christ.

Fire, allegory (1566), Giuseppe Arcimboldo. Painted for Emperor Maximillian II. Limewood, 66.5 cm × 51 cm. Inv. 1585. Kunsthistorisches Museum, Vienna. © Erich Lessing/Art Resource, New York.

So that it is not because God is unmindful of their wickedness, and does not resent it, that he does not let loose his hand and cut them off. God is not altogether such an one as themselves, though they may imagine him to be so. The wrath of God burns against them, their damnation does not slumber; the pit is prepared, the fire is made ready, the furnace is now hot, ready to receive them; the flames do now rage and glow. The glittering sword is **whet,** and held over them, and the pit hath opened its mouth under them. . . . **B**

20 Unconverted men walk over the pit of hell on a rotten covering, and there are innumerable places in this covering so weak that they will not bear their weight, and these places are not seen. The arrows of death fly unseen at noonday; the sharpest sight cannot **discern** them. God has so many different unsearchable ways of taking wicked men out of the world and sending them to hell, that there is nothing to make it appear, that God had need to be at the expense of a miracle, or go out of the ordinary course of his providence, to destroy any wicked man, at any moment. . . .

So that, thus it is that natural men[2] are held in the hand of God, over the pit of hell; they have deserved the fiery pit, and are already sentenced to it; and God is dreadfully provoked, his anger is as great towards them as to those that are actually 30 suffering the executions of the fierceness of his wrath in hell; and they have done nothing in the least to **appease** or abate that anger, neither is God in the least bound by any promise to hold them up one moment; the devil is waiting for them, hell is gaping for them, the flames gather and flash about them, and would fain[3] lay hold on them, and swallow them up; the fire pent up in their own hearts is struggling to break out: and they have no interest in any Mediator,[4] there are no means within reach that can be any security to them. In short, they have no refuge, nothing to take hold of. . . . **C**

The bow of God's wrath is bent, and the arrow made ready on the string, and justice bends the arrow at your heart, and strains the bow, and it is nothing but 40 the mere pleasure of God, and that of an angry God, without any promise or obligation at all, that keeps the arrow one moment from being made drunk with your blood. Thus all you that never passed under a great change of heart, by the mighty power of the Spirit of God upon your souls; all you that were never born again, and made new creatures, and raised from being dead in sin, to a state of new, and before altogether unexperienced light and life, are in the hands of an angry God. However you may have reformed your life in many things, and may have had religious affections, and may keep up a form of religion in your families and closets,[5] and in the house of God, it is nothing but his mere pleasure that keeps you from being this moment swallowed up in everlasting destruction. . . . **D**

50 The God that holds you over the pit of hell, much as one holds a spider, or some loathsome insect over the fire, **abhors** you, and is dreadfully provoked: his

---

2. **natural men:** people who have not been born again.

3. **would fain:** would rather.

4. **Mediator:** Jesus Christ, who mediates, or is the means of bringing about, salvation.

5. **closets:** private rooms for meditation.

whet (hwĕt) *adj.* sharpened **whet** *v.*

B EMOTIONAL APPEALS
Reread lines 14–18. What **imagery** does Edwards use to appeal to fear in these lines?

discern (dĭ-sûrn′) *v.* to perceive or recognize something

appease (ə-pēz′) *v.* to bring peace, quiet, or calm to; to soothe

C EMOTIONAL APPEALS
Loaded language, or words with strong emotional associations, can be used to influence an audience's attitude. What examples of loaded language do you see in lines 27–30?

D SERMON
Note that Edwards reveals the **purpose** of his sermon in lines 42–46. Why is he delivering this sermon?

abhor (ăb-hôr′) *v.* to regard with disgust

Babylon Burning. From the *Apocalypse of Saint John* (Revelations 18). Luther Bible, First Edition. 1530. Private collection. Photo © Art Resource, New York.

wrath towards you burns like fire; he looks upon you as worthy of nothing else, but to be cast into the fire; he is of purer eyes than to bear to have you in his sight; you are ten thousand times more **abominable** in his eyes, than the most hateful venomous serpent is in ours. You have offended him infinitely more than ever a stubborn rebel did his prince; and yet it is nothing but his hand that holds you from falling into the fire every moment. It is to be **ascribed** to nothing else, that you did not go to hell the last night; that you was suffered[6] to awake again in this world, after you closed your eyes to sleep. And there is no other reason to be 60 given, why you have not dropped into hell since you arose in the morning, but that God's hand has held you up. There is no other reason to be given why you have not gone to hell, since you have sat here in the house of God, provoking his pure eyes by your sinful wicked manner of attending his solemn worship.

abominable
(ə-bŏm′ə-nə-bəl) *adj.*
thoroughly detestable

ascribe (ə-skrīb′) *v.* to attribute to a specified cause or source

---

6. **you was suffered:** you were permitted.

Yea, there is nothing else that is to be given as a reason why you do not this very moment drop down into hell. **E**

O sinner! Consider the fearful danger you are in: it is a great furnace of wrath, a wide and bottomless pit, full of the fire of wrath, that you are held over in the hand of that God, whose wrath is provoked and **incensed** as much against you, as against many of the damned in hell. You hang by a slender thread, with the
70 flames of divine wrath flashing about it, and ready every moment to singe it, and burn it asunder;[7] and you have no interest in any Mediator, and nothing to lay hold of to save yourself, nothing to keep off the flames of wrath, nothing of your own, nothing that you ever have done, nothing that you can do, to **induce** God to spare you one moment. . . .

It is *everlasting* wrath. It would be dreadful to suffer this fierceness and wrath of Almighty God one moment; but you must suffer it to all eternity. There will be no end to this exquisite[8] horrible misery. When you look forward, you shall see a long forever, a boundless duration before you, which will swallow up your

E EMOTIONAL APPEALS
Notice the use of the **simile**, or comparison, in lines 50–65. In what way does comparing the audience to a spider appeal to both fear and vanity?

incense (ĭn-sĕns´) *v.* to cause to be extremely angry

induce (ĭn-do͞os´) *v.* to succeed in persuading someone to do something

---

7. **burn it asunder** (ə-sŭn´dər): burn it into separate parts or pieces.
8. **exquisite** (ĕk´skwĭ-zĭt): intensely felt.

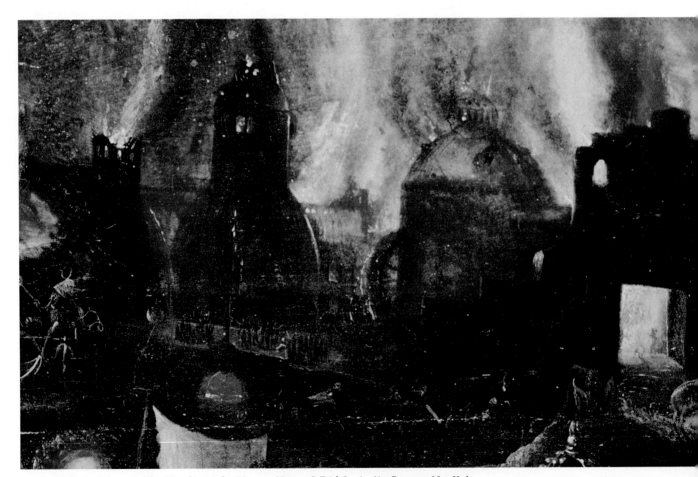

Detail of *Hell,* Hendrik met de Bles, Kunsthistorisches Museum, Vienna. © Erich Lessing/Art Resource, New York.

thoughts, and amaze your soul; and you will absolutely despair of ever having
80 any **deliverance,** any end, any **mitigation,** any rest at all. You will know certainly
that you must wear out long ages, millions of millions of ages, in wrestling and
conflicting with this almighty merciless vengeance; and then when you have so
done, when so many ages have actually been spent by you in this manner, you will
know that all is but a point to what remains. So that your punishment will indeed
be infinite. Oh, who can express what the state of a soul in such circumstances is!
All that we can possibly say about it, gives but a very feeble, faint representation
of it; it is inexpressible and inconceivable: For "who knows the power of God's
anger?"[9]

How dreadful is the state of those that are daily and hourly in the danger of
90 this great wrath and infinite misery! But this is the dismal case of every soul in this
congregation that has not been born again, however moral and strict, sober and
religious, they may otherwise be. . . . **F**

And now you have an extraordinary opportunity, a day wherein Christ has
thrown the door of mercy wide open, and stands in the door calling and crying
with a loud voice to poor sinners; a day wherein many are flocking to him, and
pressing into the kingdom of God. Many are daily coming[10] from the east, west,
north, and south; many that were very lately in the same miserable condition that
you are in, are now in a happy state, with their hearts filled with love to him who
has loved them, and washed them from their sins in his own blood, and rejoicing
100 in hope of the glory of God. How awful is it to be left behind at such a day! To
see so many others feasting, while you are pining and perishing! To see so many
rejoicing and singing for joy of heart, while you have cause to mourn for sorrow
of heart, and howl for vexation of spirit! How can you rest one moment in such a
condition? . . . **G**

Therefore, let every one that is out of Christ, now awake and fly from the wrath
to come. . . . ❧

F **SERMON**
Keep in mind that
Edwards delivers his
sermon in the **context** of
his own time and place.
In lines 90–92, in what
way does he acknowledge
the Puritan heritage of his
listeners?

G **EMOTIONAL APPEALS**
Reread lines 93–104 and
note the change in **tone.**
How might the change
in tone appeal to the
audience's pity and vanity?

deliverance (dĭ-lĭv′ər-əns)
n. rescue from danger

mitigation (mĭt-ĭ-gā′shən)
n. lessening of something
that causes suffering

---

9. **"who knows . . . anger?":** an allusion to Psalm 90:11 in the Bible—"Who knoweth the power
of thine anger?"

10. **Many . . . coming:** a reference to the hundreds of people who were being converted during
the Great Awakening.

Comprehension

1. **Recall** According to Jonathan Edwards's sermon, what is a constant threat to all human beings?

2. **Clarify** In Edwards's view, what must sinners do to save themselves?

3. **Summarize** What key image does Edwards use to frighten his audience?

Literary Analysis

4. **Analyze Emotional Appeals** Review the examples of words, phrases, and images you recorded as you read. How does this language effectively appeal to the audience's emotions and get Edwards's message across?

5. **Analyze the Sermon** Why do you think Edwards felt it was necessary to terrify his Puritan **audience** into action?

6. **Draw Conclusions** How would you describe Jonathan Edwards's view of the following? Cite specific examples for each.

   • God   • Christ   • humanity

7. **Make Judgments** Do you believe that Edwards's sermon resulted in improving the **morality** of his congregation? Explain why or why not.

8. **Compare Literary Works** Use a chart like the one shown to compare some of Jonathan Edwards's and Anne Bradstreet's attitudes and beliefs. Cite specific details from their writings to support your ideas.

	Edwards	Bradstreet
Eternal Life		
God's Relation to People		
Religious Beliefs		
Human Frailty		

Literary Criticism

9. **Historical Context** In the 18th century, many people died at a much younger age than they do today. How might awareness of the fragility of life have affected people's receptiveness to Edwards's sermon?

Vocabulary in Context

VOCABULARY PRACTICE

Decide whether the boldfaced words make the statements true or false.

1. If a movie is said to be **abominable,** you should expect to hate it.
2. A good way to **appease** a friend is to criticize her.
3. Feeding the hungry would result in the **mitigation** of their suffering.
4. If you **discern** a difference between two documents, you notice that they are not alike.
5. A person who **abhors** you is probably a close friend.
6. When you **ascribe** a motive to a crime, you explain why someone did it.
7. One way to **incense** someone is to say something complimentary.
8. If you have trouble cutting a steak, it might help to **whet** your knife.
9. An example of **deliverance** is the rescue of passengers from a sinking ship.
10. If I **induce** you to help me do a hard job, I have managed to persuade you.

VOCABULARY IN WRITING

How would people today react to a sermon like Edwards's? Using at least four vocabulary words, briefly explain your opinion and why you feel as you do. You might start like this.

> **EXAMPLE SENTENCE**
>
> I think that hearing a sermon like Edwards's would **_induce_** people to think seriously about their lives.

VOCABULARY STRATEGY: CONNOTATION

Though some words may have the same definition, their **connotations,** or shades of meaning, can vary. In Edwards's sermon, for example, the word *incense* (page 124) suggests a stronger feeling than *anger*. Being aware of words' shades of meaning can strengthen your writing as well as your reading comprehension.

PRACTICE Choose a more intense word from the following list to replace the boldfaced word in each sentence.

> antipathy   disconsolate   induce   momentous   negligible

1. Nothing could **persuade** him to run for president.
2. Getting a college degree was a very **important** event in Mom's life.
3. They expressed their **dislike** for the new law with a huge protest march.
4. Because I enjoyed my job so much, I was **sad** when I lost it.
5. The wishes of the stockholders had a **slight** effect on the board's decision.

VOCABULARY PRACTICE
For more practice, go to the **Vocabulary Center** at ClassZone.com.

Literary Analysis Workshop

American Drama

Have you ever gone to the theater or a movie and felt as if life were unfolding before you? Dramas that realistically portray events have a way of hitting a nerve. American playwrights, in particular, are known for writing dramas that reveal the truth of our everyday experience, and sometimes our not-so-everyday experience.

The Rise of American Drama

Though drama is one of the oldest forms of literature, it was one of the last of the literary genres to develop in the United States. The Puritans in New England regarded theatrical performances as frivolous, so few plays were staged in the 1600s. During the 18th and 19th centuries, drama gradually became an accepted form of entertainment. However, most of the plays performed in the United States were imported from Europe or were adapted from novels.

Eugene O'Neill's *The Iceman Cometh* became an American classic.

In 1920 the Broadway production of Eugene O'Neill's *Beyond the Horizon* marked a turning point in presenting true-to-life characters who were struggling to understand their lives. Building on O'Neill's achievement, American playwrights Thornton Wilder, Lillian Hellman, Tennessee Williams, and Arthur Miller created dramas in the 1930s and 1940s that met with critical and popular success. Following World War II, American dramatists Edward Albee and Lorraine Hansberry made significant contributions to the theater. Arthur Miller's 1953 *The Crucible* (page 134) is an example of a modern drama that portrays events from Puritan times.

Conventions of Drama

The two main types of drama are tragedy and comedy. A **tragedy** recounts the downfall of a main character, and a **comedy** is light and humorous in tone, usually ending happily. Many dramas combine elements of both. In addition, most dramas follow similar conventions, or rules, in how they are presented. An understanding of basic dramatic conventions can help you imagine the performance as you read.

PLOT AND STRUCTURE

The **plot** in drama, as in fiction, introduces events and character interactions that produce a **conflict,** or struggle between opposing forces. The conflict builds as the action intensifies throughout the play's **acts** and **scenes,** finally reaching a peak and then resolution. Each scene serves as a building block in the stages of the plot: **exposition, rising action, climax, falling action,** and **resolution.**

TYPES OF CHARACTERS

Drama has many of the same types of characters that are found in fiction. The **protagonist** is the central character of the play. This character is at the center of the conflict and often undergoes radical changes during the course of the play. The **antagonist** often opposes the protagonist, giving rise to the central conflict of the play. Some plays also include a **foil,** a minor character who provides a striking contrast to another character. Interplay among these characters heightens the dramatic tension as the play develops. The names of all a play's characters are listed in the **cast of characters** at the beginning of the play.

SPEECH DEVICES

In drama, the playwright develops the story line through the characters' actions and dialogue. Virtually everything of consequence—from the plot details to the character revelations—flows from **dialogue,** or conversation between characters. Other **speech devices** used by playwrights include

- **monologue:** a long speech spoken by a single character to the audience or another character

- **soliloquy:** a reflective speech in which a character speaks his or her private thoughts aloud, unheard by other characters.

- **aside:** a short speech or comment that is delivered by a character to the audience, but that is not heard by other characters who are present

STAGE AND SETTING

Stage directions are the italicized instructions in a play. The playwright includes the stage directions in order to describe the setting, props, lighting, scenery, sound effects, and costumes. Stage directions also describe the entrances and exits of characters and how the characters look, speak, and react to events or to others. These stage directions from *The Crucible* describe the stage set at the beginning of Act Four.

> (*A cell in Salem jail, that fall.*)
>
> (*At the back is a high barred window; near it, a great, heavy door. Along the walls are two benches.*)
>
> (*The place is in darkness but for the moonlight seeping through the bars. It appears empty. Presently footsteps are heard coming down a corridor beyond the wall, keys rattle, and the door swings open. Marshal Herrick enters with a lantern.*)
>
> —**Arthur Miller,** *The Crucible*

Close Read

Why is the description of the cell important to this scene? What effect does it have on the **mood** the scene evokes?

The Crucible

Drama by Arthur Miller

Arthur Miller

1915–2005

Author Online

For more on Arthur Miller, visit the **Literature Center** at **ClassZone.com**.

Arthur Miller once paid playwright Edward Albee a compliment, saying that his plays were "necessary." Albee replied: "I will go one step further and say that Arthur's plays are 'essential.'" Miller's plays explore family relationships, morality, and personal responsibility. Many critics consider him the greatest American dramatist of the 20th century.

A Born Playwright Miller was born in New York City in 1915 into an upper-middle-class family. However, the family's comfortable life ended in the 1930s when Miller's businessman father was hit hard by the Great Depression. Unable to afford college, Miller worked in a warehouse to earn tuition money. He eventually attended the University of Michigan.

While in college, Miller won several awards for his plays. These successes inspired him to pursue a career in the theater. His first Broadway hit, *All My Sons* (1947), was produced when Miller was still in his early 30s. However, it was his masterpiece *Death of a Salesman* that made Miller a star. The play won a Pulitzer Prize in 1949 and earned rave reviews from both critics and the public.

Dramatic Years Miller's rise to fame occurred during a difficult period in American history. In the 1940s and 1950s, a congressional committee was conducting hearings to identify suspected Communists in American society. Miller himself was called before the congressional committee and questioned about his activities with the American Communist Party. Although Miller admitted that he had attended a few meetings years earlier, he refused to implicate others. For his refusal, he was cited for contempt of Congress—a conviction that was later overturned.

The hearings provided the inspiration for his 1953 play *The Crucible,* set during the Salem, Massachusetts, witch trials of 1692. Miller wrote the play to warn against mass hysteria and to plead for freedom and tolerance.

The Curtain Closes In the 1970s, Miller's career declined a bit. The plays he wrote did not earn the critical or popular success of his earlier work. In the 1980s and 1990s, however, he enjoyed a resurgence with revivals of *Death of a Salesman* on Broadway. He even directed a production of the play in Beijing.

To the end of his life, Miller continued to write. "It is what I do," he said in an interview. "I am better at it than I ever was. And I will do it as long as I can."

● LITERARY ANALYSIS: CONVENTIONS OF DRAMA

Drama is literature in play form. It is meant to be performed and seen. However, an understanding of dramatic conventions can help you picture the performance when you read a script. As you read *The Crucible,* be aware of these drama conventions:

- **Stage directions,** which Miller uses not only to describe settings and characters but also to provide historical background in the form of expository mini-essays
- **Dialogue,** the lifeblood of drama, which moves the plot forward and reveals character traits
- **Types of characters**—heroes, villains, and foils—which Miller uses to heighten the tension of his drama
- **Plot,** which is driven by **conflict** that builds throughout each act

■ READING SKILL: DRAW CONCLUSIONS ABOUT CHARACTERS

Characters in drama reveal their personality traits through their words and actions. The descriptions in the stage directions can also provide insight into these characters. As you read *The Crucible,* **draw conclusions** about the play's main characters. Record their important traits and the evidence that reveals these traits in a chart like the one shown. Be sure to add characters to the chart as you encounter them.

	Abigail Williams	John Proctor	Reverend John Hale
Traits	proud	assertive	
Evidence			

▲ VOCABULARY IN CONTEXT

Arthur Miller uses the words shown here to help convey the atmosphere of the Salem witch trials. Place them in the following categories: words that describe character traits, words that describe actions, and words that are concepts.

WORD LIST		
adamant	corroborate	immaculate
ameliorate	deference	imperceptible
anarchy	deposition	iniquity
conciliatory	dissembling	subservient
contentious	effrontery	trepidation

What fuels a MOB?

KEY IDEA Visualize a mob of people rampaging through the streets, whipped into a frenzy by **hysteria.** The fear, anger, and panic produced by hysteria can make otherwise reasonable people do irrational things. In *The Crucible,* for example, the hysteria created by the Salem witch trials makes neighbor turn against neighbor.

DISCUSS What makes people act as a mob? What are some of the results of mob action? Think about news reports or historical accounts of mobs that you've come across. In a small group, discuss what caused these mobs to form and how they behaved.

THE
CRUCIBLE

Arthur Miller

BACKGROUND *The Crucible* is based on the witch trials that took place in the Puritan community of Salem, Massachusetts, in 1692. At these trials, spectral evidence—the testimony of a church member who claimed to have seen a person's spirit performing witchcraft—was enough to sentence the accused to death. Miller studied the court records of the trials to gain insight into his characters—all of whom were real people—and get a feel for the Puritan way of speaking. Above all, he wanted to capture the mood of a time when no one was safe.

CAST OF CHARACTERS

(in order of appearance)

Reverend Samuel Parris	Mrs. Ann Putnam	Ezekiel Cheever
Betty Parris	Thomas Putnam	Marshal Herrick
Tituba	Mercy Lewis	Judge Hathorne
Abigail Williams	Mary Warren	Martha Corey
John Proctor	Rebecca Nurse	Deputy Governor Danforth
Elizabeth Proctor	Giles Corey	Girls of Salem
Susanna Walcott	Reverend John Hale	Sarah Good
	Francis Nurse	

Act *One*

An Overture

(*A small upper bedroom in the home of* Reverend Samuel Parris, *Salem, Massachusetts, in the spring of the year 1692.*

There is a narrow window at the left. Through its leaded panes the morning sunlight streams. A candle still burns near the bed, which is at the right. A chest, a chair, and a small table are the other furnishings. At the back a door opens on the landing of the stairway to the ground floor. The room gives off an air of clean spareness. The roof rafters are exposed, and the wood colors are raw and unmellowed.

As the curtain rises, Reverend Parris *is discovered kneeling beside the bed, evidently in prayer. His daughter,* Betty Parris, *aged ten, is lying on the bed, inert.*)

At the time of these events Parris was in his middle forties. In history he cut a villainous path, and there is very little good to be said for him. He believed he was being persecuted wherever he went, despite his best efforts to win people and God to his side. In meeting, he felt insulted if someone rose to shut the door without first asking his permission. He was a widower with no interest in children, or talent with them. He regarded them as young adults, and until this strange crisis he, like the rest of Salem, never conceived that the children were anything but thankful for being permitted to walk straight, eyes slightly lowered, arms at the sides, and mouths shut until bidden to speak.

His house stood in the "town"—but we today would hardly call it a village. The meeting house[1] was nearby, and from this point outward—toward the bay or inland—there were a few small-windowed, dark houses snuggling against the raw Massachusetts winter. Salem had been established hardly forty years before. To the European world the whole province was a barbaric frontier inhabited by a sect of fanatics who, nevertheless, were shipping out products of slowly increasing quantity and value.

No one can really know what their lives were like. They had no novelists—and would not have permitted anyone to read a novel if one were handy. Their creed forbade anything resembling a theater or "vain enjoyment." They did not celebrate Christmas, and a holiday from work meant only that they must concentrate even more upon prayer.

Which is not to say that nothing broke into this strict and somber way of life. When a new farmhouse was built, friends assembled to "raise the roof," and there would be special foods cooked and probably some potent cider passed around. There was a good supply of ne'er-do-wells in Salem, who dallied at the shovelboard[2] in Bridget Bishop's tavern. Probably more than the creed, hard work kept the morals of the place from spoiling, for the people were forced

---

1. **meeting house:** the most important building in the Puritan community, used both for worship and for meetings.
2. **shovelboard:** a game in which a coin or disc is shoved across a board by hand.

Daniel Day-Lewis as John Proctor

to fight the land like heroes for every grain of corn, and no man had very much time for fooling around.

That there were some jokers, however, is indicated by the practice of appointing a two-man patrol whose duty was to "walk forth in the time of God's worship to take notice of such as either lye about the meeting house, without attending to the word and ordinances, or that lye at home or in the fields without giving good account thereof, and to take the names of such persons, and to present them to the magistrates, whereby they may be accordingly proceeded against." This predilection for minding other people's business was time-honored among the people of Salem, and it undoubtedly created many of the suspicions which were to feed the coming madness. It was also, in my opinion, one of the things that a John Proctor would rebel against, for the time of the armed camp had almost passed, and since the country was reasonably—although not wholly—safe, the old disciplines were beginning to rankle. But, as in all such matters, the issue was not clear-cut, for danger was still a possibility, and in unity still lay the best promise of safety.

The edge of the wilderness was close by. The American continent stretched endlessly west, and it was full of mystery for them. It stood, dark and threatening, over their shoulders night and day, for out of it Indian tribes marauded from time to time, and Reverend Parris had parishioners who had lost relatives to these heathen.

The parochial snobbery of these people was partly responsible for their failure to convert the Indians. Probably they also preferred to take land from heathens rather than from fellow Christians. At any rate, very few Indians were converted, and the Salem folk believed that the virgin forest was the Devil's last preserve, his home base and the citadel of his final stand. To the best of their knowledge the American forest was the last place on earth that was not paying homage to God.

For these reasons, among others, they carried about an air of innate resistance, even of persecution. Their fathers had, of course, been persecuted in England. So now they and their church found it necessary to deny any other sect its freedom, lest their New Jerusalem[3] be defiled and corrupted by wrong ways and deceitful ideas.

They believed, in short, that they held in their steady hands the candle that would light the world. We have inherited this belief, and it has helped and hurt us. It helped them with the discipline it gave them. They were a dedicated folk, by and large, and they had to be to survive the life they had chosen or been born into in this country.

The proof of their belief's value to them may be taken from the opposite character of the first Jamestown settlement, farther south, in Virginia. The Englishmen who landed there were motivated mainly by a hunt for profit. They had thought to pick off the wealth of the new country and then return rich to England. They were a band of individualists, and a much more ingratiating group than the Massachusetts men. But Virginia destroyed them. Massachusetts tried to kill off the Puritans, but they combined; they set up a communal society which, in the beginning, was little more than an armed camp with an autocratic and very devoted leadership. It was, however, an autocracy by consent, for they were united from top to bottom by a commonly held ideology whose perpetuation was the reason and justification for all their sufferings. So their self-denial, their purposefulness, their suspicion of all vain pursuits, their hard-handed justice, were altogether perfect instruments for the conquest of this space so antagonistic to man.

But the people of Salem in 1692 were not quite the dedicated folk that arrived on the *Mayflower*. A vast differentiation had taken place, and in their own time a revolution had unseated the royal government and substituted a junta which was at this

---

3. **New Jerusalem:** in Christianity, a heavenly city and the last resting place of the souls saved by Jesus. It was considered the ideal city, and Puritans modeled their communities after it.

moment in power.[4] The times, to their eyes, must have been out of joint, and to the common folk must have seemed as insoluble and complicated as do ours today. It is not hard to see how easily many could have been led to believe that the time of confusion had been brought upon them by deep and darkling forces. No hint of such speculation appears on the court record, but social disorder in any age breeds such mystical suspicions, and when, as in Salem, wonders are brought forth from below the social surface, it is too much to expect people to hold back very long from laying on the victims with all the force of their frustrations.

The Salem tragedy, which is about to begin in these pages, developed from a paradox. It is a paradox in whose grip we still live, and there is no prospect yet that we will discover its resolution. Simply, it was this: for good purposes, even high purposes, the people of Salem developed a theocracy, a combine of state and religious power whose function was to keep the community together, and to prevent any kind of disunity that might open it to destruction by material or ideological enemies. It was forged for a necessary purpose and accomplished that purpose. But all organization is and must be grounded on the idea of exclusion and prohibition, just as two objects cannot occupy the same space. Evidently the time came in New England when the repressions of order were heavier than seemed warranted by the dangers against which the order was organized. The witch-hunt was a perverse manifestation of the panic which set in among all classes when the balance began to turn toward greater individual freedom.

When one rises above the individual villainy displayed, one can only pity them all, just as we shall be pitied someday. It is still impossible for man to organize his social life without repressions, and the balance has yet to be struck between order and freedom.

The witch-hunt was not, however, a mere repression. It was also, and as importantly, a long overdue opportunity for everyone so inclined to express publicly his guilt and sins, under the cover of accusations against the victims. It suddenly became possible—and patriotic and holy—for a man to say that Martha Corey had come into his bedroom at night, and that, while his wife was sleeping at his side, Martha laid herself down on his chest and "nearly suffocated him." Of course it was her spirit only, but his satisfaction at confessing himself was no lighter than if it had been Martha herself. One could not ordinarily speak such things in public.

Long-held hatreds of neighbors could now be openly expressed, and vengeance taken, despite the Bible's charitable injunctions. Land-lust which had been expressed before by constant bickering over boundaries and deeds, could now be elevated to the arena of morality; one could cry witch against one's neighbor and feel perfectly justified in the bargain. Old scores could be settled on a plane of heavenly combat between Lucifer and the Lord; suspicions and the envy of the miserable toward the happy could and did burst out in the general revenge.

1 (*Reverend Parris is praying now, and, though we cannot hear his words, a sense of his confusion hangs about him. He mumbles, then seems about to weep; then he weeps, then prays again; but his daughter does not stir on the bed.*

The door opens, and his Negro slave enters. Tituba *is in her forties.* Parris *brought her with him from Barbados, where he spent some years as a merchant before entering the ministry. She enters as one does who*
10 *can no longer bear to be barred from the sight of her beloved, but she is also very frightened because her slave sense has warned her that, as always, trouble in this house eventually lands on her back.*)

Tituba (*already taking a step backward*). My Betty be hearty soon?

---

4. **a junta** (hōōn′tə) . . . **power:** *Junta* is a Spanish term meaning "a small, elite ruling council." The reference here is to the group that led England's Glorious Revolution of 1688–1689.

Parris. Out of here!

Tituba (*backing to the door*). My Betty not goin' die . . .

Parris (*scrambling to his feet in a fury*). Out of my
20 sight! (*She is gone.*) Out of my—(*He is overcome with sobs. He clamps his teeth against them and closes the door and leans against it, exhausted.*) Oh, my God! God help me! (*Quaking with fear, mumbling to himself through his sobs, he goes to the bed and gently takes* Betty's *hand.*) Betty. Child. Dear child. Will you wake, will you open up your eyes! Betty, little one . . .

(*He is bending to kneel again when his niece,* Abigail Williams, *seventeen, enters—a strikingly beautiful girl,*
30 *an orphan, with an endless capacity for* **dissembling**. *Now she is all worry and apprehension and propriety.*)

Abigail. Uncle? (*He looks to her.*) Susanna Walcott's here from Doctor Griggs.

Parris. Oh? Let her come, let her come.

Abigail (*leaning out the door to call to Susanna, who is down the hall a few steps*). Come in, Susanna.

(Susanna Walcott, *a little younger than* Abigail, *a nervous, hurried girl, enters.*)

Parris (*eagerly*). What does the doctor say, child?

40 **Susanna** (*craning around* Parris *to get a look at* Betty). He bid me come and tell you, reverend sir, that he cannot discover no medicine for it in his books.

Parris. Then he must search on.

Susanna. Aye, sir, he have been searchin' his books since he left you, sir. But he bid me tell you, that you might look to unnatural things for the cause of it.

Parris (*his eyes going wide*). No—no. There be no unnatural cause here. Tell him I have sent for Reverend Hale of Beverly, and Mr. Hale will surely con-
50 firm that. Let him look to medicine and put out all thought of unnatural causes here. There be none.

Susanna. Aye, sir. He bid me tell you. (*She turns to go.*)

Abigail. Speak nothin' of it in the village, Susanna.

Parris. Go directly home and speak nothing of unnatural causes.

Susanna. Aye, sir. I pray for her. (*She goes out.*)

Abigail. Uncle, the rumor of witchcraft is all about; I think you'd best go down and deny it yourself. The parlor's packed with people, sir. I'll sit with her.

60 **Parris** (*pressed, turns on her*). And what shall I say to them? That my daughter and my niece I discovered dancing like heathen in the forest?

Abigail. Uncle, we did dance; let you tell them I confessed it—and I'll be whipped if I must be. But they're speakin' of witchcraft. Betty's not witched.

Parris. Abigail, I cannot go before the congregation when I know you have not opened with me. What did you do with her in the forest?

Abigail. We did dance, uncle, and when you leaped
70 out of the bush so suddenly, Betty was frightened and then she fainted. And there's the whole of it.

Parris. Child. Sit you down.

Abigail (*quavering, as she sits*). I would never hurt Betty. I love her dearly.

Parris. Now look you, child, your punishment will come in its time. But if you trafficked with[5] spirits in the forest I must know it now, for surely my enemies will, and they will ruin me with it.

Abigail. But we never conjured spirits.

80 **Parris.** Then why can she not move herself since midnight? This child is desperate! (Abigail *lowers her eyes.*) It must come out—my enemies will bring it out. Let me know what you done there. Abigail, do you understand that I have many enemies?

Abigail. I have heard of it, uncle.

Parris. There is a faction that is sworn to drive me from my pulpit. Do you understand that?

Abigail. I think so, sir.

Parris. Now then, in the midst of such disruption,
90 my own household is discovered to be the very center of some obscene practice. Abominations are done in the forest—

---

5. **trafficked with:** met with.

Winona Ryder as Abigail Williams

Abigail. It were sport, uncle!

Parris (*pointing at* Betty). You call this sport? (*She lowers her eyes. He pleads.*) Abigail, if you know something that may help the doctor, for God's sake tell it to me. (*She is silent.*) I saw Tituba waving her arms over the fire when I came on you. Why was she doing that? And I heard a screeching and gibberish coming from her mouth. She were swaying like a dumb beast over that fire!

Abigail. She always sings her Barbados songs, and we dance.

Parris. I cannot blink what I saw, Abigail, for my enemies will not blink it. I saw a dress lying on the grass.

Abigail (*innocently*). A dress?

Parris (*It is very hard to say*). Aye, a dress. And I thought I saw—someone naked running through the trees!

Abigail (*in terror*). No one was naked! You mistake yourself, uncle!

Parris (*with anger*). I saw it! (*He moves from her. Then, resolved*) Now tell me true, Abigail. And I pray you feel the weight of truth upon you, for now my ministry's at stake, my ministry and perhaps your cousin's life. Whatever abomination you have done, give me all of it now, for I dare not be taken unaware when I go before them down there.

Abigail. There is nothin' more. I swear it, uncle.

Parris (*studies her, then nods, half convinced*). Abigail, I have fought here three long years to bend these stiff-necked people to me, and now, just now when some good respect is rising for me in the parish, you compromise my very character. I have given you a home, child, I have put clothes upon your back—now give me upright answer. Your name in the town—it is entirely white, is it not?

Abigail (*with an edge of resentment*). Why, I am sure it is, sir. There be no blush about my name.[6]

Parris (*to the point*). Abigail, is there any other cause than you have told me, for your being discharged from Goody[7] Proctor's service? I have heard it said, and I tell you as I heard it, that she comes so rarely to the church this year for she will not sit so close to something soiled. What signified that remark?

Abigail. She hates me, uncle, she must, for I would not be her slave. It's a bitter woman, a lying, cold, sniveling woman, and I will not work for such a woman!

Parris. She may be. And yet it has troubled me that you are now seven month out of their house, and in all this time no other family has ever called for your service.

Abigail. They want slaves, not such as I. Let them send to Barbados for that. I will not black my face for any of them! (*with ill-concealed resentment at him*) Do you begrudge my bed, uncle?

Parris. No—no.

Abigail (*in a temper*). My name is good in the village! I will not have it said my name is soiled! Goody Proctor is a gossiping liar!

(*Enter* Mrs. Ann Putnam. *She is a twisted soul of forty-five, a death-ridden woman, haunted by dreams.*)

Parris (*as soon as the door begins to open*). No—no, I cannot have anyone. (*He sees her, and a certain **deference** springs into him, although his worry remains.*) Why, Goody Putnam, come in.

Mrs. Putnam (*full of breath, shiny-eyed*). It is a marvel. It is surely a stroke of hell upon you.

Parris. No, Goody Putnam, it is—

Mrs. Putnam (*glancing at* Betty). How high did she fly, how high?

Parris. No, no, she never flew—

Mrs. Putnam (*very pleased with it*). Why, it's sure she did. Mr. Collins saw her goin' over Ingersoll's barn, and come down light as bird, he says!

Parris. Now, look you, Goody Putnam, she never—

---

6. **There be . . . my name:** There is nothing wrong with my reputation.

7. **Goody:** short for *Goodwife,* the Puritan equivalent of *Mrs.*

(*Enter* Thomas Putnam, *a well-to-do, hard-handed landowner, near fifty.*) Oh, good morning, Mr.
170 Putnam.

Putnam. It is a providence the thing is out now! It is a providence. (*He goes directly to the bed.*)

Parris. What's out, sir, what's—?

(Mrs. Putnam *goes to the bed.*)

Putnam (*looking down at* Betty). Why, *her* eyes is closed! Look you, Ann.

Mrs. Putnam. Why, that's strange. (*to* Parris) Ours is open.

Parris (*shocked*). Your Ruth is sick?

180 **Mrs. Putnam** (*with vicious certainty*). I'd not call it sick; the Devil's touch is heavier than sick. It's death, y'know, it's death drivin' into them, forked and hoofed.

Parris. Oh, pray not! Why, how does Ruth ail?

Mrs. Putnam. She ails as she must—she never waked this morning, but her eyes open and she walks, and hears naught, sees naught, and cannot eat. Her soul is taken, surely.

(Parris *is struck.*)

190 **Putnam** (*as though for further details*). They say you've sent for Reverend Hale of Beverly?

Parris (*with dwindling conviction now*). A precaution only. He has much experience in all demonic arts, and I—

Mrs. Putnam. He has indeed; and found a witch in Beverly last year, and let you remember that.

Parris. Now, Goody Ann, they only thought that were a witch, and I am certain there be no element of witchcraft here.

200 **Putnam.** No witchcraft! Now look you, Mr. Parris—

Parris. Thomas, Thomas, I pray you, leap not to witchcraft. I know that you—you least of all, Thomas, would ever wish so disastrous a charge laid upon me. We cannot leap to witchcraft. They will howl me out of Salem for such corruption in my house.

A word about Thomas Putnam. He was a man with many grievances, at least one of which appears justified. Some time before, his wife's brother-in-law, James Bayley, had been turned down as minister of Salem. Bayley had all the qualifications, and a two-thirds vote into the bargain, but a faction stopped his acceptance, for reasons that are not clear.

Thomas Putnam was the eldest son of the richest man in the village. He had fought the Indians at Narragansett,[8] and was deeply interested in parish affairs. He undoubtedly felt it poor payment that the village should so blatantly disregard his candidate for one of its more important offices, especially since he regarded himself as the intellectual superior of most of the people around him.

His vindictive nature was demonstrated long before the witchcraft began. Another former Salem minister, George Burroughs, had had to borrow money to pay for his wife's funeral, and, since the parish was remiss in his salary, he was soon bankrupt. Thomas and his brother John had Burroughs jailed for debts the man did not owe. The incident is important only in that Burroughs succeeded in becoming minister where Bayley, Thomas Putnam's brother-in-law, had been rejected; the motif of resentment is clear here. Thomas Putnam felt that his own name and the honor of his family had been smirched by the village, and he meant to right matters however he could.

Another reason to believe him a deeply embittered man was his attempt to break his father's will, which left a disproportionate amount to a stepbrother. As with every other public cause in which he tried to force his way, he failed in this.

So it is not surprising to find that so many accusations against people are in the handwriting of Thomas Putnam, or that his name is so often found as a witness **corroborating** the supernatural testimony, or that his daughter led the crying-out at the most opportune junctures of the trials, especially when—But we'll speak of that when we come to it.

---

8. **fought the Indians at Narragansett:** The Puritans fought a series of battles against the Narragansett Indians over territory that both groups had settled on.

Putnam (*At the moment he is intent upon getting* Parris, *for whom he has only contempt, to move toward the abyss*). Mr. Parris, I have taken your part in all contention here, and I would continue; but I cannot
210 if you hold back in this. There are hurtful, vengeful spirits layin' hands on these children.

Parris. But, Thomas, you cannot—

Putnam. Ann! Tell Mr. Parris what you have done.

Mrs. Putnam. Reverend Parris, I have laid seven babies unbaptized in the earth. Believe me, sir, you never saw more hearty babies born. And yet, each would wither in my arms the very night of their birth. I have spoke nothin', but my heart has clamored intimations.[9] And now, this year, my Ruth, my only—I see her turning
220 strange. A secret child she has become this year, and shrivels like a sucking mouth were pullin' on her life too. And so I thought to send her to your Tituba—

Parris. To Tituba! What may Tituba—?

Mrs. Putnam. Tituba knows how to speak to the dead, Mr. Parris.

Parris. Goody Ann, it is a formidable sin to conjure up the dead!

Mrs. Putnam. I take it on my soul, but who else may surely tell us what person murdered my babies?

230 **Parris** (*horrified*). Woman!

Mrs. Putnam. They were murdered, Mr. Parris! And mark this proof! Mark it! Last night my Ruth were ever so close to their little spirits; I know it, sir. For how else is she struck dumb now except some power of darkness would stop her mouth? It is a marvelous sign, Mr. Parris!

Putnam. Don't you understand it, sir? There is a murdering witch among us, bound to keep herself in the dark. (Parris *turns to* Betty, *a frantic terror rising*
240 *in him.*) Let your enemies make of it what they will, you cannot blink it more.

Parris (*to* Abigail). Then you were conjuring spirits last night.

Abigail (*whispering*). Not I, sir—Tituba and Ruth.

Parris (*turns now, with new fear, and goes to* Betty, *looks down at her, and then, gazing off*). Oh, Abigail, what proper payment for my charity! Now I am undone.

Putnam. You are not undone! Let you take hold
250 here. Wait for no one to charge you—declare it yourself. You have discovered witchcraft—

Parris. In my house? In my house, Thomas? They will topple me with this! They will make of it a—

(*Enter* Mercy Lewis, *the Putnams' servant, a fat, sly, merciless girl of eighteen.*)

Mercy. Your pardons. I only thought to see how Betty is.

Putnam. Why aren't you home? Who's with Ruth?

Mercy. Her grandma come. She's improved a little,
260 I think—she give a powerful sneeze before.

Mrs. Putnam. Ah, there's a sign of life!

Mercy. I'd fear no more, Goody Putnam. It were a grand sneeze; another like it will shake her wits together, I'm sure. (*She goes to the bed to look.*)

Parris. Will you leave me now, Thomas? I would pray a while alone.

Abigail. Uncle, you've prayed since midnight. Why do you not go down and—

Parris. No—no. (*to* Putnam) I have no answer for
270 that crowd. I'll wait till Mr. Hale arrives. (*to get* Mrs. Putnam *to leave*) If you will, Goody Ann . . .

Putnam. Now look you, sir. Let you strike out against the Devil, and the village will bless you for it! Come down, speak to them—pray with them. They're thirsting for your word, Mister! Surely you'll pray with them.

Parris (*swayed*). I'll lead them in a psalm, but let you say nothing of witchcraft yet. I will not discuss it. The cause is yet unknown. I have had enough con-
280 tention since I came; I want no more.

Mrs. Putnam. Mercy, you go home to Ruth, d'y'hear?

Mercy. Aye, mum.

(Mrs. Putnam *goes out.*)

---

9. **clamored intimations** (klăm′ərd ĭn′tə-mā′shənz): nagging suspicions.

Parris (*to* Abigail). If she starts for the window, cry for me at once.

Abigail. I will, uncle.

Parris (*to* Putnam). There is a terrible power in her arms today. (*He goes out with* Putnam.)

Abigail (*with hushed* **trepidation**). How is Ruth sick?

290 **Mercy.** It's weirdish, I know not—she seems to walk like a dead one since last night.

Abigail (*turns at once and goes to* Betty, *and now, with fear in her voice*). Betty? (Betty *doesn't move. She shakes her.*) Now stop this! Betty! Sit up now!

(Betty *doesn't stir.* Mercy *comes over.*)

Mercy. Have you tried beatin' her? I gave Ruth a good one and it waked her for a minute. Here, let me have her.

Abigail (*holding* Mercy *back*). No, he'll be comin' up.

300 Listen, now; if they be questioning us, tell them we danced—I told him as much already.

Mercy. Aye. And what more?

Abigail. He knows Tituba conjured Ruth's sisters to come out of the grave.

Mercy. And what more?

Abigail. He saw you naked.

Mercy (*clapping her hands together with a frightened laugh*). Oh, Jesus!

(*Enter* Mary Warren, *breathless. She is seventeen,*
310 *a* **subservient**, *naive, lonely girl.*)

Mary Warren. What'll we do? The village is out! I just come from the farm; the whole country's talkin' witchcraft! They'll be callin' us witches, Abby!

Mercy (*pointing and looking at* Mary Warren). She means to tell, I know it.

Mary Warren. Abby, we've got to tell. Witchery's a hangin' error, a hangin' like they done in Boston two year ago! We must tell the truth, Abby! You'll only be whipped for dancin', and the other things!

320 **Abigail.** Oh, *we'll* be whipped!

Mary Warren. I never done none of it, Abby. I only looked!

Villagers gathering to gossip

Mercy (*moving menacingly toward* Mary). Oh, you're a great one for lookin', aren't you, Mary Warren? What a grand peeping courage you have!

(Betty, *on the bed, whimpers.* Abigail *turns to her at once.*)

Abigail. Betty? (*She goes to* Betty.) Now, Betty, dear, wake up now. It's Abigail. (*She sits* Betty *up and*
330 *furiously shakes her.*) I'll beat you, Betty! (Betty *whimpers.*) My, you seem improving. I talked to your papa and I told him everything. So there's nothing to—

Betty (*darts off the bed, frightened of* Abigail, *and flattens herself against the wall*). I want my mama!

Abigail (*with alarm, as she cautiously approaches* Betty). What ails you, Betty? Your mama's dead and buried.

Betty. I'll fly to Mama. Let me fly! (*She raises her arms as though to fly, and streaks for the window, gets*
340 *one leg out.*)

Abigail (*pulling her away from the window*). I told him everything; he knows now, he knows everything we—

Betty. You drank blood, Abby! You didn't tell him that!

Abigail. Betty, you never say that again! You will never—

Betty. You did, you did! You drank a charm to kill John Proctor's wife! You drank a charm to kill Goody Proctor!

Abigail (*smashes her across the face*). Shut it! Now
350 shut it!

Betty (*collapsing on the bed*). Mama, Mama! (*She dissolves into sobs.*)

Abigail. Now look you. All of you. We danced. And Tituba conjured Ruth Putnam's dead sisters. And that is all. And mark this. Let either of you breathe a word, or the edge of a word, about the other things, and I will come to you in the black of some terrible night and I will bring a pointy reckoning that will shudder you.[10] And you know I can do it; I saw
360 Indians smash my dear parents' heads on the pillow next to mine, and I have seen some reddish work done at night, and I can make you wish you had never seen the sun go down! (*She goes to* Betty *and roughly sits her up.*) Now, you—sit up and stop this!

(*But* Betty *collapses in her hands and lies inert on the bed.*)

Mary Warren (*with hysterical fright*). What's got her? (Abigail *stares in fright at* Betty.) Abby, she's going to die! It's a sin to conjure, and we—

370 **Abigail** (*starting for* Mary). I say shut it, Mary Warren!

(*Enter* John Proctor. *On seeing him,* Mary Warren *leaps in fright.*)

Proctor was a farmer in his middle thirties. He need not have been a partisan of any faction in the town, but there is evidence to suggest that he had a sharp and biting way with hypocrites. He was the kind of man—powerful of body, even-tempered, and not easily led—who cannot refuse support to partisans without drawing their deepest resentment. In Proctor's presence a fool felt his foolishness instantly—and a Proctor is always marked for calumny[11] therefore.

But as we shall see, the steady manner he displays does not spring from an untroubled soul. He is a sinner, a sinner not only against the moral fashion of the time, but against his own vision of decent conduct. These people had no ritual for the washing away of sins. It is another trait we inherited from them, and it has helped to discipline us as well as to breed hypocrisy among us. Proctor, respected and even feared in Salem, has come to regard himself as a kind of fraud. But no hint of this has yet appeared on the surface, and as he enters from the crowded parlor below it is a man in his prime we see, with a quiet confidence and an unexpressed, hidden force. Mary Warren, his servant, can barely speak for embarrassment and fear.

---

10. **bring . . . shudder you:** inflict a terrifying punishment on you.

11. **marked for calumny** (kăl′əm-nē): singled out to have lies told about him.

Mary Warren. Oh! I'm just going home, Mr. Proctor.

Proctor. Be you foolish, Mary Warren? Be you deaf? I forbid you leave the house, did I not? Why shall I pay you? I am looking for you more often than my cows!

Mary Warren. I only come to see the great doings in the world.

Proctor. I'll show you a great doin' on your arse one
380 of these days. Now get you home; my wife is waitin' with your work! (*Trying to retain a shred of dignity, she goes slowly out.*)

Mercy Lewis (*both afraid of him and strangely titillated*). I'd best be off. I have my Ruth to watch. Good morning, Mr. Proctor.

(*Mercy sidles out. Since* Proctor's *entrance,* Abigail *has stood as though on tiptoe, absorbing his presence, wide-eyed. He glances at her, then goes to* Betty *on the bed.*)

Abigail. Gah! I'd almost forgot how strong you are,
390 John Proctor!

Proctor (*looking at* Abigail *now, the faintest suggestion of a knowing smile on his face*). What's this mischief here?

Abigail (*with a nervous laugh*). Oh, she's only gone silly somehow.

Proctor. The road past my house is a pilgrimage to Salem all morning. The town's mumbling witchcraft.

Abigail. Oh, posh! (*Winningly she comes a little closer, with a confidential, wicked air.*) We were dancin' in the woods last night, and my uncle leaped in on us.
400 She took fright, is all.

Proctor (*his smile widening*). Ah, you're wicked yet, aren't y'! (*A trill of expectant laughter escapes her, and she dares come closer, feverishly looking into his eyes.*) You'll be clapped in the stocks before you're twenty.

(*He takes a step to go, and she springs into his path.*)

Abigail. Give me a word, John. A soft word. (*Her concentrated desire destroys his smile.*)

Proctor. No, no, Abby. That's done with.

Abigail (*tauntingly*). You come five mile to see a silly
410 girl fly? I know you better.

Proctor (*setting her firmly out of his path*). I come to see what mischief your uncle's brewin' now. (*with final emphasis*) Put it out of mind, Abby.

Abigail (*grasping his hand before he can release her*). John—I am waitin' for you every night.

Proctor. Abby, I never give you hope to wait for me.

Abigail (*now beginning to anger—she can't believe it*). I have something better than hope, I think!

Proctor. Abby, you'll put it out of mind. I'll not be
420 comin' for you more.

Abigail. You're surely sportin' with me.

Proctor. You know me better.

Abigail. I know how you clutched my back behind your house and sweated like a stallion whenever I come near! Or did I dream that? It's she put me out, you cannot pretend it were you. I saw your face when she put me out, and you loved me then and you do now!

Proctor. Abby, that's a wild thing to say—

430 **Abigail.** A wild thing may say wild things. But not so wild, I think. I have seen you since she put me out; I have seen you nights.

Proctor. I have hardly stepped off my farm this sevenmonth.

Abigail. I have a sense for heat, John, and yours has drawn me to my window, and I have seen you looking up, burning in your loneliness. Do you tell me you've never looked up at my window?

Proctor. I may have looked up.

440 **Abigail** (*now softening*). And you must. You are no wintry man. I *know* you, John. I know you. (*She is weeping.*) I cannot sleep for dreamin'; I cannot dream but I wake and walk about the house as though I'd find you comin' through some door. (*She clutches him desperately*).

Proctor (*gently pressing her from him, with great sympathy but firmly*). Child—

Abigail (*with a flash of anger*). How do you call me child!

450 **Proctor.** Abby, I may think of you softly from time to time. But I will cut off my hand before I'll ever reach for you again. Wipe it out of mind. We never touched, Abby.

Abigail. Aye, but we did.

Proctor. Aye, but we did not.

Abigail (*with a bitter anger*). Oh, I marvel how such a strong man may let such a sickly wife be—

Proctor (*angered—at himself as well*). You'll speak nothin' of Elizabeth!

460 **Abigail.** She is blackening my name in the village! She is telling lies about me! She is a cold, sniveling woman, and you bend to her! Let her turn you like a—

Proctor (*shaking her*). Do you look for whippin'?

(*A psalm is heard being sung below.*)

Abigail (*in tears*). I look for John Proctor that took me from my sleep and put knowledge in my heart! I never knew what pretense Salem was, I never knew the lying lessons I was taught by all these Christian women and their covenanted[12] men! And now you **470** bid me tear the light out of my eyes? I will not, I cannot! You loved me, John Proctor, and whatever sin it is, you love me yet! (*He turns abruptly to go out. She rushes to him.*) John, pity me, pity me!

(*The words "going up to Jesus" are heard in the psalm, and* Betty *claps her ears suddenly and whines loudly.*)

Abigail. Betty? (*She hurries to* Betty, *who is now sitting up and screaming.* Proctor *goes to* Betty *as* Abigail *is trying to pull her hands down, calling* "Betty!")

Proctor (*growing unnerved*). What's she doing? Girl, **480** what ails you? Stop that wailing!

(*The singing has stopped in the midst of this, and now* Parris *rushes in.*)

Parris. What happened? What are you doing to her? Betty! (*He rushes to the bed, crying,* "Betty, Betty!" Mrs. Putnam *enters, feverish with curiosity, and with her* Thomas Putnam *and* Mercy Lewis. Parris, *at the bed, keeps lightly slapping* Betty's *face, while she moans and tries to get up.*)

Abigail. She heard you singin' and suddenly she's up **490** and screamin'.

Mrs. Putnam. The psalm! The psalm! She cannot bear to hear the Lord's name!

Parris. No. God forbid. Mercy, run to the doctor! Tell him what's happened here! (Mercy Lewis *rushes out.*)

Mrs. Putnam. Mark it for a sign, mark it!

(Rebecca Nurse, *seventy-two, enters. She is white-haired, leaning upon her walking-stick.*)

Putnam (*pointing at the whimpering* Betty). That is a notorious sign of witchcraft afoot, Goody Nurse, **500** a prodigious sign!

Mrs. Putnam. My mother told me that! When they cannot bear to hear the name of—

Parris (*trembling*). Rebecca, Rebecca, go to her, we're lost. She suddenly cannot bear to hear the Lord's—

(Giles Corey, *eighty-three, enters. He is knotted with muscle, canny, inquisitive, and still powerful.*)

Rebecca. There is hard sickness here, Giles Corey, so please to keep the quiet.

Giles. I've not said a word. No one here can testify I've **510** said a word. Is she going to fly again? I hear she flies.

Putnam. Man, be quiet now!

(*Everything is quiet.* Rebecca *walks across the room to the bed. Gentleness exudes from her.* Betty *is quietly whimpering, eyes shut.* Rebecca *simply stands over the child, who gradually quiets.*)

And while they are so absorbed, we may put a word in for Rebecca. Rebecca was the wife of Francis Nurse, who, from all accounts, was one of those men for whom both sides of the argument had to have respect. He was called upon to arbitrate disputes as though he were an unofficial judge, and

---

12. **covenanted** (kŭv′ə-nən-tĭd): In Puritan religious practice, the men of a congregation would make an agreement, or covenant, to govern the community and abide by its beliefs and practices.

Rebecca also enjoyed the high opinion most people had for him. By the time of the delusion,[13] they had three hundred acres, and their children were settled in separate homesteads within the same estate. However, Francis had originally rented the land, and one theory has it that, as he gradually paid for it and raised his social status, there were those who resented his rise.

Another suggestion to explain the systematic campaign against Rebecca, and inferentially against Francis, is the land war he fought with his neighbors, one of whom was a Putnam. This squabble grew to the proportions of a battle in the woods between partisans of both sides, and it is said to have lasted for two days. As for Rebecca herself, the general opinion of her character was so high that to explain how anyone dared cry her out for a witch—and more, how adults could bring themselves to lay hands on her—we must look to the fields and boundaries of that time.

As we have seen, Thomas Putnam's man for the Salem ministry was Bayley. The Nurse clan had been in the faction that prevented Bayley's taking office. In addition, certain families allied to the Nurses by blood or friendship, and whose farms were contiguous with the Nurse farm or close to it, combined to break away from the Salem town authority and set up Topsfield, a new and independent entity whose existence was resented by old Salemites.

That the guiding hand behind the outcry was Putnam's is indicated by the fact that, as soon as it began, this Topsfield-Nurse faction absented themselves from church in protest and disbelief. It was Edward and Jonathan Putnam who signed the first complaint against Rebecca; and Thomas Putnam's little daughter was the one who fell into a fit at the hearing and pointed to Rebecca as her attacker. To top it all, Mrs. Putnam—who is now staring at the bewitched child on the bed—soon accused Rebecca's spirit of "tempting her to **iniquity**," a charge that had more truth in it than Mrs. Putnam could know.

Mrs. Putnam (*astonished*). What have you done?

(Rebecca, *in thought, now leaves the bedside and sits.*)

Parris (*wondrous and relieved*). What do you make of it, Rebecca?

520 **Putnam** (*eagerly*). Goody Nurse, will you go to my Ruth and see if you can wake her?

Rebecca (*sitting*). I think she'll wake in time. Pray calm yourselves. I have eleven children, and I am twenty-six times a grandma, and I have seen them all through their silly seasons, and when it come on them they will run the Devil bowlegged keeping up with their mischief. I think she'll wake when she tires of it. A child's spirit is like a child, you can never catch it by running after it; you must stand 530 still, and, for love, it will soon itself come back.

Proctor. Aye, that's the truth of it, Rebecca.

Mrs. Putnam. This is no silly season, Rebecca. My Ruth is bewildered, Rebecca; she cannot eat.

Rebecca. Perhaps she is not hungered yet. (*to* Parris) I hope you are not decided to go in search of loose spirits, Mr. Parris. I've heard promise of that outside.

Parris. A wide opinion's running in the parish that the Devil may be among us, and I would satisfy them that they are wrong.

540 **Proctor.** Then let you come out and call them wrong. Did you consult the wardens[14] before you called this minister to look for devils?

Parris. He is not coming to look for devils!

Proctor. Then what's he coming for?

Putnam. There be children dyin' in the village, Mister!

Proctor. I seen none dyin'. This society will not be a bag to swing around your head, Mr. Putnam. (*to* Parris) Did you call a meeting before you—?

Putnam. I am sick of meetings; cannot the man turn 550 his head without he have a meeting?

Proctor. He may turn his head, but not to Hell!

Rebecca. Pray, John, be calm. (*Pause. He defers to her.*) Mr. Parris, I think you'd best send Reverend

---

13. **the time of the delusion:** the era of the witchcraft accusations and trials.

14. **wardens:** officers appointed to keep order.

Hale back as soon as he come. This will set us all to arguin' again in the society, and we thought to have peace this year. I think we ought rely on the doctor now, and good prayer.

Mrs. Putnam. Rebecca, the doctor's baffled!

Rebecca. If so he is, then let us go to God for the
560 cause of it. There is prodigious danger in the seeking of loose spirits. I fear it, I fear it. Let us rather blame ourselves and—

Putnam. How may we blame ourselves? I am one of nine sons; the Putnam seed have peopled this province. And yet I have but one child left of eight—and now she shrivels!

Rebecca. I cannot fathom that.

Mrs. Putnam (*with a growing edge of sarcasm*). But I must! You think it God's work you should never
570 lose a child, nor grandchild either, and I bury all but one? There are wheels within wheels in this village, and fires within fires!

Putnam (*to* Parris). When Reverend Hale comes, you will proceed to look for signs of witchcraft here.

Proctor (*to* Putnam). You cannot command Mr. Parris. We vote by name in this society, not by acreage.

Putnam. I never heard you worried so on this society, Mr. Proctor. I do not think I saw you at Sabbath meeting since snow flew.

580 **Proctor.** I have trouble enough without I come five mile to hear him preach only hellfire and bloody damnation. Take it to heart, Mr. Parris. There are many others who stay away from church these days because you hardly ever mention God any more.

Parris (*now aroused*). Why, that's a drastic charge!

Rebecca. It's somewhat true; there are many that quail to bring their children—

Parris. I do not preach for children, Rebecca. It is not the children who are unmindful of their obliga-
590 tions toward this ministry.

Rebecca. Are there really those unmindful?

Parris. I should say the better half of Salem village—

Putnam. And more than that!

Parris. Where is my wood? My contract provides I be supplied with all my firewood. I am waiting since November for a stick, and even in November I had to show my frostbitten hands like some London beggar!

Giles. You are allowed six pound a year to buy your wood, Mr. Parris.

600 **Parris.** I regard that six pound as part of my salary. I am paid little enough without I spend six pound on firewood.

Proctor. Sixty, plus six for firewood—

Parris. The salary is sixty-six pound, Mr. Proctor! I am not some preaching farmer with a book under my arm; I am a graduate of Harvard College.

Giles. Aye, and well instructed in arithmetic!

Parris. Mr. Corey, you will look far for a man of my kind at sixty pound a year! I am not used to this
610 poverty; I left a thrifty business in the Barbados to serve the Lord. I do not fathom it, why am I persecuted here? I cannot offer one proposition but there be a howling riot of argument. I have often wondered if the Devil be in it somewhere; I cannot understand you people otherwise.

Proctor. Mr. Parris, you are the first minister ever did demand the deed to this house—

Parris. Man! Don't a minister deserve a house to live in?

620 **Proctor.** To live in, yes. But to ask ownership is like you shall own the meeting house itself; the last meeting I were at you spoke so long on deeds and mortgages I thought it were an auction.

Parris. I want a mark of confidence, is all! I am your third preacher in seven years. I do not wish to be put out like the cat whenever some majority feels the whim. You people seem not to comprehend that a minister is the Lord's man in the parish; a minister is not to be so lightly crossed and contradicted—

630 **Putnam.** Aye!

Parris. There is either obedience or the church will burn like Hell is burning!

Proctor. Can you speak one minute without we land in Hell again? I am sick of Hell!

Scene Selection

The film scenes pictured here show a meeting between John Proctor and Abigail that never took place in the play, and the girls dancing in the forest, which occurs before the play begins. Why do you think such scenes were left out of the original play? Identify the advantages and disadvantages of presenting these scenes in the film version.

Parris. It is not for you to say what is good for you to hear!

Proctor. I may speak my heart, I think!

Parris (*in a fury*). What, are we Quakers?[15] We are not Quakers here yet, Mr. Proctor. And you may tell
640 that to your followers!

Proctor. My followers!

Parris (*Now he's out with it*). There is a party in this church. I am not blind; there is a faction and a party.

Proctor. Against you?

Putnam. Against him and all authority!

Proctor. Why, then I must find it and join it.

(*There is shock among the others.*)

Rebecca. He does not mean that.

Putnam. He confessed it now!

650 **Proctor.** I mean it solemnly, Rebecca; I like not the smell of this "authority."

Rebecca. No, you cannot break charity[16] with your minister. You are another kind, John. Clasp his hand, make your peace.

Proctor. I have a crop to sow and lumber to drag home. (*He goes angrily to the door and turns to* Corey *with a smile.*) What say you, Giles, let's find the party. He says there's a party.

Giles. I've changed my opinion of this man, John.
660 Mr. Parris, I beg your pardon. I never thought you had so much iron in you.

Parris (*surprised*). Why, thank you, Giles!

Giles. It suggests to the mind what the trouble be among us all these years. (*to all*) Think on it. Wherefore is everybody suing everybody else? Think on it now, it's a deep thing, and dark as a pit. I have been six time in court this year—

Proctor (*familiarly, with warmth, although he knows he is approaching the edge of* Giles' *tolerance with this*).
670 Is it the Devil's fault that a man cannot say you good morning without you clap him for defamation?[17] You're old, Giles, and you're not hearin' so well as you did.

Giles (*He cannot be crossed*). John Proctor, I have only last month collected four pound damages for you publicly sayin' I burned the roof off your house, and I—

Proctor (*laughing*). I never said no such thing, but I've paid you for it, so I hope I can call you deaf without charge. Now come along, Giles, and help
680 me drag my lumber home.

Putnam. A moment, Mr. Proctor. What lumber is that you're draggin', if I may ask you?

Proctor. My lumber. From out my forest by the riverside.

Putnam. Why, we are surely gone wild this year. What **anarchy** is this? That tract is in my bounds, it's in my bounds, Mr. Proctor.

Proctor. In your bounds! (*indicating* Rebecca) I bought that tract from Goody Nurse's husband five
690 months ago.

Putnam. He had no right to sell it. It stands clear in my grandfather's will that all the land between the river and—

Proctor. Your grandfather had a habit of willing land that never belonged to him, if I may say it plain.

Giles. That's God's truth; he nearly willed away my north pasture but he knew I'd break his fingers before he'd set his name to it. Let's get your lumber home, John. I feel a sudden will to work coming on.

700 **Putnam.** You load one oak of mine and you'll fight to drag it home!

Giles. Aye, and we'll win too, Putnam—this fool and I. Come on! (*He turns to* Proctor *and starts out.*)

Putnam. I'll have my men on you, Corey! I'll clap a writ on you!

(*Enter* Reverend John Hale *of Beverly.*)

---

15. **Quakers:** a radical English religious sect—much hated by the Puritans—who often "spoke their heart" during their religious meetings.

16. **break charity:** break off; end the relationship.

17. **clap . . . defamation** (dĕf′ə-mā′shən): imprison him for slander.

Rob Campbell as Reverend Hale

Mr. Hale is nearing forty, a tight-skinned, eager-eyed intellectual. This is a beloved errand for him; on being called here to ascertain witchcraft he felt the pride of the specialist whose unique knowledge has at last been publicly called for. Like almost all men of learning, he spent a good deal of his time pondering the invisible world, especially since he had himself encountered a witch in his parish not long before. That woman, however, turned into a mere pest under his searching scrutiny, and the child she had allegedly been afflicting recovered her normal behavior after Hale had given her his kindness and a few days of rest in his own house. However, that experience never raised a doubt in his mind as to the reality of the underworld or the existence of Lucifer's many-faced lieutenants. And his belief is not to his discredit. Better minds than Hale's were—and still are—convinced that there is a society of spirits beyond our ken. One cannot help noting that one of his lines has never yet raised a laugh in any audience that has seen this play; it is his assurance that "We cannot look to superstition in this. The Devil is precise." Evidently we are not quite certain even now whether diabolism is holy and not to be scoffed at. And it is no accident that we should be so bemused.

Like Reverend Hale and the others on this stage, we conceive the Devil as a necessary part of a respectable view of cosmology.[18] Ours is a divided empire in which certain ideas and emotions and actions are of God, and their opposites are of Lucifer. It is as impossible for most men to conceive of a morality without sin as of an earth without "sky." Since 1692 a great but superficial change has wiped out God's beard and the Devil's horns, but the world is still gripped between two diametrically opposed

---

18. **cosmology** (kŏz-mŏl′ə-jē): a branch of philosophy dealing with the structure of the universe.

absolutes. The concept of unity, in which positive and negative are attributes of the same force, in which good and evil are relative, ever-changing, and always joined to the same phenomenon—such a concept is still reserved to the physical sciences and to the few who have grasped the history of ideas. When it is recalled that until the Christian era the underworld was never regarded as a hostile area, that all gods were useful and essentially friendly to man despite occasional lapses; when we see the steady and methodical inculcation into humanity of the idea of man's worthlessness—until redeemed—the necessity of the Devil may become evident as a weapon, a weapon designed and used time and time again in every age to whip men into a surrender to a particular church or church-state.

Our difficulty in believing the—for want of a better word—political inspiration of the Devil is due in great part to the fact that he is called up and damned not only by our social antagonists but by our own side, whatever it may be. The Catholic Church, through its Inquisition,[19] is famous for cultivating Lucifer as the arch-fiend, but the Church's enemies relied no less upon the Old Boy to keep the human mind enthralled. Luther[20] was himself accused of alliance with Hell, and he in turn accused his enemies. To complicate matters further, he believed that he had had contact with the Devil and had argued theology with him. I am not surprised at this, for at my own university a professor of history—a Lutheran, by the way—used to assemble his graduate students, draw the shades, and commune in the classroom with Erasmus.[21] He was never, to my knowledge, officially scoffed at for this, the reason being that the university officials, like most of us, are the children of a history which still sucks at the Devil's teats. At this writing, only England has held back before the temptations of contemporary diabolism. In the countries of the Communist ideology, all resistance of any import is linked to the totally malign capitalist succubi,[22] and in America any man who is not reactionary in his views is open to the charge of alliance with the Red hell. Political opposition, thereby, is given an inhumane overlay which then justifies the abrogation of all normally applied customs of civilized intercourse. A political policy is equated with moral right, and opposition to it with diabolical malevolence. Once such an equation is effectively made, society becomes a congerie of plots and counterplots, and the main role of government changes from that of the arbiter to that of the scourge of God.

The results of this process are no different now from what they ever were, except sometimes in the degree of cruelty inflicted, and not always even in that department. Normally the actions and deeds of a man were all that society felt comfortable in judging. The secret intent of an action was left to the ministers, priests, and rabbis to deal with. When diabolism rises, however, actions are the least important manifests of the true nature of a man. The Devil, as Reverend Hale said, is a wily one, and, until an hour before he fell, even God thought him beautiful in Heaven.[23]

The analogy, however, seems to falter when one considers that, while there were no witches then, there are Communists and capitalists now, and in each camp there is certain proof that spies of each side are at work undermining the other. But this is a snobbish objection and not at all warranted by the facts. I have no doubt that people *were* communing with, and even worshiping, the Devil in Salem,

19. **Inquisition:** a former tribunal in the Roman Catholic Church dedicated to the discovery and punishment of heresy.

20. **Luther:** Martin Luther (1483–1546), the German theologian who led the Protestant Reformation.

21. **Erasmus** (ĭ-răz′məs): Desiderius Erasmus (1466?–1536), a Dutch scholar who sought to restore Christian faith by a study of the Scriptures and classical texts.

22. **succubi** (sŭk′yə-bī): demons that assume female form. Demons that assume male form are called incubi (ĭn′kyə-bī).

23. **The Devil . . . beautiful in Heaven:** According to Christian belief, Lucifer was God's favorite angel until the angel rebelled and was cast out of Heaven.

and if the whole truth could be known in this case, as it is in others, we should discover a regular and conventionalized propitiation of the dark spirit. One certain evidence of this is the confession of Tituba, the slave of Reverend Parris, and another is the behavior of the children who were known to have indulged in sorceries with her.

There are accounts of similar *klatches* in Europe, where the daughters of the towns would assemble at night and, sometimes with fetishes, sometimes with a selected young man, give themselves to love, with some bastardly results. The Church, sharp-eyed as it must be when gods long dead are brought to life, condemned these orgies as witchcraft and interpreted them, rightly, as a resurgence of the Dionysiac forces[24] it had crushed long before. Sex, sin, and the Devil were early linked, and so they continued to be in Salem, and are today. From all accounts there are no more puritanical mores in the world than those enforced by the Communists in Russia, where women's fashions, for instance, are as prudent and all-covering as any American Baptist would desire. The divorce laws lay a tremendous responsibility on the father for the care of his children. Even the laxity of divorce regulations in the early years of the revolution was undoubtedly a revulsion from the nineteenth-century Victorian immobility of marriage and the consequent hypocrisy that developed from it. If for no other reasons, a state so powerful, so jealous of the uniformity of its citizens, cannot long tolerate the atomization of the family. And yet, in American eyes at least, there remains the conviction that the Russian attitude toward women is lascivious. It is the Devil working again, just as he is working within the Slav[25] who is shocked at the very idea of a woman's disrobing herself in a burlesque show. Our opposites are always robed in sexual sin, and it is from this unconscious conviction that demonology gains both its attractive sensuality and its capacity to infuriate and frighten.

Coming into Salem now, Reverend Hale conceives of himself much as a young doctor on his first call. His painfully acquired armory of symptoms, catchwords, and diagnostic procedures are now to be put to use at last. The road from Beverly is unusually busy this morning, and he has passed a hundred rumors that make him smile at the ignorance of the yeomanry in this most precise science. He feels himself allied with the best minds of Europe— kings, philosophers, scientists, and ecclesiasts of all churches. His goal is light, goodness and its preservation, and he knows the exaltation of the blessed whose intelligence, sharpened by minute examinations of enormous tracts, is finally called upon to face what may be a bloody fight with the Fiend himself.

———◆◆◆———

(*He appears loaded down with half a dozen heavy books.*)

Hale. Pray you, someone take these!

710 **Parris** (*delighted*). Mr. Hale! Oh! it's good to see you again! (*taking some books*) My, they're heavy!

Hale (*setting down his books*). They must be; they are weighted with authority.

Parris (*a little scared*). Well, you do come prepared!

Hale. We shall need hard study if it comes to tracking down the Old Boy. (*noticing* Rebecca) You cannot be Rebecca Nurse?

Rebecca. I am, sir. Do you know me?

Hale. It's strange how I knew you, but I suppose you
720 look as such a good soul should. We have all heard of your great charities in Beverly.

Parris. Do you know this gentleman? Mr. Thomas Putnam. And his good wife Ann.

Hale. Putnam! I had not expected such distinguished company, sir.

---

24. **Dionysiac** (dī′ə-nĭs′ē-ăk′) **forces:** forces associated with Dionysus, the Greek god of wine and ecstasy.

25. **Slav:** a generic reference to Russians and other Slavic-speaking peoples of Eastern Europe who were under the control of the Soviet Union.

Putnam (*pleased*). It does not seem to help us today, Mr. Hale. We look to you to come to our house and save our child.

Hale. Your child ails too?

730 **Mrs. Putnam.** Her soul, her soul seems flown away. She sleeps and yet she walks . . .

Putnam. She cannot eat.

Hale. Cannot eat! (*Thinks on it. Then, to* Proctor *and* Giles Corey.) Do you men have afflicted children?

Parris. No, no, these are farmers. John Proctor—

Giles Corey. He don't believe in witches.

Proctor (*to* Hale). I never spoke on witches one way or the other. Will you come, Giles?

Giles. No—no, John, I think not. I have some few

740 queer questions of my own to ask this fellow.

Proctor. I've heard you to be a sensible man, Mr. Hale. I hope you'll leave some of it in Salem.

(Proctor *goes.* Hale *stands embarrassed for an instant.*)

Parris (*quickly*). Will you look at my daughter, sir? (*leads* Hale *to the bed*) She has tried to leap out the window; we discovered her this morning on the highroad, waving her arms as though she'd fly.

Hale (*narrowing his eyes*). Tries to fly.

Putnam. She cannot bear to hear the Lord's name,

750 Mr. Hale; that's a sure sign of witchcraft afloat.

Hale (*holding up his hands*). No, no. Now let me instruct you. We cannot look to superstition in this. The Devil is precise; the marks of his presence are definite as stone, and I must tell you all that I shall not proceed unless you are prepared to believe me if I should find no bruise of hell upon her.

Parris. It is agreed, sir—it is agreed—we will abide by your judgment.

Hale. Good then. (*He goes to the bed, looks down*

760 *at* Betty. *To* Parris.) Now, sir, what were your first warning of this strangeness?

Parris. Why, sir—I discovered her—(*indicating* Abigail) and my niece and ten or twelve of the other girls, dancing in the forest last night.

Hale (*surprised*). You permit dancing?

Parris. No, no, it were secret—

Mrs. Putnam (*unable to wait*). Mr. Parris's slave has knowledge of conjurin', sir.

Parris (*to* Mrs. Putnam). We cannot be sure of that,

770 Goody Ann—

Mrs. Putnam (*frightened, very softly*). I know it, sir. I sent my child—she should learn from Tituba who murdered her sisters.

Rebecca (*horrified*). Goody Ann! You sent a child to conjure up the dead?

Mrs. Putnam. Let God blame me, not you, not you, Rebecca! I'll not have you judging me any more! (*to* Hale) Is it a natural work to lose seven children before they live a day?

780 **Parris.** Sssh!

(Rebecca, *with great pain, turns her face away. There is a pause.*)

Hale. Seven dead in childbirth.

Mrs. Putnam (*softly*). Aye. (*Her voice breaks; she looks up at him. Silence.* Hale *is impressed.* Parris *looks to him. He goes to his books, opens one, turns pages, then reads. All wait, avidly.*)

Parris (*hushed*). What book is that?

Mrs. Putnam. What's there, sir?

790 **Hale** (*with a tasty love of intellectual pursuit*). Here is all the invisible world, caught, defined, and calculated. In these books the Devil stands stripped of all his brute disguises. Here are all your familiar spirits—your incubi and succubi; your witches that go by land, by air, and by sea; your wizards of the night and of the day. Have no fear now—we shall find him out if he has come among us, and I mean to crush him utterly if he has shown his face! (*He starts for the bed.*)

Rebecca. Will it hurt the child, sir?

800 **Hale.** I cannot tell. If she is truly in the Devil's grip we may have to rip and tear to get her free.

Rebecca. I think I'll go, then. I am too old for this. (*She rises.*)

Parris (*striving for conviction*). Why, Rebecca, we may open up the boil of all our troubles today!

Rebecca. Let us hope for that. I go to God for you, sir.

Parris (*with trepidation—and resentment*). I hope you do not mean we go to Satan here! (*slight pause*)

810 **Rebecca.** I wish I knew. (*She goes out; they feel resentful of her note of moral superiority.*)

Putnam (*abruptly*). Come, Mr. Hale, let's get on. Sit you here.

Giles. Mr. Hale, I have always wanted to ask a learned man—what signifies the readin' of strange books?

Hale. What books?

Giles. I cannot tell; she hides them.

Hale. Who does this?

Giles. Martha, my wife. I have waked at night many 820 a time and found her in a corner, readin' of a book. Now what do you make of that?

Hale. Why, that's not necessarily—

Giles. It discomfits me! Last night—mark this—I tried and tried and could not say my prayers. And then she close her book and walks out of the house, and suddenly—mark this—I could pray again!

Old Giles must be spoken for, if only because his fate was to be so remarkable and so different from that of all the others. He was in his early eighties at this time, and was the most comical hero in the history. No man has ever been blamed for so much. If a cow was missed, the first thought was to look for her around Corey's house; a fire blazing up at night brought suspicion of arson to his door. He didn't give a hoot for public opinion, and only in his last years—after he had married Martha—did he bother much with the church. That she stopped his prayer is very probable, but he forgot to say that he'd only recently learned any prayers and it didn't take much to make him stumble over them. He was a crank and a nuisance, but withal a deeply innocent and brave man. In court once, he was asked if it were true that he had been frightened by the strange behavior of a hog and had then said he knew it to be the Devil in an animal's shape. "What frighted you?" he was asked. He forgot everything but the word "frighted," and instantly replied, "I do not know that I ever spoke that word in my life."

———————

Hale. Ah! The stoppage of prayer—that is strange. I'll speak further on that with you.

Giles. I'm not sayin' she's touched the Devil, now, 830 but I'd admire to know what books she reads and why she hides them. She'll not answer me, y' see.

Hale. Aye, we'll discuss it. (*to all*) Now mark me, if the Devil is in her you will witness some frightful wonders in this room, so please to keep your wits about you. Mr. Putnam, stand close in case she flies. Now, Betty, dear, will you sit up? (*Putnam comes in closer, ready-handed. Hale sits Betty up, but she hangs limp in his hands.*) Hmmm. (*He observes her carefully. The others watch breathlessly.*) Can you hear me? I am 840 John Hale, minister of Beverly. I have come to help you, dear. Do you remember my two little girls in Beverly? (*She does not stir in his hands.*)

Parris (*in fright*). How can it be the Devil? Why would he choose my house to strike? We have all manner of licentious people in the village!

Hale. What victory would the Devil have to win a soul already bad? It is the best the Devil wants, and who is better than the minister?

Giles. That's deep, Mr. Parris, deep, deep!

850 **Parris** (*with resolution now*). Betty! Answer Mr. Hale! Betty!

Hale. Does someone afflict you, child? It need not be a woman, mind you, or a man. Perhaps some bird invisible to others comes to you—perhaps a pig, a mouse, or any beast at all. Is there some figure bids you fly? (*The child remains limp in his hands. In silence he lays her back on the pillow. Now, holding out his hands toward her, he intones.*) In nomine Domini Sabaoth sui filiique ite ad infernos.[26] (*She does not stir.* 860 *He turns to* Abigail, *his eyes narrowing.*) Abigail, what sort of dancing were you doing with her in the forest?

———————

26. **In nomine . . . infernos** *Latin:* "In the name of the Father and Son, get thee back to Hell."

Abigail. Why—common dancing is all.

Parris. I think I ought to say that I—I saw a kettle in the grass where they were dancing.

Abigail. That were only soup.

Hale. What sort of soup were in this kettle, Abigail?

Abigail. Why, it were beans—and lentils, I think, and—

Hale. Mr. Parris, you did not notice, did you, any 870 living thing in the kettle? A mouse, perhaps, a spider, a frog—?

Parris (*fearfully*). I—do believe there were some movement—in the soup.

Abigail. That jumped in, we never put it in!

Hale (*quickly*). What jumped in?

Abigail. Why, a very little frog jumped—

Parris. A frog, Abby!

Hale (*grasping Abigail*). Abigail, it may be your cousin is dying. Did you call the Devil last night?

880 **Abigail.** I never called him! Tituba, Tituba . . .

Parris (*blanched*). She called the Devil?

Hale. I should like to speak with Tituba.

Parris. Goody Ann, will you bring her up?
(Mrs. Putnam *exits.*)

Hale. How did she call him?

Abigail. I know not—she spoke Barbados.

Hale. Did you feel any strangeness when she called him? A sudden cold wind, perhaps? A trembling below the ground?

890 **Abigail.** I didn't see no Devil! (*shaking* Betty) Betty, wake up. Betty! Betty!

Hale. You cannot evade me, Abigail. Did your cousin drink any of the brew in that kettle?

Abigail. She never drank it!

Hale. Did you drink it?

Abigail. No, sir!

Hale. Did Tituba ask you to drink it?

Abigail. She tried, but I refused.

Hale. Why are you concealing? Have you sold your-
900 self to Lucifer?

Abigail. I never sold myself! I'm a good girl! I'm a proper girl!

(Mrs. Putnam *enters with* Tituba, *and instantly* Abigail *points at* Tituba.)

Abigail. She made me do it! She made Betty do it!

Tituba (*shocked and angry*). Abby!

Abigail. She makes me drink blood!

Parris. Blood!!

Mrs. Putnam. My baby's blood?

910 **Tituba.** No, no, chicken blood. I give she chicken blood!

Hale. Woman, have you enlisted these children for the Devil?

Tituba. No, no, sir, I don't truck with no Devil!

Hale. Why can she not wake? Are you silencing this child?

Tituba. I love me Betty!

Hale. You have sent your spirit out upon this child, have you not? Are you gathering souls for the Devil?

920 **Abigail.** She sends her spirit on me in church; she makes me laugh at prayer!

Parris. She have often laughed at prayer!

Abigail. She comes to me every night to go and drink blood!

Tituba. You beg *me* to conjure! She beg *me* make charm—

Abigail. Don't lie! (*to* Hale) She comes to me while I sleep; she's always making me dream corruptions!

Tituba. Why you say that, Abby?

930 **Abigail.** Sometimes I wake and find myself standing in the open doorway and not a stitch on my body! I always hear her laughing in my sleep. I hear her singing her Barbados songs and tempting me with—

Tituba. Mister Reverend, I never—

Hale (*resolved now*). Tituba, I want you to wake this child.

Tituba. I have no power on this child, sir.

Hale. You most certainly do, and you will free her from it now! When did you compact with the Devil?

940 **Tituba.** I don't compact with no Devil!

Parris. You will confess yourself or I will take you out and whip you to your death, Tituba!

Putnam. This woman must be hanged! She must be taken and hanged!

Tituba (*terrified, falls to her knees*). No, no, don't hang Tituba! I tell him I don't desire to work for him, sir.

Parris. The Devil?

Hale. Then you saw him! (Tituba *weeps*.) Now
950 Tituba, I know that when we bind ourselves to Hell it is very hard to break with it. We are going to help you tear yourself free—

Tituba (*frightened by the coming process*). Mister Reverend, I do believe somebody else be witchin' these children.

Hale. Who?

Tituba. I don't know, sir, but the Devil got him numerous witches.

Hale. Does he! *It is a clue.* Tituba, look into my eyes.
960 Come, look into me. (*She raises her eyes to his fearfully.*) You would be a good Christian woman, would you not, Tituba?

Tituba. Aye, sir, a good Christian woman.

Hale. And you love these little children?

Tituba. Oh, yes, sir, I don't desire to hurt little children.

Hale. And you love God, Tituba?

Tituba. I love God with all my bein'.

Hale. Now, in God's holy name—

970 **Tituba.** Bless Him. Bless Him. (*She is rocking on her knees, sobbing in terror.*)

Hale. And to His glory—

Tituba. Eternal glory. Bless Him—bless God . . .

Hale. Open yourself, Tituba—open yourself and let God's holy light shine on you.

Tituba. Oh, bless the Lord.

Hale. When the Devil comes to you does he ever come—with another person? (*She stares up into his face.*) Perhaps another person in the village? Some-
980 one you know.

Parris. Who came with him?

Putnam. Sarah Good? Did you ever see Sarah Good with him? Or Osburn?

Parris. Was it man or woman came with him?

Tituba. Man or woman. Was—was woman.

Parris. What woman? A woman, you said. What woman?

Tituba. It was black dark, and I—

Parris. You could see him, why could you not see
990 her?

Tituba. Well, they was always talking; they was always runnin' round and carryin' on—

Parris. You mean out of Salem? Salem witches?

Tituba. I believe so, yes, sir.

(*Now* Hale *takes her hand. She is surprised.*)

Hale. Tituba. You must have no fear to tell us who they are, do you understand? We will protect you. The Devil can never overcome a minister. You know that, do you not?

1000 **Tituba** (*kisses* Hale's *hand*). Aye, sir, oh, I do.

Hale. You have confessed yourself to witchcraft, and that speaks a wish to come to Heaven's side. And we will bless you, Tituba.

Tituba (*deeply relieved*). Oh, God bless you, Mr. Hale!

Hale (*with rising exaltation*). You are God's instrument put in our hands to discover the Devil's agents among us. You are selected, Tituba, you are chosen to help us cleanse our village. So speak utterly,
1010 Tituba, turn your back on him and face God—face God, Tituba, and God will protect you.

Tituba (*joining with him*). Oh, God, protect Tituba!

Hale (*kindly*). Who came to you with the Devil? Two? Three? Four? How many?

(Tituba *pants, and begins rocking back and forth again, staring ahead.*)

Tituba. There was four. There was four.

Parris (*pressing in on her*). Who? Who? Their names, their names!

1020 **Tituba** (*suddenly bursting out*). Oh, how many times he bid me kill you, Mr. Parris!

Parris. Kill me!

Tituba (*in a fury*). He say Mr. Parris must be kill! Mr. Parris no goodly man, Mr. Parris mean man and no gentle man, and he bid me rise out of my bed and cut your throat! (*They gasp.*) But I tell him "No! I don't hate that man. I don't want kill that man." But he say, "You work for me, Tituba, and I make you free! I give you pretty dress to wear, and put 1030 you way high up in the air, and you gone fly back to Barbados!" And I say, "You lie, Devil, you lie!" And then he come one stormy night to me, and he say, "Look! I have *white* people belong to me." And I look—and there was Goody Good.

Parris. Sarah Good!

Tituba (*rocking and weeping*). Aye, sir, and Goody Osburn.

Mrs. Putnam. I knew it! Goody Osburn were midwife to me three times. I begged you, Thomas, did 1040 I not? I begged him not to call Osburn because I feared her. My babies always shriveled in her hands!

Hale. Take courage, you must give us all their names. How can you bear to see this child suffering? Look at her, Tituba. (*He is indicating* Betty *on the bed.*) Look at her God-given innocence; her soul is so tender; we must protect her, Tituba; the Devil is out and preying on her like a beast upon the flesh of the pure lamb. God will bless you for your help.

(Abigail *rises, staring as though inspired, and cries out.*)

1050 **Abigail.** I want to open myself! (*They turn to her, startled. She is enraptured, as though in a pearly light.*) I want the light of God, I want the sweet love of Jesus! I danced for the Devil; I saw him; I wrote in his book; I go back to Jesus; I kiss His hand. I saw Sarah Good with the Devil! I saw Goody Osburn with the Devil! I saw Bridget Bishop with the Devil! (*As she is speaking,* Betty *is rising from the bed, a fever in her eyes, and picks up the chant.*)

Betty (*staring too*). I saw George Jacobs with the 1060 Devil! I saw Goody Howe with the Devil!

Parris. She speaks! (*He rushes to embrace* Betty.) She speaks!

Hale. Glory to God! It is broken, they are free!

Betty (*calling out hysterically and with great relief*). I saw Martha Bellows with the Devil!

Abigail. I saw Goody Sibber with the Devil! (*It is rising to a great glee.*)

Putnam. The marshal, I'll call the marshal!

(Parris *is shouting a prayer of thanksgiving.*)

1070 **Betty.** I saw Alice Barrow with the Devil!

(*The curtain begins to fall.*)

Hale (*as* Putnam *goes out*). Let the marshal bring irons!

Abigail. I saw Goody Hawkins with the Devil!

Betty. I saw Goody Bibber with the Devil!

Abigail. I saw Goody Booth with the Devil!

(*On their ecstatic cries, the curtain falls.*)

Comprehension

1. **Recall** What is the cause for concern in the Parris household?

2. **Clarify** What has occurred between John Proctor and Abigail Williams before the time in which the play begins?

3. **Summarize** Why does Reverend Hale come to Salem?

Literary Analysis

4. **Infer Character Motives** Reread lines 1017–1056 at the end of Act One. Why do you think Tituba and Abigail admit to having practiced witchcraft? Why do they name others?

5. **Draw Conclusions About Characters** Review the **traits** you recorded in your chart for the characters you have encountered so far. How would you describe the most important character traits of the following?

   • Abigail Williams   • John Proctor   • Reverend Hale

6. **Make Predictions** Based on what you have learned about Abigail in Act One, whom do you think she might accuse as the play goes on? Cite specific evidence to support your answer.

7. **Identify Beliefs** What do the characters in the play believe about witches? List their beliefs in a concept web like the one shown.

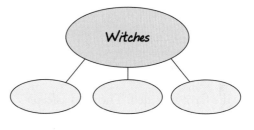

8. **Connect Setting and Mood** The setting of a literary work refers to the time and place in which the action occurs. How do you think Miller uses setting to help create mood in Act One?

9. **Analyze Conventions of Drama** Review the **stage directions** that take the form of mini-essays in Act One. What insights about America after the Second World War does Miller convey? Use details from the mini-essays in your answer.

Literary Criticism

10. **Author's Style** The mini-essays in Act One are not usually included in a stage production of *The Crucible*. Why do you think this is so? Why do you think Miller included them in his drama?

ACT *Two*

(*The common room of* Proctor's *house, eight days later.*

At the right is a door opening on the fields outside. A fireplace is at the left, and behind it a stairway leading upstairs. It is the low, dark, and rather long living room of the time. As the curtain rises, the room is empty. From above, Elizabeth *is heard softly singing to the children. Presently the door opens and* John Proctor *enters, carrying his gun. He glances about the room as he comes toward the fireplace, then halts for an instant as he hears her singing. He continues on to the fireplace, leans the gun against the wall as he swings a pot out of the fire and smells it. Then he lifts out the ladle and tastes. He is not quite pleased. He reaches to a cupboard, takes a pinch of salt, and drops it into the pot. As he is tasting again, her footsteps are heard on the stair. He swings the pot into the fireplace and goes to a basin and washes his hands and face.* Elizabeth *enters.*)

Elizabeth. What keeps you so late? It's almost dark.

Proctor. I were planting far out to the forest edge.

Elizabeth. Oh, you're done then.

Proctor. Aye, the farm is seeded. The boys asleep?

Elizabeth. They will be soon. (*And she goes to the fireplace, proceeds to ladle up stew in a dish.*)

Proctor. Pray now for a fair summer.

Elizabeth. Aye.

Proctor. Are you well today?

10 **Elizabeth.** I am. (*She brings the plate to the table, and, indicating the food.*) It is a rabbit.

Proctor (*going to the table*). Oh, is it! In Jonathan's trap?

Elizabeth. No, she walked into the house this afternoon; I found her sittin' in the corner like she come to visit.

Proctor. Oh, that's a good sign walkin' in.

Elizabeth. Pray God. It hurt my heart to strip her, poor rabbit. (*She sits and watches him taste it.*)

20 **Proctor.** It's well seasoned.

Elizabeth (*blushing with pleasure*). I took great care. She's tender?

Proctor. Aye. (*He eats. She watches him.*) I think we'll see green fields soon. It's warm as blood beneath the clods.

Elizabeth. That's well.

(Proctor *eats, then looks up.*)

Proctor. If the crop is good I'll buy George Jacob's heifer. How would that please you?

30 **Elizabeth.** Aye, it would.

Proctor (*with a grin*). I mean to please you, Elizabeth.

Elizabeth (*It is hard to say*). I know it, John.

(*He gets up, goes to her, kisses her. She receives it. With a certain disappointment, he returns to the table.*)

Proctor (*as gently as he can*). Cider?

Elizabeth (*with a sense of reprimanding herself for having forgot*). Aye! (*She gets up and goes and pours a glass for him. He now arches his back.*)

Joan Allen as Elizabeth Proctor

Proctor. This farm's a continent when you go foot
40 by foot droppin' seeds in it.

Elizabeth (*coming with the cider*). It must be.

Proctor (*drinks a long draught, then, putting the glass down*). You ought to bring some flowers in the house.

Elizabeth. Oh! I forgot! I will tomorrow.

Proctor. It's winter in here yet. On Sunday let you come with me, and we'll walk the farm together; I never see such a load of flowers on the earth. (*With good feeling he goes and looks up at the sky through the open doorway.*) Lilacs have a purple smell. Lilac is the
50 smell of nightfall, I think. Massachusetts is a beauty in the spring!

Elizabeth. Aye, it is.

(*There is a pause. She is watching him from the table as he stands there absorbing the night. It is as though she would speak but cannot. Instead, now, she takes up his plate and glass and fork and goes with them to the basin. Her back is turned to him. He turns to her and watches her. A sense of their separation rises.*)

Proctor. I think you're sad again. Are you?

60 **Elizabeth** (*She doesn't want friction, and yet she must*). You come so late I thought you'd gone to Salem this afternoon.

Proctor. Why? I have no business in Salem.

Elizabeth. You did speak of going, earlier this week.

Proctor (*He knows what she means*). I thought better of it since.

Elizabeth. Mary Warren's there today.

Proctor. Why'd you let her? You heard me forbid her go to Salem any more!

70 **Elizabeth.** I couldn't stop her.

Proctor (*holding back a full condemnation of her*). It is a fault, it is a fault, Elizabeth—you're the mistress here, not Mary Warren.

Elizabeth. She frightened all my strength away.

Proctor. How may that mouse frighten you, Elizabeth? You—

Elizabeth. It is a mouse no more. I forbid her go, and she raises up her chin like the daughter of a

prince and says to me, "I must go to Salem, Goody
80 Proctor; I am an official of the court!"

Proctor. Court! What court?

Elizabeth. Aye, it is a proper court they have now. They've sent four judges out of Boston, she says, weighty magistrates of the General Court, and at the head sits the Deputy Governor of the Province.

Proctor (*astonished*). Why, she's mad.

Elizabeth. I would to God she were. There be four-teen people in the jail now, she says. (Proctor *simply looks at her, unable to grasp it.*) And they'll be tried,
90 and the court have power to hang them too, she says.

Proctor (*scoffing, but without conviction*). Ah, they'd never hang—

Elizabeth. The Deputy Governor promise hangin' if they'll not confess, John. The town's gone wild, I think. She speak of Abigail, and I thought she were a saint, to hear her. Abigail brings the other girls into the court, and where she walks the crowd will part like the sea for Israel. And folks are brought before them, and if they scream and howl and fall to the floor—the
100 person's clapped in the jail for bewitchin' them.

Proctor (*wide-eyed*). Oh, it is a black mischief.

Elizabeth. I think you must go to Salem, John. (*He turns to her.*) I think so. You must tell them it is a fraud.

Proctor (*thinking beyond this*). Aye, it is, it is surely.

Elizabeth. Let you go to Ezekiel Cheever—he knows you well. And tell him what she said to you last week in her uncle's house. She said it had naught to do with witchcraft, did she not?

110 **Proctor** (*in thought*). Aye, she did, she did. (*now, a pause*)

Elizabeth (*quietly, fearing to anger him by prodding*). God forbid you keep that from the court, John. I think they must be told.

Proctor (*quietly, struggling with his thought*). Aye, they must, they must. It is a wonder they do believe her.

Elizabeth. I would go to Salem now, John—let you go tonight.

Proctor. I'll think on it.

120 **Elizabeth** (*with her courage now*). You cannot keep it, John.

Proctor (*angering*). I know I cannot keep it. I say I will think on it!

Elizabeth (*hurt, and very coldly*). Good, then, let you think on it. (*She stands and starts to walk out of the room.*)

Proctor. I am only wondering how I may prove what she told me, Elizabeth. If the girl's a saint now, I think it is not easy to prove she's fraud, and 130 the town gone so silly. She told it to me in a room alone—I have no proof for it.

Elizabeth. You were alone with her?

Proctor (*stubbornly*). For a moment alone, aye.

Elizabeth. Why, then, it is not as you told me.

Proctor (*his anger rising*). For a moment, I say. The others come in soon after.

Elizabeth (*quietly—she has suddenly lost all faith in him*). Do as you wish, then. (*She starts to turn.*)

Proctor. Woman. (*She turns to him.*) I'll not have 140 your suspicion any more.

Elizabeth (*a little loftily*). I have no—

Proctor. I'll not have it!

Elizabeth. Then let you not earn it.

Proctor (*with a violent undertone*). You doubt me yet?

Elizabeth (*with a smile, to keep her dignity*). John, if it were not Abigail that you must go to hurt, would you falter now? I think not.

Proctor. Now look you—

Elizabeth. I see what I see, John.

150 **Proctor** (*with solemn warning*). You will not judge me more, Elizabeth. I have good reason to think before I charge fraud on Abigail, and I will think on it. Let you look to your own improvement before you go to judge your husband any more. I have forgot Abigail, and—

Elizabeth. And I.

Proctor. Spare me! You forget nothin' and forgive nothin'. Learn charity, woman. I have gone tiptoe in this house all seven month since she is gone. I have 160 not moved from there to there without I think to please you, and still an everlasting funeral marches round your heart. I cannot speak but I am doubted, every moment judged for lies, as though I come into a court when I come into this house!

Elizabeth. John, you are not open with me. You saw her with a crowd, you said. Now you—

Proctor. I'll plead my honesty no more, Elizabeth.

Elizabeth (*now she would justify herself*). John, I am only—

170 **Proctor.** No more! I should have roared you down when first you told me your suspicion. But I wilted, and, like a Christian, I confessed. Confessed! Some dream I had must have mistaken you for God that day. But you're not, you're not, and let you remember it! Let you look sometimes for the goodness in me, and judge me not.

Elizabeth. I do not judge you. The magistrate sits in your heart that judges you. I never thought you but a good man, John—(*with a smile*)—only somewhat 180 bewildered.

Proctor (*laughing bitterly*). Oh, Elizabeth, your justice would freeze beer![1] (*He turns suddenly toward a sound outside. He starts for the door as Mary Warren enters. As soon as he sees her, he goes directly to her and grabs her by her cloak, furious.*) How do you go to Salem when I forbid it? Do you mock me? (*shaking her*) I'll whip you if you dare leave this house again!

(*Strangely, she doesn't resist him, but hangs limply by his grip.*)

190 **Mary Warren.** I am sick, I am sick, Mr. Proctor. Pray, pray, hurt me not. (*Her strangeness throws him off, and her evident pallor and weakness. He frees her.*) My insides are all shuddery; I am in the proceedings all day, sir.

---

1. **your justice . . . beer:** Alcoholic beverages freeze at very low temperatures, so Proctor is sarcastically calling his wife cold-hearted.

Proctor (*with draining anger—his curiosity is draining it*). And what of these proceedings here? When will you proceed to keep this house, as you are paid nine pound a year to do—and my wife not wholly well?

(*As though to compensate,* Mary Warren *goes to* Elizabeth *with a small rag doll.*)

Mary Warren. I made a gift for you today, Goody Proctor. I had to sit long hours in a chair, and passed the time with sewing.

Elizabeth (*perplexed, looking at the doll*). Why, thank you, it's a fair poppet.[2]

Mary Warren (*with a trembling, decayed voice*). We must all love each other now, Goody Proctor.

Elizabeth (*amazed at her strangeness*). Aye, indeed we must.

Mary Warren (*glancing at the room*). I'll get up early in the morning and clean the house. I must sleep now. (*She turns and starts off.*)

Proctor. Mary. (*She halts.*) Is it true? There be fourteen women arrested?

Mary Warren. No, sir. There be thirty-nine now— (*She suddenly breaks off and sobs and sits down, exhausted.*)

Elizabeth. Why, she's weepin'! What ails you, child?

Mary Warren. Goody Osburn—will hang!

(*There is a shocked pause, while she sobs.*)

Proctor. Hang! (*He calls into her face.*) Hang, y'say?

Mary Warren (*through her weeping*). Aye.

Proctor. The Deputy Governor will permit it?

Mary Warren. He sentenced her. He must. (*to* **ameliorate** *it*) But not Sarah Good. For Sarah Good confessed, y'see.

Proctor. Confessed! To what?

Mary Warren. That she—(*in horror at the memory*) —she sometimes made a compact with Lucifer, and wrote her name in his black book—with her blood—and bound herself to torment Christians till God's thrown down—and we all must worship Hell forevermore.

(*pause*)

Proctor. But—surely you know what a jabberer she is. Did you tell them that?

Mary Warren. Mr. Proctor, in open court she near to choked us all to death.

Proctor. How, choked you?

Mary Warren. She sent her spirit out.

Elizabeth. Oh, Mary, Mary, surely you—

Mary Warren (*with an indignant edge*). She tried to kill me many times, Goody Proctor!

Elizabeth. Why, I never heard you mention that before.

Mary Warren. I never knew it before. I never knew anything before. When she come into the court I say to myself, I must not accuse this woman, for she sleep in ditches, and so very old and poor. But then—then she sit there, denying and denying, and I feel a misty coldness climbin' up my back, and the skin on my skull begin to creep, and I feel a clamp around my neck and I cannot breathe air; and then (*entranced*) I hear a voice, a screamin' voice, and it were my voice—and all at once I remembered everything she done to me!

Proctor. Why? What did she do to you?

Mary Warren (*like one awakened to a marvelous secret insight*). So many time, Mr. Proctor, she come to this very door, beggin' bread and a cup of cider—and mark this: whenever I turned her away empty, she *mumbled.*

Elizabeth. Mumbled! She may mumble if she's hungry.

Mary Warren. But *what* does she mumble? You must remember, Goody Proctor. Last month—a Monday, I think—she walked away, and I thought my guts would burst for two days after. Do you remember it?

Elizabeth. Why—I do, I think, but—

Mary Warren. And so I told that to Judge Hathorne, and he asks her so. "Sarah Good," says he, "what curse do you mumble that this girl must fall sick after turning you away?" And then she replies

---

2. **fair poppet:** pretty doll.

(*mimicking an old crone*) "Why, your excellence, no curse at all. I only say my commandments;[3] I hope I may say my commandments," says she!

Elizabeth. And that's an upright answer.

Mary Warren. Aye, but then Judge Hathorne say, "Recite for us your commandments!" (*leaning avidly toward them*) and of all the ten she could not say a single one. She never knew no commandments, and they had her in a flat lie!

Proctor. And so condemned her?

Mary Warren (*now a little strained, seeing his stubborn doubt*). Why, they must when she condemned herself.

Proctor. But the proof, the proof!

Mary Warren (*with greater impatience with him*). I told you the proof. It's hard proof, hard as rock, the judges said.

Proctor (*pauses an instant, then*). You will not go to court again, Mary Warren.

Mary Warren. I must tell you, sir, I will be gone every day now. I am amazed you do not see what weighty work we do.

Proctor. What work you do! It's strange work for a Christian girl to hang old women!

Mary Warren. But, Mr. Proctor, they will not hang them if they confess. Sarah Good will only sit in jail some time (*recalling*) and here's a wonder for you; think on this. Goody Good is pregnant!

Elizabeth. Pregnant! Are they mad? The woman's near to sixty!

Mary Warren. They had Doctor Griggs examine her, and she's full to the brim. And smokin' a pipe all these years, and no husband either! But she's safe, thank God, for they'll not hurt the innocent child. But be that not a marvel? You must see it, sir, it's God's work we do. So I'll be gone every day for some time. I'm—I am an official of the court, they say, and I—(*She has been edging toward offstage.*)

Proctor. I'll official you! (*He strides to the mantel, takes down the whip hanging there.*)

Mary Warren (*terrified, but coming erect, striving for her authority*). I'll not stand whipping any more!

Elizabeth (*hurriedly, as Proctor approaches*). Mary, promise now you'll stay at home—

Mary Warren (*backing from him, but keeping her erect posture, striving, striving for her way*). The Devil's loose in Salem, Mr. Proctor; we must discover where he's hiding!

Proctor. I'll whip the Devil out of you! (*With whip raised he reaches out for her, and she streaks away and yells.*)

Mary Warren (*pointing at* Elizabeth). I saved her life today!

(*Silence. His whip comes down.*)

Elizabeth (*softly*). I am accused?

Mary Warren (*quaking*). Somewhat mentioned. But I said I never see no sign you ever sent your spirit out to hurt no one, and seeing I do live so closely with you, they dismissed it.

Elizabeth. Who accused me?

Mary Warren. I am bound by law, I cannot tell it. (*to* Proctor) I only hope you'll not be so sarcastical no more. Four judges and the King's deputy sat to dinner with us but an hour ago. I—I would have you speak civilly to me, from this out.

Proctor (*in horror, muttering in disgust at her*). Go to bed.

Mary Warren (*with a stamp of her foot*). I'll not be ordered to bed no more, Mr. Proctor! I am eighteen and a woman, however single!

Proctor. Do you wish to sit up? Then sit up.

Mary Warren. I wish to go to bed!

Proctor (*in anger*). Good night, then!

Mary Warren. Good night. (*Dissatisfied, uncertain of herself, she goes out. Wide-eyed, both,* Proctor *and* Elizabeth *stand staring.*)

Elizabeth (*quietly*). Oh, the noose, the noose is up!

Proctor. There'll be no noose.

---

3. **commandments:** the Ten Commandments in the Bible.

350 Elizabeth. She wants me dead. I knew all week it would come to this!

Proctor (*without conviction*). They dismissed it. You heard her say—

Elizabeth. And what of tomorrow? She will cry me out until they take me!

Proctor. Sit you down.

Elizabeth. She wants me dead, John, you know it!

Proctor. I say sit down! (*She sits, trembling. He speaks quietly, trying to keep his wits.*) Now we must be wise,
360 Elizabeth.

Elizabeth (*with sarcasm, and a sense of being lost*). Oh, indeed, indeed!

Proctor. Fear nothing. I'll find Ezekiel Cheever. I'll tell him she said it were all sport.

Elizabeth. John, with so many in the jail, more than Cheever's help is needed now, I think. Would you favor me with this? Go to Abigail.

Proctor (*his soul hardening as he senses . . .*). What have I to say to Abigail?

370 Elizabeth (*delicately*). John—grant me this. You have a faulty understanding of young girls. There is a promise made in any bed—

Proctor (*striving against his anger*). What promise!

Elizabeth. Spoke or silent, a promise is surely made. And she may dote on it now—I am sure she does— and thinks to kill me, then to take my place.

(*Proctor's anger is rising; he cannot speak.*)

Elizabeth. It is her dearest hope, John, I know it. There be a thousand names; why does she call
380 mine? There be a certain danger in calling such a name—I am no Goody Good that sleeps in ditches, nor Osburn, drunk and half-witted. She'd dare not call out such a farmer's wife but there be monstrous profit in it. She thinks to take my place, John.

Proctor. She cannot think it! (*He knows it is true.*)

Elizabeth (*"reasonably"*). John, have you ever shown her somewhat of contempt? She cannot pass you in the church but you will blush—

Proctor. I may blush for my sin.

390 Elizabeth. I think she sees another meaning in that blush.

Proctor. And what see you? What see you, Elizabeth?

Elizabeth (*"conceding"*). I think you be somewhat ashamed, for I am there, and she so close.

Proctor. When will you know me, woman? Were I stone I would have cracked for shame this seven month!

Elizabeth. Then go and tell her she's a whore. Whatever promise she may sense—break it, John, break it.

400 Proctor (*between his teeth*). Good, then. I'll go. (*He starts for his rifle.*)

Elizabeth (*trembling, fearfully*). Oh, how unwillingly!

Proctor (*turning on her, rifle in hand*). I will curse her hotter than the oldest cinder in hell. But pray, begrudge me not my anger!

Elizabeth. Your anger! I only ask you—

Proctor. Woman, am I so base? Do you truly think me base?

Elizabeth. I never called you base.

410 Proctor. Then how do you charge me with such a promise? The promise that a stallion gives a mare I gave that girl!

Elizabeth. Then why do you anger with me when I bid you break it?

Proctor. Because it speaks deceit, and I am honest! But I'll plead no more! I see now your spirit twists around the single error of my life, and I will never tear it free!

Elizabeth (*crying out*). You'll tear it free—when you
420 come to know that I will be your only wife, or no wife at all! She has an arrow in you yet, John Proctor, and you know it well!

(*Quite suddenly, as though from the air, a figure appears in the doorway. They start slightly. It is Mr. Hale. He is different now—drawn a little, and there is a quality of deference, even of guilt, about his manner now.*)

Hale. Good evening.

Proctor (*still in his shock*). Why, Mr. Hale! Good
430 evening to you, sir. Come in, come in.

Hale (*to Elizabeth*). I hope I do not startle you.

Elizabeth. No, no, it's only that I heard no horse—

Hale. You are Goodwife Proctor.

Proctor. Aye; Elizabeth.

Hale (*nods, then*). I hope you're not off to bed yet.

Proctor (*setting down his gun*). No, no. (Hale *comes
further into the room. And* Proctor, *to explain his
nervousness.*) We are not used to visitors after dark,
but you're welcome here. Will you sit you down, sir?

440 **Hale.** I will. (*He sits.*) Let you sit, Goodwife Proctor.
(*She does, never letting him out of her sight. There is
a pause as* Hale *looks about the room.*)

Proctor (*to break the silence*). Will you drink cider,
Mr. Hale?

Hale. No, it rebels[4] my stomach; I have some further
traveling yet tonight. Sit you down, sir. (Proctor
sits.) I will not keep you long, but I have some
business with you.

Proctor. Business of the court?

450 **Hale.** No—no, I come of my own, without the
court's authority. Hear me. (*He wets his lips.*) I know
not if you are aware, but your wife's name is—
mentioned in the court.

Proctor. We know it, sir. Our Mary Warren told us.
We are entirely amazed.

Hale. I am a stranger here, as you know. And in my
ignorance I find it hard to draw a clear opinion of
them that come accused before the court. And so
this afternoon, and now tonight, I go from house
460 to house—I come now from Rebecca Nurse's house
and—

Elizabeth (*shocked*). Rebecca's charged!

Hale. God forbid such a one be charged. She is,
however—mentioned somewhat.

Elizabeth (*with an attempt at a laugh*). You will never
believe, I hope, that Rebecca trafficked with the Devil.

Hale. Woman, it is possible.

Proctor (*taken aback*). Surely you cannot think so.

Hale. This is a strange time, Mister. No man may
470 longer doubt the powers of the dark are gathered
in monstrous attack upon this village. There is too
much evidence now to deny it. You will agree, sir?

Proctor (*evading*). I—have no knowledge in that line.
But it's hard to think so pious a woman be secretly
a Devil's bitch after seventy year of such good prayer.

Hale. Aye. But the Devil is a wily one, you cannot
deny it. However, she is far from accused, and I
know she will not be. (*pause*) I thought, sir, to put
some questions as to the Christian character of this
480 house, if you'll permit me.

Proctor (*coldly, resentful*). Why, we—have no fear
of questions, sir.

Hale. Good, then. (*He makes himself more comfortable.*) In the book of record that Mr. Parris keeps, I
note that you are rarely in the church on Sabbath Day.

Proctor. No, sir, you are mistaken.

Hale. Twenty-six time in seventeen month, sir. I must
call that rare. Will you tell me why you are so absent?

Proctor. Mr. Hale, I never knew I must account to
490 that man for I come to church or stay at home. My
wife were sick this winter.

Hale. So I am told. But you, Mister, why could you
not come alone?

Proctor. I surely did come when I could, and when
I could not I prayed in this house.

Hale. Mr. Proctor, your house is not a church; your
theology must tell you that.

Proctor. It does, sir, it does; and it tells me that a
minister may pray to God without he have golden
500 candlesticks upon the altar.

Hale. What golden candlesticks?

---

4. **rebels:** upsets.

Proctor. Since we built the church there were pewter candlesticks upon the altar; Francis Nurse made them, y'know, and a sweeter hand never touched the metal. But Parris came, and for twenty week he preach nothin' but golden candlesticks until he had them. I labor the earth from dawn of day to blink of night, and I tell you true, when I look to heaven and see my money glaring at his elbows—it hurt my 510 prayer, sir, it hurt my prayer. I think, sometimes, the man dreams cathedrals, not clapboard meetin' houses.

Hale (*thinks, then*). And yet, Mister, a Christian on Sabbath Day must be in church. (*pause*) Tell me— you have three children?

Proctor. Aye. Boys.

Hale. How comes it that only two are baptized?

Proctor (*starts to speak, then stops, then, as though unable to restrain this*). I like it not that Mr. Parris should lay his hand upon my baby. I see no light 520 of God in that man. I'll not conceal it.

Hale. I must say it, Mr. Proctor; that is not for you to decide. The man's ordained, therefore the light of God is in him.

Proctor (*flushed with resentment but trying to smile*).

What's your suspicion, Mr. Hale?

Hale. No, no, I have no—

Proctor. I nailed the roof upon the church, I hung the door—

Hale. Oh, did you! That's a good sign, then.

530 **Proctor.** It may be I have been too quick to bring the man to book,[5] but you cannot think we ever desired the destruction of religion. I think that's in your mind, is it not?

Hale (*not altogether giving way*). I—have—there is a softness in your record, sir, a softness.

Elizabeth. I think, maybe, we have been too hard with Mr. Parris. I think so. But sure we never loved the Devil here.

Hale (*nods, deliberating this. Then, with the voice of* 540 *one administering a secret test*). Do you know your Commandments, Elizabeth?

Elizabeth (*without hesitation, even eagerly*). I surely do. There be no mark of blame upon my life, Mr. Hale. I am a convenanted Christian woman.

Hale. And you, Mister?

Proctor (*a trifle unsteadily*). I—am sure I do, sir.

---

5. **bring the man to book:** judge the man.

John Proctor and his sons

Hale (*glances at her open face, then at* John, *then*). Let you repeat them, if you will.

Proctor. The Commandments.

550 **Hale.** Aye.

Proctor (*looking off, beginning to sweat*). Thou shalt not kill.

Hale. Aye.

Proctor (*counting on his fingers*). Thou shalt not steal. Thou shalt not covet thy neighbor's goods, nor make unto thee any graven image. Thou shalt not take the name of the Lord in vain; thou shalt have no other gods before me. (*with some hesitation*) Thou shalt remember the Sabbath Day and keep it holy. (*Pause.*
560 *Then.*) Thou shalt honor thy father and mother. Thou shalt not bear false witness. (*He is stuck. He counts back on his fingers, knowing one is missing.*) Thou shalt not make unto thee any graven image.

Hale. You have said that twice, sir.

Proctor (*lost*). Aye. (*He is flailing for it.*)

Elizabeth (*delicately*). Adultery, John.

Proctor (*as though a secret arrow had pained his heart*). Aye. (*trying to grin it away—to* Hale) You see, sir, between the two of us we do know them
570 all. (Hale *only looks at* Proctor, *deep in his attempt to define this man.* Proctor *grows more uneasy.*) I think it be a small fault.

Hale. Theology, sir, is a fortress; no crack in a fortress may be accounted small. (*He rises; he seems worried now. He paces a little, in deep thought.*)

Proctor. There be no love for Satan in this house, Mister.

Hale. I pray it, I pray it dearly. (*He looks to both of them, an attempt at a smile on his face, but his misgiv-*
580 *ings are clear.*) Well, then—I'll bid you good night.

Elizabeth (*unable to restrain herself*). Mr. Hale. (*He turns.*) I do think you are suspecting me somewhat? Are you not?

Hale (*obviously disturbed—and evasive*). Goody Proctor, I do not judge you. My duty is to add what I may to the godly wisdom of the court. I pray you

both good health and good fortune. (*to* John) Good night, sir. (*He starts out.*)

Elizabeth (*with a note of desperation*). I think you
590 must tell him, John.

Hale. What's that?

Elizabeth (*restraining a call*). Will you tell him?

(*Slight pause.* Hale *looks questioningly at* John.)

Proctor (*with difficulty*). I—I have no witness and cannot prove it, except my word be taken. But I know the children's sickness had naught to do with witchcraft.

Hale (*stopped, struck*). Naught to do—?

Proctor. Mr. Parris discovered them sportin' in the
600 woods. They were startled and took sick.

(*pause*)

Hale. Who told you this?

Proctor (*hesitates, then*). Abigail Williams.

Hale. Abigail!

Proctor. Aye.

Hale (*his eyes wide*). Abigail Williams told you it had naught to do with witchcraft!

Proctor. She told me the day you came, sir.

Hale (*suspiciously*). Why—why did you keep this?

610 **Proctor.** I never knew until tonight that the world is gone daft with this nonsense.

Hale. Nonsense! Mister, I have myself examined Tituba, Sarah Good, and numerous others that have confessed to dealing with the Devil. They have *confessed* it.

Proctor. And why not, if they must hang for denyin' it? There are them that will swear to anything before they'll hang; have you never thought of that?

Hale. I have. I—I have indeed. (*It is his own suspi-*
620 *cion, but he resists it. He glances at* Elizabeth, *then at* John.) And you—would you testify to this in court?

Proctor. I—had not reckoned with goin' into court. But if I must I will.

Hale. Do you falter here?

Proctor. I falter nothing, but I may wonder if my story will be credited in such a court. I do wonder on it, when such a steady-minded minister as you will suspicion such a woman that never lied, and cannot, and the world knows she cannot! I may falter somewhat, Mister; I am no fool.

Hale (*quietly—it has impressed him*). Proctor, let you open with me now, for I have a rumor that troubles me. It's said you hold no belief that there may even be witches in the world. Is that true, sir?

Proctor (*He knows this is critical, and is striving against his disgust with* Hale *and with himself for even answering*). I know not what I have said, I may have said it. I have wondered if there be witches in the world—although I cannot believe they come among us now.

Hale. Then you do not believe—

Proctor. I have no knowledge of it; the Bible speaks of witches, and I will not deny them.

Hale. And you, woman?

Elizabeth. I—I cannot believe it.

Hale (*shocked*). You cannot!

Proctor. Elizabeth, you bewilder him!

Elizabeth (*to* Hale). I cannot think the Devil may own a woman's soul, Mr. Hale, when she keeps an upright way, as I have. I am a good woman, I know it; and if you believe I may do only good work in the world, and yet be secretly bound to Satan, then I must tell you, sir, I do not believe it.

Hale. But, woman, you do believe there are witches in—

Elizabeth. If you think that I am one, then I say there are none.

Hale. You surely do not fly against the Gospel, the Gospel—

Proctor. She believe in the Gospel, every word!

Elizabeth. Question Abigail Williams about the Gospel, not myself!

(Hale *stares at her.*)

Proctor. She do not mean to doubt the Gospel, sir, you cannot think it. This be a Christian house, sir, a Christian house.

Hale. God keep you both; let the third child be quickly baptized, and go you without fail each Sunday in to Sabbath prayer; and keep a solemn, quiet way among you. I think—

(Giles Corey *appears in doorway.*)

Giles. John!

Proctor. Giles! What's the matter?

Giles. They take my wife.

(Francis Nurse *enters.*)

Giles. And his Rebecca!

Proctor (*to* Francis). Rebecca's in the *jail!*

Francis. Aye, Cheever come and take her in his wagon. We've only now come from the jail, and they'll not even let us in to see them.

Elizabeth. They've surely gone wild now, Mr. Hale!

Francis (*going to* Hale). Reverend Hale! Can you not speak to the Deputy Governor? I'm sure he mistakes these people—

Hale. Pray calm yourself, Mr. Nurse.

Francis. My wife is the very brick and mortar of the church, Mr. Hale (*indicating* Giles) and Martha Corey, there cannot be a woman closer yet to God than Martha.

Hale. How is Rebecca charged, Mr. Nurse?

Francis (*with a mocking, half-hearted laugh*). For murder, she's charged! (*mockingly quoting the warrant*) "For the marvelous and supernatural murder of Goody Putnam's babies." What am I to do, Mr. Hale?

Hale (*turns from* Francis, *deeply troubled, then*). Believe me, Mr. Nurse, if Rebecca Nurse be tainted, then nothing's left to stop the whole green world from burning. Let you rest upon the justice of the court; the court will send her home, I know it.

Francis. You cannot mean she will be tried in court!

Hale (*pleading*). Nurse, though our hearts break, we cannot flinch; these are new times, sir. There is a misty plot afoot so subtle we should be criminal to cling to old respects and ancient friendships. I have seen too many frightful proofs in court—the Devil is alive in Salem, and we dare not quail to follow wherever the accusing finger points!

Proctor (*angered*). How may such a woman murder children?

710 **Hale** (*in great pain*). Man, remember, until an hour before the Devil fell, God thought him beautiful in Heaven.

Giles. I never said my wife were a witch, Mr. Hale; I only said she were reading books!

Hale. Mr. Corey, exactly what complaint were made on your wife?

Giles. That bloody mongrel Walcott charge her. Y'see, he buy a pig of my wife four or five year ago, and the pig died soon after. So he come dancin' in 720 for his money back. So my Martha, she says to him, "Walcott, if you haven't the wit to feed a pig properly, you'll not live to own many," she says. Now he goes to court and claims that from that day to this he cannot keep a pig alive for more than four weeks because my Martha bewitch them with her books!

(*Enter Ezekiel Cheever. A shocked silence.*)

Cheever. Good evening to you, Proctor.

Proctor. Why, Mr. Cheever. Good evening.

Cheever. Good evening, all. Good evening, Mr. Hale.

730 **Proctor.** I hope you come not on business of the court.

Cheever. I do, Proctor, aye. I am clerk of the court now, y'know.

(*Enter Marshal Herrick, a man in his early thirties, who is somewhat shamefaced at the moment.*)

Giles. It's a pity, Ezekiel, that an honest tailor might have gone to Heaven must burn in Hell. You'll burn for this, do you know it?

Cheever. You know yourself I must do as I'm told. 740 You surely know that, Giles. And I'd as lief[6] you'd not be sending me to Hell. I like not the sound of it, I tell you; I like not the sound of it. (*He fears Proctor, but starts to reach inside his coat.*) Now believe me, Proctor, how heavy be the law, all its tonnage I do carry on my back tonight. (*He takes out a warrant.*) I have a warrant for your wife.

Proctor (*to Hale*). You said she were not charged!

Hale. I know nothin' of it. (*to Cheever*) When were she charged?

750 **Cheever.** I am given sixteen warrant tonight, sir, and she is one.

Proctor. Who charged her?

Cheever. Why, Abigail Williams charge her.

Proctor. On what proof, what proof?

Cheever (*looking about the room*). Mr. Proctor, I have little time. The court bid me search your house, but I like not to search a house. So will you hand me any poppets that your wife may keep here?

Proctor. Poppets?

760 **Elizabeth.** I never kept no poppets, not since I were a girl.

Cheever (*embarrassed, glancing toward the mantel where sits Mary Warren's poppet*). I spy a poppet, Goody Proctor.

Elizabeth. Oh! (*going for it*) Why, this is Mary's.

Cheever (*shyly*). Would you please to give it to me?

Elizabeth (*handing it to him, asks Hale*). Has the court discovered a text in poppets now?

Cheever (*carefully holding the poppet*). Do you keep 770 any others in this house?

Proctor. No, nor this one either till tonight. What signifies a poppet?

Cheever. Why, a poppet—(*He gingerly turns the poppet over.*) a poppet may signify—Now, woman, will you please to come with me?

Proctor. She will not! (*to Elizabeth*) Fetch Mary here.

Cheever (*ineptly reaching toward Elizabeth*). No, no, I am forbid to leave her from my sight.

Proctor (*pushing his arm away*). You'll leave her out 780 of sight and out of mind, Mister. Fetch Mary, Elizabeth. (*Elizabeth goes upstairs.*)

Hale. What signifies a poppet, Mr. Cheever?

---

6. **as lief** (lēf): rather.

Cheever (*turning the poppet over in his hands*). Why, they say it may signify that she—(*He has lifted the poppet's skirt, and his eyes widen in astonished fear.*) Why, this, this—

Proctor (*reaching for the poppet*). What's there?

Cheever. Why (*He draws out a long needle from the poppet.*) it is a needle! Herrick, Herrick, it is a
790 needle!

(Herrick *comes toward him.*)

Proctor (*angrily, bewildered*). And what signifies a needle!

Cheever (*his hands shaking*). Why, this go hard with her, Proctor, this—I had my doubts, Proctor, I had my doubts, but here's calamity. (*to Hale, showing the needle*) You see it, sir, it is a needle!

Hale. Why? What meanin' has it?

Cheever (*wide-eyed, trembling*). The girl, the Wil-
800 liams girl, Abigail Williams, sir. She sat to dinner in Reverend Parris's house tonight, and without word nor warnin' she falls to the floor. Like a struck beast, he says, and screamed a scream that a bull would weep to hear. And he goes to save her, and, stuck two inches in the flesh of her belly, he draw a needle out. And demandin' of her how she come to be so stabbed, she (*to Proctor now*) testify it were your wife's familiar spirit[7] pushed it in.

Proctor. Why, she done it herself! (*to Hale*) I hope
810 you're not takin' this for proof, Mister!

(Hale, *struck by the proof, is silent.*)

Cheever. 'Tis hard proof! (*to Hale*) I find here a poppet Goody Proctor keeps. I have found it, sir. And in the belly of the poppet a needle's stuck. I tell you true, Proctor, I never warranted to see such proof of Hell, and I bid you obstruct me not, for I—

(*Enter* Elizabeth *with* Mary Warren. Proctor, *seeing* Mary Warren, *draws her by the arm to* Hale.)

Proctor. Here now! Mary, how did this poppet come
820 into my house?

Mary Warren (*frightened for herself, her voice very small*). What poppet's that, sir?

Proctor (*impatiently, pointing at the doll in* Cheever's *hand*). This poppet, this poppet.

Mary Warren (*evasively, looking at it*). Why, I—I think it is mine.

Proctor. It is your poppet, is it not?

Mary Warren (*not understanding the direction of this*). It—is, sir.

830 **Proctor.** And how did it come into this house?

Mary Warren (*glancing about at the avid faces*). Why—I made it in the court, sir, and—give it to Goody Proctor tonight.

Proctor (*to* Hale). Now, sir—do you have it?

Hale. Mary Warren, a needle have been found inside this poppet.

Mary Warren (*bewildered*). Why, I meant no harm by it, sir.

Proctor (*quickly*). You stuck that needle in yourself?

840 **Mary Warren.** I—I believe I did, sir, I—

Proctor (*to* Hale). What say you now?

Hale (*watching* Mary Warren *closely*). Child, you are certain this be your natural memory? May it be, perhaps, that someone conjures you even now to say this?

Mary Warren. Conjures me? Why, no, sir, I am entirely myself, I think. Let you ask Susanna Walcott—she saw me sewin' it in court. (*or better still*) Ask Abby, Abby sat beside me when I made it.

850 **Proctor** (*to* Hale, *of* Cheever). Bid him begone. Your mind is surely settled now. Bid him out, Mr. Hale.

Elizabeth. What signifies a needle?

Hale. Mary—you charge a cold and cruel murder on Abigail.

Mary Warren. Murder! I charge no—

Hale. Abigail were stabbed tonight; a needle were found stuck into her belly—

---

7. **familiar spirit:** the spirit or demon, most usually in the form of an animal such as a black cat, that was a companion and helper to a witch.

Elizabeth. And she charges me?

Hale. Aye.

860 **Elizabeth** (*her breath knocked out*). Why—! The girl is murder! She must be ripped out of the world!

Cheever (*pointing at* Elizabeth). You've heard that, sir! Ripped out of the world! Herrick, you heard it!

Proctor (*suddenly snatching the warrant out of* Cheever's *hands*). Out with you.

Cheever. Proctor, you dare not touch the warrant.

Proctor (*ripping the warrant*). Out with you!

Cheever. You've ripped the Deputy Governor's warrant, man!

870 **Proctor.** Damn the Deputy Governor! Out of my house!

Hale. Now, Proctor, Proctor!

Proctor. Get y'gone with them! You are a broken minister.

Hale. Proctor, if she is innocent, the court—

Proctor. If *she* is innocent! Why do you never wonder if Parris be innocent, or Abigail? Is the accuser always holy now? Were they born this morning as clean as God's fingers? I'll tell you what's walking 880 Salem—vengeance is walking Salem. We are what we always were in Salem, but now the little crazy children are jangling the keys of the kingdom, and common vengeance writes the law! This warrant's vengeance! I'll not give my wife to vengeance!

Elizabeth. I'll go, John—

Proctor. You will not go!

Herrick. I have nine men outside. You cannot keep her. The law binds me, John, I cannot budge.

Proctor (*to* Hale, *ready to break him*). Will you see 890 her taken?

Hale. Proctor, the court is just—

Proctor. Pontius Pilate! God will not let you wash your hands of this![8]

Elizabeth. John—I think I must go with them. (*He cannot bear to look at her.*) Mary, there is bread enough for the morning; you will bake, in the afternoon. Help Mr. Proctor as you were his daughter— you owe me that, and much more. (*She is fighting her weeping. To* Proctor.) When the children wake, 900 speak nothing of witchcraft—it will frighten them. (*She cannot go on.*)

Proctor. I will bring you home. I will bring you soon.

Elizabeth. Oh, John, bring me soon!

Proctor. I will fall like an ocean on that court! Fear nothing, Elizabeth.

Elizabeth (*with great fear*). I will fear nothing. (*She looks about the room, as though to fix it in her mind.*) Tell the children I have gone to visit someone sick.

(*She walks out the door,* Herrick *and* Cheever *behind* 910 *her. For a moment,* Proctor *watches from the doorway. The clank of chain is heard.*)

Proctor. Herrick! Herrick, don't chain her! (*He rushes out the door. From outside.*) Damn you, man, you will not chain her! Off with them! I'll not have it! I will not have her chained!

(*There are other men's voices against his.* Hale, *in a fever of guilt and uncertainty, turns from the door to avoid the sight;* Mary Warren *bursts into tears and sits weeping.* Giles Corey *calls to* Hale.)

920 **Giles.** And yet silent, minister? It is fraud, you know it is fraud! What keeps you, man?

(Proctor *is half braced, half pushed into the room by two deputies and* Herrick.)

Proctor. I'll pay you, Herrick, I will surely pay you!

Herrick (*panting*). In God's name, John, I cannot help myself. I must chain them all. Now let you keep inside this house till I am gone! (*He goes out with his deputies.*)

(Proctor *stands there, gulping air. Horses and a wagon* 930 *creaking are heard.*)

Hale (*in great uncertainty*). Mr. Proctor—

Proctor. Out of my sight!

Hale. Charity, Proctor, charity. What I have heard in

---

8. **Pontius** (pŏn′tē-əs) **Pilate . . . hands of this:** the Roman governor who presided over the trial and sentencing of Christ. Pilate publicly washed his hands to absolve himself of responsibility for Christ's death.

her favor, I will not fear to testify in court. God help me, I cannot judge her guilty or innocent—I know not. Only this consider: the world goes mad, and it profit nothing you should lay the cause to the vengeance of a little girl.

Proctor. You are a coward! Though you be ordained in God's own tears, you are a coward now!

Hale. Proctor, I cannot think God be provoked so grandly by such a petty cause. The jails are packed—our greatest judges sit in Salem now—and hangin's promised. Man, we must look to cause proportionate. Were there murder done, perhaps, and never brought to light? Abomination? Some secret blasphemy that stinks to Heaven? Think on cause, man, and let you help me to discover it. For there's your way, believe it, there is your only way, when such confusion strikes upon the world. (*He goes to* Giles *and* Francis.) Let you counsel among yourselves; think on your village and what may have drawn from heaven such thundering wrath upon you all. I shall pray God open up our eyes.

(Hale *goes out.*)

Francis (*struck by* Hale's *mood*). I never heard no murder done in Salem.

Proctor (*He has been reached by* Hale's *words*). Leave me, Francis, leave me.

Giles (*shaken*). John—tell me, are we lost?

Proctor. Go home now, Giles. We'll speak on it tomorrow.

Giles. Let you think on it. We'll come early, eh?

Proctor. Aye. Go now, Giles.

Giles. Good night, then.

(Giles Corey *goes out. After a moment.*)

Mary Warren (*in a fearful squeak of a voice*). Mr. Proctor, very likely they'll let her come home once they're given proper evidence.

Proctor. You're coming to the court with me, Mary. You will tell it in the court.

Mary Warren. I cannot charge murder on Abigail.

Proctor (*moving menacingly toward her*). You will tell the court how that poppet come here and who stuck the needle in.

Mary Warren. She'll kill me for sayin' that! (Proctor *continues toward her.*) Abby'll charge lechery on you, Mr. Proctor!

Proctor (*halting*). She's told you!

Mary Warren. I have known it, sir. She'll ruin you with it, I know she will.

Proctor (*hesitating, and with deep hatred of himself*). Good. Then her saintliness is done with. (Mary *backs from him.*) We will slide together into our pit; you will tell the court what you know.

Mary Warren (*in terror*). I cannot, they'll turn on me—

(Proctor *strides and catches her, and she is repeating, "I cannot, I cannot!"*)

Proctor. My wife will never die for me! I will bring your guts into your mouth but that goodness will not die for me!

Mary Warren (*struggling to escape him*). I cannot do it, I cannot!

Proctor (*grasping her by the throat as though he would strangle her*). Make your peace with it! Now Hell and Heaven grapple on our backs, and all our old pretense is ripped away—make your peace! (*He throws her to the floor, where she sobs, "I cannot, I cannot . . ."* And now, half to himself, staring, and turning to the open door.*) Peace. It is a providence, and no great change; we are only what we always were, but naked now. (*He walks as though toward a great horror, facing the open sky.*) Aye, naked! And the wind, God's icy wind, will blow!

(*And she is over and over again sobbing, "I cannot, I cannot, I cannot," as the curtain falls.*)

Comprehension

1. **Recall** Why does Elizabeth want John to go to Salem?

2. **Clarify** Why does Hale come to the Proctors' home?

3. **Summarize** What proof leads to Elizabeth's arrest?

Literary Analysis

4. **Form Opinions** Do you think Reverend Hale believes that Elizabeth Proctor is practicing witchcraft? Support your opinion with specific details.

5. **Draw Conclusions About Characters** Review the **traits** you recorded in your chart for Elizabeth Proctor. How would you describe her character?

6. **Analyze Conventions of Drama** What does **dialogue** reveal about the complicated relationship between John and Elizabeth in the following scenes?

   - Elizabeth learns that John was alone with Abigail (lines 132–138)
   - Elizabeth asks John to break his unspoken promise to Abigail (lines 398–422)
   - John threatens Mary Warren (lines 990–1005)

7. **Analyze Dramatic Irony** Dramatic irony occurs when readers know more about a situation than a character does. Why is John struck by Hale's declaration that "some secret blasphemy" (lines 946–947) has caused all of the confusion?

8. **Make Judgments About a Character** How would you judge John's behavior so far? Cite evidence from the play to support your judgment.

9. **Compare Characters** Compare the following characters and determine which one has the greatest faith in the court proceedings. What accounts for their differing attitudes?

   - John Proctor   • Hale   • Cheever

Literary Criticism

10. **Historical Context** Miller wrote that during the anti-Communist hearings, "I saw accepted the notion that conscience was no longer a private matter but one of state administration." How does this notion apply to the witch-hunts in Salem?

Act *Three*

(The vestry room of the Salem meeting house, now serving as the anteroom[1] of the General Court.

As the curtain rises, the room is empty, but for sunlight pouring through two high windows in the back wall. The room is solemn, even forbidding. Heavy beams jut out, boards of random widths make up the walls. At the right are two doors leading into the meeting house proper, where the court is being held. At the left another door leads outside.

There is a plain bench at the left, and another at the right. In the center a rather long meeting table, with stools and a considerable armchair snugged up to it.

Through the partitioning wall at the right we hear a prosecutor's voice, Judge Hathorne's, *asking a question; then a woman's voice,* Martha Corey's, *replying.)*

Hathorne's Voice. Now, Martha Corey, there is abundant evidence in our hands to show that you have given yourself to the reading of fortunes. Do you deny it?

Martha Corey's Voice. I am innocent to a witch. I know not what a witch is.

Hathorne's Voice. How do you know, then, that you are not a witch?

Martha Corey's Voice. If I were, I would know it.

10 **Hathorne's Voice.** Why do you hurt these children?

Martha Corey's Voice. I do not hurt them. I scorn it!

Giles' Voice (*roaring*). I have evidence for the court!

(*Voices of townspeople rise in excitement.*)

Danforth's Voice. You will keep your seat!

Giles' Voice. Thomas Putnam is reaching out for land!

Danforth's Voice. Remove that man, Marshal!

Giles' Voice. You're hearing lies, lies!

(*A roaring goes up from the people.*)

20 **Hathorne's Voice.** Arrest him, excellency!

Giles' Voice. I have evidence. Why will you not hear my evidence?

(*The door opens and* Giles *is half carried into the vestry room by* Herrick.)

Giles. Hands off, damn you, let me go!

Herrick. Giles, Giles!

Giles. Out of my way, Herrick! I bring evidence—

Herrick. You cannot go in there, Giles; it's a court!

(*Enter* Hale *from the court.*)

30 **Hale.** Pray be calm a moment.

Giles. You, Mr. Hale, go in there and demand I speak.

---

1. **vestry room . . . anteroom:** A vestry room is a room in a church used for nonreligious meetings or church business. An anteroom is a waiting room or a room that leads into another.

Paul Scofield as Deputy Governor Danforth

Hale. A moment, sir, a moment.

Giles. They'll be hangin' my wife!

(Judge Hathorne *enters. He is in his sixties, a bitter, remorseless Salem judge.*)

Hathorne. How do you dare come roarin' into this court! Are you gone daft, Corey?

Giles. You're not a Boston judge yet, Hathorne.
40 You'll not call me daft!

(*Enter* Deputy Governor Danforth *and, behind him,* Ezekiel Cheever *and* Parris. *On his appearance, silence falls.* Danforth *is a grave man in his sixties, of some humor and sophistication that does not, however, interfere with an exact loyalty to his position and his cause. He comes down to* Giles, *who awaits his wrath.*)

Danforth (*looking directly at* Giles). Who is this man?

Parris. Giles Corey, sir, and a more **contentious**—

Giles (*to* Parris). I am asked the question, and I am
50 old enough to answer it! (*to* Danforth, *who impresses him and to whom he smiles through his strain*) My name is Corey, sir, Giles Corey. I have six hundred acres, and timber in addition. It is my wife you be condemning now. (*He indicates the courtroom.*)

Danforth. And how do you imagine to help her cause with such contemptuous riot?[2] Now be gone. Your old age alone keeps you out of jail for this.

Giles (*beginning to plead*). They be tellin' lies about my wife, sir, I—

60 **Danforth.** Do you take it upon yourself to determine what this court shall believe and what it shall set aside?

Giles. Your Excellency, we mean no disrespect for—

Danforth. Disrespect indeed! It is disruption, Mister. This is the highest court of the supreme government of this province, do you know it?

Giles (*beginning to weep*). Your Excellency, I only said she were readin' books, sir, and they come and take her out of my house for—

Danforth (*mystified*). Books! What books?

70 **Giles** (*through helpless sobs*). It is my third wife, sir; I never had no wife that be so taken with books, and I thought to find the cause of it, d'y'see, but it were no witch I blamed her for. (*He is openly weeping.*) I have broke charity with the woman, I have broke charity with her. (*He covers his face, ashamed.* Danforth *is respectfully silent.*)

Hale. Excellency, he claims hard evidence for his wife's defense. I think that in all justice you must—

Danforth. Then let him submit his evidence in
80 proper affidavit. You are certainly aware of our procedure here, Mr. Hale. (*to* Herrick) Clear this room.

Herrick. Come now, Giles. (*He gently pushes* Corey *out.*)

Francis. We are desperate, sir; we come here three days now and cannot be heard.

Danforth. Who is this man?

Francis. Francis Nurse, Your Excellency.

Hale. His wife's Rebecca that were condemned this morning.

90 **Danforth.** Indeed! I am amazed to find you in such uproar. I have only good report of your character, Mr. Nurse.

Hathorne. I think they must both be arrested in contempt, sir.

Danforth (*to* Francis). Let you write your plea, and in due time I will—

Francis. Excellency, we have proof for your eyes; God forbid you shut them to it. The girls, sir, the girls are frauds.

100 **Danforth.** What's that?

Francis. We have proof of it, sir. They are all deceiving you.

(Danforth *is shocked, but studying* Francis.)

Hathorne. This is contempt, sir, contempt!

Danforth. Peace, Judge Hathorne. Do you know who I am, Mr. Nurse?

---

2. **contemptuous** (kən-tĕmp′chōō-əs) **riot:** disrespectful, outrageous behavior.

Francis. I surely do, sir, and I think you must be a wise judge to be what you are.

Danforth. And do you know that near to four hun-
110 dred are in the jails from Marblehead to Lynn,[3] and upon my signature?

Francis. I—

Danforth. And seventy-two condemned to hang by that signature?

Francis. Excellency, I never thought to say it to such a weighty judge, but you are deceived.

(*Enter* Giles Corey *from left. All turn to see as he beck-ons in* Mary Warren *with* Proctor. Mary *is keeping her eyes to the ground;* Proctor *has her elbow as though*
120 *she were near collapse.*)

Parris (*on seeing her, in shock*). Mary Warren! (*He goes directly to bend close to her face.*) What are you about here?

Proctor (*pressing* Parris *away from her with a gentle but firm motion of protectiveness*). She would speak with the Deputy Governor.

Danforth (*shocked by this, turns to* Herrick). Did you not tell me Mary Warren were sick in bed?

Herrick. She were, Your Honor. When I go to fetch
130 her to the court last week, she said she were sick.

Giles. She has been strivin' with her soul all week, Your Honor; she comes now to tell the truth of this to you.

Danforth. Who is this?

Proctor. John Proctor, sir. Elizabeth Proctor is my wife.

Parris. Beware this man, Your Excellency, this man is mischief.

Hale (*excitedly*). I think you must hear the girl, sir,
140 she—

Danforth (*who has become very interested in* Mary Warren *and only raises a hand toward* Hale). Peace. What would you tell us, Mary Warren?

(Proctor *looks at her, but she cannot speak.*)

Proctor. She never saw no spirits, sir.

Danforth (*with great alarm and surprise, to* Mary). Never saw no spirits!

Giles (*eagerly*). Never.

Proctor (*reaching into his jacket*). She has signed a
150 **deposition,** sir—

Danforth (*instantly*). No, no, I accept no deposi-tions. (*He is rapidly calculating this; he turns from her to* Proctor.) Tell me, Mr. Proctor, have you given out this story in the village?

Proctor. We have not.

Parris. They've come to overthrow the court, sir! This man is—

Danforth. I pray you, Mr. Parris. Do you know, Mr. Proctor, that the entire contention of the state
160 in these trials is that the voice of Heaven is speaking through the children?

Proctor. I know that, sir.

Danforth (*thinks, staring at* Proctor, *then turns to* Mary Warren). And you, Mary Warren, how came you to cry out people for sending their spirits against you?

Mary Warren. It were pretense, sir.

Danforth. I cannot hear you.

Proctor. It were pretense, she says.

170 **Danforth.** Ah? And the other girls? Susanna Walcott, and—the others? They are also pretending?

Mary Warren. Aye, sir.

Danforth (*wide-eyed*). Indeed. (*Pause. He is baffled by this. He turns to study* Proctor's *face.*)

Parris (*in a sweat*). Excellency, you surely cannot think to let so vile a lie be spread in open court!

Danforth. Indeed not, but it strike hard upon me that she will dare come here with such a tale. Now, Mr. Proctor, before I decide whether I shall hear you
180 or not, it is my duty to tell you this. We burn a hot fire here; it melts down all concealment.

Proctor. I know that, sir.

---

3. **Marblehead . . . Lynn:** two coastal towns in Massachusetts, near Salem.

Danforth. Let me continue. I understand well, a husband's tenderness may drive him to extravagance in defense of a wife. Are you certain in your conscience, Mister, that your evidence is the truth?

Proctor. It is. And you will surely know it.

Danforth. And you thought to declare this revelation in the open court before the public?

190 **Proctor.** I thought I would, aye—with your permission.

Danforth (*his eyes narrowing*). Now, sir, what is your purpose in so doing?

Proctor. Why, I—I would free my wife, sir.

Danforth. There lurks nowhere in your heart, nor hidden in your spirit, any desire to undermine this court?

Proctor (*with the faintest faltering*). Why, no, sir.

Cheever (*clears his throat, awakening*). I—Your 200 Excellency.

Danforth. Mr. Cheever.

Cheever. I think it be my duty, sir—(*kindly, to* Proctor) You'll not deny it, John. (*to* Danforth) When we come to take his wife, he damned the court and ripped your warrant.

Parris. Now you have it!

Danforth. He did that, Mr. Hale?

Hale (*takes a breath*). Aye, he did.

Proctor. It were a temper, sir. I knew not what I did.

210 **Danforth** (*studying him*). Mr. Proctor.

Proctor. Aye, sir.

Danforth (*straight into his eyes*). Have you ever seen the Devil?

Proctor. No, sir.

Danforth. You are in all respects a Gospel Christian?

Proctor. I am, sir.

Parris. Such a Christian that will not come to church but once in a month!

Danforth (*restrained—he is curious*). Not come to 220 church?

Proctor. I—I have no love for Mr. Parris. It is no secret. But God I surely love.

Cheever. He plow on Sunday, sir.

Danforth. Plow on Sunday!

Cheever (*apologetically*). I think it be evidence, John. I am an official of the court, I cannot keep it.

Proctor. I—I have once or twice plowed on Sunday. I have three children, sir, and until last year my land give little.

230 **Giles.** You'll find other Christians that do plow on Sunday if the truth be known.

Hale. Your Honor, I cannot think you may judge the man on such evidence.

Danforth. I judge nothing. (*Pause. He keeps watching* Proctor, *who tries to meet his gaze.*) I tell you straight, Mister—I have seen marvels in this court. I have seen people choked before my eyes by spirits; I have seen them stuck by pins and slashed by daggers. I have until this moment not the slightest reason to 240 suspect that the children may be deceiving me. Do you understand my meaning?

Proctor. Excellency, does it not strike upon you that so many of these women have lived so long with such upright reputation, and—

Parris. Do you read the Gospel, Mr. Proctor?

Proctor. I read the Gospel.

Parris. I think not, or you should surely know that Cain were an upright man, and yet he did kill Abel.[4]

Proctor. Aye, God tells us that. (*to* Danforth) But 250 who tells us Rebecca Nurse murdered seven babies by sending out her spirit on them? It is the children only, and this one will swear she lied to you.

(Danforth *considers, then beckons* Hathorne *to him.* Hathorne *leans in, and he speaks in his ear.* Hathorne *nods.*)

---

4. **Cain . . . Abel:** According to the Book of Genesis in the Bible, Cain and Abel were the sons of Adam and Eve, the first humans.

Hathorne. Aye, she's the one.

Danforth. Mr. Proctor, this morning, your wife send me a claim in which she states that she is pregnant now.

260 **Proctor.** My wife pregnant!

Danforth. There be no sign of it—we have examined her body.

Proctor. But if she say she is pregnant, then she must be! That woman will never lie, Mr. Danforth.

Danforth. She will not?

Proctor. Never, sir, never.

Danforth. We have thought it too convenient to be credited. However, if I should tell you now that I will let her be kept another month; and if she begin to

270 show her natural signs, you shall have her living yet another year until she is delivered—what say you to that? (*John Proctor* is struck silent.) Come now. You say your only purpose is to save your wife. Good, then, she is saved at least this year, and a year is long. What say you, sir? It is done now. (*In conflict,* Proctor *glances at* Francis *and* Giles.) Will you drop this charge?

Proctor. I—I think I cannot.

Danforth (*now an almost **imperceptible** hardness in his voice*). Then your purpose is somewhat larger.

280 **Parris.** He's come to overthrow this court, Your Honor!

Proctor. These are my friends. Their wives are also accused—

Danforth (*with a sudden briskness of manner*). I judge you not, sir. I am ready to hear your evidence.

Proctor. I come not to hurt the court; I only—

Danforth (*cutting him off*). Marshal, go into the court and bid Judge Stoughton and Judge Sewall declare recess for one hour. And let them go to the tavern, if they will. All witnesses and prisoners are

290 to be kept in the building.

Herrick. Aye, sir. (*very deferentially*) If I may say it, sir, I know this man all my life. It is a good man, sir.

Danforth (*It is the reflection on himself he resents*). I am sure of it, Marshal. (Herrick *nods, then goes out.*) Now,

what deposition do you have for us, Mr. Proctor? And I beg you be clear, open as the sky, and honest.

Proctor (*as he takes out several papers*). I am no lawyer, so I'll—

Danforth. The pure in heart need no lawyers.

300 Proceed as you will.

Proctor (*handing* Danforth *a paper*). Will you read this first, sir? It's a sort of testament. The people signing it declare their good opinion of Rebecca, and my wife, and Martha Corey. (Danforth *looks down at the paper.*)

Parris (*to enlist* Danforth's *sarcasm*). Their good opinion! (*But* Danforth *goes on reading, and* Proctor *is heartened.*)

Proctor. These are all landholding farmers, mem-

310 bers of the church. (*delicately, trying to point out a paragraph*) If you'll notice, sir—they've known the women many years and never saw no sign they had dealings with the Devil.

(Parris *nervously moves over and reads over* Danforth's *shoulder.*)

Danforth (*glancing down a long list*). How many names are here?

Francis. Ninety-one, Your Excellency.

Parris (*sweating*). These people should be sum-

320 moned. (Danforth *looks up at him questioningly.*) For questioning.

Francis (*trembling with anger*). Mr. Danforth, I gave them all my word no harm would come to them for signing this.

Parris. This is a clear attack upon the court!

Hale (*to* Parris, *trying to contain himself*). Is every defense an attack upon the court? Can no one—?

Parris. All innocent and Christian people are happy for the courts in Salem! These people are gloomy for

330 it. (*to* Danforth *directly*) And I think you will want to know, from each and every one of them, what discontents them with you!

Hathorne. I think they ought to be examined, sir.

Danforth. It is not necessarily an attack, I think. Yet—

Francis. These are all covenanted Christians, sir.

Danforth. Then I am sure they may have nothing to fear. (*hands* Cheever *the paper*) Mr. Cheever, have warrants drawn for all of these—arrest for examination. (*to* Proctor) Now, Mister, what other informa-
340 tion do you have for us? (Francis *is still standing, horrified.*) You may sit, Mr. Nurse.

Francis. I have brought trouble on these people; I have—

Danforth. No, old man, you have not hurt these people if they are of good conscience. But you must understand, sir, that a person is either with this court or he must be counted against it, there be no road between. This is a sharp time, now, a precise time—we live no longer in the dusky afternoon
350 when evil mixed itself with good and befuddled the world. Now, by God's grace, the shining sun is up, and them that fear not light will surely praise it. I hope you will be one of those. (Mary Warren *suddenly sobs.*) She's not hearty,[5] I see.

Proctor. No, she's not, sir. (*to* Mary, *bending to her, holding her hand, quietly*) Now remember what the angel Raphael said to the boy Tobias.[6] Remember it.

Mary Warren (*hardly audible*). Aye.

Proctor. "Do that which is good, and no harm shall
360 come to thee."

Mary Warren. Aye.

Danforth. Come, man, we wait you.

(Marshal Herrick *returns, and takes his post at the door.*)

Giles. John, my deposition, give him mine.

Proctor. Aye. (*He hands* Danforth *another paper.*) This is Mr. Corey's deposition.

Danforth. Oh? (*He looks down at it. Now* Hathorne *comes behind him and reads with him.*)

Hathorne (*suspiciously*). What lawyer drew this,
370 Corey?

Giles. You know I never hired a lawyer in my life, Hathorne.

Danforth (*finishing the reading*). It is very well phrased. My compliments. Mr. Parris, if Mr. Putnam is in the court, will you bring him in? (Hathorne *takes the deposition, and walks to the window with it.* Parris *goes into the court.*) You have no legal training, Mr. Corey?

Giles (*very pleased*). I have the best, sir—I am thirty-
380 three time in court in my life. And always plaintiff, too.

Danforth. Oh, then you're much put-upon.

Giles. I am never put-upon; I know my rights, sir, and I will have them. You know, your father tried a case of mine—might be thirty-five year ago, I think.

Danforth. Indeed.

Giles. He never spoke to you of it?

Danforth. No, I cannot recall it.

Giles. That's strange, he give me nine pound dam-
390 ages. He were a fair judge, your father. Y'see, I had a white mare that time, and this fellow come to borrow the mare—(*Enter* Parris *with* Thomas Putnam. *When he sees* Putnam, Giles' *ease goes; he is hard.*) Aye, there he is.

Danforth. Mr. Putnam, I have here an accusation by Mr. Corey against you. He states that you coldly prompted your daughter to cry witchery upon George Jacobs that is now in jail.

Putnam. It is a lie.

400 **Danforth** (*turning to* Giles). Mr. Putnam states your charge is a lie. What say you to that?

Giles (*furious, his fists clenched*). A fart on Thomas Putnam, that is what I say to that!

Danforth. What proof do you submit for your charge, sir?

Giles. My proof is there! (*pointing to the paper*) If Jacobs hangs for a witch he forfeit up his property— that's law! And there is none but Putnam with the

---

5. **hearty:** well.

6. **what the angel said . . . Tobias:** In the Book of Tobit in the Apocrypha, Tobit's son Tobias cured his father's blindness with the help of the angel Raphael.

coin to buy so great a piece. This man is killing his neighbors for their land!

Danforth. But proof, sir, proof.

Giles (*pointing at his deposition*). The proof is there! I have it from an honest man who heard Putnam say it! The day his daughter cried out on Jacobs, he said she'd given him a fair gift of land.

Hathorne. And the name of this man?

Giles (*taken aback*). What name?

Hathorne. The man that give you this information.

Giles (*hesitates, then*). Why, I—I cannot give you his name.

Hathorne. And why not?

Giles (*hesitates, then bursts out*). You know well why not! He'll lay in jail if I give his name!

Hathorne. This is contempt of the court, Mr. Danforth!

Danforth (*to avoid that*). You will surely tell us the name.

Giles. I will not give you no name. I mentioned my wife's name once and I'll burn in hell long enough for that. I stand mute.

Danforth. In that case, I have no choice but to arrest you for contempt of this court, do you know that?

Giles. This is a hearing; you cannot clap me for contempt of a hearing.

Danforth. Oh, it is a proper lawyer![7] Do you wish me to declare the court in full session here? Or will you give me good reply?

Giles (*faltering*). I cannot give you no name, sir, I cannot.

Danforth. You are a foolish old man. Mr. Cheever, begin the record. The court is now in session. I ask you, Mr. Corey—

Proctor (*breaking in*). Your Honor—he has the story in confidence, sir, and he—

Parris. The Devil lives on such confidences! (*to Danforth*) Without confidences there could be no conspiracy, Your Honor!

Hathorne. I think it must be broken, sir.

Danforth (*to Giles*). Old man, if your informant tells the truth let him come here openly like a decent man. But if he hide in anonymity I must know why. Now sir, the government and central church demand of you the name of him who reported Mr. Thomas Putnam a common murderer.

Hale. Excellency—

Danforth. Mr. Hale.

Hale. We cannot blink it more. There is a prodigious fear of this court in the country—

Danforth. Then there is a prodigious guilt in the country. Are *you* afraid to be questioned here?

Hale. I may only fear the Lord, sir, but there is fear in the country nevertheless.

Danforth (*angered now*). Reproach me not with the fear in the country; there is fear in the country because there is a moving[8] plot to topple Christ in the country!

Hale. But it does not follow that everyone accused is part of it.

Danforth. No uncorrupted man may fear this court, Mr. Hale! None! (*to Giles*) You are under arrest in contempt of this court. Now sit you down and take counsel with yourself, or you will be set in the jail until you decide to answer all questions.

(Giles Corey *makes a rush for* Putnam. Proctor *lunges and holds him.*)

Proctor. No, Giles!

Giles (*over* Proctor's *shoulder at* Putnam). I'll cut your throat, Putnam, I'll kill you yet!

Proctor (*forcing him into a chair*). Peace, Giles, peace. (*releasing him*) We'll prove ourselves. Now we will. (*He starts to turn to* Danforth.)

---

7. **Oh . . . lawyer:** Oh, he thinks he is a real lawyer.

8. **moving:** active.

Giles. Say nothin' more, John. (*pointing at* Danforth) He's only playin' you! He means to hang us all!

(Mary Warren *bursts into sobs.*)

Danforth. This is a court of law, Mister. I'll have no **effrontery** here!

Proctor. Forgive him, sir, for his old age. Peace, Giles, we'll prove it all now. (*He lifts up* Mary's *chin.*) You cannot weep, Mary. Remember the angel, what he say
490 to the boy. Hold to it, now; there is your rock. (Mary *quiets. He takes out a paper, and turns to* Danforth.) This is Mary Warren's deposition. I—I would ask you remember, sir, while you read it, that until two week ago she were no different than the other children are today. (*He is speaking reasonably, restraining all his fears, his anger, his anxiety.*) You saw her scream, she howled, she swore familiar spirits choked her; she even testified that Satan, in the form of women now in jail, tried to win her soul away, and then when she refused—

500 **Danforth.** We know all this.

Proctor. Aye, sir. She swears now that she never saw Satan; nor any spirit, vague or clear, that Satan may have sent to hurt her. And she declares her friends are lying now.

(Proctor *starts to hand* Danforth *the deposition, and* Hale *comes up to* Danforth *in a trembling state.*)

Hale. Excellency, a moment. I think this goes to the heart of the matter.

Danforth (*with deep misgivings*). It surely does.

510 **Hale.** I cannot say he is an honest man; I know him little. But in all justice, sir, a claim so weighty cannot be argued by a farmer. In God's name, sir, stop here; send him home and let him come again with a lawyer—

Danforth (*patiently*). Now look you, Mr. Hale—

Hale. Excellency, I have signed seventy-two death warrants; I am a minister of the Lord, and I dare not take a life without there be a proof so **immaculate** no slightest qualm of conscience may doubt it.

520 **Danforth.** Mr. Hale, you surely do not doubt my justice.

Hale. I have this morning signed away the soul of Rebecca Nurse, Your Honor. I'll not conceal it, my hand shakes yet as with a wound! I pray you, sir, this argument let lawyers present to you.

Danforth. Mr. Hale, believe me; for a man of such terrible learning you are most bewildered—I hope you will forgive me. I have been thirty-two year at the bar, sir, and I should be confounded were I
530 called upon to defend these people. Let you consider, now—(*to* Proctor *and the others*) And I bid you all do likewise. In an ordinary crime, how does one defend the accused? One calls up witnesses to prove his innocence. But witchcraft is *ipso facto*,[9] on its face and by its nature, an invisible crime, is it not? Therefore, who may possibly be witness to it? The witch and the victim. None other. Now we cannot hope the witch will accuse herself; granted? Therefore, we must rely upon her victims—and they do testify, the
540 children certainly do testify. As for the witches, none will deny that we are most eager for all their confessions. Therefore, what is left for a lawyer to bring out? I think I have made my point. Have I not?

Hale. But this child claims the girls are not truthful, and if they are not—

Danforth. That is precisely what I am about to consider, sir. What more may you ask of me? Unless you doubt my probity?[10]

Hale (*defeated*). I surely do not, sir. Let you consider
550 it, then.

Danforth. And let you put your heart to rest. Her deposition, Mr. Proctor.

(Proctor *hands it to him.* Hathorne *rises, goes beside* Danforth, *and starts reading.* Parris *comes to his other side.* Danforth *looks at* John Proctor, *then proceeds to read.* Hale *gets up, finds position near the judge, reads too.* Proctor *glances at* Giles. Francis *prays silently, hands pressed together.* Cheever *waits placidly, the*

---

9. *ipso facto* Latin: by that very fact.

10. **doubt my probity:** question my integrity.

sublime official, dutiful. Mary Warren *sobs once.*

560 John Proctor *touches her head reassuringly. Presently* Danforth *lifts his eyes, stands up, takes out a kerchief and blows his nose. The others stand aside as he moves in thought toward the window.*)

Parris (*hardly able to contain his anger and fear*). I should like to question—

Danforth (*his first real outburst, in which his contempt for* Parris *is clear*). Mr. Parris, I bid you be silent! (*He stands in silence, looking out the window. Now, having established that he will set the gait.*) Mr. Cheever, will

570 you go into the court and bring the children here? (Cheever *gets up and goes out upstage.* Danforth *now turns to* Mary.) Mary Warren, how came you to this turnabout? Has Mr. Proctor threatened you for this deposition?

Mary Warren. No, sir.

Danforth. Has he ever threatened you?

Mary Warren (*weaker*). No, sir.

Danforth (*sensing a weakening*). Has he threatened you?

580 **Mary Warren.** No, sir.

Danforth. Then you tell me that you sat in my court, callously lying, when you knew that people would hang by your evidence? (*She does not answer.*) Answer me!

Mary Warren (*almost inaudibly*). I did, sir.

Danforth. How were you instructed in your life? Do you not know that God damns all liars? (*She cannot speak.*) Or is it now that you lie?

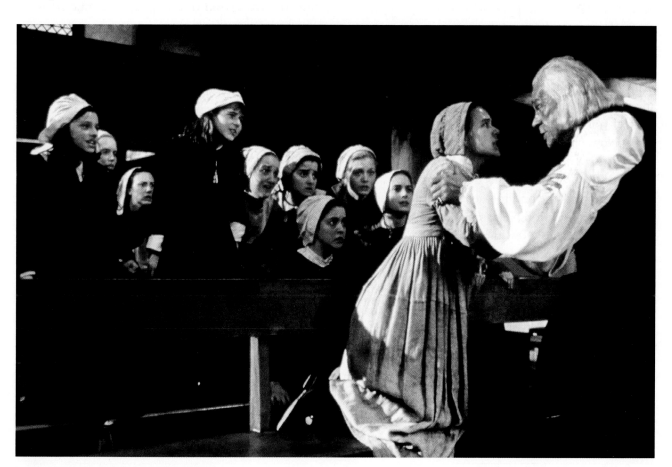

Judge Danforth questioning Mary Warren

Mary Warren. No, sir—I am with God now.

590 **Danforth.** You are with God now.

Mary Warren. Aye, sir.

Danforth (*containing himself*). I will tell you this— you are either lying now, or you were lying in the court, and in either case you have committed per- jury and you will go to jail for it. You cannot lightly say you lied, Mary. Do you know that?

Mary Warren. I cannot lie no more. I am with God, I am with God.

(*But she breaks into sobs at the thought of it, and the* 600 *right door opens, and enter* Susanna Walcott, Mercy Lewis, Betty Parris, *and finally* Abigail. Cheever *comes to* Danforth.)

Cheever. Ruth Putnam's not in the court, sir, nor the other children.

Danforth. These will be sufficient. Sit you down, children. (*Silently they sit.*) Your friend, Mary War- ren, has given us a deposition. In which she swears that she never saw familiar spirits, apparitions, nor any manifest of the Devil. She claims as well that 610 none of you have seen these things either. (*slight pause*) Now, children, this is a court of law. The law, based upon the Bible, and the Bible, writ by Almighty God, forbid the practice of witchcraft, and describe death as the penalty thereof. But likewise, children, the law and Bible damn all bearers of false witness. (*slight pause*) Now then. It does not escape me that this deposition may be devised to blind us; it may well be that Mary Warren has been con- quered by Satan, who sends her here to distract our 620 sacred purpose. If so, her neck will break for it. But if she speak true, I bid you now drop your guile and confess your pretense, for a quick confession will go easier with you. (*pause*) Abigail Williams, rise. (Abi- gail *slowly rises.*) Is there any truth in this?

Abigail. No, sir.

Danforth (*thinks, glances at* Mary, *then back to* Abigail). Children, a very auger bit[11] will now be

turned into your souls until your honesty is proved. Will either of you change your positions now, or do 630 you force me to hard questioning?

Abigail. I have naught to change, sir. She lies.

Danforth (*to* Mary). You would still go on with this?

Mary Warren (*faintly*). Aye, sir.

Danforth (*turning to* Abigail). A poppet were dis- covered in Mr. Proctor's house, stabbed by a needle. Mary Warren claims that you sat beside her in the court when she made it, and that you saw her make it and witnessed how she herself stuck her needle into it for safe-keeping. What say you to that?

640 **Abigail** (*with a slight note of indignation*). It is a lie, sir.

Danforth (*after a slight pause*). While you worked for Mr. Proctor, did you see poppets in that house?

Abigail. Goody Proctor always kept poppets.

Proctor. Your Honor, my wife never kept no pop- pets. Mary Warren confesses it was her poppet.

Cheever. Your Excellency.

Danforth. Mr. Cheever.

Cheever. When I spoke with Goody Proctor in that 650 house, she said she never kept no poppets. But she said she did keep poppets when she were a girl.

Proctor. She has not been a girl these fifteen years, Your Honor.

Hathorne. But a poppet will keep fifteen years, will it not?

Proctor. It will keep if it is kept, but Mary Warren swears she never saw no poppets in my house, nor anyone else.

Parris. Why could there not have been poppets hid 660 where no one ever saw them?

Proctor (*furious*). There might also be a dragon with five legs in my house, but no one has ever seen it.

Parris. We are here, Your Honor, precisely to dis- cover what no one has ever seen.

---

11. **auger** (ô'gər) **bit:** drill.

Proctor. Mr. Danforth, what profit this girl to turn herself about? What may Mary Warren gain but hard questioning and worse?

Danforth. You are charging Abigail Williams with a marvelous cool plot to murder, do you understand that?

670

Proctor. I do, sir. I believe she means to murder.

Danforth (*pointing at* Abigail, *incredulously*). This child would murder your wife?

Proctor. It is not a child. Now hear me, sir. In the sight of the congregation she were twice this year put out of this meetin' house for laughter during prayer.

Danforth (*shocked, turning to* Abigail). What's this? Laughter during—!

Parris. Excellency, she were under Tituba's power at that time, but she is solemn now.

680

Giles. Aye, now she is solemn and goes to hang people!

Danforth. Quiet, man.

Hathorne. Surely it have no bearing on the question, sir. He charges contemplation of murder.

Danforth. Aye. (*He studies* Abigail *for a moment, then.*) Continue, Mr. Proctor.

Proctor. Mary. Now tell the Governor how you danced in the woods.

Parris (*instantly*). Excellency, since I come to Salem this man is blackening my name. He—

690

Danforth. In a moment, sir. (*to* Mary Warren, *sternly, and surprised*) What is this dancing?

Mary Warren. I—(*She glances at* Abigail, *who is staring down at her remorselessly. Then, appealing to* Proctor.) Mr. Proctor—

Proctor (*taking it right up*). Abigail leads the girls to the woods, Your Honor, and they have danced there naked—

Parris. Your Honor, this—

700

Proctor (*at once*). Mr. Parris discovered them himself in the dead of night! There's the "child" she is!

Danforth (*It is growing into a nightmare, and he turns, astonished, to* Parris). Mr. Parris—

Parris. I can only say, sir, that I never found any of them naked, and this man is—

Danforth. But you discovered them dancing in the woods? (*Eyes on* Parris, *he points at* Abigail.) Abigail?

Hale. Excellency, when I first arrived from Beverly, Mr. Parris told me that.

710

Danforth. Do you deny it, Mr. Parris?

Parris. I do not, sir, but I never saw any of them naked.

Danforth. But she have *danced?*

Parris (*unwillingly*). Aye, sir.

(Danforth, *as though with new eyes, looks at* Abigail.)

Hathorne. Excellency, will you permit me? (*He points at* Mary Warren.)

Danforth (*with great worry*). Pray, proceed.

Hathorne. You say you never saw no spirits, Mary, were never threatened or afflicted by any manifest of the Devil or the Devil's agents.

720

Mary Warren (*very faintly*). No, sir.

Hathorne (*with a gleam of victory*). And yet, when people accused of witchery confronted you in court, you would faint, saying their spirits came out of their bodies and choked you—

Mary Warren. That were pretense, sir.

Danforth. I cannot hear you.

Mary Warren. Pretense, sir.

730

Parris. But you did turn cold, did you not? I myself picked you up many times, and your skin were icy. Mr. Danforth, you—

Danforth. I saw that many times.

Proctor. She only pretended to faint, Your Excellency. They're all marvelous pretenders.

Hathorne. Then can she pretend to faint now?

Proctor. Now?

Parris. Why not? Now there are no spirits attacking her, for none in this room is accused of witchcraft. So let her turn herself cold now, let her pretend she is attacked now, let her faint. (*He turns to* Mary Warren.) Faint!

Mary Warren. Faint?

Parris. Aye, faint. Prove to us how you pretended in the court so many times.

Mary Warren (*looking to* Proctor). I—cannot faint now, sir.

Proctor (*alarmed, quietly*). Can you not pretend it?

Mary Warren. I—(*She looks about as though searching for the passion to faint.*) I—have no *sense* of it now, I—

Danforth. Why? What is lacking now?

Mary Warren. I—cannot tell, sir, I—

Danforth. Might it be that here we have no afflicting spirit loose, but in the court there were some?

Mary Warren. I never saw no spirits.

Parris. Then see no spirits now, and prove to us that you can faint by your own will, as you claim.

Mary Warren (*stares, searching for the emotion of it, and then shakes her head*). I—cannot do it.

Parris. Then you will confess, will you not? It were attacking spirits made you faint!

Mary Warren. No, sir, I—

Parris. Your Excellency, this is a trick to blind the court!

Mary Warren. It's not a trick! (*She stands.*) I—I used to faint because I—I thought I saw spirits.

Danforth. *Thought* you saw them!

Mary Warren. But I did not, Your Honor.

Hathorne. How could you think you saw them unless you saw them?

Mary Warren. I—I cannot tell how, but I did. I—I heard the other girls screaming, and you, Your Honor, you seemed to believe them, and I—It were only sport in the beginning, sir, but then the whole world cried spirits, spirits, and I—I promise you, Mr. Danforth, I only thought I saw them but I did not.

(Danforth *peers at her.*)

Parris (*smiling, but nervous because* Danforth *seems to be struck by* Mary Warren's *story*). Surely Your Excellency is not taken by this simple lie.

Danforth (*turning worriedly to* Abigail). Abigail. I bid you now search your heart and tell me this—and beware of it, child, to God every soul is precious and His vengeance is terrible on them that take life without cause. Is it possible, child, that the spirits you have seen are illusion only, some deception that may cross your mind when—

Abigail. Why, this—this—is a base question, sir.

Danforth. Child, I would have you consider it—

Abigail. I have been hurt, Mr. Danforth; I have seen my blood runnin' out! I have been near to murdered every day because I done my duty pointing out the Devil's people—and this is my reward? To be mistrusted, denied, questioned like a—

Danforth (*weakening*). Child, I do not mistrust you—

Abigail (*in an open threat*). Let *you* beware, Mr. Danforth. Think you to be so mighty that the power of Hell may not turn *your* wits? Beware of it! There is—(*Suddenly, from an accusatory attitude, her face turns, looking into the air above—it is truly frightened.*)

Danforth (*apprehensively*). What is it, child?

Abigail (*looking about in the air, clasping her arms about her as though cold*). I—I know not. A wind, a cold wind, has come. (*Her eyes fall on* Mary Warren.)

Mary Warren (*terrified, pleading*). Abby!

Mercy Lewis (*shivering*). Your Honor, I freeze!

Proctor. They're pretending!

Hathorne (*touching* Abigail's *hand*). She is cold, Your Honor, touch her!

Mercy Lewis (*through chattering teeth*). Mary, do you send this shadow on me?

Mary Warren. Lord, save me!

Susanna Walcott. I freeze, I freeze!

Abigail (*shivering visibly*). It is a wind, a wind!

Mary Warren. Abby, don't do that!

Danforth (*himself engaged and entered by* Abigail). Mary Warren, do you witch her? I say to you, do you send your spirit out?

(*With a hysterical cry* Mary Warren *starts to run.*
820 Proctor *catches her.*)

Mary Warren (*almost collapsing*). Let me go, Mr. Proctor, I cannot, I cannot—

Abigail (*crying to Heaven*). Oh, Heavenly Father, take away this shadow!

(*Without warning or hesitation,* Proctor *leaps at* Abigail *and, grabbing her by the hair, pulls her to her feet. She screams in pain.* Danforth, *astonished, cries,* "What are you about?" *and* Hathorne *and* Parris *call,* "Take your hands off her!" *and out of it all comes*
830 Proctor's *roaring voice.*)

Proctor. How do you call Heaven! Whore! Whore!

(Herrick *breaks* Proctor *from her.*)

Herrick. John!

Danforth. Man! Man, what do you—

Proctor (*breathless and in agony*). It is a whore!

Danforth (*dumbfounded*). You charge—?

Abigail. Mr. Danforth, he is lying!

Proctor. Mark her! Now she'll suck a scream to stab me with, but—

840 **Danforth.** You will prove this! This will not pass!

Proctor (*trembling, his life collapsing about him*). I have known her, sir. I have known her.

Danforth. You—you are a lecher?

Francis (*horrified*). John, you cannot say such a—

Proctor. Oh, Francis, I wish you had some evil in you that you might know me! (*to* Danforth) A man will not cast away his good name. You surely know that.

Danforth (*dumbfounded*). In—in what time? In what place?

850 **Proctor** (*his voice about to break, and his shame great*). In the proper place—where my beasts are bedded. On the last night of my joy, some eight months past. She used to serve me in my house, sir. (*He has to clamp his jaw to keep from weeping.*) A man may think God sleeps, but God sees everything, I know it now. I beg you, sir, I beg you—see her what she is. My wife, my dear good wife, took this girl soon after, sir, and put her out on the highroad. And being what she is, a lump of vanity, sir—(*He*
860 *is being overcome.*) Excellency, forgive me, forgive me. (*Angrily against himself, he turns away from the* Governor *for a moment. Then, as though to cry out is his only means of speech left.*) She thinks to dance with me on my wife's grave! And well she might, for I thought of her softly. God help me, I lusted, and there *is* a promise in such sweat. But it is a whore's vengeance, and you must see it; I set myself entirely in your hands. I know you must see it now.

Danforth (*blanched, in horror, turning to* Abigail).
870 You deny every scrap and tittle[12] of this?

Abigail. If I must answer that, I will leave and I will not come back again!

(Danforth *seems unsteady.*)

Proctor. I have made a bell of my honor! I have rung the doom of my good name—you will believe me, Mr. Danforth! My wife is innocent, except she knew a whore when she saw one!

Abigail (*stepping up to* Danforth). What look do you give me? (Danforth *cannot speak.*) I'll not have such
880 looks! (*She turns and starts for the door.*)

Danforth. You will remain where you are! (Herrick *steps into her path. She comes up short, fire in her eyes.*) Mr. Parris, go into the court and bring Goodwife Proctor out.

Parris (*objecting*). Your Honor, this is all a—

---

12. **every scrap and tittle:** every tiny bit.

Danforth (*sharply to* Parris). Bring her out! And tell her not one word of what's been spoken here. And let you knock before you enter. (Parris *goes out.*) Now we shall touch the bottom of this swamp. (*to* Proctor) Your wife, you say, is an honest woman.

Proctor. In her life, sir, she have never lied. There are them that cannot sing, and them that cannot weep—my wife cannot lie. I have paid much to learn it, sir.

Danforth. And when she put this girl out of your house, she put her out for a harlot?[13]

Proctor. Aye, sir.

Danforth. And knew her for a harlot?

Proctor. Aye, sir, she knew her for a harlot.

Danforth. Good then. (*to* Abigail) And if she tell me, child, it were for harlotry, may God spread His mercy on you! (*There is a knock. He calls to the door.*) Hold! (*to* Abigail) Turn your back. Turn your back. (*to* Proctor) Do likewise. (*Both turn their backs—Abigail with indignant slowness.*) Now let neither of you turn to face Goody Proctor. No one in this room is to speak one word, or raise a gesture aye or nay. (*He turns toward the door, calls.*) Enter! (*The door opens. Elizabeth enters with Parris. Parris leaves her. She stands alone, her eyes looking for Proctor.*) Mr. Cheever, report this testimony in all exactness. Are you ready?

Cheever. Ready, sir.

Danforth. Come here, woman. (Elizabeth *comes to him, glancing at* Proctor's *back.*) Look at me only, not at your husband. In my eyes only.

Elizabeth (*faintly*). Good, sir.

Danforth. We are given to understand that at one time you dismissed your servant, Abigail Williams.

Elizabeth. That is true, sir.

Danforth. For what cause did you dismiss her? (*Slight pause. Then* Elizabeth *tries to glance at* Proctor.) You will look in my eyes only and not at your husband. The answer is in your memory and you need no help to give it to me. Why did you dismiss Abigail Williams?

Elizabeth (*not knowing what to say, sensing a situation, wetting her lips to stall for time*). She—dissatisfied me. (*pause*) And my husband.

Danforth. In what way dissatisfied you?

Elizabeth. She were—(*She glances at* Proctor *for a cue.*)

Danforth. Woman, look at me! (Elizabeth *does.*) Were she slovenly? Lazy? What disturbance did she cause?

Elizabeth. Your Honor, I—in that time I were sick. And I—My husband is a good and righteous man. He is never drunk as some are, nor wastin' his time at the shovelboard, but always at his work. But in my sickness—you see, sir, I were a long time sick after my last baby, and I thought I saw my husband somewhat turning from me. And this girl—(*She turns to* Abigail.)

Danforth. Look at me.

Elizabeth. Aye, sir. Abigail Williams—(*She breaks off.*)

Danforth. What of Abigail Williams?

Elizabeth. I came to think he fancied her. And so one night I lost my wits, I think, and put her out on the highroad.

Danforth. Your husband—did he indeed turn from you?

Elizabeth (*in agony*). My husband—is a goodly man, sir.

Danforth. Then he did not turn from you.

Elizabeth (*starting to glance at* Proctor). He—

Danforth (*reaches out and holds her face, then*). Look at me! To your own knowledge, has John Proctor ever committed the crime of lechery? (*In a crisis of indecision she cannot speak.*) Answer my question! Is your husband a lecher!

Elizabeth (*faintly*). No, sir.

Danforth. Remove her, Marshal.

---

13. **for a harlot:** as a woman of low morals.

960 **Proctor.** Elizabeth, tell the truth!

Danforth. She has spoken. Remove her!

Proctor (*crying out*). Elizabeth, I have confessed it!

Elizabeth. Oh, God! (*The door closes behind her.*)

Proctor. She only thought to save my name!

Hale. Excellency, it is a natural lie to tell; I beg you, stop now before another is condemned! I may shut my conscience to it no more—private vengeance is working through this testimony! From the begin-
970 ning this man has struck me true. By my oath to Heaven, I believe him now, and I pray you call back his wife before we—

Danforth. She spoke nothing of lechery, and this man has lied!

Hale. I believe him! (*pointing at* Abigail) This girl has always struck me false! She has—

(Abigail, *with a weird, wild, chilling cry, screams up to the ceiling.*)

Abigail. You will not! Begone! Begone, I say!

Danforth. What is it, child? (*But* Abigail, *pointing*
980 *with fear, is now raising up her frightened eyes, her awed face, toward the ceiling—the girls are doing the same—and now* Hathorne, Hale, Putnam, Cheever, Herrick, *and* Danforth *do the same.*) What's there? (*He lowers his eyes from the ceiling, and now he is frightened; there is real tension in his voice.*) Child! (*She is transfixed—with all the girls, she is whimpering open-mouthed, agape at the ceiling.*) Girls! Why do you—?

Mercy Lewis (*pointing*). It's on the beam! Behind the rafter!

990 **Danforth** (*looking up*). Where!

Abigail. Why—? (*She gulps.*) Why do you come, yellow bird?

Proctor. Where's a bird? I see no bird!

Abigail (*to the ceiling*). My face? My face?

Proctor. Mr. Hale—

Danforth. Be quiet!

Proctor (*to* Hale). Do you see a bird?

Danforth. Be quiet!!

Abigail (*to the ceiling, in a genuine conversation with*
1000 *the "bird," as though trying to talk it out of attacking her*). But God made my face; you cannot want to tear my face. Envy is a deadly sin, Mary.

Mary Warren (*on her feet with a spring, and horrified, pleading*). Abby!

Abigail (*unperturbed, continuing to the "bird"*). Oh, Mary, this is a black art[14] to change your shape. No, I cannot, I cannot stop my mouth; it's God's work I do.

Mary Warren. Abby, I'm *here!*

Proctor (*frantically*). They're pretending, Mr.
1010 Danforth!

Abigail (*Now she takes a backward step, as though in fear the bird will swoop down momentarily*). Oh, please, Mary! Don't come down.

Susanna Walcott. Her claws, she's stretching her claws!

Proctor. Lies, lies.

Abigail (*backing further, eyes still fixed above*). Mary, please don't hurt me!

Mary Warren (*to* Danforth). I'm not hurting her!

Danforth (*to* Mary Warren). Why does she see this
1020 vision?

Mary Warren. She sees nothin'!

Abigail (*now staring full front as though hypnotized, and mimicking the exact tone of* Mary Warren's *cry*). She sees nothin'!

Mary Warren (*pleading*). Abby, you mustn't!

Abigail and All the Girls (*all transfixed*). Abby, you mustn't!

Mary Warren (*to all the girls*). I'm here, I'm here!

Girls. I'm here, I'm here!

1030 **Danforth** (*horrified*). Mary Warren! Draw back your spirit out of them!

Mary Warren. Mr. Danforth!

---

14. **a black art:** sorcery.

Girls (*cutting her off*). Mr. Danforth!

Danforth. Have you compacted with the Devil? Have you?

Mary Warren. Never, never!

Girls. Never, never!

Danforth (*growing hysterical*). Why can they only repeat you?

1040 **Proctor.** Give me a whip—I'll stop it!

Mary Warren. They're sporting.[15] They—!

Girls. They're sporting!

Mary Warren (*turning on them all hysterically and stamping her feet*). Abby, stop it!

Girls (*stamping their feet*). Abby, stop it!

Mary Warren. Stop it!

Girls. Stop it!

Mary Warren (*screaming it out at the top of her lungs, and raising her fists*). Stop it!!

1050 **Girls** (*raising their fists*). Stop it!!

(Mary Warren, *utterly confounded, and becoming overwhelmed by Abigail's—and the girls'—utter conviction, starts to whimper, hands half raised, powerless, and all the girls begin whimpering exactly as she does.*)

Danforth. A little while ago you were afflicted. Now it seems you afflict others; where did you find this power?

Mary Warren (*staring at* Abigail). I—have no power.

Girls. I have no power.

1060 **Proctor.** They're gulling you,[16] Mister!

Danforth. Why did you turn about this past two weeks? You have seen the Devil, have you not?

Hale (*indicating* Abigail *and the girls*). You cannot believe them!

Mary Warren. I—

Proctor (*sensing her weakening*). Mary, God damns all liars!

Danforth (*pounding it into her*). You have seen the Devil, you have made compact with Lucifer, have 1070 you not?

Proctor. God damns liars, Mary!

(Mary *utters something unintelligible, staring at* Abigail, *who keeps watching the "bird" above.*)

Danforth. I cannot hear you. What do you say? (Mary *utters again unintelligibly.*) You will confess yourself or you will hang! (*He turns her roughly to face him.*) Do you know who I am? I say you will hang if you do not open with me!

Proctor. Mary, remember the angel Raphael—do 1080 that which is good and—

Abigail (*pointing upward*). The wings! Her wings are spreading! Mary, please, don't, don't—!

Hale. I see nothing, Your Honor!

Danforth. Do you confess this power! (*He is an inch from her face.*) Speak!

Abigail. She's going to come down! She's walking the beam!

Danforth. Will you speak!

Mary Warren (*staring in horror*). I cannot!

1090 **Girls.** I cannot!

Parris. Cast the Devil out! Look him in the face! Trample him! We'll save you, Mary, only stand fast against him and—

Abigail (*looking up*). Look out! She's coming down!

(*She and all the girls run to one wall, shielding their eyes. And now, as though cornered, they let out a gigantic scream, and* Mary, *as though infected, opens her mouth and screams with them. Gradually* Abigail *and the girls leave off, until only* Mary *is left there, staring* 1100 *up at the "bird," screaming madly. All watch her, horrified by this evident fit.* Proctor *strides to her.*)

Proctor. Mary, tell the Governor what they—(*He has hardly got a word out, when, seeing him coming for her, she rushes out of his reach, screaming in horror.*)

---

15. **sporting:** playing a game.

16. **gulling you:** deceiving you.

Setting and Characters

The same scene presented on stage and produced in a film may look very different. Compare these stage and film versions of the scene in which Abigail and the girls claim to see Mary Warren's spirit flying overhead. What differences do you see? What can the film version show you about the setting and characters that a stage version cannot?

Mary Warren. Don't touch me—don't touch me! (*At which the girls halt at the door.*)

Proctor (*astonished*). Mary!

Mary Warren (*pointing at* Proctor). You're the Devil's man! (*He is stopped in his tracks.*)

1110 **Parris.** Praise God!

Girls. Praise God!

Proctor (*numbed*). Mary, how—?

Mary Warren. I'll not hang with you! I love God, I love God.

Danforth (*to* Mary). He bid you do the Devil's work?

Mary Warren (*hysterically, indicating* Proctor). He come at me by night and every day to sign, to sign, to—

Danforth. Sign what?

Parris. The Devil's book? He come with a book?

1120 **Mary Warren** (*hysterically, pointing at* Proctor, *fearful of him*). My name, he want my name. "I'll murder you," he says, "if my wife hangs! We must go and overthrow the court," he says!

(Danforth's *head jerks toward* Proctor, *shock and horror in his face.*)

Proctor (*turning, appealing to* Hale). Mr. Hale!

Mary Warren (*her sobs beginning*). He wake me every night, his eyes were like coals and his fingers claw my neck, and I sign, I sign . . .

1130 **Hale.** Excellency, this child's gone wild!

Proctor (*as* Danforth's *wide eyes pour on him*). Mary, Mary!

Mary Warren (*screaming at him*). No, I love God; I go your way no more. I love God, I bless God. (*Sobbing, she rushes to* Abigail.) Abby, Abby, I'll never hurt you more! (*They all watch, as* Abigail, *out of her infinite charity, reaches out and draws the sobbing* Mary *to her, and then looks up to* Danforth.)

Danforth (*to* Proctor). What are you? (Proctor *is*
1140 *beyond speech in his anger.*) You are combined with anti-Christ,[17] are you not? I have seen your power; you will not deny it! What say you, Mister?

Hale. Excellency—

Danforth. I will have nothing from you, Mr. Hale! (*to* Proctor) Will you confess yourself befouled with Hell, or do you keep that black allegiance yet? What say you?

Proctor (*his mind wild, breathless*). I say—I say— God is dead!

1150 **Parris.** Hear it, hear it!

Proctor (*laughs insanely, then*). A fire, a fire is burning! I hear the boot of Lucifer, I see his filthy face! And it is my face, and yours, Danforth! For them that quail to bring men out of ignorance, as I have quailed, and as you quail now when you know in all your black hearts that this be fraud—God damns our kind especially, and we will burn, we will burn together!

Danforth. Marshal! Take him and Corey with him to the jail!

1160 **Hale** (*starting across to the door*). I denounce these proceedings!

Proctor. You are pulling Heaven down and raising up a whore!

Hale. I denounce these proceedings, I quit this court! (*He slams the door to the outside behind him.*)

Danforth (*calling to him in a fury*). Mr. Hale! Mr. Hale!

(*The curtain falls.*)

---

17. **combined with anti-Christ:** working with the Devil.

Comprehension

1. **Recall** Why does Mary Warren come to the court?

2. **Recall** What does John Proctor admit to the court?

3. **Clarify** Why is Proctor arrested at the end of the act?

Literary Analysis

4. **Make Inferences** What role do you suppose **hysteria** plays in the following situations? Cite specific evidence from Act Three.

   - Mary's inability to faint on command (lines 736–759)
   - Danforth's belief in the girls (lines 1030–1039)
   - the change in Mary's testimony (lines 1113–1138)

5. **Recognize Verbal Irony** Verbal irony occurs when someone states one thing and means another. According to the stage directions, Abigail draws the sobbing, repentant Mary to her side "out of her infinite charity" (lines 1136–1137). Why is this comment ironic?

6. **Draw Conclusions About Characters** Review the character traits you recorded in your chart for Danforth. How do these traits influence his relationship with the following?

   - John Proctor
   - Reverend Hale
   - Abigail Williams
   - Reverend Parris

7. **Make Judgments** What is your opinion of the way Danforth is conducting the court? Use details from the play to support your opinion.

8. **Analyze Character Motives** Why does Elizabeth lie to Danforth about her husband's relationship with Abigail?

9. **Analyze Conventions of Drama** Review the information on **types of characters** in the **Literary Analysis Workshop** on pages 128–129. Then determine the play's central character, or **protagonist,** its major **antagonists,** and **character foils.** List these characters in a chart like the one shown and take notes on their personalities and values. What effect does the interplay among these characters have on the play?

Character-Type	Personality	Values

Literary Criticism

10. **Different Perspectives** The real Abigail Williams was 11 years old in 1692 and had not had an illicit relationship with John Proctor. How would the play differ if Arthur Miller had not embellished the truth? What would be lost?

ACT *Four*

(*A cell in Salem jail, that fall.*

At the back is a high barred window; near it, a great, heavy door. Along the walls are two benches.

The place is in darkness but for the moonlight seeping through the bars. It appears empty. Presently footsteps are heard coming down a corridor beyond the wall, keys rattle, and the door swings open. Marshal Herrick *enters with a lantern.*

He is nearly drunk, and heavy-footed. He goes to a bench and nudges a bundle of rags lying on it.)

Herrick. Sarah, wake up! Sarah Good! (*He then crosses to the other bench.*)

Sarah Good (*rising in her rags*). Oh, Majesty! Comin', comin'! Tituba, he's here, His Majesty's come!

Herrick. Go to the north cell; this place is wanted now. (*He hangs his lantern on the wall.* Tituba *sits up.*)

Tituba. That don't look to me like His Majesty; look to me like the marshal.

Herrick (*taking out a flask*). Get along with you now,
10 clear this place. (*He drinks, and* Sarah Good *comes and peers up into his face.*)

Sarah Good. Oh, is it you, Marshal! I thought sure you be the devil comin' for us. Could I have a sip of cider for me goin'-away?

Herrick (*handing her the flask*). And where are you off to, Sarah?

Tituba (*as Sarah drinks*). We goin' to Barbados, soon the Devil gits here with the feathers and the wings.

Herrick. Oh? A happy voyage to you.

20 **Sarah Good.** A pair of bluebirds wingin' southerly, the two of us! Oh, it be a grand transformation, Marshal! (*She raises the flask to drink again.*)

Herrick (*taking the flask from her lips*). You'd best give me that or you'll never rise off the ground. Come along now.

Tituba. I'll speak to him for you, if you desires to come along, Marshal.

Herrick. I'd not refuse it, Tituba; it's the proper morning to fly into Hell.

30 **Tituba.** Oh, it be no Hell in Barbados. Devil, him be pleasure-man in Barbados, him be singin' and dancin' in Barbados. It's you folks—you riles him up 'round here; it be too cold 'round here for that Old Boy. He freeze his soul in Massachusetts, but in Barbados he just as sweet and—(*A bellowing cow is heard, and* Tituba *leaps up and calls to the window.*) Aye, sir! That's him, Sarah!

Sarah Good. I'm here, Majesty! (*They hurriedly pick up their rags as* Hopkins, *a guard, enters.*)

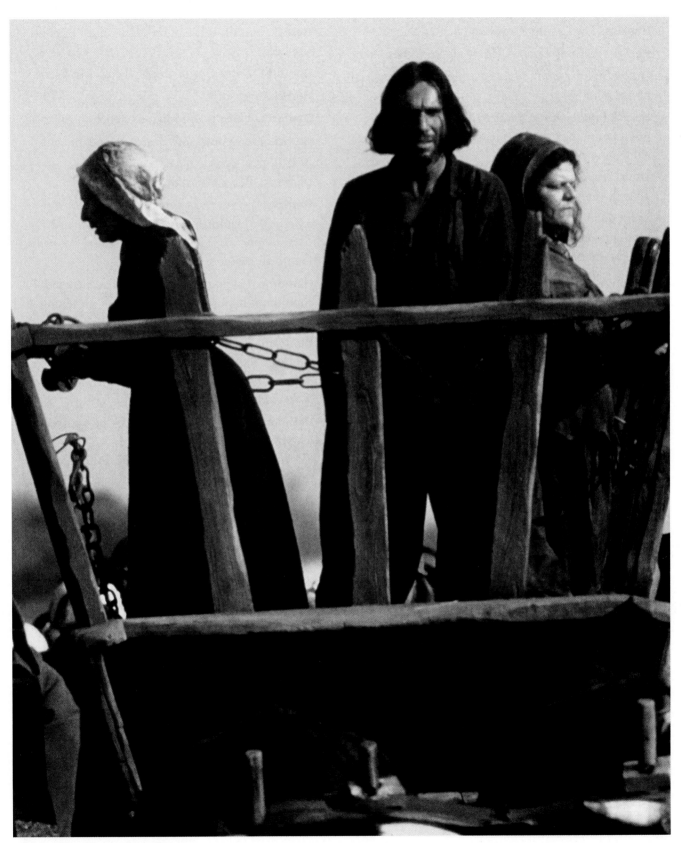
John Proctor going to the gallows

Hopkins. The Deputy Governor's arrived.

Herrick (*grabbing* Tituba). Come along, come along.

Tituba (*resisting him*). No, he comin' for me. I goin' home!

Herrick (*pulling her to the door*). That's not Satan, just a poor old cow with a hatful of milk. Come along now, out with you!

Tituba (*calling to the window*). Take me home, Devil! Take me home!

Sarah Good (*following the shouting* Tituba *out*). Tell him I'm goin', Tituba! Now you tell him Sarah Good is goin' too!

(*In the corridor outside* Tituba *calls on—"Take me home, Devil; Devil take me home!" and* Hopkins' *voice orders her to move on.* Herrick *returns and begins to push old rags and straw into a corner. Hearing footsteps, he turns, and enter* Danforth *and* Judge Hathorne. *They are in greatcoats and wear hats against the bitter cold. They are followed in by* Cheever, *who carries a dispatch case*[1] *and a flat wooden box containing his writing materials.*)

Herrick. Good morning, Excellency.

Danforth. Where is Mr. Parris?

Herrick. I'll fetch him. (*He starts for the door.*)

Danforth. Marshal. (Herrick *stops.*) When did Reverend Hale arrive?

Herrick. It were toward midnight, I think.

Danforth (*suspiciously*). What is he about here?

Herrick. He goes among them that will hang, sir. And he prays with them. He sits with Goody Nurse now. And Mr. Parris with him.

Danforth. Indeed. That man have no authority to enter here, Marshal. Why have you let him in?

Herrick. Why, Mr. Parris command me, sir. I cannot deny him.

Danforth. Are you drunk, Marshal?

Herrick. No, sir; it is a bitter night, and I have no fire here.

Danforth (*containing his anger*). Fetch Mr. Parris.

Herrick. Aye, sir.

Danforth. There is a prodigious stench in this place.

Herrick. I have only now cleared the people out for you.

Danforth. Beware hard drink, Marshal.

Herrick. Aye, sir. (*He waits an instant for further orders. But* Danforth, *in dissatisfaction, turns his back on him, and* Herrick *goes out. There is a pause.* Danforth *stands in thought.*)

Hathorne. Let you question Hale, Excellency; I should not be surprised he have been preaching in Andover[2] lately.

Danforth. We'll come to that; speak nothing of Andover. Parris prays with him. That's strange. (*He blows on his hands, moves toward the window, and looks out.*)

Hathorne. Excellency, I wonder if it be wise to let Mr. Parris so continuously with the prisoners. (Danforth *turns to him, interested.*) I think, sometimes, the man has a mad look these days.

Danforth. Mad?

Hathorne. I met him yesterday coming out of his house, and I bid him good morning—and he wept and went his way. I think it is not well the village sees him so unsteady.

Danforth. Perhaps he have some sorrow.

Cheever (*stamping his feet against the cold*). I think it be the cows, sir.

Danforth. Cows?

Cheever. There be so many cows wanderin' the highroads, now their masters are in the jails, and much disagreement who they will belong to now. I know Mr. Parris be arguin' with farmers all yesterday—

---

1. **dispatch case:** a case for carrying documents.

2. **Andover:** a town in Massachusetts northwest of Salem.

there is great contention, sir, about the cows. Contention make him weep, sir; it were always a man that weep for contention. (*He turns, as do* Hathorne *and* Danforth, *hearing someone coming up the corridor.* Danforth *raises his head as* Parris *enters. He is gaunt, frightened, and sweating in his greatcoat.*)

Parris (*to* Danforth, *instantly*). Oh, good morning, sir, thank you for coming, I beg your pardon wakin' you so early. Good morning, Judge Hathorne.

Danforth. Reverend Hale have no right to enter this—

Parris. Excellency, a moment. (*He hurries back and shuts the door.*)

Hathorne. Do you leave him alone with the prisoners?

Danforth. What's his business here?

Parris (*prayerfully holding up his hands*). Excellency, hear me. It is a providence. Reverend Hale has returned to bring Rebecca Nurse to God.

Danforth (*surprised*). He bids her confess?

Parris (*sitting*). Hear me. Rebecca have not given me a word this three month since she came. Now she sits with him, and her sister and Martha Corey and two or three others, and he pleads with them, confess their crimes and save their lives.

Danforth. Why—this is indeed a providence. And they soften, they soften?

Parris. Not yet, not yet. But I thought to summon you, sir, that we might think on whether it be not wise, to—(*He dares not say it.*) I had thought to put a question, sir, and I hope you will not—

Danforth. Mr. Parris, be plain, what troubles you?

Parris. There is news, sir, that the court—the court must reckon with. My niece, sir, my niece—I believe she has vanished.

Danforth. Vanished!

Parris. I had thought to advise you of it earlier in the week, but—

Danforth. Why? How long is she gone?

Parris. This be the third night. You see, sir, she told me she would stay a night with Mercy Lewis. And next day, when she does not return, I send to Mr. Lewis to inquire. Mercy told him she would sleep in *my* house for a night.

Danforth. They are both gone?!

Parris (*in fear of him*). They are, sir.

Danforth (*alarmed*). I will send a party for them. Where may they be?

Parris. Excellency, I think they be aboard a ship. (Danforth *stands agape.*) My daughter tells me how she heard them speaking of ships last week, and tonight I discover my—my strongbox is broke into. (*He presses his fingers against his eyes to keep back tears.*)

Hathorne (*astonished*). She have robbed you?

Parris. Thirty-one pound is gone. I am penniless. (*He covers his face and sobs.*)

Danforth. Mr. Parris, you are a brainless man! (*He walks in thought, deeply worried.*)

Parris. Excellency, it profit nothing you should blame me. I cannot think they would run off except they fear to keep in Salem any more. (*He is pleading.*) Mark it, sir, Abigail had close knowledge of the town, and since the news of Andover has broken here—

Danforth. Andover is remedied.[3] The court returns there on Friday, and will resume examinations.

Parris. I am sure of it, sir. But the rumor here speaks rebellion in Andover, and it—

Danforth. There is no rebellion in Andover!

Parris. I tell you what is said here, sir. Andover have thrown out the court, they say, and will have no part of witchcraft. There be a faction here, feeding on that news, and I tell you true, sir, I fear there will be riot here.

Hathorne. Riot! Why at every execution I have seen naught but high satisfaction in the town.

---

3. **remedied:** no longer a problem.

Parris. Judge Hathorne—it were another sort that hanged till now. Rebecca Nurse is no Bridget that lived three year with Bishop before she married him. John Proctor is not Isaac Ward that drank his family
190 to ruin. (*to* Danforth) I would to God it were not so, Excellency, but these people have great weight yet in the town. Let Rebecca stand upon the gibbet[4] and send up some righteous prayer, and I fear she'll wake a vengeance on you.

Hathorne. Excellency, she is condemned a witch. The court have—

Danforth (*in deep concern, raising a hand to* Hathorne). Pray you. (*to* Parris) How do you propose, then?

200 **Parris.** Excellency, I would postpone these hangin's for a time.

Danforth. There will be no postponement.

Parris. Now Mr. Hale's returned, there is hope, I think—for if he bring even one of these to God, that confession surely damns the others in the public eye, and none may doubt more that they are all linked to Hell. This way, unconfessed and claiming innocence, doubts are multiplied, many honest people will weep for them, and our good purpose is
210 lost in their tears.

Danforth (*after thinking a moment, then going to* Cheever). Give me the list.

(Cheever *opens the dispatch case, searches.*)

Parris. It cannot be forgot, sir, that when I summoned the congregation for John Proctor's excommunication[5] there were hardly thirty people come to hear it. That speak a discontent, I think, and—

Danforth (*studying the list*). There will be no postponement.

220 **Parris.** Excellency—

Danforth. Now, sir—which of these in your opinion may be brought to God? I will myself strive with him[6] till dawn. (*He hands the list to* Parris, *who merely glances at it.*)

Parris. There is not sufficient time till dawn.

Danforth. I shall do my utmost. Which of them do you have hope for?

Parris (*not even glancing at the list now, and in a quavering voice, quietly*). Excellency—a dagger—
230 (*He chokes up.*)

Danforth. What do you say?

Parris. Tonight, when I open my door to leave my house—a dagger clattered to the ground. (*Silence.* Danforth *absorbs this. Now* Parris *cries out.*) You cannot hang this sort. There is danger for me. I dare not step outside at night!

(Reverend Hale *enters. They look at him for an instant in silence. He is steeped in sorrow, exhausted, and more direct than he ever was.*)

240 **Danforth.** Accept my congratulations, Reverend Hale; we are gladdened to see you returned to your good work.

Hale (*coming to* Danforth *now*). You must pardon them. They will not budge.

(Herrick *enters, waits.*)

Danforth (__conciliatory__). You misunderstand, sir; I cannot pardon these when twelve are already hanged for the same crime. It is not just.

Parris (*with failing heart*). Rebecca will not confess?

250 **Hale.** The sun will rise in a few minutes. Excellency, I must have more time.

Danforth. Now hear me, and beguile yourselves no more. I will not receive a single plea for pardon or postponement. Them that will not confess will hang. Twelve are already executed; the names of

---

4. **gibbet** (jĭb′ĭt): gallows.

5. **excommunication:** banishment from a church. For the Puritans in New England, this punishment resulted in the loss of church privileges.

6. **strive with him:** struggle with him through prayer.

these seven are given out, and the village expects to see them die this morning. Postponement now speaks a floundering on my part; reprieve or pardon must cast doubt upon the guilt of them that died till now. While I speak God's law, I will not crack its voice with whimpering. If retaliation is your fear, know this—I should hang ten thousand that dared to rise against the law, and an ocean of salt tears could not melt the resolution of the statutes. Now draw yourselves up like men and help me, as you are bound by Heaven to do. Have you spoken with them all, Mr. Hale?

Hale. All but Proctor. He is in the dungeon.

Danforth (*to* Herrick). What's Proctor's way now?

Herrick. He sits like some great bird; you'd not know he lived except he will take food from time to time.

Danforth (*after thinking a moment*). His wife—his wife must be well on with child now.

Herrick. She is, sir.

Danforth. What think you, Mr. Parris? You have closer knowledge of this man; might her presence soften him?

Parris. It is possible, sir. He have not laid eyes on her these three months. I should summon her.

Danforth (*to* Herrick). Is he yet **adamant**? Has he struck at you again?

Herrick. He cannot, sir, he is chained to the wall now.

Danforth (*after thinking on it*). Fetch Goody Proctor to me. Then let you bring him up.

Herrick. Aye, sir. (Herrick *goes. There is silence.*)

Hale. Excellency, if you postpone a week and publish to the town that you are striving for their confessions, that speak mercy on your part, not faltering.

Danforth. Mr. Hale, as God have not empowered me like Joshua to stop this sun from rising,[7] so I cannot withhold from them the perfection of their punishment.

Hale (*harder now*). If you think God wills you to raise rebellion, Mr. Danforth, you are mistaken!

Danforth (*instantly*). You have heard rebellion spoken in the town?

Hale. Excellency, there are orphans wandering from house to house; abandoned cattle bellow on the highroads, the stink of rotting crops hangs everywhere, and no man knows when the harlots' cry will end his life—and you wonder yet if rebellion's spoke? Better you should marvel how they do not burn your province!

Danforth. Mr. Hale, have you preached in Andover this month?

Hale. Thank God they have no need of me in Andover.

Danforth. You baffle me, sir. Why have you returned here?

Hale. Why, it is all simple. I come to do the Devil's work. I come to counsel Christians they should belie themselves. (*His sarcasm collapses.*) There is blood on my head! Can you not see the blood on my head!!

Parris. Hush! (*For he has heard footsteps. They all face the door.* Herrick *enters with* Elizabeth. *Her wrists are linked by heavy chain, which* Herrick *now removes. Her clothes are dirty; her face is pale and gaunt.* Herrick *goes out.*)

Danforth (*very politely*). Goody Proctor. (*She is silent.*) I hope you are hearty?

Elizabeth (*as a warning reminder*). I am yet six month before my time.

Danforth. Pray be at your ease, we come not for your life. We—(*uncertain how to plead, for he is not accustomed to it.*) Mr. Hale, will you speak with the woman?

Hale. Goody Proctor, your husband is marked to hang this morning.

(*pause*)

Elizabeth (*quietly*). I have heard it.

---

7. **like Joshua . . . rising:** According to the Bible, Joshua became leader of the Israelites after Moses died. He led the people to the Promised Land while the sun stood still.

Hale. You know, do you not, that I have no connection with the court? (*She seems to doubt it.*) I come of my own, Goody Proctor. I would save your husband's life, for if he is taken I count myself his murderer. Do you understand me?

Elizabeth. What do you want of me?

Hale. Goody Proctor, I have gone this three month like our Lord into the wilderness.[8] I have sought a Christian way, for damnation's doubled on a minis-
340 ter who counsels men to lie.

Hathorne. It is no lie, you cannot speak of lies.

Hale. It is a lie! They are innocent!

Danforth. I'll hear no more of that!

Hale (*continuing to* Elizabeth). Let you not mistake your duty as I mistook my own. I came into this village like a bridegroom to his beloved, bearing gifts of high religion; the very crowns of holy law I brought, and what I touched with my bright confidence, it died; and where I turned the eye of my
350 great faith, blood flowed up. Beware, Goody Proctor—cleave to no faith when faith brings blood. It is mistaken law that leads you to sacrifice. Life, woman, life is God's most precious gift; no principle, however glorious, may justify the taking of it. I beg you, woman, prevail upon your husband to confess. Let him give his lie. Quail not before God's judgment in this, for it may well be God damns a liar less than he that throws his life away for pride. Will you plead with him? I cannot think he will
360 listen to another.

Elizabeth (*quietly*). I think that be the Devil's argument.

Hale (*with a climactic desperation*). Woman, before the laws of God we are as swine! We cannot read His will!

Elizabeth. I cannot dispute with you, sir; I lack learning for it.

Danforth (*going to her*). Goody Proctor, you are not summoned here for disputation. Be there no wifely
370 tenderness within you? He will die with the sunrise. Your husband. Do you understand it? (*She only looks at him.*) What say you? Will you contend with him? (*She is silent.*) Are you stone? I tell you true, woman, had I no other proof of your unnatural life, your dry eyes now would be sufficient evidence that you delivered up your soul to Hell! A very ape would weep at such calamity! Have the devil dried up any tear of pity in you? (*She is silent.*) Take her out. It profit nothing she should speak to him!

380 **Elizabeth** (*quietly*). Let me speak with him, Excellency.

Parris (*with hope*). You'll strive with him? (*She hesitates.*)

Danforth. Will you plead for his confession or will you not?

Elizabeth. I promise nothing. Let me speak with him.

(*A sound—the sibilance of dragging feet on stone. They turn. A pause.* Herrick *enters with* John Proctor. *His wrists are chained. He is another man, bearded, filthy,*
390 *his eyes misty as though webs had overgrown them. He halts inside the doorway, his eye caught by the sight of* Elizabeth. *The emotion flowing between them prevents anyone from speaking for an instant. Now* Hale, *visibly affected, goes to* Danforth *and speaks quietly.*)

Hale. Pray, leave them, Excellency.

Danforth (*pressing* Hale *impatiently aside*). Mr. Proctor, you have been notified, have you not? (Proctor *is silent, staring at* Elizabeth.) I see light in the sky, Mister; let you counsel with your wife,
400 and may God help you turn your back on Hell. (Proctor *is silent, staring at* Elizabeth.)

Hale (*quietly*). Excellency, let—

(Danforth *brushes past* Hale *and walks out.* Hale *follows.* Cheever *stands and follows,* Hathorne *behind.* Herrick *goes.* Parris, *from a safe distance, offers.*)

---

8. **like our Lord . . . wilderness:** According to the New Testament, Jesus spent 40 days wandering in the desert.

Parris. If you desire a cup of cider, Mr. Proctor, I am sure I—(Proctor *turns an icy stare at him, and he breaks off.* Parris *raises his palms toward* Proctor.) God lead you now. (Parris *goes out.*)

410 (*Alone.* Proctor *walks to her, halts. It is as though they stood in a spinning world. It is beyond sorrow, above it. He reaches out his hand as though toward an embodiment not quite real, and as he touches her, a strange soft sound, half laughter, half amazement, comes from his throat. He pats her hand. She covers his hand with hers. And then, weak, he sits. Then she sits, facing him.*)

Proctor. The child?

Elizabeth. It grows.

Proctor. There is no word of the boys?

420 **Elizabeth.** They're well. Rebecca's Samuel keeps them.

Proctor. You have not seen them?

Elizabeth. I have not. (*She catches a weakening in herself and downs it.*)

Proctor. You are a—marvel, Elizabeth.

Elizabeth. You—have been tortured?

Proctor. Aye. (*Pause. She will not let herself be drowned in the sea that threatens her.*) They come for my life now.

Elizabeth. I know it.

430 (*pause*)

Proctor. None—have yet confessed?

Elizabeth. There be many confessed.

Proctor. Who are they?

Elizabeth. There be a hundred or more, they say. Goody Ballard is one; Isaiah Goodkind is one. There be many.

Proctor. Rebecca?

Elizabeth. Not Rebecca. She is one foot in Heaven now; naught may hurt her more.

440 **Proctor.** And Giles?

Elizabeth. You have not heard of it?

Proctor. I hear nothin', where I am kept.

Elizabeth. Giles is dead.

(*He looks at her incredulously.*)

Proctor. When were he hanged?

Elizabeth (*quietly, factually*). He were not hanged. He would not answer aye or nay to his indictment; for if he denied the charge they'd hang him surely, and auction out his property. So he stand mute, and 450 died Christian under the law. And so his sons will have his farm. It is the law, for he could not be condemned a wizard without he answer the indictment, aye or nay.

Proctor. Then how does he die?

Elizabeth (*gently*). They press him, John.

Proctor. Press?

Elizabeth. Great stones they lay upon his chest until he plead aye or nay. (*with a tender smile for the old man*) They say he give them but two words. "More 460 weight," he says. And died.

Proctor (*numbed—a thread to weave into his agony*). "More weight."

Elizabeth. Aye. It were a fearsome[9] man, Giles Corey.

(*pause*)

Proctor (*with great force of will, but not quite looking at her*). I have been thinking I would confess to them, Elizabeth. (*She shows nothing.*) What say you? If I give them that?

Elizabeth. I cannot judge you, John.

470 (*pause*)

Proctor (*simply—a pure question*). What would you have me do?

Elizabeth. As you will, I would have it. (*slight pause*) I want you living, John. That's sure.

Proctor (*pauses, then with a flailing of hope*). Giles' wife? Have she confessed?

Elizabeth. She will not.

---

9. **fearsome:** courageous.

(*pause*)

Proctor. It is a pretense, Elizabeth.

480 **Elizabeth.** What is?

Proctor. I cannot mount the gibbet like a saint. It is a fraud. I am not that man. (*She is silent.*) My honesty is broke, Elizabeth; I am no good man. Nothing's spoiled by giving them this lie that were not rotten long before.

Elizabeth. And yet you've not confessed till now. That speak goodness in you.

Proctor. Spite only keeps me silent. It is hard to give a lie to dogs. (*Pause. For the first time he turns directly* 490 *to her.*) I would have your forgiveness, Elizabeth.

Elizabeth. It is not for me to give, John, I am—

Proctor. I'd have you see some honesty in it. Let them that never lied die now to keep their souls. It is pretense for me, a vanity that will not blind God nor keep my children out of the wind. (*pause*) What say you?

Elizabeth (*upon a heaving sob that always threatens*). John, it come to naught that I should forgive you, if you'll not forgive yourself. (*Now he turns away a little,* 500 *in great agony.*) It is not my soul, John, it is yours. (*He stands, as though in physical pain, slowly rising to his feet with a great immortal longing to find his answer. It is difficult to say, and she is on the verge of tears.*) Only be sure of this, for I know it now: Whatever you will do, it is a good man does it. (*He turns his doubting, searching gaze upon her.*) I have read my heart this three month, John. (*pause*) I have sins of my own to count. It needs a cold wife to prompt lechery.

Proctor (*in great pain*). Enough, enough—

510 **Elizabeth** (*now pouring out her heart*). Better you should know me!

Proctor. I will not hear it! I know you!

Elizabeth. You take my sins upon you, John—

Proctor (*in agony*). No, I take my own, my own!

Elizabeth. John, I counted myself so plain, so poorly made, no honest love could come to me! Suspicion kissed you when I did; I never knew how I should say my love. It were a cold house I kept! (*In fright, she swerves, as* Hathorne *enters.*)

520 **Hathorne.** What say you, Proctor? The sun is soon up.

(Proctor, *his chest heaving, stares, turns to* Elizabeth. *She comes to him as though to plead, her voice quaking.*)

Elizabeth. Do what you will. But let none be your judge. There be no higher judge under Heaven than Proctor is! Forgive me, forgive me, John—I never knew such goodness in the world! (*She covers her face, weeping.*)

(Proctor *turns from her to* Hathorne; *he is off the earth, his voice hollow.*)

530 **Proctor.** I want my life.

Hathorne (*electrified, surprised*). You'll confess yourself?

Proctor. I will have my life.

Hathorne (*with a mystical tone*). God be praised! It is a providence! (*He rushes out the door, and his voice is heard calling down the corridor.*) He will confess! Proctor will confess!

Proctor (*with a cry, as he strides to the door*). Why do you cry it? (*In great pain he turns back to her.*) It is 540 evil, is it not? It is evil.

Elizabeth (*in terror, weeping*). I cannot judge you, John, I cannot!

Proctor. Then who will judge me? (*suddenly clasping his hands*) God in Heaven, what is John Proctor, what is John Proctor? (*He moves as an animal, and a fury is riding in him, a tantalized search.*) I think it is honest, I think so; I am no saint. (*As though she had denied this he calls angrily at her.*) Let Rebecca go like a saint; for me it is fraud!

550 (*Voices are heard in the hall, speaking together in suppressed excitement.*)

Elizabeth. I am not your judge, I cannot be. (*as though giving him release*) Do as you will, do as you will!

Proctor. Would you give them such a lie? Say it. Would you ever give them this? (*She cannot answer.*) You would not; if tongs of fire were singeing you you would not! It is evil. Good, then—it is evil, and I do it!

560 (Hathorne *enters with* Danforth, *and, with them,* Cheever, Parris, *and* Hale. *It is a businesslike, rapid entrance, as though the ice had been broken.*)

Danforth (*with great relief and gratitude*). Praise to God, man, praise to God; you shall be blessed in Heaven for this. (Cheever *has hurried to the bench with pen, ink, and paper.* Proctor *watches him.*) Now then, let us have it. Are you ready, Mr. Cheever?

Proctor (*with a cold, cold horror at their efficiency*). Why must it be written?

570 **Danforth.** Why, for the good instruction of the village, Mister; this we shall post upon the church door! (*to Parris, urgently*) Where is the marshal?

Parris (*runs to the door and calls down the corridor*). Marshal! Hurry!

John and Elizabeth Proctor before the marshal

Danforth. Now, then, Mister, will you speak slowly, and directly to the point, for Mr. Cheever's sake. (*He is on record now, and is really dictating to* Cheever, *who writes.*) Mr. Proctor, have you seen the Devil in your life? (Proctor's *jaws lock.*) Come, man, there
580 is light in the sky; the town waits at the scaffold; I would give out this news. Did you see the Devil?

Proctor. I did.

Parris. Praise God!

Danforth. And when he come to you, what were his demand? (Proctor *is silent.* Danforth *helps.*) Did he bid you to do his work upon the earth?

Proctor. He did.

Danforth. And you bound yourself to his service? (Danforth *turns, as* Rebecca Nurse *enters, with*
590 Herrick *helping to support her. She is barely able to walk.*) Come in, come in, woman!

Rebecca (*brightening as she sees* Proctor). Ah, John! You are well, then, eh?

(Proctor *turns his face to the wall.*)

Danforth. Courage, man, courage—let her witness your good example that she may come to God herself. Now hear it, Goody Nurse! Say on, Mr. Proctor. Did you bind yourself to the Devil's service?

Rebecca (*astonished*). Why, John!

600 **Proctor** (*through his teeth, his face turned from* Rebecca). I did.

Danforth. Now, woman, you surely see it profit nothin' to keep this conspiracy any further. Will you confess yourself with him?

Rebecca. Oh, John—God send his mercy on you!

Danforth. I say, will you confess yourself, Goody Nurse?

Rebecca. Why, it is a lie, it is a lie; how may I damn myself? I cannot, I cannot.

610 **Danforth.** Mr. Proctor. When the Devil came to you did you see Rebecca Nurse in his company? (Proctor *is silent.*) Come, man, take courage—did you ever see her with the Devil?

Proctor (*almost inaudibly*). No.

(Danforth, *now sensing trouble, glances at* John *and goes to the table, and picks up a sheet—the list of condemned.*)

Danforth. Did you ever see her sister, Mary Easty, with the Devil?

620 **Proctor.** No, I did not.

Danforth (*his eyes narrow on* Proctor). Did you ever see Martha Corey with the Devil?

Proctor. I did not.

Danforth (*realizing, slowly putting the sheet down*). Did you ever see anyone with the Devil?

Proctor. I did not.

Danforth. Proctor, you mistake me. I am not empowered to trade your life for a lie. You have most certainly seen some person with the Devil.
630 (Proctor *is silent.*) Mr. Proctor, a score of people have already testified they saw this woman with the Devil.

Proctor. Then it is proved. Why must I say it?

Danforth. Why "must" you say it! Why, you should rejoice to say it if your soul is truly purged of any love for Hell!

Proctor. They think to go like saints. I like not to spoil their names.

Danforth (*inquiring, incredulous*). Mr. Proctor, do
640 you think they go like saints?

Proctor (*evading*). This woman never thought she done the Devil's work.

Danforth. Look you, sir. I think you mistake your duty here. It matters nothing what she thought— she is convicted of the unnatural murder of children, and you for sending your spirit out upon Mary Warren. Your soul alone is the issue here, Mister, and you will prove its whiteness or you cannot live in a Christian country. Will you tell me now what
650 persons conspired with you in the Devil's company? (Proctor *is silent.*) To your knowledge was Rebecca Nurse ever—

Proctor. I speak my own sins; I cannot judge another. (*crying out, with hatred*) I have no tongue for it.

Hale (*quickly to* Danforth). Excellency, it is enough he confess himself. Let him sign it, let him sign it.

Parris (*feverishly*). It is a great service, sir. It is a weighty name; it will strike the village that Proctor
660 confess. I beg you, let him sign it. The sun is up, Excellency!

Danforth (*considers; then with dissatisfaction*). Come, then, sign your testimony. (*to* Cheever) Give it to him. (Cheever *goes to* Proctor, *the confession and a pen in hand.* Proctor *does not look at it.*) Come, man, sign it.

Proctor (*after glancing at the confession*). You have all witnessed it—it is enough.

Danforth. You will not sign it?

670 **Proctor.** You have all witnessed it; what more is needed?

Danforth. Do you sport with me? You will sign your name or it is no confession, Mister! (*His breast heaving with agonized breathing,* Proctor *now lays the paper down and signs his name.*)

Parris. Praise be to the Lord!

(Proctor *has just finished signing when* Danforth *reaches for the paper. But* Proctor *snatches it up, and now a wild terror is rising in him, and a boundless anger.*)

680 **Danforth** (*perplexed, but politely extending his hand*). If you please, sir.

Proctor. No.

Danforth (*as though* Proctor *did not understand*). Mr. Proctor, I must have—

Proctor. No, no. I have signed it. You have seen me. It is done! You have no need for this.

Parris. Proctor, the village must have proof that—

Proctor. Damn the village! I confess to God, and God has seen my name on this! It is enough!

690 **Danforth.** No, sir, it is—

Proctor. You came to save my soul, did you not?

Here! I have confessed myself; it is enough!

Danforth. You have not con—

Proctor. I have confessed myself! Is there no good penitence but it be public? God does not need my name nailed upon the church! God sees my name; God knows how black my sins are! It is enough!

Danforth. Mr. Proctor—

Proctor. You will not use me! I am no Sarah Good or
700 Tituba, I am John Proctor! You will not use me! It is no part of salvation that you should use me!

Danforth. I do not wish to—

Proctor. I have three children—how may I teach them to walk like men in the world, and I sold my friends?

Danforth. You have not sold your friends—

Proctor. Beguile me not! I blacken all of them when this is nailed to the church the very day they hang for silence!

710 **Danforth.** Mr. Proctor, I must have good and legal proof that you—

Proctor. You are the high court, your word is good enough! Tell them I confessed myself; say Proctor broke his knees and wept like a woman; say what you will, but my name cannot—

Danforth (*with suspicion*). It is the same, is it not? If I report it or you sign to it?

Proctor (*He knows it is insane*). No, it is not the same! What others say and what I sign to is not the same!

720 **Danforth.** Why? Do you mean to deny this confession when you are free?

Proctor. I mean to deny nothing!

Danforth. Then explain to me, Mr. Proctor, why you will not let—

Proctor (*with a cry of his whole soul*). Because it is my name! Because I cannot have another in my life! Because I lie and sign myself to lies! Because I am not worth the dust on the feet of them that hang! How may I live without my name? I have given you
730 my soul; leave me my name!

Danforth (*pointing at the confession in* Proctor's *hand*). Is that document a lie? If it is a lie I will not accept it! What say you? I will not deal in lies, Mister! (Proctor *is motionless.*) You will give me your honest confession in my hand, or I cannot keep you from the rope. (Proctor *does not reply.*) Which way do you go, Mister?

(*His breast heaving, his eyes staring,* Proctor *tears the paper and crumples it, and he is weeping in fury, but* 740 *erect.*)

Danforth. Marshal!

Parris (*hysterically, as though the tearing paper were his life*). Proctor, Proctor!

Hale. Man, you will hang! You cannot!

Proctor (*his eyes full of tears*). I can. And there's your first marvel, that I can. You have made your magic now, for now I do think I see some shred of goodness in John Proctor. Not enough to weave a banner with, but white enough to keep it from such dogs.

750 (Elizabeth, *in a burst of terror, rushes to him and weeps against his hand.*) Give them no tear! Tears pleasure them! Show honor now, show a stony heart and sink them with it! (*He has lifted her, and kisses her now with great passion.*)

Rebecca. Let you fear nothing! Another judgment waits us all!

Danforth. Hang them high over the town! Who weeps for these, weeps for corruption! (*He sweeps out past them.* Herrick *starts to lead* Rebecca, *who almost* 760 *collapses, but* Proctor *catches her, and she glances up at him apologetically.*)

Rebecca. I've had no breakfast.

Herrick. Come, man.

(Herrick *escorts them out,* Hathorne *and* Cheever *behind them.* Elizabeth *stands staring at the empty doorway.*)

Parris (*in deadly fear, to* Elizabeth). Go to him, Goody Proctor! There is yet time!

(*From outside a drumroll strikes the air.* Parris *is star-* 770 *tled.* Elizabeth *jerks about toward the window.*)

Parris. Go to him! (*He rushes out the door, as though to hold back his fate.*) Proctor! Proctor!

(*again, a short burst of drums*)

Hale. Woman, plead with him! (*He starts to rush out the door, and then goes back to her.*) Woman! It is pride, it is vanity. (*She avoids his eyes, and moves to the window. He drops to his knees.*) Be his helper!— What profit him to bleed? Shall the dust praise him? Shall the worms declare his truth? Go to him, take 780 his shame away!

Elizabeth (*supporting herself against collapse, grips the bars of the window, and with a cry*). He have his goodness now. God forbid I take it from him!

(*The final drumroll crashes, then heightens violently.* Hale *weeps in frantic prayer, and the new sun is pouring in upon her face, and the drums rattle like bones in the morning air. The curtain falls.*)

Comprehension

1. **Recall** Why has Reverend Hale returned to Salem?

2. **Clarify** Why does Danforth summon Elizabeth Proctor?

3. **Summarize** What does John Proctor do when asked to sign a confession?

Literary Analysis

4. **Infer Character Motives** Explain why each of the following characters wants John and the other prisoners to confess. Support your answer with evidence.

   • Danforth   • Parris   • Hale

5. **Examine Dialogue** Reread Elizabeth Proctor's dialogue at the end of Act Four (lines 782–783) when she says of her husband, "He have his goodness now." What do you think she means? Do you agree with her?

6. **Analyze Conventions of Drama** Much of the **plot** of *The Crucible* is built around the internal and external conflicts of John Proctor. An **internal conflict** is a struggle between opposing forces within a character. An **external conflict** pits a character against nature, society, or another character. Use a chart like the one shown to show the internal and external conflicts of John Proctor. How is each resolved?

Conflict	Internal or External?	How Resolved

7. **Draw Conclusions About Characters** Refer to the chart of character traits you have created. Which characters have changed over the course of the play? How have they changed? Cite specific details from the play.

8. **Interpret Symbol** A crucible is a severe test or trial. It is also a vessel in which materials are melted at high temperatures to produce a more refined substance. What do you think a crucible might symbolize in this drama?

9. **Synthesize Themes** A theme is a central idea the writer wishes to share with the reader. This idea may be a lesson about life or about people and their actions. What do you think are some of the themes of *The Crucible*?

Literary Criticism

10. **Critical Interpretations** Many critics have observed that Miller's play goes beyond the historical events of 17th- and 20th-century America and explores universal conflicts. What universal conflicts does the play deal with?

Vocabulary in Context

WORD LIST
adamant
ameliorate
anarchy
conciliatory
contentious
corroborate
deference
deposition
dissembling
effrontery
immaculate
imperceptible
iniquity
subservient
trepidation

VOCABULARY PRACTICE

Decide whether the words in each pair are synonyms or antonyms.

1. dissembling/lying
2. iniquity/goodness
3. contentious/argumentative
4. adamant/unsure
5. immaculate/filthy
6. trepidation/bravery
7. deposition/statement
8. deference/impudence
9. conciliatory/appeasing
10. anarchy/disorder
11. ameliorate/worsen
12. effrontery/humility
13. corroborate/substantiate
14. imperceptible/unnoticeable
15. subservient/subordinate

VOCABULARY IN WRITING

Write a brief character sketch of Mary Warren, using details from the text to flesh out your portrayal of her. Include at least four vocabulary words. Here is a sample opening sentence.

> **EXAMPLE**
> Mary was a **subservient** young girl who did not know how to handle the power and attention she suddenly received.

VOCABULARY STRATEGY: CONTEXT CLUES

The words, sentences, paragraphs, and even punctuation marks that surround a word make up its **context.** Often context can help you figure out the meaning of an unfamiliar word.

PRACTICE Locate each word below in its context in the play. Then write the letter of the correct definition for each.

1. **subservient** (page 143): (a) forceful, (b) vengeful, (c) lower in importance
2. **iniquity** (page 147): (a) forgetfulness, (b) act of not caring, (c) wickedness
3. **ameliorate** (page 164): (a) improve, (b) aggravate, (c) move farther along
4. **contentious** (page 178): (a) angry, (b) generous, (c) misguided
5. **effrontery** (page 184): (a) patience, (b) presumptuousness, (c) desire to talk a lot

VOCABULARY PRACTICE
For more practice, go to the **Vocabulary Center** at **ClassZone.com.**

Reading-Writing Connection

WRITING PROMPT

ANALYZE MOTIVATIONS Why does John Proctor change his mind and tear up the confession? How does his concern for what others might think of him influence his decision? In **four or five paragraphs,** discuss Proctor's perception of a morally righteous person and how that perception affects his decision. Think about Rebecca Nurse's reaction to his confession and Elizabeth's assertion that "there be no higher judge under Heaven than Proctor is!"

SELF-CHECK

A strong analysis will . . .

- explain the choices Proctor must make to arrive at his decision
- discuss how Proctor's idea of morality differs from that of the judges
- use quotations and examples from the play to support key points

GRAMMAR AND STYLE

USE REALISTIC DIALOGUE A play consists almost entirely of dialogue; therefore, to ensure authenticity, it is important that the characters' speech match the play's setting. In *The Crucible,* Arthur Miller's **word choice** and use of **inverted sentences** accurately reflect the speech of the time, contributing to the playwright's realistic depiction of life in 17th-century Salem. Here are some examples:

> ***Parris.*** *. . . Let him look to medicine and put out all thought of unnatural causes here. There be none.*
>
> ***Susanna.*** *Aye, sir. . . .* (Act One, lines 50–52)
>
> ***Abigail.*** *Now look you. All of you. We danced. . . .* (Act One, line 353)

In the first piece of dialogue, notice how Miller uses *be* rather than *are,* the verb form that currently would be used in this context. And instead of *yes,* Miller uses the word *aye,* a word that was commonplace in the 1600s but is rarely used today.

In the second piece of dialogue, Miller forms an inverted sentence, with the verb preceding the subject. This type of inverted word order was common in 17th-century speech.

PRACTICE Rewrite the following sentences so that they better reflect the 17th-century speech patterns that Miller employs.

> **EXAMPLE**
>
> You go to the house!
> *Go you to the house!*

1. Yes, it is true I saw the devil with Rebecca Nurse.
2. Are you sure of their guilt?
3. You confess to these sins!

WRITING TOOLS
For prewriting, revision, and editing tools, visit the **Writing Center** at ClassZone.com.

The Crucible and McCarthyism

- Online Article, page 213
- Newspaper Article, page 214
- Memoir, page 216

Use with *The Crucible*, page 132.

While Arthur Miller was writing *The Crucible,* a young senator named Joseph McCarthy was conducting a campaign to root out communists in American public life. In his memoir, *Timebends,* Miller reveals that he saw a connection between the Salem witch trials and McCarthy's campaign. The following selections will help you understand that connection by providing you with information about McCarthyism and its bearing on *The Crucible.* As you read, bear in mind that you will later be asked to explain how this information affects your sense of the play.

Skill Focus: Understand Historical Context

As you may recall, the **historical context** of a literary work is the social and political conditions of the times in which the writer lived. To varying degrees, most literature reflects this context, often through its portrayal of values and conflicts.

To better grasp the historical context of *The Crucible,* take notes as you read the selections. In particular, record the significant events, values, and issues that were of primary concern in American society while Miller was writing his play. Use a chart such as the one shown here.

Source	Relevant Historical Information
"McCarthyism"	. . .
"The Demons of Salem, With Us Still"	. . .
Timebends	. . .

McCARTHYISM

Throughout the 1940s and 1950s America was overwhelmed with concerns about the threat of communism growing in Eastern Europe and China. Capitalizing on those concerns, a young Senator named Joseph McCarthy made a public accusation that more than two hundred "card-carrying" communists had infiltrated the United States government. Though

10 eventually his accusations were proven to be untrue, and he was censured by the Senate for unbecoming conduct, his zealous campaigning ushered in one of the most repressive times in 20th-century American politics. **A**

Army counsel Joseph N. Welch, left, and Senator Joseph McCarthy

While the House Un-American Activities Committee (HUAC) had been formed in 1938 as an anti-Communist organ, McCarthy's accusations heightened the political tensions of the times. Known as McCarthyism, the paranoid hunt for infiltrators was notoriously difficult on writers and entertainers, many of whom were labeled

20 communist sympathizers and were unable to continue working. Some had their passports taken away, while others were jailed for refusing to give the names of other communists. The trials, which were well publicized, could often destroy a career with a single unsubstantiated accusation. Among those well-known artists accused of communist sympathies or called before the committee were Paul Robeson, Arthur Miller, Aaron Copland, Leonard Bernstein, Charlie Chaplin and Elia Kazan. In all, three hundred and twenty artists were blacklisted, and for many of them this meant the end of exceptional and promising careers. **B**

30 During this time there were few in the press willing to stand up against McCarthy and the anti-Communist machine. Among those few were comedian Mort Sahl, and journalist Edward R. Murrow, whose strong criticisms of McCarthy are often cited as playing an important role in his eventual removal from power. By 1954, the fervor had died down and many actors and writers were able to return to work. Though relatively short, these proceedings remain one of the most shameful moments in modern U.S. history.

A HISTORICAL CONTEXT
What preoccupied Americans during the 1940s and 1950s? Record your answer on your chart.

B HISTORICAL CONTEXT
What does the term *McCarthyism* refer to? Identify the information in this paragraph that suggests a connection between McCarthyism and Miller's play.

Reprinted From **The New York Times**

Arthur Miller prepares to testify before the House Un-American Activities Commitee, 1956.

The Demons of Salem, With Us Still

by Victor Navasky

When Arthur Miller's drama *The Crucible* first opened on Broadway in 1953, the country was in a panic about the so-called Red Menace. Senator Joseph McCarthy, with his reckless charges of spies and "comsymps,"[1] occupied the front pages, while behind the scenes J. Edgar Hoover, the director of the F.B.I., presided over and
10 manipulated a vast internal security bureaucracy, issuing periodic bulletins intended to fan the flames of the domestic cold war.

In the center ring were the congressional inquisitor-investigators, asking "Are you now or have you ever been a member of the Communist Party?"

At the time, Mr. Miller and
20 Tennessee Williams were regarded as the world's two foremost playwrights. But that lofty status was an invitation rather than an obstacle to the red-hunters who wanted to talk to Mr. Miller. In fact, when he was finally summoned to appear, the committee chairman, Representative Francis Walters, let Mr. Miller know that things might go easier for him if he
30 persuaded his fiancee, Marilyn Monroe, to pose for a photograph with the chairman. Mr. Miller let that option lapse and was shortly indicted for contempt of Congress when he refused to answer the committee's questions about Communists he had known.

On the left, the hunt for subversives was routinely labeled a witch hunt, after the infamous Salem witch trials
40 of the late 17th century. And so when *The Crucible,* set in Salem in 1692 but written in the overheated atmosphere of the domestic cold war, appeared, two questions were quickly asked: Was Mr. Miller's depiction of the inhabitants and events of 1692 Salem faithful to the original? And was the original an appropriate metaphor for McCarthyism? **C**

C HISTORICAL CONTEXT
Reread lines 1–48. When *The Crucible* hit the stage, why were people so quick to ask about the connection between the play and McCarthy's campaign?

---

1. **"comsymps":** Communist sympathizers.

50 On the historical front it was generally conceded when the play was written that Mr. Miller's research was accurate. His principal changes involved fusing some characters and raising the age of John Proctor's accuser, Abigail Williams, from 11 to 17 (to accommodate Mr. Miller's story of how a liaison between Abigail and John was intertwined with the accusations of 60 witchcraft against Proctor's wife).

But even before the play was written, Mr. Miller was denounced for his metaphor. He had stopped off at the home of his friend and colleague Elia Kazan, who had directed Mr. Miller's two previous prize-winning hits, "All My Sons" and "Death of a Salesman," and who had been subpoenaed to appear before the House Committee on 70 Un-American Activities (where he ultimately named names).

They went for a walk in the Connecticut woods and discussed Mr. Kazan's dilemma. On the one hand to be an informer was unpalatable, but on the other, as Mr. Kazan put it at the time, "Secrecy serves the Communists." **D**

In his memoir *Timebends,* Mr. Miller 80 wrote that he was half inside his car when Molly, Kazan's wife, "came out and asked if I was staying at my house, half an hour away, and I said that I was on my way to Salem. She instantly understood what my destination meant, and her eyes widened in sudden apprehension and possible anger. 'You're not going to equate witches with this!'

Later, Mr. Kazan reported his wife's 90 views in his own memoir, *A Life.*

"What's going on here and now is not to be compared with the witch trials of that time," she said. "Those witches did not exist. Communists do. Here and everywhere in the world. It's a false parallel. Witch hunt! The phrase would indicate that there are no Communists in government, none in the arts, none sending money from Hollywood to 100 12th Street." **E**

For me, the parallel worked. The term "Communist" had been so demonized that like the word "witch" it signified something that didn't really exist in its popular meaning. Certainly the entertainment community Communists like Mr. Kazan (and for a brief period, Mr. Miller himself, although he never fully joined the party) 110 were not conscious agents of an international monolithic conspiracy to overthrow the Government by force and violence; they were, for the most part, do-gooders, who thought—misguidedly, most of them later concluded—that the Communist Party was the best agency to do something about the depression and racism at home and fascism abroad.

As it turned out, despite mixed 120 notices for *The Crucible,* over the years it was to become Arthur Miller's most performed play, with productions in China, Poland, Britain, high schools and repertory theaters throughout the world. Now *The Crucible* is a $25 million motion picture, under the aegis of 20th Century Fox.

Although the playwright in Mr. Miller was originally drawn to think 130 about the political and moral pressures of the domestic cold war years, when I asked him about the applicability of the play to the here and now he said:

"I have had immense confidence in the applicability of the play to almost any time, the reason being it's dealing with a paranoid situation. But that situation doesn't depend on any particular political or sociological 140 development. I wrote it blind to the world. The enemy is within, and within stays within, and we can't get out of within. It's always on the edge of our minds that behind what we see is a nefarious plot." **F**

D HISTORICAL CONTEXT
Reread lines 11–77. In light of his comment, would you say that Elia Kazan took McCarthy's mission seriously? Explain.

E HISTORICAL CONTEXT
Given her husband's role in the McCarthy hearings, why do you think Molly Kazan might have objected to Miller's comparison between HUAC and Salem?

F HISTORICAL CONTEXT
Reread Miller's final comments in lines 133–144. In the end, how would you describe his feelings about the comparison between the Salem trials and the McCarthy hearings?

TIMEBENDS

by Arthur Miller

I had known about the Salem witchcraft phenomenon since my American history class at Michigan, but it had remained in mind as one of those inexplicable mystifications of the long-dead past when people commonly believed that the spirit could leave the body, palpably and visibly. My mother might believe it still, if only in one corner of her mind, and I suspected that there were a lot of other people who, like me, were secretly open to suggestion. As though it had been ordained, a copy of Marion Starkey's book *The Devil in Massachusetts* fell into my hands, and the bizarre story came back as I had recalled it, but this time in remarkably well-organized detail. **G**

Miller at his typewriter in 1959

   At first I rejected the idea of a play on the subject. My own rationality was too strong, I thought, to really allow me to capture this wildly irrational outbreak. A drama cannot merely describe an emotion, it has to become that emotion. But gradually, over weeks, a living connection between myself and Salem, and between Salem and Washington, was made in my mind—for whatever else they might be, I saw that the hearings in Washington were profoundly and even avowedly ritualistic. After all, in almost every case the Committee knew in advance what they wanted the witness to give them; the names of his comrades in the Party. The FBI had long since infiltrated the Party, and informers had long ago identified the participants in various meetings. The main point of the hearings, precisely as in seventeenth-century Salem, was that the accused make public confession, damn his confederates as well as his Devil master, and guarantee his sterling new allegiance by breaking disgusting old vows—whereupon he was let loose to rejoin the society of extremely decent people. In other words, the same spiritual nugget lay folded within both procedures—an act of contrition done not in solemn privacy but out in the public air. The Salem prosecution was actually on more solid legal ground since the defendant, if guilty of familiarity with the Unclean One, had broken a law against the practice of witchcraft, a civil as well as a religious offense; whereas the offender against HUAC (House Un-American Activities Committee) could not be accused of any such violation but only of a spiritual crime, subservience to a political enemy's desires and ideology. He was summoned before the Committee to be called a bad name, but one that could destroy his career. **H**

G HISTORICAL CONTEXT
Reread lines 1–17. What details indicate the significance for him of finding Starkey's book?

H HISTORICAL CONTEXT
What parallels does Miller identify between the hearings in Washington and the Salem witch trials?

Comprehension

1. **Recall** What was Senator McCarthy's mission?

2. **Recall** What kinds of professionals were targeted by McCarthy's accusations?

3. **Recall** What was the catalyst for Miller's interest in the Salem witch trials?

Critical Analysis

4. **Evaluate Statements** Considering the historical context of *The Crucible* and Arthur Miller's own comments in *Timebends*, do you think Miller was really "blind to the world" when he wrote *The Crucible*? Support your opinion.

5. **Evaluate the Role of Historical Context** In your opinion, is knowing *The Crucible*'s historical context necessary to understand the playwright's message? Explain.

Read for Information: Synthesize

WRITING PROMPT

Think about the social and political conditions of the time during which Arthur Miller was writing *The Crucible*. In what ways has looking through this historical lens colored your understanding of the play? In developing your new analysis, support your thesis with information from the articles you have just read and details from the play.

To answer this prompt, follow these steps:

1. In a sentence or two, summarize how this historical information has added to or changed your understanding of the play. Consider using this summary as your thesis statement.

2. In your notes, identify elements of the play that you now view differently. How has your sense of these elements changed? For example, are there things you now see more clearly? Does the play seem more or less interesting? Note the historical details that caused you to think differently.

3. Using your thesis statement and notes, write a brief essay in which you explain how learning about the historical context of *The Crucible* affected your appreciation and understanding of the play.

from **The Crucible**

Film Clip on **MediaSmart** DVD

From Page to Screen

The Crucible is considered a modern classic of the American theater. Surprisingly, no one attempted a film version of the work in English until 1996, 43 years after the play's debut. In this lesson, view a scene from the film version to explore Arthur Miller's timeless tale in a different medium from the one originally intended.

The Filmmakers' Challenge

Translating a well-known play to the big screen poses a number of challenges for filmmakers. Writing the screenplay, perhaps the biggest hurdle, was made a little easier in the case of *The Crucible*. Arthur Miller adapted his own work and took an active role in the film's production. The playwright, consulting with the film's director, was able to take certain liberties. He could choose where a scene took place and weave in scenes not found in the original play. "I did some rewriting during production to take advantage of opportunities we had with this wonderful Hog Island [Massachusetts] location," Miller recalls.

On the set, Daniel Day-Lewis with Arthur Miller

Over the past five decades, *The Crucible*'s themes have reached far beyond the era and country in which the play was created. As Miller points out, the play's themes "find [their] relevance in every culture. I knew a woman imprisoned for six years under the [Chinese] Mao regime.... She told me that when she saw *The Crucible* in Shanghai she couldn't believe that a non-Chinese had written it, because the interrogations in *The Crucible* had been precisely the interrogations she had endured under the Cultural Revolution."

Comparing Texts: Dialogue

In taking his play from the page to the screen, Arthur Miller had to make certain decisions about how much of the original dialogue he would retain. During production, actors and directors will often make changes to the dialogue to fine-tune a scene.

Compare the dialogue from the play with the dialogue that appears in the film. Notice Miller's stage direction in the text and how actor Daniel Day-Lewis, in the role of John Proctor, interprets it.

Danforth (*with suspicion*). It is the same, is it not? If I report it or you sign it?

Proctor (*he knows it is insane*). No, it is not the same! What others say and what I sign is not the same!

5   **Danforth.** Why? Do you mean to deny this confession when you are free?

Proctor. I mean to deny nothing!

Danforth. Then explain to me, Mr. Proctor, why you will not let—

Proctor (*with a cry of his whole soul*). Because it is my name! Because I cannot have another in my life! Because I lie and sign myself to lies! Because I am
10   not worth the dust on the feet of them that hang! How may I live without my name? I have given you my soul; leave me my name!

Viewing Guide

 MediaSmart DVD

- **Film:** *The Crucible*
- **Director:** Nicholas Hytner
- **Genre:** Drama
- **Running Time:** 5 minutes

In the clip from *The Crucible*, the character John Proctor has finally agreed to sign a false confession that will save him from death.

Plan on viewing the clip several times. To help you analyze the dialogue and performance, refer to the questions.

NOW VIEW

CLOSE VIEWING: **Media Analysis**

1. **Analyze Setting** In the play, this scene is set in jail. How does moving the setting affect (or not affect) the scene?

2. **Compare Dialogue** Compare the dialogue from the play with the dialogue in the movie. Why do you think Miller changed some of his original dialogue for the movie?

3. **Evaluate Actor's Performance** Read the stage direction the playwright included for Proctor's speech. Do you think the actor playing Proctor succeeded in portraying "a cry of his whole soul"? Cite evidence from the scene to support your opinion.

[**REVIEW**]

Director Nicholas Hytner with cast

The Crucible

Peter Travers

Arthur Miller is the first to admit that *The Crucible* must stand on its own. The playwright, now 81, sat near me at a screening of the film, unwittingly intimidating all around him. For the Pulitzer Prize–winning author of *Death of a Salesman,* attention must be paid. Miller asked for none of it. He talked with boyish zest of working with director Nicholas Hytner on re-crafting *The Crucible* as a $25 million film that would allow startling imagery to resonate with his language and burst the bounds of the stage.

Does it ever. *The Crucible,* despite some damaging cuts to the text, is a seductively exciting film that crackles with visual energy, passionate provocation and incendiary acting. . . .

The great Paul Scofield is triumphant, avoiding the easy caricature of Danforth as a fanatic. He brings the role something new: wit. We laugh with this judge, which heightens the horror later when he blinds himself to truth in the name of God and his own ambition. The scene in which he ignores Rev. Hale (Rob Campbell), who knows the girls are faking, and bullies the servant Mary Warren (Karron Graves) into delusion and madness chills the blood.

As the unforgiving wife whose "justice would freeze beer," in the words of her husband, Joan Allen is an absolute stunner in an award-caliber performance that is also a surprising source of warmth. By the seashore, where the pregnant Elizabeth has come to say goodbye to her condemned husband, she tells John, "I once counted myself so plain, so poorly made, that no honest love could come to me." Elizabeth's scene of tender reconciliation is the film's moral core. John need only sign a false confession of witchcraft to save himself from the gallows. Of course, he won't. "Because it is my name," he tells Danforth simply. "Because I cannot have another in my life."

In the film's most complex role, Daniel Day-Lewis performs with quiet power. Playing nobility can make actors insufferable, but Day-Lewis keeps John Proctor human even when saddled with smudgy makeup and fake brown teeth for his final scene. *The Crucible,* for all its timely denunciation of persecution masked as piety . . . comes down to individual resistance and how you search your heart to find it. The years haven't softened the rage against self-betrayal in *The Crucible.* This stirring film lets you feel the heat of Miller's argument and the urgent power of his kick.

The Puritan Legacy

In the minds of some, Puritanism is a thing of the past—an outmoded collection of beliefs from a dour and oddly-dressed group of people. Yet others insist that the spiritual, social, and cultural principles fostered by Puritanism are stubbornly present, in one way or another, in American society today. Somewhere in the middle of this debate are literary historians Richard Ruland and Malcolm Bradbury, who insist: "Puritans considered many of the literary questions we still ask today; they answered them differently."

Writing to Analyze

We can all agree that the Puritan style of dress is out of fashion, but are Puritan ideas also outmoded? Consider these "literary questions" discussed in the selections you have just read:

What is true love?

Why do bad things happen to good people?

How can faith sustain us?

How can people best serve God?

Are people worthy?

Are people basically good or bad?

In a brief essay, explain whether you think these questions are outmoded, still relevant today, or a mixture of the two. Give specific examples from current books, television programs, or movies to support your opinions.

Consider

• each of the above questions carefully. Can you think of a current book, movie, or TV show that explores that question?

• the general thrust of today's popular culture. As a whole, what types of themes and questions do today's authors and producers seem to focus on?

Extension

SPEAKING & LISTENING

Imagine you are a Puritan villager—a contemporary of the authors in this section—who is in charge of welcoming new settlers to your community. Using the selections you've just read as your resource, write and deliver an **informal speech** to your new neighbors, welcoming them and sharing a little about the values and beliefs held by those who live in your community.

The Puritan (1883–1886), Augustus Saint-Gaudens. Bronze figure. Private collection. © Art Resource, New York.

Persuasive Rhetoric

How do you persuade someone to change his or her mind? **Persuasion** is built on the power of words—the types of words that grab your attention, keep you riveted, and finally influence what you think. **Persuasive rhetoric** is the art of using language to argue effectively for or against a set of beliefs or course of action, and to convince others to adopt a position or act in a certain way.

A Cause for Argument

America's history of persuasive rhetoric began with the impassioned pleas of statesmen, writers, and orators who held strong beliefs about the future direction of the colonized states. In the early days of the developing country, freedom—from tyranny, from taxes, and from censorship— was vigorously debated. Several writings, such as Thomas Jefferson's Declaration of Independence (page 236), were not only official state documents, but also well- crafted arguments that would set the foundation for democracy in the United States.

A 1792 British caricature of Thomas Paine, who was ridiculed in England for his appeal to overthrow the monarchy

In designing their arguments, statesmen like Jefferson, Thomas Paine, and Patrick Henry used the basic elements of an argument (see sidebar on page 223), framed them in a variety of structures, and dressed them with persuasive rhetoric to build strong, eloquent cases. The way ideas are organized in an **argument** can be key to its persuasive power. A writer can develop an argument **deductively,** by beginning with a generalization, or premise, and proceeding to marshal examples and facts that support it (as in the Declaration of Independence), or **inductively,** by beginning with examples or facts and proceeding to draw a conclusion from them.

The Power of Language

To be effective, a persuasive work should engage both the minds and the emotions of its audience. A writer may therefore use some words to arouse emotions and other words to develop sound reasoning. However, it is not the words alone that are persuasive, but how the words are put together that gives them power and strength. These **persuasive techniques** fall into three basic types.

- **Logical appeals** rely on logic and facts to support a claim. For example, "injuries and usurpations" committed by King George III are cited as evidence for the need for independence in the Declaration of Independence.

- **Emotional appeals** present ideas and images that elicit strong feelings. For example, Jefferson's statement that King George is attempting "to complete the works of death, desolation, and tyranny" would likely evoke a strong reaction from its audience.

- **Ethical appeals** use values or moral standards that are widely accepted as a way to persuade an audience. For example, to call forth his audience's sense of right, justice, and virtue, Jefferson reminded people that independence was a last resort, after the failure of other measures: "In every stage of these oppressions we have petitioned for redress, in the most humble terms; our repeated petitions have been answered only by repeated injury."

In addition to persuasive techniques, writers will often use **rhetorical devices** to enhance their arguments:

- A **rhetorical question** is a question that does not require a reply. Writers use rhetorical questions to suggest that the answer to the question is obvious or self-evident. In her letter to her husband, John Adams (page 258), Abigail Adams writes, "Shall we not be despised by foreign powers, for hesitating so long at a word?"

- **Antithesis** is a device in which contrasting ideas are expressed in a grammatically balanced statement. Notice the juxtaposition of ideas in this phrase from Thomas Paine's "The Crisis" (page 246): "I call not upon a few, but upon all."

- **Repetition** is the use of the same word or phrase more than once for emphasis. **Parallelism,** a form of repetition in which a grammatical pattern is repeated, is used effectively in this famous passage from the Declaration of Independence.

> We hold these truths to be self-evident:—That all men are created equal; that they are endowed by their Creator with certain unalienable rights; that among these are life, liberty, and the pursuit of happiness.
>
> **—Thomas Jefferson, the Declaration of Independence**

Rhetorical devices and persuasive techniques can be used to create arguments that are valid and sincere or artificial and insincere. It is up to the reader or listener to evaluate whether the argument is based on sound reasoning, and therefore credible and convincing, or whether the words and appeals are the sole strength of the argument.

To be effective, an argument should include

- a **claim,** or clear statement of a position on an issue

- **support** for the claim, which consists of reasons and evidence

- **counterarguments,** or statements that anticipate and refute opposing views

- sound **logic** and effective language

- a **conclusion** that sums up the reasons or the call for action

Close Read

In this passage, note the parallel clauses beginning with *that*. What is the effect of this **parallel structure?**

Speech in the Virginia Convention

by Patrick Henry

Virginia House of Burgesses

Patrick Henry

1736–1799

Known as "the Orator of Liberty," Patrick Henry made a name for himself with his speeches supporting American democracy. He was one of the earliest opponents of British rule in the American colonies. In 1765, after the British Parliament passed a tax bill called the Stamp Act, Henry was among the members of the Virginia legislature that challenged the legality of a British tax on the colonies. But he went farther than his colleagues by making a threat against the king. In his argument, so the story goes, he used a loaded analogy: "Caesar had his Brutus, Charles the First his Cromwell, and George III . . ."—at this point, shouts of "Treason!" erupted in the hall, but Henry continued—"may profit by their example." He ended his speech with the defiant words, "If this be treason, make the most of it." Henry did indeed make the most of his "treason," becoming a tireless and influential leader both before and after the Revolution.

Profitable Law Career Henry was born in Virginia to a prosperous landowner. His father, who had attended the University of Aberdeen in Scotland, gave him a classical education at home. His mother, Sarah Winston Syme, was from a wealthy family. Henry went out on his own at age 15. Although smart and industrious, he couldn't find success as a storekeeper or later as a tobacco planter. After marrying and starting a family, he decided to teach himself law, and in 1760, at the age of 24, he was admitted to the bar. Henry's eloquence, quick wit, and rhetorical gifts served him well, and his law practice grew increasingly profitable.

Popular Virginia Politician Henry is best known for his fervent "Speech in the Virginia Convention," which narrowly convinced the assembled leadership to prepare for war with Britain. In addition, he organized a Virginia militia that became part of the new Continental Army after independence was declared. He helped write the new state constitution and the Virginia Declaration of Rights, which was a major influence on the Bill of Rights added to the U.S. Constitution. He also served several terms as governor of Virginia and as a state legislator. Although President Washington offered him positions as secretary of state and Supreme Court justice, Henry declined and always remained suspicious of the federal government. In 1799, after being elected again to the state legislature, he died at his 700-acre plantation, Red Hill, before he could take office.

● LITERARY ANALYSIS: RHETORICAL DEVICES

Rhetorical devices are structures within language that help communicate ideas.

- A **rhetorical question** is a question to which no answer is expected. (*But when shall we be stronger?*)
- **Antithesis** expresses contrasting ideas in parallel grammatical structures. (*Give me liberty, or give me death!*)
- **Repetition** is the recurrence of words, phrases, or lines. (*Let it come! I repeat it, sir, let it come!*)
- **Parallelism** is a kind of repetition in which words or phrases in the same grammatical form connect ideas. (*Is life so dear, or peace so sweet . . .*)

As you read Henry's speech, be on the lookout for rhetorical devices and how they might have affected his audience.

▨ READING STRATEGY: READING A PERSUASIVE SPEECH

When reading a persuasive speech, imagine the techniques the speaker used to bring the speech to life, such as word emphasis, changes in pace, pauses, and changes in volume.

As you read, use a chart like the one shown to record how you would emphasize certain passages if you were Patrick Henry.

Paragraph/Line Numbers	Technique
Paragraph 1 (lines 1–14)	

▲ VOCABULARY IN CONTEXT

Use context clues to write a definition of each boldfaced word.

1. **Martial** Speech Sets Stage for War
2. **Subjugation** by Britain Called Unacceptable
3. British Claims Said Not to **Comport** with Facts
4. Colonists to **Remonstrate** with Governor Against Taxes
5. Never **Supinely** Accept Tyranny, Henry Says
6. **Invincible** Patriot Army Will Repel Attacks
7. **Insidious** Spies Reveal Patriots' Plans
8. Nothing Can **Extenuate** Tory Traitors
9. Citizens Told to Be **Vigilant**
10. America Must Remain **Inviolate**

Explore the Key Idea

When is it time to TAKE ACTION?

KEY IDEA Whether it's the winning shot in the final seconds of the game, the right moment to ask someone out, or the decision to accept a job offer—timing is everything. In the spring of 1775, Patrick Henry had had enough of compromise with the British; it was time for armed resistance. His address to the Virginia Convention turned out to be a **decisive moment** not only in his own life but in the life of the United States as well.

DISCUSS With a partner, think of examples from sports, politics, or everyday life when the time was right for decisive action. Then, for one example, analyze why it was the right action at the right time.

Example of Decisive Action:

Reasons That the Time Was Right:

SPEECH IN THE
Virginia Convention

Patrick Henry

BACKGROUND In the spring of 1775, delegates from the state of Virginia could not agree whether to press for a peaceful solution with Britain or to prepare for war. Patrick Henry introduced resolutions calling for military preparedness. After politely listening to his colleagues' objections to armed rebellion, he rose to deliver this impassioned appeal.

ANALYZE VISUALS
This painting shows Patrick Henry speaking to the Virginia House of Burgesses. What different attitudes are reflected in the faces and postures of his audience members?

March 23, 1775

Mr. President:[1] No man thinks more highly than I do of the patriotism, as well as abilities, of the very worthy gentlemen who have just addressed the House. But different men often see the same subject in different lights; and, therefore, I hope that it will not be thought disrespectful to those gentlemen, if, entertaining as I do opinions of a character very opposite to theirs, I shall speak forth my sentiments freely and without reserve. This is no time for ceremony. The question before the House is one of awful moment[2] to this country. For my own part I consider it as nothing less than a question of freedom or slavery; and in proportion to the magnitude of the subject ought to be the freedom of the debate. It is only in this
10 way that we can hope to arrive at truth, and fulfill the great responsibility which we hold to God and our country. Should I keep back my opinions at such a Ⓐ

Ⓐ RHETORICAL DEVICES
Reread lines 1–11. What are some examples of **antithesis** and what kind of emphasis does it create?

---

1. **Mr. President:** the president of the Virginia Convention, Peyton Randolph.

2. **of awful moment:** of very grave importance.

Patrick Henry Before the Virginia House of Burgesses (1851), Peter F. Rothermel. Red Hill, The Patrick Henry National Memorial, Brookneal, Virginia.

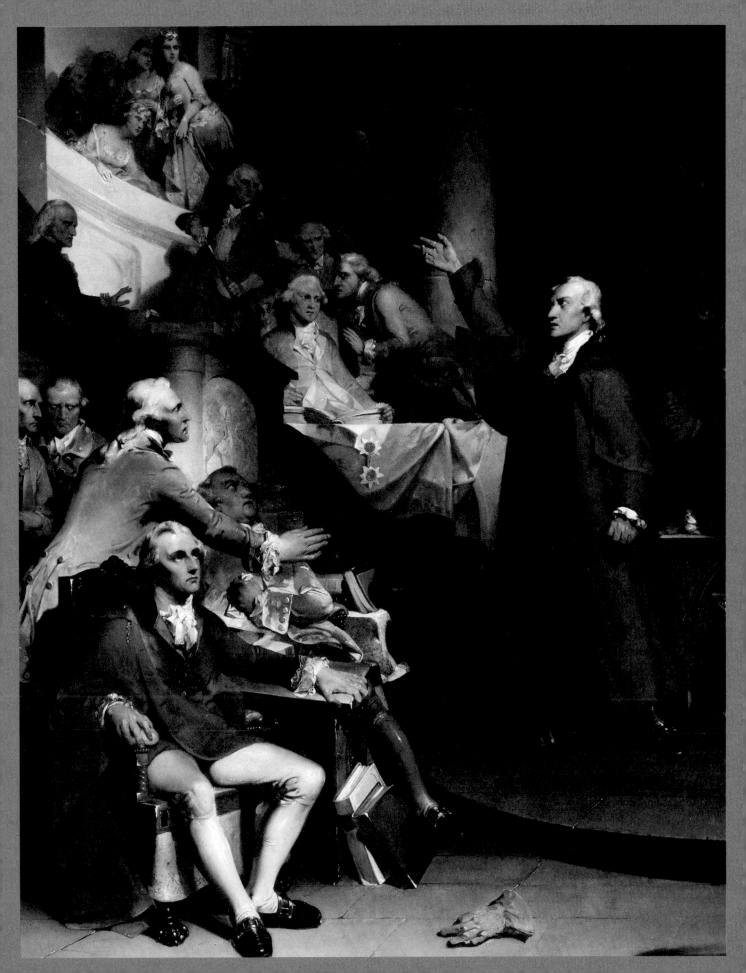

time, through fear of giving offense, I should consider myself as guilty of treason towards my country, and of an act of disloyalty towards the majesty of heaven, which I revere above all earthly kings. **B**

Mr. President, it is natural to man to indulge in the illusions of hope. We are apt to shut our eyes against a painful truth, and listen to the song of that siren, till she transforms us into beasts.[3] Is this the part of wise men, engaged in a great and arduous struggle for liberty? Are we disposed to be of the number of those who, having eyes, see not, and having ears, hear not,[4] the things which so nearly concern
20 their temporal salvation? For my part, whatever anguish of spirit it may cost, I am willing to know the whole truth—to know the worst and to provide for it. **C**

I have but one lamp by which my feet are guided; and that is the lamp of experience. I know of no way of judging of the future but by the past. And judging by the past, I wish to know what there has been in the conduct of the British ministry for the last ten years, to justify those hopes with which gentlemen have been pleased to solace themselves and the House? Is it that **insidious** smile with which our petition has been lately received? Trust it not, sir; it will prove a snare to your feet. Suffer not yourselves to be betrayed with a kiss.[5]

Ask yourselves how this gracious reception of our petition **comports** with these
30 warlike preparations which cover our waters and darken our land. Are fleets and armies necessary to a work of love and reconciliation? Have we shown ourselves so unwilling to be reconciled that force must be called in to win back our love? Let us not deceive ourselves, sir. These are the implements of war and **subjugation**— the last arguments to which kings resort. I ask gentlemen, sir, what means this **martial** array, if its purpose be not to force us to submission? Can gentlemen assign any other possible motives for it? Has Great Britain any enemy, in this quarter of the world, to call for all this accumulation of navies and armies? No, sir, she has none. They are meant for us; they can be meant for no other. They are sent over to bind and rivet upon us those chains which the British ministry
40 have been so long forging. **D**

And what have we to oppose to them? Shall we try argument? Sir, we have been trying that for the last ten years. Have we anything new to offer on the subject? Nothing. We have held the subject up in every light of which it is capable; but it has been all in vain. Shall we resort to entreaty and humble supplication? What terms shall we find which have not been already exhausted? Let us not, I beseech you, sir, deceive ourselves longer. **E**

B **PERSUASIVE SPEECH**
Henry speaks respectfully of those with whom he disagrees in lines 1–14. What words might be vocally emphasized to show respect?

C **RHETORICAL DEVICES**
What rhetorical device, besides a rhetorical question, is on display in lines 18–21? What point is he making about those who don't want to fight?

insidious (ĭn-sĭd′ē-əs) *adj.* treacherous

comport (kəm-pôrt′) *v.* to agree

subjugation (sŭb′jə-gā′shən) *n.* control by conquering

martial (mär′shəl) *adj.* warlike

D **RHETORICAL DEVICES**
Reread lines 29–40, answering each of the **rhetorical questions.** How is a listener likely to respond to Henry's final statements in lines 37–40?

E **GRAMMAR AND STYLE**
Reread lines 43–46. Notice the use of **declarative, interrogative,** and **imperative** sentences.

---

3. **the illusions of hope . . . into beasts:** In the *Odyssey* of Homer, the goddess Circe lures men to her island and then magically transforms them into pigs. Henry suggests that the "illusions of hope" may transform people in a similar way.

4. **having eyes . . . hear not:** an allusion to Ezekiel 12:2 in the Bible, which speaks of "who have eyes to see, but see not, who have ears to hear, but hear not."

5. **betrayed with a kiss:** an allusion to Luke 22:47–48 in the Bible, wherein Judas betrayed Jesus to the Roman soldiers by kissing him and thus identifying him.

The Bloody Massacre perpetrated in. . . Boston on March 5th, 1770 (1770), Paul Revere. Colored engraving. Private collection. /Art Resource, New York.

Sir, we have done everything that could be done to avert the storm which is now coming on. We have petitioned; we have **remonstrated;** we have supplicated; we have prostrated ourselves before the throne, and have implored
50 its interposition[6] to arrest the tyrannical hands of the ministry and Parliament. Our petitions have been slighted; our remonstrances have produced additional violence and insult; our supplications have been disregarded; and we have been spurned, with contempt, from the foot of the throne. In vain, after these things, may we indulge the fond hope of peace and reconciliation. There is no longer any room for hope.

remonstrate
(rĭ-mŏn′strāt′) *v.* to object; to protest strongly

---

6. **we have prostrated . . . interposition:** We have thrown ourselves at the feet of the king and have begged for intervention.

If we wish to be free—if we mean to preserve **inviolate** those inestimable privileges for which we have been so long contending—if we mean not basely to abandon the noble struggle in which we have been so long engaged, and which we have pledged ourselves never to abandon until the glorious object of our contest
60 shall be obtained, we must fight! I repeat it, sir, we must fight! An appeal to arms and to the God of Hosts is all that is left us!

They tell us, sir, that we are weak—unable to cope with so formidable an adversary. But when shall we be stronger? Will it be the next week, or the next year? Will it be when we are totally disarmed, and when a British guard shall be stationed in every house? Shall we gather strength by irresolution and inaction? Shall we acquire the means of effectual resistance, by lying **supinely** on our backs, and hugging the delusive phantom of hope, until our enemies shall have bound us hand and foot?

Sir, we are not weak, if we make a proper use of those means which the God
70 of nature hath placed in our power. Three millions of people, armed in the holy cause of liberty, and in such a country as that which we possess, are **invincible** by any force which our enemy can send against us. Besides, sir, we shall not fight our battles alone. There is a just God who presides over the destinies of nations, and who will raise up friends to fight our battles for us. The battle, sir, is not to the strong alone;[7] it is to the **vigilant,** the active, the brave. Besides, sir, we have no election.[8] If we were base enough to desire it, it is now too late to retire from the contest. There is no retreat but in submission and slavery! Our chains are forged! Their clanking may be heard on the plains of Boston! The war is inevitable—and let it come! I repeat it, sir, let it come! **G**

80 It is in vain, sir, to **extenuate** the matter. Gentlemen may cry, "Peace! peace!"—but there is no peace. The war is actually begun! The next gale that sweeps from the north[9] will bring to our ears the clash of resounding arms! Our brethren are already in the field! Why stand we here idle? What is it that gentlemen wish? What would they have? Is life so dear, or peace so sweet, as to be purchased at the price of chains and slavery? Forbid it, Almighty God! I know not what course others may take; but as for me, give me liberty, or give me death! ❧ **G**

inviolate (ĭn-vī′ə-lĭt) *adj.* not violated; intact

supinely (soō-pīn′lē) *adv.* in a manner with the face upward

invincible (ĭn-vĭn′sə-bəl) *adj.* unbeatable

vigilant (vĭj′ə-lənt) *adj.* alert; watchful

F RHETORICAL DEVICES
Why do you think Henry repeats the word *sir* so often in this paragraph? Explain the likely effect of this **repetition** as well as that of the phrase "let it come!"

extenuate (ĭk-stĕn′yoō-āt′) *v.* to lessen the seriousness of, especially by providing partial excuses

G PERSUASIVE SPEECH
How might the speaker's **pace** and **emphasis** have changed over the course of the speech? How might his audience have responded to these changes? Explain.

---

7. **battle . . . strong alone:** an allusion to Ecclesiastes 9:11 in the Bible, "the race is not to the swift, nor the battle to the strong."

8. **election:** choice.

9. **the next gale . . . north:** Some colonists in Massachusetts had already shown open resistance to the British and were on the brink of war.

Comprehension

1. **Recall** What does Patrick Henry urge the colonists to do?

2. **Paraphrase** Reread lines 22–28. What methods had the colonists already used to express their complaints against the British?

3. **Clarify** How did the British respond to those complaints?

Literary Analysis

4. **Analyze a Persuasive Speech** Look back at the chart you filled in as you read. Choose a section of Henry's speech to read aloud as he might have delivered it. How effective are the techniques you plan to use? Explain why you think so.

5. **Analyze Persuasive Strategy** Henry spends most of his speech arguing against hope, ordinarily not the best tactic when trying to inspire an audience. How does he manage to discredit hope? Why would he do this?

6. **Interpret Allusions** Review the following allusions to the *Odyssey* and the Bible that Henry uses in his speech. How does each allusion support the point Henry makes in the paragraph?

   - *Odyssey*, lines 15–17
   - Bible, lines 18–19
   - Bible, line 28
   - Bible, lines 74–75

7. **Evaluate Appeals** How does Henry convince his audience that the **decisive moment** to fight is at hand? In a chart, summarize his reasons. Then, beside each, note whether he appeals mainly to logic or emotion. Which reasons are strongest? Explain.

8. **Make Judgments About Rhetorical Devices** Review the rhetorical devices discussed on page 225. Which devices occur most frequently in Henry's speech? Do you think this is an effective way to communicate, or do you find it manipulative? Cite examples from the text to support your answer.

Reasons to Fight	Logical or Emotional
1. If we want to be free and keep the rights and privileges we have grown accustomed to, we have to fight. (lines 56–61)	logical
2.	

Literary Criticism

9. **Different Perspectives** Imagine that the following people heard Henry's speech from the visitor's gallery. How might each have reacted, and why?

   - the wife of one of the delegates
   - a farmer whose parents live in England
   - a member of the Virginia militia
   - a clergyman
   - an African enslaved in the colony

Vocabulary in Context

WORD LIST
comport
extenuate
insidious
invincible
inviolate
martial
remonstrate
subjugation
supinely
vigilant

VOCABULARY PRACTICE

Decide whether these statements about the vocabulary words are true or false.

1. A good way to **remonstrate** with someone is to plan a picnic with that person.
2. An **invincible** chess champion is one who has not been beaten.
3. A statue that is lying **supinely** is lying face down.
4. A **vigilant** guard usually takes naps while on duty.
5. Circumstances that **extenuate** a bad decision are those that make it worse.
6. A country that is overrun by armies from another land is experiencing **subjugation.**
7. An **insidious** person is unlikely to express her opinions openly.
8. A vase that has broken into several pieces may be described as **inviolate.**
9. A **martial** gathering is one that is organized by peace demonstrators.
10. If two versions of a story **comport** with each other, they are in agreement.

VOCABULARY IN WRITING

Imagine you were in the audience when Patrick Henry gave his speech. Using at least three vocabulary words, write a short explanation of why you agree or disagree with his views. Here is a sample beginning.

> **EXAMPLE SENTENCE**
>
> I cannot agree with Mr. Henry that government by our mother country can be considered **subjugation**.

VOCABULARY STRATEGY: WORDS FROM GODS AND MYTHOLOGY

A number of English words are formed from the names of Greek and Roman gods and goddesses. Usually the meanings of these words are closely related to some characteristic the deity was known for. The vocabulary word *martial*, for example, is derived from Mars, the name of the Roman god of war.

PRACTICE For each numbered word, write a sentence that shows its meaning. Use a dictionary if you need help. Then write a short explanation connecting each word's meaning to the deity whose name it is derived from.

1. saturnine
2. mercurial
3. jovial
4. nemesis
5. cupidity
6. bacchanalian

VOCABULARY PRACTICE
For more practice, go to the **Vocabulary Center** at ClassZone.com.

Reading-Writing Connection

WRITING PROMPT	SELF-CHECK

COMPOSE A PERSUASIVE SPEECH Patrick Henry's famous speech is a classic example of effective **oratory,** the art of public speaking. Using Henry's speech as a model, write a **three-to-five paragraph persuasive speech** on a topic you feel strongly about.

▶

A persuasive speech will . . .
- present a clear argument
- cite reasons and other evidence
- use rhetorical devices
- close with a strong statement

GRAMMAR AND STYLE

VARY SENTENCE TYPES Review the **Grammar and Style** note on page 228. Part of Henry's style is to vary his sentences among the four basic types:

- **Declarative,** which expresses a statement of fact, desire, intent, or feeling and ends with a period. *This is no time for ceremony.* (line 6)

- **Interrogative,** which asks a question and ends with a question mark. *Shall we try argument?* (line 41)

- **Imperative,** which gives a command, request, or direction and ends usually with a period but sometimes for emphasis with an exclamation point. *Trust it not, sir; it will prove a snare to your feet.* (lines 27–28)

- **Exclamatory,** which expresses strong emotions and always ends with an exclamation point. *I repeat it, sir, we must fight!* (line 60)

Henry's skillful use of sentence variety is emotionally expressive and compelling. It not only creates an interesting melody, but also keeps the reader engaged by calling for frequent shifts in the reader's internal responses.

PRACTICE The following excerpt is taken from Henry's speech. For each sentence in the exercise, identify the type of sentence, and then compose your own sentence following the pattern in Henry's original. The example illustrates how.

EXAMPLE

The war is actually begun!

We won the game!

---

(1) The next gale that sweeps from the north will bring to our ears the clash of resounding arms! (2) Our brethren are already in the field! (3) Why stand we here idle? (4) What is it that gentlemen wish? (5) What would they have? (6) Is life so dear, or peace so sweet, as to be purchased at the price of chains and slavery? (7) Forbid it, Almighty God!

WRITING TOOLS

For prewriting, revision, and editing tools, visit the **Writing Center** at ClassZone.com.

The Declaration of Independence

Public Document by Thomas Jefferson

Thomas Jefferson

1743–1826

Thomas Jefferson was one of the most accomplished founding fathers. Active in the cause for independence, he was governor of Virginia during the Revolutionary War and U.S. minister to France afterward. He also served the new country as the first secretary of state, the second vice-president, and the third president. As president, he acquired the vast Louisiana Territory west of the Mississippi River to the Rocky Mountains, essentially doubling the size of the country. But more important than any political office he held was the lasting impact of Jefferson's ideals of liberty and self-government so eloquently expressed in the Declaration of Independence.

Brilliant Legal Mind The son of a surveyor and gentleman farmer, Jefferson was born into a life of privilege in rural Virginia. Educated at the College of William and Mary, he was tutored in the law and practiced successfully before entering politics at age 26. As a member of the colonial Virginia legislature, he fell in with a group of radicals, among them Patrick Henry. Lacking Henry's oratorical gifts, Jefferson distinguished himself by his legal writing. Significantly, Jefferson's indelible mark on American life came largely from the many legal documents and laws he wrote promoting democracy.

Passion for Learning Jefferson had an insatiable curiosity about the world and often indulged in what he called his "canine appetite for reading." In addition to devouring works on the classics, history, law, science, and philosophy, he taught himself architecture from books. He designed his elaborate estate at Monticello and the buildings of the University of Virginia, which he also founded as the embodiment of his principles of education and individual freedom.

The Issue of Slavery Charges of hypocrisy on the issue of slavery have tarnished Jefferson's image as the "apostle of liberty." In his early writings, he denounced slavery and tried unsuccessfully to include the issue in the Declaration. Yet Jefferson always owned slaves—as many as 600 over the course of his lifetime—and in later years, he remained undecided on this issue.

A Quintessential American Jefferson's problematic stand on slavery mirrored the nation's, which took a long time to rectify. In the end, Jefferson was a man of his time who had a noble vision for the country and the genius to articulate it, even though he did not always live up to his ideals.

● LITERARY ANALYSIS: ARGUMENT

Jefferson's emphasis in the Declaration of Independence was on the logical argument to be made for independence. An **argument** expresses an opinion on an issue and supports it with reasons and evidence. Three important parts of an argument are

- **the claim:** the writer's position on an issue or problem
- **support:** reasons and evidence provided to prove a claim
- **counterargument:** arguments to answer opposing views

As you read, look for these elements of an argument.

● READING SKILL: ANALYZE TEXT STRUCTURE

The Declaration of Independence has four main parts:

1. a **preamble,** or **foreword,** that announces the reason for the document
2. a **declaration** of people's natural rights and relationship to government
3. a long **list** of complaints against George III, the British king
4. a **conclusion** that formally states America's independence

As you read, use a chart such as the one shown to indicate the line numbers for each part, as well as a brief summary of each.

Part	Summary
1 Preamble lines 1–6	When one group of people have to form their own government, it is necessary to explain why.

▲ VOCABULARY IN CONTEXT

Match each vocabulary word in the first column with the word or phrase in the second column that is closest in meaning.

1.	abdicate	**a.**	correction
2.	arbitrary	**b.**	integrity
3.	despotism	**c.**	treachery
4.	impel	**d.**	abandon
5.	mercenary	**e.**	drive
6.	perfidy	**f.**	erratic
7.	rectitude	**g.**	a taking over
8.	redress	**h.**	hired soldier
9.	unalienable	**i.**	tyranny
10.	usurpation	**j.**	unchangeable

When is REBELLION justified?

KEY IDEA Many young people harbor a spirit of **rebellion**—against parents, teachers, bosses, rules, or any situation that "just isn't fair!" But how often do you attempt to explain your rebellion logically? In June of 1776, Thomas Jefferson and other colonial leaders had decided to rebel against British rule. But they needed to justify their dangerous action—to themselves, to the king, and to the world.

DISCUSS In a small group, think of several situations in which an individual or a group rebelled against a perceived injustice. The situations could be any of the following:

- local—an incident in your school or community, for example
- global—such as demonstrations against global trade policies
- historical—such as the American, French, or Russian revolutions

Then, as a group, evaluate the reasons for each rebellion and explain which ones you think are justified.

The Declaration of *Independence*

Thomas Jefferson

BACKGROUND In September 1774, 56 delegates met in Philadelphia at the First Continental Congress to draw up a declaration of colonial rights. They agreed to reconvene in May 1775 if their demands weren't met. At this Second Continental Congress, Thomas Jefferson joined Benjamin Franklin and John Adams on the committee to draft the Declaration of Independence. The task of writing it fell to Jefferson. Although Congress made many changes to the list of grievances, Jefferson's declaration of rights remained untouched—an abiding testament to "self-evident" truths for the nation and the world.

ANALYZE VISUALS
This is an original copy of the Declaration. What might be some of the advantages of having the whole document appear on one large sheet of paper?

In Congress, July 4, 1776

When, in the course of human events, it becomes necessary for one people to dissolve the political bands which have connected them with another, and to assume, among the powers of the earth, the separate and equal station to which the laws of nature and of nature's God entitle them, a decent respect to the opinions of mankind requires that they should declare the causes which **impel** them to the separation. **Ⓐ**

We hold these truths to be self-evident:—That all men are created equal; that they are endowed by their Creator with certain **unalienable** rights; that among these are life, liberty, and the pursuit of happiness. That, to secure these
10 rights, governments are instituted among men, deriving their just powers from the consent of the governed; that, whenever any form of government becomes destructive of these ends, it is the right of the people to alter or to abolish it, and to institute a new government, laying its foundation on such principles, and organizing its powers in such form, as to them shall seem most likely to effect their safety and happiness. Prudence, indeed, will dictate that governments long established should not be changed for light and transient causes; and, accordingly,

impel (ĭm-pĕl′) *v.* to drive forward; force

Ⓐ ARGUMENT
What **claim** does Jefferson present in the preamble of the Declaration and what **support** does he say he will provide?

unalienable
(ŭn-āl′yə-nə-bəl) *adj.* not to be taken away (Today the usual form is *inalienable*.)

IN CONGRESS. JULY 4, 1776.

The unanimous Declaration of the thirteen united States of America.

all experience hath shown that mankind are more disposed to suffer, while evils are sufferable, than to right themselves by abolishing the forms to which they are accustomed. But, when a long train of abuses and **usurpations,** pursuing
20 invariably the same object, evinces a design to reduce them under absolute **despotism,** it is their right, it is their duty, to throw off such government, and to provide new guards for their future security. Such has been the patient sufferance of these colonies; and such is now the necessity that constrains them to alter their former systems of government. The history of the present King of Great Britain[1] is a history of repeated injuries and usurpations, all having, in direct object, the establishment of an absolute tyranny over these States. To prove this, let facts be submitted to a candid world. **B**

He has refused his assent to laws[2] the most wholesome and necessary for the public good. **C**

30 He has forbidden his Governors to pass laws of immediate and pressing importance, unless suspended in their operation till his assent should be obtained; and, when so suspended, he has utterly neglected to attend to them.

He has refused to pass other laws for the accommodation of large districts of people, unless these people would relinquish the right of representation in the legislature—a right inestimable to them, and formidable to tyrants only.

He has called together legislative bodies at places unusual, uncomfortable, and distant from the depository of their public records, for the sole purpose of fatiguing them into compliance with his measure.

He has dissolved representative houses repeatedly, for opposing, with manly
40 firmness, his invasions on the rights of the people.

He has refused, for a long time after such dissolutions, to cause others to be elected; whereby the legislative powers, incapable of annihilation, have returned to the people at large for their exercise; the State remaining, in the meantime, exposed to all dangers of invasion from without, and convulsions within.

He has endeavored to prevent the population[3] of these States; for that purpose obstructing the laws for the naturalization of foreigners; refusing to pass others to encourage their migration hither, and raising the conditions of new appropriations of lands.

He has obstructed the administration of justice, by refusing his assent to laws
50 for establishing judiciary powers.

He has made judges dependent on his will alone for the tenure of their offices,[4] and the amount and payment of their salaries.

He has erected a multitude of new offices, and sent hither swarms of officers to harass our people and eat out their substance.[5]

1. **the present King of Great Britain:** George III, who reigned from 1760 to 1820.
2. **refused his assent to laws:** Laws passed in the colonies needed the king's approval; sometimes it took years for laws to be approved or rejected.
3. **to prevent the population:** to keep the population from growing.
4. **the tenure of their offices:** their job security.
5. **eat out their substance:** use up their resources.

---

usurpation
(yōō´sər-pā´shən) *n.* the act of wrongfully taking over a right or power that belongs to someone else

despotism (dĕs´pə-tĭz´əm) *n.* government by a ruler with unlimited power

B **ARGUMENT**
What **counterargument** does Jefferson anticipate in lines 15–22? What **claim** does he make at the end of this paragraph and what does he say he is about to do?

C **TEXT STRUCTURE**
Why might the list of complaints make up the largest part of the four-part structure?

Declaration of Independence in Congress, at the Independence Hall, Philadelphia, July 4, 1776 (1819), John Trumbull. Oil on canvas. The Granger Collection, New York.

He has kept among us, in times of peace, standing armies, without the consent of our legislatures.

He has affected to render the military independent of, and superior to, the civil power.

He has combined with others to subject us to a jurisdiction foreign to our
60 constitutions,[6] and unacknowledged by our laws; giving his assent to their acts of pretended legislation:

For quartering large bodies of armed troops among us;

For protecting them, by a mock trial, from punishment for any murders which they should commit on the inhabitants of these States;

For cutting off our trade with all parts of the world;

For imposing taxes on us without our consent;

For depriving us, in many cases, of the benefits of trial by jury;

For transporting us beyond the seas, to be tried for pretended offenses;

For abolishing the free system of English laws in a neighboring province,[7]
70 establishing there an **arbitrary** government, and enlarging its boundaries, so as to render it at once an example and fit instrument for introducing the same absolute rule into these colonies;

For taking away our charters, abolishing our most valuable laws, and altering, fundamentally, the forms of our governments;

For suspending our own legislatures, and declaring themselves invested with power to legislate for us in all cases whatsoever. **D**

arbitrary (är′bĭ-trĕr′ē) *adj.* based on unpredictable decisions rather than law

D **TEXT STRUCTURE**
Reread lines 59–76. What is the significance of the itemized list of examples in lines 62–76?

---

6. **subject us . . . our constitutions:** Parliament had passed the Declaratory Act in 1766, stating that the king and Parliament could make laws for the colonies.

7. **a neighboring province:** the province of Quebec, which at the time extended south to the Ohio River and west to the Mississippi.

He has **abdicated** government here, by declaring us out of his protection, and waging war against us.

He has plundered our seas, ravaged our coasts, burnt our towns,[8] and destroyed
80 the lives of our people.

He is at this time transporting large armies of foreign **mercenaries** to complete the works of death, desolation, and tyranny, already begun with circumstances of cruelty and **perfidy** scarcely paralleled in the most barbarous ages, and totally unworthy the head of a civilized nation.

He has constrained our fellow citizens, taken captive on the high seas, to bear arms against their country, to become the executioners of their friends and brethren, or to fall themselves by their hands.

He has excited domestic insurrection amongst us,[9] and has endeavored to bring on the inhabitants of our frontiers the merciless Indian savages, whose known rule
90 of warfare is an undistinguished destruction of all ages, sexes, and conditions.

In every stage of these oppressions we have petitioned for **redress,** in the most humble terms; our repeated petitions have been answered only by repeated injury. A prince whose character is thus marked by every act which may define a tyrant is unfit to be the ruler of a free people.

Nor have we been wanting in our attentions to our British brethren. We have warned them, from time to time, of attempts by their legislature to extend an unwarrantable jurisdiction over us. We have reminded them of the circumstances of our emigration and settlement here. We have appealed to their native justice and magnanimity; and we have conjured them, by the ties of our common
100 kindred, to disavow these usurpations, which would inevitably interrupt our connections and correspondence. **E**

They, too, have been deaf to the voice of justice and of consanguinity.[10] We must, therefore, acquiesce in the necessity which denounces our separation; and hold them, as we hold the rest of mankind, enemies in war, in peace friends. **F**

WE, THEREFORE, THE REPRESENTATIVES OF THE UNITED STATES OF AMERICA, in General Congress assembled, appealing to the Supreme Judge of the world for the **rectitude** of our intentions, do, in the name and by the authority of the good people of these colonies, solemnly publish and declare, that these United Colonies are, and of right ought to be, Free and Independent States; that they are absolved
110 from all allegiance to the British crown, and that all political connection between them and the state of Great Britain is, and ought to be, totally dissolved; and that, as free and independent states, they have full power to levy war, conclude peace, contract alliances, establish commerce, and to do all other acts and things which independent states may of right do. And, for the support of this declaration, with a firm reliance on the protection of Divine Providence, we mutually pledge to each other our lives, our fortunes, and our sacred honor. ❧ **G**

---

8. **plundered ... our towns:** American seaports such as Norfolk, Virginia, had already been shelled.

9. **excited ... amongst us:** George III had encouraged slaves to rise up and rebel against their masters.

10. **deaf to ... consanguinity:** The British have ignored pleas based on their common ancestry with the colonists.

abdicate (ăb'dĭ-kāt') *v.* to give up responsibility for

mercenary (mûr'sə-nĕr'ē) *n.* a professional soldier hired to fight in a foreign army

perfidy (pûr'fĭ-dē) *n.* treachery

redress (rĭ-drĕs') *n.* the correction of a wrong; compensation

E GRAMMAR AND STYLE
Reread lines 98–101. Notice how Jefferson uses a **compound-complex sentence,** which has two or more independent clauses and one or more subordinate clauses, in order to show the complex relationships between ideas.

F ARGUMENT
What objections does Jefferson appear to be anticipating and refuting with **counterarguments** in lines 102–104?

rectitude (rĕk'tĭ-tōōd') *n.* morally correct behavior or thinking

G TEXT STRUCTURE
What purpose does the final paragraph serve?

Comprehension

1. **Recall** Name three complaints that the colonists had against the king.

2. **Recall** What rights are specified in the Declaration?

3. **Clarify** What does Jefferson say is the purpose of government?

4. **Clarify** According to the Declaration, who gives people their rights?

Literary Analysis

5. **Draw Conclusions** Which set of reasons for breaking away from British rule strikes you as most important, and why?

   - the colonists' philosophical ideals
   - the hardships colonists suffered as a result of British policies
   - the king's response to colonists' complaints

6. **Make Inferences** The Declaration clearly takes aim at the abuses of King George to justify the colonists' **rebellion.** But reread lines 102–104. To what extent does the document hold the British people responsible? What is the new relationship declared between Americans and their "British brethren," and how might it differ from the old?

7. **Analyze Diction** What is it about Jefferson's diction, or word choice and arrangement, that makes the declaration of rights so memorable? Explain the effects of the following words and phrases:

   - "We hold these truths to be self-evident" (line 7)
   - "endowed by their Creator" (line 8)
   - "unalienable rights" (line 8)
   - "secure these rights" (lines 9–10)

8. **Evaluate Text Structure** Review the chart you filled in. How effective is this four-part structure in stating the colonists' case? Would reordering the parts make any difference? Explain your answer.

9. **Evaluate Elements of an Argument** Identify the major claim and the support given in the Declaration. In your opinion, is the support sufficient for the claim? Does it have to be? Explain your answer.

10. **Compare Texts** Compare Jefferson's Declaration with Patrick Henry's speech in terms of the purpose of each.

Literary Criticism

11. **Historical Context** Jefferson's celebrated statement "All men are created equal" only applied to white men at the time. How has the meaning of Jefferson's statement changed over time? How has it stayed the same?

Vocabulary in Context

VOCABULARY PRACTICE

Choose the word that is not related in meaning to the other words.

1. (a) disloyalty, (b) perfidy, (c) honesty, (d) treachery
2. (a) surrendering, (b) takeover, (c) commandeering, (d) usurpation
3. (a) despotism, (b) dictatorship, (c) tyranny, (d) righteousness
4. (a) monarch, (b) ruler, (c) mercenary, (d) king
5. (a) morality, (b) rectitude, (c) virtue, (d) posture
6. (a) redress, (b) model, (c) remedy, (d) compensation
7. (a) abandon, (b) renounce, (c) confiscate, (d) abdicate
8. (a) mobilize, (b) impel, (c) propel, (d) restrain
9. (a) tardy, (b) arbitrary, (c) unpredictable, (d) capricious
10. (a) vague, (b) unclear, (c) unalienable, (d) misleading

WORD LIST

abdicate
arbitrary
despotism
impel
mercenary
perfidy
rectitude
redress
unalienable
usurpation

VOCABULARY IN WRITING

Which grievances mentioned by Jefferson seem most serious and offensive? Write a paragraph or two explaining your ideas, using three or more vocabulary words. Here is a sample opening sentence.

> **EXAMPLE SENTENCE**
>
> The **usurpation** of colonists' rights to make their own laws strikes me as particularly serious.

VOCABULARY STRATEGY: POLITICAL WORDS

Many terms are used in speaking of governing systems. Some identify specific types of government; others, like the vocabulary word *despotism,* describe the practices of a government. It is useful to understand the meaning of such terms.

PRACTICE Choose the political word described by each numbered item. Then use a dictionary to trace the etymology of each word.

> oligarchy   regency   republic   socialism   totalitarianism

1. a few people have the ruling power
2. a person rules in place of the regular ruler, who may be ill or too young
3. production of goods and services is under the control of government
4. one political group rules and suppresses all opposition, often with force
5. citizens elect representatives to manage the government

VOCABULARY PRACTICE
For more practice, go to the **Vocabulary Center** at **ClassZone.com.**

Reading-Writing Connection

GRAMMAR AND STYLE

VARY SENTENCE STRUCTURE Review the **Grammar and Style** note on page 240. Like most lawyers, who have to be precise as well as thorough, Jefferson uses **complex** and **compound-complex** sentences to pack in meaning.

- A **complex sentence** has one main clause (as in yellow), which can stand alone, and one or more subordinate clauses (as in green), which cannot.

  A prince whose character is thus marked by every act which may define a tyrant is unfit to be the ruler of a free people. (lines 93–94)

- A **compound-complex sentence** has two or more independent clauses (as in yellow) and one or more subordinate clauses (as in green).

  Such has been the patient sufferance of these colonies; and such is now the necessity that constrains them to alter their former systems of government. (lines 22–24)

PRACTICE Rewrite each pair of simple sentences as a complex or compound-complex sentence. Use the conjunction shown in parentheses. Use a comma to separate the two clauses.

EXAMPLE

The king exploits the people. The people move toward rebellion. (after)

After the king exploits the people, the people move toward rebellion.

---

1. The people declare their grievances with British rule. The British king and parliament do not listen. (when)

2. The parliament learns of the dissatisfaction of the colonists. The parliament imposes even harsher laws. (as soon as)

3. The British ignore all appeals to reason. The American colonists had attempted to seek a peaceful solution. (while)

WRITING TOOLS
For prewriting, revision, and editing tools, visit the **Writing Center** at ClassZone.com.

from **The Crisis**

Essay by Thomas Paine

Author Online

For more on Thomas Paine, visit the **Literature Center** at ClassZone.com.

Thomas Paine

1737–1809

Brash, bold, and fearless—and at times angry and offensive—Thomas Paine was the firebrand of the American Revolution. In the fall of 1775, few American leaders dared to advocate openly for independence. Not only did they risk being accused of treason, they were uncertain how the common people would react to such a radical notion. They turned to Tom Paine to test the waters. Paine had arrived in Philadelphia from London only the year before but was already gaining a reputation as a revolutionary writer. He eagerly took up the task and in a few months wrote *Common Sense* (1776), a 50-page pamphlet that attacked the injustices of hereditary rule and urged the colonists to form their own independent country where "the law is king." Paine's pamphlet sold 120,000 copies in the first three months. Six months later, the colonies declared their independence.

New Voice for a New Political Audience Paine's political ideas in *Common Sense* were not particularly new or original. In the Age of Enlightenment, intellectual circles were buzzing with talk of natural rights and democracy. What was new was Paine's voice—raw, direct, full of energy. Unlike most political writers of the day, such as Thomas Jefferson, Paine addressed common men—farmers, craftsmen, and laborers—not the educated elite. His straightforward prose reinforced his democratic message that all men were capable of understanding and participating in government. People responded because Paine spoke their language. In his native England, he had worked as sailor, teacher, customs officer, grocer, and maker of ladies' corsets. He envisioned America as the place where working men like him could have political and economic power.

Limits of Success With American independence won, Paine left for Europe in 1787 to join the reform efforts brewing there. But his outspokenness got him into trouble in both conservative England and revolutionary France. His last major work, *The Age of Reason* (1794, 1795), attacked organized religion and alienated many of his supporters. By the time he returned to the United States in 1802, few politicians wanted to associate with him. He spent his last years in poverty and obscurity.

Legacy Despite Paine's later decline, his contribution to the intellectual and cultural life of Revolutionary America is indisputable. He was the radical the country needed, the spokesman for new American values and ideals.

● LITERARY ANALYSIS: PERSUASIVE TECHNIQUES

Thomas Paine used a number of **persuasive techniques** in *The Crisis* to persuade Americans to join the cause.

- **Emotional appeals** are attempts to persuade by eliciting strong feelings, such as pity or fear.
- **Ethical appeals** call upon readers' sense of right and wrong.
- **Appeals to association** imply that one will gain acceptance or prestige by taking the writer's position.
- **Appeals to authority** call upon experts or others who warrant respect.

As you read, notice how Paine uses persuasive techniques in making various kinds of appeals to his audience.

● READING SKILL: ANALYZE MAIN IDEAS AND SUPPORT

Paine supports his main ideas with reasons and evidence. As you read, use a chart such as the one shown to record main ideas and the reasons or evidence Paine uses to support those ideas.

Main Ideas	Reasons and Evidence
I see no real cause for fear.	made an orderly retreat; kept guns and ammunition

▲ VOCABULARY IN CONTEXT

Complete each phrase with the appropriate word from the list.

WORD LIST		
ardor	infidel	repulse
celestial	prudent	tyranny
dominion	relinquish	wrangling
esteem		

1. a wise ruler with _____ over a large kingdom
2. _____ brothers who never seemed to get along
3. able to _____ the enemy with our superior weapons
4. will fight _____ and other forms of oppression
5. a _____ decision in dangerous circumstances
6. should respect and _____ one's parents
7. would not _____ control of the property
8. music so sweet it seemed _____
9. expressed his _____ in mushy love poems
10. everyone welcome, believer or _____

Whose SIDE *are you on?*

KEY IDEA **Loyalty** is a value easily expressed but often difficult to uphold. Situations change, doubts creep in, and conflicts arise that can test the strongest bonds of loyalty. Paine's essay addresses the crisis of loyalty threatening the ranks of American soldiers during the dark days of the Revolutionary War.

QUICKWRITE Think about a time when your loyalty was tested and you were tempted to switch sides or give up. In a short paragraph, briefly describe the situation and explain what you decided. What was the most crucial factor in your decision?

The CRISIS

Thomas Paine

BACKGROUND On the blustery Christmas Eve of 1776, the situation looked bleak for the Continental Army. General Washington's ragtag troops had retreated to the western banks of the Delaware River. Tom Paine was camped with them. The British were within striking distance of Philadelphia, and Washington knew he had to advance the next day or risk losing the war. To boost the morale of his ill-equipped and outnumbered soldiers, he ordered his officers to read aloud the following essay, which Paine had written the day before.

ANALYZE VISUALS
A minuteman was pledged to be ready to fight on a minute's notice. What does this suggest about the preparedness of the colonists?

tyranny (tĭr′ə-nē) *n.* cruel and oppressive government or rule

esteem (ĭ-stēm′) *v.* to set a high value on

celestial (sə-lĕs′chəl) *adj.* heavenly

Ⓐ PERSUASIVE TECHNIQUES
Identify the **loaded language**—words with strong connotations—in lines 1–12. Then paraphrase the lines using neutral language.

These are the times that try men's souls: The summer soldier and the sunshine patriot will, in this crisis, shrink from the service of his country; but he that stands it NOW, deserves the love and thanks of man and woman. **Tyranny,** like hell, is not easily conquered; yet we have this consolation with us, that the harder the conflict, the more glorious the triumph. What we obtain too cheap, we **esteem** too lightly:—' Tis dearness only that gives every thing its value. Heaven knows how to set a proper price upon its goods; and it would be strange indeed, if so **celestial** an article as FREEDOM should not be highly rated. Britain, with an army to enforce her tyranny, has declared, that she has a right (*not only to* TAX) but "to BIND us in
10 ALL CASES WHATSOEVER,"[1] and if *being bound in that manner* is not slavery, then there is not such a thing as slavery upon earth. Even the expression is impious, for so unlimited a power can only belong to God. Ⓐ

---

1. **"to BIND us in ALL CASES WHATSOEVER":** a reference to wording in the Declaratory Act of 1766, in which the British parliament asserted its "power and authority" to make and enforce laws over the American colonies.

Minute Man: Liberty or Death. Private collection.
© Scala/Art Resource, New York.

VINCE AUT MORIRE

LIBERTY OR DEATH

MINUTE MAN

1774 -75

Whether the Independence of the Continent was declared too soon, or delayed too long, I will not now enter into as an argument; my own simple opinion is, that had it been eight months earlier, it would have been much better. We did not make a proper use of last winter, neither could we, while we were in a dependant state. However, the fault, if it were one, was all our own; we have none to blame but ourselves. But no great deal is lost yet; all that Howe has been doing for this month past is rather a ravage than a conquest which the spirit of the Jerseys a year 20 ago would have quickly repulsed, and which time and a little resolution will soon recover. **B**

I have as little superstition in me as any man living, but my secret opinion has ever been, and still is, that God almighty will not give up a people to military destruction, or leave them unsupportedly to perish, who had so earnestly and so repeatedly sought to avoid the calamities of war, by every decent method which wisdom could invent. Neither have I so much of the **infidel** in me, as to suppose, that he has **relinquished** the government of the world, and given us up to the care of devils; and as I do not, I cannot see on what grounds the king of Britain can look up to heaven for help against us: A common murderer, a highwayman, or a 30 housebreaker, has as good a pretense as he. . . .

I once felt all that kind of anger, which a man ought to feel, against the mean principles that are held by the Tories:[2] A noted one, who kept a tavern at Amboy,[3] was standing at his door, with as pretty a child in his hand, about eight or nine years old, as most I ever saw, and after speaking his mind as freely as he thought was **prudent,** finished with this unfatherly expression, *"Well! give me peace in my day."* Not a man lives on the Continent but fully believes that a separation must some time or other finally take place, and a generous parent would have said, *"If there must be trouble, let it be in my day, that my child may have peace;"* and this single reflection, well applied, is sufficient to awaken every man to duty. Not a 40 place upon earth might be so happy as America. Her situation is remote from all the **wrangling** world, and she has nothing to do but trade with them. A man may easily distinguish in himself between temper and principle, and I am as confident, as I am that God governs the world, that America will never be happy until she gets clear of foreign **dominion**. Wars, without ceasing, will break out until that period arrives, and the Continent must in the end be conqueror; for, though the flame of liberty may sometimes cease to shine, the coal never can expire. . . . **C**

I turn with the warm **ardor** of a friend to those who have nobly stood, and are yet determined to stand the matter out: I call not upon a few, but upon all; not on this State or that State, but on every State; up and help us; lay your shoulders to 50 the wheel; better have too much force than too little, when so great an object is at stake. Let it be told to the future world, that in the depth of winter, when nothing but hope and virtue could survive, that the city and the country, alarmed at one

B MAIN IDEAS AND SUPPORT
How does Paine support his main idea that all is not lost for the colonists, despite their military defeats?

infidel (ĭn'fĭ-dəl) *n.* a person with no religious beliefs

relinquish (rĭ-lĭng'kwĭsh) *v.* to withdraw from; to give up

prudent (prōōd'nt) *adj.* showing caution or good judgment

wrangling (răng'glĭng) *adj.* arguing noisily **wrangle** *v.*

dominion (də-mĭn'yən) *n.* control; authority over

C PERSUASIVE TECHNIQUES
Notice that Paine makes an **ethical appeal** in lines 31–39. How does he say a parent should behave?

ardor (är'dər) *n.* intense enthusiasm; passion

---

2. **the mean principles . . . Tories:** the small-minded beliefs of those colonists who remain loyal to Great Britain.

3. **Amboy:** probably Perth Amboy, a town in New Jersey.

ANALYZE VISUALS
A broadside is a public notice printed on one side of a large sheet of paper. What feelings and emotions does this American Revolutionary War broadside appeal to?

common danger, came forth to meet and to **repulse** it. Say not, that thousands are gone, turn out your tens of thousands; throw not the burden of the day upon Providence, but *"shew your faith by your works,"* that God may bless you. It matters not where you live, or what rank of life you hold, the evil or the blessing will reach you all. The far and the near, the home counties and the back, the rich and the poor, shall suffer or rejoice alike. The heart that feels not now, is dead: The blood of his children shall curse his cowardice, who shrinks back at a time
60 when a little might have saved the whole, and made *them* happy. I love the man that can smile in trouble, that can gather strength from distress, and grow brave by reflection. 'Tis the business of little minds to shrink; but he whose heart is firm, and whose conscience approves his conduct, will pursue his principles unto death. My own line of reasoning is to myself as strait and clear as a ray of light. **D** Not all the treasures of the world, so far as I believe, could have induced me to support an offensive war, for I think it murder; but if a thief break into my house, burn and destroy my property, and kill or threaten to kill me, or those that are in it, and to *"bind me in all cases whatsoever,"* to his absolute will, am I to suffer it?

repulse (rĭ-pŭls') *v.* to drive back by force

D **PERSUASIVE TECHNIQUES**
Reread lines 58–64. Identify some examples of loaded words and phrases in this passage. What point is Paine making about those who refuse to act?

What signifies it to me, whether he who does it, is a king or a common man; my countryman or not my countryman? whether it is done by an individual villain, or an army of them? If we reason to the root of things we shall find no difference; neither can any just cause be assigned why we should punish in the one case, and pardon in the other. Let them call me rebel, and welcome, I feel no concern from it; but I should suffer the misery of devils, were I to make a whore of my soul by swearing allegiance to one, whose character is that of a sottish, stupid, stubborn, worthless, brutish man. I conceive likewise a horrid idea in receiving mercy from a being, who at the last day shall be shrieking to the rocks and mountains to cover him, and fleeing with terror from the orphan, the widow and the slain of America.

There are cases which cannot be overdone by language, and this is one. There are persons too who see not the full extent of the evil that threatens them; they solace themselves with hopes that the enemy, if they succeed, will be merciful. It is the madness of folly to expect mercy from those who have refused to do justice; and even mercy, where conquest is the object, is only a trick of war: The cunning of the fox is as murderous as the violence of the wolfe; and we ought to guard equally against both. Howe's first object is partly by threats and partly by promises, to terrify or seduce the people to deliver up their arms, and receive mercy. The ministry recommended the same plan to Gage, and this is what the Tories call making their peace; *"a peace which passeth all understanding" indeed!* A peace which would be the immediate forerunner of a worse ruin than any we have yet thought of. Ye men of Pennsylvania, do reason upon those things! Were the back counties to give up their arms, they would fall easy prey to the Indians, who are all armed: This perhaps is what some Tories would not be sorry for. Were the home counties to deliver up their arms, they would be exposed to the resentment of the back counties, who would then have it at their power to chastise their defection at pleasure. And were any one State to give up its arms, that State must be garrisoned by all Howe's army of Britons and Hessians to preserve it from the anger of the rest. Mutual fear is a principal link in the chain of mutual love, and woe be the State that breaks the compact. Howe is mercifully inviting you to barbarous destruction, and men must be either rogues or fools that will not see it. I dwell not upon the vapours of imagination; I bring reason to your ears; and in language, as plain as A, B, C, hold up truth to your eyes. **E**

I thank God that I fear not. I see no real cause for fear. I know our situation well, and can see the way out of it. While our army was collected, Howe dared not risk a battle, and it is no credit to him that he decamped from the White Plains, and waited a mean opportunity to ravage the defenceless Jersies; but it is great credit to us, that, with an handful of men, we sustained an orderly retreat for near an hundred miles, brought off our ammunition, all our field-pieces, the greatest part of our stores, and had four rivers to pass. None can say that our retreat was

E PERSUASIVE TECHNIQUES
Reread lines 79–101. What statement does Paine make about the use of language at the beginning of this paragraph? What does this tell you about his use of **emotional appeals** and loaded language in this piece?

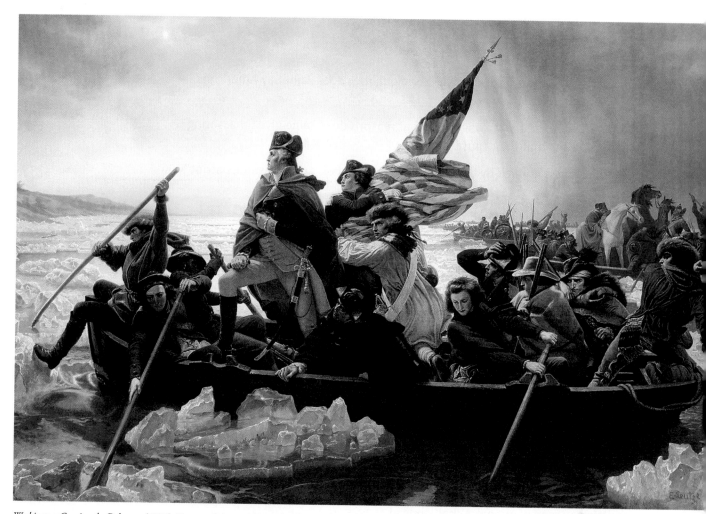

Washington Crossing the Delaware (1851), Eastman Johnson. Copy after the Emmanuel Leutze painting in the Metropolitan Museum, New York. Private collection. © Art Resource, New York.

ANALYZE VISUALS
What figures and objects are emphasized by the **composition,** or the arrangement of shapes? Consider what this emphasis adds to the painting's meaning.

precipitate, for we were near three weeks in performing it, and the country might
110 have time to come in. Twice we marched back to meet the enemy and remained out till dark. The sign of fear was not seen in our camp, and had not some of the cowardly and disaffected inhabitants spread false alarms through the country, the Jersies had never been ravaged. Once more we are again collected and collecting; our new army at both ends of the Continent is recruiting fast, and we shall be able to open the next campaign with sixty thousand men, well armed and clothed. This is our situation, and who will may know it. By perseverance and fortitude we have the prospect of a glorious issue; by cowardice and submission, the sad choice of a variety of evils—a ravaged country—a depopulated city—habitations without safety, and slavery without hope—our homes turned into barracks and
120 bawdy-houses for Hessians, and a future race to provide for whose fathers we shall doubt of. Look on this picture, and weep over it!—and if there yet remains one thoughtless wretch who believes it not, let him suffer it unlamented. ∾ **F**

F MAIN IDEAS AND SUPPORT
The main idea is stated in the first line of this paragraph. What evidence does Paine give to support the idea that there is no cause for fear?

Comprehension

1. **Recall** At the end of the essay, what two qualities does Paine say American troops need to win the war?

2. **Summarize** In the third paragraph, what reasons does Paine give for assuring the Americans that their cause is right?

3. **Clarify** What is implied by the terms "summer soldier" and "sunshine patriot" in the first paragraph?

Literary Analysis

4. **Interpret Metaphor** A metaphor is a figure of speech that equates two unlike things. Explain what Paine means by the metaphor in lines 45–46: "for, though the flame of liberty may sometimes cease to shine, the coal can never expire." How might this metaphor serve to inspire the troops' **loyalty?**

5. **Analyze Main Ideas and Support** Review the chart of main ideas and support you completed as you read. What kind of support does Paine primarily use—reasons, facts, or expert testimony? Explain why you think this is so.

6. **Analyze Persuasive Techniques** Review the different persuasive techniques explained on page 245. Then, go back through the essay and find six examples of Paine's strong persuasive appeals. In a chart, record your examples and briefly explain the type of appeal. What kinds of techniques does Paine favor in his essay?

Example from "The Crisis"	Kind of Appeal
Those soldiers who stand firm in the "service of [their] country" deserve the "love and thanks of man and woman." (lines 2–3)	ethical appeal of "service to country" plus emotional appeal of love and gratitude
"God almighty will not give up a people to military destruction...." (lines 23–24)	appeal to authority—in this case, the ultimate authority

7. **Evaluate Analogy** More detailed than a metaphor, an **analogy** is a point-by-point comparison in which an unfamiliar subject is explained in terms of a familiar one. Reread lines 65–68. Explain the analogy of the thief in terms of the following four points. In your opinion, does the analogy adequately justify the war? Explain why or why not.

   • breaking and entering   • threatening to kill
   • destroying property   • binding to his will

Literary Criticism

8. **Critical Interpretations** John Adams, second U.S. president and no fan of Paine's, nonetheless acknowledged his crucial influence: "Without the pen of Paine the sword of Washington would have been wielded in vain." Use information from Paine's essay, as well as facts from his biography on page 244, to support Adams's assessment.

Vocabulary in Context

WORD LIST

ardor

celestial

dominion

esteem

infidel

prudent

relinquish

repulse

tyranny

wrangling

VOCABULARY PRACTICE

Choose the letter of the phrase that defines or is related to the boldfaced word.

1. **celestial:** (a) an instrument, (b) a star in the sky, (c) a slogan
2. **tyranny:** (a) a country with no freedoms, (b) an old bicycle, (c) a relay race
3. **repulse:** (a) a long-winded speaker, (b) a resisted enemy, (c) a favorite shirt
4. **esteem:** (a) a temperature drop, (b) a cousin, (c) an honored guest
5. **ardor:** (a) a grove of trees, (b) a passion for justice, (c) an accounting mistake
6. **infidel:** (a) a religious skeptic, (b) a lieutenant, (c) a television game show
7. **dominion:** (a) a landlocked country, (b) a public garden, (c) a control freak
8. **relinquish:** (a) a building site, (b) a surrender of territory, (c) a bad argument
9. **prudent:** (a) a cautious investor, (b) a distant relative, (c) car insurance
10. **wrangling:** (a) a favor, (b) a rowing machine, (c) towns with border disputes

VOCABULARY IN WRITING

What emotions does Paine try to elicit from his readers in this essay? Using three or more vocabulary words, write a brief discussion of at least two emotions and the methods Paine uses to elicit them. You might start like this.

> **EXAMPLE SENTENCE**
>
> *Paine primarily wanted to stir up revolutionary **ardor** in his audience.*

VOCABULARY STRATEGY: WORDS FROM MIDDLE ENGLISH

Middle English was the language spoken in England roughly between A.D. 1100 and 1500. This form of English evolved after the Norman French, led by William the Conqueror, invaded and conquered England in 1066. Many modern words that first occurred in Middle English, such as the vocabulary word *ardor,* were derived from French. Others continued from Old English, the earliest recognized form of the language.

PRACTICE The boldfaced words in these sentences have their origins in Middle English. Use context clues to create a definition of each. Then check a dictionary etymology to find out the word's original meaning.

1. He demonstrated his athletic **prowess** by participating in the triathlon.
2. She has been a **recluse** ever since the death of her husband.
3. Her **fulsome** praise of his decision greatly embarrassed him.
4. He had the perfect **rejoinder** for every accusation of the committee.
5. The garden held a **plenitude** of rare plants and flowers.

VOCABULARY PRACTICE
For more practice, go to the **Vocabulary Center** at **ClassZone.com.**

Letter to the Reverend Samson Occom

by Phillis Wheatley

Phillis Wheatley

c. 1753–1784

NOTABLE QUOTE

"Some view our sable race with scornful eye . . .
Remember, Christians, Negroes, black as Cain,
May be refin'd, and join th' angelic train."

Phillis Wheatley became the first African-American poet to be published. Moreover, her unusual life is the stuff that movies are made of. Kidnapped at age seven in West Africa, she was sold to the prosperous Wheatley family at a Boston slave auction. Within 16 months, the precocious child had mastered English and could read the Bible. She then went on to learn Latin and Greek well enough to read the classics.

Startling Success Story With the encouragement of the Wheatley family, she started writing poetry as a teenager. She gained considerable fame both in the colonies and in England when newspapers began publishing her poems, most of them on moral and religious subjects. While in London in 1773 to publish her book of poetry, Wheatley was the toast of society, which included many nobles and dignitaries and the visiting American patriot Ben Franklin.

Life as a Free Black Woman By 1778, Wheatley had gained her freedom and married a free black man. Their life together was a losing struggle against poverty, however, for in many respects living as a free black in a colonial city was as bad as being a slave. In late 1779, Wheatley tried to get a second book of her poems published, but war-torn, financially strapped Boston had lost interest in her.

Letter to John Adams

by Abigail Adams

Abigail Adams

1744–1818

NOTABLE QUOTE

"Remember all Men would be tyrants if they could."

Abigail Adams was the wife of the second U.S. president, John Adams, and mother of the sixth, John Quincy Adams. But she is equally well-known for her outspoken opinions as expressed in thousands of personal letters.

Intelligent and Competent The daughter of a wealthy minister, young Abigail read extensively in her father's well-stocked library. After marrying John Adams, she moved with him to a farm in Braintree, Massachusetts. As John became increasingly involved in colonial politics and the struggle for independence, Abigail took over management of the household and farm as well as John's business affairs.

An Early Feminist? Because of her support for women's education and her acute awareness of men's "absolute power," many have championed Abigail Adams as an early advocate of women's rights. However, although her thinking was clearly advanced for her time—she also favored the abolition of slavery—she held quite conventional views about a woman's subordinate role in society.

Author Online

For more on Wheatley and Adams, visit the **Literature Center** at ClassZone.com.

LITERARY ANALYSIS: DICTION

Diction is a writer's choice of words. Diction includes both vocabulary (words) and syntax (arrangement of words). Diction can be formal or informal, common or technical, abstract or concrete. Note the formal diction in this excerpt from the letter written by Abigail Adams:

How many are the solitary hours I spend, ruminating upon the past, and anticipating the future, whilst you, overwhelmed with the cares of state, have but a few moments you can devote to any individual.

Writers often communicate **tone,** or attitude toward a subject, through their diction. As you read the letters, notice words and phrases that reveal each writer's attitude toward the issues of liberty and freedom.

READING STRATEGY: READING PRIMARY SOURCES

Primary sources are materials written or made by people who took part in or witnessed the events portrayed. These sources can provide unique insights on a subject. To get the most out of a primary source, consider the following:

- Who was the writer? The age, nationality, and social class of the writer can influence the point of view.
- What is the form of the document: letter, diary, speech? How might the form have affected the content?
- When and where was it written? The time and place of a primary source's writing can provide clues to the culture and history of the period.
- Who is the intended audience? In a private letter to a loved one, a writer might voice thoughts and feelings more freely than in an open letter to a public audience.

For help analyzing the letters of Wheatley and Adams, complete a chart such as the one shown here as you read each letter.

Writer:
Form:
When and Where Written:
Intended Purpose/Audience:

Explore the Key Idea

Who gets to make the RULES?

KEY IDEA Those in **authority** make the rules for others—whether it's in the halls of Congress or the classroom. The authors of these two letters, while agreeing wholeheartedly with the patriot cause, still felt left out of the process and the benefits of the American Revolution.

DISCUSS People today have not only more freedom than people did in colonial times but also more ways to change the laws. Think of at least three situations in which rules directly impact your life. Then for each situation, discuss ways that are available to change or modify those rules.

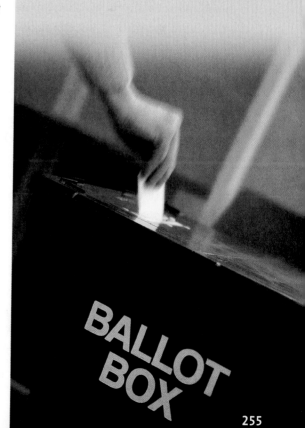

BALLOT BOX

Letter to the Reverend Samson Occom

Phillis Wheatley

BACKGROUND The Reverend Samson Occom was a Mohegan Indian who became a minister after converting to Christianity. In a letter to Phillis Wheatley, he had criticized some of his fellow ministers for owning slaves. Wheatley's response to her friend, dated February 11, 1774, was later published in colonial newspapers.

Reverend and honored sir,

I have this day received your obliging kind epistle, and am greatly satisfied with your reasons respecting the negroes, and think highly reasonable what you offer in vindication of their natural rights: Those that invade them cannot be insensible that the divine light is chasing away the thick darkness which broods over the land of Africa;[1] and the chaos which has reigned so long, is converting into beautiful order, and reveals more and more clearly the glorious dispensation of civil and religious liberty, which are so inseparably united, that there is little or no enjoyment of one without the other: Otherwise, perhaps, the Israelites had been less solicitous for their freedom from Egyptian slavery;[2] I do not say they would
10 have been contented without it, by no means; for in every human breast God has implanted a principle, which we call love of freedom; it is impatient **Ⓐ** of oppression, and pants for deliverance; and by the leave of our modern Egyptians[3] I will assert, that the same principle lives in us. God grant deliverance in his own way and time, and get him honor upon all those whose avarice impels them to countenance and help forward the calamities of their fellow creatures. This I desire not for their hurt, but to convince them of the strange absurdity of their conduct, whose words and actions are so diametrically opposite. How well the cry for liberty, and the reverse disposition for the exercise of oppressive power over others agree—I humbly think it does not require the penetration[4] of a
20 philosopher to determine.— **Ⓑ**

Phillis Wheatley

---

1. **insensible . . . the land of Africa:** unaware that Christianity is spreading throughout Africa.

2. **Israelites . . . Egyptian slavery:** a biblical allusion to the Israelites who were led out of Egypt by Moses.

3. **modern Egyptians:** the owners of African slaves.

4. **penetration:** understanding; insight.

ANALYZE VISUALS
This image shows a slave auction in New Amsterdam (New York). What does this tell you about slavery in colonial America?

Ⓐ DICTION
Describe Wheatley's **diction** in lines 1–11. How do you think her way of writing might have struck white readers at the time?

Ⓑ PRIMARY SOURCES
Does Wheatley's letter deal with private or public issues? What are they?

First Slave Auction in New Amsterdam, 1655.
The Granger Collection, New York.

Letter to JOHN ADAMS

Abigail Adams

> **BACKGROUND** In March of 1776, while John Adams was in Philadelphia with other delegates drafting a code of laws for the new independent country, Abigail wrote a letter asking him to "remember the ladies" in the new laws: "Be more generous and favorable to them than your ancestors. Do not put such unlimited power into the hands of husbands." John's response was to laugh and remark, "You are so saucy." The following is the next letter she sent to him.

Braintree, 7, May, 1776

How many are the solitary hours I spend, ruminating upon the past, and anticipating the future, whilst you, overwhelmed with the cares of state, have but a few moments you can devote to any individual. All domestic pleasures and enjoyments are absorbed in the great and important duty you owe your country, "for our country is, as it were, a secondary god, and the first and greatest parent. It is to be preferred to parents, wives, children, friends, and all things, the gods only excepted; for, if our country perishes, it is as impossible to save an individual, as to preserve one of the fingers of a mortified hand." Thus do I suppress every wish, and silence every murmur, acquiescing in a painful separation from the
10 companion of my youth, and the friend of my heart. **C**

I believe 't is near ten days since I wrote you a line. I have not felt in a humor to entertain you if I had taken up my pen. Perhaps some unbecoming invective[1] might have fallen from it. The eyes of our rulers have been closed, and a lethargy has seized almost every member. I fear a fatal security has taken possession of them. Whilst the building is in flames, they tremble at the expense of water to quench it. In short, two months have elapsed since the evacuation of Boston,[2] and very little has been done in that time to secure it, or the harbor, from future

ANALYZE VISUALS
These pastel portraits of Abigail and John Adams were done in 1766, about two years after their marriage. How do these portraits compare with those that might be done today of a young couple?

C PRIMARY SOURCES
Does Adams's letter concern itself with private or public issues in lines 1–10? What does she say about the relationship between the private and the public?

---

1. **unbecoming invective:** inappropriate abusive language.

2. **two months . . . Boston:** British troops under General William Howe and more than a thousand Loyalists evacuated Boston on March 17, 1776.

invasion. The people are all in a flame, and no one among us, that I have heard of, even mentions expense. They think, universally, that there has been an amazing
20 neglect somewhere. Many have turned out as volunteers to work upon Noddle's Island, and many more would go upon Nantasket,[3] if the business was once set on foot. "'T is a maxim of state, that power and liberty are like heat and moisture. Where they are well mixed, every thing prospers; where they are single, they are destructive."

A government of more stability is much wanted in this colony, and they are ready to receive it from the hands of the Congress. And since I have begun with maxims of state,[4] I will add another, namely, that a people may let a king fall, yet still remain a people; but, if a king let his people slip from him, he is no longer a king.[5] And as this is most certainly our case, why not proclaim to the world, in
30 decisive terms, your own importance? **D**

Shall we not be despised by foreign powers, for hesitating so long at a word?

I cannot say that I think you are very generous to the ladies; for, whilst you are proclaiming peace and good-will to men, emancipating all nations, you insist upon retaining an absolute power over wives. But you must remember, that arbitrary power is like most other things which are very hard, very liable to be broken; and, notwithstanding all your wise laws and maxims, we have it in our power, not only to free ourselves, but to subdue our masters, and, without violence, throw both your natural and legal authority at our feet;—

"Charm by accepting, by submitting sway,
40   Yet have our humor most when we obey."[6] **E**

I thank you for several letters which I have received since I wrote last; they alleviate a tedious absence, and I long earnestly for a Saturday evening, and experience a similar pleasure to that which I used to find in the return of my friend upon that day after a week's absence. The idea of a year dissolves all my philosophy.

Our little ones, whom you so often recommend to my care and instruction, shall not be deficient in virtue or probity,[7] if the precepts of a mother have their desired effect; but they would be doubly enforced, could they be indulged with the example of a father alternately before them. I often point them to their sire,
50 "engaged in a corrupted state,
    Wrestling with vice and faction."[8] **F**

A. Adams

D DICTION
Reread lines 25–30. What words suggest a concern with political issues? What does this diction tell you about the writer's comfort with discussing the subject of government?

E PRIMARY SOURCES
What inconsistency in the attitudes of the times does Abigail Adams point out in lines 32–40?

F DICTION
Reread lines 46–51. What does the formal language used to discuss both public and private matters tell you about family relations at the time?

---

3. **Noddle's Island . . . Nantasket:** sites near the city of Boston. Noddle's Island is now called East Boston.

4. **maxims of state:** rules or short sayings related to government.

5. **king:** a reference to King George III, who ignored colonists' protests and put Massachusetts under military rule.

6. **"Charm . . . obey":** a couplet taken from Alexander Pope's poem *Moral Essays*.

7. **deficient . . . probity:** lacking in goodness or integrity.

8. **"engaged . . . faction":** lines taken from Joseph Addison's play *Cato*. Cato (234–149 B.C.) was a Roman politician who fought for high moral standards in the Roman Senate.

Comprehension

1. **Recall** What does Phillis Wheatley praise the Reverend Occom for doing?

2. **Clarify** In Wheatley's opinion, what is the cause of slavery?

3. **Recall** Why does Abigail Adams put her country before personal happiness?

4. **Clarify** What is the situation in Massachusetts that Adams complains to her husband about?

Literary Analysis

5. **Compare and Contrast** In both letters, Wheatley and Adams reveal their powerlessness to change what they clearly see as wrong. How do they personally deal with this lack of **authority?** Discuss how they cope with the following situations:

   - slavery
   - lack of security due to inaction
   - absolute power of men

6. **Analyze Diction** For each letter, look for examples of diction that reveal the writer's **tone.** Then compare and contrast the tone of each, explaining possible reasons for any differences you find.

7. **Analyze Primary Sources** What are some of the advantages and disadvantages of these personal letters as historical documents? For example, what insights do they provide that more formal documents, such as the Declaration of Independence, do not? How are the letters useful or limited in their historical value? How does the identity of the writer influence the content? Draw upon your chart to cite examples from the letters to prove your points.

8. **Evaluate Argument** Each woman makes an argument in her letter: Wheatley against slavery, and Adams against the "arbitrary power" of men. In your opinion, who presents the stronger case? Cite evidence to support your opinion.

Literary Criticism

9. **Historical Context** Personal letters, even ones such as Wheatley's that were later published in newspapers, offer a rare opportunity to hear women's voices from the past. What distinguishes Wheatley's and Adams's writing from the rhetoric of Patrick Henry, Thomas Jefferson, and Tom Paine? What do their letters reveal about how women were expected to behave in early America?

from The Autobiography

by Benjamin Franklin

Benjamin Franklin

1706–1790

Printer, publisher, writer, scientist, inventor, businessman, philosopher, statesman—Benjamin Franklin's numerous roles only hint at the man's tremendous versatility and talent. As the oldest founding father, Franklin had already lived a full life when at the age of 70 he joined 40-year-old John Adams and 33-year-old Thomas Jefferson to draft the Declaration of Independence. Soon afterward, he loaned Congress a large sum of his own money and sailed on a leaky ship to France to arrange for more loans and a crucial alliance to fight the British. His masterly efforts abroad on behalf of the American cause earned him a reputation as one of the most successful American diplomats of all time. Only a few years before he died, his presence at the Constitutional Convention helped unify the delegates. So great was his influence that he is credited with convincing them to approve the final document by a vote of 39 to 3. A man of great integrity, intelligence, and charm, Ben Franklin embodied the best of the new nation and became its first celebrity.

Pulling Himself Up Born in Boston as the youngest of 15 children, Franklin did not want to follow in his father's footsteps to become a candle and soap maker. Instead, he joined his brother in the printing business as an apprentice. With only two years of formal education, Franklin taught himself to write by imitating the great essayists of his day. At the age of 16, he was contributing satirical pieces to his brother's newspaper. By his own account "too saucy and provoking" as a youth, he soon quarreled with his brother and struck out on his own for Philadelphia. Franklin did very well in Philadelphia, prospering in his own printing business, running the successful *Pennsylvania Gazette* newspaper, writing his popular *Poor Richard's Almanack* for 26 years, and being active in colonial politics.

Citizen of the World Franklin's writing—from humorous satires and wise sayings to serious political essays and scientific observations on electricity—as well as his diplomacy and charismatic personality made him an international celebrity. Although respected by the great minds of his age, he never lost his connection to the common people. In the words of John Adams: "His reputation is greater than that of Newton, Frederick the Great or Voltaire, his character more revered than all of them. There's scarcely a coachman or a footman or scullery maid who does not consider him a friend of all mankind."

FEBRUA

Ve fmile at Florifts, we
And think their Hearts en
ut are thofe wifer, who
urvey with Envy, and purfue with Fire?
Vhat's he, who fights for Wealth, or Fame, or Power?
nother *Florio*, doating on a Flower,
fhort-liv'd Flower, and which has often fprung.

New ☽ 25 2 mo.

☾ ♑ 9 Deg.

LITERARY ANALYSIS: CHARACTERISTICS OF AUTOBIOGRAPHY

An **autobiography** is the story of a person's life, written by that person. As you read this excerpt from Franklin's autobiography, notice the following characteristics of autobiography:

- **First person:** The author of an autobiography usually writes from the first-person point of view.
- **Dual perspective:** Often the author of an autobiography writes as an older person looking back on him- or herself as a younger person, providing opportunities for reflection.
- **Significant moments:** Autobiographies may vary from straightforward chronological accounts to impressionistic narratives. In either case, especially important events and people in the author's life are highlighted.

READING SKILL: MAKE INFERENCES ABOUT THE AUTHOR

Making inferences means "reading between the lines"— making logical guesses based on evidence in the text to figure out what is not directly stated. As you read the *Autobiography*, make inferences about the values and motives that seem characteristic of Franklin's personality. Use a chart like the one shown to record details from the text about the 13 virtues he hopes to acquire and how he goes about doing so. What inferences can you make about him?

Details or Evidence from Text	Inference

Review: **Connect**

VOCABULARY IN CONTEXT

Franklin uses the following boldfaced words in describing his efforts to improve himself. Restate each phrase, using a different word or words for the boldfaced term.

1. **unremitting** storms that went on for weeks
2. **felicity** over her great good luck
3. a mansion as one symbol of **affluence**
4. dreamed up an **artifice** to avoid doing his job
5. **incorrigible** behavior that disgraced the family
6. a **trifling** problem, easily cleared up
7. would often **contrive** to secretly meet his friends
8. worked to **eradicate** smallpox around the world

Is PERFECTION *possible?*

KEY IDEA As a young man, Benjamin Franklin believed that human beings could actually achieve perfection in a given area. All you needed was a reasonable plan and a lot of self-discipline. Many people today also aim for perfection, although their quest may take a different path. Bookstores have whole sections devoted to **self-improvement** in a variety of areas, including diet, exercise, careers, and dating.

QUICKWRITE Do you think perfection is possible or at least worth striving for? If you think so, outline a self-improvement plan that shows how you might achieve your goal. If you don't think perfection is possible, write a paragraph in which you explain why you think it is unattainable.

THE *Autobiography*

BENJAMIN FRANKLIN

BACKGROUND Franklin was a prolific writer, producing volumes of essays, travel journals, newspaper articles, satires, speeches, almanacs, letters, and even ballads. But his great masterpiece was his *Autobiography,* which is still very popular today. The following excerpt details Franklin's plan to achieve moral perfection. He was about 20 years old when he first conceived the idea on one of his long, trans-Atlantic voyages. The plan reveals his faith in reason, order, and human perfectibility, which was typical of 18th-century thought.

It was about this time I conceived the bold and arduous project of arriving at moral perfection. I wished to live without committing any fault at any time; I would conquer all that either natural inclination, custom, or company might lead me into. As I knew, or thought I knew, what was right and wrong, I did not see why I might not always do the one and avoid the other. But I soon found I had undertaken a task of more difficulty than I had imagined. While my care was employed in guarding against one fault, I was often surprised by another; habit took the advantage of inattention; inclination was sometimes too strong for reason. I concluded, at length, that the mere speculative conviction that it was our
10 interest to be completely virtuous, was not sufficient to prevent our slipping; and that the contrary habits must be broken, and good ones acquired and established, before we can have any dependence on a steady, uniform rectitude of conduct. For this purpose I therefore contrived the following method. **Ⓐ**

In the various enumerations of the moral virtues I had met with in my reading, I found the catalogue more or less numerous, as different writers included more or

ANALYZE VISUALS
What do the details of this famous painting suggest about Franklin?

Ⓐ AUTOBIOGRAPHY
What characteristics of autobiography do you find in the first paragraph of this selection?

Benjamin Franklin (1767), David Martin. Oil on canvas.
© White House Historical Association, Washington, D.C.

fewer ideas under the same name. Temperance, for example, was by some confined to eating and drinking, while by others it was extended to mean the moderating every other pleasure, appetite, inclination, or passion, bodily or mental, even to our avarice and ambition. I proposed to myself, for the sake of clearness, to use rather more names, with fewer ideas annexed to each, than a few names with more ideas; and I included under thirteen names of virtues all that at that time occurred to me as necessary or desirable, and annexed to each a short precept, which fully expressed the extent I gave to its meaning.

These names of virtues, with their precepts were:

1. **TEMPERANCE.** Eat not to dullness; drink not to elevation.

2. **SILENCE.** Speak not but what may benefit others or yourself; avoid **trifling** conversation.

3. **ORDER.** Let all your things have their places; let each part of your business have its time.

4. **RESOLUTION.** Resolve to perform what you ought; perform without fail what you resolve.

5. **FRUGALITY.** Make no expense but to do good to others or yourself; *i.e.,* waste nothing.

6. **INDUSTRY.** Lose no time; be always employed in something useful; cut off all unnecessary actions.

7. **SINCERITY.** Use no hurtful deceit; think innocently and justly; and, if you speak, speak accordingly.

8. **JUSTICE.** Wrong none by doing injuries, or omitting the benefits that are your duty.

9. **MODERATION.** Avoid extremes; forbear resenting injuries so much as you think they deserve.

10. **CLEANLINESS.** Tolerate no uncleanliness in body, clothes, or habitation.

11. **TRANQUILLITY.** Be not disturbed at trifles, or at accidents common or unavoidable.

12. **CHASTITY.** Rarely use venery but for health or offspring, never to dulness, weakness, or the injury of your own or another's peace or reputation.

13. **HUMILITY.** Imitate Jesus and Socrates.[1] **B**

My intention being to acquire the *habitude* of all these virtues, I judged it would be well not to distract my attention by attempting the whole at once, but to fix it on one of them at a time; and, when I should be master of that, then to proceed to another, and so on, till I should have gone through the thirteen; and, as the previous acquisition of some might facilitate the acquisition of certain others, I arranged them with that view, as they stand above. Temperance first, as it tends to

trifling (trī'flǐng) *adj.* frivolous; inconsequential **trifle** v.

B MAKE INFERENCES
Based on Franklin's list of virtues, what inference can you make about his view of his own moral character? Explain.

---

1. **Socrates** (sŏk'rə-tēz'): Greek philosopher (470?–399 B.C.) who believed that true knowledge comes through dialogue and systematic questioning of ideas; he was executed for his beliefs.

procure that coolness and clearness of head, which is so necessary where constant vigilance was to be kept up, and guard maintained against the **unremitting** attraction of ancient habits, and the force of perpetual temptations. This being acquired and established, Silence would be more easy; and my desire being to gain knowledge at the same time that I improved in virtue, and considering that in conversation it was obtained rather by the use of the ears than of the tongue, and therefore wishing to break a habit I was getting into of prattling, punning, and joking, which only made me acceptable to trifling company, I gave *Silence* the second place. This and the next, *Order,* I expected would allow me more time for
40 attending to my project and my studies. *Resolution,* once become habitual, would keep me firm in my endeavors to obtain all the subsequent virtues; *Frugality* and Industry freeing me from my remaining debt, and producing **affluence** and independence, would make more easy the practice of Sincerity and Justice, etc., etc. Conceiving then, that, agreeably to the advice of Pythagoras in his Golden Verses,[2] daily examination would be necessary, I **contrived** the following method for conducting that examination. **C**

I made a little book, in which I allotted a page for each of the virtues. I ruled each page with red ink, so as to have seven columns, one for each day of the week, marking each column with a letter for the day. I crossed these columns with
50 thirteen red lines, marking the beginning of each line with the first letter of one of the virtues, on which line, and in its proper column, I might mark, by a little black spot, every fault I found upon examination to have been committed respecting that virtue upon that day.

I determined to give a week's strict attention to each of the virtues successively. Thus, in the first week,
60 my great guard was to avoid every[3] the least offense against *Temperance,* leaving the other virtues to their ordinary chance, only marking every evening the faults of the day. Thus, if in the first week I could keep my first line, marked T, clear of spots, I supposed the habit of that virtue so much strengthened, and its opposite weakened, that I might venture
70 extending my attention to include the next, and for the following week keep both lines clear of spots. Proceeding

unremitting
(ŭn′rĭ-mĭt′ĭng) *adj.* constant; never stopping

affluence (ăf′lōō-əns) *n.* wealth

contrive (kən-trīv′) *v.* to plan skillfully; to design

C MAKE INFERENCES
What can you infer from lines 25–46 about Franklin's approach to problems?

Form of the pages.

TEMPERANCE							
eat not to dullness; drink not to elevation.							
	S.	M.	T.	W.	T.	F.	S.
T.							
S.	•	•		•		•	
O.	••	•	•		•	•	•
R.			•			•	
F.		•			•		
I.			•	•			
S.							
J.							
M.							
C.							
T.							
C.							
H.							

---

2. **Pythagoras** (pĭ-thăg′ər-əs)... **Golden Verses:** Pythagoras was a Greek philosopher and mathematician (580?–500? B.C.).

3. **every:** even.

thus to the last, I could go through a course complete in thirteen weeks, and four courses in a year. And like him who, having a garden to weed, does not attempt to **eradicate** all the bad herbs at once, which would exceed his reach and his strength, but works on one of the beds at a time, and, having accomplished the first, proceeds to a second, so I should have, I hoped, the encouraging pleasure of seeing on my pages the progress I made in virtue, by clearing successively my lines of their spots, till in the end, by a number of courses, I should be happy in
80 viewing a clean book, after thirteen weeks' daily examination. . . . **D**

The precept of *Order* requiring that *every part of my business should have its allotted time,* one page in my little book contained the following scheme of employment for the twenty-four hours of a natural day.

eradicate (ĭ-răd'ĭ-kāt') *v.* to destroy completely

D AUTOBIOGRAPHY
In what way do lines 47–80 provide an example of Franklin's **dual perspective?**

The Morning.	5	Rise, wash, and address
Question. What good shall I do this day?	6	*Powerful Goodness!* Contrive day's business, and take the resolution of the day; prosecute the present
	7	study, and breakfast.
	8	
	9	Work.
	10	
	11	
Noon.	12	Read, or overlook
	1	my accounts, and dine.
	2	
	3	Work.
	4	
	5	
Evening.	6	Put things in their places. Supper.
Question. What good have I done today?	7	Music or diversion, or conversation.
	8	Conversation. Examination of
	9	the day.
	10	
	11	
	12	
Night.	1	Sleep.
	2	
	3	
	4	

I entered upon the execution of this plan for self-examination, and continued it with occasional intermissions for some time. I was surprised to find myself so much fuller of faults than I had imagined; but I had the satisfaction of seeing them diminish. To avoid the trouble of renewing now and then my little book, which, by scraping out the marks on the paper of old faults to make room for new ones in a new course, became full of holes, I transferred my tables and precepts to the ivory leaves of a memorandum book, on which the lines were drawn with red ink, that made a durable stain, and on those lines I marked my faults with a black-lead pencil, which marks I could easily wipe out with a wet sponge. After a while I went through one course only in a year, and afterward only one in several years, till at length I omitted them entirely, being employed in voyages and business abroad, with a multiplicity of affairs that interfered; but I always carried my little book with me. **E**

My scheme of *Order* gave me the most trouble; and I found that, though it might be practicable where a man's business was such as to leave him the disposition of his time, that of a journeyman printer, for instance, it was not possible to be exactly observed by a master, who must mix with the world, and often receive people of business at their own hours. *Order,* too, with regard to places for things, papers, etc., I found extremely difficult to acquire. I had not been early accustomed to it, and, having an exceeding good memory, I was not so sensible of the inconvenience attending want of method. This article, therefore, cost me so much painful attention, and my faults in it vexed me so much, and I made so little progress in amendment, and had such frequent relapses, that I was almost ready to give up the attempt, and content myself with a faulty character in that respect, like the man who, in buying an ax of a smith, my neighbor, desired to have the whole of its surface as bright as the edge. The smith consented to grind it bright for him if he would turn the wheel; he turned, while the smith pressed the broad face of the ax hard and heavily on the stone, which made the turning of it very fatiguing. The man came every now and then from the wheel to see how the work went on, and at length would take his ax as it was, without farther grinding. "No," said the smith, "turn on, turn on; we shall have it bright by-and-by; as yet, it is only speckled." "Yes," says the man, *"but I think I like a speckled ax best."* And I believe this may have been the case with many, who, having, for want of some such means as I employed, found the difficulty of obtaining good and breaking bad habits in other points of vice and virtue, have given up the struggle, and concluded that *"a speckled ax was best;"* for something, that pretended to be reason, was every now and then suggesting to me that such extreme nicety as I exacted of myself might be a kind of foppery in morals,[4] which, if it were known, would make me ridiculous; that a perfect character might be attended with the inconvenience of being envied and hated; and that a benevolent man should allow a few faults in himself, to keep his friends in countenance. **F**

In truth, I found myself **incorrigible** with respect to Order; and now I am grown old, and my memory bad, I feel very sensibly the want of it. But, on the whole, though I never arrived at the perfection I had been so ambitious of

E MAKE INFERENCES
Reread lines 84–95. What can you infer about Franklin's persistence in pursuing his goals?

F CONNECT
What insight does Franklin come to about his quest for perfection? Consider what you have learned in your own life about perfection. Does his insight seem reasonable?

incorrigible
(ĭn-kôr′ĭ-jə-bəl) *adj.*
incapable of being reformed or corrected

---

4. **foppery in morals:** excessive regard for and concern about one's moral appearance.

obtaining, but fell short of it, yet I was, by the endeavor, a better and a happier man than I otherwise should have been if I had not attempted it; as those who aim at perfect writing by imitating the engraved copies, though they never reach the wished-for excellence of those copies, their hand is mended by the endeavor, and is tolerable while it continues fair and legible. **G**

It may well be my posterity should be informed that to this little **artifice,** with the blessing of God, their ancestor owed the constant **felicity** of his life, down to his 79th year, in which this is written. What reverses may attend the reminder is in the hand of Providence; but, if they arrive, the reflection on past happiness enjoyed ought to help his bearing them with more resignation. To Temperance he ascribes his long-continued health, and what is still left to him of a good constitution; to Industry and Frugality, the early easiness of his circumstances and acquisition of his fortune, with all that knowledge that enabled him to be a useful citizen, and obtained for him some degree of reputation among the learned; to Sincerity and Justice, the confidence of his country, and the honorable employs it conferred upon him; and to the joint influence of the whole mass of the virtues, even in the the imperfect state he was able to acquire them, all that evenness of temper, and that cheerfulness in conversation, which makes his company still sought for, and agreeable even to his younger acquaintance. I hope, therefore, that some of my descendants may follow the example and reap the benefit. ∿

G **AUTOBIOGRAPHY**
What **significant moment** or insight is described in this paragraph?

artifice (är′tə-fĭs) *n.* a clever means to an end

felicity (fĭ-lĭs′ĭ-tē) *n.* great happiness

from Poor Richard's Almanack

BENJAMIN FRANKLIN

He that cannot obey cannot command.

Don't count your chickens before they are hatched.

A mob's a monster; heads enough but no brains.

Well done is better than well said.

Lost time is never found again.

Early to bed, early to rise, makes a man healthy, wealthy and wise.

If you would know the worth of money, go and try to borrow some.

A friend in need is a friend indeed.

Fish and visitors smell in three days.

Love your neighbor; yet don't pull down your hedge.

God helps them that help themselves.

If you would keep your secret from an enemy, tell it not to a friend.

Be slow in choosing a friend, slower in changing.

Don't throw stones at your neighbors', if your own windows are glass.

Eat to live and not live to eat.

Love your enemies, for they tell you your faults.

Better slip with foot than tongue.

Three may keep a secret, if two of them are dead.

Never leave that till tomorrow, which you can do today.

A penny saved is a penny earned.

A rolling stone gathers no moss.

Make hay while the sun shines.

Beware of little expenses; a small leak will sink a great ship.

He that goes a borrowing goes a sorrowing.

Honesty is the best policy.

Little strokes fell big oaks.

He that lies down with dogs shall rise up with fleas.

Comprehension

1. **Recall** Name seven of Franklin's virtues.

2. **Recall** Who are Franklin's models for the virtue of humility?

3. **Clarify** Why does Franklin list the virtues in the order he does?

4. **Summarize** What is Franklin's method for acquiring the 13 virtues?

Literary Analysis

5. **Make Inferences About the Author** Look at the details and inferences you recorded in your chart. Now assign each of Franklin's 13 virtues to one of the following categories. What can you infer about Franklin's beliefs and values in general from his list of virtues?

   • healthful living   • succeeding in the world   • getting along with others

6. **Analyze Autobiography** Like most autobiographies, Franklin's has a dual perspective in which he is both main character and narrator. Go back through the excerpt to find characterizations of Franklin as a young man and as an older man looking back on his life. Record your answers in two charts as shown. What differences do you find?

Young Franklin	
Character Trait	Evidence in Text
1. Ambitious	1. "I conceived the bold and arduous project of arriving at moral perfection." (lines 1–2)
2.	

Old Franklin	
Character Trait	Evidence in Text
1. Honest	1. "In truth, I found myself incorrigible with respect to Order, and now I am grown old, . . . I feel very sensibly the want of it." (lines 124–125)
2.	

7. **Interpret Analogy** Reread lines 105–115. How does the analogy about the man buying an ax help explain Franklin's problems with order? How is Franklin like or different from the man with the ax?

8. **Evaluate Conclusions** Franklin ultimately fails to achieve moral perfection. What conclusions does he draw about his original plan? In terms of **self-improvement,** is it better to aim high and fall short or to set a lower goal?

Literary Criticism

9. **Critical Interpretations** Throughout history, Franklin has had his detractors as well as his admirers. Some consider him self-righteous and materialistic; others have ridiculed his plan for moral perfection as too regimented and superficial. Do you find any evidence for these charges in the excerpt? Explain.

Vocabulary in Context

VOCABULARY PRACTICE

Show your understanding of the vocabulary words by answering these questions.

1. Which would cause **felicity,** doing well on a test or having trouble sleeping?
2. If someone created an **artifice,** would that person be shrewd or naïve?
3. If you want to **eradicate** the weeds in your yard, should you use a plant book or a garden tool?
4. To **contrive,** would you act impulsively or by plan?
5. Who is more likely **incorrigible,** a person with five parking tickets or one with five burglary convictions?
6. Is a **trifling** problem one you should ignore or act on immediately?
7. If you wanted to hide your **affluence,** would you probably drive an inexpensive car or take a trip around the world?
8. Is a person with **unremitting** joy constantly happy or never happy?

> **WORD LIST**
> affluence
> artifice
> contrive
> eradicate
> felicity
> incorrigible
> trifling
> unremitting

VOCABULARY IN WRITING

Choose a virtue from Franklin's list on page 266 that you have trouble with in your own life. Using at least two vocabulary words, write a brief plan explaining steps you could take to improve in this area. Here is a sample beginning.

> **EXAMPLE SENTENCE**
> *Like Franklin, I need to **contrive** a plan to become more frugal.*

VOCABULARY STRATEGY: THE LATIN ROOT *fic*

You are probably familiar with the Latin root *fac,* which means "make" or "do." Another common spelling of this root is *fic,* as in the vocabulary word *artifice.* Identifying a word's roots, as well as looking at context and at the other parts of the word, can often help you to figure out the word's meaning.

PRACTICE Choose the word from the word web that best completes each sentence. Use context clues to help you or consult a dictionary.

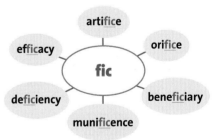

1. Who is the _____ on Grandma's life insurance policy?
2. A _____ in vitamin D can lead to rickets, a disease of the bones.
3. One_____ in the pipe was blocked, causing water to back up into it.
4. Due to the _____ of the Kelly family, the town has the money to build a new pool.
5. The speaker described the _____ of acupuncture as a treatment for several ailments.

VOCABULARY PRACTICE
For more practice, go to the **Vocabulary Center** at **ClassZone.com.**

MAGAZINE ARTICLE Benjamin Franklin's drive for self-improvement may seem a little excessive, but it remains a great American ideal. This article looks at the continuing American urge to change oneself for the better.

50 Ways to Fix Your Life

by Carolyn Kleiner Butler

Americans have long been captivated by the notion of self-improvement—none more so than Benjamin Franklin. An accomplished printer, author, postmaster, scientist, inventor, and diplomat who taught himself to speak five languages, this Founding Father "conceiv'd the bold and arduous project of arriving at moral perfection."

Today, self-help is not just a way of life—it's practically a national obsession. There are 7,500 books on the topic on amazon.com alone, covering just about every imaginable bad habit or dilemma.

Such offerings "appeal to the deeply felt American idea of 'before and after,'" says Robert Thompson, professor of media and popular culture at Syracuse University in New York, who points out the underlying similarities between Franklin and, say, Dr. Phil. "If you were born a peasant in a medieval village, you knew who you were and it was very hard to change that, but here there is fluidity of class, and entire industries pop up that reflect the ultimate optimism that really anybody can be a 'swan' and completely turn [his or her] life around."

Time to change. The hard truth is that lasting change doesn't usually happen in a single TV season. In reality, of the 40 to 45 percent of people who will make New Year's resolutions come January, fewer than half will succeed within six months, according to John Norcross, professor of psychology at the University of Scranton in Pennsylvania and coauthor of *Changing for Good*. But the fact is that when someone makes a serious commitment to transform his or her life, it is possible.

How can you cross that far-off finish line? First and foremost, you really have to be ready to do it and understand that the pros outweigh the cons. Also, research shows that keeping track of your development in a visible way—charting your weight loss, for one, or graphing your heart rate and stamina—is associated with sustainable lifestyle change, as is social support, whether in the form of friends, online discussion groups, or reliable, proven, self-help books.

Lastly, and most important, don't give up if you tumble off the wagon now and then. Triumphant changers often see a setback as a reason to recommit to their goal, and they get back on the horse immediately.

In the end, simply making a concerted effort to improve your lifestyle can have lasting benefits, no matter what the final result. Indeed, Franklin recounts, "On the whole, tho' I never arrived at . . . perfection . . . I was, by the endeavour, a better and happier man than I otherwise should have been if I had not attempted it."

Revolutionary Ideas

For colonists living in the 1770s, there was one topic around which most conversation and writing revolved: the Revolution. The writing of this period was political, and it was persuasive. It had a life-and-death purpose: to win over the hearts and minds of American colonists—and the rest of the world—to the belief that rebellion was necessary.

Writing to Persuade

Reflect briefly on each of the pieces you have just read, and select one or two you find particularly persuasive. Then, imagine you are a colonist of the time and write a letter to your local paper in which you voice your support for the ideas of the writer or writers chosen. Be sure to cite specific phrases or lines that you find convincing. Add your own thoughts and opinions to try to further persuade readers to support the rebellion.

Consider

- thought-provoking or incendiary sentences or passages
- your opinions on the issues discussed in the selections
- how to express your viewpoint clearly and convincingly

Extension

SPEAKING & LISTENING Imagine yourself on the village green, part of an impassioned gathering of colonists arguing both sides of independence from England. Recast your letter as a **speech** and deliver it to your friends, neighbors, and political opponents.

Give Me Liberty or Give Me Death. Patrick Henry delivering his great speech on the *Rights of the Colonies* before the Virginia Assembly, Richmond, March 23, 1775. The Granger Collection, New York.

Writing Workshop

Persuasive Essay

Here's an opportunity to think about what you believe in—and to persuade readers to agree with you and take action. Follow the **Writer's Road Map** to get started on a persuasive essay that will help you make your own mark on the world.

WRITER'S ROAD MAP

Persuasive Essay

WRITING PROMPT 1

Writing for the Real World Sometimes an issue affects you so strongly that you want to convince others to act in a certain way. Write a persuasive essay on an issue that is important to you.

Issues to Consider

• a local political issue, such as a curfew
• issues involving the environment or social justice
• freedoms and responsibilities of the media

WRITING PROMPT 2

Writing from Literature Choose an issue from Unit 1 that you feel strongly about. Write a persuasive essay that explains the issue and mentions the literary work in which you found it.

Literature to Consider

• Patrick Henry's speech to the Virginia Convention (What is liberty worth?)
• Benjamin Franklin's proverbs (Is honesty always the best policy?)
• *The Way to Rainy Mountain* (How can oppression be stopped?)
• The Declaration of Independence (When is it right to rebel?)

WRITING TOOLS
For prewriting, revision, and editing tools, visit the **Writing Center at ClassZone.com.**

KEY TRAITS

1. IDEAS
• Clearly identifies the **issue**
• Presents a **thesis statement** that makes a clear, logical, and forceful **claim**
• Uses relevant and convincing **evidence** to **support** the position
• Anticipates and answers **opposing arguments** and counterclaims

2. ORGANIZATION
• **Introduces** the issue in an attention-getting way
• Connects ideas with **transitional words and phrases**
• **Concludes** with a summary or a call to action

3. VOICE
• Captures an appropriate **tone** for the subject matter

4. WORD CHOICE
• Addresses the **audience** directly, using appropriate language
• Uses **persuasive techniques** effectively

5. SENTENCE FLUENCY
• Employs **rhetorical devices** such as parallelism and repetition
• Varies **sentence types and lengths**

6. CONVENTIONS
• Employs **correct grammar and usage**

Part 1: Analyze a Student Model

Bruce Lomibao
Plainview High School

Cell Phone Use in Cars: Hang Up—Don't Bang Up!

Picture this: a man gets into a car, puts on a blindfold, starts the engine, puts his foot on the gas, and takes his hands off the wheel. That would never happen, you say? Maybe not, but something just as dangerous is happening all around you every day. Every time a motorist carries on a
5 cellular-phone conversation, that person is endangering not only his or her own life but also the lives of everyone else walking, bicycling, or driving nearby. Using cell phones while driving must be banned—now.

A new study by the Cellular Telecommunications & Internet Association found that more than 200 million Americans use cellular
10 telephones. People talk on the phone while watching a ballgame, walking the dog, washing the dishes, or driving to work. Although talking on a cell phone distracts people from what they are doing in each of these cases, this distraction can have serious—even fatal—consequences for drivers. I have just learned to drive myself, so I know how complicated it is and how much
15 concentration it takes. "It's absolutely clear from the research literature that talking on a cell phone while driving does elevate the risk of a crash," said Dr. Donald Reinfurt of the University of North Carolina's Highway Safety Research Center. "Using cell phones slows reaction times and degrades drivers' tracking abilities."

20 Do these slowed reflexes cause accidents? According to a study that Dr. Reinfurt conducted, about one of every 600 driving accidents involved the use of a cell phone. However, he believes that "cell phones are involved in many more crashes" because most drivers won't admit to police officers that they were on the phone at the time of the crash. According to a study of
25 drivers in Canada, "the risk of a collision when using a cellular telephone was four times higher than the risk when a cellular telephone was not being used."

KEY TRAITS IN ACTION

Memorable title identifies the **issue.** The parallelism and repetition of "Hang Up—Don't Bang Up!" is an effective **rhetorical device.**

Introduces the issue with a startling idea.

Strong words (*every time, endangering, must*) help to establish a serious **tone. Thesis statement** forcefully states a specific **claim.**

Relevant and convincing **evidence,** including an expert opinion and a statistic, add **support.**

Despite these frightening statistics, some people may say their time is so valuable that they absolutely need to talk while driving. What they fail to consider is how much time they'd lose if they were injured—or worse—in a car accident. Others might argue that if lawmakers ban talking on a cell phone while driving, they will also have to ban other distractions such as eating, listening to music, and talking to passengers in the car. However, the Insurance Information Institute reports that "there is increasing evidence that the dangers associated with cell-phone use outweigh those of other distractions." One reason may be that talking on a cell phone takes the driver's hands, mind, and even eyes away from the car and the road for extended periods. What about hands-free phones, then? In 2004, the National Highway Traffic Safety Administration found that drivers using hands-free sets had to redial their calls more than twice as often as those using handheld phones. They also braked more slowly and were less aware of other drivers, pedestrians, and roadside landmarks.

Obviously, many people are already aware of this problem. But what are governments doing about it? Nearly 50 countries from Australia to Zimbabwe have banned or restricted the use of cell phones while driving. In the United States, three states and the District of Columbia have forbidden motorists from driving while talking on the telephone, and four states have declared that only mature drivers may do so. More than two-thirds of the states and the federal government are considering legislation related to cell phones and driving.

You could be the next victim of a driver distracted by a cell-phone conversation. So before that happens, remember: "Hang up—don't bang up!" Send letters or e-mails to your local, state, and federal legislators urging them to ban the use of these devices in cars. Do it today.

Transitional word (*Despite*) tells the reader that the writer is about to discuss and rebut **opposing arguments** and counterclaims.

Varied **sentence types and lengths** throughout the essay give the message maximum impact.

Strong **conclusion** addresses the **audience** directly. The appeal to fear (*You could be the next victim*) is a dramatic **persuasive technique.** The last two sentences are a call to action.

2

Part 2: Apply the Writing Process

PREWRITING

What Should I Do?	**What Does It Look Like?**

1. Make sure you understand the prompt.
Reread the prompt you chose on page 276. Underline the type of writing you will do and circle the purpose of that writing. Look for information about your audience. If that information is not given, you can assume that your teacher and your classmates are your audience.

▶ **WRITING PROMPT** Sometimes an issue affects you so strongly that you want to convince others to act in a certain way. Write a persuasive essay to convince your readers to agree with your point of view.

I should write about something that really matters to me. But what?

2. Think of issues that you truly care about.
Use a graphic organizer to help you examine your opinion—and opposing viewpoints—about issues that concern you. Put an asterisk by the issue you want to write about.

TIP Be sure that there are two ways to look at your issue. There's no need to persuade people if everyone already agrees.

▶

Issue	My View	Opposing Views
lower voting age to 16	many teens work, pay taxes	16-year-olds not mature enough
use of cell phones while driving*	extremely dangerous	necessary in this busy world
freedom of speech on the Internet	a right we should protect	should be limited—some ideas too dangerous

3. Write a working thesis statement.
Focus on your **claim**—the main idea that you want to persuade readers about. Then express that idea clearly in a sentence or two. You can modify your statement as you gather evidence and start drafting.

▶ *It would be a good idea to consider banning the use of cell phones while driving. If we don't, who knows how many innocent people will be injured or killed?*

4. Collect support for your claim.
Search the Internet and talk to experts to find facts, statistics, and other details that strengthen and clarify your ideas.

See pages 1270–1273: Choosing the Right Research Tools

▶
- *My own experience: Driving takes focus and concentration.*
- *University study: Using cell phones slows drivers' reaction times.*
- *Canadian study: Using a cell phone makes crash risk four times higher!*

What Should I Do?	**What Does It Look Like?**

1. Put your ideas in a sensible order. First, introduce the issue. Next, present your thesis statement. As you plan the rest of your essay, be sure to think of opposing arguments. Make sure that you think of at least one answer, or counterclaim, for every opposing argument. To be certain that you include all the points you want to make, you may want to create an outline before you start writing.	I. Introduction
	II. Evidence that the problem is widespread
	  A. Many people use cell phones. (How many?)
	  B. Driving takes concentration. I know from experience.
	III. Evidence that cell phone users cause accidents
	  A. Cite statistic from university study.
	  B. Cite statistic from Canadian study.
	IV. Opposing arguments (and counterclaims)
	  A. Time is valuable. (lose time in an accident)
	  B. Other distractions (phones even more distracting)
	  C. Hands-free phones (users brake slowly)
	V. Legislation passed or pending
	  A. In other countries
	  B. Within the United States
	VI. Conclusion

2. Support your statements with reasons and evidence. Include logical reasons for your point of view. Quote experts and share facts and statistics that make your position convincing. Explain how each piece of evidence backs up your claim.	This distraction can have serious—even fatal—consequences. ⎤ Main idea "It's absolutely clear from the research literature that talking on a cell phone while driving does elevate the risk of a crash," said Dr. Donald Reinfurt of the University of North Carolina's Highway Safety Research Center. ⎤ Support: expert opinion
3. Use persuasive techniques. Depending on your topic and your audience, you might appeal to readers' ethics or to their emotions. However, no one likes to feel bullied. Choose words that are strong but not overbearing. **See page 245:** Persuasive Techniques	Every time a motorist carries on a cellular-phone conversation, that person is ~~dooming everyone who comes near~~ endangering not only his or her own life but also the lives of everyone else walking, bicycling, or driving nearby.

REVISING AND EDITING

What Should I Do?	*What Does It Look Like?*

1. Energize your language.
- Read your draft aloud. [Bracket] words that sound vague or hesitant: *a good idea, fairly important, maybe, kind of,* and *possibly.*
- Replace these words with ones that appropriately express your strong feelings: imperatives such as *should* and *must,* adjectives such as *crucial,* and adverbs such as *immediately.*

▶ ~~It would be [a good idea] to [consider] banning the use of cell phones while driving.~~

Using cell phones while driving must be banned—now.

2. Prop up any weak arguments.
- Reread your essay, <u>underlining</u> statements that have few or no supporting details or explanations.
- Think of clear, convincing reasons to strengthen your position. Add facts, statistics, or other evidence.

▶ Others might argue that if lawmakers ban talking on a cell phone while driving, they will also have to ban other distractions such as eating, listening to music, and talking to passengers in the car. ~~How ridiculous can you get?~~ However, the Insurance Information Institute reports that "there is increasing evidence that the dangers associated with cell-phone use outweigh those of other distractions."

3. Watch for mistakes in logic.
- Ask a peer reader to (circle) any illogical statements in your essay. For example, have him or her look for words such as *all, every, no one,* and *never,* which often signal overgeneralizations.
- Instead, make accurate statements.

See page 282: Errors in Reasoning

▶ Nearly 50 countries from Australia to Zimbabwe have
(~~Every country outside of the United States has~~) banned or restricted the use of cell phones while driving.

4. Conclude concisely.
- Have a peer reader review your concluding paragraph. Does it sum up the issue? Does it spell out what you want him or her to do?
- Add information that summarizes the issue or makes a clear call for specific action.

See page 282: Ask a Peer Reader

▶ You could be the next victim of a driver distracted by a cell-phone conversation. So before that happens, remember: "Hang up—don't bang up!" Send letters or e-mails to your local, state, and federal legislators urging them to ban the use of these devices in cars. Do it today.

Persuasive Essay

Apply the Rubric

A strong persuasive essay . . .

- ☑ has a compelling introduction
- ☑ identifies the issue and the writer's claim in a strong thesis statement
- ☑ persuasively supports the claim with reasons, facts, or statistics
- ☑ presents and answers opposing arguments
- ☑ connects ideas clearly with transitional words and phrases
- ☑ varies sentence types and lengths
- ☑ is targeted to a specific audience and addresses that audience directly
- ☑ maintains an appropriate tone
- ☑ concludes with a summary or a call to action

Ask a Peer Reader

- Did my essay change your position on the issue? Why or why not?
- How could I strengthen the reasons and support in my essay?
- How could I improve my conclusion?

Errors in Reasoning

Circular reasoning: supporting an idea by simply restating it ("Cell phones are distracting because they divert drivers' attention.")

Overgeneralization: making a statement that is too broad or general to be proved ("Everyone has a cell phone nowadays.")

Either/or fallacy: ignoring possible alternate outcomes of an action ("Either you stop phoning while driving, or you'll have an accident.")

False cause: assuming that an event that follows another was the result of the first event ("Countries that have banned phone use in cars have experienced economic growth.")

See page R22: Identifying Faulty Reasoning

Check Your Grammar

Use parallel structure to express similar ideas.

> Picture this: a man gets into a car, puts on a
> blindfold, starts the engine, ~~putting~~ *puts* his foot
> on the gas, and ~~his hands are off~~ *takes* the wheel.

See page R68: Parallel Structure

Writing On|ine

PUBLISHING OPTIONS
For publishing options, visit the **Writing Center** at ClassZone.com.

ASSESSMENT PREPARATION
For writing and grammar assessment practice, go to the **Assessment Center** at ClassZone.com.

Presenting a Persuasive Speech

You've spent time and effort crafting an outstanding persuasive essay. Now put your words into action by presenting a speech on the same topic.

Planning the Speech

1. **Remember your purpose and audience.** Review the reason you wrote your essay, and think about the readers you were originally addressing. Then consider what the audience for your speech might know about the issue. Will you speak to the audience as an authority or as a peer? If necessary, collect additional background information or consider eliminating specific points.

2. **Turn your essay into a script.** Mark up a copy of your essay indicating where to insert or delete information. Highlight statements you want to stress and indicate how you want to stress them—for example, by slowing down, raising your voice, or including gestures. Also think of helpful visuals to include, such as posters or video clips. Mark your script to indicate when you want to show them.

3. **Fine-tune your speech.** Practice in front of a mirror and with friends and family. Smoothly integrate the visuals with the speech. Ask for feedback and suggestions.

Delivering the Speech

1. **Look at your audience.** As you deliver your speech and display the visuals you have created, focus on different people throughout the room. This will show your audience that you are addressing everyone, even people who may not agree with your stance on the issue.

2. **Make your voice, facial expressions, and gestures work for you.** Vary your pace, tone of voice, and volume to hold your audience's attention and emphasize your points. Augment your message with appropriate facial expressions and gestures. For example, you might frown slightly when describing an opposing argument.

3. **Stay relaxed and responsive to audience reactions.** Remind yourself to stand naturally and speak slowly. Calmly respond to talking or fidgeting in the audience by picking up the pace or speaking more loudly and clearly.

See page R82: Evaluate a Persuasive Speech

Reading Comprehension

DIRECTIONS *Read these selections and answer the questions that follow.*

from Defense of the Constitutions of Government in Massachusetts During the Revolution

John Adams

   It is become a kind of fashion among writers, to admit, as a maxim, that if you could be always sure of a wise, active, and virtuous prince, monarchy would be the best of governments. But this is so far from being admissible, that it will forever remain true, that a free government has a great advantage over a simple monarchy. The best and wisest prince, by means of a freer communication with his people, and the greater opportunities to collect the best advice from the best of his subjects, would have an immense advantage in a free state over a monarchy. A senate consisting of all that is most noble, wealthy, and able in the nation, with a right to counsel the crown at all times, is a check to ministers, and a security
10 against abuses, such as a body of nobles who never meet, and have no such right, can never supply. Another assembly, composed of representatives chosen by the people in all parts, gives free access to the whole nation, and communicates all its wants, knowledge, projects, and wishes to government; it excites emulation among all classes, removes complaints, redresses grievances, affords opportunities of exertion to genius, though in obscurity, and gives full scope to all the faculties of man; it opens a passage for every speculation to the legislature, to administration, and to the public; it gives a universal energy to the human character, in every part of the state, such as never can be obtained in a monarchy.
   There is a third particular which deserves attention both from governments
20 and people. In a simple monarchy, the ministers of state can never know their friends from their enemies; secret cabals undermine their influence, and blast their reputation. This occasions a jealousy ever anxious and irritated, which never thinks the government safe without an encouragement of informers and spies, throughout every part of the state, who interrupt the tranquillity of private life, destroy the confidence of families in their own domestics and in one another, and poison freedom in its sweetest retirements. In a free government, on the contrary, the ministers can have no enemies of consequence but among the members of the great or little council, where every man is obliged to take his side, and declare his opinion, upon every question. This circumstance alone, to every manly mind,
30 would be sufficient to decide the preference in favor of a free government.

from Boston Tea Party

George Hewes

It was now evening, and I immediately dressed myself in the costume of an Indian, equipped with a small hatchet, which I and my associates denominated the tomahawk, with which, and a club, after having painted my face and hands with coal dust in the shop of a blacksmith, I repaired to Griffin's wharf, where the ships lay that contained the tea. When I first appeared in the street after being thus disguised, I fell in with many who were dressed, equipped and painted as I was, and who fell in with me and marched in order to the place of our destination. . . .

We then were ordered by our commander to open the hatches and take out all the chests of tea and throw them overboard, and we immediately proceeded to
10 execute his orders, first cutting and splitting the chests with our tomahawks, so as thoroughly to expose them to the effects of the water.

In about three hours from the time we went on board, we had thus broken and thrown overboard every tea chest to be found in the ship, while those in the other ships were disposing of the tea in the same way, at the same time. We were surrounded by British armed ships, but no attempt was made to resist us.

We then quietly retired to our several places of residence, without having any conversation with each other, or taking any measures to discover who were our associates; nor do I recollect of our having had the knowledge of the name of a single individual concerned in that affair, except that of Leonard Pitt, the
20 commander of my division, whom I have mentioned. There appeared to be an understanding that each individual should volunteer his services, keep his own secret, and risk the consequence for himself. No disorder took place during that transaction, and it was observed at that time that the stillest night ensued that Boston had enjoyed for many months. . . .

Another attempt was made to save a little tea from the ruins of the cargo by a tall, aged man who wore a large cocked hat and white wig, which was fashionable at that time. He had sleightly slipped a little into his pocket, but being detected, they seized him and, taking his hat and wig from his head, threw them, together with the tea, of which they had emptied his pockets, into the water. In
30 consideration of his advanced age, he was permitted to escape, with now and then a slight kick.

The next morning, after we had cleared the ships of the tea, it was discovered that very considerable quantities of it were floating upon the surface of the water; and to prevent the possibility of any of its being saved for use, a number of small

GO ON ➤

boats were manned by sailors and citizens, who rowed them into those parts of the harbor wherever the tea was visible, and by beating it with oars and paddles so thoroughly drenched it as to render its entire destruction inevitable.

Comprehension

DIRECTIONS *Answer these questions about the excerpt from "Defense of the Constitutions of Government in Massachusetts During the Revolution."*

1. Which position on government does Adams favor?

   A Monarchies are the best form of government because they have wise and virtuous rulers.

   B Writers should be consulted when a country forms its government because they are well informed.

   C A free state is the best form of government because its ideas and opinions come from the people.

   D Only the best and wisest prince who communicates with his subjects should rule a nation.

2. The words *enemies, informers,* and *spies* in lines 20–26 appeal to the emotion of

   A excitement   C anger

   B fear   D guilt

3. Which claim does Adams make about a free government in lines 26–29?

   A The best way to run a free government is with a large assembly and a small one.

   B Members of a free government often take a tough-minded approach to governing.

   C People who serve in a free government often express strong opinions.

   D The leaders in a free government usually have few hidden enemies.

4. "Every manly mind" in line 29 is an example of which persuasive technique?

   A an appeal by association

   B an appeal to authority

   C an ethical appeal

   D loaded language

5. Which quote contains loaded language?

   A "monarchy would be the best of governments" (lines 2–3)

   B "such as a body of nobles who never meet" (line 10)

   C "gives free access to the whole nation" (line 12)

   D "poison freedom in its sweetest retirements" (line 26)

6. This excerpt reflects the view of colonists who

   A believed that political rivalries would destroy the British monarchy

   B questioned British rule and tried to form a new government

   C upheld the ideals of a monarchy

   D had simple ideas about government

DIRECTIONS *Answer these questions about the excerpt from "Boston Tea Party."*

7. Which descriptive details most clearly place this account in its historical context?

   A tomahawk, chests of tea, coal dust

   B armed ships, hatches, small boats

   C evening, three hours, next morning

   D sailors, citizens, aged man

8. This narrative is a primary source because it is

   A a political argument

   B a participant's report

   C an accurate history

   D a published document

9. This account by a colonial shoemaker calls attention to

   A an alliance between Native Americans and tradespeople

   B a lack of leadership during the Revolutionary War

   C the tension between wealthy and poor people in the colonies

   D the role of the common people in the Revolution

10. The colonists most likely dressed as Native Americans to

   A honor Native American traditions

   B forge an alliance against the British

   C protect themselves from the British

   D cause economic problems in the colonies

11. The descriptive anecdote in lines 25–31 suggests that

   A tea was a prized commodity among the colonists in Boston

   B the elderly were treated with disrespect in colonial times

   C many participants thought the Boston Tea Party was amusing

   D violent attacks were characteristic of the Boston Tea Party

12. The descriptive details in this account emphasize that the Boston Tea Party was

   A poorly planned

   B carried out in secret

   C led by Native Americans

   D authorized by the British

DIRECTIONS *Answer this question about both selections.*

13. Both primary sources give the reader insight into the

   A origins of the United States

   B benefits of a constitution

   C advantages of a monarchy

   D fashions of the period

Written Response

SHORT RESPONSE *Write three or four sentences to answer this question.*

14. Cite three details from George Hewes's account that identify it as a primary source.

EXTENDED RESPONSE *Write two or three paragraphs to answer this question.*

15. What argument does John Adams make in lines 11–18 in favor of an assembly of representatives? Cite three reasons he gives to support his argument.

Vocabulary

DIRECTIONS *Use context clues and your knowledge of specialized vocabulary to answer the following questions about political words in the excerpt from "Defense of the Constitutions of Government in Massachusetts During the Revolution."*

1. What is the most likely meaning of the word *monarchy* as it is used in line 2?

   "It is become a kind of fashion among writers, to admit, as a maxim, that if you could be always sure of a wise, active, and virtuous prince, <u>monarchy</u> would be the best of governments."

   A a state headed by a leader who usually rules by hereditary right

   B a body of elected officials who hold the supreme power in a nation

   C a small group of persons or a family who rule together

   D a government that shares power with the people

2. What is the most likely meaning of the word *cabals* as it is used in line 21?

   " . . . secret <u>cabals</u> undermine their influence, and blast their reputation."

   A social clubs

   B religious denominations

   C groups of conspirators

   D military organizations

3. What is the most likely meaning of the word *ministers* as it is used in line 27?

   "In a free government, on the contrary, the <u>ministers</u> can have no enemies of consequence. . . ."

   A church leaders   **C** foreign diplomats

   B public officials   **D** business tycoons

DIRECTIONS *Use context clues and your knowledge of multiple-meaning words to answer the following questions based on the excerpt from "Boston Tea Party."*

4. Which meaning of the word *execute* is used in line 10?

   " . . . and we immediately proceeded to <u>execute</u> his orders, first cutting and splitting the chests with our tomahawks, so as thoroughly to expose them to the effects of the water."

   A create

   B carry out

   C kill

   D validate

5. Which meaning of the word *several* is used in line 16?

   "We then quietly retired to our <u>several</u> places of residence. . . ."

   A same

   B separate

   C small number of

   D more than two or three

6. Which meaning of the word *measures* is used in line 17?

   " . . . without having any conversation with each other, or taking any <u>measures</u> to discover who were our associates . . ."

   A actions

   B dimensions

   C quantities

   D legislative bills

Writing & Grammar

DIRECTIONS *Read this passage and answer the questions that follow.*

(1) George Washington hired engineer Pierre L'Enfant to plan a new capital city. (2) The new capital would be called Federal City and would be located in Maryland. (3) L'Enfant was later fired. (4) Surveyor Andrew Ellicott redrew the plans but upheld much of L'Enfant's vision. (5) By 1800, President John Adams had moved into the White House. (6) It was far from finished. (7) It was damp. (8) The city was later renamed. (9) Today, Washington, D.C., reflects L'Enfant's vision of a city of open space.

1. How might you rewrite sentence 1 by using an adverb clause?

   A George Washington hired engineer Pierre L'Enfant to plan a new capital city, which would be situated between two rivers.

   B In 1791, George Washington hired engineer Pierre L'Enfant to plan a new capital city.

   C When George Washington decided to establish a new capital city in 1791, he hired engineer Pierre L'Enfant to do the planning.

   D Excited about the prospect of a new capital city, George Washington hired engineer Pierre L'Enfant to plan it.

2. How might you combine sentences 3 and 4 to form a compound-complex sentence?

   A L'Enfant was later fired, but when surveyor Andrew Ellicott redrew the plans, he upheld much of L'Enfant's vision.

   B L'Enfant was later fired, and surveyor Andrew Ellicott redrew the plans but upheld much of L'Enfant's vision.

   C When redrawing the plans, surveyor Andrew Ellicott upheld much of L'Enfant's vision, even though L'Enfant was fired.

   D Much of L'Enfant's vision was upheld by surveyor Andrew Ellicott, who redrew the plans after L'Enfant was fired.

3. How might you combine sentences 5 and 6 to form a complex sentence?

   A By 1800, President John Adams had moved into the White House, even though it was far from finished.

   B By 1800, President John Adams had moved into the White House, but it was far from finished.

   C By 1800, President John Adams had moved into the White House; however, it was far from finished.

   D By 1800, President John Adams had moved into the White House; it was far from finished.

4. Identify a prepositional phrase that would add descriptive detail to the end of sentence 7.

   A and leaked incessantly

   B in many of the rooms

   C because the plaster was wet

   D and very musty

5. Identify a prepositional phrase that would add descriptive detail to the end of sentence 8.

   A even as it grew

   B to reflect Washington's involvement

   C Washington, D.C.

   D after Washington's death

STOP

Ideas for Independent Reading

Continue exploring the Questions of the Times on pages 16–17 with these additional works.

Who owns the LAND?

The Narrative of the Captivity and Restoration of Mrs. Mary Rowlandson
by Mary Rowlandson

In February 1676, during a land dispute called King Philip's War, a minister's wife named Mary Rowlandson was taken hostage by Wampanoag warriors. Packed with violence, cruelty, piety, and anger, Rowlandson's account of her three-month captivity became one of the first bestsellers in colonial America.

The Portable North American Indian Reader
edited by Fredrick W. Turner

As an introduction to the verbal art of Native Americans, this anthology has few equals. It includes myths, tales, poetry, and speeches from the many diverse Native American cultures who thrived before, during, and after contact with European explorers and settlers. Modern selections show how traditional Indian kinship with the land continues to the present day.

Finding the Center: The Art of the Zuni Storyteller
translated by Dennis Tedlock

Thought to have descended from the Anasazi, a cliff-dwelling people of 1,000 years ago, the Zuni of present-day New Mexico enjoy a rich oral heritage handed down from long before the first Europeans arrived. The folklorist Dennis Tedlock has collected, translated, and transcribed many key Zuni stories in this volume, placing the words on the page in a manner that mimics their oral performance.

What makes an EXPLORER?

The Four Voyages
by Christopher Columbus

In these journals and eyewitness accounts, Christopher Columbus comes across as a complex, driven, yet entirely understandable person. In place of the confident adventurer of story, we see a man of mixed motives, influenced equally by greed, religious passion, and scientific curiosity. These journals shed light on the impulses that pushed Columbus to make the most significant journeys of his time.

Love and Hate in Jamestown
by David Price

In 1607, 105 Englishmen arrived in what would become the Virginia settlement of Jamestown. They came seeking gold, a route to the Orient, and survivors from the lost Roanoke Colony. What they found instead were Native American people—some friendly, some brutally hostile—and day after day of challenges, hardship, and misery.

Voyages and Discoveries
by Richard Hakluyt

Early English explorers were a fascinating breed. These sailors were willing—even eager—to face unknown dangers for the sake of their country and the glory and adventure it would bring. Using ships' records, charts, and logs, Richard Hakluyt pulls together the stories of such adventurers as Sir Francis Drake, whose yen for exploration enabled the European settlement of America.

Are people basically GOOD?

The Diary and Life of Samuel Sewall
edited by Mel Yazawa

Samuel Sewall served as one of the judges in the Salem witchcraft trials, voting to hang 19 people for wholly imaginary offenses. Yet in his diary, we see another side of this forbidding figure. He wrestles with lingering guilt over his role in that public hysteria, feels remorse over the unfair treatment of the Indians, recalls the pleasures of food and marriage, and grieves bitterly over the loss of friends and family.

A Short Account of the Destruction of the Indies
by Bartolomé de Las Casas

A Spanish priest and missionary, Las Casas was appalled by the abuse and enslavement of Native Americans. He dedicated himself to their emancipation, returning to Spain to plead their case before the king, then going back to the New World to serve as their official protector.

Letters from an American Farmer
by Michel Guillaume Jean de Crèvecœur

Crèvecœur's "letters," originally written as essays, paint a mesmerizing portrait of a fertile country populated with rough-mannered yet skilled and kindhearted people. Crèvecœur addresses such difficult topics as the hardships of the frontier, the plight of women, and the evils of slavery. Yet such problems fade before his faith in the righteousness of American individualism.

Who has the right to RULE?

1776
by David McCullough

How did a ragtag group of farmers manage to defeat the world's most powerful army? That is the question historian David McCullough explores in this fascinating look at one pivotal year in our nation's history. Persistence, optimism, ingenuity, leadership, luck, and weather are the elements to which McCullough attributes the colonists' success in the Revolutionary War.

The Puritan Dilemma: The Story of John Winthrop
by Edmund S. Morgan

As the leader of Massachusetts Bay Colony for nearly 20 years, John Winthrop spent his life combining religious devotion with power politics. This biography shines a spotlight upon issues that mattered most to Winthrop: the relationship between individual liberties and community harmony, and the legitimacy of political authority.

The Adams-Jefferson Letters
edited by Lester J. Cappon

Divided by political party and regional affiliation, Thomas Jefferson of Virginia and John Adams of Massachusetts were united in their love of country and their concern for the future of democracy. This collection of letters, including contributions by Abigail Adams (John Adams's gifted wife), touches upon virtually every major issue that faced the young republic.

UNIT 2

Preview Unit Goals

LITERARY ANALYSIS
- Understand romanticism as a literary movement
- Identify elements of transcendentalism
- Identify and analyze blank verse
- Identify and examine stanza, rhyme scheme, and meter
- Analyze elements used to create mood
- Identify and evaluate sound devices and imagery
- Interpret symbol and allegory
- Identify and analyze satire and unity of effect
- Analyze elements of an essay

READING
- Paraphrase main ideas; summarize information; take notes
- Clarify meaning of archaic vocabulary; examine complex sentences

WRITING AND GRAMMAR
- Write a reflective essay
- Use rhetorical questions
- Identify and use parallelism and adjective clauses
- Use imperative sentences and dashes

SPEAKING, LISTENING, AND VIEWING
- Conduct an interview
- Analyze how meaning is conveyed in visual media

VOCABULARY
- Use knowledge of word roots and affixes to determine word meaning
- Research word origins

ACADEMIC VOCABULARY
- romanticism
- allegory
- blank verse
- symbol
- satire
- transcendentalism

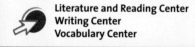

Literature and Reading Center
Writing Center
Vocabulary Center

American Romanticism

Nathaniel
Hawthorne

1800–1855
CELEBRATING THE INDIVIDUAL

- The Early Romantics
- The Transcendentalists
- The Fireside Poets
- American Gothic

UNIT 2

Questions of the Times

DISCUSS In small groups or as a class, discuss the following questions. Then read on to learn how writers—and other Americans—grappled with these issues during the **American romantic** period.

Is the price of progress ever TOO HIGH?

During the romantic period, America seemed limitless—new frontiers were being explored every day, and inventions advanced both farming and industry. Yet to many people, life felt frantic and soulless. Is progress always worth its price?

Is it patriotic to protest one's GOVERNMENT?

Democracy was flourishing in the early 19th century and citizens felt optimistic about their country. Yet the problems of the age—slavery, women's disenfranchisement, the mistreatment of workers—were severe, and protestors agitated for change. What role do you think activism plays in a democracy? Under what circumstances, if any, should citizens lose their right to protest?

Does everyone have a "DARK SIDE"?

Although most romantic writers reflected the optimism of their times, some pondered the darker side of human nature. Edgar Allan Poe, for example, conjectured that in extreme situations people would reveal their true, evil natures. Do you think everyone has a dark side? What might make the dark side prevail?

Where do people look for TRUTH?

To escape the materialism and hectic pace of industrialization, many writers of the age turned to nature and to the self for simplicity, truth, and beauty. In earlier centuries, people had looked to reason or to God for answers. Where do you think people turn to make sense of their lives today?

American Romanticism
1800–1855

Celebrating
the Individual

*Patriotic and individualistic,
urban and untamed, wealthy and
enslaved—Americans in the first half
of the 19th century embodied a host
of contradictions. Struggling to make
sense of their complex, inconsistent
society, writers of the period turned
inward for a sense of truth. Their
movement, known as romanticism,
explored the glories of the individual
spirit, the beauty of nature, and the
possibilities of the imagination.*

Romanticism: Historical Context

KEY IDEAS Historical forces clearly shaped the literature of the American romantic period. Writers responded—positively and negatively—to the country's astonishing growth and to the booming Industrial Revolution.

The Spirit of Exploration

WESTWARD EXPANSION Writers of the romantic period were witness to a period of great growth and opportunity for the young American nation. With that growth, however, came a price. In 1803, the Louisiana Purchase doubled the country's size. In the years that followed, explorers and settlers pushed farther and farther west. Settlers moved for largely practical reasons: to make money and to gain land. But each bit of land settled by white Americans was taken from Native American populations who had lived there for generations. The Indian Removal Act of 1830, for example, required Native Americans to relocate west. As whites invaded their homelands, many Native Americans saw no choice but to comply. And those who did not were simply—and often brutally—forced to leave.

Toward the middle of the century, Americans embraced the notion of **"manifest destiny"**—the idea that it was the destiny of the United States to expand to the Pacific Ocean and into Mexican territory. Mexicans disagreed, of course. When Texas was annexed from Mexico by the United States in 1845, it set off the Mexican-American War. Many Americans, including writer **Henry David Thoreau,** found the war to be immoral—a war fought mainly to expand slavery. "Can there not be a government," he wrote, "in which majorities do not virtually decide right and wrong, but conscience?" In the end, the United States defeated Mexico and, through treaties and subsequent land purchases from the Mexican government, established the current borders of the 48 contiguous United States.

Growth of Industry

The stories and essays of the romantic period reflect an enormous shift in the attitudes and working habits of many Americans. When the War of 1812 interrupted trade with the British, Americans were suddenly forced to produce many of the goods they had previously imported. The **Industrial Revolution** began, changing the country from a largely agrarian economy to an industrial powerhouse.

The factory system changed the way of life for many Americans, but not always for the better. People left their farms for the cities, working long hours for low wages in harsh conditions. In addition, Northeastern textile mills' demand for cotton played a role in the expansion of slavery in the South. Writers of this period reacted to the negative effects of industrialization—the commercialism, hectic pace, and lack of conscience—by turning to nature and to the self for simplicity, truth, and beauty.

▶ **TAKING NOTES**

Outlining As you read this introduction, use an outline to record the main ideas about the characteristics and the literature of the period. You can use article headings, boldfaced terms, and the information in these boxes as starting points. (See page R49 in the **Research Handbook** for more help with outlining.)

I. *Historical Context*
   A. *Spirit of Exploration*
      1. *Westward Expansion*
      2. *Manifest Destiny*
   B. *Growth of Industry*

ADDITIONAL BACKGROUND For more on the American romantic period, visit the **Literature Center** at ClassZone.com.

Cultural Influences

KEY IDEAS Many romantic writers were outspoken in their support for human rights. Their works created awareness of the injustice of slavery and called for reform in many other areas as well.

This antislavery medal was created to help grow support for the abolition movement.

The Tragedy of Slavery

From 1793 to 1860, cotton production rose greatly, due to the invention of the cotton gin and other farming machinery. So did the number of enslaved workers. Plantation owners were the wealthiest and most powerful people in the South, yet they were relatively few in number. Most Southern farmers held few or no slaves, but they aspired to. They felt that slavery had become necessary for increasing profits.

For slaves, life was brutal. Field workers—men, women, and children—rose before dawn and worked in the fields until bedtime. Many were beaten or otherwise abused. And worst of all, family members were sold away from one another. Often family members attempted to escape to be with one another again. Unfortunately, escapes were rarely successful.

Tension over slavery increased between the North and the South. Many in the North saw slavery as immoral and worked to have it abolished. Others worried as the balance of power between free and slave states shifted with each new state entering the Union. Romantic poets **James Russell Lowell** and **John Greenleaf Whittier** wrote abolitionist journalism and poetry, and even **Henry Wadsworth Longfellow** published a volume of antislavery poems. Perhaps the greatest social achievement of the romantics was to create awareness of slavery's cruelty.

> **A Voice from the Times**
>
> *Men! Whose boast it is that ye*
> *Come of fathers brave and free,*
> *If there breathe on earth a slave,*
> *Are ye truly free and brave?*
> *If ye do not feel the chain,*
> *When it works a brother's pain,*
> *Are ye not base slaves indeed,*
> *Slaves unworthy to be freed?*
>
> —James Russell Lowell
> *from* "Stanzas on Freedom"

Call for Social Reform

By the mid-19th century, many Americans had joined together to fight slavery and the other social ills of the time. Many leading writers of the romantic movement were outspoken in their support for human rights. **William Cullen Bryant** and **James Russell Lowell,** for example, were prominent abolitionists who also supported workers' and women's rights.

The abolition movement began by advocating resettlement of blacks in Africa. But most enslaved African Americans had been born and raised in the United States and resented the idea of being forced to leave. Instead, white and black abolitionists (including women) began to join together to work for emancipation. They formed societies, spoke at conventions, published newspapers, and swamped Congress with petitions to end slavery.

In the 1830s and 1840s, workers began to agitate as well, protesting low wages and deteriorating working conditions. Many struck, but few were successful—a large pool of immigrants was always ready to take their places. Still, workers began forming unions, and slowly conditions improved.

Women in the early 19th century found much to protest. They could neither vote nor sit on juries. Their education rarely extended beyond elementary school. When they married, their property and money became their husband's. Many even lacked guardianship rights over their children. Throughout this period, women worked for change, gathering in 1848 at Seneca Falls, New York, to continue their long fight for women's rights.

Ideas of the Age

KEY IDEAS Reflecting the optimism of their growing country, American romantic writers forged a national literature for the very first time. Yet sectionalism threatened to tear the nation apart.

Nationalism vs. Sectionalism

In the early 1800s, many Supreme Court decisions strengthened the federal government's power over the states. At the same time, Secretary of State John Quincy Adams established a foreign policy guided by **nationalism**—the belief that national interests should be placed ahead of regional concerns or the interests of other countries. Reflecting the national pride and optimism of the American people, writers of this age forged a literature entirely the nation's own. For the first time, writers were not imitating their European counterparts, but were listening to their own voices and writing with a distinctly American accent.

However, this new spirit of nationalism was challenged by the question of slavery. Up until 1818, the United States had consisted of ten free and ten slave states. As new territories tried to enter the Union, the North and South wrangled over the balance of power between free and slave states. Economic interests also challenged nationalism. Tariffs on manufactured goods from Britain forced Southerners to buy more expensive, Northern-manufactured goods. From the South's point of view, the North was getting rich at the South's expense. Sectionalism, or the placing of the interests of one's own region ahead of the nation as a whole, began to take hold.

The Hudson River School

The paintings on pages 296 and 300 are excellent examples of the works of the Hudson River School artists. This group of landscape painters flourished between 1825 and 1870. The artists knew one another and used similar techniques for portraying nature scenes.

American Style Thomas Cole painted *A View of the Mountain Pass Called the Notch of the White Mountains* (1839), shown here and on page 293. He and the other Hudson River artists created passionate wilderness scenes that appealed to the imagination and made earlier American landscapes seem weak and unobserved. Like the American romantic writers of the time, the Hudson River School artists made a conscious effort to create an American style—one based on nature and the emotions.

Real-Life Inspiration The painting shown in detail here has an interesting history. Author Nathaniel Hawthorne wrote a short story about a real-life landslide at Crawford Notch that took the lives of nine people. The story may have piqued Cole's interest in the scene. In the painting Cole highlights the insignificance and vulnerability of the human figures in the face of the coming storm. One barely notices the settlers' homes or the rider, who seems oblivious to the ominous clouds gathering at the upper left—hinting of disaster to come.

Romantic Literature

KEY IDEAS Themes of individualism and nature unified the writing of the American romantic movement, despite dramatic differences in the writers' focus and style.

The Early Romantics

The early American romantic writers may have been influenced more by the literature of another continent than by that of their own. **Romanticism** had first emerged in Europe in the late 18th century, in reaction to the neoclassicism of the period that had preceded it. Where neoclassical writers admired and imitated classical forms, the romantics looked to nature for inspiration. Where neoclassicists valued reason, the romantics celebrated emotions and the imagination. The first American romantic writers grew

▶ *For Your Outline*

THE EARLY ROMANTICS

- were inspired by the beauty of nature
- emphasized emotions and the imagination over reason
- celebrated the individual spirit

Kindred Spirits (1849), Asher B. Durand. © Francis G. Mayer/Corbis.

ANALYZE VISUALS
This painting is a memorial to painter Asher B. Durand's friend and fellow Hudson River School artist Thomas Cole (here shown with romantic poet William Cullen Bryant).

Although Durand was influenced by Cole, his works express stillness and a realistic imitation of nature, in contrast to Cole's more expressive rendering. Compare this painting with Cole's on the previous page. How are they similar? How are they different?

A collection of major works by early American romantics

out of this European tradition, shaping and molding it to fit their unique American identity. They too were reacting to what had come before—the rationality of the Age of Reason and the strict doctrines of Puritanism.

Indeed, much had changed since the Puritan era in America, and the writers of the early romantic period reflected the more modern sensibilities of their day. As the U.S. population exploded and the country's borders moved westward, American writers aimed to capture the energy and character of their growing country. They saw the limits of reason and instead celebrated the glories of the individual spirit, the emotions, and the imagination as basic elements of human nature. The splendors of nature inspired the romantics more than the fear of God, and some of them felt a fascination with the supernatural.

William Cullen Bryant's 1817 poem "Thanatopsis" went a long way toward establishing romanticism as the major force in the literature of mid-19th century America. Bryant followed the trend of the English romantics by celebrating nature in his work. Romanticism was not only a movement in poetry, however. **Washington Irving,** the first American writer esteemed abroad, pioneered the short story as a literary form. He put America on the literary map and also influenced other writers, particularly Nathaniel Hawthorne. **James Fenimore Cooper** is remembered for writing the first truly original American novel. He celebrated the American spirit in all his frontier novels, known as *The Leatherstocking Tales.* The early romantic writers were the pioneers of America's national literature, setting the course for those who would follow.

A Voice from the Times

To him who in the love of Nature holds
Communion with her visible forms, she speaks
A various language; for his gayer hours
She has a voice of gladness, and a smile
And eloquence of beauty, and she glides
Into his darker musings, with a mild
And healing sympathy, that steals away
Their sharpness, ere he is aware. . . .

—William Cullen Bryant
from "Thanatopsis"

The legendary Hiawatha, memorialized in Longfellow's poem "The Song of Hiawatha"

The Fireside Poets

Other writers influential in forging an American literature were the Fireside Poets, a group of New England poets whose work was morally uplifting and romantically engaging. The group's name came from the family custom of reading poetry aloud beside a fire, a common form of entertainment in the 19th century. With the Fireside Poets, the poetry of American writers was, for the first time, on equal footing with that of their British counterparts.

Henry Wadsworth Longfellow, the best-known member of the group, stressed individualism and an appreciation of nature in his work. His poems took for their subject matter the more colorful aspects of America's past. "Evangeline," for example, tells of lovers who are separated during the French and Indian War, while "The Song of Hiawatha" takes its themes from Native American folklore. Longfellow's fame was so great that after his death, he was honored with a plaque in Poets' Corner of Westminster Abbey in London—the only American poet ever to receive such an honor.

The other Fireside Poets, **James Russell Lowell, Oliver Wendell Holmes,** and **John Greenleaf Whittier,** were strongly committed to using poetry to bring about social reform. They were interested in such issues as abolition, women's rights, improvement of factory conditions, and temperance. They also championed the common person—perhaps as an outgrowth of the form of democracy that had been sweeping the land since President Jackson took office in 1829. Jackson had crusaded against control of the government by the wealthy and promised to look out for the interests of common people. One can see this regard for the common person in the work of Whittier, for example, who wrote of farmers, lumbermen, migrants, and the poor.

> ▶ *For Your Outline*
>
> **THE FIRESIDE POETS**
>
> - emphasized moral themes in work
> - were viewed as equals of British poets of the day
> - stressed individualism and an appreciation of nature
> - were committed to social reform

The Transcendentalists

By the mid-1800s, Americans were taking new pride in their emerging culture. **Ralph Waldo Emerson,** a New England writer, nurtured this pride. Emerson led a group practicing **transcendentalism**—a philosophical and literary movement that emphasized living a simple life and celebrating the truth found in nature and in personal emotion and imagination. Exalting the dignity of the individual, the transcendentalist stressed American ideas of optimism, freedom, and self-reliance.

The term transcendentalism came from Immanuel Kant, a German philosopher who wrote of "transcendent forms" of knowledge that exist beyond reason and experience. Emerson gave this philosophy a peculiarly American spin: he said that every individual is capable of discovering this higher truth on his or her own, through intuition. The transcendentalists believed that people are inherently good and should follow their own beliefs, however different these beliefs may be from the norm. Both Emerson's essay "Self-Reliance" and **Henry David Thoreau's** "Civil Disobedience" address this faith in the integrity of the individual.

Not surprisingly, a major target for the transcendentalists' criticism was their Puritan heritage, with its emphasis on material prosperity and rigid obedience to the laws of society. The transcendentalists disliked the commercial, financial side of American life and stressed instead spiritual well-being, achieved through intellectual activity and a close relationship to nature. Thoreau put his beliefs into practice by building a small cabin on Walden Pond and living there for two years, writing and studying nature.

Transcendental ideas lived on in American culture in the works of later poets such as Walt Whitman, Robert Frost, and Wallace Stevens and through the civil rights movement of the 20th century. In the short term, however, transcendentalists' optimism began to fade when confronted with the persistence of slavery and the difficulty in abolishing it.

▶ *For Your Outline*

THE TRANSCENDENTALISTS

- emphasized living a simple life
- stressed a close relationship to nature
- celebrated emotions and the imagination
- stressed individualism and self-reliance
- believed intuition can lead to knowledge
- believed in the inherent goodness of people
- encouraged spiritual well-being over financial well-being

A replica of Thoreau's 10-by-15-foot cabin on the shore of Walden Pond

A Voice from the Times

Go confidently in the direction of your dreams! Live the life you've imagined. As you simplify your life, the laws of the universe will be simpler.

—Henry David Thoreau

American Gothic: The "Brooding" Romantics

Not all American romantics were optimistic or had faith in the innate goodness of humankind, however. Three other giants from this period, **Edgar Allan Poe, Nathaniel Hawthorne,** and **Herman Melville** are what have been called **"brooding" romantics** or **"anti-transcendentalists."** Theirs is a complex philosophy, filled with dark currents and a deep awareness of the human capacity for evil. While Irving had been satisfied if his work kept "mankind in good humor with one another," Hawthorne, Melville, and Poe were haunted by a darker vision of human existence. Their stories are characterized by a probing of the inner life of their characters, and examination of the complex and often mysterious forces that motivate human behavior. They are romantic, however, in their emphasis on emotion, nature, the individual, and the unusual.

EXPLORING THE DARKNESS Poe and Hawthorne, and to a lesser extent Melville, used **gothic** elements such as grotesque characters, bizarre situations, and violent events in their fiction. The gothic tradition had begun in Europe, perhaps inspired by the gothic architecture of the Middle Ages. European writers of the 19th century, such as Mary Shelley, author of *Frankenstein,* delighted readers with their deliciously creepy accounts of monsters, vampires, and humans with a large capacity for evil. The romantic movement itself also gave rise to gothic literature. Once the romantics freed the imagination from the restrictions of reason, they could follow it wherever it might go. For the dark romantics, the imagination led to the threshold of the unknown—that shadowy region where the fantastic, the demonic, and the insane reside.

Edgar Allan Poe, of course, was the master of the gothic form in the United States. He explored human psychology from the inside, using first-person narrators who were sometimes criminal or even insane. His plots involved extreme situations—not just murder, but live burials, physical and mental torture, and retribution from beyond the grave.

Nathaniel Hawthorne agreed with the romantic emphasis on emotion and the individual. However, he did not see these as completely positive forces. His works, such as *The Scarlet Letter* and "The Minister's Black Veil," examine the darker facets of the human soul—for example, the psychological effects sin and guilt may have on human life.

Herman Melville's early works were mostly adventure stories set in the South Pacific. *Moby Dick,* however, departed from that pattern. By concentrating on a ship's captain's obsessive quest for the whale that took his leg, Melville explores such issues as madness and the conflict of good and evil. Later, in "Bartleby the Scrivener," Melville

> ▶ *For Your Outline*
>
> **AMERICAN GOTHIC: THE "BROODING" ROMANTICS**
>
> - did not believe in the innate goodness of people
> - explored the human capacity for evil
> - probed the inner life of characters
> - explored characters' motivations
> - agreed with romantic emphasis on emotion, nature, and the individual
> - included elements of fantasy and the supernatural in works

> ## A Voice from the Times
>
> *I looked upon the scene before me—upon the mere house, and the simple landscape features of the domain—upon the bleak walls—upon the vacant eye-like windows—upon a few rank sedges—and upon a few white trunks of decayed trees—with an utter depression of soul which I can compare to no earthly sensation more properly than to the after-dream of the reveller upon opium—the bitter lapse into every-day life—the hideous dropping off of the veil.*
>
> **—Edgar Allan Poe**
> *from* "The Fall of the House of Usher"

Like an Open-Doored Marble Tomb, George Klauba. Acrylic on panel, 18″ × 14.5″. Courtesy Ann Nathan Gallery, Chicago. © George Klamba.

reveals the dark side of material prosperity by exploring how the struggle for material gain affects the individual.

Perhaps the dark vision of Hawthorne, Melville, and Poe foreshadowed the tumult and tragedy that was soon to erupt in civil war in America. There is no question that these three writers profoundly affected the development of the American literary voice throughout the remainder of the 19th century.

Connecting Literature, History, and Culture

Use this timeline and the questions on the next page to gain insight about how developments during the American romantic period reflected what was happening in the world as a whole.

AMERICAN LITERARY MILESTONES

1800

1806 Noah Webster's first dictionary is published. It includes 5,000 words related to American customs that have never before been collected.

1809 Washington Irving publishes *A History of New York*, satirizing the young nation.

1810

1817 "Thanatopsis," composed by William Cullen Bryant at age 18, is published in *The North American Review.* ▼

1820

1824 Irving's "The Devil and Tom Walker" is published.

1826 James Fenimore Cooper writes *The Last of the Mohicans*.

1827 *Freedom's Journal,* the first African-American newspaper, is founded. ▼

FREEDOM'S JOURNAL.

HISTORICAL CONTEXT

1800

1803 Thomas Jefferson doubles ▲ the country's size by buying Louisiana Territory from France.

1807 Robert Fulton launches *Clermont,* the first steamboat.

1808 United States bans slave trade.

1810

1812 United States declares war ▲ on Great Britain. American industry booms.

1815 Quaker Levi Coffin establishes the Underground Railroad.

1820

1820 Missouri Compromise prohibits slavery in western territories but allows slavery in Arkansas Territory and Louisiana.

1823 The Monroe Doctrine bans European colonization in the Americas.

1825 The Erie Canal is opened, linking Lake Erie with the Hudson River.

1828 Construction begins on the first railroad in the United States.

WORLD CULTURE AND EVENTS

1800

1804 Napoleon is crowned emperor of France.

1806 The Holy Roman Empire reaches its last days.

1807 British slave trade is abolished.

1810

1813 Jane Austen publishes *Pride and Prejudice*.

1816 Rossini writes the comic opera *The Barber of Seville*.

1819 Factory work is outlawed in England for children under nine years old.

1820

1821 Venezuela and Mexico declare independence from Spain. ▶

1823 Beethoven completes his Ninth Symphony.

1829 Slavery is abolished in Mexico.

MAKING CONNECTIONS

- Which European authors were contemporaries of American romantic writers?
- What evidence do you see that slavery was not only an American problem?
- What nations were battling for independence or dealing with its challenges?
- What inventions were moving the world into a more technological age?

1830

1835 Emerson, Thoreau, Margaret Fuller, and others form the Transcendental Club.

1838 Henry Wadsworth Longfellow's "A Psalm of Life" is published.

1839 Edgar Allan Poe's "The Fall of the House of Usher" is published.

1840

1845 Henry David Thoreau moves to Walden Pond.

1846 Herman Melville's first novel, *Typee,* is published. ▼

1850

1850 Nathaniel Hawthorne's *The Scarlet Letter* is published.

1851 Sojourner Truth delivers her "Ain't I a Woman?" speech to the Women's Rights Convention in Akron, Ohio. ▶

1852 Harriet Beecher Stowe publishes *Uncle Tom's Cabin.*

1830

1830 Indian Removal Act authorizes relocation of southeastern Native American tribes to territories west of Mississippi River.

1832 Samuel B. Morse invents the telegraph. ▼

1840

1845 Florida and Texas become the 27th and 28th states.

1848 Gold discoveries in California lead to first gold rush. ▼

1850

1850 Congress passes the Fugitive Slave Act, forcing officials in Northern states to return escaped slaves to their owners.

1851 Isaac Singer devises the sewing machine. ▼

1830

1838 Slaves mutiny aboard the ▲ Spanish ship *Amistad.*

1840

1843 Charles Dickens writes *A Christmas Carol.*

1847 Emily Brontë publishes *Wuthering Heights.*

1848 Karl Marx and Friedrich Engels publish *The Communist Manifesto.*

1850

1852 Dr. Livingston explores Zambesi.

1853 Verdi's opera *La Traviata* is first performed in Venice; Crimean War begins, involving Turkey, Russia, Britain, and France.

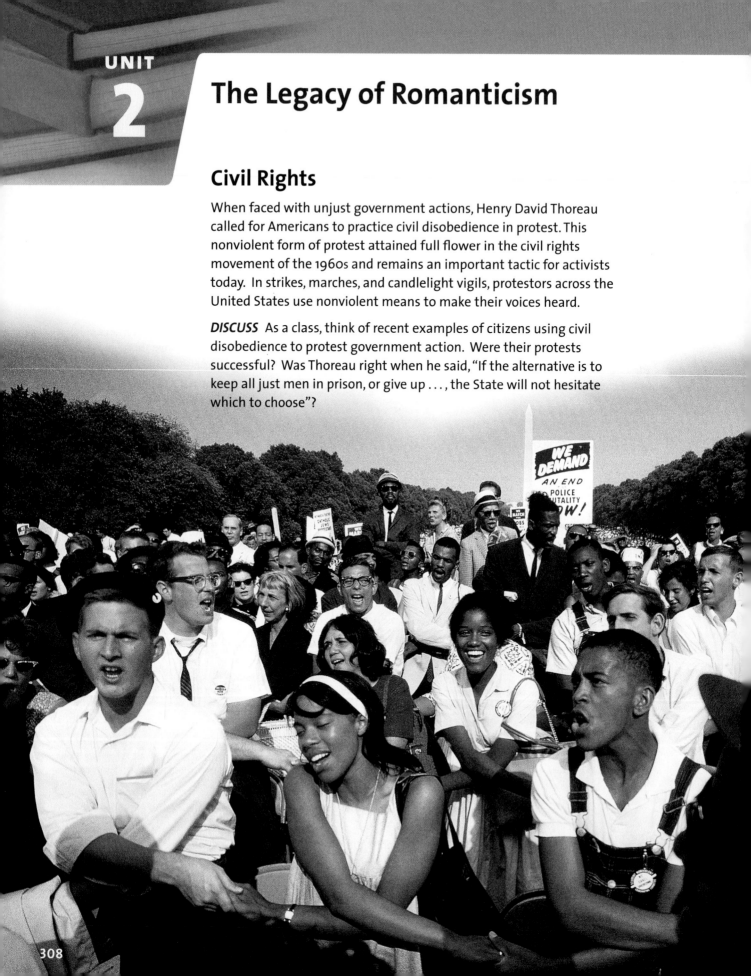

The Legacy of Romanticism

Civil Rights

When faced with unjust government actions, Henry David Thoreau called for Americans to practice civil disobedience in protest. This nonviolent form of protest attained full flower in the civil rights movement of the 1960s and remains an important tactic for activists today. In strikes, marches, and candlelight vigils, protestors across the United States use nonviolent means to make their voices heard.

DISCUSS As a class, think of recent examples of citizens using civil disobedience to protest government action. Were their protests successful? Was Thoreau right when he said, "If the alternative is to keep all just men in prison, or give up . . . , the State will not hesitate which to choose"?

Modern Gothic

The influence of Edgar Allan Poe is alive and well—make that undead and decaying—in the works of modern horror authors such as Stephen King and Anne Rice, and in many of the graphic novels lining today's bookstore shelves. Though their settings may be modern, these works share Poe's fascination with the dark side of humankind.

QUICKWRITE Why do you think people enjoy being frightened? Write a paragraph or two giving your reasons why so many people read gothic literature and enjoy films written in this same tradition.

The Romantic Hero

The romantic writers' focus on the individual led to the creation of a different kind of hero: unique, bold, sometimes brooding or eccentric. From the obsessed Captain Ahab, searching for his white whale in *Moby Dick,* to *The Last of the Mohicans'* noble Natty Bumppo, living on the fringes of society as both a white man and a Native American, romantic heroes were often larger than life, and always unforgettable. Their stories are still told today, and they have inspired a modern array of equally vivid characters.

CREATE With a small group, brainstorm a memorable hero for a new novel, TV show, or movie. Your hero should exemplify key aspects of the romantic spirit and must be utterly unique, a dynamic or mesmerizing individual who would capture people's imaginations.

Indiana Jones, from the movie *Raiders of the Lost Ark*, is a typical romantic hero.

The Devil and Tom Walker

Short Story by Washington Irving

Washington Irving
1783–1859

The Headless Horseman has thundered through readers' nightmares for nearly 200 years. Rip Van Winkle has been inspiring laughter for just as long. These characters, along with scores of others that populate his writing, helped make Washington Irving the first American writer to achieve an international reputation.

A Reluctant Lawyer Born when the nation was new and patriotism at its fiercest, Washington Irving was named for the country's first president. He began studying law at 16 but never showed much enthusiasm for it. He did, however, have a passion for writing, a playful mind, and keen powers of observation. "I was always fond of visiting new scenes and observing strange characters and manners," he once wrote. In 1807, he began publishing light satirical pieces about New York politics, culture, and theater.

Also Known As . . . In 1809, Irving penned *A History of New York from the Beginning of Time Through the End of the Dutch Dynasty,* a satire of both historical texts and the local politics they chronicled. It was considered a comic masterpiece, but for a time no one knew who had written it—the manuscript was said to have been left at an inn by an old lodger named Diedrich Knickerbocker. Knickerbocker was one of many eccentric narrators created by Irving, who didn't sign his own name to his works until he was over 40.

American Abroad In 1815, Irving began traveling through Europe, remaining there for 17 years. With the encouragement of Sir Walter Scott—the author of *Ivanhoe* and a fan of Irving's *History*—he began writing a series of stories that blended the legends of Europe with the tales he had heard while wandering as a young man through New York's Catskill Mountains and Hudson Valley. The stories, including both "The Legend of Sleepy Hollow" and "Rip Van Winkle," appeared in 1820 as *The Sketch-Book of Geoffrey Crayon, Gent.* The collection was wildly successful. However, in 1824, Irving published *Tales of a Traveller* (which contained "The Devil and Tom Walker"), and the book was not well received. In fact, the criticism was so harsh that Irving stopped writing fiction altogether.

Irving returned to America in 1832 to live with his brother on the Sunnyside estate. He died at the age of 76 and was buried near the haunting ground of his famous horseman—in New York's Sleepy Hollow Cemetery.

Sleepy Hollow Cemetery

● LITERARY ANALYSIS: SATIRE

Irving was a master of **satire,** a literary device in which people, customs, or institutions are ridiculed with the purpose of improving society. In this passage, Irving pokes fun at quarrelsome, complaining women:

> *. . . Though a female scold is generally considered to be a match for the devil, yet in this instance she appears to have had the worst of it.*

Satire is often subtle, so as you read, watch for its indicators: humor, exaggeration, absurd situations, and irony.

● READING SKILL: INTERPRET IMAGERY

Through the creative use of **imagery**—words and phrases that appeal to the five senses—Irving develops his characters and establishes mood.

> *. . . There lived near this place a meager, miserly fellow, of the name of Tom Walker. He had a wife as miserly as himself. . . . They lived in a forlorn-looking house that stood alone and had an air of starvation.*

As you read, use a chart like the one shown to record images that support the story's characterization and mood.

Images	Characterization	Mood
house with a look of starvation	Tom and his wife are miserly.	depressing

Review: **Make Inferences**

▲ VOCABULARY IN CONTEXT

The following words are critical to the story of a miser who would trade his soul for money. Check your understanding of each one by rewording the sentence in which it appears.

1. The **melancholy** sight of the graveyard chilled him.
2. The **persecution** of the Puritans went unchallenged.
3. The mention of gold awakened his **avarice.**
4. The corrupt **usurer** charged 20 percent interest.
5. **Speculating** in land deals held the promise of quick profits.
6. Hard economic times are **propitious** for moneylenders.
7. People who flaunt their wealth are guilty of **ostentation.**
8. He was a strict **censurer** of other people's vices.

Explore the Key Idea

Are you willing to
PAY ANY PRICE?

KEY IDEA People who'll stop at nothing to achieve wealth, success, or fame are often said to have "sold their soul." In other words, they have sacrificed something important—moral beliefs, privacy, family—in order to get what they want. Consider this kind of trade-off. Do you think it might ever be worth the **consequences?**

DISCUSS Working with a partner, list several people—real or fictional—who fit this profile. Then pick one such person and list his or her gains and their consequences. Assign a value to each item and decide whether, overall, the prize was worth the price. Share your conclusions with the rest of the class.

The DEVIL *and* Tom Walker

WASHINGTON IRVING

> **BACKGROUND** The story of Tom Walker is a variation on the legend of Faust, a 16th-century magician and astrologer who was said to have sold his soul to the devil for wisdom, money, and power. Washington Irving reinvented the tale, setting it in the 1720s in an area of New England settled by Quakers and Puritans. In Irving's comic retelling of the legend, the writer satirizes people who present a pious public image as they "sell their soul" for money.

A few miles from Boston in Massachusetts, there is a deep inlet, winding several miles into the interior of the country from Charles Bay, and terminating in a thickly wooded swamp or morass. On one side of this inlet is a beautiful dark grove; on the opposite side the land rises abruptly from the water's edge into a high ridge, on which grow a few scattered oaks of great age and immense size. Under one of these gigantic trees, according to old stories, there was a great amount of treasure buried by Kidd the pirate. The inlet allowed a facility to bring the money in a boat secretly and at night to the very foot of the hill; the elevation of the place permitted a good lookout to be kept that no one was at hand; while 10 the remarkable trees formed good landmarks by which the place might easily be found again. The old stories add, moreover, that the devil presided at the hiding of the money and took it under his guardianship; but this, it is well-known, he always does with buried treasure, particularly when it has been ill-gotten. Be that as it may, Kidd never returned to recover his wealth; being shortly after seized at Boston, sent out to England, and there hanged for a pirate. **A**

About the year 1727, just at the time that earthquakes were prevalent in New England, and shook many tall sinners down upon their knees, there lived near this place a meager, miserly fellow, of the name of Tom Walker. He had a wife as miserly as himself: they were so miserly that they even conspired to cheat each other.
20 Whatever the woman could lay hands on, she hid away; a hen could not cackle but she was on the alert to secure the new-laid egg. Her husband was continually prying about to detect her secret hoards, and many and fierce were the conflicts that took place about what ought to have been common property. They lived in a forlorn-looking house that stood alone and had an air of starvation. A few straggling savin trees, emblems of sterility, grew near it; no smoke ever curled from its chimney; no traveler stopped at its door. A miserable horse, whose ribs were as articulate as the bars of a gridiron,[1] stalked about a field, where a thin carpet of moss, scarcely covering the ragged beds of puddingstone,[2] tantalized and balked his hunger; and sometimes he would lean his head over the fence, look piteously
30 at the passerby and seem to petition deliverance from this land of famine. **B**

The house and its inmates had altogether a bad name. Tom's wife was a tall termagant,[3] fierce of temper, loud of tongue, and strong of arm. Her voice was often heard in wordy warfare with her husband; and his face sometimes showed signs that their conflicts were not confined to words. No one ventured, however, to interfere between them. The lonely wayfarer shrunk within himself at the horrid clamor and clapper-clawing;[4] eyed the den of discord askance;[5] and hurried on his way, rejoicing, if a bachelor, in his celibacy. **C**

One day that Tom Walker had been to a distant part of the neighborhood, he took what he considered a shortcut homeward, through the swamp. Like most
40 shortcuts, it was an ill-chosen route. The swamp was thickly grown with great gloomy pines and hemlocks, some of them ninety feet high, which made it dark at noonday, and a retreat for all the owls of the neighborhood. It was full of pits and quagmires, partly covered with weeds and mosses, where the green surface often betrayed the traveler into a gulf of black, smothering mud; there were also dark and stagnant pools, the abodes of the tadpole, the bullfrog, and the water snake; where the trunks of pines and hemlocks lay half-drowned, half-rotting, looking like alligators sleeping in the mire. **D**

Tom had long been picking his way cautiously through this treacherous forest; stepping from tuft to tuft of rushes and roots, which afforded precarious footholds
50 among deep sloughs; or pacing carefully, like a cat, along the prostrate trunks of trees; startled now and then by the sudden screaming of the bittern,[6] or the quacking of wild duck rising on the wind from some solitary pool. At length he arrived at a firm piece of ground, which ran out like a peninsula into the deep bosom of the swamp. It had been one of the strongholds of the Indians during their wars

---

B IMAGERY
Identify the images in lines 16–30 that help to characterize Tom and his wife. What **character traits** do these images reveal?

C SATIRE
In lines 31–37, Irving satirizes scolding women and the institution of marriage. What humorous details indicate this satire?

D IMAGERY
What kind of **mood** is established by the description of the swamp in lines 40–47?

---

1. **as articulate . . . gridiron:** as clearly separated as the bars of a grill.
2. **puddingstone:** a rock consisting of pebbles and gravel cemented together.
3. **termagant** (tûr´mə-gənt): a quarrelsome, scolding woman.
4. **clapper-clawing:** scratching or clawing with the fingernails.
5. **eyed . . . askance** (ə-skăns´): looked disapprovingly at the house filled with arguing.
6. **bittern:** a wading bird with mottled, brownish plumage and a deep, booming cry.

with the first colonists. Here they had thrown up a kind of fort, which they had looked upon as almost impregnable, and had used as a place of refuge for their squaws and children.

Nothing remained of the old Indian fort but a few embankments, gradually sinking to the level of the surrounding earth, and already overgrown in part by
60 oaks and other forest trees, the foliage of which formed a contrast to the dark pines and hemlocks of the swamp.

It was late in the dusk of evening when Tom Walker reached the old fort, and he paused there awhile to rest himself. Anyone but he would have felt unwilling to linger in this lonely, **melancholy** place, for the common people had a bad opinion of it, from the stories handed down from the time of the Indian wars, when it was asserted that the savages held incantations[7] here, and made sacrifices to the evil spirit.

Tom Walker, however, was not a man to be troubled with any fears of the kind. He reposed himself for some time on the trunk of a fallen hemlock, listening to
70 the boding cry of the tree toad, and delving with his walking staff into a mound of black mold at his feet. As he turned up the soil unconsciously, his staff struck against something hard. He raked it out of the vegetable mold, and lo! a cloven skull, with an Indian tomahawk buried deep in it, lay before him. The rust on the weapon showed the time that had elapsed since this death-blow had been given. It was a dreary memento of the fierce struggle that had taken place in this last foothold of the Indian warriors.

"Humph!" said Tom Walker, as he gave it a kick to shake the dirt from it. **E**

"Let that skull alone!" said a gruff voice. Tom lifted up his eyes, and beheld a great black man seated directly opposite him, on the stump of a tree. He was ex-
80 ceedingly surprised, having neither heard nor seen anyone approach; and he was still more perplexed on observing, as well as the gathering gloom would permit, that the stranger was neither Negro nor Indian. It is true he was dressed in a rude half-Indian garb, and had a red belt or sash swathed round his body; but his face was neither black nor copper-color, but swarthy and dingy, and begrimed with soot, as if he had been accustomed to toil among fires and forges. He had a shock of coarse black hair, that stood out from his head in all directions, and bore an ax on his shoulder.

He scowled for a moment at Tom with a pair of great red eyes.

"What are you doing on my grounds?" said the black man, with a hoarse,
90 growling voice.

"Your grounds!" said Tom, with a sneer, "no more your grounds than mine; they belong to Deacon Peabody."

"Deacon Peabody be d—d," said the stranger, "as I flatter myself he will be, if he does not look more to his own sins and less to those of his neighbors. Look yonder, and see how Deacon Peabody is faring."

---

melancholy
(mĕl′ən-kŏl´ē) *adj.*
gloomy; sad

E MAKE INFERENCES
Look again at lines 68 and 77. What can you infer about Tom Walker from his reaction to the swamp and to his grisly discovery of the skull?

---

7. **incantations:** verbal charms or spells recited to produce a magic effect.

The Devil and Tom Walker (1856), John Quidor. Oil on canvas, 68.8 cm × 86.6 cm.
© The Cleveland Museum of Art, Mr. and Mrs. William H. Marlatt Fund, 1967.18.

ANALYZE VISUALS
This Quidor painting illustrates the first meeting between Tom and the devil. In your opinion, how well do the artist's choices of color and shading and his depiction of Tom's **character** match the story? Explain.

Tom looked in the direction that the stranger pointed, and beheld one of the great trees, fair and flourishing without, but rotten at the core, and saw that it had been nearly hewn through, so that the first high wind was likely to blow it down. On the bark of the tree was scored the name of Deacon Peabody, an eminent man, who had waxed wealthy by driving shrewd bargains with the Indians. He now looked around, and found most of the tall trees marked with the name of some great man of the colony, and all more or less scored by the ax. The one on which he had been seated, and which had evidently just been hewn down, bore the name of Crowninshield; and he recollected a mighty rich man of that name, who made a vulgar display of wealth, which it was whispered he had acquired by buccaneering.[8] **F**

"He's just ready for burning!" said the black man, with a growl of triumph. "You see, I am likely to have a good stock of firewood for winter."

"But what right have you," said Tom, "to cut down Deacon Peabody's timber?"

"The right of a prior claim," said the other. "This woodland belonged to me long before one of your white-faced race put foot upon the soil."

"And pray, who are you, if I may be so bold?" said Tom.

"Oh, I go by various names. I am the wild huntsman in some countries; the black miner in others. In this neighborhood I am he to whom the red men consecrated this spot, and in honor of whom they now and then roasted a white man, by way of sweet-smelling sacrifice. Since the red men have been exterminated by you white savages, I amuse myself by presiding at the **persecutions** of Quakers and Anabaptists;[9] I am the great patron and prompter of slave dealers, and the grand master of the Salem witches." **G**

"The upshot of all which is that, if I mistake not," said Tom, sturdily, "you are he commonly called Old Scratch."[10]

"The same, at your service!" replied the black man, with a half-civil nod.

Such was the opening of this interview, according to the old story; though it has almost too familiar an air to be credited. One would think that to meet with such a singular personage, in this wild, lonely place, would have shaken any man's nerves; but Tom was a hard-minded fellow, not easily daunted, and he had lived so long with a termagant wife that he did not even fear the devil.

It is said that after this commencement they had a long and earnest conversation together, as Tom returned homeward. The black man told him of great sums of money buried by Kidd the pirate, under the oak trees on the high ridge, not far from the morass. All these were under his command, and protected by his power, so that none could find them but such as propitiated his favor. These he offered to place within Tom Walker's reach, having conceived an especial kindness for him; but they were to be had only on certain conditions. What these conditions were may be easily surmised, though Tom never disclosed them publicly. They must have been very hard, for he required time to think of them, and he was not a man

F MAKE INFERENCES
Reread lines 96–105. Why do you think the trees are marked with the men's names

persecution
(pûr´sĭ-kyōo͞'shən) n. the act or practice of oppressing or harassing with ill-treatment, especially because of race, religion, gender, or beliefs

G SATIRE
Reread lines 115–118. What do they tell you about the author's attitude toward the activities of the early settlers? What led you to make that inference?

8. **buccaneering:** robbing ships at sea; piracy.

9. **presiding . . . Anabaptists:** exercising authority over the oppression of Christian groups that the Puritans considered heretical.

10. **Old Scratch:** a nickname for the devil.

Forest Landscape (1800s), Asher Brown Durand. Oil on canvas, 76.2 cm × 66 cm. © Brooklyn Museum of Art/ Bridgeman Art Library.

to stick at trifles when money was in view. When they had reached the edge of the swamp, the stranger paused. "What proof have I that all you have been telling me is true?" said Tom. "There's my signature," said the black man, pressing his finger on Tom's forehead. So saying, he turned off among the thickets of the swamp, and
140 seemed, as Tom said, to go down, down, down, into the earth, until nothing but his head and shoulders could be seen, and so on, until he totally disappeared.

When Tom reached home, he found the black print of a finger burnt, as it were, into his forehead, which nothing could obliterate.

The first news his wife had to tell him was the sudden death of Absalom Crowninshield, the rich buccaneer. It was announced in the papers with the usual flourish that "a great man had fallen in Israel."[11]

---

11. **a great man . . . Israel:** a biblical reference—"Know ye not that there is a prince and a great man fallen this day in Israel?" (2 Samuel 3:38)—used, with unconscious irony, by the papers to mean that an important member of God's people on earth had passed away.

Tom recollected the tree which his black friend had just hewn down and which was ready for burning. "Let the freebooter[12] roast," said Tom; "who cares!" He now felt convinced that all he had heard and seen was no illusion.

150   He was not prone to let his wife into his confidence; but as this was an uneasy secret, he willingly shared it with her. All her **avarice** was awakened at the mention of hidden gold, and she urged her husband to comply with the black man's terms, and secure what would make them wealthy for life. However Tom might have felt disposed to sell himself to the devil, he was determined not to do so to oblige his wife; so he flatly refused, out of the mere spirit of contradiction. Many and bitter were the quarrels they had on the subject; but the more she talked, the more resolute was Tom not to be damned to please her.

    At length she determined to drive the bargain on her own account, and if she succeeded, to keep all the gain to herself. Being of the same fearless temper as her
160 husband, she set off for the old Indian fort toward the close of a summer's day. She was many hours absent. When she came back, she was reserved and sullen in her replies. She spoke something of a black man, whom she met about twilight hewing at the root of a tall tree. He was sulky, however, and would not come to terms; she was to go again with a propitiatory offering, but what it was she forbore to say.

    The next evening she set off again for the swamp, with her apron heavily laden. Tom waited and waited for her, but in vain; midnight came, but she did not make her appearance; morning, noon, night returned, but still she did not come. Tom now grew uneasy for her safety, especially as he found she had carried off in her apron the silver teapot and spoons, and every portable article of value. Another night elapsed,
170 another morning came; but no wife. In a word, she was never heard of more.

    What was her real fate nobody knows, in consequence of so many pretending to know. It is one of those facts which have become confounded by a variety of historians. Some asserted that she lost her way among the tangled mazes of the swamp, and sank into some pit or slough; others, more uncharitable, hinted that she had eloped with the household booty and made off to some other province; while others surmised that the tempter had decoyed her into a dismal quagmire, on the top of which her hat was found lying. In confirmation of this, it was said a great black man, with an ax on his shoulder, was seen late that very evening coming out of the swamp, carrying a bundle tied in a check apron, with an air
180 of surly triumph. ◆

    The most current and probable story, however, observes that Tom Walker grew so anxious about the fate of his wife and his property that he set out at length to seek them both at the Indian fort. During a long summer's afternoon he searched about the gloomy place, but no wife was to be seen. He called her name repeatedly, but she was nowhere to be heard. The bittern alone responded to his voice, as they flew screaming by; or the bullfrog croaked dolefully from a neighboring pool. At length, it is said, just in the brown hour of twilight, when the owls began to hoot, and the bats to flit about, his attention was attracted by the clamor of carrion crows[13] hovering about a cypress tree. He looked up, and beheld a bundle tied in a

avarice (ăv′ə-rĭs) *n.* immoderate desire for wealth; greed

◆ GRAMMAR AND STYLE
Irving emphasizes ideas and creates lyricism through the use of **parallelism,** the repetition of grammatical structures. In lines 173–177, for example, the writer uses parallelism to present three possible fates of Tom's wife.

---

12. **freebooter:** pirate.

13. **carrion crows:** crows that feed on dead or decaying flesh.

190 check apron, and hanging in the branches of the tree, with a great vulture perched
hard by, as if keeping watch upon it. He leaped with joy; for he recognized his
wife's apron and supposed it to contain the household valuables. **I**

"Let us get hold of the property," said he consolingly to himself, "and we will
endeavor to do without the woman."

As he scrambled up the tree, the vulture spread its wide wings, and sailed off
screaming into the deep shadows of the forest. Tom seized the checked apron, but,
woeful sight! found nothing but a heart and liver tied up in it!

Such, according to this most authentic old story, was all that was to be found
of Tom's wife. She had probably attempted to deal with the black man as she had
200 been accustomed to deal with her husband; but though a female scold is generally considered a match for the devil, yet in this instance she appears to have had
the worst of it. She must have died game, however; for it is said Tom noticed
many prints of cloven feet stamped upon the tree, and found handfuls of hair
that looked as if they had been plucked from the coarse black shock of the woodman. Tom knew his wife's prowess by experience. He shrugged his shoulders, as
he looked at the signs of a fierce clapper-clawing. "Egad," said he to himself, "Old
Scratch must have had a tough time of it!" **J**

Tom consoled himself for the loss of his property with the loss of his wife, for
he was a man of fortitude. He even felt something like gratitude towards the black
210 woodman, who, he considered, had done him a kindness. He sought, therefore,
to cultivate a further acquaintance with him, but for some time without success;
the old blacklegs played shy, for, whatever people may think, he is not always to be
had for calling for: he knows how to play his cards when pretty sure of his game.

At length, it is said, when delay had whetted Tom's eagerness to the quick, and
prepared him to agree to anything rather than not gain the promised treasure, he met
the black man one evening in his usual woodsman's dress, with his ax on his shoulder,
sauntering along the swamp, and humming a tune. He affected to receive Tom's advances with great indifference, made brief replies, and went on humming his tune.

By degrees, however, Tom brought him to business, and they began to haggle
220 about the terms on which the former was to have the pirate's treasure. There was
one condition which need not be mentioned, being generally understood in all
cases where the devil grants favors; but there were others about which, though of
less importance, he was inflexibly obstinate. He insisted that the money found
through his means should be employed in his service. He proposed, therefore,
that Tom should employ it in the black traffic; that is to say, that he should fit
out a slave ship. This, however, Tom resolutely refused: he was bad enough in
all conscience; but the devil himself could not tempt him to turn slave trader.

Finding Tom so squeamish on this point, he did not insist upon it, but proposed, instead, that he should turn **usurer;** the devil being extremely anxious for
230 the increase of usurers, looking upon them as his peculiar people.

To this no objections were made, for it was just to Tom's taste.

"You shall open a broker's shop in Boston next month," said the black man.

"I'll do it tomorrow, if you wish," said Tom Walker.

"You shall lend money at two percent a month."

"Egad, I'll charge four!" replied Tom Walker.

I IMAGERY
Which images in lines
189–192 suggest that
Tom's discovery won't
be a pleasant one?

J SATIRE
How does Irving use
humor and **exaggeration**
to satirize a "female
scold" in lines 199–207?

usurer (yo͞o′zhər-ər) *n.*
one who lends money, at
interest, especially at an
unusually or unlawfully
high rate of interest

"You shall extort bonds, foreclose mortgages, drive the merchants to bankruptcy—"

"I'll drive them to the d——l," cried Tom Walker.

"You are the usurer for my money!" said blacklegs with delight. "When will you want the rhino?"[14]

"This very night."

"Done!" said the devil.

"Done!" said Tom Walker. So they shook hands and struck a bargain. **K**

A few days' time saw Tom Walker seated behind his desk in a countinghouse[15] in Boston.

His reputation for a ready-moneyed man, who would lend money out for a good consideration, soon spread abroad. Everybody remembers the time of Governor Belcher, when money was particularly scarce. It was a time of paper credit. The country had been deluged with government bills; the famous Land Bank[16] had been established; there had been a rage for **speculating;** the people had run mad with schemes for new settlements; for building cities in the wilderness; land-jobbers[17] went about with maps of grants, and townships, and Eldorados[18] lying nobody knew where, but which everybody was ready to purchase. In a word, the great speculating fever, which breaks out every now and then in the country, had raged to an alarming degree, and everybody was dreaming of making sudden fortunes from nothing. As usual the fever had subsided; the dream had gone off, and the imaginary fortunes with it; the patients were left in doleful plight, and the whole country resounded with the consequent cry of "hard times."

At this **propitious** time of public distress did Tom Walker set up as usurer in Boston. His door was soon thronged by customers. The needy and adventurous, the gambling speculator, the dreaming land-jobber, the thriftless tradesman, the merchant with cracked credit; in short, everyone driven to raise money by desperate means and desperate sacrifices hurried to Tom Walker.

Thus Tom was the universal friend of the needy and acted like a "friend in need"; that is to say, he always exacted good pay and good security. In proportion to the distress of the applicant was the hardness of his terms. He accumulated bonds and mortgages; gradually squeezed his customers closer and closer; and sent them at length, dry as a sponge, from his door.

In this way he made money hand over hand, became a rich and mighty man, and exalted his cocked hat upon 'Change.[19] He built himself, as usual, a vast

K SATIRE
Reread lines 232–243. How does Tom compare with the devil in terms of his greed and mercilessness? Decide what comment Irving is making about usurers in general.

speculating
(spĕk'yə- lā´tĭng) *n.* engaging in risky business transactions on the chance of a quick or considerable profit

propitious
(prə-pĭsh'əs) *adj.* helpful or advantageous; favorable

---

14. **rhino:** a slang term for money.

15. **countinghouse:** an office in which a business firm conducts its bookkeeping, correspondence, and similar activities.

16. **Land Bank:** Boston merchants organized the Land Bank in 1739. Landowners could take out mortgages on their property and then repay the loans with cash or manufactured goods. When the Land Bank was outlawed in 1741, many colonists lost money.

17. **land-jobbers:** people who buy and sell land for profit.

18. **Eldorados:** places of fabulous wealth or great opportunity. Early Spanish explorers sought a legendary country named El Dorado, which was rumored to be rich with gold.

19. **exalted . . . 'Change:** proudly raised himself to a position of importance as a trader on the stock exchange.

house, out of **ostentation;** but left the greater part of it unfinished and unfurnished, out of parsimony. He even set up a carriage in the fullness of his vainglory,[20] though he nearly starved the horses which drew it; and as the ungreased
wheels groaned and screeched on the axletrees, you would have thought you heard
the souls of the poor debtors he was squeezing. **L**

As Tom waxed old, however, he grew thoughtful. Having secured the good
things of this world, he began to feel anxious about those of the next. He thought
with regret on the bargain he had made with his black friend, and set his wits to
work to cheat him out of the conditions. He became, therefore, all of a sudden,
280 a violent churchgoer. He prayed loudly and strenuously, as if heaven were to be
taken by force of lungs. Indeed, one might always tell when he had sinned most
during the week, by the clamor of his Sunday devotion. The quiet Christians who
had been modestly and steadfastly traveling Zionward[21] were struck with self-
reproach at seeing themselves so suddenly outstripped in their career by this new-
made convert. Tom was as rigid in religious as in money matters; he was a stern
supervisor and **censurer** of his neighbors, and seemed to think every sin entered
up to their account became a credit on his own side of the page. He even talked of
the expediency of reviving the persecution of Quakers and Anabaptists. In a word,
Tom's zeal became as notorious as his riches. **M**

290 Still, in spite of all this strenuous attention to forms, Tom had a lurking dread
that the devil, after all, would have his due.[22] That he might not be taken unawares, therefore, it is said he always carried a small Bible in his coat pocket. He
had also a great folio Bible on his countinghouse desk, and would frequently be
found reading it when people called on business; on such occasions he would lay
his green spectacles in the book, to mark the place, while he turned round to drive
some usurious bargain.

Some say that Tom grew a little crackbrained in his old days, and that fancying
his end approaching, he had his horse new shod, saddled and bridled, and buried
with his feet uppermost; because he supposed that at the last day the world would
300 be turned upside down; in which case he should find his horse standing ready for
mounting, and he was determined at the worst to give his old friend a run for it.
This, however, is probably a mere old wives' fable. If he really did take such a precaution, it was totally superfluous; at least so says the authentic old legend, which
closes his story in the following manner:

One hot summer afternoon in the dog days, just as a terrible black thundergust
was coming up, Tom sat in his countinghouse, in his white linen cap and India
silk morning gown. He was on the point of foreclosing a mortgage, by which he
would complete the ruin of an unlucky land speculator for whom he had pro-
fessed the greatest friendship. The poor land-jobber begged him to grant a few
310 months' indulgence. Tom had grown testy and irritated, and refused another day.

---

20. **vainglory:** boastful, undeserved pride in one's accomplishments or qualities.

21. **Zionward:** toward heaven.

22. **the devil . . . due:** a reference to the proverb "Give the devil his due," used to mean "Give even a
disagreeable person the credit he or she deserves." Here, of course, the expression is used literally
rather than figuratively.

---

ostentation
(ŏs′ tĕn-tā′shən) *n.*
display meant to
impress others; boastful
showiness

L IMAGERY
Find the images in lines
264–275 that are used to
describe both Tom and
his clients. What do these
images tell you about
Tom and his methods?

censurer
(sĕn′shər-ər) *n.* one
who expresses strong
disapproval or harsh
criticism

M SATIRE
What kind of churchgoer
is represented by Tom
in lines 276–289? Think
about what Irving is
suggesting about this
kind of individual.

"My family will be ruined and brought upon the parish," said the land-jobber. "Charity begins at home," replied Tom; "I must take care of myself in these hard times."

"You have made so much money out of me," said the speculator.

Tom lost his patience and his piety. "The devil take me," said he, "if I have made a farthing!"[23]

Just then there were three loud knocks at the street door. He stepped out to see who was there. A black man was holding a black horse, which neighed and stamped with impatience.

320   "Tom, you're come for," said the black fellow, gruffly. Tom shrank back, but too late. He had left his little Bible at the bottom of his coat pocket, and his big Bible on the desk buried under the mortgage he was about to foreclose; never was a sinner taken more unawares. The black man whisked him like a child into the saddle,

Tom Walker's Flight (about 1856), John Quidor. Oil on canvas, 26³/₄″ × 33³/₄″. The Fine Arts Museums of San Francisco, Gift of Mr. and Mrs. John D. Rockefeller 3rd, 1979.7.84.

ANALYZE VISUALS
What elements in this painting by Quidor emphasize the human fear of the supernatural and the consequences of greed? Explain.

gave the horse the lash, and away he galloped, with Tom on his back, in the midst of the thunderstorm. The clerks stuck their pens behind their ears, and stared after him from the windows. Away went Tom Walker, dashing down the streets; his white cap bobbing up and down, his morning gown fluttering in the wind, and his steed striking fire out of the pavement at every bound. When the clerks turned to look for the black man, he had disappeared.

330   Tom Walker never returned to foreclose the mortgage. A countryman, who lived on the border of the swamp, reported that in the height of the thundergust he had heard a great clattering of hoofs and a howling along the road, and running to the window caught sight of a figure, such as I have described, on a horse that galloped like mad across the fields, over the hills, and down into the black hemlock swamp toward the old Indian fort; and that shortly after a thunderbolt falling in that direction seemed to set the whole forest in a blaze.

        The good people of Boston shook their heads and shrugged their shoulders, but had been so much accustomed to witches and goblins, and tricks of the devil, in all kinds of shapes, from the first settlement of the colony, that they were not
340 so much horror-struck as might have been expected. Trustees were appointed to take charge of Tom's effects. There was nothing, however, to administer upon. On searching his coffers[24] all his bonds and mortgages were found reduced to cinders. In place of gold and silver, his iron chest was filled with chips and shavings; two skeletons lay in his stable instead of his half-starved horses, and the very next day his great house took fire and burnt to the ground. **N**

        Such was the end of Tom Walker and his ill-gotten wealth. Let all griping money brokers lay this story to heart. The truth of it is not to be doubted. The very hole under the oak trees whence he dug Kidd's money is to be seen to this day; and the neighboring swamp and old Indian fort are often haunted in stormy nights
350 by a figure on horseback, in morning gown and white cap, which is doubtless the troubled spirit of the usurer. In fact the story has resolved itself into a proverb so prevalent throughout New England, of "The Devil and Tom Walker." ∾

N IMAGERY
Reread lines 341–345. What **message** do these images suggest about material possessions and those who seek them?

---

24. **coffers:** safes or strongboxes designed to hold money or other valuable items.

Comprehension

1. **Recall** What character traits do Tom Walker and his wife share?

2. **Recall** What bargain does Tom make with the stranger in the forest?

3. **Summarize** How does Tom try to avoid fulfilling his end of the bargain?

Literary Analysis

4. **Compare Character Traits** As Tom gets older, he begins to worry about his actions and becomes "a violent churchgoer." But does he really change? Support your opinion with examples from the story. Use a chart like the one shown to collect evidence.

	Before the Bargain	As He Ages
Attitude		
Statements		
Actions		

5. **Draw Conclusions** In your opinion, is there any way Tom could have escaped the **consequences** of his deal with the devil? Use evidence from the story and your own knowledge of human nature to support your answer.

6. **Interpret Imagery** Review the examples of images you recorded as you read the story. How does Irving use each of the following images to support characterization and mood?

   - the description of the trees and the swamp (lines 40–47)
   - the description of the hewn trees (lines 96–102)
   - the description of Tom's new house (lines 270–272)
   - the description of Tom as a churchgoer (lines 279–289)

7. **Analyze Satire** Through statements he makes about Tom Walker, his wife, and his community, what messages is Irving communicating about

   - women (lines 31–37)?
   - the Puritan attitude (lines 115–118)?
   - the slave trade (lines 224–227)?
   - moneylenders (lines 228–230)?

8. **Analyze Irony** Much of the humor in this tale is based on irony, where what happens or is said is the opposite of what one would expect. Look again at lines 290–296. What is ironic about Tom's mix of Bible study and business?

Literary Criticism

9. **Critical Interpretations** The story of Tom Walker engaged readers both here and in Europe for many different, and sometimes conflicting, reasons. Look at the story again through the eyes of each of the following people. What reasons would you give for recommending the story to others?

   - businessman
   - banker
   - English critic
   - revolutionary
   - Puritan
   - American politician

Vocabulary in Context

VOCABULARY PRACTICE

Choose the vocabulary word that best matches each description below.

1. someone who loves to nag, criticize, and sneer
2. your mood if you suddenly lost your job, your best friend, or your dog
3. what a hot day is to lemonade vendors
4. a pretentious display that is meant to impress others
5. what the Bill of Rights was written to prevent
6. what someone who buys stock in a struggling company is doing
7. a person you don't want to have help you out of financial difficulties
8. a feeling that can make someone drool in a department store

VOCABULARY IN WRITING

Using at least four vocabulary words, write an obituary that might have been published after the death of Tom Walker. Remember as you write that he was not a well-loved figure, so there is no need to be diplomatic. An example beginning is shown below.

EXAMPLE SENTENCE

Tom Walker, the corrupt __usurer__ who has been the source of much misery in this town, disappeared last week and is presumed dead.

VOCABULARY STRATEGY: THE LATIN ROOT *spec*

When Tom Walker's neighbors speculated in land, they were hoping to spot opportunities for a quick profit. The Latin root *spec* in the word *speculating* actually means "to look at" or "to see or behold." Words containing this root, or the related forms *spect* and *spic,* usually have something to do with light, sight, or clarity.

PRACTICE Match each definition below with the appropriate word from the word web, considering what you know about the Latin root *spec* and the other word parts shown.

1. tending to look within, at one's own thoughts or feelings
2. an observer of an event
3. a ghostly sight or apparition
4. showing unwillingness to act rashly; prudent
5. a point of view
6. a range of colored light

WORD LIST

avarice
censurer
melancholy
ostentation
persecution
propitious
speculating
usurer

VOCABULARY PRACTICE
For more practice, go to the **Vocabulary Center** at **ClassZone.com**.

Reading-Writing Connection

WRITING PROMPT

WRITE A STORY An archetypal plot is a basic storyline that serves as a frame for stories across time and cultures. Any Faust-like tale of a person who "sells his soul" for personal gain is based on an archetype. The story of Cinderella also has its origins in an archetype.

Choose a contemporary situation, such as a political race, or a well-known character type, such as a social climber. Write a **one-to-three-page story** around it that fits the Faustian archetype. Be sure to show the consequences of the main character's actions.

SELF-CHECK

A successful story will . . .

- have a well-developed main character
- clearly show the character's goals and choices
- effectively portray the consequences of the choices
- reflect the Faustian archetype

GRAMMAR AND STYLE

RECOGNIZE PARALLELISM Review the **Grammar and Style** note on page 319. One of the many delights of Irving's style is his use of parallelism—the repetition of grammatical structures—to create emphasis or to add rhythm. Here is an example from the story:

> *Tom's wife was a tall termagant, fierce of temper, loud of tongue, and strong of arm.* (lines 31–32)

Notice that each of the highlighted phrases contains an adjective (*fierce, loud,* and *strong*) followed by a prepositional phrase (*of temper, of tongue,* and *of arm*). Read the sentence aloud. How does it sound? How does the parallelism affect the description of Tom's wife?

PRACTICE Write down each of the following sentences from the selection. Then identify the parallel elements from each sentence as shown and write your own sentence with similar parallel elements.

EXAMPLE

. . . No smoke ever curled from its chimney; no traveler stopped at its door.

No frown ever crossed his face; no complaint crossed his lips.

---

1. "Oh, I go by various names. I am the wild huntsman in some countries; the black miner in others. . . . I am the great patron and prompter of slave dealers, and the grand master of the Salem witches."

2. . . . Midnight came, but she did not make her appearance; morning, noon, night returned, but still she did not come.

3. He built himself, as usual, a vast house, out of ostentation; but left the greater part of it unfinished and unfurnished, out of parsimony.

WRITING TOOLS
For prewriting, revision, and editing tools, visit the **Writing Center** at ClassZone.com.

Thanatopsis

Poem by William Cullen Bryant

William Cullen Bryant
1794–1878

In his own day, William Cullen Bryant was a literary superstar. Schoolchildren recited his poetry. Adults pored over his newspaper editorials. And other writers praised his genius. James Fenimore Cooper even went so far as to call Bryant "the author of America" for helping to create a distinctive American literature.

All-American Poet Born in 1794 in Cummington, Massachusetts, Bryant began his writing career at an early age. At 10, he translated poems written in Latin; at 13, he published "The Embargo," a poem satirizing the policies of President Thomas Jefferson.

But the young Bryant was most inspired to write poetry about the natural world. As a boy, he spent hours exploring the forests and hills near his home. His earliest efforts reflected the influence of the English romantic poets.

In time, however, Bryant discovered his American voice. At the ripe old age of 18, he wrote "Thanatopsis," a poem inspired by his wanderings in the countryside. The American editor who published the poem was so struck by its brilliance that he asserted, "No one on this side of the Atlantic is capable of writing such a verse."

Career Moves At his father's urging, Bryant attended law school and spent ten years as a lawyer in Plainsfield, Massachusetts. But he was destined for a career in literature and writing. Leaving behind the "disagreeable drudgery" of his law practice, Bryant moved to New York City in 1825 to become a journalist.

Eventually, he became the editor-in-chief of the *New York Evening Post,* a position he held until his death. A committed political and social activist, Bryant used the newspaper to advocate for human rights and the protection of the environment.

Lifelong Naturalist Unfortunately, Bryant's journalistic work took a toll on his poetry. Nonetheless, Bryant left his mark on American literature as one of the first poets to overthrow what he called the "servile habit of copying" English poets.

Above all, Bryant is celebrated for his power to portray the wild American landscape. Walking up to 40 miles a day, he developed a deep knowledge of America's forests, streams, mountains, and valleys. "Even as an old man," noted one critic, "Bryant was never content unless he knew the name of every tree, bush, and weed in sight."

● LITERARY ANALYSIS: BLANK VERSE

William Cullen Bryant wrote "Thanatopsis" in a verse form known as blank verse. **Blank verse** is unrhymed poetry written in **iambic pentameter.** In this meter, each line has five iambic feet, a pattern consisting of an unstressed syllable (˘) followed by a stressed syllable (´). Read the following lines from "Thanatopsis" aloud to hear the rhythm:

˘ ´ ˘ ´ ˘ ´ ˘ ´ ˘ ´
To him who in the love of Nature holds
˘ ´ ˘ ´ ˘ ´ ˘ ´ ˘ ´
Communion with her visible forms, she speaks

Notice that the lines do not have a singsong quality as some lines of rhymed poetry do. In fact, good blank verse imitates the natural rhythms of spoken English and so sounds very much like the way people talk. Bryant also achieves this effect through the use of **enjambment,** which means that one line ends without a pause and continues into the next line for its meaning. As you read "Thanatopsis," notice how the poem's rhythm imitates natural speech.

● READING SKILL: UNDERSTAND STRUCTURE

In poetry, **structure** is the arrangement of words and lines to produce a desired effect. The structure of a poem usually emphasizes important aspects of content and can help a poet indicate shifts in mood. Use the following strategies to help you understand the structure and effects of Bryant's poem:

- Notice the indented line that indicates the beginning of each of the three verse sections in the poem.
- Summarize each section to understand the content and central ideas.
- Look for details and word choices that convey mood.

As you read "Thanatopsis," use a chart like the one shown to record the ideas and mood evoked in each section of the poem.

Section	Ideas	Mood
1st	Death comes to everyone.	bleak
2nd		
3rd		

What can DEATH teach us about life?

KEY IDEA Some people view death as the ultimate enemy. Others, however, consider it a natural part of life. Acceptance of that fact is a theme of William Cullen Bryant's "Thanatopsis." But death—and life—have other important **lessons** to teach us. One is recognizing that death, since it comes to us all, makes us all equal. What are some other important life lessons?

SURVEY With a partner, conduct a survey among your classmates, friends, and family and ask them to name the five greatest lessons that life—or death—has taught them. Compile the results and share them with the rest of the class.

329

Thanatopsis

William Cullen Bryant

To him who in the love of Nature holds
Communion with her visible forms, she speaks
A various language; for his gayer hours
She has a voice of gladness, and a smile
5 And eloquence of beauty, and she glides
Into his darker musings, with a mild
And healing sympathy, that steals away
Their sharpness, ere he is aware. When thoughts **Ⓐ**
Of the last bitter hour come like a blight
10 Over thy spirit, and sad images
Of the stern agony, and shroud, and pall,
And breathless darkness, and the narrow house,
Make thee to shudder, and grow sick at heart;—
Go forth, under the open sky, and list
15 To Nature's teachings, while from all around—
Earth and her waters, and the depths of air—
Comes a still voice—Yet a few days, and thee
The all-beholding sun shall see no more
In all his course; nor yet in the cold ground,
20 Where thy pale form was laid, with many tears,
Nor in the embrace of ocean, shall exist
Thy image. Earth, that nourished thee, shall claim
Thy growth, to be resolved to earth again,
And, lost each human trace, surrendering up
25 Thine individual being, shalt thou go
To mix forever with the elements,
To be a brother to the insensible rock
And to the sluggish clod, which the rude swain
Turns with his share, and treads upon. The oak
30 Shall send his roots abroad, and pierce thy mold. **Ⓑ**

Yet not to thine eternal resting-place
Shalt thou retire alone—nor couldst thou wish
Couch more magnificent. Thou shalt lie down
With patriarchs of the infant world—with kings,
35 The powerful of the earth—the wise, the good,
Fair forms, and hoary seers of ages past,
All in one mighty sepulcher.—The hills
Rock-ribbed and ancient as the sun,—the vales

2 **communion:** a close relationship.

Ⓐ **BLANK VERSE**
Reread lines 1–8 aloud. Identify the places where a phrase begins at the end of a line and continues on the next line. How does this **enjambment** affect the flow of the lines?

11–12 **shroud . . . the narrow house:** A shroud is a burial garment, while a pall is a heavy garment draped over a coffin. The narrow house is the grave or coffin.

28–29 **the sluggish clod . . . share:** the heavy mass of earth, which the farmer loosens with his plow.

Ⓑ **STRUCTURE**
What is the central idea of the poem's first section, lines 1–30?

33 **couch:** bed.

36 **hoary seers:** ancient wise men.

37 **sepulcher:** grave.

Stretching in pensive quietness between;
40 The venerable woods—rivers that move
In majesty, and the complaining brooks
That make the meadows green; and, poured round all,
Old ocean's gray and melancholy waste,—
Are but the solemn decorations all
45 Of the great tomb of man. The golden sun, **C**
The planets, all the infinite host of heaven,
Are shining on the sad abodes of death,
Through the still lapse of ages. All that tread
The globe are but a handful to the tribes
50 That slumber in its bosom.—Take the wings
Of morning—and the Barcan desert pierce,
Or lose thyself in the continuous woods
Where rolls the Oregon, and hears no sound,
Save his own dashings—yet—the dead are there;
55 And millions in those solitudes, since first
The flight of years began, have laid them down
In their last sleep—the dead reign there alone.
So shalt thou rest—and what if thou withdraw
Unheeded by the living—and no friend
60 Take note of thy departure? All that breathe
Will share thy destiny. The gay will laugh
When thou art gone, the solemn brood of care
Plod on, and each one as before will chase
His favorite phantom; yet all these shall leave
65 Their mirth and their employments, and shall come
And make their bed with thee. As the long train **D**
Of ages glide away, the sons of men,
The youth in life's green spring, and he who goes
In the full strength of years, matron and maid,
70 The speechless babe, and the gray-headed man—
Shall one by one be gathered to thy side,
By those, who in their turn shall follow them.

    So live, that when thy summons comes to join
The innumerable caravan, which moves
75 To that mysterious realm, where each shall take
His chamber in the silent halls of death,
Thou go not, like the quarry-slave at night,
Scourged to his dungeon, but, sustained and soothed
By unfaltering trust, approach thy grave,
80 Like one who wraps the drapery of his couch
About him, and lies down to pleasant dreams. **E**

40 **venerable:** impressive and worthy of respect because of age.

C STRUCTURE
Identify the **mood** in lines 31–45. How does it contrast with the mood in the first section?

51 **Barcan desert:** a desert region in northern Africa.

53 **Oregon:** old name for the Columbia River, which flows between the states of Washington and Oregon.

D BLANK VERSE
Tap your foot to the rhythm as you read lines 61–66. Note the motion described in these lines. How does the rhythm suggest this motion?

E STRUCTURE
Reread the last section of the poem, lines 73–81. How would you **summarize** these lines?

Comprehension

1. **Recall** According to the speaker, how does nature help people cope during times of sadness?

2. **Recall** According to lines 22–30, what happens to people when they die?

3. **Clarify** Why, according to the speaker, should people greet death without fear?

Literary Analysis

4. **Analyze Title** The title of the poem combines the Greek words *thanatos* ("death") and *opsis* ("a vision"). Cite specific details from the poem to explain the vision of death presented in "Thanatopsis."

5. **Understand Structure** Review the notes you recorded in your chart on the ideas and mood in each section of "Thanatopsis." Identify the central idea in each section, and explain how the poem's structure helps develop an overall message.

6. **Draw Conclusions About Tone** A writer establishes his or her tone, or attitude toward a subject, through a variety of language choices. Use a chart to jot down important examples of Bryant's word choices, details, and direct statements. Then draw conclusions about the poem's tone.

Examples	Tone

7. **Interpret Ideas** Use details from the poem to determine what **lessons** Bryant conveys about

   • life   • nature   • religion

8. **Evaluate Blank Verse** How would the impact of Bryant's message differ if he had used a fixed meter and regular rhythm in his poem? Evaluate whether his use of blank verse is an effective or pleasing way to express his ideas. Give reasons for your opinion.

9. **Recognize Characteristics of Romanticism** How does "Thanatopsis" reflect Romantic notions of nature and democratic values?

Literary Criticism

10. **Different Perspectives** Bryant wrote "Thanatopsis" when he was a very young man. He was also greatly influenced by the English romantic poets. Given what you have learned about the Puritans and the romantic poets, how do you think the following people might have reacted to the poem?

    • Bryant at age 70   • a Puritan   • an English romantic poet

Elements of Romantic Style

On the surface, it seems as if William Cullen Bryant's "Thanatopsis" and Washington Irving's "The Devil and Tom Walker" could hardly be more different. One is an elegant nature poem written in formal language.

> *Go forth, under the open sky, and List / To Nature's teachings*
>
> from "Thanatopsis"

The other is a short story about strange, supernatural deeds and is written in a down-to-earth, casual style.

> *Tom's wife was a tall termagant, fierce of temper, loud of tongue, and strong of arm.*
>
> from "The Devil and Tom Walker"

But with a more careful reading, one can find elements of romanticism in each work.

Writing to Analyze

In general, America's romantic writers shared several characteristics. They looked to nature for inspiration, they celebrated individualism, they valued emotion and the imagination, and they sometimes explored the supernatural in their work. Which of these elements can you find in the two works you've just read? Create a chart like the one here, and use it to write a brief essay explaining why these two very different writers were each good examples of the romantic movement.

Element	Selection(s)	Example(s)
nature	"Thanatopsis"	"To him who in the love of Nature holds / Communion with her visible forms, she speaks / A various language"
	"The Devil and Tom Walker"	"On one side of this inlet is a beautiful dark grove; on the opposite side the land rises abruptly from the water's edge into a high ridge, on which grow a few scattered oaks of great age and immense size."
individualism		
emotion or passion		
imagination		
supernatural		

Extension

VIEWING & REPRESENTING

Romanticism was not only a literary movement; it was a movement of the other arts as well. Romantic artists shared many of the same concerns as writers of the day. Examine the painting shown here. (If you have trouble making out the painting's details, turn to page 318, where you can view it in a larger format.) With a partner, discuss what elements you think might indicate that the work is a good example of a romantic painting.

A Psalm of Life
The Tide Rises, the Tide Falls
Poetry by Henry Wadsworth Longfellow

Henry Wadsworth Longfellow
1807–1882

For nearly 150 years, Longfellow's "Paul Revere's Ride" has captivated readers. Its lines are as familiar as a nursery rhyme, and the image of Revere galloping into danger is imprinted on our minds. This poem, along with a number of others, made Henry Wadsworth Longfellow one of America's most popular poets.

Boy Genius Longfellow grew up in a literary household in Portland, Maine. His mother, Zilpah Wadsworth, often read aloud to him, while his father, Stephen, supplied him with numerous books. An exceptionally intelligent child, Longfellow entered school at the age of three and at six received this flattering report: "Master Henry Longfellow is one of the best boys we have in school. He spells and reads very well. He can also add and multiply numbers. His conduct is very correct and amiable."

Professor and Poet At age 13 Longfellow became a published poet, and at 15 he entered Bowdoin College in Maine where, like his classmate Nathaniel Hawthorne, he decided to devote his life to writing. While in college, he published poems in national magazines. Longfellow studied a number of foreign languages, including French, Spanish, and Italian. He was such a gifted translator that the college offered him upon graduation the first professorship in modern languages. Longfellow taught at Bowdoin until 1834, when he transferred to Harvard. He remained there until 1854.

Voice of America Although he worked hard to introduce European literature to an American audience, Longfellow wrote about American subjects. He sought inspiration in American history and lore, as well as in the country's landscape. A poet, argued Longfellow, should take his subjects from "nature and not from books" and should try to "fathom the recesses of his own mind, and bring up rich pearls from the secret depths of thought."

Literary Fame With the publication of his books *Evangeline, A Tale of Acadie* (1847) and *The Song of Hiawatha* (1855), Longfellow became a household name. Personal tragedy, however, cast a shadow over his achievement. His first wife died following a miscarriage and his second wife was fatally burned in a fire. Longfellow coped by immersing himself in his work. In his final years, Longfellow was showered with accolades. When he died, he became the first American writer to be honored with a bust in Poets' Corner of London's Westminster Abbey.

● LITERARY ANALYSIS: STANZA AND RHYME SCHEME

Poets often organize their ideas and images in compact units known as **stanzas**—groups of lines sometimes characterized by a repeated pattern of rhyme and number of lines. Each stanza generally develops a separate idea, image, or example of figurative language; recognizing stanzas will help you trace this development.

A **rhyme scheme** is the pattern of end rhyme in a stanza or an entire poem. Rhyme helps to make the words of a poem memorable and is often used to emphasize important words in the poem.

> *Life is real! Life is earnest!*
>   *And the grave is not its goal;*
> *Dust thou art, to dust returnest,*
>   *Was not spoken of the soul.*

Here the rhyme scheme is *abab*; that is, the first and third lines (*a* and *a*) rhyme, as do the second and fourth lines (*b* and *b*).

As you read, note how Longfellow makes use of these conventions to organize his thoughts about life and express them in a form that the reader will remember.

● READING STRATEGY: READING TRADITIONAL POETRY

To appreciate the musical qualities of these Longfellow poems, try the following strategies:

- Read each poem silently to interpret the basic meaning.
- Then, read them aloud, listening for the end rhyme. Notice which words are emphasized by rhyme.

In a web diagram like the one shown, note some important words that are emphasized through rhyme. You will need a separate diagram for each poem.

Explore the Key Idea

What gives life PURPOSE?

KEY IDEA People who live with **purpose** may be more likely to feel a sense of satisfaction or accomplishment. What is it that gives life value or meaning? Is it self-expression, creativity, following one's dream, or serving humanity? In the poems that follow, Longfellow offers his thoughts about how to lead a purposeful life.

QUICKWRITE Think of a person you know or have read about who has led a life you truly admire. How has this person made a difference in the world? Describe his or her impact on family, community, or country in a short paragraph.

335

A Psalm of Life

Henry Wadsworth Longfellow

What the Heart of the Young Man
Said to the Psalmist[1]

Tell me not, in mournful numbers,[2]
    Life is but an empty dream!—
For the soul is dead that slumbers,
    And things are not what they seem.

5 Life is real! Life is earnest!
    And the grave is not its goal;
Dust thou art, to dust returnest,
    Was not spoken of the soul. **Ⓐ**

Not enjoyment, and not sorrow,
10   Is our destined end or way;
But to act, that each tomorrow
    Find us farther than today.

Art is long, and Time is fleeting,
    And our hearts, though stout[3] and brave,
15 Still, like muffled drums, are beating
    Funeral marches to the grave.

In the world's broad field of battle,
    In the bivouac[4] of Life,
Be not like dumb, driven cattle!
20   Be a hero in the strife!

Ⓐ STANZA AND RHYME SCHEME
Review the rhyme scheme of the first two stanzas. How does the rhyme scheme contribute to the poem's **tone,** or attitude? Explain.

---

1. **Psalmist** (sä′mĭst): the author of the poems in the biblical Book of Psalms, many of which comment on the fleeting nature of life. King David of Israel is regarded as the author of most of the psalms.

2. **numbers:** metrical feet or lines; verses.

3. **stout:** strong.

4. **bivouac** (bĭv′o͞o-ak′): a temporary encampment of troops.

The Calm After the Storm (1866), Edward Moran. Oil on canvas. Private collection. © SuperStock, Inc./SuperStock.

Trust no Future, howe'er pleasant!
    Let the dead Past bury its dead!
Act,—act in the living Present!
    Heart within, and God o'erhead!

25 Lives of great men all remind us
    We can make our lives sublime,
And, departing, leave behind us
    Footprints on the sands of time; **B**

Footprints, that perhaps another,
30   Sailing o'er life's solemn main,[5]
A forlorn and shipwrecked brother,
    Seeing, shall take heart again.

Let us, then, be up and doing,
    With a heart for any fate;
35 Still achieving, still pursuing,
    Learn to labor and to wait.

---

5. **main:** open ocean.

ANALYZE VISUALS
How might the title of this painting (*The Calm After the Storm*) connect to the **theme** of this poem?

B TRADITIONAL POETRY
Note the word emphasized by the end rhyme in lines 25 and 27. What might be the significance of this word?

THE TIDE RISES,
The Tide Falls

Henry Wadsworth Longfellow

The tide rises, the tide falls,
The twilight darkens, the curlew[1] calls;
Along the sea sands damp and brown
The traveler hastens toward the town,
5   And the tide rises, the tide falls. **C**

Darkness settles on roofs and walls,
But the sea in the darkness calls and calls;
The little waves, with their soft white hands,
Efface[2] the footprints in the sands,
10   And the tide rises, the tide falls.

The morning breaks; the steeds in their stalls
Stamp and neigh, as the hostler[3] calls;
The day returns, but nevermore
Returns the traveler to the shore,
15   And the tide rises, the tide falls. **D**

---

1. **curlew:** a type of large bird often found along the shoreline.
2. **efface:** to wear away; wipe out.
3. **hostler:** person who takes care of horses.

C **STANZA AND RHYME SCHEME**
What rhyme occurs in three of the five lines of each stanza? What word is emphasized by this repeated rhyme? Consider the impact of this technique on the poem's meaning.

D **TRADITIONAL POETRY**
In terms of basic meaning, what is the difference between the day and the traveler in lines 13–14?

Singing Beach, Manchester (1863), Martin Johnson Heade. Oil on canvas, 50.8 cm × 91.4 cm. The Fine Arts Museums of San Francisco, Gift of Mr. and Mrs. John D. Rockefeller, 3rd, 1993.35.12.

Comprehension

1. **Recall** What record does the traveler leave behind in "The Tide Rises, the Tide Falls"? What happens to this record and to the traveler?

2. **Recall** What, according to the speaker of "A Psalm of Life," is "our destined end" or purpose?

3. **Paraphrase** What does the speaker say about the value of the lives of great people in "A Psalm of Life"?

Literary Analysis

4. **Draw Conclusions About Traditional Poetry** Review the emphasized words you recorded in your web diagram for "A Psalm of Life." What can you conclude about the relationship between the poem's sound and its meaning?

5. **Analyze Metaphor** A metaphor compares two things that seem dissimilar. Think about the metaphor in lines 17–18 of "A Psalm of Life." What is Longfellow saying about the world and life by comparing them to a battlefield and a bivouac?

6. **Examine Stanza and Rhyme Scheme** Identify the rhyme scheme used in "The Tide Rises, the Tide Falls." How does this rhyme scheme reflect the poem's central image?

7. **Interpret Repetition** Longfellow repeats the line "the tide rises, the tide falls" throughout his poem. What idea is he trying to emphasize about the difference between nature and human life through this repetition?

8. **Compare and Contrast** Reread lines 8–10 in "The Tide Rises . . ." and 25–32 in "A Psalm of Life." Consider what happens to the footprints in each poem. Based on this and other images, how would you say Longfellow's outlook on life and death in each poem is similar? In what way is it different? Use a Venn diagram like the one shown to organize your thoughts.

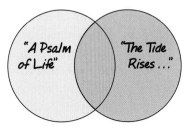

9. **Evaluate the Author's Message** According to the speaker of "A Psalm of Life," what should people do to give their lives value, or **purpose?** Do you agree or disagree? Cite evidence to support your conclusions.

Literary Criticism

10. **Critical Interpretations** "Longfellow," writes critic Alan Trachtenberg, "remains one of the nation's abidingly popular poets; more poems of his are probably still taken to heart and committed to memory than those of any of his more luminous 19th century peers. . . ." Based on the two poems you've read, why do you think Longfellow was, and continues to be, so popular? Cite evidence to support your conclusions.

The Chambered Nautilus
Old Ironsides

Poetry by Oliver Wendell Holmes

Oliver Wendell Holmes
1809–1894

Many people climb the ladder of success, but few make their mark in two very different fields. Oliver Wendell Holmes was both a prize-winning physician and a wildly popular poet. His discovery of the contagious nature of puerperal ("childbed") fever changed the practice of medicine. And his verse was so beloved that he was frequently called upon to write poems for public occasions.

A Cultural Elite Holmes grew up in a family steeped in history and tradition. He was descended from prominent Boston families and early Dutch settlers. His father, a Calvinist minister in Cambridge, Massachusetts, nurtured his interests in books, religion, and nature. "I am very thankful," wrote Holmes, "that the first part of my life was not passed shut in between high walls and treading the unimpressible and unsympathetic pavement."

Literary Triumph At 15, Holmes enrolled at Phillips Andover Academy, where he impressed his teachers by translating the Roman poet Virgil's *Aeneid.* After receiving a bachelor's degree and a medical degree from Harvard University, he entered private practice in Boston. Holmes achieved literary stardom at the age of 21 with the appearance of his poem "Old Ironsides." Written to protest the planned destruction of a ship that fought in the War of 1812, the poem won Holmes instant fame. Following its publication, the USS *Constitution* was returned to active duty.

Talent for Talk After his first book of poems was published in 1836, Holmes joined the lecture circuit, where he entranced audiences with his ready wit. He was equally charming in the classroom, causing his students at Harvard Medical School to greet his lectures with "a mighty shout and stamp of applause." Holmes's eloquence was also on display at the Saturday Club, a group including Ralph Waldo Emerson and Nathaniel Hawthorne. The writers met regularly to share their latest works.

Renaissance Man In addition to poetry, Holmes wrote three novels, a biography of Emerson, and numerous essays. Many of the essays appeared in *The Atlantic Monthly,* a magazine edited by Holmes's friend James Russell Lowell. Printed under the title "The Autocrat of the Breakfast Table," these essays combined prose and poetry and explored the themes of human destiny and freedom.

LITERARY ANALYSIS: METER

Meter is one of the tools used by poets to make language memorable and pleasing to the ear. It is defined as the repetition of a regular rhythmic unit in a line of poetry. Each unit, known as a **foot,** has one stressed syllable (indicated by a ´) and either one or two unstressed syllables (indicated by a ˘). The two basic types of metrical feet used by Holmes in these poems are the **iamb,** in which an unstressed syllable is followed by a stressed syllable (˘´), and the **trochee,** in which a stressed syllable is followed by an unstressed syllable (´˘). Two words are used to describe the meter of a line. The first word identifies the type of metrical foot—iambic, trochaic— and the second word indicates the number of feet in a line: **monometer** (one), **dimeter** (two), **trimeter** (three), **tetrameter** (four), **pentameter** (five), **hexameter** (six), and so forth. Here is a line from "Old Ironsides" with the meter marked:

Her deck, once red with heroes' blood

As you read these two poems by Holmes, note the meter in each and consider what it contributes to the poem's meaning and aesthetic appeal.

READING SKILL: MAKE INFERENCES

Making inferences involves "reading between the lines"— making logical guesses based on evidence in the text to figure out what is not directly stated. As you read these two poems by Holmes, you will need to make inferences to get at the author's meaning. For each poem, create a chart like the one shown.

"The Chambered Nautilus"		
Details or Evidence from Text	What I Know from Experience	Ideas Inferred
"Year after year beheld the silent toil / that spread his lustrous coil"	It takes a lot of practice to become good at a sport.	Change requires effort.

Explore the Key Idea

When is it time to MOVE ON?

KEY IDEA Sometimes people have to choose between cherishing the past and looking toward the future. For example, when you move out of your parents' house, will you expect them to keep your room exactly as it is or to convert it to a home office? **Change** can produce a renewed sense of well-being as well as a sense of loss.

DISCUSS Working with a partner, list situations or occasions in life when one must decide between holding on to the past and making a change. In each case, what are the benefits of either choice? After discussing this question with your partner, share your conclusions with others.

341

The Chambered Nautilus

Oliver Wendell Holmes

This is the ship of pearl, which, poets feign,[1]
    Sails the unshadowed main,—
    The venturous bark that flings
On the sweet summer wind its purpled wings
5 In gulfs enchanted, where the Siren[2] sings,
    And coral reefs lie bare,
Where the cold sea-maids rise to sun their streaming hair.

Its webs of living gauze no more unfurl;
    Wrecked is the ship of pearl!
10   And every chambered cell,
Where its dim dreaming life was wont to dwell,
As the frail tenant shaped his growing shell,
    Before thee lies revealed,—
Its irised ceiling rent,[3] its sunless crypt unsealed! Ⓐ

15 Year after year beheld the silent toil
    That spread his lustrous coil;
    Still, as the spiral grew,
He left the past year's dwelling for the new,
Stole with soft step its shining archway through,
20   Built up its idle door,
Stretched in his last-found home, and knew the old no more.

Thanks for the heavenly message brought by thee,
    Child of the wandering sea,
    Cast from her lap, forlorn!
25 From thy dead lips a clearer note is born

Ⓐ **METER**
Although the basic meter of this poem is **iambic,** what kind of **foot** is substituted for the iamb at the beginning of many of the lines? How does this variation affect the feel of these lines?

---

1. **feign:** imagine.

2. **Siren:** a partly human female creature in Greek mythology that lured sailors to destruction with sweet, magical songs.

3. **its irised ceiling rent:** its rainbow-colored ceiling ripped apart.

ANALYZE VISUALS
As the nautilus grows, it adds a new chamber to its spiral shell, abandoning the old chamber for the new one. What might this process of growth suggest about the role of change in life?

Than ever Triton blew from wreathèd horn![4]
    While on mine ear it rings,
Through the deep caves of thought I hear a voice that sings:—

Build thee more stately mansions, O my soul,
30   As the swift seasons roll!
    Leave thy low-vaulted past!
Let each new temple, nobler than the last,
Shut thee from heaven with a dome more vast,
    Till thou at length art free,
35 Leaving thine outgrown shell by life's unresting sea! **B**

B **MAKE INFERENCES**
Reread lines 29–35. What inference can you make about what it might mean for the soul to escape its shell?

---

4. **Triton . . . wreathèd horn:** Triton, a sea god in Greek mythology, is usually pictured blowing a wreathed, or coiled, conch-shell horn.

OLD IRONSIDES
Oliver Wendell Holmes

Ay, tear her tattered ensign[1] down!
    Long has it waved on high,
And many an eye has danced to see
    That banner in the sky;
5 Beneath it rung the battle shout,
    And burst the cannon's roar;—
The meteor of the ocean air
    Shall sweep the clouds no more.

Her deck, once red with heroes' blood,
10   Where knelt the vanquished foe,
When winds were hurrying o'er the flood,
    And waves were white below,
No more shall feel the victor's tread,
    Or know the conquered knee;—
15 The harpies[2] of the shore shall pluck
    The eagle of the sea! **C**

Oh, better that her shattered hulk
    Should sink beneath the wave;
Her thunders shook the mighty deep,
20   And there should be her grave;
Nail to the mast her holy flag,
    Set every threadbare sail,
And give her to the god of storms,
    The lightning and the gale! **D**

---

1. **ensign:** flag.
2. **harpies:** evil monsters from Greek mythology that are half woman and half bird.

ANALYZE VISUALS
What **mood** is suggested by this image of the USS *Constitution* ("Old Ironsides") in the mist in Boston Harbor?

C METER
What is the basic meter of this poem? Notice which lines are longer and which are shorter.

D MAKE INFERENCES
Reread the third stanza. Based on what has been said in previous stanzas about the ship's gloried past, do you think the speaker is being sincere or **ironic** about the fate of Old Ironsides? Explain.

Comprehension

1. **Recall** What event involving Old Ironsides took place during the war?

2. **Recall** According to the speaker, what should be the ship's fate?

3. **Summarize** In lines 1–14 of "The Chambered Nautilus," what does the speaker imagine and notice about the nautilus?

Literary Analysis

4. **Analyze Symbol** What do you think the chambered nautilus **symbolizes,** or represents, for the speaker of the poem? Cite evidence to support your answer.

5. **Make Inferences** Look back at the inferences and evidence you recorded as you read. What ideas about **change** does Holmes convey in "The Chambered Nautilus"? How does Holmes use each of the following images to express his thoughts about change?

   • the shell's appearance in the speaker's hands (lines 8–14)
   • the growth of the shell (lines 15–21)
   • the message the shell conveys (lines 29–35)

6. **Identify Tone** The attitude that a writer takes toward a particular subject is called **tone.** How would you describe the tone of each poem? What words and figures of speech help establish this tone? Use a chart like the one shown to record your answers.

   > "Old Ironsides"
   >
   > **Tone:** sardonic
   >
   > **Words:** "Oh, better that her shattered hulk / Should sink beneath the wave" (lines 17–18)
   >
   > "The Chambered Nautilus"
   >
   > **Tone:**
   >
   > **Words:**

7. **Interpret Meter** Review the metric pattern you identified in "Old Ironsides." Then read the poem aloud. How does this meter reflect the poem's subject matter? Explain.

Literary Criticism

8. **Author's Style** Recall from Holmes's biography on page 340 that the poem "Old Ironsides" was instrumental in saving the USS *Constitution*. What techniques and details used in the poem might have motivated readers to act? Cite evidence to support your answer.

John Greenleaf Whittier

1807–1892

NOTABLE QUOTE
"Beauty seen is never lost."

from Snowbound

Poem by John Greenleaf Whittier

John Greenleaf Whittier embodied the idealism of his age, which combined social activism and literary activity. He devoted most of his waking hours to the abolition of slavery, even risking his own life for the cause. Yet he also managed to write hundreds of poems. Many express an idyllic view of rural life and a profound moral aversion to slavery.

Rural Childhood Whittier's social consciousness derived from his modest background. Born to devout Quakers, Whittier was taught to believe in the equality of all men and women, the immorality of war, and the importance of thrift. Working long days on his family's farm in Haverhill, Massachusetts, Whittier also learned about the cycles of nature.

Poet and Politician Unlike most of his literary contemporaries, Whittier received little formal schooling. He was, however, an avid reader, devouring books by John Milton, Robert Burns, and other poets. Burns's poems about rural life inspired Whittier to write his own. When he was 19, his poetry was discovered by the abolitionist and editor William Lloyd Garrison. In the years that followed, Whittier contributed poems to various newspapers. He was also a founding member of the Republican Party and of the American Anti-Slavery Society.

James Russell Lowell

1819–1891

NOTABLE QUOTE
"All the beautiful sentiments in the world weigh less than a single lovely action."

The First Snowfall

Poem by James Russell Lowell

To his contemporaries, James Russell Lowell was the quintessential New England man of letters. He wrote poetry that stirred the emotions, newspaper editorials that influenced public opinion, and literary criticism.

Rebel with a Cause Lowell was born into a prominent New England family. In 1834, he entered Harvard, where he exasperated his teachers with his spoiled, immature behavior. His flouting of school rules and his disregard for his studies eventually led to his suspension. In 1844, Lowell married Maria White, who set her husband on the path to more mature behavior. In later years, Lowell published several volumes of verse and numerous articles in support of the abolitionist movement. He opposed slavery, the Mexican War, and corruption in politics.

Poet and Diplomat Lowell's talents were not limited to writing. He served as editor of *The Atlantic Monthly,* as an American diplomat in Spain, and as ambassador to Great Britain. While he enjoyed much public success in these roles, Lowell is today best remembered for his poetry.

Author Online

For more on these poets, visit the
Literature Center at **ClassZone.com.**

LITERARY ANALYSIS: MOOD

Mood is the feeling or atmosphere that a writer creates for the reader. Although it may seem that mood is simply inherent in a piece, it is actually achieved through the use of various devices, such as the following:

- **figurative language:** language that communicates ideas beyond the literal meaning of words
- **imagery:** descriptive words and phrases a writer uses to re-create sensory experiences
- **meter:** repetition of a regular rhythmic unit in a line of poetry
- **rhyme:** similarity of sound between two words

Notice, for example, how Lowell uses all four devices in the following stanza from "The First Snowfall":

I stood and watched by the window
*   The noiseless work of the sky,*
And the sudden flurries of snowbirds,
*   Like brown leaves whirling by.*

As you read the poems by Lowell and Whittier, look for the devices that help to create a different mood in each poem.

READING STRATEGY: PARAPHRASE

Sometimes, the surest way to get through a difficult passage is to **paraphrase** it, or restate the ideas in simpler words. To paraphrase a line or stanza in a poem, determine its main idea and replace difficult words with easier ones. In some cases, footnotes will help you clarify meaning. Consider the following lines from Lowell's poem "The First Snowfall":

And the poorest twig on the elm-tree
*   Was ridged inch deep with pearl.*

Here is a paraphrase of the same lines that restates the poet's idea in simpler language:

An inch of snow covered the slender twig on the elm tree.

As you read, use a chart like the one shown to record difficult words or phrases and how you might paraphrase them.

Original Word(s)	My Paraphrase

Review: **Make Inferences**

Explore the Key Idea

What can NATURE *teach us?*

KEY IDEA What lessons about life have you learned from **nature?** Perhaps waiting out a thunderstorm taught you something about patience. Or maybe watching monkeys at the zoo helped you to understand group behavior. The selections that follow describe kernels of wisdom two poets gleaned from the natural world.

QUICKWRITE In your notebook, list some insights you have gained from nature. How could you apply these insights to your own life? Write down your thoughts and ideas in a short paragraph.

Scene or Event	Insights
thunderstorm	Nature puts things in perspective.

SNOWBOUND
A Winter Idyll

John Greenleaf Whittier

The sun that brief December day
Rose cheerless over hills of gray,
And, darkly circled, gave at noon
A sadder light than waning[1] moon.
5 Slow tracing down the thickening sky
Its mute and ominous prophecy,
A portent[2] seeming less than threat,
It sank from sight before it set. **Ⓐ**
A chill no coat, however stout,
10 Of homespun stuff could quite shut out,
A hard, dull bitterness of cold,
That checked, mid-vein, the circling race
Of lifeblood in the sharpened face,
The coming of the snowstorm told.
15 The wind blew east; we heard the roar
Of Ocean on his wintry shore,
And felt the strong pulse throbbing there
Beat with low rhythm our inland air.

Meanwhile we did our nightly chores,—
20 Brought in the wood from out of doors,
Littered the stalls, and from the mows
Raked down the herd's grass for the cows:
Heard the horse whinnying for his corn;
And, sharply clashing horn on horn,
25 Impatient down the stanchion rows[3]

Ⓐ MOOD
Think about the mood
of these first eight lines.
What **imagery** helps to set
this mood?

---

1. **waning:** lessening in intensity.
2. **portent:** omen.
3. **stanchion** (stăn′chən) **rows:** lines of devices that fit loosely around the necks of animals such as cows in order to limit their motion.

ANALYZE VISUALS
To what senses does this
photograph appeal, in
addition to sight?

The cattle shake their walnut bows;
While, peering from his early perch
Upon the scaffold's pole of birch,
The cock his crested helmet bent
30 And down his querulous[4] challenge sent.

Unwarmed by any sunset light
The gray day darkened into night,
A night made hoary with the swarm
And whirl-dance of the blinding storm,
35 As zigzag, wavering to and fro,
Crossed and recrossed the wingëd snow:
And ere the early bedtime came
The white drift piled the window frame,
And through the glass the clothesline posts
40 Looked in like tall and sheeted ghosts. **B**

So all night long the storm roared on:
The morning broke without a sun;
In tiny spherule[5] traced with lines
Of Nature's geometric signs,
45 In starry flake, and pellicle,[6]
All day the hoary meteor fell;
And, when the second morning shone,
We looked upon a world unknown,
On nothing we could call our own.
50 Around the glistening wonder bent
The blue walls of the firmament,
No cloud above, no earth below—
A universe of sky and snow! **C**
The old familiar sights of ours
55 Took marvelous shapes; strange domes and towers
Rose up where sty or corncrib stood,
Or garden wall, or belt of wood;
A smooth white mound the brush pile showed,
A fenceless drift what once was road;
60 The bridle post an old man sat
With loose-flung coat and high cocked hat;
The well curb[7] had a Chinese roof;

B **MOOD**
A **simile** is a figure of speech comparing two things using the words *like* or *as*. What mood does the poet create with the simile in lines 39–40?

C **PARAPHRASE**
How has the world been transformed by snow in lines 50–53?

---

4. **querulous** (kwĕr′ə-ləs): complaining.

5. **spherule** (sfîr′ool): a little sphere.

6. **pellicle:** a thin film or skin.

7. **well curb:** framing around the neck of a well.

And even the long sweep,[8] high aloof,
In its slant splendor, seemed to tell
65 Of Pisa's leaning miracle.[9]

A prompt, decisive man, no breath
Our father wasted: "Boys, a path!"
Well pleased, (for when did farmer boy
Count such a summons less than joy?)
70 Our buskins[10] on our feet we drew;
With mittened hands, and caps drawn low,
To guard our necks and ears from snow,
We cut the solid whiteness through.
And, where the drift was deepest, made
75 A tunnel walled and overlaid
With dazzling crystal: we had read
Of rare Aladdin's wondrous cave,[11]
And to our own his name we gave,
With many a wish the luck were ours
80 To test his lamp's supernal[12] powers.
We reached the barn with merry din,
And roused the prisoned brutes within.
The old horse thrust his long head out,
And grave with wonder gazed about;
85 The cock his lusty greeting said,
And forth his speckled harem led;
The oxen lashed their tails, and hooked,
And mild reproach of hunger looked;
The hornëd patriarch of the sheep,
90 Like Egypt's Amun[13] roused from sleep,
Shook his sage head with gesture mute,
And emphasized with stamp of foot. **D**

All day the gusty north wind bore
The loosening drift its breath before;
95 Low circling round its southern zone,
The sun through dazzling snow-mist shone.
No church bell lent its Christian tone

D MOOD
Identify examples of **figurative language** and **imagery** in lines 66–92. What is the mood created by this language?

---

8. **sweep:** a long pole connected to a bucket, used for raising water from a well.

9. **Pisa's leaning miracle:** the Leaning Tower of Pisa, Italy.

10. **buskins:** high leather boots.

11. **Aladdin's wondrous cave:** In *The Thousand and One Nights*, the boy Aladdin used a magic lamp to discover a treasure in a cave.

12. **supernal:** heavenly; supernatural.

13. **Amun** (ä′mən): the supreme god of the ancient Egyptians, often represented as having a ram's head.

To the savage air, no social smoke
Curled over woods of snow-hung oak.
100 A solitude made more intense
By dreary-voicëd elements,
The shrieking of the mindless wind,
The moaning tree boughs swaying blind,
And on the glass the unmeaning beat
105 Of ghostly fingertips of sleet.
Beyond the circle of our hearth
No welcome sound of toil or mirth
Unbound the spell, and testified
Of human life and thought outside. **E**

110 We minded that the sharpest ear
The buried brooklet could not hear,
The music of whose liquid lip
Had been to us companionship,
And, in our lonely life, had grown
115 To have an almost human tone.

As night drew on, and, from the crest
Of wooded knolls that ridged the west,
The sun, a snow-blown traveler, sank
From sight beneath the smothering bank,
120 We piled, with care, our nightly stack
Of wood against the chimney back,—
The oaken log, green, huge, and thick,
And on its top the stout backstick;
The knotty forestick laid apart,
125 And filled between with curious art
The ragged brush; then, hovering near,
We watched the first red blaze appear,
Heard the sharp crackle, caught the gleam
On whitewashed wall and sagging beam,
130 Until the old, rude-furnished room
Burst, flowerlike, into rosy bloom;
While radiant with a mimic flame
Outside the sparkling drift became,
And through the bare-boughed lilac tree
135 Our own warm hearth seemed blazing free.
The crane and pendent trammels showed,
The Turks' heads on the andirons[14] glowed;

E **PARAPHRASE**
Reread lines 106–109.
What effect does the
snowstorm have on the
family's sense of itself and
the world outside?

---

14. **The crane . . . the andirons:** The crane was the movable arm
on which the trammels, or adjustable pothooks, hung. The
andirons, or metal supports holding the fireplace wood, were
topped with turbanlike knots.

While childish fancy, prompt to tell
The meaning of the miracle,
140 Whispered the old rhyme: *"Under the tree,*
When fire outdoors burns merrily,
There the witches are making tea." **F**

The moon above the eastern wood
Shone at its full; the hill range stood
145 Transfigured in the silver flood,
Its blown snows flashing cold and keen,
Dead white, save where some sharp ravine
Took shadow, or the somber green
Of hemlocks turned to pitchy black
150 Against the whiteness at their back.
For such a world and such a night
Most fitting that unwarming light,
Which only seemed where'er it fell
To make the coldness visible.

155 Shut in from all the world without,
We sat the clean-winged hearth[15] about,
Content to let the north wind roar
In baffled rage at pane and door,
While the red logs before us beat
160 The frost line back with tropic heat; **G**
And ever, when a louder blast
Shook beam and rafter as it passed,
The merrier up its roaring draught
The great throat of the chimney laughed;
165 The house dog on his paws outspread
Laid to the fire his drowsy head,
The cat's dark silhouette on the wall
A couchant[16] tiger's seemed to fall;
And, for the winter fireside meet,
170 Between the andirons' straddling feet,
The mug of cider simmered slow,
The apples sputtered in a row,
And, close at hand, the basket stood
With nuts from brown October's wood.

F MOOD
In lines 116–142, what techniques does the poet use to create a mood of security and warmth in the midst of nature's cold and snow?

G MAKE INFERENCES
Reread lines 155–160. Why is the north wind baffled?

---

15. **clean-winged hearth:** Hearths were commonly swept with a turkey wing.

16. **couchant** (kou'chənt): lying down, but with head raised.

THE FIRST SNOWFALL

James Russell Lowell

The snow had begun in the gloaming,[1]
    And busily all the night
Had been heaping field and highway
    With a silence deep and white.

5 Every pine and fir and hemlock
    Wore ermine[2] too dear for an earl,
And the poorest twig on the elmtree
    Was ridged inch deep with pearl.

From sheds new-roofed with Carrara[3]
10   Came Chanticleer's[4] muffled crow,
The stiff rails softened to swan's-down,
    And still fluttered down the snow.

I stood and watched by the window
    The noiseless work of the sky,
15 And the sudden flurries of snowbirds,
    Like brown leaves whirling by. ⓗ

I thought of a mound in sweet Auburn[5]
    Where a little headstone stood;
How the flakes were folding it gently,
20   As did robins the babes in the wood. ⓘ

Up spoke our own little Mabel,
    Saying, "Father, who makes it snow?"
And I told of the good All-father
    Who cares for us here below.

ⓗ **MOOD**
Reread lines 1–16. How would you describe the mood created by the poet's use of **rhyme** and **meter?** Explain your answer.

ⓘ **PARAPHRASE**
Paraphrase lines 17–20. How does the mood shift in these lines?

---

1. **gloaming:** twilight.
2. **ermine:** the expensive white fur of a type of weasel.
3. **Carrara:** Carrara marble, a white marble named after the Italian city where it is mined.
4. **Chanticleer's:** a rooster's.
5. **Auburn:** Mount Auburn Cemetery, located in Cambridge, Massachusetts.

ANALYZE VISUALS
This photograph shows
Mount Auburn Cemetery,
which is mentioned in
the poem. What **mood**
is suggested by the
photograph, what details
support the mood, and
how does the mood of
the picture match that of
the poem?

25 Again I looked at the snowfall,
    And thought of the leaden sky
That arched o'er our first great sorrow,
    When that mound was heaped so high. **J**

    I remembered the gradual patience
30   That fell from that cloud like snow,
    Flake by flake, healing and hiding
        The scar that renewed our woe.

    And again to the child I whispered,
        "The snow that husheth all,
35 Darling, the merciful Father
        Alone can make it fall!" **K**

    Then, with eyes that saw not, I kissed her;
        And she, kissing back, could not know
    That *my* kiss was given to her sister,
40   Folded close under deepening snow.

J **MAKE INFERENCES**
In line 17, "mound" refers
to the daughter's grave.
What else does "mound"
refer to in line 28?

K **MOOD**
What mood does the
speaker create at the end
of the poem by invoking
the "merciful Father"?

Comprehension

1. **Recall** In what ways does the family in "Snowbound" prepare for and cope with the storm?

2. **Clarify** How does the family in "Snowbound" feel about being snowed in?

3. **Summarize** How does the snowfall transform the landscape in lines 1–14 of "The First Snowfall"?

4. **Clarify** In "The First Snowfall," what has happened to the family?

Literary Analysis

5. **Make Inferences** How do the speaker and family in "Snowbound" respond to the storm? What do their responses suggest about their relationship to one another and to **nature?**

6. **Interpret Figurative Language** Reread lines 29–32 of "The First Snowfall." What does the figurative language in this stanza suggest about the family's grief and the relation of their sorrow to the natural world?

7. **Paraphrase to Draw Conclusions** Review the paraphrases you made in your chart as you read Lowell's poem. Describe Lowell's religious beliefs. How do they help the poet cope with his pain?

8. **Analyze Mood** Poets can use a variety of devices to establish mood, including **figurative language, imagery, rhyme,** and **meter.** In each of the poems, identify two devices used to create mood, giving examples. For each poem, which device would you say is the more important? Explain.

9. **Associate Ideas** In these poems and elsewhere, snow is often referred to as having a quieting effect. What are some common metaphors or images used to express our associations with these other kinds of weather?

   - downpour
   - windstorm
   - torrid heat
   - Indian summer

Literary Criticism

10. **Historical Context** Whittier and Lowell were two of a group known as the Fireside Poets. (See page 302.) This name refers to a popular family pastime of the period: reading poetry aloud in front of the fireplace after dinner. The poems of the group were very popular and read as entertainment not only in homes but also in schools. Why might the poetry of this group have played such an important role in people's lives? Support your opinion.

The Fireside Poets were extremely popular in their day. Indeed, they were so beloved that many families read their works aloud by the fire as a form of nightly entertainment. They were respected as well, becoming the first poets to be considered on equal footing with their British counterparts. Over the years, however, the group's works fell out of favor with critics, who began to look upon them with more affection than respect. Only in recent years have critics again begun to appreciate the craft of the Fireside Poets.

Writing to Evaluate

With a group of classmates, come up with several criteria for evaluating the poems on pages 336–355. Then use your criteria to write a brief evaluation of the work of the Fireside Poets as a whole.

Consider

- what elements (vivid imagery, precise word choice, or thought-provoking themes) you think distinguish "good" poetry from "bad"
- whether the poems contain those elements
- whether your opinion of the poems changed upon rereading

Extension

SPEAKING & LISTENING

Perform an **oral interpretation** of one poem from this group of Fireside Poets' work. Let your opinion of the Fireside Poets in general and of this work in particular inform your reading. For example, if you admire a particular poem, you may wish to read it in a lively and engaging voice. If, on the other hand, you found a poem too sentimental, let your reading reflect this judgment.

The Art of the Essay

When you write an essay for class, you are taking part in a literary tradition that goes back hundreds of years. In classroom writing, the essay may have many rules governing its structure and topic, but in the literary world, essays come in all shapes and sizes, accommodate any topic, and can be found in books, magazines, and daily newspapers.

First Attempts

An **essay** is a short work of nonfiction that offers a writer's opinion on a particular subject. The length can vary greatly. Some are personal, while others are coldly factual. The essay originated with the 16th-century French philosopher Michel de Montaigne, who first introduced the form when he published a collection of writings entitled *Essais,* a French word meaning "attempts." English writers began using the form, and eventually it became commonplace.

Two masters of the American essay in the 19th century were Ralph Waldo Emerson and Henry David Thoreau. These writers used the form to express their philosophies and personal views on a variety of topics, from the ideal lifestyle to the beauty of nature. Using notes he recorded in his journals, Emerson created essays that gave his ideas structure and refined his concepts. In turn they became the cornerstone of **transcendentalism,**

Thoreau's Walden Pond today, located just outside Concord, Massachusetts.

a literary and philosophical movement that emphasized individualism and intuition as a means to understanding reality. Among Thoreau's works is a series of essays, entitled *Walden,* in which he describes his experience of living out the ideals of individualism at Walden Pond (see page 372).

Emerson and Thoreau laid the groundwork for the American essay. Since then, numerous writers have gained reputations as respected authors of the form, including H. L. Mencken, Ernest Hemingway, E. B. White, Joan Didion, and Amy Tan.

The Craft of Expressing Ideas

Essays generally fall into one of two traditions. **Formal essays** explore topics in a serious and organized manner. **Informal essays** adopt a more casual tone and may include humor and unconventional topics. These essays are often more personal in nature. Emerson's "Self-Reliance" (see page 362) is a formal essay, whereas Thoreau's *Walden* essays are more informal.

Whether the essay's purpose is to be **persuasive, expository, descriptive,** or **narrative,** essayists typically rely on these elements to express their ideas:

- **Organization** is the arrangement of the main ideas and supporting details. Some essays may be narratives that read like a story, while others may follow a strict pattern of organization, such as **cause-and-effect** or **compare-and-contrast.**

- **Supporting details** include facts, opinions, reasons, sensory details, anecdotes, and examples that support the **main idea,** the most important idea about a topic.

- **Diction** is the way a writer uses and arranges language. Some writers use simple and casual words and sentences that may create a personal voice. Others are more formal, using elevated language and complex sentence structures.

- **Tone** is the expression of a writer's attitude toward a subject and may be described as serious, humorous, sarcastic, and so on. The writer's diction and details will provide clues to his or her tone.

"Self-Reliance" is a carefully constructed argument in the form of an essay. Emerson organizes his ideas step by step, leading the reader to the conclusion he wants them to reach—an understanding of his philosophy of individualism. Note Emerson's **opinions,** abstract **language,** and formal **tone** in this passage from "Self-Reliance":

> There is a time in every man's education when he arrives at the conviction that envy is ignorance; that imitation is suicide; that he must take himself for better for worse as his portion . . . .
>
> —**Ralph Waldo Emerson, "Self-Reliance"**

Close Read

What ideas does Emerson introduce in this sentence? Paraphrase his ideas in your own words.

Thoreau, on the other hand, takes a more personal and informal approach in *Walden.* Even though his **sentence structure** is complicated and lengthy, the **language** is simple, and the **details** are concrete.

> When first I took up my abode in the woods, that is, began to spend my nights as well as days there, which, by accident, was on Independence day, or the fourth of July 1845, my house was not finished for winter, but was merely a defense against the rain, without plastering or chimney, the walls being of rough weather-stained boards, with wide chinks, which made it cool at night.
>
> —**Henry David Thoreau, *Walden***

Close Read

Note the **diction** and **details** in this passage. What do they reveal about Thoreau's **tone?**

from **Self-Reliance**
from **Nature**

Essays by Ralph Waldo Emerson

Old North Bridge, Concord, Massachusetts

Ralph Waldo Emerson
1803–1882

As the acknowledged leader of the transcendentalists, Ralph Waldo Emerson, poet, essayist, and lecturer, was a towering figure in the 19th-century literary world. He helped shape a new, uniquely American body of literature and is often cited as one of the most significant writers in American history. "All life is an experiment," the radical thinker and writer once said. "The more experiments you make, the better."

An Average Student Emerson was born in Boston, Massachusetts. His father, a prominent Unitarian minister, died when Emerson was eight, plunging the family into financial trouble. Although money was tight, funds were found to enroll Emerson at Harvard. When he graduated in 1821, ranked 30th out of a class of 59, there was little indication that Emerson would soon become one of the most celebrated literary figures of all time.

Spiritual Crisis In 1825, Emerson returned to Harvard to study for the Unitarian ministry and was ordained in 1829. Just over a year later, his beloved wife, Ellen, died of tuberculosis. Ellen's death threw Emerson into a state of spiritual crisis, causing him to question many aspects of the Christian tradition and his duties as a minister. In 1832, after much consideration, Emerson resigned his post.

The Voice of Transcendentalism Following his wife's death, Emerson settled in Concord, Massachusetts, and devoted himself to the study of philosophy, religion, and literature. In 1836 Emerson published *Nature,* in which he eloquently articulated his transcendental philosophy, an outgrowth of European romanticism. That same year, Emerson formed the Transcendental Club with a group of like-minded friends, including Henry David Thoreau and Margaret Fuller. *Nature,* with its emphasis on self-reliance and individuality, became the group's unofficial manifesto.

The Sage of Concord Those who met Emerson in person often thought him a rather stiff and formal person, dressed always in black. He reserved his passion for the page and the podium, where he elaborated upon his ideas in essays and a series of popular lectures. By the 1840s the Sage of Concord, as he was known, had become a major literary force whose influence is still evident in American culture today.

● LITERARY ANALYSIS: TRANSCENDENTALISM

Ralph Waldo Emerson's motto was "Trust thyself." This principle lies at the heart of **transcendentalism,** an intellectual movement that emphasized the dignity of the individual and advocated a simple, mindful life. The transcendentalists, led by Emerson himself, wanted to transcend—or go beyond—the limitations of the senses and everyday experience. Key tenets of transcendentalism include

- a theory that "transcendent forms" of truth exist beyond reason and experience; every individual is capable of discovering this truth on his or her own, through intuition
- a conviction that people are inherently good and should follow their own beliefs, however controversial they may be
- a belief that humankind, nature, and God are all interconnected

As you read, consider how Emerson's writing articulates his belief in the importance of the individual as well as his ideas about humankind's relationship to the natural world.

● READING SKILL: IDENTIFY APHORISMS

An **aphorism** is a brief statement, usually one sentence long, that expresses a general principle or truth about life. Benjamin Franklin's famous declaration "Honesty is the best policy" is one example of an aphorism. As you read, use a chart to record aphorisms that stand out to you. Think about how these statements reflect Emerson's transcendentalist ideals.

"Self-Reliance"	Nature
"Trust thyself: every heart vibrates to that iron string."	

▲ VOCABULARY IN CONTEXT

Emerson uses these words to state his convictions. Test your knowledge by deciding which word is suggested by each phrase.

WORD LIST	aversion	exhilaration	nonconformist
	decorum	importune	occult

1. a food you can't stand
2. a race you have just won
3. a well-behaved crowd
4. a nagging younger sibling

What is your MOTTO?

KEY IDEA The ancient Roman poet Horace gravely advised, "Never despair." Modern comedian Woody Allen quipped that the secret to success in life is simple: "Eighty percent of success is showing up." Each of these mottos captures an individual's attitude toward life in one pithy phrase. Ralph Waldo Emerson's motto, "Trust thyself," distills the essence of the **ideals** he expressed in his essays and lectures.

QUICKWRITE Create your own personal motto. To get started, consider the traits or resources that helped you solve a difficult problem, or the best advice you've ever given a friend. Use your answers to develop a personal motto that is short and to the point.

live the life you have imagined

Self-Reliance

RALPH WALDO EMERSON

There is a time in every man's education when he arrives at the conviction that envy is ignorance; that imitation is suicide; that he must take himself for better for worse as his portion; that though the wide universe is full of good, no kernel of nourishing corn can come to him but through his toil bestowed on that plot of ground which is given to him to till. . . .

Trust thyself: every heart vibrates to that iron string. Accept the place the divine providence has found for you, the society of your contemporaries, the connection of events. Great men have always done so, and confided themselves childlike to the genius of their age, betraying their perception that the absolutely trustworthy[1]
10 was seated at their heart, working through their hands, predominating[2] in all their being. . . . **Ⓐ**

Whoso would be a man, must be a **nonconformist.** He who would gather immortal palms[3] must not be hindered by the name of goodness, but must explore if it be goodness. Nothing is at last sacred but the integrity of your own mind. Absolve you to yourself, and you shall have the suffrage[4] of the world. I remember an answer which when quite young I was prompted to make to a valued adviser

ANALYZE VISUALS
What elements of **transcendentalism** are reflected in the painting on page 363?

Ⓐ TRANSCENDENTALISM
Summarize the ideas Emerson presents in lines 1–11. After reading these lines, how would you define self-reliance?

nonconformist
(nŏn′kən-fôr′mĭst) *n.* one who does not follow generally accepted beliefs, customs, or practices

1. **the absolutely trustworthy:** God.
2. **predominating:** being predominant, or having controlling influence.
3. **immortal palms:** everlasting triumph and honor. In ancient times, people carried palm leaves as a symbol of victory, success, or joy.
4. **suffrage:** approval; support.

Wanderer Above the Sea of Fog (1818), Caspar David Friedrich. Oil on canvas, 94.8 cm × 74.8 cm.

who was wont to **importune** me with the dear old doctrines of the church. On my saying, "What have I to do with the sacredness of traditions, if I live wholly from within?" my friend suggested—"But these impulses may be from below, not from
20 above." I replied, "They do not seem to me to be such; but if I am the Devil's child, I will live then from the Devil." No law can be sacred to me but that of my nature. Good and bad are but names very readily transferable to that or this; the only right is what is after my constitution;[5] the only wrong what is against it. . . . **B**

What I must do is all that concerns me, not what the people think. This rule, equally arduous in actual and in intellectual life, may serve for the whole distinction between greatness and meanness.[6] It is the harder because you will always find those who think they know what is your duty better than you know it. It is easy in the world to live after the world's opinion; it is easy in solitude to live after our own; but the great man is he who in the midst of the crowd keeps with
30 perfect sweetness the independence of solitude. . . . **C**

For nonconformity the world whips you with its displeasure. And therefore a man must know how to estimate a sour face. The by-standers look askance on him in the public street or in the friend's parlor. If this **aversion** had its origin in contempt and resistance like his own he might well go home with a sad countenance; but the sour faces of the multitude, like their sweet faces, have no deep cause, but are put on and off as the wind blows and a newspaper directs. . . .

The other terror that scares us from self-trust is our consistency; a reverence for our past act or word because the eyes of others have no other data for computing our orbit than our past acts, and we are loth to disappoint them. . . .
40 A foolish consistency is the hobgoblin[7] of little minds, adored by little statesmen and philosophers and divines.[8] With consistency a great soul has simply nothing to do. He may as well concern himself with his shadow on the wall. Speak what you think now in hard words and tomorrow speak what tomorrow thinks in hard words again, though it contradict everything you said today.—"Ah, so you shall be sure to be misunderstood."— Is it so bad then to be misunderstood? Pythagoras was misunderstood, and Socrates, and Jesus, and Luther, and Copernicus, and Galileo, and Newton,[9] and every pure and wise spirit that ever took flesh. To be great is to be misunderstood. ∿ **D**

importune (ĭm′pôr-tōōn′) v. to ask urgently or repeatedly; to annoy or trouble

B TRANSCENDENTALISM
Transcendentalists believed in disregarding external authority in favor of one's own experience and intuition. What is implied by the word *sacred* in line 21?

C GRAMMAR AND STYLE
Emerson adds detail and precision to his writing by using **adjective clauses,** which modify nouns and pronouns. In line 27 and lines 29–30, he uses adjective clauses beginning with "who" to describe specific types of people.

aversion (ə-vûr′zhən) n. a strong dislike

D IDENTIFY APHORISMS
Identify at least one aphorism in lines 40–48. How does that aphorism reflect Emerson's transcendentalist ideals?

---

5. **after my constitution:** consistent with my nature.

6. **meanness:** the state of being inferior in quality, character, or value.

7. **hobgoblin:** a source of fear or dread.

8. **divines:** religious leaders.

9. **Pythagoras** (pĭ-thăg′ər-əs) . . . **Newton:** great thinkers whose radical theories and viewpoints caused controversy.

Nature

RALPH WALDO EMERSON

Nature is a setting that fits equally well a comic or a mourning piece. In good health, the air is a cordial of incredible virtue. Crossing a bare common, in snow puddles, at twilight, under a clouded sky, without having in my thoughts any occurrence of special good fortune, I have enjoyed a perfect **exhilaration.** I am glad to the brink of fear. In the woods too, a man casts off his years, as the snake his slough,[1] and at what period soever of life, is always a child. In the woods, is perpetual youth. Within these plantations of God, a **decorum** and sanctity reign, a perennial festival is dressed, and the guest sees not how he should tire of them in a thousand years. In the woods, we return to reason and faith. There I feel that
10 nothing can befall me in life,—no disgrace, no calamity, (leaving me my eyes,) which nature cannot repair. Standing on the bare ground,—my head bathed by the blithe air, and uplifted into infinite space,—all mean egotism vanishes. I become a transparent eye-ball; I am nothing; I see all; the currents of the Universal Being circulate through me; I am part or particle of God. The name of the nearest friend sounds then foreign and accidental: to be brothers, to be acquaintances,— master or servant, is then a trifle and a disturbance. I am the lover of uncontained and immortal beauty. In the wilderness, I find something more dear and connate[2] than in streets or villages. In the tranquil landscape, and especially in the distant line of the horizon, man beholds somewhat as beautiful as his own nature. **ⓔ**

exhilaration
(ĭg-zĭl′ə-rā′shən) *n.* a feeling of high spirits or lively joy

decorum (dĭ-kôr′əm) *n.* good taste in conduct or appearance

ⓔ TRANSCENDENTALISM
Review the elements of transcendentalism listed on page 361. Which aspect of transcendentalist thought is reflected in lines 12–19?

---

1. **slough** (slŭf): the cast-off skin of a snake.

2. **connate:** agreeable; able to be related to.

20   The greatest delight which the fields and woods minister, is the suggestion
of an **occult** relation between man and the vegetable. I am not alone and
unacknowledged. They nod to me, and I to them. The waving of the boughs in
the storm, is new to me and old. It takes me by surprise, and yet is not unknown.
Its effect is like that of a higher thought or a better emotion coming over me,
when I deemed I was thinking justly or doing right.

        Yet it is certain that the power to produce this delight, does not reside in
nature, but in man, or in a harmony of both. It is necessary to use these pleasures
with great temperance. For, nature is not always tricked[3] in holiday attire, but the
same scene which yesterday breathed perfume and glittered as for the frolic of the
30 nymphs, is overspread with melancholy today. Nature always wears the colors of
the spirit. To a man laboring under calamity, the heat of his own fire hath sadness
in it. Then, there is a kind of contempt of the landscape felt by him who has just
lost by death a dear friend. The sky is less grand as it shuts down over less worth
in the population. ∞ **F**

---

3. **tricked:** dressed.

occult (ə-kŭlt′) *adj.* secret
or hidden from view

F **TRANSCENDENTALISM**
Reread lines 30–34. What
is Emerson saying about
our perception of the
natural world?

ANALYZE VISUALS
Emerson says that
"nature always wears the
colors of the spirit." What
mood does this painting
convey? Describe the
elements of the painting
that establish this mood.

Ben Lomond (1829–1830), Thomas Doughty. Oil on canvas. © Christie's Images/SuperStock.

Comprehension

1. **Recall** According to "Self-Reliance," what is the only law that Emerson can hold sacred?

2. **Summarize** What are three ways the woods can transform a man, according to Emerson in *Nature?*

3. **Clarify** In *Nature,* Emerson discusses the "delight" the natural world often inspires. What does Emerson think this power to delight comes from?

Critical Analysis

4. **Draw Conclusions** Reread lines 37–48 of "Self-Reliance." What is Emerson speaking of when he mentions consistency, and why does he berate it as "the hobgoblin of little minds"? Consider the following examples of Emerson's statements as you formulate your response:

    - "Good and bad are but names very readily transferable to that or this. . . ."
    - ". . . The sour faces of the multitude . . . have no deep cause, but are put on and off as the wind blows. . . ."

5. **Identify Elements of Transcendentalism** Review the elements of transcendentalism listed on page 361. Then reexamine "Self-Reliance" and *Nature,* identifying key ideas that reflect each tenet of transcendentalism. Record your answer in a chart like the one shown.

Element of Transcendentalism	Example from the Text
Every individual is capable of discovering higher truths on his or her own, through intuition.	"Nothing is at last sacred but the integrity of your own mind." ("Self-Reliance," line 14)

6. **Synthesize Ideas** Which **ideals** do the essays celebrate that reflect Emerson's motto, "Trust thyself"? Citing specific lines from both essays, explain how Emerson's main principles relate to his famous motto.

7. **Evaluate Aphorisms** Review the aphorisms you recorded as you read. Choose three or four that you found meaningful or evocative and explain whether or not they have stood the test of time.

Literary Criticism

8. **Critical Interpretation** Writer Henry James argued that Emerson had no concept of the evil that exists in the world. In James's words, it was "a side of life as to which Emerson's eyes were thickly bandaged. . . . He had no great sense of wrong . . . no sense of the dark, the foul, the base." In your opinion, is this a valid criticism of Emerson? Citing evidence, explain why or why not.

Vocabulary in Context

VOCABULARY PRACTICE

Choose the vocabulary word that best completes each sentence.

WORD LIST
aversion
decorum
exhilaration
importune
nonconformist
occult

1. An unexpected tragedy can quickly turn_____ into grief.
2. To constantly _____ a friend for favors can destroy the friendship.
3. One should act with _____ on serious or formal occasions.
4. It is not wise to pry into the _____ intrigues of others.
5. Certain values are held by every person, whether a traditionalist or a(n) _____.
6. It makes sense to avoid anything to which one has a(n) _____.

VOCABULARY IN WRITING

Find a statement in these selections that you strongly agree or disagree with. Identify the statement and, using two or more vocabulary words, explain your views on it. Here is a sample beginning.

EXAMPLE SENTENCE

*I share Emerson's **exhilaration** at walking in the woods, and I, too, see woods as a source of "reason and faith."*

VOCABULARY STRATEGY: WORDS WITH MULTIPLE AFFIXES

You can decipher many long words if you are able to locate a recognizable base word within them. Removing the prefix and the suffix from the vocabulary word *nonconformist,* for example, reveals the base word *conform.* What meanings do the affixes add to the base word? Analyze similar words by separating them into a base word and affixes. Remember that many base words drop the final *e* before suffixes are added.

PRACTICE Write the base word and the affixes that make up each word listed. Then write a sentence that demonstrates the meaning of the longer word.

1. prefabricated
2. undiversified
3. disreputable
4. repagination
5. indefatigable
6. abnegation

VOCABULARY PRACTICE
For more practice, go to the **Vocabulary Center** at **ClassZone.com.**

Reading-Writing Connection

GRAMMAR AND STYLE

USE DESCRIPTIVE DETAILS Review the **Grammar and Style** note on page 364. The power and precision of Emerson's prose owes a good deal to his skillful use of **adjective clauses**—subordinate clauses that, like adjectives, add important detail about nouns and pronouns. An adjective clause usually follows the word it modifies and is introduced by words such as *when, who, whom, whose, that,* and *which.* Here is an example from "Self-Reliance":

> There is a time in every man's education *when he arrives at the conviction that envy is ignorance; that imitation is suicide; that he must take himself for better for worse as his portion.* . . . (lines 1–3)

Notice that each of the highlighted phrases offers information about the word it modifies. The first phrase tells you about the "time in every man's education" Emerson is discussing. The second, third, and fourth clauses explain what kind of convictions he embraces at this time.

PRACTICE Identify the adjective clause in each sentence from Emerson's work. Then write your own sentences, using adjective clauses as Emerson does.

> **EXAMPLE**
>
> He *who would gather immortal palms* must not be hindered by the name of goodness, but must explore if it be goodness.
>
> *Those who wish to make a true difference cannot worry what others might say behind their backs.*

1. There is a kind of contempt of the landscape felt by him who has just lost by death a dear friend.

2. Nature is a setting that fits equally well a comic or a mourning piece.

3. There I feel that nothing can befall me in life,—no disgrace, no calamity, (leaving my eyes,) which nature cannot repair.

WRITING TOOLS
For prewriting, revision, and editing tools, visit the **Writing Center** at ClassZone.com.

from **Walden**
from **Civil Disobedience**

Essays by Henry David Thoreau

Henry David Thoreau
1817–1862

Henry David Thoreau (thə-rō′) advocated simple, mindful living and rejected a lifestyle dedicated to the pursuit of wealth. Thoreau spent much of his life writing and observing nature, devoting only a minimum of time to earning a wage. He published just two books, both of which sold very poorly in his own lifetime. Few of his contemporaries would have judged him much of a success. In the years since his death, however, his reputation has grown tremendously. Today, he is regarded as a writer of uncommon vision and remembered as one of the first environmentalists.

Independent Spirit Thoreau was born and raised in Concord, Massachusetts, and attended Harvard University. After graduating, he returned to Concord to teach school. Though some of Thoreau's neighbors viewed him as eccentric, he was a careful observer and a deep thinker. Taking to heart the ideas of his friend Ralph Waldo Emerson, Thoreau tried to live by his own values, often doing odd jobs that would earn him just enough money to meet his own modest needs.

Defiant Nonconformist Thoreau's life was full of examples of his nonconformity to society's norms. As a Harvard student, he was required to wear a black coat but sported a green one instead. In his first year of teaching, he refused to punish his students physically, a harsh but common practice of the time, and resigned his post. In 1845, he conducted his famous experiment, living simply and frugally in a small cabin on the shores of Walden Pond. In 1846, he was arrested and spent a night in jail for refusing to pay a poll tax, an act of protest against the U.S. government's war with Mexico and its support of slavery. This exercise of conscience over law later became known as civil disobedience.

Influential Thinker At the time of Thoreau's death from tuberculosis at age 44, he was viewed as an unsuccessful nature writer. Today, however, he is known as the father of American nature writing and an important political thinker. His observations about the natural world and the value of the simple life, as well as his promotion of nonviolent protest, have helped bring about great societal change. He has provided inspiration to many, including conservationist John Muir and civil rights leader Martin Luther King Jr.

SITE OF
THOREAU'S
CABIN

DISCOVERED
NOV 11 1945
BY
ROLAND WELLS ROBBINS

● LITERARY ANALYSIS: ESSAY

An **essay** is a work of nonfiction that usually deals with a single main subject. Though essays can be formal or informal, they are often loosely structured and contain the personal views of the writer. To analyze an essay, pay careful attention to

- the writer's **tone,** or attitude toward his or her subject
- **figurative language** that makes abstract concepts more understandable and emphasizes ideas
- **anecdotes,** or short accounts of personal incidents
- **imagery** that creates vivid impressions for the reader

As you read, consider how these elements illuminate Thoreau's ideas and give readers a glimpse into his personality.

Review: **Transcendentalism**

● READING SKILL: EVALUATE IDEAS

When you **evaluate** a writer's ideas, you examine them carefully and then make judgments about their value. Before you can judge a writer's ideas, however, you have to identify and understand them. **Summarizing** can help. As you read *Walden,* use a chart like the one shown to briefly restate Thoreau's philosophical ideas in your own words. As you tackle "Civil Disobedience," summarize the author's main political beliefs. After you summarize each idea, note your reaction to it.

	Thoreau's Ideas and Beliefs	My Reactions
Walden		
"Civil Disobedience"		

▲ VOCABULARY IN CONTEXT

Thoreau uses the following words to present his theories about simple, principled living. To see how many you know, choose the word that is closest in meaning to each numbered term.

WORD LIST	abject	impetuous	pervade
	congenial	misgiving	transgress
	deliberately	perturbation	

1. err
2. disturbance
3. doubt
4. wretched
5. friendly
6. permeate
7. impulsive
8. thoughtfully

Do you chart your own COURSE?

KEY IDEA "Cranks," "crackpots," "oddballs"—society is quick to apply a negative label to people outside the mainstream. Although Thoreau was probably never called an "oddball," he was certainly regarded as an eccentric. **Nonconformity** has never been an easy choice, as people often condemn nonconformists without bothering to find out why they embrace a different set of values. Nevertheless, history has shown that many nonconformists, like Thoreau, are often simply ahead of their time.

DISCUSS With a small group of classmates, create a list of famous nonconformists. How did the individuals you listed depart from the norms of their time? Were they punished for their actions? Were they able to win others to their point of view? Discuss these questions with your group.

WALDEN

Henry David Thoreau

> **BACKGROUND** Like Ralph Waldo Emerson and other transcendentalists, Thoreau felt a need to affirm his unity with nature. On July 4, 1845, he began an experiment in what he thought of as "essential living"—living simply, studying the natural world, and seeking truth within himself. On land owned by Emerson near Concord, Massachusetts, Thoreau built a small cabin by Walden Pond and lived there for more than two years, writing and studying nature. *Walden* is the record of his experiences.

from WHERE I LIVED, AND WHAT I LIVED FOR

When first I took up my abode in the woods, that is, began to spend my nights as well as days there, which, by accident, was on Independence day, or the fourth of July, 1845, my house was not finished for winter, but was merely a defense against the rain, without plastering or chimney, the walls being of rough weather-stained boards, with wide chinks, which made it cool at night. The upright white hewn studs and freshly planed door and window casings gave it a clean and airy look, especially in the morning, when its timbers were saturated with dew, so that I fancied that by noon some sweet gum would exude from them. . . . **Ⓐ**

10   I was seated by the shore of a small pond, about a mile and a half south of the village of Concord and somewhat higher than it, in the midst of an extensive wood between that town and Lincoln, and about two miles south of that our only field known to fame, Concord Battle Ground; but I was so low in the woods that the opposite shore, half a mile off, like the rest, covered with wood, was my most distant horizon. For the first week, whenever I looked out on the pond it impressed me like a tarn high up

ANALYZE VISUALS
Consider the tranquil scene depicted in the photograph on page 373. What aspect of the photograph is most responsible for conveying this sense of tranquility, and why?

Ⓐ ESSAY
Think about Thoreau's **tone** as he describes his crude, unfinished house. What sense of the writer's views or personality do you get from these opening lines?

16 tarn: a small mountain lake or pool.

on the side of a mountain, its bottom far above the surface of other lakes, and, as the sun arose, I saw it throwing off its nightly clothing of mist, and here and there, by degrees, its soft ripples or its smooth reflecting surface
20 was revealed, while the mists, like ghosts, were stealthily withdrawing in every direction into the woods, as at the breaking up of some nocturnal conventicle. The very dew seemed to hang upon the trees later into the day than usual, as on the sides of mountains. . . .

I went to the woods because I wished to live **deliberately,** to front only the essential facts of life, and see if I could not learn what it had to teach, and not, when I came to die, discover that I had not lived. I did not wish to live what was not life, living is so dear; nor did I wish to practice resignation, unless it was quite necessary. I wanted to live deep and suck out all the marrow of life, to live so sturdily and Spartan-like as to put to rout all that
30 was not life, to cut a broad swath and shave close, to drive life into a corner, and reduce it to its lowest terms, and, if it proved to be mean, why then to get the whole and genuine meanness of it, and publish its meanness to the world; or if it were sublime, to know it by experience, and be able to give a true account of it in my next excursion. For most men, it appears to me, are in a strange uncertainty about it, whether it is of the devil or of God, and have *somewhat hastily* concluded that it is the chief end of man here to "glorify God and enjoy him forever." **B**

Still we live meanly, like ants; though the fable tells us that we were long ago changed into men; like pygmies we fight with cranes; it is error
40 upon error, and clout upon clout, and our best virtue has for its occasion a superfluous and evitable wretchedness. Our life is frittered away by detail. An honest man has hardly need to count more than his ten fingers, or in extreme cases he may add his ten toes, and lump the rest. Simplicity, simplicity, simplicity! I say, let your affairs be as two or three, and not a hundred or a thousand; instead of a million count half a dozen, and keep your accounts on your thumbnail. In the midst of this chopping sea of civilized life, such are the clouds and storms and quicksands and thousand-and-one items to be allowed for, that a man has to live, if he would not founder and go to the bottom and not make his port at all, by dead
50 reckoning, and he must be a great calculator indeed who succeeds. Simplify, simplify. Instead of three meals a day, if it be necessary eat but one; instead of a hundred dishes, five; and reduce other things in proportion. . . . **C**

Why should we live with such hurry and waste of life? We are determined to be starved before we are hungry. Men say that a stitch in time saves nine, and so they take a thousand stitches today to save nine to-morrow. As for *work,* we haven't any of any consequence. We have the Saint Vitus' dance, and cannot possibly keep our heads still. If I should only give a few pulls at the parish bell-rope, as for a fire, that is, without setting the bell, there is hardly a man on his farm in the outskirts of Concord, notwithstanding that
60 press of engagements which was his excuse so many times this morning,

22 **conventicle:** a secret religious meeting.

deliberately (dĭ-lĭb′ər-ĭt-lē) *adv.* in an unhurried and thoughtful manner

29 **Spartan-like:** in a simple and disciplined way, like the inhabitants of the ancient city-state of Sparta.

B EVALUATE IDEAS
Reread lines 24–37. **Summarize** Thoreau's reasons for moving to the woods. What do you think of these reasons?

41 **evitable:** avoidable.

C ESSAY
In this essay, Thoreau often uses **figurative language** to present his observations. In lines 46–50, he likens civilized life to a rough sea. What might "the clouds and storms and quicksand" of life be? How might one "founder," or sink, in civilized life?

56 **Saint Vitus' dance:** a disorder of the nervous system, characterized by rapid, jerky, involuntary movements.

nor a boy, nor a woman, I might almost say, but would forsake all and follow that sound, not mainly to save property from the flames, but, if we will confess the truth, much more to see it burn, since burn it must, and we, be it known, did not set it on fire,—or to see it put out, and have a hand in it, if that is done as handsomely; yes, even if it were the parish church itself. Hardly a man takes a half hour's nap after dinner, but when he wakes he holds up his head and asks, "What's the news?" as if the rest of mankind had stood his sentinels. Some give directions to be waked every half hour, doubtless for no other purpose; and then, to pay for it, they tell

70 what they have dreamed. After a night's sleep the news is as indispensable as the breakfast. "Pray tell me any thing new that has happened to a man any where on this globe,"—and he reads it over his coffee and rolls, that a man has had his eyes gouged out this morning on the Wachito River; never dreaming the while that he lives in the dark unfathomed mammoth cave of this world, and has but the rudiment of an eye himself. **D**

For my part, I could easily do without the post-office. I think that there are very few important communications made through it. To speak critically, I never received more than one or two letters in my life—I wrote this some years ago—that were worth the postage. The penny-post is, commonly,

80 an institution through which you seriously offer a man that penny for his thoughts which is so often safely offered in jest. And I am sure that I never read any memorable news in a newspaper. If we read of one man robbed, or murdered, or killed by accident, or one house burned, or one vessel wrecked, or one steamboat blown up, or one cow run over on the Western Railroad, or one mad dog killed, or one lot of grasshoppers in the winter,—we never need read of another. One is enough. . . .

Let us spend one day as deliberately as Nature, and not be thrown off the track by every nutshell and mosquito's wing that falls on the rails. Let us rise early and fast, or break fast, gently and without **perturbation;** let

90 company come and let company go, let the bells ring and the children cry,— determined to make a day of it. . . .

Time is but the stream I go a-fishing in. I drink at it; but while I drink I see the sandy bottom and detect how shallow it is. Its thin current slides away, but eternity remains. I would drink deeper; fish in the sky, whose bottom is pebbly with stars. I cannot count one. I know not the first letter of the alphabet. I have always been regretting that I was not as wise as the day I was born. The intellect is a cleaver; it discerns and rifts its way into the secret of things. I do not wish to be any more busy with my hands than is necessary. My head is hands and feet. I feel all my best faculties concentrated

100 in it. My instinct tells me that my head is an organ for burrowing, as some creatures use their snout and fore-paws, and with it I would mine and burrow my way through these hills. I think that the richest vein is somewhere hereabouts; so by the divining rod and thin rising vapors I judge; and here I will begin to mine. **E**

D ESSAY
What situation does Thoreau exaggerate in lines 66–75? Would you respond differently to Thoreau's point if he simply stated his views on this subject?

79–81 penny-post . . . jest: Thoreau jokingly connects the postage rate at the time (a penny per letter) with the phrase "a penny for your thoughts."

perturbation (pûr′tər-bā′shən) *n.* disturbance of the emotions; agitation; uneasiness

E EVALUATE IDEAS
Summarize lines 87–104. What does Thoreau want to spend his time trying to understand, and how does he plan to achieve this understanding? Decide what you think about this desire.

from SOLITUDE

This is a delicious evening, when the whole body is one sense, and imbibes delight through every pore. I go and come with a strange liberty in Nature, a part of herself. As I walk along the stony shore of the pond in my shirt sleeves, though it is cool as well as cloudy and windy, and I see nothing special to attract me, all the elements are unusually **congenial** to me. The
110 bullfrogs trump to usher in the night, and the note of the whippoorwill is borne on the rippling wind from over the water. Sympathy with the fluttering alder and poplar leaves almost takes away my breath; yet, like the lake, my serenity is rippled but not ruffled. These small waves raised by the evening wind are as remote from storm as the smooth reflecting surface. Though it is now dark, the wind still blows and roars in the wood, the waves still dash, and some creatures lull the rest with their notes. The repose is never complete. The wildest animals do not repose, but seek their prey now; the fox, and skunk, and rabbit, now roam the fields and woods without fear. They are Nature's watchmen,—links which connect the days
120 of animated life. . . .

Men frequently say to me, "I should think you would feel lonesome down there, and want to be nearer to folks, rainy and snowy days and nights especially." I am tempted to reply to such,—This whole earth which we inhabit is but a point in space. How far apart, think you, dwell the two most distant inhabitants of yonder star, the breadth of whose disk cannot be appreciated by our instruments? Why should I feel lonely? Is not our planet in the Milky Way? This which you put seems to me not to be the most important question. What sort of space is that which separates a man from his fellows and makes him solitary? I have found that no exertion of the legs
130 can bring two minds much nearer to one another. . . . **F**

congenial (kən-jēn'yəl) *adj.* suited to one's needs or nature; agreeable

F **EVALUATE IDEAS**
Reread lines 121–130. **Summarize** Thoreau's ideas about loneliness. Do you agree with his assessment of this condition? Explain your answer.

from THE POND IN WINTER

Every winter the liquid and trembling surface of the pond, which was so sensitive to every breath, and reflected every light and shadow, becomes solid to the depth of a foot or a foot and a half, so that it will support the heaviest teams, and perchance the snow covers it to an equal depth, and it is not to be distinguished from any level field. Like the marmots in the surrounding hills, it closes its eye-lids and becomes dormant for three months or more. Standing on the snow-covered plain, as if in a pasture amid the hills, I cut my way first through a foot of snow, and then a foot of ice, and open a window under my feet, where, kneeling to drink, I look down into the quiet
140 parlor of the fishes, **pervaded** by a softened light as through a window of

135 marmots: burrowing rodents that hibernate in winter; also known as groundhogs or woodchucks.

pervade (pər-vād') *v.* to spread through every part of

ground glass, with its bright sanded floor the same as in summer; there a perennial waveless serenity reigns as in the amber twilight sky, corresponding to the cool and even temperament of the inhabitants. Heaven is under our feet as well as over our heads. . . . **G**

G TRANSCENDENTALISM
What transcendentalist ideal is reflected in lines 143–144?

from SPRING

One attraction in coming to the woods to live was that I should have leisure and opportunity to see the spring come in. The ice in the pond at length begins to be honey-combed, and I can set my heel in it as I walk. Fogs and rains and warmer suns are gradually melting the snow; the days have grown sensibly longer; and I see how I shall get through the winter without adding
150 to my woodpile, for large fires are no longer necessary. I am on the alert for the first signs of spring, to hear the chance note of some arriving bird, or the striped squirrel's chirp, for his stores must be now nearly exhausted, or see the woodchuck venture out of his winter quarters. . . .

149 **sensibly:** noticeably.

The change from storm and winter to serene and mild weather, from dark and sluggish hours to bright and elastic ones, is a memorable crisis which all things proclaim. It is seemingly instantaneous at last. Suddenly an influx of light filled my house, though the evening was at hand, and the clouds of winter still overhung it, and the eaves were dripping with sleety rain. I looked out the window, and lo! where yesterday was cold gray ice there lay
160 the transparent pond already calm and full of hope as in a summer evening, reflecting a summer evening sky in its bosom, though none was visible overhead, as if it had intelligence with some remote horizon. . . . **H**

H ESSAY
Imagery is a common feature of nature writing. Identify details in lines 145–162 that recreate sensory experiences for the reader. In what ways does this descriptive language enhance your mental picture of Walden Pond?

from CONCLUSION

I left the woods for as good a reason as I went there. Perhaps it seemed to me that I had several more lives to live, and could not spare any more time for that one. It is remarkable how easily and insensibly we fall into a particular route, and make a beaten track for ourselves. I had not lived there a week before my feet wore a path from my door to the pond-side; and though it is five or six years since I trod it, it is still quite distinct. It is true, I fear that others may have fallen into it, and so helped to keep it open. The surface of
170 the earth is soft and impressible by the feet of men; and so with the paths which the mind travels. How worn and dusty, then, must be the highways of the world, how deep the ruts of tradition and conformity! I did not wish to take a cabin passage, but rather to go before the mast and on the deck of

172–175 On a sailing ship, passengers stayed in private compartments, or cabins, near the middle of the ship, while the crew shared living quarters at the front, where more was visible.

the world, for there I could best see the moonlight amid the mountains. I do not wish to go below now. **I**

I learned this, at least, by my experiment; that if one advances confidently in the direction of his dreams, and endeavors to live the life which he has imagined, he will meet with a success unexpected in common hours. He will put some things behind, will pass an invisible boundary; new, universal,
180 and more liberal laws will begin to establish themselves around and within him; or the old laws be expanded, and interpreted in his favor in a more liberal sense, and he will live with the license of a higher order of beings. In proportion as he simplifies his life, the laws of the universe will appear less complex, and solitude will not be solitude, nor poverty poverty, nor weakness weakness. If you have built castles in the air, your work need not be lost; that is where they should be. Now put the foundations under them. . . .

Why should we be in such desperate haste to succeed, and in such desperate enterprises? If a man does not keep pace with his companions,
190 perhaps it is because he hears a different drummer. Let him step to the music which he hears, however measured or far away. It is not important that he should mature as soon as an appletree or an oak. Shall he turn his spring into summer? If the condition of things which we were made for is not yet, what were any reality which we can substitute? We will not be shipwrecked on a vain reality. Shall we with pains erect a heaven of blue glass over ourselves, though when it is done we shall be sure to gaze still at the true ethereal heaven far above, as if the former were not? . . . **J**

However mean your life is, meet it and live it; do not shun it and call it hard names. It is not so bad as you are. It looks poorest when you are richest.
200 The fault-finder will find faults even in paradise. Love your life, poor as it is. You may perhaps have some pleasant, thrilling, glorious hours, even in a poorhouse. The setting sun is reflected from the windows of the almshouse as brightly as from the rich man's abode; the snow melts before its door as early in the spring. I do not see but a quiet mind may live as contentedly there, and have as cheering thoughts, as in a palace. The town's poor seem to me often to live the most independent lives of any. May be they are simply great enough to receive without **misgiving.** Most think that they are above being supported by the town; but it oftener happens that they are not above supporting themselves by dishonest means, which should be
210 more disreputable. Cultivate poverty like a garden herb, like sage. Do not trouble yourself much to get new things, whether clothes or friends. Turn the old; return to them. Things do not change; we change. Sell your clothes and keep your thoughts. God will see that you do not want society. If I were confined to a corner of a garret all my days, like a spider, the world would be just as large to me while I had my thoughts about me. The philosopher said: "From an army of three divisions one can take away its general, and put it in disorder; from the man the most **abject** and vulgar one cannot take away his thought." Do not seek so anxiously to be developed, to subject

I **ESSAY**
To what does Thoreau compare life in lines 172–175? Explain how this **metaphor** conveys Thoreau's reasons for leaving Walden.

189–191 If a man . . . away: This is one of Thoreau's most famous passages. The "different drummer" evolved from a journal entry describing how he fell asleep to the sound of someone beating a drum "alone in the silence and the dark." The phrase "marching to the beat of a different drummer" became popular during the 1960s and 1970s.

J **TRANSCENDENTALISM**
What key feature of transcendentalism does Thoreau embrace in lines 189–191?

misgiving (mĭs-gĭv′ĭng) *n.* a feeling of doubt, mistrust, or uncertainty

215 the philosopher: Confucius (551–479 B.C.), Chinese teacher of moral living, who had an influence on Thoreau's ideas.

abject (ăb′jĕkt′) *adj.* low; contemptible; wretched

yourself to many influences to be played on; it is all dissipation. Humility like darkness reveals the heavenly lights. The shadows of poverty and meanness gather around us, "and lo! creation widens to our view." We are often reminded that if there were bestowed on us the wealth of Croesus, our aims must still be the same, and our means essentially the same. Moreover, if you are restricted in your range by poverty, if you cannot buy books and newspapers, for instance, you are but confined to the most significant and vital experiences; you are compelled to deal with the material which yields the most sugar and the most starch. It is life near the bone where it is sweetest. You are defended from being a trifler. No man loses ever on a lower level by magnanimity on a higher. Superfluous wealth can buy superfluities only. Money is not required to buy one necessary of the soul. . . . **K**

The life in us is like the water in the river. It may rise this year higher than man has ever known it, and flood the parched uplands; even this may be the eventful year, which will drown out all our muskrats. It was not always dry land where we dwell. I see far inland the banks which the stream anciently washed, before science began to record its freshets. Every one has heard the story which has gone the rounds of New England, of a strong and beautiful bug which came out of the dry leaf of an old table of apple-tree wood, which had stood in a farmer's kitchen for sixty years, first in Connecticut, and afterward in Massachusetts,—from an egg deposited in the living tree many years earlier still, as appeared by counting the annual layers beyond it; which was heard gnawing out for several weeks, hatched perchance by the heat of an urn. Who does not feel his faith in a resurrection and immortality strengthened by hearing of this? Who knows what beautiful and winged life, whose egg has been buried for ages under many concentric layers of woodenness in the dead dry life of society, deposited at first in the alburnum of the green and living tree, which has been gradually converted into the semblance of its well-seasoned tomb,—heard perchance gnawing out now for years by the astonished family of man, as they sat round the festive board,—may unexpectedly come forth from amidst society's most trivial and handselled furniture, to enjoy its perfect summer life at last!

I do not say that John or Jonathan will realize all this; but such is the character of that morrow which mere lapse of time can never make to dawn. The light which puts out our eyes is darkness to us. Only that day dawns to which we are awake. There is more day to dawn. The sun is but a morning star. ❧

220

230

240

250

222 Croesus (krē′səs): an ancient king legendary for his great wealth.

K **EVALUATE IDEAS**
Summarize Thoreau's ideas about poverty. Do you think his view of the poor and the lives they lead is realistic? Record your thoughts in your chart.

235 freshets: overflowings of a stream caused by heavy rain or melting snow.

245 alburnum (ăl-bûr′nəm): the part of a tree's trunk through which sap flows.

251 John or Jonathan: the common man (as in the more current expression "Tom, Dick, and Harry").

Comprehension

1. **Recall** What were Thoreau's reasons for moving to the woods?

2. **Recall** What does Thoreau advise people to do to ensure their lives are not "frittered away by detail"?

3. **Summarize** What are Thoreau's views on correspondence and the daily news?

Critical Analysis

4. **Make Inferences** Thoreau rejects many things as inessential or unimportant. List at least three things that *were* important to him, citing specific lines from the essay to support your answer.

5. **Analyze the Essay** Thoreau was a poet as well as an essayist, and in *Walden*, he uses **figurative language** to express abstract concepts. Complete the chart by finding examples of such language. Use your completed chart to describe what you think Thoreau's use of figurative language adds to this essay.

Type of Figurative Language	Examples from *Walden*
metaphor	"Time is but the stream I go a-fishing in."
simile	
personification	

6. **Analyze Transcendentalism** Thoreau practiced many of the transcendentalist ideals Emerson promoted. What connections do you see between the ideas Thoreau expresses in *Walden* and the ideas Ralph Waldo Emerson presents in "Self-Reliance" and *Nature?* Cite evidence to support your answer.

7. **Evaluate Ideas** Review the philosophical ideas you summarized as you read. Choose one idea—Thoreau's view of the poor, for example, or the way he feels about civilized life. Explain whether or not you think the idea you chose has merit, citing reasons for your opinion.

8. **Compare Texts** In "Thoreau Still Beckons, *if* I Can Take My Laptop" on page 381, Cynthia G. La Ferle argues that "making choices is so much more difficult in a culture fueled by sheer busyness and commercialism. There are few places ... where one can escape." Do you agree that it would be more challenging for a modern American to live as Thoreau did? Explain why or why not, using details from both texts to support your opinion.

Literary Criticism

9. **Critical Interpretations** According to Frank Stewart, author of *A Natural History of Nature Writing*, nature writers are "moved by the joyous, wild, and dazzling beauty in the world." Do you think this comment applies to Thoreau? Cite examples from *Walden* to support your opinion.

MAGAZINE ARTICLE Thoreau's call for a simpler life continues to resonate with Americans. Those struggling with a hectic lifestyle may recall his words with a particular sense of longing. Read on to hear one busy woman's reflection on the topic.

THOREAU STILL BECKONS,
if I Can Take My Laptop

By Cynthia G. La Ferle

Thanks to the wonders of modern technology, I now have a mind-boggling array of options.

I can shop for birthday gifts on the Internet, watch a funeral in Britain on "live" television, and order a complete wardrobe from a computer catalog. . . .

Every day I have more choices than I can reasonably consider. And so, like other tired Americans, I carry the burden of complexity—a burden so overwhelming, in fact, that there are times when I imagine trading places with Henry David Thoreau.

It's only fitting that I rediscovered Thoreau the week I purged my home office with a dust rag and a vacuum cleaner. The autumn mornings felt ripe for pitching and sorting. "Walden," Thoreau's famous treatise on simple living, was jammed behind a pile of unread paperbacks. . . .

It occurred to me that things were vastly different for Thoreau. The "comforts of life" in the 1840s were not exactly cushy by today's standards. His concept of luxury might have been taking tea in his mother's bone china saucers. So what had he given up to commune with nature?

Even before he moved to Walden Pond, Thoreau hadn't accumulated three television sets or a closetful of designer clothes. He didn't own several pairs of expensive athletic shoes for all those philosophical walks he took. His cot in the cabin couldn't have been more lumpy than the straw-filled mattresses in most mid-19th-century homes. And Thoreau never had to trade a personal computer for a pencil.

With all due respect, I wonder, how tough was Thoreau's two-year sabbatical with simplicity? Is it true that he occasionally walked from Walden Pond back to Concord, where Emerson's wife had a home-cooked supper waiting for him? . . .

And yet, just as Thoreau did, I'd like to weed out, pare down, live deliberately, be a resident philosopher. . . .

Visiting the "real" Walden Pond this fall, I was amazed and disappointed to find the place overrun. Locals were strewn on its small beach. You couldn't walk the path around the pond without rubbing shoulders with other sightseers; there wasn't a spot left for solitary reflection.

If nothing else, my rendezvous with Thoreau got me thinking. What—and how much—do I really need? What price have I paid for modern technology and "convenience"? In which landfill will all my stuff end up? . . .

Could I survive in a one-room cabin with barely more than a chair, a wooden table, a bowlful of raw vegetables, and my laptop? Honestly, I wish I could.

Civil DISOBEDIENCE
Henry David Thoreau

BACKGROUND Thoreau put into practice the ideas expressed in Ralph Waldo Emerson's "Self-Reliance." In 1846, he spent a night in jail for refusing to pay a poll tax—a tax one had to pay in order to vote—as an act of protest against the U.S. government. Thoreau was enraged by the government's support of slavery and its war against Mexico, which he viewed as a case of a stronger country overpowering a weaker one simply to expand its own borders. Inspired by his experience in jail, Thoreau wrote this essay.

ANALYZE VISUALS
The photographer who created the image on page 383 made a deliberate choice to focus not on the people in the crowd, but on their shadows. Why might she have made this choice?

I heartily accept the motto, "That government is best which governs least;" and I should like to see it acted up to more rapidly and systematically. Carried out, it finally amounts to this, which also I believe,—"That government is best which governs not at all;" and when men are prepared for it, that will be the kind of government which they will have. Government is at best but an expedient; but most governments are usually, and all governments are sometimes, inexpedient. The objections which have Ⓐ been brought against a standing army, and they are many and weighty, and deserve to prevail, may also at last be brought against a standing
10 government. The standing army is only an arm of the standing government. The government itself, which is only the mode which the people have chosen to execute their will, is equally liable to be abused and perverted before the people can act through it. Witness the present Mexican war, the work of comparatively a few individuals using the standing government as their tool; for, in the outset, the people would not have consented to this measure. . . .

But, to speak practically and as a citizen, unlike those who call themselves no-government men, I ask for, not at once no government, but *at once* a

Ⓐ EVALUATE IDEAS
Reread lines 1–7. What effect might these lines have on Thoreau's readers?

13 the present Mexican war: the 1846–1848 war between Mexico and the United States.

better government. Let every man make known what kind of government
20 would command his respect, and that will be one step toward obtaining it.

After all, the practical reason why, when the power is once in the hands
of the people, a majority are permitted, and for a long period continue,
to rule is not because they are most likely to be in the right, nor because
this seems fairest to the minority, but because they are physically the
strongest. But a government in which the majority rule in all cases cannot
be based on justice, even as far as men understand it. Can there not be a
government in which majorities do not virtually decide right and wrong,
but conscience?—in which majorities decide only those questions to which
the rule of expediency is applicable? Must the citizen ever for a moment,
30 or in the least degree, resign his conscience to the legislator? Why has every
man a conscience, then? I think that we should be men first, and subjects
afterward. It is not desirable to cultivate a respect for the law, so much as for
the right. The only obligation which I have a right to assume is to do at any
time what I think right. It is truly enough said, that a corporation has no
conscience; but a corporation of conscientious men is a corporation *with* a
conscience. Law never made men a whit more just; and, by means of their
respect for it, even the well-disposed are daily made the agents of injustice. **B**
A common and natural result of an undue respect for law is, that you may
see a file of soldiers, colonel, captain, corporal, privates, powder-monkeys,
40 and all, marching in admirable order over hill and dale to the wars, against
their wills, ay, against their common sense and consciences, which makes it
very steep marching indeed, and produces a palpitation of the heart. They
have no doubt that it is a damnable business in which they are concerned;
they are all peaceably inclined. Now, what are they? Men at all? or small
movable forts and magazines, at the service of some unscrupulous man
in power? Visit the Navy-Yard, and behold a marine, such a man as an
American government can make, or such as it can make a man with its black
arts—a mere shadow and reminiscence of humanity, a man laid out alive
and standing, and already, as one may say, buried under arms with funeral
50 accompaniments, though it may be,—

> "Not a drum was heard, not a funeral note,
> As his corse to the rampart we hurried;
> Not a soldier discharged his farewell shot
> O'er the grave where our hero we buried."

The mass of men serve the state thus, not as men mainly, but as
machines, with their bodies. They are the standing army, and the militia,
jailers, constables, *posse comitatus,* etc. In most cases there is no free exercise
whatever of the judgment or of the moral sense; but they put themselves
on a level with wood and earth and stones; and wooden men can perhaps
60 be manufactured that will serve the purpose as well. Such command no
more respect than men of straw or a lump of dirt. They have the same sort
of worth only as horses and dogs. Yet such as these even are commonly

B **EVALUATE IDEAS**
Reread lines 21–37. What
position does Thoreau take on
the conflict between majority
rule and individual conscience?
On your chart, **summarize** and
react to his position.

39 powder-monkeys: boys with
the job of carrying gunpowder to
artillery crews.

45 magazines: places where
ammunition is stored.

47–48 black arts: witchcraft.

51–54 "Not a drum . . . we buried":
opening lines of "The Burial of Sir
John Moore After Corunna" by the
Irish poet Charles Wolfe (1791–1823).

57 *posse comitatus* (pŏs'ē
kŏm-ə-tā'-təs): group of people that
can be called on by the sheriff to help
enforce the law [*Latin,* literally, the
power of the county].

esteemed good citizens. Others—as most legislators, politicians, lawyers, ministers, and office-holders—serve the state chiefly with their heads; and, as they rarely make any moral distinctions, they are as likely to serve the Devil, without *intending* it, as God. A very few—as heroes, patriots, martyrs, reformers in the great sense, and *men*—serve the state with their consciences also, and so necessarily resist it for the most part; and they are commonly treated as enemies by it. . . . **C**

70 Unjust laws exist: shall we be content to obey them, or shall we endeavor to amend them, and obey them until we have succeeded or shall we **transgress** them at once? Men generally, under such a government as this, think that they ought to wait until they have persuaded the majority to alter them. They think that, if they should resist, the remedy would be worse than the evil. But it is the fault of the government itself that the remedy *is* worse than the evil. *It* makes it worse. Why is it not more apt to anticipate and provide for reform? Why does it not cherish its wise minority? Why does it cry and resist before it is hurt? Why does it not encourage its citizens to be on the alert to point out its faults, and *do* better than it would have them? Why

80 does it always crucify Christ, and excommunicate Copernicus and Luther, and pronounce Washington and Franklin rebels? . . . **D**

If the injustice is part of the necessary friction of the machine of government, let it go, let it go: perchance it will wear smooth, certainly the machine will wear out. If the injustice has a spring, or a pulley, or a rope, or a crank, exclusively for itself, then perhaps you may consider whether the remedy will not be worse than the evil; but if it is of such a nature that it requires you to be the agent of injustice to another, then, I say, break the law. Let your life be a counter-friction to stop the machine. What I have to do is to see, at any rate, that I do not lend myself to the wrong which

90 I condemn. . . .

I meet this American government, or its representative, the state government, directly, and face to face, once a year—no more—in the person of its tax-gatherer; this is the only mode in which a man situated as I am necessarily meets it; and it then says distinctly, Recognize me; and the simplest, most effectual, and, in the present posture of affairs, the indispensablest mode of treating with it on this head, of expressing your little satisfaction with and love for it, is to deny it then. My civil neighbor, the tax-gatherer, is the very man I have to deal with,—for it is, after all, with men and not with parchment that I quarrel,—and he has voluntarily

100 chosen to be an agent of the government. How shall he ever know well what he is and does as an officer of the government, or as a man, until he is obliged to consider whether he shall treat me, his neighbor, for whom he has respect, as a neighbor and well-disposed man, or as a maniac and disturber of the peace, and see if he can get over this obstruction to his neighborliness without a ruder and more **impetuous** thought or speech corresponding with his action. I know this well, that if one thousand, if one hundred, if ten men

C EVALUATE IDEAS
Reread lines 55–69. Which way of serving the state does Thoreau approve of? Which ways does he condemn? Decide whether you agree with his assessment of soldiers and others who serve.

transgress (trăns-grĕs′) *v.* to violate a command or law

80 Copernicus (kō-pûr′nə-kəs) and Luther: Radicals in their time, Polish astronomer Nicolaus Copernicus theorized that the sun rather than the earth was the center of our planetary system; German theologian Martin Luther was a leader in the Protestant Reformation.

D GRAMMAR AND STYLE
In lines 70–81, Thoreau adds emphasis and emotion to his writing by asking **rhetorical questions**—questions that don't require a reply because the writer assumes the answers are obvious.

95 posture of affairs: situation.

impetuous (ĭm-pĕch′o͞o-əs) *adj.* acting with sudden or rash energy; hasty

Left: London police arresting a suffragist, 1914; *center:* Gandhi marching to the sea, in defiance of the British salt monopoly

whom I could name,—if ten *honest* men only,—ay, if *one* honest man, in this State of Massachusetts, *ceasing to hold slaves,* were actually to withdraw from this copartnership, and be locked up in the county jail therefor, it
110 would be the abolition of slavery in America. For it matters not how small the beginning may seem to be: what is once well done is done forever. But we love better to talk about it: that we say is our mission. Reform keeps many scores of newspapers in its service, but not one man. . . .

Under a government which imprisons any unjustly, the true place for a just man is also a prison. The proper place today, the only place which Massachusetts has provided for her freer and less desponding spirits, is in her prisons, to be put out and locked out of the State by her own act, as they have already put themselves out by their principles. It is there that the fugitive slave, and the Mexican prisoner on parole, and the Indian come to
120 plead the wrongs of his race should find them; on that separate, but more free and honorable ground, where the State places those who are not *with* her, but *against* her,—the only house in a slave State in which a free man can abide with honor. If any think that their influence would be lost there, and their voices no longer afflict the ear of the State, that they would not be as an enemy within its walls, they do not know by how much truth is stronger than error, nor how much more eloquently and effectively he can combat injustice who has experienced a little in his own person. Cast your whole vote, not a strip of paper merely, but your whole influence. A minority is powerless while it conforms to the majority; it is not even a minority then;
130 but it is irresistible when it clogs by its whole weight. If the alternative is to keep all just men in prison, or give up war and slavery, the State will not hesitate which to choose. If a thousand men were not to pay their tax bills

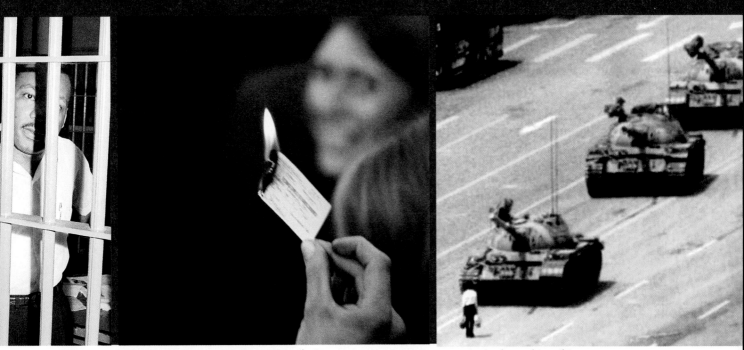

Left: Dr. Martin Luther King Jr., jailed for civil disobedience; *center:* Vietnam war protester burns his military draft card; *right:* Beijing man stands in front of tanks during the 1989 Tiananmen Square uprising.

this year, that would not be a violent and bloody measure, as it would be to pay them, and enable the State to commit violence and shed innocent blood. This is, in fact, the definition of a peaceable revolution, if any such is possible. If the tax-gatherer, or any other public officer, asks me, as one has done, "But what shall I do?" my answer is, "If you really wish to do anything, resign your office." When the subject has refused allegiance, and the officer has resigned his office, then the revolution is accomplished. But
140 even suppose blood should flow. Is there not a sort of blood shed when the conscience is wounded? Through this wound a man's real manhood and immortality flow out, and he bleeds to an everlasting death. I see this blood flowing now. . . . **E**

I have paid no poll-tax for six years. I was put into a jail once on this account, for one night; and, as I stood considering the walls of solid stone, two or three feet thick, the door of wood and iron, a foot thick, and the iron grating which strained the light, I could not help being struck with the foolishness of that institution which treated me as if I were mere flesh and blood and bones, to be locked up. I wondered that it should have concluded
150 at length that this was the best use it could put me to, and had never thought to avail itself of my services in some way. I saw that, if there was a wall of stone between me and my townsmen, there was a still more difficult one to climb or break through before they could get to be as free as I was. I did not for a moment feel confined, and the walls seemed a great waste of stone and mortar. I felt as if I alone of all my townsmen had paid my tax. They plainly did not know how to treat me, but behaved like persons who are underbred. In every threat and in every compliment there was a blunder; for they thought that my chief desire was to stand the other side of

E EVALUATE IDEAS
Thoreau holds an **assumption**—an opinion or belief that is taken for granted—that civil disobedience is the only sensible and moral course to take. Reread lines 114–143. How convincing are the reasons Thoreau gives in support of his belief?

157 underbred: ill-mannered.

that stone wall. I could not but smile to see how industriously they locked
160 the door on my meditations, which followed them out again without let or
hindrance, and *they* were really all that was dangerous. As they could not
reach me, they had resolved to punish my body; just as boys, if they cannot
come at some person against whom they have a spite, will abuse his dog. I
saw that the State was half-witted, that it was timid as a lone woman with
her silver spoons, and that it did not know its friends from its foes, and
I lost all my remaining respect for it, and pitied it. **F**

Thus the State never intentionally confronts a man's sense, intellectual
or moral, but only his body, his senses. It is not armed with superior wit or
honesty, but with superior physical strength. I was not born to be forced.
170 I will breathe after my own fashion. Let us see who is the strongest. What
force has a multitude? They only can force me who obey a higher law than I.
They force me to become like themselves. I do not hear of *men* being *forced*
to live this way or that by masses of men. What sort of life were that to live?
When I meet a government which says to me, "Your money or your life,"
why should I be in haste to give it my money? It may be in a great strait, and
not know what to do: I cannot help that. It must help itself; do as I do. It is
not worth the while to snivel about it. I am not responsible for the successful
working of the machinery of society. I am not the son of the engineer. I
perceive that, when an acorn and a chestnut fall side by side, the one does
180 not remain inert to make way for the other, but both obey their own laws,
and spring and grow and flourish as best they can, till one, perchance,
overshadows and destroys the other. If a plant cannot live according to its
nature, it dies; and so a man. ∾ **G**

160–161 **without let or hindrance:**
without encountering obstacles.

F **ESSAY**
Why do you think Thoreau
includes this personal **anecdote**
about his night in jail? Consider
why he feels free as he stands in
his cell, contemplating his own
imprisonment.

G **ESSAY**
What **message** does Thoreau
convey through his example of
the acorn and the chestnut?

Comprehension

1. **Recall** According to Thoreau, what should be respected more than the law?

2. **Summarize** What should a citizen do about an unjust law?

3. **Clarify** List the three ways Thoreau says a citizen may serve the state. With which did Thoreau agree?

Critical Analysis

4. **Make Judgments** Consider the **historical context** of Thoreau's essays. Would it be easier or more difficult to practice his brand of **nonconformity** today? Consider the possible contemporary consequences of the following:

   - refusing to pay a tax ("Civil Disobedience," lines 144–166)
   - going to live alone in the woods (*Walden,* lines 1–37)
   - celebrating or "cultivating" poverty (*Walden,* lines 198–230)

5. **Analyze Essays** Even when they discuss serious or even lofty ideas, essays are often loosely structured and highly personal. **Skim** *Walden* and "Civil Disobedience," noting passages in which Thoreau refers to himself. Identify his personal feelings and instances when he shares his own experiences, such as the night he spent in jail. How do these passages influence your acceptance of his arguments? Explain, citing specific lines from both essays.

6. **Interpret Paradox** A paradox is a statement that seems to contradict itself but may nevertheless suggest an important truth. Reexamine both selections and record in a chart the examples of paradox you find. Then explain what truth or idea each paradox illustrates.

Paradox	Explanation
"I did not wish to live what was not life...." (*Walden,* lines 26–27)	

7. **Evaluate Ideas** Ralph Waldo Emerson said of Thoreau, "No truer American ever lived." Review the political ideas you summarized as you read "Civil Disobedience." Do you consider Thoreau's arguments to be those of a patriot or those of a traitor? In your response, consider Thoreau's points on

   - the necessity of government
   - majority rule
   - how unjust laws may be changed

Literary Criticism

8. **Critical Interpretations** Critic Andrew Delbanco has asserted that Thoreau is, "despite all the barricades he erected around himself, an irresistible writer; to read him is to feel wrenched away from the customary world and delivered into a place we fear as much as we need." What does Delbanco mean when he says we both need and fear the world Thoreau creates? After you interpret the critic's statement, explain whether or not you agree with him.

Vocabulary in Context

WORD LIST
abject
congenial
deliberately
impetuous
misgiving
perturbation
pervade
transgress

VOCABULARY PRACTICE

Decide whether each statement is true or false.

1. If an odor were to **pervade** a room, it would be escaping through a chimney.
2. A person who is experiencing **perturbation** usually feels relaxed and confident.
3. An **impetuous** act is one that you do on the spur of the moment.
4. If you have some **misgiving** about attending a party, you should consider not going.
5. A **congenial** person usually gets along with others.
6. If you act **deliberately,** you act with haste and lack of concern.
7. **Abject** sorrow is sadness that will pass quickly.
8. If you **transgress** a law, you break it.

VOCABULARY IN WRITING

Do you agree that the only place to experience nature is in a remote rural setting? Using two or more vocabulary words, write a short explanation of your opinion and what you base it on. You might start like this.

> **EXAMPLE SENTENCE**
> Peace and quiet may not **_pervade_** most urban settings, but there are still ways to commune with nature in the city.

VOCABULARY STRATEGY: THE PREFIXES *ab-* AND *per-*

Though the prefixes *ab-* and *per-* are sometimes combined with recognizable base words, often they are attached to Latin roots, as in the vocabulary words *abject* and *pervade*. When you think you recognize the prefix *ab-* or *per-* in a word, look for context clues that support your guess. Then use the meaning of the prefix—and of the root, if you know it—to decipher the word's definition.

Prefix	Meaning
ab-	"away"; "away from"
per-	"through"; "thoroughly, very"

PRACTICE The prefix *ab-* or *per-* occurs in each boldfaced word below. Use context clues and root and prefix meanings—or a dictionary, if necessary—to define each word.

1. That man's **pernicious** lies have totally destroyed his son's reputation.
2. To get out of debt, I have decided to **abjure** going to the mall for three months.
3. The recruits immediately obeyed the officer's **peremptory** command.
4. **Abstemious** eating habits can help a person lose weight.
5. His **perfunctory** effort to learn who had **absconded** with the money was unsuccessful.

VOCABULARY PRACTICE
For more practice, go to the **Vocabulary Center** at **ClassZone.com.**

Reading-Writing Connection

WRITING PROMPT

WRITE A LETTER TO THE EDITOR Thoreau proposed radical ideas in "Civil Disobedience." Some people found them thrilling; others found them threatening. Choose one of the ideas proposed in "Civil Disobedience." Write a **three-paragraph letter** to the editor of a local newspaper in which you explain the idea and argue for or against implementing it.

SELF-CHECK

A successful letter to the editor will . . .

- state the issue and your position on the issue
- support your position with reasons and examples
- use rhetorical devices that will help reinforce your position

GRAMMAR AND STYLE

ASK RHETORICAL QUESTIONS Review the **Grammar and Style** note on page 385. Thoreau asks a number of thought-provoking questions in "Civil Disobedience." But he's not expecting any answers. The questions he asks are **rhetorical questions;** they don't require a reply, because the answers are considered obvious. Writers often use these types of **interrogative sentences** to drive home a point or evoke an emotional response. Here is an example from the text:

> *But even suppose blood should flow. Is there not a sort of blood shed when the conscience is wounded?* (lines 139–141)

Read this passage aloud. Consider how it would sound if it lacked a rhetorical question—if the second sentence read, "A sort of blood flows when the conscience is wounded." Do you think the rhetorical question makes Thoreau's argument more compelling?

PRACTICE Rewrite the following paragraph, changing some sentences to rhetorical questions.

> Thoreau suggests that if citizens disagree with their government's actions, they should stop paying taxes. However, if a large number of Americans refused to pay their taxes this year, the results would be disastrous. Public schools would collapse, salaries for police officers and firefighters would go unpaid, and services from public transportation to public hospitals would crumble. I do not see how a good citizen could allow this to happen. I do not see the honor in such an act.

WRITING TOOLS
For prewriting, revision, and editing tools, visit the **Writing Center** at ClassZone.com.

On *Civil Disobedience*

Mohandas K. Gandhi

> **BACKGROUND** Mohandas K. Gandhi (1869–1948), called Mahatma ("Great Soul"), helped free India of British rule. As a student, he greatly admired Thoreau's essay "Civil Disobedience." Thoreau's ideas helped shape Gandhi's key principle—*satyagraha* (sə-tyä′grə-hə), or "truth-force." In the following excerpt from a 1916 speech, Gandhi describes this powerful weapon for fighting oppression.

July 27, 1916

There are two ways of countering injustice. One way is to smash the head of the man who perpetrates injustice and to get your own head smashed in the process. All strong people in the world adopt this course. Everywhere wars are fought and millions of people are killed. The consequence is not the progress of a nation but its decline. . . . No country has ever become, or will ever become, happy through victory in war. A nation does not rise that way, it only falls further. In fact, what comes to it is defeat, not victory. And if, perchance, either our act or our purpose was ill-conceived, it brings disaster to both belligerents.[1]

10   But through the other method of combating injustice, we alone suffer the consequences of our mistakes, and the other side is wholly spared. This other method is *satyagraha*.[2] One who resorts to it does not have to break another's head; he may merely have his own head broken. He has to be prepared to die himself, suffering all the pain. In opposing the atrocious laws of the Government of South Africa,[3] it was this method that we adopted. We made it clear to the said Government that we would never bow to its outrageous laws. No clapping is possible without two hands to do it, and no quarrel without two persons to make it. Similarly, no State is possible without two entities, the rulers and the ruled. You are our sovereign, our Government, only so long as we consider ourselves your subjects. When we are not subjects, you are not the

20 sovereign either. So long as it is your endeavour to control us with justice and love, we will let you to do so. But if you wish to strike at us from behind, we cannot permit it. Whatever you do in other matters, you will have to ask our opinion about the laws that concern us. If you make laws to keep us suppressed in a wrongful manner and without taking us into confidence, these laws will merely adorn the statute-books. We will never obey them. Award us for it what punishment you like, we will put up with it. Send us to prison and we will live there as in a paradise. Ask us to mount the

---

1. **belligerents:** participants in a war.

2. **satyagraha** (sə-tyä′grə-hə) *Sanskrit:* insistence on truth. Gandhi used this term to describe his policy of seeking reform by means of nonviolent resistance.

3. **atrocious laws . . . South Africa:** Gandhi led the Indian community in opposition to racial discrimination in South Africa, where he lived for several years.

Gandhi in 1948, after ending a six-day hunger strike for peace

scaffold[4] and we will do so laughing. Shower what sufferings you like upon us, we will calmly endure all and not hurt a hair of your body. We will gladly die and will not so much as touch you. But so long as there is yet life in these our bones, we will never 30 comply with your arbitrary laws. ✍

---

4. **mount the scaffold:** ascend the platform on which one is executed by hanging.

Literary Analysis

1. **Summarize** What two ways of countering injustice does Gandhi describe? Explain which approach Gandhi adopted.

2. **Interpret** Reread lines 16–20. What point is Gandhi making about the relationship between a government and its citizens?

3. **Compare Texts** Henry David Thoreau's ideas influenced many 20th-century reformers, including Gandhi. What connections do you see between the views Thoreau presents in *Walden* and "Civil Disobedience" and Gandhi's beliefs? Cite evidence from both texts to support your answer.

from **Woman in the Nineteenth Century**

Nonfiction by Margaret Fuller

Margaret Fuller
1810–1850

Margaret Fuller spent much of her life fighting to make women equal members of society. At a time when a woman's only place was thought to be the small sphere of the home, Fuller became a respected author, a commanding public speaker, a popular journalist, and a key figure in the transcendentalist movement. One literary historian observed that Fuller "transcended virtually every stereotype American women had to endure in the first half of the 19th century."

A Demanding Childhood Sarah Margaret Fuller was born in Cambridgeport, Massachusetts. Her father, a stern and formidable man, had high expectations for her. When she was only 10 years old, he counseled that excelling "in all things should be your constant aim." As a teenager, Fuller typically started her studies at five in the morning and sometimes did not finish until eleven at night.

Coming into Her Own Fuller's father died suddenly when she was 25, and she became a teacher to help support her family. Through a mutual acquaintance, she met Ralph Waldo Emerson, who was much impressed by her intelligence and wit. She began attending meetings of the Transcendental Club. In 1840, Fuller became the editor of *The Dial,* a short-lived but highly influential literary magazine. Fuller solicited poems, essays, and fiction from leading transcendentalists and wrote much of the content herself.

An Influential Voice In 1844, Fuller started writing the literary column for the *New York Tribune,* perhaps the most widely read newspaper of its day. In addition to reviewing literary works, she addressed social issues such as poverty and slavery. In 1845, Fuller published *Woman in the Nineteenth Century,* a revolutionary feminist work that paid tribute to women's intellectual and creative abilities and declared that women must be accepted as equal to men. The first edition sold out in two weeks.

Romance and Tragedy In 1846, the *New York Tribune* sent Fuller to cover civil unrest in Europe. She settled in Rome, where she fell in love with and married Italian aristocrat Giovanni Angelo Ossoli. When revolution broke out in Rome in 1848, Fuller supported the cause by volunteering at a hospital while her husband fought for the republic. The revolution failed, and Fuller, Ossoli, and their young son sailed to the United States in 1850. With New York City almost in sight, their ship hit a sandbar and sank. Fuller, Ossoli, and their son drowned.

• LITERARY ANALYSIS: AUTHOR'S PERSPECTIVE

You know that people often look at a subject from different perspectives. For example, a Vietnam War veteran would bring a unique set of ideas and experiences to a discussion of that war. A person who spent the 1960s protesting that same war would approach the discussion with an entirely different set of beliefs. **Author's perspective** refers to the distinct combination of ideas, values, and beliefs that influence the way a writer looks at a topic. An author's perspective is rarely stated; instead, you have to look closely at details within the text. To determine an author's perspective, examine

- the writer's **tone,** or attitude toward the subject
- **details** the writer chooses to include or focus on
- how the writer portrays specific individuals

As you read the excerpt from *Woman in the Nineteenth Century,* use these elements to help you analyze Margaret Fuller's perspective.

• READING STRATEGY: PARAPHRASE MAIN IDEAS

When you read challenging texts like this one, it is important to pay careful attention to the author's **main ideas.** One way to make sure you're understanding these key points is to **paraphrase** them, or restate the information in your own words. A good paraphrase is about the same length as the original text but is written in simpler language. As you read, paraphrase the annotated passages to achieve a better understanding of Fuller's main ideas. Record your work in a chart like the one shown.

Fuller's Main Ideas	My Paraphrases
"I was talking on this subject with Miranda, a woman, who, if any in the world could, might speak without heat or bitterness of the position of her sex."	I spoke about this with Miranda. If any woman can talk about gender issues calmly and rationally, Miranda can.

*W*oman
in the Nineteenth Century

MARGARET FULLER

BACKGROUND From 1839 to 1844, Fuller led a series of seminars for women called "Conversations." She lectured on topics ranging from ethics to art and then asked her listeners to discuss each topic, thus helping the women to recognize their own intellectual abilities. The sessions led Fuller to write *Woman in the Nineteenth Century*, in which she insists society accept women and men as equals. Here, Fuller presents her views as a dialogue between herself and the fictional "Miranda," a woman who, like Fuller, had from childhood been encouraged to exercise her mind.

I was talking on this subject with Miranda, a woman, who, if any in the world could, might speak without heat and bitterness of the position of her sex. Her father was a man who cherished no sentimental reverence for woman, but a firm belief in the equality of the sexes. She was his eldest child, and came to him at an age when he needed a companion. From the time she could speak and go alone, he addressed her not as a plaything, but as a living mind. Among the few verses he ever wrote was a copy addressed to this child, when the first locks were cut from her head, and the reverence expressed on this occasion for that cherished head, he never belied. It was to him the temple of immortal intellect. He respected his child, however, too much
10 to be an indulgent parent. He called on her for clear judgment, for courage, for honor and fidelity; in short, for such virtues as he knew. In so far as he possessed the keys to the wonders of this universe, he allowed free use of them to her, and by the incentive of a high expectation, he forbade, as far as possible, that she should let the privilege lie idle. **A**

Thus this child was early led to feel herself a child of the spirit. She took her place easily, not only in the world of organized being, but in the world of mind. A dignified sense of self-dependence was given as all her portion,[1] and she found it a

ANALYZE VISUALS
In your opinion, what **traits** does the subject of this portrait project? After you've read the selection, revisit your answer. Tell whether you think the woman in the portrait might share any of Miranda's qualities.

A **PARAPHRASE MAIN IDEAS**
Paraphrase lines 2–4. What were Miranda's father's views on gender equality?

---

1. **all her portion:** something that she had a right to expect.

Portrait of Ann Cochrells (1848), David Parr. Oil on canvas, 9″ × 11″. © Christie's Images Ltd.

sure anchor. Herself securely anchored, her relations with others were established with equal security. She was fortunate in a total absence of those charms which
20 might have drawn to her bewildering flatteries, and in a strong electric nature, which repelled those who did not belong to her; and attracted those who did. With men and women her relations were noble,—affectionate without passion, intellectual without coldness. The world was free to her, and she lived freely in it. Outward adversity came, and inward conflict, but that faith and self-respect had early been awakened which must always lead at last, to an outward serenity and an inward peace. **B**

Of Miranda I had always thought as an example, that the restraints upon the sex were insuperable[2] only to those who think them so, or who noisily strive to break them. She had taken a course of her own, and no man stood in her way.
30 Many of her acts had been unusual, but excited no uproar. Few helped, but none checked her, and the many men, who knew her mind and her life, showed to her confidence, as to a brother, gentleness as to a sister. And not only refined, but very coarse men approved and aided one in whom they saw resolution and clearness of design. Her mind was often the leading one, always effective. **C**

When I talked with her upon these matters, and had said very much what I have written, she smilingly replied: "and yet we must admit that I have been fortunate, and this should not be. My good father's early trust gave the first bias, and the rest followed of course. It is true that I have had less outward aid, in after years, than most women, but that is of little consequence. Religion was early
40 awakened in my soul, a sense that what the soul is capable to ask it must attain, and that, though I might be aided and instructed by others, I must depend on myself as the only constant friend. This self dependence, which was honored in me, is deprecated as a fault in most women. They are taught to learn their rule from without, not to unfold it from within. **D**

"This is the fault of man, who is still vain, and wishes to be more important to woman than, by right, he should be."

"Men have not shown this disposition toward you," I said.

"No! because the position I early was enabled to take was one of self-reliance. And were all women as sure of their wants as I was, the result would be the same.
50 But they are so overloaded with precepts by guardians, who think that nothing is so much to be dreaded for a woman as originality of thought or character, that their minds are impeded by doubts till they lose their chance of fair free proportions. The difficulty is to get them to the point from which they shall naturally develop self-respect, and learn self-help. **E**

"Once I thought that men would help to forward this state of things more than I do now. I saw so many of them wretched in the connections they had formed in weakness and vanity. They seemed so glad to esteem women whenever they could.

"'The soft arms of affection,' said one of the most discerning spirits, 'will not suffice for me, unless on them I see the steel bracelets of strength.'"

B **AUTHOR'S PERSPECTIVE**
Consider Fuller's **tone** in lines 15–26. What can you **infer** about the traits Fuller found admirable?

C **PARAPHRASE MAIN IDEAS**
Paraphrase the main idea Fuller states in lines 27–29. Of what does Fuller see Miranda as an "example"?

D **PARAPHRASE MAIN IDEAS**
Paraphrase lines 42–44. How is Miranda different from most women of her time?

E **AUTHOR'S PERSPECTIVE**
Consider the **details** Fuller chooses to focus on. By contrasting Miranda's upbringing with that of most 19th-century women, what type of upbringing is Fuller advocating?

---

2. **insuperable:** incapable of being overcome.

60   But early I perceived that men never, in any extreme of despair, wished to be women. On the contrary they were ever ready to taunt one another at any sign of weakness, with,

Art thou not like the women, who—

The passage ends various ways, according to the occasion and rhetoric of the speaker. When they admired any woman they were inclined to speak of her as "above her sex." Silently I observed this, and feared it argued a rooted scepticism, which for ages had been fastening on the heart, and which only an age of miracles could eradicate. Ever I have been treated with great sincerity; and I look upon it as a signal instance of this, that an intimate friend of the other sex said, in a fervent

70   moment, that I "deserved in some star to be a man." He was much surprised when I disclosed my view of my position and hopes, when I declared my faith that the feminine side, the side of love, of beauty, of holiness, was now to have its full chance, and that, if either were better, it was better now to be a woman, for even the slightest achievement of good was furthering an especial work of our time. He smiled incredulously. "She makes the best she can of it," thought he. "Let Jews believe the pride of Jewry, but I am of the better sort, and know better."[3] ⓕ

Another used as highest praise, in speaking of a character in literature, the words "a manly woman."

"So in the noble passage of Ben Jonson:

80   *'I meant the day-star should not brighter ride,*
        Nor shed like influence from its lucent seat;
    I meant she should be courteous, facile, sweet,
        Free from that solemn vice of greatness, pride;
    I meant each softest virtue there should meet,
        Fit in that softer bosom to abide,
    Only a learned and a manly *soul,*
        I purposed her, that should with even powers,
    The rock, the spindle, and the shears control
        Of destiny, and spin her own free hours.'"[4]

90   "Methinks," said I, "you are too fastidious in objecting to this. Jonson in using the word 'manly' only meant to heighten the picture of this, the true, the intelligent fate, with one of the deeper colors."

"And yet," said she, "so invariable is the use of this word where a heroic quality is to be described, and I feel so sure that persistence and courage are the most womanly no less than the most manly qualities, that I would exchange these words for others of a larger sense at the risk of marring the fine tissue of the verse. Read 'A heavenward and instructed soul,' and I should be satisfied. Let it not be said, wherever there is energy or creative genius, 'She has a masculine mind.'" ∽

ⓕ **PARAPHRASE MAIN IDEAS**
Paraphrase lines 65–68 in your chart. What way of thinking does Miranda describe, and how easy does she think it will be to reverse?

---

3. **'She makes . . . know better':** Miranda's male friend uses a religious slur to discount women.

4. **'I meant . . . free hours':** These lines are taken from the poem "On Lucy, Countess of Bedford." Their author, Ben Jonson (1573?–1637), was an English playwright and poet.

Comprehension

1. **Recall** What did Miranda's father believe in regard to the equality of the sexes?

2. **Summarize** According to Miranda, how did her relationship with her father shape her character?

3. **Clarify** What do the men Miranda describes mean when they comment that a woman they admire is "above her sex"?

Literary Analysis

4. **Analyze Main Ideas** Examine the main ideas you **paraphrased** as you read. Then reread the selection's last two paragraphs. What is Fuller's main point about "heroic" qualities such as persistence, confidence, and creativity? Use your own paraphrases as well as specific lines from the text to support your answer.

5. **Examine Author's Perspective** Recall that Fuller was in the Transcendental Club, and think about the ideals that this group embraced. Through her description of Miranda, what was Fuller saying about the traits a woman needed in order to transcend society's **expectations?** Restate Fuller's perspective in one or two sentences. Consider the following as you formulate your answer:

   • Miranda's statement that women "are taught to learn their rule without, not to unfold it from within." (lines 43–44)

   • The contrast between Miranda's upbringing and that of women "so overloaded with precepts by guardians . . . that their minds are impeded by doubts." (lines 50–52)

6. **Draw Conclusions About the Author's Technique** Why might Fuller have chosen to present her views as a dialogue between herself and the fictional Miranda, instead of simply stating her beliefs outright? Explain how the dialogue format helps the author achieve her **purpose.** Cite at least one example from the text to support your analysis.

7. **Compare Texts** Compare Fuller's main ideas with the beliefs Ralph Waldo Emerson sets forth in "Self-Reliance" (page 360). What common elements do the two texts share? In what ways does their focus differ? Cite examples.

Literary Criticism

8. **Historical Context** A friend of Fuller's once described her as possessing "what in woman is generally called a masculine mind; that is, its action was determined by ideas rather than sentiments." Was this just a 19th-century attitude, or is it still prevalent today? Do contemporary Americans still believe that men are governed by reason while women are driven by emotion? Explain your answer.

The Transcendental Spirit

In the 19th century, transcendentalism emerged as a fresh intellectual framework for addressing social, economic, political, and cultural changes in America's increasingly complex society. Many of the issues writers of the day struggled with continue to be relevant today. Get into a "transcendental" frame of mind by taking the following quiz.

How TRANSCENDENTAL Are You?

* ✳ Do you ever take a walk with no destination in mind?   ☐ yes ☐ no

* ✳ Do you express your opinions even when they aren't popular?   ☐ yes ☐ no

* ✳ Would you accept very low pay for a job that you loved?   ☐ yes ☐ no

* ✳ Do you think there are too many gadgets and gizmos in modern life and that we should all aim to simplify?   ☐ yes ☐ no

* ✳ Would you go to jail rather than conform to a law that goes against your conscience?   ☐ yes ☐ no

Extension Online

INQUIRY & RESEARCH Search the Internet for evidence of Henry David Thoreau's legacy. Use the key words *Thoreau* and *Walden* to find several different types of memorials for one of transcendentalism's greatest thinkers. You will find many nonprofit organizations, projects, schools, and centers dedicated to promoting or remembering Thoreau's ideas. Choose three of the most interesting to **report** back to the class on.

Writing to Reflect

Select one of the questions above and respond to it in a focused, well-developed paragraph. Give at least one example from your life to support your answer. Then write one more paragraph exploring how one of the transcendental writers whose work you've just read might have responded to the same question.

Consider

* which question resonated with you the most
* what example(s) from your life might best reveal your beliefs to your audience
* how particular sentences or passages in the readings relate to the question you chose

The Fall of the House of Usher

Short Story by Edgar Allan Poe

FYI

Did you know that Edgar Allan Poe . . .

- invented the modern detective story?
- inspired the name of the Baltimore Ravens football team?
- briefly wrote a literary gossip column?
- publicly denounced the work of Henry Wadsworth Longfellow?

Author Online

For more on Edgar Allan Poe, visit the **Literature Center** at ClassZone.com.

Baltimore, Maryland, scene of Poe's mysterious death

Edgar Allan Poe
c. 1809–1849

"The Raven" has been called the best-known poem in American literature; "The Fall of the House of Usher" is a masterpiece of Gothic horror. Both of these works were the creation of one feverish imagination, that of poet, critic, and fiction innovator Edgar Allan Poe.

Haunted by Death Once called one of literature's "most brilliant, but erratic, stars," Poe is as well-known for his unstable life as for his formidable talent. Abandoned by his father as an infant, Poe lost his mother to tuberculosis by the age of 3. He was taken in by John Allan, a wealthy Virginia businessman, but the two had a stormy relationship. At age 18, Poe got himself thrown out of college for gambling debts, beginning a lifelong pattern of self-sabotage. Estranged from Allan as a young man, Poe formed a new family with his aunt and his young cousin, Virginia Clemm. In 1836, he and Virginia married publicly, although they had probably married in secret the year before, when she was only 13. She died 11 years later, and the devastated Poe died 2 years after. Theories about the cause of his death range from alcohol poisoning to brain lesions to rabies.

Making Ends Meet For much of his adult life, Poe struggled to support his family. He landed promising positions at a series of literary magazines, spoiling one opportunity after another with his erratic behavior. At the same time, his scathing reviews made him a feared and respected critic, and his inventive short stories brought him acclaim. Although his life matched the Romantic ideal of the starving artist who suffered for the purity of his art, Poe's stories were designed to reach a wide audience. His successes with horror, science fiction, and detective stories proved his mastery of popular genres.

Tortured Soul Poe's distinctive themes included madness, untimely death, and obsession. Given his troubled life, many critics have interpreted Poe's deranged narrators as reflections of the author's own state of mind. But Poe was a brilliant and controlled stylist, whose theories of art championed rigorous structure, careful use of language, and the masterful creation of a single, calculated effect. His fascination with the macabre was equaled by his interest in logic; his supremely rational detective C. Auguste Dupin inspired Sir Arthur Conan Doyle's scientific sleuth Sherlock Holmes. Poe's life and work exemplify the deepest divisions of the self: the conflict of beautiful ideals and dark impulses.

LITERARY ANALYSIS: UNITY OF EFFECT

Some writers insist that plot or character drives a story. Edgar Allan Poe wanted his stories to achieve a **unity of effect,** where every element—plot, character, setting, and imagery—helped create a single effect, or **mood,** as in this opening sentence from the selection:

During the whole of a dull, dark, and soundless day in the autumn of the year, when the clouds hung oppressively low . . .

The ominous details set a scene of instant gloom. As you read, note the choices Poe makes to achieve his intended effect.

READING SKILL: UNDERSTAND COMPLEX SENTENCES

Poe's sentences have a nervous, excited quality: they pile on details and jump from one subject to another. Use these strategies to help you understand Poe's complex sentences:

- Focus on the main idea. Finding the main subject and verb of a sentence can help you identify its main idea.

- Break long sentences into shorter ones that focus on one idea. Group modifiers with the words they describe.

- Keep reading. Poe often restates ideas, and a confusing sentence might be followed by one easier to understand.

Apply these strategies as you read. Using a chart like the one shown, paraphrase five especially complex sentences.

Line Numbers for Poe's Sentence	My Paraphrase

VOCABULARY IN CONTEXT

Poe was fascinated with unusual language. Review the vocabulary words, noting any familiar roots, prefixes, or suffixes that might help you unlock the meanings of the words.

WORD LIST		
affinity	demeanor	insipid
alleviation	equivocal	pertinacity
anomaly	inordinate	vagary
apathy		

Where does TERROR *begin?*

KEY IDEA Fear can be a reasonable response to an immediate danger, like the instant alarm you would feel upon seeing a car racing toward you. But some of the things we find most **terrifying** don't present any real threat. A strange noise in the night, a creepy phone call, a creaking door slowly opening—what makes us afraid of things that can't really hurt us?

QUICKWRITE Recall times when you were frightened for no good reason: a walk in a familiar place that seemed strangely spooky or a sudden paranoia about being home alone. Describe what triggered your fear and why. How much of your terror was the result of your own imagination?

THE FALL OF THE
House of Usher

Edgar Allan Poe

Son coeur est un luth suspendu;
Sitôt qu'on le touche il résonne.
                    —De Béranger

"His heart is a hanging lute; / As soon as one touches it, it sounds" (lines from a poem by the 19th-century French poet Pierre Jean de Béranger).

During the whole of a dull, dark, and soundless day in the autumn of the year, when the clouds hung oppressively low in the heavens, I had been passing alone, on horseback, through a singularly dreary tract of country, and at length found myself, as the shades of the evening drew on, within view of the melancholy House of Usher. I know not how it was—but, with the first glimpse of the building, a sense of insufferable gloom pervaded my spirit. I say insufferable; for the feeling was unrelieved by any of that half-pleasurable, because poetic, sentiment with which the mind usually receives even the sternest natural images of the desolate or terrible. I looked
10 upon the scene before me—upon the mere house, and the simple landscape features of the domain—upon the bleak walls—upon the vacant, eye-like windows—upon a few rank sedges—and upon a few white trunks of decayed trees—with an utter depression of soul which I can compare to no earthly sensation more properly than to the after-dream of the reveller

ANALYZE VISUALS
What mood does this image convey? Identify specific elements, such as color, texture, and composition, that contribute to this mood.

12 rank sedges: overgrown grassy plants.

Illustrations by Shane Rebenscheid.

upon opium—the bitter lapse into everyday life—the hideous dropping off of the veil. There was an iciness, a sinking, a sickening of the heart—an unredeemed dreariness of thought which no goading of the imagination could torture into aught of the sublime. What was it—I paused to think—what was it that so unnerved me in the contemplation of the House of Usher? It was a mystery all insoluble; nor could I grapple with the shadowy fancies that crowded upon me as I pondered. I was forced to fall back upon the unsatisfactory conclusion, that while, beyond doubt, there *are* combinations of very simple natural objects which have the power of thus affecting us, still the analysis of this power lies among considerations beyond our depth. It was possible, I reflected, that a mere different arrangement of the particulars of the scene, of the details of the picture, would be sufficient to modify, or perhaps to annihilate its capacity for sorrowful impression; and, acting upon this idea, I reined my horse to the precipitous brink of a black and lurid tarn that lay in unruffled lustre by the dwelling, and gazed down—but with a shudder even more thrilling than before—upon the remodelled and inverted images of the grey sedge, and the ghastly tree-stems, and the vacant and eye-like windows. **Ⓐ**

Nevertheless, in this mansion of gloom I now proposed to myself a sojourn of some weeks. Its proprietor, Roderick Usher, had been one of my boon companions in boyhood; but many years had elapsed since our last meeting. A letter, however, had lately reached me in a distant part of the country—a letter from him—which, in its wildly importunate nature, had admitted of no other than a personal reply. The MS. gave evidence of nervous agitation. The writer spoke of acute bodily illness—of a mental disorder which oppressed him—and of an earnest desire to see me, as his best, and indeed his only personal friend, with a view of attempting, by the cheerfulness of my society, some **alleviation** of his malady. It was the manner in which all this, and much more, was said—it was the apparent *heart* that went with his request—which allowed me no room for hesitation; and I accordingly obeyed forthwith what I still considered a very singular summons.

Although, as boys, we had been even intimate associates, yet I really knew little of my friend. His reserve had been always excessive and habitual. I was aware, however, that his very ancient family had been noted, time out of mind, for a peculiar sensibility of temperament, displaying itself, through long ages, in many works of exalted art, and manifested, of late, in repeated deeds of munificent yet unobtrusive charity, as well as in a passionate devotion to the intricacies, perhaps even more than to the orthodox and easily recognizable beauties, of musical science. I had learned, too, the very remarkable fact, that the stem of the Usher race, all time-honored as it was, had put forth, at no period, any enduring branch; in other words, that the entire family lay in the direct line of descent, and had always, with very trifling and very temporary variation, so lain. It was this

28–29 precipitous...tarn: steep bank of a small black, repulsive-looking mountain lake.

Ⓐ UNITY OF EFFECT
Reread lines 16–32. Describe the **mood** of the scene. What details of the narrator's reactions contribute to this effect?

38 had admitted of no other than: had required; **MS.:** an abbreviation of *manuscript*.

alleviation (ə-lē′vē-ā′shən) *n.* relief

52 munificent yet unobtrusive: generous yet inconspicuous.

deficiency, I considered, while running over in thought the perfect keeping
60 of the character of the premises with the accredited character of the people,
and while speculating upon the possible influence which the one, in the
long lapse of centuries, might have exercised upon the other—it was this
deficiency, perhaps, of collateral issue, and the consequent undeviating
transmission, from sire to son, of the patrimony with the name, which had, at
length, so identified the two as to merge the original title of the estate in the
quaint and **equivocal** appellation of the "House of Usher"—an appellation
which seemed to include, in the minds of the peasantry who used it, both
the family and the family mansion. **B**

I have said that the sole effect of my somewhat childish experiment—that
70 of looking down within the tarn—had been to deepen the first singular
impression. There can be no doubt that the consciousness of the rapid increase
of my superstition—for why should I not so term it?—served mainly to
accelerate the increase itself. Such, I have long known, is the paradoxical law of
all sentiments having terror as a basis. And it might have been for this reason
only, that, when I again uplifted my eyes to the house itself, from its image
in the pool, there grew in my mind a strange fancy—a fancy so ridiculous,
indeed, that I but mention it to show the vivid force of the sensations which
oppressed me. I had so worked upon my imagination as really to believe that
about the whole mansion and domain there hung an atmosphere peculiar
80 to themselves and their immediate vicinity—an atmosphere which had no
affinity with the air of heaven, but which had reeked up from the decayed
trees, and the gray wall, and the silent tarn—a pestilent and mystic vapor, dull,
sluggish, faintly discernible, and leaden-hued.

Shaking off from my spirit what *must* have been a dream, I scanned
more narrowly the real aspect of the building. Its principal feature seemed
to be that of an excessive antiquity. The discoloration of ages had been
great. Minute fungi overspread the whole exterior, hanging in a fine tangled
web-work from the eaves. Yet all this was apart from any extraordinary
dilapidation. No portion of the masonry had fallen; and there appeared to
90 be a wild inconsistency between its still perfect adaptation of parts, and the
crumbling condition of the individual stones. In this there was much that
reminded me of the specious totality of old wood-work which has rotted
for long years in some neglected vault, with no disturbance from the breath
of the external air. Beyond this indication of extensive decay, however,
the fabric gave little token of instability. Perhaps the eye of a scrutinizing
observer might have discovered a barely perceptible fissure, which, extending
from the roof of the building in front, made its way down the wall in a
zigzag direction, until it became lost in the sullen waters of the tarn. **C**

Noticing these things, I rode over a short causeway to the house. A
100 servant in waiting took my horse, and I entered the Gothic archway of the
hall. A valet, of stealthy step, thence conducted me, in silence, through
many dark and intricate passages in my progress to the *studio* of his master.

62–63 **this deficiency . . . issue:** for
some reason, the Ushers have few
descendants.

equivocal (ĭ-kwĭv′ə-kəl) *adj.*
ambiguous

B **COMPLEX SENTENCES**
Identify the main idea of lines
62–68. What are the two
meanings of the phrase "the
House of Usher"?

affinity (ə-fĭn′ĭ-tē) *n.* a kinship
or likeness

92 **specious totality:** false
appearance of soundness.

96 **fissure:** long narrow crack.

C **GRAMMAR AND STYLE**
Reread lines 95–98. Note
how Poe uses the **participle**
"scrutinizing" and the **participial
phrase** "extending from the
roof of the building in front"
as modifiers.

Much that I encountered on the way contributed, I know not how, to heighten the vague sentiments of which I have already spoken. While the objects around me—while the carvings of the ceilings, the sombre tapestries of the walls, the ebon blackness of the floors, and the phantasmagoric armorial trophies which rattled as I strode, were but matters to which, or to such as which, I had been accustomed from my infancy—while I hesitated not to acknowledge how familiar was all this—I still wondered to find how unfamiliar were the fancies which ordinary images were stirring up. On one of the staircases, I met the physician of the family. His countenance, I thought, wore a mingled expression of low cunning and perplexity. He accosted me with trepidation and passed on. The valet now threw open a door and ushered me through into the presence of his master.

The room in which I found myself was very large and lofty. The windows were long, narrow, and pointed, and at so vast a distance from the black oaken floor as to be altogether inaccessible from within. Feeble gleams of encrimsoned light made their way through the trellissed panes, and served to render sufficiently distinct the more prominent objects around; the eye, however, struggled in vain to reach the remoter angles of the chamber, or the recesses of the vaulted and fretted ceiling. Dark draperies hung upon the walls. The general furniture was profuse, comfortless, antique, and tattered. Many books and musical instruments lay scattered about, but failed to give any vitality to the scene. I felt that I breathed an atmosphere of sorrow. An air of stern, deep, and irredeemable gloom hung over and pervaded all.

Upon my entrance, Usher arose from a sofa on which he had been lying at full length, and greeted me with a vivacious warmth which had much in it, I at first thought, of an overdone cordiality—of the constrained effort of the *ennuyé* man of the world. A glance, however, at his countenance convinced me of his perfect sincerity. We sat down; and for some moments, while he spoke not, I gazed upon him with a feeling of half pity, half of awe. Surely, man had never before so terribly altered, in so brief a period, as had Roderick Usher! It was with difficulty that I could bring myself to admit the identity of the wan being before me with the companion of my early boyhood. Yet the character of his face had been at all times remarkable. A cadaverousness of complexion; an eye large, liquid, and luminous beyond comparison; lips somewhat thin and very pallid, but of a surpassingly beautiful curve; a nose of a delicate Hebrew model, but with a breadth of nostril unusual in similar formations; a finely moulded chin, speaking, in its want of prominence, of a want of moral energy; hair of a more than web-like softness and tenuity; these features, with an **inordinate** expansion above the regions of the temple, made up altogether a countenance not easily to be forgotten. And now in the mere exaggeration of the prevailing character of these features, and of the expression they were wont to convey, lay so much of change that I doubted to whom I spoke. The now ghastly pallor of the skin, and the now miraculous lustre of the eye, above all things startled and

106–107 phantasmagoric (făn-tăz′mə-gôr′ĭk) **armorial trophies:** fantastic wall decorations bearing coats of arms.

121 vaulted and fretted: arched and decorated with interlaced designs.

129 *ennuyé* (äɴ-nwē-yā′) *French:* bored.

136 cadaverousness of complexion: a corpselike appearance.

inordinate (ĭn-ôr′dn-ĭt) *adj.* exceeding reasonable limits; excessive even awed me. The silken hair, too, had been suffered to grow all unheeded, and as, in its wild gossamer texture, it floated rather than fell about the face, I could not, even with effort, connect its Arabesque expression with any idea of simple humanity. **D**

150

In the manner of my friend I was at once struck with an incoherence—an inconsistency; and I soon found this to arise from a series of feeble and futile struggles to overcome an habitual trepidancy—an excessive nervous agitation. For something of this nature I had indeed been prepared, no less by his letter, than by reminiscences of certain boyish traits, and by conclusions deduced from his peculiar physical conformation and temperament. His action was alternately vivacious and sullen. His voice varied rapidly from a tremulous indecision (when the animal spirits seemed utterly in abeyance) to that species of energetic concision—that abrupt, weighty, unhurried, and hollow-sounding enunciation—that leaden, self-balanced, and perfectly modulated guttural utterance, which may be observed in the lost drunkard, or the irreclaimable eater of opium, during the periods of his most intense excitement.

160

It was thus that he spoke of the object of my visit, of his earnest desire to see me, and of the solace he expected me to afford him. He entered, at some length, into what he conceived to be the nature of his malady. It was, he said, a constitutional and a family evil, and one for which he despaired to find a remedy—a mere nervous affection, he immediately added, which would undoubtedly soon pass off. It displayed itself in a host of unnatural sensations. Some of these, as he detailed them, interested and bewildered me; although, perhaps, the terms and the general manner of their narration had their weight. He suffered much from a morbid acuteness of the senses; the most **insipid** food was alone endurable; he could wear only garments of certain texture; the odors of all flowers were oppressive; his eyes were tortured by even a faint light; and there were but peculiar sounds, and these from stringed instruments, which did not inspire him with horror.

170

To an anomalous species of terror I found him a bounden slave. "I shall perish," said he, "I *must* perish in this deplorable folly. Thus, thus, and not otherwise, shall I be lost. I dread the events of the future, not in themselves, but in their results. I shudder at the thought of any, even the most trivial, incident, which may operate upon this intolerable agitation of soul. I have, indeed, no abhorrence of danger, except in its absolute effect—in terror. In this unnerved—in this pitiable, condition—I feel that the period will sooner or later arrive when I must abandon life and reason together, in some struggle with the grim phantasm, FEAR." **E**

180

I learned, moreover, at intervals, and through broken and equivocal hints, another singular feature of his mental condition. He was enchained by certain superstitious impressions in regard to the dwelling which he tenanted, and whence, for many years, he had never ventured forth—in regard to an influence whose supposititious force was conveyed in terms too

190

149 Arabesque (ăr′a-bĕsk′): intricately interwoven, like the design of an Oriental rug.

D **UNITY OF EFFECT**
Reread lines 132–150. Poe often uses **exaggeration** to add drama to his descriptions. Which details of Roderick's appearance show this technique at work?

159 concision: terseness; brevity in use of words.

insipid (ĭn-sĭp′ĭd) *adj.* lacking in flavor; bland

175 but peculiar: only certain.

E **COMPLEX SENTENCES**
Reread the description of Roderick's state of mind in lines 177–185, and identify the idea that is repeatedly emphasized. What does Roderick seem to be afraid of?

190 supposititious: supposed.

shadowy here to be re-stated—an influence which some peculiarities in the mere form and substance of his family mansion had, by dint of long sufferance, he said, obtained over his spirit—an effect which the *physique* of the gray walls and turrets, and of the dim tarn into which they all looked down, had, at length, brought about upon the *morale* of his existence.

He admitted, however, although with hesitation, that much of the peculiar gloom which thus afflicted him could be traced to a more natural and far more palpable origin—to the severe and long-continued illness—indeed to the evidently approaching dissolution—of a tenderly beloved
200 sister—his sole companion for long years—his last and only relative on earth. "Her decease," he said, with a bitterness which I can never forget, "would leave him (him, the hopeless and the frail) the last of the ancient race of the Ushers." While he spoke, the lady Madeline (for so she was called) passed through a remote portion of the apartment, and, without having noticed my presence, disappeared. I regarded her with an utter astonishment not unmingled with dread—and yet I found it impossible to account for such feelings. A sensation of stupor oppressed me as my eyes followed her retreating steps. When a door, at length, closed upon her, my glance sought instinctively and eagerly the countenance of the brother—but he had buried
210 his face in his hands, and I could only perceive that a far more than ordinary wanness had overspread the emaciated fingers through which trickled many passionate tears.

The disease of the lady Madeline had long baffled the skill of her physicians. A settled **apathy**, a gradual wasting away of the person, and frequent although transient affections of a partially cataleptical character were the unusual diagnosis. Hitherto she had steadily borne up against the pressure of her malady, and had not betaken herself finally to bed; but on the closing in of the evening of my arrival at the house, she succumbed (as her brother told me at night with inexpressible agitation) to the prostrating
220 power of the destroyer; and I learned that the glimpse I had obtained of her person would thus probably be the last I should obtain—that the lady, at least while living, would be seen by me no more.

For several days ensuing, her name was unmentioned by either Usher or myself; and during this period I was busied in earnest endeavors to alleviate the melancholy of my friend. We painted and read together, or I listened, as if in a dream, to the wild improvisations of his speaking guitar. And thus, as a closer and still closer intimacy admitted me more unreservedly into the recesses of his spirit, the more bitterly did I perceive the futility of all attempt at cheering a mind from which darkness, as if an inherent positive
230 quality, poured forth upon all the objects of the moral and physical universe in one unceasing radiation of gloom. **F**

I shall ever bear about me a memory of the many solemn hours I thus spent alone with the master of the House of Usher. Yet I should fail in any attempt to convey an idea of the exact character of the studies, or of the

ANALYZE VISUALS
What techniques has the artist used to create contrast between Madeline and the two men?

apathy (ăp'ə-thē) *n.* lack of feeling or interest

215 transient . . . cataleptical (kăt'l-ĕp'tĭ-kəl) **character:** temporary episodes of a trancelike condition.

F COMPLEX SENTENCES
Reread lines 226–231. **Paraphrase** this sentence by breaking it into two shorter sentences, each beginning with the word *I*. What has changed in the narrator's relationship with Roderick?

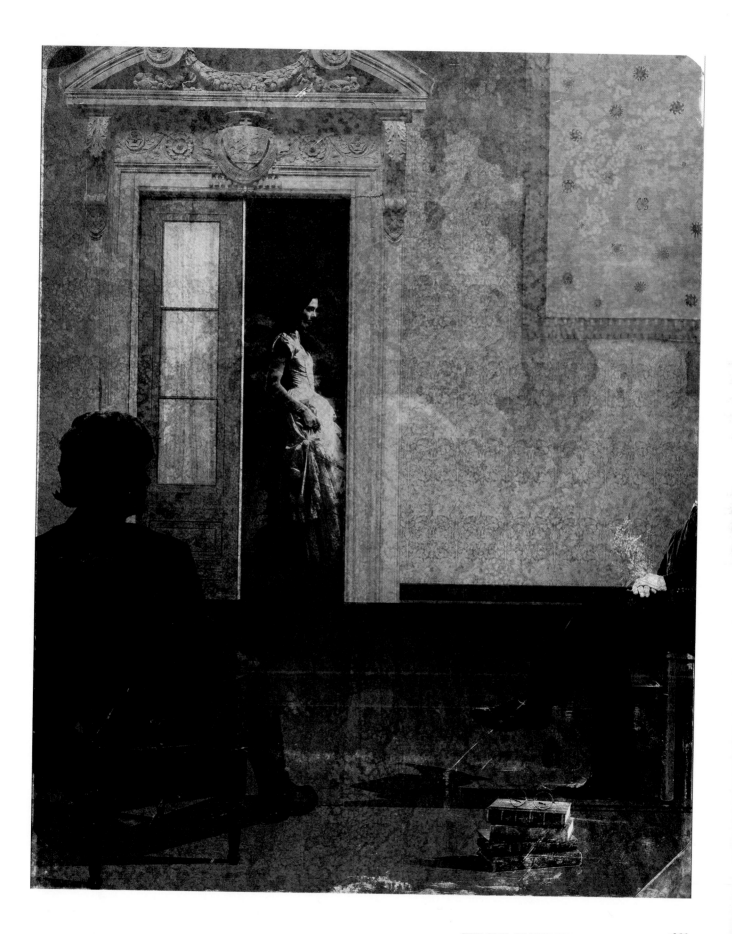

occupations, in which he involved me, or led me the way. An excited and highly distempered ideality threw a sulphureous lustre over all. His long improvised dirges will ring forever in my ears. Among other things, I hold painfully in mind a certain singular perversion and amplification of the wild air of the last waltz of Von Weber. From the paintings over which his
240 elaborate fancy brooded, and which grew, touch by touch, into vagueness at which I shuddered the more thrillingly, because I shuddered knowing not why,—from these paintings (vivid as their images now are before me) I would in vain endeavor to educe more than a small portion which should lie within the compass of merely written words. By the utter simplicity, by the nakedness of his designs, he arrested and over-awed attention. If ever mortal painted an ideal, that mortal was Roderick Usher. For me at least— in the circumstances then surrounding me—there arose out of the pure abstractions which the hypochondriac contrived to throw upon his canvas, an intensity of intolerable awe, no shadow of which felt I ever yet in the
250 contemplation of the certainly glowing yet too concrete reveries of Fuseli.

One of the phantasmagoric conceptions of my friend, partaking not so rigidly of the spirit of abstraction, may be shadowed forth, although feebly, in words. A small picture presented the interior of an immensely long and rectangular vault or tunnel, with low walls, smooth, white, and without interruption or device. Certain accessory points of the design served well to convey the idea that this excavation lay at an exceeding depth below the surface of the earth. No outlet was observed in any portion of its vast extent, and no torch or other artificial source of light was discernable; yet a flood of intense rays rolled throughout, and bathed the whole in a ghastly and
260 inappropriate splendor.

I have just spoken of that morbid condition of the auditory nerve which rendered all music intolerable to the sufferer, with the exception of certain effects of stringed instruments. It was, perhaps, the narrow limits to which he thus confined himself upon the guitar which gave birth, in great measure, to the fantastic character of his performances. But the fervid *facility* of his *impromptus* could not be so accounted for. They must have been, and were, in the notes, as well as in the words of his wild fantasias (for he not unfrequently accompanied himself with rhymed verbal improvisations), the result of that intense mental collectedness and concentration to which
270 I have previously alluded as observable only in particular moments of the highest artificial excitement. The words of one of these rhapsodies I have easily remembered. I was, perhaps, the more forcibly impressed with it as he gave it, because, in the under or mystic current of its meaning, I fancied that I perceived, and for the first time, a full consciousness on the part of Usher of the tottering of his lofty reason upon her throne. The verses, which were entitled "The Haunted Palace," ran very near, if not accurately, thus:—

236 distempered . . . sulphureous (sŭl-fər′ē-əs) **lustre:** diseased creativity gave a nightmarish quality.

239 Von Weber (vŏn vā′bər): the German romantic composer Karl Maria von Weber (1786–1826).

250 Fuseli (fyōō′zə-lē′): the Swiss-born British painter Henry Fuseli (1741–1825), many of whose works feature fantastic or gruesome elements.

266 *impromptus* (ăɴ-prôɴp-tü′) *French:* musical pieces made up as they are played.

I

In the greenest of our valleys,
By good angels tenanted,
Once a fair and stately palace—
280   *Radiant palace—reared its head.*
In the monarch Thought's dominion—
It stood there!
Never seraph spread a pinion
    Over fabric half so fair.

II

Banners yellow, glorious, golden,
    On its roof did float and flow;
(This—all this—was in the olden
    Time long ago)
And every gentle air that dallied,
290   *In that sweet day,*
Along the ramparts plumed and pallid,
    A winged odor went away.

III

Wanderers in that happy valley
    Through two luminous windows saw
Spirits moving musically
    To a lute's well-tunèd law,
Round about a throne, where sitting
    (Porphyrogene!)
In state his glory well befitting,
300   *The ruler of the realm was seen.*

IV

And all with pearl and ruby glowing
    Was the fair palace door,
Through which came flowing, flowing, flowing
    And sparkling evermore,
A troop of Echoes whose sweet duty
    Was but to sing,
In voices of surpassing beauty,
    The wit and wisdom of their king.

V

But evil things, in robes of sorrow,
    Assailed the monarch's high estate;
(Ah, let us mourn, for never morrow
    Shall dawn upon him, desolate!)
And, round about his home, the glory
    That blushed and bloomed
Is but a dim-remembered story
    Of the old time entombed.

310

VI

And travellers now within that valley,
    Through the red-litten windows see
Vast forms that move fantastically
    To a discordant melody;
While, like a rapid ghastly river,
    Through the pale door,
A hideous throng rush out forever,
    And laugh—but smile no more.

320

I well remember that suggestions arising from this ballad led us into
a train of thought wherein there became manifest an opinion of Usher's
which I mention not so much on account of its novelty (for other men have
thought thus), as on account of the **pertinacity** with which he maintained
it. This opinion, in its general form, was that of the sentience of all vegetable
330 things. But, in his disordered fancy, the idea had assumed a more daring
character, and trespassed, under certain conditions, upon the kingdom of
inorganization. I lack words to express the full extent, of the earnest *abandon*
of his persuasion. The belief, however, was connected (as I have previously
hinted) with the gray stones of the home of his forefathers. The conditions
of the sentience had been here, he imagined, fulfilled in the method of
collocation of these stones—in the order of their arrangement, as well as
in that of the many *fungi* which overspread them, and of the decayed trees
which stood around—above all, in the long undisturbed endurance of
this arrangement, and in its reduplication in the still waters of the tarn. Its
340 evidence—the evidence of the sentience—was to be seen, he said (and I here
stared as he spoke), in the gradual yet certain condensation of an atmosphere
of their own about the waters and the walls. The result was discoverable,
he added, in that silent yet importunate and terrible influence which for
centuries had moulded the destinies of his family, and which made *him* what
I now saw him—what he was. Such opinions need no comment, and I will
make none.

    Our books—the books which, for years, had formed no small portion of
the mental existence of the invalid—were, as might be supposed, in strict
keeping with this character of phantasm. We pored together over such works

pertinacity (pûr′tn-ăs′ĭ-tē) *n.*
stubbornness; persistence

329–330 sentience (sĕn′shəns) **of all
vegetable things:** consciousness of
all growing things.

350 as the Ververt et Chartreuse of Gresset; the Belphegor of Machiavelli; the
Heaven and Hell of Swedenborg; the Subterranean Voyage of Nicholas
Klimm by Holberg; the Chiromancy of Robert Flud, of Jean D'Indaginé,
and of De la Chambre; the Journey into the Blue Distance of Tieck; and
the City of the Sun of Campanella. Our favorite volume was a small octavo
edition of the *Directorium Inquisitorium*, by the Dominican Eymeric de
Gironne; and there were passages in Pomponius Mela, about the old African
Satyrs and Aegipans, over which Usher would sit dreaming for hours. His
chief delight, however, was found in the perusal of an exceedingly rare and
curious book in quarto Gothic—the manual of a forgotten church—the
360 *Vigiliae Mortuorum secundum Chorum Ecclesiae Maguntinae.*

350–356 **Ververt et Chartreuse
. . . Pomponius Mela:** extravagantly
imaginative works of fiction,
theology, philosophy, and geography.

360 *Vigiliae Mortuorum secundum
Chorum Ecclesiae Maguntinae* Latin:
Wakes for the Dead, in the Manner
of the Choir of the Church of Mainz.

   I could not help thinking of the wild ritual of this work, and of its
probable influence upon the hypochondriac, when, one evening, having
informed me abruptly that the lady Madeline was no more, he stated his
intention of preserving her corpse for a fortnight (previously to its final
interment), in one of the numerous vaults within the main walls of the
building. The worldly reason, however, assigned for this singular proceeding,
was one which I did not feel at liberty to dispute. The brother had been led
to his resolution (so he told me) by consideration of the unusual character
of the malady of the deceased, of certain obtrusive and eager inquiries on
370 the part of her medical men, and of the remote and exposed situation of the
burial-ground of the family. I will not deny that when I called to mind the
sinister countenance of the person whom I met upon the staircase, on the
day of my arrival at the house, I had no desire to oppose what I regarded
as at best but a harmless, and by no means an unnatural, precaution.

364–365 **for a fortnight . . .
interment:** for two weeks prior to its
final burial.

   At the request of Usher, I personally aided him in the arrangements for
the temporary entombment. The body having been encoffined, we two
alone bore it to its rest. The vault in which we placed it (and which had
been so long unopened that our torches, half smothered in its oppressive
atmosphere, gave us little opportunity for investigation) was small, damp,
380 and entirely without means of admission for light; lying, at great depth,
immediately beneath that portion of the building in which was my own
sleeping apartment. It had been used, apparently, in remote feudal times, for
the worst purposes of a donjonkeep, and, in later days, as a place of deposit
for powder, or some other highly combustible substance, as a portion of its
floor, and the whole interior of a long archway through which we reached
it, were carefully sheathed with copper. The door, of massive iron, had been,
also, similarly protected. Its immense weight caused an unusually sharp,
grating sound, as it moved upon its hinges. **G**

383 **donjonkeep** (dŏn'jən-kēp):
dungeon.

   Having deposited our mournful burden upon tressels within this region
390 of horror, we partially turned aside the yet unscrewed lid of the coffin,
and looked upon the face of the tenant. A striking similitude between the
brother and sister now first arrested my attention; and Usher, divining,
perhaps, my thoughts, murmured out some few words from which I learned

G UNITY OF EFFECT
Reread lines 377–388. Why might
Poe have provided so much **detail**
about the structure of the vault?

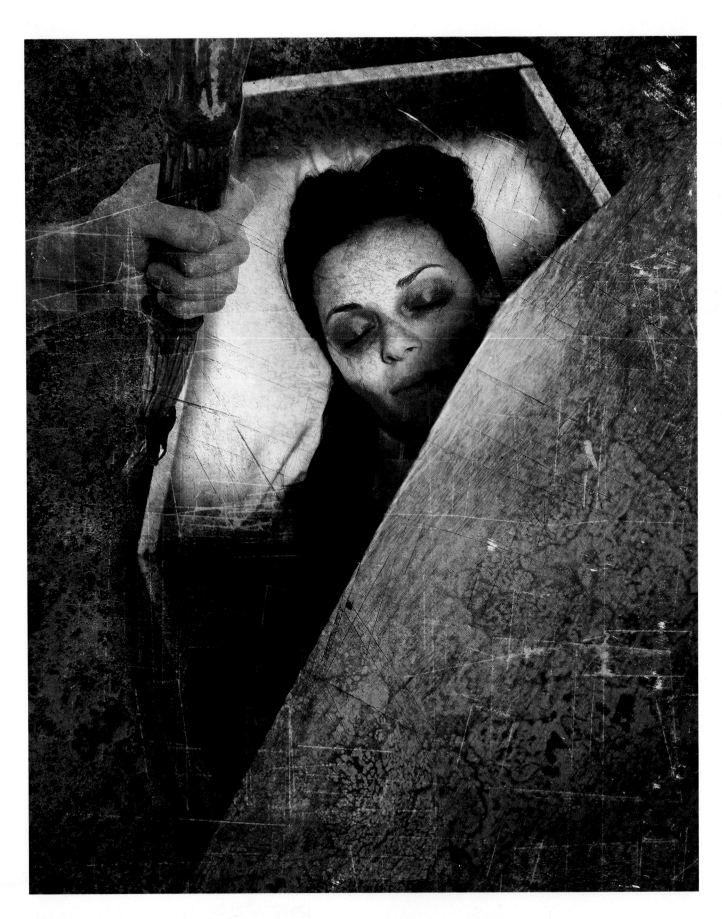

that the deceased and himself had been twins, and that sympathies of a scarcely intelligible nature had always existed between them. Our glances, however, rested not long upon the dead—for we could not regard her unawed. The disease which had thus entombed the lady in the maturity of her youth, had left, as usual in all maladies of a strictly cataleptical character, the mockery of a faint blush upon the bosom and the face, and that suspiciously lingering smile upon the lip which is so terrible in death. We replaced and screwed down the lid, and, having secured the door of iron, made our way, with toil, into the scarcely less gloomy apartments of the upper portion of the house.

And now, some days of bitter grief having elapsed, an observable change came over the features of the mental disorder of my friend. His ordinary manner had vanished. His ordinary occupations were neglected or forgotten. He roamed from chamber to chamber with hurried, unequal, and objectless step. The pallor of his countenance had assumed, if possible, a more ghastly hue—but the luminousness of his eye had utterly gone out. The once occasional huskiness of his tone was heard no more; and a tremulous quaver, as if of extreme terror, habitually characterized his utterance. There were times, indeed, when I thought his unceasingly agitated mind was laboring with some oppressive secret, to divulge which he struggled for the necessary courage. At times, again, I was obliged to resolve all into the mere inexplicable **vagaries** of madness, for I beheld him gazing upon vacancy for long hours, in an attitude of the profoundest attention, as if listening to some imaginary sound. It was no wonder that his condition terrified—that it infected me. I felt creeping upon me, by slow yet certain degrees, the wild influences of his own fantastic yet impressive superstitions.

It was, especially, upon retiring to bed late in the night of the seventh or eighth day after the placing of the lady Madeline within the donjon, that I experienced the full power of such feelings. Sleep came not near my couch—while the hours waned and waned away. I struggled to reason off the nervousness which had dominion over me. I endeavored to believe that much, if not all of what I felt, was due to the bewildering influence of the gloomy furniture of the room—of the dark and tattered draperies, which, tortured into motion by the breath of a rising tempest, swayed fitfully to and fro upon the walls, and rustled uneasily about the decorations of the bed. But my efforts were fruitless. An irrepressible tremor gradually pervaded my frame; and, at length, there sat upon my very heart an incubus of utterly causeless alarm. Shaking this off with a gasp and a struggle, I uplifted myself upon the pillows, and, peering earnestly within the intense darkness of the chamber, hearkened—I know not why, except that an instinctive spirit prompted me—to certain low and indefinite sounds which came, through the pauses of the storm, at long intervals, I knew not whence. Overpowered by an intense sentiment of horror, unaccountable yet unendurable, I threw on my clothes with haste (for I felt that I should sleep no more during the night), and endeavored to arouse myself from the pitiable condition into which I had fallen, by pacing rapidly to and fro through the apartment. **H**

vagary (vā′gə-rē) *n.* strange idea

423 **couch:** bed.

430 **incubus:** something that burdens like a nightmare.

H COMPLEX SENTENCES
Reread lines 431–435. Identify the main subject and verb of the sentence. Which participial phrases modify this subject?

440   I had taken but a few turns in this manner, when a light step on an adjoining staircase arrested my attention. I presently recognized it as that of Usher. In an instant afterward he rapped, with a gentle touch, at my door, and entered, bearing a lamp. His countenance was, as usual, cadaverously wan—but, moreover, there was a species of mad hilarity in his eyes—an evidently restrained *hysteria* in his whole **demeanor.** His air appalled me— but any thing was preferable to the solitude which I had so long endured, and I even welcomed his presence as a relief.

    "And you have not seen it?" he said abruptly, after having stared about him for some moments in silence—"you have not then seen it?—but, stay! 450 you shall." Thus speaking, and having carefully shaded his lamp, he hurried to one of the casements, and threw it freely open to the storm.

    The impetuous fury of the entering gust nearly lifted us from our feet. It was, indeed, a tempestuous yet sternly beautiful night, and one wildly singular in its terror and its beauty. A whirlwind had apparently collected its force in our vicinity; for there were frequent and violent alterations in the direction of the wind; and the exceeding density of the clouds (which hung so low as to press upon the turrets of the house) did not prevent our perceiving the lifelike velocity with which they flew careering from all points against each other, without passing away into the distance. I say that even 460 their exceeding density did not prevent our perceiving this—yet we had no glimpse of the moon or stars, nor was there any flashing forth of lightning. But the under surfaces of the huge masses of agitated vapor, as well as the terrestrial objects immediately around us, were glowing in the unnatural light of a faintly luminous and distinctly visible gaseous exhalation which hung about and enshrouded the mansion.

    "You must not—you shall not behold this!" said I, shuddering, to Usher, as I led him, with a gentle violence, from the window to a seat. "These appearances, which bewilder you, are merely electrical phenomena not uncommon—or it may be that they have their ghastly origin in the rank 470 miasma of the tarn. Let us close this casement;—the air is chilling and dangerous to your frame. Here is one of your favorite romances. I will read, and you shall listen;—and so we will pass away this terrible night together."

    The antique volume which I had taken up was the "Mad Trist" of Sir Launcelot Canning; but I had called it a favorite of Usher's more in sad jest than in earnest; for, in truth, there is little in its uncouth and unimaginative prolixity which could have had interest for the lofty and spiritual ideality of my friend. It was, however, the only book immediately at hand; and I indulged a vague hope that the excitement which now agitated the hypochondriac, might find relief (for the history of mental disorder is full of 480 similar **anomalies**) even in the extremeness of the folly which I should read. Could I have judged, indeed, by the wild overstrained air of vivacity with which he hearkened, or apparently hearkened, to the words of the tale, I might well have congratulated myself upon the success of my design.

demeanor (dĭ-mē′nər) *n.* behavior

458 **careering:** going at top speed.

462–463 **huge masses ... terrestrial objects:** the huge, fast-moving clouds, as well as the objects on the ground.

470 **miasma** (mī-ăz′mə): poisonous vapors.

475–476 **uncouth ... prolixity** (prōlĭk′sĭ-tē): clumsy and unimaginative wordiness.

anomaly (ə-nŏm′ə-lē) *n.* departure from the normal rules

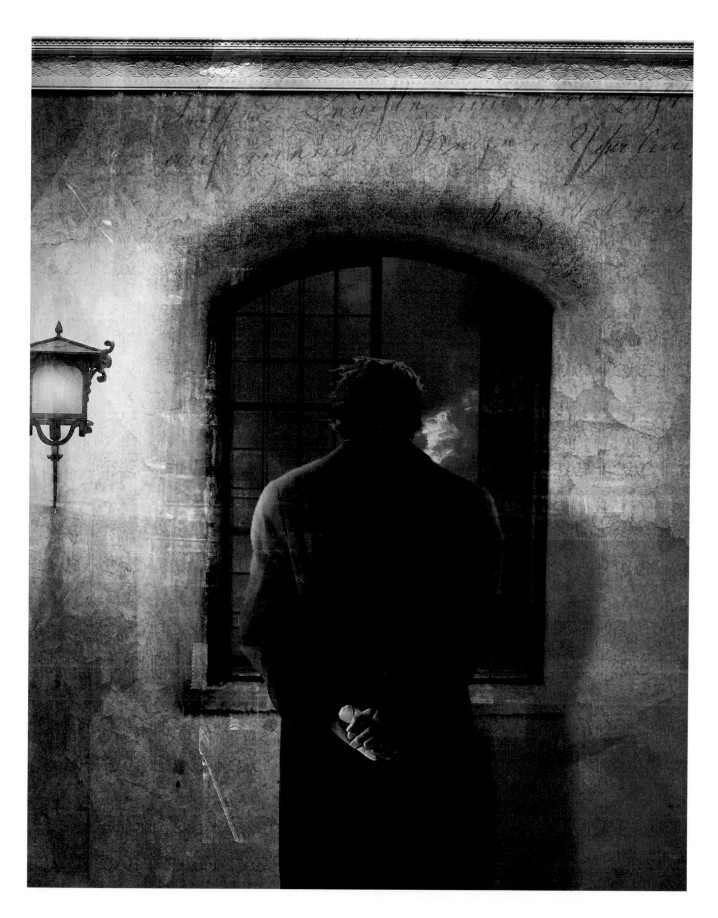

I had arrived at that well-known portion of the story where Ethelred, the hero of the Trist, having sought in vain for peaceable admission into the dwelling of the hermit, proceeds to make good an entrance by force. Here, it will be remembered, the words of the narrative run thus:

"And Ethelred, who was by nature of a doughty heart, and who was now mighty withal, on account of the powerfulness of the wine which he had drunken, waited no longer to hold parley with the hermit, who, in sooth, was of an obstinate and maliceful turn, but, feeling the rain upon his shoulders, and fearing the rising of the tempest, uplifted his mace outright, and, with blows, made quickly room in the plankings of the door for his gauntleted hand; and now pulling therewith sturdily, he so cracked, and ripped, and tore all asunder, that the noise of the dry and hollow-sounding wood alarumed and reverberated throughout the forest."

490

At the termination of this sentence I started and, for a moment, paused; for it appeared to me (although I at once concluded that my excited fancy had deceived me)—it appeared to me that, from some very remote portion of the mansion, there came, indistinctly, to my ears, what might have been, in its exact similarity of character, the echo (but a stifled and dull one certainly) of the very cracking and ripping sound which Sir Launcelot had so particularly described. It was, beyond doubt, the coincidence alone which had arrested my attention; for, amid the rattling of the sashes of the casements, and the ordinary commingled noises of the still increasing storm, the sound, in itself, had nothing, surely, which should have interested or disturbed me. I continued the story:

500

"But the good champion Ethelred, now entering within the door, was sore enraged and amazed to perceive no signal of the maliceful hermit; but, in the stead thereof, a dragon of scaly and prodigious demeanor, and of a fiery tongue, which sate in guard before a palace of gold, with a floor of silver; and upon the wall there hung a shield of shining brass with this legend enwritten—

510

Who entereth herein, a conqueror hath bin;
Who slayeth the dragon, the shield he shall win;

And Ethelred uplifted his mace, and struck upon the head of the dragon, which fell before him, and gave up his pesty breath, with a shriek so horrid and harsh, and withal so piercing, that Ethelred had fain to close his ears with his hands against the dreadful noise of it, the like whereof was never before heard."

520

Here again I paused abruptly, and now with a feeling of wild amazement—for there could be no doubt whatever that, in this instance, I did actually hear (although from what direction it proceeded I found it impossible to say) a low and apparently distant, but harsh, protracted, and most unusual screaming or grating sound—the exact counterpart of what

492–494 uplifted his mace . . . gauntleted hand: raised his spiked club and cut a space in the door for his armored, gloved hand.

517 pesty: poisonous.

my fancy had conjured up for the dragon's unnatural shriek as described by the romancer. ❶

Oppressed, as I certainly was, upon the occurrence of this second and most extraordinary coincidence, by a thousand conflicting sensations, in which wonder and extreme terror were predominant, I still retained sufficient presence of mind to avoid exciting, by any observation, the sensitive nervousness of my companion. I was by no means certain that he had noticed the sounds in question; although, assuredly, a strange alteration had, during the last few minutes, taken place in his demeanor. From a position fronting my own, he had gradually brought round his chair, so as to sit with his face to the door of the chamber; and thus I could but partially perceive his features, although I saw that his lips trembled as if he were murmuring inaudibly. His head had dropped upon his breast—yet I knew that he was not asleep, from the wide and rigid opening of the eye as I caught a glance of it in profile. The motion of his body, too, was at variance with this idea—for he rocked from side to side with a gentle yet constant and uniform sway. Having rapidly taken notice of all this, I resumed the narrative of Sir Launcelot, which thus proceeded:

"And now, the champion, having escaped from the terrible fury of the dragon, bethinking himself of the brazen shield, and of the breaking up of the enchantment which was upon it, removed the carcass from out of the way before him, and approached valorously over the silver pavement of the castle to where the shield was upon the wall; which in sooth tarried not for his full coming, but fell down at his feet upon the silver floor, with a mighty great and terrible ringing sound."

No sooner had these syllables passed my lips, than—as if a shield of brass had indeed, at the moment, fallen heavily upon a floor of silver—I became aware of a distinct, hollow, metallic, and clangorous, yet apparently muffled, reverberation. Completely unnerved, I leaped to my feet; but the measured rocking movement of Usher was undisturbed. I rushed to the chair in which he sat. His eyes were bent fixedly before him, and throughout his whole countenance there reigned a stony rigidity. But, as I placed my hand upon his shoulder, there came a strong shudder over his whole person; a sickly smile quivered about his lips; and I saw that he spoke in a low, hurried, and gibbering murmur, as if unconscious of my presence. Bending closely over him, I at length drank in the hideous import of his words.

"Not hear it?—yes, I hear it, and *have* heard it. Long—long—long—many minutes, many hours, many days, have I heard it—yet I dared not—oh, pity me, miserable wretch that I am!—I dared not—I *dared* not speak! *We have put her living in the tomb!* Said I not that my senses were acute? I *now* tell you that I heard her first feeble movements in the hollow coffin. I heard them—many, many days ago—yet I dared not—*I dared not speak!* And now—to-night—Ethelred—ha ha!—the breaking of the hermit's door, and the death-cry of the dragon, and the clangor of the shield!—say, rather, the

❶ UNITY OF EFFECT
Reread lines 521–527. What coincidence is repeated?

570 rending of her coffin, and the grating of the iron hinges of her prison, and her struggles within the coppered archway of the vault! Oh! whither shall I fly? Will she not be here anon? Is she not hurrying to upbraid me for my haste? Have I not heard her footstep on the stair? Do I not distinguish that heavy and horrible beating of her heart? MADMAN!"—here he sprang furiously to his feet, and shrieked out his syllables, as if in the effort he were giving up his soul—"MADMAN! I TELL YOU THAT SHE NOW STANDS WITHOUT THE DOOR!" **J**

As if in the superhuman energy of his utterance there had been found the potency of a spell, the huge antique panels to which the speaker pointed threw slowly back, upon the instant, their ponderous and ebony jaws. It 580 was the work of the rushing gust—but then without those doors there did stand the lofty and enshrouded figure of the lady Madeline of Usher. There was blood upon her white robes, and the evidence of some bitter struggle upon every portion of her emaciated frame. For a moment she remained trembling and reeling to and fro upon the threshold—then, with a low moaning cry, fell heavily inward upon the person of her brother, and in her violent and now final death-agonies, bore him to the floor a corpse, and a victim to the terrors he had anticipated.

From the chamber, and from that mansion, I fled aghast. The storm was still abroad in all its wrath as I found myself crossing the old causeway. 590 Suddenly there shot along the path a wild light, and I turned to see whence a gleam so unusual could have issued; for the vast house and its shadows were alone behind me. The radiance was that of the full, setting, and blood-red moon, which now shone vividly through that once barely discernible fissure, of which I have before spoken as extending from the roof of the building, in a zigzag direction, to the base. While I gazed, the fissure rapidly widened—there came a fierce breath of the whirlwind—the entire orb of the satellite burst at once upon my sight—my brain reeled as I saw the mighty walls rushing asunder—there was a long tumultuous shouting sound like the voice of a thousand waters—and the deep and dank tarn at my feet closed 600 sullenly and silently over the fragments of the "HOUSE OF USHER." ❧

J **UNITY OF EFFECT**
Reread lines 568–571. Recall the description of the vault you read earlier. In what way does that description help set up the situation of the story's **climax?**

ANALYZE VISUALS
Compare the image on page 423 with the description in lines 581–587. Is the artist's interpretation of the scene effective? Why or why not?

Comprehension

1. **Recall** Why does the narrator come to the House of Usher?

2. **Recall** What change in Madeline's condition occurs shortly after the narrator's arrival?

3. **Clarify** What are Roderick's reasons for placing Madeline in the vault below the house?

Literary Analysis

4. **Examine Complex Sentences** Review the chart you created as you read. Compare your paraphrases with Poe's original sentences. Without Poe's elaborate language, does the story have the same **mood?** Explain.

5. **Draw Conclusions about Point of View** Explain what each of the following reveals about the narrator's changing response to the house and its inhabitants. How does Poe's use of the first-person point of view help communicate the experience of **terror?**

   - the narrator's response to the house (lines 63–83)
   - his opinion of Roderick (lines 186–195)
   - Roderick's influence on the narrator (lines 417–419)
   - his efforts to calm his own fears (lines 423–431)

6. **Interpret Title** Reread lines 58–68. Based on this passage, explain two possible meanings of the story's title. In what ways does the title help you anticipate the ending of the story?

7. **Analyze Unity of Effect** In what way does each of the following demonstrate Poe's principle of the single effect? Cite key details that show Poe's use of the specified story element to build **mood.**

   - setting (lines 115–125)
   - character traits (lines 172–176)
   - plot developments (lines 216–222)
   - imagery (lines 452–465)

8. **Evaluate Author's Technique** In your opinion, does Poe's technique of the unified effect accomplish its intended purpose? What, if any, are the disadvantages of his approach? Explain.

Literary Criticism

9. **Critical Interpretations** The literary critic Cleanth Brooks dismissed "The Fall of the House of Usher" as an "essentially meaningless" exercise in horror for its own sake. Considering your own reading of the story, do you agree or disagree with this opinion? Cite details to support your answer.

Vocabulary in Context

VOCABULARY PRACTICE

Choose the word that is not related in meaning to the other words.

1. (a) dull, (b) uninteresting, (c) insipid, (d) insecure
2. (a) demeanor, (b) antique, (c) manner, (d) interaction
3. (a) conception, (b) delusion, (c) vagary, (d) tome
4. (a) connection, (b) disturbance, (c) affinity, (d) relationship
5. (a) deviation, (b) oddity, (c) representative, (d) anomaly
6. (a) bureaucratic, (b) extravagant, (c) extreme, (d) inordinate
7. (a) apathy, (b) ecstasy, (c) indifference, (d) unconcern
8. (a) agony, (b) torment, (c) alleviation, (d) anguish
9. (a) persistence, (b) perseverance, (c) pretense, (d) pertinacity
10. (a) hazy, (b) ambiguous, (c) contentious, (d) equivocal

VOCABULARY IN WRITING

The narrator describes Usher's instability, but how stable was the narrator himself? Write an explanation of your opinion, using evidence from the story. Include at least three vocabulary words. Here is a sample beginning.

> **EXAMPLE SENTENCE**
>
> The narrator's __inordinate__ attention to the Ushers' quirks can be seen as one sign of his own instability.

VOCABULARY STRATEGY: THE GREEK ROOT *path*

The vocabulary word *apathy* contains the Greek root *path,* which means "feel" or "suffer." This root is found in a number of English words. To understand words with *path,* use context clues as well as your knowledge of the root's meaning.

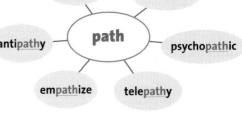

apathy pathos antipathy **path** psychopathic empathize telepathy

PRACTICE Choose the word from the word web that best completes each sentence. Consider what you know about the Greek root and the other word parts shown. If necessary, consult a dictionary.

1. Her brother's cruel actions caused her to feel a strong _____ for him.
2. The characters' tearful farewell evoked a sense of _____ in the audience.
3. Their thoughts were so aligned that it seemed they could communicate by _____.
4. Many criminals' behavior tends to be _____.
5. Parents are often able to _____ with their children's problems and frustrations.

VOCABULARY PRACTICE
For more practice, go to the **Vocabulary Center** at ClassZone.com.

Reading-Writing Connection

GRAMMAR AND STYLE

ADD DESCRIPTIVE DETAILS Review the **Grammar and Style** note on page 407. Poe is a master of elaborate, ornate descriptions that are packed with details. Some of his descriptive words are **participles,** verb forms that function as adjectives, as in this example:

> *His long improvised dirges will ring forever in my ears.* (lines 236–237)

Participles usually end in *-ing* or *-ed* and can be combined with modifiers and complements to make **participial phrases.**

PRACTICE Read each of the following sentences from Poe's story, noting the boldfaced participle or participial phrase. Then, write your own sentence, using a participle as instructed in parentheses. An example has been done for you.

EXAMPLE

His countenance, I thought, wore a **mingled** expression of low cunning and perplexity. (Use a past participle, one that ends with *-ed.*)

The cat, I noticed, carried a mangled mouse in her jaws.

---

1. A sensation of stupor oppressed me as my eyes followed her **retreating** steps. (Use a present participle, one that ends with *-ing.*)

2. **Shaking off from my spirit what *must* have been a dream,** I scanned more narrowly the real aspect of the building. (Use a participial phrase to begin your sentence. Make sure your phrase modifies the subject.)

3. Minute fungi overspread the whole exterior, **hanging in a fine tangled web-work from the eaves.** (Use a participial phrase at the end of your sentence. Make sure the phrase modifies the subject.)

WRITING TOOLS

For prewriting, revision, and editing tools, visit the **Writing Center** at ClassZone.com.

The Masque of the Red Death

Short Story by
Edgar Allan Poe

● LITERARY ANALYSIS: ALLEGORY

You can enjoy this story by Poe for its thrills, or you can read it as an **allegory,** a work of art with two levels of meaning. In an allegory, characters and objects stand for ideas outside the work, such as good and evil. Often meant to teach moral lessons, allegories typically feature simple characters and unnamed settings, somewhat like fairy tales.

The "Red Death" had long devastated the country.

In early allegories, ideas were **personified** as characters and given proper names (Good, Evil). As you read, note how Poe uses allegorical elements to suggest a moral lesson.

● READING STRATEGY: CLARIFY MEANING

Poe's unusual, archaic vocabulary reinforces this story's feeling of antiquity. The following strategies can help you clarify the meaning of difficult words and phrases:

- Consult the side notes for helpful information.
- Use **context clues** in surrounding phrases to figure out unfamiliar words.
- **Paraphrase** difficult passages, using simpler language.

As you read, pause to write summarizes of each paragraph. Note which parts of the story require further clarifying.

▲ VOCABULARY IN CONTEXT

Poe used the following words in his eerie tale. Complete each phrase with an appropriate word from the list.

WORD LIST	blasphemous	disapprobation	propriety
	cessation	impede	reverie

1. wandered the halls lost in a _____
2. a peace treaty following the _____ of hostilities
3. her friends' _____ after her unwise decision
4. tried not to _____ the flow of traffic
5. deeply offended by his _____ arguments
6. acted with decorum and _____

Explore the Key Idea

Is SAFETY an illusion?

KEY IDEA We like to feel that there are steps we can take to keep ourselves safe. To protect ourselves from theft, we can install an alarm or add high-security locks. To protect our health, we can exercise and eat healthy food. But do our precautions really keep danger away, or do they just give us an illusion of **safety?**

PRESENT Work with a small group to develop an argument for or against the question, *Is safety an illusion?* Choose at least two examples to support your argument. Then, taking turns with other groups, present your case to the class.

POSITION:

Safety is NOT an illusion.

ARGUMENT:

People can take steps to protect themselves from danger.

EXAMPLE:

A vaccine can provide nearly complete protection from a disease.

THE
Masque
OF THE
RED DEATH

Edgar Allan Poe

> **BACKGROUND** Around 1350, Europe was struck by an epidemic of bubonic plague (Black Death) that killed more than a quarter of its population. The plague killed its victims quickly—within three to five days—and there was no cure. Artwork from that time is full of haunting symbols like the Dance of Death, where Death, personified as a skeleton, whirls anonymous figures to their graves. These grisly allegorical images spoke to the deepest fears of their audience, for whom death was a nearby presence. Note how Poe borrows from this history in his own tale of death.

The "Red Death" had long devastated the country. No pestilence had ever been so fatal, or so hideous. Blood was its Avatar and its seal—the redness and horror of blood. There were sharp pains, and sudden dizziness, and then profuse bleeding at the pores, with dissolution. The scarlet stains upon the body, and especially upon the face of the victim, were the pest ban which shut him out from the aid and from the sympathy of his fellow men. And the whole seizure, progress, and termination of the disease were the incidents of half an hour. **A**

But the Prince Prospero was happy and dauntless and sagacious. When his
10 dominions were half depopulated, he summoned to his presence a thousand hale and lighthearted friends from among the knights and dames of his court,

2 **Avatar** (ăv'ə-tär'): the physical form of an unseen force.

5 **pest ban:** announcement of infection with the plague.

A CLARIFY MEANING
Use the **side notes** to help you restate lines 1–8. What can you **infer** about the mood of the country from this description?

and with these retired to the deep seclusion of one of his castellated abbeys. This was an extensive and magnificent structure, the creation of the prince's own eccentric yet august taste. A strong and lofty wall girdled it in. This wall had gates of iron. The courtiers, having entered, brought furnaces and massy hammers and welded the bolts. They resolved to leave means neither of ingress or egress to the sudden impulses of despair or of frenzy from within. The abbey was amply provisioned. With such precautions the courtiers might bid defiance to contagion. The external world could take care of itself. In the meantime 20 it was folly to grieve, or to think. The prince had provided all the appliances of pleasure. There were buffoons, there were improvisatori, there were ballet-dancers, there were musicians, there was Beauty, there was wine. All these and security were within. Without was the "Red Death." **B**

It was toward the close of the fifth or sixth month of his seclusion, and while the pestilence raged most furiously abroad, that the Prince Prospero entertained his thousand friends at a masked ball of the most unusual magnificence.

It was a voluptuous scene, that masquerade. But first let me tell of the rooms in which it was held. There were seven—an imperial suite. In many palaces, however, such suites form a long and straight vista, while the folding 30 doors slide back nearly to the walls on either hand, so that the view of the whole extent is scarcely **impeded.** Here the case was very different; as might have been expected from the duke's love of the *bizarre.* The apartments were so irregularly disposed that the vision embraced but little more than one at a time. There was a sharp turn at every twenty or thirty yards, and at each turn a novel effect. To the right and left, in the middle of each wall, a tall and narrow Gothic window looked out upon a closed corridor which pursued the windings of the suite. These windows were of stained glass whose color varied in accordance with the prevailing hue of the decorations of the chamber into which it opened. That at the eastern extremity was 40 hung, for example, in blue—and vividly blue were its windows. The second chamber was purple in its ornaments and tapestries, and here the panes were purple. The third was green throughout, and so were the casements. The fourth was furnished and lighted with orange—the fifth with white—the sixth with violet. The seventh apartment was closely shrouded in black velvet tapestries that hung all over the ceiling and down the walls, falling in heavy folds upon a carpet of the same material and hue. But in this chamber only, the color of the windows failed to correspond with the decorations. The panes here were scarlet—a deep blood color. Now in no one of the seven apartments were there any lamp or candelabrum amid the profusion 50 of golden ornaments that lay scattered to and fro or depended from the roof. There was no light of any kind emanating from lamp or candle within the suite of chambers. But in the corridors that followed the suite, there stood, opposite to each window, a heavy tripod, bearing a brazier of fire that projected its rays through the tinted glass and so glaringly illuminated the room. And thus were produced a multitude of gaudy and fantastic appearances. But in the western or black chamber the effect of the firelight that streamed upon the dark hangings through the blood-tinted panes, was

12 **castellated abbeys** (kăs′tə-lā′tĭd ăb′ēz): castle-like buildings once used as monasteries ("abbeys").

16–17 **ingress** (ĭn′grĕs′) **or egress** (ē′grĕs′): entry or exit.

18 **provisioned:** stocked with supplies.

21 **improvisatori** (ĭm-prŏv′ĭ-zə-tôr′ē): poets who compose verses aloud.

B **ALLEGORY**
Reread lines 9–23. Which details suggest a mythical or fairy-tale **setting?**

impede (ĭm-pēd′) *v.* to interfere with or slow the progress of

53 **brazier** (brā′zhər): metal pan for holding a fire.

ghastly in the extreme, and produced so wild a look upon the countenances of those who entered, that there were few of the company bold enough to set foot within its precincts at all.

It was in this apartment, also, that there stood against the western wall a gigantic clock of ebony. Its pendulum swung to and fro with a dull, heavy, monotonous clang; and when the minute hand made the circuit of the face, and the hour was to be stricken, there came from the brazen lungs of the clock a sound which was clear and loud and deep and exceedingly musical, but of so peculiar a note and emphasis that, at each lapse of an hour, the musicians of the orchestra were constrained to pause, momentarily, in their performance, to hearken to the sound; and thus the waltzers perforce ceased their evolutions; and there was a brief disconcert of the whole gay company; and, while the chimes of the clock yet rang, it was observed that the giddiest turned pale, and the more aged and sedate passed their hands over their

58 countenances (koun′tə-nəns-əz): faces.

62 ebony (ĕb′ə-nē): a hard, very dark wood.

64 brazen: brass.

69 evolutions: intricate patterns of movement; **disconcert:** state of confusion.

brows as if in confused **reverie** or meditation. But when the echoes had fully ceased, a light laughter at once pervaded the assembly; the musicians looked at each other and smiled as if at their own nervousness and folly, and made whispering vows, each to the other, that the next chiming of the clock should produce in them no similar emotion; and then, after the lapse of sixty minutes (which embrace three thousand and six hundred seconds of the Time that flies), there came yet another chiming of the clock, and then were the same disconcert and tremulousness and meditation as before. **C**

80   But, in spite of these things, it was a gay and magnificent revel. The tastes of the duke were peculiar. He had a fine eye for colors and effects. He disregarded the *decora* of mere fashion. His plans were bold and fiery, and his conceptions glowed with barbaric lustre. There are some who would have thought him mad. His followers felt that he was not. It was necessary to hear and see and touch him to be *sure* that he was not.

He had directed, in great part, the movable embellishments of the seven chambers, upon occasion of this great *fête;* and it was his own guiding taste which had given character to the masqueraders. Be sure they were grotesque. There were much glare and glitter and piquancy and phantasm—much of

90 what has been seen since in *Hernani*. There were arabesque figures with unsuited limbs and appointments. There were delirious fancies such as the madman fashions. There was much of the beautiful, much of the wanton, much of the *bizarre,* something of the terrible, and not a little of that which might have excited disgust. To and fro in the seven chambers there stalked, in fact, a multitude of dreams. And these—the dreams—writhed in and about, taking hue from the rooms, and causing the wild music of the orchestra to seem as the echo of their steps. And, anon, there strikes the ebony clock which stands in the hall of velvet. And then, for a moment, all is still, and all is silent save the voice of the clock. The dreams are stiff-

100 frozen as they stand. But the echoes of the chime die away—they have endured but an instant—and a light, half-subdued laughter floats after them as they depart. And now again the music swells, and the dreams live, and writhe to and fro more merrily than ever, taking hue from the many-tinted windows through which stream the rays of the tripods. But to the chamber which lies most westwardly of the seven, there are now none of the maskers who venture; for the night is waning away; and there flows a ruddier light through the blood-colored panes; and the blackness of the sable drapery appalls; and to him whose foot falls upon the sable carpet, there comes from the near clock of ebony a muffled peal more solemnly emphatic than

110 any which reaches *their* ears who indulge in the more remote gaieties of the other apartments. **D**

But these other apartments were densely crowded, and in them beat feverishly the heart of life. And the revel went whirlingly on, until at length there commenced the sounding of midnight upon the clock. And then the music ceased, as I have told; and the evolutions of the waltzes were quieted; and there was an uneasy **cessation** of all things as before. But now there were twelve strokes to be sounded by the bell of the clock; and thus

reverie (rĕv′ə-rē) *n.* daydream

C ALLEGORY
Identify the idea that is **personified** in lines 61–79. What object does Poe use to represent this concept?

82 *decora:* fine things.

90 *Hernani* (ĕr′nä-nē): a play by French writer Victor Hugo, first staged in 1830 and notable for its use of color and spectacle; **arabesque** (ăr′ə-bĕsk′): intricately designed.

D CLARIFY MEANING
Paraphrase lines 104–111. Why do none of the guests venture into the seventh room?

cessation (sĕ-sā′shən) *n.* a coming to an end; a stopping

it happened, perhaps, that more of thought crept, with more of time, into the meditations of the thoughtful among those who reveled. And thus, too, it happened, perhaps, that before the last echoes of the last chime had utterly sunk into silence, there were many individuals in the crowd who had found leisure to become aware of the presence of a masked figure which had arrested the attention of no single individual before. And the rumor of this new presence having spread itself whisperingly around, there arose at length from the whole company a buzz, or murmur, expressive of **disapprobation** and surprise—then, finally of terror, of horror, and of disgust.

In an assembly of phantasms such as I have painted, it may well be supposed that no ordinary appearance could have excited such sensation. In truth the masquerade license of the night was nearly unlimited; but the figure in question had out-Heroded Herod, and gone beyond the bounds of even the prince's indefinite decorum. There are chords in the hearts of the most reckless which cannot be touched without emotion. Even with the utterly lost, to whom life and death are equally jests, there are matters of which no jest can be made. The whole company, indeed, seemed now deeply to feel that in the costume and bearing of the stranger neither wit nor **propriety** existed. The figure was tall and gaunt, and shrouded from head to foot in the habiliments of the grave. The mask which concealed the visage was made so nearly to resemble the countenance of a stiffened corpse that the closest scrutiny must have had difficulty in detecting the cheat. And yet all this might have been endured, if not approved, by the mad revellers around. But the mummer had gone so far as to assume the type of the Red Death. His vesture was dabbled in *blood*—and his broad brow, with all the features of the face, was besprinkled with the scarlet horror. **E**

When the eyes of Prince Prospero fell upon this spectral image (which with a slow and solemn movement, as if more fully to sustain its *role,* stalked to and fro among the waltzers), he was seen to be convulsed, in the first moment with a strong shudder either of terror or distaste; but, in the next, his brow reddened with rage.

"Who dares?" he demanded hoarsely of the courtiers who stood near him—"who dares insult us with this **blasphemous** mockery? Seize him and unmask him—that we may know whom we have to hang at sunrise, from the battlements!"

It was in the eastern or blue chamber in which stood the Prince Prospero as he uttered these words. They rang throughout the seven rooms loudly and clearly—for the prince was a bold and robust man, and the music had become hushed at the waving of his hand.

It was in the blue room where stood the prince, with a group of pale courtiers by his side. At first, as he spoke, there was a slight rushing movement of this group in the direction of the intruder, who at the moment was also near at hand, and now, with deliberate and stately step, made closer approach to the speaker. But from a certain nameless awe with which the mad assumptions of the mummer had inspired the whole party, there

disapprobation
(dĭs-ăp′rə-bā′shən)
n. disapproval

130 out-Heroded Herod: been more extreme than the biblical King Herod, who ordered the deaths of all male babies in order to kill the infant Jesus. This expression is also used in Shakespeare's *Hamlet.*

propriety (prə-prī′ĭ-tē) *n.*
the quality of being proper; appropriateness

137 habiliments (hə-bĭl′ə-mənts): clothing.

E **CLARIFY MEANING**
Reread lines 127–143. Use **context clues** to determine the meaning of the words *decorum, visage,* and *vesture.* What details help explain why the figure's appearance is so shocking?

blasphemous (blăs′fə-məs) *adj.*
disrespectful or offensive

162 mummer: a person dressed for a masquerade.

were found none who put forth hand to seize him; so that, unimpeded, he passed within a yard of the prince's person; and, while the vast assembly, as if with one impulse, shrank from the centers of the rooms to the walls, he made his way uninterruptedly, but with the same solemn and measured step which had distinguished him from the first, through the blue chamber to the purple—through the purple to the green—through the green to the orange—through this again to the white—and even thence to the violet,
170 ere a decided movement had been made to arrest him. It was then, however, that the Prince Prospero, maddening with rage and the shame of his own momentary cowardice, rushed hurriedly through the six chambers while none followed him on account of a deadly terror that had seized upon all. He bore aloft a drawn dagger, and had approached, in rapid impetuosity, to within three or four feet of the retreating figure, when the latter, having attained the extremity of the velvet apartment, turned suddenly and confronted his pursuer. There was a sharp cry—and the dagger dropped gleaming upon the sable carpet, upon which, instantly afterwards, fell prostrate in death the Prince Prospero. Then, summoning the wild courage
180 of despair, a throng of the revellers at once threw themselves into the black apartment, and seizing the mummer, whose tall figure stood erect and motionless within the shadow of the ebony clock, gasped in unutterable horror at finding the grave-cerements and corpselike mask, which they handled with so violent a rudeness, untenanted by any tangible form. **F**

And now was acknowledged the presence of the Red Death. He had come like a thief in the night. And one by one dropped the revellers in the blood-bedewed halls of their revel, and died each in the despairing posture of his fall. And the life of the ebony clock went out with that of the last of the gay. And the flames of the tripods expired. And Darkness and Decay and the Red
190 Death held illimitable dominion over all. ❧

183–184 **finding the . . . form:** ripping off the figure's burial garments and mask to find nothing underneath.

F **ALLEGORY**
The prince's name suggests prosperity, or good fortune. Given this suggestion, what is **ironic,** or unexpected, about his fate?

190 **illimitable dominion**
(ĭ-lĭm′ĭ-tə-bəl də-mĭn′yən): unlimited power.

Comprehension

1. **Recall** Why does Prince Prospero seal himself and his guests in the abbey?

2. **Recall** What effect does the striking of the clock have on the revellers?

3. **Summarize** What happens after the mysterious figure is unmasked?

Literary Analysis

4. **Make Inferences** What does each of the following reveal about Prince Prospero?

   - his response to the crisis in his country (lines 1–12)
   - his solution to the threat of disease (lines 15–23)
   - his plans for the masquerade (lines 86–94)
   - his response to the masked figure (lines 144–152)

5. **Clarify Meaning** Recall the summaries you wrote to help clarify each paragraph of the story. Which proved more difficult to understand, the events in the story or the descriptions that set the scene? Explain your answer.

6. **Analyze Descriptive Details** For each of the following examples, identify the contrast drawn between the seventh room and the rest of Prince Prospero's suite. Based on these contrasts, what might the seventh room represent?

   - its decorations (lines 44–48)
   - its location (lines 104–105)
   - its atmosphere (lines 56–60)
   - what occurs there (lines 174–179)

7. **Interpret Allegory** Using a chart like the one shown, identify a possible meaning for each character or object and list details from the text that support your interpretation. Based on your answers, what lesson is Poe's allegory intended to teach?

Main Story Elements	Possible Meaning	Supporting Details
Prince Prospero		
the abbey		
the series of seven rooms		
the clock		
the masked stranger		

8. **Evaluate Characters' Actions** Consider the desperate measures the characters take to achieve **safety**. In what ways, if any, do their behaviors reflect real-world responses to a deadly threat? Support your answer with details.

Literary Criticism

9. **Critical Interpretations** Some critics have argued that "The Masque of the Red Death" takes place in Prospero's mind. Cite details from the story that support this interpretation. How does this view change the story's meaning?

Vocabulary in Context

VOCABULARY PRACTICE

Show you understand the vocabulary words by answering these questions.

1. Will an attempt to **impede** the passage of a law speed up the process or slow it down?
2. Would a **blasphemous** comment be considered controversial or appeasing?
3. Which would more likely result in a parent's **disapprobation**—a detention or a school award?
4. Would someone's **reverie** make them attentive or distracted?
5. If I act with **propriety,** am I being polite or asking uncomfortable questions?
6. Which would cause the **cessation** of a conversation—one participant nodding in agreement or one participant walking away?

WORD LIST

blasphemous

cessation

disapprobation

impede

propriety

reverie

VOCABULARY IN WRITING

Poe's formal language echoes his story's setting in a royal court. Using at least two vocabulary words, write a royal declaration for your subjects to obey. You might start like this.

> **EXAMPLE SENTENCE**
>
> *I order the immediate **cessation** of this unlicensed and unauthorized behavior.*

VOCABULARY STRATEGY: AFFIXES AND SPELLING CHANGES

Some base words are hard to recognize because they are spelled differently when affixes are added. For example, the vocabulary word *cessation* includes the base word *cease* and the suffix *-ation*. Note how the spelling of the base word changes in the new word. These spelling changes may reflect the word's etymology (its history and origins), or they may simply reflect new pronunciation that made the word easier to say. To decipher words of this type, look for related base words and use context clues to unlock meaning.

PRACTICE Identify the appropriate base word for each of the following examples. Then write a sentence that demonstrates the meaning of each numbered word. Finally, use a dictionary to research the word's origins. Did the spelling change as a result of the word's history?

1. derisive
2. contentious
3. impermeable
4. pomposity
5. acclamation
6. irrevocable
7. despicable
8. incessant
9. sobriety
10. commensurate

VOCABULARY PRACTICE
For more practice, go to the **Vocabulary Center** at ClassZone.com.

The Raven

Poem by
Edgar Allan Poe

● LITERARY ANALYSIS: SOUND DEVICES

First published in 1845, "The Raven" became an instant hit. Part of the poem's popularity was due to Poe's clever use of **sound devices**, patterns of word sounds used to create musical effects.

- **Rhyme,** the repetition of similar sounds, is one of the easiest sound devices to spot. Poe adds variety by using **internal rhyme,** rhyming words that fall inside a line.

  Ah, distinctly I <u>remember</u> it was in the bleak <u>December</u>;

- **Repetition,** of rhymes and of words and phrases, helps give "The Raven" its distinctive rhythm.

  As of someone gently <u>rapping</u>, <u>rapping</u> at my chamber door.

- **Alliteration,** the repetition of initial consonant sounds, is used to create rhythm or to stress key words.

  While I <u>n</u>odded, <u>n</u>early <u>n</u>apping . . .

- **Onomatopoeia** is the use of words that sound like their meaning, such as the word *rustling* in this example:

  And the silken, sad, uncertain rustling of each purple curtain

As you read, note how Poe combines these sound devices to form complex rhythmic patterns. Reading aloud will help you appreciate Poe's ingenious use of sound effects.

Review: **Stanza and Rhyme Scheme**

● READING SKILL: MAKE INFERENCES

"The Raven" tells a story without directly stating all of the important details. You'll need to use clues in the poem to **make inferences** about the speaker's situation as the poem opens and about his state of mind during the events of the poem. As you read, use a chart like the one shown to record your inferences and the clues that helped you. By the end of the poem, you'll be able to **draw conclusions** about what the speaker experiences.

	Inferences About the Speaker	Clues
State of Mind		
Recent Experiences		

Explore the Key Idea

How do people handle LOSS?

KEY IDEA At some point in our lives, we all face loss—of someone we love, our favorite pet, or even a cherished dream. But even though the experience of loss is universal, people can choose many different ways to cope with the sadness and **grief** they feel. What do people need to do to face their grief and move on?

DISCUSS Working in small groups, think about some ways people respond to a serious loss. Discuss how they express their own feelings and what they do to adjust to the changes that the loss creates. What patterns can you identify?

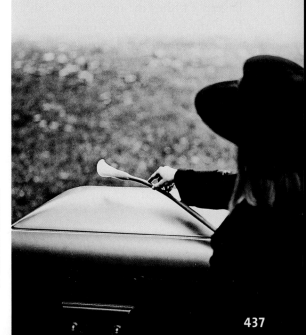

The *Raven*

Edgar Allan Poe

Once upon a midnight dreary, while I pondered, weak and weary,
Over many a quaint and curious volume of forgotten lore—
While I nodded, nearly napping, suddenly there came a tapping,
As of someone gently rapping, rapping at my chamber door.
5 "'Tis some visitor," I muttered, "tapping at my chamber door—
    Only this and nothing more." **A**

Ah, distinctly I remember it was in the bleak December;
And each separate dying ember wrought its ghost upon the floor.
Eagerly I wished the morrow;—vainly I had sought to borrow
10 From my books surcease[1] of sorrow—sorrow for the lost Lenore—
For the rare and radiant maiden whom the angels name Lenore—
    Nameless *here* forevermore. **B**

And the silken, sad, uncertain rustling of each purple curtain
Thrilled me—filled me with fantastic terrors never felt before;
15 So that now, to still the beating of my heart, I stood repeating
"'Tis some visitor entreating entrance at my chamber door;—
Some late visitor entreating entrance at my chamber door;—
    That it is and nothing more."

1. **surcease:** an end.

ANALYZE VISUALS
What techniques has the photographer used that make the raven on page 439 seem mysterious?

A **SOUND DEVICES**
Reread lines 1–6. What pattern of **internal rhyme** does Poe establish in the first stanza?

B **MAKE INFERENCES**
Reread lines 9–12. What does this passage imply about Lenore's connection to the speaker and the reason for her absence? Give details to support your answer.

Presently my soul grew stronger; hesitating then no longer,
20 "Sir," said I, "or Madam, truly your forgiveness I implore;
But the fact is I was napping, and so gently you came rapping,
And so faintly you came tapping, tapping at my chamber door,
That I scarce was sure I heard you"—here I opened wide the door;—
     Darkness there and nothing more. **C**

25 Deep into that darkness peering, long I stood there wondering, fearing,
Doubting, dreaming dreams no mortal ever dared to dream before;
But the silence was unbroken, and the stillness gave no token,
And the only word there spoken was the whispered word, "Lenore!"
This I whispered, and an echo murmured back the word "Lenore!"
30   Merely this and nothing more.

Back into the chamber turning, all my soul within me burning,
Soon again I heard a tapping somewhat louder than before.
"Surely," said I, "surely that is something at my window lattice;
Let me see, then, what thereat is, and this mystery explore—
35 Let my heart be still a moment and this mystery explore;—
     'Tis the wind and nothing more!"

Open here I flung the shutter, when, with many a flirt and flutter,
In there stepped a stately Raven of the saintly days of yore.[2]
Not the least obeisance[3] made he; not a minute stopped or stayed he;
40 But, with mien[4] of lord or lady, perched above my chamber door—
Perched upon a bust of Pallas[5] just above my chamber door—
     Perched, and sat, and nothing more. **D**

Then this ebony bird beguiling my sad fancy into smiling,
By the grave and stern decorum of the countenance it wore,
45 "Though thy crest be shorn and shaven, thou," I said, "art sure no craven,[6]
Ghastly grim and ancient Raven wandering from the Nightly shore—
Tell me what thy lordly name is on the Night's Plutonian[7] shore!"
     Quoth the Raven, "Nevermore." **E**

Much I marveled this ungainly fowl to hear discourse so plainly,
50 Though its answer little meaning—little relevancy bore;
For we cannot help agreeing that no living human being

C STANZA AND RHYME SCHEME
Recall that a poem's rhyme scheme is its pattern of **end rhyme**. Describe the rhyme scheme of this poem. How does Poe use **repetition** as part of the rhyme scheme?

D SOUND DEVICES
Reread lines 37–38. What example of **onomatopoeia** can you find?

E SOUND DEVICES
Identify the **alliteration** in lines 45–46. What words are emphasized by using this technique?

2. **days of yore:** days of long ago.
3. **obeisance** (ō-bā′səns): a gesture of respect.
4. **mien** (mēn): appearance.
5. **bust of Pallas:** statue of the head and shoulders of Pallas Athena, Greek goddess of wisdom.
6. **craven:** coward.
7. **Plutonian:** having to do with Pluto, Roman god of the dead and ruler of the underworld.

Ever yet was blessed with seeing bird above his chamber door—
Bird or beast upon the sculptured bust above his chamber door,
     With such name as "Nevermore."

55 But the Raven, sitting lonely on the placid bust, spoke only
That one word, as if his soul in that one word he did outpour.
Nothing farther then he uttered—not a feather then he fluttered—
Till I scarcely more than muttered "Other friends have flown before—
On the morrow *he* will leave me, as my hopes have flown before."
60   Then the bird said, "Nevermore." **F**

Startled at the stillness broken by reply so aptly spoken,
"Doubtless," said I, "what it utters is its only stock and store
Caught from some unhappy master whom unmerciful Disaster
Followed fast and followed faster till his songs one burden[8] bore—
65 Till the dirges[9] of his Hope that melancholy burden bore
     Of 'Never—nevermore.'"

But the Raven still beguiling all my fancy into smiling,
Straight I wheeled a cushioned seat in front of bird, and bust and door;
Then, upon the velvet sinking, I betook myself to linking
70 Fancy unto fancy, thinking what this ominous bird of yore—
What this grim, ungainly, ghastly, gaunt, and ominous bird of yore
     Meant in croaking, "Nevermore." **G**

This I sat engaged in guessing, but no syllable expressing
To the fowl whose fiery eyes now burned into my bosom's core;
75 This and more I sat divining,[10] with my head at ease reclining
On the cushion's velvet lining that the lamp-light gloated o'er,
But whose velvet violet lining with the lamp-light gloating o'er,
     She shall press, ah, nevermore!

Then, methought, the air grew denser, perfumed from an unseen censer
80 Swung by Seraphim[11] whose foot-falls tinkled on the tufted floor.
"Wretch," I cried, "thy God hath lent thee—by these angels he hath sent thee
Respite—respite and nepenthe[12] from thy memories of Lenore;
Quaff,[13] oh quaff this kind nepenthe and forget this lost Lenore!"
     Quoth the Raven, "Nevermore."

F MAKE INFERENCES
Reread lines 58–59.
What does this
comment suggest
about the speaker's past
experiences and his
current mood? Explain.

G SOUND DEVICES
Identify the sound device
used in lines 71–72. What
qualities of the raven are
emphasized by the use of
this device?

---

8. **burden:** the chorus or refrain of a song.

9. **dirges:** songs of mourning.

10. **divining:** guessing from incomplete evidence.

11. **censer / Swung by Seraphim** (sĕr′ə-fĭm): container of sweet burning incense swung by angels of the highest rank.

12. **respite . . . and nepenthe** (nĭ-pĕn′thē): temporary relief and a forgetfulness that eases grief.

13. **quaff:** drink deeply.

85 "Prophet!" said I, "thing of evil!—prophet still, if bird or devil!—
   Whether Tempter[14] sent, or whether tempest tossed thee here ashore,
   Desolate yet all undaunted, on this desert land enchanted—
   On this home by Horror haunted—tell me truly, I implore—
   Is there—*is* there balm in Gilead?[15]—tell me—tell me, I implore!"
90   Quoth the Raven, "Nevermore."

   "Prophet!" said I, "thing of evil!—prophet still, if bird or devil!
   By that Heaven that bends above us—by that God we both adore—
   Tell this soul with sorrow laden if, within the distant Aidenn,[16]
   It shall clasp a sainted maiden whom the angels name Lenore—
95 Clasp a rare and radiant maiden whom the angels name Lenore."
       Quoth the Raven, "Nevermore." **H**

   "Be that word our sign of parting, bird or fiend!" I shrieked, upstarting—
   "Get thee back into the tempest and the Night's Plutonian shore!
   Leave no black plume as a token of that lie thy soul hath spoken!
100 Leave my loneliness unbroken!—quit the bust above my door!
   Take thy beak from out my heart, and take thy form from off my door!"
       Quoth the Raven, "Nevermore."

   And the Raven, never flitting, still is sitting, *still* is sitting
   On the pallid bust of Pallas just above my chamber door;
105 And his eyes have all the seeming of a demon's that is dreaming,
   And the lamp-light o'er him streaming throws his shadow on the floor;
   And my soul from out that shadow that lies floating on the floor
       Shall be lifted—nevermore!

H MAKE INFERENCES
Given the bird's repeated response, what does the speaker's persistent questioning of the raven suggest about his state of mind? Explain your answer.

---

14. **Tempter:** the devil.

15. **balm** (bäm) **in Gilead** (gĭl′ē-əd): relief from suffering.

16. **Aidenn** (ād′n): heaven (from the Arabic form of the word *Eden*).

Comprehension

1. **Recall** Where and when do the events of the poem take place?

2. **Recall** What is the raven's response to all of the speaker's questions?

3. **Clarify** What is the speaker's explanation of the raven's one response?

Literary Analysis

4. **Draw Conclusions** Review the **inferences** you made as you read. What conclusions did you draw about the speaker and his emotional state?

5. **Examine Tone** For each of the following passages, describe the speaker's tone, or attitude, toward the raven. What explains the speaker's changing responses to his mysterious visitor?

   - the raven's first appearance (lines 43–44)
   - the thoughts the raven inspires (lines 71–74)
   - the purpose the speaker attributes to the raven (lines 81–84)
   - the speaker's command to the raven (lines 97–98)

6. **Compare and Contrast Imagery** Poe uses imagery to create a stark contrast between Lenore and the raven. Using a chart like the one shown, list images used to describe each character. Based on these images, what main feeling or quality is each character used to communicate? Cite evidence.

Lenore	Raven

7. **Evaluate Sound Devices** Reread lines 79–84. Identify the sound devices used in this stanza, and give examples of each technique. Which of these devices do you find most compelling or effective? Explain your answer.

8. **Make Judgments** Consider the speaker's changing responses to the raven and the conclusions you drew about his state of mind. What does the speaker's **conflict** with the raven suggest about the behavior of people who are struggling with **grief**? Support your answer with details.

Literary Criticism

9. **Author's Style** In an essay about "The Raven," Poe claimed that he started with the word *nevermore* (he liked its vowel sounds), then added the death of a beautiful woman ("the most poetical topic in the world"). Only later did he invent the story and characters that readers have found so moving and memorable. Poe seems to have been more interested in form than content. Which do you find more important in this poem? Cite details in your answer.

Reading-Writing Connection

WRITE A MONOLOGUE In a monologue, a character expresses thoughts in an uninterrupted flow, with no other character's words intervening. Monologues in literature often explore a character's feelings. They may be addressed to an absent or abstract listener, or they may be more random, following a person's train of thought.

Write a **one-page prose monologue,** in your own voice or that of a fictional character, that explores an emotion, such as grief, anger, or joy. Use your monologue to reveal details about your speaker's personality and the reasons for his or her emotional response.

A successful monologue will . . .

- reflect the clearly defined voice of the speaker
- effectively convey the speaker's emotional state
- establish a convincing motivation for the speaker's feelings

GRAMMAR AND STYLE

CRAFT EFFECTIVE SENTENCES Poe uses **imperative sentences**—sentences that give orders or make requests—and **dashes** to convey his character's excitable state. The use of dashes and a tone of breathless urgency are distinctive features of Poe's style.

> *"Be that word our sign of parting, bird or fiend!" I shrieked, upstarting—*
> *"Get thee back into the tempest and the Night's Plutonian shore!"* (lines 97–98)

PRACTICE Using the following verse from "The Raven" as a model, compose your own stanza in the style of Poe, incorporating dashes and imperative sentences. Feel free to choose a different subject, but make sure to follow Poe's rhyme scheme and to echo his tone. A sample beginning is provided for you.

EXAMPLE

"Prophet!" said I, "thing of evil!—prophet still, if bird or devil!—
"You pest, begone!" I cried—near choking. "Take from me your wretched joking!"

"Prophet!" said I, "thing of evil!—prophet still, if bird or devil!—
Whether Tempter sent, or whether tempest tossed thee here ashore,
Desolate yet all undaunted, on this desert land enchanted—
On this home by Horror haunted—tell me truly, I implore—
Is there—*is* there balm in Gilead?—tell me—tell me, I implore!"
    Quoth the Raven, "Nevermore."

WRITING TOOLS
For prewriting, revision, and editing tools, visit the **Writing Center** at ClassZone.com.

PARODY Like other well-known and well-loved works of literature, "The Raven" has inspired many a **parody**—a comic imitation of another work or type of literature. As you read the following parody, note the points of imitation in form or content. In what ways does the parodist turn Poe's ideas to comic effect?

What Troubled Poe's Raven

John Bennett

Could Poe walk again to-morrow, heavy with
 dyspeptic sorrow,
While the darkness seemed to borrow darkness
 from the night before,
From the hollow gloom abysmal, floating
 downward, grimly dismal,
Like a pagan curse baptismal from the bust above
 the door,
5 He would hear the Raven croaking from the dusk
 above the door,
  "Never, never, nevermore!"

And, too angry to be civil, "Raven," Poe would
 cry "or devil,
Tell me why you will persist in haunting Death's
 Plutonian shore?"
Then would croak the Raven gladly, "I will tell
 you why so sadly,
10 I so mournfully and madly, haunt you, taunt you,
 o'er and o'er,
Why eternally I haunt you, daunt you, taunt you,
 o'er and o'er —
  Only this, and nothing more.

"Forty-eight long years I've pondered, forty-eight
 long years I've wondered,
How a poet ever blundered into a mistake so sore.
15 How could lamp-light from your table ever in the
 world be able,
From *below*, to throw my sable shadow 'streaming
 on the floor,'
When I perched up here on Pallas, high above
 your chamber-door?
  Tell me that — if nothing more!"

Then, like some wan, weeping willow, Poe
 would bend above his pillow,
20 Seeking surcease in the billow where mad
 recollections drown,
And in tearful tones replying, he would groan
 "There's no denying
Either I was blindly lying, or the world was
 upside down—
Say, by Joe!—it was just midnight—so the
 world *was* upside down—
  Aye, the world was upside down!"

Illustrations Inspired by Poe

Image Collection on ⊙ **MediaSmart** DVD

What does GOTHIC *look like?*

KEY IDEA Shadows and gargoyles and pervading gloom all evoke the **gothic spirit** that Edgar Allan Poe depicted so well in his stories and poems. Countless artists have been inspired by Poe's works—writers, musicians, architects, and certainly visual artists. British illustrator Arthur Rackham had a particular affinity for Poe's writing. In examining Rackham's illustrations in this lesson, you'll see how an artist influenced by Poe's gothic style expresses his own personal interpretation.

Background

American Gothic It's not simply the plots and characters Poe created that have mesmerized readers and artists over time. It's what his writing revealed of our dark side, of our capacity for decadence and even insanity, that has given him such lasting influence. Though the term *gothic* has been applied to other art forms such as architecture and music, it is in Poe's writing that the psychological elements of gothic are most sharply defined.

At the time Poe's work was first published, illustrators were regularly hired to create images to accompany his text. As Poe's reputation grew and more people read his often disturbing stories, painters and artists found great imaginative fodder in Poe's phantasmagorical tales. You can see his influence in the work of countless illustrators over the past 150 years, including Poe contemporary Gustave Doré, Arthur Rackham, Edward Gorey, Charles Addams (creator of "The Addams Family" cartoon), and even popular children's book illustrator Stephen Gammell. Many of today's graphic novelists are heavily influenced by Poe's sense of gothic.

Media Literacy: Art Elements in Illustrations

In Edgar Allan Poe's writing, he often expresses his style through imagery that re-creates certain sensory experiences. In "The Fall of the House of Usher," Poe's description of the house is one of decay and desolation. In order to translate such descriptions into a visual image, an illustrator relies on the art elements of **color, line, shape,** and **texture** to evoke similar feelings. Another aspect of visual art is **dominance,** which is created when one or more parts of an image are given more importance than the others.

Consider these elements when analyzing this 1935 Arthur Rackham illustration for "The Fall of the House of Usher." Think about the deliberate stylistic choices made by the illustrator to match the mood and tone of Poe's writing.

STRATEGIES FOR ANALYZING ILLUSTRATIONS

1 Color is used to highlight important aspects and create mood in an image. To analyze an illustrator's use of color, think about the overall mood of the image. Are the colors warm (red and orange) or cool (blue and green)? Do the muted colors in this image seem to reflect Poe's descriptions?

2 Line is a stroke or a mark. Vertical, horizontal, jagged, curved—lines have expressive qualities. Look at the style of lines an artist uses. Here, for example, the vertical lines are strong and varied and suggest the dreary atmosphere of Poe's setting.

3 Shape is the outline of an object in an image. Notice the tension created by the strong yet warped lines of the dead trees against the severe lines of the house.

4 Texture is the surface quality of an image. Examine how this artist manipulates visual elements to create different textures. Ask yourself: If I could touch this image, how would it feel?

5 Be aware of the primary object that draws your eye. Here the house of Usher is the dominant image.

- **Selection 1:** "The Fall of The House of Usher"
- **Selection 2:** "The Pit and the Pendulum"
- **Type:** Illustration
- **Illustrator:** Arthur Rackham

Illustrations Inspired by Poe

Access the full-sized images on the DVD. Examine each image carefully, jotting down your initial impressions. Look for common elements, themes, and subjects in the images. To help you analyze each image in terms of color, shape, line, texture, and dominance, use the viewing strategies detailed on page 447. You can also refer to the Illustrations and Photographs section of the Media Handbook (pages R94–R95). Answer the questions to help you analyze the images.

NOW VIEW

FIRST VIEWING: Comprehension

1. **Describe** Where does the narrator of "The Fall of the House of Usher" appear in Rackham's illustration?
2. **Identify** Where is the man standing in "The Pit and the Pendulum" illustration?

CLOSE VIEWING: Media Literacy

3. **Analyze Color** What colors does Rackham use in the "House of Usher" illustration, and what mood do these create? Explain your answer.
4. **Compare Line** Look carefully at the way line is used in both illustrations. In which image is line used most effectively? Explain.
5. **Compare Dominance** Consider the images for "The Fall of the House of Usher" and "The Pit and the Pendulum." One part of each image is dominant. How does the illustrator achieve this effect? Think about
   - the use of shape in the images
   - how color is used to create dominance

Write or Discuss

Describe Unity of Effect Poe believed in writing to achieve "unity of effect," in which every detail of a work contributes to a single overall feeling. This idea guided his word choices, sentence structures, and subject matter. Look at the two Rackham illustrations in this Media Study. How do you think Rackham's decisions as an artist create unity of effect? Write a brief description of what Rackham achieves with these gothic images. Consider these elements:

- Rackham's use of color, line, shape, and texture in the images
- the parts of Poe's stories that each work depicts
- the overall mood of each illustration

Produce Your Own Media

Create Gothic Artwork How would you visually represent something in the gothic style? Use your understanding of the term to create a gothic piece of **artwork.** It can be a photograph, a painting, a computer-generated image, a drawing, even a collage of magazine clippings.

HERE'S HOW Here are a few suggestions for creating gothic visual art:

- No matter what type of gothic piece you will create, make notes on your intentions and how you plan to achieve them.
- Decide on the psychological mood you want to express.
- Keep in mind the visual art elements.
- Consider what colors you'll need to use. If creating a gothic photograph, consider the lighting effects you might employ, or whether to use color or black-and-white film.
- Try to establish a dominant element in your piece, something that the viewer will quickly focus on.

MEDIA TOOLS

For help creating gothic art, visit the **Media Center** at **ClassZone.com.**

Tech Tip

If available, use a design program to turn a photograph of a happy occasion into a gothic representation.

Further Exploration

Contrasting Styles Revisit the variety of additional Poe-inspired images on the DVD, or look for other examples on your own. Explore how these works are all influenced by Poe's writing in some way. What Poe-inspired similarities can you find between the images? Cite specific elements from the images. Think about

- line, shape, color, and texture
- how the images reflect a gothic sensibility
- how the images express the psychological

Find the Gothic in Your Life Think about other art forms—movies, music, live theater—where you find gothic elements. Describe a movie, song, or play in which you can identify these elements.

from
Danse Macabre

Essay by Stephen King

> **BACKGROUND** Stephen King may well be the best-known writer of horror fiction since Edgar Allan Poe. In 1981, after writing a number of best-selling novels, King wrote *Stephen Kings's Danse Macabre*, a nonfiction work in which he discussed horror in literature and film and examined the psychology of terror. The book's title is a reference to the "Dance of Death," a symbolic representation of death, in the form of a skeleton, leading people to their graves. This dance was commonly depicted on cemetery walls and in the European art of the Middle Ages and the Renaissance.

I want to say something about imagination purely as a tool in the art and science of scaring people. The idea isn't original with me; I heard it expressed by William F. Nolan at the 1979 World Fantasy Convention. Nothing is so frightening as what's behind the closed door, Nolan said. You approach the door in the old, deserted house, and you hear something scratching at it. The audience holds its breath along with the protagonist as she or he (more often she) approaches that door. The protagonist throws it open, and there is a ten-foot-tall bug. The audience screams, but this particular scream has an oddly relieved sound to it. "A bug ten feet tall is pretty horrible," the audience thinks, "but I can deal with
10 a ten-foot-tall bug. I was afraid it might be a *hundred* feet tall.". . .

Bill Nolan was speaking as a screenwriter when he offered the example of the big bug behind the door, but the point applies to all media. What's behind the door or lurking at the top of the stairs is never as frightening as the door or the staircase itself. And because of this, comes the paradox: the artistic work of horror is almost always a disappointment. It is the classic no-win situation. You can scare people with the unknown for a long, long time (the classic example, as Bill Nolan also pointed out, is the Jacques Tourneur film with Dana Andrews, *Curse of the Demon*), but sooner or later, as in poker, you have to turn your down cards up. You have to open the door and show the audience what's behind it. And if what happens to be behind it is a bug,
20 not ten but a hundred feet tall, the audience heaves a sigh of relief (or utters a scream of relief) and thinks, "A bug a hundred feet tall is pretty horrible, but I can deal with that. I was afraid it might be a *thousand* feet tall." . . .

The danse macabre is a waltz with death. This is a truth we cannot afford to shy away from.

Like the rides in the amusement park which mimic violent death, the tale of horror is a chance to examine what's going on behind doors which we usually keep double-locked. Yet the human imagination is not content with locked doors.

Somewhere there is another dancing partner, the imagination whispers in the night—a partner in a rotting ball gown, a partner with empty eyesockets, green mold growing on her elbow-length gloves, maggots squirming in the thin remains of her hair. To hold such a creature in our arms? Who, you ask me, would be so mad? Well . . . ?

"You will not want to open this door," Bluebeard tells his wife in that most horrible of all horror stories, "because your husband has forbidden it." But this, of course, only makes her all the more curious . . . and at last, her curiosity is satisfied.

"You may go anywhere you wish in the castle," Count Dracula tells Jonathan Harker, "except where the doors are locked, where of course you will not wish to go." But Harker goes soon enough.

And so do we all. Perhaps we go to the forbidden door or window willingly because we understand that a time comes when we must go whether we want to or not . . . and not just to look, but to be pushed through. Forever. ❧

Literary Analysis

1. **Summarize** According to King, what makes a closed door so frightening?

2. **Interpret Metaphor** Why does King compare the suspenseful experience of watching the forbidden door to a waltz with death?

3. **Compare Texts** What elements in "The Fall of the House of Usher" and "The Masque of the Red Death" might be considered analogous to King's metaphor of the closed, forbidden door? In these cases, do you agree with King's idea that the revelation of the unknown is a letdown? Explain, citing evidence.

Moby Dick

Herman Melville

Herman Melville
1819–1891

ABOUT THE AUTHOR Herman Melville was known during his lifetime as "the man who had lived among cannibals" because of his best-selling novels of the South Seas, *Typee* and *Omoo*. These novels fictionalized his experiences in the Marquesas Islands among the supposedly cannibalistic Typee people. But how did Melville come to be in such a place? The early death of his father and the loss of the family fortune had led Melville to try for a life at sea. He spent years as a young man working a variety of ships, including a whaling vessel. His experiences—jumping ship, living with the Typee people, taking part in a mutiny, and spending time in a Tahitian jail—provided vivid fodder for his later writing, and the reading public loved him for it. By the 1840s Melville was among the most celebrated of American authors.

Ironically, when Melville turned to more serious works, including the great American novel *Moby Dick,* his public deserted him. After a series of critical and financial failures, Melville saw his career in ruins, eventually abandoning the novel for poetry and a job as a customs inspector. Melville never regained his earlier popularity during his lifetime, but later critics and readers have embraced him as one of the greatest of American writers.

ABOUT THE NOVEL "Call me Ishmael," says the narrator of *Moby Dick* in the novel's famous opening words. Ishmael, the sole survivor of the lost whaling ship the *Pequod,* goes on to tell the story of his sea captain's obsessive hunting of the great white whale, Moby Dick. An adventure tale at its core, *Moby Dick* is also many other things—a discourse on whales and whaling, a critique of commercial expansion at sea, a tragedy of human obsession, and an examination of the conflicts between the individual and society, society and nature, and fate and free will. No wonder D. H. Lawrence once said of *Moby Dick:* "[It] commands a stillness in the soul, an awe. . . . [It is] one of the strangest and most wonderful books in the world." In the following passage, the ship's crew learns for the first time that their captain, Ahab, sees the voyage as his own personal quest for revenge.

"Whosoever of ye raises me a white-headed whale with a wrinkled brow and a crooked jaw; whosoever of ye raises me that white-headed whale, with three holes punctured in his starboard fluke—look ye, whosoever of ye raises me that same white whale, he shall have this gold ounce, my boys!"

"Huzza! huzza!" cried the seamen, as with swinging tarpaulins they hailed the act of nailing the gold to the mast.

"It's a white whale, I say," resumed Ahab, as he threw down the top-maul; "a white whale. Skin your eyes for him, men; look sharp for white water; if ye see but a bubble, sing out."

10   All this while Tashtego, Daggoo, and Queequeg had looked on with even more intense interest and surprise than the rest, and at the mention of the wrinkled brow and crooked jaw they had started as if each was separately touched by some specific recollection.

    "Captain Ahab," said Tashtego, "that white whale must be the same that some call Moby Dick."

    "Moby Dick?" shouted Ahab. "Do ye know the white whale then, Tash?"

    "Does he fan-tail a little curious, sir, before he goes down?" said the Gay-Header deliberately.

    "And has he a curious spout, too," said Daggoo, "very bushy, even for a
20 parmacetty, and mighty quick, Captain Ahab?"

    "And he have one, two, tree-oh! good many iron in him hide, too, Captain," cried Queequeg disjointedly, "all twisketee be-twisk, like him—him—" faltering hard for a word, and screwing his hand round and round as though uncorking a bottle— "like him—him—"

    "Corkscrew!" cried Ahab, "aye, Queequeg, the harpoons lie all twisted and wrenched in him; aye, Daggoo, his spout is a big one, like a whole shock of wheat, and white as a pile of our Nantucket wool after the great annual sheep-shearing; aye, Tashtego, and he fan-tails like a split jib in a squall. Death and devils! men, it is Moby Dick ye have seen—Moby Dick—Moby Dick!"

30   "Captain Ahab," said Starbuck, who with Stubb and Flask, had thus far been eyeing his superior with increasing surprise, but at last seemed struck with a thought which somewhat explained all the wonder. "Captain Ahab, I have heard of Moby Dick—but it was not Moby Dick that took off thy leg?"

    "Who told thee that?" cried Ahab; then pausing, "Aye, Starbuck, aye, my hearties all round; it was Moby Dick that dismasted me; Moby Dick that brought me to this dead stump I stand on now. Aye, aye," he shouted with a terrific, loud, animal sob, like that of a heart-stricken moose; "Aye, aye! it was that accursed white whale that razed me; made a poor pegging lubber of me forever and a day!" Then tossing both arms, with measureless imprecations he shouted out: "Aye, aye! and I'll chase him
40 round Good Hope, and round the Horn, and round the Norway Maelstrom, and round perdition's flames before I give him up. And this is what ye have shipped for, men! to chase that white whale on both sides of land, and over all sides of earth, till he spouts black blood and rolls fin out. What say ye, men, will ye splice hands on it, now? I think ye do look brave."

    "Aye, aye!" shouted the harpooneers and seamen, running closer to the excited old man: "A sharp eye for the White Whale; a sharp lance for Moby Dick!"

The Scarlet Letter

Nathaniel Hawthorne

Nathaniel Hawthorne
1804–1864

ABOUT THE AUTHOR The descendant of a judge at the Salem witchcraft trials, Nathaniel Hawthorne was haunted by his Puritan ancestors' intolerance. He wrote *The Scarlet Letter* in part to absolve his guilt, saying in his introduction to the novel: "I take shame upon myself for their sakes and pray that any curse incurred by them . . . may be now and henceforth removed." Yet it seems Hawthorne bore no love for the people living in Salem in his day either, once commenting: "I detest this town so much that I hate to go into the streets, or to have the people see me. . . . I feel an infinite contempt for them, and probably have expressed more of it than I intended; for my preliminary chapter [of *The Scarlet Letter*] has caused the greatest uproar that ever happened here since witch-times." The novel, as well as most of Hawthorne's other writing, depicts human beings as imperfect and imperfectible, with a dark side to their natures—ironically, a view more in keeping with that of Hawthorne's detested Puritan ancestors than with the optimistic spirit of his times.

ABOUT THE NOVEL Published in 1850, *The Scarlet Letter* is a short historical novel set in Salem in the earliest days of the Massachusetts Bay colony. Vividly re-creating the world of Puritan New England, the novel explores universal themes of sin, retribution, and forgiveness. It traces the story of Hester Prynne, who commits the sin of adultery and is publicly punished for it, and the two men in her life—her one-time lover and her vengeful husband—who keep their own sins hidden from public view. Part of Hester's punishment is to wear, for all her life, a scarlet letter *A* sewn onto the bodice of her gown.

LEGACY OF A MASTERPIECE "The publication of *The Scarlet Letter* was in the United States a literary event of the first importance," wrote author and critic Henry James. The carefully crafted novel, with its serious themes and complex symbolism, showed that writers in the young nation could produce literature equal to that of Britain and could draw on America's history and heritage in producing it. In the following scene from the novel's opening, Hester Prynne is about to appear in public for the first time with the scarlet letter on her gown. Waiting for her appearance outside the jail door, members of the community heap their scorn on the sinner.

"Goodwives," said a hard-featured dame of fifty, "I'll tell ye a piece of my mind. It would be greatly for the public behoof, if we women, being of mature age and church-members in good repute, should have the handling of such malefactresses as this Hester Prynne. What think ye, gossips? If the hussy stood up for judgment before us five, that are now here in a knot together, would she come off with such a sentence as the worshipful magistrates have awarded? Marry, I trow not!"

"People say," said another, "that the Reverend Master Dimmesdale, her godly pastor, takes it very grievously to heart that such a scandal should have come upon 10 his congregation."

"The magistrates are God-fearing gentlemen, but merciful overmuch, — that is a truth," added a third autumnal matron. "At the very least, they should have put the brand of a hot iron on Hester Prynne's forehead. Madam Hester would have winced at that, I warrant me. But she, — the naughty baggage, — little will she care what they put upon the bodice of her gown! Why, look you, she may cover it with a brooch, or such like heathenish adornment, and so walk the streets as brave as ever!"

"Ah, but," interposed, more softly, a young wife, holding a child by the hand, "let her cover the mark as she will, the pang of it will be always in her heart."

"What do we talk of marks and brands, whether on the bodice of her gown, 20 or the flesh of her forehead?" cried another female, the ugliest as well as the most pitiless of these self-constituted judges. "This woman has brought shame upon us all, and ought to die. Is there not law for it? Truly there is, both in the Scripture and the statute-book. Then let the magistrates, who have made it of no effect, thank themselves if their own wives and daughters go astray!"

"Mercy on us, goodwife," exclaimed a man in the crowd, "is there no virtue in woman, save what springs from a wholesome fear of the gallows? That is the hardest word yet! Hush, now, gossips; for the lock is turning in the prison-door, and here comes Mistress Prynne herself."

The Minister's Black Veil

Short Story by Nathaniel Hawthorne

Nathaniel Hawthorne
c. 1804–1864

FYI
Did you know that Nathaniel Hawthorne . . .

- achieved his first literary success writing stories for children?
- was a mentor to Herman Melville, who dedicated *Moby Dick* to him?
- wrote a campaign biography for his college friend Franklin Pierce, who became the 14th U.S. president ?

Author Online

For more on Nathaniel Hawthorne, visit the **Literature Center** at ClassZone.com.

An intensely private man who allowed few to know him well, Nathaniel Hawthorne was fascinated by the dark secrets of human nature. In his greatest novels and short stories, including his masterpieces *The Scarlet Letter* and *The House of the Seven Gables,* he explored such themes as sin, hypocrisy, and guilt. One of the first American writers to explore his characters' hidden motivations, Hawthorne broke new ground in American literature with his morally complex characters.

Legacy of Guilt Born in Salem, Hawthorne was a descendant of the Puritan settlers of Massachusetts. His great-great-grandfather was a judge at the infamous Salem witch trials—the only one who refused to apologize for his role in sentencing innocent people to death. Though he tried to distance himself from his family's dark legacy, Hawthorne shared the Puritan belief that people are basically sinful. But where Puritans believed that society could be purified by the actions of a righteous few, Hawthorne was more pessimistic: he believed that perfection was impossible and remained skeptical of all attempts to reform or improve society.

Difficult Compromises Throughout his life, Hawthorne was torn between his literary calling and his desire for a stable, respectable profession. By the time he left for Bowdoin College in 1821, Hawthorne knew he wanted to write. After graduation, he lived alone for 12 years, dedicated to building his literary career. By 1842, he had achieved some success and had married his great love, Sophia Peabody. Their otherwise happy marriage was constantly shadowed by financial woes. When times were tough, Hawthorne had well-connected friends set him up with government jobs, whose dull routines choked his imagination and limited his time to write. Although he never stopped writing, work, illness, and family duties dominated Hawthorne's later years. He died in 1864 of a sudden illness.

Challenging Questions One of Hawthorne's great talents was his mastery of symbolism. He often chose symbols whose meaning was ambiguous, forcing readers to think deeply about his characters and their conflicts. Despite his pessimism, he found hope in the redeeming power of love, a theme he developed in his mature works. Hawthorne's efforts to come to terms with his own past inspired profound reflections on American identity that still resonate today.

● LITERARY ANALYSIS: SYMBOL

A **symbol** is something concrete—a person, a place, an object, or an action—used to stand for an abstract idea or feeling. In some works, symbols may be subtle and hard to identify. In this story, Hawthorne identifies his main symbol outright:

Know, then, this veil is a type and a symbol . . .

The challenge, then, is to decide what the symbol means. A rich symbol has many possible interpretations rather than a single precise meaning. To interpret a symbol, pay close attention to its context in the work, including

- what ideas and feelings are associated with it
- its impact on characters and events

As you read, use a concept map to note details about the minister's black veil, the main symbol in this story.

■ READING SKILL: IDENTIFY CULTURAL CHARACTERISTICS

The characters' reactions to the events of this story may not make sense to a modern reader. Keep in mind that the story is set in an 18th-century Puritan town. The parishioners' responses to their minister are meant to illustrate the traits that, in Hawthorne's eyes, define Puritan culture. As you read, think about the values, beliefs, and social constraints that are revealed by the parishioners' behavior.

▲ VOCABULARY IN CONTEXT

The boldfaced words helped Hawthorne tell his tale of Puritan life. Use context clues to write a definition of each.

1. messages filled with confusion and **ambiguity**
2. a **zealous** speaker whose eyes blazed intensely
3. a tale of sin and **iniquity**
4. an event so unusual that it seemed **preternatural**
5. an **ostentatious** costume that made people stare
6. **imbued** with great hopes for the future
7. her **tremulous** voice that revealed her nervousness
8. a sign that might **portend** trouble ahead

How does someone become a STRANGER?

KEY IDEA Your best friend suddenly doesn't like the things she's always liked. Your brother comes home from college with a new haircut, listening to strange new music. What happens when someone you thought you knew changes the way they act or look? Can you still recognize the person you knew, or do his or her new behaviors lead to **estrangement**?

QUICKWRITE Recall a time when someone close to you changed in a way that made him or her seem like a different person. Write a paragraph to describe the change. Explain why it made you see the person so differently.

457

THE MINISTER'S BLACK VEIL

Nathaniel Hawthorne

BACKGROUND In the Puritan town of 18th-century Massachusetts, the meetinghouse was the center of the community life. Used for both religious and civil gatherings, meetinghouses were simple and plain, with no obviously religious decorations. Families did not sit together during religious services, which lasted most of the day on Sundays. Men and women sat on opposite sides, and worshipers were seated according to their age and social standing. The oldest and most distinguished citizens were rewarded with seats closest to the pulpit, the raised platform from which the pastor delivered his sermons. As services began, all eyes turned expectantly toward the pulpit, awaiting the pastor's entrance.

ANALYZE VISUALS
Simplicity was a central value of Puritan life. What elements of this painting help create its simple style? Consider the use of color, line, and texture, as well as the composition of the image, in your answer.

The sexton[1] stood in the porch of Milford meetinghouse, pulling lustily at the bell rope. The old people of the village came stooping along the street. Children, with bright faces, tripped merrily beside their parents, or mimicked a graver gait,[2] in the conscious dignity of their Sunday clothes. Spruce bachelors looked sidelong at the pretty maidens, and fancied that the Sabbath sunshine made them prettier than on weekdays. When the throng had mostly streamed into the porch, the sexton began to toll the bell, keeping his eye on the Reverend Mr. Hooper's door. The first glimpse of the clergyman's figure was the signal for the bell to cease its summons. **A**

A CULTURAL CHARACTERISTICS
Reread lines 1–9. What details reveal the importance of Sunday worship for the people of Milford?

---

1. **sexton:** church employee who takes care of church property and performs various other duties.
2. **mimicked a graver gait:** followed their parents' example and walked in a more dignified way.

Church at Head Tide #2 (1938–1940), Marsden Hartley. Oil on academy board, 37 $1/4$″ × 31 $1/4$″ × 2 $1/4$″. Gift of Mr. and Mrs. John Cowles. The Minneapolis Institute of Arts.

10   "But what has good Parson Hooper got upon his face?" cried the sexton in astonishment.

All within hearing immediately turned about, and beheld the semblance of Mr. Hooper, pacing slowly his meditative way towards the meetinghouse. With one accord they started, expressing more wonder than if some strange minister were coming to dust the cushions of Mr. Hooper's pulpit.

"Are you sure it is our parson?" inquired Goodman[3] Gray of the sexton.

"Of a certainty it is good Mr. Hooper," replied the sexton. "He was to have exchanged pulpits with Parson Shute of Westbury; but Parson Shute sent to excuse himself yesterday, being to preach a funeral sermon."

20   The cause of so much amazement may appear sufficiently slight. Mr. Hooper, a gentlemanly person about thirty, though still a bachelor, was dressed with due clerical neatness, as if a careful wife had starched his band, and brushed the weekly dust from his Sunday's garb. There was but one thing remarkable in his appearance. Swathed about his forehead, and hanging down over his face, so low as to be shaken by his breath, Mr. Hooper had on a black veil. On a nearer view, it seemed to consist of two folds of crape,[4] which entirely concealed his features, except the mouth and chin, but probably did not intercept his sight, farther than to give a darkened aspect to all living and inanimate things. With this gloomy shade before him, good Mr. Hooper walked onward, at a slow and quiet pace,
30   stooping somewhat and looking on the ground, as is customary with abstracted[5] men, yet nodding kindly to those of his parishioners who still waited on the meetinghouse steps. But so wonder-struck were they that his greeting hardly met with a return.

"I can't really feel as if good Mr. Hooper's face was behind that piece of crape," said the sexton.

"I don't like it," muttered an old woman, as she hobbled into the meetinghouse. "He has changed himself into something awful, only by hiding his face."

"Our parson has gone mad!" cried Goodman Gray, following him across the threshold.

40   A rumor of some unaccountable phenomenon had preceded Mr. Hooper into the meetinghouse, and set all the congregation astir. Few could refrain from twisting their heads towards the door; many stood upright, and turned directly about; while several little boys clambered upon the seats, and came down again with a terrible racket. There was a general bustle, a rustling of the women's gowns and shuffling of the men's feet, greatly at variance with that hushed repose which should attend the entrance of the minister. But Mr. Hooper appeared not to notice the perturbation of his people. He entered with an almost noiseless step, bent his head mildly to the pews on each side, and bowed as he passed his oldest parishioner, a white-haired great-grandsire, who occupied an armchair in the
50   centre of the aisle. It was strange to observe how slowly this venerable man became conscious of something singular in the appearance of his pastor. He seemed not

---

3. **Goodman:** the Puritan equivalent of Mr.

4. **crape** (krāp): a piece of dark material worn as a sign of mourning. Also called *crepe*.

5. **abstracted:** preoccupied, or lost in thought.

fully to partake of the prevailing wonder till Mr. Hooper had ascended the stairs, and showed himself in the pulpit, face-to-face with his congregation, except for the black veil. That mysterious emblem was never once withdrawn. It shook with his measured breath as he gave out the psalm; it threw its obscurity between him and the holy page, as he read the Scriptures; and while he prayed, the veil lay heavily on his uplifted countenance. Did he seek to hide from the dread Being[6] whom he was addressing?

60 Such was the effect of this simple piece of crape, that more than one woman of delicate nerves was forced to leave the meetinghouse. Yet perhaps the pale-faced congregation was almost as fearful a sight to the minister as his black veil to them.

Mr. Hooper had the reputation of a good preacher, but not an energetic one: he strove to win his people heavenward by mild persuasive influences, rather than to drive them thither by the thunders of the Word. The sermon which he now delivered was marked by the same characteristics of style and manner as the general series of his pulpit oratory. But there was something, either in the sentiment of the discourse itself, or in the imagination of the auditors, which made it greatly the most powerful effort that they had ever heard from their pastor's lips. It was tinged, rather more darkly than usual, with the gentle gloom
70 of Mr. Hooper's temperament. The subject had reference to secret sin, and those sad mysteries which we hide from our nearest and dearest, and would fain conceal from our own consciousness, even forgetting that the Omniscient[7] can detect them. A subtle power was breathed into his words. Each member of the congregation, the most innocent girl, and the man of hardened breast, felt as if the preacher had crept upon them, behind his awful veil, and discovered their hoarded **iniquity** of deed or thought. Many spread their clasped hands on their bosoms. There was nothing terrible in what Mr. Hooper said; at least, no violence; and yet, with every tremor of his melancholy voice, the hearers quaked. An unsought pathos came hand in hand with awe. So sensible were the audience of some
80 unwonted attribute in their minister, that they longed for a breath of wind to blow aside the veil, almost believing that a stranger's visage would be discovered, though the form, gesture and voice were those of Mr. Hooper. **B**

At the close of the services, the people hurried out with indecorous confusion, eager to communicate their pent-up amazement, and conscious of lighter spirits the moment they lost sight of the black veil. Some gathered in little circles, huddled closely together, with their mouths all whispering in the centre; some went homeward alone, wrapped in silent meditation; some talked loudly, and profaned the Sabbath day with **ostentatious** laughter. A few shook their sagacious heads, intimating that they could penetrate the mystery; while one or two affirmed that
90 there was no mystery at all, but only that Mr. Hooper's eyes were so weakened by the midnight lamp as to require a shade. After a brief interval, forth came good Mr. Hooper also, in the rear of his flock. Turning his veiled face from one group to another, he paid due reverence to the hoary heads, saluted the middle-aged with kind dignity, as their friend and spiritual guide, greeted the young with mingled

iniquity (ĭ-nĭk'wĭ-tē) *n.* wickedness

B SYMBOL
Reread lines 62–82. Describe the change that occurs in Mr. Hooper's preaching. What seems to cause the listeners' unusual response?

ostentatious
(ŏs'tĕn-tā'shəs) *adj.* loud; overdone

---

6. **the dread Being:** the awe-inspiring God.
7. **the Omniscient:** a title for God, signifying that he is all-knowing.

authority and love, and laid his hands on the little children's heads to bless them. Such was always his custom on the Sabbath day. Strange and bewildered looks repaid him for his courtesy. None, as on former occasions, aspired to the honor of walking by their pastor's side. Old Squire Saunders, doubtless by an accidental lapse of memory, neglected to invite Mr. Hooper to his table, where the good clergyman 100 had been wont to bless the food almost every Sunday since his settlement. He returned, therefore, to the parsonage, and at the moment of closing the door, was observed to look back upon the people, all of whom had their eyes fixed upon the minister. A sad smile gleamed faintly from beneath the black veil, and flickered about his mouth, glimmering as he disappeared. **C**

"How strange," said a lady, "that a simple black veil, such as any woman might wear on her bonnet, should become such a terrible thing on Mr. Hooper's face!"

"Something must surely be amiss with Mr. Hooper's intellects," observed her husband, the physician of the village. "But the strangest part of the affair is the effect of this vagary, even on a sober-minded man like myself. The black veil,

C CULTURAL CHARACTERISTICS
Reread lines 92–100. Identify details that convey Mr. Hooper's social status in Milford. What does the change in the villagers' behavior toward the minister suggest about their values?

The Last Halt: Stop of Hooker's Band in East Hartford before Crossing River (1939), Alton S. Tobey. Study for East Hartford, Connecticut Postal Office. Oil on fiberboard, 26" x 44¹/₈". Transfer from General Services Administration. Smithsonian American Art Museum, Washington, D.C. Photo © Smithsonian American Art Museum, Washington, D.C./Art Resource, New York. © Alton Tobey Collection/www.altontobey.org.

110 though it covers only our pastor's face, throws its influence over his whole person, and makes him ghost-like from head to foot. Do you not feel it so?"

"Truly do I," replied the lady; "and I would not be alone with him for the world. I wonder he is not afraid to be alone with himself!"

"Men sometimes are so," said her husband.

The afternoon service was attended with similar circumstances. At its conclusion, the bell tolled for the funeral of a young lady. The relatives and friends were assembled in the house, and the more distant acquaintances stood about the door, speaking of the good qualities of the deceased, when their talk was interrupted by the appearance of Mr. Hooper, still covered with his black veil. It was now an

120 appropriate emblem. The clergyman stepped into the room where the corpse was laid, and bent over the coffin, to take a last farewell of his deceased parishioner. As he stooped, the veil hung straight down from his forehead so that, if her eyelids had not been closed forever, the dead maiden might have seen his face. Could Mr. Hooper be fearful of her glance, that he so hastily caught back the black veil? A person, who watched the interview between the dead and the living, scrupled not to affirm that, at the instant when the clergyman's features were disclosed, the corpse had slightly shuddered, rustling the shroud[8] and muslin cap, though the countenance retained the composure of death. A superstitious old woman was the only witness of this prodigy. From the coffin, Mr. Hooper passed into the chamber

130 of the mourners, and thence to the head of the staircase, to make the funeral prayer. It was a tender and heart-dissolving prayer, full of sorrow, yet so **imbued** with celestial hopes, that the music of the heavenly harp, swept by the fingers of the dead, seemed faintly to be heard among the saddest accents of the minister. The people trembled, though they but darkly understood him, when he prayed that they, and himself, and all of mortal race might be ready, as he trusted this young maiden had been, for the dreadful hour that should snatch the veil from their faces. The bearers went heavily forth, and the mourners followed, saddening all the street, with the dead before them, and Mr. Hooper in his black veil behind. **D**

"Why do you look back?" said one in the procession to his partner.

140 "I had a fancy," replied she, "that the minister and the maiden's spirit were walking hand in hand."

"And so had I, at the same moment," said the other.

That night, the handsomest couple in Milford village were to be joined in wedlock. Though reckoned a melancholy man, Mr. Hooper had a placid cheerfulness for such occasions, which often excited a sympathetic smile, where livelier merriment would have been thrown away. There was no quality of his disposition which made him more beloved than this. The company at the wedding awaited his arrival with impatience, trusting that the strange awe, which had gathered over him throughout the day, would now be dispelled. But such was

150 not the result. When Mr. Hooper came, the first thing that their eyes rested on was the same horrible black veil, which had added deeper gloom to the funeral, and could **portend** nothing but evil to the wedding. Such was its immediate effect on the guests, that a cloud seemed to have rolled duskily from beneath the

---

imbued (ĭm-byōo'd) adj. deeply influenced by imbue v.

D SYMBOL
Paraphrase lines 133–138. In this context, what could Mr. Hooper mean when he refers to "the dreadful hour that should snatch the veil from their faces"?

portend (pôr-tĕnd') v. to serve as an omen of; to signify

---

8. **shroud:** burial garment.

black crape, and dimmed the light of the candles. The bridal pair stood up before the minister. But the bride's cold fingers quivered in the **tremulous** hand of the bridegroom, and her death-like paleness caused a whisper that the maiden who had been buried a few hours before was come from her grave to be married. If ever another wedding were so dismal, it was that famous one where they tolled the wedding knell.[9] After performing the ceremony, Mr. Hooper raised a glass
160 of wine to his lips, wishing happiness to the new-married couple, in a strain of mild pleasantry that ought to have brightened the features of the guests, like a cheerful gleam from the hearth. At that instant, catching a glimpse of his figure in the looking glass, the black veil involved his own spirit in the horror with which it overwhelmed all others. His frame shuddered—his lips grew white—he spilt the untasted wine upon the carpet—and rushed forth into the darkness. For the Earth, too, had on her Black Veil. **E**

The next day, the whole village of Milford talked of little else than Parson Hooper's black veil. That, and the mystery concealed behind it, supplied a topic for discussion between acquaintances meeting in the street, and good women
170 gossiping at their open windows. It was the first item of news that the tavern keeper told to his guests. The children babbled of it on their way to school. One imitative little imp covered his face with an old black handkerchief, thereby so affrighting his playmates that the panic seized himself, and he well-nigh lost his wits by his own waggery.[10]

It was remarkable that, of all the busybodies and impertinent people in the parish, not one ventured to put the plain question to Mr. Hooper, wherefore he did this thing. Hitherto, whenever there appeared the slightest call for such interference, he had never lacked advisers, nor shown himself averse to be guided by their judgment. If he erred at all, it was by so painful a degree of self-distrust
180 that even the mildest censure would lead him to consider an indifferent action as a crime. Yet, though so well acquainted with this amiable weakness, no individual among his parishioners chose to make the black veil a subject of friendly remonstrance. There was a feeling of dread, neither plainly confessed nor carefully concealed, which caused each to shift the responsibility upon another, till at length it was found expedient to send a deputation to the church, in order to deal with Mr. Hooper about the mystery, before it should grow into a scandal. Never did an embassy so ill discharge its duties. The minister received them with friendly courtesy, but became silent, after they were seated, leaving to his visitors the whole burden of introducing their important business. The topic, it might be supposed,
190 was obvious enough. There was the black veil, swathed round Mr. Hooper's forehead, and concealing every feature above his placid mouth, on which, at times, they could perceive the glimmering of a melancholy smile. But that piece of crape, to their imagination, seemed to hang down before his heart, the symbol of a fearful secret between him and them. Were the veil but cast aside, they might speak freely of it, but not till then. Thus they sat a considerable time, speechless,

tremulous (trĕm′yə-ləs)
adj. trembling; quivering

E SYMBOL
Reread lines 162–166. Compare the references to veils in this passage with the earlier reference in lines 133–138. In what ways has the veil's meaning become more ambiguous, or unclear?

---

9. **If . . . the wedding knell:** a reference to "The Wedding Knell," a story by Hawthorne in which a bell-tolling appropriate for a funeral is sounded at a wedding.

10. **waggery:** mischievous merriment.

confused, and shrinking uneasily from Mr. Hooper's eye, which they felt to be fixed upon them with an invisible glance. Finally, the deputies returned abashed to their constituents, pronouncing the matter too weighty to be handled, except by a council of the churches, if, indeed, it might not require a general synod.[11] **F**

200   But there was one person in the village unappalled by the awe with which the black veil had impressed all beside herself. When the deputies returned without an explanation, or even venturing to demand one, she, with the calm energy of her character, determined to chase away the strange cloud that appeared to be settling round Mr. Hooper, every moment more darkly than before. As his plighted wife,[12] it should be her privilege to know what the black veil concealed. At the minister's first visit, therefore, she entered upon the subject, with a direct simplicity, which made the task easier both for him and her. After he had seated himself, she fixed her eyes steadfastly upon the veil, but could discern nothing of the dreadful gloom that had so overawed the multitude: it was but a double fold of crape, hanging

210 down from his forehead to his mouth, and slightly stirring with his breath. **G**

"No," said she aloud, and smiling, "there is nothing terrible in this piece of crape except that it hides a face which I am always glad to look upon. Come, good sir, let the sun shine from behind the cloud. First lay aside your black veil: then tell me why you put it on."

Mr. Hooper's smile glimmered faintly.

"There is an hour to come," said he, "when all of us shall cast aside our veils. Take it not amiss, beloved friend, if I wear this piece of crape till then."

"Your words are a mystery too," returned the young lady. "Take away the veil from them, at least."

220   "Elizabeth, I will," said he, "so far as my vow may suffer me. Know, then, this veil is a type and a symbol, and I am bound to wear it ever, both in light and darkness, in solitude and before the gaze of multitudes, and as with strangers, so with my familiar friends. No mortal eye will see it withdrawn. This dismal shade must separate me from the world: even you, Elizabeth, can never come behind it!"

"What grievous affliction hath befallen you," she earnestly inquired, "that you should thus darken your eyes forever?"

"If it be a sign of mourning," replied Mr. Hooper, "I, perhaps, like most other mortals, have sorrows dark enough to be typified by a black veil."

"But what if the world will not believe that it is the type of an innocent
230 sorrow?" urged Elizabeth. "Beloved and respected as you are, there may be whispers that you hide your face under the consciousness of secret sin. For the sake of your holy office, do away this scandal!"

The color rose into her cheeks, as she intimated the nature of the rumors that were already abroad in the village. But Mr. Hooper's mildness did not forsake him. He even smiles again—that same sad smile, which always appeared like a faint glimmering of light proceeding from the obscurity beneath the veil.

"If I hide my face for sorrow, there is cause enough," he merely replied; "and if I cover it for secret sin, what mortal might not do the same?"

F CULTURAL CHARACTERISTICS
Paraphrase lines 175–186. Explain what motivates the parishioners to confront Mr. Hooper. What do their fears reveal about Puritan culture?

G SYMBOL
Reread lines 200–210. Contrast the response of the minister's fiancée to the veil with the responses of the other villagers. What might explain the difference in her response?

---

11. **a general synod:** a meeting of the governing body of the churches.

12. **plighted wife:** fiancée.

Portrait of Alice Irene Harvey (1912), Mark Gertler. Oil on canvas, 60.9 cm × 50.8 cm. © Leeds Museums and Galleries, Leeds, United Kingdom/Bridgeman Art Library.

And with this gentle but unconquerable obstinacy did he resist all her
240 entreaties. At length Elizabeth sat silent. For a few moments she appeared lost in
thought, considering, probably, what new methods might be tried to withdraw
her lover from so dark a fantasy, which, if it had no other meaning, was perhaps a
symptom of mental disease. Though of a firmer character than his own, the tears
rolled down her cheeks. But, in an instant, as it were, a new feeling took the place
of sorrow: her eyes were fixed insensibly on the black veil, when, like a sudden
twilight in the air, its terrors fell around her. She arose, and stood trembling
before him.

"And do you feel it then at last?" said he mournfully.

She made no reply, but covered her eyes with her hand, and turned to leave
250 the room. He rushed forward and caught her arm.

"Have patience with me, Elizabeth!" cried he passionately. "Do not desert
me, though this veil must be between us here on earth. Be mine, and hereafter
there shall be no veil over my face, no darkness between our souls! It is but a
mortal veil—it is not for eternity! Oh! you know not how lonely I am, and how
frightened to be alone behind my black veil. Do not leave me in this miserable
obscurity forever!"

"Lift the veil but once, and look me in the face," said she.

"Never! It cannot be!" replied Mr. Hooper.

"Then, farewell!" said Elizabeth.

260 She withdrew her arm from his grasp and slowly departed, pausing at the door
to give one long, shuddering gaze that seemed almost to penetrate the mystery of
the black veil. But even amid his grief, Mr. Hooper smiled to think that only a
material emblem had separated him from happiness, though the horrors which
it shadowed forth must be drawn darkly between the fondest of lovers.

From that time no attempts were made to remove Mr. Hooper's black veil or,
by a direct appeal, to discover the secret which it was supposed to hide. By persons
who claimed a superiority to popular prejudice, it was reckoned merely an eccentric
whim, such as often mingles with the sober actions of men otherwise rational, and
tinges them all with its own semblance of insanity. But with the multitude, good
270 Mr. Hooper was irreparably a bugbear.[13] He could not walk the streets with any
peace of mind, so conscious was he that the gentle and timid would turn aside to
avoid him, and that others would make it a point of hardihood to throw themselves
in his way. The impertinence of the latter class compelled him to give up his
customary walk, at sunset, to the burial ground, for when he leaned pensively over
the gate, there would always be faces behind the gravestones, peeping at his black
veil. A fable went the rounds that the stare of the dead people drove him thence.
It grieved him to the very depth of his kind heart to observe how the children
fled from his approach, breaking up their merriest sports, while his melancholy
figure was yet afar off. Their instinctive dread caused him to feel, more strongly
280 than aught else, that a **preternatural** horror was interwoven with the threads of

---

13. **bugbear:** a source of dread or fear.

ANALYZE VISUALS
In what ways does the
woman depicted in the
painting on page 466
reflect the character of
Elizabeth as described
in lines 240–244? What
could the woman's white
dress **symbolize**?

preternatural
(prē'tər-năch'ər-əl) *adj.*
supernatural

the black crape. In truth, his own antipathy to the veil was known to be so great that he never willingly passed before a mirror, nor stooped to drink at a still fountain, lest, in its peaceful bosom, he should be affrighted by himself. This was what gave plausibility to the whispers that Mr. Hooper's conscience tortured him for some great crime too horrible to be entirely concealed, or otherwise than so obscurely intimated. Thus, from beneath the black veil there rolled a cloud into the sunshine, an **ambiguity** of sin or sorrow, which enveloped the poor minister, so that love or sympathy could never reach him. It was said that ghost and fiend consorted with him there. With self-shudderings and outward terrors, he walked
290 continually in its shadow, groping darkly within his own soul, or gazing through a medium that saddened the whole world. Even the lawless wind, it was believed, respected his dreadful secret, and never blew aside the veil. But still good Mr. Hooper sadly smiled at the pale visages of the worldly throng as he passed by.

Among all its bad influences, the black veil had the one desirable effect, of making its wearer a very efficient clergyman. By the aid of his mysterious emblem—for there was no other apparent cause—he became a man of awful power, over souls that were in agony for sin. His converts always regarded him with a dread peculiar to themselves, affirming, though but figuratively, that before he brought them to celestial light, they had been with him behind the
300 black veil. Its gloom, indeed, enabled him to sympathize with all dark affections. Dying sinners cried aloud for Mr. Hooper, and would not yield their breath till he appeared; though ever, as he stooped to whisper consolation, they shuddered at the veiled face so near their own. Such were the terrors of the black veil, even when Death had bared his visage! Strangers came long distances to attend service at his church, with the mere idle purpose of gazing at his figure, because it was forbidden them to behold his face. But many were made to quake ere they departed! Once, during Governor Belcher's[14] administration, Mr. Hooper was appointed to preach the election sermon. Covered with his black veil, he stood before the chief magistrate, the council, and the representatives, and wrought so
310 deep an impression that the legislative measures of that year were characterized by all the gloom and piety of our earliest ancestral sway. [15] **H**

In this manner Mr. Hooper spent a long life, irreproachable in outward act, yet shrouded in dismal suspicions; kind and loving, though unloved, and dimly feared; a man apart from men, shunned in their health and joy, but ever summoned to their aid in moral anguish. As years wore on, shedding their snows above his sable veil, he acquired a name throughout the New England churches, and they called him Father Hooper. Nearly all his parishioners, who were of a mature age when he was settled, had been borne away by many a funeral: he had one congregation in the church, and a more crowded one in the churchyard; and
320 having wrought so late into the evening, and done his work so well, it was now good Father Hooper's turn to rest.

---

ambiguity
(ăm′bĭ-gyōō′ĭ-tē) *n.*
unclearness; uncertainty

H CULTURAL CHARACTERISTICS
Once Mr. Hooper is perceived to have intimate knowledge of sin, he becomes a famous and respected clergyman. Based on this fact, what would you conclude is the main concern of Puritan worshipers?

---

14. **Governor Belcher's:** referring to Governor Jonathan Belcher (1682–1757), colonial governor of the Massachusetts Bay Colony from 1730 to 1741, and later of New Jersey.

15. **earliest ancestral sway:** the Puritans who held power in 17th-century America.

Several persons were visible by the shaded candlelight in the death chamber of the old clergyman. Natural connections[16] he had none. But there was the decorously grave, though unmoved physician, seeking only to mitigate the last pangs of the patient whom he could not save. There were the deacons, and other eminently pious members of his church. There, also, was the Reverend Mr. Clark, of Westbury, a young and <u>zealous</u> divine, who had ridden in haste to pray by the bedside of the expiring minister. There was the nurse, no hired handmaiden of death, but one whose calm affection had endured thus long, in secrecy, in solitude, amid the chill of age, and would not perish, even at the dying hour. Who, but Elizabeth! And there lay the hoary head of good Father Hooper upon the death pillow, with the black veil still swathed about his brow and reaching down over his face, so that each more difficult gasp of his faint breath caused it to stir. All through life that piece of crape had hung between him and the world: it had separated him from cheerful brotherhood and woman's love, and kept him in that saddest of all prisons, his own heart; and still it lay upon his face, as if to deepen the gloom of his darksome chamber, and shade him from the sunshine of eternity.

For some time previous, his mind had been confused, wavering doubtfully between the past and the present, and hovering forward, as it were, at intervals, into the indistinctness of the world to come. There had been feverish turns, which tossed him from side to side and wore away what little strength he had. But in the most convulsive struggles, and in the wildest vagaries of his intellect, when no other thought retained its sober influence, he still showed an awful solicitude lest the black veil should slip aside. Even if his bewildered soul could have forgotten, there was a faithful woman at his pillow, who, with averted eyes, would have covered that aged face, which she had last beheld in the comeliness of manhood. At length the death-stricken old man lay quietly in the torpor of mental and bodily exhaustion, with an imperceptible pulse, and breath that grew fainter and fainter, except when a long, deep, and irregular inspiration seemed to prelude the flight of his spirit.

The minister of Westbury approached the bedside.

"Venerable Father Hooper," said he, "the moment of your release is at hand. Are you ready for the lifting of the veil, that shuts in time from eternity?"

Father Hooper at first replied merely by a feeble motion of his head; then, apprehensive, perhaps, that his meaning might be doubtful, he exerted himself to speak.

"Yea," said he, in faint accents, "my soul hath a patient weariness until that veil be lifted."

"And is it fitting," resumed the Reverend Mr. Clark, "that a man so given to prayer, of such a blameless example, holy in deed and thought, so far as mortal judgment may pronounce; is it fitting that a father in the church should leave a shadow on his memory that may seem to blacken a life so pure? I pray you, my venerable brother, let not this thing be! Suffer us to be gladdened by your

zealous (zĕl′əs) *adj.*
eager and enthusiastic

16. **natural connections:** relatives.

triumphant aspect, as you go to your reward. Before the veil of eternity be lifted, let me cast aside this black veil from your face!"

And thus speaking, the Reverend Mr. Clark bent forward to reveal the mystery of so many years. But, exerting a sudden energy that made all the beholders stand aghast, Father Hooper snatched both his hands from beneath the bedclothes and pressed them strongly on the black veil, resolute to struggle, if the minister of Westbury would contend with a dying man.

370 "Never!" cried the veiled clergyman. "On earth, never!"

"Dark old man!" exclaimed the affrighted minister, "with what horrible crime upon your soul are you now passing to the judgment?"

Father Hooper's breath heaved; it rattled in his throat; but with a mighty effort, grasping forward with his hands, he caught hold of life, and held it back till he should speak. He even raised himself in bed; and there he sat shivering, with the arms of death around him, while the black veil hung down, awful, at that last moment, in the gathered terrors of a lifetime. And yet the faint, sad smile, so often there, now seemed to glimmer from its obscurity, and linger on Father Hooper's lips.

"Why do you tremble at me alone?" cried he, turning his veiled face round
380 the circle of pale spectators. "Tremble also at each other! Have men avoided me, and women shown no pity, and children screamed and fled, only for my black veil? What, but the mystery which it obscurely typifies, has made this piece of crape so awful? When the friend shows his inmost heart to his friend; the lover to his best beloved; when man does not vainly shrink from the eye of his Creator, loathsomely treasuring up the secret of his sin; then deem me a monster, for the symbol beneath which I have lived, and die! I look around me, and, lo! On every visage a Black Veil!" ❶

While his auditors shrank from one another, in mutual affright, Father Hooper fell back upon his pillow, a veiled corpse, with a faint smile lingering on his lips.
390 Still veiled, they laid him in his coffin, and a veiled corpse they bore him to the grave. The grass of many years has sprung up and withered on that grave, the burial stone is moss-grown, and good Mr. Hooper's face is dust; but awful is still the thought, that it mouldered beneath the Black Veil! ❧

❶ **SYMBOL**
Explain Father Hooper's reproach in lines 380–387. What do his comments suggest about the meaning of the veil?

Comprehension

1. **Recall** What is the topic of the first sermon Mr. Hooper gives while wearing the veil?

2. **Recall** What reason does Mr. Hooper give Elizabeth for wearing the veil?

3. **Summarize** As time goes by, how do Mr. Hooper's relationships change?

Literary Analysis

4. **Identify Cultural Characteristics** What does the story reveal about Puritan religious beliefs, rules of behavior, and values and ideals?

5. **Interpret Symbol** Review the concept map you created as you read. Based on this information, what does the black veil represent? Explain your answer.

6. **Analyze Irony** To highlight his criticisms of Puritan society, Hawthorne uses verbal irony, where what is stated differs from what is really meant. In each of the following examples, explain what is ironic about the narrator's comments. What behavior, value, or belief is being criticized?

   - Squire Saunders's insult to Mr. Hooper (lines 98–100)
   - wild rumors (lines 125–129)
   - the deputation's visit to the minister (lines 195–199)
   - Mr. Hooper's new reputation (lines 295–297)

7. **Examine Character Ambiguity** The minister is an ambiguous character: he can be seen as an innocent victim of others' fears or as a man driven to isolate himself, convinced of his own moral superiority. Identify at least two details that support each perspective. Which interpretation do you find more compelling? Give reasons for your answer.

8. **Make Judgments About Character Motivations** Mr. Hooper's wearing of the black veil leads to his **estrangement** from his congregation. Based on the following passages, what argument would you make about the real causes of the villagers' discomfort in the minister's presence?

   - the first sighting of the minister (lines 34–39)
   - parishioners' comments after services (lines 105–113)
   - his arrival at the wedding (lines 147–152)
   - the attempt to confront him (lines 190–197)

Literary Criticism

9. **Biographical Context** Reread the biography of Hawthorne on page 456. Explain the personal motives that inspired Hawthorne's critical portrayal of Puritan culture. In what ways might Mr. Hooper represent Hawthorne's struggle with his own guilt?

Vocabulary in Context

WORD LIST

ambiguity

imbued

iniquity

ostentatious

portend

preternatural

tremulous

zealous

VOCABULARY PRACTICE

Decide whether the words in each pair are synonyms or antonyms.

1. ostentatious/discreet
2. ambiguity/clarity
3. portend/predict
4. iniquity/vice
5. zealous/halfhearted
6. imbued/infused
7. preternatural/ordinary
8. tremulous/quaking

VOCABULARY IN WRITING

Assume the role of the minister's fiancée, and write a journal entry to describe your feelings at some point after the breakup. Use at least two vocabulary words in your entry. You might begin like this.

> **EXAMPLE SENTENCE**
>
> It has been eight months now, and I still am **tremulous** and weepy whenever I think of Mr. Hooper.

VOCABULARY STRATEGY: THE LATIN ROOT *ambi*

The vocabulary word *ambiguity* contains the Latin root *ambi*. This root, which can mean either "both" or "around," can be found in many English words. When you encounter *ambi* in a word, you can often use context clues to determine which meaning of the root is involved.

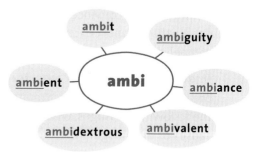

PRACTICE Choose the word from the word web that best completes each sentence. Consider what you know about the Latin root and the other word parts shown. If necessary, consult a dictionary.

1. Because Peter was _____, he could write with either hand.
2. Their home had a pleasant and gracious _____.
3. Beth was_____ about joining the group and could not make up her mind.
4. The _____ of their property extends to that line of trees.
5. Too much _____ noise can interfere with the quality of a recording.

VOCABULARY PRACTICE

For more practice, go to the **Vocabulary Center** at ClassZone.com.

The Gothic Perspective

Although the romantic period was mostly characterized by a feeling of optimism, American gothic literature showed a fascination with the dark side of human nature. Sin, deception, hedonism, guilt, death—all are subjects upon which gothic writers based their dark tales, as illustrated beautifully in this excerpt from Edgar Allan Poe's "The Masque of the Red Death."

> *"The 'Red Death' had long devastated the country. No pestilence had ever been so fatal, or so hideous. Blood was its Avatar and its seal—the redness and horror of blood. There were sharp pains, and sudden dizziness, and then profuse bleeding at the pores, with dissolution. . . .*
>
> *But the Prince Prospero was happy and dauntless and sagacious. When his dominions were half depopulated, he summoned to his presence a thousand hale and lighthearted friends from among the knights and dames of his court, and with these retired to the deep seclusion of one of his castellated abbeys."*

Literary critic Paul Zweig has a few words to say about the importance of Poe's dark perspective.

> *"Poe's achievement . . . was to give literary expression to the dread that haunted America's dream of success in the 19th century. If anything was possible in this land of wealth and change, then personal failure, even simple unhappiness, was obscene, a skeleton in the cellar of democracy."*

Writing to Analyze

Nathaniel Hawthorne is also a master of the gothic genre. Do you think Zweig's comments about Poe can apply to Hawthorne's work as well? Write a brief response, citing evidence from "The Minister's Black Veil" to support your opinion.

Consider

- characters' personal failings
- characters' unhappiness or fears
- the message you take away from the story

© Gary Kelley, 1996.

Extension

SPEAKING & LISTENING

Although Poe and Hawthorne both wrote gothic literature, the nature of their work differs quite a bit. While Poe was the master of supernatural horror, Hawthorne focused on more everyday, realistic fears. With your classmates, **discuss** what frightens you more—the fantastic or the realistic?

Writing Workshop

Reflective Essay

In this unit, you have read Ralph Waldo Emerson's and Henry David Thoreau's reflections about life, based on their own experiences. Now you will reflect on and write about an experience that changed you significantly.

WRITER'S ROAD MAP

Reflective Essay

WRITING PROMPT 1

Writing from Your Life Write an essay in which you reflect on an experience that taught you an important lesson. Include details that help your reader understand the people and events you are writing about. Explain how the experience changed you.

Experiences to Consider

- a victory or a defeat in a competition
- an incident that strongly affected you, such as a "random act of kindness" or a conflict

WRITING PROMPT 2

Writing from Literature Choose a quotation from a literary work in this unit. Write a reflective essay that relates the quotation to an event in your life. Your essay should tell why the event matters to you and explain whether you agree or disagree with the author.

Quotations to Consider

- "If a man does not keep pace with his companions, perhaps it is because he hears a different drummer." (*Walden*)
- "...though I might be aided and instructed by others, I must depend on myself as the only constant friend." (*Woman in the Nineteenth Century*)

 WRITING TOOLS
For prewriting, revision, and editing tools, visit the **Writing Center** at **ClassZone.com.**

KEY TRAITS

1. IDEAS
- Focuses on a single, well-defined **experience**
- Maintains a **balance** between describing the experience and explaining personal beliefs or ideas

2. ORGANIZATION
- Intrigues the reader with a fresh, original **introduction**
- Has a clear **sequence**
- **Concludes** by summarizing the **significance** of the experience

3. VOICE
- Has an individual **style** that shows the writer's beliefs and personality
- Maintains a **tone** that is appropriate for the audience, purpose, and subject matter

4. WORD CHOICE
- **Re-creates** the experience for the reader by using elements such as figurative language, sensory details, or dialogue

5. SENTENCE FLUENCY
- Structures sentences using the **active voice**

6. CONVENTIONS
- Employs **correct grammar and usage**

Part 1: Analyze a Student Model

Ashley Jackson
Carlisle High School

Learning to Trust Myself

What has eight legs and only one head? The answer is a group of four girls in middle school. At least that was true of the group I formed four years ago with my so-called friends Annie, Selina, and Madison. Although I didn't realize it at the time, I understand now that from the moment we
5 banded together in seventh grade, it was a disaster in the making.

Looking back on that year, I see four girls who regarded being alone as a dreaded disease. We did everything together, including shopping, going to games and dances, and doing homework. Whenever one of us had to go somewhere or needed something, it meant that all of us did. "We're all in
10 this together," we would say.

Unfortunately, our togetherness extended into some dark corners. One night, Annie stole money from her mother's wallet, and we all went to LaRusso's Pizza and spent it. When Madison lost her math book, we chatted with Jason Villalta while she swiped his book, and he ended up
15 paying the fine for lost school property. We laughed about these events as if they were amusing or unimportant, but they bothered me. Still, we never visited the land of separate opinions. We were unanimous about our ideas, or we kept them to ourselves.

One night, Selina's mom dropped us off at Crosstown Mall. We spent
20 most Friday nights there, and this one was no different until Annie smirked at Selina and said, "I dare you to steal a pair of sunglasses off that cart in front of Bath & Bubble!"

Selina laughed and said, "Why should I do that?"

Annie answered, "Well, when you bring the glasses back, then you get
25 to dare someone else! We'll play a game and see who's chicken first."

Did Selina hesitate? When I reflect on that moment, I want to believe that she did. Nevertheless, she smiled and said, "No problem, Annie!" Then

KEY TRAITS IN ACTION

Surprising, unusual **introduction** helps to create a distinctive writing **style.**

The entire essay strikes a **balance** between retelling and reflecting. (The reflective parts of this paragraph are highlighted.)

Focuses on a single, well-defined **experience** (a conflict among friends) and relates it in the **active voice.**

Uses **dialogue** to **re-create** the experience.

the three of us stared dumbfounded as she shoplifted a pair of sunglasses. After showing them to us, she dropped them in the trash, clearly very
30 pleased with herself, and then she pointed triumphantly to me.

"Ashley, you are next, girl!" she grinned. "How 'bout you get me one of those little pink bears off the Cuddle Teddy cart?"

"I don't think so," I said, as shy as a mouse trying to please a cat.

"Oh, but you *do* think so," Selina crooned. "I can just *tell* you think so.
35 And, hey, we're all in this together," she added.

Quickly sizing up the cart, I noticed that the woman who ran it had only a limited view of all the goods she sold. With the throngs of kids and shoppers around, the woman wouldn't notice if I grabbed something small and inconsequential from the far edge. Almost as if I were hypnotized, I
40 turned and started walking toward the cart.

When I got there, however, I just kept going. I didn't want a pink teddy bear, I didn't want to play this juvenile game, and, most of all, I didn't want to steal. Knowing that I was leaving my so-called friends forever, I took out my cell phone and asked my dad to take me home.

45 In school the next Monday, Selina, Annie, and Madison taunted me. For a few days, they hissed "Chicken!" and made little "bawk, bawk, bawk" sounds when they saw me, but soon they acted as if I didn't exist. It was a long time before I made new friends or felt a sense of belonging.

Presents a clear **sequence** of events.

Eventually, however, I began to feel proud of being independent. Over
50 time, I met other people who weren't scared to be alone. I gradually realized that the friendships I formed with these people weren't mindless loyalty pacts; instead, they were built on mutual respect.

Uses a serious **tone** that is appropriate to the topic.

That day at the mall marked the beginning of my adult life. On that day, I had to make a decision that mattered, and I had to make it alone. I
55 trusted myself then to distinguish between my values and those that others wanted to impose on me, and I stayed true to myself. I still trust myself to know the difference between right and wrong.

Explores the **significance** of the experience in the **conclusion**.

2

Part 2: Apply the Writing Process

PREWRITING

What Should I Do?	What Does It Look Like?

1. Travel to your past to find a topic.
To go back in time, look through your old photographs, ticket stubs, Weblog entries, and souvenirs. Or use a chart like this one to trigger memories. Highlight the experience you want to write about.

TIP If you can't think of an event to write about, reread the bulleted lists under each prompt on page 474.

Types of Experiences	My Experiences
a victory or a defeat	won the camp diving contest
an incident that strongly affected me	volunteered at a soup kitchen
a conflict	realized I had to say no to my friends when they started shoplifting

2. Freewrite about the experience.
Your freewriting might include what you said, what others said, your feelings, and even the sounds, sights, and smells of the experience. To refresh your memory, consider interviewing a friend or family member who was present. See page ooo for interviewing tips.

TIP If your story is too personal to share with an audience, choose a different topic from the chart you created in step 1.

It was a Friday night . . . the mall was really crowded . . . lots of kids running around, crabby shoppers . . . I can still hear the stupid tinkly music they used to play there . . . Selina walked up to one of those carts and grabbed a pair of sunglasses. Nobody even saw her . . . except us!!
She looked so proud of herself.
Then she dumped the glasses in the trash and pointed to me.

3. Reflect on why the experience matters to you.
Put your topic to the test before you start drafting. Ask yourself:
- Will this event interest my audience?
- Was it truly meaningful in my life?
- What did I learn?
- How did I change?

Try using a chart like this one.

What Happened?	Why Does It Matter?
I hung out with three friends.	I stopped being myself; I was scared to be on my own.
My friends dared me to shoplift.	I had to decide which was more important: honesty or popularity.
I refused to steal.	I learned to be independent. I started to grow up.

DRAFTING

What Should I Do?	**What Does It Look Like?**

1. Outline your essay.
You have two important goals in this essay: to retell an experience and to explain what you learned from it. Creating an outline can help you meet both requirements. Here is one basic plan for a reflective essay:

- Introduce the issue, hinting at the lesson you learned.
- Retell the experience.
- Reflect on how you have changed.

Notice how the writer of this outline balanced reflection and retelling.

TIP Make sure your outline includes a clear sequence of events. Your reader shouldn't have to ask what happened or when events took place.

▶

Intro:
  1. Get audience attention.
  2. Reflect on what I understand now: that group was not good for me.

Body:
  1. Describe who we were.
  2. Reflect on what being together all the time meant, including doing sneaky things.
  3. Describe the night at the mall.
    A. Annie suggests an "I dare you" game.
    B. Selina takes the dare, then dares me.
    C. I walk away.
  4. Describe and reflect on what happened after.

Conclusion: Reflect on how the experience changed me.

2. Craft a stylish introduction.
Your introduction should grab your reader's attention and hint at your overall reflection about the experience. Consider including a surprising contrast, a memorable description, or a joke, a riddle, or some other bit of humor.

▶

Contrast
Crosstown Mall is a brightly lit, busy place where dark deeds can occur.

Humor
What has eight legs and only one head? The answer is a group of four girls in middle school.

3. Include the thoughts and feelings you experienced at the time.
Avoid a bare-bones account: "First I did this, then I did that." Instead, describe what you thought and how you felt. Consider using **interior monologue**—presenting your thoughts as you might have said them to yourself.

▶

Writer's thoughts and feelings
I noticed that the woman who ran the cart had only a limited view of what she sold. Almost as if I were hypnotized, I turned and started walking toward the cart.

Interior monologue
Could I really do this? I asked myself.

REVISING AND EDITING

What Should I Do?	*What Does It Look Like?*

1. Show, don't tell.
- Reread your draft, looking for vivid descriptions.
- If your writing seems boring, consider adding similes (comparisons that use *like* or *as*) or metaphors (comparisons that do not use *like* or *as*).

See page 111: Literary Analysis: Figurative Language

▶

Tells: *"I don't think so," I said, scared.*

Shows with a simile: *"I don't think so," I said, as shy as a mouse trying to please a cat.*

Tells: *We never disagreed.*

Shows with a metaphor: *We never visited the land of separate opinions.*

2. Use the active voice.
- ⬭ (Circle) examples of the passive voice.
- To make your essay livelier, use the active voice whenever possible.

TIP Passive voice is acceptable when the doer of the action is not important (The house *was built* in 1920) or when the doer is unknown (The money *was stolen* last night).

▶

They bothered me.
I was bothered by them.

We kept our ideas to ourselves.
Our ideas were kept to ourselves.

3. Keep a consistent tone.
- Have a peer reader draw a ▭ box around passages that shift in tone. For example, parts of your essay may contain too much slang or jargon.
- Decide whether your overall tone is appropriate to your topic. For example, if you are writing about a tragic event, your tone should be serious.

See page 480: Ask a Peer Reader

▶

When I got there, however, I just kept going.
Then it totally hit me: no way was I gonna do this! I was SO out of there. I didn't want . . .

Quickly sizing up the cart,
Hastily assessing the parameters of my hypothetical mission, I noticed . . .

4. Make sure your conclusion specifies why the experience matters.
- Avoid vague or overused statements such as "It's hard to grow up" or "Honesty is the best policy."
- Make your conclusion forceful and specific.

▶

That day at the mall marked the beginning of my adult life. On that day, I had to make a decision that mattered, and I had to make it alone. I trusted myself then to distinguish between my values and those that others wanted to impose on me, and I stayed true to myself. I still trust myself to know the difference between right and wrong.

Apply the Rubric

A strong reflective essay . . .

- ☑ has a creative, attention-getting introduction
- ☑ retells a single experience and reflects on why it was important
- ☑ keeps a balance between retelling and reflecting
- ☑ makes people, places, and events vivid by using dialogue, figurative language, or sensory details
- ☑ presents a clear sequence
- ☑ has an appropriate tone
- ☑ has a fresh, individual style
- ☑ uses the active voice
- ☑ ends with a summary of the event's significance

Ask a Peer Reader

- In your own words, why was this experience significant to me?
- How would you describe my tone?
- Where could I use more or better dialogue, figurative language, or sensory details?

Check Your Grammar

- When you write dialogue, enclose each speaker's words in quotation marks. Each time the speaker changes, begin a new paragraph.

> "I don't think so," I said, as shy as a mouse trying to please a cat.
> "Oh, but you _do_ think so," Selina crooned.

- End punctuation goes inside the quotation marks.

> "Why should I do that?"

See page R54: Quick Reference: Punctuation

- For events from the past, maintain the past tense. For present-day reflections, however, you may need to use the present tense.

> **Consistent Past:**
> I noticed that the woman who ran the cart had only a limited view of all the goods she sold. I saw the throngs of kids and shoppers.
> **Present:**
> I still trust myself to know the difference between right and wrong.

See pages R59–R60: Verb Tense

Writing On|ine

PUBLISHING OPTIONS
For publishing options, visit the **Writing Center** at ClassZone.com.

ASSESSMENT PREPARATION
For writing and grammar assessment practice, go to the **Assessment Center** at ClassZone.com.

Conducting an Interview

Conducting an interview can help you recall your own history. It can also allow you to discover another person's perspective of a past event.

Planning the Interview

1. **Choose someone to interview.** You might interview someone who experienced an important event with you or someone who lived through an exciting historical event or time.
2. **Seek permission.** Begin by explaining your purpose and the incident or topic you want to focus on. Then set up a time and place. You can interview someone by telephone, by e-mail, by fax, or in person. Choose a setting that has few distractions. If you want to make a video or audio recording of the interview, discuss that in advance with your interviewee.
3. **Plan ahead.** First, research or reflect on the topic so you know enough to ask interesting questions. Then write down some open-ended questions. Such questions cannot be answered with a simple yes or no. Instead, they ask why or say, "Tell me about when . . . ," and ideally they lead to full, rich answers.

Conducting the Interview

1. **Ask your planned questions, and follow up when necessary.** Ask about facts before asking about personal matters and opinions. Whenever you receive a particularly interesting answer, you can always add, "Could you tell me more about that?"
2. **Inquire about photographs and other items.** Ask if your interviewee has any photographs, newspaper clippings, awards, or other items related to the topic of your interview. These mementoes can improve your understanding of the topic and the person.

See pages R85–R86: Interviews

Reading Comprehension

DIRECTIONS *Read these poems and answer the questions that follow.*

A Dream Within a Dream

Edgar Allan Poe

Take this kiss upon the brow!
And, in parting from you now,
Thus much let me avow—
You are not wrong, who deem
5 That my days have been a dream;
Yet if Hope has flown away
In a night, or in a day,
In a vision, or in none,
Is it therefore the less *gone*?
10 *All* that we see or seem
Is but a dream within a dream.

I stand amid the roar
Of a surf-tormented shore,
And I hold within my hand
15 Grains of the golden sand—
How few! yet how they creep
Through my fingers to the deep,
While I weep—while I weep!
O God! can I not grasp
20 Them with a tighter clasp?
O God! can I not save
One from the pitiless wave?
Is *all* that we see or seem
But a dream within a dream?

The Fire of Driftwood

Henry Wadsworth Longfellow

Devereux Farm near Marblehead

We sat within the farmhouse old,
    Whose windows, looking o'er the bay,
Gave to the sea-breeze damp and cold,
    An easy entrance, night and day.

5 Not far away we saw the port,
    The strange, old-fashioned, silent town,
The lighthouse, the dismantled fort,
    The wooden houses, quaint and brown.

We sat and talked until the night,
10   Descending, filled the little room;
Our faces faded from the sight,
    Our voices only broke the gloom.

We spake of many a vanished scene,
    Of what we once had thought and said,
15 Of what had been, and might have been,
    And who was changed, and who was dead;

And all that fills the hearts of friends,
    When first they feel, with secret pain,
Their lives thenceforth have separate ends,
20   And never can be one again;

The first slight swerving of the heart,
    That words are powerless to express,
And leave it still unsaid in part,
    Or say it in too great excess.

25 The very tones in which we spake
    Had something strange, I could but mark;
The leaves of memory seemed to make
    A mournful rustling in the dark.

Oft died the words upon our lips,
30   As suddenly, from out the fire
Built of the wreck of stranded ships,
    The flames would leap and then expire.

And, as their splendor flashed and failed,
    We thought of wrecks upon the main,
35 Of ships dismasted, that were hailed
    And sent no answer back again.

The windows, rattling in their frames,
    The ocean, roaring up the beach,
The gusty blast, the bickering flames,
40   All mingled vaguely in our speech;

Until they made themselves a part
   Of fancies floating through the brain,
The long-lost ventures of the heart,
    That send no answers back again.

45 O flames that glowed! O hearts that yearned!
   They were indeed too much akin,
The driftwood fire without that burned,
    The thoughts that burned and glowed within.

Comprehension

DIRECTIONS *Answer these questions about "A Dream Within a Dream."*

1. Which statement is the best paraphrase of lines 6–9?

  A There is no time left to hope for the future.

  B Some people have hope, while others have none.

  C If you are not careful, hope can disappear overnight.

  D Once hope has disappeared, it doesn't matter how it was lost.

2. Which lines contain internal rhyme?

  A lines 1–2

  B lines 4–5

  C lines 10–11

  D lines 21–22

3. In lines 7–8, the repetition of the words "in a" calls attention to

  A shifting moods

  B contrasting images

  C childlike expressions

  D symbolic meanings

4. The "pitiless wave" in line 22 most likely symbolizes the

  A passage of time

  B changing shoreline

  C force of a storm

  D speaker's thoughts

5. Which line best expresses the melancholy mood of the poem?

  A "Take this kiss upon the brow!" (line 1)

  B "In a night, or in a day" (line 7)

  C "Grains of the golden sand" (line 15)

  D "While I weep—while I weep!" (line 18)

DIRECTIONS *Answer these questions about "The Fire of Driftwood."*

6. Longfellow's poem is written in tetrameter lines. Each line contains how many feet?

  A two   **C** four

  B three   **D** five

7. The first two stanzas establish the

  A symbolism   **C** main theme

  B setting   **D** speaker's identity

8. Which idea about friendship is expressed in lines 17–24?

   A Friends communicate best by sitting together quietly.

   B Grievances among friends are hard to resolve.

   C It is sad to realize that friends have grown apart.

   D People find comfort in talking with old friends.

9. Which line best conveys the melancholy mood of "The Fire of Driftwood"?

   A "An easy entrance, night and day" (line 4)

   B "The wooden houses, quaint and brown" (line 8)

   C "The ocean, roaring up the beach" (line 38)

   D "The long-lost ventures of the heart" (line 43)

10. Which statement most accurately paraphrases lines 27–28?

   "The leaves of memory seemed to make
     A mournful rustling in the dark."

   A Dried leaves made a sad sound.

   B Darkness brought on vivid memories.

   C The best memories were from long ago.

   D The friends were haunted by memories.

11. The "wreck of stranded ships" in line 31 most likely symbolizes

   A losses in life   **C** sinister forces

   B wasted lives   **D** desires for adventure

12. The alliteration of the phrase "fancies floating" in line 42 suggests the sound of a

   A pounding wave   **C** gentle breeze

   B gathering storm   **D** crackling fire

13. Which line contains an example of onomatopoeia?

   A "Our faces faded from the sight" (line 11)

   B "And who was changed, and who was dead" (line 16)

   C "The windows, rattling in their frames" (line 37)

   D "O flames that glowed! O hearts that yearned!" (line 45)

DIRECTIONS *Answer this question about both poems.*

14. Which setting do both poets use to create a mournful mood?

   A farmhouse   **C** campfire

   B seashore   **D** dream

Written Response

SHORT RESPONSE *Write three or four sentences to answer each question.*

15. Which of the two poems has a more varied rhyme scheme, stanza structure, and meter? Give an example of these devices from each poem to support your answer.

16. What effect does Poe achieve in "A Dream Within a Dream" by repeating the statement in lines 10–11 as a question at the end of the poem?

EXTENDED RESPONSE *Write two or three paragraphs to answer this question.*

17. What might the grains of sand and the driftwood symbolize in the two poems? Support your ideas with details from the poems.

GO ON ➡

Writing & Grammar

DIRECTIONS *Read this passage and answer the questions that follow.*

> (1) The honeybee is well known for its production of honey and beeswax. (2) But it is also esteemed for its exceptional memory and its language system, which is complex. (3) The honeybee has an excellent short-term memory. (4) It remembers where the best food sources are, knows when their quality is best, and they will seek out these sources. (5) The honeybee locates these food sources by remembering the color and scent of the flowers. (6) The honeybee forms a short-term memory of the flower's color. (7) It converts this initial memory to a long-term memory through a biological process. (8) Even after winter hibernation, these foragers go right to the flowers they visited the summer before. (9) One group of honeybees was even able to fly through a maze!

1. How might you add a participle to sentence 1?

 A Change "The honeybee" to "The industrious honeybee."

 B Change "is well known" to "is often known."

 C Change "its production" to "its complicated production."

 D Change "honey and beeswax" to "sweet honey and beeswax."

2. How might you best rewrite sentence 2 to make its elements parallel?

 A But it is also renowned for its exceptional memory and complex language system.

 B But it is also renowned for its exceptional memory; also, its language system is complex.

 C But it is also renowned for its exceptional memory and has a language system that is complex.

 D But it is also renowned for its memory, which is exceptional, and it has a complex language system.

3. How might you add details to sentence 3 by using an adjective clause?

 A The small honeybee has an excellent short-term memory.

 B The honeybee has an excellent short-term memory, which scientists have studied in great detail.

 C To learn about the honeybee's short-term memory, scientists have studied it in great detail.

 D Scientists have carefully studied the honeybee's excellent short-term memory.

4. How might you best rewrite sentence 4 to make its elements parallel?

 A It remembers where the best food sources are and knows when their quality is best and will seek out these sources.

 B It remembers where the best food sources are, knows when their quality is best, and seeks out these sources.

 C It remembers the best food locations, knowing when their quality is best, seeking out these sources.

 D Remembering the best food sources, they know when their quality is best, and they will seek out these sources.

5. How might you add details to sentence 5 by using an adjective clause?

A The honeybee dutifully locates these food sources by remembering the color and scent of the flowers.

B The honeybee locates these food sources by remembering the rich color and aromatic scent of the flowers.

C The honeybee locates these food sources by remembering the color and scent of the flowers that provide the best pollen and nectar.

D The honeybee locates these food sources by remembering the best pollen and nectar food sources and the color and scent of the flowers.

6. How might you change sentence 6 to include a participial phrase?

A In its approach to the flower, the honeybee forms a short-term memory of its color.

B As it approaches the flower, the honeybee forms a short-term memory of its color.

C The honeybee approaches the flower and forms a short-term memory of its color.

D Approaching the flower, the honeybee forms a short-term memory of its color.

7. How might you add details to sentence 7 by using an adjective clause?

A It converts this initial memory to a long-term memory by cleverly using a biological process.

B Like many mammals, it converts this initial memory to long-term memory through a biological process.

C It converts this initial memory to long-term memory through a biological process that is similar to memory formation in higher mammals.

D Through a biological process, it converts this initial memory to a long-term memory and uses it to navigate to various food sources.

8. How might you add a participle to sentence 8?

A Change "winter hibernation" to "a long, cold hibernation."

B Change "these foragers" to "these emerging foragers."

C Change "go right to the flowers" to "go directly to the flowers."

D Change "they visited the summer before" to "they remember from last summer."

9. How might you add a participial phrase to sentence 9?

A One group of honeybees even followed a trail of dots and was able to fly through a maze!

B Following a trail of dots, one group of honeybees was even able to fly through a maze!

C A trail of dots was used by one group of honeybees to learn how to fly through a maze!

D One large group of honeybees followed a trail of dots through a maze!

STOP

Ideas for Independent Reading

Continue exploring the Questions of the Times with these additional works.

Is the price of progress ever TOO HIGH?

Rip Van Winkle and Other Stories
by Washington Irving

Behind the high jinks and folklore of the stories in this collection, there lurks a mingled sense of wonder and worry at the rapid changes taking place in America in the early 19th century. In the title tale, for example, Rip Van Winkle falls asleep in a British colony and wakes 20 years later in a new nation, his village's statue of King George replaced with one of George Washington. With insight and humor, Irving makes a profound social comment on the changes taking place in his time.

The Last of the Mohicans
by James Fenimore Cooper

The hero of this story, Natty Bumppo, lives on the borderline between two cultures—admired by both Indians and whites, but truly at home with neither. Here, Natty and his Indian friend Chingachgook escort two British maidens through hostile territory during the French and Indian War. Breathtaking chases and gun battles ensue. Yet through the course of the story a deeper theme emerges: that the United States, in its desire for wealth, may have forsaken the rewards of living in harmony with nature.

Is it patriotic to protest one's GOVERNMENT?

Uncle Tom's Cabin
by Harriet Beecher Stowe

Written toward the end of the romantic period, Stowe's novel changed history. Appalled by the institution of slavery, Stowe set out to make whites see slaves as human beings—mothers, fathers, children, *people* with hearts and souls like any other. Her work became immensely popular and did in fact influence opinions and garner support for the abolitionist movement. Indeed, the novel had so great an impact that it has often been cited as one of the causes of the Civil War.

The Night Thoreau Spent in Jail
by Jerome Lawrence and Robert E. Lee

Issues of moral and civic responsibility take center stage in this play dramatizing the risks Thoreau took to follow his conscience. As the curtain rises, Thoreau is behind bars—his punishment for committing an act of civil disobedience. When Ralph Waldo Emerson visits, Thoreau challenges him to defy a government that fosters injustice.

The Poetry of John Greenleaf Whittier: A Readers' Edition
by John Greenleaf Whittier

John Greenleaf Whittier was committed to using poetry to bring about social reform. This anthology includes several poems that explore the evils of slavery. One such poem, "Ichabod," savaged real-life senator Daniel Webster for his support of the Missouri Compromise and the Fugitive Slave Act.

Does everyone have a "DARK SIDE"?

The Fall of the House of Usher and Other Writings
by Edgar Allan Poe

Does everyone have a "dark side"? Over and over again, Poe answered that question with a resounding yes. In so doing, he helped establish the modes of horror and fantasy, which to this day dominate much of American culture. For an overview of the best of Poe's writing, this edition is the book to read. Murderous delusions, decadent appetites, and unspeakable cruelty pepper the stories and poems found here.

The House of the Seven Gables
by Nathaniel Hawthorne

This gothic romance tells of the Pyncheon family (owners of "the house of the seven gables"), whose ancestor Colonel Pyncheon has cursed them with his wicked deeds. In the book's preface, Hawthorne conveys its theme: "The wrong-doing of one generation lives into the successive ones, and . . . becomes a pure and uncontrollable mischief."

American Gothic Tales
edited by Joyce Carol Oates

Oates's anthology of haunting tales shows the far reaches of the gothic imagination in American literature. The collection includes short stories from over 40 of the best American horror writers of the past 200 years, ranging from Washington Irving to Stephen King.

Where do people look for TRUTH?

The Portable Thoreau
by Henry David Thoreau

An icon of individualism, Henry David Thoreau looked for the truth in two main places: nature and himself. Generations of readers have concluded not only that those are good places to search for the truth, but also that Thoreau—for all his peculiarities—did a fine job of finding it. This edition contains the full text of *Walden,* as well as poems, notebooks, journal entries, and essays such as "Civil Disobedience." These works allow readers to see past the confident sage of Walden to the prickly, affectionate, politically motivated man beneath.

The Essential Transcendentalists
edited by Richard G. Geldard

America's best transcendentalist thinkers and writers grappled with many questions of their day: What is woman's role in society? When and how should a person protest the government? How can we live ethical lives? Where can one find the truth? The works in this collection explore these and many other ideas as relevant today as they were nearly 200 years ago.

UNIT 3

Preview Unit Goals

LITERARY ANALYSIS	• Understand the historical and cultural contexts of romanticism and realism; understand realism as a literary movement
	• Analyze tone
	• Analyze and evaluate free verse
	• Analyze elements of style, including tone, sentence structure, figurative language, and dialogue
	• Analyze the styles of Whitman and Dickinson
	• Analyze narrative elements, including conflict and characterization
	• Analyze the relationship between audience and form and the ways in which form influences a message
READING	• Analyze primary sources
	• Analyze author's purpose and beliefs; analyze structure of a work
	• Take notes; synthesize information
WRITING AND GRAMMAR	• Make effective word choices; use vivid verbs
	• Use language that conveys tone
	• Write a biographical narrative
SPEAKING, LISTENING, AND VIEWING	• Compare and contrast print and film versions of a work
	• Produce a video documentary
VOCABULARY	• Use knowledge of Latin roots to understand word meaning
ACADEMIC VOCABULARY	• romanticism • free verse • primary source
	• realism • style

Literature and Reading Center
Writing Center
Vocabulary Center

From Romanticism to Realism

Frederick Douglass

1855–1870
AN AGE OF TRANSITION

- Brilliant Mavericks: Whitman and Dickinson
- Literature of the Civil War

Questions of the Times

DISCUSS After reading these questions and talking about them with a partner, share your views with the class as a whole. Then read on to explore the ways in which writers of the Civil War era dealt with the same issues.

What DIVIDES *a nation?*

In the years leading up to the Civil War, the agrarian South, whose economy depended upon slave labor, and the industrialized North, which became increasingly opposed to slavery, began to see each other as enemies. Slavery was one of many issues that divided Americans of the day. What issues or beliefs typically cause conflict between citizens? What divides Americans today?

Is anything worth DYING FOR?

During the Civil War, boys and young men on both sides of the conflict marched off to war with visions of becoming heroes in the service of a great cause. Hundreds of thousands never returned home. Was their sacrifice worthwhile? Would you ever be willing to risk your life for a flag, a group, or an idea?

Why do people BREAK RULES?

Poets Walt Whitman and Emily Dickinson broke well-established rules about poetic form and content, and today they are celebrated for their ingenuity. Yet, during their lives few readers recognized their genius because their work was radically different from the popular poetry of the day. Why do you think people break the rules if they will not be rewarded for it? Do artists, especially, tend to break the rules?

Is it important to FACE REALITY?

After the horrors of the Civil War, romantic attitudes no longer captured the spirit of America. Instead, artists and writers turned to a new movement known as realism, which reflected a different view of life—unsentimental, honest, and often harsh or even ugly. Do you think writers and artists should deal with life's realities or take us away from them?

From Romanticism to Realism
1855–1870

An Age of Transition

The Civil War was a violent clash, not just of armies, but of ideas. Who was right, and who was wrong? What did it mean to be an American? Was any price too high to pay to keep the nation whole? There was nothing theoretical about the conflict—real people died, hundreds of thousands of them: fathers, sons, and brothers. But the war began before a single shot was ever fired. Writers served as its first soldiers, and the battle lines were drawn in ink.

Emerging Realism:
Historical Context

KEY IDEAS The central influence on literature of this period was
the conflict between North and South that ended in the Civil War.
Although romantic attitudes helped push the nation into war, four
years of bitter fighting led to a new realism.

A Cultural Divide

"A house divided against itself cannot stand," wrote **Abraham Lincoln** in
1858, referring to the bitterly divided United States. Since colonial times,
the South and the North had shown strong regional differences. Most
of the manufacturing and financial services of the nation were located in
the North, whose economy was based primarily on trade and industry. In
contrast, the South had developed an agricultural way of life—growing
cotton, tobacco, and sugar cane for export to the North and Europe—that
relied on the labor of nearly four million slaves. Most Southerners opposed
any interference with slavery by the federal government because of the
region's economic dependence on it, the widespread fear of slave unrest,
and the belief that states should control their own affairs.

SLAVERY DIVIDES THE NATION Although national political leaders tried
to sidestep the slavery issue, growing Northern opposition to slavery and its
expansion into the West made confrontation inevitable. In the 1850s, several
events moved the country to its breaking point. In Kansas, the vote over
whether to join the Union as a free state or a slave state turned deadly when
gun-toting mobs swarmed over the border from Missouri to cast illegal ballots
in favor of slavery. Continuing violence between proslavery and antislavery
settlers led people to begin calling the territory **Bleeding Kansas.** Abolitionist
John Brown played a role in Bleeding Kansas in 1856, killing five proslavery
men as revenge for the sacking of the antislavery town of Lawrence. Three
years later, Brown again shocked the nation when he led a bloody raid on
the federal arsenal at Harpers Ferry, hoping to spark a slave uprising. Writer
Henry David Thoreau called Brown "an angel of light"; but fellow writer
Nathaniel Hawthorne retorted, "No man was ever more justly hanged."

CONFLICT REACHES THE GOVERNMENT Even the floor of the U.S. Senate
became a battleground. In 1856, Massachusetts senator Charles Sumner
gave an impassioned speech against slavery, berating his colleagues for two
days for their support of slavery. A few days later, Carolina congressman
Preston S. Brooks retaliated by attacking Sumner with his cane, beating the
Massachusetts senator unconscious. When writer **William Cullen Bryant**
heard about the caning, he was outraged. "Has it come to this," he asked
in the *New York Evening Post,* "that we must speak with bated breath in the
presence of our Southern masters? . . . Are we, too, slaves, slaves for life, a

Battle for the Shenandoah © Mort Künstler, Inc.

target for their brutal blows, when we do not comport ourselves to please them?" Meanwhile, newspapers across the South applauded the attack, describing abolitionists as unruly dogs to be collared and disciplined. Such angry name-calling and accusations reflected—and added to—the growing sense on both sides that Northerners and Southerners were no longer simply Americans from different regions, but foreigners and enemies.

SOUTHERN CHIVALRY — ARGUMENT versus CLUB'S.

An 1856 cartoon of Congressman Preston S. Brooks attacking Senator Charles Sumner on the Senate floor.

In 1857, the Supreme Court entered the fray by hearing the case of **Dred Scott,** a slave whose owner had taken him to spend several years in a free state. Scott argued that living in a free state made him free; the Supreme Court ruled against him. Worse, it went on to say that even free blacks "had no rights which a white man was bound to respect." The *Dred Scott* decision sent shock waves through the already divided nation. Northerners were outraged and alarmed. Was the South's "peculiar institution" of slavery to become the law of the whole land?

The Civil War

Ironically, none of these acts led to the final break. Instead, the lawful election in 1860 of a politically moderate U.S. president, Abraham Lincoln ignited war. Enraged at Lincoln's pledge to stop the western spread of slavery, the Southern states seceded to form the **Confederate States of America.**

For a generation that had grown up on the literary ideal of the brave, dashing **Romantic hero,** the booming of Confederate cannons firing on Fort Sumter in the spring of 1861 was a call to glory. Boys and young men rushed off to join the Union or Confederate army. Southerners boasted that a single one of them could lick ten Yankees; Northerners were sure that "Johnny Reb" would turn and run at the first shot. For many, the biggest fear was that the war would end too soon and they would miss their chance to become heroes.

The mood was nearly festive on the sunny July day when fresh Union forces marched south into Virginia to confront the rebels at Bull Run. Soldiers wandered from their lines to pick blackberries and drink cool water from the creek, and the cream of Washington society drove down in carriages with bottles of champagne and picnic baskets to enjoy the spectacle.

REALITY STRIKES By late afternoon, thousands of dead and wounded soldiers lay near the banks of Bull Run. On the losing side, panic-stricken Union soldiers stumbled away from the battlefield, their feet tangling in shawls and parasols that had been dropped by terrified civilians as they fled. The party was over.

A Voice from the Times

Future years will never know the seething hell and the black infernal background of countless minor scenes and interiors, (not the official surface courteousness of the Generals, not the few great battles) . . . the real war will never get in the books.

—Walt Whitman

The blood-soaked **Battle of Bull Run** gave everyone (especially the losing Union side) a taste of the reality of war, but it was only the beginning. Four long years of fighting followed. Names of battle sites became synonymous with death: Shiloh, Antietam, Fredericksburg, Gettysburg, Vicksburg. When the war ended at last, in April 1865, with **General Robert E. Lee's** surrender to **General Ulysses S. Grant** at Appomattox Courthouse, approximately 618,000 men had died—nearly as many as have died in all other wars that the United States has ever fought. Much of the South lay in ruins, scarred by gutted plantation houses, burned bridges, and uprooted railroad lines.

Ideas of the Age

KEY IDEAS Americans in the postwar period embraced notions of freedom and unity. At the same time, they lost their taste for romanticism, having been confronted with the harsh realities of war.

Freedom and Unity

The United States was changed by the Civil War. It had suffered bitterly and was now a wiser, more somber nation. Yet the ideals of America's founders had survived the devastation of war. For the first time, the Declaration of Independence's notions of equality and liberty for all were brought closer to fruition. Slavery was dead— outlawed by Lincoln's bold **Emancipation Proclamation** and the **Thirteenth Amendment** to the Constitution. "We shout for joy that we live to record this righteous decree," said **Frederick Douglass.** "Free Forever!"

The Civil War had divided the country; its end brought the country back together. This time the country was united in a new way. Before the war, people were used to saying "The United States *are . . . ,*" with the emphasis on the individual states more than on the united interests of all. After the war, people began saying "The United States *is . . . .*" A group of independent states had become one nation, indivisible, with the goal of liberty for all.

The Civil War changed not only American society but its literary culture as well. In the years following the war, American readers and writers found they had lost their taste for romanticism. Many had witnessed war's grim nature firsthand, and it shaped their view of life. Gallant heroism and adventure no longer suited America's tastes; nor did meditations on the beauty of nature or the worth of the individual. Writing became more honest, unsentimental, and ironic. A new style, **realism,** would predominate in the years to come.

Abraham Lincoln Reading the Emancipation Proclamation Before His Cabinet Members, undated color illustration after painting by Francis Bicknell Carpenter. © Bettmann/Corbis.

Literature of the Times

KEY IDEAS The Civil War was a transitional period for writers of the day. Groundbreaking poets, former slaves, famous public figures and everyday people all contributed their ideas as the country and its literature moved from romanticism to realism.

Brilliant Mavericks: Whitman and Dickinson

In 1842, when the conflicts leading to the Civil War were just beginning to brew and the romantic movement was going strong, writer **Ralph Waldo Emerson** issued a challenge to America. The nation needed a poet worthy of itself—a truly fresh voice with limitless passion and originality. "I look in vain," lamented Emerson, "for the poet whom I describe. We do not with sufficient plainness, or sufficient profoundness, address ourselves to life. . . ." In the coming decades, two poets would answer Emerson's bold call: **Walt Whitman** and **Emily Dickinson.**

Outwardly, Whitman and Dickinson had little in common. Whitman, big, bearded, and outspoken, was always in the thick of things and wrote many poems about current issues and events, from the sad plight of the slave to the shocking assassination of President Lincoln. Dickinson, on the other hand, was shy and reclusive, living her whole life in her native New England, and finding inspiration for her poetry in her own thoughts.

RULE-BREAKERS The two, however, were not entirely unalike. Both felt hemmed in by conventional ideas of how poems ought to look and what poems ought to say. Both wrote poetry so radical in form and content that it took many years for readers to appreciate it. (In Dickinson's case, appreciation didn't come until after her death.) Together, they broke poetry wide open, creating the most remarkable work of the Civil War era.

In 1855, Whitman published at his own expense a book of poetry called *Leaves of Grass*. The book was small, but it contained a huge ambition. Whitman saw America as a great poem, the greatest in the world, and his job was to capture it on paper. A sprawling, rowdy, vigorous young nation, he believed, could not be squeezed into traditional poetic forms. Instead, he wrote in **free verse,** unconfined by formal patterns of rhyme and meter. His lines were loose and rambling, his language colorful and vigorous, and he refused to limit himself to "poetic" subjects. If it was a part of American life, it was his to write about, even if it was a topic others might consider common or vulgar.

Emily Dickinson also found traditional poetic forms inadequate. Yet, where Whitman's poems were expansive, hers were terse and compressed—a few brief lines packed with complex, original images. Her subject matter was intensely personal, and her themes

▶ *For Your Outline*

BRILLIANT MAVERICKS

- Whitman and Dickinson answered Emerson's call for a national poet.
- Whitman was gregarious and outspoken; Dickinson, shy and reclusive.
- Both broke conventional rules of poetry.
- Whitman used free verse to write about everything American.
- Dickinson used compressed lines and complex imagery to explore personal themes.
- Both poets can be seen as transitional.

Emily Dickinson

Walt Whitman

© Tom Gauld/Heart USA Inc.

were the great themes of life: love, death, immortality, and nature. Although she wrote nearly 1,800 poems, only a handful appeared in print during her lifetime. In fact, she was virtually unknown in her time, living a reclusive life that belied the intense creative fervor of her inner world.

Neither Dickinson nor Whitman can be easily categorized. Although Whitman can be considered a romantic poet because of his emphasis on individualism, emotion, and nature, his exploration of topics others found vulgar was certainly not romantic. Dickinson, too, could be aggressively unromantic, with her images of ordinary household items and her abrupt, unemotional tone. Perhaps both poets can be seen as transitional, moving with Americans of the day from romanticism to realism.

Literature of the Civil War

Of all human actions, none speaks so dramatically nor so violently as war. Of all wars, civil war by its very nature divides a nation's voice into factions. Among the diverse literary voices heard during the Civil War, some of the most powerful were African American.

Often at the urging of abolitionists, former slaves who escaped to the North published **slave narratives** detailing their experiences. These tales of suffering were immensely important to the cause of antislavery. Not simply autobiography, they were testimony, giving lie to Southern claims that slaves were happy and well-treated, that slavery was a "positive good" for both master and slave, and that people of African descent were inferior to whites. More than that, the narratives made readers *care* by showing that slaves were real human beings who suffered and wept and longed for freedom.

▶ *For Your Outline*

LITERATURE OF THE CIVIL WAR

- Slave narratives revealed the true nature of slavery and made readers care.
- Diaries and letters gave personal responses to historical events.
- Public documents influenced a large audience.
- Later fiction moved toward realism.

Fugitive slaves flee a Southern plantation at night in an attempt to reach the North.

Personal experience was central to the literature of the time, because everyday life now had great historical significance. Writers—male and female, white and black, from the highest-ranking general down to the common foot soldier—shared "their" Civil War in **diaries** and **letters**.

> **Voices from the Times**
>
> *Many times I sat down in the mud determined to go no further, and willing to die to end my misery. But soon a friend would pass and urge me to make another effort, and I would stagger a mile further.*
>
> **—Union soldier Elisha Rhodes**
>
> *I daily part with my raiment for food. We find no one who will exchange eatables for Confederate money. So we are devouring our clothes.*
>
> **—Southern diarist Mary Chesnut**

While these writers addressed their words to friends and family (or even to themselves), others, such as President **Abraham Lincoln,** wrote for a larger audience. Still, Lincoln underestimated the reach of his words. "The world will little note, nor long remember, what we say here," he proclaimed in his **Gettysburg Address,** which in fact proved to be one of the most enduring works of the Civil War era.

Lincoln's speech, with its inspiring message and elevated language, represents the highest ideals of the period. The fiction created after the war by realistic writers such as **Ambrose Bierce** and **Stephen Crane,** however, shows the period in a harsher light. Their stories focus on the human tragedy of a war that destroyed hundreds of thousands of American lives, even as it freed many more.

In the years to come, **realism** would grow and refine itself to include the work of writers countrywide, from the frozen arctic north of Jack London to the plains of Willa Cather's frontier. It would develop to include the work of naturalist writers who viewed human beings as passive victims of their environment. Brought on by the brutalities of the Civil War, realism would become the form that to some extent still dominates American literature today.

THE ARTISTS' GALLERY

Prisoners from the Front (1866), Winslow Homer. Oil on canvas, 24″ × 38″. The Metropolitan Museum of Art, Gift of Mrs. Frank B. Porter, 1922 (22.207). Photo © 1995 The Metropolitan Museum of Art, New York.

Winslow Homer

Known for his bold technique and unsentimental style, **Winslow Homer** was one of the most admired artists of the 19th century. He first rose to acclaim during the Civil War.

Behind Union Lines When war broke out, *Harper's Weekly* sent Homer south, to draw illustrations for the magazine. The young artist camped out with the Union army and shared the soldiers' hardships, from meager rations to the deadly threat of typhoid fever.

Homer rarely drew a battle scene, spurning the romantic elements of high drama and heroism. Instead, he recorded the reality of everyday life in camp—the boredom and sadness of men far from home. In 1863, a critic praised him as "the first of our artists who has endeavored to tell us any truth about the war."

Civil War Masterpiece At first glance, the painting shown here might seem like nothing special, just soldiers standing in an empty field. Yet *Prisoners from the Front*, painted just after the war ended, won acclaim as the most powerful painting of the war. Why?

For Americans, this work had a deep symbolic meaning. In the soldiers, Homer conveys two opposing worldviews: the romantic, long-haired Southern officer confronts his Northern counterpart, who eyes him coolly. Behind them, the devastated landscape of the South tells the story of how the Civil War ends.

Connecting Literature, History, and Culture

As you read this timeline and answer the questions on the next page, think about the ways in which American literature was influenced by—and itself influenced—national and world events.

AMERICAN LITERARY MILESTONES

1855

1855 Frederick Douglass's autobiographical slave narrative, *My Bondage and My Freedom*, is published; Walt Whitman publishes the first edition of *Leaves of Grass* at his own expense.

1857 The *Atlantic Monthly*, a journal of literature and opinion, is founded. Over the years, Emerson, Longfellow, and other writers and editors will contribute to the magazine.

1859

1859 Henry David Thoreau writes "A Plea for Captain John Brown," in which he refers to the condemned abolitionist as "an angel of light."

1861 The first autobiography by a formerly enslaved woman, Harriet Jacobs's *Incidents in the Life of a Slave Girl*, is published. ▶

1862 Emily Dickinson writes 366 poems within the year.

HISTORICAL CONTEXT

1855

1856 Preston S. Brooks beats Massachusetts senator Charles Sumner with a cane on the floor of the Senate in retaliation for Sumner's antislavery speech.

1857 Supreme Court's *Dred Scott* decision declares that slaves and former slaves are not U.S. citizens and thus not entitled to basic rights. ▶

1859

1859 Abolitionist John Brown is hanged for treason after leading a raid on the federal arsenal at Harpers Ferry.

1860 Abraham Lincoln is elected president; in response, South Carolina secedes from the Union, followed eventually by ten other Southern states.

1861 Confederate guns fire on Fort Sumter, launching the Civil War. ▶

WORLD CULTURE AND EVENTS

1855

1855 British nurse Florence Nightingale introduces hygienic standards into military hospitals during the Crimean War. ▶

1856 Two states of Australia introduce the voting procedure known as the Australian, or secret, ballot.

1857 Indians rebel against British occupation of the subcontinent.

1859

1859 British naturalist Charles Darwin publishes *Origin of Species*, giving his theory of evolution.

1861 Czar Alexander II of Russia frees serfs; in England, Charles Dickens publishes *Great Expectations*.

1862 French physicist Jean Foucault calculates the speed of light; Victor Hugo publishes *Les Misérables*.

MAKING CONNECTIONS

- What examples do you see of American writers being influenced by political events?
- What evidence shows that the nation was sharply divided before the Civil War?
- How did African Americans contribute to the literary culture of America during this period?
- What important scientific theories and discoveries arose during this period?

1863

1863 Abraham Lincoln delivers Gettysburg Address. ▶

1864 The *New Orleans Tribune,* one of the first daily newspapers produced by African Americans, begins publication.

1865 Walt Whitman pens his classic ode to Abraham Lincoln, "When Lilacs Last in the Dooryard Bloom'd."

1867

1867 Mark Twain publishes *The Celebrated Jumping Frog of Calaveras County, and Other Sketches.*

1868 Part 1 of *Little Women,* Louisa May Alcott's classic novel about four sisters, is published. ▶

1870 Bret Harte publishes story collection *The Luck of Roaring Camp and Other Sketches.*

1863

1863 Lincoln signs Emancipation Proclamation; the 54th Massachusetts Volunteer Infantry, one of the first African-American regiments, is founded. ▶

1864 Union general William Tecumseh Sherman marches from Atlanta to the Atlantic Ocean.

1865 Civil War ends; Lincoln is assassinated; 13th Amendment abolishes slavery.

1867

1867 United States buys Alaska from Russia.

1868 Congress passes 14th Amendment, prohibiting discrimination against African Americans.

1869 The hammering of a golden spike at Promontory Point, Utah, marks completion of the transcontinental railroad. ▼

1870 The first African-American senator, Hiram R. Revels, takes his seat.

1863

1863 Leo Tolstoy publishes *War and Peace.*

1864 Louis Pasteur invents pasteurization.

1865 Telegraph cable is laid across the Atlantic Ocean. ▶

1866 Fyodor Dostoyevsky publishes *Crime and Punishment.*

1867

1868 Remains of Cro-Magnon man discovered in Europe; Meiji era in Japan begins period of modernization.

1869 Suez Canal is completed in Egypt.

1870 After a troubled reign, Queen Isabella II of Spain abdicates throne in favor of her son, Alfonso XII.

UNIT 3

The Legacy of the Era

War Stories

Before the Civil War, most American writers depicted war romantically, focusing on the glory of a battle, the justness of a cause, or the heroism of a leader. Later, writers such as Stephen Crane began to depict war in all its grim reality, uncovering the daily discomforts of military life, the horrors of the battlefield, and the lasting and unexpected consequences of war. Americans today are still drawn to war stories of all kinds.

DISCUSS As a class, discuss which elements in current war stories (novels, movies, TV shows, news reports) are realistic and which are romantic in nature. Give specific examples.

Steven Spielberg's 1998 movie *Saving Private Ryan* was noted for its realistic portrayal of battle.

Artistic Innovators

Who are the blue men in this picture, and what do they have to do with Walt Whitman and Emily Dickinson? The Blue Man Group is just one example of many current artistic innovators who can tip their hats to the mavericks of an earlier era: Whitman and Dickinson. Since Whitman and Dickinson's bold experiments with poetic form and content in the 19th century, writers, musicians, and artists have increasingly pushed the limits of what is considered art, broadening Americans' tastes and imaginations in the process.

QUICKWRITE With your classmates, list as many artistic innovators as you can think of from the Civil War period to today. What do they have in common? What value do they bring to our society?

African-American Influence

One lasting legacy of the Civil War period has been the rise of African Americans to leadership positions and levels of prominence. Beginning with abolitionists such as Sojourner Truth and Frederick Douglass, African Americans have made their way into all spheres of American public life, from politics, education, and the sciences to the arts and entertainment.

CREATE With a partner, create a poster high-lighting the achievements of three African American leaders today. Include photographs of three leaders who are working in different fields, and list their accomplishments along with quotations by or about each person.

From top, Scientist George Washington Carver, activist Rosa Parks, Senator Barack Obama, writer Maya Angelou, activist Martin Luther King Jr., media mogul Oprah Winfrey

Form and Content in Poetry

Do you think everything has already been said? Throughout American history, poets have prided themselves on finding new ways to say things, as well as inventing new poetic forms in which to say them.

Form and Function

All works of art have **form,** a particular organization of parts that makes a whole. In poetry, form is referred to as **poetic structure:** the way words are arranged in lines, lines are arranged in stanzas, and units of sound are organized to achieve rhythm and rhyme. In general, poetic forms fall into two categories, traditional and organic. Poems in **traditional form** follow certain fixed rules. For example, they can have a limited number of lines, a specified meter and rhyme scheme, and a definite structure. Such poems are also called **fixed form** poems and include the **sonnet,** the **ballad,** the **epic,** the **elegy,** the **ode,** the **villanelle,** and **blank verse.** Often, poets choose a form that fits the subject matter. For example, a sonnet was originally intended only for the subject of love. The great English poets, such as William Shakespeare and John Milton, used traditional poetic forms, as did many early American poets.

Engraving of Walt Whitman by Max Beerbohm, 1904

The **organic form** of poetry, also known as **irregular form,** developed in the early 19th century. The English romantic poets wanted more flexible verse forms to fit the new content of their poetry. Unlike traditional forms, which provide an ideal pattern for poems to follow, organic form takes its shape and pattern from the content of the poem itself. That is, the form of a poem "grows" naturally out of what the poem says. A poem in organic form may have meter and rhyme, but the poet may vary the rhythm and rhyme scheme in irregular and unexpected ways. In searching for ways to find new expression, several American poets, such as Walt Whitman and Emily Dickinson, began experimenting with organic form.

Poetic Form in Action

One way to understand the difference between traditional and organic forms is to compare the poetry of Henry Wadsworth Longfellow and Emily Dickinson. Longfellow was somewhat conventional in most of his poems, using a predictable alternating rhyme scheme and punctuation. The excerpted lines shown here from Longfellow's "Psalm of Life" have a regular meter (even the dash in the second line counts as an unstressed syllable).

Tell me not, in mournful numbers,   *a*

Life is but an empty dream!—   *b*

For the soul is dead that slumbers,   *a*

And things are not what they seem.   *b*

—Henry Wadsworth Longfellow, "A Psalm of Life"

Close Read

Note that the metrical pattern of this passage is **trochaic tetrameter** (four stressed syllables in a line, with each accent followed by an unstressed syllable). Study the pattern of rhythm in the first two lines, and then sound out and note the stressed and unstressed syllables in lines 3 and 4.

Now look at the first stanza of a poem by Dickinson. She also used meter and rhyme, but she added rhythmical variations, which characterize it as organic. The first line has four accents plus an unaccented dash, while the next three lines each has three accented syllables and is an **enjambed,** or **run-on,** line— a line that ends without a grammatical or normal speech pause.

My life closed twice before its close—   *a*

It yet remains to see   *b*

If Immortality unveil   *c*

A third event to me   *b*

—Emily Dickinson, "My life closed twice before its close"

Close Read

Notice the difference in rhythm between line 1 and lines 2–4. What effect does this shift have on the way the poem sounds? How might the change in rhythm emphasize the writer's meaning?

Free verse is an organic form that lacks regular meter and rhyme. Although free verse still has rhythm and may include an occasional rhyme within a line, it does not follow any strict rules. Like all forms of poetry, however, it may include a variety of sound devices, such as repetition and alliteration, to achieve a musical quality.

The great master of free verse in American poetry was Walt Whitman. At a time when American poetry followed traditional forms, Whitman went his own way and created a form that grew purely out of the ideas expressed. In this passage from "I Hear America Singing," notice the language and sound devices that create a poetic effect in sentences that are almost like those in prose.

I hear America singing, the varied carols I hear,
Those of mechanics, each one singing his as it should be blithe and strong,
The carpenter singing his as he measures his plank or beam,

—Walt Whitman, "I Hear America Singing"

Close Read

Examine and compare the three examples on this page. How do they vary in content?

Selected Poetry

by Walt Whitman

Walt Whitman
1819–1892

When Walt Whitman's book of poems *Leaves of Grass* first appeared, many people were shocked by its controversial content and revolutionary form. Of the 800 copies printed, most were eventually thrown away. However, a few readers recognized the poet's genius. In a letter to Whitman, Ralph Waldo Emerson called *Leaves of Grass* "the most extraordinary piece of wit and wisdom that America has yet contributed."

The Making of a Poet Nothing Whitman wrote before *Leaves of Grass* contained any hint of what was to come. He burst onto the literary scene full-bodied and brash, like one of his poems.

His early years offered little in the way of preparation. Born in 1819, Whitman grew up in rural Long Island and crowded Brooklyn. He held a series of jobs including office boy, typesetter, printer, newspaper editor, school teacher, carpenter, and journalist.

In the 1840s, Whitman published a number of poems and short stories—and even a fairly successful novel—but these were conventional efforts.

Apparently, however, Whitman was just waiting for the proper inspiration. Upon reading Emerson, he realized that he could celebrate all aspects of nature and humanity by using spiritual language. "I was simmering, simmering, simmering," he once declared. "Emerson brought me to a boil."

An American Bard In the early 1850s, Whitman quit his job as a journalist and worked on *Leaves of Grass.* Declaring a kind of literary Independence Day, he printed his 12-poem book on July 4, 1855, at his own expense; he even set some of the type himself. Throughout his lifetime, Whitman would continue to rewrite, revise, and expand *Leaves of Grass.* The ninth and final edition, published in 1892, contained nearly 400 poems.

Unfettered by traditional poetic conventions and grammatical structures, Whitman captured the vitality, optimism, and voice of his native land. He celebrated all aspects of American life—the unique and the commonplace, the beautiful and the ugly.

Whitman once claimed that "the proof of a poet is that his country absorbs him as affectionately as he has absorbed it." By that measure and any other, Whitman is one of the most successful poets in history. Today *Leaves of Grass* is widely regarded as the most influential book of poetry in American literature.

● POETIC FORM: FREE VERSE

Walt Whitman is the great master of free verse in American poetry. **Free verse** is poetry that does not contain regular patterns of rhyme and meter. The lines in free verse often flow more naturally than do rhymed, metrical lines and so sound more like everyday speech. Note, however, that Whitman does use the following poetic devices to create rhythm:

- **cataloging:** frequent lists of people, things, and attributes

  The shoemaker singing as he sits on his bench, the hatter singing as he stands

- **repetition:** repeated words or phrases at the beginning of two or more lines

  Beat! beat! drums!—blow! bugles! blow!

- **parallelism:** related ideas phrased in similar ways

  Born here of parents born here from parents the same, and their parents the same

As you read the poems, notice how Whitman uses these devices to achieve rhythm, musical effects, and a style all his own.

● READING SKILL: ANALYZE TONE

To help you understand Whitman's poems, pay attention to their tone. **Tone** is an expression of a writer's attitude toward his or her subject. For example, a writer's tone might be respectful, angry, or amused. Tone can be communicated through choice of words and details. Notice the triumphant tone in these lines from "Song of Myself":

I celebrate myself, and sing myself,
And what I assume you shall assume,
For every atom belonging to me as good belongs to you.

As you read Whitman's poems, jot down examples of words and details that communicate tone in a chart like the one shown.

	Examples	Tone
"I Hear America Singing"	"blithe and strong"	happy, confident
"Song of Myself"		
"A Noiseless Patient Spider"		
"Beat! Beat! Drums!"		

Explore the Key Idea

What does AMERICA *look like?*

KEY IDEA What images come to mind when you think about **America?** Maybe you see big cities or rolling farmland. Maybe you picture the mountains or the coasts. Or maybe you focus on the people rather than the land. Many of Walt Whitman's poems contain vivid images of America in the mid-1800s. What—and who—captures America's spirit and reality today?

DISCUSS Imagine that you have been asked to design a poster that will help introduce tourists and newcomers to America. Get together in a small group and discuss the images that represent the people and places of America. Be sure to include images that symbolize all aspects of the country.

I Hear America Singing

Walt Whitman

I hear America singing, the varied carols I hear,
Those of mechanics, each one singing his as it should be blithe
    and strong,
The carpenter singing his as he measures his plank or beam, **Ⓐ**
The mason singing his as he makes ready for work, or leaves off
    work,
5 The boatman singing what belongs to him in his boat, the
    deckhand singing on the steamboat deck,
The shoemaker singing as he sits on his bench, the hatter singing
    as he stands,
The wood-cutter's song, the ploughboy's on his way in the
    morning, or at noon intermission or at sundown,
The delicious singing of the mother, or of the young wife at work,
    or of the girl sewing or washing,
Each singing what belongs to him or her and to none else,
10 The day what belongs to the day—at night the party of young
    fellows, robust, friendly,
Singing with open mouths their strong melodious songs. **Ⓑ**

Ⓐ FREE VERSE
Notice the use of **cataloging** throughout the poem. What rhythmic effect does the poet create with his list of the men and women at work in America?

Ⓑ ANALYZE TONE
Reread lines 10–11. What attitude does the speaker express toward the young men? Note the words and details that help convey that attitude.

Literary Analysis

1. **Summarize** What types of workers does Whitman celebrate in this poem?

2. **Clarify** What do you think singing represents in the poem?

3. **Make Inferences** Why do you think Whitman does not mention wealthy entrepreneurs, prominent leaders, or powerful politicians?

The Reaper (1878), Winslow Homer.
Watercolor. Private collection.
Photo © Art Resource, New York.

Song of Myself

Walt Whitman

1

I celebrate myself, and sing myself,
And what I assume you shall assume,
For every atom belonging to me as good belongs to you. **C**

I loaf and invite my soul,
5 I lean and loaf at my ease observing a spear of summer grass.

My tongue, every atom of my blood, form'd from this soil, this air,
Born here of parents born here from parents the same, and their
    parents the same,
I, now thirty-seven years old in perfect health begin,
Hoping to cease not till death.

10 Creeds and schools in abeyance,
Retiring back a while sufficed at[1] what they are, but never
    forgotten,
I harbor for good or bad, I permit to speak at every hazard,
Nature without check with original energy. **D**

6

A child said *What is the grass?* fetching it to me with full hands,
15 How could I answer the child? I do not know what it is any more
    than he.
I guess it must be the flag of my disposition, out of hopeful green
    stuff woven.

Or I guess it is the handkerchief of the Lord,
A scented gift and remembrancer designedly dropt,[2]

C **FREE VERSE**
Read lines 1–3 aloud and listen to the rhythm created by **parallelism.** In what ways does the use of this technique reflect the relationship between the speaker and the reader?

D **ANALYZE TONE**
Compare the tone in lines 4–5 with that in lines 12–13. How does the tone change? How is the tone in both pairs of lines similar?

---

1. **sufficed at:** satisfied with.
2. **remembrancer designedly dropt:** a purposely dropped token of affection.

Boys in Pasture, Winslow Homer. © Burstein Collection/Corbis.

Bearing the owner's name someway in the corners, that we may see
    and remark, and say *Whose?*

20 Or I guess the grass is itself a child, the produced babe of the
    vegetation.

Or I guess it is a uniform hieroglyphic,[3] **E**
And it means, Sprouting alike in broad zones and narrow zones,
Growing among black folks as among white,
Kanuck, Tuckahoe, Congressman, Cuff,[4] I give them the same, I
    receive them the same.

25 And now it seems to me the beautiful uncut hair of graves.

Tenderly will I use you curling grass,
It may be you transpire[5] from the breasts of young men,
It may be if I had known them I would have loved them,
It may be you are from old people, or from offspring taken soon
    out of their mothers' laps,
30 And here you are the mothers' laps. **F**

E FREE VERSE
Be aware of the **repetition** in lines 16–21. What is the relationship between the repeated elements?

F ANALYZE TONE
What attitude does the speaker express toward the dead in lines 25–30?

---

3. **hieroglyphic:** a system of symbols that represent meanings or speech sounds.

4. **Kanuck, Tuckahoe, . . . Cuff:** slang terms for various groups of people. A Kanuck (now spelled Canuck) is a Canadian, especially a French Canadian; a Tuckahoe is someone from the coast of Virginia; a Cuff is an African American.

5. **transpire:** emerge; ooze out.

This grass is very dark to be from the white heads of old mothers,
Darker than the colorless beards of old men,
Dark to come from under the faint red roofs of mouths.

O I perceive after all so many uttering tongues,
35 And I perceive they do not come from the roofs of mouths for
    nothing.

I wish I could translate the hints about the dead young men and
    women,
And the hints about old men and mothers, and the offspring taken
    soon out of their laps.

What do you think has become of the young and old men?
And what do you think has become of the women and children?

40 They are alive and well somewhere,
The smallest sprout shows there is really no death,
And if ever there was it led forward life, and does not wait at the
    end to arrest it,
And ceas'd the moment life appear'd.

All goes onward and outward, nothing collapses,
45 And to die is different from what any one supposed, and luckier. **G**

52

The spotted hawk swoops by and accuses me, he complains of my
    gab and my loitering.

I too am not a bit tamed, I too am untranslatable,
I sound my barbaric yawp[6] over the roofs of the world. **H**

The last scud[7] of day holds back for me,
50 It flings my likeness after the rest and true as any on the shadow'd
    wilds,
It coaxes me to the vapor and the dusk.

I depart as air, I shake my white locks at the runaway sun,
I effuse my flesh in eddies,[8] and drift it in lacy jags.

---

6. **yawp:** loud, rough speech.
7. **scud:** wind-blown cloud.
8. **effuse . . . eddies:** scatter my flesh in swirling currents.

G ANALYZE TONE
What words would you use to describe the tone in lines 38–45, where the speaker discusses life and death?

H FREE VERSE
Reread lines 47–48. What **poetic devices** in these lines emphasize the speaker's untamed nature?

I bequeath[9] myself to the dirt to grow from the grass I love,
55 If you want me again look for me under your boot-soles. **1**

You will hardly know who I am or what I mean,
But I shall be good health to you nevertheless,
And filter and fibre your blood.

Failing to fetch me at first keep encouraged,
60 Missing me one place search another,
I stop somewhere waiting for you.

---

9. **bequeath:** hand over, as if in a will.

1 ANALYZE TONE
What words and details does the poet use in lines 49–55 to create a defiant tone?

Literary Analysis

1. **Clarify** According to the speaker, in lines 40–43, why is there "really no death"?

2. **Summarize** To what does the speaker compare himself in section 52?

3. **Analyze Symbols** What do you think grass symbolizes in this poem?

ANALYZE VISUALS
This painting by American artist Elliott Daingerfield shows a man returning home after working on his farm. What **images** in the painting are similar to those described in the poem?

Return from the Farm (1915–1920), Elliott Daingerfield. Smithsonian American Art Museum, Washington, D.C. Photo © Smithsonian American Art Museum/Art Resource, New York.

Crossing the Spider Web, Victor Hugo. Watercolor. Maison Victor Hugo. Musée de la Ville de Paris. Photo © Giraudon/Art Resource, New York.

A Noiseless **Patient Spider**

Walt Whitman

A noiseless patient spider,
I mark'd where on a little promontory[1] it stood isolated,
Mark'd how to explore the vacant vast surrounding,
It launch'd forth filament, filament, filament, out of itself,
5 Ever unreeling them, ever tirelessly speeding them.

And you O my soul where you stand,
Surrounded, detached, in measureless oceans of space,
Ceaselessly musing, venturing, throwing, seeking the spheres to
    connect them, **J**
Till the bridge you will need be form'd, till the ductile[2] anchor
    hold,
10 Till the gossamer[3] thread you fling catch somewhere, O my soul. **K**

J FREE VERSE
Compare the use of **parallelism** in lines 5 and 8. What do these parallel elements suggest about the relationship between the spider and speaker?

K ANALYZE TONE
What is the overall tone of the poem? What details communicate that tone?

---

1. **promontory:** a high ridge of land or rock jutting out over water or land.
2. **ductile:** capable of being drawn or stretched out.
3. **gossamer:** extremely light or fine.

Beat! Beat! Drums!

Walt Whitman

Beat! beat! drums!—blow! bugles! blow!
Through the windows—through doors—burst like a ruthless force,
Into the solemn church, and scatter the congregation,
Into the school where the scholar is studying;
5   Leave not the bridegroom quiet—no happiness must he have now
        with his bride,
Nor the peaceful farmer any peace, ploughing his field or
        gathering his grain,
So fierce you whirr and pound you drums—so shrill you bugles
        blow. **L**

Beat! beat! drums!—blow! bugles! blow!
Over the traffic of cities—over the rumble of wheels in the streets;
10 Are beds prepared for sleepers at night in the houses? no sleepers
        must sleep in those beds,
No bargainers' bargains by day—no brokers or speculators—
        would they continue?
Would the talkers be talking? would the singer attempt to sing?
Would the lawyer rise in the court to state his case before the
        judge?
Then rattle quicker, heavier drums—you bugles wilder blow.

15 Beat! beat! drums!—blow! bugles! blow!
Make no parley—stop for no expostulation,[1]
Mind not the timid—mind not the weeper or prayer,
Mind not the old man beseeching the young man,
Let not the child's voice be heard, nor the mother's entreaties,
20 Make even the trestles[2] to shake the dead where they lie awaiting
        the hearses,
So strong you thump O terrible drums—so loud you bugles blow. **M**

L ANALYZE TONE
Describe the tone in lines 1–7. Why is this tone appropriate for the subject matter?

M FREE VERSE
Notice the **parallel structure** in the last line of each stanza. What impact does this device have on the poem's message?

---

1. **parley:** a discussion or conference; **expostulation:** argument.
2. **trestles:** tables, in this case, upon which coffins sit until the undertaker comes to take them away.

ESSAY Among the most important themes of Walt Whitman's poetry is the magnificence of America as seen in the nation's common people. In his preface to *Leaves of Grass,* his great life work, he introduces this idea quite emphatically.

from the Preface to
Leaves of GRASS

Walt Whitman

The Americans of all nations at any time upon the earth have probably the fullest poetical nature. The United States themselves are essentially the greatest poem. In the history of the earth hitherto the largest and most stirring appear tame and orderly to their ampler largeness and stir. Here at last is something in the doings of man that corresponds with the broadcast doings of the day and night. Here is not merely a nation but a teeming nation of nations. Here is action untied from strings necessarily blind to particulars and details magnificently moving in vast masses. Here is the hospitality which forever indicates heroes. . . . Here are the roughs and beards and space and ruggedness and nonchalance that the soul loves. Here the performance disdaining the trivial unapproached in the tremendous audacity of its crowds and groupings and the push of its perspective spreads with crampless and flowing breadth and showers its prolific and splendid extravagance. One sees it must indeed own the riches of the summer and winter, and need never be bankrupt while corn grows from the ground or the orchards drop apples or the bays contain fish or men beget children upon women.

Other states indicate themselves in their deputies . . . but the genius of the United States is not best or most in its executives or legislatures, nor in its ambassadors or authors or colleges or churches or parlors, nor even in its newspapers or inventors . . . but always most in the common people. Their manners speech dress friendships— the freshness and candor of their physiognomy—the picturesque looseness of their carriage . . . their deathless attachment to freedom—their aversion to anything indecorous or soft or mean—the practical acknowledgment of the citizens of one state by the citizens of all other states—the fierceness of their roused resentment— their curiosity and welcome of novelty—their self-esteem and wonderful sympathy— their susceptibility to a slight—the air they have of persons who never knew how it felt to stand in the presence of superiors—the fluency of their speech—their delight in music, the sure symptom of manly tenderness and native elegance of soul . . . their good temper and openhandedness—the terrible significance of their elections—the President's taking off his hat to them not they to him—these too are unrhymed poetry. It awaits the gigantic and generous treatment worthy of it.

Comprehension

1. **Recall** What two things does Whitman compare in "A Noiseless Patient Spider"?

2. **Summarize** In "Beat! Beat! Drums!" whom do the drums and bugles call to action?

3. **Paraphrase** How would you paraphrase lines 16–19 of "Beat! Beat! Drums!"?

Literary Analysis

4. **Examine Imagery** Think about the images of mid-19th-century **America** that Whitman conveys in his poems. How do these images compare with what America looks like today? Cite specific details from the poems to support your comparisons.

5. **Analyze Tone** Review the examples of tone that you recorded as you read the poems. What can you conclude about Whitman's attitude toward the following?

   • manual labor   • the soul   • himself   • war

6. **Analyze Metaphor** Reread lines 16–25 of "Song of Myself." What metaphors does the speaker use to describe what grass means to him? What ideas does each metaphor suggest?

7. **Compare Poems** Use a chart like the one shown to compare the **images** and **mood** of "A Noiseless Patient Spider" and "Beat! Beat! Drums!" Based on your notes, what is the overall impact of each poem?

	Images	Mood
"A Noiseless Patient Spider"		
"Beat! Beat! Drums!"		

8. **Compare Texts** In what ways are the pronouncements made in Whitman's preface (page 518) reflected in his poems? Consider the content of what he says as well as the manner in which he states it. Provide details to support your ideas.

9. **Evaluate Free Verse** Why is free verse an appropriate form for Whitman's poems? Support your opinion.

Literary Criticism

10. **Author's Style** In another section of "Song of Myself," Whitman writes: "He most honors my style who learns under it to destroy the teacher." What does he mean? Do you think Whitman encourages this position in the poems you have read? Use evidence from the poems to support your opinion.

Ode to Walt Whitman

PABLO NERUDA

BACKGROUND Pablo Neruda (1904–1973), a Nobel Prize–winning poet from Chile, was greatly inspired by Walt Whitman's poetry. In a speech delivered in 1972, he said, "I was barely 15 when I discovered Walt Whitman, my primary creditor. I stand among you today still owing this marvelous debt that has helped me live." In the following poem, Neruda echoes Whitman's joyful exuberance.

I do not remember
at what age
nor where:
in the great damp South
5 or on the fearsome
coast, beneath the brief
cry of the seagulls,
I touched a hand and it was
the hand of Walt Whitman.
10 I trod the ground
with bare feet,
I walked on the grass,
on the firm dew
of Walt Whitman.

15 During
my entire
youth
I had the company of that hand,
that dew,
20 its firmness of patriarchal pine, its
    prairie-like expanse,
and its mission of circulatory peace.

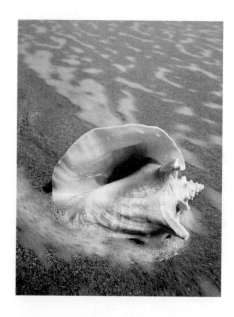

Not
disdaining
the gifts
25 of the earth,
nor the copious
curving of the column's capital,
nor the purple
initial
30 of wisdom,
you taught me
to be an American,
you raised
my eyes
35 to books,
towards
the treasure
of the grains:
broad,
40 in the clarity
of the plains,
you made me see
the high
tutelary
45 mountain. From subterranean
echoes,
you gathered
for me
everything;
50 everything that came forth
was harvested by you,
galloping in the alfalfa,
picking poppies for me,
visiting
55 the rivers,
coming into the kitchens
in the afternoon.

But not only
soil
60 was brought to light
by your spade:
you unearthed
man,
and the
65 slave
who was humiliated
with you, balancing
the black dignity of his stature,
walked on, conquering
70 happiness.

To the fireman
below,
in the stoke-hole,
you sent
75 a little basket
of strawberries.
To every corner of your town
a verse
of yours arrived for a visit,
80 and it was like a piece
of clean body,
the verse that arrived,
like
your own fisherman beard
85 or the solemn tread of your acacia
legs.

Your silhouette
passed among the soldiers:
the poet, the wound-dresser,
the night attendant
90 who knows
the sound
of breathing in mortal agony
and awaits with the dawn
the silent
95 return
of life.

Good baker!
Elder first cousin
of my roots,
100 araucaria's
cupola,
it is
now
a hundred
105 years
that over your grass
and its germinations,
the wind
passes
110 without wearing out your eyes

New
and cruel years in your Fatherland:
persecutions,
tears,
115 prisons,
poisoned weapons
and wrathful wars
have not crushed
the grass of your book;
120 the vital fountainhead
of its freshness.
And, alas!
those
who murdered
125 Lincoln
now
lie in his bed.
They felled
his seat of honor
130 made of fragrant wood,
and raised a throne
spattered
with misfortune and blood.

View from Neruda's house on Isla Negra, Chile, with antique sailboat figureheads
hanging in the window

But
135 your voice
sings
in the suburban
stations,
in
140 the
vespertine
wharfs,
your word
splashes
145 like
dark water.
Your people,
white
and black,
150 poor
people,
simple people
like
all

155 people
do not forget
your bell:
They congregate singing
beneath
160 the magnitude
of your spacious life.
They walk among the peoples with your
love
caressing
the pure development
165 of brotherhood on earth.

Literary Analysis

1. **Analyze Metaphor** Neruda uses various metaphors to characterize Whitman's poems. What does each of these metaphors suggest about Whitman's verse?

   - Whitman's hand (lines 8–9)
   - Whitman as harvester (lines 47–70)
   - a basket of strawberries (lines 71–76)
   - a bell (lines 147–157)

2. **Compare Texts** Neruda has acknowledged Whitman's influence on his own verse. What elements of "Ode to Walt Whitman" reveal this influence? Be specific, citing evidence from this poem as well as from the Whitman poems you read on pages 510–517.

Selected Poetry

by Emily Dickinson

Author Online

For more on Emily Dickinson, visit the **Literature Center** at ClassZone.com.

Emily Dickinson

1830–1886

Emily Dickinson rarely ventured beyond the confines of her family home in Amherst, Massachusetts, but her restless mind and creativity knew no such boundaries. In her bedroom overlooking the village graveyard, Dickinson meditated on life and death and wrote about these subjects with startling originality. Today she and Walt Whitman are considered the greatest American poets of the 19th century.

Family Ties Dickinson was born in 1830 into a well-to-do family, which would become the center of her existence. She stood in awe of her father, a stern, imposing man committed to Puritan ideals, and felt estranged from her mother, who "did not," Dickinson once commented in a letter, "care for thought." However, she had a close relationship with her older brother, Austin, and her younger sister, Vinnie.

In 1847, Dickinson left home to attend Mount Holyoke Female Seminary in nearby South Hadley, but she left after just one year. She missed her family, but she also resented the intense pressure she felt there to join the church. All her life, Dickinson felt torn between her own convictions and the religious beliefs of those around her. This conflict is reflected in many of her poems.

A Writer's Life In the 1850s, Dickinson began to devote herself to poetry. Late at night, she wrote by candlelight. During the day, she jotted down her thoughts between household chores. Inspired by her own observations and experiences, Dickinson composed a remarkable number of profound, gemlike poems.

Perhaps because of this newfound focus on her writing, Dickinson gradually withdrew from the world. However, she did not become a total recluse. She entertained occasional visitors in her home and maintained contact with friends and family by means of a lively correspondence.

Poetic Legacy Early in 1886, Dickinson wrote a letter to her cousins that simply read "Called back." She seemed to have realized that she was dying. Following her death, her sister Vinnie discovered a box full of Dickinson's poems bound into neat booklets. As a result of Vinnie's perseverance, the first volume of Dickinson's poetry appeared four years after the poet's death. Her poems—1,775 in all—finally revealed to the world the passionate, witty woman who never flinched from the truth.

● LITERARY ANALYSIS: AUTHOR'S STYLE

Emily Dickinson's style is as unique and personal as her observations about the world. Here are some of the distinctive stylistic elements you will find in Dickinson's poetry:

- dense **quatrains,** or four-line stanzas, that echo the simple rhythms of church hymns
- **slant rhymes,** or words that do not exactly rhyme ("chill"/ "Tulle")
- inventive punctuation and sentence structure, including the use of dashes to highlight important words and break up the rhythm of her poems
- irregular capitalization and inverted syntax to emphasize words
- surprisingly unconventional **figurative language,** including similes, metaphors, and personification

As you read, think about the effect of these style elements in Dickinson's poems.

● READING STRATEGY: READING DICKINSON'S POETRY

To get the most out of Emily Dickinson's poetry, try reading each poem three times.

- The first time, read for an overall impression. Pause when you encounter dashes, and be aware of the poem's **rhythm.**
- The second time, note the use of **imagery** and **figurative language.** Pay attention to the words capitalized for emphasis.
- The third time, read the poem aloud. Think about what the imagery and figurative language convey about meaning.

Use a chart like the one shown for each poem. Jot down your thoughts and ideas after each reading.

"Because I could not stop for Death"		
1st Reading	2nd Reading	3rd Reading
Poem has a calm, reflective mood.	Images of death are not frightening.	Poem suggests that death and dying are not frightening.

What are life's ESSENTIAL TRUTHS?

KEY IDEA Love, loss. Joy, death. When you focus on life's real meaning, you explore its **essential truths.** These truths, of course, are the natural focus of poets. For instance, in the poems that follow, Emily Dickinson has a great deal to say about death and dying. But does she—or any other poet—speak for you? What do you think about such weighty matters as death, success, and solitude? What is your truth?

QUICKWRITE Create your own top-five list of life's essential truths. Begin with number five and work your way up to number one. Feel free to express your truths in statements, phrases, questions, or any form you want.

Because I could not stop for Death—

EMILY DICKINSON

Because I could not stop for Death—
He kindly stopped for me—
The Carriage held but just Ourselves—
And Immortality. **A**

5 We slowly drove—He knew no haste
And I had put away
My labor and my leisure too,
For His Civility[1]—

We passed the School, where Children strove
10 At Recess—in the Ring—
We passed the Fields of Gazing Grain[2]—
We passed the Setting Sun—

Or rather—He passed Us—
The Dews drew quivering and chill—
15 For only Gossamer,[3] my Gown—
My Tippet—only Tulle[4]—

We paused before a House that seemed
A Swelling of the Ground—
The Roof was scarcely visible—
20 The Cornice[5]—in the Ground— **B**

Since then—'tis Centuries—and yet
Feels shorter than the Day
I first surmised the Horses' Heads
Were toward Eternity—

---

1. **Civility:** politeness.
2. **Gazing Grain:** grain leaning toward the sun.
3. **Gossamer:** a thin, light cloth.
4. **My Tippet—only Tulle** (tōōl): My shawl was only a fine net cloth.
5. **Cornice** (kôr′nĭs): the molding around the top of a building.

A **AUTHOR'S STYLE**
Reread lines 1–4 and notice the use of **personification,** a figure of speech in which an object, animal, or idea is given human characteristics. How is Death personified?

B **DICKINSON'S POETRY**
Note the **imagery** used to describe the house in lines 17–20. What do you think the house represents?

ANALYZE VISUALS
Why might the artist have chosen to keep this photograph out of focus?

Success is counted sweetest

EMILY DICKINSON

Success is counted sweetest
By those who ne'er succeed.
To comprehend a nectar[1]
Requires sorest need.

5 Not one of all the purple Host[2]
Who took the Flag[3] today
Can tell the definition
So clear of Victory

As he defeated—dying—
10 On whose forbidden ear
The distant strains of triumph
Burst agonized and clear!

C DICKINSON'S POETRY
Read lines 9–12 aloud.
What elements create the
rhythm in these lines?

---

1. **To comprehend a nectar:** to fully appreciate
   a delicious beverage.
2. **Host:** army.
3. **took the Flag:** captured the enemy's flag as
   a token of victory.

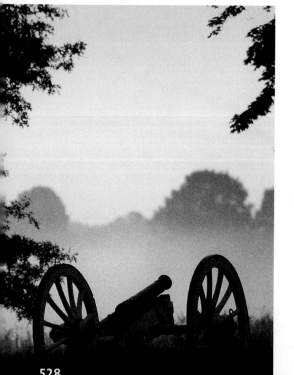

Literary Analysis

1. **Clarify** Who is the "purple Host" in line 5?

2. **Paraphrase** Reread lines 9–12. How would you
   paraphrase these lines?

3. **Form Opinions** Do you agree that those who fail
   are better able to appreciate success than those
   who win? Explain your answer.

Much Madness is divinest Sense—

EMILY DICKINSON

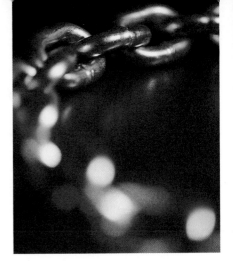

Much Madness is divinest Sense—
To a discerning Eye—
Much Sense—the starkest Madness— **D**
'Tis the Majority
5 In this, as All, prevail—
Assent—and you are sane—
Demur[1]—you're straightway dangerous—
And handled with a Chain[2]—

---

1. **demur** (dĭ-mûr'): voice opposition; object.
2. **handled with a Chain:** In the 19th century, those who were considered insane were often kept chained in asylums.

D AUTHOR'S STYLE
Pay attention to the use of capitalization in lines 1–3. Which two words are twice capitalized? Why do you think Dickinson chose to capitalize those words?

My life closed twice before its close—

EMILY DICKINSON

My life closed twice before its close—
It yet remains to see
If Immortality unveil
A third event to me

5 So huge, so hopeless to conceive
As these that twice befell.
Parting is all we know of heaven,
And all we need of hell. **E**

E DICKINSON'S POETRY
After your first reading of the poem, what is your overall impression of its subject?

The Soul selects her own Society—

Emily Dickinson

The Soul selects her own Society—
Then—shuts the Door—
To her divine Majority[1]—
Present no more—

5 Unmoved—she notes the Chariots[2]—pausing—
At her low Gate—
Unmoved—an Emperor be kneeling
Upon her Mat— **F**

I've known her—from an ample nation—
10 Choose One—
Then—close the Valves of her attention—
Like Stone— **G**

---

1. **divine Majority:** other souls.
2. **the Chariots:** the Emperor's chariots.

F DICKINSON'S POETRY
Reread lines 5–8. What are some of the effects of the dashes and the poet's abbreviated use of words?

G AUTHOR'S STYLE
A **simile** is a figure of speech that compares two things that have something in common, using *like* or *as*. What images does the comparison in the last quatrain suggest?

Literary Analysis

1. **Summarize** How would you summarize the second quatrain?

2. **Paraphrase** Reread lines 9–10. How would you paraphrase these lines?

3. **Draw Conclusions** What do you think the speaker means by "Society"?

I heard a *Fly buzz—when I died—*

EMILY DICKINSON

I heard a Fly buzz—when I died—
The Stillness in the Room
Was like the Stillness in the Air—
Between the Heaves[1] of Storm— **H**

5 The Eyes around—had wrung them dry—
And Breaths were gathering firm
For that last Onset—when the King[2]
Be witnessed—in the Room—

I willed my Keepsakes—Signed away
10 What portion of me be
Assignable—and then it was
There interposed[3] a Fly—

With Blue—uncertain stumbling Buzz—
Between the light—and me—
15 And then the Windows failed—and then
I could not see to see— **I**

---

1. **Heaves:** risings and fallings.
2. **the King:** God.
3. **interposed:** came between.

H AUTHOR'S STYLE
Notice the **simile** in the first quatrain. What is being compared? Why is this comparison appropriate?

I DICKINSON'S POETRY
Reread lines 13–16. What final images does the speaker describe? What is ironic about this **imagery?**

My Life had stood— a Loaded Gun—   EMILY DICKINSON

My Life had stood—a Loaded Gun—
In Corners—till a Day
The Owner passed—identified—
And carried Me away— **J**

5 And now We roam in Sovereign Woods[1]—
And now We hunt the Doe—
And every time I speak for Him—
The Mountains straight reply—

And do I smile, such cordial light
10 Upon the Valley glow—
It is as a Vesuvian[2] face
Had let its pleasure through—

And when at Night—Our good Day done—
I guard My Master's Head—
15 'Tis better than the Eider-Duck's
Deep Pillow—to have shared—

To foe of His—I'm deadly foe—
None stir the second time—
On whom I lay a Yellow Eye—
20 Or an emphatic Thumb—

Though I than He—may longer live
He longer must—than I—
For I have but the power to kill,
Without—the power to die— **K**

J AUTHOR'S STYLE
Remember that a
metaphor is a figure of
speech that compares
two things directly,
without using *like* or *as*.
What is surprising about
the metaphor introduced
in lines 1–4?

K DICKINSON'S POETRY
Read the final quatrain
aloud. What do the
lines suggest about the
relationship between the
gun and its owner?

---

1. **Sovereign** (sŏv′ər-ĭn) **Woods:** God's woods.

2. **Vesuvian** (vĭ-soo′vē-ən): marked by sudden or violent outbursts;
   after the volcano Mount Vesuvius, which erupted and destroyed
   Pompeii in A.D. 79.

Letter to Mr. T. W. Higginson

April 15, 1862

Mr Higginson,

Are you too deeply occupied to say if my Verse is alive?

The Mind is so near itself—it cannot see,
distinctly—and I have none to ask—

Should you think it breathed—and had you the leisure to tell
me, I should feel quick gratitude—

If I make the mistake—that you dared to tell me—
would give me sincerer honor—toward you—

I enclose my name—asking you, if you please—
Sir—to tell me what is true?

That you will not betray me—it is needless to ask—
since Honor is it's own pawn—

Miss Emily E. Dickinson

Comprehension

1. **Recall** What has happened to the speaker in "Because I could not stop for Death—"?

2. **Clarify** What do you think is the speaker's attitude toward the Majority in "Much Madness is divinest Sense"?

3. **Summarize** How would you summarize lines 5–8 of "I heard a Fly buzz—when I died—"?

Literary Analysis

4. **Make Inferences** What **essential truths** about death and dying does Dickinson convey in the following poems? Cite specific details.

   - "Because I could not stop for Death—"
   - "My life closed twice before its close—"
   - "I heard a Fly buzz—when I died—"

5. **Analyze Author's Style** What ideas are emphasized by the unusual use of capitalization in the following poems? Be specific.

   - "Success is counted sweetest"
   - "Much Madness is divinest Sense"
   - "The Soul selects her own Society—"

6. **Analyze Dickinson's Poetry** Review the thoughts and ideas you recorded as you read and reread the poems. Based on Dickinson's **imagery** and **figurative language,** how would you characterize the overall **tone** of her poems?

7. **Evaluate Paradox** A paradox is a statement that seems to contradict itself but may nevertheless suggest an important truth. Use a diagram like the one shown to identify the paradoxes in

   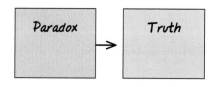

   "Success is counted sweetest," "Much Madness is divinest Sense," and "My Life had stood—a Loaded Gun—." What truth does each paradox convey?

8. **Compare Texts** What style elements of the poet do you recognize in Emily Dickinson's letter to Thomas Wentworth Higginson (page 533)?

Literary Criticism

9. **Different Perspectives** Until 1955, editors published "corrected" versions of Dickinson's poems in which dashes had been deleted, rhyme and meter had been made regular, and metaphors replaced with more conventional figures of speech. Imagine what corrections might have been made. What would have been lost? Use details from the poems to support your ideas. Why do you think the editors might have decided to change the original versions?

The Innovations of Whitman and Dickinson

Although Emily Dickinson and Walt Whitman were both revolutionary in their approach to poetic form and content, their poems look quite different. Dickinson wrote short and concise lines; Whitman, long and sprawling ones.

> *Success is counted sweetest*
> *By those who ne'er succeed.*
>
> **—Emily Dickinson**
>
> *I wish I could translate the hints about the dead young men*
>   *and women,*
> *And the hints about old men and mothers, and the offspring taken*
>   *soon out of their laps.*
>
> **—Walt Whitman**

Dickinson concentrated on private and personal experiences; Whitman, on representative experiences of the American people.

> *I heard a Fly buzz—when I died—*
>
> **—Emily Dickinson**
>
> *I hear America singing, the varied carols I hear,*
>
> **—Walt Whitman**

Writing to Compare

Write an essay to further compare the work of Dickinson and Whitman. Cite specific lines from the poems on page 510 through 532 to support your comparison.

Consider

- each poet's style and form (that is, word choice, imagery, line length, stanzas, rhythm, rhyme)
- the poems' subject matter and general themes
- which words, lines, or stanzas will provide you with effective evidence and details

© Mike Caplanis/Luminarygraphics.com.

Extension

SPEAKING & LISTENING With a partner, imagine a dialogue that might have occurred between Whitman and Dickinson had they had a chance meeting. Create the dialogue of this momentous literary conversation, in which the poets discuss their topics, themes, and techniques. Then, **perform** your conversation for the class. Try to use speaking styles that you think are appropriate for the two poets.

from **Narrative of the Life of Frederick Douglass, an American Slave**

Slave Narrative by Frederick Douglass

Frederick Douglass

c. 1817–1895

Frederick Douglass endured 21 years of slavery before he escaped to freedom in the North, where he became an outspoken and influential abolitionist. In the years leading up to the Civil War, his powerful speeches spurred the nation to move against slavery and to extend equal rights to all its citizens.

Forbidden Education As a boy, Douglass worked as a slave in the home of Hugh and Sophia Auld of Baltimore, Maryland. Although it was against the law, Mrs. Auld taught Douglass how to read. After Mr. Auld commanded his wife to stop her lessons, Douglass educated himself in secret, studying from a textbook on public speaking titled *The Columbian Orator.*

From Slave to Abolitionist Douglass escaped and in 1838 settled in New Bedford, Massachusetts. Three years later, he spoke so eloquently to the Massachusetts Anti-Slavery Society that they hired him to lecture about his experiences. Proslavery hecklers frequently attacked him, hurling insults and even rotten eggs and vegetables, but Douglass continued, undeterred.

In 1845, with the publication of his autobiography, *Narrative of the Life of Frederick Douglass, an American Slave,* Douglass rose to international fame—dangerous attention for a runaway slave. To avoid being recaptured, Douglass left for a two-year speaking tour of Great Britain. During the trip, two friends raised the money to purchase his freedom.

Tireless Reformer Returning to the United States as a free man, Douglass settled in Rochester, New York, and founded an antislavery newspaper, the *North Star.* During the Civil War, he advised President Abraham Lincoln and helped recruit the first African-American soldiers for the Union army. For Douglass, the end of slavery was only a first step to achieving a greater goal: full and equal civil rights for African Americans.

In the years after the Civil War, Douglass was appointed to several government posts, including U.S. marshal for the District of Columbia and minister to Haiti. To the end of his life, he continued his fight for full citizenship for African Americans and his support for other causes, including women's rights, land reform, and public education.

LITERARY ANALYSIS: STYLE

Style is a writer's distinctive way of expressing ideas—not what is said, but how it is said. Douglass uses a formal, elegant style that demonstrates his masterful command of language.

After running thus for a considerable distance, they finally upset the cart, dashing it with great force against a tree, and threw themselves into a dense thicket.

Elements that characterize style include

- **tone,** conveyed by choice of words and details
- **sentence patterns and structures**
- use of **figurative language**
- use of **dialogue**

Douglass combines crisp, factual narration with bursts of poetic language. As you read, note the choices Douglass makes that contribute to his sophisticated style.

READING SKILL: ANALYZE AUTHOR'S PURPOSE

An author creates a work to achieve a specific **purpose,** or goal. In general, an author writes to inform, to express thoughts or feelings, to persuade, or to entertain. However, a complex work will often have more than one purpose.

Frederick Douglass wrote his autobiography mainly to persuade readers that slavery should be abolished. To achieve his purpose, he describes the physical realities that slaves endure and his responses to his life as a slave.

We were often in the field from the first approach of day till its last lingering ray had left us . . .

As you read, use a chart like the one shown to take notes on Douglass's experiences. Notice when he provides factual details about the general conditions of slave life and when he describes his personal responses to his situation.

Physical Realities	Responses to Situation

Explore the Key Idea

Can you set yourself FREE?

KEY IDEA Separated from his parents, denied the right to an education, and moved from place to place at the convenience of his owners, Frederick Douglass learned that nothing in his life was under his control. Rejecting the injustice of slavery, he risked his life to escape. With his decision to set himself free, he claimed the right to **self-determination:** he would be a man and not a slave.

QUICKWRITE Without mentioning any names, contrast two people you know of—one who has self-determination and one who does not. Would you attribute the differences beween them more to circumstances or to attitude?

A—	M—
stands up to defend the rights of others	afraid to disagree with her boyfriend

Narrative of the Life of Frederick Douglass

Frederick Douglass

> **BACKGROUND** Douglass wrote his autobiography to convince skeptics that such an eloquent speaker had indeed once been a slave. His book became one of the most famous slave narratives ever published and played an enormous role in rallying support for the abolition of slavery. This excerpt recounts a period in Douglass's life during which his owner, Hugh Auld's brother, Thomas, had hired him out to a man with a reputation as a "slave breaker."

I left Master Thomas's house, and went to live with Mr. Covey, on the 1st of January, 1833. I was now, for the first time in my life, a field hand. In my new employment, I found myself even more awkward than a country boy appeared to be in a large city. I had been at my new home but one week before Mr. Covey gave me a very severe whipping, cutting my back, causing the blood to run, and raising ridges on my flesh as large as my little finger. The details of this affair are **Ⓐ** as follows: Mr. Covey sent me, very early in the morning of one of our coldest days in the month of January, to the woods, to get a load of wood. He gave me a team of unbroken oxen. He told me which was the in-hand ox, and which the off-
10 hand[1] one. He then tied the end of a large rope around the horns of the in-hand ox, and gave me the other end of it, and told me, if the oxen started to run, that

ANALYZE VISUALS
Describe the **style** of this painting. What impression of its subject does the painting convey?

Ⓐ STYLE
Explain what Douglass means by "this affair" in line 6. What is surprising about his **word choice?**

---

1. **in-hand . . . off-hand:** In a team of animals trained to pull loads, the in-hand animal is the one on the left; the animal on the right is the off-hand one.

Panel 30 from *The Frederick Douglass Series* (1938–1939), Jacob Lawrence. Hampton University Museum. © 2007 The Jacob and Gwendolyn Lawrence Foundation, Seattle/ Artists Rights Society (ARS), New York.

The Life of Harriet Tubman, #9 (1940), Jacob Lawrence. Casein tempera on hardboard, 12" x 17⅞". Hampton University Museum. Photo courtesy of Gwendolyn Knight Lawrence/Art Resource, New York. © 2007 The Jacob and Gwendolyn Lawrence Foundation, Seattle/Artists Rights Society (ARS), New York.

I must hold on upon the rope. I had never driven oxen before, and of course I was very awkward. I, however, succeeded in getting to the edge of the woods with little difficulty; but I had got a very few rods[2] into the woods, when the oxen took fright, and started full tilt, carrying the cart against trees, and over stumps, in the most frightful manner. I expected every moment that my brains would be dashed out against the trees. After running thus for a considerable distance, they finally upset the cart, dashing it with great force against a tree, and threw themselves into a dense thicket.

20 How I escaped death, I do not know. There I was, entirely alone, in a thick wood, in a place new to me. My cart was upset and shattered, my oxen were entangled among the young trees, and there was none to help me. After a long spell of effort, I succeeded in getting my cart righted, my oxen disentangled, and again yoked to the cart. I now proceeded with my team to the place where I had, the day before, been chopping wood, and loaded my cart pretty heavily, thinking in this way to tame my oxen. I then proceeded on my way home. I had now

ANALYZE VISUALS
Identify details in this painting that are used to represent the experience of slavery. What effects are achieved by centering the image of the figures' feet?

---

2. **rods:** units of length equal to 5 1/2 yards.

consumed one half of the day. I got out of the woods safely, and now felt out of danger. I stopped my oxen to open the woods gate; and just as I did so, before I could get hold of my ox rope, the oxen again started, rushed through the gate,
30 catching it between the wheel and the body of the cart, tearing it to pieces, and coming within a few inches of crushing me against the gate-post. Thus twice, in one short day, I escaped death by the merest chance. On my return, I told Mr. Covey what had happened, and how it happened. He ordered me to return to the woods again immediately. I did so, and he followed on after me. Just as I got into the woods, he came up and told me to stop my cart, and that he would teach me how to trifle away my time, and break gates. He then went to a large gum-tree, and with his axe cut three large switches, and, after trimming them up neatly with his pocket-knife, he ordered me to take off my clothes. I made him no answer, but stood with my clothes on. He repeated his order. I still made him no answer,
40 nor did I move to strip myself. Upon this he rushed at me with the fierceness of a tiger, tore off my clothes, and lashed me till he had worn out his switches, cutting me so savagely as to leave the marks visible for a long time after. This whipping was the first of a number just like it, and for similar offenses. **B**

I lived with Mr. Covey one year. During the first six months, of that year, scarce a week passed without his whipping me. I was seldom free from a sore back. My awkwardness was almost always his excuse for whipping me. We were worked fully up to the point of endurance. Long before day we were up, our horses fed, and by the first approach of day we were off to the field with our hoes and ploughing teams. Mr. Covey gave us enough to eat, but scarce time to eat it. We were often
50 less than five minutes taking our meals. We were often in the field from the first approach of day till its last lingering ray had left us; and at saving-fodder time, midnight often caught us in the field binding blades.[3] **C**

Covey would be out with us. The way he used to stand it, was this. He would spend the most of his afternoons in bed. He would then come out fresh in the evening, ready to urge us on with his words, example, and frequently with the whip. Mr. Covey was one of the few slaveholders who could and did work with his hands. He was a hard-working man. He knew by himself just what a man or a boy could do. There was no deceiving him. His work went on in his absence almost as well as in his presence; and he had the faculty of making us feel that he was ever
60 present with us. This he did by surprising us. He seldom approached the spot where we were at work openly, if he could do it secretly. He always aimed at taking us by surprise. Such was his cunning, that we used to call him, among ourselves, "the snake." When we were at work in the cornfield, he would sometimes crawl on his hands and knees to avoid detection, and all at once he would rise nearly in our midst, and scream out, "Ha, ha! Come, come! Dash on, dash on!" This being **D** his mode of attack, it was never safe to stop a single minute. His comings were like a thief in the night. He appeared to us as being ever at hand. He was under every

B STYLE
Reread lines 31–43. What is the effect of Douglass's choice to use little imagery or figurative language in his narration?

C AUTHOR'S PURPOSE
Reread lines 46–52. What details does Douglass use to inform his readers about the working conditions of slaves?

D GRAMMAR AND STYLE
Reread lines 63–65. Note how Douglass uses the **vivid verbs** *crawl* and *scream* to characterize Covey's menacing behavior.

---

3. **saving- fodder . . . binding blades:** They are gathering and bundling ("binding") corn-plant leaves ("blades") to use for livestock ("fodder").

tree, behind every stump, in every bush, and at every window, on the plantation.
He would sometimes mount his horse, as if bound to St. Michael's,⁴ a distance of
70 seven miles, and in half an hour afterwards you would see him coiled up in the
corner of the wood-fence, watching every motion of the slaves. He would, for this
purpose, leave his horse tied up in the woods. Again, he would sometimes walk
up to us, and give us orders as though he was upon the point of starting on a long
journey, turn his back upon us, and make as though he was going to the house
to get ready; and, before he would get half way thither, he would turn short and
crawl into a fence-corner, or behind some tree, and there watch us till the going
down of the sun. . . .

If at any one time of my life more than another, I was made to drink the bitterest
dregs of slavery, that time was during the first six months of my stay with Mr.
80 Covey. We were worked in all weathers. It was never too hot or too cold; it could
never rain, blow, hail, or snow, too hard for us to work in the field. Work, work,
work, was scarcely more the order of the day than of the night. The longest days
were too short for him, and the shortest nights too long for him. I was somewhat
unmanageable when I first went there, but a few months of this discipline tamed
me. Mr. Covey succeeded in breaking me. I was broken in body, soul, and spirit.
My natural elasticity was crushed, my intellect languished, the disposition to read
departed, the cheerful spark that lingered about my eye died; the dark night of
slavery closed in upon me; and behold a man transformed into a brute! ⓔ

Sunday was my only leisure time. I spent this in a sort of beast-like stupor,
90 between sleep and wake, under some large tree. At times I would rise up, a flash
of energetic freedom would dart through my soul, accompanied with a faint beam
of hope, that flickered for a moment, and then vanished. I sank down again,
mourning over my wretched condition. I was sometimes prompted to take my
life, and that of Covey, but was prevented by a combination of hope and fear. My
sufferings on this plantation seem now like a dream rather than a stern reality. . . .

I have already intimated that my condition was much worse, during the first
six months of my stay at Mr. Covey's, than in the last six. The circumstances
leading to the change in Mr. Covey's course toward me form an epoch in my
humble history. You have seen how a man was made a slave; you shall see how a
100 slave was made a man. On one of the hottest days of the month of August, 1833,
Bill Smith, William Hughes,⁵ a slave named Eli, and myself, were engaged in
fanning wheat.⁶ Hughes was clearing the fanned wheat from before the fan. Eli
was turning, Smith was feeding, and I was carrying wheat to the fan. The work
was simple, requiring strength rather than intellect; yet, to one entirely unused to
such work, it came very hard. About three o'clock of that day, I broke down; my
strength failed me; I was seized with a violent aching of the head, attended with

---

4. **St. Michael's:** a town southeast of Baltimore, on the east side of the Chesapeake Bay.

5. **Bill Smith, William Hughes:** Bill Smith was a hired man, and William Hughes was Mr. Covey's cousin.

6. **fanning wheat:** using a machine that blows air to separate grains of wheat from the unusable husks.

extreme dizziness; I trembled in every limb. Finding what was coming, I nerved myself up, feeling it would never do to stop work. I stood as long as I could stagger to the hopper[7] with grain. When I could stand no longer, I fell, and felt as if held down by an immense weight. The fan of course stopped; every one had his own work to do; and no one could do the work of the other, and have his own go on at the same time.

   Mr. Covey was at the house, about one hundred yards from the treading-yard where we were fanning. On hearing the fan stop, he left immediately, and came to the spot where we were. He hastily inquired what the matter was. Bill answered that I was sick, and there was no one to bring wheat to the fan. I had by this time crawled away under the side of the post and rail-fence by which the yard was enclosed, hoping to find relief by getting out of the sun. He then asked where I was. He was told by one of the hands. He came to the spot, and, after looking at me awhile, asked me what was the matter. I told him as well as I could, for I scarce had strength to speak. He then gave me a savage kick in the side, and told me to get up. I tried to do so, but fell back in the attempt. He gave me another kick, and again told me to rise. I again tried, and succeeded in gaining my feet; but, stooping to get the tub with which I was feeding the fan, I again staggered and fell. While down in this situation, Mr. Covey took up the hickory slat with which Hughes had been striking off the half-bushel measure, and with it gave me a heavy blow upon the head, making a large wound, and the blood ran freely; and with this again told me to get up. I made no effort to comply, having now made up my **F** mind to let him do his worst. In a short time after receiving this blow, my head grew better. Mr. Covey had now left me to my fate. At this moment I resolved, for the first time, to go to my master, enter a complaint, and ask his protection. In order to do this, I must that afternoon walk seven miles; and this, under the circumstances, was truly a severe undertaking. I was exceedingly feeble; made so as much by the kicks and blows which I received, as by the severe fit of sickness to which I had been subjected. I, however, watched my chance, while Covey was looking in an opposite direction, and started for St. Michael's. I succeeded in getting a considerable distance on my way to the woods, when Covey discovered me, and called after me to come back, threatening what he would do if I did not come. I disregarded both his calls and his threats, and made my way to the woods as fast as my feeble state would allow; and thinking I might be overhauled by him if I kept the road,[8] I walked through the woods, keeping far enough from the road to avoid detection, and near enough to prevent losing my way. I had not gone far before my little strength again failed me. I could go no farther. I fell down, and lay for a considerable time. The blood was yet oozing from the wound on my head. For a time I thought I should bleed to death; and think now that I should have done so, but that the blood so matted my hair as to stop the wound. After lying there about three quarters of an hour, I nerved myself up again, and started on my

F AUTHOR'S PURPOSE
Reread lines 121–128. Why might Douglass have chosen not to include details about his own reactions to the events he describes? Explain.

---

7. **hopper:** a funnel-shaped container for storing grain.
8. **kept the road:** stayed on the road.

way, through bogs and briers, barefooted and bareheaded, tearing my feet
sometimes at nearly every step; and after a journey of about seven miles,
150 occupying some five hours to perform it, I arrived at master's store. I then
presented an appearance enough to affect any but a heart of iron. From the crown
of my head to my feet, I was covered with blood. My hair was all clotted with dust
and blood; my shirt was stiff with blood. My legs and feet were torn in sundry
places with briers and thorns, and were also covered with blood. I suppose I
looked like a man who had escaped a den of wild beasts, and barely escaped them.
In this state I appeared before my master, humbly entreating him to interpose his
authority for my protection. I told him all the circumstances as well as I could,
and it seemed, as I spoke, at times to affect him. He would then walk the floor,
and seek to justify Covey by saying he expected I deserved it. He asked me what I
160 wanted. I told him, to let me get a new home; that as sure as I lived with Mr.
Covey again, I should live with but to die with him; that Covey would surely kill
me; he was in a fair way for it. Master Thomas ridiculed the idea that there was
any danger of Mr. Covey's killing me, and said that he knew Mr. Covey; that he
was a good man, and that he could not think of taking me from him; that, should
he do so, he would lose the whole year's wages; that I belonged to Mr. Covey for
one year, and that I must go back to him, come what might; and that I must not
trouble him with any more stories, or that he would himself *get hold of me*. After **G**
threatening me thus, he gave me a very large dose of salts,[9] telling me that I might
remain in St. Michael's that night, (it being quite late,) but that I must be off back
170 to Mr. Covey's early in the morning; and that if I did not, he would get *hold of me,*
which meant that he would whip me. I remained all night, and, according to his
orders, I started off to Covey's in the morning, (Saturday morning,) wearied in
body and broken in spirit. I got no supper that night, or breakfast that morning. I
reached Covey's about nine o'clock; and just as I was getting over the fence that
divided Mrs. Kemp's fields from ours, out ran Covey with his cowskin, to give me
another whipping. Before he could reach me, I succeeded in getting to the
cornfield; and as the corn was very high, it afforded me the means of hiding. He
seemed very angry, and searched for me a long time. My behavior was altogether
unaccountable. He finally gave up the chase, thinking, I suppose, that I must
180 come home for something to eat; he would give himself no further trouble in
looking for me. I spent that day mostly in the woods, having the alternative before
me,—to go home and be whipped to death, or stay in the woods and be starved to
death. That night, I fell in with Sandy Jenkins, a slave with whom I was somewhat
acquainted. Sandy had a free wife who lived about four miles from Mr. Covey's;
and it being Saturday, he was on his way to see her. I told him my circumstances,
and he very kindly invited me to go home with him. I went home with him, and
talked this whole matter over, and got his advice as to what course it was best for
me to pursue. I found Sandy an old adviser. He told me, with great solemnity, I

G **STYLE**
Reread lines 159–167.
Note that Douglass
chooses to convey this
dialogue without the
use of quotations. What
effect does he achieve
instead by repeating the
word *that*?

---

9. **salts:** mineral salts used to relieve faintness and headache or to reduce swelling.

Panel #10 from *The Frederick Douglass Series of 1938-1940,* Jacob Lawrence. © 2007 The Jacob and Gwendolyn Lawrence Foundation, Seattle/Artists Rights Society (ARS), New York

must go back to Covey; but that before I went, I must go with him into another
190 part of the woods, where there was a certain *root,* which, if I would take some of it
with me, carrying it *always on my right side,* would render it impossible for Mr.
Covey, or any other white man, to whip me. He said he had carried it for years;
and since he had done so, he had never received a blow, and never expected to
while he carried it. I at first rejected the idea, that the simple carrying of a root in
my pocket would have any such effect as he had said, and was not disposed to take
it; but Sandy impressed the necessity with much earnestness, telling me it could
do no harm, if it did no good. To please him, I at length took the root, and,
according to his direction, carried it upon my right side. This was Sunday
morning. I immediately started for home; and upon entering the yard gate, out
200 came Mr. Covey on his way to meeting.[10] He spoke to me very kindly, made me
drive the pigs from a lot near by, and passed on towards the church. Now, this
singular conduct of Mr. Covey really made me begin to think that there was
something in the *root* which Sandy had given me; and had it been on any other
day than Sunday, I could have attributed the conduct to no other cause than the
influence of that root; and as it was, I was half inclined to think the *root* to be
something more than I at first had taken it to be. All went well till Monday
morning. On this morning, the virtue of the *root* was fully tested. Long before
daylight, I was called to go and rub, curry, and feed, the horses. I obeyed, and was
glad to obey. But whilst thus engaged, whilst in the act of throwing down some
210 blades from the loft, Mr. Covey entered the stable with a long rope; and just as I
was half out of the loft, he caught hold of my legs, and was about tying me. As
soon as I found what he was up to, I gave a sudden spring, and as I did so, he
holding to my legs, I was brought sprawling on the stable floor. Mr. Covey seemed
now to think he had me, and could do what he pleased; but at this moment—
from whence came the spirit I don't know—I resolved to fight; and, suiting my
action to the resolution, I seized Covey hard by the throat; and as I did so, I rose.
He held on to me, and I to him. My resistance was so entirely unexpected, that
Covey seemed taken all aback. He trembled like a leaf. This gave me assurance,
and I held him uneasy, causing the blood to run where I touched him with the
220 ends of my fingers. Mr. Covey soon called out to Hughes for help. Hughes came,
and, while Covey held me, attempted to tie my right hand. While he was in the
act of doing so, I watched my chance, and gave him a heavy kick close under the
ribs. This kick fairly sickened Hughes, so that he left me in the hands of Mr.
Covey. This kick had the effect of not only weakening Hughes, but Covey also.
When he saw Hughes bending over with pain, his courage quailed. He asked me if
I meant to persist in my resistance. I told him I did, come what might; that he
had used me like a brute for six months, and that I was determined to be used so
no longer. With that, he strove to drag me to a stick that was lying just out of the
stable door. He meant to knock me down. But just as he was leaning over to get

---

10. **meeting:** church service.

230 the stick, I seized him with both hands by his collar, and brought him by a
sudden snatch to the ground. By this time, Bill came. Covey called upon him
for assistance. Bill wanted to know what he could do. Covey said, "Take hold of
him, take hold of him!" Bill said his master hired him out to work, and not to
help to whip me; so he left Covey and myself to fight our own battle out. We
were at it for nearly two hours. Covey at length let me go, puffing and blowing
at a great rate, saying that if I had not resisted, he would not have whipped me
half so much. The truth was, that he had not whipped me at all. I considered
him as getting entirely the worst end of the bargain; for he had drawn no blood
from me, but I had from him. The whole six months afterwards, that I spent
240 with Mr. Covey, he never laid the weight of his finger upon me in anger. He
would occasionally say, he didn't want to get hold of me again. "No," thought I,
"you need not; for you will come off worse than you did before."

   This battle with Mr. Covey was the turning-point in my career as a slave. It
rekindled the few expiring embers of freedom, and revived within me a sense
of my own manhood. It recalled the departed self-confidence, and inspired me
again with a determination to be free. The gratification afforded by the triumph
was a full compensation[11] for whatever else might follow, even death itself. He
only can understand the deep satisfaction which I experienced, who has himself
repelled by force the bloody arm of slavery. I felt as I never felt before. It was
250 a glorious resurrection, from the tomb of slavery, to the heaven of freedom.
My long-crushed spirit rose, cowardice departed, bold defiance took its place;
and I now resolved that, however long I might remain a slave in form, the day
had passed forever when I could be a slave in fact. I did not hesitate to let it be
known of me, that the white man who expected to succeed in whipping, must
also succeed in killing me. **H**

   From this time I was never again what might be called fairly whipped,
though I remained a slave four years afterwards. I had several fights, but was
never whipped. ❧

H **AUTHOR'S PURPOSE**
Reread lines 243–253.
What effect might this
description have had on
Douglass's readers?

---

11. **compensation:** payment; something of equivalent value.

Comprehension

1. **Recall** What was Covey's first reason for beating Douglass?

2. **Summarize** How did Master Thomas respond when Douglass asked for protection from Covey?

3. **Clarify** How was the battle with Covey a turning point in Douglass's life as a slave?

Literary Analysis

4. **Analyze Author's Purpose** Review the chart you created as you read. Given his main purpose, why might Douglass have chosen to include both kinds of detail in his narrative? Explain your answer.

5. **Analyze Style** Describe the main elements of Douglass's style. Which elements, if any, help Douglass establish himself as a credible **narrator?** Support your answer with details.

6. **Examine Rhetorical Devices** Douglass was a great orator, and his style was influenced by his mastery of rhetorical devices. One of his signature techniques was his use of **inverted parallelism,** a reversal of ideas expressed in parallel phrases or clauses: "The longest days were too short for him, and the shortest nights too long for him." Identify the inverted parallelism in lines 99–100. In what ways does this reversal of ideas summarize Douglass's emotional experiences in this selection?

7. **Make Generalizations from Conflicts** What do the conflicts between Douglass and Covey reveal about slavery's effects on both slaves and masters? Use a chart like the one shown to make generalizations about slavery based on Douglass's experiences.

Conflicts with Covey		Generalizations About Slavery
•		**Effects on Slaves:**
•		
•		**Effects on Masters:**

8. **Draw Conclusions** Consider how Douglass portrays his triumphant moment of **self-determination.** In what ways does his experience illustrate each of the following classic American ideas? Support your answers with details.

   • individual rights   • self-reliance   • resistance to tyranny

Literary Criticism

9. **Different Perspectives** In what ways might a slave narrative written by an enslaved woman differ from Douglass's account? Explain your answer.

Reading-Writing Connection

WRITING PROMPT

DESCRIBE A TURNING POINT Douglass viewed his fight with the cowardly overseer Covey as a turning point in his life. Think of an episode from your own life that you would describe as a turning point. Write a **three-paragraph description** of the episode. Make effective word choices to convey the significance of the event to your readers.

SELF-CHECK

A strong description will . . .
- have a clear focus
- use descriptive details and precise words to create a vivid image
- clearly demonstrate the significance of the event

GRAMMAR AND STYLE

MAKE EFFECTIVE WORD CHOICES Review the **Grammar and Style** note on page 541. To convey the brutal conditions he endured as a slave, Douglass used **vivid verbs,** ones that convey precise actions or emotions and draw readers into the reality of his experiences.

> *I was seized with a violent aching of the head, attended with extreme dizziness; I trembled in every limb. Finding what was coming, I nerved myself up, feeling it would never do to stop work. I stood as long as I could stagger to the hopper with grain.* (lines 106–109)

The verbs *seized, trembled, nerved,* and *stagger* help communicate the urgency of Douglass's situation.

PRACTICE Rewrite each sentence, replacing the boldfaced words with vivid verbs. An example has been done for you.

> **EXAMPLE**
>
> I **walked** into the room where the baby was **crying** and **helped** her back to sleep.
>
> *I crept into the room where the baby was whimpering and coaxed her back to sleep.*

1. The wind **blew** as he **walked** through the dark forest.

2. A sudden wave of illness made me **hold** my stomach.

3. The waves **moved** the ship back and forth as the storm **continued.**

WRITING TOOLS
For prewriting, revision, and editing tools, visit the **Writing Center** at ClassZone.com.

from **Incidents in the Life of a Slave Girl**

Slave Narrative by Harriet Jacobs

Harriet Jacobs

1813–1897

Harriet Jacobs's *Incidents in the Life of a Slave Girl* is one of the few slave narratives to recount the anguish of slavery from a female point of view. The book ranks as one of the most powerful and important examples of the slave narrative genre.

Defying Her Owner Jacobs was born into slavery in Edenton, North Carolina. Her first owner was a relatively kind woman who taught her to read and sew. When Jacobs was 12, the woman died, and Jacobs was willed to the 3-year-old daughter of Dr. James Norcom—the man she calls "Dr. Flint" in her autobiography. Norcom began making sexual advances toward Jacobs when she was in her teens. Jacobs resisted him and instead started a relationship with Norcom's neighbor, a white lawyer named Samuel Sawyer ("Mr. Sands" in the narrative), hoping the relationship would put a stop to Norcom's unwanted attentions. Jacobs had two children with Sawyer, but Norcom continued harassing her. Infuriated by her refusals, he punished Jacobs by sending her and her young children to work for his son ("Mr. Flint"), who he hoped would be able to break her resistance.

Seven Years in Hiding Shortly after arriving at the son's plantation, Jacobs made the painful decision to run away and leave her children behind. She hoped that her leaving would make the Norcoms sell the children to their father, Sawyer. Unlike many runaways, Jacobs did not immediately flee north. She hid in a tiny attic space in her grandmother's house. She remained there for seven years, but was able to take comfort in the knowledge that her children had been bought by Sawyer and saved from plantation life. In 1842, friends arranged for Jacobs to escape to New York. Once there, she found work as a nanny for a white family. Even so, Jacobs was always in danger of losing her freedom. Fugitive slave laws allowed for slave catchers to capture slaves who had escaped to the North and return them to slavery in the South. Fortunately, in 1852, Jacobs's employer purchased Jacobs's freedom and that of her two children.

Abolitionist and Author In the North, Jacobs became involved in the abolitionist movement. Abolitionist friends encouraged her to write *Incidents in the Life of a Slave Girl,* which she published in 1861 under the pseudonym Linda Brent, the name she uses to refer to herself in the narrative.

LITERARY ANALYSIS: NARRATIVE ELEMENTS

The events in Jacobs's autobiography are true, not fictional, yet she selects and arranges them to tell a compelling story. Critics have noted, not always admiringly, how much her book resembles a novel. As you read, notice the following narrative characteristics:

- Linda, the main character, experiences internal and external **conflicts** resulting from slavery. An **internal conflict** is a struggle within a character; an **external conflict** is a struggle between a character and an outside force.

- These conflicts result in **suspense,** or excitement and tension, as readers wonder about the outcome of events.

- Direct comments and telling details build the strong **characterizations** of Linda and the slave owners, making their personalities clear yet complex.

READING STRATEGY: READING A NARRATIVE

Numerous characters are mentioned in this selection, and because the excerpt is from the middle of the book, it is not always clear who they are. Some are never given names. Study Jacobs's biography on page 550, then match characters in the narrative to the actual figures in Jacobs's life. Pay attention to the background paragraphs that precede each part of the selection. As you read, use a graphic organizer to keep track of the characters and their relation to the narrator. Note whether they support or oppose her.

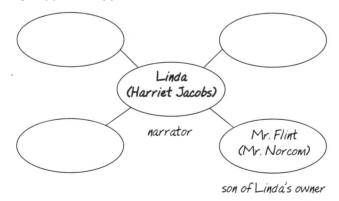

Linda
(Harriet Jacobs)

narrator

Mr. Flint
(Mr. Norcom)

son of Linda's owner

Explore the Key Idea

What is the PRICE of freedom?

KEY IDEA Parents often put their children's welfare before their own. In Harriet Jacobs's case, the **sacrifice** she made for her children was tremendous. Running away put her at risk of being caught and severely beaten, jailed, or sold. In addition, she deprived herself of the opportunity to play a role in the raising of her own children.

DISCUSS Think about sacrifices people have made for their own or their children's freedom. Discuss examples from the past or the present with a group of classmates. Can the price of freedom ever be too high?

The Ride for Freedom, The Fugitive Slaves (1862), Eastman Johnson. Oil. The Granger Collection, New York.

Incidents *in the* Life *of a* Slave Girl

Harriet Jacobs

BACKGROUND At this point in the narrative, Linda has spent six weeks at the plantation of old Dr. Flint's son, Mr. Flint, making the house ready for his new bride, who is now at the house. Mr. Flint has said openly that he plans to break Linda's willful spirit, as his father had not been able to do. In addition, Linda has learned that the next day, her children are to be brought from their grandmother's house, where they are loved, to the plantation, where they will be put to work and used to keep Linda in line. Be warned that this selection contains a racial slur.

The Flight

MR. FLINT was hard pushed for house servants, and rather than lose me he had restrained his malice. I did my work faithfully, though not, of course, with a willing mind. They were evidently afraid I should leave them. Mr. Flint wished that I should sleep in the great house instead of the servants' quarters. His wife agreed to the proposition, but said I mustn't bring my bed into the house, because it would scatter feathers on her carpet. I knew when I went there that they would never think of such a thing as furnishing a bed of any kind for me and my little one. I therefore carried my own bed, and now I was forbidden to use it. I did as I **A** was ordered. But now that I was certain my children were to be put in their power,

10 in order to give them a stronger hold on me, I resolved to leave them that night. I remembered the grief this step would bring upon my dear old grandmother; and nothing less than the freedom of my children would have induced me to disregard her advice. I went about my evening work with trembling steps. Mr. Flint twice called from his chamber door to inquire why the house was not locked up. I replied that I had not done my work. "You have had time enough to do it," said he. "Take care how you answer me!"

ANALYZE VISUALS
What can you **infer** about the enslaved family pictured in this photograph from South Carolina?

A **NARRATIVE ELEMENTS**
Notice how the details in lines 1–8 build the **characterization** of the Flints. What kind of people are they?

I shut all the windows, locked all the doors, and went up to the third story, to wait till midnight. How long those hours seemed, and how fervently I prayed that God would not forsake me in this hour of utmost need! I was about to risk
20 everything on the throw of a die; and if I failed, O what would become of me and my poor children? They would be made to suffer for my fault. **B**

At half past twelve I stole softly down stairs. I stopped on the second floor, thinking I heard a noise. I felt my way down into the parlor, and looked out of the window. The night was so intensely dark that I could see nothing. I raised the window very softly and jumped out. Large drops of rain were falling, and the darkness bewildered me. I dropped on my knees, and breathed a short prayer to God for guidance and protection. I groped my way to the road, and rushed towards the town with almost lightning speed. I arrived at my grandmother's house, but dared not see her. She would say, "Linda, you are killing me;" and I
30 knew that would unnerve me. I tapped softly at the window of a room, occupied by a woman, who had lived in the house several years. I knew she was a faithful friend, and could be trusted with my secret. I tapped several times before she heard me. At last she raised the window, and I whispered, "Sally, I have run away. Let me in, quick." She opened the door softly, and said in low tones, "For God's sake, don't. Your grandmother is trying to buy you and de chillern. Mr. Sands was here last week. He tole her he was going away on business, but he wanted her to go ahead about buying you and de chillern, and he would help her all he could. Don't run away, Linda. Your grandmother is all bowed down wid trouble now." **C**

I replied, "Sally, they are going to carry my children to the plantation to-
40 morrow; and they will never sell them to any body so long as they have me in their power. Now, would you advise me to go back?"

"No, chile, no," answered she. "When dey finds you is gone, dey won't want de plague[1] ob de chillern; but where is you going to hide? Dey knows ebery inch ob dis house."

I told her I had a hiding-place, and that was all it was best for her to know. I asked her to go into my room as soon as it was light, and take all my clothes out of my trunk, and pack them in hers; for I knew Mr. Flint and the constable would be there early to search my room. I feared the sight of my children would be too much for my full heart; but I could not go out into the uncertain future without
50 one last look. I bent over the bed where lay my little Benny and baby Ellen. Poor little ones! fatherless and motherless! Memories of their father came over me. He wanted to be kind to them; but they were not all to him, as they were to my womanly heart. I knelt and prayed for the innocent little sleepers. I kissed them lightly, and turned away. **D**

As I was about to open the street door, Sally laid her hand on my shoulder, and said, "Linda, is you gwine all alone? Let me call your uncle. "

"No, Sally," I replied, "I want no one to be brought into trouble on my account."

---

1. **plague:** nuisance.

B NARRATIVE ELEMENTS
Describe the **conflicts** presented in lines 9–21. Which lines build **suspense?**

C READING A NARRATIVE
Reread lines 28–38. Who are Sally and Mr. Sands? Refer to Jacobs's biography on page 550 if necessary.

D GRAMMAR AND STYLE
Examine lines 50–54. Notice how the writer uses emotionally charged **adjectives** to express the depth of her despair.

I went forth into the darkness and rain. I ran on till I came to the house of the friend who was to conceal me.

60   Early the next morning Mr. Flint was at my grandmother's inquiring for me. She told him she had not seen me, and supposed I was at the plantation. He watched her face narrowly, and said, "Don't you know any thing about her running off?" She assured him that she did not. He went on to say, "Last night she ran off without the least provocation. We had treated her very kindly. My wife liked her. She will soon be found and brought back. Are her children with you?" When told that they were, he said, "I am very glad to hear that. If they are here, she cannot be far off. If I find out that any of my niggers have had any thing to do with this damned business, I'll give 'em five hundred lashes." As he started to go to his father's, he turned round and added, persuasively, "Let her be brought back, 70 and she shall have her children to live with her."

    The tidings made the old doctor rave and storm at a furious rate. It was a busy day for them. My grandmother's house was searched from top to bottom. As my trunk was empty, they concluded I had taken my clothes with me. Before

ten o'clock every vessel northward bound was thoroughly examined, and the law against harboring[2] fugitives was read to all on board. At night a watch was set over the town. Knowing how distressed my grandmother would be, I wanted to send her a message; but it could not be done. Every one who went in or out of her house was closely watched. The doctor said he would take my children, unless she became responsible for them; which of course she willingly did. The next day was
80 spent in searching. Before night, the following advertisement was posted at every corner, and in every public place for miles round:—

> *$300 REWARD! Ran away from the subscriber,[3] an intelligent, bright, mulatto[4] girl, named Linda, 21 years of age. Five feet four inches high. Dark eyes, and black hair inclined to curl; but it can be made straight. Has a decayed spot on a front tooth. She can read and write, and in all probability will try to get to the Free States. All persons are forbidden, under penalty of the law, to harbor or employ said slave. $150 will be given to whoever takes her in the state, and $300 if taken out of the state and delivered to me, or lodged in jail. DR. FLINT.*

For a week, Linda hides in the house of an unnamed friend. Her pursuers come so close to finding her that she rushes from the house into the bushes, where she is bitten by a poisonous snake or lizard. She suffers greatly until an old woman treats her with a folk remedy. Vowing "give me liberty or death," she refuses to return to the Flints. Then a sympathetic white woman, an old friend of her grandmother's, offers to conceal Linda in a small storage room in her house. The woman makes them promise never to tell, as she is the wife of a prominent slaveholder. The woman sends her cook, Linda's friend Betty, to meet Linda and take her to the house.

Months of Peril

90 I went to sleep that night with the feeling that I was for the present the most fortunate slave in town. Morning came and filled my little cell with light. I thanked the heavenly Father for this safe retreat. Opposite my window was a pile of feather beds. On the top of these I could lie perfectly concealed, and command a view of the street through which Dr. Flint passed to his office. Anxious as I was, I felt a gleam of satisfaction when I saw him. Thus far I had outwitted him, and I triumphed over it. Who can blame slaves for being cunning? They are constantly compelled to resort to it. It is the only weapon of the weak and oppressed against the strength of their tyrants. **E**

E NARRATIVE ELEMENTS
Consider the **characterization** of Linda in this paragraph. How are readers likely to feel toward her?

---

2. **harboring:** sheltering or protecting.

3. **the subscriber:** the person placing the notice, Dr. Flint.

4. **mulatto:** of mixed black and white ancestry.

I was daily hoping to hear that my master had sold my children; for I knew
who was on the watch to buy them. But Dr. Flint cared even more for revenge
than he did for money. My brother William, and the good aunt who had served
in his family twenty years, and my little Benny, and Ellen, who was a little over
two years old, were thrust into jail, as a means of compelling my relatives to give
some information about me. He swore my grandmother should never see one of
them again till I was brought back. They kept these facts from me for several days.
When I heard that my little ones were in a loathsome jail, my first impulse was to
go to them. I was encountering dangers for the sake of freeing them, and must I
be the cause of their death? The thought was agonizing. My benefactress[5] tried to
soothe me by telling me that my aunt would take good care of the children while
they remained in jail. But it added to my pain to think that the good old aunt,
who had always been so kind to her sister's orphan children, should be shut up in
prison for no other crime than loving them. I suppose my friends feared a reckless
movement on my part, knowing, as they did, that my life was bound up in my
children. I received a note from my brother William. It was scarcely legible, and
ran thus: "Wherever you are, dear sister, I beg of you not to come here. We are all
much better off than you are. If you come, you will ruin us all. They would force
you to tell where you had been, or they would kill you. Take the advice of your
friends; if not for the sake of me and your children, at least for the sake of those
you would ruin." **F**

Poor William! He also must suffer for being my brother. I took his advice and
kept quiet. My aunt was taken out of jail at the end of a month, because Mrs.
Flint could not spare her any longer. She was tired of being her own housekeeper.
It was quite too fatiguing to order her dinner and eat it too. My children remained
in jail, where brother William did all he could for their comfort. Betty went to see
them sometimes, and brought me tidings. She was not permitted to enter the jail;
but William would hold them up to the grated window while she chatted with
them. When she repeated their prattle, and told me how they wanted to see their
ma, my tears would flow. Old Betty would exclaim, "Lors, chile! what's you crying
'bout? Dem young uns vil kill you dead. Don't be so chick'n hearted! If you does,
you vil nebber git thro' dis world." ❧ **G**

F NARRATIVE ELEMENTS
What new **conflict**
is presented in this
paragraph?

G READING A NARRATIVE
Review the paragraph
that begins "For a
week…" on page 556.
Who is Betty, mentioned
in lines 124–130?

---

5. **benefactress:** a woman who gives aid.

Comprehension

1. **Recall** What prompts Linda to make the decision to escape?

2. **Summarize** What actions do the Flints take after they find out Linda has left?

3. **Clarify** Why does Linda want the Flints to sell her children?

Literary Analysis

4. **Reading a Narrative** Review the web you made as you read. Which characters support Linda and which oppose her? Share questions you have about them.

5. **Examine Narrative Elements** Describe different **conflicts**—internal and external—that Linda faces in this excerpt. What do these conflicts reveal about the institution of slavery and the **sacrifices** forced by it?

6. **Analyze Characterization** How does the writer present herself? Discuss what you learn about her character and values from

   - her attitude toward her work (lines 2–3)
   - her thoughts as she visits her children (lines 48–54)
   - her insistence upon escaping alone (line 57)

7. **Contrast Characterizations** Contrast the writer's portrayal of herself with her portrayal of the Flints. What does she reveal about the Flints' character and values?

8. **Draw Conclusions** How might the writer's political purpose and the knowledge that she was writing for an audience of Northern white women have influenced her characterizations?

9. **Compare Texts** Read "Free Labor" and "Go Down, Moses" on pages 560 and 561. How do they compare with Harriet Jacobs's narrative in their **tone** and their messages about slavery?

Literary Criticism

10. **Author's Style** Jacobs's style was influenced by the literature popular in her time. Nineteenth-century women's novels were melodramatic, arousing readers' emotions with suspenseful plots that usually involved virtuous characters pitted against evil villains. *Uncle Tom's Cabin,* an immensely popular antislavery novel, included such elements as well. It also rendered the speech of slave characters in heavy dialect, a convention of the time. How do you, as a modern reader, respond to Jacobs's style? Evaluate the effects of her style on the power of her narrative.

Reading-Writing Connection

WRITING PROMPT

EXPLORE POINT OF VIEW *Incidents in the Life of a Slave Girl* is told from the first-person point of view and thus focuses on the thoughts, words, and actions of the narrator, Linda (Harriet Jacobs). Choose one of the other people mentioned in the narrative—Sally, or Linda's grandmother, aunt, or brother. Write a **three-paragraph response,** told from that character's point of view, reacting to the news that Linda has run away. As a starting point, reread Linda's descriptions of how any of these characters did or would react.

SELF-CHECK

An effective response will...
- have a clear focus
- establish a consistent tone and point of view
- use precise words to convey the character's emotions
- establish a mood

GRAMMAR AND STYLE

ESTABLISH TONE Review the **Grammar and Style** note on page 554. Tone is a writer's attitude toward a subject. In Jacobs's compelling narrative, she uses emotionally charged language to establish a tone of melancholy and desperation. In the following example, the **adjectives** *loathsome* and *agonizing* succinctly convey the turmoil and conflict the narrator is experiencing and help elicit empathy from her readers.

> *When I heard my little ones were in a loathsome jail, my first impulse was to go to them. I was encountering dangers for the sake of freeing them, and must I be the cause of their death? The thought was agonizing.* (lines 106–108)

PRACTICE Copy the sentences in the example. Then rewrite them, using adjectives, verbs, and additional phrases to effectively convey a tone of fear or sorrow. A sample answer has been done for you.

EXAMPLE

I fainted when I heard Linda had run off, leaving her children behind.

I collapsed to the floor when I heard poor Linda had run off, tearing herself away from the dear babies she cherished.

---

1. I'm an old woman, but I tried to be strong as Mr. Flint asked me questions about Linda.

2. The children cried when they heard their mother had left them behind.

3. It made me sad to see them feeling so bad. It is very hard for the little children.

WRITING TOOLS
For prewriting, revision, and editing tools, visit the **Writing Center** at ClassZone.com.

Free Labor

Frances Ellen Watkins Harper

I wear an easy garment,
   O'er it no toiling slave
Wept tears of hopeless anguish,
   In his passage to the grave.

5 And from its ample folds
   Shall rise no cry to God,
Upon its warp and woof shall be
   No stain of tears and blood.

Oh, lightly shall it press my form,
10   Unladened with a sigh,
I shall not 'mid its rustling hear,
   Some sad despairing cry.

This fabric is too light to bear
   The weight of bondsmen's tears,
15 I shall not in its texture trace
   The agony of years.

Too light to bear a smother'd sigh,
   From some lorn woman's heart,
Whose only wreath of household love
20   Is rudely torn apart.

Then lightly shall it press my form,
   Unburden'd by a sigh;
And from its seams and folds shall rise,
   No voice to pierce the sky,

25 And witness at the throne of God,
   In language deep and strong,
That I have nerv'd Oppression's hand,
   For deeds of guilt and wrong.

Go Down, Moses

Traditional Spiritual

When Israel was in Egypt's land,
Let my people go!
Oppressed so hard they could not stand
Let my people go!

5 Go down, Moses
'Way down in Egypt's land,
Tell old Pharoah, "Let my people go!"

"Thus saith the Lord" bold Moses said,
Let my people go!
10 "If not I'll smite your first-born dead"
Let my people go!

Go down, Moses
'Way down in Egypt's land,
Tell old Pharoah, "Let my people go!"

15 No more in bondage shall they toil,
Let my people go!
Let them come out with Egypt's spoil
Let my people go!

Go down, Moses
20 'Way down in Egypt's land,
Tell old Pharoah, "Let my people go!"

The Gettysburg Address
Speech by Abraham Lincoln
The Emancipation Proclamation
Proclamation by Abraham Lincoln

View of Washington, D.C.

Abraham Lincoln
1809–1865

Abraham Lincoln led the United States during its greatest crisis—the Civil War. Dedicated to keeping the nation together, Lincoln guided the country toward a new national identity, that of a nation committed to the principle of union, in which slavery no longer had a place.

Humble Origins Born on the Kentucky frontier to illiterate parents, Lincoln rarely went to school and was largely self-educated. As a young man, he moved with his family to Illinois, where he worked as a shopkeeper, rail-splitter, and surveyor and studied law. He served in the state legislature from 1834 to 1841, becoming a lawyer in 1836.

Evolving Views Although Lincoln opposed slavery as "injustice and bad policy," he was not an abolitionist; he preferred to free slaves gradually. In 1854, he began a vigorous public campaign to block the expansion of slavery to the western territories. His eloquent speeches and famous debates with Senator Stephen A. Douglas raised his political profile and strengthened his opposition to slavery.

A House Divided In 1860, Lincoln was elected president on his antislavery platform, prompting seven Southern states to secede from the Union before he even took office. In 1861, two months after his inauguration, the Civil War began.

As the fighting wore on, Lincoln faced increasing pressure to move against slavery while he struggled to keep the loyalty of the Union states that permitted slavery within their borders. After nearly two years of fighting, Lincoln issued the Emancipation Proclamation, which freed slaves in the rebelling states.

Tragic Ending Throughout the war, Lincoln faced opposition and ridicule from the public, his generals, and his own cabinet. The prospect of a Union victory, however, earned him reelection, and the Confederate armies surrendered weeks into his second term. Just five days later, Lincoln was assassinated, the first such occurrence in American history. His shocking murder and the end of war made him an instant hero. Today, he is one of the country's most widely respected presidents.

LITERARY ANALYSIS: AUDIENCE AND FORM

Lincoln was a master orator and an expert lawyer. He was keenly aware that the **form** a piece of writing takes affects what the writer can say to his or her **audience.**

- A **speech,** such as the Gettysburg Address, is often prepared for a specific audience. The speaker chooses details and language appropriate for the occasion so that the audience will be moved.

  We have come to dedicate a portion of that field as a final resting place for those who here gave their lives . . .

- A **proclamation,** such as the Emancipation Proclamation, is a legal document that announces official state business. As with any legal document, the writer is a person of authority and addresses the general public using precise language that can be clearly interpreted in a court of law.

  I, Abraham Lincoln, President of the United States, by virtue of the power in me vested as Commander-in-Chief . . .

As you read these two works of Lincoln's, note how the conventions of each form shape the way Lincoln expresses his message.

READING SKILL: ANALYZE AN AUTHOR'S BELIEFS

A thoughtful, principled man, Lincoln tried to act in accordance with his beliefs. To identify those beliefs in his writing, consider the ideals he invokes, the actions he takes, and the reasons he gives for his actions. As you read, note details that reveal

- the reason he felt the war was necessary
- his views on the responsibilities of the president
- the reasons he opposed slavery

Use a chart like the one shown to record your notes.

Beliefs About . . .	Gettysburg Address	Emancipation Proclamation
the necessity of war		
the duties of the president		
slavery		

Explore the Key Idea

What makes a great LEGACY?

KEY IDEA Washington, Jefferson, Lincoln—these legendary figures top most lists of greatest American presidents. In each case, the **legacy** is more complicated than the heroic myths suggest. What are the real reasons some leaders hold such a prominent place in history?

TEST YOURSELF What ideas come to mind when you think of Abraham Lincoln and the times in which he lived? Decide whether each statement is fact or myth.

Myth or History?

1. Hard-working Abe Lincoln was a poor country boy who rose to become president.
   ☐ TRUE   ○ FALSE

2. Lincoln led the fight to abolish slavery.
   ☐ TRUE   ○ FALSE

3. The Civil War was fought to free the slaves.
   ☐ TRUE   ○ FALSE

4. The Emancipation Proclamation ended slavery in the United States.
   ☐ TRUE   ○ FALSE

5. All of the Union states opposed slavery.
   ☐ TRUE   ○ FALSE

The GETTYSBURG ADDRESS

Abraham Lincoln

> **BACKGROUND** The Battle of Gettysburg was fought July 1–3, 1863. The victory for Union forces marked a turning point in the Civil War, but the losses on both sides were staggering: 28,000 Confederate soldiers and 23,000 Union soldiers were killed or wounded. Lincoln delivered his Gettysburg Address on November 19, 1863, at a ceremony dedicating a national cemetery on the battle site.

Four score and seven years ago[1] our fathers brought forth on this continent a new nation, conceived in liberty, and dedicated to the proposition that all men are created equal.

Now we are engaged in a great civil war, testing whether that nation, or any nation so conceived and so dedicated, can long endure. We are met on a great battlefield of that war. We have come to dedicate a portion of that field as a final resting place for those who here gave their lives that that nation might live. It is altogether fitting and proper that we should do this. **Ⓐ**

But, in a larger sense, we cannot dedicate—we cannot consecrate—we cannot
10 hallow[2]—this ground. The brave men, living and dead, who struggled here have consecrated it far above our poor power to add or detract. The world will little note nor long remember what we say here, but it can never forget what they did **Ⓑ** here. It is for us, the living, rather, to be dedicated here to the unfinished work which they who fought here have thus far so nobly advanced. It is rather for us to be here dedicated to the great task remaining before us—that from these honored dead we take increased devotion to that cause for which they gave the last full measure of devotion; that we here highly resolve that these dead shall not have died in vain; that this nation, under God, shall have a new birth of freedom; and that government of the people, by the people, for the people, shall not perish from
20 the earth. ☙ **Ⓒ**

---

1. **four score . . . ago:** 87 years ago—that is, in 1776. (*Score* means "a group of 20.")
2. **hallow:** set apart as holy.

Ⓐ AUDIENCE AND FORM
Describe the **tone** of lines 1–8. What details help convey the importance of the occasion?

Ⓑ GRAMMAR AND STYLE
Reread lines 9–13. Note how **repetition** emphasizes the verbs *dedicate and consecrate*.

Ⓒ AUTHOR'S BELIEFS
What is the "great task" Lincoln mentions in line 15?

The Emancipation Proclamation

January 1, 1863

Abraham Lincoln

BACKGROUND The Emancipation Proclamation was more of a symbolic gesture than an enforceable law. The document applied only to territory the Union did not control; it did not free slaves held by states that were loyal to the Union. Though the proclamation had little immediate legal impact, its promises inspired nearly 200,000 African Americans to join the Union army. Their efforts helped the North win the war.

A Transcription By the President of the United States of America:
A Proclamation.

Whereas, on the twenty-second day of September, in the year of our Lord one thousand eight hundred and sixty-two, a proclamation was issued by the President of the United States, containing, among other things, the following, to wit: **D**

"That on the first day of January, in the year of our Lord one thousand eight hundred and sixty-three, all persons held as slaves within any State or designated part of a State, the people whereof shall then be in rebellion against the United States, shall be then, thenceforward, and forever free; and the Executive Government of the United States, including the military and naval authority thereof, will recognize and maintain the freedom of such persons, and will do no
10 act or acts to repress such persons, or any of them, in any efforts they may make for their actual freedom.

"That the Executive will, on the first day of January aforesaid,[1] by proclamation, designate the States and parts of States, if any, in which the people thereof, respectively, shall then be in rebellion against the United States; and the fact that any State, or the people thereof, shall on that day be, in good faith, represented in the Congress of the United States by members chosen thereto at elections wherein a majority of the qualified voters of such State shall have participated, shall, in the absence of strong countervailing[2] testimony, be deemed conclusive evidence that such State, and the people thereof, are not then in
20 rebellion against the United States." **E**

Now, therefore I, Abraham Lincoln, President of the United States, by virtue of the power in me vested as Commander-in-Chief, of the Army and Navy of

D AUDIENCE AND FORM
Describe the word choice and sentence structure of lines 1–3. In what ways does the form of the writing—namely, a presidential proclamation—affect Lincoln's **diction?**

E AUDIENCE AND FORM
Paraphrase lines 12–20. What is the **purpose** of the complicated and careful definitions in this paragraph?

---

1. **aforesaid:** mentioned earlier.
2. **countervailing:** contradicting.

the United States in time of actual armed rebellion against the authority and government of the United States, and as a fit and necessary war measure for suppressing said rebellion, do, on this first day of January, in the year of our Lord one thousand eight hundred and sixty-three, and in accordance with my purpose so to do publicly proclaimed for the full period of one hundred days, from the day first above mentioned, order and designate as the States and parts of States wherein the people thereof respectively, are this day in rebellion against the United
30 States, the following, to wit:

Arkansas, Texas, Louisiana, (except the Parishes of St. Bernard, Plaquemines, Jefferson, St. John, St. Charles, St. James Ascension, Assumption, Terrebonne, Lafourche, St. Mary, St. Martin, and Orleans, including the City of New Orleans)[3] Mississippi, Alabama, Florida, Georgia, South Carolina, North Carolina, and Virginia, (except the forty-eight counties designated as West Virginia,[4] and also the counties of Berkley, Accomac, Northampton, Elizabeth City, York, Princess Ann, and Norfolk, including the cities of Norfolk and Portsmouth), and which excepted parts, are for the present, left precisely as if this proclamation were not issued.

40 And by virtue of the power, and for the purpose aforesaid, I do order and declare that all persons held as slaves within said designated States, and parts of States, are, and henceforward shall be free; and that the Executive government of the United States, including the military and naval authorities thereof, will recognize and maintain the freedom of said persons.

And I hereby enjoin upon[5] the people so declared to be free to abstain from all violence, unless in necessary self-defence; and I recommend to them that, in all cases when allowed, they labor faithfully for reasonable wages.

And I further declare and make known, that such persons of suitable condition, will be received into the armed service of the United States to garrison[7] forts,
50 positions, stations, and other places, and to man vessels of all sorts in said service.

And upon this act, sincerely believed to be an act of justice, warranted by the Constitution, upon military necessity, I invoke the considerate judgment of mankind, and the gracious favor of Almighty God. **F**

In witness whereof, I have hereunto set my hand and caused the seal of the United States to be affixed.

Done at the City of Washington, this first day of January, in the year of our Lord one thousand eight hundred and sixty three, and of the Independence of the United States of America the eighty-seventh.

By the President: ABRAHAM LINCOLN
WILLIAM H. SEWARD, Secretary of State.

F **AUTHOR'S BELIEFS**
Reread lines 51–53.
What reasons does
Lincoln give for freeing
the slaves?

---

3. **except the Parishes . . . New Orleans:** Parishes, or counties, occupied by Union forces.

4. **the forty-eight . . . Virginia:** the western counties of Virginia broke from the Confederacy to form a new state. West Virginia joined the Union as a slave state in 1863.

5. **enjoin upon:** to direct.

6. **garrison:** to occupy as troops.

Comprehension

1. **Recall** For what occasion did Lincoln deliver the Gettysburg Address?

2. **Clarify** According to Lincoln, for what cause or idea was the Battle of Gettysburg fought?

3. **Recall** What authority does Lincoln claim for issuing the Emancipation Proclamation?

4. **Summarize** What exceptions limit the effect of Lincoln's proclamation?

Literary Analysis

5. **Examine Historical Context** Using details from the author's biography on page 562 and from the background paragraphs on pages 564 and 566, describe the historical context of each document. What political pressures influenced Lincoln's public statements?

6. **Compare Audience and Form** Use a chart to compare and contrast Lincoln's two works. In what ways does the form used influence Lincoln's message?

7. **Draw Conclusions About Author's Beliefs** Review the chart you created as you read. Based on your answers, what would you consider to be Lincoln's fundamental values? Cite evidence to support your answer.

	Gettysburg Address	Emancipation Proclamation
Form		
Audience		
Diction		
Tone		

8. **Evaluate Form** Which of the two works better conveys each of the following ideas? Support your answers with details.

   - a sense of presidential authority
   - the urgency of the national crisis
   - the value of freedom
   - Lincoln's personal voice

9. **Synthesize Details** Review your answers to the quiz about Lincoln's life and times that you took before reading these works. Based on your reading and the historical information provided, explain which aspects of Lincoln's **legacy** are fact and which are myth. In your opinion, should Lincoln be considered a great leader? Give reasons for your answer.

Literary Criticism

10. **Critical Interpretations** Often critical of Lincoln's policies, Frederick Douglass also spoke warmly of his honesty and moral conviction. He stated, "The image of the man went out with his words, and those who read them knew him." Based on your own reading, what impressions do you have of Lincoln's character? Explain your answer.

Reading-Writing Connection

WRITE A LETTER Knowing he'd be speaking to an audience of people mourning the tremendous losses of the Civil War, Lincoln chose his words carefully. To show his respect for their heavy sacrifices, he used elevated language that conveyed a sense of their importance in history.

Imagine that you are a parent who lost a son at Gettysburg, fighting for either the Union or the Confederate army. Write a **three-paragraph letter** to Lincoln explaining your response to the Gettysburg Address.

A successful letter will

- clearly state its purpose
- use precise words to express emotion
- convey a sense of historic importance
- use an appropriate tone

GRAMMAR AND STYLE

USE LANGUAGE EFFECTIVELY Review the **Grammar and Style** note on page 564. In the Gettysburg Address, Lincoln makes effective use of the rhetorical device of **repetition.** Here is an example:

> *It is for us, the living, rather, to be dedicated here to the unfinished work which they who fought here have thus far so nobly advanced. It is rather for us to be here dedicated to the great task remaining before us . . .* (lines 13–15)

To emphasize the purpose of the solemn occasion, Lincoln repeats the word *dedicate,* as well as other verbs and abstract nouns, throughout his address. As he repeats words, he sometimes introduces subtle shifts in their meaning, encouraging reflection among the mourners.

PRACTICE Rewrite the following paragraph, incorporating repetition to emphasize key points.

> I was among the mourners who heard your eloquent and inspiring speech at Gettysburg. It made me want to write to you, and it caused me to think about what we are fighting for. My son was 19 years old when he enlisted. He was 20 when he was killed. My family and I can hardly bear the loss, but we have no other choice. We can only hope that his death—and the loss of thousands of others—will not have been in vain. As a parent, it is my sincere hope this is true. Speaking as a citizen of the United States, I can only pray the soldiers have not died for nothing.

WRITING TOOLS
For prewriting, revision, and editing tools, visit the **Writing Center** at ClassZone.com.

Voices from the Civil War

- Letter, page 571
- Letter, page 572
- Diary Entry, page 573
- Speech, page 574

Use with the Gettysburg Address, page 564.

Abraham Lincoln delivered the Gettysburg Address to an audience gathered in honor of fallen Union soldiers. How do you think they reacted to it? Might the same speech have been received differently by a Southern audience? The following documents can give you some insight into differing perspectives on the Civil War. After reading each text, take a moment to imagine how each author might have responded to Lincoln's message; later, you'll be asked to write such a response.

Skill Focus: Analyze Primary Sources

As you know, **primary sources** are materials written or made by people who took part in or witnessed the events portrayed. As such, these sources give you something you would probably miss if you read a more removed account. Many primary sources describe individual, personal experiences expressed in the writers' own voices.

The letters, diary entry, and speech you are about to read are all primary sources of information on the Civil War. Read the background paragraph before each document as well as its title and date, noting

- the form of the document (letter, diary entry, or speech)
- when and where it was written or delivered
- whether it was intended for a public or private audience
- some of the details that shaped the author's perspective

Record what you learn on a chart such as the one shown here. Then, as you read the texts, consider how these factors may have influenced the content.

Author	Form of Writing	Time & Place Created	Intended Audience	Relevant Details About the Author
Robert E. Lee				
Sullivan Ballou				
Mary Chesnut				
Sojourner Truth				

Robert E. Lee had a distinguished career in the U.S. Army until his home state of Virginia seceded from the Union. At that point, his loyalty to Virginia compelled him to join the Confederate army, where he became a general and one of the Confederacy's greatest heroes.

Letter to His Son

January 23, 1861

. . . The South, in my opinion, has been aggrieved by the acts of the North, as you say. I feel the aggression, and am willing to take every proper step for redress. It is the principle I contend for, not individual or private gain. As an American citizen, I take pride in my country, her prosperity and institutions, and would defend any State if her rights were invaded. But I can anticipate no greater calamity for the country than a dissolution of the Union. It would be an accumulation of all the evils we complain of, and I am willing to sacrifice everything but honor for its preservation. I hope, therefore, that all constitutional means will be exhausted before there is a recourse to force. Secession is nothing but revolution. The framers of our **A**
10 Constitution never exhausted so much labor, wisdom and forbearance in its formation, and surrounded it with so many guards and securities, if it was intended to be broken by every member of the Confederacy at will. It was intended for 'perpetual union' so expressed in the preamble, and for the establishment of a government, not a compact, which can only be dissolved by revolution, or the consent of all the people in convention assembled. It is idle to talk of secession. Anarchy would have been established, and not a government by Washington, Hamilton, Jefferson, Madison, and the other patriots of the Revolution. . . . Still, a Union that can only be maintained by swords and bayonets, and in which strife and civil war are to take the place of brotherly love
20 and kindness, has no charm for me. I shall mourn for my country and for the welfare and progress of mankind. If the Union is dissolved, and the Government disrupted, I shall return to my native State and share the miseries of my people, and save in defence will draw my sword on none. **B**

A PRIMARY SOURCES
Reread lines 5–8. What does Lee want to preserve at any cost but his honor? What is his view of secession?

B PRIMARY SOURCES
Based on lines 18–21, how does Lee feel about maintaining the Union "by swords and bayonets"? Why?

Major Sullivan Ballou of the Second Rhode Island Regiment wrote the following letter to his wife on July 14, 1861. He was killed about a week later, at the first battle of Bull Run.

Letter to Sarah Ballou

My very dear Sarah:

The indications are very strong that we shall move in a few days—perhaps tomorrow. Lest I should not be able to write again, I feel impelled to write a few lines that may fall under your eye when I shall be no more. . . .

I have no misgivings about, or lack of confidence in the cause in which I am engaged, and my courage does not halt or falter. I know how strongly American Civilization now leans on the triumph of the Government, and how great a debt we owe to those who went before us through the blood and sufferings of the Revolution. And I am willing—perfectly willing—to lay down all my joys in this life, to help maintain this Government, and to pay that debt. . . .

10   Sarah my love for you is deathless, it seems to bind me with mighty cables that nothing but Omnipotence could break; and yet my love of Country comes over me like a strong wind and bears me unresistibly on with all these chains to the battlefield. **C**

The memories of the blissful moments I have spent with you come creeping over me, and I feel most gratified to God and to you that I have enjoyed them so long. And hard it is for me to give them up and burn to ashes the hopes of future years, when, God willing, we might still have lived and loved together, and seen our sons grown up to honorable manhood, around us. I have, I know, but few and small claims upon Divine Providence, but something whispers to me—

20 perhaps it is the wafted prayer of my little Edgar, that I shall return to my loved ones unharmed. If I do not my dear Sarah, never forget how much I love you, and when my last breath escapes me on the battlefield, it will whisper your name. Forgive my many faults, and the many pains I have caused you. How thoughtless and foolish I have often times been! How gladly would I wash out with my tears every little spot upon your happiness. . . .

But, O Sarah! If the dead can come back to this earth and flit unseen around those they loved, I shall always be near you; in the gladdest days and in the darkest nights . . . always, always, and if there be a soft breeze upon your cheek, it shall be my breath, as the cool air fans your throbbing temple, it shall be my spirit

30 passing by. Sarah do not mourn me dead; think I am gone and wait for thee, for we shall meet again. . . .

C PRIMARY SOURCES
How committed is Ballou to the cause for which he is fighting? What reasons does he give for this degree of commitment?

Wife of a former South Carolina senator, James Chesnut, and a member of the Southern gentility, Mary Chesnut socialized with many prominent Confederates. In her extensive diaries, she kept notes on the social and political conditions in the wartime South.

A Diary from Dixie

1864

September 1st — The battle is raging at Atlanta, our fate hanging in the balance.

September 2nd — Atlanta is gone. Well that agony is over. Like David, when the child was dead, I will get up from my knees, will wash my face and comb my hair. There is no hope, but we will try to have no fear. . . . **D**

September 21st — The President has gone West. He sent for Mr. Chesnut. I went with Mrs. Rhett to hear Dr. Palmer. I did not know before how utterly hopeless was our situation. This man is so eloquent; it was hard to listen and not give way. Despair was his word, and martyrdom. He offered us nothing more in this world than the martyr's crown. He is not for slavery, he says; he is for freedom, 10 the freedom to govern our own country as we see fit. He is against foreign interference in our state matters. That is what Mr. Palmer went to war for, it appears. Every day shows that slavery is doomed the world over. For that he thanked God. He spoke of this time of our agony; and then came the cry: "Help us, Oh God! Vain is the help of man." So we came away shaken to the depths. . . .

The end has come, no doubt of the fact. Our Army has so moved as to uncover Macon and Augusta. We are going to be wiped off the face of the earth. Now what is there to prevent Sherman taking General Lee in the rear. We have but two armies, and Sherman is between them now. **E**

September 29th — These stories of our defeats in the Valley fall like blows upon 20 a dead body. Since Atlanta, I have felt as if all were dead within me, forever. Captain Ogden of General Chesnut's staff dined here today. Had ever a Brigadier with little or no brigade so magnificent a staff? The reserves, as somebody said, are gathered by robbing the cradle and the grave of men too old and boys too young. . . .

General Chesnut was away in Camden, but I could not wait. I gave the beautiful bride, Mrs. Darby, a dinner which was simply perfect. I was satisfied for once in my life with my own table, and I know pleasanter guests were never seated around any table whatsoever in the world. My house is always crowded. After all, what a number of pleasant people are thrown by war's catastrophes into Columbia. I call such society glorious. It is the wind-up, the Cassandra in me says; and the 30 old life means to die royally.

D PRIMARY SOURCES
What does Chesnut feel after the fall of Atlanta?

E PRIMARY SOURCES
According to Chesnut, why did Dr. Palmer go to war? What did he not fight for?

An advocate for the rights of blacks and women, and herself a former slave, Sojourner Truth delivered this candid address to a progressive audience not long after the signing of the Emancipation Proclamation.

Speech to the American Equal Rights Association

May 9, 1867

My friends, I am rejoiced that you are glad, but I don't know how you will feel when I get through. I come from another field—the country of the slave. They have got their liberty—so much good luck to have slavery partly destroyed; not entirely. I want it root and branch destroyed. Then we will all be free indeed. I feel that if I have to answer for the deeds done in my body just as much as a man, I have a right to have just as much as a man. There is a great stir about colored men getting their rights, but not a word about the colored women; and if colored men get their rights, and not colored women theirs, you see the colored men will be masters over the women, and it will be just as bad as it was before. So I am for keeping the thing going while things are stirring; because if we
10 wait till it is still, it will take a great while to get it going again. . . . I want women to have their rights. In the courts women have no right, no voice; nobody speaks for them. I wish woman to have her voice there among the pettifoggers. If it is not a fit place for women, it is unfit for men to be there. **F**

   I am above eighty years old; it is about time for me to be going. I have been forty years a slave and forty years free, and would be here forty years more to have equal rights for all. I suppose I am kept here because something remains for me to do; I suppose I am yet to help to break the chain. I have done a great deal of work; as much as a man, but did not get so much pay. I used to work in the field and bind grain, keeping up with the cradler; but men doing no more, got twice as much pay; so with
20 the German women. They work in the field and do as much work, but do not get the pay. We do as much, we eat as much, we want as much. I suppose I am about the only colored woman that goes about to speak for the rights of the colored women. I want to keep the thing stirring, now that the ice is cracked. What we want is a little money. You men know that you get as much again as women when you write, or for what you do. When we get our rights we shall not have to come to you for money, for then we shall have money enough in our own pockets; and may be you will ask us for money. But help us now until we get it. It is a good consolation to know that when we have got this battle fought we shall not be coming to you any more. You have been having our rights so long, that you think, like a slaveholder, that you own us. I know that it is hard for
30 one who has held the reins for so long to give up; it cuts like a knife. It will feel all the better when it closes up again. I have been in Washington about three years, seeing about these colored people. Now colored men have the right to vote. There ought to be equal rights now more than ever, since colored people have got their freedom. **G**

Comprehension

1. **Recall** How did Robert E. Lee plan to respond if the Union was dissolved?

2. **Recall** What did Sullivan Ballou think would be his fate in battle?

3. **Recall** How did Mary Chesnut spend her time during the month of September 1864?

4. **Summarize** In the primary sources you just read, Union and Confederate soldiers and civilians reveal some of the motives they had for engaging in the Civil War. Summarize these motives.

Critical Analysis

5. **Analyze Author's Purpose** Think about what Ballou shares with his wife, Sarah. For what purpose—or purposes—would you say he is writing to her? Explain.

6. **Analyze Primary Sources** For each document, speculate on how the private or public nature of its intended audience may have affected its content.

7. **Analyze Author's Perspective** An author's perspective is the combination of life experiences, culture, values, and beliefs that influences his or her view on a topic. Drawing upon the information you recorded on your chart, describe each author's perspective on the Civil War.

Read for Information: Synthesize

WRITING PROMPT

Choose one of the four writers whose documents you just read, and imagine how this person might have responded to Lincoln's Gettysburg Address. Then summarize the imagined response, and support your ideas with evidence from the text.

To answer this prompt, choose a writer whose perspective on the war you think you understand well. Then follow these steps:

1. Reread the Gettysburg Address to remind yourself of Lincoln's message.

2. Bearing in mind the personal experiences and loyalties of your chosen writer and the thoughts and feelings he or she expresses about the war, imagine how he or she might have reacted to Lincoln's speech. Summarize this imaginary response.

3. Support your notion of that person's response with evidence from your chart and from the primary source written by that individual.

Realism

Most modern readers expect stories to be like real life. In the mid-19th century, however, a "realistic" story was considered radical and was even criticized. Despite this outcry, several famous American writers persevered, and in doing so, they initiated one of the most enduring movements in literary history.

The Rise of Realism

Realism in literature refers to writing that offers an accurate and detailed portrayal of actual life. It also refers to a literary movement that first developed in France in the mid-19th century and then spread to England, Russia, and the United States. Realism was born as a reaction to **romanticism,** an artistic and literary movement that glorified the individual and celebrated the emotions and imagination; it dominated literature during the early 19th century. Unlike the romantics, realists did not want to glorify anything. They simply wanted to depict reality, no matter how ordinary the characters or their circumstances. In basing their literature on careful observations of commonplace events and people, the realists believed they could shed light on greater social issues and concerns.

New York City sweatshop, circa 1912

In the United States, realism was also the product of a rapidly changing society. By the end of the Civil War in 1865, America was changing from a predominantly rural society to an urban one and was experiencing the effects of the Industrial Revolution. Many writers were inspired to depict the effects of these dramatic social changes on the average citizen. The first American writers to experiment with realism—in the 1870s and 1880s—were Mark Twain, William Dean Howells, and Henry James. In the following decades, the realist movement spawned several related movements, such as **naturalism, regionalism,** and **local color** (see pages 632–633).

Characteristics of Realism

COMPLEX CHARACTERS IN ORDINARY PLACES

In realist fiction, character exploration and development became more important than plot. Often the characters were laborers, businessmen, or housewives from the lower and middle classes. Exploring details of a personality or a relationship could reveal important complexities, contradictions, and ironies, especially those related to social or economic issues.

The realist writer might write long, involved descriptions of a character's inner thoughts, usually focused on personal concerns or the mundane events of his or her everyday life. Realist fiction would typically

- focus on **complex characters** who are ordinary people, not heroes or villains
- portray ordinary **settings,** especially those that allow for accurate depictions of society and culture
- depict true-to-life **dialogue** that captures the dialects and idioms of conversation

DETACHED NARRATION

Realist writers adopted the scientific method of detached observation. This allows the narrator of a story to sound unbiased and distant, as if simply recording the complete facts of the story. The reader is then allowed to draw his or her own conclusions. Notice the detached perspective of the narrator and the detailed **description** in this passage.

> A man stood upon a railroad bridge in northern Alabama, looking down into the swift water twenty feet below. The man's hands were behind his back, the wrists bound with a cord. A rope closely encircled his neck.
>
> —Ambrose Bierce, "An Occurrence at Owl Creek Bridge"

SOCIAL THEMES

The literature of realism sought to explore the key issues of the time: What are the implications of modern technology? What are the effects of urbanization? Realist **themes** are typically concerned with class conflicts, urbanization, marriage, and family life. In his novel *The Rise of Silas Lapham,* author William Dean Howells tells the story of a family coming to terms with new wealth, acquisition, and corruption. In the following passage, Howells relates the family's initial responses to their newfound wealth.

> Their first years there were given to careful getting on Lapham's part, and careful saving on his wife's. Suddenly the money began to come so abundantly that she need not save; and then they did not know what to do with it. A certain amount could be spent on horses, and Lapham spent it; his wife spent on rich and rather ugly clothes and a luxury of household appointments. Lapham had not yet reached the picture-buying stage of the rich man's development, but they decorated their house with the costliest and most abominable frescoes. . . .
>
> —William Dean Howells, *The Rise of Silas Lapham*

ROMANTICISM VS. REALISM

To understand the different perspectives and subject matter of romanticism and realism, consider these two prose examples:

Romanticism
In that moment of the afternoon, the sun fell upon the snow drifts in an ethereal light, and all the heavens seemed to shine down upon the frozen fields, as if promising, one day, the ascent of spring.

Realism
At 4:00 each afternoon, the sunlight cast long shadows along the frozen landscape. The whistle of the clothing factory would blow, and the workers would stream out from the opened doors and squint into the last light of the day.

Close Read

What effect does the detached perspective in Bierce's passage have on the reader? From these few lines, what is your reaction to this character?

Close Read

What do you think might happen to the Laphams, given what you know about the typical **themes** in realism?

The Red Badge of Courage

Stephen Crane

Stephen Crane
1871–1900

ABOUT THE AUTHOR Stephen Crane had a knack for writing about his experiences—before he even had them! His first novel, *Maggie: A Girl of the Streets,* for example, exposed the brutal realities of New York slum life. Yet Crane wrote its first draft while still in college, *before* moving to the slums himself in search of work as a journalist. Similarly, Crane wrote *The Red Badge of Courage,* a Civil War novel acclaimed by soldiers and veterans for presenting combat realistically, having never seen battle himself. When asked how he knew so much about war, Crane once stated that he learned what it meant to fight while playing football as a boy. He also learned about war from his brother William, an expert on the battles of Chancellorsville and Gettysburg.

After *The Red Badge of Courage* became a hit, newspapers were eager to hire Crane. He was taken on as a war correspondent to cover the Greco-Turkish War and the Spanish-American War and was finally able to observe battle himself. However, Crane nearly drowned when his ship capsized on the way to Cuba to report on the insurrection there. The incident inspired his famous story "The Open Boat" (page 712); it also contributed to the poor health that claimed his life at the age of 28.

ABOUT THE NOVEL In *The Red Badge of Courage,* Crane focuses on a single, unnamed Civil War battle—the details suggest Chancellorsville—seen from the viewpoint of Henry Fleming, a young private who had recently enlisted in the Union army. Through Henry's eyes the reader experiences the long, tedious wait for battle; the utter chaos once the fighting begins; and the ironic twists of fate that determine who will survive and who will perish. Much of the "action" takes place in Henry's mind as he struggles to adapt to his environment, tries to comprehend his new experiences, and worries about whether he will prove courageous or cowardly.

LEGACY OF A MASTERPIECE "There was no real literature of our Civil War," Ernest Hemingway once observed, "until Stephen Crane wrote *The Red Badge of Courage.*" Crane's great novel is considered a pioneering work of realistic war fiction, breaking with tradition in a number of ways. First, it focuses not on kings or generals but on a lowly private caught up in the action. Second, it ignores the great sweep of history and deals instead with one character's impressions. Finally, the novel is almost completely devoid of heroics. "The idea of falling like heroes on ceremonial battlefields," remarked novelist and critic Ford Madox Ford, "was gone forever."

In the following passage, Henry Fleming (referred to as "the youth") gets his first real taste of battle.

"Here they come! Here they come!" Gun locks clicked.

Across the smoke-infested fields came a brown swarm of running men who were giving shrill yells. They came on, stooping and swinging their rifles at all angles. A flag, tilted forward, sped near the front.

As he caught sight of them the youth was momentarily startled by a thought that perhaps his gun was not loaded. He stood trying to rally his faltering intellect so that he might recollect the moment when he had loaded, but he could not.

A hatless general pulled his dripping horse to a stand near the colonel of the
10 304th. He shook his fist in the other's face. "You've got to hold 'em back!" he shouted, savagely; "you've got to hold 'em back!"

In his agitation the colonel began to stammer. "A-all r-right, General, all right, by Gawd! We-we'll do our—we-we'll d-d-do—do our best, General." The general made a passionate gesture and galloped away. The colonel, perchance to relieve his feelings, began to scold like a wet parrot. The youth, turning swiftly to make sure that the rear was unmolested, saw the commander regarding his men in a highly resentful manner, as if he regretted above everything his association with them.

The man at the youth's elbow was mumbling, as if to himself: "Oh, we're in for it now! oh, we're in for it now!"

20 The captain of the company had been pacing excitedly to and fro in the rear. He coaxed in schoolmistress fashion, as to a congregation of boys with primers. His talk was an endless repetition. "Reserve your fire, boys—don't shoot till I tell you—save your fire—wait till they get close up—don't be damned fools—"

Perspiration streamed down the youth's face, which was soiled like that of a weeping urchin. He frequently, with a nervous movement, wiped his eyes with his coat sleeve. His mouth was still a little way open.

He got the one glance at the foe-swarming field in front of him, and instantly ceased to debate the question of his piece being loaded. Before he was ready to begin—before he had announced to himself that he was about to fight—he threw
30 the obedient, well-balanced rifle into position and fired a first wild shot. Directly he was working at his weapon like an automatic affair.

He suddenly lost concern for himself, and forgot to look at a menacing fate. He became not a man, but a member. He felt that something of which he was a part— a regiment, an army, a cause, or a country—was in a crisis. He was welded into a common personality which was dominated by a single desire. For some moments he could not flee, no more than a little finger can commit a revolution from a hand.

An Occurrence at Owl Creek Bridge

Short Story by Ambrose Bierce

Union soldiers

Ambrose Bierce

1842–c. 1914

As a Civil War soldier, Ambrose Bierce was an eyewitness to the harsh realities of war. The brutal contrast between soldiers' dreams of glory and the senselessness of warfare became a recurring theme in Bierce's postwar short stories, including his suspenseful tale "An Occurrence at Owl Creek Bridge."

In the Line of Fire Born into a poor, intensely religious family, Bierce spent his early years on an Indiana farm. At age 15, he left home for a job at a newspaper, where he set type. Three years later, the Civil War broke out, and the idealistic Bierce immediately volunteered for the Union army. Fighting in some of the war's bloodiest battles, Bierce watched many of his comrades die and nearly died himself from a head wound.

When the war was over, Bierce moved to San Francisco, which was then the literary center of the West. Determined to become a writer, Bierce took a job as a night watchman, which allowed him ample time for reading and for polishing his writing skills. He started writing a regular newspaper column and became infamous for exposing bigotry, hypocrisy, and corruption with razor-sharp satire. His cutting wit earned him the title "the Wickedest Man in San Francisco." Such a reputation delighted Bierce, who kept on his desk a human skull that he claimed belonged to one of his critics.

A Morbid Imagination Bierce began publishing short stories in the 1870s, when realism was becoming the dominant literary style in American fiction. Although Bierce's true-to-life war stories inspired realist writers like Stephen Crane, his fiction often included surreal or ghostly events. Like Edgar Allan Poe, to whom he was often compared, Bierce was fascinated with strange and horrible deaths, and he described them with his characteristic dark humor and a sense of irony. Bierce also went beyond realism in his experiments with narration, pioneering the use of multiple points of view in a single story.

Vanished At 71, Bierce revisited Civil War battle sites where he had fought and then went to Mexico to report on the Mexican Revolution as an observer with Pancho Villa's rebel army. He never returned to the United States, and no trace of him was found. Before he left, he wrote to a niece, "If you hear of my being stood up against a Mexican stone wall and shot to rags, please know that I think that a pretty good way to depart this life. It beats old age, disease or falling down the cellar stairs."

● LITERARY ANALYSIS: POINT OF VIEW

Because the narrator is the voice that tells a story, the reader only knows what the narrator is able to tell. Therefore, the narrator's role in the story's events and his or her range of knowledge about the characters help reveal the story's point of view. Types of **point of view** include

- **first person:** told by a character in the work whose knowledge is limited to his or her own experiences
- **third-person omniscient:** told by a voice outside the story who reveals the thoughts and feelings of all the characters
- **third-person limited:** told by a voice outside the story who focuses on one character's thoughts and feelings

As you read, look for clues in the narration that help identify the point of view in Ambrose Bierce's story.

● READING SKILL: ANALYZE STRUCTURE

To analyze the **structure** of a literary work, you examine the relationship between its parts and its content. This story is divided into three numbered sections, each of which occurs at a different point in time. After you read each section, summarize the events that occur and note when they take place. Use a chart like the one shown to record your notes.

	What Happens	When
Section 1		

▲ VOCABULARY IN CONTEXT

Bierce used the words in Column A in his tale of a man facing death. Test your knowledge by matching each vocabulary word with its synonym in Column B.

Column A	Column B
1. interminable	a. swaying
2. poignant	b. painful
3. ineffable	c. predicting
4. summarily	d. unending
5. oscillation	e. indescribable
6. ludicrous	f. evil
7. presaging	g. immediately
8. malign	h. laughable

Can we escape the INEVITABLE?

KEY IDEA "An Occurrence at Owl Creek Bridge" opens with an execution about to take place. Standing on an isolated, heavily guarded bridge, with a noose around his neck, the protagonist is doomed. There is no **escape.** Or is there?

DISCUSS In a small group, list ways people respond when faced with a bad situation they cannot change. Classify each response as useful or destructive. When does it make sense to look for a way out, and when is it time to accept the inevitable?

An Occurrence at Owl Creek Bridge

Ambrose Bierce

I

A man stood upon a railroad bridge in northern Alabama, looking down into the swift water twenty feet below. The man's hands were behind his back, the wrists bound with a cord. A rope closely encircled his neck. It was attached to a stout cross-timber above his head and the slack fell to the level of his knees. Some loose boards laid upon the sleepers[1] supporting the metals of the railway supplied a footing for him and his executioners—two private soldiers of the Federal army, directed by a sergeant who in civil life may have been a deputy sheriff. At a short remove upon the same temporary platform was an officer in the uniform of his rank, armed. He was a captain. A sentinel at each end of the bridge stood with his
10 rifle in the position known as "support," that is to say, vertical in front of the left shoulder, the hammer resting on the forearm thrown straight across the chest—a formal and unnatural position, enforcing an erect carriage of the body. It did not appear to be the duty of these two men to know what was occurring at the center of the bridge; they merely blockaded the two ends of the foot planking that traversed it. **Ⓐ**

Beyond one of the sentinels nobody was in sight; the railroad ran straight away into a forest for a hundred yards, then, curving, was lost to view. Doubtless there was an outpost farther along. The other bank of the stream was open ground—a gentle acclivity[2] topped with a stockade of vertical tree trunks, loopholed for rifles,
20 with a single embrasure[3] through which protruded the muzzle of a brass cannon commanding the bridge. Midway of the slope between bridge and fort were the spectators—a single company of infantry in line, at "parade rest," the butts of the rifles on the ground, the barrels inclining slightly backward against the right

ANALYZE VISUALS
Based on this image, what do you predict will happen in the story?

Ⓐ POINT OF VIEW
Identify the point of view used in lines 1–15. What does the **tone** of the description tell you about the narrator's perspective?

1. **sleepers:** railroad ties.
2. **acclivity:** an upward slope.
3. **embrasure:** a flared opening in a wall for a gun, with sides angled so that the inside opening is larger than that on the outside.

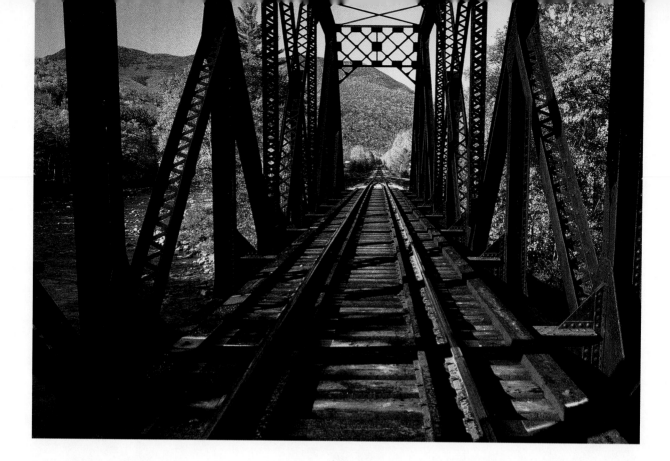

shoulder, the hands crossed upon the stock.[4] A lieutenant stood at the right of the line, the point of his sword upon the ground, his left hand resting upon his right. Excepting the group of four at the center of the bridge, not a man moved. The company faced the bridge, staring stonily, motionless. The sentinels, facing the banks of the stream, might have been statues to adorn the bridge. The captain stood with folded arms, silent, observing the work of his subordinates, but making
30 no sign. Death is a dignitary who when he comes announced is to be received with formal manifestations of respect, even by those most familiar with him. In the code of military etiquette silence and fixity are forms of deference.

The man who was engaged in being hanged was apparently about thirty-five years of age. He was a civilian, if one might judge from his habit, which was that of a planter. His features were good—a straight nose, firm mouth, broad forehead, from which his long, dark hair was combed straight back, falling behind his ears to the collar of his well-fitting frock-coat. He wore a mustache and pointed beard, but no whiskers; his eyes were large and dark gray, and had a kindly expression which one would hardly have expected in one whose neck was in the hemp.
40 Evidently this was no vulgar assassin. The liberal military code makes provision for hanging many kinds of persons, and gentlemen are not excluded.

The preparations being complete, the two private soldiers stepped aside and each drew away the plank upon which he had been standing. The sergeant turned to the captain, saluted and placed himself immediately behind that officer, who in

---

4. **stock:** the wooden part of the rifle that serves as a handle.

turn moved apart one pace. These movements left the condemned man and the sergeant standing on the two ends of the same plank, which spanned three of the cross-ties of the bridge. The end upon which the civilian stood almost, but not quite, reached a fourth. This plank had been held in place by the weight of the captain; it was now held by that of the sergeant. At a signal from the former the latter would step aside, the plank would tilt and the condemned man go down between two ties. The arrangement commended itself to his judgment as simple and effective. His face had not been covered nor his eyes bandaged. He looked a moment at his "unsteadfast footing," then let his gaze wander to the swirling water of the stream racing madly beneath his feet. A piece of dancing driftwood caught his attention and his eyes followed it down the current. How slowly it appeared to move! What a sluggish stream! **B**

He closed his eyes in order to fix his last thoughts upon his wife and children. The water, touched to gold by the early sun, the brooding mists under the banks at some distance down the stream, the fort, the soldiers, the piece of drift—all had distracted him. And now he became conscious of a new disturbance. Striking through the thought of his dear ones was a sound which he could neither ignore nor understand, a sharp, distinct, metallic percussion like the stroke of a blacksmith's hammer upon the anvil; it had the same ringing quality. He wondered what it was, and whether immeasurably distant or near by—it seemed both. Its recurrence was regular, but as slow as the tolling of a death knell.[5] He awaited each stroke with impatience and—he knew not why—apprehension. The intervals of silence grew progressively longer; the delays became maddening. With their greater infrequency the sounds increased in strength and sharpness. They hurt his ear like the thrust of a knife; he feared he would shriek. What he heard was the ticking of his watch.

He unclosed his eyes and saw again the water below him. "If I could free my hands," he thought, "I might throw off the noose and spring into the stream. By diving I could evade the bullets and, swimming vigorously, reach the bank, take to the woods and get away home. My home, thank God, is as yet outside their lines; my wife and little ones are still beyond the invader's farthest advance."

As these thoughts, which have here to be set down in words, were flashed into the doomed man's brain rather than evolved from it the captain nodded to the sergeant. The sergeant stepped aside. **C**

II

Peyton Farquhar was a well-to-do planter, of an old and highly respected Alabama family. Being a slave owner and like other slave owners a politician he was naturally an original secessionist and ardently devoted to the Southern cause. Circumstances of an imperious nature, which it is unnecessary to relate here, had prevented him from taking service with the gallant army that had fought the disastrous campaigns ending with the fall of Corinth,[6] and he chafed under the

---

5. **the tolling of a death knell:** the slow, steady ringing of a bell at a funeral or to indicate death.

6. **Corinth:** a town in Mississippi that was the site of a Civil War battle in 1862.

inglorious restraint, longing for the release of his energies, the larger life of the soldier, the opportunity for distinction. That opportunity, he felt, would come, as it comes to all in war time. Meanwhile he did what he could. No service was too humble for him to perform in aid of the South, no adventure too perilous for him to undertake if consistent with the character of a civilian who was at heart a soldier, and who in good faith and without too much qualification assented to at least a part of the frankly villainous dictum that all is fair in love and war.

One evening while Farquhar and his wife were sitting on a rustic bench near the entrance to his grounds, a gray-clad soldier rode up to the gate and asked for a drink of water. Mrs. Farquhar was only too happy to serve him with her own white hands. While she was fetching the water her husband approached the dusty horseman and inquired eagerly for news from the front.

"The Yanks are repairing the railroads," said the man, "and are getting ready for another advance. They have reached the Owl Creek bridge, put it in order and built a stockade on the north bank. The commandant has issued an order, which is posted everywhere, declaring that any civilian caught interfering with the railroad, its bridges, tunnels or trains will be **summarily** hanged. I saw the order." **D**

"How far is it to the Owl Creek bridge?" Farquhar asked.

"About thirty miles."

"Is there no force on this side the creek?"

"Only a picket post[7] half a mile out, on the railroad, and a single sentinel at this end of the bridge."

"Suppose a man—a civilian and student of hanging—should elude the picket post and perhaps get the better of the sentinel," said Farquhar, smiling, "what could he accomplish?"

The soldier reflected. "I was there a month ago," he replied. "I observed that the flood of last winter had lodged a great quantity of driftwood against the wooden pier at this end of the bridge. It is now dry and would burn like tow."[8]

The lady had now brought the water, which the soldier drank. He thanked her ceremoniously, bowed to her husband and rode away. An hour later, after nightfall, he repassed the plantation, going northward in the direction from which he had come. He was a Federal scout. **E**

III

As Peyton Farquhar fell straight downward through the bridge he lost consciousness and was as one already dead. From this state he was awakened— ages later, it seemed to him—by the pain of a sharp pressure upon his throat, followed by a sense of suffocation. Keen, **poignant** agonies seemed to shoot from his neck downward through every fiber of his body and limbs. These pains appeared to flash along well-defined lines of ramification[9] and to beat with an inconceivably rapid periodicity. They seemed like streams of pulsating fire heating

summarily (sə-mĕr′ə-lē) *adv.* quickly and without ceremony

D ANALYZE STRUCTURE
Compare lines 97–101 with the description in lines 1–21. What details connect these two sections of the story?

E POINT OF VIEW
Reread lines 113–116. Explain what the reader knows that Peyton Farquhar does not. Which type of third-person point of view allows the author to give the reader details that are hidden from the characters?

poignant (poin′yənt) *adj.* physically or mentally painful

---

7. **picket post:** the camp of soldiers who are assigned to guard against a surprise attack.

8. **tow** (tō): coarse, dry fiber.

9. **flash . . . ramification:** spread out rapidly along branches from a central point.

him to an intolerable temperature. As to his head, he was conscious of nothing but a feeling of fullness—of congestion. These sensations were unaccompanied by thought. The intellectual part of his nature was already effaced; he had power only to feel, and feeling was torment. He was conscious of motion. Encompassed in a luminous cloud, of which he was now merely the fiery heart, without material substance, he swung through unthinkable arcs of **oscillation,** like a vast

130 pendulum. Then all at once, with terrible suddenness, the light about him shot upward with the noise of a loud plash; a frightful roaring was in his ears, and all was cold and dark. The power of thought was restored; he knew that the rope had broken and he had fallen into the stream. There was no additional strangulation; the noose about his neck was already suffocating him and kept the water from his lungs. To die of hanging at the bottom of a river!—the idea seemed to him **ludicrous.** He opened his eyes in the darkness and saw above him a gleam

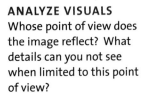

oscillation (ŏs′ə-lā′shən) *n.* the action of swinging back and forth

ludicrous (lōō′dĭ-krəs) *adj.* laughably absurd; ridiculous

ANALYZE VISUALS
Whose point of view does the image reflect? What details can you not see when limited to this point of view?

of light, but how distant, how inaccessible! He was still sinking, for the light became fainter and fainter until it was a mere glimmer. Then it began to grow and brighten, and he knew that he was rising toward the surface—knew it with reluctance, for he was now very comfortable. "To be hanged and drowned," he thought, "that is not so bad; but I do not wish to be shot. No; I will not be shot; that is not fair." **F**

He was not conscious of an effort, but a sharp pain in his wrist apprised him that he was trying to free his hands. He gave the struggle his attention, as an idler might observe the feat of a juggler, without interest in the outcome. What splendid effort!—what magnificent, what superhuman strength! Ah, that was a fine endeavor! Bravo! The cord fell away; his arms parted and floated upward, the hands dimly seen on each side in the growing light. He watched them with a new interest as first one and then the other pounced upon the noose at his neck.
They tore it away and thrust it fiercely aside, its undulations resembling those of a water-snake. "Put it back, put it back!" He thought he shouted these words to his hands, for the undoing of the noose had been succeeded by the direst pang that he had yet experienced. His neck ached horribly; his brain was on fire; his heart, which had been fluttering faintly, gave a great leap, trying to force itself out at his mouth. His whole body was racked and wrenched with an insupportable anguish![10] But his disobedient hands gave no heed to the command. They beat the water vigorously with quick, downward strokes, forcing him to the surface. He felt his head emerge; his eyes were blinded by the sunlight; his chest expanded convulsively, and with a supreme and crowning agony his lungs engulfed a great draught of air, which instantly he expelled in a shriek!

He was now in full possession of his physical senses. They were, indeed, preternaturally keen and alert. Something in the awful disturbance of his organic system had so exalted and refined them that they made record of things never before perceived. He felt the ripples upon his face and heard their separate sounds as they struck. He looked at the forest on the bank of the stream, saw the individual trees, the leaves and the veining of each leaf—saw the very insects upon them: the locusts, the brilliant-bodied flies, the gray spiders stretching their webs from twig to twig. He noted the prismatic colors in all the dewdrops upon a million blades of grass. The humming of the gnats that danced above the eddies of the stream, the beating of the dragon-flies' wings, the strokes of the water-spiders' legs, like oars which had lifted their boat—all these made audible music. A fish slid along beneath his eyes and he heard the rush of its body parting the water.

He had come to the surface facing down the stream; in a moment the visible world seemed to wheel slowly round, himself the pivotal point, and he saw the bridge, the fort, the soldiers upon the bridge, the captain, the sergeant, the two privates, his executioners. They were in silhouette against the blue sky. They shouted and gesticulated, pointing at him. The captain had drawn his pistol, but did not fire; the others were unarmed. Their movements were grotesque and horrible, their forms gigantic.

F POINT OF VIEW
Contrast the point of view used in lines 137–142 with that used in the opening of the story. What effect does this shift in perspective have on the reader's experience of the story?

---

10. **racked ... anguish:** stretched and twisted with unendurable physical pain.

180　　Suddenly he heard a sharp report and something struck the water smartly within a few inches of his head, spattering his face with spray. He heard a second report, and saw one of the sentinels with his rifle at his shoulder, a light cloud of blue smoke rising from the muzzle. The man in the water saw the eye of the man on the bridge gazing into his own through the sights of the rifle. He observed that it was a gray eye and remembered having read that gray eyes were keenest, and that all famous marksmen had them. Nevertheless, this one had missed.

　　A counter-swirl had caught Farquhar and turned him half round; he was again looking into the forest on the bank opposite the fort. The sound of a clear, high voice in a monotonous singsong now rang out behind him and came across the

190　　water with a distinctness that pierced and subdued all other sounds, even the beating of the ripples in his ears. Although no soldier, he had frequented camps enough to know the dread significance of that deliberate, drawling, aspirated chant; the lieutenant on shore was taking a part in the morning's work. How coldly and pitilessly—with what an even, calm intonation, **presaging,** and enforcing tranquillity in the men—with what accurately measured intervals fell those cruel words:

　　"Attention, company! . . . Shoulder arms! . . . Ready! . . . Aim! . . . Fire!"

presaging (prĕsʹĭj-ĭng)
adj. predicting **presage** *v.*

Farquhar dived—dived as deeply as he could. The water roared in his ears like the voice of Niagara, yet he heard the dulled thunder of the volley and, rising
200 again toward the surface, met shining bits of metal, singularly flattened, oscillating slowly downward. Some of them touched him on the face and hands, then fell away, continuing their descent. One lodged between his collar and neck; it was uncomfortably warm and he snatched it out.

As he rose to the surface, gasping for breath, he saw that he had been a long time under water; he was perceptibly farther down stream—nearer to safety. The soldiers had almost finished reloading; the metal ramrods flashed all at once in the sunshine as they were drawn from the barrels, turned in the air, and thrust into their sockets. The two sentinels fired again, independently and ineffectually.

The hunted man saw all this over his shoulder; he was now swimming
210 vigorously with the current. His brain was as energetic as his arms and legs; he thought with the rapidity of lightning.

"The officer," he reasoned, "will not make that martinet's[11] error a second time. It is as easy to dodge a volley as a single shot. He has probably already given the command to fire at will. God help me, I cannot dodge them all!"

An appalling plash within two yards of him was followed by a loud, rushing sound, *diminuendo*,[12] which seemed to travel back through the air to the fort and died in an explosion which stirred the very river to its deeps! A rising sheet of water curved over him, fell down upon him, blinded him, strangled him! The cannon had taken a hand in the game. As he shook his head free from the
220 commotion of the smitten water he heard the deflected shot humming through the air ahead, and in an instant it was cracking and smashing the branches in the forest beyond.

"They will not do that again," he thought; "the next time they will use a charge of grape.[13] I must keep my eye upon the gun; the smoke will apprise me—the report arrives too late; it lags behind the missile. That is a good gun."

Suddenly he felt himself whirled round and round—spinning like a top. The water, the banks, the forests, the now distant bridge, fort and men—all were commingled and blurred. Objects were represented by their colors only; circular horizontal streaks of color—that was all he saw. He had been caught in a vortex
230 and was being whirled on with a velocity of advance and gyration that made him giddy and sick. In a few moments he was flung upon the gravel at the foot of the left bank of the stream—the southern bank—and behind a projecting point which concealed him from his enemies. The sudden arrest of his motion, the abrasion of one of his hands on the gravel, restored him, and he wept with delight. He dug his fingers into the sand, threw it over himself in handfuls and audibly blessed it. It looked like diamonds, rubies, emeralds; he could think of nothing beautiful which it did not resemble. The trees upon the bank were giant garden plants; he

---

11. **martinet's:** alluding to a strict disciplinarian or person who demands that regulations be followed exactly.

12. *diminuendo* (dĭ-mĭn′yo͞o-ĕn′dō) *Italian:* gradually decreasing in loudness.

13. **grape:** short for grapeshot, a cluster of several small iron balls fired in one shot from a cannon.

noted a definite order in their arrangement, inhaled the fragrance of their blooms.
A strange, roseate light shone through the spaces among their trunks and the wind
240 made in their branches the music of æolian harps.[14] He had no wish to perfect his
escape—was content to remain in that enchanting spot until retaken.

A whiz and rattle of grapeshot among the branches high above his head roused
him from his dream. The baffled cannoneer had fired him a random farewell. He
sprang to his feet, rushed up the sloping bank, and plunged into the forest.

All that day he traveled, laying his course by the rounding sun. The forest
seemed **interminable;** nowhere did he discover a break in it, not even a
woodman's road. He had not known that he lived in so wild a region. There was
something uncanny in the revelation.

interminable
(ĭn-tûr′mə-nə-bol)
adj. endless

---

14. **music of æolian** (ē-ō′lē-ən) **harps:** heavenly, or unearthly, music.

By night fall he was fatigued, footsore, famishing. The thought of his wife
250 and children urged him on. At last he found a road which led him in what he
knew to be the right direction. It was as wide and straight as a city street, yet it
seemed untraveled. No fields bordered it, no dwelling anywhere. Not so much as
the barking of a dog suggested human habitation. The black bodies of the trees
formed a straight wall on both sides, terminating on the horizon in a point, like
a diagram in a lesson in perspective. Overhead, as he looked up through this
rift in the wood, shone great golden stars looking unfamiliar and grouped in
strange constellations. He was sure they were arranged in some order which had
a secret and **malign** significance. The wood on either side was full of singular
noises, among which—once, twice, and again, he distinctly heard whispers in an
260 unknown tongue.

His neck was in pain and lifting his hand to it he found it horribly swollen.
He knew that it had a circle of black where the rope had bruised it. His eyes felt
congested; he could no longer close them. His tongue was swollen with thirst; he
relieved its fever by thrusting it forward from between his teeth into the cold air.
How softly the turf had carpeted the untraveled avenue—he could no longer feel
the roadway beneath his feet!

Doubtless, despite his suffering, he had fallen asleep while walking, for now he
sees another scene—perhaps he has merely recovered from a delirium. He stands
at the gate of his own home. All is as he left it, and all bright and beautiful in the
270 morning sunshine. He must have traveled the entire night. As he pushes open
the gate and passes up the wide white walk, he sees a flutter of female garments;
his wife, looking fresh and cool and sweet, steps down from the veranda to meet
him. At the bottom of the steps she stands waiting, with a smile of **ineffable** joy,
an attitude of matchless grace and dignity. Ah, how beautiful she is! He springs
forward with extended arms. As he is about to clasp her he feels a stunning blow
upon the back of the neck; a blinding white light blazes all about him with a
sound like the shock of a cannon—then all is darkness and silence!

Peyton Farquhar was dead; his body, with a broken neck, swung gently from
side to side beneath the timbers of the Owl Creek bridge. ∿ **G**

malign (mə-līn′) *adj.* evil;
harmful

ineffable (ĭn-ĕf′ə-bəl)
adj. beyond description;
inexpressible

G POINT OF VIEW
Describe the change
in point of view that
occurs in lines 275–279.
What impact does this
change have on your
understanding of
the story?

Comprehension

1. **Summarize** What is Peyton Farquhar's background?

2. **Recall** How does Farquhar die?

3. **Clarify** Why did the soldier who visited Farquhar give him such detailed information about the bridge?

Literary Analysis

4. **Make Inferences** What is the Union soldiers' reason for hanging Farquhar? Cite evidence to support your inference.

5. **Analyze Structure** Review the chart you created as you read. How would the story be different if it were told in chronological order?

6. **Examine Point of View** Citing at least two examples from the story, explain how the shifts in point of view affect the level of **suspense**. What would be different about the story if it were told entirely from the **third-person omniscient** point of view?

7. **Make Judgments About Sensory Details** Bierce uses sensory details to provide clues to Farquhar's state of mind. In each of the following episodes, what sensory details suggest that Farquhar's perceptions may be unreliable?

   - on the bridge (lines 60–70)
   - in the river (lines 161–172)
   - reaching land (lines 231–240)
   - in the woods (lines 255–260)

8. **Interpret Themes** Reread lines 80–91. Based on the contrast between Farquhar's dreams of wartime glory and his ultimate fate, what point might Bierce be making about

   - heroism
   - the realities of war
   - the dangers of fantasy

9. **Evaluate Narrative Devices** In your opinion, did Bierce intend Farquhar's miraculous **escape** to seem believable? Cite evidence from the story to support your view.

Literary Criticism

10. **Author's Style** Compare Bierce's use of realistic and fantastic elements in this story. Which label—realistic or fantastic—best describes Bierce's style? Support your answer with details.

Vocabulary in Context

Decide whether these statements using the vocabulary words are true or false.

1. A **ludicrous** TV show would probably make you cry.
2. A job that is performed **summarily** tends to take a long time.
3. An **ineffable** pleasure is likely to leave you speechless with joy.
4. A **malign** decision could cause others pain and suffering.
5. Climbing a very steep ladder is an example of **oscillation.**
6. You would typically describe a standup comic's performance as **poignant.**
7. Messages **presaging** happiness tend to make a fortuneteller popular.
8. If a school day seems **interminable,** it feels like it will never be over.

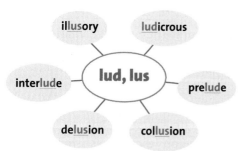

WORD LIST
ineffable
interminable
ludicrous
malign
oscillation
poignant
presaging
summarily

VOCABULARY IN WRITING

Looking back over this story, you might find several clues hinting at its ending. Using three or more vocabulary words, write a brief description of those clues. You might start like this.

EXAMPLE SENTENCE

*Both physical and psychological clues **presaging** Farquhar's fate are revealed through careful rereading of the story.*

VOCABULARY STRATEGY: THE LATIN ROOT *lud*

The vocabulary word *ludicrous* contains the Latin root *lud,* meaning "play." This root, which may also be spelled *lus,* can be found in a number of English words. To understand words with *lud* or *lus,* use context clues as well as your knowledge of the meaning of the root.

PRACTICE Choose the word from the word web that best completes each sentence. Consider what you know about the Latin root and the other word parts shown. If necessary, consult a dictionary.

1. In the _____ between the scenes, a violinist performed for the audience.
2. He suffers from the _____ that he is a good golfer.
3. Though she dresses expensively, her wealth is more _____ than real.
4. As a _____ to the main act, a young, inexperienced band played.
5. As a result of the two guards' _____, a prisoner was allowed to escape.

illusory ludicrous
interlude **lud, lus** prelude
delusion collusion

VOCABULARY PRACTICE
For more practice, go to the **Vocabulary Center** at **ClassZone.com.**

Voices of the Civil War

Near the outbreak of the Civil War, writer Ralph Waldo Emerson remarked, "All arts disappear in the one art of war." In other words, the necessities of warfare—military, political, economic, and social—act somehow to discourage or diminish the creation of what might be termed "serious literature." Yet fine nonfiction writing about searing national issues emerged in the years prior to, during, and immediately following the Civil War.

The selections beginning on page 538 include many forms of nonfiction: autobiography, speeches, documents, letters, and diaries. Perhaps these forms served as better vehicles than poems or short stories might have for the people of the day who wanted to explore their personal responses to the war. In any case, the nonfiction here is valuable for several reasons:

- It gives readers a glimpse into the events and culture of the writers' troubled time.
- It provides each writer's personal response to what was happening all around.
- It presents a good overview of the many different factions that made up the country at the time.

Writing to Synthesize

Write an essay describing both the historical and the personal insights you gained from reading the nonfiction in this unit.

Consider

- the historical facts you learned from the selections (important figures, dates, battles, and so forth)
- the personal concerns of the writers (their opinions, worries, pride, and so forth)
- what you can infer about the country as a whole from the many voices of its writers

Lincoln at Gettysburg II (1939–1942), William H. Johnson. Gouache and pen and ink on paper, 19 3/4″ × 17 1/16″.

Extension

VIEWING & REPRESENTING

Perhaps the most important writer of this period was Abraham Lincoln. Presented with a divided nation, Lincoln took on the task of uniting all of its various factions. Examine the image of Lincoln shown here. Based upon your reading and your prior knowledge of President Lincoln, give a brief **oral critique** of how he is portrayed in this painting. Discuss the style of the work as a whole, Lincoln's placement in relation to other figures in the painting, the colors used, and any other aspects you consider important.

from **An Occurrence at Owl Creek Bridge**

Film Clips on (o) *MediaSmart* DVD

From Page to Screen

Since 1932, the short story "An Occurrence at Owl Creek Bridge" has been adapted for the screen at least four times. Its Civil War setting, heart-pounding suspense, and surprise ending make it an ideal story to adapt to film. In this lesson, you'll view three clips from the 2005 version to explore one of the ways Ambrose Bierce's tale has been adapted for the big screen.

The Filmmaker's Challenge

The fact that the main action of the story takes place in the mind of the character Peyton Farquhar creates a challenge for a filmmaker. To reveal a character's thoughts, a filmmaker must rely on such devices as **voice-over narration,** in which the character speaks his or her thoughts, and **flashbacks,** which present a scene from the character's memory.

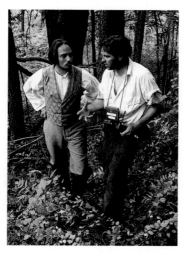

Brian James Egen directs an actor on location.

In his film, director Brian James Egen provided only subtle clues that what the audience sees is not what is actually happening. "I had to create a feeling," Egen says, "from the time the rope breaks to the end, as if it was real. I wanted the audience to be taken completely by surprise, so we created the scenes as realistically as possible."

Comparing Texts: Point of View

Point of view in film can be either objective or subjective. In the **objective point of view,** the camera acts as a neutral recorder of action. It is used to show scenes as they would occur in reality. In the **subjective point of view,** the camera becomes a participant in the scene and seems to get inside a character's head by showing the viewer exactly what the character sees.

Read the following passage from the story and visualize the events. When you view the clips, pay special attention to this moment in the film. How close does the film come to the scene as you imagined it? Compare Bierce's use of the **third-person limited point of view** with the point of view used by the filmmaker. Notice the ways in which both the story and the film emphasize this moment.

> He felt his head emerge; his eyes were blinded by the sunlight; his chest expanded convulsively, and with a supreme and crowning agony his lungs engulfed a great draught of air, which instantly he expelled in a shriek!
>
> He was now in full possession of his physical senses. They were, indeed, pre-
> 5 ternaturally keen and alert. Something in the awful disturbance of his organic system had so exalted and refined them that they made record of things never before perceived. He felt the ripples upon his face and heard their separate sounds as they struck. He looked at the forest on the bank of the stream, saw the individual trees, the leaves and the veining of each leaf—saw the very
> 10 insects upon them: the locusts, the brilliant-bodied flies, the gray spiders stretching their webs from twig to twig. He noted the prismatic colors in all the dewdrops upon a million blades of grass.

Viewing Guide

🔘 **MediaSmart** DVD

- **Film:** *An Occurrence at Owl Creek Bridge*
- **Director:** Brian James Egen
- **Genre:** Historical thriller
- **Running Time:** 14 minutes

The three clips you'll view from *An Occurrence at Owl Creek Bridge* include Farquhar's hanging and escape, his long walk through the night to reach his wife, and, of course, the sudden ending. You may want to watch the clips more than once in order to analyze them.

NOW VIEW

CLOSE VIEWING: Media Analysis

1. **Compare Point of View** Think about the scene in the film that corresponds to the passage shown from the story. Did the filmmaker use the **objective** or **subjective point of view?** What is the effect of this point of view in comparison with Bierce's use of the **third-person limited?**

2. **Analyze Montage** A **montage** is a succession of shots, often short and without dialogue, intended to create a particular effect or suggest meaning. What do you think the filmmaker wanted to convey with the montage of Farquhar's family and home in the third clip?

3. **Evaluate the Adaptation** How effective do you think the filmmaker was in adapting Bierce's story to the big screen? Think about the following:
   - the rising suspense in the hanging scene
   - the voice-over narration
   - moments in the film that do not appear in the story

Writing Workshop

Biographical Narrative

People and ideas like the ones you've read about in this unit are what change our world. To investigate how someone has influenced your life, write your own biographical narrative.

WRITER'S ROAD MAP

Biographical Narrative

WRITING PROMPT 1

Writing from Your Life Write a biographical narrative about a person who you believe is important or influential. Include anecdotes and details to help your reader visualize the person clearly. Make sure your reader understands why the person is important to you.

People to Write About
- a friend who taught you something important
- a teacher who made a difference to you
- a relative who helped you

WRITING PROMPT 2

Writing from Literature Writing about another person can give you insight into that person's life and his or her significance. Do some research and write a biographical narrative about one of the writers in this unit whose life inspires or intrigues you.

Writers to Consider
- Frederick Douglass
- Abraham Lincoln
- Sojourner Truth
- Mary Chesnut

 WRITING TOOLS
For prewriting, revision, and editing tools, visit the **Writing Center** at **ClassZone.com.**

KEY TRAITS

1. IDEAS
- Provides a **dominant impression** of a clearly identified person
- Includes **anecdotes** to describe the person
- Uses **dialogue** to show the subject's personality

2. ORGANIZATION
- Draws the reader in with an intriguing **introduction**
- Provides **background information** about the person as needed
- **Concludes** by showing the significance of the person

3. VOICE
- Uses a **tone** that clearly conveys the writer's attitude toward the person

4. WORD CHOICE
- Includes **sensory details** to help readers get a focused impression of the person
- Uses **precise words** to describe the person's physical appearance, personality traits, and actions

5. SENTENCE FLUENCY
- Varies **sentence beginnings and structures**

6. CONVENTIONS
- Employs **correct grammar and usage**

Part 1: Analyze a Student Model

Travis Saelzler
Fayetteville High School

A Mentor to Remember

The first time I saw him, he was running down the hall with one end of his tie over his shoulder, his arms overflowing with books and notes, leaving papers fluttering to the floor behind him. He disappeared into Room 203, tie flapping. "That," I muttered to myself, "can only be Mr. Moore." A
5   school legend, Mr. Moore has become my most memorable teacher and mentor.

Mr. Moore was in a class by himself. That doesn't mean his classes were poorly attended. On the contrary, they were always filled to capacity. English, Russian, French, American history, world religions, Western
10   civilization—no matter what he taught, he made learning an exciting experience. That's because what mattered most to him wasn't the subject but the students. Mr. Moore respected and understood us and helped us understand ourselves.

One way we learned who we were was by just watching him be himself.
15   When the other teachers wore jeans and flannel shirts to class, he dressed in a suit and tie, "to be suitable," he punned. Because he was comfortable with who he was, it didn't matter to him that he looked somewhat out of place.

He was also endearingly absent-minded. I'll never forget the time the announcement came over the loudspeaker: "Anyone knowing about a car
20   abandoned by the side of the road a few blocks from the school should contact the office immediately."

"Oh! Well! I'll be back in just a moment!" Mr. Moore said as he scurried from the classroom.

"I bet that's Mr. Moore's car," I said, and several of my classmates
25   agreed. We just figured he had run out of gas and left the car where it had coughed to a stop. And that's exactly what had happened.

KEY TRAITS IN ACTION

Lively **introduction** uses **precise words** and strong **sensory details.**

The writer supplies helpful **background information** about Mr. Moore's classes and begins building a **dominant impression** of him: he is an unusual but talented teacher.

Reveals Mr. Moore's character by quoting **dialogue** and sharing an **anecdote.**

Even though Mr. Moore seemed unaware of what others thought of him, he cared deeply about us and what we thought of ourselves. He knew exactly how to draw students out and encourage us to participate. The

30   way he listened carefully and found something valuable in every question made us feel important. When just learning the Russian alphabet gave me nightmares, Mr. Moore calmed me down, then found a student in his advanced class who agreed to tutor me in exchange for extra credit. When a student in our world religions class developed severe complications from

35   diabetes, Mr. Moore visited her in the hospital. He encouraged interaction, questions, debate, and different ways of looking at things, and his lessons addressed every possible learning style. In our Western civilization class, for example, we held a council of Greek gods and goddesses, made mobiles tracing the theme of guilt through history, and presented a song, poem,

40   dance, or pantomime depicting our visions of the future. After struggling with that last activity, I thought, "We're not just studying history, but learning to make it by figuring out what kind of world we want to help create."

Then there were Mr. Moore's tests. All his exams were open-book, and

45   we could bring along whatever additional materials we wanted. That's because he wasn't as interested in getting answers as he was in getting us to ask our own questions and come up with new ideas. For me, the only way to study for his tests was to freewrite about the material, letting my mind wander and make its own connections. His respect and trust meant more

50   than any grade I've ever gotten.

That gift will always be with Mr. Moore's students. Even if we forget who won the Trojan War or how to spell Thucydides, we will remember how Mr. Moore helped us get to know ourselves. He's already so much more than a teacher to me; I'm sure he will be a lifelong mentor. What

55   more can a teacher do for his or her students?

Overall **tone** is respectful and admiring.

Uses interior monologue to illustrate Mr. Moore's impact on the writer.

A variety of **sentence beginnings and structures** hold the reader's interest.

Conclusion shows Mr. Moore's lasting significance in the writer's life and leaves readers with a question to ponder.

2

Part 2: Apply the Writing Process

PREWRITING

What Should I Do?	What Does It Look Like?

1. Analyze the prompt.
Choose one of the prompts on page 598 and read it at least twice. Circle the phrase that tells you the kind of writing you will be doing. Underline phrases that tell you what you must include. Also, think about your audience. Will you be writing just for your teacher or for your classmates as well?

▶ **WRITING PROMPT** Write a (biographical) (narrative about a person who you believe is) (important or influential.) Include <u>anecdotes and details</u> to help your reader visualize the person clearly. <u>Make sure your reader understands why the person is important to you.</u>

> *Once I choose my subject, I should think about what my teacher and my classmates already know about him or her.*

2. Choose your subject.
Brainstorm a list of people who would be interesting to write about. Put an asterisk by the person you choose.

▶ *Grandma Freddi—taught me to be less judgmental*
*Mr. Moore—respected me, made class fun
Ed—my best friend for three years, helped me when I was in a car accident

3. Describe the person.
How does (or did) he or she look, behave, speak, and interact with others? Which characteristics make the person so special? List those traits. Decide on a **dominant impression**—the main opinion or idea you want your reader to learn about this person.

TIP If you have selected Prompt 2, you will need to research the person you have chosen.

▶ *Mr. Moore's traits*
- *absent-minded*
- *does things his own way*
- *really cares about students*
- *helps us learn who we are*

Dominant impression: unusual but talented teacher

4. Gather typical anecdotes and incidents.
Think of stories about the person that support the dominant impression you want to convey. Use a graphic organizer to record specific sensory details.

TIP Choose stories and details that reveal something significant about your subject.

▶

What Should I Do?	What Does It Look Like?

1. Plan your narrative.
Decide which points you want to make about your subject to convey a dominant impression of him or her. Make a chart of those points and the details or anecdotes that support them.

▶

Characteristic	Supporting Details
absent-mindedness	leaving car at side of road
being his own person	wearing suit and tie "to be suitable"
caring about students	arranging for tutoring, visiting student in hospital
helping us know ourselves	involving us in subject matter (visions-of-future assignment)

2. Craft an intriguing introduction.
Begin with a few well-chosen details or with an anecdote. Your goal is to "hook" your reader and give clues about your subject's values or personality.

TIP As you draft, avoid **clichés** (overused expressions). See page 604 for a list of clichés and suggestions for original alternatives.

▶

Intriguing details

The first time I saw him, he was running down the hall with one end of his tie over his shoulder, his arms overflowing with books and notes, leaving papers fluttering to the floor behind him.

A relevant anecdote

I'll never forget the time the announcement came over the loudspeaker: "Anyone knowing about a car abandoned by the side of the road a few blocks from the school should contact the office. . . ."

3. End forcefully.
Make sure your conclusion reinforces the dominant impression and leaves readers with something to think about. You might include a memorable quotation or question.

TIP Before revising, consult the **key traits on page 598** and the **rubric and peer-reader questions on page 604**.

▶

A quotation

"The ability to learn is a gift," Mr. Moore used to tell us. That gift will always be with me.

A thoughtful question

He's already so much more than a teacher to me; I'm sure he will be a lifelong mentor. What more can a teacher do for his or her students?

REVISING AND EDITING

What Should I Do?

1. Include rich sensory details.
- Circle words that refer to sight, smell, touch, taste, or sound.
- If your draft doesn't have many circles, add fresh, inventive sensory details.

2. Delete irrelevant information.
- Underline details, anecdotes, descriptions, and dialogue that describe your subject.
- Review what you underlined, deleting material that doesn't support the dominant impression you want to get across.

3. Add background information.
- Ask a peer reader to point out statements that need more explanation.
- Weave in necessary background information.

See page 604: Ask a Peer Reader

4. Make the significance clear.
- Put [brackets] around passages that explain what makes this person interesting or significant.
- If you don't have many brackets, add details about your subject's importance to you.

What Does It Look Like?

~~I watched him close the door.~~
He disappeared into Room 203, tie flapping.

We just figured that he had run out of gas and left the car where it ~~was~~ had coughed to a stop.

He knew exactly how to draw students out and encourage us to participate. ~~Once, when he pointed with a piece of chalk at someone who wanted to speak, it flew out of his hand and hit the window.~~ The way he listened carefully and found something valuable in every question made us feel important.

Peer reader's question: What subjects did Mr. Moore teach?

English, Russian, French, American history, world religions, Western civilization—no matter what he taught, He made learning an exciting experience.

[One way we learned who we were was by just watching him be himself.] When the other teachers wore jeans and flannel shirts to class, he dressed in a suit and tie, "to be suitable," he punned. Because he was comforable with who he was, it didn't matter to him that he looked somewhat out of place.

All his exams were open-book, and we could bring along whatever additional materials we wanted. That's because he wasn't as interested in getting answers as he was in getting us to ask our own questions and come up with new ideas.

Biographical Narrative

Apply the Rubric

A strong biographical narrative . . .

- ☑ introduces the person in a way that makes the reader want to know more
- ☑ clearly identifies the person
- ☑ uses detailed descriptions, sensory details, anecdotes, and dialogue to give a dominant impression of the person
- ☑ weaves in background information to provide context and clarity
- ☑ reveals the writer's attitude toward the person through precise words and an appropriate tone
- ☑ includes a variety of sentence beginnings and structures
- ☑ concludes memorably by summarizing the significance of the person to the writer

Ask a Peer Reader

- How would you describe this person in your own words?
- What details, if any, do I need to add?
- Why is this person meaningful to me?

Avoid Clichés

Cliché	Creative Alternative
He had his head in the clouds.	He was endearingly absent-minded.
He was a people person.	What mattered most to him wasn't the subject but the students.
He was one in a million.	His respect and trust meant more than any grade I've ever gotten.
I am his number-one fan.	I'm sure he will be a lifelong mentor.

Check Your Grammar

Do not shift verb tenses needlessly. Inconsistent tenses can confuse your reader.

> All his exams were open-book, and we ~~can~~ ∧*could*
> bring along whatever additional materials
> we ~~want~~ ∧*wanted*.

See pages R59–R60: Verbs

Writing Online

PUBLISHING OPTIONS
For publishing options, visit the **Writing Center** at ClassZone.com.

ASSESSMENT PREPARATION
For writing and grammar assessment practice, go to the **Assessment Center** at ClassZone.com.

Producing a Video Documentary

Here's your chance to sit in the director's chair. Use your biographical narrative as the basis for a video documentary.

Planning the Documentary

1. **Look for audio and visual materials.** Can you interview the person on tape or video? Find out if he or she has photographs, newspaper clippings, or other visuals that you could use. If you wrote about a historical figure, you might look for an expert to interview about that person.

2. **Create a script.** Using your narrative as a starting point, create a **script** for your documentary. Think about where to use voice-over narration, interview footage, and music. Consider including opening and closing credits.

3. **Develop a storyboard.** Plan what your audience will see and hear shot by shot. Include several types of camera positions, such as **establishing shots** (wide-angle shots that set the scene), **medium shots,** and **close-ups.**

Voice-over *A school legend, Mr. Moore has become my most memorable teacher and mentor.*

Excerpt from interview *"My job is to get students to come up with new ideas and learn to evaluate their own work."*

Producing the Documentary

1. **Find out what equipment is available.** Your school may have a camcorder that you can borrow. If you have video editing software, you can record scenes in any order; if not, you will have to film each scene sequentially.

2. **Record the video and the voice-overs.** Follow your script and storyboard carefully.

3. **Pull it together.** Review your footage, reshooting as necessary. When you are satisfied, screen your documentary for neighbors or classmates. Ask for specific feedback so you can make your next documentary even better.

Reading Comprehension

DIRECTIONS *Read these poems and answer the questions that follow.*

The Wind begun to knead the Grass—

Emily Dickinson

The Wind begun to knead the Grass—
As Women do a Dough—
He flung a Hand full at the Plain—
A Hand full at the Sky—
5 The Leaves unhooked themselves from Trees—
And started all abroad—
The Dust did scoop itself like Hands—
And throw away the Road—

The Wagons quickened on the Street—
10 The Thunders gossiped low—
The Lightning showed a Yellow Head—
And then a livid Toe—
The Birds put up the Bars to Nests—
The Cattle flung to Barns—
15 Then came one drop of Giant Rain—
And then, as if the Hands
That held the Dams—had parted hold—
The Waters Wrecked the Sky—
But overlooked my Father's House—
20 Just Quartering a Tree—

ASSESSMENT ONLINE
For more assessment practice and test-taking tips, go to the **Assessment Center** at ClassZone.com.

Patroling Barnegat

Walt Whitman

Wild, wild the storm, and the sea high running,
Steady the roar of the gale, with incessant undertone muttering,
Shouts of demoniac laughter fitfully piercing and pealing,
Waves, air, midnight, their savagest trinity lashing,
5 Out in the shadows there milk-white combs careering,
On beachy slush and sand spirts of snow fierce slanting,
Where through the murk the easterly death-wind breasting,
Through cutting swirl and spray watchful and firm advancing,
(That in the distance! is that a wreck? is the red signal flaring?)
10 Slush and sand of the beach tireless till daylight wending,
Steadily, slowly, through hoarse roar never remitting,
Along the midnight edge by those milk-white combs careering,
A group of dim, weird forms, struggling, the night confronting,
That savage trinity warily watching.

Comprehension

DIRECTIONS *Answer these questions about "The Wind begun to knead the Grass—."*

1. What effect do the dashes have on your reading and understanding of the poem?

   A They tell you to read some words without emphasis because they are less important to the poem's meaning.

   B They show where similes and metaphors occur and help convey their meaning.

   C They help establish the poem's rhythm and indicate a pause after each description.

   D They call attention to rhyming words and mark the end of sentences within the poem.

2. What does the simile in lines 1–2 suggest about the wind?

   A The wind is gently ruffling the grass.

   B A windy day is a good day for baking.

   C The direction of the wind is inconsistent.

   D The wind is strong as it pushes against the grass.

3. Dickinson uses similes and personification to describe different aspects of

   A someone's personality

   B a thunderstorm

   C a dam breaking

   D small-town life

4. The personification of the wind, the leaves, and the dust conveys a sense of

   A natural order

   B gentle guidance

   C unpredictable power

   D domestic happiness

5. The slant rhyme of *abroad* and *road* in lines 6 and 8 draws attention to the

   A wagons hurrying on the road

   B chaotic unruliness of the wind

   C travelers caught by the weather

   D contrast of the leaves against the dust

6. Which words best describe the speaker's tone in lines 1–18?

   A fearful and serious

   B gloomy and somber

   C exhilarated and playful

   D optimistic and confident

7. Dickinson most likely uses irregularly capitalized words in this poem to emphasize

   A key words that tell the story

   B the rhythm of the rain

   C her opinion of the events

   D emotions conveyed in the poem

8. Dickinson personifies the "Thunders" in line 10 as people who gossip to call attention to thunder's

   A dramatic display

   B sinister rumbling

   C meaningless noise

   D frightening power

DIRECTIONS *Answer these questions about "Patroling Barnegat."*

9. Which poetic devices does Whitman use in line 1 to make a dramatic exclamation?

   A cataloging and parallelism

   B simile and personification

   C repetition and inverted word order

   D slant rhymes and inventive punctuation

10. By ending each line with a participle, Whitman is using

   A imagery to convey an idea

   B parallelism to create rhythm

   C details to communicate tone

   D personification to describe an object

11. Whitman uses the irregular meter of free verse to

   A convey the wildness of the storm

   B present a contrast with the subject

   C suggest daily life near the sea

   D establish movement in the poem

12. The effect of Whitman's catalog of sights and sounds on the beach is to

   A build tension

   B emphasize ideas

   C honor people

   D celebrate everyday diction

13. What effect does Whitman achieve by repeating the word *through* in lines 7–11?

   A He interrupts the chronological order of events.

   B He mimics the sound of the wind blowing across the beach.

   C He emphasizes the relentlessness of the darkness, the waves, and the wind.

   D He focuses attention on how a storm damages the surrounding area.

14. Which word best describes the tone Whitman creates in lines 1–8?

   A tragic   **C** triumphant

   B hysterical   **D** suspenseful

DIRECTIONS *Answer this question about both poems.*

15. Which statement best contrasts the tone at the end of the two poems?

   A The Dickinson poem is factual; the Whitman poem is reflective.

   B The Dickinson poem is sad; the Whitman poem is exuberant.

   C The Dickinson poem is peaceful; the Whitman poem is frantic.

   D The Dickinson poem is menacing; the Whitman poem is distant.

Written Response

SHORT RESPONSE *Write three or four sentences to answer this question.*

16. Whitman often repeats words and phrases in his poetry. What effect does he achieve in "Patroling Barnegat" by writing the phrases "savagest trinity" in line 4, "savage trinity" in line 14, and "milk-white combs careering" in lines 5 and 12?

EXTENDED RESPONSE *Write two or three paragraphs to answer this question.*

17. Compare Whitman's and Dickinson's writing styles. Which poetic devices does Dickinson use to describe a storm? Which poetic devices does Whitman use?

GO ON ➡

Vocabulary

DIRECTIONS *Use context clues and the Latin word and root definitions to answer the following questions about words in the two poems.*

1. The Latin word *livere* means "to be bluish." The most likely meaning of the word *livid* as it is used line 12 of "The Wind begun to knead the Grass—" is

   A extremely furious

   B very pale

   C in a state of shock

   D leaden colored

2. The Latin prefix *in-* means "not" and the Latin word *cessare* means "to stop." The most likely meaning of the word *incessant* as it is used in line 2 of "Patroling Barnegat" is

   A continuing without interruption

   B concluding a recent action

   C pausing periodically

   D resuming activity

3. The word *remit* comes from the Latin prefix *re-,* which means "backward," and the Latin word *mittere,* which means "to send." The most likely meaning of the word *remitting* as it is used in line 11 of "Patroling Barnegat" is

   A letting up

   B waiting

   C forgiving

   D restoring

DIRECTIONS *Use context clues to answer the following questions about words in the two poems.*

4. The most likely meaning of the word *quartering* as it is used in line 20 of "The Wind begun to knead the Grass—" is

   A. locating

   B. measuring

   C. splitting into parts

   D. making visible

5. What is the most likely meaning of *demoniac* as it is used in line 3 of "Patroling Barnegat"?

   A. thunderous

   B. fiendish

   C comical

   D sincere

6. What is the most likely meaning of the word *careering* as it is used in lines 5 and 12 of "Patroling Barnegat"?

   A pounding

   B growing

   C rushing

   D falling

Writing & Grammar

DIRECTIONS *Read this passage and answer the questions that follow.*

(1) With a weight of 13,632 tons and a length of 729 feet, the *Edmund Fitzgerald* was the largest carrier on the Great Lakes when it first sailed in 1958. (2) <u>Seventeen years later, the ship</u> would sink in Lake Superior. (3) At 2:20 P.M. on November 9th, 1975, the *Fitzgerald* departed Superior, Wisconsin, destined for Detroit. (4) Shortly afterwards, the National Weather Service issued gale warnings for the area. (5) The next day, winds gusting up to 70 knots and waves cresting as high as 30 feet <u>shook</u> the ship. (6) Water <u>came</u> onto the deck. (7) At approximately 7:15 that evening, the ship vanished from radar observation, and <u>all 29 crew members were lost.</u> (8) It was later discovered that the ship had <u>dropped</u> about 530 feet to the bottom of Lake Superior. (9) <u>That day</u> of November 10, 1975, will always be remembered.

1. Choose the best way to rewrite the underlined portion of sentence 2 to convey a more somber tone.

   A Seventeen years later, the hefty ship

   B Seventeen short years later, the ship

   C Seventeen productive years later, the ship

   D Seventeen years later, the doomed ship

2. Choose the best example of a vivid verb to replace the underlined word in sentence 5.

   A pushed   **C** propelled

   B stirred   **D** battered

3. Choose the best example of a vivid verb to replace the underlined word in sentence 6.

   A splashed   **C** crashed

   B washed   **D** seeped

4. Choose the best way to rewrite the underlined portion of sentence 7 to convey a more somber tone.

   A all 29 crew members were tragically lost.

   B all 29 crew members were unfortunately lost.

   C all 29 crew members were suddenly lost.

   D all 29 crew members were definitely lost.

5. Choose the best example of a vivid verb to replace the underlined word in sentence 8.

   A fallen   **C** sunk

   B plunged   **D** floated

6. Choose the best way to rewrite the underlined portion of sentence 9 to convey a more somber tone.

   A That unexpected day

   B That memorable day

   C That fateful day

   D That historic day

Ideas for Independent Reading

Continue exploring the Questions of the Times on pages 492–493 with these additional works.

What DIVIDES *a nation?*

Classic Slave Narratives
edited by Henry Louis Gates Jr.

This collection of classic slave narratives provides testimony to the horrors of bondage and sheds light on the American slave experience. The volume contains two of the best-known examples of "literature of escape"—the stories of Frederick Douglass and Olaudah Equiano—as well as two narratives by women—Harriet Jacobs and Mary Prince.

Battle Cry of Freedom
by James M. McPherson

This history of the Civil War brings all aspects of the conflict to vivid life, from the momentous episodes that preceded the war, to the battles, politics, and personalities of the war itself. James McPherson provides readers with the framework they need to understand the complex economic, political, and social forces that divided the nation and led the country to war.

Journal of a Residence on a Georgian Plantation in 1838–1839
by Frances Anne Kemble

After her marriage, Fanny Kemble discovered the source of her wealthy husband's income: rice plantations that depended upon the labor of more than 600 slaves. This journal, published after her divorce, describes the appalling conditions Fanny found on one of the plantations and her attempts to improve life for the slaves there.

Is anything worth DYING FOR?

The Personal Memoirs of Ulysses S. Grant
by Ulysses S. Grant

Dying of throat cancer, Ulysses S. Grant spent his last days looking back upon the most important years of his life—the years he spent as the commander of the Union army in the Civil War. Here, in what Mark Twain called "the best [memoirs] of any general's since Caesar," Grant recalls how he managed to defeat Robert E. Lee and the Confederate army.

Co. Aytch: A Confederate Memoir of the Civil War
by Sam R. Watkins

Sam Watkins was 21 years old when the Civil War broke out. A native of Columbia, Tennessee, he didn't want to miss out on the "big show." Volunteering as a private, he served in Company H of the Maury Grays, First Tennessee Regiment. From that lowly position, Watkins fought in almost every major clash, from the battle of Shiloh to the battle of Nashville.

Lincoln
by David Herbert Donald

Pulitzer Prize–winning author David Donald tells the story of Abraham Lincoln, the man who managed to hold together a nation of vastly differing regional interests during the turmoil and tragedy of the Civil War. Donald's Lincoln emerges as ambitious yet fallible, with a remarkable capacity for growth—a man who spent his whole life learning and growing to eventually become one of our nation's greatest presidents.

Why do people BREAK RULES?

Leaves of Grass
by Walt Whitman

Walt Whitman created a daring new kind of poetry that would become a major force in the world of literature. Whitman first published this volume himself, in 1855, with only 12 poems. He expanded and revised the book over the course of his life as his experiences and the nation's history changed and grew.

Letters of Emily Dickinson
by Emily Dickinson

Emily Dickinson's ingenuity, sensitivity, and wit course through her letters as well as her poetry. Compiled by a close friend, Dickinson's letters were first published in 1894, eight years after her death. Although she became increasingly reclusive and rarely saw her friends in her later years, this volume of letters shows that she thought of them often and affectionately.

Daisy Miller
by Henry James

In this short novel, a wealthy young woman named Daisy Miller takes the grand tour of Europe. In the 19th century, such a long trip was a rite of passage for well-to-do young Americans. In Rome, Daisy's friendship with an Italian man, though innocent, causes her to be shunned by her peers. Yet she refuses to change her carefree ways. By disregarding the social rules of her community, Daisy sets herself up for tragedy.

Is it important to FACE REALITY?

Shiloh: A Novel
by Shelby Foote

This modern novel gives readers an up-close impression of the battle of Shiloh from the perspectives of many different soldiers who fought in it. Each chapter consists of the first-person accounts of various narrators, Union and Confederate, telling of what transpires in their own little corner of the battle.

Ambrose Bierce's Civil War
by Ambrose Bierce, edited by William McCann

Ambrose Bierce is one of the few writers of his day who actually fought in the Civil War. As a result, his gritty depictions of battle and close observation of soldiers' daily lives have the ring of authenticity. This collection includes both personal memoirs and fictional accounts of the war.

Life in the Iron Mills
by Rebecca Harding Davis

Decades before most Americans took notice, Rebecca Harding Davis unveiled the human costs of industrialism in *Life in the Iron Mills*. She concentrated on the stunted lives of factory workers, showing the dirty hovels where they lived, their unwholesome food, their constant labor, and their lack of education. Her story was one of the first works of American fiction to acknowledge such realities. Yet Davis also looked beyond social conditions to explore her characters' hidden yearnings for artistic expression and lasting love.

UNIT 4

Preview Unit Goals

LITERARY ANALYSIS	• Analyze descriptive language, including imagery, figurative language, repetition, and diction
	• Understand regionalism and naturalism as literary movements
	• Analyze characteristics of regionalism and naturalism
	• Identify and analyze literary elements, including setting, plot, conflict, theme, and tone
	• Analyze irony
READING	• Make inferences and draw conclusions about characters
	• Analyze author's perspective
	• Analyze primary sources
	• Analyze how an author's choice of genre affects the expression of a theme or topic
WRITING AND GRAMMAR	• Write a literary analysis paper
	• Use gerunds and gerund phrases
	• Use passive and active voice effectively
SPEAKING, LISTENING, AND VIEWING	• Interpret and evaluate messages in photography and fine art
	• Create a visual representation
	• Create a power presentation
VOCABULARY	• Use knowledge of Latin roots to understand word meaning
	• Discriminate between connotative and denotative meanings of words
	• Read and understand analogies
ACADEMIC VOCABULARY	• regionalism • analogy • irony
	• naturalism • descriptive language • author's perspective

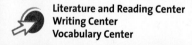

Literature and Reading Center
Writing Center
Vocabulary Center

Regionalism and Naturalism

Willa Cather

1870–1910
CAPTURING THE AMERICAN LANDSCAPE

- Regionalism and Local Color Writing
- A New Role for Women
- The Rise of Naturalism

Questions of the Times

DISCUSS Consider the following questions with your classmates. Then read on to learn how these issues affected people living during this period and how the questions were reflected in the writing of the time.

What makes a place UNIQUE?

In the post–Civil War years, the United States was growing and changing at such a rapid pace that many Americans felt they were losing their regional identities. People were proud of the things they felt made them unique, and writers responded to this impulse by attempting to record the character of the country's distinct regions. What is it exactly that makes a place unique?

Does the universe CARE?

Life was quite difficult for many Americans during this period. Native Americans, African Americans, immigrants, factory workers, laborers, and farmers struggled daily against poverty and oppression. To many, it seemed that life was unfair—that despite their efforts, they could not escape their fate. Do you think people can control their destiny, or are they simply victims of circumstance?

How are women's ROLES CHANGING?

Women of this era were becoming more educated, politically aware, and ambitious. Yet they were not allowed to vote, and those who stepped outside their homes to become artists, writers, and reformers faced strong disapproval and warnings that such activities were "unnatural" for women. How have women's roles evolved over the years?

Why are there "haves" and "HAVE-NOTS"?

This period was a time of harsh extremes. Industry was controlled by a handful of businesses owned by a few people who became very wealthy. These businesses were supported by countless laborers who worked long hours for low wages in dangerous conditions. Why do some people reap huge benefits while others are locked into hardship? Should the government ensure opportunity for all?

Regionalism and Naturalism
1870–1910
Capturing the American Landscape

Vast, varied, filled with seemingly limitless possibility—that was the United States in the years following the Civil War. Yet, all around them in this land of hope and opportunity, writers saw fellow Americans living lives of hardship and even despair. Regionalism tried to capture the reality of ordinary people's lives; naturalism searched for explanations.

Regionalism and Naturalism: Historical Context

KEY IDEAS The post–Civil War period saw the nation reunited and transformed. Writers responded by attempting to preserve in their writing the distinct character of America's regions and to come to terms with some of its harsh new realities.

Reconstruction's Failures and Successes

The Civil War left the South in ruins. Its primary labor system, slavery, had been abolished. Freed African Americans lacked money, property, education, and opportunity. Farms, factories, and plantations had been destroyed, and rail lines were unusable. The federal government had to come up with a plan to solve these problems and to readmit the Southern states to the union. That plan was **Reconstruction.**

Reconstruction did not go smoothly. The president and Congress clashed over how to best carry it out. Southern states resisted many of the protections granted to newly freed blacks, while blacks felt that too little was being done to ensure their civil rights and economic independence. However, Reconstruction did succeed in a few significant ways. African Americans gained citizenship and equal protection under the law as well as the right to vote, and all of the Confederate states returned to the Union.

Although Americans were glad to move past the divisiveness of the war years, they regretted losing their regional identities and were unsettled by the many changes taking place in the country. These circumstances influenced writers of the time to begin trying to capture the customs, character, and landscapes of the nation's distinct regions—a type of writing that would come to be called **regionalism.**

A Nation Transformed

In the decades following the Civil War, the country as a whole changed radically. In 1869, the first **transcontinental railroad** was completed. It was an event of huge importance. The railroad brought a flood of new settlers west—so many, in fact, that in 1890 the government announced the closing of the frontier. This westward expansion was yet another influence on writers of the time. It created an appreciation for America's diversity, which was celebrated by **local color writers** such as **Mark Twain** and **Bret Harte.**

The railroad also expanded industry. By 1885, four transcontinental lines had been completed, creating manufacturing hubs in Pittsburgh, Cleveland, Detroit, and Chicago. In turn, cities grew exponentially as more and more people came looking for work. In 1850, Chicago was a small town of 20,000; by 1910, the population was more than 2 million. Yet although new technologies and industrial modernization ensured the nation's prosperity, much of its wealth lay in the hands of only a few.

Country Fair, New England (1890), Childe Hassam. 24 ¼″ × 20 ⅛″.
© Manoogian Collection, Taylor, Michigan.

► TAKING NOTES

Outlining As you read this introduction, use an outline to record the main ideas about the characteristics and literature of the period. You can use headings, boldfaced terms, and the information in these boxes as starting points. (See page R49 in the **Research Handbook** for more help with outlining.)

I. Historical Context
A. Reconstruction
  1. Failures
  2. Successes
  3. Effect on writers
B. Transformed Nation

ADDITIONAL BACKGROUND
For more on this period, visit the **Literature Center** at ClassZone.com.

The Hatch Family (1871), Eastman Johnson. Oil on canvas, 48″ × 73 ³⁄₈″. The Metropolitan Museum of Art, Gift of Frederic H. Hatch, 1926 (26.97. Photo © 1999 The Metropolitan Museum of Art.

ANALYZE VISUALS
What might have been the artist's purpose in rendering the scene in this painting? How would you describe the photographer's purpose for capturing the image on page 621?

Cultural Influences

KEY IDEAS Industry's success created a better life for many Americans. For a few, it brought great wealth, but others suffered poverty and hardship. Both regional and naturalist writers were influenced by these developments.

The Gilded Age

As the 1800s drew to an end, a very small group of men controlled the vast majority of industry, including the enormously profitable steel, railroad, oil, and meatpacking sectors. Captains of industry such as John D. Rockefeller, the oil tycoon, and Cornelius Vanderbilt, the railroad magnate, enjoyed showing off the vast fortunes they had made. They built palatial mansions, draped their wives and daughters in diamonds, and threw extravagant parties (at one, guests were handed silver shovels and invited to dig in a sandbox filled with jewels)—in short, they did everything but actually coat themselves in gold. When writers **Mark Twain** and **Charles Dudley Warner** dubbed this period "the Gilded Age," they did not exaggerate. It was a time of sparkle and glitter, luxury and excess.

Many ordinary people had more money too and all sorts of new things to spend it on. They could take the train to an amusement park and ride the Ferris wheel, then snack on soda and a candy bar. City dwellers could shop in the new department stores, while country folks pored over the mail-order catalog from Sears, Roebuck (known as "the wish book," it offered everything from skin lotion to bicycles, and even an entire house—assembly required).

> **A Voice from the Times**
>
> *The only way not to think about money is to have a great deal of it.*
>
> —Edith Wharton

There were telephones now, thanks to Alexander Graham Bell. In 1908 Henry Ford brought out the first Model T, a "horseless carriage" cheap enough for his own factory workers to buy. Thomas Edison alone patented more than 1,000 inventions, from the phonograph to the electric light bulb.

The Have-Nots

Unfortunately, the Gilded Age was not so shiny for many other Americans. The settling of the West forced Native Americans off their land and onto reservations. Although Native Americans fought back—among them **Chief Joseph** of the Nez Perce and the legendary Sioux warriors Crazy Horse and Sitting Bull—there was no stopping the tide.

Life was hard for freed African Americans as well. The failures of Reconstruction in the South left many poor and powerless, held down by segregationist Jim Crow laws and forced to work as sharecroppers under conditions much like slavery.

Others who found themselves facing hard times during this period were many immigrants who had come to America in search of freedom and opportunity. Russian, Italian, Scandinavian, German, Dutch, and Japanese immigrants—all were seeking a better life. Some joined the settlers heading west; others stayed in the cities, where they lived in crowded tenements and found work in factories. Unfortunately, many of these new city-dwelling Americans found themselves working 16-hour days in airless sweatshops for subsistence wages.

> ### A Voice from the Times
>
> *Hear me, my chiefs! I am tired; my heart is sick and sad. From where the sun now stands I will fight no more forever.*
>
> **—Chief Joseph of the Nez Perce,**
> from his 1877 surrender speech

Child Coal Mine Workers in Hughestown, Pennsylvania (1911). Lewis Wickes Hine/© Corbis.

Even independent farmers faced hard times. They borrowed money from the banks for new machinery that made them more productive than ever before; but high yields meant low prices, and when they couldn't pay back their loans they lost their farms.

People knew that they were missing out on the prosperity that others were enjoying, and it made them angry. Workers began to form **labor unions;** many farmers, white and black, joined the **Populist Party,** hoping to make the government more responsive to workers' needs. However, the opposition had money and power, and these early efforts often ended in bitter defeat.

More and more, the individual seemed helpless, at the mercy of forces beyond his or her understanding or control. Life became a constant struggle, and the world appeared to be a harsh, uncaring place. These feelings found their voice in a literary movement called **naturalism.** Naturalist writers, such as **Stephen Crane,** were concerned with the impact of social and natural forces on the individual. These writers tended to portray characters victimized by brutal forces and unable to control their lives.

Ideas of the Age

KEY IDEAS During this period, some Americans believed in "survival of the fittest," while others worked for social justice.

Laissez Faire vs. Progressivism

Many of the naturalists' ideas corresponded to new scientific, political, and economic theories emerging at the time. Various thinkers of the day felt that Charles Darwin's theory of natural selection could be applied to human society. An English philosopher named Herbert Spencer called this idea **survival of the fittest,** claiming that those who rose to the top of society were "fit," while those who suffered at the bottom were best left to die out. **Social Darwinists** used these ideas to justify the huge gap between rich and poor and to push a governmental policy of **laissez faire** (French for "allow to do"), meaning that business should not be regulated, because the law of nature would ensure success for the "fittest" and inevitable failure for everyone else.

This self-serving philosophy infuriated many Americans. A **progressive movement** emerged, which aimed to restore economic opportunities and correct injustices in American life. The progressives did not see inequality as the way of the world. They believed that social change was possible and necessary and that it was the job of the government to make laws to protect people.

Industrialist John D. Rockefeller is portrayed as a wealthy king, with the oil and railroad industries as the "jewels" in his crown.

A Voice from the Times

Let no one underestimate the need of pity. We live in a stony universe whose hard, brilliant forces rage fiercely.

—Theodore Dreiser

Regional and Naturalist Literature

KEY IDEAS The country's rapid growth and change was reflected in new literary movements and voices, including regionalism, naturalism, and women's writing.

Regionalism and Local Color Writing

The end of the Civil War, the country's rapid expansion, and the growth of industry all led to the birth of local color writing, a form of regionalism. Aware of the speed with which the nation was changing, regional writers sought to record for the future the unique character of their areas.

Prominent among the early local colorists were **Bret Harte** and **Mark Twain.** Their versions of life on the frontier captured the imagination of readers in the more settled communities of the East, Midwest, and South. For those who could not hop aboard the new transcontinental train and see the country for themselves, reading all about it was the next best thing. Americans were endlessly fascinated by tales of life in the mining camps, on the cattle ranches, and in the frontier towns. The new regionalist literature satisfied this curiosity with its honest portrayals of the people and their way of life in different areas of the country, especially the West. Writers carefully recorded how ordinary people spoke, dressed, acted, thought, and looked, from the knobby, roughened hands of a Nebraska farm woman to the dust-covered boots of a California gambler.

AN OUTGROWTH OF REALISM Regionalism, with its emphasis on everyday experience and accuracy, grew out of **realism.** Many regionalist writers, such as **Willa Cather,** shared the realist goal of showing ordinary lives as they

▶ *For Your Outline*

REGIONALISM AND LOCAL COLOR WRITING

- Writing was influenced by end of Civil war, country's expansion, and industry's growth.

- Regionalists sought to record for the future the unique character of a region.

- Regionalists captured life on the frontier and in other regions.

- Regionalsim was an outgrowth of realism.

- Native American oral literature was a form of regionalism.

- *Huckleberry Finn* is a masterpiece of regionalism.

Deadwood in 1876.

623

were, without romance or sentimentality. Cather's story, "A Wagner Matinee," for example, gives a very unromantic view of life on the plains. Other writers tended to exaggerate a bit, either for comic effect—as in Twain's "The Notorious Jumping Frog of Calaveras County"—or to make their stories livelier. Our national legend of the Wild West, with its gunslingers, saloons, and sheriffs, had its origins in the picturesque settings and characters of writers like **Bret Harte.**

NATIVE AMERICAN LITERATURE While this kind of regional literature thrived, another was under siege. For generations, Native American tribes had passed down from one generation to the next folk tales, legends, and other **oral literature,** relying on the memories of traditional storytellers and their audiences. Now, the tribes found themselves scattered. Children were forcibly taken from their elders and sent away to "Indian schools," where teachers demanded they forget their language and heritage and assimilate into American society. Entire cultures were rapidly disappearing. However, through the efforts of Native Americans and sympathetic outsiders who helped them write their stories down, some of the literature was saved, thus giving another view of life in the West.

AN "AMERICAN" NOVEL With the publication in 1884 of Mark Twain's *The Adventures of Huckleberry Finn,* regionalism and local color writing reached a zenith. *Huckleberry Finn* was the first novel written entirely in "American"—that is, it was told in the colorful, colloquial, and often ungrammatical voice of its young narrator, Huck. Twain was known for using his gift of humor to make a serious point, and in this novel he used biting satire to tackle the issue of racism in America. Despite Twain's immense popularity with readers worldwide, critics of the time dismissed *Huckleberry Finn,* calling it vulgar and immoral, and libraries banned the book from their shelves as "the veriest trash." Today, many consider it not only Twain's finest work but possibly the best book ever written by an American author. The novel had a huge influence on later writers, among them Ernest Hemingway, who said, "All modern American literature comes from one book by Mark Twain called *Huckleberry Finn.* There was nothing before. There has been nothing as good since."

The Rise of Naturalism

As the 19th century came to a close, several factors led to the rise of a literary movement called **naturalism.** The final decades of the century were a time of rapid change and sharp contrasts—a time when "captains of industry" amassed vast fortunes by exploiting the cheap labor of immigrants and other workers who flooded the cities in search of work. By 1916, the majority of American workers were industrial laborers in factories.

WRITING REFLECTS REALITY The work of naturalist writers, such as Theodore Dreiser, reflected this harsh new reality. In the first pages of his novel *The Financier,* for example, a boy named Frank stares through the window of a fish shop at a lobster and a squid that have been placed together in a tank. Day after day, the two creatures battle it out, the sharp-clawed lobster attacking, the squid fighting for its life. At last, the lobster devours the squid. That's the way of the world, Frank thinks—one creature lives off another. When Frank grows up and becomes a banker, he applies this lesson to the ruthless world of business.

Why do people do the things they do? Are humans capable of choice, or do they act on instinct, like other animals? Is life a losing battle? Looking to the theories of Darwin and other scientists, naturalists such as **Dreiser, Frank Norris, Jack London,** and **Stephen Crane** saw human beings as helpless creatures moved by forces beyond their understanding or control.

Despite this grim attitude, many naturalist writers were quite popular. Some, like Frank Norris, gave a voice to ordinary people and portrayed the rich and influential in an unflattering light, as in his famous 1901 novel *The Octopus,* which attacked the railroad interests in his home state of California. Jack London, on the other hand, captured readers with his tales of an arctic world entirely outside their everyday experience. Riveted by the exotic setting and thrilling action of novels such as *White Fang* and *The Call of the Wild,* readers were willing to accept less-than-happy endings.

▶ *For Your Outline*

THE RISE OF NATURALISM

- Naturalism reflected time of rapid changes and sharp contrasts, when wealth was concentrated in few hands.
- Naturalists saw humans as helpless from forces beyond their control.

A New Role for Women

Women writing in this period in the United States tended to be realists. Some were regionalists and others embraced naturalist themes, but all were breaking barriers as women's roles slowly shifted. "The power of a woman is in her refinement, gentleness, and elegance; it is she who makes etiquette, and it is she who preserves the order and decency of society." So said a popular book of etiquette in 1880, voicing a widely held notion about women's place in society.

At the same time, however, the movement to give women the **right to vote** was reemerging after a period of inactivity in the years immediately following the Civil War, when male reformers argued that black and white women should wait until black men gained their rights. Women were growing impatient, not just for the vote, but to have a larger voice in every aspect of public life, from politics to literature.

▶ *For Your Outline*

A NEW ROLE FOR WOMEN

- Women writers tended to be realists, whether working as regionalists or naturalists.
- They broke barriers as women's roles shifted.
- The women's suffrage movement reemerged.
- University education became more available to women.
- Women's writing reflected society's limitations.

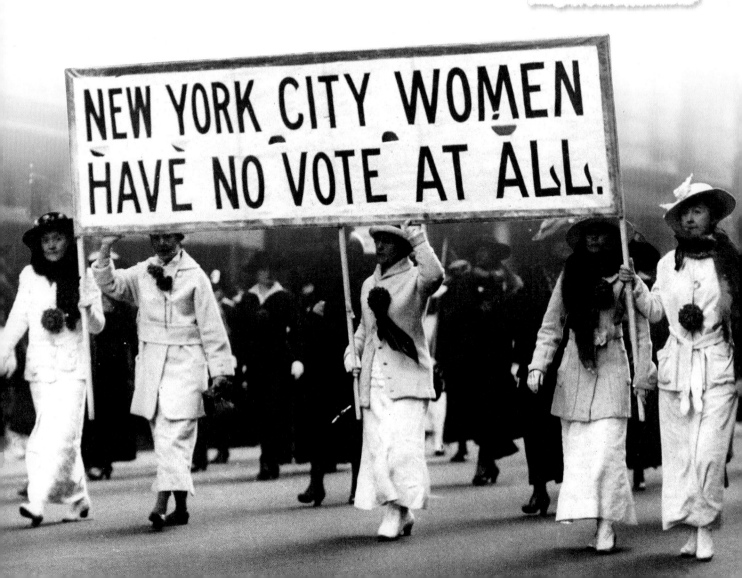

One important factor in the growth of the women's movement was the spread of **university education** among women of the era. Newspapers of the day trumpeted the dangers of this development. An 1896 *New York Journal* headline proclaimed: "Are We Destroying Woman's Beauty? The Startling Warning of a Great English Physician Against Higher Education of Women. How Intellectual Work Destroys Beauty." Despite such dire warnings, women continued to seek education. Then they found that the limited roles assigned them did not make full use of their abilities and knowledge.

BREAKTHROUGH WRITERS Charlotte Perkins Gilman— related on her father's side to a noted family of writers and social reformers that included Harriet Beecher Stowe, the author of *Uncle Tom's Cabin*—became one of the most well-known advocates for women. Fleeing a repressive marriage, **Gilman** moved from the East Coast to California, where she wrote and spoke out on behalf of women's rights and against male domination. One of her most famous stories is "The Yellow Wallpaper," about a woman writer who, as treatment for her "nervous condition," is forbidden to write.

Kate Chopin wrote fiction that articulates the frustrations of generations of women confined to a sort of extended childhood by the men in their lives. Her gentle stories depicting some of the most obvious of women's troubles were extremely popular in the 1890s. Her 1899 novel *The Awakening,* however, stepped over the line in its portrayal of a woman's hidden passion, arousing a public protest so vigorous that Chopin ceased writing completely.

Works by women of this period often end tragically, in madness, ruin, scandal, and death. In part, this was a reflection of their **naturalist** leanings; at the same time, though, it grew out of their own experiences in a culture that did not encourage women's artistic goals. **Edith Wharton,** who in novels such as *The Age of Innocence* and *The House of Mirth* decried the stifling small-mindedness of upper-class society, made her own escape by running off to Paris, only to have her marriage fall apart. Facing overwhelming obstacles, women writers fought with, in the words of New England's local color writer **Mary Wilkins Freeman**, "little female weapons." When the weapon was a pen, the impact could be revolutionary.

As the country moved farther into the 20th century, writers would begin to turn from regionalism and naturalism to the more experimental works that characterize modernism. Thankfully Twain, London, Chopin, and the other writers of their time captured for future generations the unique spirit of late 19th- and early 20th-century America.

American Impressionism

During this period, the revolutionary style pioneered by French painters such as Claude Monet and Auguste Renoir made its mark in the United States. American artists took the basic goal of **impressionism**—to capture reality as we actually see it in the moment, not as formal rules of art say we should see it—and adapted it to their own situation.

Style and Subject Like their European counterparts, American impressionists focused on the effects of light and color and liked to paint outdoors. Often they painted what a new American leisure class wanted to buy: idyllic landscapes that let them "get away" and portraits of themselves relaxing in their homes or picnicking at the seaside. Paintings like these were not only a pleasure to look at but a status symbol too—proof that the owner (perhaps the son or grandson of a penniless immigrant) had acquired taste and culture.

Progressive Woman One of the few women who exhibited with the impressionists in Paris was an American artist named **Mary Cassatt,** whose work *In the Garden* (1904) is shown here. At a time when no respectable woman traveled alone, lived alone, or pursued a career in art, Cassatt did all three. Known as "a painter of mothers and children," her works reflect a surprisingly modern sensibility. Though her paintings show women in conventional settings, she gives them a new sense of purpose. Cassatt's women do not exist just to be looked at; they are the heroes of their own lives.

Connecting Literature, History, and Culture

Use the timeline and the questions on the next page to gain insight about how developments in the United States during this period reflected those in the world as a whole.

AMERICAN LITERARY MILESTONES

1870

1870 Bret Harte publishes his story collection *The Luck of Roaring Camp and Other Sketches.* ▶

1876 Mark Twain completes *The Adventures of Tom Sawyer* and begins writing *The Adventures of Huckleberry Finn.*

1880

1881 Henry James publishes *The Portrait of a Lady.*

1883 Mark Twain's *Life on the Mississippi* is published. ▶

1885 Libraries across America ban Mark Twain's *The Adventures of Huckleberry Finn,* published the previous year; William Dean Howells publishes *The Rise of Silas Lapham.*

1887 Diary of Chief Seattle is published.

HISTORICAL CONTEXT

1870

1872 Susan B. Anthony is arrested and fined for leading a group of women to test their right to vote. ▶

1876 Alexander Graham Bell patents first telephone; at Battle of Little Bighorn, 1,500 Sioux and Cheyenne warriors defeat and kill about 200 U.S. Army troops, commanded by George A. Custer.

1877 Chief Joseph of the Nez Perce tribe surrenders to U.S. Army; Thomas Edison invents the phonograph.

1880

1880 John D. Rockefeller's Standard Oil Company of Ohio controls U.S. refining; George Eastman patents his rolled camera film.

1883 The first metal-framed skyscraper, ten stories high, is built in Chicago.

1886 The Statue of Liberty, a gift from France to the United States, is dedicated in New York Harbor. ▶

WORLD CULTURE AND EVENTS

1870

1871 Franco-Prussian War ends and Germany is unified; French naturalist writer Émile Zola publishes the first book in his 20-novel series *Les Rougon-Macquart.*

1872 Critics coin the term *impressionism* after viewing Claude Monet's painting *Impression: Sunrise.*

1879 The British defeat the Zulus in South Africa.

1880

1883 The Orient Express makes its first rail run from Paris to Istanbul.

1887 Fictional detective Sherlock Holmes makes his first appearance in *A Study in Scarlet,* by Sir Arthur Conan Doyle. ▶

1889 The Eiffel Tower is completed in Paris.

MAKING CONNECTIONS

- Who were some inventors at work in Europe and the United States?
- How did American women fare in gaining the right to vote as compared with New Zealand women?
- What evidence do you see that the United States was becoming an imperial power?
- Name two works of American literature from this period that describe real people or events.

1890

1890 Charlotte Perkins Gilman describes the emotional and intellectual decline of a young wife and mother in "The Yellow Wallpaper."

1893 Stephen Crane publishes *Maggie: A Girl of the Streets;* Paul Laurence Dunbar publishes his first volume of poetry, *Oak and Ivy,* while working as an elevator operator.

1899 Kate Chopin publishes her novel *The Awakening.*

1900

1900 Theodore Dreiser publishes *Sister Carrie.*

1901 Booker T. Washington publishes *Up From Slavery: An Autobiography.*

1903 Jack London publishes *The Call of the Wild;* W. E. B. Du Bois publishes *The Souls of Black Folk.*

1905 Edith Wharton publishes *The House of Mirth.*

1906 Upton Sinclair's *The Jungle* ▶ exposes dangerous conditions in meatpacking factories.

THE JUNGLE

UPTON SINCLAIR

1890

1892 New York's Ellis Island becomes entry point for European immigrants.

1896 Supreme Court upholds "separate but equal" doctrine of Jim Crow laws, widely used to discriminate against African Americans; the Klondike gold rush begins in Alaska and Canada.

1898 The Spanish-American War results in United States gaining control of Guam, Puerto Rico, and the Philippines; U.S. also annexes Hawaii.

1900

1901 William McKinley is assassinated; Theodore Roosevelt becomes president of the United States.

1903 Near Kitty Hawk, North Carolina, Orville and Wilbur Wright make first flight in engine-powered airplane.

1906 Earthquake and fire destroy much of San Francisco.

1908 Ford Motor Company brings out the first Model T automobile.

1890

1893 New Zealand becomes first country to grant women suffrage.

1894 Rudyard Kipling publishes *The Jungle Book.*

1896 Italian physicist Guglielmo Marconi invents first radio; first modern Olympic games are held in Athens.

1897 Edmond Rostand publishes *Cyrano de Bergerac.*

1900

1900 The Boxer Rebellion protests foreign influence in China.

1901 After 64 years as ruler of Great Britain, Queen Victoria dies. ▶

1902 Joseph Conrad publishes *Heart of Darkness.*

1904 James Joyce begins *Dubliners.*

1905 Albert Einstein formulates his theory of relativity.

The Legacy of the Era

The Wild, Wild West

It's high noon and two cowboys face off on a deserted street, spurs jingling, fingers twitching. Sound familiar? Although the real Wild West lasted just a few decades, it lives on today in Westerns—a genre of novels, television shows, and movies inspired originally by the stories of Bret Harte and other regionalist writers such as Zane Grey and Owen Wister.

QUICKWRITE What is it about the Wild West that makes it so appealing to Americans? Write a paragraph or two explaining why, in your opinion, the legend lives on.

The Labor Movement

In the post–Civil War period, many laborers, unhappy with the appalling working conditions of their day, began to join unions and strike for better wages and conditions. Business leaders feared the growth of unions and tried to break their power with lockouts, firings, and even violence. Slowly, however, unions increased their membership and their power, eventually changing the way many Americans worked.

ONLINE RESEARCH Today, workers consider 8 hours a full day. Contrast that with the 10 to 12 hours typically worked in the 19th century, and you will see one benefit won by early unions. What issues are today's unions focusing on? Visit the Web site of a modern labor union, and report to the class on its top concerns.

Regionalism Today

Local color writing is still very popular in America. Writers such as Garrison Keillor, Larry McMurtry, and Fannie Flagg capture regions as we know them today, from small-town Minnesota to the great spaces of Texas to sleepy towns of the South.

REPORT Do some research to find out if there are any writers working today who are capturing the flavor of the region in which you live. Report to the class on the writer or writers you discover. What have they written? Is their work well-known? Do they write in dialect, describe landscapes or towns, work in fiction or nonfiction? Explore these and any other questions that arise as you research.

Garrison Keillor

Setting in Regional Literature

Many places in the world are fascinating, but some of the most ordinary places can be interesting, too, if you notice what is unique about them. In the last half of the 19th century, regional writers in the United States strove to depict in their stories the unique aspects of a specific place and of its people. These enduring tales give readers a glimpse into the past and inspire a tradition that continues to this day.

The Growth of Regional Literature

Regional literature arose from an effort to accurately represent the speech, manners, habits, history, folklore, and beliefs of people in specific geographical areas. Although regionalism is considered an offshoot of realism, it has been part of American literature from the beginning. Washington Irving's tales of Dutch New York and Nathaniel Hawthorne's stories of Puritan New England are just two examples. After the Civil War, however, when realism became the dominant literary movement, writers began to focus on the lives of ordinary people and to avoid the supernaturalism and sentimentality found in much of the work of Irving, Hawthorne, and Edgar Allan Poe.

Mark Twain relaxes on a ship's deck.

A factor that contributed to the growth of regional writing was the boom in publishing in the late 1800s. Popular magazines sprang up all over the United States to meet the demand for information about the rest of the country. Mark Twain's "The Notorious Jumping Frog of Calaveras County," for example, was first published in a New York magazine and became an immediate sensation.

The Importance of Setting

The effectiveness of regional writing depends to a large extent on the depiction of **setting,** the time and place in which a story's events occur. Key elements of setting in regional literature include the following:

- geographical location and physical features, such as a river, a camp, a house, or a mode of transportation

- the time in which the events take place—a season of the year or a historical period

- the jobs and daily activities of the characters

- the culture of the characters, including their religious and moral beliefs and the social and economic conditions in which they live

Two means of conveying setting that are commonly found in regional literature are the use of **dialects**—distinctive forms of language spoken in particular areas or by particular groups of people—and **detailed descriptions** of location. Take a look at the beginning of Simon Wheeler's rambling tale in Twain's "The Notorious Jumping Frog of Calaveras County" (page 660).

> "Rev. Leonidas W. H'm, Reverend Le— Well, there was a feller here once by the name of Jim Smiley, in the winter of '49—or maybe it was the spring of '50—I don't recollect exactly, somehow, though what makes me think it was one or the other is because I remember the big flume warn't finished when he first come to the camp. . . ."
>
> **—Mark Twain, "The Notorious Jumping Frog of Calaveras County"**

The pronunciations indicated by the spellings *feller* and *warn't,* the expression "I don't recollect," and the use of *come* rather than *came* all contribute to the regional flavor of the piece.

Now look at this description from Willa Cather's "A Wagner Matinee" (page 694), in which the narrator recalls the Nebraska farm where he grew up. Notice the harshness and the lack of color in the setting described; both the landscape and the evidence of human habitation are black, pitted, and bare.

> I saw again the tall, naked house on the prairie, black and grim as a wooden fortress; the black pond where I had learned to swim, its margin pitted with sun-dried cattle tracks; the rain gullied clay banks about the naked house, the four dwarf ash seedlings where the dish-cloths were always hung to dry before the kitchen door.
>
> **—Willa Cather, "A Wagner Matinee"**

In regional literature, setting, characters, and plot are usually inseparable. As you read regional writing, notice the relationship between the characters and the setting. Ask yourself how the characters react to the setting. Then decide how this relationship is significant to the story's plot.

LOCAL COLOR REALISM

Prospectors pan for gold during the gold rush, 1889.

In 1868, a popular story about the California gold rush—Bret Harte's "The Luck of Roaring Camp"—launched a specific form of regional writing called **local color writing.** Mark Twain, with his memorable characters, was a master of this form. Other local color realists of the time include Joel Chandler Harris in the South and Sarah Orne Jewett and Mary Wilkins Freeman in New England. Later regional writers, such as Willa Cather, William Faulkner, and Flannery O'Connor, developed sophisticated ways of making universal statements about the human condition while focusing on the local and the particular.

Close Read

What feeling about life on the frontier do you get from the description? How could you rewrite the passage to change that feeling?

from **The Autobiography of Mark Twain**

by Mark Twain

FYI

Did you know that Mark Twain . . .

- used multiple pen names, including S. L. C., Josh, and Thomas Jefferson Snodgrass?
- served briefly in the Confederate Army?
- took his name from a nautical term for water depth meaning "two fathoms deep"?

Author Online

For more on Mark Twain, visit the **Literature Center** at **ClassZone.com.**

Mark Twain

1835–1910

Readers of all ages have followed the youthful adventures of Huck Finn and Tom Sawyer for more than 100 years. Many have also enjoyed the witty and sharp social commentary in Mark Twain's lectures and journalism. A man who found humor in a life filled with tragedy, Mark Twain remains one of America's greatest literary voices.

Life on the River Samuel Langhorne Clemens—as Twain was named at birth—grew up in the Mississippi River town of Hannibal, Missouri. The river and the town shaped young Clemens's early years. After his father's death, he began working at an early age to help support his family. Work for a printer and a newspaper began a lifelong connection to journalism and led to his first published writing—a humorous sketch. Planning to write travel sketches, Clemens signed on with a river pilot. He spent four years on the river, where he met many different kinds of people. After the Civil War, river travel was largely replaced by railroad travel, but Clemens remembered the river's lessons as he took the pen name by which his readers came to know him.

On the Move Twain kept traveling, first to the American West, where he panned for gold. He gained literary recognition with his tall tale "The Notorious Jumping Frog of Calaveras County," set in California. Twain also traveled the world, sharing his experiences in sketches, letters, and lectures. Travel writings such as *The Innocents Abroad* artfully combined wit and serious information and were vastly popular.

Twain's Great Legacy After his 1870 marriage, Twain based his growing family in Hartford, Connecticut, where he produced his most lasting works, *The Adventures of Tom Sawyer* and *The Adventures of Huckleberry Finn*. These books secured Twain's place as a great American novelist.

Tragedy Haunts the Later Years Despite literary success, Twain found himself in debt from unsuccessful business ventures. Facing bankruptcy in 1893, he traveled once again, delivering humorous lectures amidst the great personal sorrow of two daughters' deaths and his wife's fading health. Twain's last works reflect the sorrow and anger of this period, which lasted until his death.

● LITERARY ANALYSIS: IRONY

One of the most distinctive elements of Twain's style is his use of **irony**—the contrast between appearance and actuality. In general, there are three types of irony:

- **situational irony**—a contrast between what is expected to happen and what actually does happen
- **dramatic irony**—when readers know more about a situation or character than the characters do
- **verbal irony**—a contrast between what is stated and what is meant

In this selection, Twain uses primarily two of the three types of irony. Watch for examples of them as you read and notice how they add tension and humor to the writing.

● READING SKILL: PREDICT

When you **predict,** you use text clues to make a reasonable guess about what will happen in a story. Sometimes a story will surprise you with a plot twist; sometimes your predictions will hit the mark. Either way, watching for text clues can help you find the situational irony in Twain's story. As you read, use a chart like the one shown to record your predictions and the clues from the text that that led you to make your educated guess.

Predictions	Text Clues
I predict he'll find a way to get involved.	Narrator says he can't resist the temptation to be a subject.

▲ VOCABULARY IN CONTEXT

Match each vocabulary word in the first column with the word in the second column that is closest in meaning.

1. unassailable
2. multifariously
3. minutest
4. implacable
5. credulity
6. rapt
7. nettled
8. gullible

a. trust
b. peeved
c. spellbound
d. overtrusting
e. tiniest
f. unquestionable
g. unyielding
h. variously

Explore the Key Idea

Have you ever put on an ACT?

KEY IDEA Occasionally we are tempted to try to fool others into thinking we are smarter, cooler, richer, or more popular than we really are. Sometimes it's as simple as putting on a new pair of sunglasses or pretending to know more about something than we really do. In his autobiography, Mark Twain recalls from his youth a more extreme version of this kind of **deception.**

DISCUSS With your classmates, come up with a list of ways in which people pretend to be something they're not. Examples can range from simple social posing to more outrageous, even criminal, forms of falsified identity. Then review these examples, considering people's motives for such deception.

The Autobiography of Mark Twain

Mark Twain

> **BACKGROUND** This excerpt from Mark Twain's autobiography focuses on a traveling show that visits Twain's small town around 1850. These entertainment shows were popular in a time before radio, television, or computers. They featured magic acts, ventriloquists, and mesmerizers (or hypnotists). Hypnotists placed people in suggestible, trancelike states and then ordered them to perform various antics.

An exciting event in our village was the arrival of the mesmerizer.[1] I think the year was 1850. As to that I am not sure but I know the month—it was May; that detail has survived the wear of fifty years. A pair of connected little incidents of that month have served to keep the memory of it green for me all this time; incidents of no consequence and not worth embalming,[2] yet my memory has preserved them carefully and flung away things of real value to give them space and make them comfortable. The truth is, a person's memory has no more sense than his conscience and no appreciation whatever of values and proportions. However, never mind those trifling incidents; my subject is the mesmerizer now. Ⓐ

10   He advertised his show and promised marvels. Admission as usual: 25 cents, children half price. The village had heard of mesmerism in a general way but had not encountered it yet. Not many people attended the first night but next day they had so many wonders to tell that everybody's curiosity was fired and after

ANALYZE VISUALS
Look at the poster on page 637, especially at the image in the top circle. What can you **infer** about the mesmerizer depicted?

Ⓐ **PREDICT**
Based on the clues presented in this first paragraph, what can you predict about what might happen in the story?

---

1. **mesmerizer:** hypnotist; from the name of an Austrian physician, Franz Anton Mesmer, who popularized hypnotism in the 1770s.
2. **embalming:** preserving.

THE MESMERIZER

that for a fortnight[3] the magician had prosperous times. I was fourteen or fifteen years old, the age at which a boy is willing to endure all things, suffer all things short of death by fire, if thereby he may be conspicuous and show off before the public; and so, when I saw the "subjects" perform their foolish antics on the platform and make the people laugh and shout and admire I had a burning desire to be a subject myself.

20   Every night for three nights I sat in the row of candidates on the platform and held the magic disk[4] in the palm of my hand and gazed at it and tried to get sleepy, but it was a failure; I remained wide awake and had to retire defeated, like the majority. Also, I had to sit there and be gnawed with envy of Hicks, our journeyman;[5] I had to sit there and see him scamper and jump when Simmons the enchanter exclaimed, "See the snake! See the snake!" and hear him say, "My, how beautiful!" in response to the suggestion that he was observing a splendid sunset; and so on—the whole insane business. I couldn't laugh, I couldn't applaud; it filled me with bitterness to have others do it and to have people make a hero of Hicks and crowd around him when the show was over and ask him for more and
30 more particulars of the wonders he had seen in his visions and manifest in many ways that they were proud to be acquainted with him. Hicks—the idea! I couldn't stand it; I was getting boiled to death in my own bile.

    On the fourth night temptation came and I was not strong enough to resist. When I had gazed at the disk a while I pretended to be sleepy and began to nod. Straightway came the professor and made passes over my head and down my body and legs and arms, finishing each pass with a snap of his fingers in the air to discharge the surplus electricity;[6] then he began to "draw" me with the disk, holding it in his fingers and telling me I could not take my eyes off it, try as I might; so I rose slowly, bent and gazing, and followed that disk all over the place,
40 just as I had seen the others do. Then I was put through the other paces. Upon suggestion I fled from snakes, passed buckets at a fire, became excited over hot steamboat-races, made love to imaginary girls and kissed them, fished from the platform and landed mud cats that outweighed me—and so on, all the customary marvels. But not in the customary way. I was cautious at first and watchful, being afraid the professor would discover that I was an impostor and drive me from the platform in disgrace; but as soon as I realized that I was not in danger, I set myself the task of terminating Hicks's usefulness as a subject and of usurping his place. **B**

    It was a sufficiently easy task. Hicks was born honest, I without that incumbrance[7]—so some people said. Hicks saw what he saw and reported
50 accordingly, I saw more than was visible and added to it such details as could help. Hicks had no imagination; I had a double supply. He was born calm, I was

B IRONY
Reread lines 33–47. Identify the **dramatic irony** in this paragraph. What sort of tension does this create?

---

3. **fortnight:** 14 days.

4. **magic disk:** the object used by the mesmerizer to focus a subject's attention, helping him or her to achieve a hypnotic state.

5. **journeyman:** a competent and experienced, but not brilliant, craftsman.

6. **discharge . . . electricity:** It was once erroneously believed that hypnosis was linked to electricity and magnetism.

7. **incumbrance:** earlier spelling of *encumbrance*, here meaning "burden; obligation."

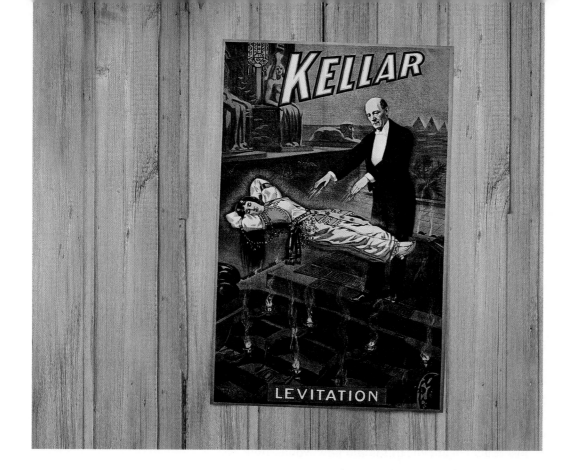

born excited. No vision could start a rapture in him and he was constipated as to language, anyway; but if I saw a vision I emptied the dictionary onto it and lost the remnant of my mind into the bargain.

At the end of my first half-hour Hicks was a thing of the past, a fallen hero, a broken idol, and I knew it and was glad and said in my heart, "Success to crime!" Hicks could never have been mesmerized to the point where he could kiss an imaginary girl in public or a real one either, but I was competent. Whatever Hicks had failed in, I made it a point to succeed in, let the cost be what it might,
60 physically or morally. He had shown several bad defects and I had made a note of them. For instance, if the magician asked, "What do you see?" and left him to invent a vision for himself, Hicks was dumb and blind, he couldn't see a thing nor say a word, whereas the magician soon found out that when it came to seeing visions of a stunning and marketable sort I could get along better without his help than with it.

Then there was another thing: Hicks wasn't worth a tallow dip[8] on mute mental suggestion. Whenever Simmons stood behind him and gazed at the back of his skull and tried to drive a mental suggestion into it, Hicks sat with vacant face and never suspected. If he had been noticing he could have seen by
70 the **rapt** faces of the audience that something was going on behind his back that required a response. Inasmuch as I was an impostor I dreaded to have this test put upon me, for I knew the professor would be "willing" me to do something, and as

rapt (răpt) *adj.* deeply moved, delighted, or absorbed

---

8. **wasn't worth a tallow dip:** wasn't any good. A tallow dip was an inexpensive candle.

I couldn't know what it was, I should be exposed and denounced. However, when my time came, I took my chance. I perceived by the tense and expectant faces of the people that Simmons was behind me willing me with all his might. I tried my best to imagine what he wanted but nothing suggested itself. I felt ashamed and miserable then. I believed that the hour of my disgrace was come and that in another moment I should go out of that place disgraced. I ought to be ashamed to confess it but my next thought was not how I could win the compassion of kindly
80 hearts by going out humbly and in sorrow for my misdoings, but how I could go out most sensationally and spectacularly. **C**

There was a rusty and empty old revolver lying on the table among the "properties" employed in the performances. On May Day two or three weeks before there had been a celebration by the schools and I had had a quarrel with a big boy who was the school bully and I had not come out of it with credit.[9] That boy was now seated in the middle of the house, halfway down the main aisle. I crept stealthily and impressively toward the table, with a dark and murderous scowl on my face, copied from a popular romance, seized the revolver suddenly, flourished it, shouted the bully's name, jumped off the platform and made a
90 rush for him and chased him out of the house before the paralyzed people could interfere to save him. There was a storm of applause, and the magician, addressing the house, said, most impressively—

"That you may know how really remarkable this is and how wonderfully developed a subject we have in this boy, I assure you that without a single spoken word to guide him he has carried out what I mentally commanded him to do, to the **minutest** detail. I could have stopped him at a moment in his vengeful career by a mere exertion of my will, therefore the poor fellow who has escaped was at no time in danger."

So I was not in disgrace. I returned to the platform a hero and happier than
100 I have ever been in this world since. As regards mental suggestion, my fears of it were gone. I judged that in case I failed to guess what the professor might be willing me to do, I could count on putting up something that would answer just as well. I was right, and exhibitions of unspoken suggestion became a favorite with the public. Whenever I perceived that I was being willed to do something I got up and did something—anything that occurred to me—and the magician, not being a fool, always ratified it. When people asked me, "How *can* you tell what he is willing you to do?" I said, "It's just as easy," and they always said admiringly, "Well, it beats *me* how you can do it."

Hicks was weak in another detail. When the professor made passes over him
110 and said "his whole body is without sensation now—come forward and test him, ladies and gentlemen," the ladies and gentlemen always complied eagerly and stuck pins into Hicks, and if they went deep Hicks was sure to wince, then that poor professor would have to explain that Hicks "wasn't sufficiently under the influence." But I didn't wince; I only suffered and shed tears on the inside. The miseries that a conceited boy will endure to keep up his "reputation"! And so

---

9. **credit:** honor or distinction.

minutest (mī-nōō′tĭst) *adj.* smallest; most precise

will a conceited man; I know it in my own person and have seen it in a hundred thousand others. That professor ought to have protected me and I often hoped he would, when the tests were unusually severe, but he didn't. It may be that he was deceived as well as the others, though I did not believe it nor think it possible.

120 Those were dear good people but they must have carried simplicity and **credulity** to the limit. They would stick a pin in my arm and bear on it until they drove it a third of its length in, and then be lost in wonder that by a mere exercise of will power the professor could turn my arm to iron and make it insensible to pain. Whereas it was not insensible at all; I was suffering agonies of pain.

After that fourth night, that proud night, that triumphant night, I was the only subject. Simmons invited no more candidates to the platform. I performed alone every night the rest of the fortnight. Up to that time a dozen wise old heads, the intellectual aristocracy of the town, had held out as **implacable** unbelievers. I was as hurt by this as if I were engaged in some honest occupation. There is

130 nothing surprising about this. Human beings feel dishonor the most, sometimes, when they most deserve it. That handful of overwise old gentlemen kept on shaking their heads all the first week and saying they had seen no marvels there that could not have been produced by collusion; and they were pretty vain of their unbelief too and liked to show it and air it and be superior to the ignorant and the **gullible.** Particularly old Dr. Peake, who was the ringleader of the irreconcilables and very formidable; for he was an F.F.V.,[10] he was learned, white-haired and venerable, nobly and richly clad in the fashions of an earlier and a courtlier day, he was large and stately, and he not only seemed wise but was what he seemed in that regard. He had great influence and his opinion upon any matter was worth much

140 more than that of any other person in the community. When I conquered him at last, I knew I was undisputed master of the field; and now after more than fifty years I acknowledge with a few dry old tears that I rejoiced without shame. **D**

In 1847 we were living in a large white house on the corner of Hill and Main Streets—a house that still stands but isn't large now although it hasn't lost a plank; I saw it a year ago and noticed that shrinkage. My father died in it in March of the year mentioned but our family did not move out of it until some months afterward. Ours was not the only family in the house; there was another, Dr. Grant's. One day Dr. Grant and Dr. Reyburn argued a matter on the street with sword canes and Grant was brought home **multifariously** punctured. Old Dr.

150 Peake caulked the leaks and came every day for a while to look after him.

The Grants were Virginians, like Peake, and one day when Grant was getting well enough to be on his feet and sit around in the parlor and talk, the conversation fell upon Virginia and old times. I was present but the group were probably unconscious of me, I being only a lad and a negligible quantity. Two of

credulity (krĭ-dōō′lĭ-tē) *n.* an inclination to believe too readily

implacable (ĭm-plăk′ə-bəl) *adj.* impossible to satisfy

gullible (gŭl′ə-bəl) *adj.* easily deceived or tricked

D IRONY
Reread lines 125–131. Identify the **situational irony** in Twain's reaction to the skeptical wise old men in the crowd. What does this suggest about him?

multifariously
(mŭl′tə-fâr′ē-əs-lē) *adv.* in many and various ways

---

10. **F.F.V.:** First Family of Virginia. Dr. Peake has high social status because his ancestors were among the first settlers of Virginia.

the group—Dr. Peake and Mrs. Crawford, Mrs. Grant's mother—had been of the audience when the Richmond theater burned down thirty-six years before, and they talked over the frightful details of that memorable tragedy. These were eyewitnesses, and with their eyes I saw it all with an intolerable vividness: I saw the black smoke rolling and tumbling toward the sky, I saw the flames burst
160 through it and turn red, I heard the shrieks of the despairing, I glimpsed their faces at the windows, caught fitfully through the veiling smoke, I saw them jump to their death or to mutilation worse than death. The picture is before me yet and can never fade.

In due course they talked of the colonial mansion of the Peakes, with its stately columns and its spacious grounds, and by odds and ends I picked up a clearly defined idea of the place. I was strongly interested, for I had not before heard of such palatial things from the lips of people who had seen them with their own eyes. One detail, casually dropped, hit my imagination hard. In the wall by the great front door there was a round hole as big as a saucer—a British cannon ball
170 had made it in the war of the Revolution. It was breathtaking; it made history real; history had never been real to me before.

Very well, three or four years later, as already mentioned, I was king bee and sole "subject" in the mesmeric show; it was the beginning of the second week; the performance was half over; just then the majestic Dr. Peake with his ruffled bosom and wrist-bands and his gold-headed cane entered, and a deferential citizen vacated his seat beside the Grants and made the great chief take it. This happened while I was trying to invent something fresh in the way of vision, in response to the professor's remark—

"Concentrate your powers. Look—look attentively. There—don't you see
180 something? Concentrate—concentrate! Now then—describe it." **E**

Without suspecting it, Dr. Peake, by entering the place, had reminded me of the talk of three years before. He had also furnished me capital and was become my confederate, an accomplice in my frauds. I began on a vision, a vague and dim one (that was part of the game at the beginning of a vision; it isn't best to see it too clearly at first, it might look as if you had come loaded with it). The vision developed by degrees and gathered swing, momentum, energy. It was the Richmond fire. Dr. Peake was cold at first and his fine face had a trace of polite scorn in it; but when he began to recognize that fire, that expression changed and his eyes began to light up. As soon as I saw that, I threw the valves wide open and
190 turned on all the steam and gave those people a supper of fire and horrors that was calculated to last them one while! They couldn't gasp when I got through—they were petrified. Dr. Peake had risen and was standing—and breathing hard. He said, in a great voice:

"My doubts are ended. No collusion could produce that miracle. It was totally impossible for him to know those details, yet he has described them with the clarity of an eyewitness —and with what **unassailable** truthfulness God knows I know!" **F**

I saved the colonial mansion for the last night and solidified and perpetuated

E PREDICT
Predict how Twain will win over the wise old men of the town.

unassailable
(ŭn′ə-sā′lə-bəl) *adj.*
impossible to dispute or disprove

F IRONY
What do you know that Dr. Peake doesn't? Explain how this **dramatic irony** affects your impression of the characters involved, including young Twain.

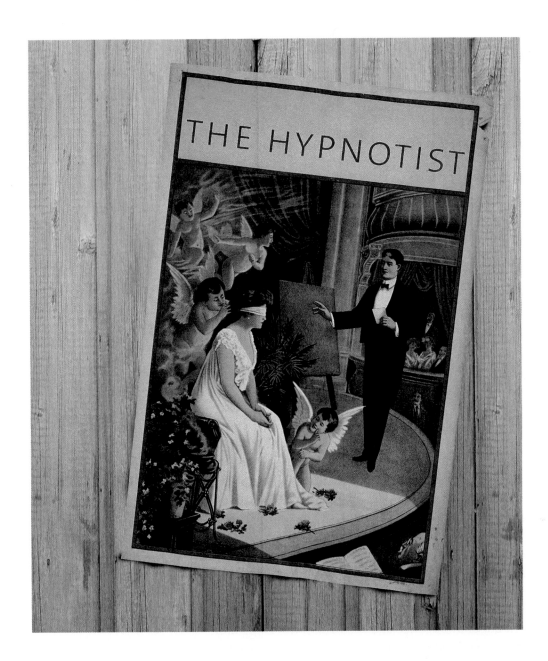

Dr. Peake's conversion with the cannon-ball hole. He explained to the house that
200 I could never have heard of that small detail, which differentiated this mansion
from all other Virginian mansions and perfectly identified it, therefore the fact
stood proven that I had *seen* it in my vision. Lawks![11]

It is curious. When the magician's engagement closed there was but one person
in the village who did not believe in mesmerism and I was the one. All the others
were converted but I was to remain an implacable and unpersuadable disbeliever
in mesmerism and hypnotism for close upon fifty years. This was because I never
would examine them, in after life. I couldn't. The subject revolted me. Perhaps it
brought back to me a passage in my life which for pride's sake I wished to forget;

---

11. **Lawks!:** an expression of wonder or amusement, shortened from "Lord, have mercy!"

though I thought, or persuaded myself I thought, I should never come across a
210 "proof" which wasn't thin and cheap and probably had a fraud like me behind it.

The truth is I did not have to wait long to get tired of my triumphs. Not thirty days, I think. The glory which is built upon a lie soon becomes a most unpleasant incumbrance. No doubt for a while I enjoyed having my exploits told and retold and told again in my presence and wondered over and exclaimed about, but I quite distinctly remember that there presently came a time when the subject was wearisome and odious to me and I could not endure the disgusting discomfort of it. I am well aware that the world-glorified doer of a deed of great and real splendor has just my experience; I know that he deliciously enjoys hearing about it for three or four weeks and that pretty soon after that he begins to dread the
220 mention of it and by and by wishes he had been with the damned before he ever thought of doing that deed. I remember how General Sherman[12] used to rage and swear over "While we were marching through Georgia," which was played at him and sung at him everywhere he went; still, I think I suffered a shade more than the legitimate hero does, he being privileged to soften his misery with the reflection that his glory was at any rate golden and reproachless in its origin, whereas I had no such privilege, there being no possible way to make mine respectable.

How easy it is to make people believe a lie and how hard it is to undo that work again! Thirty-five years after those evil exploits of mine I visited my old mother, whom I had not seen for ten years; and being moved by what seemed
230 to me a rather noble and perhaps heroic impulse, I thought I would humble myself and confess my ancient fault. It cost me a great effort to make up my mind; I dreaded the sorrow that would rise in her face and the shame that would look out of her eyes; but after long and troubled reflection, the sacrifice seemed due and right and I gathered my resolution together and made the confession. **G**

To my astonishment there were no sentimentalities, no dramatics, no George Washington effects; she was not moved in the least degree; she simply did not believe me and said so! I was not merely disappointed, I was **nettled** to have my costly truthfulness flung out of the market in this placid and confident way when I was expecting to get a profit out of it. I asserted and reasserted, with rising heat,
240 my statement that every single thing I had done on those long-vanished nights was a lie and a swindle; and when she shook her head tranquilly and said she knew better, I put up my hand and *swore* to it—adding a triumphant, "*Now* what do you say?"

It did not affect her at all; it did not budge her the fraction of an inch from her position. If this was hard for me to endure, it did not begin with the blister she put upon the raw[13] when she began to put my sworn oath out of court with *arguments* to prove that I was under a delusion and did not know what I was talking about. Arguments! Arguments to show that a person on a man's outside can know better what is on his inside than he does himself. I had cherished some

G PREDICT
Reread lines 227–234. How do you think Twain's mother will respond to his confession? Explain why you think this.

nettled (nĕt′əld) *adj.* irritated; annoyed **nettle** *v.*

12. **General Sherman:** William Tecumseh Sherman, Union commander who led a destructive march in 1864 from Atlanta, Georgia, to the Atlantic, cutting the Confederacy in two.

13. **the blister . . . raw:** a bad thing made even worse.

250 contempt for arguments before, I have not enlarged my respect for them since. She refused to believe that I had invented my visions myself; she said it was folly: that I was only a child at the time and could not have done it. She cited the Richmond fire and the colonial mansion and said they were quite beyond my capacities. Then I saw my chance! I said she was right—I didn't invent those, I got them from Dr. Peake. Even this great shot did not damage. She said Dr. Peake's evidence was better than mine, and he had said in plain words that it was impossible for me to have heard about those things. Dear, dear, what a grotesque and unthinkable situation: a confessed swindler convicted of honesty and condemned to acquittal by circumstantial evidence furnished by the swindled! **H**

260 I realized with shame and with impotent vexation that I was defeated all along the line. I had but one card left but it was a formidable one. I played it and stood from under. It seemed ignoble to demolish her fortress after she had defended it so valiantly but the defeated know not mercy. I played that master card. It was the pin-sticking. I said solemnly—

"I give you my honor, a pin was never stuck into me without causing me cruel pain."

She only said—

"It is thirty-five years. I believe you do think that now but I was there and I know better. You never winced."

270 She was so calm! and I was so far from it, so nearly frantic.

"Oh, my goodness!" I said, "let me *show* you that I am speaking the truth. Here is my arm; drive a pin into it—drive it to the head—I shall not wince."

She only shook her gray head and said with simplicity and conviction—

"You are a man now and could dissemble the hurt; but you were only a child then and could not have done it."

And so the lie which I played upon her in my youth remained with her as an unchallengeable truth to the day of her death. Carlyle[14] said "a lie cannot live." It shows that he did not know how to tell them. If I had taken out a life policy on this one the premiums would have bankrupted me ages ago. ❧

H IRONY
Reread lines 244–259. Identify the **situational irony** that underlies Twain's confession to his mother. What statement is Twain making about honesty and deception?

---

14. **Carlyle:** Thomas Carlyle, a British historian and essayist.

A popular writer and a sought-after public speaker, Mark Twain was full of witty remarks. What do these **epigrams**—short, clever, and sometimes paradoxical statements—reveal about Twain's view of human nature?

Epigrams
Mark Twain

Don't, like the cat, try to get more out of an experience than there is in it. The cat, having sat upon a hot stove lid, will not sit upon a hot stove lid again. Nor upon a cold stove lid.

· · · · · · · · ·

It is by the goodness of God that in our country we have those three unspeakably precious things: freedom of speech, freedom of conscience, and the prudence never to practice either of them.

· · · · · · · · ·

Man is the only animal that blushes. Or needs to.

· · · · · · · · ·

I am an old man and have known a great many troubles, but most of them have never happened.

· · · · · · · · ·

Nothing so needs reforming as other people's habits.

· · · · · · · · ·

When I was a boy of fourteen, my father was so ignorant I could hardly stand to have the old man around. But when I got to be twenty-one, I was astonished at how much the old man had learned in seven years.

· · · · · · · · ·

Put all your eggs in one basket, and—watch the basket.

There are several good protections against temptations, but the surest is cowardice.

· · · · · · · · ·

If you pick up a starving dog and make him prosperous, he will not bite you. This is the principal difference between a dog and a man.

· · · · · · · · ·

Good breeding consists in concealing how much we think of ourselves and how little we think of the other person.

· · · · · · · · ·

To promise not to do a thing is the surest way in the world to make a body want to go and do that very thing.

· · · · · · · · ·

Habit is habit, and not to be flung out of the window by any man, but coaxed downstairs a step at a time.

· · · · · · · · ·

One of the most striking differences between a cat and a lie is that a cat only has nine lives.

· · · · · · · · ·

Each person is born to one possession which outvalues all the others—his last breath.

· · · · · · · · ·

Everyone is a moon, and has a dark side which he never shows to anybody.

Comprehension

1. **Recall** What position or role does young Twain want to have? Why?

2. **Summarize** What weaknesses made Hicks a bad subject?

3. **Clarify** What does Twain do to get the mesmerizer to choose him?

Literary Analysis

4. **Examine Predictions** Review your list of predictions and clues. Were you able to correctly predict everything that happened? Or were you surprised by how some aspects of the story developed? Cite details from the story in your answer.

5. **Contrast Characters** To become the mesmerizer's subject, Twain must displace Hicks. Twain presents himself as very different from Hicks. Based on this contrast, what does Twain seem to value and admire in a person? Use a chart like the one shown to collect evidence.

Hicks	Twain

6. **Analyze Irony** By its very nature, irony presents a degree of tension wherever it appears—the tension between expectations and reality. In many cases, it also adds humor. Review Twain's use of irony in the following passages. What's funny about them?

   - "Hicks was born honest, I without that incumbrance [burden]—so some people said." (lines 48–49)
   - Young Twain is genuinely hurt by those who do not believe his performances. (lines 127–129)
   - Twain identifies with great heroes who tire of hearing their praises sung. (lines 213–223)

7. **Draw Conclusions About Changing Perspective** In writing this piece, the adult Twain had a different view of himself, his boyhood **deception**, and the people of his hometown than he had as a young boy. What does this dual perspective show you about his growth from boyhood to adulthood?

Literary Criticism

8. **Author's Perspective** Reread Twain's epigrams on page 646. What view of human nature do you find in these sayings? Explain how this view is played out in this episode of the *Autobiography*, giving evidence from both texts to support your answer.

Vocabulary in Context

WORD LIST

credulity

gullible

implacable

minutest

multifariously

nettled

rapt

unassailable

VOCABULARY PRACTICE

Decide whether these statements about the vocabulary words are true or false.

1. Someone with many career changes can be said to have worked **multifariously.**

2. Believing everything a fortuneteller tells you is an example of **credulity.**

3. A person who pays **rapt** attention to a performance is probably bored with it.

4. You might feel **nettled** if it rains on your picnic.

5. If you are **gullible,** you have an enormous appetite for sweet foods.

6. A defendant with an **unassailable** alibi should feel confident testifying in court.

7. If you record the **minutest** facts about an event, you are noting how long it took.

8. A person with **implacable** demands is not likely to be easily satisfied.

VOCABULARY IN WRITING

Would people today be taken in by Twain's performance? Use two or more vocabulary words in a paragraph telling your opinion. You could start this way.

> **EXAMPLE SENTENCE**
>
> *I think the average person is as **gullible** as ever.*

VOCABULARY STRATEGY: WORDS PRONOUNCED DIFFERENTLY

Some words are spelled the same but have different meanings and may have different pronunciations. An example is *minute* (mī-nōōt′), meaning "small," and *minute* (mĭn′ĭt), meaning "60 seconds." When these words also have different etymologies, they are called homographs, from the Latin root *graph* ("written") and prefix *homo-* ("the same"). Most dictionaries give homographs separate entries and mark them with superscripts: minute¹, minute².

Other words have multiple pronunciations depending on their part of speech. *Progress*, for example, is pronounced (prŏg′rĕs′) when used as a noun and (prə-grĕs′) when used as a verb.

PRACTICE Write the letter of the correct pronunciation for each boldfaced word; then define the word. Write *H* after the definition of any homograph.

1. take the household **refuse** to the dump   **a.** (rĭ-fyōōz′)   **b.** (rĕf′yōōs)

2. the band has a new upright **bass** player   **a.** (băs)   **b.** (bās)

3. crushed stone used in an **aggregate**   **a.** (ăg′rĭ-gĭt)   **b.** (ăg′rĭ-gāt′)

4. allowed the wind to **buffet** the boat   **a.** (bə-fā′)   **b.** (bŭf′ĭt)

5. proposed a theoretical **construct**   **a.** (kən-strŭkt′)   **b.** (kŏn′strŭkt′)

VOCABULARY PRACTICE
For more practice, go to the **Vocabulary Center** at ClassZone.com.

from **Life on the Mississippi**

Memoir by
Mark Twain

● LITERARY ANALYSIS: VOICE

Voice is a writer's unique use of language. It allows a reader to "hear" the writer's personality in his or her writing. Mark Twain's distinctive voice is full of dry wit.

Here was something fresh—this thing of getting up in the middle of the night. . . . It was a detail . . . that had never occurred to me at all. I knew that boats ran all night, but somehow I had never happened to reflect that somebody had to get up out of a warm bed to run them.

A writer's voice is established through **diction,** or word choice and order, and **tone,** or attitude toward the subject. As you read, look for Twain's ironic or humorous tone.

● READING STRATEGY: PARAPHRASE

Twain's readers enjoy his deadpan humor and insights. However, it can take some digging through difficult sentences to figure out just what he's saying. **Paraphrasing** can help; if you can slow down and restate hard sentences in simpler language, you'll find it easier to follow him. And by recognizing his use of **understatement** (downplaying the importance of things) or his use of **hyperbole** (exaggeration) and other figures of speech, you can paraphrase better.

Within ten seconds more I was set aside in disgrace, and Mr. Bixby was . . . flaying me alive with abuse of my cowardice.

With a dictionary, you can paraphrase this sentence.

1. **Paraphrase it literally:** "I was promptly disgraced, and Mr. Bixby was skinning me alive and calling me a coward."

2. **Notice where Twain is stretching the truth:** Bixby is not really skinning him alive, but abusing him verbally.

Your final paraphrase can read, "Soon I had gotten into trouble and Mr. Bixby was shouting at me, calling me a coward." Record your paraphrases in a chart like the one shown.

Difficult Passage	Literal Paraphrase	Final Paraphrase (when appropriate)

Explore the Key Idea

Is **IGNORANCE** *really bliss?*

KEY IDEA People who don't pay attention to the news or world affairs are sometimes described as burying their heads in the sand. This is not a compliment. However, it's also acknowledged that these people are sometimes happier or less worried than those who **experience** more. Mark Twain discovers that his experiences on the Mississippi River come at a price.

PRESENT Consider people you know who seek varied experiences and others who prefer to remain sheltered. Then list the advantages and disadvantages of each approach. Decide which approach makes the most sense to you, and identify two reasons for your choice. Share your conclusions with the class.

Life on the Mississippi

Mark Twain

BACKGROUND In this excerpt from his memoir, Mark Twain describes his first days as an apprentice riverboat pilot. Piloting a paddle steamboat was dangerous and tricky, because the Mississippi was constantly changing. The powerful current moved from one side to the other, especially in the windy parts of the river. Along this twisting course lurked hidden sandbars and submerged wrecks. Riverboat pilots gathered—and exchanged—precious information about the river's changing current.

A Cub-Pilot's Experience

What with lying on the rocks four days at Louisville, and some other delays, the poor old *Paul Jones* fooled away about two weeks in making the voyage from Cincinnati to New Orleans. This gave me a chance to get acquainted with one of the pilots, and he taught me how to steer the boat, and thus made the fascination of river life more potent than ever for me. . . .

I soon discovered two things. One was that a vessel would not be likely to sail for the mouth of the Amazon under ten or twelve years; and the other was that the nine or ten dollars still left in my pocket would not suffice for so impossible an exploration[1] as I had planned, even if I could afford to wait for a ship. Therefore
10 it followed that I must contrive a new career. The *Paul Jones* was now bound for

---

1. **mouth of the Amazon . . . exploration:** Twain, having read that an American expedition had been unable to finish its exploration of the Amazon River, went to New Orleans with the idea that he would be able to travel to South America and complete the job.

ANALYZE VISUALS
What does this illustrated map tell you about the size of the Mississippi River compared with the town on its banks? What other impressions of the river do you glean?

St. Louis. I planned a siege against my pilot, and at the end of three hard days he surrendered. He agreed to teach me the Mississippi River from New Orleans to St. Louis for five hundred dollars, payable out of the first wages I should receive after graduating. I entered upon the small enterprise of "learning" twelve or thirteen hundred miles of the great Mississippi River with the easy confidence of my time of life. If I had really known what I was about to require of my faculties, I should not have had the courage to begin. I supposed that all a pilot had to do was to keep his boat in the river, and I did not consider that that could be much of a trick, since it was so wide. **Ⓐ**

20   The boat backed out from New Orleans at four in the afternoon, and it was "our watch" until eight. Mr. Bixby, my chief, "straightened her up," plowed her along past the sterns of the other boats that lay at the Levee,[2] and then said, "Here, take her; shave those steamships as close as you'd peel an apple." I took the wheel, and my heartbeat fluttered up into the hundreds; for it seemed to me that we were about to scrape the side off every ship in the line, we were so close. I held my breath and began to claw the boat away from the danger; and I had my own opinion of the pilot who had known no better than to get us into such peril, but I was too wise to express it. In half a minute I had a wide margin of safety intervening between the *Paul Jones* and the ships; and within ten seconds more I
30 was set aside in disgrace, and Mr. Bixby was going into danger again and flaying me alive with abuse of my cowardice. I was stung, but I was obliged to admire the easy confidence with which my chief loafed from side to side of his wheel, and trimmed the ships so closely that disaster seemed ceaselessly imminent. When he had cooled a little he told me that the easy water was close ashore and the current outside, and therefore we must hug the bank, upstream, to get the benefit of the former, and stay well out, downstream, to take advantage of the latter. In my own mind I resolved to be a downstream pilot and leave the upstreaming to people dead to prudence.[3] **Ⓑ**

        Now and then Mr. Bixby called my attention to certain things. Said he, "This
40 is Six-Mile Point." I assented. It was pleasant enough information, but I could not see the bearing of it. I was not conscious that it was a matter of any interest to me. Another time he said, "This is Nine-Mile Point." Later he said, "This is Twelve-Mile Point." They were all about level with the water's edge; they all looked about alike to me; they were monotonously unpicturesque. I hoped Mr. Bixby would change the subject. But no; he would crowd up around a point, hugging the shore with affection, and then say: "The slack water ends here, abreast this bunch of China trees; now we cross over." So he crossed over. He gave me the wheel once or twice, but I had no luck. I either came near chipping off the edge of a sugar plantation, or I yawed[4] too far from shore, and so dropped back into disgrace
50 again and got abused.

        The watch was ended at last, and we took supper and went to bed. At midnight the glare of a lantern shone in my eyes, and the night watchman said, "Come!"

Ⓐ **VOICE**
Reread lines 6–19. What does Twain's **tone** suggest about his youthful confidence?

Ⓑ **PARAPHRASE**
Reread and paraphrase lines 33–38. What does Twain learn about the upstream and downstream currents? What decision does he make about the future?

2. **Levee** (lĕv′ē): a landing place for boats on a river.

3. **dead to prudence:** lacking good judgment.

4. **yawed:** swerved.

Turn out!" And then he left. I could not understand this extraordinary procedure; so I presently gave up trying to, and dozed off to sleep. Pretty soon the watchman was back again, and this time he was gruff. I was annoyed. I said,

"What do you want to come bothering around here in the middle of the night for? Now, as like as not, I'll not get to sleep again to-night."

The watchman said, "Well, if this ain't good, I'm blessed."

The "offwatch"[5] was just turning in, and I heard some brutal laughter from them, and such remarks as "Hello, watchman! ain't the new cub turned out yet? He's delicate, likely. Give him some sugar in a rag, and send for the chambermaid to sing 'Rock-a-by Baby' to him." **C**

About this time Mr. Bixby appeared on the scene. Something like a minute later I was climbing the pilothouse steps with some of my clothes on and the rest in my arms. Mr. Bixby was close behind, commenting. Here was something fresh—this thing of getting up in the middle of the night to go to work. It was a detail in piloting that had never occurred to me at all. I knew that boats ran all night, but somehow I had never happened to reflect that somebody had to get up out of a warm bed to run them. I began to fear that piloting was not quite so romantic as I had imagined it was; there was something very real and worklike about this new phase of it. . . .

M r. Bixby made for the shore and soon was scraping it, just the same as if it had been daylight. And not only that, but singing:

Father in heaven, the day is declining, etc.

It seemed to me that I had put my life in the keeping of a peculiarly reckless outcast. Presently he turned on me and said, "What's the name of the first point above New Orleans?"

I was gratified to be able to answer promptly, and I did. I said I didn't know.

"Don't *know?*"

This manner jolted me. I was down at the foot[6] again, in a moment. But I had to say just what I had said before.

"Well, you're a smart one!" said Mr. Bixby. "What's the name of the *next* point?" Once more I didn't know.

"Well, this beats anything. Tell me the name of *any* point or place I told you."

I studied awhile and decided that I couldn't.

"Look here! What do you start out from, above Twelve-Mile Point, to cross over?"

"I—I—don't know."

"You—you—don't know?" mimicking my drawling manner of speech. "What *do* you know?"

"I—I—nothing, for certain."

"By the great Caesar's ghost, I believe you! You're the stupidest dunderhead I ever saw or ever heard of, so help me Moses! The idea of *you* being a pilot—*you!* Why, you don't know enough to pilot a cow down a lane."

C PARAPHRASE
Twain's frequent use of **dialogue** and **dialect,** or regional speech, is one of the challenging qualities about his writing. Paraphrase the dialogue in lines 51–61. What are the other crew members saying about him?

---

5. **"offwatch"**: those sailors who had just completed their watch.

6. **down at the foot**: at the bottom of the class.

Oh, but his wrath was up! He was a nervous man, and he shuffled from one side of his wheel to the other as if the floor was hot. He would boil awhile to himself, and then overflow and scald me again.

"Look here! What do you suppose I told you the names of those points for?"

I tremblingly considered a moment, and then the devil of temptation provoked me to say, "Well to—to—be entertaining, I thought."

100 This was a red rag to the bull.[7] He raged and stormed so (he was crossing the river at the time) that I judged it made him blind, because he ran over the steering oar of a trading scow.[8] Of course the traders sent up a volley of red-hot profanity. Never was a man so grateful as Mr. Bixby was, because he was brimful, and here were subjects who could *talk back.* He threw open a window, thrust his head out, and such an irruption followed as I never had heard before. The fainter and farther away the scowmen's curses drifted, the higher Mr. Bixby lifted his voice and the weightier his adjectives grew. When he closed the window he was empty. You could have drawn a seine[9] through his system and not caught curses enough to disturb your mother with. Presently he said to me in the gentlest way, "My boy,
110 you must get a little memorandum book; and every time I tell you a thing, put it down right away. There's only one way to be a pilot, and that is to get this entire river by heart. You have to know it just like A B C." **D**

That was a dismal revelation to me, for my memory was never loaded with anything but blank cartridges. However, I did not feel discouraged long. I judged that it was best to make some allowances, for doubtless Mr. Bixby was "stretching." . . .[10]

By the time we had gone seven or eight hundred miles up the river, I had learned to be a tolerably plucky upstream steersman, in daylight; and before we reached St. Louis I had made a trifle of progress in night work, but only a trifle.
120 I had a notebook that fairly bristled with the names of towns, "points," bars, islands, bends, reaches, etc.; but the information was to be found only in the notebook—none of it was in my head. It made my heart ache to think I had only got half of the river set down; for as our watch was four hours off and four hours on, day and night, there was a long four-hour gap in my book for every time I had slept since the voyage began. . . . **E**

The face of the water, in time, became a wonderful book—a book that was a dead language to the uneducated passenger, but which told its mind to me without reserve, delivering its most cherished secrets as clearly as if it uttered them with a voice. And it was not a book to be read once and thrown aside, for
130 it had a new story to tell every day. Throughout the long twelve hundred miles there was never a page that was void of interest, never one that you could leave unread without loss, never one that you would want to skip, thinking you could find higher enjoyment in some other thing. There never was so wonderful a book

---

7. **a red rag to the bull:** Bullfighters wave capes to both provoke and distract the bull.

8. **scow:** a flat-bottomed boat used chiefly to transport freight.

9. **seine** (sān): large fishing net.

10. **"stretching":** exaggerating.

D VOICE
Reread this paragraph, focusing on lines 104–112. Notice the elaborate **diction** Twain uses to describe Mr. Bixby's behavior, especially as Mr. Bixby finally quiets down. How does this choice of language affect the pacing and humor of this paragraph?

E VOICE
Reread lines 117–125. What **tone** does Twain take here in describing his own progress? Give details from the text to support your answer.

written by man; never one whose interest was so absorbing, so unflagging, so sparklingly renewed with every reperusal.[11] The passenger who could not read it was charmed with a peculiar sort of faint dimple on its surface (on the rare occasions when he did not overlook it altogether); but to the pilot that was an *italicized* passage; indeed, it was more than that, it was a legend of the largest capitals,[12] with a string of shouting exclamation points at the end of it, for it
140 meant that a wreck or a rock was buried there that could tear the life out of the strongest vessel that ever floated. It is the faintest and simplest expression the water ever makes, and the most hideous to a pilot's eye. In truth, the passenger who could not read this book saw nothing but all manner of pretty pictures in it,

---

11. **reperusal** (rē'pə-rōo'zal): rereading.

12. **a legend of the largest capitals:** an inscription in large capital letters.

painted by the sun and shaded by the clouds, whereas to the trained eye these were not pictures at all, but the grimmest and most dead earnest of reading matter.

Now when I had mastered the language of this water, and had come to know every trifling feature that bordered the great river as familiarly as I knew the letters of the alphabet, I had made a valuable acquisition. But I had lost something, too. I had lost something which could never be restored to me while I lived. All the
150 grace, the beauty, the poetry, had gone out of the majestic river! I still keep in mind a certain wonderful sunset which I witnessed when steamboating was new to me. A broad expanse of the river was turned to blood; in the middle distance the red hue brightened into gold, through which a solitary log came floating, black and conspicuous; in one place a long, slanting mark lay sparkling upon the water; in another the surface was broken by boiling, tumbling rings, that were as many-tinted as an opal; where the ruddy flush was faintest, was a smooth spot that was covered with graceful circles and radiating lines, ever so delicately traced; the shore on our left was densely wooded, and the somber shadow that fell from this forest was broken in one place by a long, ruffled trail that shone like silver; and high
160 above the forest wall a clean-stemmed dead tree waved a single leafy bough that glowed like a flame in the unobstructed splendor that was flowing from the sun. There were graceful curves, reflected images, woody heights, soft distances; and over the whole scene, far and near, the dissolving lights drifted steadily, enriching it every passing moment with new marvels of coloring. **F**

F VOICE
Consider Twain's **tone** and **diction** earlier in the selection, as he was first learning his way around the ship. Then reread lines 126–164. How does Twain's voice change as he explains his increased knowledge of the river? Give details.

Champions of the Mississippi, Currier and Ives. Lithograph. Museum of the City of New York, New York. © Scala/Art Resource, New York.

I stood like one bewitched. I drank it in, in a speechless rapture. The world was new to me, and I had never seen anything like this at home. But as I have said, a day came when I began to cease from noting the glories and the charms which the moon and the sun and the twilight wrought upon the river's face; another day came when I ceased altogether to note them. Then, if that sunset scene had been repeated, I should have looked upon it without rapture, and should have commented upon it, inwardly, after this fashion: "This sun means that we are going to have wind tomorrow; that floating log means that the river is rising, small thanks to it; that slanting mark on the water refers to a bluff reef[13] which is going to kill somebody's steamboat one of these nights, if it keeps on stretching out like that; those tumbling 'boils' show a dissolving bar and a changing channel there; the lines and circles in the slick water over yonder are a warning that that troublesome place is shoaling up[14] dangerously; that silver streak in the shadow of the forest is the 'break' from a new snag, and he has located himself in the very best place he could have found to fish for steamboats; that tall dead tree, with a single living branch, is not going to last long, and then how is a body ever going to get through this blind place at night without the friendly old landmark?"

No, the romance and beauty were all gone from the river. All the value any feature of it had for me now was the amount of usefulness it could furnish toward compassing the safe piloting of a steamboat. Since those days, I have pitied doctors from my heart. What does the lovely flush in a beauty's cheek mean to a doctor but a "break" that ripples above some deadly disease? Are not all her visible charms sown thick with what are to him the signs and symbols of hidden decay? Does he ever see her beauty at all, or doesn't he simply view her professionally, and comment upon her unwholesome condition all to himself? And doesn't he sometimes wonder whether he has gained most or lost most by learning his trade? ✺ **G**

G **PARAPHRASE**
Reread lines 184–190 and paraphrase the comments about what a doctor sees. What parallel is Twain drawing between the doctor's plight and his own?

---

13. **bluff reef:** an underwater ridge of rock.

14. **shoaling up:** becoming too shallow for safe navigation because of a buildup of sand or silt in the riverbed.

Comprehension

1. **Recall** What new job does Mark Twain begin?

2. **Recall** How does Twain react to Mr. Bixby's initial instruction?

3. **Summarize** As Twain's training continues, what does he learn?

Literary Analysis

4. **Examine Paraphrases** Review the paraphrases you recorded as you read. In the end, what were the most difficult aspects of Twain's writing? Explain.

5. **Analyze Humor** In any piece of humorous writing, the humor usually springs from a general underlying attitude toward the subject. Review the following humorous passages from the selection and in each case identify the attitude expressed. What do the passages have in common?

   • Twain tries to steer the boat for the first time (lines 23–38)
   • Twain fails to show up for his first night watch (lines 51–71)
   • Twain learns that he has to learn the entire river by heart (lines 75–112)

6. **Analyze Voice** Twain's voice undergoes a distinct change at line 126. Describe his voice both up to and after this point in terms of its **diction** and **tone.** What change in attitude is reflected by this change in voice?

7. **Draw Conclusions** In this selection, Twain develops an **extended metaphor** comparing the river with a book. In a chart like this one, identify the points of this comparison. Through this metaphor, what is he saying about the river and his **experience** as a student pilot?

Line Numbers	Passage	What It Says About the River
126–127	"The face of the water … became a wonderful book—a book that was a dead language to the uneducated passenger"	It's "wonderful" but cannot be understood by the uneducated.

8. **Compare Literary Works** How does the humorous attitude you described in answer to question 5 compare with that expressed in Twain's *Autobiography?* Which piece do you think is funnier? Cite details to support your answer.

Literary Criticism

9. **Author's Style** *Life on the Mississippi* first appeared serially in the *Atlantic Monthly* magazine in 1875. In 1874, Twain wrote the magazine's editor that he liked writing for the audience of the *Atlantic* "for the simple reason that it don't require a 'humorist' to paint himself stripèd and stand on his head every fifteen minutes." In other words, he liked an audience that appreciated subtle humor. Do you find this sensibility reflected in the selection you have just read? Explain.

The Notorious Jumping Frog of Calaveras County

Short Story
by Mark Twain

● LITERARY ANALYSIS: TALL TALE

The **tall tale** is a distinctively American form of storytelling featuring outlandish characters and events, often with a comic effect. Based on oral tradition, the tall tale generally aims to fool or impress the listener or reader, using various devices. Look for these techniques and consider their impact:

- **Hyperbole**—a figure of speech exaggerating the truth
- **Understatement**—the technique of downplaying the significance of the outlandish, often to ironic or humorous effect
- **Local color**—writing that brings a region alive by portraying its dress, mannerisms, customs, character types, and speech

● READING SKILL: UNDERSTAND DIALECT

Dialect is the distinct form of a language spoken in one geographic area or by a particular group. Writers use dialect to establish setting, provide local color, and develop characters. In this story, Twain uses a frontier dialect. Because of its unfamiliar idioms and strange spellings, dialect can be hard to read. These strategies will help:

- **Read slowly**—Try reading aloud to help you recognize words you may have heard but don't normally see in print.
- **Use context clues**—When Twain writes, "You'd see that frog whirling in the air like a doughnut—see him turn one summerset," context tells you that *summerset* must mean the same as *somersault*.

As you read, jot down unfamiliar words and what you think they mean.

▲ VOCABULARY IN CONTEXT

Which of the following words do you know? Write definitions for the words and then check the definitions as you read.

WORD LIST		
cavorting	enterprising	infamous
conjecture	garrulous	tranquil
dilapidated	indifferent	

Explore the Key Idea

Can you spot a TALL TALE?

KEY IDEA You listen to a friend recount the events of the weekend and you're pretty sure the story is way too wild to be true. You hear a politician describe great accomplishments and you just know it's a stretch. These situations inspire the **skepticism** you need to read about a frog that turns somersaults.

DISCUSS Work with a small group to play the game "Two Truths and a Lie." Take a few minutes for each of you to come up with two truths and one lie. The statements can be about anything from personal experience to oddball facts. Take turns sharing statements. Can you guess which are the lies and which are the truths? Compare your answers and explain what made you believe or disbelieve each statement.

The Notorious JUMPING FROG of Calaveras County

Mark Twain

BACKGROUND Twain got the idea for this story during his days panning for gold in California. Local storytellers told this tale without cracking a smile, teaching Twain two important lessons about humor: one, that the manner in which a person tells a story is what makes it funny, and two, that a humorist should always pretend to be dead serious.

ANALYZE VISUALS
What techniques in this illustration can be compared with the storytelling techniques of a tall tale? Explain.

In compliance with the request of a friend of mine who wrote me from the East, I called on good-natured, <u>garrulous</u> old Simon Wheeler and inquired after my friend's friend, Leonidas W. Smiley, as requested to do, and I hereunto append[1] the result. I have a lurking suspicion that *Leonidas W.* Smiley is a myth, that my friend never knew such a personage, and that he only <u>conjectured</u> that if I asked old Wheeler about him, it would remind him of his <u>infamous</u> *Jim* Smiley and he would go to work and bore me to death with some exasperating reminiscence of him as long and as tedious as it should be useless to me. If that was the design, it succeeded.

garrulous (găr′ə-ləs) *adj.* extremely talkative

conjecture (kən-jĕk′chər) *v.* to guess

infamous (ĭn′fə-məs) *adj.* having a very bad reputation; disgraceful

---

1. **hereunto append:** add to this document.

W.J.WELCH.83

10   I found Simon Wheeler dozing comfortably by the barroom stove of the **dilapidated** tavern in the decayed mining camp of Angel's, and I noticed that he was fat and baldheaded and had an expression of winning gentleness and simplicity upon his **tranquil** countenance. He roused up and gave me good day. I told him that a friend of mine had commissioned me to make some inquiries about a cherished companion of his boyhood named *Leonidas W.* Smiley—*Rev. Leonidas W.* Smiley, a young minister of the Gospel, who he had heard was at one time a resident of Angel's Camp. I added that if Mr. Wheeler could tell me anything about this Rev. Leonidas W. Smiley, I would feel under many obligations to him.

    Simon Wheeler backed me into a corner and blockaded me there with his chair,
20 and then sat down and reeled off the monotonous narrative which follows this paragraph. He never smiled, he never frowned, he never changed his voice from the gentle-flowing key to which he tuned his initial sentence, he never betrayed the slightest suspicion of enthusiasm, but all through the interminable narrative there ran a vein of impressive earnestness and sincerity which showed me plainly that, so far from his imagining that there was anything ridiculous or funny about his story, he regarded it as a really important matter and admired its two heroes as men of transcendent genius in *finesse.*[2] I let him go on in his own way and never interrupted him once. **Ⓐ**

    "Rev. Leonidas W. H'm, Reverend Le—Well, there was a feller here once by
30 the name of *Jim* Smiley, in the winter of '49—or maybe it was the spring of '50—I don't recollect exactly, somehow, though what makes me think it was one or the other is because I remember the big flume[3] warn't finished when he first come to the camp; but anyway, he was the curiousest man about always betting on anything that turned up you ever see, if he could get anybody to bet on the other side, and if he couldn't he'd change sides. Any way that suited the other man would suit *him*—any way just so's he got a bet, *he* was satisfied. But still he was lucky, uncommon lucky; he most always come out winner. He was always ready and laying for a chance; there couldn't be no solit'ry thing mentioned but that feller'd offer to bet on it and take ary side you please, as I was just telling you. If
40 there was a horse race, you'd find him flush or you'd find him busted at the end of it; if there was a dogfight, he'd bet on it; if there was a cat fight, he'd bet on it; if there was a chicken fight, he'd bet on it; why, if there was two birds setting on a fence, he would bet you which one would fly first; or if there was a camp meeting, he would be there reg'lar to bet on Parson Walker, which he judged to be the best exhorter about here, and so he was too, and a good man. If he even see a straddlebug[4] start to go anywheres, he would bet you how long it would take him to get to—to wherever he was going to, and if you took him up, he would foller that straddlebug to Mexico but what he would find out where he was bound for and how long he was on the road. Lots of the boys here has seen that Smiley and
50 can tell you about him. Why, it never made no difference to *him*—he'd bet on

---

2. **men of . . . finesse:** exceptionally brilliant men.

3. **flume:** a wooden trough built as a channel for running water—used in gold mining for separating particles of gold.

4. **straddlebug:** a long-legged beetle.

dilapidated
(dĭ-lăp'ĭ-dā'tĭd) *adj.*
in a state of disrepair;
rundown **dilapidate** *v.*

tranquil (trăng'kwəl) *adj.*
undisturbed; peaceful

Ⓐ **TALL TALE**
Reread lines 19–28, and describe Simon Wheeler's manner of storytelling. What does the narrator suggest about the relationship between Wheeler's manner and the substance of his story?

any thing—the dangdest feller. Parson Walker's wife laid very sick once for a good while, and it seemed as if they warn't going to save her; but one morning he come in and Smiley up and asked him how she was, and he said she was considerable better—thank the Lord for his inf'nite mercy—and coming on so smart that with the blessing of Prov'dence she'd get well yet; and Smiley, before he thought, says, 'Well, I'll resk two-and-a-half she don't anyway.' **B**

"Thish-yer Smiley had a mare—the boys called her the fifteen-minute nag but that was only in fun, you know, because of course she was faster than that—and he used to win money on that horse, for all she was so slow and always had the asthma, or the distemper, or the consumption,[5] or something of that kind. They used to give her two or three hundred yards' start and then pass her under way, but always at the fag end[6] of the race she'd get excited and desperatelike, and come **cavorting** and straddling up and scattering her legs around limber, sometimes in the air and sometimes out to one side among the fences, and kicking up m-o-r-e dust and raising m-o-r-e racket with her coughing and sneezing and blowing her nose—and always fetch up at the stand just about a neck ahead, as near as you could cipher it down.[7]

"And he had a little small bull-pup, that to look at him you'd think he warn't worth a cent but to set around and look ornery and lay for a chance to steal something. But as soon as money was up on him he was a different dog; his underjaw'd begin to stick out like the fo'castle[8] of a steamboat and his teeth would uncover and shine like the furnaces. And a dog might tackle him and bullyrag[9] him, and bite him and throw him over his shoulder two or three times, and Andrew Jackson—which was the name of the pup—Andrew Jackson would never let on but what *he* was satisfied and hadn't expected nothing else—and the bets being doubled and doubled on the other side all the time, till the money was all up; and then all of a sudden he would grab that other dog jest by the j'int of his hind leg and freeze to it—not chaw, you understand, but only just grip and hang on till they throwed up the sponge,[10] if it was a year. Smiley always come out winner on that pup till he harnessed a dog once that didn't have no hind legs, because they'd been sawed off in a circular saw, and when the thing had gone along far enough and the money was all up and he come to make a snatch for his pet holt,[11] he see in a minute how he'd been imposed on and how the other dog had him in the door, so to speak, and he 'peared surprised, and then he looked sorter discouragedlike and didn't try no more to win the fight, and so he got shucked out bad. He give Smiley a look, as much as to say his heart was broke, and it was *his* fault for putting up a dog that hadn't no hind legs for him to take holt of, which was his main dependence in a fight, and

5. **distemper . . . consumption:** Distemper is a viral disease caught by dogs and other four-legged mammals. Consumption is an old-fashioned name for tuberculosis.

6. **fag end:** final part.

7. **cipher** (sī′fər) **it down:** calculate it; figure it.

8. **fo'castle** (fōk′səl): forecastle—here, the protruding front deck of a steamboat.

9. **bullyrag:** harass.

10. **throwed up the sponge:** gave up.

11. **pet holt:** favorite grip.

B DIALECT
Paraphrase the passage written in dialect in lines 29–56. What point is Simon Wheeler making about Smiley?

cavorting (kə-vôr′tĭng) *adj.* prancing about in a playful manner **cavort** *v.*

then he limped off a piece and laid down and died. It was a good pup, was that Andrew Jackson, and would have made a name for hisself if he'd lived, for the stuff was in him and he had genius—I know it, because he hadn't no opportunities to speak of, and it don't stand to reason that a dog could make such a fight as he could under them circumstances if he hadn't no talent. It always makes me feel sorry when I think of that last fight of his'n and the way it turned out. **C**

    "Well, thish-yer Smiley had rat terriers, and chicken cocks, and tomcats and all them kind of things till you couldn't rest, and you couldn't fetch nothing for him to bet on but he'd match you. He ketched a frog one day and took him home, and said he cal'lated[12] to educate him; and so he never done nothing for three months but set in his back yard and learn that frog to jump. And you bet you he *did* learn him, too. He'd give him a little punch behind, and the next minute you'd see that frog whirling in the air like a doughnut—see him turn one summerset, or maybe a couple if he got a good start, and come down flatfooted and all right, like a cat. He got him up so in the matter of ketching flies, and kep' him in practice so constant, that he'd nail a fly every time as fur as he could see him. Smiley said all a frog wanted was education and he could do 'most anything—and I believe him. Why, I've seen him set Dan'l Webster down here on this floor—Dan'l Webster was the name of the frog—and sing out, 'Flies, Dan'l, flies!' and quicker'n you could wink he'd spring straight up and snake a fly off'n the counter there, and flop down on the floor ag'in as solid as a gob of mud, and fall to scratching the side of his head with his hind foot as **indifferent** as if he hadn't no idea he'd been doin' any more'n any frog might do. You never see a frog so modest and straight-for'ard as he was, for all he was so gifted. And when it come to fair and square jumping on a dead level, he could get over more ground at one straddle than any animal of his breed you ever see. Jumping on a dead level was his strong suit, you understand; and when it come to that, Smiley would ante up money on him as long as he had a red.[13] Smiley was monstrous proud of his frog, and well he might be for fellers that had traveled and been everywheres all said he laid over any frog that ever *they* see. **D**

    "Well, Smiley kep' the beast in a little lattice box, and he used to fetch him downtown sometimes and lay for a bet. One day a feller—a stranger in the camp, he was—come acrost him with his box and says:

    "'What might it be that you've got in the box?'

    "And Smiley says, sorter indifferent-like, 'It might be a parrot, or it might be a canary, maybe, but it ain't—it's only just a frog.'

    "And the feller took it and looked at it careful, and turned it round this way and that, and says, 'H'm—so 'tis. Well, what's *he* good for?'

    "'Well,' Smiley says, easy and careless, 'he's good enough for *one* thing, I should judge—he can outjump any frog in Calaveras County.'

    "The feller took the box again and took another long, particular look, and give it back to Smiley and says, very deliberate, 'Well,' he says, 'I don't see no p'ints[14] about that frog that's any better'n any other frog.'

---

12. **cal'lated:** calculated; intended.

13. **a red:** a red cent (slang for a penny).

14. **p'ints:** points.

C TALL TALE
Reread lines 68–93. What device characteristic of the tall tale is on display in this paragraph?

indifferent (ĭn-dĭf′ər-ənt) *adj.* having no particular interest

D DIALECT
Reread lines 110–111. How does the dialect in this sentence, and throughout the paragraph, help to characterize the frog?

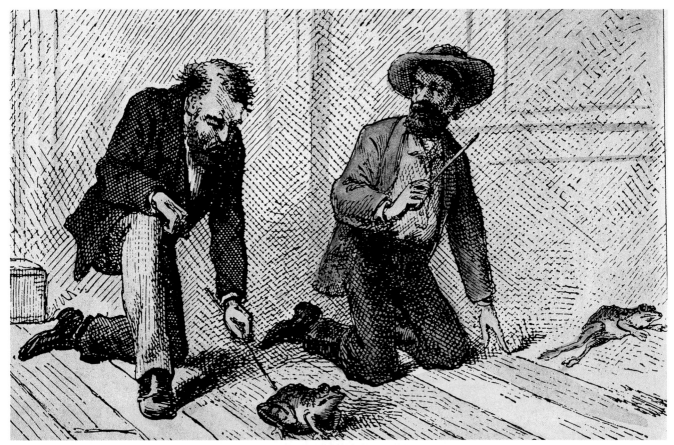

Frog of Calaveras County. The Granger Collection, New York.

130   "'Maybe you don't,' Smiley says. 'Maybe you understand frogs and maybe you don't understand 'em; maybe you've had experience and maybe you ain't only a amature, as it were. Anyways, I've got *my* opinion, and I'll resk forty dollars that he can outjump any frog in Calaveras County.'

   "And the feller studied a minute and then says, kinder sad-like, 'Well, I'm only a stranger here and I ain't got no frog; but if I had a frog, I'd bet you.'

   "And then Smiley says, 'That's all right—that's all right—if you'll hold my box a minute, I'll go and get you a frog.' And so the feller took the box and put up his forty dollars along with Smiley's, and set down to wait. **E**

   "So he set there a good while thinking and thinking to himself, and then he got
140 the frog out and prized his mouth open and took a teaspoon and filled him full of quail shot[15]—filled him pretty near up to his chin—and set him on the floor. Smiley he went to the swamp and slopped around in the mud for a long time, and finally he ketched a frog and fetched him in and give him to this feller, and says:

   "'Now, if you're ready, set him alongside of Dan'l, with his forepaws just even with Dan'l's, and I'll give the word.' Then he says, 'One—two—three—*git!*' and him and the feller touched up the frogs from behind, and the new frog hopped off

E TALL TALE
Reread the dialogue in lines 120–138. What does the straightfaced understatement reveal about the two characters?

---

15. **quail shot:** small lead pellets for firing from a shotgun.

lively, but Dan'l give a heave and hysted up his shoulders—so—like a Frenchman, but it warn't no use—he couldn't budge; he was planted as solid as a church, and he couldn't no more stir than if he was anchored out. Smiley was a good deal surprised, and he was disgusted too, but he didn't have no idea what the matter was, of course.

"The feller took the money and started away, and when he was going out at the door, he sorter jerked his thumb over his shoulder—so—at Dan'l and says again, very deliberate, 'Well,' he says, '*I* don't see no p'ints about that frog that's any better'n any other frog.'

"Smiley he stood scratching his head and looking down at Dan'l a long time, and at last he says, 'I do wonder what in the nation that frog throw'd off for—I wonder if there ain't something the matter with him—he 'pears to look mighty baggy, somehow.' And he ketched Dan'l by the nap of the neck and hefted him, and says, 'Why, blame my cats if he don't weigh five pound!' and turned him upside down and he belched out a double handful of shot. And then he see how it was, and he was the maddest man—he set the frog down and took out after that feller, but he never ketched him. And—"

[Here Simon Wheeler heard his name called from the front yard and got up to see what was wanted.] And turning to me as he moved away, he said: "Just set where you are, stranger, and rest easy—I ain't going to be gone a second."

But, by your leave, I did not think that a continuation of the history of the **enterprising** vagabond *Jim* Smiley would be likely to afford me much information concerning the Rev. *Leonidas W.* Smiley and so I started away.

At the door I met the sociable Wheeler returning, and he buttonholed me and recommenced:[16]

"Well, thish-yer Smiley had a yaller one-eyed cow that didn't have no tail, only just a short stump like a bannanner, and—"

However, lacking both time and inclination, I did not wait to hear about the afflicted cow but took my leave. ✎

F GRAMMAR AND STYLE
Reread lines 144–151. Notice how Twain uses **coordinating conjunctions** and **dashes** to convey Simon's breathless retelling of the story.

enterprising
(ĕn'tər-prī'zǐng) *adj.*
possessing imagination and initiative

---

16. **buttonholed . . . recommenced:** detained me for conversation and began talking again.

Comprehension

1. **Recall** How does the narrator hear the story of the jumping frog?

2. **Recall** What is Smiley always willing to do?

3. **Summarize** What happens to Smiley's frog?

Literary Analysis

4. **Make Inferences About Characters** What can you infer about Jim Smiley based on each of the following examples?

   • Smiley betting on the health of the parson's wife

   • Smiley spending three months teaching a frog to jump

   • Smiley studying why the frog couldn't jump

5. **Understand Dialect** Review the dialect and translations you recorded as you read. In general, what does the use of dialect contribute to **characterization** and **setting** in this story? Cite specific examples.

6. **Analyze Hyperbole** Simon Wheeler makes liberal use of hyperbole in describing Jim Smiley; some of what he says is totally improbable, and some is simply a bit of a stretch. List five to ten examples of this hyperbole and rate each on a scale of one to five, with five being the most outrageous. At any point, did your **skepticism** prevent you from enjoying the story? Explain.

7. **Make Judgments About the Tall Tale** Twain sets this story in a **frame**—a story within a story—in which the first-person narrator asks about a man named Leonidas Smiley but gets a story about Jim Smiley instead. In the end, the narrator makes a show of going away disappointed. How does this device contribute to the impact of the tall tale? Explain how the story would be different if the original first-person narrator had simply told the story in his own voice, or if Wheeler himself were the first-person narrator. Do you think this is an effective technique? Why or why not?

Literary Criticism

8. **Critical Interpretations** According to one critic, Twain's organization of this tale "seems wholly directionless," yet "actually it is carefully molded for climax." Do you agree? Look back at the story and explain how the elaborate setup affects the impact of the story's punchline. Use examples from the story to support your ideas.

Vocabulary in Context

cavorting
conjecture
dilapidated
enterprising
garrulous
indifferent
infamous
tranquil

VOCABULARY PRACTICE

Choose the word that is not related in meaning to the other words.

1. (a) dilapidated, (b) decaying, (c) neglected, (d) lonesome
2. (a) chatty, (b) argumentative, (c) garrulous, (d) verbose
3. (a) serene, (b) tranquil, (c) unhappy, (d) placid
4. (a) unusual, (b) infamous, (c) disreputable, (d) notorious
5. (a) comfort, (b) condolence, (c) consolation, (d) conjecture
6. (a) imaginative, (b) expensive, (c) enterprising, (d) resourceful
7. (a) unconcerned, (b) detached, (c) indifferent, (d) unnoticeable
8. (a) cavorting, (b) trembling, (c) shaking, (d) jarring

VOCABULARY IN WRITING

If you had seen the jumping frog contest, would you have found it humorous or foolish? Write a short description of the event, making your attitude clear. Use two or more vocabulary words. Here is a sample opening.

> **EXAMPLE SENTENCE**
>
> *Enterprising* people can always find ways to cheat and win. But filling a frog with shot seems especially cruel.

VOCABULARY STRATEGY: WORDS WITH MISLEADING PREFIXES

The prefix *in-* (and its variant *im-*) generally has a negative meaning, as do the prefixes *un-* and *non-*. When you see these prefixes attached to a base word, it is usually easy to figure out the meaning of the new word. Sometimes, though, the process doesn't quite work: *infamous,* for example, doesn't mean "not famous." Using context clues is one way of understanding words that are not quite what they seem.

PRACTICE Use context clues, or if necessary a dictionary, to help you create a definition of each boldfaced word.

1. The bill collector tried to **unnerve** Mom with his threats.
2. Jason is **indisposed** with a chest cold.
3. Her letter described the **insufferable** heat of Texas in July.
4. The old building has been there since time **immemorial**.
5. Everyone was **nonplused** by the surprising turn of events.

VOCABULARY PRACTICE
For more practice, go to the **Vocabulary Center** at ClassZone.com.

Reading-Writing Connection

WRITING PROMPT

WRITE A DIALOGUE A **conversation** can reveal a great deal about its participants. Character's words and gestures as well as the pace and flow of their speech all make a story character believable.

Write a **one-page conversation** between two real people or fictional characters. Like Twain, have them share amazing—and possibly exaggerated—experiences.

SELF-CHECK

A successful conversation will...

• be written for two speakers
• reveal attitudes and background
• include a natural flow of ideas and informal language
• use correct punctuation

GRAMMAR AND STYLE

CREATE REALISTIC CHARACTERS Review the **Grammar and Style** note on page 666. Mark Twain creates convincing dialogue to help establish the character of Simon Wheeler. Look at this example from the story:

> *And a dog might tackle him and <u>bullyrag</u> him, and bite him and throw him over his shoulder two or three times, and Andrew Jackson—which was the name of the pup—Andrew Jackson would never let on but what he was satisfied and hadn't expected nothing else....* (lines 72–75)

Notice how Twain uses the highlighted **coordinating conjunctions** to construct long, rambling sentences that reflect Simon's chatty nature. He also uses **dashes** to show how Simon will interrupt himself. Finally, the underlined text demonstrates elements of dialect, which shows that Simon is rooted in his local culture.

PRACTICE Revise the dialogue you wrote in response to the writing prompt, this time writing it in dialect. You may wish to use the same Western dialect that Twain uses in his short story, or use another dialect that is familiar to you. Make use of coordinating conjunctions, dashes, and regional vocabulary, as well as any special spellings or contractions that will help your reader "hear" the rhythm and pronunciation of the dialect as it would be spoken aloud.

EXAMPLE

"My goodness! If I had known you felt that way about it, I never would have said anything in the first place."

"Well, shet my mouth! If I'da known you felt that way 'bout it, I never woulda said nothin' in th' first place."

WRITING TOOLS
For prewriting, revision, and editing tools, visit the **Writing Center** at ClassZone.com.

The Adventures of Huckleberry Finn

Mark Twain

Mark Twain
1835–1910

ABOUT THE AUTHOR "Half twain! Quarter twain! Mark twain!"—such were the cries of 19th-century Mississippi riverboatmen, indicating that the water was deep enough to cross. Samuel Clemens heard those cries as a boy growing up in Hannibal, Missouri, and as a young man working as a riverboat pilot. Later he chose the cry of "Mark twain!" for his pen name. Although Twain first won fame as a Western humorist writing about life in the California gold-mining camps, he drew on his Missouri childhood for many of his best-known works. These include *The Adventures of Tom Sawyer* (1876), his popular tale of a boy growing up in a town not unlike Hannibal; *Life on the Mississippi* (1883), his memoir of his days as a riverboat pilot; and *The Adventures of Huckleberry Finn* (1884), Tom Sawyer's more mature sequel.

ABOUT THE NOVEL *The Adventures of Huckleberry Finn* takes place in the years before the Civil War, when slavery was still legal in Missouri, where the novel opens. Huck Finn, a friend of Tom Sawyer's, is the son of an abusive, drunken lout and has been taken in by the kindly Widow Douglas and her sister, Miss Watson. Huck's neglectful father appears and steals Huck away, taking the boy to live with him in an isolated cabin. Huck escapes to Jackson's Island, where he meets Jim, Miss Watson's runaway slave. Fleeing together down the Mississippi River on a raft in an attempt to reach Ohio and freedom, the two outcasts form a close friendship and experience all sorts of strange adventures.

LEGACY OF A MASTERPIECE Regarded as the quintessential American coming-of-age novel, *The Adventures of Huckleberry Finn* is also a scathing satire of 19th-century social institutions and a pioneering work of American regionalism. In *Huck Finn,* Twain brilliantly captures the flavor of a particular time and place. During the journey down the Mississippi, for example, Huck meets a wide variety of characters whom Twain used to portray nearly every social class living on or along the river in that day. In addition, in Huck's speech, Twain manages to capture the dialect of an uneducated Missouri boy while still being able to humorously and vividly describe scenes and characters. In the end, though, it may be best to enjoy the novel—in the words of Huck's friend Tom Sawyer—for "the *adventure* of it."

In the following excerpt, Huck has just done what his society has taught him is the right thing to do: he has written a note to Miss Watson, reporting the whereabouts of her runaway slave, Jim. However, Huck has deep misgivings about this action.

I felt good and all washed clean of sin for the first time I had ever felt so in my life, and I knowed I could pray now. But I didn't do it straight off, but laid the paper down and set there thinking—thinking how good it was all this happened so, and how near I come to being lost and going to hell. And went on thinking. And got to thinking over our trip down the river; and I see Jim before me, all the time, in the day, and in the nighttime, sometimes moonlight, sometimes storms, and we a floating along, talking, and singing, and laughing. But somehow I couldn't seem to strike no places to harden me against him, but only

10 the other kind. I'd see him standing my watch on top of his'n, stead of calling me, so I could go on sleeping; and see him how glad he was when I come back out of the fog; and when I come to him again in the swamp, up there where the feud was; and such-like times; and would always call me honey, and pet me, and do everything he could think of for me, and how good he always was; and at last I struck the time I saved him by telling the men we had small-pox aboard, and he was so grateful, and said I was the best friend old Jim ever had in the world, and the only one he's got now; and then I happened to look around, and see that paper.

It was a close place. I took it up, and held it in my hand. I was a trembling, because I'd got to decide, forever, betwixt two things, and I knowed it. I studied

20 a minute, sort of holding my breath, and then says to myself:

"All right, then, I'll *go* to hell"—and tore it up.

It was awful thoughts, and awful words, but they was said. And I let them stay said; and never thought no more about reforming. I shoved the whole thing out of my head; and said I would take up wickedness again, which was in my line, being brung up to it, and the other warn't. And for a starter, I would go to work and steal Jim out of slavery again; and if I could think up anything worse, I would do that, too; because as long as I was in, and in for good, I might as well go the whole hog.

Then I set to thinking over how to get at it, and turned over considerable many ways in my mind; and at last fixed up a plan that suited me. So then I took the

30 bearings of a woody island that was down the river a piece, and as soon as it was fairly dark I crept out with my raft and went for it, and hid it there, and then turned in. I slept the night through, and got up before it was light, and had my breakfast, and put on my store clothes, and tied up some others and one thing or another in a bundle, and took the canoe and cleared for shore. I landed below where I judged was Phelps's place, and hid my bundle in the woods, and then filled up the canoe with water, and loaded rocks into her and sunk her where I could find her again when I wanted her, about a quarter mile below a little steam sawmill that was on the bank.

The Outcasts of Poker Flat

Short Story by Bret Harte

Bret Harte
1836–1902

NOTABLE QUOTE

"Luck is a mighty queer thing. All you know about it for certain is that it's bound to change."

FYI

Did you know that Bret Harte . . .

- was called "Dickens among the pines" for the vivid and recognizable characters he created?

- worked as a shotgun rider on a California stagecoach?

- worked as an abolitionist during the Civil War, often speaking out against the harsh treatment of minorities?

Author Online

For more on Bret Harte, visit the **Literature Center** at ClassZone.com.

Many of the familiar characters in Western stories and films—saloon keepers, fallen ladies, hard-bitten gamblers, mining prospectors, and dewy-eyed youngsters—can be found in the stories of Bret Harte. Harte's colorful writing helped shape the Western genre. It also inspired emigration to the developing region of the American west. Harte's writing made him—for a short while—one of America's most popular and highly paid literary figures.

A Man of Many Hats Born into an educated but financially struggling family, Bret Harte moved often during his childhood. Although the frequent moves and his poor health kept him from formal schooling, he read widely on his own and published his first writing at age 11. After his father died, Harte began working—first for a pharmacist, then a lawyer, and later as a tutor, a miner, and finally a journalist for a newspaper in California, where the family had moved after his mother's remarriage. It was at this newspaper that Harte began to publish his stories and articles.

Good Times In the early 1860s, Harte moved to San Francisco and began to hone his literary craft. He wrote and edited stories, articles, humor, and literary criticism for two newspapers, the *Golden Era* and then the *Californian*. At the *Californian*, Harte helped along the career of a young, unknown Mark Twain. Becoming founding editor of the *Overland Monthly*, Harte soon wrote and published "The Luck of Roaring Camp" and "The Outcasts of Poker Flat," stories of outcasts with hearts of gold. These stories put him on the literary map. Suddenly, he was the talk of the town with his work much discussed, often imitated, and highly sought after. When the *Atlantic Monthly* in Boston offered Harte an annual contract with a big salary, he moved his family back east.

. . . And Bad Times Harte was careless about fulfilling his *Atlantic Monthly* contract, and it was not renewed. He tried lecturing, novel writing (*Gabriel Conroy*), and playwriting with Mark Twain (*Ah Sin*), but was left with a failing literary career. His marriage had also deteriorated. Finally, in 1877, friends helped Harte get an appointment as U.S. consul in Germany. By 1885 he had landed in London. Bret Harte, who played a key role in creating the popular portrait of the Old West, lived in London for the rest of his life, dying there in 1902.

● LITERARY ANALYSIS: REGIONALISM

Regionalism was a literary movement of the 19th century that strove to accurately represent the speech, manners, habits, history, and beliefs of people in a specific geographic area. A natural outgrowth of realism, regionalism often focused on the lives of ordinary people. As you read Bret Harte's famous story, note his use of the following characteristics of regional literature:

- detailed description of the physical features of **setting**
- attention to the specific time in which events occur, for example, a season of the year or a historical period
- depiction of the social and economic conditions of the **characters,** as well as any religious or moral beliefs that become apparent
- the use of **dialect,** which reflects the unique speech of a region during a particular time

● READING SKILL: CLARIFY MEANING

Harte's style of writing can pose challenges to any reader. As you read this story, make sure to **clarify** any portions of the story that seem unclear on first reading. Stop and ask yourself questions such as these:

- What just happened?
- What do the characters' words and actions reveal about them?
- What meaning can be extracted from the narrator's comments and expressions?

▲ VOCABULARY IN CONTEXT

Harte uses a rich and challenging vocabulary in this story of the Old West. Choose the word from the list that you would associate with or use to describe an individual who

1. can see into the future
2. is constantly joking
3. criticizes others
4. complains all the time
5. utters a curse
6. is friendly to everyone
7. is an exile
8. has a steady outlook
9. weeps in sad movies
10. is avoided by others

WORD LIST	amicable	jocular	prescience
	anathema	maudlin	querulous
	equanimity	pariah	vituperative
	expatriated		

Explore the Key Idea

What does it mean to be an OUTCAST?

KEY IDEA In ancient times, people were sent into **exile** as a form of punishment. They were cast out of society and set adrift, often in harsh and dangerous wilderness. In "The Outcasts of Poker Flat," the characters are exiled into the California mountains, where they face both psychological and physical challenges. Consider why exile might be such an effective and extreme punishment.

DEBATE In a small group, prepare arguments for or against the statement "We need society to live." In developing your argument, consider the various consequences of living outside of society. After the debate, discuss whether you would support exile as a form of modern punishment.

The Outcasts *of* Poker Flat

Bret Harte

> **BACKGROUND** Many of Bret Harte's stories highlighted both the lure of gold in California and the challenge of battling a harsh landscape of huge spaces and towering mountains. During the California Gold Rush, which began in 1848, thousands of people poured into the state, creating towns such as the one in this story. These towns, which developed from miners' camps, were often rough and featured the homemade style of justice that sets this story's events in motion.

As Mr. John Oakhurst, gambler, stepped into the main street of Poker Flat on the morning of the twenty-third of November, 1850, he was conscious of a change in its moral atmosphere since the preceding night. Two or three men, conversing earnestly together, ceased as he approached, and exchanged significant glances. There was a Sabbath lull in the air, which, in a settlement unused to Sabbath influences, looked ominous. **A**

Mr. Oakhurst's calm, handsome face betrayed small concern in these indications. Whether he was conscious of any predisposing cause, was another question. "I reckon they're after somebody," he reflected; "likely it's me." He
10 returned to his pocket the handkerchief with which he had been whipping away the red dust of Poker Flat from his neat boots, and quietly discharged his mind of any further conjecture.

In point of fact, Poker Flat was "after somebody." It had lately suffered the loss of several thousand dollars, two valuable horses, and a prominent citizen. It was experiencing a spasm of virtuous reaction, quite as lawless and ungovernable as any of the acts that had provoked it. A secret committee had determined to rid the town of all improper persons. This was done permanently in regard of two

ANALYZE VISUALS
Describe the sense of time and place conveyed in this image. What details give you this sense?

A CLARIFY MEANING
Reread the first paragraph. What has happened thus far?

Deadwood, South Dakota, 1877. The Granger Collection, New York.

men who were then hanging from the boughs of a sycamore in the gulch, and temporarily in the banishment of certain other objectionable characters. I regret
20 to say that some of these were ladies. It is but due to the sex, however, to state that their impropriety was professional, and it was only in such easily established standards of evil that Poker Flat ventured to sit in judgment. **B**

Mr. Oakhurst was right in supposing that he was included in this category. A few of the committee had urged hanging him as a possible example, and a sure method of reimbursing themselves from his pockets of the sums he had won from them. "It's agin justice," said Jim Wheeler, "to let this yer young man from Roaring Camp[1]—an entire stranger—carry away our money." But a crude sentiment of equity residing in the breasts of those who had been fortunate enough to win from Mr. Oakhurst overruled this narrower local prejudice. **C**

30 Mr. Oakhurst received his sentence with philosophic calmness, none the less coolly that he was aware of the hesitation of his judges. He was too much of a gambler not to accept Fate. With him life was at best an uncertain game, and he recognized the usual percentage in favor of the dealer.

A body of armed men accompanied the deported wickedness of Poker Flat to the outskirts of the settlement. Besides Mr. Oakhurst, who was known to be a coolly desperate man, and for whose intimidation the armed escort was intended, the **expatriated** party consisted of a young woman familiarly known as "The Duchess," another who had won the title of "Mother Shipton,"[2] and "Uncle Billy," a suspected sluice-robber[3] and confirmed drunkard. The cavalcade
40 provoked no comments from the spectators, nor was any word uttered by the escort. Only, when the gulch which marked the uttermost limit of Poker Flat was reached, the leader spoke briefly and to the point. The exiles were forbidden to return at the peril of their lives.

As the escort disappeared, their pent-up feelings found vent in a few hysterical tears from the Duchess, some bad language from Mother Shipton, and a Parthian volley of expletives[4] from Uncle Billy. The philosophic Oakhurst alone remained silent. He listened calmly to Mother Shipton's desire to cut somebody's heart out, to the repeated statements of the Duchess that she would die in the road, and to the alarming oaths that seemed to be bumped out of Uncle Billy as he
50 rode forward. With the easy good-humor characteristic of his class, he insisted upon exchanging his own riding-horse, "Five Spot," for the sorry mule which the Duchess rode. But even this act did not draw the party into any closer sympathy. The young woman readjusted her somewhat draggled plumes with a feeble, faded coquetry; Mother Shipton eyed the possessor of "Five Spot" with malevolence, and Uncle Billy included the whole party in one sweeping **anathema**. **D**

---

1. **Roaring Camp:** name applied to a wild California settlement that was established in the 1830s by Isaac Graham. Harte used the name in his story "The Luck of Roaring Camp."
2. **"Mother Shipton":** originally, a 16th-century English woman who was accused of being a witch.
3. **sluice-robber** (slōōs′rŏb-ər): a person who steals gold from sluices, or the water troughs used by miners to sift gold.
4. **Parthian volley of expletives:** crude or hostile remarks made when leaving. Soldiers from the ancient Asian land of Parthia typically shot at their enemies while pretending to retreat on horseback.

B CLARIFY MEANING
Reread lines 13–22. What is the narrator's attitude toward the "virtuous reaction" of Poker Flat?

C REGIONALISM
What can you infer about life in Poker Flat?

expatriated
(ĕk-spā′trē-ā′tĭd) *adj.* sent out of a country or area; banished **expatriate** *v.*

anathema (ə-năth′ə-mə) *n.* a strong denunciation; a curse

D CLARIFY MEANING
Reread lines 44–55. What is your impression of Oakhurst at this point in the story? Compare him with the other outcasts.

The road to Sandy Bar—a camp that, not having as yet experienced the regenerating influences of Poker Flat, consequently seemed to offer some invitation to the emigrants—lay over a steep mountain range. It was distant a day's severe travel. In that advanced season, the party soon passed out of the moist, 60 temperate regions of the foot-hills into the dry, cold, bracing air of the Sierras.[5] The trail was narrow and difficult. At noon the Duchess, rolling out of her saddle upon the ground, declared her intention of going no farther, and the party halted.

The spot was singularly wild and impressive. A wooded amphitheatre, surrounded on three sides by precipitous cliffs of naked granite, sloped gently toward the crest of another precipice that overlooked the valley. It was, undoubtedly, the most suitable spot for a camp, had camping been advisable. But Mr. Oakhurst knew that scarcely half the journey to Sandy Bar was accomplished, and the party were not equipped or provisioned for delay. This fact he pointed out to his companions curtly, with a philosophic commentary on the folly of 70 "throwing up their hand before the game was played out." But they were furnished with liquor, which in this emergency stood them in place of food, fuel, rest, and **prescience.** In spite of his remonstrances, it was not long before they were more or less under its influence. Uncle Billy passed rapidly from a bellicose state into one of stupor, the Duchess became **maudlin,** and Mother Shipton snored. Mr. Oakhurst alone remained erect, leaning against a rock, calmly surveying them.

Mr. Oakhurst did not drink. It interfered with a profession which required coolness, impassiveness, and presence of mind, and, in his own language, he "couldn't afford it." As he gazed at his recumbent fellow-exiles, the loneliness begotten of his **pariah**-trade, his habits of life, his very vices, for the first time 80 seriously oppressed him. He bestirred himself in dusting his black clothes, washing his hands and face, and other acts characteristic of his studiously neat habits, and for a moment forgot his annoyance. The thought of deserting his weaker and more pitiable companions never perhaps occurred to him. Yet he could not help feeling the want of that excitement which, singularly enough, was most conducive to that calm **equanimity** for which he was notorious. He looked at the gloomy walls that rose a thousand feet sheer above the circling pines around him; at the sky, ominously clouded; at the valley below, already deepening into shadow. And, doing so, suddenly he heard his own name called. **Ⓔ**

A horseman slowly ascended the trail. In the fresh, open face of the new-comer 90 Mr. Oakhurst recognized Tom Simson, otherwise known as "The Innocent" of Sandy Bar. He had met him some months before over a "little game," and had, with perfect equanimity, won the entire fortune—amounting to some forty dollars—of that guileless youth. After the game was finished, Mr. Oakhurst drew the youthful speculator behind the door and thus addressed him: "Tommy, you're a good little man, but you can't gamble worth a cent. Don't try it over again." He then handed him his money back, pushed him gently from the room, and so made a devoted slave of Tom Simson.

prescience (prĕsh'əns) *n.* knowledge of events before they occur

maudlin (môd'lĭn) *adj.* excessively sentimental

pariah (pə-rī'ə) *n.* an outcast, someone or something looked down on by others

equanimity (ē'kwə-nĭm'ĭ-tē) *n.* evenness of temper, especially under stress

Ⓔ REGIONALISM Reread lines 56–88. In what way is this passage typical of regionalist writing?

---

5. **Sierras:** the Sierra Nevada range of mountains, in eastern California.

There was a remembrance of this in his boyish and enthusiastic greeting of Mr. Oakhurst. He had started, he said, to go to Poker Flat to seek his fortune. "Alone?" No, not exactly alone; in fact (a giggle), he had run away with Piney Woods. Didn't Mr. Oakhurst remember Piney? She that used to wait on the table at the Temperance House?[6] They had been engaged a long time, but old Jake Woods had objected, and so they had run away, and were going to Poker Flat to be married, and here they were. And they were tired out, and how lucky it was they had found a place to camp and company. All this the Innocent delivered rapidly, while Piney, a stout, comely damsel of fifteen, emerged from behind the pine tree, where she had been blushing unseen, and rode to the side of her lover.

Mr. Oakhurst seldom troubled himself with sentiment, still less with propriety; but he had a vague idea that the situation was not fortunate. He retained, however, his presence of mind sufficiently to kick Uncle Billy, who was about to say something, and Uncle Billy was sober enough to recognize in Mr. Oakhurst's kick a superior power that would not bear trifling. He then endeavored to dissuade Tom Simson from delaying further, but in vain. He even pointed out the fact that there was no provision, nor means of making a camp. But, unluckily, the Innocent met this objection by assuring the party that he was provided with an extra mule loaded with provisions, and by the discovery of a rude attempt at a log house near the trail. "Piney can stay with Mrs. Oakhurst," said the Innocent, pointing to the Duchess, "and I can shift for myself."

---

6. **Temperance House:** a place where customers could not drink.

Nothing but Mr. Oakhurst's admonishing foot saved Uncle Billy from bursting
120 into a roar of laughter. As it was, he felt compelled to retire up the canyon until
he could recover his gravity. There he confided the joke to the tall pine trees, with
many slaps of his leg, contortions of his face, and the usual profanity. But when
he returned to the party, he found them seated by a fire—for the air had grown
strangely chill and the sky overcast—in apparently **amicable** conversation. Piney
was actually talking in an impulsive, girlish fashion to the Duchess, who was
listening with an interest and animation she had not shown for many days. The
Innocent was holding forth, apparently with equal effect, to Mr. Oakhurst and
Mother Shipton, who was actually relaxing into amiability. "Is this yer a d—d
picnic?" said Uncle Billy, with inward scorn, as he surveyed the sylvan group, the
130 glancing firelight, and the tethered animals in the foreground. Suddenly an idea
mingled with the alcoholic fumes that disturbed his brain. It was apparently of
a **jocular** nature, for he felt impelled to slap his leg again and cram his fist into
his mouth. **F**

As the shadows crept slowly up the mountain, a slight breeze rocked the tops
of the pine trees, and moaned through their long and gloomy aisles. The ruined
cabin, patched and covered with pine boughs, was set apart for the ladies. As
the lovers parted, they unaffectedly exchanged a kiss, so honest and sincere
that it might have been heard above the swaying pines. The frail Duchess and
the malevolent Mother Shipton were probably too stunned to remark upon this
140 last evidence of simplicity, and so turned without a word to the hut. The fire was
replenished, the men lay down before the door, and in a few minutes were asleep. **G**

Mr. Oakhurst was a light sleeper. Toward morning he awoke benumbed and
cold. As he stirred the dying fire, the wind, which was now blowing strongly,
brought to his cheek that which caused the blood to leave it—snow!

He started to his feet with the intention of awakening the sleepers, for there
was no time to lose. But turning to where Uncle Billy had been lying, he found
him gone. A suspicion leaped to his brain and a curse to his lips. He ran to the
spot where the mules had been tethered; they were no longer there. The tracks
were already rapidly disappearing in the snow.

150 The momentary excitement brought Mr. Oakhurst back to the fire with his
usual calm. He did not waken the sleepers. The Innocent slumbered peacefully,
with a smile on his good-humored, freckled face; the virgin Piney slept beside her
frailer sisters as sweetly as though attended by celestial guardians, and Mr. Oakhurst,
drawing his blanket over his shoulders, stroked his mustaches and waited for the
dawn. It came slowly in a whirling mist of snowflakes, that dazzled and confused the
eye. What could be seen of the landscape appeared magically changed. He looked
over the valley, and summed up the present and future in two words—"snowed in!"

A careful inventory of the provisions, which, fortunately for the party, had
been stored within the hut, and so escaped the felonious fingers of Uncle Billy,
160 disclosed the fact that with care and prudence they might last ten days longer.

amicable (ăm′ĭ-kə-bəl)
adj. characterized by
friendly goodwill

jocular (jŏk′yə-lər) *adj.*
humorous

F CLARIFY MEANING
Reread lines 117–133.
What effect has the
arrival of Tom and Piney
had on the outcasts?

G GRAMMAR AND STYLE
Reread lines 134–135.
Note that the **verbs** *crept*
and *moaned* are used to
personify the shadows
and the breeze.

"That is," said Mr. Oakhurst, *sotto voce*[7] to the Innocent, "if you're willing to board us." If you ain't—and perhaps you'd better not—you can wait till Uncle Billy gets back with provisions." For some occult reason, Mr. Oakhurst could not bring himself to disclose Uncle Billy's rascality, and so offered the hypothesis that he had wandered from the camp and had accidentally stampeded the animals. He dropped a warning to the Duchess and Mother Shipton, who of course knew the facts of their associate's defection. "They'll find out the truth about us *all* when they find out anything," he added, significantly, "and there's no good frightening them now."

170   Tom Simson not only put all his worldly store at the disposal of Mr. Oakhurst, but seemed to enjoy the prospect of their enforced seclusion. "We'll have a good camp for a week, and then the snow'll melt, and we'll all go back together." The cheerful gaiety of the young man and Mr. Oakhurst's calm infected the others. The Innocent, with the aid of pine boughs, extemporized a thatch for the roofless cabin, and the Duchess directed Piney in the rearrangement of the interior with a taste and tact that opened the blue eyes of that provincial maiden to their fullest extent. "I reckon now you're used to fine things at Poker Flat," said Piney. The Duchess turned away sharply to conceal something that reddened her cheeks through its professional tint, and Mother Shipton requested Piney not to "chatter." But when Mr. Oakhurst returned
180 from a weary search for the trail, he heard the sound of happy laughter echoed from the rocks. He stopped in some alarm, and his thoughts first naturally reverted to the whiskey, which he had prudently cached.[8] "And yet it don't somehow sound like whiskey," said the gambler. It was not until he caught sight of the blazing fire through the still-blinding storm and the group around it that he settled to the conviction that it was "square fun." **H**

        Whether Mr. Oakhurst had cached his cards with the whiskey as something debarred the free access of the community, I cannot say. It was certain that, in Mother Shipton's words, he "didn't say cards once" during the evening. Haply the time was beguiled by an accordion, produced somewhat ostentatiously by
190 Tom Simson from his pack. Notwithstanding some difficulties attending the manipulation of this instrument, Piney Woods managed to pluck several reluctant melodies from its keys, to an accompaniment by the Innocent on a pair of bone castanets. But the crowning festivity of the evening was reached in a rude camp-meeting hymn, which the lovers, joining hands, sang with great earnestness and vociferation. I fear that a certain defiant tone and Covenanter's swing[9] to its chorus, rather than any devotional quality, caused it speedily to infect the others, who at last joined the refrain:

> "I'm proud to live in the service of the Lord,
> And I'm bound to die in His army."[10] **I**

---

7. **sotto voce** (sŏt′ō vō′chē) *Italian*: in a low voice.

8. **prudently cached** (kă-shād′): wisely hidden away.

9. **Covenanter's swing:** the strong rhythms of songs sung by Scottish Presbyterians, who made covenants or agreements to oppose the Church of England.

10. **"I'm proud . . . army":** lines from the early American spiritual "Service of the Lord."

H CLARIFY MEANING
Reread lines 170–185. What is Piney's impression of the Duchess? of Poker Flat?

I REGIONALISM
Reread lines 186–199. From the information given, what can you **infer** about the characters and the culture to which they belong?

200 The pines rocked, the storm eddied and whirled above the miserable group, and the flames of their altar leaped heavenward, as if in token of the vow.

At midnight the storm abated, the rolling clouds parted, and the stars glittered keenly above the sleeping camp. Mr. Oakhurst, whose professional habits had enabled him to live on the smallest possible amount of sleep, in dividing the watch with Tom Simson, somehow managed to take upon himself the greater part of that duty. He excused himself to the Innocent, by saying that he had "often been a week without sleep." "Doing what?" asked Tom. "Poker!" replied Oakhurst, sententiously; "when a man gets a streak of luck, he don't get tired. The luck gives in first. Luck," continued the gambler, reflectively, "is a mighty queer thing. All
210 you know about it for certain is that it's bound to change. And it's finding out when it's going to change that makes you. We've had a streak of bad luck since we left Poker Flat—you come along, and slap you get into it, too. If you can hold your cards right along you're all right. For," added the gambler, with cheerful irrelevance,

> "I'm proud to live in the service of the Lord,
> And I'm bound to die in His army."

The third day came, and the sun, looking through the white-curtained valley, saw the outcasts divide their slowly decreasing store of provisions for the morning meal. It was one of the peculiarities of that mountain climate that its rays diffused
220 a kindly warmth over the wintry landscape, as if in regretful commiseration of the past. But it revealed drift on drift of snow piled high around the hut—a hopeless, uncharted, trackless sea of white lying below the rocky shores to which the castaways still clung. Through the marvelously clear air the smoke of the pastoral village of Poker Flat rose miles away. Mother Shipton saw it, and from a remote pinnacle of her rocky fastness, hurled in that direction a final malediction.[11] It was her last **vituperative** attempt, and perhaps for that reason was invested with a certain degree of sublimity. It did her good, she privately informed the Duchess. "Just you go out there and cuss, and see." She then set herself to the task of amusing "the child," as she and the Duchess were pleased to call Piney. Piney was
230 no chicken, but it was a soothing and original theory of the pair thus to account for the fact that she didn't swear and wasn't improper.

When night crept up again through the gorges, the reedy notes of the accordion rose and fell in fitful spasms and long-drawn gasps by the flickering campfire. But music failed to fill entirely the aching void left by insufficient food, and a new diversion was proposed by Piney—storytelling. Neither Mr. Oakhurst nor his female companions caring to relate their personal experiences, this plan would have failed, too, but for the Innocent. Some months before he had chanced upon a stray copy of Mr. Pope's ingenious translation of the *Iliad*.[12] He now proposed

vituperative
(vī-tōō′pər-ə-tĭv) *adj.*
abusively critical

---

11. **malediction:** curse.
12. **Mr. Pope's . . . *Iliad*:** British poet Alexander Pope published his translation of Homer's *Iliad* in 1720.

to narrate the principal incidents of that poem—having thoroughly mastered the
240 argument and fairly forgotten the words—in the current vernacular of Sandy Bar.
And so for the rest of that night the Homeric demigods again walked the earth.
Trojan bully and wily Greek wrestled in the winds, and the great pines in the
canyon seemed to bow to the wrath of the son of Peleus.[13] Mr. Oakhurst listened
with quiet satisfaction. Most especially was he interested in the fate of "Ash-heels,"
as the Innocent persisted in denominating the "swift-footed Achilles."

So with small food and much of Homer and the accordion, a week passed over
the heads of the outcasts. The sun again forsook them, and again from leaden skies
the snowflakes were sifted over the land. Day by day closer around them drew
the snowy circle, until at last they looked from their prison over drifted walls of
250 dazzling white, that towered twenty feet above their heads. It became more and
more difficult to replenish their fires, even from the fallen trees beside them, now
half hidden in the drifts. And yet no one complained. The lovers turned from the
dreary prospect and looked into each other's eyes, and were happy. Mr. Oakhurst
settled himself coolly to the losing game before him. The Duchess, more cheerful
than she had been, assumed the care of Piney. Only Mother Shipton—once the
strongest of the party—seemed to sicken and fade. At midnight on the tenth day
she called Oakhurst to her side. "I'm going," she said, in a voice of **querulous**
weakness, "but don't say anything about it. Don't waken the kids. Take the bundle
from under my head and open it." Mr. Oakhurst did so. It contained Mother
260 Shipton's rations for the last week, untouched. "Give 'em to the child," she said,
pointing to the sleeping Piney. "You've starved yourself," said the gambler. "That's

J REGIONALISM
Reread lines 246–250.
What words used to
describe the characters'
physical surroundings
seem especially
descriptive of their
situation?

querulous (kwĕr′ə-ləs)
adj. complaining

---

13. **son of Peleus** (pē′lē-əs): Achilles (ə-kĭl′ēz), the Greek hero in the *Iliad*. Tom Simson mispronounces his
name as "Ash-heels."

what they call it," said the woman, querulously, as she lay down again, and, turning her face to the wall, passed quietly away. **K**

The accordion and the bones were put aside that day, and Homer was forgotten. When the body of Mother Shipton had been committed to the snow, Mr. Oakhurst took the Innocent aside, and showed him a pair of snowshoes, which he had fashioned from the old pack saddle. "There's one chance in a hundred to save her yet," he said, pointing to Piney; "but it's there," he added, pointing toward Poker Flat. "If you can reach there in two days she's safe." "And
270 you?" asked Tom Simson. "I'll stay here," was the curt reply.

The lovers parted with a long embrace. "You are not going, too?" said the Duchess, as she saw Mr. Oakhurst apparently waiting to accompany him. "As far as the canyon," he replied. He turned suddenly, and kissed the Duchess, leaving her pallid face aflame, and her trembling limbs rigid with amazement.

Night came, but not Mr. Oakhurst. It brought the storm again and the whirling snow. Then the Duchess, feeding the fire, found that someone had quietly piled beside the hut enough fuel to last a few days longer. The tears rose to her eyes, but she hid them from Piney.

The women slept but little. In the morning, looking into each other's faces,
280 they read their fate. Neither spoke; but Piney, accepting the position of the stronger, drew near and placed her arm around the Duchess's waist. They kept this attitude for the rest of the day. That night the storm reached its greatest fury, and, rendering asunder[14] the protecting pines, invaded the very hut.

Toward morning they found themselves unable to feed the fire, which gradually died away. As the embers slowly blackened, the Duchess crept closer to Piney, and broke the silence of many hours: "Piney, can you pray?" "No, dear," said Piney,

K CLARIFY MEANING
What happens to Mother Shipton? Explain whether or not you were surprised by this development, and why or why not.

---

14. **rending asunder:** forcefully ripping apart.

simply. The Duchess, without knowing exactly why, felt relieved, and, putting her head upon Piney's shoulder, spoke no more. And so reclining, the younger and purer pillowing the head of her soiled sister upon her virgin breast, they fell asleep.

290   The wind lulled as if it feared to waken them. Feathery drifts of snow, shaken from the long pine boughs, flew like white-winged birds, and settled about them as they slept. The moon through the rifted clouds looked down upon what had been the camp. But all human stain, all trace of earthly travail, was hidden beneath the spotless mantle mercifully flung from above.

    They slept all that day and the next, nor did they waken when voices and footsteps broke the silence of the camp. And when pitying fingers brushed the snow from their wan faces, you could scarcely have told from the equal peace that dwelt upon them, which was she that had sinned. Even the law of Poker Flat recognized this, and turned away, leaving them still locked in each other's arms. **L**

300   But at the head of the gulch, on one of the largest pine trees, they found the deuce of clubs[15] pinned to the bark with a bowie-knife. It bore the following, written in pencil, in a firm hand:

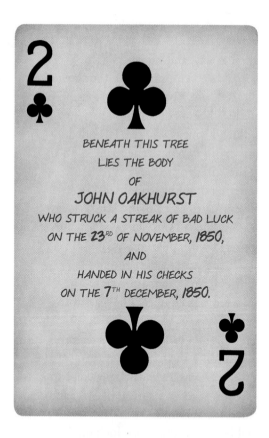

BENEATH THIS TREE
LIES THE BODY
OF
JOHN OAKHURST
WHO STRUCK A STREAK OF BAD LUCK
ON THE 23RD OF NOVEMBER, 1850,
AND
HANDED IN HIS CHECKS
ON THE 7TH DECEMBER, 1850.

    And pulseless and cold, with a Derringer[16] by his side and a bullet in his heart, though still calm as in life, beneath the snow lay he who was at once the strongest and yet the weakest of the outcasts of Poker Flat. **M**

> **L** CLARIFY MEANING
> **Summarize** what has happened to the Duchess and Piney. What point does the narrator seem to be making in lines 279–299?

> **M** CLARIFY MEANING
> Why has Oakhurst committed this final act?

---

15. **deuce of clubs:** the lowest card in a deck of playing cards—thus a loser's card.

16. **Derringer:** a short-barreled pistol invented by American gunsmith Henry Derringer.

Comprehension

1. **Recall** Why do Mr. Oakhurst and the others leave Poker Flat?

2. **Recall** Who joins the traveling group at their camp?

3. **Summarize** What happens to the travelers at the camp?

Literary Analysis

4. **Clarify Meaning** Review the following quotations within the context of the story and summarize what they mean:

   - "There was a Sabbath lull in the air, which, in a settlement unused to Sabbath influences, looked ominous." (lines 5–6)

   - "Mr. Oakhurst seldom troubled himself with sentiment, still less with propriety; but he had a vague idea that the situation was not fortunate." (lines 108–109)

   - "...Beneath the snow lay he who was at once the strongest and yet the weakest of the outcasts of Poker Flat." (lines 304–305)

5. **Examine the Main Character** Bret Harte was known for portraying outcast characters with hearts of gold. How does John Oakhurst fit this formula of the character with contradictory traits? Use a chart to explore this question.

Outcast Traits	Virtuous Traits

6. **Interpret Author's Perspective** Personal experience and historical context influence the characters and conflicts that a writer chooses to depict. Based on events in this story and their outcome, how would you describe Harte's opinion of the following?

   - John Oakhurst
   - society in the Old West
   - human nature
   - the other outcasts
   - the young couple

7. **Analyze Theme** In your opinion, what message does this story convey?

8. **Evaluate Use of Regionalism** The goal of regionalists was to capture life at a particular time in history. In your opinion, how well did Harte convey the region, the people, and the times in "The Outcasts of Poker Flat"? Cite evidence to support your view.

Literary Criticism

9. **Critical Interpretations** Mark Twain said that it was Bret Harte who "trimmed and schooled me patiently until he changed me from an awkward utterer of coarse grotesqueness to a writer of paragraphs and chapters." Harte also influenced Ambrose Bierce and Rudyard Kipling. Why do you think Harte might have had a strong impact on so many writers?

Vocabulary in Context

WORD LIST

amicable

anathema

equanimity

expatriated

jocular

maudlin

pariah

prescience

querulous

. vituperative

VOCABULARY PRACTICE

Show you understand the vocabulary words by answering these questions.

1. If I handled a situation with **equanimity,** would I be upset about it or calm?
2. Which could be considered **maudlin,** a stern lecture or a mushy love story?
3. Would a **querulous** person be more likely to enjoy a party or find fault with it?
4. If I am **expatriated,** am I living in exile or returning to my own country?
5. Is a party host or a prosecuting lawyer more likely to be **amicable?**
6. Is a **pariah** shunned or welcomed into gatherings?
7. If a person utters an **anathema,** is he or she expressing anger or compassion?
8. Who is more likely to be **jocular,** a runner or a comedian?
9. Does someone with **prescience** predict future events or excel in chemistry?
10. Would a **vituperative** tutor encourage her students or scold them?

VOCABULARY IN WRITING

In your opinion, which character in this story proves to be most admirable? Identify the character and defend your ideas, using events in the story. Include at least three vocabulary words. You might start this way.

> **EXAMPLE SENTENCE**
>
> *Though hard and **querulous**, Mother Shipton ultimately proved to have a better heart than any of the others.*

VOCABULARY STRATEGY: THE LATIN ROOT *equ*

The vocabulary word *equanimity* contains the Latin root *equ*, which means "even," "just," or "equal." This root, which is occasionally spelled *iqu*, is found in a number of English words. In its prefix form *equi*, it is sometimes combined with existing words to form new words, as in *equiprobable*. To understand words with *equ*, use context clues as well as your knowledge of the meaning of the root.

PRACTICE Apply what you know about *equ*, *equi*, and other word parts to help you understand the words in the web. Then choose the word that best completes each sentence. If necessary, consult a dictionary.

1. If you _____, it may be said that you are talking out of both sides of your mouth.
2. What town is _____ between Chicago and Milwaukee?
3. The accident affected her _____, and she often felt dizzy.
4. Passing a high school _____ test can take the place of actually graduating.

VOCABULARY PRACTICE
For more practice, go to the **Vocabulary Center** at **ClassZone.com.**

Reading-Writing Connection

WRITING PROMPT

WRITE A DESCRIPTION Choose a real or fictional society—one from history, for example, or one crafted entirely from imagination. Write a **three-or four-paragraph description** of the society that reflects the perspective of one who has been sent into **exile.**

SELF-CHECK

A successful description will describe . . .

- the society's institutions
- the interactions of people
- the society's buildings
- the society's holidays

GRAMMAR AND STYLE

ADD DESCRIPTIVE DETAILS Review the **Grammar and Style** note on page 679. Harte uses **personification**—the attribution of human qualities to objects or ideas—to enliven his descriptions of inanimate objects. Here is an example from the story:

> *The third day came, and the sun, looking through the white-curtained valley, saw the outcasts divide their slowly decreasing store of provisions for the morning meal.* (lines 217–219)

Harte's use of the highlighted **participial phrase** and **verb** creates an ethereal image of the sun "watching" the outcasts.

PRACTICE Rewrite each of the following sentences to include personification.

EXAMPLE

We could see the town at the top of the mountain but couldn't see most of its buildings.

The town seemed to turn its back on us, hiding its buildings from our view down in the valley.

---

1. The mountain was solid rock, very steep, and very tall.

2. Lights were shining in some of the windows.

3. Snow began to fall, making it harder to see the town way above us.

WRITING TOOLS
For prewriting, revision, and editing tools, visit the **Writing Center** at **ClassZone.com.**

from Lake Wobegon Days

GARRISON KEILLOR

BACKGROUND Garrison Keillor has been classed with such great American humorists as Ring Lardner, James Thurber, and Mark Twain. A Minnesota native, he began his career in radio. He made a name for himself with his weekly radio variety show, *A Prairie Home Companion,* which began in 1974 and, after one six-year hiatus, continued to run into the 21st century. Among the show's most beloved features has been Keillor's weekly monologue in which he delivers the news from Lake Wobegon, a fictionalized version of his hometown in Minnesota. *Lake Wobegon Days* is a novel based on this small town in America's heartland and its earnest, hard-working inhabitants.

People who visit Lake Wobegon come to see somebody, otherwise they missed the turn on the highway and are lost. *Ausländers,* the Germans call them. They don't come for Toast 'n Jelly Days, or the Germans' quadrennial Gesuffa Days, or Krazy Daze, or the Feast Day of St. Francis, or the three-day Mist County Fair with its exciting Death Leap from the top of the grandstand to the arms of the haystack for only ten cents. What's special about here isn't special enough to draw a major crowd, though Flag Day—you could drive a long way on June 14 to find another like it.

    Flag Day, as we know it, was the idea of Herman Hochstetter, Rollie's dad, who ran the dry goods store and ran Armistice Day, the Fourth of July, and Flag Day. For the
10 Fourth, he organized a double-loop parade around the block which allowed people to take turns marching and watching. On Armistice Day, everyone stepped outside at 11 A.M and stood in silence for two minutes as Our Lady's bell tolled eleven times.

Flag Day was his favorite. For a modest price, he would install a bracket on your house to hold a pole to hang your flag on, or he would drill a hole in the sidewalk in the front of your store with his drill gun powered by a .22 shell. *Bam!* And in went the flag. On patriotic days, flags flew all over; there were flags on the tall poles, flags on the short, flags in the brackets on the pillars and the porches, and if you were flagless you could expect to hear from Herman. His hairy arm around your shoulder, his poochlike face close to yours, he would say how proud he was
20 that so many people were proud of their country, leaving you to see the obvious, that you were a gap in the ranks.

In June 1944, the day after D-Day, a salesman from Fisher Hat called on Herman and offered a good deal on red and blue baseball caps. "Do you have white also?" Herman asked. The salesman thought that white caps could be had for the same wonderful price. Herman ordered two hundred red, two hundred white, and one hundred blue. By the end of the year, he still had four hundred and eighty-six caps. The inspiration of the Living Flag was born from that overstock.

On June 14, 1945, a month after V-E Day, a good crowd assembled in front of the Central Building in response to Herman's ad in the paper:

30   Honor "AMERICA" June 14 AT 4 P.M. Be proud
              of "Our Land & People". Be part of the "LIVING
              FLAG". Don't let it be said that Lake Wobegon was
              "Too Busy". Be on time. 4 P.M. "Sharp".

His wife Louise handed out the caps, and Herman stood on a stepladder and told people where to stand. He lined up the reds and whites into stripes, then got the blues into their square. Mr. Hanson climbed up on the roof of the Central Building and took a photograph, they sang the national anthem, and then the Living Flag dispersed. The photograph appeared in the paper the next week. Herman kept the caps.
40   In the flush of victory, people were happy to do as told and stand in place, but in 1946 and 1947, dissension cropped up in the ranks: people complained about the heat and about Herman—what gave *him* the idea he could order *them* around? "People! Please! I need your attention! You blue people, keep your hats on! Please! Stripe No. 4, you're sagging! You reds, you're up here! We got too many white people, we need more red ones! Let's do this without talking, people! I can't get you straight if you keep moving around! Some of you are not paying attention! Everybody shut up! Please!"

One cause of resentment was the fact that none of them got to see the Flag they were in; the picture in the paper was black and white. Only Herman and Mr. Hanson
50 got to see the real Flag, and some boys too short to be needed down below. People wanted a chance to go up to the roof and witness the spectacle for themselves.

"How can you go up there if you're supposed to be down here?" Herman said. "You go up there to look, you got nothing to look at. Isn't it enough that you're doing your part?"

On Flag Day, 1949, just as Herman said, "That's it! Hold it now!" one of the reds made a break for it—dashed up four flights of stairs to the roof and leaned over and had a long look. Even with the hole he left behind, it was a magnificent sight. The

Living Flag filled the street below. A perfect Flag! The reds so brilliant! He couldn't take his eyes off it. "Get down here! We need a picture!" Herman yelled up to him.
60 "How does it look?" people yelled up to him. "Unbelievable! I can't describe it!" he said.

So then everyone had to have a look. "No!" Herman said, but they took a vote and it was unanimous. One by one, members of the Living Flag went up to the roof and admired it. It *was* marvelous! It brought tears to the eyes, it made one reflect on this great country and on Lake Wobegon's place in it. One wanted to stand up there all afternoon and just drink it in. So, as the first hour passed, and only forty of the five hundred had been to the top, the others got more and more restless. "Hurry up! Quit dawdling! *You've* seen it! Get down here and give someone else a chance!" Herman sent people up in groups of four, and then ten, but after two hours, the Living Flag
70 became the Sitting Flag and then began to erode, as the members who had had a look thought about heading home to supper, which infuriated the ones who hadn't. "Ten more minutes!" Herman cried, but ten minutes became twenty and thirty, and people snuck off and the Flag that remained for the last viewer was a Flag shot through by cannon fire.

In 1950, the Sons of Knute took over Flag Day. Herman gave them the boxes of caps. Since then, the Knutes have achieved several good Flags, though most years the attendance was poor. You need at least four hundred to make a good one. Some years the Knutes made a "no-look" rule, other years they held a lottery. One year they experimented with a large mirror held by two men over the edge of the roof, but
80 when people leaned back and looked up, the Flag disappeared, of course. ❧

Literary Analysis

1. **Analyze Local Color** One of the primary characteristics of regional writing is **local color,** or writing that portrays the customs, character types, mannerisms, and speech of a region. What elements of local color do you find in this excerpt? Citing evidence from the text, characterize the residents of small-town Minnesota as portrayed by Keillor.

2. **Compare Texts** As Twain does in the excerpt from his *Autobiography* and in "The Notorious Jumping Frog of Calaveras County," Keillor depicts a community event in a small town. Which author takes a more mocking **tone,** and which is gentler? In either case, do you think that one of the authors is writing with a greater degree of affection for the people portrayed? Explain, citing evidence from the texts.

A Wagner Matinee

Short Story by Willa Cather

Willa Cather
1873–1947

Willa Cather believed that "the most basic material a writer works with is acquired before the age of 15." Indeed, it was the American West of Cather's early years that inspired the majority of her literary successes.

The Power of Place At age nine, Virginia-born Willa Cather moved to Nebraska with her family. The prairie challenged Cather—and almost all other settlers—with its "erasure of personality" and made her feel that she "would go under." But after a difficult transition, Cather grew to love the harsh prairie and to admire the immigrants—especially women—who struggled daily against an unforgiving climate. Though they lived by hard physical labor, many of these immigrants were educated people. They introduced Cather to French and German literature, also teaching her Latin and Greek. Nebraska and Cather's childhood neighbors —whose stories "went round and round in [her] head"— dramatically influenced her writing.

Seeing the World After college, where she did some writing, Cather went back east and worked as a journalist, teacher, and magazine editor. During this time, she met her best friend, Isabelle McClung, who sparked in her a lifelong interest in music, which can be seen in "A Wagner Matinee." She also formed lifelong relationships with her companion Edith Lewis and writer Sarah Orne Jewett. Cather also saw something of the world on several trips to France and then to the American Southwest.

Developing a Voice Around 1906, Cather moved to New York City and began a full-time writing career. Though she never lived in Nebraska again, the prairie was never far from her work. Many of her 12 novels and 58 stories had prairie settings or immigrant characters, showing Cather's respect for the grit needed to endure everyday life. Some of these characters were directly drawn from real people Cather had known, such as childhood friend Annie (Anna) who formed the basis of the main character in her novel *My Ántonia*.

Choices Willa Cather chose an artist's life rather than the everyday family life she so closely observed in her Nebraska neighbors. She once said to a friend that "nothing mattered to her but writing books, and living the kind of life that makes it possible to write them." Willa Cather lived that life until her death in 1947.

● LITERARY ANALYSIS: SETTING

In Willa Cather's fiction, the development of the plot and characters is heavily influenced by the **setting,** or the time and place in which the story occurs. In "A Wagner Matinee," the narrator's aunt has moved from Boston to the Nebraska frontier; these places determine the kind of person she becomes. Setting can also serve as a **symbol.** As you read, note the details of each location and what they seem to represent.

● READING SKILL: DRAW CONCLUSIONS ABOUT CHARACTER

Understanding a character in a story is like getting to know a real person. You **draw conclusions,** or make reasonable judgments, about the person by combining the impressions you have already formed with new facts you discover. To become better acquainted with Aunt Georgiana, the main character in "A Wagner Matinee," look closely at the details as you read the story. Create a chart like the one shown, using it to record details and **make inferences** about Aunt Georgiana. At the end of the story, you will use these specific inferences to draw larger conclusions about her character.

Observations About . . .	What They Reveal
physical appearance: • •	
major decision: • •	
actions and reactions: • •	

▲ VOCABULARY IN CONTEXT

Cather uses the listed words to develop setting and character. Choose a word from the list to complete each phrase.

WORD LIST	callow	overture	tentatively
	excruciatingly	somnambulant	veritable
	myriad	sordid	

1. _____ employees with more bravado than experience
2. _____ tasks to complete—almost too many to count
3. living in _____, disgusting conditions
4. agreed _____ to take on the additional work

Explore the Key Idea

Does it matter where we **LIVE?**

KEY IDEA Imagine life on an island with only a few dozen other people. How would it shape your social life? your work habits? your relationship to nature? Now think about life in a big city. How would these things be different? The **places** we live really shape our personality and values.

DISCUSS As a class, choose two very different places and discuss the lifestyles of the people who live there. Then consider how life in each place would shape the personalities of its inhabitants.

A Wagner Matinee

Willa Cather

BACKGROUND "A Wagner Matinee" takes place in Nebraska and Boston around 1900. At the time, Bostonians could attend concerts of works by European composers such as Richard Wagner (väg′nər). Americans who moved west, such as Willa Cather's family and Aunt Georgiana in this story, left such worldly pleasures behind. Instead, the settlers endured long hours of strenuous labor, and natural disasters such as drought, flood, and prairie fires.

ANALYZE VISUALS
Look at the painting on page 695. What might souvenirs like this signify to a settler who left the city for life on the prairie? Explain.

I received one morning a letter, written in pale ink on glassy, blue-lined note-paper, and bearing the postmark of a little Nebraska village. This communication, worn and rubbed, looking as though it had been carried for some days in a coat pocket that was none too clean, was from my Uncle Howard and informed me that his wife had been left a small legacy by a bachelor relative who had recently died, and that it would be necessary for her to go to Boston to attend to the settling of the estate. He requested me to meet her at the station and render her whatever services might be necessary. On examining the date indicated as that of her arrival, I found it no later than tomorrow. He had characteristically delayed writing until, had I been away from home for a day, I must have missed the good woman altogether. Ⓐ

The name of my Aunt Georgiana called up not alone her own figure, at once pathetic and grotesque, but opened before my feet a gulf of recollection so wide and deep, that, as the letter dropped from my hand, I felt suddenly a stranger to all the present conditions of my existence, wholly ill at ease and out of place amid the familiar surroundings of my study. I became, in short, the gangling farmer-boy

Ⓐ **SETTING**
What does the **description** of the letter tell you about the place from which it was sent? What does it suggest about the place it is sent to? Give details to support your answer.

Old Souvenirs (about 1881–1901), John F. Peto. Bequest of Oliver Burr Jennings, 1968 (68.205.3). Metropolitan Museum of Art, New York.

my aunt had known, scourged with chilblains[1] and bashfulness, my hands cracked
and sore from the corn husking. I felt the knuckles of my thumb **tentatively,** as
though they were raw again. I sat again before her parlor organ, fumbling the
20 scales with my stiff, red hands, while she, beside me, made canvas mittens for the
huskers.[2]

The next morning, after preparing my landlady somewhat, I set out for the
station. When the train arrived I had some difficulty in finding my aunt. She was
the last of the passengers to alight, and it was not until I got her into the carriage
that she seemed really to recognize me. She had come all the way in a day coach;
her linen duster[3] had become black with soot and her black bonnet grey with dust
during the journey. When we arrived at my boarding-house the landlady put her
to bed at once and I did not see her again until the next morning.

Whatever shock Mrs. Springer experienced at my aunt's appearance, she
30 considerately concealed. As for myself, I saw my aunt's misshapen figure with
that feeling of awe and respect with which we behold explorers who have left
their ears and fingers north of Franz-Josef-Land, or their health somewhere along
the Upper Congo.[4] My Aunt Georgiana had been a music teacher at the Boston
Conservatory, somewhere back in the latter sixties. One summer, while visiting
in the little village among the Green Mountains[5] where her ancestors had dwelt

tentatively
(tĕn′tə-tĭv-lē) *adv.* in a
hesitant or uncertain
manner

---

1. **scourged with chilblains:** tormented with painful swelling or sores on the hands or feet caused by
   exposure to the cold.
2. **huskers:** farm workers who remove cornhusks by hand.
3. **duster:** a long, lightweight overgarment to protect clothing from dust
4. **Franz-Josef-Land . . . Upper Congo:** Franz-Josef-Land is a group of small, mostly ice-covered islands
   in the Arctic Ocean, north of Russia. The Upper Congo, in central Africa, is now called the Zaire River.
5. **Green Mountains:** a mountain range in Vermont.

Family and Their Dugout (1870s), Anonymous. Photo 11″ × 14″. Near McCook, Nebraska. © Nebraska State Historical
Society, Lincoln, Nebraska.

for generations, she had kindled the **callow** fancy of the most idle and shiftless of all the village lads, and had conceived for this Howard Carpenter one of those extravagant passions which a handsome country boy of twenty-one sometimes inspires in an angular, spectacled woman of thirty. When she returned to her
40 duties in Boston, Howard followed her, and the upshot of this inexplicable infatuation was that she eloped with him, eluding the reproaches of her family and the criticisms of her friends by going with him to the Nebraska frontier. Carpenter, who, of course, had no money, had taken a homestead in Red Willow County,[6] fifty miles from the railroad. There they had measured off their quarter section themselves by driving across the prairie in a wagon, to the wheel of which they had tied a red cotton handkerchief, and counting off its revolutions. They built a dugout in the red hillside, one of those cave dwellings whose inmates so often reverted to primitive conditions. Their water they got from the lagoons where the buffalo drank, and their slender stock of provisions was always at the
50 mercy of bands of roving Indians. For thirty years my aunt had not been further than fifty miles from the homestead. **B**

But Mrs. Springer knew nothing of all this, and must have been considerably shocked at what was left of my kinswoman. Beneath the soiled linen duster which, on her arrival, was the most conspicuous feature of her costume, she wore a black stuff[7] dress, whose ornamentation showed that she had surrendered herself unquestioningly into the hands of a country dressmaker. My poor aunt's figure, however, would have presented astonishing difficulties to any dressmaker. Originally stooped, her shoulders were now almost bent together over her sunken chest. She wore no stays, and her gown, which trailed unevenly behind, rose in a sort
60 of peak over her abdomen. She wore ill-fitting false teeth, and her skin was as yellow as a Mongolian's from constant exposure to a pitiless wind and to the alkaline water which hardens the most transparent cuticle into a sort of flexible leather. **C**

I owed to this woman most of the good that ever came my way in my boyhood, and had a reverential affection for her. During the years when I was riding herd for my uncle, my aunt, after cooking the three meals—the first of which was ready at six o'clock in the morning—and putting the six children to bed, would often stand until midnight at her ironing-board, with me at the kitchen table beside her, hearing me recite Latin declensions and conjugations,[8] gently shaking me when my drowsy head sank down over a page of irregular verbs. It was to her, at her ironing
70 or mending, that I read my first Shakespeare, and her old text-book on mythology was the first that ever came into my empty hands. She taught me my scales and exercises, too—on the little parlor organ, which her husband had bought her after fifteen years, during which she had not so much as seen any instrument, but an accordion that belonged to one of the Norwegian farmhands. She would sit beside me by the hour, darning and counting while I struggled with the "Joyous Farmer,"[9] but she seldom talked to me about music, and I understood why. She was a pious

callow (kăl′ō) *adj.* lacking adult experience; immature

B SETTING
Consider the **description** of the homestead in lines 43–51. How do you think life in such a place might affect a woman with Aunt Georgiana's background?

C DRAW CONCLUSIONS
Reread lines 52–62. What can you **infer** about Aunt Georgiana based upon her appearance?

---

6. **Red Willow County:** county in southwestern Nebraska, bordering on Kansas.

7. **stuff:** a woolen material.

8. **Latin declensions and conjugations:** forms of Latin nouns and verbs representing different cases and tenses.

9. **"Joyous Farmer":** one of a series of musical pieces for children by German composer Robert Schumann.

woman; she had the consolations of religion and, to her at least, her martyrdom was not wholly **sordid.** Once when I had been doggedly beating out some easy passages from an old score of *Euryanthe*[10] I had found among her music books, she came up
80 to me and, putting her hands over my eyes, gently drew my head back upon her shoulder, saying tremulously, "Don't love it so well, Clark, or it may be taken from you. Oh! dear boy, pray that whatever your sacrifice may be, it be not that." **D**

When my aunt appeared on the morning after her arrival, she was still in a semi-**somnambulant** state. She seemed not to realize that she was in the city where she had spent her youth, the place longed for hungrily half a lifetime. She had been so wretchedly train-sick throughout the journey that she had no recollection of anything but her discomfort, and, to all intents and purposes, there were but a few hours of nightmare between the farm in Red Willow County and my study on Newbury Street. I had planned a little pleasure for her that
90 afternoon, to repay her for some of the glorious moments she had given me when we used to milk together in the straw-thatched cowshed and she, because I was more than usually tired, or because her husband had spoken sharply to me, would tell me of the splendid performance of the *Huguenots*[11] she had seen in Paris, in her youth. At two o'clock the Symphony Orchestra was to give a Wagner program, and I intended to take my aunt; though, as I conversed with her, I grew doubtful about her enjoyment of it. Indeed, for her own sake, I could only wish her taste for such things quite dead, and the long struggle mercifully ended at last. I suggested our visiting the Conservatory and the Common[12] before lunch, but she seemed altogether too timid to wish to venture out. She questioned me
100 absently about various changes in the city, but she was chiefly concerned that she had forgotten to leave instructions about feeding half-skimmed milk to a certain weakling calf, "old Maggie's calf, you know, Clark," she explained, evidently having forgotten how long I had been away. She was further troubled because she had neglected to tell her daughter about the freshly-opened kit of mackerel in the cellar, which would spoil if it were not used directly.

I asked her whether she had ever heard any of the Wagnerian operas,[13] and found that she had not, though she was perfectly familiar with their respective situations, and had once possessed the piano score of *The Flying Dutchman.* I began to think it would have been best to get her back to Red Willow County
110 without waking her, and regretted having suggested the concert.

From the time we entered the concert hall, however, she was a trifle less passive and inert, and for the first time seemed to perceive her surroundings. I had felt some trepidation lest she might become aware of the absurdities of her attire, or might experience some painful embarrassment at stepping suddenly into the world to which she had been dead for a quarter of a century. But, again, I found how superficially I

sordid (sôr'dĭd) *adj.* wretched; dirty; morally degraded

D DRAW CONCLUSIONS
Reread lines 63–82. What does Aunt Georgiana's treatment of her nephew reveal about her?

somnambulant (sŏm-năm'byə-lənt') *adj.* sleepwalking

---

10. *Euryanthe* (yŏŏr'ē-än'thē): an opera by German composer Carl Maria von Weber.

11. *Huguenots* (hyŏŏ'gə-nŏts'): an opera by German composer Giacomo Meyerbeer.

12. **the Common:** Boston Common, a public park.

13. **Wagnerian operas:** The orchestra will play selections from several operas composed by Wagner, including *The Flying Dutchman, Tannhäuser, Tristan and Isolde,* and a cycle of four operas called *The Ring of the Nibelung.*

698 UNIT 4: REGIONALISM AND NATURALISM

had judged her. She sat looking about her with eyes as impersonal, almost as stony, as those with which the granite Rameses[14] in a museum watches the froth and fret that ebbs and flows[15] about his pedestal—separated from it by the lonely stretch of centuries. I have seen this same aloofness in old miners who drift into the Brown
120 hotel at Denver, their pockets full of bullion,[16] their linen soiled, their haggard faces unshaven; standing in the thronged corridors as solitary as though they were still in a frozen camp on the Yukon, conscious that certain experiences have isolated them from their fellows by a gulf no haberdasher[17] could bridge.

We sat at the extreme left of the first balcony, facing the arc of our own and the balcony above us, **veritable** hanging gardens, brilliant as tulip beds. The matinée audience was made up chiefly of women. One lost the contour of faces and figures, indeed any effect of line whatever, and there was only the color of bodices past counting, the shimmer of fabrics soft and firm, silky and sheer; red, mauve, pink, blue, lilac, purple, ecru, rose, yellow, cream, and white, all the colors that an
130 impressionist[18] finds in a sunlit landscape, with here and there the dead shadow of a frock coat. My Aunt Georgiana regarded them as though they had been so many daubs of tube-paint on a palette.

When the musicians came out and took their places, she gave a little stir of anticipation and looked with quickening interest down over the rail at that invariable grouping, perhaps the first wholly familiar thing that had greeted her eye since she had left old Maggie and her weakling calf. I could feel how all those details sank into her soul, for I had not forgotten how they had sunk into mine when I came fresh from ploughing forever and forever between green aisles of corn, where, as in a treadmill, one might walk from daybreak to dusk without
140 perceiving a shadow of change. The clean profiles of the musicians, the gloss of their linen, the dull black of their coats, the beloved shapes of the instruments, the patches of yellow light thrown by the green shaded lamps on the smooth, varnished bellies of the 'cellos and the bass viols in the rear, the restless, wind-tossed forest of fiddle necks and bows—I recalled how, in the first orchestra I had ever heard, those long bow strokes seemed to draw the heart out of me, as a conjurer's stick reels out yards of paper ribbon from a hat. **E**

The first number was the *Tannhauser* **overture.** When the horns drew out the first strain of the Pilgrim's chorus, my Aunt Georgiana clutched my coat sleeve. Then it was I first realized that for her this broke a silence of thirty years; the
150 inconceivable silence of the plains. With the battle between the two motives, with the frenzy of the Venusberg theme and its ripping of strings, there came to me an overwhelming sense of the waste and wear we are so powerless to combat;

veritable (vĕr´ĭ-tə-bəl) *adj.* true; not unreal or imaginary

E SETTING
Reread lines 133–146. How does Aunt Georgiana respond to the setting of the Boston concert hall?

overture (ō´vər-chŏŏr´) *n.* the orchestral introduction to a musical dramatic work

---

14. **Rameses** (răm´ĭ-sēz´): one of the ancient kings of Egypt of that name.

15. **froth . . . flows:** happiness and sadness that come and go.

16. **bullion:** gold.

17. **haberdasher:** a dealer in men's clothing and accessories.

18. **impressionist:** a follower of a movement in French painting that emphasized the play of light and color.

and I saw again the tall, naked house on the prairie, black and grim as a wooden fortress; the black pond where I had learned to swim, its margin pitted with sun-dried cattle tracks; the rain-gullied clay banks about the naked house, the four dwarf ash seedlings where the dish-cloths were always hung to dry before the kitchen door. The world there was the flat world of the ancients; to the east, a cornfield that stretched to daybreak; to the west, a corral that reached to sunset; between, the conquests of peace, dearer bought than those of war.

160   The overture closed, my aunt released my coat sleeve, but she said nothing. She sat staring at the orchestra through a dullness of thirty years, through the films made little by little by each of the three hundred and sixty-five days in every one of them. What, I wondered, did she get from it? She had been a good pianist in her day I knew, and her musical education had been broader than that of most music teachers of a quarter of a century ago. She had often told me of Mozart's operas and Meyerbeer's, and I could remember hearing her sing, years ago, certain melodies of Verdi's. When I had fallen ill with a fever in her house she used to sit by my cot in the evening—when the cool, night wind blew in through the faded mosquito netting tacked over the window and I lay watching a certain bright
170 star that burned red above the cornfield—and sing "Home to our mountains, O, let us return!" in a way fit to break the heart of a Vermont boy near dead of homesickness already.

I watched her closely through the prelude to *Tristan and Isolde,* trying vainly to conjecture what that seething turmoil of strings and winds might mean to her, but she sat mutely staring at the violin bows that drove obliquely downward, like the pelting streaks of rain in a summer shower. Had this music any message for her? Had she enough left to at all comprehend this power which had kindled the world since she had left it? I was in a fever of curiosity, but Aunt Georgiana sat silent upon her peak in Darien.[19] She preserved this utter immobility throughout
180 the number from *The Flying Dutchman,* though her fingers worked mechanically upon her black dress, as though, of themselves, they were recalling the piano score they had once played. Poor old hands! They had been stretched and twisted into mere tentacles to hold and lift and knead with; the palms unduly swollen, the fingers bent and knotted—on one of them a thin, worn band that had once been a wedding ring. As I pressed and gently quieted one of those groping hands, I remembered with quivering eyelids their services for me in other days.

Soon after the tenor began the "Prize Song," I heard a quick drawn breath and turned to my aunt. Her eyes were closed, but the tears were glistening on her cheeks, and I think, in a moment more, they were in my eyes as well. It never
190 really died, then—the soul that can suffer so **excruciatingly** and so interminably; it withers to the outward eye only; like that strange moss which can lie on a dusty shelf half a century and yet, if placed in water, grows green again. She wept so throughout the development and elaboration of the melody. **F**

excruciatingly
(ĭk-skrōō'shē-ā'tĭng-lē)
adv. in a way that causes great pain or distress

F DRAW CONCLUSIONS
Reread lines 187–193. What **inferences** can you make about Aunt Georgiana's feeling for music, based upon her reaction to it?

---

19. **peak in Darien:** a mountain in what is now Panama, referred to in English poet John Keats's "On First Looking into Chapman's Homer" as a place where the Pacific was contemplated with silence and awe by Spanish explorers.

During the intermission before the second half of the concert, I questioned my aunt and found that the "Prize Song" was not new to her. Some years before there had drifted to the farm in Red Willow County a young German, a tramp cow puncher, who had sung the chorus at Bayreuth,[20] when he was a boy, along with the other peasant boys and girls. Of a Sunday morning he used to sit on his gingham-sheeted bed in the hands' bedroom which opened off the kitchen, cleaning the leather of his boots and saddle, singing the "Prize Song," while my aunt went about her work in the kitchen. She had hovered about him until she had prevailed upon him to join the country church, though his sole fitness for this step, in so far as I could gather, lay in his boyish face and his possession of this divine melody. Shortly afterward he had gone to town on the Fourth of July, been drunk for several days, lost his money at a faro table, ridden a saddled Texas steer on a bet, and disappeared with a fractured collar-bone. All this my aunt told me huskily, wanderingly, as though she were talking in the weak lapses of illness. **G**

G **DRAW CONCLUSIONS**
Reread lines 194–207. Explain Aunt Georgiana's poignant association with the "Prize Song." Why do you think it causes her to weep?

20. **Bayreuth** (bī-roit'): a town in the Bavarian region of Germany where annual Wagner music festivals are held.

Two on the Aisle (1927), Edward Hopper © Francis G. Mayer/Corbis. © Heirs of Josephine N. Hopper, licensed by the Whitney Museum of American Art.

"Well, we have come to better things than the old *Trovatore*[21] at any rate, Aunt Georgie?" I queried, with a well meant effort at jocularity.

210 Her lip quivered and she hastily put her handkerchief up to her mouth. From behind it she murmured, "And you have been hearing this ever since you left me, Clark?" Her question was the gentlest and saddest of reproaches.

The second half of the program consisted of four numbers from the *Ring*, and closed with Siegfried's funeral march. My aunt wept quietly, but almost continuously, as a shallow vessel overflows in a rainstorm. From time to time her dim eyes looked up at the lights which studded the ceiling, burning softly under their dull glass globes; doubtless they were stars in truth to her. I was still perplexed as to what measure of musical comprehension was left to her, she who had heard nothing but the singing of Gospel Hymns at Methodist services in the
220 square frame school-house on Section Thirteen for so many years. I was wholly unable to gauge how much of it had been dissolved in soapsuds, or worked into bread, or milked into the bottom of a pail. **H**

The deluge of sound poured on and on; I never knew what she found in the shining current of it; I never knew how far it bore her, or past what happy islands. From the trembling of her face I could well believe that before the last numbers she had been carried out where the **myriad** graves are, into the grey, nameless burying grounds of the sea; or into some world of death vaster yet, where, from the beginning of the world, hope has lain down with hope and dream with dream and, renouncing, slept.

230 The concert was over; the people filed out of the hall chattering and laughing, glad to relax and find the living level again, but my kinswoman made no effort to rise. The harpist slipped its green felt cover over his instrument; the flute-players shook the water from their mouthpieces; the men of the orchestra went out one by one, leaving the stage to the chairs and music stands, empty as a winter cornfield.

I spoke to my aunt. She burst into tears and sobbed pleadingly. "I don't want to go, Clark, I don't want to go!"

I understood. For her, just outside the door of the concert hall, lay the black pond with the cattle-tracked bluffs; the tall, unpainted house, with weather-curled boards;
240 naked as a tower, the crook-backed ash seedlings where the dish-cloths hung to dry; the gaunt, molting turkeys picking up refuse about the kitchen door. ❧

H SETTING
Reread lines 220–222. What does this **metaphor** suggest about how a place might affect one's appreciation of music?

myriad (mîr′ē-əd) *adj.* exceedingly numerous

---

21. **Trovatore** (trō′vä-tôr′ĕ): *Il Trovatore* is an opera by the Italian composer Giuseppe Verdi.

Comprehension

1. **Recall** Why does Aunt Georgiana travel to Boston?

2. **Recall** Why does Clark take his aunt to the concert?

3. **Summarize** How do Clark and his aunt respond to the concert?

Literary Analysis

4. **Predict Events** In your opinion, will Aunt Georgiana return to Nebraska, or will she stay in Boston? Give evidence to support your answer.

5. **Make Inferences** Aunt Georgiana warns Clark, "Don't love it so well, Clark, or it may be taken from you." What does this suggest about the role of music in her own life?

6. **Draw Conclusions About Character** Look back at the **inferences** you recorded in your chart as you read. Judging from the choices that Aunt Georgiana has made in her life, what conclusions can you draw about her character? What emotions does she seem to experience, and how does she handle them?

7. **Contrast Settings** The two settings in this story—the Nebraska prairie and the Boston concert hall—are both significant for Aunt Georgiana. What do they **symbolize?** Support your answer with details from the story.

8. **Make Judgments** How might Aunt Georgiana be different if she had stayed in Boston? Use examples from the story and your views about the importance of **place** to support your answer.

Literary Criticism

9. **Biographical Context** "A Wagner Matinee" created a stir when it appeared in 1904. Cather's family objected to the fictional portrait of her real-life aunt Franc. One of her friends remarked: "The stranger to this state will associate Nebraska with the aunt's wretched figure, her ill-fitting false teeth, her skin yellowed by the weather." Do you agree? Examine the **imagery** and **figurative language** used to describe the people and scenes of Nebraska. Do you think Cather's Nebraska relatives were justified in taking offense? Cite evidence from the story to support your answer.

Vocabulary in Context

WORD LIST

callow
excruciatingly
myriad
overture
somnambulant
sordid
tentatively
veritable

VOCABULARY PRACTICE

Choose the word from the list that best completes each sentence.

1. Though uncertain whether Aunt Georgiana would enjoy the concert, Clark _____ made plans to go.
2. Earlier, his aunt had seemed dazed, walking around in an almost _____ state.
3. Her life on the farm, while not _____, was certainly harsh and difficult.
4. She was worn down from the _____ jobs she performed from dawn to dusk.
5. But Aunt Georgiana was not a(n) _____ young girl with no experience or culture.
6. She was a(n) _____ treasure chest of musical knowledge.
7. When the _____ was played, she became a new woman.
8. Yet she found it _____ difficult to listen to the beautiful music.

VOCABULARY IN WRITING

Using two or more vocabulary words, assume the role of Aunt Georgiana and describe your experience in Boston in a few paragraphs. Here is a sample beginning.

> **EXAMPLE SENTENCE**
>
> It had been years since I'd been in Boston, and I was unprepared for its **myriad** sights and sounds.

VOCABULARY STRATEGY: MUSIC TERMINOLOGY

The world of classical music employs its own specialized vocabulary to help describe the people, the musical forms, and the expressive qualities it comprises. The vocabulary word *overture,* for example, refers in music to the introductory piece at the beginning of an opera or other musical drama. Becoming familiar with musical terminology can not only enhance your vocabulary; it can also increase both your understanding of classical music and your cultural literacy in general.

PRACTICE Match each term in the lefthand column with its definition in the righthand column. Research the origin of each word to see which words, as they are used today, have retained their Italian spelling.

1. concerto
2. contralto
3. aria
4. diva
5. andante
6. tenor

a. an elaborate melody in an opera, sung by one person
b. a moderately slow tempo, or pace
c. a man who sings with a higher voice
d. a woman who sings with a lower voice
e. a leading woman soloist in an opera company
f. a piece in which a soloist performs with an orchestra

VOCABULARY PRACTICE
For more practice, go to the **Vocabulary Center** at **ClassZone.com.**

Indiana author Edward Eggleston made this claim in 1892.

"It used to be a matter of no little jealousy to us, I remember, that the manners, customs, thoughts and feelings of New England country people filled so large a place in books, while our life, not less interesting, not less romantic, and certainly not less filled with humorous and grotesque material, had no place in literature. It was as though we were shut out of good society."

By the end of the 19th century, however, virtually every region of the country—from the cities of the Northeast, to the mining camps of California, to the Southern bayou, to the northern plains—had its own local colorist capturing the region's distinctive features in writing. These local color writers portrayed the dialects, dress, mannerisms, customs, character types, and landscapes of their regions with an eye for accurate detail.

Writing to Synthesize

Make a chart like the one shown, listing each of the selections you've read in this section (pages 634–704). On your chart, note what you've learned about the way the people in each region speak, the way they dress, their customs, and their landscapes. Then use your chart to write a one-paragraph description of each region you've encountered in your reading.

	How People Speak	How People Dress	Local Customs	Local Landscape
The Autobiography of Mark Twain				

Extension

VIEWING & REPRESENTING
Create a **single-frame cartoon** to represent the region you live in. You may want to focus on the way people speak and dress, or you may prefer to characterize the landscape.

A homesteader's dugout house in Pie Town, New Mexico

American Landscapes

Image Collection on ⊙ *MediaSmart* DVD

Can pictures DEVELOP *new frontiers?*

KEY IDEA Paintings and photographs can have a profound effect on us. They can enlighten us, frighten us, elicit our sympathies, even inspire us. In this lesson, you'll examine the landscape work of two 19th-century artists and discover how paintings and photographs helped to spur **Western expansion.**

Background

Framing New Views In the late 1800s, at a time when writer Mark Twain portrayed a romanticized view of the West, the new medium of photography gained popularity for revealing American life as it really was. For many painters of the day, photography posed a new challenge. While some saw it as displacing traditional forms of representation, others embraced it as a liberating artistic force.

Photography was also having an impact on the mass media. Because people were increasingly interested in facts and in realistic portrayals of events, they turned to the burgeoning newspaper industry and the day's more "realistic" writers. With the portability of cameras, photographers could supply newspapers, magazines, and advertisers with images in a short period of time, exposing viewers to faraway locations.

At the same time, Western expansion was being promoted by the federal government and by land developers from the East and Midwest. Photographic images of the new frontier were frequently used by advertisers and marketers to entice Americans to go West and settle the sparsely populated territory. In 1871, painter Thomas Moran joined forces with photographer William Henry Jackson and embarked on a geological expedition to document Western lands. These two artists found inspiration in surroundings of astounding natural beauty. Examples of their work appear in this lesson.

Media Literacy: Photographs and Paintings

The paintings of Thomas Moran and the photographs of William Henry Jackson were instrumental in convincing Congress to declare Yellowstone, in 1872, the country's first national park. Shown here are a painting by Moran and a photograph by Jackson of a canyon scene. Analyze these images by considering how each artist used certain elements to achieve compelling landscape art.

STRATEGIES FOR ANALYZING PHOTOGRAPHS AND PAINTINGS

Composition is the arrangement of subject elements within an image. Scan each image from top to bottom, side to side, and corner to corner, noting how each artist has arranged the elements in the frame. Ask yourself: Where is the **focal point,** or main focus, of the painting and of the photograph? What section of the image first catches my eye? In both of these images, the focal point is the waterfall.

For painters, **perspective** is a technique that creates the illusion of depth, making objects look three-dimensional. To determine the perspective of an image, try to identify the **horizon line,** the horizontal section that appears to your eye to be at the farthest distance in a landscape. In both of these images, the horizon line appears near the top, where the sky meets the uppermost part of the valley.

Depth of field is the area in front of and behind a focused subject in which the image appears sharp. Photographers achieved this effect by adjusting camera lenses. Notice in the photograph how depth of field creates an impression of distance.

Texture is the surface quality of an image—what the image would feel like if we could touch it. Ask yourself:
• What materials or techniques did the photographer use to create a sense of texture?
• With paintings, where does the paint seem to rise slightly from the canvas?
   In these canyon images, your own knowledge of what is being depicted adds to your interpretation and appreciation of the textures conveyed.

⊙ **MediaSmart** DVD

Paintings by Thomas Moran
- **Selection 1:** "Grand Canyon of the Yellowstone"
- **Selection 4:** "Castle Geyser"

Paintings by William Henry Jackson
- **Selection 2:** "The Grand Canyon of the Yellowstone"
- **Selection 3:** "Castle Geyser"

American Landscape Artists

Look at the full-sized images on the DVD. Examine each image carefully, jotting down your initial impressions. To help you analyze the paintings of Thomas Moran and the photographs of William Henry Jackson in terms of certain design elements, refer to the details on page 707. You can also refer to the Illustrations and Photographs section of the Media Handbook (pages R94–R95) to review the visual art elements of color, shape, line, and texture. Then consider these questions to help you analyze the images.

NOW VIEW

FIRST VIEWING: Comprehension

1. **Identify** In both Grand Canyon images, what elements of nature do you see?

2. **Clarify** Which Grand Canyon image has people in it?

CLOSE VIEWING: Media Literacy

3. **Analyze Composition** In each of the Grand Canyon images, the artist chose to depict the widest possible view. Through this composition, what effect do you think each artist was trying to achieve?

4. **Compare Texture** Consider both Moran paintings. Which appears to have more texture? Explain your choice.

5. **Analyze Perspective** In the color painting "Castle Geyser" by Thomas Moran, find the horizon line. Name whatever objects you can that rise up from this line.

6. **Compare Images** Both the painting and the photograph of the geyser on this page have an otherworldly look and feel. Which image looks more alien to you? Support your response in terms of your view of

   - in the painting, the stark color contrast between the deep blue of the pool and the lighter tone of the sky
   - in the photograph, the placement of the camera and the lens to make the pool seem as large as possible

Write or Discuss

Judge an Image The landscape paintings and photographs of this lesson not only inspired thousands to journey to the West but also inspired the protection of one of America's most striking natural regions. Among these four images, pick one that you think is the most interesting. In a short evaluation, describe what elements it has that make it a fine example of landscape art. Base your criteria on these considerations

- the **composition** and **perspective** in the paintings or the effect of the **depth of field** in the photographs
- the aim of Thomas Moran and William Henry Jackson to capture stunning scenes of natural beauty
- the aspects of the painting or photograph that especially appeal to you (for example, the specific subject matter, use or absence of color, overall mood or feeling)

Produce Your Own Media

MEDIA TOOLS

For help with creating a landscape image, visit the **Media Center** at **ClassZone.com**.

Create Your Personal Landscape Think of a favorite place. How would you represent it visually? Create a landscape image of your choice. It can be a photograph, a painting, a computer-generated image, or a drawing.

HERE'S HOW Decide what landscape you want to capture and which medium you want to use. Here are some things to keep in mind

- Be aware of composition. What you show and don't show in an image defines your vision of the landscape. Is there a dominant element you want to focus on?
- Try to provide some texture to your image regardless of the medium you've chosen.
- Give your work a horizontal landscape orientation. Experiment with giving your image an illusion of depth. For a drawing or painting, determine where to position the lines that will establish the perspective. For a photograph, determine the depth of field by adjusting lenses or camera position.
- No matter what type of image you create, make notes on what your intentions were and how you planned to create it.

Tech Tip

Use a software program to experiment with various effects.

Further Exploration

View More Photographs The equipment the early photographers used was quite unwieldy. Photographers had to carry their big box cameras and heavy film plates to their subjects, so you can imagine the rigors of filming a vast and remote landscape like the Grand Canyon.

Look at the early photographs housed on the DVD or find examples of early photography through your own research, and choose an image that most interests you.

The Open Boat

Short Story by Stephen Crane

Stephen Crane
1871–1900

When Crane's novel *The Red Badge of Courage* was published in 1895, it caused a literary sensation. Critics hailed its unromanticized portrayal of a young soldier's struggles during one battle of the Civil War. As one reviewer exclaimed, "The style is as rough as it is direct. . . . But the original power of the book is great enough to set a new fashion in literature." War veterans, unimpressed by literary fashion, were struck by the graphic depiction of combat. So vivid was the battlefield experience in the novel that they assumed the story was a factual eyewitness account. But the author was only 23 years old at the time and had not yet seen war. Such was the power of Crane's imagination that he was able in his short life to create works of great integrity as well as artistic force.

Living on the Edge Born in Newark, New Jersey, the youngest of 14 children, Stephen Crane came from a family of writers. His father, a Methodist minister, and his mother both wrote religious articles, and two of his brothers were journalists. A stint in military school nourished the teenage Crane's interest in the Civil War, but college life bored him. "Not that I disliked books," he insisted, but that "humanity was a much more interesting study." And study it he did—first as a freelance journalist living in the slums of New York City's Bowery, then as a reporter traveling in Mexico and the American Wild West, and finally as a war correspondent shipping out to hot spots in Cuba and Greece. Twelve years of living on the edge gave Crane material not only for numerous news articles but also for three novels, several volumes of poetry, and some of the best-known short stories in American literature, including "The Open Boat," "The Blue Hotel," and "The Bride Comes to Yellow Sky."

The Cost of Adventure Adventure often comes at a price. Biographers cite the deprivations of Crane's years in the New York slums, the dangers of traveling to far-off places, and his own neglect of his health as contributing to his death from tuberculosis at age 28. But Crane had matured far beyond his years. True to his early intentions, he was a great student of humanity, and he developed a philosophy described by one critic as a "bold and robust humanism." As a naturalist writer, Crane believed that nature was a powerful force that shaped our lives. But as a humanist, he also had faith in his fellow humans' ability to act responsibly and honestly.

● LITERARY ANALYSIS: NATURALISM

Naturalism is an offshoot of **realism,** the 19th-century literary movement that featured detailed portrayals of life. Naturalist writers sought to describe the effect of natural and social forces on the individual. Naturalism typically

- renders common people and life accurately
- shows that environment and instinct determine behavior
- paints human destiny as beyond the control of the individual
- uses setting, theme, irony, and conflict to convey these ideas

As you read, look for characteristics of naturalism in the story and consider what they lend to the story's impact.

● READING SKILL: ANALYZE DESCRIPTIVE LANGUAGE

Naturalist writers made great use of **descriptive language,** lending vivid qualities to scenes, events, and characters. Effective description relies on various literary elements.

- **imagery**—descriptive words that create sensory experiences
- **figurative language**—language that goes beyond the literal
- **repetition**—recurrence of words, phrases, or lines
- **diction**—a writer's choice of words and word order
- **tone**—a writer's attitude toward the subject
- **mood**—the feeling the writer creates for the reader

As you read, record examples of Crane's use of these elements.

▲ VOCABULARY IN CONTEXT

Match each vocabulary word in the first column with the word or phrase in the second column that is closest in meaning.

1.	dearth	**a.**	comply
2.	ingenuously	**b.**	abnormality
3.	opprobrious	**c.**	raucous
4.	acquiesce	**d.**	compel
5.	motley	**e.**	insulting
6.	epithet	**f.**	relief
7.	respite	**g.**	insulting name
8.	obstreperous	**h.**	naively
9.	coerce	**i.**	assorted
10.	aberration	**j.**	shortage

Explore the Key Idea

Does **NATURE** *play fair?*

KEY IDEA A lioness kills an antelope. An earthquake destroys one small town and leaves other nearby towns untouched. Diseases kill millions worldwide. Does this seem fair? Does **nature** stack the deck against certain creatures? As one of the leading writers in the naturalist movement, Stephen Crane addresses this issue in "The Open Boat."

DISCUSS With a small group, discuss how you explain the inequities found in nature. First, list some specific natural disasters or dangers that you know of. Then, discuss the reasons why each one may have happened the way it did.

THE OPEN BOAT

STEPHEN CRANE

> **BACKGROUND** On New Year's Eve, 1896, Stephen Crane was traveling on the ship *Commodore* to Cuba to report on an impending revolution. Loaded with ammunition and Cuban rebels, the ship was damaged by a sandbar outside of Jacksonville, Florida, and two days later sank in the open sea. Most survivors filled the lifeboats, but Crane and four others ended up in a much smaller boat. This is the story he wrote about his harrowing ordeal. It has been called one of the world's great short stories.

A tale intended to be after the fact. Being the experience of four men from the sunk steamer *Commodore*.

I

None of them knew the color of the sky. Their eyes glanced level, and were fastened upon the waves that swept toward them. These waves were the hue of slate, save for the tops, which were of foaming white, and all of the men knew the colors of the sea. The horizon narrowed and widened, and dipped and rose, and at all times its edge was jagged with waves that seemed thrust up in points like rocks. **A**

Many a man ought to have a bathtub larger than the boat which here rode
10 upon the sea. These waves were most wrongfully and barbarously abrupt and tall, and each froth top was a problem in small boat navigation.

ANALYZE VISUALS
Look at the art on page 713. Apart from the men's appearance, what do the colors of the water and the sky suggest about their situation? Explain.

A DESCRIPTIVE LANGUAGE
The first paragraph is not really about the color of the sky. What does Crane emphasize by beginning the story this way?

German Shipwreck Survivors (image manipulated), Achille Beltrame. Engraving in Italian newspaper *La Domenica del Corriere,* February 1941. © Dagli Orti/The Art Archive.

The cook squatted in the bottom and looked with both eyes at the six inches of gunwale[1] which separated him from the ocean. His sleeves were rolled over his fat forearms, and the two flaps of his unbuttoned vest dangled as he bent to bail out the boat. Often he said: "Gawd! That was a narrow clip." As he remarked it he invariably gazed eastward over the broken sea.

The oiler,[2] steering with one of the two oars in the boat, sometimes raised himself suddenly to keep clear of water that swirled in over the stern. It was a thin little oar and it seemed often ready to snap.

20 The correspondent, pulling at the other oar, watched the waves and wondered why he was there.

The injured captain, lying in the bow, was at this time buried in that profound dejection and indifference which comes, temporarily at least, to even the bravest and most enduring when, willy nilly, the firm fails, the army loses, the ship goes down. The mind of the master of a vessel is rooted deep in the timbers of her, though he command for a day or a decade, and this captain had on him the stern impression of a scene in the grays of dawn of seven turned faces, and later a stump of a topmast with a white ball on it that slashed to and fro at the waves, went low and lower, and down. Thereafter there was something strange in his voice. 30 Although steady, it was deep with mourning, and of a quality beyond oration or tears. **B**

"Keep'er a little more south, Billie," said he.

"'A little more south,' sir," said the oiler in the stern.

A seat in this boat was not unlike a seat upon a bucking bronco, and, by the same token, a bronco is not much smaller. The craft pranced and reared, and plunged like an animal. As each wave came, and she rose for it, she seemed like a horse making at a fence outrageously high. The manner of her scramble over these walls of water is a mystic thing, and, moreover, at the top of them were ordinarily these problems in white water, the foam racing down from the summit 40 of each wave, requiring a new leap, and a leap from the air. Then, after scornfully bumping a crest, she would slide, and race, and splash down a long incline and arrive bobbing and nodding in front of the next menace. **C**

A singular disadvantage of the sea lies in the fact that after successfully surmounting one wave you discover that there is another behind it just as important and just as nervously anxious to do something effective in the way of swamping boats. In a ten-foot dinghy[3] one can get an idea of the resources of the sea in the line of waves that is not probable to the average experience, which is never at sea in a dinghy. As each slaty wall of water approached, it shut all else from the view of the men in the boat, and it was not difficult to imagine that 50 this particular wave was the final outburst of the ocean, the last effort of the grim water. There was a terrible grace in the move of the waves, and they came in silence, save for the snarling of the crests.

B NATURALISM
Reread lines 22–31. What can you **infer** about the "seven turned faces" and the "stump of a topmast"? Consider what these things tell you about the captain's recent experience.

C DESCRIPTIVE LANGUAGE
Notice the descriptive language in lines 34–42. What quality of the boat is emphasized by the bronco **metaphor?**

---

1. **gunwale** (gŭn'əl): the upper edge of a boat.

2. **oiler:** a worker who cares for the machinery in the engine room of a ship.

3. **dinghy** (dĭng'ē): a small open boat.

In the wan light, the faces of the men must have been gray. Their eyes must have glinted in strange ways as they gazed steadily astern. Viewed from a balcony, the whole thing would doubtlessly have been weirdly picturesque. But the men in the boat had no time to see it, and if they had had leisure there were other things to occupy their minds. The sun swung steadily up the sky, and they knew it was broad day because the color of the sea changed from slate to emerald green, streaked with amber lights, and the foam was like tumbling snow. The process of the breaking day was unknown to them. They were aware only of this effect upon the color of the waves that rolled toward them. **D**

In disjointed sentences the cook and the correspondent argued as to the difference between a lifesaving station and a house of refuge. The cook had said: "There's a house of refuge just north of the Mosquito Inlet Light, and as soon as they see us, they'll come off in their boat and pick us up."

"As soon as who see us?" said the correspondent.

"The crew," said the cook.

"Houses of refuge don't have crews," said the correspondent. "As I understand them, they are only places where clothes and grub are stored for the benefit of shipwrecked people. They don't carry crews."

"Oh, yes, they do," said the cook.

"No, they don't," said the correspondent.

"Well, we're not there yet, anyhow," said the oiler, in the stern.

"Well," said the cook, "perhaps it's not a house of refuge that I'm thinking of as being near Mosquito Inlet Light. Perhaps it's a lifesaving station."

"We're not there yet," said the oiler, in the stern.

II

As the boat bounced from the top of each wave, the wind tore through the hair of the hatless men, and as the craft plopped her stern down again the spray slashed past them. The crest of each of these waves was a hill, from the top of which the men surveyed, for a moment, a broad tumultuous expanse, shining and wind-riven. It was probably splendid. It was probably glorious, this play of the free sea, wild with lights of emerald and white and amber.

"Bully good thing it's an on-shore wind,"[4] said the cook. "If not, where would we be? Wouldn't have a show."

"That's right," said the correspondent.

The busy oiler nodded his assent.

Then the captain, in the bow, chuckled in a way that expressed humor, contempt, tragedy, all in one. "Do you think we've got much of a show, now, boys?" said he.

Whereupon the three were silent, save for a trifle of hemming and hawing. To express any particular optimism at this time they felt to be childish and stupid, but they all doubtless possessed this sense of the situation in their mind. A young man thinks doggedly at such times. On the other hand, the ethics of their condition was decidedly against any open suggestion of hopelessness. So they were silent.

D **DESCRIPTIVE LANGUAGE**
In lines 53–61, how does the author describe the dawn? Explain what this description tells you about the men and their state of mind.

---

4. **on-shore wind:** wind that blows toward the shore.

"Oh, well," said the captain, soothing his children, "we'll get ashore all right."

But there was that in his tone which made them think, so the oiler quoth: "Yes! If this wind holds!"

The cook was bailing. "Yes! If we don't catch hell in the surf."

Canton flannel gulls[5] flew near and far. Sometimes they sat down on the sea,
100 near patches of brown seaweed that rolled over the waves with a movement like carpets on a line in a gale. The birds sat comfortably in groups, and they were envied by some in the dinghy, for the wrath of the sea was no more to them than it was to a covey of prairie chickens a thousand miles inland. Often they came very close and stared at the men with black bead-like eyes. At these times they were uncanny and sinister in their unblinking scrutiny, and the men hooted angrily at them, telling them to be gone. One came, and evidently decided to alight on the top of the captain's head. The bird flew parallel to the boat and did not circle, but made short sidelong jumps in the air in chicken fashion. His black eyes were wistfully fixed upon the captain's head. "Ugly brute," said the oiler to the bird.
110 "You look as if you were made with a jackknife." The cook and the correspondent swore darkly at the creature. The captain naturally wished to knock it away with the end of the heavy painter,[6] but he did not dare do it, because anything resembling an emphatic gesture would have capsized this freighted boat, and so with his open hand, the captain gently and carefully waved the gull away. After it had been discouraged from the pursuit the captain breathed easier on account of his hair, and others breathed easier because the bird struck their minds at this time as being somehow gruesome and ominous. **E**

In the meantime the oiler and the correspondent rowed. And also they rowed.

They sat together in the same seat, and each rowed an oar. Then the oiler
120 took both oars; then the correspondent took both oars; then the oiler; then the correspondent. They rowed and they rowed. The very ticklish part of the business was when the time came for the reclining one in the stern to take his turn at the oars. By the very last star of truth, it is easier to steal eggs from under a hen than it was to change seats in the dinghy. First the man in the stern slid his hand along the thwart[7] and moved with care, as if he were of Sèvres.[8] Then the man in the rowing seat slid his hand along the other thwart. It was all done with the most extraordinary care. As the two sidled past each other, the whole party kept watchful eyes on the coming wave, and the captain cried: "Look out now! Steady there!"

The brown mats of seaweed that appeared from time to time were like islands,
130 bits of earth. They were traveling, apparently, neither one way nor the other. They were, to all intents, stationary. They informed the men in the boat that it was making progress slowly toward the land.

The captain, rearing cautiously in the bow, after the dinghy soared on a great swell, said that he had seen the lighthouse at Mosquito Inlet. Presently the cook

E NATURALISM
Reread lines 99–117. How does the author suggest the indifference or even hostility of nature in these lines?

---

5. **canton flannel gulls:** gulls looking as if they were made of canton flannel, a heavy type of cotton that is soft on one side and ribbed on the other.

6. **painter:** a line used for towing or securing a boat.

7. **thwart:** a seat that extends across a boat.

8. **Sèvres:** a type of fine china made in Sèvres, France.

remarked that he had seen it. The correspondent was at the oars, then, and for some reason he too wished to look at the lighthouse, but his back was toward the far shore and the waves were important, and for some time he could not seize an opportunity to turn his head. But at last there came a wave more gentle than the others, and when at the crest of it he swiftly scoured the western horizon.

140   "See it?" said the captain.

"No," said the correspondent, slowly, "I didn't see anything."

"Look again," said the captain. He pointed. "It's exactly in that direction."

At the top of another wave, the correspondent did as he was bid, and this time his eyes chanced on a small still thing on the edge of the swaying horizon. It was precisely like the point of a pin. It took an anxious eye to find a lighthouse so tiny.

"Think we'll make it, Captain?"

"If this wind holds and the boat don't swamp, we can't do much else," said the captain.

The little boat, lifted by each towering sea, and splashed viciously by the crests,
150 made progress that in the absence of seaweed was not apparent to those in her. She seemed just a wee thing wallowing, miraculously, top up, at the mercy of five oceans. Occasionally, a great spread of water, like white flames, swarmed into her. **F**

"Bail her, cook," said the captain, serenely.

"All right, Captain," said the cheerful cook.

III

It would be difficult to describe the subtle brotherhood of men that was here established on the seas. No one said that it was so. No one mentioned it. But it dwelt in the boat, and each man felt it warm him. They were a captain, an oiler, a cook, and a correspondent, and they were friends, friends in a more curiously ironbound degree than may be common. The hurt captain, lying against the
160 water jar in the bow, spoke always in a low voice and calmly, but he could never command a more ready and swiftly obedient crew than the **motley** three of the dinghy. It was more than a mere recognition of what was best for the common safety. There was surely in it a quality that was personal and heartfelt. And after this devotion to the commander of the boat there was this comradeship that the correspondent, for instance, who had been taught to be cynical of men, knew even at the time was the best experience of his life. But no one said that it was so. No one mentioned it.

"I wish we had a sail," remarked the captain. "We might try my overcoat on the end of an oar and give you two boys a chance to rest." So the cook and the
170 correspondent held the mast and spread wide the overcoat. The oiler steered, and the little boat made good way with her new rig. Sometimes the oiler had to scull[9] sharply to keep a sea from breaking into the boat, but otherwise sailing was a success.

Meanwhile the lighthouse had been growing slowly larger. It had now almost assumed color, and appeared like a little gray shadow on the sky. The man at the

F NATURALISM
In lines 149–152, what images, words, and phrases suggest the overwhelming power of nature and the smallness of humanity?

motley (mŏt′lē) *adj.* composed of diverse, often mismatched elements

---

9. **scull:** to propel a boat by rowing from side to side, reversing the oar at each turn.

The Much Resounding Sea (1884), Thomas Moran. 25″ × 62″.

oars could not be prevented from turning his head rather often to try for a glimpse of this little gray shadow.

At last, from the top of each wave the men in the tossing boat could see land. Even as the lighthouse was an upright shadow on the sky, this land seemed but a 180 long black shadow on the sea. It certainly was thinner than paper. "We must be about opposite New Smyrna,"[10] said the cook, who had coasted this shore often in schooners. "Captain, by the way, I believe they abandoned that lifesaving station there about a year ago."

"Did they?" said the captain.

The wind slowly died away. The cook and the correspondent were not now obliged to slave in order to hold high the oar. But the waves continued their old

---

10. **New Smyrna:** New Smyrna Beach, a city on the eastern coast of Florida, about 15 miles south of Daytona Beach.

impetuous swooping at the dinghy, and the little craft, no longer under way, struggled woundily over them. The oiler or the correspondent took the oars again.

Shipwrecks are *apropos* of nothing. If men could only train for them
190 and have them occur when the men had reached pink condition, there would be less drowning at sea. Of the four in the dinghy none had slept any time worth mentioning for two days and two nights previous to embarking in the dinghy, and in the excitement of clambering about the deck of a foundering[11] ship they had also forgotten to eat heartily. **G**

For these reasons, and for others, neither the oiler nor the correspondent was fond of rowing at this time. The correspondent wondered **ingenuously** how in the name of all that was sane could there be people who thought it amusing to row a boat. It was not an amusement; it was a diabolical punishment, and even

G **NATURALISM**
In lines 189–194, the author uses **verbal irony**, suggesting something different from what is literally meant. In this paragraph, what is Crane suggesting about the timing of shipwrecks? Explain.

ingenuously
(ĭn-jĕn'yōō-əs-lē) *adv.* in a manner showing childlike innocence or simplicity

---

11. **foundering:** sinking.

a genius of mental **aberrations** could never conclude that it was anything but a horror to the muscles and a crime against the back. He mentioned to the boat in general how the amusement of rowing struck him, and the weary-faced oiler smiled in full sympathy. Previously to the foundering, by the way, the oiler had worked double watch in the engine room of the ship.

"Take her easy, now, boys," said the captain. "Don't spend yourselves. If we have to run a surf[12] you'll need all your strength, because we'll sure have to swim for it. Take your time."

Slowly the land arose from the sea. From a black line it became a line of black and a line of white—trees and sand. Finally, the captain said that he could make out a house on the shore. "That's the house of refuge, sure," said the cook. "They'll see us before long, and come out after us."

The distant lighthouse reared high. "The keeper ought to be able to make us out now, if he's looking through a glass," said the captain. "He'll notify the lifesaving people."

"None of those other boats could have got ashore to give word of the wreck," said the oiler, in a low voice. "Else the lifeboat would be out hunting us."

Slowly and beautifully the land loomed out of the sea. The wind came again. It had veered from the northeast to the southeast. Finally, a new sound struck the ears of the men in the boat. It was the low thunder of the surf on the shore. "We'll never be able to make the lighthouse now," said the captain. "Swing her head a little more north, Billie."

"'A little more north' sir," said the oiler.

Whereupon the little boat turned her nose once more down the wind, and all but the oarsman watched the shore grow. Under the influence of this expansion doubt and direful apprehension was leaving the minds of the men. The management of the boat was still most absorbing, but it could not prevent a quiet cheerfulness. In an hour, perhaps, they would be ashore.

Their backbones had become thoroughly used to balancing in the boat and they now rode this wild colt of a dinghy like circus men. The correspondent thought that he had been drenched to the skin, but happening to feel in the top pocket of his coat, he found therein eight cigars. Four of them were soaked with seawater; four were perfectly scatheless. After a search, somebody produced three dry matches, and thereupon the four waifs rode impudently in their little boat, and with an assurance of an impending rescue shining in their eyes, puffed at the big cigars and judged well and ill of all men. Everybody took a drink of water. **H**

aberration (ăb'ə-rā'shən)
n. a disorder of the mind

IV

"Cook," remarked the captain, "there don't seem to be any signs of life about your house of refuge."

"No," replied the cook. "Funny they don't see us!"

A broad stretch of lowly coast lay before the eyes of the men. It was of dunes topped with dark vegetation. The roar of the surf was plain, and sometimes they

H **DESCRIPTIVE LANGUAGE**
Reread lines 227–234. Cite examples of the author's language that suggests the assurance of the men might be premature.

---

12. **run a surf:** row through the surf to get to shore.

240 could see the white lip of a wave as it spun up the beach. A tiny house was blocked
out black upon the sky. Southward, the slim lighthouse lifted its little gray length.

Tide, wind, and waves were swinging the dinghy northward. "Funny they don't
see us," said the men.

The surf's roar here dulled, but its tone was, nevertheless, thunderous and
mighty. As the boat swam over the great rollers, the men sat listening to this roar.
"We'll swamp sure," said everybody.

It is fair to say here that there was not a lifesaving station within twenty miles
in either direction, but the men did not know this fact and in consequence they
made dark and **opprobrious** remarks concerning the eyesight of the nation's
250 lifesavers. Four scowling men sat in the dinghy and surpassed records in the
invention of **epithets.**

"Funny they don't see us."

The lightheartedness of a former time had completely faded. To their sharpened
minds it was easy to conjure pictures of all kinds of incompetency and blindness
and, indeed, cowardice. There was the shore of the populous land, and it was
bitter and bitter to them that from it came no sign. ❶

"Well," said the captain, ultimately, "I suppose we'll have to make a try for
ourselves. If we stay out here too long, we'll none of us have strength left to swim
after the boat swamps."

260 And so the oiler, who was at the oars, turned the boat straight for the shore.
There was a sudden tightening of muscles. There was some thinking.

"If we don't all get ashore—" said the captain. "If we don't all get ashore, I
suppose you fellows know where to send news of my finish?"

They then briefly exchanged some addresses and admonitions. As for the
reflections of the men, there was a great deal of rage in them. Perchance they
might be formulated thus: "If I am going to be drowned—if I am going to be
drowned—if I am going to be drowned, why, in the name of the seven mad gods
who rule the sea,[13] was I allowed to come thus far and contemplate sand and trees?
Was I brought here merely to have my nose dragged away as I was about to nibble
270 the sacred cheese of life? It is preposterous. If this old ninny-woman, Fate, cannot
do better than this, she should be deprived of the management of men's fortunes.
She is an old hen who knows not her intention. If she has decided to drown me,
why did she not do it in the beginning and save me all this trouble. The whole
affair is absurd. . . . But, no, she cannot mean to drown me. She dare not drown
me. She cannot drown me. Not after all this work." Afterward the man might
have had an impulse to shake his fist at the clouds. "Just you drown me, now, and
then hear what I call you!" ❷

The billows that came at this time were more formidable. They seemed always
just about to break and roll over the little boat in a turmoil of foam. There was
280 a preparatory and long growl in the speech of them. No mind unused to the sea
would have concluded that the dinghy could ascend these sheer heights in time.

---

opprobrious (ə-prō′brē-əs)
adj. scornful; derogatory

epithet (ĕp′ə-thĕt′) *n.* an
abusive word or phrase

❶ **NATURALISM**
Dramatic irony is the
technique of allowing
the reader to know more
than the characters do
about their own situation.
What does the author
emphasize with his use
of dramatic irony in lines
247–256?

❷ **NATURALISM**
Reread lines 264–277.
What techniques does
the author use to here
suggest the indifference
or hostility of nature?

---

13. **seven mad . . . the sea:** possibly a reference to the gods of the seven major seas of the world.

The shore was still afar. The oiler was a wily surfman. "Boys," he said, swiftly, "she won't live there minutes more and we're too far out to swim. Shall I take her to sea again, Captain?"

"Yes! Go ahead!" said the captain.

This oiler, by a series of quick miracles, and fast and steady oarsmanship, turned the boat in the middle of the surf and took her safely to sea again.

There was a considerable silence as the boat bumped over the furrowed sea to deeper water. Then somebody in gloom spoke. "Well, anyhow, they must have seen us from the shore by now."

290

The gulls went in slanting flight up the wind toward the gray desolate east. A squall, marked by dingy clouds, and clouds brick-red, like smoke from a burning building, appeared from the southeast.

"What do you think of those lifesaving people? Ain't they peaches?"

"Funny they haven't seen us."

"Maybe they think we're out here for sport! Maybe they think we're fishin'. Maybe they think we're damned fools."

It was a long afternoon. A changed tide tried to force them southward, but wind and wave said northward. Far ahead, where coastline, sea, and sky formed their mighty angle, there were little dots which seemed to indicate a city on the shore.

300

"St. Augustine?"[14]

The captain shook his head. "Too near Mosquito Inlet."

And the oiler rowed, and then the correspondent rowed. Then the oiler rowed. It was a weary business. The human back can become the seat of more aches and pains than are registered in books for the composite anatomy of a regiment. It is a limited area, but it can become the theatre of innumerable muscular conflicts, tangles, wrenches, knots, and other comforts.

"Did you ever like to row, Billie?" asked the correspondent.

310

"No," said the oiler. "Hang it."

When one exchanged the rowing seat for a place in the bottom of the boat, he suffered a bodily depression that caused him to be careless of everything save an obligation to wiggle one finger. There was cold seawater swashing to and fro in the boat, and he lay in it. His head, pillowed on a thwart, was within an inch of the swirl of a wave crest, and sometimes a particularly **obstreperous** sea came inboard and drenched him once more. But these matters did not annoy him. It is almost certain that if the boat had capsized he would have tumbled comfortably out upon the ocean as if he felt sure that it was a great soft mattress.

"Look! There's a man on the shore!"

320

"Where?"

"There! See 'im? See 'im?"

"Yes, sure! He's walking along."

"Now he's stopped. Look! He's facing us!"

"He's waving at us!"

obstreperous
(ŏb-strĕp′ər-əs) *adj.* very noisy and unruly

---

14. **St. Augustine:** a city about 65 miles north of New Smyrna Beach, along the northeastern coast of Florida.

"So he is! By thunder!"

"Ah, now, we're all right! Now we're all right! There'll be a boat out here for us in half an hour."

"He's going on. He's running. He's going up to that house there."

The remote beach seemed lower than the sea, and it required a searching glance to discern the little black figure. The captain saw a floating stick and they rowed to it. A bath towel was by some weird chance in the boat, and, tying this on the stick, the captain waved it. The oarsman did not dare turn his head, so he was obliged to ask questions.

"What's he doing now?"

"He's standing still again. He's looking, I think. . . . There he goes again. Toward the house. . . . Now he's stopped again."

"Is he waving at us?"

"No, not now! He was, though."

"Look! There comes another man!"

"He's running."

"Look at him go, would you."

"Why, he's on a bicycle. Now he's met the other man. They're both waving at us. Look!"

"There comes something up the beach."

"What the devil is that thing?"

"Why, it looks like a boat."

"Why, certainly it's a boat."

"No, it's on wheels."

"Yes, so it is. Well, that must be the lifeboat. They drag them along shore on a wagon."

"That's the lifeboat, sure."

"No, by——it's—it's an omnibus."[15]

"I tell you it's a lifeboat."

"It is not! It's an omnibus. I can see it plain. See? One of those big hotel omnibuses."

"By thunder, you're right. It's an omnibus, sure as fate. What do you suppose they are doing with an omnibus? Maybe they are going around collecting the lifecrew, hey?"

"That's it, likely. Look! There's a fellow waving a little black flag. He's standing on the steps of the omnibus. There come those two other fellows. Now they're all talking together. Look at the fellow with the flag. Maybe he ain't waving it!"

"That ain't a flag, is it? That's his coat. Why, certainly, that's his coat."

"So it is. It's his coat. He's taken it off and is waving it around his head. But would you look at him swing it!"

"Oh, say, there isn't any lifesaving station there. That's just a winter resort hotel omnibus that has brought over some of the boarders to see us drown."

"What's that idiot with the coat mean? What's he signaling, anyhow?"

"It looks as if he were trying to tell us to go north. There must be a lifesaving

---

15. **omnibus:** bus. At this time, a bus would have been pulled by horses.

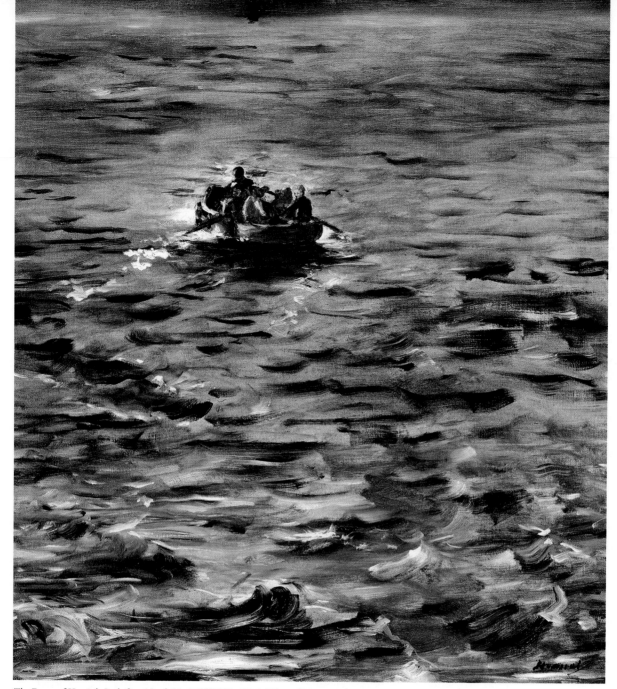

The Escape of Henri de Rochefort, March 20, 1874 (1880–1881), Edouard Manet. Oil on canvas, 80 cm × 73 cm. Musée d'Orsay, Paris.
© Bridgeman Art Library.

station up there."

370   "No! He thinks we're fishing. Just giving us a merry hand. See? Ah, there, Willie."

    "Well, I wish I could make something out of those signals. What do you suppose he means?"

    "He don't mean anything. He's just playing."

    "Well, if he'd just signal us to try the surf again, or to go to sea and wait, or go north, or go south, or go to hell—there would be some reason in it. But look at him. He just stands there and keeps his coat revolving like a wheel. The ass!"

    "There come more people."

    "Now there's quite a mob. Look! Isn't that a boat?"

380 "Where? Oh, I see where you mean. No, that's no boat."

"That fellow is still waving his coat."

"He must think we like to see him do that. Why don't he quit it. It don't mean anything."

"I don't know. I think he is trying to make us go north. It must be that there's a lifesaving station there somewhere."

"Say, he ain't tired yet. Look at 'im wave."

"Wonder how long he can keep that up. He's been revolving his coat ever since he caught sight of us. He's an idiot. Why aren't they getting men to bring a boat out. A fishing boat—one of those big yawls[16]—could come out here all right.
390 Why don't he do something?"

"Oh, it's all right, now."

"They'll have a boat out here for us in less than no time, now that they've seen us."

A faint yellow tone came into the sky over the low land. The shadows on the sea slowly deepened. The wind bore coldness with it, and the men began to shiver.

"Holy smoke!" said one, allowing his voice to express his impious mood, "if we keep on monkeying out here! If we've got to flounder out here all night!"

"Oh, we'll never have to stay here all night! Don't you worry. They've seen us now, and it won't be long before they'll come chasing out after us."

400 The shore grew dusky. The man waving a coat blended gradually into this gloom, and it swallowed in the same manner the omnibus and the group of people. The spray, when it dashed uproariously over the side, made the voyagers shrink and swear like men who were being branded. **K**

"I'd like to catch the chump who waved the coat. I feel like soaking him one, just for luck."

"Why? What did he do?"

"Oh, nothing, but then he seemed so damn cheerful."

In the meantime the oiler rowed, and then the correspondent rowed, and then the oiler rowed. Gray-faced and bowed forward, they mechanically, turn by turn,
410 plied the leaden oars. The form of the lighthouse had vanished from the southern horizon, but finally a pale star appeared, just lifting from the sea. The streaked saffron in the west passed before the all-merging darkness, and the sea to the east was black. The land had vanished, and was expressed only by the low and drear thunder of the surf.

"If I am going to be drowned—if I am going to be drowned—if I am going to be drowned, why, in the name of the seven mad gods who rule the sea, was I allowed to come thus far and contemplate sand and trees? Was I brought here merely to have my nose dragged away as I was about to nibble the sacred cheese of life?" **L**

420 The patient captain, drooped over the water jar, was sometimes obliged to speak to the oarsman.

K DESCRIPTIVE LANGUAGE
What mood is established by the **description** in lines 394–403?

L NATURALISM
Reread lines 416–419. There is something almost comical about the repeated image of a man "about to nibble the sacred cheese of life." Why do you think Crane might have chosen to strike such a **tone** in reference to such a serious topic? Explain.

---

16. **yawls:** sailboats with two masts.

"Keep her head up! Keep her head up!"

"'Keep her head up,' sir." The voices were weary and low.

This was surely a quiet evening. All save the oarsman lay heavily and listlessly in the boat's bottom. As for him, his eyes were just capable of noting the tall black waves that swept forward in a most sinister silence, save for an occasional subdued growl of a crest.

The cook's head was on a thwart, and he looked without interest at the water under his nose. He was deep in other scenes. Finally he spoke. "Billie," he 430 murmured, dreamfully, "what kind of pie do you like best?"

V

"Pie," said the oiler and the correspondent, agitatedly. "Don't talk about those things, blast you!"

"Well," said the cook, "I was just thinking about ham sandwiches, and—"

A night on the sea in an open boat is a long night. As darkness settled finally, the shine of the light, lifting from the sea in the south, changed to full gold. On the northern horizon a new light appeared, a small bluish gleam on the edge of the waters. These two lights were the furniture of the world. Otherwise there was nothing but waves.

Two men huddled in the stern, and distances were so magnificent in the dinghy 440 that the rower was enabled to keep his feet partly warmed by thrusting them under his companions. Their legs indeed extended far under the rowing seat until they touched the feet of the captain forward. Sometimes, despite the efforts of the tired oarsman, a wave came piling into the boat, an icy wave of the night, and the chilling water waked them anew. They would twist their bodies for a moment and groan, and sleep the dead sleep once more, while the water in the boat gurgled about them as the craft rocked.

The plan of the oiler and the correspondent was for one to row until he lost the ability, and then arouse the other from his seawater couch in the bottom of the boat.

450 The oiler plied the oars until his head drooped forward, and the overpowering sleep blinded him. And he rowed yet afterward. Then he touched a man in the bottom of the boat, and called his name. "Will you spell me for a little while?" he said, meekly.

"Sure, Billie," said the correspondent, awakening and dragging himself to a sitting position. They exchanged places carefully, and the oiler, cuddling down in the seawater at the cook's side, seemed to go to sleep instantly.

The particular violence of the sea had ceased. The waves came without snarling. The obligation of the man at the oars was to keep the boat headed so that the tilt of the rollers would not capsize her, and to preserve her from filling when the 460 crests rushed past. The black waves were silent and hard to be seen in the darkness. Often one was almost upon the boat before the oarsman was aware.

In a low voice the correspondent addressed the captain. He was not sure that the captain was awake, although this iron man seemed to be always awake. "Captain, shall I keep her making for that light north, sir?"

The same steady voice answered him. "Yes. Keep it about two points off the port bow."[17]

The cook had tied a life belt around himself in order to get even the warmth which this clumsy cork contrivance could donate, and he seemed almost stovelike when a rower, whose teeth invariably chattered wildly as soon as he ceased his labor, dropped down to sleep.

The correspondent, as he rowed, looked down at the two men sleeping under foot. The cook's arm was around the oiler's shoulders, and, with their fragmentary clothing and haggard faces, they were the babes of the sea, a grotesque rendering of the old babes in the wood.[18]

Later he must have grown stupid at his work, for suddenly there was a growling of water, and a crest came with a roar and a swash into the boat, and it was a wonder that it did not set the cook afloat in his life belt. The cook continued to sleep, but the oiler sat up, blinking his eyes and shaking with the new cold. **M**

"Oh, I'm awfully sorry, Billie," said the correspondent, contritely.

"That's all right, old boy," said the oiler, and lay down again and was asleep.

Presently it seemed that even the captain dozed, and the correspondent thought that he was the one man afloat on all the oceans. The wind had a voice as it came over the waves, and it was sadder than the end.

There was a long, loud swishing astern of the boat, and a gleaming trail of phosphorescence, like blue flame, was furrowed on the black waters. It might have been made by a monstrous knife.

Then there came a stillness, while the correspondent breathed with the open mouth and looked at the sea.

Suddenly there was another swish and another long flash of bluish light, and this time it was alongside the boat, and might almost have been reached with an oar. The correspondent saw an enormous fin speed like a shadow through the water, hurling the crystalline spray and leaving the long glowing trail.

The correspondent looked over his shoulder at the captain. His face was hidden, and he seemed to be asleep. He looked at the babes of the sea. They certainly were asleep. So, being bereft of sympathy, he leaned a little way to one side and swore softly into the sea.

But the thing did not then leave the vicinity of the boat. Ahead or astern, on one side or the other, at intervals long or short, fled the long sparkling streak, and there was to be heard the whiroo of the dark fin. The speed and power of the thing was greatly to be admired. It cut the water like a gigantic and keen projectile. **N**

The presence of this biding thing did not affect the man with the same horror that it would if he had been a picnicker. He simply looked at the sea dully and swore in an undertone.

475
470
480
490
500

M GRAMMAR AND STYLE
Reread lines 475–478. With his unusual use of the **gerund phrase** "a growling of water," Crane characterizes the sea as a wild or angry animal, emphasizing its danger.

N NATURALISM
Reread lines 484–501. What might the shark symbolize? Consider what this symbol contributes to the development of the **theme.**

---

17. **two points off the port bow:** two compass points, or a total of 45 degrees, to the left.

18. **babes in the wood:** a reference to an old nursery rhyme in which two children are abandoned in the woods and die there in the night.

Nevertheless, it is true that he did not wish to be alone with the thing. He wished one of his companions to awaken by chance and keep him company with it. But the captain hung motionless over the water jar and the oiler and the cook in the bottom of the boat were plunged in slumber.

VI

"If I am going to be drowned—if I am going to be drowned—if I am going to be
510 drowned, why, in the name of the seven mad gods who rule the sea, was I allowed to come thus far and contemplate sand and trees?" **◯**

During this dismal night, it may be remarked that a man would conclude that it was really the intention of the seven mad gods to drown him, despite the abominable injustice of it. For it was certainly an abominable injustice to drown a man who had worked so hard, so hard. The man felt it would be a crime most unnatural. Other people had drowned at sea since galleys[19] swarmed with painted sails, but still—

When it occurs to a man that nature does not regard him as important, and that she feels she would not maim the universe by disposing of him, he at first
520 wishes to throw bricks at the temple, and he hates deeply the fact that there are no bricks and no temples. Any visible expression of nature would surely be pelleted with his jeers. **◉**

Then, if there be no tangible thing to hoot he feels, perhaps, the desire to confront a personification and indulge in pleas, bowed to one knee, and with hands supplicant, saying: "Yes, but I love myself."

A high cold star on a winter's night is the word he feels that she says to him. Thereafter he knows the pathos of his situation.

The men in the dinghy had not discussed these matters, but each had, no doubt, reflected upon them in silence and according to his mind. There was
530 seldom any expression upon their faces save the general one of complete weariness. Speech was devoted to the business of the boat.

To chime the notes of his emotion, a verse mysteriously entered the correspondent's head. He had even forgotten that he had forgotten this verse, but it suddenly was in his mind.

> *A soldier of the Legion lay dying in Algiers,*
> *There was lack of woman's nursing, there was **dearth** of woman's tears;*
> *But a comrade stood beside him, and he took that comrade's hand,*
> *And he said: "I never more shall see my own, my native land."*[20]

In his childhood, the correspondent had been made acquainted with the fact
540 that a soldier of the Legion lay dying in Algiers, but he had never regarded it as important. Myriads of his schoolfellows had informed him of the soldier's plight, but the dinning had naturally ended by making him perfectly indifferent. He had never considered it his affair that a soldier of the Legion lay dying in Algiers, nor

◯ NATURALISM
What is the tone of this third repetition of the men's outcry against fate?

◉ NATURALISM
What does the author say about nature's regard for the individual in lines 518–522?

dearth (dûrth) *n.* lack

---

19. **galleys:** large medieval ships propelled by sails and oars.

20. **A soldier . . . native land:** condensed first stanza of Caroline E. S. Norton's poem "Bingen on the Rhine." The Legion is the French Foreign Legion; Algiers is the capital city of the African nation Algeria.

had it appeared to him as a matter for sorrow. It was less to him than the breaking of a pencil's point.

Now, however, it quaintly came to him as a human, living thing. It was no longer merely a picture of a few throes in the breast of a poet, meanwhile drinking tea and warming his feet at the grate; it was actuality—stern, mournful, and fine.

The correspondent plainly saw the soldier. He lay on the sand with his feet out
550 straight and still. While his pale left hand was upon his chest in an attempt to thwart the going of his life, the blood came between his fingers. In the far Algerian distance, a city of low square forms was set against a sky that was faint with the last sunset hues. The correspondent, plying the oars and dreaming of the slow and slower movements of the lips of the soldier, was moved by a profound and perfectly impersonal comprehension. He was sorry for the soldier of the Legion who lay dying in Algiers. **Q**

The thing which had followed the boat and waited had evidently grown bored at the delay. There was no longer to be heard the slash of the cutwater,[21] and there was no longer the flame of the long trail. The light in the north still glimmered,
560 but it was apparently no nearer to the boat. Sometimes the boom of the surf rang in the correspondent's ears, and he turned the craft seaward then and rowed harder. Southward, some one had evidently built a watch fire on the beach. It was too low and too far to be seen, but it made a shimmering, roseate reflection upon the bluff back of it, and this could be discerned from the boat. The wind came stronger, and sometimes a wave suddenly raged out like a mountain-cat and there was to be seen the sheen and sparkle of a broken crest.

The captain, in the bow, moved on his water jar and sat erect. "Pretty long night," he observed to the correspondent. He looked at the shore. "Those lifesaving people take their time."
570 "Did you see that shark playing around?"

"Yes, I saw him. He was a big fellow, all right."

"Wish I had known you were awake."

Later the correspondent spoke into the bottom of the boat.

"Billie!" There was a slow and gradual disentanglement. "Billie, will you spell me?"

"Sure," said the oiler.

As soon as the correspondent touched the cold comfortable seawater in the bottom of the boat, and had huddled close to the cook's life belt he was deep in sleep, despite the fact that his teeth played all the popular airs. This sleep was so
580 good to him that it was but a moment before he heard a voice call his name in a tone that demonstrated the last stages of exhaustion. "Will you spell me?"

"Sure, Billie."

The light in the north had mysteriously vanished, but the correspondent took his course from the wide-awake captain.

Later in the night they took the boat farther out to sea, and the captain directed the cook to take one oar at the stern and keep the boat facing the seas. He was to

Q DESCRIPTIVE LANGUAGE
The description in lines 549–556 paints the correspondent's mental picture of the soldier in the poem. What does this **imagery** suggest about the correspondent's own plight?

call out if he should hear the thunder of the surf. This plan enabled the oiler and the correspondent to get **respite** together. "We'll give those boys a chance to get into shape again," said the captain. They curled down and, after a few preliminary
590　chatterings and trembles, slept once more the dead sleep. Neither knew they had bequeathed to the cook the company of another shark, or perhaps the same shark.

　　As the boat caroused on the waves, spray occasionally bumped over the side and gave them a fresh soaking, but this had no power to break their repose. The ominous slash of the wind and the water affected them as it would have affected mummies.

　　"Boys," said the cook, with the notes of every reluctance in his voice, "she's drifted in pretty close. I guess one of you had better take her to sea again." The correspondent, aroused, heard the crash of the toppled crests.

　　As he was rowing, the captain gave him some whiskey and water, and this
600　steadied the chills out of him. "If I ever get ashore and anybody shows me even a photograph of an oar—"

　　At last there was a short conversation.

　　"Billie. . . . Billie, will you spell me?"

　　"Sure," said the oiler.

VII

When the correspondent again opened his eyes, the sea and the sky were each of the gray hue of the dawning. Later, carmine and gold was painted upon the waters. The morning appeared finally, in its splendor, with a sky of pure blue, and the sunlight flamed on the tips of the waves. **R**

　　On the distant dunes were set many little black cottages, and a tall white
610　windmill reared above them. No man, nor dog, nor bicycle appeared on the beach. The cottages might have formed a deserted village.

　　The voyagers scanned the shore. A conference was held in the boat. "Well," said the captain, "if no help is coming, we might better try a run through the surf right away. If we stay out here much longer we will be too weak to do anything for ourselves at all." The others silently **acquiesced** in this reasoning. The boat was headed for the beach. The correspondent wondered if none ever ascended the tall wind tower, and if then they never looked seaward. This tower was a giant, standing with its back to the plight of the ants. It represented in a degree, to the correspondent, the serenity of nature amid the struggles of the individual—nature
620　in the wind, and nature in the vision of men. She did not seem cruel to him then, nor beneficent, nor treacherous, nor wise. But she was indifferent, flatly indifferent. It is, perhaps, plausible that a man in this situation, impressed with the unconcern of the universe, should see the innumerable flaws of his life and have them taste wickedly in his mind and wish for another chance. A distinction between right and wrong seems absurdly clear to him, then, in this new ignorance of the grave edge, and he understands that if he were given another opportunity he would mend his conduct and his words, and be better and brighter during an introduction, or at a tea. **S**

respite (rĕs′pĭt) *n.* a period of rest or relief

R DESCRIPTIVE LANGUAGE
Note the change in mood. What descriptive language has been used to achieve this?

acquiesce (ăk′wē-ĕs′) *v.* to comply or give in

S NATURALISM
Reread lines 612–628. Which sentence in this paragraph do you think most effectively expresses the indifference of nature to the struggles of the individual? Explain.

Moonlit Shipwreck at Sea (1901), Thomas Moran. 30″ × 40 ¼″. © Christie's Images Limited.

"Now, boys," said the captain, "she is going to swamp sure. All we can do is to
630 work her in as far as possible, and then when she swamps, pile out and scramble
for the beach. Keep cool now, and don't jump until she swamps sure."

The oiler took the oars. Over his shoulders he scanned the surf. "Captain,"
he said, "I think I'd better bring her about, and keep her head-on to the seas and
back her in."

"All right, Billie," said the captain. "Back her in." The oiler swung the boat then
and, seated in the stern, the cook and the correspondent were obliged to look over
their shoulders to contemplate the lonely and indifferent shore.

The monstrous inshore rollers[22] heaved the boat high until the men were
again enabled to see the white sheets of water scudding up the slanted beach.
640 "We won't get in very close," said the captain. Each time a man could wrest his

---

22. **inshore rollers:** long waves swelling close to the shore.

ANALYZE VISUALS
In your opinion, how well
does this painting reflect
the men's situation?
Reread the description of
the waves on this page
and compare them to the
waves as portrayed by
the artist.

attention from the rollers, he turned his glance toward the shore, and in the expression of the eyes during this contemplation there was a singular quality. The correspondent, observing the others, knew that they were not afraid, but the full meaning of their glances was shrouded.

As for himself, he was too tired to grapple fundamentally with the fact. He tried to **coerce** his mind into thinking of it, but the mind was dominated at this time by the muscles, and the muscles said they did not care. It merely occurred to him that if he should drown it would be a shame.

There were no hurried words, no pallor, no plain agitation. The men simply
650　looked at the shore. "Now, remember to get well clear of the boat when you jump," said the captain.

Seaward the crest of a roller suddenly fell with a thunderous crash, and the long white comber[23] came roaring down upon the boat.

"Steady now," said the captain. The men were silent. They turned their eyes from the shore to the comber and waited. The boat slid up the incline, leaped at the furious top, bounced over it, and swung down the long back of the wave. Some water had been shipped and the cook bailed it out.

But the next crest crashed also. The tumbling boiling flood of white water caught the boat and whirled it almost perpendicular. Water swarmed in from all
660　sides. The correspondent had his hands on the gunwale at this time, and when the water entered at that place he swiftly withdrew his fingers, as if he objected to wetting them.

The little boat, drunken with this weight of water, reeled and snuggled deeper into the sea. **T**

"Bail her out, cook! Bail her out," said the captain.

"All right, Captain," said the cook.

"Now, boys, the next one will do for us, sure," said the oiler. "Mind to jump clear of the boat."

The third wave moved forward, huge, furious, implacable. It fairly swallowed
670　the dinghy, and almost simultaneously the men tumbled into the sea. A piece of life belt had lain in the bottom of the boat, and as the correspondent went overboard he held this to his chest with his left hand.

The January water was icy, and he reflected immediately that it was colder than he had expected to find it off the coast of Florida. This appeared to his dazed mind as a fact important enough to be noted at the time. The coldness of the water was sad; it was tragic. This fact was somehow so mixed and confused with his opinion of his own situation that it seemed almost a proper reason for tears. The water was cold.

When he came to the surface he was conscious of little but the noisy water.
680　Afterward he saw his companions in the sea. The oiler was ahead in the race. He was swimming strongly and rapidly. Off to the correspondent's left, the cook's great white and corked back bulged out of the water, and in the rear the captain was hanging with his one good hand to the keel of the overturned dinghy.

T **NATURALISM**
What is **ironic** about the description of the correspondent and then the boat in lines 660–664? Consider the impact of this tone on these paragraphs.

---

23. **comber:** a large wave that breaks on a beach.

There is a certain immovable quality to a shore, and the correspondent wondered at it amid the confusion of the sea.

It seemed also very attractive, but the correspondent knew that it was a long journey, and he paddled leisurely. The piece of life preserver lay under him, and sometimes he whirled down the incline of a wave as if he were on a hand sled.

But finally he arrived at a place in the sea where travel was beset with difficulty. He did not pause swimming to inquire what manner of current had caught him, but there his progress ceased. The shore was set before him like a bit of scenery on a stage, and he looked at it and understood with his eyes each detail of it.

As the cook passed, much farther to the left, the captain was calling to him, "Turn over on your back, cook! Turn over on your back and use the oar."

"All right, sir." The cook turned on his back, and, paddling with an oar, went ahead as if he were a canoe.

Presently the boat also passed to the left of the correspondent with the captain clinging with one hand to the keel. He would have appeared like a man raising himself to look over a board fence, if it were not for the extraordinary gymnastics of the boat. The correspondent marveled that the captain could still hold to it.

They passed on, nearer to shore—the oiler, the cook, the captain—and following them went the water jar, bouncing gaily over the seas.

The correspondent remained in the grip of this strange new enemy—a current. The shore, with its white slope of sand and its green bluff, topped with little silent cottages, was spread like a picture before him. It was very near to him then, but he was impressed as one who in a gallery looks at a scene from Brittany[24] or Holland.

He thought: "I am going to drown? Can it be possible? Can it be possible? Can it be possible?" Perhaps an individual must consider his own death to be the final phenomenon of nature. **U**

But later a wave perhaps whirled him out of this small deadly current, for he found suddenly that he could again make progress toward the shore. Later still, he was aware that the captain, clinging with one hand to the keel of the dinghy, had his face turned away from the shore and toward him, and was calling his name. "Come to the boat! Come to the boat!"

In his struggle to reach the captain and the boat, he reflected that when one gets properly wearied, drowning must really be a comfortable arrangement, a cessation of hostilities accompanied by a large degree of relief, and he was glad of it, for the main thing in his mind for some moments had been horror of the temporary agony. He did not wish to be hurt.

Presently he saw a man running along the shore. He was undressing with most remarkable speed. Coat, trousers, shirt, everything flew magically off him.

"Come to the boat," called the captain.

"All right, Captain." As the correspondent paddled, he saw the captain let himself down to bottom and leave the boat. Then the correspondent performed his one little marvel of the voyage. A large wave caught him and flung him with

U NATURALISM
Reread lines 707–709. How does the correspondent come to view death as he is faced with the prospect of drowning?

---

24. **Brittany:** a region in northwestern France.

ease and supreme speed completely over the boat and far beyond it. It struck him even then as an event in gymnastics, and a true miracle of the sea. An overturned boat in the surf is not a plaything to a swimming man.

The correspondent arrived in water that reached only to his waist, but his
730 condition did not enable him to stand for more than a moment. Each wave knocked him into a heap, and the undertow pulled at him.

Then he saw the man who had been running and undressing, and undressing and running, come bounding into the water. He dragged ashore the cook, and then waded toward the captain, but the captain waved him away, and sent him to the correspondent. He was naked, naked as a tree in winter, but a halo was about his head, and he shone like a saint. He gave a strong pull, and a long drag, and a bully heave at the correspondent's hand. The correspondent, schooled in the minor formulæ, said: "Thanks, old man." But suddenly the man cried: "What's that?" He pointed a swift finger. The correspondent said: "Go."
740 In the shallows, face downward, lay the oiler. His forehead touched sand that was periodically, between each wave, clear of the sea.

The correspondent did not know all that transpired afterward. When he achieved safe ground he fell, striking the sand with each particular part of his body. It was as if he had dropped from a roof, but the thud was grateful to him.

It seems that instantly the beach was populated with men with blankets, clothes, and flasks, and women with coffeepots and all the remedies sacred to their minds. The welcome of the land to the men from the sea was warm and generous, but a still and dripping shape was carried slowly up the beach, and the land's welcome for it could only be the different and sinister hospitality of the grave.
750 When it came night, the white waves paced to and fro in the moonlight, and the wind brought the sound of the great sea's voice to the men on shore, and they felt that they could then be interpreters. ☙

Comprehension

1. **Recall** Which character in the story doesn't survive?

2. **Clarify** Why don't the men row the boat directly onto the beach?

3. **Clarify** Why don't the people on shore rescue the men?

Literary Analysis

4. **Draw Conclusions About Conflict** The sea is the great **antagonist** in Crane's story. Are the men saved primarily by their own efforts or by chance? Think about the following dangers the men face in the open boat and what they do to combat the dangers:

   - distance from shore
   - size of waves
   - sharks
   - exposure to weather
   - exhaustion

5. **Examine Naturalism** Reread lines 509–522 at the beginning of section VI, where the correspondent rails against the "abominable injustice" of **nature.** Is nature really unjust in the story? What characteristics of nature are suggested in these lines and in other places in the story?

6. **Examine Dramatic Irony** Naturalistic writers generally apply heavy doses of irony to express their worldview. Find two instances in "The Open Boat" in which the characters' perceptions don't match the reality of the situation. Then, explain how the two examples of irony contribute to Crane's naturalistic theme.

7. **Analyze Tone** The narrative voice of this story is quite detached, relating highly dramatic events with a mild and even slightly humorous tone. Find examples of this detachment. How does this tone affect the story's message or overall impact? Explain.

8. **Evaluate Descriptive Language** Identify the section of the story (a page or more) that you find most compelling. Now review the examples of descriptive elements that you recorded as you read. What role does descriptive writing play in this passage? How do you think the description affects your feelings about it? Cite details from the text to support your answer.

Literary Criticism

9. **Author's Style** One writer described Stephen Crane's stories as "intensely realistic." He attributed this realism to Crane's training as a reporter, saying "his English flow[s] simple and pure." Do you agree? Explain why or why not, citing evidence from the story to support your answer.

Vocabulary in Context

VOCABULARY PRACTICE

Choose the letter of the phrase that defines or is related to the boldfaced word.

1. **coerce:** (a) someone being robbed, (b) someone singing, (c) someone writing
2. **epithet:** (a) a sincere apology, (b) a two-handed card game, (c) a show of anger
3. **motley:** (a) polka dots with plaid, (b) a portrait of twins, (c) a thunderstorm
4. **obstreperous**: (a) a severe cold, (b) a noisy argument, (c) a lazy summer day
5. **dearth:** (a) a large fireplace, (b) a song played at funerals, (c) a shortage of good ideas
6. **respite:** (a) halftime at a game, (b) jealous anger, (c) paying back a debt
7. **aberration:** (a) a pilot in training, (b) a small city park, (c) the habits of an eccentric
8. **ingenuously:** (a) a sudden change in weather, (b) a believer in fairy tales, (c) a clever invention
9. **opprobrious:** (a) a clever comedian, (b) a scornful laugh, (c) a wildlife refuge
10. **acquiesce:** (a) an army's surrender, (b) a child's naptime, (c) a bird's piercing call

WORD LIST

aberration
acquiesce
coerce
dearth
epithet
ingenuously
motley
obstreperous
opprobrious
respite

VOCABULARY IN WRITING

How did the correspondent's attitude about his situation change through the story? Using three or more vocabulary words, describe the changes in his state of mind. You could start like this.

> **EXAMPLE SENTENCE**
>
> *The correspondent experienced a fair range of emotions, but ultimately he seemed willing to* **acquiesce** *to the sea.*

VOCABULARY STRATEGY: THE GREEK PREFIX *epi-*

The vocabulary word *epithet* contains the Greek prefix *epi-*, which means "upon," "among," or "in addition." This prefix is found in a number of English words, both scientific and nonscientific. To understand words with *epi-*, look for context clues and also use your knowledge of the meaning of the prefix.

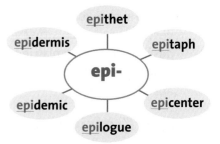

PRACTICE Choose the word from the word web that best completes each sentence. Consider what you know about the Greek prefix and the other word parts shown. If necessary, consult a dictionary.

1. The _____ of the earthquake was 200 miles from the city.
2. The top layer of skin in humans is called the _____.
3. The _____ spread illness and disease throughout the region.

VOCABULARY PRACTICE
For more practice, go to the **Vocabulary Center** at **ClassZone.com**.

Reading-Writing Connection

WRITE A CHARACTER SKETCH The sea in "The Open Boat" is the most compelling character in the story. It is more fully described than any of the four humans in the boat. Crane frequently uses **personification,** a figure of speech in which an object is given human characteristics, in order to describe the sea.

Write a **three-paragraph character sketch** of the sea in "The Open Boat." You might look through the story for examples of personification to form the basis of your character sketch.

A successful character sketch will...

- characterize the sea as a human being
- describe how the sea is perceived by the human characters
- give examples, quotations, and other evidence from the story to support your interpretation

GRAMMAR AND STYLE

USE EFFECTIVE DESCRIPTION Review the **Grammar and Style** note on page 727. Crane uses gerunds and gerund phrases in some unusual ways, creating energetic phrases and sentences. A **gerund** is a verb form that ends in *-ing* and functions as a noun. A **gerund phrase** includes a gerund and its modifiers and complements. In this example from "The Open Boat," notice how "snarling of the crests" functions as a noun in the sentence:

> *There was a terrible grace in the move of the waves, and they came in silence, save for the snarling of the crests.* (lines 51–52)

The gerund emphasizes the action of the waves more than the simple noun *snarl* would. It's a subtle difference that, when used strategically in your writing, can have a cumulative impact.

PRACTICE Rewrite each of the following sentences so that it contains a gerund phrase. You may want to change an existing verb into a gerund or add an entirely new idea. (Remember that a participial phrase, which also uses the *-ing* form of a verb, is used as an adjective, whereas a gerund phrase is used as a noun.)

EXAMPLE

The sun sank gradually, and their hearts sank soon after.

The gradual sinking of the sun was followed by the sinking of their hearts.

---

1. The surf roared, announcing the nearness of the shore.

2. The gulls cried and gave voice to their own despair.

3. The men looked warily at the shark fin as it coolly sliced the water.

WRITING TOOLS
For prewriting, revision, and editing tools, visit the **Writing Center** at ClassZone.com.

The Wreck of the *Commodore*
Newspaper Articles

Use with "The Open Boat," page 712.

"The Open Boat" was based on Stephen Crane's experience with the wreck of the *Commodore*, a ship on a private mission to arm rebels fighting in the Cuban civil war. Crane had joined these filibusters, as these men were known, in search of adventure and a good story. When the ship went down, however, he acted as far more than a journalist. You'll now read news stories about this sensational event, including an account by Crane himself.

Skill Focus: Analyze Primary Sources

The 1897 articles about the wreck of the *Commodore* are **primary sources** of information on that event. You can also look to them as evidence of the kind of writing that appeared in newspapers of the day. As you read each article, make notes about your impressions of it. Keep the following questions in mind:

- Who is the intended **audience**?
- What techniques are used to capture the readers' interest?
- What is the **tone** of the piece?
- What is its **scope** and **focus**? In other words, how much is covered, and what in the piece is most important?
- How much **imagery** or other colorful language does it contain?
- How does the piece differ from something you might find in a newspaper today?

Note your observations and impressions in a chart such as this one.

"The Commodore Sinks at Sea"	"More of the Filibusters Safe"	"Stephen Crane and His Work"	"Stephen Crane's Own Story"
lots of stacked headlines	.		

THE FLORIDA TIMES-UNION

SUNDAY, JANUARY 3, 1897   PRICE 5 CENTS.

THE COMMODORE SINKS AT SEA

The Little Vessel Lost with Her Cargo of Arms and Ammunition

HER NUMEROUS COMPANY REACH LAND IN SAFETY

They are Compelled to Take to the Boats and Abandon the Sinking Vessel

An Overload of Coal the Probable Cause **A**

THE STEAMER COMMODORE, which left here Thursday night with an expedition for the Cuban insurgents, is now resting on the bottom of the sea, twenty fathoms below the surface, about eighteen miles northeast of Mosquito Inlet.

All of the men on the vessel, twenty-eight in number, reached the
10 shore in safety, and twelve of them arrived in Jacksonville last night over the Florida East Coast railway. The other sixteen are still down the coast, but are expected to arrive here on a special train this morning. . . .

DETAILS OF THE ACCIDENT

About 12 o'clock Friday night it was discovered that the boat was leaking badly. The swash of the water in the hold as the vessel rolled from side to side
20 soon alarmed everyone on board. A panic ensued, but Captain Murphy, Stephen Crane, R. A. Delgado and one or two others soon quieted the excitement and put everybody to work on the pumps and with buckets. The steam pump was started and for two hours the water was poured over the sides in streams.

At 2:30 A.M., it was seen that the
30 water was steadily gaining, and it was decided to abandon the vessel.

IN THE BOATS

Paul Rojo, R. A. Delgado, Franco Blanco, the old Cuban pilot, and nine other men took one of the boats and left the steamer. Captain Murphy, the first and second mate, the engineer and assistant, Stephen Crane and ten men took the large yawl boat, and at 3 o'clock they left the Commodore to
40 her fate. The night was dark and they could not see what became of her, but as she was rapidly filling with water, they are all confident that she is now resting on the bottom, and old Neptune has been supplied with enough arms and ammunition to blow up the island of Cuba. . . . **B**

A PRIMARY SOURCES
Compare these headlines with those in papers today. Why do you think there are so many?

B PRIMARY SOURCES
Reread lines 43–47. What does the writer mean by this comment?

The New York Press

MONDAY, JANUARY 4, 1897   SECTION 1

MORE OF THE FILIBUSTERS SAFE

STEPHEN CRANE, NOVELIST, SWIMS ASHORE

DAYTONA, Fla., Jan. 3.—"That newspaper feller was a nervy man," said the cook of the ill-fated Commodore to-night in reference to Stephen Crane, the novelist, who is after material for stories. "He didn't seem to know what fear was. When we started out he insisted upon doing a seaman's work, and he did it well, too.

10 "When the boats were launched he was the last one, except Captain Murphy, to get in, and his nerve greatly encouraged all hands. In the small dingy he rowed as well as the others, notwithstanding he was so worn out that he could hardly hold his oar straight in the terrific seas.

SAVES A DROWNING MAN

"Both he and Captain Murphy were thrown out on the same side. Crane was 20 partially thrown under the overturned boat and but for Captain Murphy's readiness in catching him by the collar he would have gone under. We all battled there in the water for hours, it seemed to us. Crane was a good swimmer, and he really saved one of the sailors, as the man could not swim a stroke, and Crane had to keep him up by the aid of an oar. These newspaper 30 fellers have got spunk, if they do tell such awful woppers at times," concluded the cook, as he took another big swig of the "life preservative" provided by the good people here. . . . **C**

STEPHEN CRANE AND HIS WORK
How He Came to Be on the Unlucky Commodore

TO WRITE FOR THE PRESS
Brilliant Author Not of the Sort to Give Up His Cuban Letters Because of Shipwreck

STEPHEN CRANE, the writer, is safe and readers of The Press may expect in a short time a treat from his versatile pen. . . .

Mr. Crane was on the way to Cuba to write about the war there. He will get to Cuba as soon as he can. He is not of the sort who are frightened by an experience in a lifeboat. His letters will 10 appear in The Press as soon as they arrive.

Mr. Crane has not intimated just what he is going to write; probably he does not know himself. But that his letters will be intensely interesting and true to life readers of his stories, "The Red Badge of Courage," "The Third Violet," "George's Mother" and "Maggie, a Girl of the Streets," feel 20 assured. **D**

C **PRIMARY SOURCES**
Note that this article consists entirely of a quotation by the cook. Why do you think the writer of this article chose to quote him at such length?

D **PRIMARY SOURCES**
This paper portrays Crane as quite a hero, citing his bravery and pluck. In this article, why do you think the editors have chosen to make so much of his "Cuban letters," or his work as a foreign correspondent?

The New York Press

THURSDAY, JANUARY 7, 1897   SECTION 1

STEPHEN CRANE'S OWN STORY

JACKSONVILLE, FLA., Jan. 6.—It was the afternoon of New Year's. The Commodore lay at her dock in Jacksonville and negro stevedores processioned steadily toward her with box after box of ammunition and bundle after bundle of rifles. Her hatch, like the mouth of a monster, engulfed them. It might have been the feeding
10 time of some legendary creature of the sea. It was in broad daylight and the crowd of gleeful Cubans on the pier did not forbear to sing the strange patriotic ballads of their island. . . . The revenue cutter Boutwell, the old isosceles triangle that protects United States interests in the St. John's, lay at anchor, with no sign of excitement aboard her. **E**

SLEEP IMPOSSIBLE

As darkness came upon the waters,
20 the Commodore was a broad, flaming path of blue and silver phosphorescence, and as her stout bow lunged at the great black waves she threw flashing, roaring cascades to either side. And all that was to be heard was the rhythmical and mighty pounding of the engines.

THE COOK IS HOPEFUL

The cook was asleep on a bench in the galley. He woke as I entered the galley and delivered himself of some
30 dolorous sentiments: "I don't feel right about this ship, somehow. It strikes me that something is going to happen to us. I don't know what it is, but the old ship is going to get it in the neck, I think."

Author Stephen Crane

"Well, how about the men on board of her?" said I. "Are any of us going to get out, prophet?"

"Yes," said the cook. "Sometimes I have these damned feelings come over
40 me, and they are always right, and it seems to me, somehow, that you and I will both get [out] and meet again somewhere, down at Coney Island, perhaps, or some place like that."

Here I first came to know a certain young oiler named Billy Higgins. He was sloshing around this inferno filling buckets with water and passing them to a chain of men that extended up the
50 ship's side.

A WHISTLE OF DESPAIR

Now the whistle of the Commodore had been turned loose, and if there ever was a voice of despair and death, it was in the voice of this whistle. It had gained a new tone. It was as if its throat was already choked by the water, and this cry on the sea at night, with a wind blowing

continued

E **PRIMARY SOURCES**
Note that this article is written by Crane himself. How, if at all, has the style of writing changed from that in the previous articles? Explain.

the spray over the ship, and the waves roaring over the bow, and swirling white 60 along the decks, was to each of us probably a song of man's end. The boat moved at last and swung down toward the water. **F**

IN THE TEN-FOOT DINGY

The captain was just about to swing over the rail when a dark form came forward and a voice said: "Captain, I go with you."

The captain answered: "Yes, Billy; get in."

HIGGINS LAST TO LEAVE SHIP

70　It was Billy Higgins, the oiler. Billy dropped into the boat and a moment later the captain followed, bringing with him an end of about forty yards of lead line. The other end was attached to the rail of the ship.

As we swung back to leeward the captain said: "Boys, we will stay right near the ship till she goes down."

This cheerful information, of course, 80 filled us all with glee.

When came the gray shade of dawn, the form of the Commodore grew slowly clear to us as our little ten-foot boat rose over each swell. She was floating with such an air of buoyancy that we laughed when we had time, and said "What a gag it would be on those other fellows if she didn't sink at all."

But later we saw men aboard of her, 90 and later still they began to hail us.

We rowed back to the ship, but did not approach too near, because we were four men in a ten-foot boat, and we knew that the touch of a hand on our gunwale would assuredly swamp us. . . .

THE COMMODORE SINKS

The cook let go of the line. We rowed around to see if we could not get a line from the chief engineer, and

all this time, mind, there were no 100 shrieks, no groans, but silence, silence and silence, and then the Commodore sank. **G**

She lurched to windward, then swung afar back, righted and dove into the sea, and rafts were suddenly swallowed by this frightful maw of the ocean. And then by the men of the ten-foot dingy were words said that were still not words—something far beyond 110 words.

The lighthouse of Mosquito Inlet stuck up above the horizon like the point of a pin. We turned our dingy toward the shore.

The history of life in an open boat for thirty hours would no doubt be instructive for the young, but none is to be told here and now. For my part I would prefer to tell the story at once, 120 because from it would shine the splendid manhood of Captain Edward Murphy and of William Higgins, the oiler, but let it suffice at this time to say that when we were swamped in the surf and making the best of our way toward the shore the captain gave orders amid the wildness of the breakers as clearly as if he had been on the quarter deck of a battleship.

130　John Kitchell of Daytona came running down the beach, and as he ran the air was filled with clothes. If he had pulled a single lever and undressed, even as the fire horses harness, he could not seem to me to have stripped with more speed. He dashed into the water and dragged the cook. Then he went after the captain, but the captain sent him to me, and then it was that he saw Billy 140 Higgins lying with his forehead on sand that was clear of the water, and he was dead. **H**

STEPHEN CRANE

F **PRIMARY SOURCES**
Reread lines 51–63. Identify the **imagery** used to characterize the *Commodore*. What **mood** does Crane achieve with this language?

G **PRIMARY SOURCES**
Reread lines 81–102. What happened to the men still aboard the ship?

H **PRIMARY SOURCES**
What **tone** does Crane adopt in the last paragraph? Explain how this tone affects your perception of these events.

Comprehension

1. **Clarify** Over how many days did these articles appear in the newspapers?

2. **Summarize** What happened to the *Commodore* and her crew?

Critical Analysis

3. **Examine Text Features** Review the headlines of these articles. Consider their content and number. What **tone** do they convey? Explain.

4. **Analyze Primary Sources** Consider the headlines, contents, and tone of the articles. Based on these examples, what general statements might you make about 19th-century journalism? Cite evidence to support your generalization.

Read for Information: Compare Forms

WRITING PROMPT

In Stephen Crane's article about the wreck of the *Commodore*, he wrote:

The history of life in an open boat for thirty hours would no doubt be instructive for the young, but none is to be told here and now. . . . I would prefer to tell the story at once, because from it would shine the splendid manhood of Captain Edward Murphy and of William Higgins, the oiler.

Based on your reading of "The Open Boat" and "Stephen Crane's Own Story," why might Crane have reserved the tale of the open boat for a short story? What does he do with the short story that he can't or doesn't do in the article?

The following steps will help you answer the prompt:

1. Compare the short story and the article, considering the following elements:

	Article	Short Story
Audience and Purpose	to describe shipwreck for newspaper readers	
Character Development		
Coverage of Events		
Imagery and Figurative Language		
Theme and Main Idea		

2. Based on this comparison, consider why Crane may have made the choices he did in writing each piece.

3. Finally, try to explain Crane's decision to write "The Open Boat" by evaluating the strengths of the short story over the article. Support your ideas with details from each text.

The Law of Life

Short Story by Jack London

Jack London
1876–1916

According to critic Alfred Kazin, The greatest story Jack London ever wrote was the story he lived." Before London had turned 21 he had had more adventures than a Hollywood action hero. Once he began publishing stories about his experiences, he became an international celebrity. His works, many set in the wilds of Alaska and the American West, brought before the reading public a fresh style and subject matter that proved popular and profitable.

The Call of Adventure Born in San Francisco, Jack London grew up in Oakland, California. Disowned by his biological father, he took the name of his stepfather, John London. Although a decent man, the stepfather couldn't make much of a living, so London spent much of his youth working. Periods of backbreaking manual labor—in factories, canneries, a power plant, and a laundry—alternated with high adventure. The 16-year-old Jack became an oyster pirate in San Francisco Bay before switching sides to join the shore police. At age 17, he boarded a ship for a seal-hunting expedition to the Bering Sea. At 18, he quit work altogether to travel the country as a hobo. These escapades came to an abrupt halt when he was arrested for vagrancy in New York State and jailed for 30 days. Moved by the hard-luck stories of the men he had met on the road and in prison, London could see where his life was heading and decided to turn it around. I ran back to California and opened the books," he explained. By the time he was 20, he had enrolled at the University of California at Berkeley and become a writer.

From Rags to Riches Although writing steadily, London could get nothing published. News of the Klondike Gold Rush in 1897 inspired him to head to Alaska in hopes of striking it rich. Instead of finding gold, however, he got a bad case of scurvy and returned home after less than a year. Still, London admitted, It was in the Klondike that I found myself." Equally important, he found a wealth of material and formulated the naturalistic philosophy that would make him a blockbuster writer. He shot to international fame with *The Call of the Wild* (1903), and within six years had produced most of his greatest works—*The Sea Wolf* (1904), *White Fang* (1906), *The Road* (1907), the autobiographical *Martin Eden* (1909), and several collections of short stories. London inspired many in the next generation of writers, including Ernest Hemingway, Jack Kerouac, and Norman Mailer.

● LITERARY ANALYSIS: THEME

Theme is the central message communicated by a literary work. It may not be explicit but often emerges as a set of ideas expressed through literary elements. The answers to certain questions can help you identify a story's theme.

- What is the resolution of the primary **conflict?**
- What traits do the main **characters** display?
- What about the physical or cultural **setting** is significant?
- What **point of view** is used to describe the experiences of the main character?
- What objects or figures have **symbolic** meaning?
- What does the **title** refer to?

Ask yourself these questions as you read "The Law of Life," recording the answers and other details in a chart.

Details Revealing Theme					
Conflict	Character	Setting	Point of View	Symbol	Title

Review: **Naturalism**

● READING SKILL: ANALYZE AUTHOR'S PERSPECTIVE

An **author's perspective** is the unique combination of background, experiences, beliefs, and values that influences the way a writer looks at a topic. "The Law of Life" contains echoes of of London's own life experiences in Alaska and the Klondike, where he had gone in hopes of striking it rich in the goldfields. Carefully read London's biography on page 744. As you read the story, draw on what you know of London's life to help you understand his perspective on such subjects as youth and old age, strength and weakness, survival and death.

▲ VOCABULARY IN CONTEXT

Restate each phrase, using a different word or words for the boldfaced term.

1. need to **replenish** the water supply
2. a **slovenly** fellow, with dirty hair and unshined shoes
3. the **inexorable** passage of time
4. willing to **attest** to his honesty
5. a cat attempting to **harry** the mouse it caught

How do people face DEATH?

KEY IDEA **Death** comes to all of us, but different cultures approach the inevitable end in various ways. The death described in London's story may seem cruel to you, but consider the cultural context of the community described in the story.

QUICKWRITE Think about how your own culture treats people who are dying. Are they treated with indifference or respect? In a more hostile environment, such as a natural disaster, do you think society could maintain the same customs? In your notebook, jot down your thoughts about these issues.

THE
LAW
OF
LIFE

JACK LONDON

BACKGROUND Written when London was about 25 years old, this story was included in his second collection of short stories about Alaska, *Children of the Frost* (1902). The characters are members of a nomadic native tribe whose customs are shaped by the harsh conditions of the Arctic. The law they live by expresses London's naturalistic vision at its most brutal.

ANALYZE VISUALS
Look at the image on page 747. What elements of the man's clothing and facial expression give clues to the photo's **setting?** Explain.

Old Koskoosh listened greedily. Though his sight had long since faded, his hearing was still acute, and the slightest sound penetrated to the glimmering intelligence which yet abode behind his withered forehead, but which no longer gazed forth upon the things of the world. Ah! that was Sit-cum-to-ha, shrilly anathematizing the dogs as she cuffed and beat them into the harness. Sit-cum-to-ha was his daughter's daughter, but she was too busy to waste a thought upon her broken grandfather, sitting alone there in the snow, forlorn and helpless. Camp must be broken. The long trail waited while the short day refused to linger. Life called her, and the duties of life, not death. And he was very close to death now. Ⓐ

10   The thought made the old man panicky for the moment, and he stretched forth a palsied hand which wandered tremblingly over the small heap of dry wood beside him. Reassured that it was indeed there, his hand returned to the shelter of his mangy furs, and he again fell to listening. The sulky crackling of half-frozen hides told him that the chief's moose-skin lodge had been struck, and

Ⓐ THEME
What is significant about the **setting** described in the first paragraph, and what **mood** does it create?

even then was being rammed and jammed into portable compass. The chief was his son, stalwart and strong, head man of the tribesmen, and a mighty hunter. As the women toiled with the camp luggage, his voice rose, chiding them for their slowness. Old Koskoosh strained his ears. It was the last time he would hear that voice. There went Geehow's lodge! And Tusken's! Seven, eight, nine; only
20 the shaman's[1] could be still standing. There! They were at work upon it now. He could hear the shaman grunt as he piled it on the sled. A child whimpered, and a woman soothed it with soft, crooning gutturals.[2] Little Koo-tee, the old man thought, a fretful child, and not overstrong. It would die soon, perhaps, and they would burn a hole through the frozen tundra and pile rocks above to keep the wolverines away. Well, what did it matter? A few years at best, and as many an empty belly as a full one. And in the end, Death waited, ever-hungry and hungriest of them all. **B**

What was that? Oh, the men lashing the sleds and drawing tight the thongs. He listened, who would listen no more. The whip-lashes snarled and bit among
30 the dogs. Hear them whine! How they hated the work and the trail! They were off! Sled after sled churned slowly away into the silence. They were gone. They had passed out of his life, and he faced the last bitter hour alone. No. The snow crunched beneath a moccasin; a man stood beside him; upon his head a hand rested gently. His son was good to do this thing. He remembered other old men whose sons had not waited after the tribe. But his son had. He wandered away into the past, till the young man's voice brought him back.

"Is it well with you?" he asked.

And the old man answered, "It is well."

"There be wood beside you," the younger man continued, "and the fire burns
40 bright. The morning is gray, and the cold has broken. It will snow presently. Even now it is snowing."

"Ay, even now it is snowing."

"The tribesmen hurry. Their bales are heavy, and their bellies flat with lack of feasting. The trail is long and they travel fast. I go now. It is well?"

"It is well. I am as a last year's leaf, clinging lightly to the stem. The first breath that blows, and I fall. My voice is become like an old woman's. My eyes no longer show me the way of my feet, and my feet are heavy, and I am tired. It is well."

He bowed his head in content till the last noise of the complaining snow had died away, and he knew his son was beyond recall. Then his hand crept out in
50 haste to the wood. It alone stood between him and the eternity that yawned in upon him. At last the measure of his life was a handful of fagots.[3] One by one they would go to feed the fire, and just so, step by step, death would creep upon him. When the last stick had surrendered up its heat, the frost would begin to gather strength. First his feet would yield, then his hands; and the numbness would travel, slowly, from the extremities to the body. His head would fall forward upon his knees, and he would rest. It was easy. All men must die. **C**

---

1. **shaman's:** belonging to a priest who uses magic to cure the sick or predict events.

2. **gutturals:** sounds that are made in the throat.

3. **fagots:** sticks of wood.

B THEME
Reread lines 10–27. From whose **point of view** are we experiencing the events described? What are some of the contrasting ideas running through this character's head?

C AUTHOR'S PERSPECTIVE
Reread the biography on page 744 and consider the experience that forced London to leave Alaska. How might this experience be reflected in lines 48–56? Explain.

He did not complain. It was the way of life, and it was just. He had been born close to the earth, close to the earth had he lived, and the law thereof was not new to him. It was the law of all flesh. Nature was not kindly to the flesh. She had no concern for that concrete thing called the individual. Her interest lay in the species, the race. This was the deepest abstraction old Koskoosh's barbaric mind was capable of, but he grasped it firmly. He saw it exemplified in all life. The rise of the sap, the bursting greenness of the willow bud, the fall of the yellow leaf—in this alone was told the whole history. But one task did Nature set the individual. Did he not perform it, he died. Did he perform it, it was all the same, he died. Nature did not care; there were plenty who were obedient, and it was only the obedience in this matter, not the obedient, which lived and lived always. The tribe of Koskoosh was very old. The old men he had known when a boy, had known old men before them. Therefore it was true that the tribe lived, that it stood for the obedience of all its members, way down into the forgotten past, whose very resting-places were unremembered. They did not count; they were episodes. They had passed away like clouds from a summer sky. He also was an episode, and would pass away. Nature did not care. To life she set one task, gave one law. To perpetuate was the task of life, its law was death. A maiden was a good creature to look upon, full-breasted and strong, with spring to her step and light in her eyes. But her task was yet before her. The light in her eyes brightened, her step quickened, she was now bold with the young men, now timid, and she gave them of her own unrest. And ever she grew fairer and yet fairer to look upon, till some hunter, able no longer to withhold himself, took her to his lodge to cook and toil for him and to become the mother of his children. And with the coming of her offspring her looks left her. Her limbs dragged and shuffled, her eyes dimmed and bleared, and only the little children found joy against the withered cheek of the old squaw by the fire. Her task was done. But a little while, on the first pinch of famine or the first long trail, and she would be left, even as he had been left, in the snow, with a little pile of wood. Such was the law. **D**

He placed a stick carefully upon the fire and resumed his meditations. It was the same everywhere, with all things. The mosquitoes vanished with the first frost. The little tree-squirrel crawled away to die. When age settled upon the rabbit it became slow and heavy, and could no longer outfoot its enemies. Even the big bald-face grew clumsy and blind and quarrelsome, in the end to be dragged down by a handful of yelping huskies. He remembered how he had abandoned his own father on an upper reach of the Klondike one winter, the winter before the missionary came with his talk-books and his box of medicines. Many a time had Koskoosh smacked his lips over the recollection of that box, though now his mouth refused to moisten. The "painkiller" had been especially good. But the missionary was a bother after all, for he brought no meat into the camp, and he ate heartily, and the hunters grumbled. But he chilled his lungs on the divide by the Mayo,[4] and the dogs afterwards nosed the stones away and fought over his bones.

D NATURALISM
Reread lines 57–85. In one or two sentences, summarize the relationship between nature and the individual expressed in this paragraph.

---

4. **the Mayo:** a small river in the Yukon Territory in northwestern Canada.

100   Koskoosh placed another stick on the fire and harked back deeper into the past. There was the time of the Great Famine, when the old men crouched empty-bellied to the fire, and let fall from their lips dim traditions of the ancient day when the Yukon ran wide open for three winters, and then lay frozen for three summers. He had lost his mother in that famine. In the summer the salmon run had failed, and the tribe looked forward to the winter and the coming of the caribou. Then the winter came, but with it there were no caribou. Never had the like been known, not even in the lives of the old men. But the caribou did not come, and it was the seventh year, and the rabbits had not **replenished,** and the dogs were naught but bundles of bones. And through the long darkness the

110 children wailed and died, and the women, and the old men; and not one in ten of the tribe lived to meet the sun when it came back in the spring. That *was* a famine!

    But he had seen times of plenty, too, when the meat spoiled on their hands, and the dogs were fat and worthless with overeating—times when they let the game go unkilled, and the women were fertile, and the lodges were cluttered with sprawling men-children and women-children. Then it was the men became high-stomached, and revived ancient quarrels, and crossed the divides to the south to kill the Pellys, and to the west that they might sit by the dead fires of the Tananas.[5] He remembered, when a boy, during a time of plenty, when he saw a moose pulled

120 down by the wolves. Zing-ha lay with him in the snow and watched—Zing-ha, who later became the craftiest of hunters, and who, in the end, fell through an air-hole on the Yukon. They found him, a month afterward, just as he had crawled halfway out and frozen stiff to the ice.

    But the moose. Zing-ha and he had gone out that day to play at hunting after the manner of their fathers. On the bed of the creek they struck the fresh track of a moose, and with it the tracks of many wolves. "An old one," Zing-ha, who was quicker at reading the sign, said—"an old one who cannot keep up with the herd. The wolves have cut him out from his brothers, and they will never leave him." And it was so. It was their way. By day and by night, never resting, snarling on his

130 heels, snapping at his nose, they would stay by him to the end. How Zing-ha and he felt the blood-lust quicken! The finish would be a sight to see! **E**

    Eager-footed, they took the trail, and even he, Koskoosh, slow of sight and an unversed tracker, could have followed it blind, it was so wide. Hot were they on the heels of the chase, reading the grim tragedy, fresh-written, at every step. Now they came to where the moose had made a stand. Thrice the length of a grown man's body, in every direction, had the snow been stamped about and uptossed. In the midst were the deep impressions of the splay-hoofed game, and all about, everywhere, were the lighter footmarks of the wolves. Some, while their brothers **harried** the kill, had lain to one side and rested. The full-stretched impress of their

140 bodies in the snow was as perfect as though made the moment before. One wolf had been caught in a wild lunge of the maddened victim and trampled to death. A few bones, well picked, bore witness.

---

5. **Pellys . . . Tananas:** *Pellys* probably refers to native peoples who lived near the Pelly River. The Tananas are native people who traditionally lived in areas of Alaska and the Yukon.

replenish (rĭ-plĕn'ĭsh) *v.* to fill up again

E THEME
In lines 124–131, the third-person limited point of view reveals Koskoosh's memory of the old moose and his own reaction at the time. What is **ironic** about this recollection?

harry (hăr'ē) *v.* to torment, often by constant attack

Again, they ceased the uplift of their snowshoes at a second stand. Here the great animal had fought desperately. Twice had he been dragged down, as the snow **attested,** and twice had he shaken his assailants clear and gained footing once more. He had done his task long since, but none the less was life dear to him. Zing-ha said it was a strange thing, a moose once down to get free again; but this one certainly had. The shaman would see signs and wonders in this when they told him. **F**

150 And yet again, they came to where the moose had made to mount the bank and gain the timber. But his foes had laid on from behind, till he reared and fell back upon them, crushing two deep into the snow. It was plain the kill was at hand, for their brothers had left them untouched. Two more stands were hurried past, brief in time-length and very close together. The trail was red now, and the clean stride of the great beast had grown short and **slovenly.** Then they heard the first sounds of the battle—not the full-throated chorus of the chase, but the short, snappy bark which spoke of close quarters and teeth to flesh. Crawling up the wind, Zing-ha bellied it through the snow, and with him crept he, Koskoosh, who was to be chief of the tribesmen in the years to come. Together they shoved aside the under 160 branches of a young spruce and peered forth. It was the end they saw.

The picture, like all of youth's impressions, was still strong with him, and his dim eyes watched the end played out as vividly as in that far-off time. Koskoosh

attest (ə-tĕst′) v. to affirm to be true; to be proof of

F THEME
Reread lines 143–149. What is surprising about the moose's struggle with the wolves? Consider the significance of this **conflict.**

slovenly (slŭv′ən-lē) *adj.* untidy in personal appearance marvelled at this, for in the days which followed, when he was a leader of men and a head of councillors, he had done great deeds and made his name a curse in the mouths of the Pellys, to say naught of the strange white man he had killed, knife to knife, in open fight. **G**

For long he pondered on the days of his youth, till the fire died down and the frost bit deeper. He replenished it with two sticks this time, and gauged his grip on life by what remained. If Sit-cum-to-ha had only remembered her grandfather,
170 and gathered a larger armful, his hours would have been longer. It would have been easy. But she was ever a careless child, and honored not her ancestors from the time the Beaver, son of the son of Zing-ha, first cast eyes upon her. Well, what mattered it? Had he not done likewise in his own quick youth? For a while he listened to the silence. Perhaps the heart of his son might soften, and he would come back with the dogs to take his old father on with the tribe to where the caribou ran thick and the fat hung heavy upon them.

He strained his ears, his restless brain for the moment stilled. Not a stir, nothing. He alone took breath in the midst of the great silence. It was very lonely. Hark! What was that? A chill passed over his body. The familiar, long-drawn howl
180 broke the void, and it was close at hand. Then on his darkened eyes was projected the vision of the moose—the old bull moose—the torn flanks and bloody sides, the riddled mane, and the great branching horns, down low and tossing to the last. He saw the flashing forms of gray, the gleaming eyes, the lolling tongues, the slavered fangs. And he saw the **inexorable** circle close in till it became a dark point in the midst of the stamped snow. **H**

A cold muzzle thrust against his cheek, and at its touch his soul leaped back to the present. His hand shot into the fire and dragged out a burning fagot. Overcome for the nonce[6] by his hereditary fear of man, the brute retreated, raising a prolonged call to his brothers; and greedily they answered, till a ring of
190 crouching, jaw-slobbered gray was stretched round about. The old man listened to the drawing in of this circle. He waved his brand wildly, and sniffs turned to snarls; but the panting brutes refused to scatter. Now one wormed his chest forward, dragging his haunches after, now a second, now a third; but never a one drew back. Why should he cling to life? he asked, and dropped the blazing stick into the snow. It sizzled and went out. The circle grunted uneasily, but held its own. Again he saw the last stand of the old bull moose, and Koskoosh dropped his head wearily upon his knees. What did it matter after all? Was it not the law of life? ∾

<table>
<tr><td>**G** AUTHOR'S PERSPECTIVE</td></tr>
</table>

G AUTHOR'S PERSPECTIVE
Reread lines 162–166. What sensibility about human relationships is revealed in the struggle described here? Consider how this sensibility might be rooted in London's life experience.

inexorable
(ĭn-ĕk′sər-ə-bəl) *adj.*
relentless

H THEME
Reread lines 177–185. What does the old bull moose represent? Consider the thematic message suggested by this **symbol**.

---

6. **for the nonce:** for the time being.

Comprehension

1. **Recall** How does Koskoosh die?

2. **Clarify** How has he expected to die?

3. **Summarize** Describe the conditions of life for the tribe.

Literary Analysis

4. **Interpret Theme** Look back at the details about narrative elements you recorded in your chart as you read. Taken together, what do these details suggest about the fate of Koskoosh and all humans?

5. **Analyze Cultural Context** Explain how each of the following factors might contribute to the tribe's attitude about **death:**

   - the tribe's connection "to the earth" (lines 57–67)
   - what the tribe sees as "the task of life" (lines 73–85)
   - the Arctic environment (lines 101–123)

6. **Analyze Point of View** Imagine that this story had been written without any insight into Koskoosh's thoughts. What information or ideas would be missing? With this in mind, explain whether or not you think the point of view plays a crucial role in expressing the story's **theme.** Cite evidence from the story to support your view.

7. **Examine Author's Perspective** In your opinion, has London created a credible portrayal of the native American tribe and their values? How do you think this portrayal reflects London's own life experiences? In developing your answer, give details from the story as well as from the biography on page 744.

8. **Compare Expressions of Naturalism** Compare and contrast London's portrayal of nature in this story with Crane's in "The Open Boat." Consider in particular the characters' fates and any differences in tone. Record your answers with evidence from the stories in a Venn diagram. In which version of nature would you prefer to live? Explain.

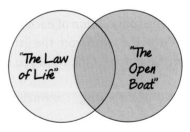

Literary Criticism

9. **Critical Interpretation** The writer E. L. Doctorow said, "It was Jack London's capacity for really living in the world, for taking it on in self-conscious and often reckless acts of courage, that made him our first writer-hero." Given what you have read in London's biography and your reading of "The Law of Life," do you agree with the notion of London as a hero? Explain.

Vocabulary in Context

VOCABULARY PRACTICE

Determine the relationship between the first pair of words in each analogy.
Then choose the vocabulary word that best completes the second pair.

1. *Nurse* is to *care* as *pest* is to _____.
2. *Impressive* is to *splendid* as _____ is to *unyielding*.
3. *Agree* is to *contradict* as _____ is to *deplete*.
4. *Well-groomed* is to *dandy* as _____ is to *slob*.
5. *Refuse* is to *decline* as _____ is to *declare*.

> **WORD LIST**
> attest
> harry
> inexorable
> replenish
> slovenly

VOCABULARY IN WRITING

Make a case for or against leaving the elderly to die in a society such as the
one in this story, and write a short defense of your opinion. Use one or two
vocabulary words. Here is a sample beginning.

> **EXAMPLE SENTENCE**
> *Death is certainly **inexorable**, but it should be delayed as long as possible.*

VOCABULARY STRATEGY: DENOTATION AND CONNOTATION

Every word has a **denotation,** or basic dictionary meaning. Some words have
certain **connotations,** or additional shades of meaning. For example, the word
slovenly means "untidy," but it has a more strongly negative connotation. When
you encounter a new word, be sure to consider whether its connotation fits
the context.

PRACTICE The connotation of each boldfaced word makes it inappropriate in the
context. Write the word from the list provided that would be more suitable in
each case. Explain why the word you chose is a better match for the context.

> charlatan   discriminating   ostentatious   resolute   subservient   traditional

1. His **picky** taste was evident in his beautiful suits and well-chosen ties.
2. That **beguiler!** She convinced the children that she was their long-lost aunt.
3. I admire **inflexible** leaders who make hard decisions and then stick with them.
4. Her **humble** attitude impressed her employers, but behind their backs she
   belittled them constantly.
5. The **elegant** ballroom had more than its share of gold chandeliers, gaudy silk
   couches, and overly elaborate draperies.
6. The mayor espouses **reactionary** values such as hard work and love of family.

VOCABULARY PRACTICE
For more practice, go
to the **Vocabulary Center**
at **ClassZone.com.**

Naturalistic Perspectives

As illustrated in the short stories by Stephen Crane and Jack London you have just read, the central assumption of naturalism is that human beings have very little control over their own lives, but instead are at the mercy of the natural world and the impersonal force of fate. The following quotations all explore a similarly naturalistic attitude.

"Nature, to be commanded, must be obeyed."

—**Sir Francis Bacon**

"It clearly matters very little to nature whether man has a mind or not."

—**Eugène Delacroix**

"At no time and in no place, will nature ever ask your permission."

—**Fyodor Dostoyevsky**

"Man and nature have such different views about the good of the world."

—**George Gissing**

"In nature there are neither rewards nor punishments—there are consequences."

—**R. G. Ingersoll**

Extension Online

INQUIRY & RESEARCH A tornado demolishes a house yet skips its neighbor; a marathon runner dies of a heart attack; a woman loses her retirement fund after working loyally for a company for 25 years. Every day it seems there is another story in the newspaper about the randomness of nature or the inability of humans to control their own lives. **Search** three online newspapers for stories that seem to support the naturalistic viewpoint. Print out one story to share with your classmates.

Writing to Evaluate

Choose the quotation on this page that you think best represents the theme of "The Open Boat" or "The Law of Life." Write an essay defending your choice, using details from the story as support.

Consider

- the main message of each story
- the subtle and sometimes not-so-subtle differences between the quotations
- which details from the story support your choice of quotation

Social Themes in Fiction

People often talk about social issues—such as poverty, racism, or crime—in a general sense, but how do these issues affect individuals' lives in reality? In 19th-century America, writers began to explore these issues in fiction.

Dramatizing Social Issues

Typical themes in literature deal with issues that are common to most people, such as the loss of innocence, difficult family relationships, or a new love. **Social themes,** however, deal with issues that concern a particular group of people, such as those in a certain neighborhood, geographical region, or religious community. These issues are usually specific to a time and place, but they may echo in other cultures and times as well. For example, the dynamics of Puritan society inspired a number of great literary works with social themes, from Nathaniel Hawthorne's *The Scarlet Letter* (1850) to Arthur Miller's *The Crucible* (1953). While Hawthorne explored the effects of Puritan morality on individual lives, Miller chose to expose the wrongs committed in the name of righteousness during the Salem witch trials as a way to explore parallel events of his own time.

Two suffragettes, circa 1905, stand on an American city street, promoting women's rights.

In the late 19th and early 20th centuries, novels and short stories with a contemporary social theme typically dealt with issues that generated strong public reaction and debate for that era. These issues included industrialism, urbanization, and the displacement of Native Americans. In this way, literature became a powerful tool for social change.

Identifying Social Themes

Novels and short stories of the period often portray characters struggling against poverty, prejudice, and other social obstacles. One social issue in particular that emerged in the second half of the 19th century was the role of women in society. This issue preoccupied writers of many nationalities during this time and inspired feminist writers in the 20th century. All of the stories in this part of Unit 4 address this issue in one way or another. To help you identify the social themes in these and other stories, consider the following:

- Look for **characters** who have little control over their fate, and ask yourself what **social factors** contribute to their situation.

- Clarify the **conflicts** in the story and determine to what extent they are caused by forces beyond a character's control.

- Examine direct statements of a **character's or narrator's opinions** to see whether these provide clues to a theme.

- Think about the **author's reason** for writing the story. What was he or she trying to achieve?

Works that address social issues often focus on people who have few, if any, rights and privileges in society. The first-person narrator of "The Yellow Wallpaper" (page 768), although comfortably middle-class, has no control over her life. Early in the story, she explains her complete submission to her doctor and her husband.

> So I take phosphates . . . and tonics, and journeys, and air, and exercise, and am absolutely forbidden to "work" until I am well again.
>
> Personally, I disagree with their ideas.
>
> Personally, I believe that congenial work, with excitement and change, would do me good.
>
> But what is one to do?
>
> **—Charlotte Perkins Gilman, "The Yellow Wallpaper"**

Close Read

Based on the narrator's statements in this passage, how would you describe her relationship with the doctor and her husband?

In "The Story of an Hour" (page 760), the main character, after hearing that her husband is dead, reflects on the control he has exercised over her. Notice how her thoughts are a statement on the relationships between men and women in general.

> There would be no one to live for her during those coming years; she would live for herself. There would be no powerful will bending hers in that blind persistence with which men and women believe they have a right to impose a private will upon a fellow creature.
>
> **—Kate Chopin, "The Story of an Hour"**

Close Read

How is this character's attitude different from that expressed in "The Yellow Wallpaper"?

The Story of an Hour

Short Story by Kate Chopin

Kate Chopin

1850–1904

When her second volume of short stories was published in 1897, Kate Chopin's literary career was already thriving. Critics had praised her first collection, *Bayou Folk,* for its local-color realism, calling her tales "charming" and "quaint." Two years later came the bombshell: Chopin published *The Awakening,* a novel about a housewife's sexual and artistic awakening, complete with an adulterous affair and suicide as a last, desperate act of freedom. A chorus of outraged reviewers reviled the novel as immoral, drowning out the few brave enough to praise it. No publisher would touch her next collection, *A Vocation and a Voice,* which included "The Story of an Hour." Chopin died soon after, and *The Awakening* languished out of print for 50 years.

Faithful Wife and Mother Chopin was born Catherine O'Flaherty in St. Louis, Missouri, to a socially prominent family.

Esteemed for her beauty, intelligence, and ready wit, she fell in love with and married Oscar Chopin when she was 19. The Chopins settled in New Orleans, where their six children were born. Kate Chopin had no difficulty in reconciling the demands of her family with her strong independent streak. With the support of her husband, she smoked cigarettes and explored the city unescorted—scandalous behavior for an upper-class woman at the time.

A Budding Writer Chopin started writing at the age of 32. After her husband died, she returned to St. Louis, where her doctor suggested she write stories to work through her grief. Encouraged that her very first story was published, Chopin studied the work of French short story master Guy de Maupassant and honed her craft. She gradually developed an interest in complex issues such as the longing for freedom and self-fulfillment among women.

A Late-Blooming Classic Though *The Awakening* ended its author's career, it went on, after her death, to become a classic. Critics in the 1950s rediscovered the novel and, proclaiming Chopin "ahead of her time," sparked renewed interest in her modern sensibilities. Of *The Awakening*'s heroine, Edna Pontellier, Chopin once said, "I never dreamed of Mrs. Pontellier making such a mess of things. . . . If I had the slightest intimation of such a thing I would have excluded her from the company." The controversial heroine made Chopin a legend. Today, *The Awakening* is among the five most-read American novels in colleges and universities.

LITERARY ANALYSIS: PLOT AND CONFLICT

What makes a great story? The power of a literary work comes partly from its **plot,** or sequence of actions and events. These events are often external—maybe one character rescues another, or the sky opens up with a ferocious downpour. They might also take place internally. These events invariably lead to both **internal** and **external conflict,** and it is this conflict that drives the plot to its **climax,** or turning point, and **resolution,** in which the conflict is settled one way or another.

The plot of "The Story of an Hour" begins with an external event that propels the main character into a dramatic inner conflict.

She was beginning to recognize this thing that was approaching to possess her, and she was striving to beat it back with her will. . . .

As you read this story, pay attention to the relationship between external and internal events and conflicts. In particular, look to see just how the conflict is resolved.

READING STRATEGY: PREDICT

Making accurate **predictions** as you read is not always easy—especially when certain elements in a story are not as straightforward as they initially seem. To create surprising plot twists, a writer often uses **situational irony,** a contrast between what readers expect to happen and what actually does happen. Other times, a writer lets the reader know more about a character or situation in the story than the characters themselves know. This is called **dramatic irony.**

As you read this story, note details that seem to reveal something important about a character or **foreshadow** an upcoming event, giving hints about what will take place. Use these clues to predict what will happen next. As events unfold, note whether your expectations were met or you were taken by surprise.

Clues from the Text	My Predictions	Actual Outcome
"Great care" is taken to delicately break the news of Mr. Mallard's death to his widow, who has a weak heart.		

Explore the Key Idea

Do all CAGES *have bars?*

KEY IDEA Prisons and detention centers, animal cages, even children's playpens—all have bars to keep their inhabitants from escaping. But are these the only kinds of **constraints** that restrict freedom? In "The Story of an Hour," Kate Chopin explores just how restrictive invisible bars can be.

PRESENT With a partner, brainstorm a list of different circumstances in which people can become trapped or otherwise kept from fulfilling themselves. Share your list with the class and explain which constraint you think is the biggest threat to an individual's freedom today.

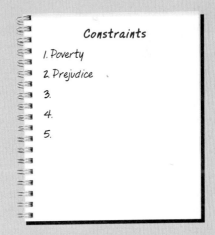

Constraints
1. Poverty
2. Prejudice
3.
4.
5.

The Story of an HOUR

KATE CHOPIN

BACKGROUND This story takes place around 1900, when the status of women was radically different than it is today. Because women could not vote, they had almost no political or legal power; because they could not own property and had few chances to gain education or employment, they had little or no financial independence. Few careers were open to middle- and upper-class women, who were expected to be supported by their husbands. In most American marriages of the time, the husband was the undisputed head of the household.

Knowing that Mrs. Mallard was afflicted with a heart trouble, great care was taken to break to her as gently as possible the news of her husband's death. **A**

It was her sister Josephine who told her, in broken sentences; veiled hints that revealed in half concealing. Her husband's friend Richards was there, too, near her. It was he who had been in the newspaper office when intelligence of the railroad disaster was received, with Brently Mallard's name leading the list of "killed." He had only taken the time to assure himself of its truth by a second telegram, and had hastened to forestall any less careful, less tender friend in bearing the sad message.

ANALYZE VISUALS
In the era in which this story is set, women were deemed fragile, sensitive, and submissive. What artistic elements help to convey these attributes in the painting?

A PREDICT
What might this early mention of Mrs. Mallard's illness **foreshadow?** Use this clue to predict how she will react to the news of her husband's death. Record your prediction in your chart.

A Sketch of a Faraway Look, Herman Jean Joseph Richir. Bonhams, London. © Bridgeman Art Library/SuperStock.

She did not hear the story as many women have heard the same, with a
10 paralyzed inability to accept its significance. She wept at once, with sudden, wild
abandonment, in her sister's arms. When the storm of grief had spent itself she
went away to her room alone. She would have no one follow her.

There stood, facing the open window, a comfortable, roomy armchair. Into
this she sank, pressed down by a physical exhaustion that haunted her body and
seemed to reach into her soul.

She could see in the open square before her house the tops of trees that were
all aquiver with the new spring life. The delicious breath of rain was in the air. In
the street below a peddler was crying his wares. The notes of a distant song which
someone was singing reached her faintly, and countless sparrows were twittering
20 in the eaves.

There were patches of blue sky showing here and there through the clouds that
had met and piled one above the other in the west facing her window.

She sat with her head thrown back upon the cushion of the chair, quite
motionless, except when a sob came up into her throat and shook her, as a child
who has cried itself to sleep continues to sob in its dreams.

She was young, with a fair, calm face, whose lines bespoke repression and even
a certain strength. But now there was a dull stare in her eyes, whose gaze was
fixed away off yonder on one of those patches of blue sky. It was not a glance of
reflection, but rather indicated a suspension of intelligent thought.

30   There was something coming to her and she was waiting for it, fearfully. What
was it? She did not know; it was too subtle and elusive to name. But she felt it,
creeping out of the sky, reaching toward her through the sounds, the scents, the
color that filled the air. **B**

Now her bosom rose and fell tumultuously. She was beginning to recognize this
thing that was approaching to possess her, and she was striving to beat it back with
her will—as powerless as her two white slender hands would have been. **C**

When she abandoned herself a little whispered word escaped her slightly parted
lips. She said it over and over under her breath: "free, free, free!" The vacant stare
and the look of terror that had followed it went from her eyes. They stayed keen
40 and bright. Her pulses beat fast, and the coursing blood warmed and relaxed every
inch of her body. **D**

She did not stop to ask if it were or were not a monstrous joy that held her.
A clear and exalted perception enabled her to dismiss the suggestion as trivial.

She knew that she would weep again when she saw the kind, tender hands
folded in death; the face that had never looked save with love upon her, fixed and
gray and dead. But she saw beyond that bitter moment a long procession of years
to come that would belong to her absolutely. And she opened and spread her arms
out to them in welcome.

B GRAMMAR AND STYLE
Reread lines 30–33.
Notice how Chopin uses
the **active voice,** with the
subjects performing the
action in the sentences.
Contrast this with her use
of the **passive voice** in the
first sentence of the story.

C PLOT AND CONFLICT
Reread lines 34–36. With
what is Mrs. Mallard
struggling? Explain
whether her conflict is
internal or **external.**

D PREDICT
Did Mrs. Mallard respond
to the revelation as you
predicted she would?
What is **ironic** about her
reaction?

There would be no one to live for her during those coming years; she would
50 live for herself. There would be no powerful will bending hers in that blind
persistence with which men and women believe they have a right to impose a
private will upon a fellow creature. A kind intention or a cruel intention made
the act seem no less a crime as she looked upon it in that brief moment of
illumination.

And yet she had loved him—sometimes. Often she had not. What did it matter!
What could love, the unsolved mystery, count for in face of this possession of self-
assertion which she suddenly recognized as the strongest impulse of her being!

"Free! Body and soul free!" she kept whispering.

Josephine was kneeling before the closed door with her lips to the keyhole,
60 imploring for admission. "Louise, open the door! I beg; open the door—you will
make yourself ill. What are you doing, Louise? For heaven's sake open the door."

"Go away. I am not making myself ill." No; she was drinking in a very elixir
of life[1] through that open window.

Her fancy was running riot along those days ahead of her. Spring days, and
summer days, and all sorts of days that would be her own. She breathed a quick
prayer that life might be long. It was only yesterday she had thought with a
shudder that life might be long. **E**

She arose at length and opened the door to her sister's importunities. There was
a feverish triumph in her eyes, and she carried herself unwittingly like a goddess
70 of Victory. She clasped her sister's waist, and together they descended the stairs.
Richards stood waiting for them at the bottom.

Someone was opening the front door with a latchkey. It was Brently Mallard
who entered, a little travel-stained, composedly carrying his grip-sack[2] and
umbrella. He had been far from the scene of accident, and did not even know
there had been one. He stood amazed at Josephine's piercing cry; at Richards'
quick motion to screen him from the view of his wife.

But Richards was too late.

When the doctors came they said she had died of heart disease—of joy that
kills. ❧

E **PLOT AND CONFLICT**
Consider the feelings
Mrs. Mallard struggles
to repress when she first
enters her room. How, in
lines 42–67, is this conflict
resolved?

---

1. **elixir of life:** a medicine that restores vigor or the essence of life.
2. **grip-sack:** a small traveling bag or satchel.

Comprehension

1. **Recall** What illness afflicts Mrs. Mallard?

2. **Summarize** Describe the news Mrs. Mallard receives at the beginning of the story and explain how she reacts.

3. **Clarify** What happens at the end of the story?

Literary Analysis

4. **Analyze Plot and Conflict** The plot of "The Story of an Hour" is driven by Mrs. Mallard's **internal conflict.** Describe her conflict; then explain how this secret inner struggle sets up the story's **surprise ending.**

5. **Examine Predictions** Review the chart you filled in as you read. Were your predictions accurate? Consider how Chopin uses **irony** to play on readers' expectations and deliver surprise plot twists in each of the following cases. Does this manipulation increase or decrease your enjoyment of the story?

   • Mrs. Mallard's reaction to the news that her husband is dead (lines 34–58)
   • Mrs. Mallard's wish that "life might be long" (lines 64–67)
   • the doctor's explanation of the cause of Mrs. Mallard's death (lines 78–79)

6. **Interpret Imagery** Reread lines 16–22. How does Chopin's use of imagery contribute to your understanding of Mrs. Mallard's character and situation? Did the imagery make you more or less sympathetic toward her? Explain, citing specific lines from the story that influenced your response.

7. **Compare Characters** Both Mrs. Mallard and Aunt Georgiana in "A Wagner Matinee" by Willa Cather (page 694) face **constraints** that confine them to a specific way of life. In a Venn diagram like the one shown, compare and contrast these two characters' situations. Use your completed diagram to explain what message each author might be trying to convey through her main character.

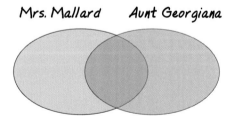

Mrs. Mallard   Aunt Georgiana

Literary Criticism

8. **Social Context** Women's roles have certainly changed since Chopin wrote this story, but has the institution of marriage? Reread lines 49–54 of "The Story of an Hour." Is the imposition of will by both men and women that Chopin describes still an issue in contemporary marriages? Explain your opinion.

Reading-Writing Connection

WRITING PROMPT

COMPOSE A JOURNAL ENTRY "The Story of an Hour" focuses on Mrs. Mallard's conflicted feelings about her husband's rumored death. Think about the moment her feelings suddenly shift from sorrow to joy. What are some of the possibilities she thinks her newfound "freedom" might offer her? How does she foresee her life changing? Imagine you are Mrs. Mallard. Write a **three-paragraph journal entry** in which you detail some of the thoughts that might have gone through her mind as she pondered a future free of **constraints**.

SELF-CHECK

A strong journal entry will . . .

- reflect Mrs. Mallard's initial struggle with her feelings
- give concrete examples of how she believes her life might change
- use language and sentence types that capture her emotions

GRAMMAR AND STYLE

USE EFFECTIVE VOICE Review the **Grammar and Style** note on page 762. The **active voice** indicates that the subject of a sentence is *performing* the action. It is the voice writers use most of the time. The **passive voice** indicates that the subject of a sentence is *receiving* the action. Though the passive voice is generally avoided in formal writing, writers will sometimes use it to create a particular effect or to indicate that the performer of an action is indefinite or unknown. Here are examples of each type of voice:

Active: *Someone was opening the front door with a latchkey.* (line 72)

Passive: *It was he who had been in the newspaper office when intelligence of the railroad disaster was received....* (lines 5–6)

Kate Chopin effectively uses the active and passive voices to mirror her character's emotional transition from repression to liberation. She begins the story in the passive voice, when Mrs. Mallard is still under constraint, but later switches to the active voice as Mrs. Mallard begins to acknowledge her own identity.

PRACTICE Change the voice of the following sentences as indicated in parentheses.

> **EXAMPLE**
>
> He gave me my freedom. (Change to the passive voice.)
>
> *Freedom was given to me.*

1. A life of adventure is desired by everyone. (Change to the active voice.)

2. I will spend my days as I wish. (Change to the passive voice.)

3. No one will be consulted about my plans. (Change to the active voice.)

WRITING TOOLS
For prewriting, revision, and editing tools, visit the **Writing Center** at ClassZone.com.

The Yellow Wallpaper
Short Story by Charlotte Perkins Gilman

Charlotte Perkins Gilman
1860–1935

As a feminist writer, social activist, public lecturer, editor, and publisher, Charlotte Perkins Gilman rode the wave of reform that washed over the United States in the late 19th and early 20th centuries. Her 1898 landmark study, *Women and Economics*—called "the Bible of the woman's movement" at the time—argued persuasively that women's economic dependence on men made them veritable slaves in U.S. society. To rectify the inequities, she advocated child-care centers and communal kitchens so that women could earn money outside the home. In addition, her startlingly original story "The Yellow Wallpaper," published in 1892, discredited a popular treatment for women's so-called "nervous disorders." Looking beyond suffrage, Gilman sought to free women from domestic servitude and foster their intellectual and emotional growth.

Formative Early Years Gilman got a rather shaky start in life. Her father abandoned the family shortly after her birth in Hartford, Connecticut. Her mother, possibly in reaction to her dire circumstances, adopted the odd child-rearing habits of withholding affection and forbidding her daughter to read fiction or form close friendships. Fortunately, financial hardship forced the family to live with relatives, the most prominent among them being Harriet Beecher Stowe, the abolitionist author of *Uncle Tom's Cabin*, and the feminists Catherine Beecher and Isabella Beecher Hooker. Guided by her strong, successful aunts, young Charlotte grew into a well-adjusted, independent woman.

Sweetening Reform with Humor Gilman's first published work was a volume of poetry, *In This Our World*, which attracted attention for the humorous way she ridiculed social injustice and inequality. *Women and Economics* garnered similar praise despite its frontal assault on conventional marriage. One reviewer praised the "wit and sarcasm" that made Gilman's "profound social philosophy" such an entertaining read. After publishing several more sociological studies, Gilman returned to writing fiction. *Herland* (1915) is a science-fiction satire about the comic misadventures of three men who stumble upon an all-female society. Still, Gilman's most popular work continues to be "The Yellow Wallpaper," the grim but fascinating portrait of a woman's descent into madness. The one-of-a-kind story has never gone out of print.

● LITERARY ANALYSIS: FIRST-PERSON NARRATOR

A story's narrator—the character or voice that relates events to the reader—can have a marked effect on how you perceive those events. A **first-person narrator** is a character in the story. "The Yellow Wallpaper" is narrated by an unnamed woman diagnosed with a "nervous condition"; readers get to know her through her journal entries. As you read, allow yourself to perceive things as she does. Occasionally, though, stand back to examine her perceptions and actions with a critical eye.

● READING SKILL: UNDERSTAND SOCIAL CONTEXT

The **social context** of a work is the social conditions that inspired or influenced its creation. You know that in 1892, when this story was written, women held a drastically different place in society than they do today. Use your prior knowledge, as well as the background on page 768, to analyze the social context of this story as you read. Note what the annotated passages reveal about how women were treated and how they were expected to behave. Consider what Gilman may have thought about these conditions and how she responds to them in "The Yellow Wallpaper."

Story Passages	Notes on Social Context
"John laughs at me, of course, but one expects that in marriage."	The narrator does not expect that a husband would take his wife's ideas seriously. At this time, men wielded the power in most American households.

▲ VOCABULARY IN CONTEXT

Gilman uses these words in her harrowing story of stress and power. Determine the meaning of each word from its context.

1. doctor's orders **misconstrued** because of their complexity
2. a **recurrent** ailment, returning every few months
3. a delicate **temperament,** prone to worrying
4. disturbed by intense, **lurid** dreams
5. flashy, **flamboyant** drawings representing her state of mind
6. **undulating** patterns that made her feel seasick
7. a twisted **convolution** of nightmarish thoughts
8. feared the **derision** of cruel household help
9. a **patent** lie that fooled no one
10. ignorant remarks that demonstrated her **fatuity**

Explore the Key Idea

What if no one took you SERIOUSLY?

KEY IDEA A friend rolls his or her eyes in disbelief as you tell a story. Your parents don't believe that you really *are* sick, not just feigning illness to get out of a test. A teacher or coach refuses to listen to your perspective before launching into a lecture. On at least one occasion, you've probably felt the sting of someone dismissing your feelings or refusing to listen to you. An isolated instance is bad enough, but if everyone around you refused to take you seriously, you might feel utterly **powerless.**

QUICKWRITE Try to imagine a whole day during which, no matter what happened, no one took you seriously. Envision yourself in the middle of such a day; then write a journal entry describing your reaction.

The Yellow WALLPAPER

CHARLOTTE PERKINS GILMAN

BACKGROUND If a woman sought medical treatment for a disorder such as depression or anxiety in 1892, her ills were often diagnosed as trivial "nervous conditions," curable through isolation and prolonged rest. Today it is believed that some of these disorders were caused in part by the stress of living within the rigid social roles to which women were confined. Doctors of the time, however, typically felt that their patients' gender lay at the root of the problem. Many saw women as weak and emotionally unstable, and thus predisposed to illness.

ANALYZE VISUALS
Examine this painting. Describe the woman's size, position, and coloring relative to the flowers in the foreground. How does she look next to the flowers? Explain.

It is very seldom that mere ordinary people like John and myself secure ancestral halls for the summer.

A colonial mansion, a hereditary estate, I would say a haunted house, and reach the height of romantic felicity—but that would be asking too much of fate!

Still I will proudly declare that there is something queer about it.

Else, why should it be let so cheaply? And why have stood so long untenanted?

John laughs at me, of course, but one expects that in marriage.

John is practical in the extreme. He has no patience with faith, an intense horror of superstition, and he scoffs openly at any talk of things not to be felt and 10 seen and put down in figures.

John is a physician, and *perhaps*—(I would not say it to a living soul, of course, but this is dead paper and a great relief to my mind)—*perhaps* that is one reason I do not get well faster.

You see he does not believe I am sick!

And what can one do? **A**

A SOCIAL CONTEXT
Consider what you learned from the background paragraph at the top of this page. How does Gilman convey the belief prevalent in her time that women were emotionally unstable and prone to illness?

Geraniums (1888), Childe Hassam. 18 1/4″ × 12 7/8″. The Hyde Collection, Glens Falls, New York. Photo © Michael Fredericks.

If a physician of high standing, and one's own husband, assures friends and relatives that there is really nothing the matter with one but temporary nervous depression—a slight hysterical[1] tendency—what is one to do?

My brother is also a physician, and also of high standing, and he says the same thing.

So I take phosphates or phosphites—whichever it is, and tonics, and journeys, and air, and exercise, and am absolutely forbidden to "work" until I am well again.

Personally, I disagree with their ideas.

Personally, I believe that congenial work, with excitement and change, would do me good.

But what is one to do?

I did write for a while in spite of them; but it *does* exhaust me a good deal—having to be so sly about it, or else meet with heavy opposition.

I sometimes fancy that in my condition if I had less opposition and more society and stimulus—but John says the very worst thing I can do is to think about my condition, and I confess it always makes me feel bad.

So I will let it alone and talk about the house.

The most beautiful place! It is quite alone, standing well back from the road, quite three miles from the village. It makes me think of English places that you read about, for there are hedges and walls and gates that lock, and lots of separate little houses for the gardeners and people.

There is a *delicious* garden! I never saw such a garden—large and shady, full of box-bordered paths, and lined with long grape-covered arbors with seats under them.

There were greenhouses, too, but they are all broken now.

There was some legal trouble, I believe, something about the heirs and coheirs; anyhow, the place has been empty for years.

That spoils my ghostliness, I am afraid, but I don't care—there is something strange about the house—I can feel it.

I even said so to John one moonlight evening, but he said what I felt was a *draft*, and shut the window.

I get unreasonably angry with John sometimes. I'm sure I never used to be so sensitive. I think it is due to this nervous condition.

But John says if I feel so, I shall neglect proper self-control; so I take pains to control myself—before him, at least, and that makes me very tired. **B**

I don't like our room a bit. I wanted one downstairs that opened on the piazza and had roses all over the window, and such pretty old-fashioned chintz hangings![2] but John would not hear of it.

He said there was only one window and not room for two beds, and no near room for him if he took another.

He is very careful and loving, and hardly lets me stir without special direction.

B FIRST-PERSON NARRATOR
What, in addition to her writing, is the narrator hiding from her husband? Explain how her opinion of the cure for her disorder differs from his.

---

1. **hysterical:** Hysteria is the presence of a physical ailment with no underlying physical cause.
2. **chintz hangings:** curtains made out of chintz, a printed cotton fabric.

I have a schedule prescription for each hour in the day; he takes all care from me, and so I feel basely ungrateful not to value it more.

He said we came here solely on my account, that I was to have perfect rest and all the air I could get. "Your exercise depends on your strength, my dear," said he, "and your food somewhat on your appetite; but air you can absorb all the time." So we took the nursery at the top of the house.

It is a big, airy room, the whole floor nearly, with windows that look all ways, and air and sunshine galore. It was nursery first and then playroom and gymnasium, I should judge; for the windows are barred for little children, and there are rings and things in the walls.

The paint and paper look as if a boys' school had used it. It is stripped off—the paper—in great patches all around the head of my bed, about as far as I can reach, and in a great place on the other side of the room low down. I never saw a worse paper in my life.

One of those sprawling **flamboyant** patterns committing every artistic sin.

It is dull enough to confuse the eye in following, pronounced enough to constantly irritate and provoke study, and when you follow the lame uncertain curves for a little distance they suddenly commit suicide—plunge off at outrageous angles, destroy themselves in unheard of contradictions.

The color is repellent, almost revolting; a smouldering unclean yellow, strangely faded by the slow-turning sunlight.

It is a dull yet **lurid** orange in some places, a sickly sulphur tint in others.

No wonder the children hated it! I should hate it myself if I had to live in this room long.

There comes John, and I must put this away, —he hates to have me write a word.

We have been here two weeks, and I haven't felt like writing before, since that first day.

I am sitting by the window now, up in this atrocious nursery, and there is nothing to hinder my writing as much as I please, save lack of strength. ©

John is away all day, and even some nights when his cases are serious.

I am glad my case is not serious!

But these nervous troubles are dreadfully depressing.

John does not know how much I really suffer. He knows there is no *reason* to suffer, and that satisfies him.

Of course it is only nervousness. It does weigh on me so not to do my duty in any way!

I meant to be such a help to John, such a real rest and comfort, and here I am a comparative burden already!

Nobody would believe what an effort it is to do what little I am able,—to dress and entertain, and order things.

flamboyant (flăm-boi′ənt) *adj.* marked by strikingly elaborate or colorful display

lurid (lŏor′ĭd) *adj.* shocking; gruesome

© **GRAMMAR AND STYLE** Notice that Gilman chose to tell this story in the **present tense.** This lends the narrative a sense of immediacy and allows readers to feel as though they're witnessing new developments in the narrator's condition as they unfold.

It is fortunate Mary is so good with the baby. Such a dear baby!

And yet I *cannot* be with him, it makes me so nervous.

I suppose John never was nervous in his life. He laughs at me so about this
100 wallpaper!

At first he meant to repaper the room, but afterwards he said that I was letting
it get the better of me, and that nothing was worse for a nervous patient than to
give way to such fancies.

He said that after the wallpaper was changed it would be the heavy bedstead, and
then the barred windows, and then that gate at the head of the stairs, and so on.

"You know the place is doing you good," he said, "and really, dear, I don't care
to renovate the house just for a three months' rental."

"Then do let us go downstairs," I said, "there are such pretty rooms there."

Then he took me in his arms and called me a blessed little goose, and said he

A Woman Seated at a Table by a Window, Carl Holsoe. Oil on canvas. © SuperStock.

ANALYZE VISUALS
How would you describe
the **mood** of this
painting? In your opinion,
is it similar to or different
from the mood of the
story? Explain, citing
specific details from each
that influenced your
answer.

110 would go down to the cellar, if I wished, and have it whitewashed into the bargain. **D**

But he is right enough about the beds and windows and things.

It is an airy and comfortable room as anyone need wish, and, of course, I would not be so silly as to make him uncomfortable just for a whim.

I'm really getting quite fond of the big room, all but that horrid paper.

Out of one window I can see the garden, those mysterious deepshaded arbors, the riotous old-fashioned flowers, and bushes and gnarly trees.

Out of another I get a lovely view of the bay and a little private wharf belonging to the estate. There is a beautiful shaded lane that runs down there from the house. I always fancy I see people walking in these numerous paths and arbors,
120 but John has cautioned me not to give way to fancy in the least. He says that with my imaginative power and habit of story-making, a nervous weakness like mine is sure to lead to all manner of excited fancies, and that I ought to use my will and good sense to check the tendency. So I try.

I think sometimes that if I were only well enough to write a little it would relieve the press of ideas and rest me.

But I find I get pretty tired when I try.

It is so discouraging not to have any advice and companionship about my work. When I get really well, John says we will ask Cousin Henry and Julia down for a long visit; but he says he would as soon put fireworks in my pillowcase as to
130 let me have those stimulating people about now.

I wish I could get well faster.

But I must not think about that. This paper looks to me as if it *knew* what a vicious influence it had!

There is a **recurrent** spot where the pattern lolls like a broken neck and two bulbous eyes stare at you upside down.

I get positively angry with the impertinence of it and the everlastingness. **E** Up and down and sideways they crawl, and those absurd, unblinking eyes are everywhere. There is one place where two breadths didn't match, and the eyes go all up and down the line, one a little higher than the other.

140 I never saw so much expression in an inanimate thing before, and we all know how much expression they have! I used to lie awake as a child and get more entertainment and terror out of blank walls and plain furniture than most children could find in a toy store.

I remember what a kindly wink the knobs of our big, old bureau used to have, and there was one chair that always seemed like a strong friend.

I used to feel that if any of the other things looked too fierce I could always hop into that chair and be safe.

The furniture in this room is no worse than inharmonious, however, for we had to bring it all from downstairs. I suppose when this was used as a playroom they
150 had to take the nursery things out, and no wonder! I never saw such ravages as the children have made here.

D SOCIAL CONTEXT
Reread lines 99–110 and describe the relationship between the narrator and her husband. What might Gilman be saying about how women were viewed in the late 1800s?

recurrent (rĭ-kûr′ənt) *adj.* occurring time after time

E FIRST-PERSON NARRATOR
How are the narrator's feelings about the wallpaper changing? Explain whether or not her response to the room's décor seems rational to you.

The wallpaper, as I said before, is torn off in spots, and it sticketh closer than a brother—they must have had perseverance as well as hatred.

Then the floor is scratched and gouged and splintered, the plaster itself is dug out here and there, and this great heavy bed which is all we found in the room, looks as if it had been through the wars.

But I don't mind it a bit—only the paper.

There comes John's sister. Such a dear girl as she is, and so careful of me! I must not let her find me writing.

160 She is a perfect and enthusiastic housekeeper, and hopes for no better profession. I verily believe she thinks it is the writing which made me sick!

But I can write when she is out, and see her a long way off from these windows. **F**

There is one that commands the road, a lovely shaded winding road, and one that just looks off over the country. A lovely country, too, full of great elms and velvet meadows.

This wallpaper has a kind of sub-pattern in a different shade, a particularly irritating one, for you can only see it in certain lights, and not clearly then.

But in the places where it isn't faded and where the sun is just so—I can see a strange, provoking, formless sort of figure, that seems to skulk about behind that 170 silly and conspicuous front design.

There's sister on the stairs!

Well, the Fourth of July is over! The people are all gone and I am tired out. John thought it might do me good to see a little company, so we just had mother and Nellie and the children down for a week.

Of course I didn't do a thing. Jennie sees to everything now.

But it tired me all the same.

John says if I don't pick up faster he shall send me to Weir Mitchell[3] in the fall.

But I don't want to go there at all. I had a friend who was in his hands once, and she says he is just like John and my brother, only more so! **G**

180 Besides, it is such an undertaking to go so far.

I don't feel as if it was worth while to turn my hand over for anything, and I'm getting dreadfully fretful and querulous.

I cry at nothing, and cry most of the time.

Of course I don't when John is here, or anybody else, but when I am alone.

And I am alone a good deal just now. John is kept in town very often by serious cases, and Jennie is good and lets me alone when I want her to.

So I walk a little in the garden or down that lovely lane, sit on the porch under the roses, and lie down up here a good deal.

I'm getting really fond of the room in spite of the wallpaper. Perhaps *because* 190 of the wallpaper.

It dwells in my mind so!

I lie here on this great immovable bed—it is nailed down, I believe—and

3. **Weir Mitchell:** Dr. Silas Weir Mitchell, a physician famous for his "rest cure" for nervous diseases, which is no longer considered effective.

774   UNIT 4: REGIONALISM AND NATURALISM

F SOCIAL CONTEXT
Consider the narrator's description of John's sister in lines 158–162. What information does her description offer about a woman's accepted roles in society?

G SOCIAL CONTEXT
Explain what the narrator means by this description of Dr. Mitchell. What is suggested or highlighted by the fact that all the male characters in the story share common opinions and **traits?**

follow that pattern about by the hour. It is as good as gymnastics, I assure you. I start, we'll say, at the bottom, down in the corner over there where it has not been touched, and I determine for the thousandth time that I *will* follow that pointless pattern to some sort of a conclusion.

I know a little of the principle of design, and I know this thing was not arranged on any laws of radiation, or alternation, or repetition, or symmetry, or anything else that I ever heard of.

200   It is repeated, of course, by the breadths, but not otherwise.

Looked at in one way each breadth stands alone, the bloated curves and flourishes—a kind of "debased Romanesque" with *delirium tremens*[4]—go waddling up and down in isolated columns of **fatuity**.

fatuity (fə-tōō′ĭ-tē) *n.* something foolish or stupid

But, on the other hand, they connect diagonally, and the sprawling outlines run off in great slanting waves of optic horror, like a lot of wallowing seaweeds in full chase.

The whole thing goes horizontally, too, at least it seems so, and I exhaust myself in trying to distinguish the order of its going in that direction.

They have used a horizontal breadth for a frieze, and that adds wonderfully to
210   the confusion.

There is one end of the room where it is almost intact, and there, when the crosslights fade and the low sun shines directly upon it, I can almost fancy radiation after all,—the interminable grotesques seem to form around a common center and rush off in headlong plunges of equal distraction.

It makes me tired to follow it. I will take a nap I guess.

I don't know why I should write this.

I don't want to.

I don't feel able.

And I know John would think it absurd. But I *must* say what I feel and think
220   in some way—it is such a relief!

But the effort is getting to be greater than the relief.

Half the time now I am awfully lazy, and lie down ever so much.

John says I mustn't lose my strength, and has me take cod liver oil and lots of tonics and things, to say nothing of ale and wine and rare meat.

Dear John! He loves me very dearly, and hates to have me sick. I tried to have a real earnest reasonable talk with him the other day, and tell him how I wish he would let me go and make a visit to Cousin Henry and Julia.

But he said I wasn't able to go, nor able to stand it after I got there; and I did not make out a very good case for myself, for I was crying before I had finished. ⒣

230   It is getting to be a great effort for me to think straight. Just this nervous weakness I suppose.

And dear John gathered me up in his arms, and just carried me upstairs and laid me on the bed, and sat by me and read to me till it tired my head.

⒣ **FIRST-PERSON NARRATOR**
Imagine the "real earnest reasonable talk" the narrator describes. How might the account of this scene be different if John were the narrator?

---

4. **"debased Romanesque" with *delirium tremens*:** Romanesque is an artistic style characterized by simple ornamentation. *Delirium tremens* refers to violent trembling and hallucinations caused by excessive drinking.

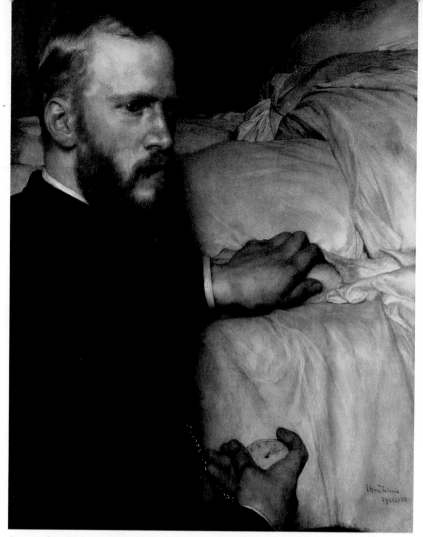

Portrait of Dr. Washington Epps, My Doctor (1885), Sir Lawrence Alma-Tadema. Oil on canvas, 64.2 cm × 51 cm. Private collection. © Bridgeman Art Library.

ANALYZE VISUALS
Study this painting, then describe the emotion conveyed by the subject's facial expression. Does this image make you feel more or less sympathetic toward John, the narrator's husband? Explain your answer.

He said I was his darling and his comfort and all he had, and that I must take care of myself for his sake, and keep well.

He says no one but myself can help me out of it, that I must use my will and self-control and not let any silly fancies run away with me.

There's one comfort, the baby is well and happy, and does not have to occupy this nursery with the horrid wallpaper.

240   If we had not used it, that blessed child would have! What a fortunate escape! Why, I wouldn't have a child of mine, an impressionable little thing, live in such a room for worlds.

I never thought of it before, but it is lucky that John kept me here after all, I can stand it so much easier than a baby, you see.

Of course I never mention it to them any more—I am too wise,—but I keep watch of it all the same.

There are things in that paper that nobody knows but me, or ever will.

Behind that outside pattern the dim shapes get clearer every day.

It is always the same shape, only very numerous.

250 And it is like a woman stooping down and creeping about behind that pattern. I don't like it a bit. I wonder—I begin to think—I wish John would take me away from here!

It is so hard to talk with John about my case, because he is so wise, and because he loves me so.

But I tried it last night.

It was moonlight. The moon shines in all around just as the sun does.

I hate to see it sometimes, it creeps so slowly, and always comes in by one window or another.

John was asleep and I hated to waken him, so I kept still and watched the
260 moonlight on that **undulating** wallpaper till I felt creepy.

The faint figure behind seemed to shake the pattern, just as if she wanted to get out.

I got up softly and went to feel and see if the paper *did* move, and when I came back John was awake.

"What is it, little girl?" he said. "Don't go walking about like that—you'll get cold."

I thought it was a good time to talk, so I told him that I really was not gaining here, and that I wished he would take me away.

"Why darling!" said he, "our lease will be up in three weeks, and I can't see how
270 to leave before.

"The repairs are not done at home, and I cannot possibly leave town just now. Of course if you were in any danger, I could and would, but you really are better, dear, whether you can see it or not. I am a doctor, dear, and I know. You are gaining flesh and color, your appetite is better, I feel really much easier about you."

"I don't weigh a bit more," said I, "nor as much; and my appetite may be better in the evening when you are here, but it is worse in the morning when you are away!"

"Bless her little heart!" said he with a big hug, "she shall be as sick as she pleases! But now let's improve the shining hours[5] by going to sleep, and talk about it in the morning!"

280 "And you won't go away?" I asked gloomily.

"Why, how can I, dear? It is only three weeks more and then we will take a nice little trip of a few days while Jennie is getting the house ready. Really dear you are better!"

"Better in body perhaps—" I began, and stopped short, for he sat up straight and looked at me with such a stern, reproachful look that I could not say another word.

"My darling," said he, "I beg of you, for my sake and for our child's sake, as well as for your own, that you will never for one instant let that idea enter your mind! There is nothing so dangerous, so fascinating, to a **temperament** like yours. It is a false and foolish fancy. Can you not trust me as a physician when I tell you so?"

undulating (ŭn'jə-lā'tĭng) *adj.* appearing to move in waves **undulate** *v.*

temperament (tĕm'prə-mənt) *n.* a person's characteristic mode of emotional response

---

5. **improve the shining hours:** make good use of time—an allusion to the poem "Against Idleness and Mischief" by Isaac Watts.

290 So of course I said no more on that score, and we went to sleep before long. He thought I was asleep first, but I wasn't, and lay there for hours trying to decide whether that front pattern and the back pattern really did move together or separately.

On a pattern like this, by daylight, there is a lack of sequence, a defiance of law, that is a constant irritant to a normal mind. ❶

The color is hideous enough, and unreliable enough, and infuriating enough, but the pattern is torturing.

You think you have mastered it, but just as you get well underway in following, it turns a back-somersault and there you are. It slaps you in the face, knocks you 300 down, and tramples upon you. It is like a bad dream.

The outside pattern is a florid arabesque,[6] reminding one of a fungus. If you can imagine a toadstool in joints, an interminable string of toadstools, budding and sprouting in endless **convolutions**—why, that is something like it.

That is, sometimes!

There is one marked peculiarity about this paper, a thing nobody seems to notice but myself, and that is that it changes as the light changes.

When the sun shoots in through the east window—I always watch for that first long, straight ray—it changes so quickly that I never can quite believe it.

That is why I watch it always.

310 By moonlight—the moon shines in all night when there is a moon—I wouldn't know it was the same paper.

At night in any kind of light, in twilight, candle light, lamplight, and worst of all by moonlight, it becomes bars! The outside pattern I mean, and the woman behind it is as plain as can be.

I didn't realize for a long time what the thing was that showed behind, that dim sub-pattern, but now I am quite sure it is a woman.

By daylight she is subdued, quiet. I fancy it is the pattern that keeps her so still. It is so puzzling. It keeps me quiet by the hour.

I lie down ever so much now. John says it is good for me, and to sleep all I can.

320 Indeed he started the habit by making me lie down for an hour after each meal.

It is a very bad habit I am convinced, for you see I don't sleep.

And that cultivates deceit, for I don't tell them I'm awake—O no!

The fact is I am getting a little afraid of John.

He seems very queer sometimes, and even Jennie has an inexplicable look.

It strikes me occasionally, just as a scientific hypothesis,—that perhaps it is the paper!

I have watched John when he did not know I was looking, and come into the room suddenly on the most innocent excuses, and I've caught him several times *looking at the paper!* And Jennie too. I caught Jennie with her hand on it once.

330 She didn't know I was in the room, and when I asked her in a quiet, a very quiet voice, with the most restrained manner possible, what she was doing with

---

6. **florid arabesque:** an elaborate interwoven pattern.

❶ FIRST-PERSON NARRATOR
Consider the narrator's statement in lines 294–295. Based on her description of the wallpaper, would you say she has "a normal mind"? Explain your answer.

convolution
(kŏn′və-loo′shən) *n.*
a form or shape that is folded into curved, complicated windings

the paper—she turned around as if she had been caught stealing, and looked quite angry—asked me why I should frighten her so!

Then she said that the paper stained everything it touched, that she had found yellow smooches[7] on all my clothes and John's, and she wished we would be more careful!

Did not that sound innocent? But I know she was studying that pattern, and I am determined that nobody shall find it out but myself! **J**

Life is very much more exciting now than it used to be. You see I have something
340   more to expect, to look forward to, to watch. I really do eat better, and am more quiet than I was.

John is so pleased to see me improve! He laughed a little the other day, and said I seemed to be flourishing in spite of my wallpaper.

I turned it off with a laugh. I had no intention of telling him it was *because* of the wallpaper—he would make fun of me. He might even want to take me away.

I don't want to leave now until I have found it out. There is a week more, and I think that will be enough.

'm feeling ever so much better! I don't sleep much at night, for it is so interesting to watch developments; but I sleep a good deal in the daytime.
350   In the daytime it is tiresome and perplexing.

There are always new shoots on the fungus, and new shades of yellow all over it. I cannot keep count of them, though I have tried conscientiously.

It is the strangest yellow, that wallpaper! It makes me think of all the yellow things I ever saw—not beautiful ones like buttercups, but old foul, bad yellow things.

But there is something else about that paper—the smell! I noticed it the moment we came into the room, but with so much air and sun it was not bad. Now we have had a week of fog and rain, and whether the windows are open or not, the smell is here.

It creeps all over the house.
360   I find it hovering in the dining room, skulking in the parlor, hiding in the hall, lying in wait for me on the stairs.

It gets into my hair.

Even when I go to ride, if I turn my head suddenly and surprise it—there is that smell!

Such a peculiar odor, too! I have spent hours in trying to analyze it, to find what it smelled like.

It is not bad—at first, and very gentle, but quite the subtlest, most enduring odor I ever met.

In this damp weather it is awful, I wake up in the night and find it hanging
370   over me.

It used to disturb me at first. I thought seriously of burning the house—to reach the smell.

J **FIRST-PERSON NARRATOR**
Reread lines 323–338. How has the narrator's attitude toward John and Jennie changed? What do you think they might say about her feelings if they were aware of them?

---

7. **smooches:** smudges.

In Bed (1878), Federico Zandomeneghi. Oil on canvas, 60.5 cm × 73.5 cm. Galleria d'Arte Moderna, Florence. © Alinari/Art Resource, New York.

But now I am used to it. The only thing I can think of that it is like is the *color* of the paper! A yellow smell. **K**

There is a very funny mark on this wall, low down, near the mopboard. A streak that runs round the room. It goes behind every piece of furniture, except the bed, a long, straight, even *smooch*, as if it had been rubbed over and over.

I wonder how it was done and who did it, and what they did it for. Round and round and round—round and round and round—it makes me dizzy!

380 I really have discovered something at last.

Through watching so much at night, when it changes so, I have finally found out. The front pattern *does* move—and no wonder! The woman behind shakes it!

Sometimes I think there are a great many women behind, and sometimes only one, and she crawls around fast, and her crawling shakes it all over.

K FIRST-PERSON NARRATOR
Describe the woman's state of mind at this point as an impartial, **omniscient narrator** might describe it.

Then in the very bright spots she keeps still, and in the very shady spots she just takes hold of the bars and shakes them hard.

And she is all the time trying to climb through. But nobody could climb through that pattern—it strangles so; I think that is why it has so many heads.

They get through, and then the pattern strangles them off and turns them
390 upside down, and makes their eyes white!

If those heads were covered or taken off it would not be half so bad.

I think that woman gets out in the daytime!

And I'll tell you why—privately—I've seen her!

I can see her out of every one of my windows!

It is the same woman, I know, for she is always creeping, and most women do not creep by daylight.

I see her on that long road under the trees, creeping along, and when a carriage comes she hides under the blackberry vines.

I don't blame her a bit. It must be very humiliating to be caught creeping by
400 daylight!

I always lock the door when I creep by daylight. I can't do it at night, for I know John would suspect something at once.

And John is so queer now, that I don't want to irritate him. I wish he would take another room! Besides, I don't want anybody to get that woman out at night but myself.

I often wonder if I could see her out of all the windows at once.

But, turn as fast as I can, I can only see out of one at one time.

And though I always see her, she *may* be able to creep faster than I can turn!

I have watched her sometimes away off in the open country, creeping as fast
410 as a cloud shadow in a high wind.

If only that top pattern could be gotten off from the under one! I mean to try it, little by little.

I have found out another funny thing, but I shan't tell it this time! It does not do to trust people too much.

There are only two more days to get this paper off, and I believe John is beginning to notice. I don't like the look in his eyes.

And I heard him ask Jennie a lot of professional questions about me. She had a very good report to give.

She said I slept a good deal in the daytime.

420 John knows I don't sleep very well at night, for all I'm so quiet!

He asked me all sorts of questions, too, and pretended to be very loving and kind.

As if I couldn't see through him! ❶

❶ FIRST-PERSON NARRATOR
Consider the narrator's statements in lines 403–404 and line 423. Why is she turning against her husband? Explain what John's real concerns might be.

Still, I don't wonder he acts so, sleeping under this paper for three months.

It only interests me, but I feel sure John and Jennie are secretly affected by it.

Hurrah! This is the last day, but it is enough. John to stay in town overnight, and won't be out until this evening.

Jennie wanted to sleep with me—the sly thing! but I told her I should undoubtedly rest better for a night all alone.

That was clever, for really I wasn't alone a bit! As soon as it was moonlight and that poor thing began to crawl and shake the pattern, I got up and ran to help her.

I pulled and she shook, I shook and she pulled, and before morning we had peeled off yards of that paper.

A strip about as high as my head and half around the room.

And then when the sun came and that awful pattern began to laugh at me, I declared I would finish it today!

We go away tomorrow, and they are moving all my furniture down again to leave things as they were before.

Jennie looked at the wall in amazement, but I told her merrily that I did it out of pure spite at the vicious thing.

She laughed and said she wouldn't mind doing it herself, but I must not get tired.

How she betrayed herself that time! **(M)**

But I am here, and no person touches this paper but me,—not *alive!*

She tried to get me out of the room—it was too **patent!** But I said it was so quiet and empty and clean now that I believed I would lie down again and sleep all I could; and not to wake me even for dinner—I would call when I woke.

So now she is gone, and the servants are gone, and the things are gone, and there is nothing left but that great bedstead nailed down, with the canvas mattress we found on it.

We shall sleep downstairs tonight, and take the boat home tomorrow.

I quite enjoy the room, now it is bare again.

How those children did tear about here!

This bedstead is fairly gnawed!

But I must get to work.

I have locked the door and thrown the key down into the front path.

I don't want to go out, and I don't want to have anybody come in, till John comes.

I want to astonish him.

I've got a rope up here that even Jennie did not find. If that woman does get out, and tries to get away, I can tie her!

But I forgot I could not reach far without anything to stand on!

This bed will *not* move!

I tried to lift and push it until I was lame, and then I got so angry I bit off a little piece at one corner—but it hurt my teeth.

Then I peeled off all the paper I could reach standing on the floor. It sticks horribly and the pattern just enjoys it! All those strangled heads and bulbous eyes and waddling fungus growths just shriek with **derision!**

(M) FIRST-PERSON NARRATOR
Explain what the narrator means when she says that Jennie has "betrayed herself." Do you think her assessment of Jennie's **motives** is accurate?

patent (păt'nt) *adj.* obvious; apparent

derision (dĭ-rĭzh'ən) *n.* harsh ridicule or mockery; scorn

I am getting angry enough to do something desperate. To jump out of the window would be admirable exercise, but the bars are too strong even to try.

Besides I wouldn't do it. Of course not. I know well enough that a step like that is improper and might be **misconstrued.**

I don't like to *look* out of the windows even—there are so many of those creeping women, and they creep so fast.

I wonder if they all come out of that wallpaper as I did? **N**

But I am securely fastened now by my well-hidden rope—you don't get *me* out in the road there!

I suppose I shall have to get back behind the pattern when it comes night, and that is hard!

It is so pleasant to be out in this great room and creep around as I please!

I don't want to go outside. I won't, even if Jennie asks me to.

For outside you have to creep on the ground, and everything is green instead of yellow.

But here I can creep smoothly on the floor, and my shoulder just fits in that long smooch around the wall, so I cannot lose my way.

Why there's John at the door!

It is no use, young man, you can't open it!

How he does call and pound!

Now he's crying for an axe.

It would be a shame to break down that beautiful door!

"John dear!" said I in the gentlest voice, "the key is down by the front steps, under a plantain leaf!"

That silenced him for a few moments.

Then he said—very quietly indeed, "Open the door, my darling!"

"I can't," said I. "The key is down by the front door under a plantain leaf!"

And then I said it again, several times, very gently and slowly, and said it so often that he had to go and see, and he got it of course, and came in. He stopped short by the door.

"What is the matter?" he cried. "What are you doing!"

I kept on creeping just the same, but I looked at him over my shoulder.

"I've got out at last," said I, "in spite of you and Jane.[8] And I've pulled off most of the paper, so you can't put me back!"

Now why should that man have fainted? But he did, and right across my path by the wall, so that I had to creep over him every time! ❧

8. **in spite of you and Jane:** As Jane is, previously unmentioned, the name may be a typographical error by the original printer of the story in place of the name of the housekeeper, Jennie, or Cousin Julia; or it may denote the narrator herself, freed from her commonplace, wifely, "Jane" persona.

misconstrued
(mĭs′kən-strood′)
adj. misunderstood; misinterpreted
misconstrue *v.*

N **FIRST-PERSON NARRATOR**
What does the narrator now believe about the wallpaper?

JOURNAL ARTICLE Charlotte Perkins Gilman herself suffered a profound depression and was prescribed a "rest cure" by a noted neurologist of the day. In this 1913 article from her feminist journal *Forerunner,* she says she wrote "The Yellow Wallpaper" to bear witness to the horrors of this "cure" and to attest to her recovery.

THE FORERUNNER

A MONTHLY MAGAZINE

CHARLOTTE PERKINS GILMAN

WHY I WROTE "THE YELLOW WALLPAPER"

Many and many a reader has asked that. When the story first came out, in the *New England Magazine* about 1891, a Boston physician made protest in *The Transcript.* Such a story ought not to be written, he said; it was enough to drive anyone mad to read it.

Another physician, in Kansas I think, wrote to say that it was the best description of incipient insanity he had ever seen, and—begging my pardon—had I been there?

Now the story of the story is this:

For many years I suffered from a severe and continuous nervous breakdown tending to melancholia—and beyond. During about the third year of this trouble I went, in devout faith and some faint stir of hope, to a noted specialist in nervous diseases, the best known in the country. This wise man put me to bed and applied the rest cure, to which a still good physique responded so promptly that he concluded there was nothing much the matter with me, and sent me home with solemn advice to "live as domestic a life as far as possible," to "have but two hours' intellectual life a day," and "never to touch pen, brush or pencil again as long as I lived." This was in 1887.

I went home and obeyed those directions for some three months, and came so near the border line of utter mental ruin that I could see over.

Then, using the remnants of intelligence that remained, and helped by a wise friend, I cast the noted specialist's advice to the winds and went to work again—work, the normal life of every human being; work, in which is joy and growth and service, without which one is a pauper and a parasite; ultimately recovering some measure of power.

Being naturally moved to rejoicing by this narrow escape, I wrote *The Yellow Wallpaper,* with its embellishments and additions to carry out the ideal (I never had hallucinations or objections to my mural decorations) and sent a copy to the physician who so nearly drove me mad. He never acknowledged it.

The little book is valued by alienists and as good a specimen of one kind of literature. It has to my knowledge saved one woman from a similar fate—so terrifying her family that they let her out into normal activity and she recovered.

But the best result is this. Many years later I was told that the great specialist had admitted to friends of his that he had altered his treatment of neurasthenia since reading *The Yellow Wallpaper.*

It was not intended to drive people crazy, but to save people from being driven crazy, and it worked.

Comprehension

1. **Summarize** Describe the "rest cure" treatment and explain why it is prescribed for the narrator.

2. **Recall** Why does the narrator hate the wallpaper at first?

3. **Clarify** Who does the narrator think she is at the end of the story?

Literary Analysis

4. **Examine Character Change** How does the narrator change once she "discovers" the woman in the wallpaper? At what point does she begin to lose her grip on reality? Citing examples from both the beginning and the end of the story, explain how the writing style reflects her psychological transformation.

5. **Analyze First-Person Narrator** The narrator of this story is **unreliable**—you can't always trust that what she says is true. What are the advantages and disadvantages of using a first-person narrator to tell this story, especially in light of her condition?

6 **Interpret Symbolism** Reread lines 380–391 and consider the narrator's **powerlessness.** What might the yellow wallpaper symbolize in the story? Consider the following as you formulate your answer:

   - the narrator's attitude toward both her "condition" and her marriage
   - what she sees in the "strangling" pattern of the paper
   - her exhilaration when she rips the wallpaper off the wall

7. **Understand Social Context** Examine the chart you filled in as you read. What conclusions can you draw about the social conditions that shaped Gilman's work? Citing evidence from both the short story and "Why I Wrote 'The Yellow Wallpaper'" on page 784, explain

   - how wives were expected to behave in the 1890s
   - how women seem to have been treated by the men—husbands, brothers, doctors—who cared for them
   - what Gilman thought about women being denied meaningful work and personal power, and how she addresses these issues in this story

Literary Criticism

8. **Different Perspectives** At the time it was published, most critics read "The Yellow Wallpaper" as a horror tale about madness or, after Gilman's explanation appeared in 1913, as an exposé of women's medical treatment. Only a few saw what feminists in the 1970s would interpret as Gilman's **political assumptions.** They viewed the story as a harsh criticism of marriage and the oppression of women. Explain which of these interpretations you favor, citing evidence from the text.

Vocabulary in Context

VOCABULARY PRACTICE

Choose the word that is not related in meaning to the other words.

1. (a) extravagant, (b) showy, (c) flamboyant, (d) lowly
2. (a) undulating, (b) flying, (c) soaring, (d) gliding
3. (a) mockery, (b) derision, (c) decision, (d) contempt
4. (a) consideration, (b) convolution, (c) intricacy, (d) complexity
5. (a) clear-cut, (b) reserved, (c) patent, (d) evident
6. (a) periodic, (b) repeated, (c) refused, (d) recurrent
7. (a) fatuity, (b) favor, (c) silliness, (d) folly
8. (a) miscellaneous, (b) misconstrued, (c) various, (d) diversified
9. (a) vivid, (b) lurid, (c) sensational, (d) vapid
10. (a) humidity, (b) personality, (c) disposition, (d) temperament

WORD LIST

convolution
derision
fatuity
flamboyant
lurid
misconstrued
patent
recurrent
temperament
undulating

VOCABULARY IN WRITING

How is John, the narrator's husband, portrayed in this story? Write a short description of his personality, using three or more vocabulary words.

> **EXAMPLE SENTENCE**
>
> *John seems to have a pleasant* **temperament***, but in many ways he treats his wife like a foolish child.*

VOCABULARY STRATEGY: TEMPERAMENT WORDS

The vocabulary word *temperament* can relate to personality study, which has fascinated people since ancient times. One theory popular into the Middle Ages classified people into four basic personality types—choleric, phlegmatic, sanguine, and melancholic—depending on how much of certain body fluids, such as blood and bile, they possessed. Modern medicine has debunked this theory, but the terms are still used to define certain temperament traits today.

PRACTICE Read each personality description and then choose the word from the list provided that identifies it. Use a dictionary to define the terms if you need to.

> melancholic   phlegmatic   sanguine   choleric

1. Mrs. Peabody flies into a rage every time someone disagrees with her.
2. Even a tornado tearing the roof off his house could not upset Dr. Lewis.
3. No matter how far behind schedule a project runs, Ms. Tenny is always optimistic that it will be finished on time.
4. The only movies Mr. Ioacca wants to watch are those with unhappy endings.

VOCABULARY PRACTICE
For more practice, go to the **Vocabulary Center** at ClassZone.com.

Reading-Writing Connection

WRITE A PERSONAL RESPONSE Although most contemporary readers respond positively to "The Yellow Wallpaper," the editor of the *Atlantic Monthly* in 1892 rejected it for publication. By way of explanation, he offered this candid reaction: "I could not forgive myself if I made others as miserable as I have made myself." How did the story affect you? Write a **three-to-five-paragraph personal response** explaining your own thoughts and feelings about the story.

A strong personal response will . . .

- identify the story and clearly state your overall response to it in the introduction
- give specific reasons for your response or more detailed reactions to specific aspects of the story
- support your statements with details, examples, and quotations from the story

GRAMMAR AND STYLE

CHOOSE EFFECTIVE VERB TENSE Review the **Grammar and Style** note on page 771. The immediacy and power of "The Yellow Wallpaper" comes in part from Gilman's choice to have the narrator tell the story mostly in the **present tense** as though writing in a diary. In this way, the reader plunges directly into the narrator's mind and follows its dark descent. Notice the use of **present-tense verbs** in this chilling example from the end of the story:

> But I *am* securely *fastened* now by my well-hidden rope—you *don't get* me *out* in the road there! (lines 475–476)

PRACTICE The following paragraph is a sample from another short story. Notice how the past-tense verbs create a certain distance between the reader and the events. Revise the paragraph, writing it in the present tense to achieve a different effect.

> I threw another log on the fire, waiting for Ahmer to come home. Dinner sat on the table, growing cold. Ahmer had been gone for hours and I was sure he had left with hurt feelings. Why did we always argue this way on special occasions? It was as though we didn't really want to celebrate, or didn't know how.

WRITING TOOLS
For prewriting, revision, and editing tools, visit the **Writing Center** at ClassZone.com.

Ethan Frome

Edith Wharton

Edith Wharton
1862–1937

ABOUT THE AUTHOR In the late 19th century, it was sometimes said that only 400 people really "mattered" in New York society—the number of people who could fit into millionaire socialite Caroline Astor's posh Fifth Avenue ballroom. Edith Wharton grew up in this rarefied society and wrote about it in most of her novels. Yet *Ethan Frome,* her best-known work, was not set in uppercrust New York society, but rather in a poor New England village. Wharton got her first taste of New England at the fashionable resort of Newport, Rhode Island, where families like hers and the Astors summered when she was a girl. However, Wharton also observed a different side of New England—its world of tiny villages and hardscrabble farms where poor families eked out a living from the bleak landscape. After she and her husband purchased an estate in the Berkshire Mountains of western Massachusetts, Wharton was inspired to write about that very different world in her novel *Ethan Frome.*

ABOUT THE NOVEL So short that it is sometimes called a novella, *Ethan Frome* is set in a Massachusetts village called Starkfield, the name clearly evoking the bleak lifestyle that Wharton wished to portray. The story is told by an engineer who visits Starkfield and grows interested in a "ruin of a man" he sees there named Ethan Frome. Frome himself, we learn, had always wanted to be an engineer and to live in cities, "where there were lectures and big libraries." Instead, poverty and tradition have restricted him to a barren farm and an equally barren marriage. A visit from his sickly wife Zeena's young cousin, Mattie Silver, brings a spark of joy into Frome's grim life. His tragic attempt to grasp that joy forms the central conflict of the tale.

LEGACY OF A MASTERPIECE *Ethan Frome* was not a huge success when it first appeared in 1911, but in time it became Wharton's best-known work. Told in prose as spare and lean as the New England farm on which it is set, its style is in sharp contrast to Wharton's lushly detailed portraits of Gilded Age Manhattan. Though different in style and setting, *Ethan Frome* is similar to Wharton's other books, however, in that its characters seem to have very little control over their own lives. In this resepct, Wharton was a naturalist writer exploring the power that environment holds over human beings.

The following passage describes Ethan Frome's changing relationship with Mattie Silver and the strong emotions that she has awakened in him.

Frome was in the habit of walking into Starkfield to fetch home his wife's cousin, Mattie Silver, on the rare evenings when some chance of amusement drew her to the village. It was his wife who had suggested, when the girl came to live with them, that such opportunities should be put in her way. Mattie Silver came from Stamford, and when she entered the Fromes' household to act as her cousin Zeena's aid it was thought best, as she came without pay, not to let her feel too sharp a contrast between the life she had left and the isolation of a Starkfield farm. But for this—as Frome sardonically reflected—it would hardly have occurred
10 to Zeena to take any thought for the girl's amusement.

When his wife first proposed that they should give Mattie an occasional evening out he had inwardly demurred at having to do the extra two miles to the village and back after his hard day on the farm; but not long afterward he had reached the point of wishing that Starkfield might give all its nights to revelry.

Mattie Silver had lived under his roof for a year, and from early morning till they met at supper he had frequent chances of seeing her; but no moments in her company were comparable to those when, her arm in his, and her light step flying to keep time with his long stride, they walked back through the night to the farm. He had taken to the girl from the first day, when he had driven over to the Flats to
20 meet her, and she had smiled and waved to him from the train, crying out, "You must be Ethan!" as she jumped down with her bundles, while he reflected, looking over her slight person: "She don't look much on housework, but she ain't a fretter, anyhow." But it was not only that the coming to his house of a bit of hopeful young life was like the lighting of a fire on a cold hearth. The girl was more than the bright serviceable creature he had thought her. She had an eye to see and an ear to hear: he could show her things and tell her things, and taste the bliss of feeling that all he imparted left long reverberations and echoes he could wake at will.

It was during their night walks back to the farm that he felt most intensely the sweetness of this communion. He had always been more sensitive than the people
30 about him to the appeal of natural beauty. His unfinished studies had given form to this sensibility and even in his unhappiest moments field and sky spoke to him with a deep and powerful persuasion. But hitherto the emotion had remained in him as a silent ache, veiling with sadness the beauty that evoked it. He did not even know whether any one else in the world felt as he did, or whether he was the sole victim of this mournful privilege. Then he learned that one other spirit had trembled with the same touch of wonder: that at his side, living under his roof and eating his bread, was a creature to whom he could say: "That's Orion down yonder; the big fellow to the right is Aldebaran, and the bunch of little ones—like bees swarming—they're the Pleiades . . . ."

April Showers

Short Story by Edith Wharton

Edith Wharton
1862–1937

Author Online

For more on Edith Wharton, visit the **Literature Center** at ClassZone.com.

To understand Edith Wharton is to know something about the insular upper-class society that produced her. Rich and fashionable "old New York" consisted of established families, like Wharton's own, descended from English and Dutch colonists and having inherited "old money" made in banking, shipping, and real estate. For Wharton, it was a restrictive world of narrow minds and rigid, arbitrary rules, where "'bad manners' were the supreme offense." It was a world already starting to disintegrate in the late 19th and early 20th century as new immigrants poured into New York and "new money" was being made in industry and manufacturing. But it was the world Wharton struggled with and wrote about with the satiric wit of an insider who had found a way to be free.

The Compensations of Wealth Wharton was educated at home by governesses and spent her youth as expected, traveling with her parents to Europe and dutifully attending the lavish balls and dinners during New York's social season. Her happiest times, however, were spent in her father's large library, reading and writing. Her cold, domineering mother thwarted the young Edith's literary ambitions by limiting her supply of paper and forcing her to marry a rich banker 12 years her senior. Depressed by her empty marriage and frivolous social life, Wharton used her characteristic moral strength and imaginative powers to break out. She had her own country estate built in Lenox, Massachusetts, where she could associate with people who shared her interests in art and literature. She also escaped to Europe each winter, where she cultivated friendships with famous artists and writers, such as her mentor, rival, and long-time friend, Henry James. Ultimately, she divorced her husband and moved permanently to France, living alternately outside Paris and on the Riviera.

Fame and Fulfillment? The novel that brought Wharton her first great success was *The House of Mirth* (1905), the story of a young woman crushed by the ranks of old New York when she tries to live by her own moral standards. Many of Wharton's other novels and stories sympathetically portray individuals who try but fail to find happiness in unconventional ways. *Ethan Frome* (1911), perhaps her best-known novel, depicts a doomed pair of lovers in a poor farming community. Wharton was the most celebrated American woman writer of her time but had a rather skeptical view of personal fulfillment. "If only we'd stop trying to be happy," she once said, "we could have a pretty good time."

● LITERARY ANALYSIS: TONE

Occasionally, a writer's **tone,** or attitude toward a subject, is so recognizable that it leaps out from the first sentence. Usually, however, tone is more subtle. Readers must analyze the writer's choice of words and details to determine whether his or her tone is somber or playful, sarcastic or admiring. As you read this story, consider how Wharton describes different characters and their actions. Try to detect the writer's attitude toward her characters, particularly Theodora, a young woman who is attempting to become a writer herself.

● READING SKILL: MAKE INFERENCES ABOUT CHARACTERS

You know that writers don't state everything about their characters directly. Instead, they often leave it up to the reader to **make inferences,** or logical assumptions, about characters based on how those characters think and behave. To be logical, inferences must be supported by evidence from the text. As you read, jot down telling actions and dialogue. Note what you can infer about each character from his or her behavior.

Evidence from the Text	My Inferences
"Lingeringly, tenderly she gathered up the pages of her novel . . . and tied them with the blue satin ribbon. . . . She had meant to wear the ribbon with her new dotted muslin on Sundays, but this was putting it to a nobler use. She bound it round her manuscript, tying the ends in a pretty bow."	Theodora cares more abut her novel than she does about her clothes. But she's also dressing up the novel like a doll, not just sending it out, as a serious, more experienced writer would do.

▲ VOCABULARY IN CONTEXT

Wharton uses these words in her story about a writer waiting for a lucky break. Choose the word that completes each phrase.

WORD LIST	admonitory	harassing	predecessor
	commiseration	impending	retrospective
	dastardly	interrogation	

1. wrote stories of evil villains and their _____ deeds
2. ignored _____ advice that success doesn't come overnight
3. modeled herself after her famous _____
4. sent impatient letters _____ those reviewing her work
5. feared _____ failure when no one responded

What is your DREAM JOB?

KEY IDEA You've probably answered the question "What do you want to be when you grow up?" more than a few times. But take a minute to think about your ultimate **ambition.** What is it about your dream job that's so appealing? Money? Fame? The thrill of doing something you love? The main character in this story dreams of becoming a writer, but does she have what it takes?

QUICKWRITE Imagine you're filling out an application for your dream job (even if your chosen job—be it rock star or international soccer sensation—isn't one you'd typically fill out an application to get). What skills or traits make you the perfect candidate for the job? Why do you want it? What are you willing to do to get it?

April Showers

EDITH WHARTON

BACKGROUND By the turn of the 20th century, popular magazines—*Scribner's, Harper's, Century,* the *Atlantic Monthly,* and *Ladies' Home Journal*—paid good money to publish short stories, essays, and also longer works in serial form as, say, several chapters per issue. Edith Wharton first published her stories in magazines and serialized her Pulitzer Prize–winning novel, *The Age of Innocence,* as well as her autobiography. Such a publishing bonanza was great encouragement for writers of varying degrees of talent.

ANALYZE VISUALS
Describe the **mood** suggested in this painting. Which is more responsible for conveying the mood, the subject's pose and expression, or the artist's use of light and shadow? Explain your choice

"But Guy's heart slept under the violets on Muriel's grave."

It was a beautiful ending; Theodora had seen girls cry over last chapters that weren't half as pathetic. She laid her pen aside and read the words over, letting her voice linger on the fall of the sentence; then, drawing a deep breath, she wrote across the foot of the page the name by which she had decided to become known in literature—Gladys Glyn. **Ⓐ**

Downstairs the library clock struck two. Its muffled thump sounded like an **admonitory** knock against her bedroom floor. Two o' clock! and she had promised her mother to be up early enough to see that the buttons were sewn
10 on Johnny's reefer, and that Kate had her cod-liver oil[1] before starting for school!

Lingeringly, tenderly she gathered up the pages of her novel—there were five hundred of them—and tied them with the blue satin ribbon that her Aunt Julia had given her. She had meant to wear the ribbon with her new dotted muslin on Sundays, but this was putting it to a nobler use. She bound it round her manuscript, tying the ends in a pretty bow. Theodora was clever at making bows, and could have trimmed hats beautifully, had not all her spare moments been given to literature. Then, with a last look at the precious pages, she sealed and addressed the package. She meant to send it off next morning to the *Home Circle.*[2] She knew it would be hard to obtain access to a paper which numbered so many popular authors among
20 its contributors, but she had been encouraged to make the venture by something her Uncle James had said the last time he had come down from Boston.

Ⓐ TONE
Consider the literary merit of the last sentence of Theodora's novel, and think about the way in which she reads it out loud. Do you think Wharton's tone is entirely serious in these lines? Explain why or why not.

admonitory
(ăd-mŏn′ĭ-tôr′ē) *adj.* warning

---

1. **cod-liver oil:** a foul-tasting liquid once commonly taken as a source of vitamins A and D.
2. *Home Circle:* a magazine popular in the late 19th and early 20th centuries.

Girl Reading (1909), Edmund Charles Tarbell. Oil on canvas, 32 ¹/₄″ × 28 ¹/₂″. The Hayden Collection, Charles Henry Hayden Fund 09.209. © Museum of Fine Arts, Boston.

He had been telling his brother, Doctor Dace, about his new house out at Brookline.[3] Uncle James was prosperous, and was always moving into new houses with more "modern improvements." Hygiene was his passion, and he migrated in the wake of sanitary plumbing.

"The bathrooms alone are worth the money," he was saying, cheerfully, "although it *is* a big rent. But then, when a man's got no children to save up for—" he glanced compassionately round Doctor Dace's crowded table "—and it *is* something to be in a neighborhood where the drainage is A-one. That's what
30 I was telling our neighbor. Who do you suppose she is, by the way?" He smiled at Theodora. "I rather think that young lady knows all about her. Ever heard of Kathleen Kyd?"

Kathleen Kyd! The famous "society novelist," the creator of more "favorite heroines" than all her **predecessors** put together had ever turned out, the author of *Fashion and Passion, An American Duchess, Rhona's Revolt.* Was there any intelligent girl from Maine to California whose heart would not have beat faster at the mention of that name? **B**

"Why, yes," Uncle James was saying, "Kathleen Kyd lives next door. Frances G. Wollop is her real name, and her husband's a dentist. She's a very pleasant, sociable
40 kind of woman; you'd never think she was a writer. Ever hear how she began to write? She told me the whole story. It seems she was a saleswoman in a store, working on starvation wages, with a mother and a consumptive[4] sister to support. Well, she wrote a story one day, just for fun, and sent it to the *Home Circle.* They'd never heard of her, of course, and she never expected to hear from them. She did, though. They took the story and passed their plate for more. She became a regular contributor and eventually was known all over the country. Now she tells me her books bring her in about ten thousand a year. Rather more than you and I can boast of, eh, John? Well, I hope *this* household doesn't contribute to her support." He glanced sharply at Theodora. "I don't believe in feeding youngsters
50 on sentimental trash; it's like sewer gas—doesn't smell bad, and infects the system without your knowing it." **C**

Theodora listened breathlessly. Kathleen Kyd's first story had been accepted by the *Home Circle,* and they had asked for more! Why should Gladys Glyn be less fortunate? Theodora had done a great deal of novel reading—far more than her parents were aware of—and felt herself competent to pronounce upon the quality of her own work. She was almost sure that "April Showers" was a remarkable book. If it lacked Kathleen Kyd's lightness of touch, it had an emotional intensity never achieved by that brilliant writer. Theodora did not care to amuse her readers; she left that to more frivolous talents. Her aim was to stir the depths of human nature,
60 and she felt she had succeeded. It was a great thing for a girl to be able to feel that about her first novel. Theodora was only seventeen; and she remembered, with a touch of **retrospective** compassion, that George Eliot[5] had not become famous till she was nearly forty.

---

3. **Brookline:** a town in Massachusetts, just west of Boston.

4. **consumptive:** having consumption, or tuberculosis.

5. **George Eliot:** the pseudonym of the great 19th-century English novelist Mary Ann Evans.

---

predecessor (prĕd′ĭ-sĕs′ər) *n.* a person who precedes or comes before

B TONE
Judging from the stories' titles, describe the kind of writer you think Kathleen Kyd might be. What is Wharton's tone as she describes Theodora's reaction to the news about Kyd?

C MAKE INFERENCES
Why does Uncle James distinguish between "pleasant, sociable" women and female writers? Explain what you can infer about his character from these lines.

retrospective
(rĕt′rə-spĕk′tĭv) *adj.* looking back into the past

No, there was no doubt about the merit of "April Showers." But would not an inferior work have had a better chance of success? Theodora recalled the early struggles of famous authors, the notorious antagonism of publishers and editors to any new writer of exceptional promise. Would it not be wiser to write the book down to the average reader's level, reserving for some later work the great "effects" into which she had thrown all the fever of her imagination? The thought was sacrilege! Never would she lay hands on the sacred structure she had reared; never would she resort to the inartistic expedient of modifying her work to suit the popular taste. Better obscure failure than a vulgar triumph. The great authors never stooped to such concessions, and Theodora felt herself included in their ranks by the firmness with which she rejected all thought of conciliating an unappreciative public. The manuscript should be sent as it was. **D**

She woke with a start and a heavy sense of apprehension. The *Home Circle* had refused "April Showers"! No, that couldn't be it; there lay the precious manuscript, waiting to be posted. What was it, then? Ah, that ominous thump below stairs—nine o'clock striking! It was Johnny's buttons!

She sprang out of bed in dismay. She had been so determined not to disappoint her mother about Johnny's buttons! Mrs. Dace, helpless from chronic rheumatism, had to entrust the care of the household to her eldest daughter; and Theodora honestly meant to see that Johnny had his full complement of buttons, and that Kate and Bertha went to school tidy. Unfortunately, the writing of a great novel leaves little time or memory for the lesser obligations of life, and Theodora usually found that her good intentions matured too late for practical results.

Her contrition was softened by the thought that literary success would enable her to make up for all the little negligences of which she was guilty. She meant to spend all her money on her family; and already she had visions of a wheeled chair for her mother, a fresh wallpaper for the doctor's shabby office, bicycles for the girls, and Johnny's establishment at a boarding school where sewing on his buttons would be included in the curriculum. If her parents could have guessed her intentions, they would not have found fault with her as they did; and Doctor Dace, on this particular morning, would not have looked up to say, with his fagged, ironical air:

"I suppose you didn't get home from the ball till morning?"

Theodora's sense of being in the right enabled her to take the thrust with a dignity that would have awed the unfeeling parent of fiction.

"I'm sorry to be late, father," she said.

Doctor Dace, who could never be counted on to behave like a father in a book, shrugged his shoulders impatiently.

"Your sentiments do you credit, but they haven't kept your mother's breakfast warm." **E**

"Hasn't mother's tray gone up yet?"

"Who was to take it, I should like to know? The girls came down so late that

D MAKE INFERENCES
Consider Theodora's sympathy for George Eliot in lines 61–63 and her opinion of the "average reader." What inferences can you make about Theodora's character based on her thoughts about her own work?

E MAKE INFERENCES
Theodora muses repeatedly that Dr. Dace does not act as a father in a work of fiction would. What does she mean by this?

I had to hustle them off before they'd finished breakfast, and Johnny's hands were so dirty that I sent him back to his room to make himself decent. It's a pretty thing for the doctor's children to be the dirtiest little savages in Norton!"

Theodora had hastily prepared her mother's tray, leaving her own breakfast
110 untouched. As she entered the room upstairs, Mrs. Dace's patient face turned to her with a smile much harder to bear than her father's reproaches.

"Mother, I'm *so* sorry—"

"No matter, dear. I suppose Johnny's buttons kept you. I can't think what that boy does to his clothes!"

Theodora sat the tray down without speaking. It was impossible to own to having forgotten Johnny's buttons without revealing the cause of her forgetfulness. For a few weeks longer she must bear to be misunderstood; then—ah, then if her novel were accepted, how gladly would she forget and forgive! But what if it were refused? She turned aside to hide the dismay that flushed her face. Well, then
120 she would admit the truth—she would ask her parents' pardon, and settle down without a murmur to an obscure existence of mending and combing.

She had said to herself that after the manuscript had been sent, she would have time to look after the children and catch up with the mending; but she had reckoned without the postman. He came three times a day; for an hour before each ring she was too excited to do anything but wonder if he would bring an answer this time, and for an hour afterward she moved about in a leaden stupor of disappointment. The children had never been so trying. They seemed to be always coming to pieces, like cheap furniture; one would have supposed they had been put together with bad glue. Mrs. Dace worried herself ill over Johnny's tatters,
130 Bertha's bad marks at school, and Kate's open abstention from cod-liver oil; and Doctor Dace, coming back late from a long round of visits to a fireless office with a smoky lamp, called out furiously to know if Theodora would kindly come down and remove the "East, West, home's best" that hung above the empty grate.

In the midst of it all, Miss Sophy Brill called. It was very kind of her to come, for she was the busiest woman in Norton. She made it her duty to look after other people's affairs, and there was not a house in town but had the benefit of her personal supervision. She generally came when things were going wrong, and the sight of her bonnet on the doorstep was a surer sign of calamity than a crepe bow on the bell.[6] After she left, Mrs. Dace looked very sad, and the doctor punished
140 Johnny for warbling down the entry:

> "Miss Sophy Brill
> Is a bitter pill!"

while Theodora, locking herself in her room, resolved with tears that she would never write another novel. **F**

The week was a long nightmare. Theodora could neither eat nor sleep. She was up early enough, but instead of looking after the children and seeing that breakfast

F TONE
What kind of person is Miss Brill? Describe Wharton's tone as she introduces this character, and point out the phrases and details that help establish this tone.

---

6. **crepe bow on the bell:** a signal that someone had died. Clothing made from black crepe (a silk material used to be worn by those in mourning).

was ready, she wandered down the road to meet the postman, and came back wan and empty-handed, oblivious of her morning duties. She had no idea how long the suspense would last; but she didn't see how authors could live if they were kept 150 waiting more than a week.

Then suddenly, one afternoon—she never quite knew how or when it happened—she found herself with a *Home Circle* envelope in her hands, and her dazzled eyes flashing over a wild dance of words that wouldn't settle down and make sense.

"Dear Madam:" (They called her *Madam!* And then; yes, the words were beginning to fall into line now.) "Your novel, 'April Showers,' has been received, and we are glad to accept it on the usual terms. A serial on which we were counting for immediate publication has been delayed by the author's illness, and the first chapters of 'April Showers' will therefore appear in our midsummer number. Thanking you 160 for favoring us with your manuscript, we remain," and so forth.

Theodora found herself in the wood beyond the schoolhouse. She was kneeling on the ground, brushing aside the dead leaves and pressing her lips to the little bursting green things that pushed up eager tips through last year's decay. It was spring—spring! Everything was crowding toward the light and in her own heart hundreds of germinating hopes had burst into sudden leaf. She wondered if the thrust of those little green fingers hurt the surface of the earth as her springing raptures hurt—yes, actually hurt!—her hot, constricted breast! She looked up through interlacing boughs at a tender, opaque blue sky full of the coming of a milky moon. She seemed enveloped in an atmosphere of loving comprehension. 170 The brown earth throbbed with her joy, the treetops trembled with it, and a sudden star broke through the branches like an audible "I know!"

Theodora, on the whole, behaved very well. Her mother cried, her father whistled and said he supposed he must put up with grounds in his coffee now, and be thankful if he ever got a hot meal again; while the children took the most deafening and **harassing** advantage of what seemed a sudden suspension of the laws of nature.

harassing (hə-răs'ĭng) *adj.* persistently annoying **harass** *v.*

Within a week everybody in Norton knew that Theodora had written a novel, and that it was coming out in the *Home Circle*. On Sundays, when she walked up the aisle, her friends dropped their prayer books and the soprano sang false in 180 her excitement. Girls with more pin money than Theodora had ever dreamed of copied her hats and imitated her way of speaking. The local paper asked her for a poem; her old school teachers stopped to shake hands and grew shy over their congratulations; and Miss Sophy Brill came to call. She had put on her Sunday bonnet and her manner was almost abject. She ventured, very timidly, to ask her young friend how she wrote, whether it "just came to her," and if she had found that the kind of pen she used made any difference; and wound up by begging Theodora to write a sentiment in her album.

Even Uncle James came down from Boston to talk the wonder over. He called Theodora a "sly baggage," and proposed that she should give him her earnings to invest in a new patent grease-trap company. From what Kathleen Kyd had told him, he thought Theodora would probably get a thousand dollars for her story. He concluded by suggesting that she should base her next romance on the subject of sanitation, making the heroine nearly die of sewer gas poisoning because her parents won't listen to the handsome young doctor next door, when he warns them that their plumbing is out of order. That was a subject that would interest everybody, and do a lot more good than the sentimental trash most women wrote.

At last the great day came. Theodora had left an order with the bookseller for the midsummer number of the *Home Circle* and before the shop was open she was waiting on the sidewalk. She clutched the precious paper and ran home without opening it. Her excitement was almost more than she could bear. Not heeding her father's call to breakfast, she rushed upstairs and locked herself in her room. Her hands trembled so that she could hardly turn the pages. At last—yes, there it was: "April Showers."

The paper dropped from her hands. What name had she read beneath the title? Had her emotion blinded her?

"April Showers, by *Kathleen Kyd*."

Kathleen Kyd! Oh, cruel misprint! Oh, **dastardly** typographer! Through tears of rage and disappointment Theodora looked again; yes, there was no mistaking the hateful name. Her glance ran on. She found herself reading a first paragraph

dastardly (dăs′tərd-lē)
adj. characterized by underhandedness or treachery

In the Station Waiting Room, Boston (1915), Edmund Charles Tarbell. Oil on canvas, 24 ³/₈″ × 32″. Gift of Dr. Joseph R. Fazzano. © Crocker Art Museum, Sacramento, California.

210 that she had never seen before. She read farther. All was strange. The horrible truth burst upon her: *It was not her story!*

She never knew how she got back to the station. She struggled through the crowd on the platform, and a gold-banded arm pushed her into the train just starting for Norton. It would be dark when she reached home; but that didn't matter—nothing mattered now. She sank into her seat, closing her eyes in the vain attempt to shut out the vision of the last few hours; but minute by minute memory forced her to relive it; she felt like a rebellious school child dragged forth to repeat the same detested "piece."

220 Although she did not know Boston well, she had made her way easily enough to the *Home Circle* building; at least, she supposed she had, since she remembered nothing till she found herself ascending the editorial stairs as easily as one does incredible things in dreams. She must have walked very fast, for her heart was beating furiously, and she had barely breath to whisper the editor's name to a young man who looked out at her from a glass case, like a zoological specimen. The young man led her past other glass cases containing similar specimens to an inner enclosure which seemed filled by an enormous presence. Theodora felt herself enveloped in the presence, submerged by it, gasping for air as she sank under its rising surges.

Gradually fragments of speech floated to the surface. "'April Showers?' Mrs.
230 Kyd's new serial? *Your* manuscript, you say? You have a letter from me? The name, please? Evidently some unfortunate misunderstanding. One moment." And then a bell ringing, a zoological specimen ordered to unlock a safe, her name asked for again, the manuscript, her own precious manuscript, tied with Aunt Julia's ribbon, laid on the table before her, and her outcries, her protests, her **interrogations,** drowned in a flood of bland apology: "An unfortunate accident—Mrs. Kyd's manuscript received the same day—extraordinary coincidence in the choice of a title—duplicate answers sent by mistake—Miss Dace's novel hardly suited to their purpose—should of course have been returned—regrettable oversight—accidents would happen—sure she understood."

240 The voice went on, like the steady pressure of a surgeon's hand on a shrieking nerve. When it stopped she was in the street. A cab nearly ran her down, and a car bell jangled furiously in her ears. She clutched her manuscript, carrying it tenderly through the crowd, like a live thing that had been hurt. She could not bear to look at its soiled edges and the ink stain on Aunt Julia's ribbon. **G**

The train stopped with a jerk and she opened her eyes. It was dark, and by the windy flare of gas on the platform she saw the Norton passengers getting out. She stood up stiffly and followed them. A warm wind blew into her face the fragrance of the summer woods, and she remembered how, two months earlier, she had knelt among the dead leaves, pressing her lips to the first shoots of green. Then
250 for the first time she thought of home. She had fled away in the morning without a word, and her heart sank at the thought of her mother's fears. And her father—how angry he would be! She bent her head under the coming storm of his derision.

interrogation
(ĭn-tĕr′ə-gā′shən) *n.* a questioning

G TONE
Compare Wharton's tone in earlier descriptions of Theodora with the tone she adopts in lines 240–244. How has Wharton's tone changed?

The night was cloudy, and as she stepped into the darkness beyond the station a hand was slipped in hers. She stood still, too weary to feel frightened, and a voice said, quietly:

"Don't walk so fast, child. You look tired."

"Father!" Her hand dropped from his, but he recaptured it and drew it through his arm. When she found voice, it was to whisper, "You were at the station?"

"It's such a good night I thought I'd stroll down and meet you."

260   Her arm trembled against his. She could not see his face in the dimness, but the light of his cigar looked down on her like a friendly eye, and she took courage to falter out: "Then you knew—"

"That you'd gone to Boston? Well, I rather thought you had."

They walked on slowly, and presently he added, "You see, you left the *Home Circle* lying in your room."

How she blessed the darkness and the muffled sky! She could not have borne the scrutiny of the tiniest star.

"Then mother wasn't very much frightened?"

"Why, no, she didn't appear to be. She's been busy all day over some toggery 270 of Bertha's."

Theodora choked. "Father, I'll—" She groped for words, but they eluded her. "I'll do things—differently; I haven't meant—" Suddenly she heard herself bursting out: "It was all a mistake, you know—about my story. They didn't want it; they won't have it!" and she shrank back involuntarily from his **impending** mirth.

She felt the pressure of his arm, but he didn't speak, and she figured his mute hilarity. They moved on in silence. Presently he said:

"It hurts a bit just at first, doesn't it?"

"O father!"

He stood still, and the gleam of his cigar showed a face of unexpected 280 participation.

"You see I've been through it myself."

"You, father? You?"

"Why, yes. Didn't I ever tell you? I wrote a novel once. I was just out of college, and didn't want to be a doctor. No; I wanted to be a genius, so I wrote a novel."

The doctor paused, and Theodora clung to him in a mute passion of **commiseration.** It was as if a drowning creature caught a live hand through the murderous fury of the waves.

"Father—O father!"

"It took me a year—a whole year's hard work; and when I'd finished it the 290 public wouldn't have it, either; not at any price and that's why I came down to meet you, because I remembered my walk home." ❧ 🄷

impending (ĭm-pĕn′dĭng) *adj.* to be about to occur **impend** *v.*

commiseration (kə-mĭz′ə-rā′shən) *n.* a feeling of sympathy or pity

🄷 **TONE**
Has the change in Wharton's tone affected how you feel about her characters? Explain whether you view Theodora or her father differently, and cite the lines that changed your opinion.

Comprehension

1. **Summarize** Describe Theodora's family situation and responsibilities.

2. **Recall** What does Theodora plan to do with the money she expects to earn?

3. **Clarify** How does the *Home Circle* editor explain the mix-up?

4. **Clarify** What does Theodora's father reveal to her at the end of the story?

Literary Analysis

5. **Draw Conclusions** Does this story have a happy ending? What kind of life does Theodora have to look forward to now that her **ambition** has been thwarted? Cite evidence from the story to support your conclusion.

6. **Analyze Tone** Reread lines 52–75. How does Wharton's tone in these lines let readers know that Theodora might not be the "great author" she thinks herself to be? Describe Wharton's tone, pointing out the words and details she employs to achieve it.

7. **Make Inferences About Characters** Review the inferences you recorded as you read, and recall Theodora's disappointment that her father does not act the way she thinks the parent in a novel would. How might their relationship change as a result of the disastrous "April Showers" incident?

8. **Interpret Satire** A satire ridicules ideas and behavior to expose human faults or weakness. Satire is sometimes hard to detect, but a writer's tone is often an indication—reading a satire can feel as though the author were winking at you while telling the story. Explain what characters and behavior Wharton satirizes in this story by filling out a chart like the one shown.

Character	Satirized for ...	Evidence in Story
Uncle James	being crude and materialistic	• talks obsessively about indoor plumbing and "sewer gas" at the dinner table (lines 24–51) • brags about his money and even asks Theodora to invest the money from her novel in one of his schemes (lines 26–29, 188–196)

Literary Criticism

9. **Historical Context** A contemporary critic commented, "When we look beneath the high surface gloss of Wharton's world, we see a marketplace, pure and simple. Hers is an almost purely economic conception of life." What insights does this story give you into the economic position of women at the turn of the 20th century? What kinds of work were available to them, and at what kinds of wages? Is it surprising that an educated young woman would try to make money by writing? Support your answer with evidence.

Vocabulary in Context

VOCABULARY PRACTICE

Show you understand the vocabulary words by answering these questions.

1. Which is a **dastardly** deed, betraying a friend or voting in an election?
2. If an investigation is **impending,** is it over or about to happen?
3. Would an artist have a **retrospective** exhibit early or late in his or her career?
4. What is the intent of a **harassing** letter, to schedule an appointment or to irritate the recipient into action?
5. If I make an **admonitory** statement, do I expect you to laugh or take it seriously?
6. Is an **interrogation** intended to get information or rehearse a performance?
7. Which would be a gesture of **commiseration,** sending flowers or watching a lengthy movie?
8. Who would be your mother's **predecessor** in life, you or your grandmother?

VOCABULARY IN WRITING

What was Theodora's state of mind after she submitted her manuscript? Write a short explanation of how she felt , including at least two vocabulary words.

> **EXAMPLE SENTENCE**
> Waiting for **impending** news of the fate of her manuscript almost drove Theodora crazy.

VOCABULARY STRATEGY: THE LATIN ROOT *rog*

The vocabulary word *interrogation* contains the Latin root *rog*, which means "ask," "ask for," or "propose." This root is found in several English words. To understand words built around *rog*, use your knowledge of the meaning of the root as well as context clues.

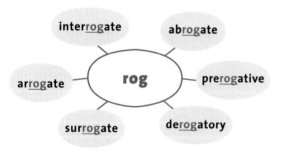

PRACTICE Apply what you know about the Latin root *rog* and the other word parts to help you understand the words in the web. Then choose the word that best completes each sentence. If necessary, consult a dictionary.

1. It is the race winner's _____ to wear the yellow jersey.
2. The official could not attend the ceremony, so he sent a(n) _____.
3. They feared that the new judge would _____ to herself powers that belonged to the legislature.
4. Jake tends to make _____ remarks about people he does not like.
5. People _____ their responsibility when they do not care for their pets.

VOCABULARY PRACTICE
For more practice, go to the **Vocabulary Center** at **ClassZone.com.**

Women's Changing Roles

A woman's role in American society was rigidly defined in the late 19th and early 20th centuries. Women of this period could not vote, few owned businesses, and few gained a higher education. Yet women were increasingly agitating for change in both big and small ways. The writers in this section (pages 758–802) gave voice to the struggles of women attempting to fashion a new role for themselves and break free from restricting social expectations. As critic Richard Gray noted, "Humanity, if it is repressed, will always have its revenge."

Writing to Compare

Think about how women's roles have changed since the times of Kate Chopin and Edith Wharton. Using the stories you have just read and your knowledge of American society today, write a comparison of women's roles then and now.

Consider

- what each selection tells you about society's expectations for women at that time
- how things have or have not changed since the days these writers were working
- what details from the selections best illustrate women's roles in the past
- what examples from today best illustrate women's roles now

Extension

SPEAKING & LISTENING

With a partner, **role-play** a conversation between two of the main characters from this section of the book. Discuss your family life, your work, your frustrations, and so on. Alternatively, role-play two of the main characters' husbands or fathers discussing the women in their lives.

Writing Workshop

Literary Analysis

As you have seen in this unit, literature often reflects what is happening in the world and in the author's imagination. Analyzing how authors use literary elements will give you a better understanding and appreciation of what you read. The **Writer's Road Map** will guide you as you write a literary analysis.

WRITER'S ROAD MAP

Literary Analysis

WRITING PROMPT 1

Writing from Literature Analyzing a literary work can help you understand it more deeply. Write an essay in which you focus on one or more literary elements, such as setting, characters, or plot details, in a work of fiction. Explain how the element or elements contribute to the meaning.

Literature to Consider

- theme in "The Open Boat"
- setting in "The Law of Life"
- humor in "The Outcasts of Poker Flat"

WRITING PROMPT 2

Writing from the Real World Choose a story you have viewed or read that you just can't stop thinking about. Write an essay that briefly summarizes the story and examines its meaning. Focus on specific elements that make the story meaningful and memorable.

Sources of Stories

- television shows that use suspense or conflict
- movies that have strong characters
- magazines that publish fictional or real-life adventure stories

 WRITING TOOLS
For prewriting, revision, and editing tools, visit the **Writing Center** at **ClassZone.com**.

KEY TRAITS

1. IDEAS
- Presents a **thesis statement** that clearly identifies the key points of the discussion
- Uses **evidence** from the text to support each key point

2. ORGANIZATION
- Attention-getting **introduction** identifies the title and author of the work
- Consistent **organizational pattern** includes **transitions** to connect ideas
- **Conclusion** summarizes ideas and discusses the overall meaning of the work

3. VOICE
- **Tone** is appropriate for the audience and purpose

4. WORD CHOICE
- Uses **precise language** to examine and explain the work

5. SENTENCE FLUENCY
- Varies **sentence structures and lengths**

6. CONVENTIONS
- Employs **correct grammar and usage**

Part 1: Analyze a Student Model

Amanda Olivares
Jackson Regional High School

"The Story of an Hour": Shock and Self-Discovery

How would you react if a friend came to you with a shocking piece of news? The first sentence of "The Story of an Hour" reveals that the main character's husband has died. As this short story develops, we find out her complicated and conflicting reactions to this tragedy. Throughout the story,
5   author Kate Chopin uses symbolism and irony to tell the tale of a woman's short-lived self-discovery.

Chopin wastes no words. The first several paragraphs give almost no details about the main character. Although we know that she is "afflicted" with a mysterious "heart trouble," we aren't told what her personality is
10 like, where she lives, or what she looks like. We don't even know her first name; she is simply "Mrs. Mallard." This lack of detail symbolizes how little the main character knows about her feelings and her identity. It also shows how women of that time period (the late 19th century) were portrayed—as selfless, dependent wives and mothers, devoted to their
15 families. Based on the story's beginning, we assume that Mrs. Mallard is a stereotypical woman of the era. However, as we read further, our impression of her begins to change.

It is only when the main character is alone that Chopin begins to reveal rich and symbolic details. "Pressed down by a physical exhaustion," Mrs.
20 Mallard sinks into an armchair and looks out an open window. Chopin writes, "She could see in the open square before her house the tops of trees that were all aquiver with the new spring life. The delicious breath of rain was in the air. . . . The notes of a distant song which someone was singing reached her faintly. . . ." By describing this "new spring life" in exquisite
25 detail, Chopin changes the pace of the story and symbolizes the new beginning that is now available to the main character.

KEY TRAITS IN ACTION

Intriguing **introduction** identifies the literary work.

Presents the key points of the analysis in a clear **thesis statement.**

Varied **sentence structures and lengths** maintain the reader's interest.

Uses **evidence** (details and quotations from the story) to illustrate and support statements. The writer of this analysis carefully assesses how subtle details affect the story's meaning.

As we learn more about Mrs. Mallard's thoughts and hopes, the story takes an ironic turn. At first the new widow is stunned and exhausted, with an increasing feeling of dread. Because her husband has just died and she has "heart trouble," we can assume that she will be utterly miserable. She might even die of grief. Instead, however, she repeats a single word under her breath: "free, free, free!" Her husband was always kind and loving to her, but his death means that "there would be no one to live for her during those coming years; she would live for herself." Ironically, the event that readers think will ruin her life actually brings her "a monstrous joy." Brently Mallard's death has given his wife a chance at freedom and independence.

Transformed by "self-assertion which she suddenly recognized as the strongest impulse of her being," Mrs. Mallard comes out of her room to rejoin the world "like a goddess of Victory." As she goes back downstairs, she sees her husband coming in the door, as alive as ever. The resulting shock is too much for her to bear. Everyone assumes that Mrs. Mallard dies of the "joy that kills." Ironically, she actually dies because she cannot stand the idea of losing her independence, even though she experienced it for just one hour.

From the title of this short story to its last words, Kate Chopin uses irony and symbolism to describe a woman's discovery—and loss—of her own identity. As we follow the surprising twists and turns of "The Story of an Hour," we can't help thinking, what shocks and self-discoveries might the hours of our own lives have in store?

> Logical **organizational pattern** follows order of events in the story. **Transitions** show how ideas are related.

> **Tone** is formal without being stuffy.

> **Conclusion** uses **precise language** to summarize the main points of the analysis and identify its effect on readers. Repetition of words from the essay title create a feeling of closure.

2

Part 2: Apply the Writing Process

PREWRITING

What Should I Do?	What Does It Look Like?

1. Revisit the work you're analyzing.
Reading or viewing the work several times will reveal details you may have missed the first time around. Note your thoughts about the characters, events, dialogue, or style in a learning log.

▶

Details from the Story	My Thoughts
Mrs. Mallard's "heart trouble"	could have two meanings—physical or emotional (or both)
Husband's death makes her feel free.	We expect her to be unhappy.
He's really alive.	turns everything in the story upside down

2. Freewrite to explore your ideas.
As you freewrite, don't worry about spelling, grammar, or organization. Just let the comments and ideas flow freely.

See page 810: Review Literary Terms

▶

Lots of surprises in this story ... Mrs. M seems to care about her husband, but when she thinks he's dead, she's sort of glad because now she can be independent. But he's NOT really dead, and she's so shocked that <u>she</u> dies when she learns this. That's called irony, I think.

3. Develop a working thesis statement.
Review your learning log and your freewriting. Decide on the main idea you want to make about the work and condense it into a sentence or two. You can refine this statement as you draft your analysis.

▶

Working thesis statement:

In "The Story of an Hour," Kate Chopin tells the tale of a woman's self-discovery. The author uses symbolism and irony to help explain what happens to the woman and why.

4. Find evidence to support your key points.
Carefully read through the work again. List quotations, details, and other examples that back up the main ideas in your working thesis statement.

TIP Focus on how one or two elements help get the meaning of the work across. The writer of the student model focused on symbolism and irony.

▶

Evidence	How It Conveys Meaning
The reader doesn't know Mrs. Mallard's first name until late in the story.	symbolizes her lack of identity
"the tops of trees that were all aquiver with the new spring life"	symbolizes Mrs. Mallard's self-discovery
She dies of "joy that kills."	ironic, since she really dies from grief for herself

DRAFTING

What Should I Do?	What Does It Look Like?

1. Plan your organization.
Experiment with different ways of presenting your ideas. You might want to discuss your points in the order that they appear in the work, as Amanda Olivares did (Pattern 1). You could also discuss the end of the work first and then trace how that ending came about (Pattern 2).

PATTERN 1

Introduction and thesis

1. Beginning of story: lack of first name symbolizes character's lack of identity
2. Middle: "new spring life" symbolizes her new life
3. Middle: ironic that tragic event brings joy
4. End: ironic that she dies from lack of independence, not from joy

Conclusion

PATTERN 2

Introduction and thesis

A. Irony
   1. The main character dies from lack of independence, not from "joy that kills."
   2. Why would a tragic event bring joy?
B. Symbolism
   1. Lack of first name at beginning of story symbolizes lack of identity.
   2. "New spring life" parallels her new life.

Conclusion

2. Back up your key points with evidence from the work.
Choose examples, details, and quotations that clearly support your ideas.

TIP Remember, you don't have to—and shouldn't—discuss every detail of the work.

His death means that "there would be no one to live for her during those coming years; she would live for herself." Ironically, the event that readers think will ruin her life actually brings her "a monstrous joy." — Explanations and quotations

Brently Mallard's death has given his wife a chance at freedom and independence. — Key point

3. Create a strong, thoughtful conclusion.
Summarize the ideas you've discussed and leave your reader with something more to think about—maybe a way to relate the overall message of the work to his or her own life.

TIP Before revising, consult the key traits on page 804 and the rubric and peer-reader questions on page 810.

From the title of this short story to its last words, Kate Chopin uses irony and symbolism to describe a woman's discovery—and loss—of her own identity. — Summary

As we follow the surprising twists and turns of "The Story of an Hour," we can't help thinking, what shocks and self-discoveries might the hours of our own lives have in store? — Relating the work to reader's life

REVISING AND EDITING

What Should I Do?	*What Does It Look Like?*

1. Enliven your introduction.
- Read your introduction aloud. (Circle) statements that seem dull or unclear.
- Recast these sentences so they immediately capture the reader's attention.

▶

How would you react if a friend came to you with a shocking piece of news? The first sentence of "The Story of an Hour" reveals ~~"The Story of an Hour" is a short story by Kate Chopin.~~ We learn in the first sentence that the main character's husband has died. As this short story develops, we find out her complicated and conflicting reactions to this tragedy.

2. Use exact, specific words.
- Have a peer reader <u>underline</u> words that are too general or that should be replaced with precise literary terms.
- Substitute lively language and specific terms.

▶

It is only when the ~~woman~~ *main character* is alone that Chopin ~~adds details,~~ begins to reveal rich and symbolic details.

As we learn more about ~~her~~ *Mrs. Mallard's thoughts and hopes,* the story ~~changes,~~ takes an ironic turn.

3. Vary your sentence structures and lengths.
- Are many of your sentences short and choppy or long and droning? Draw a box around sentences that are of similar lengths or that have the same structure.
- Combine or separate some sentences to give your readers variety.

▶

~~She goes downstairs. She sees her husband come in. He is alive! It is a terrible shock.~~

As she goes back downstairs, she sees her husband coming in the door, as alive as ever. The resulting shock is too much for her to bear.

4. Emphasize the meaning.
- Ask a peer reader to highlight sentences that explain the author's message.
- If your analysis has little or no highlighting, add information about the story's significance.

See page 810: Ask a Peer Reader

▶

Although we know that she is "afflicted" with a mysterious "heart trouble," we aren't told what her personality is like, where she lives, or what she looks like. We don't even know her first name; she is simply "Mrs. Mallard." *This lack of detail symbolizes how little the main character knows about her feelings and her identity. It also shows how women of that time period (the late 19th century) were portrayed—as selfless, dependent wives and mothers, devoted to their families.*

Apply the Rubric

A strong literary analysis . . .

- ☑ identifies the author and the work in an interesting introduction
- ☑ gives the key points of the analysis in a clear thesis statement
- ☑ organizes ideas sensibly, using appropriate transitions
- ☑ supports statements with specific details, examples, quotations, and other information from the text
- ☑ uses a tone suited to the purpose and audience
- ☑ maintains interest by varying the structures and lengths of sentences and by using precise language
- ☑ concludes with a summary of the key points and a discussion of the work's overall meaning

Ask a Peer Reader

- What did you learn from my analysis?
- Do my statements need more explanation? If so, which ones?
- Are there places where I retell events without explaining their significance? If so, where?

Review Literary Terms

Irony: a contrast between appearance and actuality (In "The Story of an Hour," the husband's death brings the wife joy, not misery.)

Point of view: the perspective from which a story is told (Chopin's story has a third-person omniscient narrator. See "Point of view" on page Rooo to learn more.)

Symbolism: the use of one idea or object to represent another (The buds on the trees symbolize Mrs. Mallard's new life.)

Theme: an underlying message about life or human nature that the writer wants readers to understand (Some critics say the theme of Chopin's story is "Women crave independence.")

Check Your Grammar

Make sure modifiers are placed as close as possible to the words they modify.

> As she goes back downstairs, (as alive as ever) she sees her husband coming in the door.

See page R63: Misplaced Modifiers

Writing Online

PUBLISHING OPTIONS
For publishing options, visit the
Writing Center at ClassZone.com.

ASSESSMENT PREPARATION
For writing and grammar assessment practice,
go to the **Assessment Center** at ClassZone.com.

Producing a Power Presentation

Share your literary analysis by turning it into a power presentation—a series of slides that you create using computer software.

Planning the Presentation

1. **Focus on your main ideas.** Sketch out at least one slide apiece for your introduction, your conclusion, and every key point you made. Each sketch should include a headline and three to five short bullet points.

2. **Decide on a design.** Choose one of the templates available with the software program you are using. Or, if you prefer, choose your own fonts and colors. Your slides must be readable throughout the room, so use type that is 14 points or larger.

3. **Spice it up.** Create or find visuals that illustrate your points. Consider adding music or sound effects.

4. **Practice and fine-tune.** If possible, run through your presentation with the equipment and in the room you will be using. Otherwise, use a printed copy of the slides to present to friends and family. Make sure information is logical and in order, quotations are accurate, and spelling is correct.

Symbolism of View from Window

- Mrs. Mallard sees trees "aquiver with the new spring life"

- Changes the pace of the story

- Symbolizes her new beginning

Delivering the Presentation

1. **Make it a presentation, not a reading.** Maintain eye contact with your audience most of the time. Elaborate on each point with additional details and evidence from the work to strengthen your statements.

2. **Ask for feedback.** Create a simple questionnaire on the content and style of your presentation. Distribute copies of the questionnaire to audience members. Use the feedback to power up your next power presentation.

Reading Comprehension

DIRECTIONS *Read these selections and answer the questions that follow.*

These two selections represent the end of one way of life and the beginning of another at the close of the 19th century. Chief Joseph delivered his surrender speech in 1877, as the Nez Perce were being relocated to a reservation. Dreiser's novel, set in 1889, recounts the experiences of Carrie Meeber, a fictional character based on the thousands of rural Americans who came to industrial cities (like Chicago) in search of new opportunities.

I Will Fight No More Forever
Chief Joseph

Tell General Howard I know his heart. What he told me before, I have in my heart. I am tired of fighting. Our chiefs are killed. Looking Glass is dead. Toohoolhoolzote is dead. The old men are all dead. It is the young men who say yes or no. He who led on the young men is dead. It is cold and we have no blankets. The little children are freezing to death. My people, some of them, have run away to the hills, and have no blankets, no food; no one knows where they are—perhaps freezing to death. I want to have time to look for my children and see how many of them I can find. Maybe I shall find them among the dead. Hear me, my chiefs! I am tired; my heart is sick and sad. From where the sun now
10 stands I will fight no more forever.

from Sister Carrie
Theodore Dreiser

With the wane of the afternoon went her hopes, her courage and her strength. She had been astonishingly persistent. So earnest an effort was well deserving of a better reward. On every hand, to her fatigued senses, the great business portion grew larger, harder, more stolid in its indifference. It seemed as if it was all closed to her, that the struggle was too fierce for her to hope to do anything at all. Men and women hurried by in long, shifting lines. She felt the flow of the tide of effort and interest, felt her own helplessness without quite realizing the wisp on the tide that she was. She cast about vainly for some possible place to apply but found no door which she had the courage to enter. It would be the same thing
10 all over. The old humiliation of her pleas rewarded by curt denial. Sick at heart and in body, she turned to the west, the direction of Minnie's flat, which she had now fixed in mind, and began that wearisome, baffled retreat which the seeker for

employment at nightfall too often makes. In passing through Fifth Avenue, south towards Van Buren Street, where she intended to take a car, she passed the door of a large wholesale shoe house, through the plate glass window of which she could see a middle-aged gentleman sitting at a small desk. One of those forlorn impulses which often grow out of a fixed sense of defeat, the last sprouting of a baffled and uprooted growth of ideas, seized upon her. She walked deliberately through the door and up to the gentleman who looked at her weary face with partially

20 awakened interest.

"What is it?" he said.

"Can you give me something to do?" asked Carrie.

"Now I really don't know," he said kindly. "What kind of work is it you want— you're not a typewriter, are you?"

"Oh, no," answered Carrie.

"Well, we only employ book keepers and typewriters here. You might go round to the side and inquire upstairs. They did want some help upstairs a few days ago. Ask for Mr. Brown."

She hastened around to the side entrance and was taken up by the elevator to

30 the fourth floor.

"Call Mr. Brown, Willie," said the elevator man to a boy near by.

Willie went off and presently returned with the information that Mr. Brown said she should sit down and that he would be around in a little while.

It was a portion of a stock room which gave no idea of the general character of the floor, and Carrie could form no opinion of the nature of the work.

"So you want something to do," said Mr. Brown, after he inquired concerning the nature of her errand. "Have you ever been employed in a shoe factory before?"

"No sir," said Carrie.

"What is your name?" he inquired, and being informed, "Well, I don't know as

40 I have anything for you. Would you work for four and a half a week?"

Carrie was too worn by defeat not to feel that it was considerable. She had not expected that he would offer her less than six. She acquiesced, however, and he took her name and address.

"Well," he said finally—"you report here at eight o'clock Monday morning. I think I can find something for you to do."

He left her revived by the possibilities, sure that she had found something to do at last. Instantly the blood crept warmly over her body. Her nervous tension relaxed. She walked out into the busy street and discovered a new atmosphere. Behold, the throng was moving with a lightsome step. She noticed that men

50 and women were smiling. Scraps of conversation and notes of laughter floated

to her. The air was light. People were already pouring out of the buildings, their labor ended for the day. She noticed that they were pleased, and thoughts of her sister's home, and the meal that would be awaiting her, quickened her steps. She hurried on, tired perhaps, but no longer weary of foot. What would not Minnie say! Ah, long the winter in Chicago—the lights, the crowd, the amusement. This was a great, pleasing metropolis after all. Her new firm was a goodly institution. Its windows were of huge plate glass. She could probably do well there. Thoughts of Drouet returned, of the things he had told her. She now felt that life was better. That it was livelier, sprightlier. She boarded a car in the best of spirits, feeling her
60 blood still flowing pleasantly. She would live in Chicago, her mind kept saying to itself. She would have a better time than she ever had before—she would be happy.

Comprehension

DIRECTIONS *Answer these questions about "I Will Fight No More Forever."*

1. Which words best describes Chief Joseph's tone?

   A brash and ironic

   B weary and heavy-hearted

   C self-pitying and imploring

   D suspicious and angry

2. Reread lines 2–4. The repetition in Chief Joseph's roll call of the dead emphasizes the

   A losses suffered in the conflict with U.S. troops

   B risks incurred in relocating to a reservation

   C honor bestowed on the Nez Perce warriors

   D shame associated with the Nez Perce's defeat

3. Chief Joseph's phrase "From where the sun now stands" emphasizes

   A a measured distance

   B the change of seasons

   C an exact point in time

   D his geographic location

DIRECTIONS *Answer these questions about the excerpt from* Sister Carrie.

4. Dreiser's description in lines 3–10 reflects the naturalist theme that the world is

   A safe and predictable

   B indifferent to the individual

   C filled with economic opportunities

   D fast-paced and exciting

5. Which word best describes how Carrie feels in the business district in lines 3–10?

   A energized   **C** homesick

   B powerless   **D** comfortable

6. Which event exemplifies the naturalist view that humans are controlled by impulses?

   A Carrie's long and fruitless search for a job

   B Carrie's decision to ask for work in the shoe house

   C Mr. Brown's offer of four and a half dollars a week

   D people leaving work at the end of the day

7. Which of these forces does Carrie struggle with in this excerpt?

   A inner anger

   B unfair competition

   C political corruption

   D economic need

8. By revealing Carrie's innermost thoughts and impressions the narrator

   A creates a realistic scenario

   B emphasizes her bewilderment

   C undermines her credibility

   D highlights class conflict

9. In lines 48–52, Carrie now perceives Chicago's business district as

   A stifling   C well lit

   B friendly   D chaotic

10. Why does Carrie see the business district differently at the end of the excerpt?

    A It is late in the day.

    B The air is clear.

    C The street is busy.

    D She just got a job.

11. The characters in this excerpt typify naturalism's focus on what kind of people?

    A common men and women

    B young job seekers

    C business professionals

    D strong individualists

12. Which image suggests that human destiny is shaped by forces beyond our control?

    A "fatigued senses" (line 3)

    B "wisp on the tide" (lines 7–8)

    C "baffled retreat" (line 12)

    D "great, pleasing metropolis" (line 56)

13. From Carrie's experience in this excerpt, you might infer that newcomers to cities in the late 19th century

    A received an enthusiastic welcome

    B caused problems for local officials

    C often had to accept low-paying jobs

    D were ridiculed for their behavior

DIRECTIONS *Answer this question about both selections.*

14. Which statement accurately compares the diction used in the two selections?

    A Both selections rely on nature imagery.

    B The speech uses comparisons; the excerpt does not.

    C The speech is spare and simple; the excerpt is formal and literary.

    D The speech uses abstract language; the excerpt uses colorful language.

Written Response

SHORT RESPONSE *Write three or four sentences to answer each question.*

15. What is unusual about Chef Joseph's diction in the statement "I will fight no more forever"? What effect does he achieve with that choice of words?

16. Dreiser depicts Chicago as what type of city? Cite three details to support your answer.

17. Identify one theme that emerges in the excerpt from *Sister Carrie*.

EXTENDED RESPONSE *Write two or three paragraphs to answer this question.*

18. Materialism is a recurring theme in Theodore Dreiser's works. Which details in this excerpt illustrate that theme?

GO ON ➡

Vocabulary

DIRECTIONS *Use context clues and your knowledge of denotation and connotation to answer the following questions about words from* Sister Carrie.

1. What connotation does the word *persistent* have in line 2?

   A arrogance

   B determination

   C pessimism

   D ruthlessness

2. What connotation does the word *wisp* have in line 7?

   A freedom

   B openness

   C steadiness

   D insignificance

3. What connotation does the word *forlorn* have in line 16?

   A uniqueness

   B swiftness

   C abandonment

   D spirituality

4. What connotation does the word *acquiesced* have in line 42?

   A wariness

   B submissiveness

   C hostility

   D enthusiasm

DIRECTIONS *Use context clues and your knowledge of Latin words and roots to answer the following questions about words from* Sister Carrie.

5. The word *curt* derives from the Latin word *curtus,* which means "shortened." What is the most likely meaning of *curt* as it is used in line 10?

   A grammatically incorrect

   B rudely brief

   C unusually direct

   D watered down

6. The word *impulses* derives from the Latin prefix *in-,* which means "into," and the Latin root *pel,* which means "to push or drive." What is the most likely meaning of *impulses* as it is used in line 16?

   A changes in momentum produced by the force in a time interval

   B surges of electrical power in one direction

   C sudden urges that prompt unplanned acts

   D motion produced by strong forces

7. The word *sprightlier* derives from the Latin word *spiritus,* which means "vigor" or "breath." What is the most likely meaning of *sprightlier* as it is used in line 59?

   A more full of vitality

   B breathing more heavily

   C cleaner than in the past

   D in need of more fresh air

Writing & Grammar

DIRECTIONS *Read this passage and answer the questions that follow.*

> (1) In the 1770s, the first permanent settlement in Chicago was established by a Haitian trader named Jean Baptiste Point du Sable. (2) The community developed slowly at first. (3) The growth of Chicago was spurred by the construction of railroads in the mid-1800s. (4) Unfortunately, its progress came to a halt when <u>the city was destroyed by a fire in 1871</u>. (5) <u>Organizations immediately offered aid</u>, however. (6) Triumphantly, the city bounced back. (7) In 1893, Chicago hosted the World's Fair.

1. Choose the correct way to rewrite sentence 1 in the active voice.

  A In the 1770s, a Haitian trader named Jean Baptiste Point du Sable established the first permanent settlement in Chicago.

  B The first permanent settlement in Chicago was established in the 1770s by a Haitian trader named Jean Baptiste Point du Sable.

  C In Chicago in the 1770s, the first permanent settlement was established by a Haitian trader named Jean Baptiste Point du Sable.

  D The first permanent settlement in Chicago was established by a Haitian trader named Jean Baptiste Point du Sable in the 1770s.

2. Choose the correct way to rewrite sentence 3 in the active voice.

  A The growth of Chicago was spurred in the mid-1800s by railroads that were constructed.

  B The growth of Chicago was spurred by railroads that were constructed in the mid-1800s.

  C The construction of railroads in the mid-1800s spurred the growth of Chicago.

  D Railroads were constructed in the mid-1800s, spurring the growth of Chicago.

3. Choose the correct way to rewrite the underlined part of sentence 4 in the active voice.

  A in 1871, the destruction of the city was caused by a fire

  B in 1871, the city was destroyed by a fire

  C the city's ruin was caused by a fire in 1871

  D a fire destroyed the city in 1871

4. Choose the correct way to rewrite the underlined part of sentence 5 by using a gerund phrase.

  A Organizations immediately started forming relief and clean-up crews

  B Organizations immediately started to arrange cleaning crews to assist the city

  C Organizations immediately helped

  D Assisting organizations immediately helped

5. Choose the correct way to rewrite sentence 6 by using a gerund phrase.

  A Triumphantly, the city began reconstructing itself.

  B The city was hoping to triumph.

  C Triumphantly, the city was determining its future.

  D The city, a lightning force, was triumphant.

Ideas for Independent Reading

Continue exploring the Questions of the Times on pages 616–617 with these additional works.

What makes a place UNIQUE?

My Ántonia
by Willa Cather

This novel, recognized as Willa Cather's finest, depicts through the voice of the immigrant Ántonia Shimerda the hardships and rewards of pioneer life and the strength of America's frontier women. As Ántonia grows into womanhood, she overcomes poverty, disappointment, and family tragedy to become a mother and a successful farmer—a woman who "had not lost the fire of life."

American Indian Stories, Legends, and Other Writings
by Zitkala-Sa

This collection of works by Sioux writer and activist Zitkala-Sa (1876–1938) contains retellings of traditional Native American legends as well as stories, poems, essays, and speeches focused on the Native American experience.

The Virginian: A Horseman of the Plains
by Owen Wister

The strong-but-silent cowboy, the saintly schoolmarm, the climactic shootout—all have become standards of American Westerns but were brand-new ideas when Owen Wister penned *The Virginian* in 1902. His story of "the Virginian," a man torn between his love for a woman and his quest for justice, was the first true American Western.

Does the universe CARE?

Sister Carrie
by Theodore Dreiser

Carrie Meeber arrives in Chicago filled with vague hopes of fun and comfort. Meanwhile, across town, George Hurstwood, a well-to-do restaurant manager, is living the life of his dreams, respected by his peers and hobnobbing with famous actors. In *Sister Carrie,* Dreiser brings these two people together and lets us watch, amazed and appalled, as Carrie is taken to heights of glory while Hurstwood falls to the depths of despair.

The Best Short Stories of Jack London
by Jack London

No issue engaged writer Jack London more consistently than the clash between a seemingly uncaring natural world and the striving creatures who inhabit it. Intense, thrilling, and thought-provoking, the ten short stories in this collection show why London was so popular in his day and remains one of the most widely read of all American authors.

McTeague: A Story of San Francisco
by Frank Norris

Frank Norris set the literary establishment on its ear when he published *McTeague,* a naturalistic story of a San Francisco dentist. The title character, spurred by a strange force of self-destruction, makes one bad decision after another. Finally, he commits a murder and winds up fighting for his life in the harsh alkali deserts of California.

How are women's ROLES CHANGING?

The Awakening
by Kate Chopin

Causing a storm of controversy when published in 1899, *The Awakening* follows the daily life of an attractive, well-to-do New Orleans matron named Edna Pontellier. Married into a prominent family, Edna leads a very comfortable existence, with good friends, a fine house, and nothing very pressing to do. Yet Edna is assailed by a nameless discontent. Although she cannot articulate exactly what she wants, she knows that the options open to women in her society are slowly making her die inside.

The House of Mirth
by Edith Wharton

The daughter of a failed New York businessman, Lily Bart is pretty, independent-minded, and cultivated. She is also penniless. Living with her rich yet miserly aunt, she spends her time socializing with New York's aristocrats. In such a situation, Lily's course of action is obvious to everyone. If she wants to maintain her lifestyle, she must find a rich man and marry him. Yet selling her beauty to the highest bidder strikes Lily as savage. Unable to find a path that would bring her both self-respect and material comfort, Lily drifts from party to party, trying not to think about what is going to happen to her. Lily's ultimately tragic fate is clearly the blame of a society that values wealth and convention above all.

Why are there "haves" and "HAVE-NOTS"?

The Jungle
by Upton Sinclair

No other novel in American literature has had a more direct impact upon daily life than *The Jungle*. Based upon extensive research conducted in Chicago's slaughterhouses, Sinclair's novel was intended to turn a blinding light on unfair labor practices and rally readers to the cause of socialism. Instead, its descriptions of unclean meatpacking practices caused a steep decline in the sales of beef and pork and brought about federal laws to keep food healthy. "I aimed at the public's heart, and by accident hit it in the stomach," Sinclair ruefully remarked. Nevertheless, *The Jungle* remains jarring in its description of the appalling conditions laborers were forced to endure.

A Hazard of New Fortunes
by William Dean Howells

In this novel of class conflict, a mild-mannered editor moves to New York from Boston, looking to enhance his career. He takes charge of a magazine sponsored by a ruthless financier and comes into contact with his old German tutor, who has become a political radical. Torn between his sympathy for the working poor and his need to stay on good terms with his rich patron, the editor does not know what to do. When a violent streetcar strike breaks out, he can no longer remain a bystander. He has to decide whether to support what he knows is right or to play it safe and keep his job.

Preview Unit Goals

LITERARY ANALYSIS	• Understand Harlem Renaissance and modernism as literary movements
	• Identify and analyze literary elements, including tone, theme, diction, voice, mood, irony, imagery, and character traits and motives
	• Identify and analyze form and meaning in poetry
	• Identify and analyze individual styles, including Frost's and Hemingway's
	• Analyze and interpret modern, narrative, and imagist poetry
READING	• Make inferences and draw conclusions
	• Identify and analyze author's purpose and position
	• Distinguish literal from figurative meaning
	• Identify explicit and implicit main ideas
WRITING AND GRAMMAR	• Write a comparison-contrast essay
	• Craft effective sentences by using vivid language, phrases, and coordinating conjunctions
SPEAKING, LISTENING, AND VIEWING	• Interpret and evaluate the way events and information are presented in media
	• Analyze and evaluate persuasive techniques in print advertising
	• Deliver an oral interpretation
VOCABULARY	• Use knowledge of Latin and Greek word roots to understand word meaning
	• Research word origins to understand historical influences in English
ACADEMIC VOCABULARY	• Harlem Renaissance • tone • form in poetry
	• modernism • irony • meaning in poetry
	• imagery

Online LITERATURE CLASSZONE.COM

Literature and Reading Center
Writing Center
Vocabulary Center

The Harlem Renaissance & Modernism

Langston Hughes

1910–1940
A CHANGING AWARENESS

- **The Harlem Renaissance**
- **The New Poetry**
- **The Modern Short Story**
- **Journalism as Literature**

Questions of the Times

DISCUSS Share your views about the following questions with a small group or in a whole-class discussion. As you read the selections in this unit, reflect on how the writing of the **Harlem Renaissance** and the **modernist period** was shaped by these questions.

What is MODERN?

Americans in the first half of the 20th century consciously moved away from the traditions of their past and embraced all things modern. From the shiny new automobiles rolling off Henry Ford's assembly line to the esoteric poetry of T. S. Eliot—Americans' love affair with modernism was in full swing. What does *modern* mean to you? Why do you think people like to be on the "cutting edge"?

Can ideals survive CATASTROPHE?

The years between 1910 and 1940 were scarred by two historical events: World War I and the Great Depression. Faced with a world at war followed by deep economic instability at home, many American writers began to see the world with a new cynicism. How can people hold on to their idealism in light of dire events? Is it even possible?

How can people honor their HERITAGE?

The writers of the Harlem Renaissance were quite diverse stylistically, yet they shared a pride in their heritage that shines through their work. Why do you think writing might be a good vehicle for honoring one's past? How else do people honor their heritage?

What drives HUMAN BEHAVIOR?

Newly familiar with Sigmund Freud's groundbreaking work in human psychology, American writers of this period began to examine the unconscious motivations that affect human behavior. Do you think people regulate their behavior through reason and understanding, or are they driven by unconscious desires?

The Harlem Renaissance and Modernism

1910–1940

A Changing Awareness

Change was the only constant for Americans in the early 20th century. In 30 short years, they faced a world war, an economic boom followed by the Great Depression, shifting attitudes toward women's place in society, and a mass culture that isolated and alienated the individual. In this swirl of uncertainty, traditional values seemed to slip out of reach or were actively discarded as Americans—writers and nonwriters alike—searched for truths in what felt like a whole new world.

The Harlem Renaissance and Modernism: Historical Context

KEY IDEAS Catastrophic historical events—including a devastating war and a deep economic depression—as well as rapid societal change profoundly affected the writing of this period.

A World at War

World War I—the **Great War**—was perhaps the most influential force on American writers of the early 20th century. The war broke out in Europe in 1914; before it ended in 1918, it involved 32 nations, including the United States, and took the lives of over 20 million people. It was a new kind of war, waged on a massive scale with terrible new weapons that reflected the technological advances of the time—machine guns, poison gases, airplane bombers, and submarines. Old ideals about the purposes and meaning of war were destroyed in the carnage. As Lieutenant Frederic Henry, a character in **Ernest Hemingway's** 1929 novel *A Farewell to Arms,* observed: "Words such as glory, honor, courage, or hallow were obscene." For many Americans, the war signaled an end to idealism and ushered in an era marked by hedonism, political corruption, and ruthless business practices.

The Jazz Age

Some Americans, disillusioned with the traditional values that had led to war, sought escape in the pleasures of entertainment and good times. The 1920s, with its booming economy, became known as the **Roaring Twenties.** Writer **F. Scott Fitzgerald** called this decade "the greatest, gaudiest spree in history." As incomes rose, people were able to spend more money on goods and leisure activities. In addition, many young people began, for the first time, to rebel as a group against the values of the past and the authority of their elders. They experimented with new fashions and new attitudes, actively seeking out fun and freedom.

A NEW ERA FOR WOMEN Women of the period saw their lives change in fundamental ways. In 1920, the passage of the **19th Amendment** finally gave women the right to vote. But the vote was just one facet of the changing nature of womanhood. The 1920s saw the emergence of the **flapper,** an emancipated young woman who embraced new fashions and the urban attitudes of the day. By 1930, ten million American women were earning wages in the workplace—another new frontier. In addition, family life was made increasingly easier by technological innovations, from ready-made clothes to sliced bread. Many women writers, such as **Edna St. Vincent Millay** and **Dorothy Parker,** were celebrated as much for their modern lifestyles as for their writing. In turn, they often wrote about the clash between traditional and modern values, celebrating youth, independence, and freedom from social constraints.

> ▶ **TAKING NOTES**
>
> **Outlining** As you read each section of this introduction, add the information you learn to an outline like the one started for you here. You can use headings, boldfaced terms, and the information in these boxes as starting points. (See page R49 in the **Research Handbook** for more help with outlining.)
>
> I. *Historical Context*
>
>   A. *A World at War*
>   *1. influence on writers*
>   *2. affected millions*
>   *3. new kind of war*
>   *4. destroyed ideals*
>   B. *The Jazz Age*

ADDITIONAL BACKGROUND for more on the Harlem Renaissance and modernism, visit the **Literature Center** at ClassZone.com.

The City from Greenwich Village (1922), John Sloan. Gift of Helen Farr Sloan. © 2006 Board of Trustees, National Gallery of Art, Washington, D.C. 1970.1.1 Photo © Superstock.

JAZZ CULTURE This period also saw the passage of **Prohibition** (1920–1933), in which alcohol was made illegal. In defiance of this restriction, many people drank in illegal nightclubs called speakeasies, as gangsters made fortunes running and supplying the clubs. At the fancy Cotton Club in New York's Harlem neighborhood, the guests—all whites—rubbed shoulders with celebrities and gangsters as they listened to the great jazz performers—all blacks—who helped give the era its name: the **Jazz Age.**

The Great Depression

The good times came to a dramatic end when the stock market crashed in October 1929, plunging the nation into economic depression. During the **Great Depression**, so called for its length and severity, many banks failed, businesses floundered, and workers lost their jobs. By 1933, the unemployment rate had grown to 25 percent. Unable to pay their bills, thousands of people lost their homes, and millions went hungry.

THE DUST BOWL A severe drought that began in the early 1930s added to the nation's pain. When the drought began, winds picked up dirt from the dry, exhausted fields of the Great Plains. Huge dust storms arose, damaging farms across a 150,000-square-mile region called the **Dust Bowl.**

Ruined farmers set off with their families to find work, many traveling west to California. Unfortunately, little work was to be found in California, for it, like the rest of the nation, was suffering through the Great Depression. Writers such as **John Steinbeck** captured the uncertainty and despair of the times: "Carloads, caravans, homeless and hungry; twenty thousand and fifty thousand and a hundred thousand and two hundred thousand. They streamed over the mountains, hungry and restless—restless as ants, scurrying to find work to do."

THE NEW DEAL The country was desperate for help. During his presidential campaign in 1932, Franklin Delano Roosevelt pledged to give the country a "new deal." When elected, he fulfilled his promise by enacting various **New Deal** programs—relief for the homeless and hungry, recovery for agriculture and business, and various economic reforms to prevent such a severe depression from occurring again. Yet in truth, it was the massive spending and production spurred by World War II that finally brought the economic crisis to an end.

Migrant Mother by Dorothea Lange, 1936. This photograph of Florence Owens Thompson with her children came to symbolize the Great Depression for many Americans.

Cultural Influences

KEY IDEAS A developing mass culture and ideas that challenged traditional thought provided fodder for writers of the time.

New Directions

MASS CULTURE The 1920s was the first decade to be significantly shaped by **mass media.** New goods—from cars to toasters to beauty products—were flooding the market, and businesses relied on advertising to sell them. Thanks to advertising, items people had formerly considered luxuries were now deemed necessities. Mass media quickly became the ultimate source for this manufacturing of desire.

   Mass production quickly and efficiently produced Americans' newfound necessities, but efficiency came with a price. Henry Ford perfected the assembly-line system, but its repetitiveness and monotony reduced workers to nameless, faceless cogs in the production process. And its products, efficiently mass-produced, led to the homogenization of American culture. **Sinclair Lewis** and many other significant writers of the day were alienated by the new values and lifestyles of their peers and soon began to criticize what they saw as Americans' conformity and materialism.

NEW IDEAS The writers of this period were also influenced by exciting new ideas that were challenging Americans' traditional views. A literary technique called **stream of consciousness** developed from the psychoanalytic theories of **Sigmund Freud,** who proposed that unconscious forces drive human beings and that the key to understanding behavior lay in this deeper realm of the mind. **Karl Marx's** socioeconomic theories—that history is a constant struggle between classes, for example—found their way into some of the literature of the day, mainly that of Depression-era writers. And **Albert Einstein's** theory that everything is relative, that there are no absolutes, offered writers a fresh new way of looking at the world.

Print advertisements from the 1920s and 1930s

A Voice from the Times

It's the fellow with four to ten thousand a year . . . and an automobile and a nice little family in a bungalow . . . that makes the wheels of progress go round! That's the type of fellow that's ruling America today[!]

—Sinclair Lewis
from *Babbitt*

Modern Literature and the Harlem Renaissance

KEY IDEAS The writers of this period, working in a variety of genres and focusing on discrete themes, were markedly influenced by the events and culture of the day. Many responded by embracing all things new, while others celebrated their heritage.

The New Poetry

At the beginnning of the century, rapid industrialization and urbanization caused many Americans to feel that the social order governing their lives was crumbling. Poets of the day began to explore in their work the impact of rapid change and uncertainty on the individual.

Edgar Lee Masters, in his famous collection *Spoon River Anthology,* used free verse to probe the discontent beneath the apparent stability of small-town life in the United States. *Spoon River Anthology* found a wide audience, in part because it voiced concerns shared by many Americans about the transformation from a rural to an industrialized society. Like Masters, **Edwin Arlington Robinson** also exposed the tensions underlying small-town life. His poems draw psychological portraits of characters isolated in the midst of American society. In portraying their isolation, Robinson was a forerunner of the modernist movement. These poets charted new territory by challenging conventional attitudes.

Others, such as **Carl Sandburg, Robert Frost,** and **Edna St. Vincent Millay,** seemed to be more connected to earlier traditions that focused on nature and common people. Yet they, too, revealed an awareness of the changes sweeping the American landscape. For this reason, Millay, Sandburg, and Frost can be called transitional poets, those who connect past traditions with modern thought.

MODERNISM Other poets of this period belong to the literary movement called **modernism** (see page 894). Modernism arose as a direct response to the social and intellectual forces shaping the 20th century. Modernist writers, many of whom were expatriates living in Europe, responded to the loss of idealism they felt in the wake of World War I. Living abroad, they experienced both the immediate and the long-term effects of World War I more acutely than did Americans at home. Most modernists also saw mass society as a threat to the individual, especially the artist. They felt that the standardization of culture resulted in alienation—a theme they captured in their work.

Experimentation was a distinguishing characteristic of these writers. "Make it new," extolled **Ezra Pound** as he urged fellow poets to abandon the artifice of past forms and search for their individual voices. **Harriet Monroe,** editor of *Poetry* magazine, wrote that the new poetry "has set before itself an ideal of absolute simplicity and sincerity—an ideal which implies an individual, unstereotyped diction; and an individual, unstereotyped rhythm." The lack of

Works by transitional poets Millay, Frost, and Sandburg

▶ *For Your Outline*

THE NEW POETRY

- Poets began to challenge conventional thought.
- Modernists responded to historical forces such as WWI and an increasing mass society.
- Experimentation characterized modernism.
- Imagists believed that poetry should be expressed through the "rendering of concrete objects."
- Imagists favored free verse.
- In objectivist poetry, objects speak for themselves.

"stereotypes," however, made any recognizable movement hard to sustain: as soon as a style became accepted, it also became a new standard against which to rebel. The result was that modernist poetry as a body of work is as fragmented as many of its individual poems.

IMAGISM Many of the so-called new poets did, however, share the belief that poetry is most profoundly expressed through the "rendering of concrete objects." Ezra Pound called this kind of poetry **imagism** because it sought to re-create an image—not comment on it, not interpret it, but just present it. Pound became the center of a circle of poets, including **H. D.** (Hilda Doolittle) and **Amy Lowell,** who cast off the sentimentality, formal structures, and rhyme schemes of their predecessors and exploded into **free verse** (poetry without a predictable rhyme or metric scheme). Ezra Pound was especially taken with the poetry of **T. S. Eliot,** whose *The Waste Land* is considered one of the most representative and influential of modernist poems.

OBJECTIVISM One modernist poet, **William Carlos Williams,** however, vehemently disliked *The Waste Land* for its intellectualism and its references to classical literature. In response to Eliot's complex ideas and academic references, Williams famously stated that there are "no ideas but in things." Williams became the center of a new movement in modernist poetry called **objectivism,** in which poets let the objects they rendered speak for themselves. These poets invited readers to experience the homely simplicity of an object for no other reason than to understand its "this-ness."

The modernist movement had an enormous impact on later poets. Many poets today prefer to communicate through images rather than direct statements. They believe in economy of words and continue to experiment with free verse. Poetry had been altered irrevocably.

> **A Voice from the Times**
>
> *so much depends*
> *upon*
>
> *a red wheel*
> *barrow*
>
> *glazed with rain*
> *water*
>
> *beside the white*
> *chickens.*
>
> **—William Carlos Williams**
> "The Red Wheelbarrow"

Sculpture inspired by William Carlos Williams's poem

The Red Wheelbarrow (1992), Frank Jensen. © Frank Jensen.

The Modern Short Story

Poetry was not the only form popular during this period. In fact, the period from 1890 to 1930 has been called "the Age of the Short Story" in American literature. The great popularity of the short story has often been attributed to the American temperament. Americans living in the first half of the 20th century were too impatient and too much in a hurry to read longer works. They wanted "fast" literature, just as Americans today want fast food.

Other factors contributed to the popularity of the short story as well. New methods of advertising had brought about a boom in magazine publication. As the number of magazines grew, so did the demand for short stories. In turn, magazines paid their writers handsome fees. At one point, **F. Scott Fitzgerald** was receiving as much as $4,000 for a single story. **William Faulkner,** who complained that writing short stories interfered with his more serious, longer works, earned more from the sale of four short stories to the *Saturday Evening Post* than he did from his first four novels.

THEMES PULLED FROM LIFE The upheavals of this period in American history provided rich fodder for short story writers. World War I turned many Americans' idealism into uncertainty. Civilization as people had known it was being destroyed, and writers sought to capture in their work the resulting alienation and confusion. Indeed, World War I shook the ideological foundations of some young American writers so profoundly that **Gertrude Stein,** an American writer living in Paris, called them **"the lost generation."**

These alienated writers broke with the traditions of the past, turning to new methods and stylistic devices to carry their themes. **Ernest Hemingway** and other writers composed short, fragmentary stories without traditional beginnings or endings. They left out a narrrative voice, leaving readers alone to figure out what might be going on or what a character might be feeling. "I always try to write on the principle of the iceberg," Hemingway said. "There is seven-eighths of it under water for every part that shows."

The boom years of the Roaring Twenties inspired its own literature. Writers such as **F. Scott Fitzgerald** revealed the negative side of the period's gaiety and freedom by portraying wealthy and attractive people leading empty lives in their gilded surroundings. Writer **John Steinbeck** is most closely identified with the bust years of the Great Depression. Declaring that a writer's duty is to "set down his time as nearly as he can understand it," Steinbeck managed to tell, perhaps better than anyone else, the stories of ordinary people caught up

▶ *For Your Outline*

MODERN SHORT STORY

- 1890–1930 called the "Age of the Short Story"
- stories' popularity due to American temperament and growth of magazines
- "lost generation" alienated by WWI
- wrote fragmentary stories without traditional beginning or ending

THE HARLEM RENAISSANCE

- a flowering of African-American arts
- expressions of what it meant to be black in a white-dominated world
- came to an end with the Great Depression

An illustration of the Roaring Twenties high life, which served as inspiration for writers such as F. Scott Fitzgerald in the Great Depression and lost from the devastation of the Dust Bowl.

Steinbeck, **Eudora Welty,** and many other writers of the time were beneficiaries of one of President Roosevelt's New Deal programs, the Works Progress Administration (WPA). The WPA was set up to create as many jobs as possible, as quickly as possible, including work for the nation's artists and writers. As the head of the WPA put it, "They've got to eat just like other people." Eudora Welty traveled around Mississippi for the WPA, writing articles about various projects under way in the state. She later said that these travels introduced her to the very different ways in which people lived, inspiring her later writing.

The Harlem Renaissance

Beginning in 1916 and continuing throughout the 1920s, in what came to be known as the **Great Migration,** millions of black farmers and sharecroppers moved to the urban North in search of opportunity and freedom from oppression and racial hostility. Thousands of these migrants settled in Harlem, a New York City neighborhood that quickly became the cultural center of African-American life.

Soon, the very air in Harlem seemed charged with creativity as black men and women drew on their own cultural resources—their folk traditions as well as a new urban awareness—to produce unique forms of expression. Harlem attracted worldly and race-conscious African Americans who nurtured each other's artistic, musical, and literary talents and created a flowering of African-American arts known as the **Harlem Renaissance.**

A LITERARY MOVEMENT The event that unofficially kicked off the Harlem Renaissance as a literary movement was a dinner given on March 21, 1924. Some of the nation's most celebrated writers and thinkers, black and white, gathered at New York City's Civic Club. The sponsors of the dinner— an older generation of African-American intellectuals that included **W. E. B. Du Bois, James Weldon Johnson,** and **Charles S. Johnson**—had begun organizations such as the National Urban League and the National Association for the Advancement of Colored People to promote equality for African Americans. These organizations published journals in which the writings of a younger generation were first published. **Countee Cullen, Zora Neale Hurston,** and **Langston Hughes** were among the young writers who received recognition and sometimes cash awards for

The Migration of the Negro Panel no. 1 (1940–1941), Jacob Lawrence. Casein tempera on hardboard, 12″ x 18″. Acquired 1942. The Phillips Collection, Washington, D.C. © The Estate of Gwendolyn Knight Lawrence/Artist Rights Society (ARS), New York.

Jacob Lawrence

The Harlem Renaissance was not only a literary movement but a flourishing movement of the visual arts as well. Since it was difficult for black Americans of the day to attend art academies as their white counterparts did, the art schools and workshops of Harlem provided vital training for many of America's finest black artists. Jacob Lawrence was one of the first to be educated by the African-American community in Harlem.

Harlem as Muse Lawrence found inspiration in the streets of Harlem. His early work depicted the community—its people, sidewalks, streets, and storefronts—in bold colors and elemental shapes. He once said that 1930s "was actually a wonderful period in Harlem.... There was real vitality in the community." Lawrence rubbed elbows there with writers and artists such as Langston Hughes, Claude McKay, Romare Bearden, and Augusta Savage, all of whom emphasized their cultural identity in their work.

The Migration Series The painting shown here was the first in a 60-panel series on the Great Migration. It shows a crowd of Southern migrants about to embark on a journey to three Northern cities. Lawrence's decision to show no faces but only the shapes of hats and coats and luggage enhances the viewer's sense of a crowd surging as one entity toward the station. Lawrence based the paintings in this series on the experiences of his family and other members of his community who took part in the Great Migration.

their work in these journals, and many were present at this "coming-out party" for the writers of the Harlem Renaissance.

These young writers considered themselves the founders of a new era in literature. They looked inward and expressed what it meant to be black in a white-dominated world. They represented what came to be called "the New Negro," a sophisticated and well-educated African American with strong racial pride and self-awareness. In fact, connections made at that dinner led to a popular and enduring anthology of writing, published in 1925, titled *The New Negro.*

MANY VOICES Yet this new generation of writers did not speak with only one voice. Harvard-educated **Countee Cullen,** for example, used a classical style to explore the black struggle. Others cast off more formal language and styles and wrote with the pulse of jazz rhythms. "Jazz is a heartbeat," wrote Langston Hughes, "and its heartbeat is yours." Some, like Jamaican-born **Claude McKay,** were militant. McKay's poem "If We Must Die," written after race riots in 1919, ends with an image of African Americans "pressed to the wall, dying, but fighting back!" Others, such as **Jean Toomer,** were more interested in exploring their own identities than the concerns of a whole race. "I was inescapably myself," he wrote. Despite their varied perspectives, however, these writers shared a deep pride in their heritage and asserted their cultural identity through their work.

Zora Neale Hurston, Harlem Renaissance writer

The Harlem Renaissance was brought to a premature end by the economic collapse of the Great Depression. Many of the writers who had gathered in Harlem were forced to scatter and take other jobs to support themselves. Nevertheless, their work planted seeds that continue to generate important writing from the African-American perspective.

Journalism as Literature

In the early decades of the 20th century, journalism came into its own as an influential part of the literary scene (see page 1046). The sensationalism and reckless misinterpretation of facts that had characterized journalism in the last decades of the 19th century were being replaced by an interest in stylistic quality and the recognition that there was more to news than scandal. Many of the writers who were to become major figures in American literature learned their craft—and developed some of their most compelling subjects—writing for newspapers or magazines.

REPORTING THE ERA Fresh out of high school in 1917, **Ernest Hemingway** worked as a reporter for the *Kansas City Star.* The newspaper's strict rules of

▶ *For Your Outline*

JOURNALISM AS LITERATURE

- Journalism turned from sensationalism.
- Writers honed their craft at newspapers and magazines.
- Hemingway, Porter, and Steinbeck reported on the day's big news
- White, Thurber, and Parker built their reputations at *New Yorker.*

style helped him develop the clear, provocative prose that characterizes his work: "Use short sentences. Use short first paragraphs. Use vigorous English. Be positive, not negative." Hemingway was also a war correspondent who reported on the Spanish Civil War, and he was the first Allied journalist to enter Paris on August 25, 1944—the day it was liberated from Nazi control.

Some other writers who became well-known for their fiction produced fine journalism as well. **Katherine Anne Porter,** for example, worked for several newspapers and magazines. On assignment in 1920, she traveled to Mexico and arrived in the middle of a revolution. Her observations of this conflict later became the subject of several short stories in a collection called *Flowering Judas* (1930), which launched her literary career. **John Steinbeck** turned his hand to journalism as well, reporting in 1936 for the *San Francisco News* about the plight of California's migrant farm workers and working in 1943 as a war correspondent for the *New York Herald Tribune*.

MAGAZINES ON THE RISE In the first decades of the 20th century, the popular magazine came into its own as new magazines were created to satisfy every taste and interest. The *New Yorker,* which first appeared in 1925, was founded by one-time newspaperman **Harold Ross.** To staff his new magazine, Ross sought writers with newspaper experience, writers who could grind out "the gleams and sparkles of humor and satire from the grist of human nature and the news of the world." Among them were **E. B. White, James Thurber,** and **Dorothy Parker,** who went on to write poetry, short stories, and novels. Yet these writers' reputations as witty, satiric observers of contemporary society were built on the essays, commentary, and book and theater reviews (and in the case of Thurber, cartoons too) that they contributed to the *New Yorker*.

Like poetry and short stories, literary journalism continues to be popular. Today's writers can thank the innovators of the modernist movement, America's giants of the short story form, the groundbreaking writers of the Harlem Renaissance, and the literary journalists of this earlier era for many of the themes, styles, and forms currently in use.

Herbert Hoover and Franklin Delano Roosevelt on the cover of the *New Yorker*, 1933

Connecting Literature, History, and Culture

The literature and culture of the United States during this period reflect developments occurring elsewhere in the world. Use the timeline and the questions on the next page to find connections.

AMERICAN LITERARY MILESTONES

1910

1912 Harriet Monroe founds *Poetry: A Magazine of Verse*; Edna St. Vincent Millay publishes "Renascence."

1913 Ezra Pound forms a group of imagist poets in London.

1915

1915 Edgar Lee Masters examines small-town life in *Spoon River Anthology*.

1916 Carl Sandburg publishes *Chicago Poems*.

1919 Claude McKay publishes his militant "If We Must Die."

1920

1920 Edith Wharton's *The Age of Innocence* is published.

1921 Langston Hughes's poem "The Negro Speaks of Rivers" appears in *The Crisis* magazine.

1922 T. S. Eliot's *The Waste Land* captures modern sensibilities.

1924 Robert Frost wins the first of his four Pulitzer Prizes.

HISTORICAL CONTEXT

1910

1911 The National Urban League is founded.

1912 The *Titanic* sinks, killing more than 1,500 people.

1913 The Armory Show in New York City introduces European modernist paintings and sculpture to shocked Americans.

1915

1916 Jeannette Rankin of Montana becomes the first woman elected to the U.S. House of Representatives.

1917 The United States enters World War I. ▶

1919 Race riots break out in 25 U.S. cities.

1920

1920 The 18th Amendment ushers in the era of Prohibition, and the 19th Amendment assures women of the right to vote.

1921 Albert Einstein presents a lecture in New York City about his theory of relativity. ▶

1924 Native Americans win full citizenship.

WORLD CULTURE AND EVENTS

1910

1911 Marie Curie wins the Nobel Prize in chemistry. ▶

1914 World War I begins with the assassination of Archduke Francis Ferdinand of Austria.

1915

1915 The short story "Rashomon" by Japanese modernist writer Akutagawa Ryunosuke is published.

1918 A flu pandemic kills more than 20 million people worldwide.

1919 The Treaty of Versailles spells out the peace terms for the end of World War I.

1920

1922 James Joyce publishes his masterpiece, *Ulysses*.

1923 Sigmund Freud publishes *The Ego and the Id*, examining the causes of human behavior. ▶

MAKING CONNECTIONS

- Why was the year 1913 an important one for poetry and art?
- Violence stirred in the years between 1910 and 1940. Give an example from each of the three main sections of the timeline that support this observation.
- Name three women of this period who were gaining recognition or breaking barriers in literature, politics, and science.

1925

1925 F. Scott Fitzgerald's *The Great Gatsby* explores the American dream.

1926 Ernest Hemingway's novel *The Sun Also Rises* chronicles expatriates after WWI.

1929 William Faulkner's *The Sound and the Fury* experiments with stream of consciousness and multiple viewpoints.

1930

1930 *Flowering Judas* by Katherine Anne Porter is published. ▶

1932 Pearl S. Buck wins a Pulitzer Prize for *The Good Earth*.

1933 William Faulkner's *A Green Bough* is published.

1935

1936 Margaret Mitchell publishes *Gone with the Wind*.

1937 Zora Neale Hurston's *Their Eyes Were Watching God* is published.

1940 Richard Wright's *Native Son* is published.

1925

1927 Charles Lindbergh makes his historic solo nonstop flight from New York to Paris; the first talking movie, *The Jazz Singer*, stars Al Jolson.

1929 The Wall Street stock market crashes and the Great Depression begins. ▼

1930

1931 The Empire State building is completed. ▶

1932 Franklin Delano Roosevelt is elected president for the first of his four terms.

1933 Roosevelt's New Deal tries to put Americans back to work.

1935

1938 The Fair Labor Standards Act sets a minimum wage and limits the workweek to 40 hours.

1939 Judy Garland stars in *The Wizard of Oz*. ▼

1925

1925 Virginia Woolf's innovative novel *Mrs. Dalloway* is published in England.

1928 Joseph Stalin becomes dictator of Communist Russia. Chiang Kai-shek becomes head of the Nationalist government in China.

1930

1930 Mahatma Gandhi leads a nonviolent march to protest British taxes.

1932 Japan takes control of Manchuria.

1933 Adolf Hitler takes control of Germany.

1935

1936 The Spanish Civil War breaks out.

1937 Japan invades China.

1939 World War II begins with the German invasion of Poland.

UNIT 5

The Legacy of the Era

Mass Culture

Many American writers of the early 20th century were reacting against a rising mass culture and the conformity and materialism they saw as its inevitable effects. These writers would likely be astounded to see the extent to which mass culture has overtaken the United States today. From the restaurant business, with nationwide chains replacing family-owned places, to a fashion scene in which only a very few styles (and sizes) are considered desirable—mass culture is everywhere you look.

DISCUSS In small groups, brainstorm ten examples of our current mass culture. Then discuss what you see as the effects—positive and negative—of mass culture on our society as a whole.

Trends in Journalism

Many of the best writers of the early 20th century, such as Ernest Hemingway, E. B. White, and William Faulkner, sharpened their skills writing for newspapers and magazines. Today there is no shortage of talented journalists, yet the nature of the business has changed. Thousands of newspapers and magazines—one for nearly every conceivable interest—are printed every day. Twenty-four-hour news stations and Web sites give minute-by-minute accounts of current events, and blogs allow people to respond personally to the news.

QUICKWRITE With all of the venues available for today's writers to publish their ideas, how much of it is worthwhile literature? Is some simply a lot of hot air? Write several paragraphs sharing your opinions about today's journalists and the everyday people who, thanks to the Internet, can reach the masses with their words.

The New Deal Today

Several of President Roosevelt's New Deal programs remain in place today: Social Security (to pay out retirement pensions), the FDIC (to insure bank deposits), agricultural price supports (to protect farmers from price devaluation), and the SEC (to regulate the stock market). Yet some of these long-running programs have become politically controversial in today's world.

RESEARCH With a partner, research one of these programs. Summarize for your class why the program is politically controversial, what suggestions have been made to reform or eliminate it, and your opinion of its merit.

Selected Poetry

by Langston Hughes

Langston Hughes
1902–1967

Langston Hughes was one of the leading poets of the Harlem Renaissance as well as an accomplished novelist, playwright, and essayist. His writings center on poor and working-class African Americans, a group whom literature had generally ignored.

Early Inspirations James Mercer Langston Hughes started writing poetry in seventh grade, when his classmates elected him class poet. He admired the work of Paul Laurence Dunbar and Carl Sandburg, two poets known for their efforts to capture the voices of everyday Americans. After graduating from high school, Hughes went to live with his father in Mexico, where he became fluent in Spanish. On the train journey south, he composed what would become one of his most famous poems, "The Negro Speaks of Rivers."

Busboy Poet In 1921, Hughes enrolled at Columbia University in New York City. He left after one year to travel the world as a cook's assistant aboard a ship. In 1925, Hughes settled in Washington, D.C., and took a job busing tables at a hotel restaurant. One day Vachel Lindsay, a well-known poet, came to the hotel. Hughes mustered the courage to slip three of his poems, including "The Weary Blues," beside Lindsay's plate. Lindsay liked the poems, and the next morning's newspapers reported Lindsay's discovery of the "busboy poet."

A year later, Hughes published his first poetry collection, *The Weary Blues.* His gritty depiction of "workers, roustabouts, and singers and job hunters" angered some African-American critics who felt that members of the race should always be portrayed in the best possible light. Hughes responded to these criticisms, saying, "I knew only the people I had grown up with, and they weren't people whose shoes were always shined. . . . But they seemed to me good people, too."

Poet Laureate of Harlem As a poet, Hughes kept his language direct; he made no attempt to be obscure or pretentious. He celebrated the lively nightlife and the everyday experiences of working-class African Americans, often re-creating the structures and rhythms of blues and jazz music in works such as *Montage of a Dream Deferred* (1951), a book-length suite of related poems. Hughes became informally known as the Poet Laureate of Harlem and today is universally recognized as the most influential voice of the Harlem Renaissance.

LITERARY ANALYSIS: SPEAKER

You know that the **speaker** of a poem, like the narrator of a story, is the voice that talks to the reader. In his poems, Langston Hughes created speakers who represented important aspects of African-American culture. Sometimes his speaker is the voice of the culture itself.

I've known rivers ancient as the world and older than the
   flow of human blood in human veins.

Hughes also uses his speakers to portray the joys and struggles of working-class African Americans.

In a deep song voice with a melancholy tone
I heard that Negro sing, that old piano moan—

As you read each poem, try to identify the speaker of the poem and what aspects of African-American life the speaker describes.

READING SKILL: ANALYZE RHYTHM AND REPETITION

When Hughes began writing, most African-American poets tried to sound like the white poets they read in school. Instead, Hughes drew his inspiration from jazz and blues music, using the rhythm and repetition of these musical forms to structure his poetry. Musical elements found in Hughes's poetry include

- jazz-influenced **rhythm** (the pattern of stressed and unstressed syllables) that features strong accents, quick changes in rhythm, and irregular beats

- rhythmic **repetition** of words and phrases, like that used in blues lyrics

- the **refrain,** one or more repeated lines of poetry that function like the chorus of a song

As you read each poem, use a chart like the one shown to record examples of these musical patterns.

Rhythm	Repetition	Refrain

Explore the Key Idea

What shapes your IDENTITY?

KEY IDEA Hughes wrote poetry to honor his African-American heritage, but he didn't limit himself to great heroes and historical events. For Hughes, it was the vibrant culture of everyday people—their music, their slang, and their experiences of life in the city—that shaped his sense of **identity.**

DISCUSS What everyday experiences help shape your identity? List images and activities that characterize the way you live: the sounds and smells of your neighborhood, the places you go, the foods you eat, and so on. In a small group, compare your answers. Which experiences, if any, do group members have in common?

Harlem

Langston Hughes

What happens to a dream deferred?

    Does it dry up
    like a raisin in the sun?
    Or fester like a sore—
5   And then run?
    Does it stink like rotten meat?
    Or crust and sugar over—
    like a syrupy sweet? **A**

    Maybe it just sags
10   like a heavy load.

    Or does it explode?

ANALYZE VISUALS
What elements of this painting help capture the thriving street life in Harlem?

A RHYTHM AND REPETITION
Identify the pattern of stresses in lines 2–8. Which words are emphasized by this rhythm?

Literary Analysis

1. **Clarify** What does the speaker mean by "a dream deferred"?

2. **Make Inferences** What social or political consequences are hinted at in the poem's last line?

3. **Interpret Figurative Language** List the **similes** the speaker uses to describe the effect of a deferred dream. What do these comparisons reveal about the speaker's attitude?

Street Shadows (1959), Jacob Lawrence. Egg tempera on hardboard, 24″ × 30″. Private collection, New York. Photograph courtesy of Gwendolyn Knight Lawrence/Art Resource, New York. © 2007, The Jacob and Gwendolyn Lawrence Foundation, Seattle/ Artists Rights Society (ARS), New York.

The Negro Speaks of Rivers

Langston Hughes

The Negro Speaks of Rivers (1998), Phoebe Beasley. Silkscreen. © Phoebe Beasley.

I've known rivers:
I've known rivers ancient as the world and older than the
    flow of human blood in human veins. **B**

My soul has grown deep like the rivers.

5 I bathed in the Euphrates[1] when dawns were young.
I built my hut near the Congo and it lulled me to sleep.
I looked upon the Nile and raised the pyramids above it.
I heard the singing of the Mississippi when Abe Lincoln
    went down to New Orleans,[2] and I've seen its muddy
10   bosom turn all golden in the sunset.

I've known rivers:
Ancient, dusky[3] rivers.

My soul has grown deep like the rivers. **C**

B **SPEAKER**
Reread lines 1–3. What traits of the speakers are emphasized by Hughes's word choice?

C **RHYTHM AND REPETITION**
Reread the poem. Which line serves as the poem's **refrain?**

---

1. **Euphrates** (yōō-frā′tēz): a river flowing through present-day Turkey, Syria, and Iraq. The valley between the Tigris and Euphrates rivers was the site of one of the world's earliest civilizations.

2. **when Abe Lincoln went down to New Orleans:** Lincoln's first glimpse of the horrors of slavery reportedly came on his trip to New Orleans as a young man.

3. **dusky:** dark; shadowy.

I, Too

Langston Hughes

I, too, sing America.

I am the darker brother.
They send me to eat in the kitchen
When company comes,
5   But I laugh,
And eat well,
And grow strong. **D**

Tomorrow,
I'll be at the table
10 When company comes.
Nobody'll dare
Say to me,
"Eat in the kitchen,"
Then.

15 Besides,
They'll see how beautiful I am
And be ashamed—

I, too, am America.

D SPEAKER
Reread lines 1–7. Identify the speaker of the poem. What aspects of the African-American experience does the speaker describe?

Literary Analysis

1. **Summarize** In "I, Too," what is the speaker's attitude toward America?

2. **Interpret Imagery** What is the significance of the four rivers mentioned in "The Negro Speaks of Rivers"?

3. **Compare and Contrast Speakers** What qualities do the speakers of both poems share? In what ways are they different?

The *Weary* Blues

Langston Hughes

Droning a drowsy syncopated[1] tune,
Rocking back and forth to a mellow croon,
    I heard a Negro play.
Down on Lenox Avenue[2] the other night
5 By the pale dull pallor[3] of an old gas light
    He did a lazy sway. . . .
    He did a lazy sway. . . .
To the tune o' those Weary Blues.
With his ebony hands on each ivory key
10 He made that poor piano moan with melody.
    O Blues!
Swaying to and fro on his rickety stool
He played that sad raggy tune like a musical fool.
    Sweet Blues!
15 Coming from a black man's soul.
    O Blues!
In a deep song voice with a melancholy tone
I heard that Negro sing, that old piano moan—
    "Ain't got nobody in all this world,
20   Ain't got nobody but ma self.
    I's gwine to quit ma frownin'
    And put ma troubles on the shelf."
Thump, thump, thump, went his foot on the floor.
He played a few chords then he sang some more— **E**
25   "I got the Weary Blues
    And I can't be satisfied.
    Got the Weary Blues
    And can't be satisfied—
    I ain't happy no mo'
30   And I wish that I had died."
And far into the night he crooned that tune.
The stars went out and so did the moon.
The singer stopped playing and went to bed
While the Weary Blues echoed through his head.
35 He slept like a rock or a man that's dead.

E **RHYTHM AND REPETITION**
Identify three examples of repetition in the poem thus far. Which line or phrase might be considered the poem's refrain?

---

1. **syncopated** (sĭng′kə-pā′tĭd): characterized by a shifting of stresses from normally strong to normally weak beats.
2. **Lenox Avenue:** a main north-south street in Harlem.
3. **pallor** (păl′ər): lack of color.

Comprehension

1. **Clarify** What hope does the speaker of "I, Too" express?

2. **Recall** Who are the individuals described in "The Weary Blues"?

3. **Summarize** What happens to the speaker of "The Weary Blues"?

Literary Analysis

4. **Identify Sensory Details** Many of Hughes's poems are rich in details that appeal to the five senses. Reread "Harlem" and "The Weary Blues." For each poem, use a chart like the one shown to record examples of each kind of sensory detail. Which example did you find especially vivid? Explain your answer.

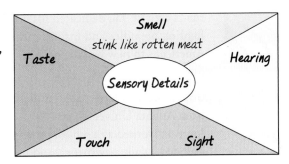

5. **Analyze Rhythm and Repetition** Review the chart you created while you read the poems. Which poem seems most influenced by the rhythms of jazz music? Support your answer with details.

6. **Examine Style** Describe the differences between the two blues verses in "The Weary Blues" (lines 19–22 and 25–30) and the other lines of the poem. In your opinion, do the two styles work well together? Explain your answer.

7. **Draw Conclusions About Author's Perspective** Use the events, situations, and ideas presented in each of Hughes's poems to draw conclusions about his views on African-American **identity.** In Hughes's eyes, what characteristics define African-American culture?

8. **Evaluate Speakers** Consider the four poems you read. In your opinion, which speaker best achieves each of the following goals? Cite details from the poems in your answers.

   - captures Hughes's pride in African-American culture
   - reflects the everyday life of African Americans
   - conveys the sounds of African-American speech
   - represents the feelings of African Americans today

Literary Criticism

9. **Critical Interpretations** In a review of Hughes's poetry collection *The Weary Blues,* poet Countee Cullen criticized Hughes for "too much emphasis on strictly Negro themes" and questioned whether jazz poems belong to "that select and austere circle of high literary expression which we call poetry." Do you agree with Cullen's concerns? Why or why not?

James Weldon Johnson
1871–1938

My City
Poem by James Weldon Johnson

A leading light of the Harlem Renaissance, James Weldon Johnson was also a lawyer, teacher, songwriter, diplomat, and civil rights activist. He dedicated his life to fighting prejudice and inspiring African Americans to new heights of social and literary achievement.

Unstoppable Talent After graduating from Atlanta University in 1894, Johnson worked as a school principal, founded a daily newspaper, and became the first African-American lawyer since Reconstruction to be admitted to the Florida bar. In 1901, the restless Johnson traveled to New York, where he and his younger brother became successful Broadway songwriters. One of their early songs, "Lift Every Voice and Sing," eventually became known as the African-American national anthem.

Renaissance Man Johnson also published works in many genres of literature. Among his best-known works are his novel *The Autobiography of an Ex-Colored Man,* his poetry collection *God's Trombones,* and a cultural history, *Black Manhattan.* He also edited several groundbreaking collections of African-American poetry and spirituals.

Claude McKay
c. 1890–1948

If We Must Die
Poem by Claude McKay

Hailed by James Weldon Johnson as "the poet of rebellion," Jamaican-born Festus Claudius McKay made his name as a fierce critic of racism in the United States. His poetry collection *Harlem Shadows,* published in 1922, is considered one of the founding works of the Harlem Renaissance.

Poet of Rebellion Already established as a poet, 23-year-old McKay arrived in the United States in 1912. In 1919, the country was torn apart by a wave of violent attacks against African Americans. Racial tensions erupted into 26 riots across the country during a period known as the Red Summer. "If We Must Die" was McKay's anguished response, which became instantly popular among African Americans.

Enduring Message During World War II, the poem took on new meaning when British Prime Minister Sir Winston Churchill quoted from it during a speech. The poem went on to become a battle cry for the Allies in their fight against the Nazis. McKay often complained that the fame of this one poem had overshadowed his other work, which included the novels *Home to Harlem* and *Banana Bottom.*

Author Online
For more on James Weldon Johnson and Claude McKay, visit the **Literature Center** at ClassZone.com.

● LITERARY ANALYSIS: SONNET

New ideas help keep poetic traditions alive. The centuries-old **sonnet,** a 14-line lyric poem with specific patterns of rhythm and rhyme, has been reimagined by many poets. The poems in this lesson are based on two classic types of sonnets.

- The **Italian,** or **Petrarchan, sonnet** is divided into two parts: an **octave,** or eight-line grouping, and a **sestet,** or six-line grouping. The usual rhyme scheme for the octave is *abbaabba.* The rhyme scheme for the sestet varies but is often *cdccde* or *cdccdc.*

- The **English,** or **Shakespearean, sonnet** has a rhyme scheme of *abab cdcd efef gg.* This divides the poem into four distinct line groups: three **quatrains,** or four-line units, followed by a **couplet,** a pair of rhymed lines.

Sonnets are often written in **iambic pentameter.** In this meter, each line includes five pairs of syllables, the first unstressed, the second stressed. However, modern poets often break the rules when writing sonnets. As you read, note how each poet adapts this classic form to a modern message.

● READING SKILL: UNDERSTAND FORM AND MEANING

Understanding a sonnet's structure can help you interpret its meaning. Keep in mind the following:

- In many sonnets, quatrains, octaves, and other line groupings are not set apart by stanza breaks. Use the rhyme scheme to determine the poem's line groupings.

- Each line grouping usually expresses one main idea.

- The first line grouping of the sonnet describes the speaker's situation or problem. The last line grouping resolves, concludes, or reacts to that situation.

As you begin to read each sonnet, identify the line groupings, listing them in a chart like the one shown. Also record in your chart the main idea expressed in each line grouping.

Title:	
Line Grouping	Main Idea
1st quatrain	

Explore the Key Idea

When does old become NEW *again?*

KEY IDEA When CDs came on the market, vinyl records seemed doomed. Then, hip-hop artists made the scratching of a needle on vinyl the signature sound of a new style of music. Artists often bring back old ideas to give them new meaning. Poets James Weldon Johnson and Claude McKay did just that with their **revival** of the sonnet, breathing new life into a 700-year-old poetic form.

PRESENT Think of an artist, a musician, or a writer from the past whose work you admire. Create a plan to adapt this person's work to make a creation of your own, and present your plan to the class.

My City

James Weldon Johnson

When I come down to sleep death's endless night,
The threshold of the unknown dark to cross,
What to me then will be the keenest loss,
When this bright world blurs on my fading sight?
5 Will it be that no more I shall see the trees
Or smell the flowers or hear the singing birds
Or watch the flashing streams or patient herds?
No, I am sure it will be none of these. **A**

But, ah! Manhattan's sights and sounds, her smells,
10 Her crowds, her throbbing force, the thrill that comes
From being of her a part, her subtle spells,
Her shining towers, her avenues, her slums—
O God! the stark, unutterable pity,
To be dead, and never again behold my city! **B**

ANALYZE VISUALS
What details in this photo correspond to the poet's vision of his city?

A FORM AND MEANING
Use the **stanza break** to identify the line groupings of this poem. What is the main idea of lines 1–8?

B SONNET
Judging from its line groupings, what type of sonnet is this?

View of Broadway near Times Square in Manhattan, 1920s

If We Must Die

Claude McKay

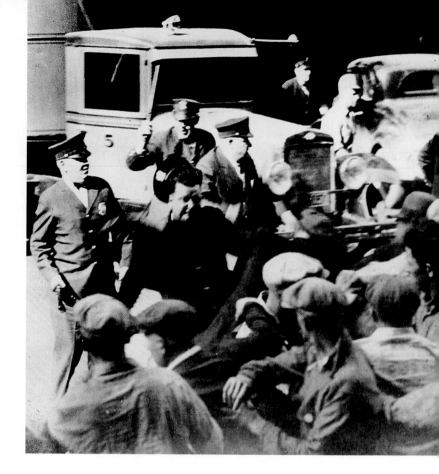

If we must die, let it not be like hogs
Hunted and penned in an inglorious[1] spot,
While round us bark the mad and hungry dogs,
Making their mock at our accursed lot.
5 If we must die, O let us nobly die,
So that our precious blood may not be shed
In vain; then even the monsters we defy
Shall be constrained[2] to honor us though dead! **C**
O kinsmen! we must meet the common foe!
10 Though far outnumbered let us show us brave,
And for their thousand blows deal one deathblow!
What though before us lies the open grave?
Like men we'll face the murderous, cowardly pack,
Pressed to the wall, dying, but fighting back! **D**

C SONNET
State the **rhyme scheme** of lines 1–8. Considering the rhyme scheme, what type of sonnet is this?

D FORM AND MEANING
By the end of the poem, what resolution has the speaker reached?

---

1. **inglorious:** shameful; disgraceful.
2. **constrained:** forced.

Comprehension

1. **Recall** In "My City," what will the speaker most regret about death?

2. **Clarify** In "If We Must Die," what type of death does the speaker argue for?

3. **Paraphrase** In "If We Must Die," what is the meaning of the phrase "making their mock at our accursed lot"?

Literary Analysis

4. **Identify Form** McKay's poem closely follows the conventions of a traditional sonnet. Which kind of sonnet is it? Explain your answer.

5. **Make Inferences About Audience** Recall the events that inspired McKay to write "If We Must Die." What audience can you infer the speaker is addressing? Describe the speaker's relationship to this audience.

6. **Classify Sonnet** Johnson's poem includes features of both Shakespearean and Petrarchan sonnets. Using a chart like the one shown, decide whether each listed feature of the poem's structure is characteristic of Shakespearean sonnets, Petrarchan sonnets, or both. Based on your answers, which label is the better description of Johnson's sonnet?

	Shakespearean	Petrarchan
Structure		
Rhyme Scheme		
Meter		
Final Couplet		

7. **Analyze Form and Meaning** Review the chart you completed as you read. Notice Johnson's use of a stanza break, whereas McKay uses none. In your opinion, how does this choice contribute to each poem's meaning? Explain.

8. **Examine Author's Purpose** Consider the motives that might have inspired African-American poets to express themselves in European poetic forms. What artistic and social messages are suggested by the Harlem Renaissance **revival** of the sonnet?

9. **Evaluate Style** In your opinion, which poem more successfully updates the sonnet for a modern audience? Include details in your answer.

Literary Criticism

10. **Critical Interpretations** Claude McKay once stated that he hoped his poems could convey universal meaning. Reread the background on "If We Must Die" included in the author biography. Does the poem's history suggest McKay was successful in his goal? Explain your answer.

Any Human to Another

Poem by Countee Cullen

Countee Cullen
1903–1946

In 1925, while still an undergraduate at New York University, Countee Cullen (kŭl′ən) published his first poetry collection, *Color,* which won immediate critical acclaim.

Cullen's greatest poetic influences were the English Romantic poets, especially John Keats. Although some of Cullen's poetry deals directly with experiences specific to African Americans, much of his work addresses universal concerns such as love and faith. Cullen adamantly believed that poetry could break down racial barriers and disliked being pigeonholed, once stating, "If I am going to be a poet at all, I am going to be a Poet and not a Negro Poet."

Storm Ending

Poem by Jean Toomer

Jean Toomer
1894–1967

Born in Washington, D.C., Nathan Eugene Toomer grew up in a prominent, racially mixed family. Toomer could pass for white, and as a young man, often changed his racial identification from white to black and back again. As an adult, he rejected the concept of race altogether and embraced an idealistic vision of himself as a founder of a "united human race."

Toomer was drawn to Eastern philosophy and Imagist poetry—poetry that conveys meaning through the use of precise, striking images. His reputation rests mainly on his novel *Cane* (1923), an experimental work exploring the African-American experience through fragments of poetry and prose.

A Black Man Talks of Reaping

Poem by Arna Bontemps

Arna Bontemps
1902–1973

After graduating from college in 1923, Arna Bontemps (bôn-tăn′) discovered a thriving literary scene in Harlem that he called a "foretaste of paradise." Despite his love for the bustle of the Northern cities, Bontemps was most deeply inspired by the Southern roots of African-American culture. Nearly all of his stories, novels, and plays are set in the South and provide vivid portrayals of rural life.

Bontemps, who earned his living as an educator, left Harlem in 1931 and spent most of his career in the South. His major works include the short story collection *The Old South* and the novel *God Sends Sunday,* which is often cited as the final work of the Harlem Renaissance.

Author Online

For more on these poets, visit the **Literature Center** at ClassZone.com.

● LITERARY ANALYSIS: THEME

In poetry, the speaker's descriptions of the world will often help you identify a poem's **theme,** its underlying message about life or human nature. In most works, the theme is implied, rather than directly stated. Consider these lines:

Your grief and mine
Must intertwine

The speaker might be talking to a loved one or making a general point about sorrow. To uncover the message of a poem, use these strategies:

- Consider the title. What information does it reveal?
- Identify the speaker. Is the speaker the voice of an individual or of a group?
- Notice key images and think about their meaning.
- Consider the mood, or feeling, the speaker conveys.

Readers notice different details and often find different themes in the same work. As you read, try to draw your own conclusions about each poet's message.

● READING SKILL: DISTINGUISH FIGURATIVE FROM LITERAL MEANING

You've learned that poets use **figurative language,** such as similes, metaphors, and personification, to go beyond the literal meaning of words. Use these steps to uncover this extra level of meaning:

- Read each poem once to grasp its overall meaning.
- Reread the poem, noting important words and phrases.
- Ask questions about comparisons you notice. What is being compared, and how are these things alike?
- Uncover hidden metaphors by noting descriptive details. What do these details remind you of?

As you read each poem, record examples of figurative language in a chart like the one shown. Then, jot down some of the impressions created by the words the poet chooses.

Example	Impressions
like an arrow	

How do you VIEW *the world?*

KEY IDEA You can see a glass as half empty or half full. You can see a pile of old newspapers as trash to be thrown away or as the makings of papier-mâché. The way you see things—your **outlook**—says a lot about who you are.

QUICKWRITE Many factors shape your outlook—your personality, your life experiences, your state of mind. Write one or two sentences describing your outlook. Then, explain the factors you think have most influenced the way you look at the world.

Any Human *to Another*

Countee Cullen

The ills I sorrow at
Not me alone
Like an arrow,
Pierce to the marrow,
5 Through the fat
And past the bone.

Your grief and mine
Must intertwine
Like sea and river,
10 Be fused and mingle,
Diverse yet single,
Forever and forever. **A**

Let no man be so proud
And confident,
15 To think he is allowed
A little tent
Pitched in a meadow
Of sun and shadow
All his little own.

20 Joy may be shy, unique,
Friendly to a few,
Sorrow never scorned to speak
To any who
Were false or true. **B**

25 Your every grief
Like a blade
Shining and unsheathed[1]
Must strike me down.
Of bitter aloes[2] wreathed,
30 My sorrow must be laid
On your head like a crown.

A THEME
Reread lines 1–12.
Consider the title of the
poem. Based on the title,
what message about
sorrow is expressed in
these lines?

B FIGURATIVE
MEANING
Identify two examples of
personification in lines
20–24. What qualities are
indicated by these lines?

---

1. **unsheathed:** removed from its protective case.
2. **bitter aloes:** spiny-leafed plants whose juice is
   used to make a bad-tasting medicine.

Storm Ending

Jean Toomer

Thunder blossoms gorgeously above our heads,
Great, hollow, bell-like flowers,
Rumbling in the wind,
Stretching clappers to strike our ears . . **C**
5 Full-lipped flowers
Bitten by the sun
Bleeding rain
Dripping rain like golden honey—
And the sweet earth flying from the thunder.

C **FIGURATIVE MEANING**
What is thunder compared to in lines 1–4? Explain what qualities are emphasized by this comparison.

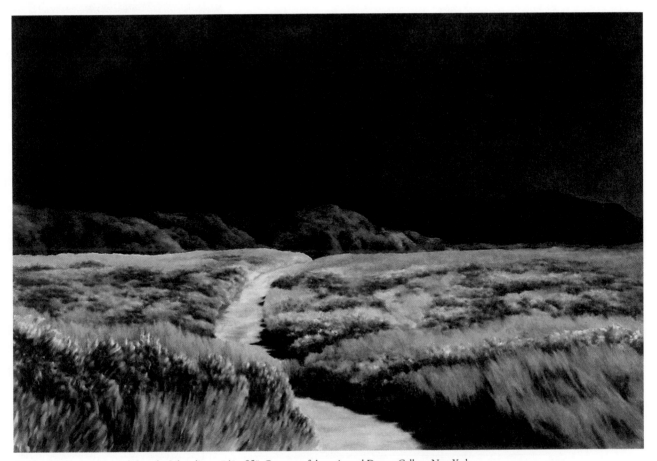

Field and Storm (2003), April Gornik. Oil on linen, 74″ × 95″. Courtesy of the artist and Danese Gallery, New York.

Sunflowers, Charly Palmer. Mixed media collage on canvas, 48″ × 24″. © Charly Palmer.

A Black Man Talks of Reaping

Arna Bontemps

I have sown beside all waters in my day.
I planted deep, within my heart the fear
That wind or fowl would take the grain away.
I planted safe against this stark, lean year. **D**

5   I scattered seed enough to plant the land
In rows from Canada to Mexico,
But for my reaping[1] only what the hand
Can hold at once is all that I can show.

Yet what I sowed and what the orchard yields
10 My brother's sons are gathering stalk and root,
Small wonder then my children glean[2] in fields
They have not sown, and feed on bitter fruit. **E**

---

1. **reaping:** harvesting grain.
2. **glean:** gather grain left behind by reapers.

ANALYZE VISUALS
What elements of this painting reflect the theme of the poem?

D **FIGURATIVE MEANING**
Reread lines 1–4. What idea do the words *sown, planted,* and *grain* have in common?

E **THEME**
In lines 11–12, why are the children's gleanings described as "bitter fruit"?

Comprehension

1. **Summarize** In "Any Human to Another," what comparisons does the speaker use to describe grief?

2. **Clarify** In "Storm Ending," what event is described in the last line of the poem?

3. **Clarify** In "A Black Man Talks of Reaping," how much has the speaker reaped from all the seed he has scattered?

Literary Analysis

4. **Distinguish Figurative from Literal Meaning** Review the notes you took on Bontemps's poem. Bontemps uses an **extended metaphor,** a lengthy comparison of two things that have many points in common. Identify the extended metaphor Bontemps uses. What is this metaphor meant to suggest?

5. **Examine Imagery** "Storm Ending" includes several examples of **synesthesia,** imagery that uses one type of sensory experience to describe a different one—for example, a sound decribed as a smell. Identify two examples of synesthesia in the poem. Which two senses are combined in each image?

6. **Compare and Contrast Tone** Describe the tone, or attitude toward the subject, of Cullen's and Bontemps's poems. What **outlook** on the prospects for social equality does each poem suggest?

7. **Analyze Theme** Complete a chart like the one shown for each poem. What do you conclude is the theme of each poem?

Title Reveals:	Speaker's Identity:
Key Images:	Mood:

Literary Criticism

8. **Biographical Context** Reread the author biographies on page 852. In each case, what connections can you make between the poet's life story and the worldview expressed in his work? Be specific.

How It Feels to Be Colored Me

Essay by Zora Neale Hurston

FYI

Did you know that Zora Neale Hurston . . .

- dressed so flamboyantly that one acquaintance referred to her as a "macaw of brilliant plumage"?
- shocked some people by wearing pants in public?
- became a fan of British poet John Milton after rescuing one of his books from the trash?

Author Online

For more on Zora Neale Hurston, visit the **Literature Center** at ClassZone.com.

Zora Neale Hurston

c. 1891–1960

Raised in the all-black town of Eatonville, Florida, Zora Neale Hurston followed her mother's advice to "jump at de sun"—to follow her dreams, no matter how impossible they seemed. In 1925, she arrived in New York with "$1.50, no job, no friends, and a lot of hope." Hurston's flair, talent, and sheer nerve soon made her one of the leading African-American novelists of the 1930s.

Early Days When Hurston was 13 years old, her family life fell apart. Her mother died, her father remarried, and by the age of 14, Hurston was on her own. Working an endless series of menial jobs, Hurston tried for years to earn enough money to send herself back to school. After 12 years of trials and adventures, she finally completed high school and scraped together a year's tuition for Howard University, "the Negro Harvard," where in 1921 she published her first story.

Collector of Stories By 1925, Hurston's efforts began to pay off. She won a scholarship to Barnard College, where she studied with the renowned anthropologists Franz Boas and Ruth Benedict. After graduating from Barnard in 1928—the first known African American to do so—Hurston returned to the South to collect African-American folklore. "I had to go back, dress as they did, talk as they did, live their life," she said, "so I could get into my stories the world I knew as a child." The lively, hilarious stories she collected soon became material for her own fiction. In the 1930s and '40s, she published a series of major works, including the folklore collection *Mules and Men* (1935), the novel *Their Eyes Were Watching God* (1937), and her autobiography, *Dust Tracks on a Road* (1942).

Down But Not Out Hurston often came under fire by African-American writers who felt she minimized the seriousness of racial prejudice. By the late 1940s, her books had fallen out of favor and out of print. During the last 20 years of her life, Hurston struggled to earn a living, once again working as a maid to pay her bills. In 1960, Hurston died in a welfare home, poor and nearly forgotten, and was buried in an unmarked grave in Fort Pierce, Florida. Thanks to the efforts of author Alice Walker, Hurston's work was rediscovered in the 1970s. Hurston is now acknowledged as an influential figure in the history of African-American literature.

● LITERARY ANALYSIS: TONE

Famously outspoken, Zora Neale Hurston wasn't afraid to stand out from the crowd. In this essay, she writes about race with a distinctive **tone,** or attitude toward the topic, that sets her apart from other Harlem Renaissance writers.

I do not belong to that sobbing school of Negrohood who hold that nature somehow has given them a lowdown dirty deal....

A writer establishes tone through choice of words and details. Note Hurston's use of informal language (*lowdown*) and her flippant reference to other African-American writers (*sobbing school of Negrohood*). As you read the essay, think about her choice of words and details and the tone they create.

● READING SKILL: IDENTIFY MAIN IDEAS

You know that the **main idea** of a paragraph is the basic point it makes. Sometimes, the main idea is **explicit,** or directly stated in the text. However, main ideas may also be only **implicit**—suggested or hinted at by the details in the text. In such cases, you'll need to analyze the details the author presents to discover the main idea.

As you read, use a chart like the one shown to record the main idea of each paragraph. If the main idea is implicit, note key details that helped you identify the main idea.

Paragraph	Main Idea	Key Details
1	I'm not ashamed to be colored.	offers no "extenuating circumstances"

▲ VOCABULARY IN CONTEXT

Hurston uses the following words to make her points about African-American identity. Restate each phrase, using a different word or words for the boldfaced term.

1. collected a **miscellany** of objects on her travels
2. did not use **pigmentation** to judge character
3. excused from penalties because of **extenuating** factors
4. dressed in colorful **raiment**
5. spoke **exultingly** of her triumphs
6. saw herself as **cosmic** rather than small and narrow

Explore the Key Idea

What makes you YOU?

KEY IDEA Think of the things that make you unique: your style, your sense of humor, the way you keep your head (or don't) when things get tense. Of all the qualities and behaviors that make you who you are, which ones do you think best define your **personality?**

SURVEY Of the things you do, what best expresses your personality? Create a snapshot of yourself by completing each statement in the following quiz.

The Insider's Guide to Me

1. To find me in a crowd, look/ listen for _____

2. The story my friends/family all tell about me is _____

3. Most people in school know me as _____

4. The thing I do that is most "me" is _____

How It Feels to Be Colored Me

Zora Neale Hurston

BACKGROUND Between 1865 and 1900, more than 100 independent towns were founded by African Americans trying to escape racial prejudice. Eatonville, Florida, a small town just north of Orlando, was the oldest of these self-governing black communities. Growing up in Eatonville, Zora Neale Hurston was sheltered from the experiences of exclusion and contempt that shaped the lives of many African Americans. As you read this essay, think about how these early experiences influenced Hurston's opinions on race.

ANALYZE VISUALS
What words would you use to describe the girl in the painting? Identify the techniques or elements that lend her these qualities.

I am colored but I offer nothing in the way of **extenuating** circumstances except the fact that I am the only Negro in the United States whose grandfather on the mother's side was *not* an Indian chief.

I remember the very day that I became colored. Up to my thirteenth year I lived in the little Negro town of Eatonville, Florida. It is exclusively a colored town. The only white people I knew passed through the town going to or coming from Orlando. The native whites rode dusty horses, the Northern tourists chugged down the sandy village road in automobiles. The town knew the Southerners and never stopped cane chewing when they passed. But the Northerners were something
10 else again. They were peered at cautiously from behind curtains by the timid. The more venturesome would come out on the porch to watch them go past and got just as much pleasure out of the tourists as the tourists got out of the village. **A**

The front porch might seem a daring place for the rest of the town, but it was a gallery seat to me. My favorite place was atop the gate-post. Proscenium box for a born first-nighter.[1] Not only did I enjoy the show, but I didn't mind the actors knowing that I liked it. I actually spoke to them in passing. I'd wave at them and when they returned my salute, I would say something like this: "Howdy-do-well-

extenuating
(ĭk-stĕn′yōo-a′tĭng) *adj.*
lessening the severity of
extenuate *v.*

A TONE
Describe the tone of lines 1–12. What does Hurston's tone reveal about the way she sees herself?

Girl in a Red Dress (1934), Charles Alston. Oil on canvas, 71″ × 55.9″. © The Harmon and Harriet Kelley Collection of African American Art. © Estate of Charles Alston. Courtesy of Michael Rosenfeld Gallery, LLC, New York.

---

1. **proscenium . . . first-nighter:** A proscenium box is a box seat near the stage. A first-nighter is a person who attends the opening night of a performance.

I-thank-you-where-you-goin'?" Usually automobile or the horse paused at this, and after a queer exchange of compliments, I would probably "go a piece of the way" with them, as we say in farthest Florida. If one of my family happened to come to the front in time to see me, of course negotiations would be rudely broken off. But even so, it is clear that I was the first "welcome-to-our-state" Floridian, and I hope the Miami Chamber of Commerce will please take notice.

During this period, white people differed from colored to me only in that they rode through town and never lived there. They liked to hear me "speak pieces" and sing and wanted to see me dance the parse-me-la,[2] and gave me generously of their small silver for doing these things, which seemed strange to me for I wanted to do them so much that I needed bribing to stop. Only they didn't know it. The colored people gave no dimes. They deplored any joyful tendencies in me, but I was their Zora nevertheless. I belonged to them, to the nearby hotels, to the county—everybody's Zora.

But changes came in the family when I was thirteen, and I was sent to school in Jacksonville. I left Eatonville, the town of the oleanders,[3] as Zora. When I disembarked from the riverboat at Jacksonville, she was no more. It seemed that I had suffered a sea change.[4] I was not Zora of Orange County any more, I was now a little colored girl. I found it out in certain ways. In my heart as well as in the mirror, I became a fast brown—warranted not to rub nor run.

But I am not tragically colored. There is no great sorrow dammed up in my soul, nor lurking behind my eyes. I do not mind at all. I do not belong to the sobbing school of Negrohood who hold that nature somehow has given them a low-down dirty deal and whose feelings are all hurt about it. Even in the helter-skelter skirmish that is my life, I have seen that the world is to the strong regardless of a little **pigmentation** more or less. No, I do not weep at the world—I am too busy sharpening my oyster knife.[5] **B**

Someone is always at my elbow reminding me that I am the grand-daughter of slaves. It fails to register depression with me. Slavery is sixty years in the past. The operation was successful and the patient is doing well, thank you. The terrible struggle that made me an American out of a potential slave said "On the line!" The Reconstruction said "Get set!"; and the generation before said "Go!" I am off to a flying start and I must not halt in the stretch to look behind and weep. Slavery is the price I paid for civilization, and the choice was not with me. It is a bully adventure and worth all that I have paid through my ancestors for it. No one on earth ever had a greater chance for glory. The world to be won and nothing to be lost. It is thrilling to think—to know that for any act of mine, I shall get twice as much praise or twice as much blame. It is quite exciting to hold the center of the national stage, with the spectators not knowing whether to laugh or to weep. **C**

---

2. **parse-me-la:** a dance movement popular with Southern African Americans of the period.

3. **oleanders** (ō'lē-ăn'dərz): evergreen shrubs with fragrant flowers.

4. **sea change:** complete transformation.

5. **oyster knife:** a reference to the saying "The world is my oyster," implying that the world contains treasure waiting to be taken, like the pearl in an oyster.

pigmentation
(pĭg'mən-tā'shən) *n.*
coloring

B **MAIN IDEAS**
State the main idea of lines 38–44. What criticism is implied by the author's statement?

C **TONE**
Reread lines 51–52. Explain what is unusual about Hurston's tone. What effect might this comment have on an African-American reader? a white reader?

Empress of the Blues (1974), Romare Bearden. Collage, 36″ × 48″. Photo © Smithsonian American Art Museum/Art Resource, New York. © The Romare Bearden Foundation/Licensed by VAGA, New York.

The position of my white neighbor is much more difficult. No brown specter pulls up a chair beside me when I sit down to eat. No dark ghost thrusts its leg against mine in bed. The game of keeping what one has is never so exciting as the
60 game of getting.

I do not always feel colored. Even now I often achieve the unconscious Zora of Eatonville before the Hegira.[6] I feel most colored when I am thrown against a sharp white background.

For instance at Barnard. "Beside the waters of the Hudson"[7] I feel my race. Among the thousand white persons, I am a dark rock surged upon, overswept by a creamy sea. I am surged upon and overswept, but through it all, I remain myself. When covered by the waters, I am; and the ebb but reveals me again.

Sometimes it is the other way around. A white person is set down in our midst, but the contrast is just as sharp for me. For instance, when I sit in the
70 drafty basement that is The New World Cabaret with a white person, my color comes. We enter chatting about any little nothing that we have in common and are seated by the jazz waiters. In the abrupt way that jazz orchestras have, this one plunges into a number. It loses no time in circumlocutions, but gets right down to business. It constricts the thorax and splits the heart with its tempo and narcotic harmonies. This orchestra grows rambunctious, rears on its hind legs and attacks the tonal veil with primitive fury, rending it, clawing it until it breaks through

---

6. **Hegira** (hĭ-jī′rə): journey (from the name given to Muhammad's journey from Mecca to Medina in 622).

7. **Barnard . . . Hudson":** Barnard is the college in New York City from which Hurston graduated in 1928. "Beside the waters . . ." is a reference to the first line of the college song.

the tonal veil with primitive fury, rending it, clawing it until it breaks through to the jungle beyond. I follow those heathen—follow them **exultingly.** I dance wildly inside myself; I yell within, I whoop; I shake my assegai[8] above my head, I hurl it true to the mark *yeeeeooww!* I am in the jungle and living in the jungle

80 way. My face is painted red and yellow, and my body is painted blue. My pulse is throbbing like a war drum. I want to slaughter something—give pain, give death to what, I do not know. But the piece ends. The men of the orchestra wipe their lips and rest their fingers. I creep back slowly to the veneer we call civilization with the last tone and find the white friend sitting motionless in his seat, smoking calmly.

"Good music they have here," he remarks, drumming the table with his fingertips.

Music! The great blobs of purple and red emotion have not touched him. He has only heard what I felt. He is far away and I see him but dimly across the ocean

90 and the continent that have fallen between us. He is so pale with his whiteness then and I am *so* colored. **D**

At certain times I have no race, I am *me.* When I set my hat at a certain angle and saunter down Seventh Avenue, Harlem City, feeling as snooty as the lions in front of the Forty-Second Street Library, for instance. So far as my feelings are concerned, Peggy Hopkins Joyce on the Boule Mich[9] with her gorgeous **raiment,** stately carriage, knees knocking together in a most aristocratic manner, has nothing on me. The **cosmic** Zora emerges. I belong to no race nor time, I am the eternal feminine with its string of beads.

I have no separate feeling about being an American citizen and colored. I

100 am merely a fragment of the Great Soul that surges within the boundaries. My country, right or wrong.

Sometimes, I feel discriminated against, but it does not make me angry. It merely astonishes me. How *can* any deny themselves the pleasure of my company! It's beyond me.

But in the main, I feel like a brown bag of **miscellany** propped against a wall. Against a wall in company with other bags, white, red, and yellow. Pour out the contents, and there is discovered a jumble of small things priceless and worthless. A first-water[10] diamond, an empty spool, bits of broken glass, lengths of string, a key to a door long since crumbled away, a rusty knife-blade, old shoes saved for

110 a road that never was and never will be, a nail bent under the weight of things too heavy for any nail, a dried flower or two, still a little fragrant. In your hand is the **E** brown bag. On the ground before you is the jumble it held—so much like the jumble in the bags, could they be emptied, that all might be dumped in a single heap and the bags refilled without altering the content of any greatly. A bit of colored glass more or less would not matter. Perhaps that is how the Great Stuffer of Bags filled them in the first place—who knows? ∾

exultingly (ĭg-zŭlt′ĭng-lē)
adv. joyfully

D MAIN IDEAS
Describe the two responses that are contrasted in lines 88–91. What does this contrast imply about the differences between whites and blacks?

raiment (rā′mənt) *n.* clothing; garments

cosmic (kŏz′mĭk) *adj.* of or relating to the universe

miscellany (mĭs′ə-lā′nē)
n. a mixture of various things

E GRAMMAR AND STYLE
Reread lines 105–111. Note how Hurston uses **sentence fragments** to highlight specific details in her description.

---

8. **assegai** (ăs′ə-gī′): a type of light spear used in southern Africa.

9. **Peggy . . . Boule Mich:** a wealthy woman of Hurston's day, walking along the Boulevard Saint-Michel in Paris.

10. **first-water:** of the highest quality or purity.

Comprehension

1. **Recall** In Hurston's description, what kind of community was Eatonville?

2. **Recall** What was the big change Hurston experienced at age 13?

3. **Paraphrase** What is Hurston's view on slavery?

Literary Analysis

4. **Identify Main Ideas** Review the chart you created as you read. What is the main idea of the essay? In what ways does race shape Hurston's sense of identity?

5. **Analyze Tone** Describe the tone of this essay. What point does Hurston make by choosing this tone to discuss the subject of race?

6. **Make Inferences** Judging from the anecdotes Hurston includes in her essay, what experiences and traits does she consider distinctively African-American? Support your answer with details.

7. **Interpret Analogy** An analogy is a point-by-point comparison that uses one thing or idea to make sense of another. Reread the analogy Hurston develops in lines 105–116. What message does this comparison convey? In your response, explain the meaning of each part of the analogy, including

   • the colored bags   • the "Great Stuffer of Bags"   • the bags' contents

8. **Compare and Contrast Author's Perspectives** Hurston's views set her apart from most of her Harlem Renaissance contemporaries. Choose one of the poets you have read in this unit, and use a chart like the one shown to contrast his perspectives with Hurston's. What similarities and differences do you find?

	Hurston's Views	_____'s Views
What Defines Black Identity		
Goals of Black Writers		
Opinions of Whites		

9. **Synthesize Details** Reread the author biography on page 858 and the background on page 860. What connections can you draw between Hurston's **personality,** her life experiences, and her unique perspective on race?

Literary Criticism

10. **Critical Interpretations** The author Alice Walker, one of Hurston's greatest admirers, finds Hurston's views sometimes "exasperating." She notes that this essay "presents two stereotypes: the 'happy darky' who sings and dances for white folks, for money and for joy; and the educated black person who is, underneath the thin veneer of civilization, still a 'heathen.'" Do you agree with Walker's views? Why or why not? Be specific in your response.

Vocabulary in Context

VOCABULARY PRACTICE

Choose the word that is not related in meaning to the other words.

1. (a) collection, (b) miscellany, (c) regulation, (d) assortment
2. (a) apparel, (b) clothing, (c) weathering, (d) raiment
3. (a) vast, (b) cosmic, (c) universal, (d) fictional
4. (a) shading, (b) pigmentation, (c) zoology, (d) coloration
5. (a) determinedly, (b) exultingly, (c) delightedly, (d) ecstatically
6. (a) extenuating, (b) moderating, (c) mitigating, (d) exaggerating

WORD LIST

cosmic

extenuating

exultingly

miscellany

pigmentation

raiment

VOCABULARY IN WRITING

What about Hurston's personality most impressed you? Using at least two vocabulary words, write a brief explanation of your opinion. Here is a sample beginning.

> **EXAMPLE SENTENCE**
>
> I was impressed that Hurston spoke **exultingly** of her good experiences and seemed to ignore any bad ones.

VOCABULARY STRATEGY: THE GREEK ROOT *COSM* OR *COSMO*

The vocabulary word *cosmic* is derived from the Greek word *kosmos,* which means "world" or "universe." This root, which is spelled *cosm* or *cosmo* in English, is found in a number of words, both scientific and nonscientific. To understand words with *cosm* or *cosmo,* use your knowledge of the root as well as any context clues provided.

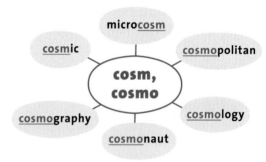

microcosm

cosmic

cosmopolitan

cosm, cosmo

cosmography

cosmology

cosmonaut

PRACTICE Apply what you know about the Greek root *cosm* or *cosmo* to the words in the web. Then, choose the word from the web that best completes each sentence. If you need to, consult a dictionary.

1. Many myths of creation also include a _____, or a theory of the universe.

2. A _____ is an explorer of outer space.

3. The science called _____ includes astronomy, geography, and geology.

4. A _____ can be any type of miniature community or world.

5. A _____ person tends to have a sophisticated view of the world.

VOCABULARY PRACTICE
For more practice, go to the **Vocabulary Center** at **ClassZone.com.**

Reading-Writing Connection

GRAMMAR AND STYLE

VARY SENTENCE STRUCTURE Review the **Grammar and Style** note on page 864. Zora Neale Hurston's independent and unconventional personality shines through in her writing style. She wasn't afraid to bend the rules of formal writing, adding punch and emphasis through the use of **sentence fragments.** Here are two examples from the essay:

> *I feel most colored when I am thrown against a sharp white background. For instance at Barnard.* (lines 62–64)

> *"Good music they have here," he remarks, drumming the table with his fingertips. Music! The great blobs of purple and red emotion have not touched him.* (lines 86–88)

The single-word fragment "Music" brings the reader to an abrupt halt, creating a dramatic pause before the exuberant description of the music's effects. The change in sentence rhythm helps emphasize the cultural gulf between Hurston and her white companion.

PRACTICE Rewrite the following paragraph in Zora Neale Hurston's style, incorporating one or two intentional sentence fragments. Add or delete any words as necessary.

> My parents were always finding opportunities to point out how much the world owed to China. We learned that our Chinese ancestors had invented paper, books, kites, gunpowder, compasses, fishing reels, and umbrellas. Was there anything that hadn't been invented by the Chinese? One day we went to eat at an Italian restaurant. As I dug into my plate of pasta, I told my mom, "Well, here's one thing the Chinese didn't invent." I was wrong! The Chinese invented pasta, she explained, and they invented restaurants, too!

WRITING TOOLS
For prewriting, revision, and editing tools, visit the **Writing Center** at ClassZone.com.

Thoughts on the African-American Novel

Literary Criticism by Toni Morrison

NOTABLE QUOTE

"The ability of writers to imagine what is not the self, to familiarize the strange and mystify the familiar, is the test of their power."

FYI

Did you know that Toni Morrison . . .

- was once a textbook editor?

- raised two sons as a single mother after her first marriage ended?

- changed her first name in college because "Chloe" was hard to pronounce?

- was the first African American to win the Nobel Prize in literature?

Author Online

For more on Toni Morrison, visit the **Literature Center** at ClassZone.com.

Toni Morrison
born 1931

Toni Morrison was born Chloe Anthony Wofford in Lorain, Ohio. This working-class town had a small, close-knit African-American community with a vibrant oral culture. In stories, songs, and everyday speech, Morrison heard an imaginative blend of biblical phrases, rhetorical devices, slang, and conventional English. This early awareness of the power of language and storytelling was a powerful influence on Morrison's work.

Accidental Novelist After earning a bachelor's degree from Howard University (1953) and a master's in English from Cornell University (1955), Morrison embarked on a teaching career. While teaching at Howard, she joined a writers' group for fun, showing up at meetings with what she called "old junk" that she'd written in high school. When she ran out of "junk" before one meeting, she quickly scribbled down a story—a story that later inspired her first novel, *The Bluest Eye.* Published in 1969, the book recounts the story of a troubled African-American girl who, conditioned by white society's ideals of beauty, longs to have blue eyes. The novel's themes, such as the trauma of racism and the importance of community, set the stage for Morrison's later work.

A Major Literary Force The novels *Sula* (1973), *Song of Solomon* (1977), and *Tar Baby* (1981) established Morrison as a major author with a unique voice. Her novels typically have richly symbolic plots that include supernatural or fantastic elements. Within this imaginative context, Morrison provides a realistic treatment of social issues. Her characters, who often have allegorical or biblical names, confront the central struggles of African-American life: the impact of violence and injustice on their lives and the search for cultural identity.

Morrison has been nominated for every major literary honor; she has received, among others, the National Book Critics Circle Award, the Pulitzer Prize, and the Nobel Prize in Literature. She has written several novels and numerous works of commentary and cultural analysis. More recent novels include *Paradise* (1998) and *Love* (2003). Morrison lectures and teaches at various universities across the country. She is widely considered one of the most innovative stylists in contemporary American literature.

● LITERARY ANALYSIS: LITERARY CRITICISM

If you've ever read a book review, you're already familiar with **literary criticism,** writing that focuses on literary works, genres, and ideas. Works of literary criticism, which are most often essays or book reviews, are written to make readers more knowledgeable about, and appreciative of, the literature they read. Typically, these works

- describe a specific aspect—such as origins, characteristics, or impact—of a literary work, genre, or idea
- provide a historical or literary context for their subject
- describe standards for measuring the excellence of literary works

As you read, see what features of literary criticism you can identify in this essay.

● READING SKILL: IDENTIFY AUTHOR'S POSITION

Works of literary criticism are written to communicate a position, or an opinion, on a topic. To identify an author's **position,** look for direct statements that express the author's viewpoint, such as the following:

I don't regard Black literature as simply books written by *Black people, or simply as literature written* about *Black people . . .*

You'll also want to look for the specific reasons and evidence the writer presents to support his or her opinion. As you read, identify Morrison's position on the importance of the novel to society and on the characteristics that define the African-American novel. In a chart like the one shown, record the reasons and evidence she uses to support her positions. Consider whether you find these positions persuasive.

	Position	Reasons and Evidence
Importance of the Novel		
What Defines the African-American Novel		

Can CULTURE *be captured in words?*

KEY IDEA You can think of **culture** as the things people make, such as food, books, music, and crafts. But culture is also the things people do: the way they talk, the relationships they build, the values they hold dear. In this essay, Toni Morrison talks about her struggle to capture the essence of African-American culture on the printed page.

QUICKWRITE Think about the cultures you belong to—your ethnicity, your religion, even your region or town. If you were writing about one of these cultures, what would you need to include? List three or more features you would use to capture the experience of that culture.

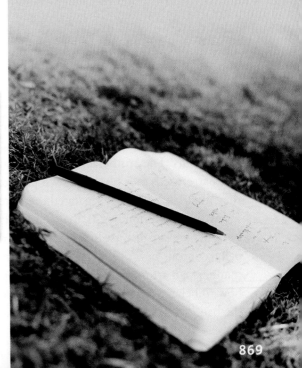

Thoughts
on the
African-American
Novel

Toni Morrison

The label "novel" is useful in technical terms because I write prose that is longer than a short story. My sense of the novel is that it has always functioned for the class or the group that wrote it. The history of the novel as a form began when there was a new class, a middle class, to read it, it was an art form that they needed. The lower classes didn't need novels at that time because they had an art form already: they had songs, and dances, and ceremony, and gossip, and celebrations. The aristocracy didn't need it because they had the art that they had patronized, they had their own pictures painted, their own houses built, and they made sure their art separated them from the rest of the world. But when the
10 industrial revolution began, there emerged a new class of people who were neither peasants nor aristocrats. In large measure they had no art form to tell them how to behave in this new situation. So they produced an art form: we call it the novel of manners, an art form designed to tell people something they didn't know. That is, how to behave in this new world, how to distinguish between the good guys and the bad guys. How to get married. What a good living was. What would happen

ANALYZE VISUALS
Read lines 1–15. How might the painting on page 871 be compared with the "novel of manners" referred to in lines 12–13? Explain.

Family (1955), Charles H. Alston. Oil on canvas, 48¼″ × 35¾″. Whitney Museum of American Art, New York. Purchase, with funds from the Artists and Students Assistance Fund 55.47. © Estate of Charles H. Alston.

if you strayed from the fold. So that early works such as *Pamela,* by Samuel
Richardson, and the Jane Austen material[1] provided social rules and explained
behavior, identified outlaws, identified the people, habits, and customs that one
should approve of. They were didactic[2] in that sense. That, I think, is probably
20 why the novel was not missed among the so-called peasant cultures. They didn't
need it, because they were clear about what their responsibilities were and who
and where was evil, and where was good. **Ⓐ**

   But when the peasant class, or lower class, or what have you, confronts the
middle class, the city, or the upper classes, they are thrown a little bit into disarray.
For a long time, the art form that was healing for Black people was music. That
music is no longer *exclusively* ours, we don't have exclusive rights to it. Other
people sing it and play it; it is the mode of contemporary music everywhere. So
another form has to take that place, and it seems to me that the novel is needed
by African-Americans now in a way that it was not needed before—and it is
30 following along the lines of the function of novels everywhere. We don't live in
places where we can hear those stories anymore; parents don't sit around and
tell their children those classical, mythological archetypal[3] stories that we heard
years ago. But new information has got to get out, and there are several ways to
do it. One is in the novel. I regard it as a way to accomplish certain very strong
functions—one being the one I just described. **Ⓑ**

   It should be beautiful, and powerful, but it should also *work.* It should have
something in it that enlightens; something in it that opens the door and points
the way. Something in it that suggests what the conflicts are, what the problems
are. But it need not solve those problems because it is not a case study,[4] it is not a
40 recipe. There are things that I try to incorporate into my fiction that are directly
and deliberately related to what I regard as the major characteristics of Black art,
wherever it is. One of which is the ability to be both print and oral literature: to
combine those two aspects so that the stories can be read in silence, of course, but
one should be able to hear them as well. It should try deliberately to make you
stand up and make you feel something profoundly in the same way that a Black
preacher requires his congregation to speak, to join him in the sermon, to behave
in a certain way, to stand up and to weep and to cry and to accede or to change
and to modify—to expand on the sermon that is being delivered. In the same way
that a musician's music is enhanced when there is a response from the audience.
50 Now in a book, which closes, after all—it's of some importance to me to try to
make that connection—to try to make that happen also. And, having at my
disposal only the letters of the alphabet and some punctuation, I have to provide
the places and spaces so that the reader can participate. Because it is the affective

Ⓐ LITERARY CRITICISM
Reread lines 1–22.
Summarize Morrison's
account of the origins of
the novel. What was the
genre's original purpose?

Ⓑ AUTHOR'S POSITION
Reread lines 23–35.
Which sentence is
the best statement of
Morrison's opinion on the
importance of the novel?

---

1. **the Jane Austen material:** Jane Austen (1775–1817) wrote several novels focused on middle-class
   life in her era.
2. **didactic** (dī-dăk′tĭk): intended to instruct.
3. **archetypal** (är′kĭ-tī′pəl): serving as a pattern for later examples.
4. **case study:** an intensive analysis of a group, individual or unit and its development.

and participatory relationship between the artist or the speaker and the audience that is of primary importance, as it is in these other art forms that I have described. **C**

To make the story appear oral, meandering, effortless, spoken—to have the reader *feel* the narrator without *identifying* that narrator, or hearing him or her knock about, and to have the reader work *with* the author in the construction
60 of the book—is what's important. What is left out is as important as what is there. To describe sexual scenes in such a way that they are not clinical, not even explicit[5]—so that the reader brings his own sexuality to the scene and thereby participates in it in a very personal way. And owns it. To construct the dialogue so that it is heard. So that there are no adverbs attached to them: "loudly," "softly," "he said menacingly." The menace should be in the sentence. To use, even formally, a chorus. The real presence of a chorus. Meaning the community or the reader at large, commenting on the action as it goes ahead.

In the books that I have written, the chorus has changed but there has always been a choral note, whether it is the "I" narrator of *Bluest Eye,* or the town
70 functioning as a character in *Sula,* or the neighborhood and the community that responds in the two parts of town in *Solomon.*[6] Or, as extreme as I've gotten, all of nature thinking and feeling and watching and responding to the action going on in *Tar Baby,* so that they are in the story: the trees hurt, fish are afraid, clouds report, and the bees are alarmed. Those are the ways in which I try to incorporate, into that traditional genre the novel, unorthodox novelistic characteristics—so that it is, in my view, Black, because it uses the characteristics of Black art. I am not suggesting that some of these devices have not been used before and elsewhere—only the reason why I do. I employ them as well as I can. And those are just some; I wish there were ways in which such things could be talked about
80 in the criticism. My general disappointment in some of the criticism that my work has received has nothing to do with approval. It has something to do with the vocabulary used in order to describe these things. I don't like to find my books condemned as bad or praised as good, when that condemnation or that praise is based on criteria from other paradigms.[7] I would much prefer that they were dismissed or embraced based on the success of their accomplishment within the culture out of which I write. **D**

I don't regard Black literature as simply books written *by* Black people, or simply as literature written *about* Black people, or simply as literature that uses a certain mode of language in which you just sort of drop *g*'s. There is something
90 very special and very identifiable about it and it is my struggle to *find* that elusive but identifiable style in the books. My joy is when I think that I have approached it; my misery is when I think I can't get there. ❧

5. **not clinical, not even explicit:** not coldly impersonal or even clearly detailed.

6. *Solomon:* Morrison's novel *Song of Solomon.*

7. **paradigms** (păr'ə-dīmz'): theoretical frameworks or patterns.

C LITERARY CRITICISM
What does Morrison regard as the main characteristic of African-American art?

D AUTHOR'S POSITION
Reread lines 68–86. What examples from her own work does Morrison cite as **evidence** for her position?

Comprehension

1. **Recall** With what social class does Morrison associate the novel?

2. **Clarify** According to Morrison, why is the novel especially important for African Americans?

3. **Clarify** Why is it important to Morrison to include a chorus in her fiction?

Literary Analysis

4. **Examine Author's Position** Review the chart you created as you read. In your opinion, does Morrison provide compelling support for her positions? Explain your answer.

5. **Analyze Literary Criticism** Review the bulleted list on page 869. In what ways is Morrison's essay typical of a work of literary criticism? Support your answer with details.

6. **Analyze Details** Explain the comparison Morrison makes in lines 44–48. What does this comparison reveal about the way Morrison views her work?

7. **Compare and Contrast Authors' Perspectives** Consider the aspects of African-American culture Morrison tries to capture in her novels. What artistic goals does Morrison share with the writers of the Harlem Renaissance? How does her vision of black culture compare with theirs? Explain your answer.

8. **Evaluate Author's Purpose** Literary criticism has three main purposes: to inform readers, to express the writer's opinions, and to persuade readers to accept those opinions. Based on your reading, which of these purposes was Morrison trying to achieve with her essay? Which, if any, did she achieve? Support your answer with details.

Literary Criticism

9. **Critical Interpretations** Consider the qualities Morrison identifies as characteristic of African-American art forms. Which of the Harlem Renaissance works you read would meet Morrison's criteria for African-American art? Cite details in your answer.

Perspectives on the Harlem Renaissance

Literary historian Richard Gray states the following about the writers of the Harlem Renaissance.

> *"[W]hat is notable about them is how they explored different literary forms to express the condition of African Americans in their times. Facing a racial experience the determining feature of which was that it was mixed and conflicted, they were prepared individually to confront and collectively to debate the question of just how their experience should be turned into literature."*

Because the experiences of the Harlem Renaissance writers were "mixed and conflicted," their works naturally examined different aspects of African-American life.

Writing to Analyze

Imagine that you are a publisher who is planning to print the works beginning on page 840 in a slim anthology called *The Harlem Renaissance*. You'd like to organize the works into thematic groupings to help your readers gain a sense of some of the issues and concerns that these writers, despite their varied experiences, collectively held in common. With a partner, work together to create a table of contents for your book, with the works grouped under thematic headings, such as "Social Protest" or "Reflections on Heritage." Then write a brief explanation of why you grouped the works as you did.

Consider

- which selections deal with similar topics or themes (some selections may explore several themes, giving you the option to group them in more than one way)
- what overarching phrases might best express those topics or themes
- what, specifically, from each selection led you to place it in its particular grouping

Writers Jessie Fauset, Langston Hughes, and Zora Neale Hurston

Extension Online

RESEARCH Go online to find two additional works by Harlem Renaissance writers to add to your anthology. You may choose works by writers already represented in your anthology, or works by other Harlem Renaissance writers, such as Paul Laurence Dunbar or Helene Johnson. Give an **oral reading** for the class, and explain where you would place the works in your anthology.

Jump at the Sun

Documentary on ● **MediaSmart** DVD

How do you DOCUMENT *a life?*

KEY IDEA Think about how you would tell the story of your life. What events would you include to help someone understand the essential you? What would you leave out? Filmmakers face similar questions when they make a biographical **documentary.** The many details of a person's life must be boiled down to the key events that influenced and shaped that person. As you view *Jump at the Sun,* notice the details chosen to tell Zora Neale Hurston's life story.

Background

A Vibrant Life Zora Neale Hurston lived her life fully by following her mother's advice. "Mama exhorted her children at every opportunity to 'jump at de sun,'" Hurston explained. "We might not land on the sun, but at least we would get off the ground."

Hurston was a passionate woman who celebrated her role as a black female writer at a time when that was not an easy role to play. She was confident and proud of her heritage, making no apologies for who she was or what she did.

Hurston's dazzling personality and the dynamic times she lived through made her an ideal subject for a documentary film. Thus, the idea for *Jump at the Sun* was born. The filmmakers faced a challenge, though—Hurston died nearly a half-century ago, and film footage of her was not available. The filmmakers, therefore, had to find a way to bring her strong personality to life for the viewer, relying primarily on photographs, paintings, music, and readings from Hurston's own work. The filmmakers' challenge was to shape this material into a coherent and interesting film that tells the story of her life and work.

Jump at the Sun imparts to the viewer both the facts—the actual events that made up Hurston's life—and the exuberance of her personality. As you study the film, you'll explore the techniques used to bring life to the Harlem Renaissance and one of its most spirited writers.

Zora Neale Hurston

Media Literacy: Documentary

A **documentary** is a nonfiction film that often presents social, political, or historical subject matter. Prominent people make good subjects, as they allow the filmmaker to explore both an interesting life and its greater social context.

Feature filmmakers and other storytellers often repeat an old adage: "Show, don't tell." Many documentary filmmakers follow the same principle, presenting their material as a story that unfolds before the viewer's eyes. The use of **primary sources,** which include photographs, film clips, letters, and eyewitness accounts, helps to immerse the viewer in the subject's world.

DOCUMENTARY TOOLS AND TECHNIQUES

Visual

- **Footage** is recorded material used to reveal information about a subject. It includes film clips, news reports, photographs, interviews, and text. Footage can be used to create a visual and emotional impression of the times.
- **Camera movement**—such as zooming in from a long shot to a close-up, and tracking shots, which move the camera parallel to the object being filmed—can give a dynamic feel to a still picture.

> ▶ **RACE RIOTERS FIRE AND SHOOT OR HA DEAD ESTIMATE**
>
> MANY BODIES IN THE RUINS | *More Sto*

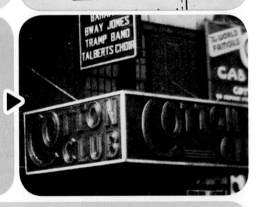

Sound

- **Voice-over narration** is the voice of an unseen speaker that can be heard in a documentary.
- The style and tempo of the **music** will generally match the mood of the story and signal transitions to different settings or time periods.
- **Sound effects** are often used to help re-create a scene. For example, filmmakers may add crowd and traffic noise over a picture of a city.

STRATEGIES FOR VIEWING

As you view a documentary, consider the filmmakers' purpose in creating the film. Realize that documentaries reflect the point of view of the filmmaker. They do not always represent objective truth.

- Notice the different types of **footage** used in a documentary. Pay special attention to the use of **primary sources.** Note how they help to bring the story to life by using the "show, don't tell" principle.
- Listen to the different types of **voice-over narration.** In this documentary, the main narrator provides the facts of the subject's life story. The second narrator evokes Hurston's personality with a lively reading of her work.
- Consider how the **visual** and **sound techniques** work together. Think about why the particular footage was chosen to accompany each type of voice-over narration. Notice how the music changes with each major shift in the story.

MediaSmart DVD
- **Film:** *Jump at the Sun*
- **Genre:** Documentary
- **Voice-Over Narrator:** Veronica Chambers
- **Running Time:** 9 minutes

Jump at the Sun

Filmmakers face a difficult challenge when they set out to tell a true story. They must carefully choose which details are necessary to bring the tale to life. Consider the documentary techniques you examined as you view the Zora Neale Hurston biography. Think about how each element contributes to the story being told. You may need to watch the documentary more than once in order to analyze it properly.

NOW VIEW

FIRST VIEWING: Comprehension

1. **Recall** What poet's work so influenced Hurston that she was moved to devote herself to literature?
2. **Clarify** What were Hurston's feelings about whether African-American writers have a duty to write about race relations?

CLOSE VIEWING: Media Literacy

3. **Identify Filmmakers' Purpose** Documentaries are made for a variety of purposes. For example, they can educate, inform, or influence opinion. What do you think the makers of *Jump at the Sun* wanted to achieve? Explain.
4. **Analyze the Voice-Over** The documentary is narrated by the writer Veronica Chambers. Why do you think the filmmakers chose a young writer to narrate the story of Hurston's life?
5. **Analyze Visuals** What types of images are shown to depict Hurston's hometown? Why do you think this type of footage was chosen?
6. **Evaluate Technique** In your opinion, which of the techniques in *Jump at the Sun* is the most effective in conveying Hurston's personality? Cite evidence from the film to support your opinion. Think about
   - the use of such **primary sources** as photographs, film clips, and the actual text read from Hurston's *Dust Tracks on a Road*
   - **music** that suggests the 1920s
   - the two types of **voice-over narration**

Write or Discuss

Compare the Texts Zora Neale Hurston was known for her unique personality. Think about the most memorable parts of Hurston's essay "How It Feels to Be Colored Me." Now consider the ways Hurston is depicted in the documentary. Write a paragraph that compares the Zora portrayed in the film with the Zora you know from the text. Think about

- the tone evident in the essay and in the documentary
- the quotes from Hurston's work that are included in the film, and the style in which they're read
- the selection of images and music in the film

Produce Your Own Media

Plan a Documentary Imagine you are making a documentary about someone you know well. Gather the materials you'll need to film your documentary and present them to the class. They should include **primary source material** from your subject's life, **interviews** with friends or family members, and a script for the **voice-over narration.**

HERE'S HOW Write interview questions about your subject for two or three friends or family members to answer. Write a script for the voice-over narration that gives a brief overview of the life you're describing. Collect your primary source material. Consider these suggestions:

- Choose photographs or home video footage.
- Find out about the people or events that have had the greatest impact on your subject's life. Find ways to represent them visually.
- Decide what music might be appropriate. Match it to the events you'll cover.

Further Exploration

Create a Shooting Plan Now that you've gathered the materials for your documentary, plan how you will shoot it. Decide on the best image to start your film. Plan where you'll use the interviews you conducted, and over what images the voice-over narration will play. Think about when you'll play the music you've chosen. Remember that your film should both inform the audience and keep them interested throughout. Write a description of your film that includes the order in which you'll present your footage, the sounds that will accompany each segment, and the types of shots you'll use.

 MEDIA TOOLS

For help with creating a documentary, visit the **Media Center** at **ClassZone.com.**

Tech Tip

If a video camera is available, film your documentary.

Richard Cory
Miniver Cheevy
Poetry by Edwin Arlington Robinson

Edwin Arlington Robinson
1869–1935

NOTABLE QUOTE
"He knows much of what men paint themselves would blister in the light of what they are."

Failure is a familiar subject in the poetry of Edwin Arlington Robinson, and one the artist knew well. Robinson wrote poetry for years before achieving recognition, and he witnessed family members suffer one personal defeat after another.

A Difficult Youth His father's financial struggles forced Robinson to curtail his studies at Harvard University. The family's fortunes continued to decline and Robinson's mother died of diphtheria in 1896. In addition, he lost both of his brothers to fatal addictions.

Devotion to His Craft Despite his tragic past and his own struggles with alcoholism, Robinson devoted his life to his craft. Over time he gained a reputation as one of the country's most accomplished narrative poets.

Reflections of the Past Robinson's best known poems explore the inner lives of the citizens of Tilbury Town, a fictional community modeled on Robinson's hometown of Gardiner, Maine. Many poems grew out of the tragic experiences of his family and childhood acquaintances. Often, the poems focus on individuals who are brought low because of their own personal failings and the town's repressive, materialistic culture.

Lucinda Matlock
Poetry by Edgar Lee Masters

Edgar Lee Masters
1868–1950

NOTABLE QUOTE
"How shall the soul of man be larger than the life he has lived?"

When his brilliant portrait of rural life, *Spoon River Anthology*, first appeared in 1915, Edgar Lee Masters became a literary sensation. Both the general public and renowned critics embraced the book, making it an American classic.

The Making of a Poet The book grew out of Masters's memories of growing up in the central Illinois towns of Lewiston and Petersburg. Living on his grandparents' farm in Petersburg and in the semi-industrialized Lewiston, Masters acquired both an appreciation and a distaste for rural culture. While he admired the hard work and resilience of rural folk, he despised their small-mindedness and bigotry. Eventually Masters left rural Illinois for the big city, residing in Chicago and New York City.

Literary Masterpiece Masters remains most famous for his *Spoon River Anthology*. In this book, 244 deceased inhabitants of the fictional town of Spoon River deliver monologues in which they bare their souls. The cast of characters is varied, ranging from prostitutes and thieves to librarians and Masters's own grandmother Lucinda, the model for "Lucinda Matlock."

Author Online
For more on these poets, visit the **Literature Center** at ClassZone.com.

LITERARY ANALYSIS: CHARACTERIZATION IN NARRATIVE POETRY

While most modernist poets turned their efforts to lyric poetry, Edward Arlington Robinson and Edgar Lee Masters continued to develop the tradition of narrative poetry, often telling stories of interesting characters in the context of their communities. Like fiction, **narrative poetry** tells a story using elements of plot, character, and setting. To develop character, poets may adapt methods of **characterization** typically used in fiction.

- physical description of the character, including vivid **imagery**
- the character's own actions, words, thoughts, and feelings
- comments, thoughts, or actions of other characters
- direct comments about the character by the poem's speaker

As you read these poems, pay attention to the methods used by the poet to develop the characters.

Review: **Meter**

READING SKILL: ANALYZE SPEAKER'S ATTITUDE

In many poems, the **speaker** has a persona that is distinct from the poet. It is the speaker's **attitude** that shapes our view of the poem's subject. In each of the following poems, a speaker delivers a character sketch; in one case, the speaker is describing herself. By noticing the details and phrases the speaker uses to describe the character, we can learn about his or her attitude not only toward the character but toward life.

To analyze the speaker's attitude toward the character in each poem, use a chart like the one shown. As you read, jot down the details and phrases from each poem that reflect that attitude. One example has been filled in for you.

Details and Phrases Reflecting Speaker's Attitude		
"Richard Cory"	"Miniver Cheevy"	"Lucinda Matlock"
"He was a gentleman from sole to crown"		

Explore the Key Idea

What makes for a FULL LIFE?

KEY IDEA Everyone wants to be happy, but happiness comes more easily to some people than to others. What is the secret? Some seek happiness in close, loving relationships. Others pursue their dreams and try to remain true to their inner voice. Still others strive for the comforts of material success and prosperity. The following poems portray characters who have met with varying degrees of success in their search for **contentment**.

DISCUSS With a partner, make a list of some different ways in which people seek happiness. Which are the most likely to succeed? Which are the least likely? After discussing these questions, present your conclusions to the class.

RICHARD CORY

Edwin Arlington Robinson

Whenever Richard Cory went down town,
We people on the pavement looked at him:
He was a gentleman from sole to crown,
Clean favored,[1] and imperially slim.

5 And he was always quietly arrayed,
And he was always human when he talked;
But still he fluttered pulses when he said,
"Good-morning," and he glittered when he walked. **A**

And he was rich—yes, richer than a king—
10 And admirably schooled in every grace:[2]
In fine,[3] we thought that he was everything
To make us wish that we were in his place.

So on we worked, and waited for the light,
And went without the meat, and cursed the bread;
15 And Richard Cory, one calm summer night,
Went home and put a bullet through his head. **B**

A CHARACTERIZATION
Reread lines 1–8. Describe Richard Cory's appearance and manners. What do you think the speaker means by "he fluttered pulses" and "he glittered when he walked"?

B SPEAKER'S ATTITUDE
Reread lines 11–14. What contrast does the speaker draw between Richard Cory and the townspeople? How do they seem to regard him?

1. **clean favored:** having a tidy appearance.
2. **schooled in every grace:** extremely well-mannered and cultured.
3. **in fine:** in short.

Sir Philip Sassoon (1923), John Singer Sargent. Oil on canvas, 95.2 cm x 57.8 cm. Tate Gallery, London. © Tate Gallery, London/Art Resource, New York.

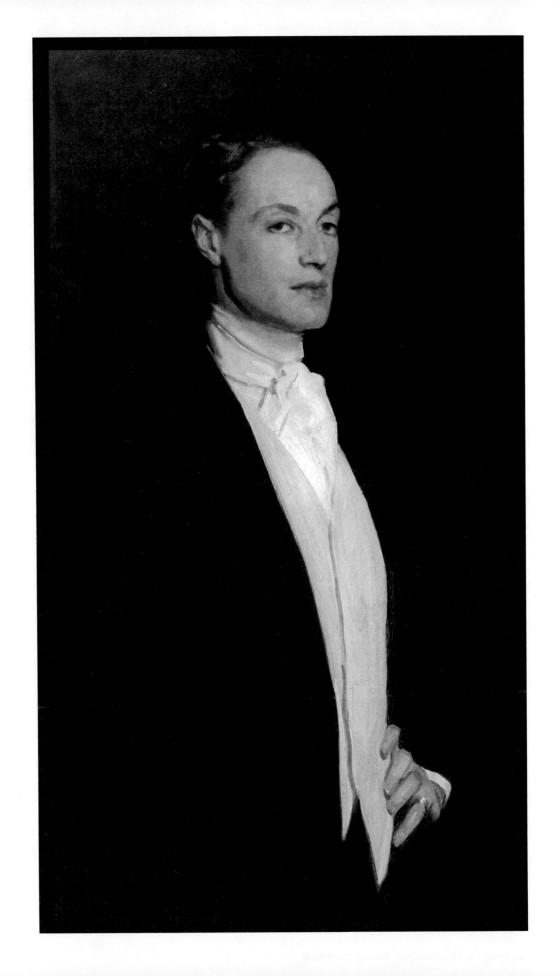

Miniver Cheevy

Edwin Arlington Robinson

Reading in a Study, Walt Louderback. Oil on plywood, 76.2 cm × 59.7 cm. Pri[…]
collection. Photo ©Bridgeman Art Library.

Miniver Cheevy, child of scorn,
    Grew lean while he assailed[1] the seasons;
He wept that he was ever born,
    And he had reasons.

5 Miniver loved the days of old
    When swords were bright and steeds
        were prancing;
The vision of a warrior bold
    Would set him dancing. **C**

Miniver sighed for what was not,
10   And dreamed, and rested from his labors;
He dreamed of Thebes and Camelot,
    And Priam's neighbors.[2]

Miniver mourned the ripe renown
    That made so many a name so fragrant;
15 He mourned Romance, now on the town,
    And Art, a vagrant.

Miniver loved the Medici,[3]
    Albeit[4] he had never seen one;
He would have sinned incessantly
20   Could he have been one. **D**

C METER
Reread lines 1–8. In each stanza, which line has a meter that stands out from the others? What emphasis is achieved by this change in **rhythm?**

D CHARACTERIZATION
Reread lines 9–20. Identify the primary means of characterization in these lines. What is the main **trait** conveyed here?

---

1. **assailed:** attacked violently, in this case with words.

2. **Thebes** (thēbz) . . . **Camelot** . . . **Priam's** (prī'əmz) **neighbors:** Thebes was an ancient Greek city, the setting of many famous legends; Camelot was the site of King Arthur's legendary court; Priam's neighbors were participants in the Trojan War, during which Priam was king of Troy.

3. **Medici** (měd'ə-chē): a powerful Italian family that funded the arts and ruled Florence, sometimes with cruel and immoral leaders, during the Renaissance.

4. **albeit** (ôl-bē'ĭt): even though.

Miniver cursed the commonplace
    And eyed a khaki suit with loathing;
He missed the medieval grace
    Of iron clothing. **E**

25 Miniver scorned the gold he sought,
    But sore annoyed was he without it;
Miniver thought, and thought, and thought,
    And thought about it.

    Miniver Cheevy, born too late,
30   Scratched his head and kept on thinking;
Miniver coughed, and called it fate,
    And kept on drinking. **F**

E SPEAKER'S ATTITUDE
Identify the **irony** in lines 23–24. What does this irony suggest about the speaker's attitude toward Miniver's love of the medieval?

F METER
How does the last line of the poem change your understanding of Miniver? Recall your earlier analysis of the poem's meter, and explain its effect in this stanza.

Literary Analysis

1. **Recall** What is the townspeople's initial impression of Richard Cory?

2. **Recall** Why does Miniver Cheevy claim to be unhappy?

3. **Compare Texts** What is similar about the ways the two poems end? In each case, how do the last two lines change your view of the character?

LUCINDA MATLOCK

Edgar Lee Masters

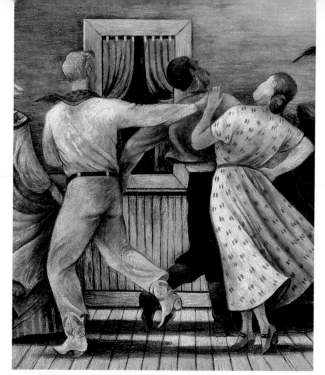

Detail of *Cowboy Dance* (mural study, Anson, Texas, post office) (1941), Jenne Magafan. Oil on fiberboard. Photo © Smithsonian American Art Museum, Washington, D.C./Art Resource, New York.

I went to the dances at Chandlerville,
And played snap-out[1] at Winchester.
One time we changed partners,
Driving home in the moonlight of middle June,
5 And then I found Davis.
We were married and lived together for seventy years,
Enjoying, working, raising the twelve children,
Eight of whom we lost
Ere I had reached the age of sixty.
10 I spun, I wove, I kept the house, I nursed the sick,
I made the garden, and for holiday
Rambled over the fields where sang the larks,
And by Spoon River gathering many a shell,
And many a flower and medicinal weed—
15 Shouting to the wooded hills, singing to the green valleys. **G**
At ninety-six I had lived enough, that is all,
And passed to a sweet repose.[2]
What is this I hear of sorrow and weariness,
Anger, discontent and drooping hopes?
20 Degenerate[3] sons and daughters,
Life is too strong for you—
It takes life to love Life. **H**

---

1. **snap-out:** a game in which players join hands in a line, then run about trying to shake off those at the end of the line.

2. **repose:** here, the peaceful sleep of death.

3. **degenerate** (dĭ-jĕn′ər-ĭt): showing a decline in vigor or moral strength.

ANALYZE VISUALS
What qualities do you sense in the dancers portrayed in this painting? Do you find them to have anything in common with Lucinda Matlock? Explain.

G CHARACTERIZATION
Reread lines 1–15. What does the speaker's behavior reveal about her?

H SPEAKER'S ATTITUDE
Whom do you think the speaker is addressing in lines 18–22? How does she seem to feel about them? Explain.

Comprehension

1. **Recall** What pleasures and sorrows did Lucinda Matlock experience in her life?

2. **Clarify** Overall, was Lucinda content with the life she lived?

Literary Analysis

3. **Compare Characters** Richard Cory, Miniver Cheevy, and Lucinda Matlock have found widely varying degrees of **contentment.** In your view, what is the primary reason for each character's happiness or unhappiness? Give details to support your answer.

4. **Examine Characterization in Narrative Poetry** What details does Robinson use to reveal each of the following character traits of Richard Cory and Miniver Cheevy? What impact does this characterization have on your sympathy or distaste for the characters? Explain.

   - Richard's perfectionism
   - Richard's self-restraint
   - Miniver's laziness
   - Miniver's romanticism

5. **Analyze Speaker's Attitude** Review the chart you created as you read. What attitude does the speaker of each poem express toward the main character? Would you say that the speaker is sympathetic to or critical of the character described? In each case, what does this attitude tell you about the speaker's own personality and values? Give evidence to support your answer.

6. **Evaluate Author's Style** Robinson's poems use **rhyme, meter,** and **humor** in a playful way that is somewhat at odds with the grim revelations made in the last lines. How does this playfulness shape the impact of these final lines? Explain whether or not you find this an effective technique, and why.

Literary Criticism

7. **Critical Interpretations** Literary critic Bill Peschel has said that in Robinson's Tilbury Town poems, "the town's Puritan ethic, portrayed as repressive and critical, combined with the materialistic aspects of society, conspires to bring down its citizens." Do you find evidence of this repressive Puritan ethic in the attitudes of the speakers in the Robinson poems? Explain why or why not.

Chicago
Grass

Poetry by Carl Sandburg

Carl Sandburg

1878–1967

When Carl Sandburg died in 1967, President Lyndon Johnson was among the first to sing his praises. "Carl Sandburg," the president declared, "was more than the voice of America, more than the poet of its strength and genius. He was America." Johnson's feelings were not unique. Americans everywhere cherished Sandburg, believing his verse celebrated their spirit and speech as well as championed their cause.

A Hobo at Heart Sandburg grew up in America's heartland in Galesburg, Illinois. From his Swedish immigrant parents, August and Clara Sandburg, he learned to value hard work and education. His family's poverty, however, forced Sandburg to curtail his schooling at 13 in order to go to work. He labored at various jobs, ranging from shining shoes to delivering milk. When he turned 19, he left home to explore the American West, becoming one of the many hoboes who hopped freight trains in order to travel free.

Social Activist When the Spanish-American War erupted in 1898, Sandburg served for eight months in Puerto Rico. After his return, he studied at Lombard College but left without receiving a diploma. Overtaken once again by wanderlust, he rambled about the country, soaking up America's sights and songs. When he ran out of money, he returned to the Midwest, writing for journals in Chicago and joining the lecture circuit. His skill as an orator eventually earned him a job in Milwaukee as an organizer for the Wisconsin Social-Democratic Party. While living there, he married Lillian Steichen, who, like Sandburg, was committed to fighting social injustice.

Literary Celebrity In 1912, the couple moved to Chicago, where Sandburg became a reporter, editorial writer, and columnist for the *Chicago Daily News.* Two years later, his verse began to appear in *Poetry,* a prominent literary magazine. With the publication of his poetry collections *Chicago Poems, Cornhuskers,* and *Smoke and Steel,* Sandburg gained a reputation as the poet of the common people. The poetry readings he gave further heightened his popularity. Interspersing poetry with commentary and folk songs sung in his melodious baritone, Sandburg enthralled audiences wherever he went.

Sandburg won a number of awards and honors, including the 1951 Pulitzer Prize for poetry for *Complete Poems* and the 1939 Pulitzer Prize for history for *Abraham Lincoln: The War Years,* the last volume in a six-volume biography.

● LITERARY ANALYSIS: TONE AND DICTION

Some poems exhibit a subtle tone that is difficult to perceive and nearly impossible to describe. Others practically break forth with trumpets in the first stanza. Whether gently or boldly, poets generally convey tone, or attitude toward the subject, through **diction** (word choice and syntax) and choice of details. In the first lines of "Chicago," Carl Sandburg's diction creates a tone of admiration for a hard-working city:

Hog Butcher for the World,
Tool Maker, Stacker of Wheat,
Player with Railroads and the Nation's Freight Handler;
Stormy, husky, brawling,
City of the Big Shoulders. . . .

Read these two poems by Sandburg aloud to help you identify the tone of each. If you read with emotion, your tone of voice may provide you with clues to the poem's tone.

Review: **Personification**

● READING SKILL: SYNTHESIZE DETAILS

In "Chicago," Sandburg presents a long list, or catalog, of qualities, images, and statements about the city. It is the accumulation of these listed items that creates such a strong portrait of the city. As you read, pay attention to each item and allow yourself to absorb the ideas and images presented. After you read the poem, you'll be asked to **synthesize** numerous **details** into a single, coherent impression.

Would you rather live in the CITY or the COUNTRY?

KEY IDEA "If you would be known, and not know, vegetate in a village; if you would know, and not be known, live in a city," wrote the poet Reverend Charles Caleb Colton. What benefits and drawbacks do you associate with city living? with country living? What kind of **place** inspires you the most? In the poems that follow, Carl Sandburg explores different settings that have affected him.

QUICKWRITE Think about a city or a place in the country where you would like to live. What aspects of this setting particularly appeal to you? How might living there enrich your life? Spend a few minutes writing in response to these questions.

Chicago

Carl Sandburg

Hog Butcher for the World,
Tool Maker, Stacker of Wheat,
Player with Railroads and the Nation's Freight Handler;
Stormy, husky, brawling,
5   City of the Big Shoulders: **Ⓐ**

They tell me you are wicked and I believe them, for I
    have seen your painted women under the gas lamps
    luring the farm boys.
And they tell me you are crooked and I answer: Yes, it
    is true I have seen the gunman kill and go free to
    kill again.
And they tell me you are brutal and my reply is: On the
    faces of women and children I have seen the marks
    of wanton[1] hunger.
And having answered so I turn once more to those who
    sneer at this my city, and I give them back the sneer
    and say to them:
10 Come and show me another city with lifted head singing
    so proud to be alive and coarse and strong and cunning. **Ⓑ**
Flinging magnetic curses amid the toil of piling job on
    job, here is a tall bold slugger set vivid against the
    little soft cities;
Fierce as a dog with tongue lapping for action, cunning
    as a savage pitted against the wilderness,
        Bareheaded,
        Shoveling,

Ⓐ SYNTHESIZE DETAILS
The brief descriptive phrases in lines 1–5, also known as **epithets,** are almost like nicknames; in fact, some of them have come into common use. What do they tell you about the city's economy and industry?

Ⓑ TONE AND DICTION
Lines 6–8 contain harsh words such as *wicked* and *brutal.* Identify the language in lines 9–10 that counters this harshness. What does it reveal about Sandburg's feelings toward the city as well as its critics?

---

1. **wanton:** without limitation.

South of the Loop (1936), Charles Turzak. Color woodcut, Image 10²/₃″ × 11³/₄″, sheet 11¹/₄″ × 15″. Mary and Leigh Block Museum of Art, Northwestern University, 1992.73 © Joan Turzak Van Hees.

15   Wrecking,
           Planning,
           Building, breaking, rebuilding,

Under the smoke, dust all over his mouth, laughing with
    white teeth,
Under the terrible burden of destiny laughing as a young
    man laughs,
20 Laughing even as an ignorant fighter laughs who has
    never lost a battle,
Bragging and laughing that under his wrist is the pulse, and
    under his ribs the heart of the people,
                      Laughing!
Laughing the stormy, husky, brawling laughter of
    Youth, half-naked, sweating, proud to be Hog
    Butcher, Tool Maker, Stacker of Wheat, Player with
    Railroads and Freight Handler to the Nation.

ANALYZE VISUALS
What qualities of the city are emphasized by both the horizontal and the vertical lines in this woodcut? Refer to specific areas of the print when giving your answer.

Grass

Carl Sandburg

Pile the bodies high at Austerlitz and Waterloo.[1]
Shovel them under and let me work—
       I am the grass; I cover all. **C**

And pile them high at Gettysburg
5 And pile them high at Ypres and Verdun.[2]
Shovel them under and let me work.
Two years, ten years, and passengers ask the conductor:
       What place is this?
       Where are we now?

10   I am the grass.
       Let me work. **D**

---

1. **Austerlitz** (ô′stər-lĭts′) **and Waterloo:** sites of significant battles during the Napoleonic Wars (1800–1815).

2. **Ypres** (ē′prə) **and Verdun** (vər-dŭn′): sites of significant battles during World War I.

C PERSONIFICATION
Reread lines 1–3. Sandburg uses personification in establishing the speaker for this poem. Who is the speaker and what is its role in these scenes?

D TONE AND DICTION
Identify several examples of **repetition** in this poem. What **tone** is established by the repetition of these words and/or phrases?

Le Plateau de Bolante (1917), Félix Vallotton. Oil on canvas. Musée d'Histoire Contemporaine, Paris. © Musée d'Histoire Contemporaine-BDIC.

Comprehension

1. **Recall** What negative aspects of Chicago are presented in lines 6–8?
2. **Clarify** What scenes are referred to in "Grass"?

Literary Analysis

3. **Synthesize Details** Think about the **litany,** or list, of images and ideas in "Chicago." Based on the accumulation of detail in this poem, what general statement can you make about the people who live and work in the city?

4. **Compare Tone and Diction** Identify the tone of each poem. Are the tones similar or different? Cite at least three examples of diction that reveal tone in each poem.

5. **Evaluate Personification** Sandburg uses personification in "Chicago" as well as in "Grass," giving human characteristics to objects, animals, or ideas. Describe the figure who personifies Chicago. What words and phrases capture his most important traits?

6. **Analyze Style** What poetic or other stylistic devices underscore Sandburg's characterization of Chicago as a brash, brawling, vibrant city? Consider such elements as line and stanza shape, rhythm, and other formal conventions. Be specific, citing examples from the text.

7. **Interpret Setting and Theme** Both "Chicago" and "Grass" depict a strong sense of place, each containing some contradiction. For each poem, identify this contradiction and use it to help you formulate a theme statement. Give evidence to support your answers.

8. **Compare and Contrast Writers** Carl Sandburg was greatly influenced by the poetry of Walt Whitman (see page 508). Compare and contrast the two poets in terms of the following points, citing specific lines from their work. Can you see Whitman's influence in Sandburg's poems? Explain why or why not.

   - use of **catalog** or **litany**
   - **tone** and **diction**
   - use of **repetition** and **parallelism**
   - ideas about America

Literary Criticism

9. **Critical Interpretations** Imagist poet William Carlos Williams once criticized Sandburg's poetry as "formless." Even some of Sandburg's supporters conceded that this was true. Do you agree or disagree? Cite evidence to support your response, also explaining whether you would count yourself among his supporters or his critics, and why.

Modernism

In 1860, most Americans lived their entire lives without using a powered machine of any sort. By 1940, nearly everyone used or owned radios, cars, telephones, or appliances. With the Industrial Revolution, the modern world had come into being. It was a world of contradictions: disillusion and hope, self-doubt and self-discovery, crumbling traditions and explosive creative energy. In response to these forces, there arose a literary and cultural movement known as **modernism.**

Making It New

Poet Ezra Pound is credited with bringing the techniques of literary modernism to the United States in the early 20th century. He urged his literary colleagues to "make it new": to experiment with literary forms, subjects, themes, and structure. The result of this experimentation was a diverse flowering of literary achievement, which became known as the modernist movement.

Experimental photograph of Ezra Pound, 1916

Though modernism as a literary movement had its seeds in the late 19th century, it did not flourish until the early decades of the 20th century and throughout World War II. Prose writers Ernest Hemingway, F. Scott Fitzgerald, William Faulkner, and Katherine Anne Porter and poets Ezra Pound, T. S. Eliot, H. D. (Hilda Doolittle), and William Carlos Williams were part of a generation of writers who created new ways of writing to respond to the post–World War I realities and the loss of stability felt so strongly between 1914 and 1945.

The Defining Features of Modernism

Modernism comprises a diversity of individual styles. Yet there are some common defining features of the literature that show a distinct break with the past.

- Modernists rejected traditional **subject matter** and **themes.** Instead of love, many modernists wrote of the inability to commit to, or even communicate with, others. For most modernists, nothing lasted, and therefore themes frequently focused on impermanence and change.

- Instead of "heroes" who stood for the values of society, modernists focused on alienated individuals. The **protagonist** of T. S. Eliot's poem "The Love Song of J. Alfred Prufrock" (page 930) is no heroic explorer but an insecure, lonely man who is consumed by self-doubt.

- Modernists revealed important emotions and ideas with **understatement** and **irony**. They no longer felt confident directly stating universal truths in their works as the romantics and transcendentalists had before them.

- Rather than directly state meaning, modernists typically used **symbols** and **images** to suggest meaning. The speaker in Frost's "Acquainted with the Night" (page 898) never admits he's lonely or sad; the images, however, show this.

Although modernist writers often describe their characters' actions, feelings, and thoughts, they do not interpret them for the reader. A comparison of Ernest Hemingway's writing with Willa Cather's can help you see the difference between a modernist work and a more traditional one. Note how Cather's narrator in "A Wagner Matinee" (page 694) directly explains the significance of his relationship with his aunt.

> I owed to this woman most of the good that ever came my way in my boyhood, and had a reverential affection for her. During the years when I was riding herd for my uncle, my aunt, after cooking three meals . . . and putting the six children to bed, would often stand until midnight at her ironing-board with me at the kitchen table beside her, hearing me recite Latin declensions and conjugations, gently shaking me when my drowsy head sank down over a page of irregular verbs.
>
> —**Willa Cather, "A Wagner Matinee"**

In this excerpt from "In Another Country" (page 970), Hemingway's narrator, in contrast, does not explain the emotional significance of his relationships to the other characters, and the reader is left to infer how the characters feel about each other. Hemingway once explained such omissions this way: "I always try to write on the principle of the iceberg. There is seven-eighths of it under water for every part that shows."

> There were three boys who came each day who were about the same age I was. They were all three from Milan, and one of them was to be a lawyer, and one was to be a painter, and one had intended to be a soldier, and after we were finished with the machines, sometimes we walked back together to the Café Cova, which was next door to the Scala.
>
> —**Ernest Hemingway, "In Another Country"**

AMERICANS IN PARIS

French painter Henri Matisse was an inspiration to American writers in Paris.

At loose ends after World War I, many disillusioned Americans remained in Europe, often settling in the Left Bank district of Paris, where they were joined by numerous writers and artists. Ezra Pound, Ernest Hemingway, Gertrude Stein, F. Scott Fitzgerald, James Joyce, and George Orwell were just some of the many writers who lived for a time in Paris during the 1920s. Many of the expatriate community saw it as a place where they could be more open to life—in a way that was impossible in the United States. For others, it served for inspiration: The simplicity of both Ernest Hemingway's and Gertrude Stein's styles is said to have been inspired by the art of French painters Paul Cezanne and Henri Matisse. Ironically, Paris became known as the place where American literary style was cultivated and crafted.

Close Read

In Cather's passage, what details explain the aunt's character and the narrator's feelings about her? What do the details in Hemingway's passage reveal about his narrator?

Selected Poetry

by Robert Frost

NOTABLE QUOTE

"Poetry is a way of taking life by the throat."

FYI

Did you know that Robert Frost...

- was unable to read a poem at John F. Kennedy's inauguration because of bright sunlight and so recited one from memory?

- won 44 honorary degrees from prestigious universities but never earned a college degree himself?

Author Online

For more on Robert Frost, visit the **Literature Center** at ClassZone.com.

Robert Frost

1874–1963

Robert Frost once remarked that his life's goal was to write "a few poems it will be hard to get rid of." Undoubtedly, he succeeded. Frost's best poems lodge themselves in the reader's imagination and refuse to go away. As a result, Frost is one of the most beloved American poets.

Awakening to Poetry Although Frost is associated with rural New England, he spent his first 11 years in San Francisco. Following his father's death in 1885, Frost's mother brought her two children east, eventually settling in the industrial city of Lawrence, Massachusetts. As a boy, Frost developed a passion for baseball and poetry. By the time he graduated from high school, he knew he would be a poet.

Aimless Years Frost's early manhood was nonetheless filled with change. He enrolled at both Dartmouth College and Harvard University but did not remain at either place, tiring of the routine of college life. For several years he drifted working as a mill hand, a school teacher, and a reporter. One stabilizing event in his life was his marriage in 1895 to Elinor White, his high school sweetheart.

Voice of New England In 1900, Frost abandoned the indoor life of teaching for the outdoor life of farming. During the day Frost worked his poultry farm, and at night he wrote. The 11 years Frost spent farming were some of his most creative. Inspired by the rugged New Hampshire countryside and its plain-spoken inhabitants, Frost wrote poems that probed the mysteries of nature and the human heart.

Literary Acclaim At the age of 38, Frost moved his family to England, where he could "write and be poor." Less than two months later, a London publisher accepted the manuscript of *A Boy's Will* (1913) for publication. By the time Frost returned to the United States in 1915, he was hailed as a leading American poet.

In 1924, Frost's collection *New Hampshire* won a Pulitzer Prize, the first of four that he would receive. His public success, however, was overshadowed by personal tragedy. Between 1934 and 1940, Frost lost a daughter, his wife, and a son; another daughter was institutionalized for mental illness. As a result, his later poems often convey a bleak outlook on life.

LITERARY ANALYSIS: FROST'S STYLE

Some of Robert Frost's poems seem so simple, yet they move people deeply. Why? It certainly has something to do with his powerful choice of theme and subject matter, but it's also a matter of his unique **style**—the distinctive way in which he uses words and poetic devices. For one thing, he makes skillful use of traditional rhyme, meter, and stanza form. He also uses other elements in a distinctive way.

- **Diction**—word choice and syntax, or word order
- **Imagery**—the descriptive phrases that appeal to the senses
- **Mood**—the overall feeling or atmosphere that a writer creates for the reader (often created with imagery)

Notice these elements in the opening lines of "'Out, Out—'":

The buzz saw snarled and rattled in the yard
And made dust and dropped stove-length sticks of wood,
Sweet-scented stuff when the breeze drew across it.

As you read these poems by Frost, pay close attention to his diction and his use of imagery and mood.

READING SKILL: RECOGNIZE AMBIGUITY

Many people approach poems like riddles; they are certain that the true meaning must lie in a single interpretation. This approach fails to take into account the **ambiguity** that lends richness and beauty to so many poems. Ambiguous works of literature contain more than one meaning; they are open to various, even opposing, interpretations, as in the opening lines of "Nothing Gold Can Stay."

Nature's first green is gold,
Her hardest hue to hold.

Are these lines referring to a golden hue of green, or are they making the point that nature's first green is precious, like gold? You don't have to choose between these meanings; skilled readers of poetry recognize ambiguity and live with it, even enjoy it, as they read and consider a poem. As you read, record different interpretations of lines from each poem.

"Acquainted with the Night"	"Nothing Gold Can Stay"	"'Out, Out—'"
	lines 1–2: • *golden shade of green* • *green is precious, like gold*	

What does it mean to be ALONE?

KEY IDEA Does **solitude** make you lonely? Or is it precious to you? It's a powerful idea, being alone. Some people can't get enough of it, and others have it in painful abundance. In any event, it offers opportunity for reflection. In "Acquainted with the Night," Robert Frost explores one person's emotional reaction to being alone.

QUICKWRITE What images and feelings does the word *solitude* evoke in you? Write a short poem describing a moment alone.

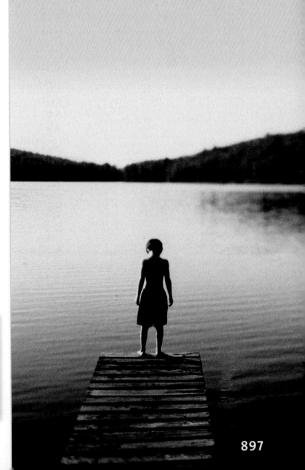

Acquainted
with the Night

Robert Frost

I have been one acquainted with the night.
I have walked out in rain—and back in rain.
I have outwalked the furthest city light.

I have looked down the saddest city lane.
5 I have passed by the watchman on his beat
And dropped my eyes, unwilling to explain.

I have stood still and stopped the sound of feet
When far away an interrupted cry
Came over houses from another street,

10 But not to call me back or say good-by; **Ⓐ**
And further still at an unearthly height
One luminary¹ clock against the sky

Proclaimed the time was neither wrong nor right.
I have been one acquainted with the night. **Ⓑ**

ANALYZE VISUALS
Notice the shadowy human figures in relation to other objects in the photograph. What mood is established by the **composition,** or arrangement of shapes? How do the figures appear in relation to each other? Explain.

Ⓐ FROST'S STYLE
Reread lines 7–10. In what way does line 7 set the stage for lines 8–10? Identify the **mood** evoked by the **image** of the interrupted cry.

Ⓑ RECOGNIZE AMBIGUITY
Reread lines 11–14. Identify at least two possible meanings of "the time was neither wrong nor right." What does this proclamation suggest about the "luminary clock"? Explain.

---

1. **luminary:** giving off light.

The Flatiron Building, Evening from *Camera Work,* April, 1906, Edward Steichen © Carousel Research © Réunion des Musées Nationaux/ Art Resource, New York.

Nothing Gold Can Stay

Robert Frost

Haystacks and Barn (1909), George Wesley Bellows. Oil on canvas, 56.5 cm × 71.4 cm. © Museum of Fine Arts, Houston, Texas/Bridgeman Art Library.

Nature's first green is gold,
Her hardest hue to hold.
Her early leaf's a flower;
But only so an hour.
5 Then leaf subsides to leaf.
So Eden[1] sank to grief,
So dawn goes down to day.
Nothing gold can stay. **C**

---

1. **Eden:** the biblical Garden of Eden, from which Adam and Eve were expelled for disobeying God.

C FROST'S STYLE
What is the **mood** of this poem? Identify the **diction** or **imagery** that most strongly establishes this mood for you.

Literary Analysis

1. **Clarify** What does the speaker of the first poem mean when he says he's been "acquainted with the night"?

2. **Summarize** What does the speaker of "Acquainted with the Night" see and hear on his walk?

3. **Interpret Analogies** In "Nothing Gold Can Stay," how is the fate of a leaf similar to that of the Garden of Eden?

"Out, Out—"

Robert Frost

The buzz saw snarled and rattled in the yard
And made dust and dropped stove-length sticks of wood,
Sweet-scented stuff when the breeze drew across it.
And from there those that lifted eyes could count
5 Five mountain ranges one behind the other
Under the sunset far into Vermont.
And the saw snarled and rattled, snarled and rattled, **D**
As it ran light, or had to bear a load.
And nothing happened: day was all but done.
10 Call it a day, I wish they might have said
To please the boy by giving him the half hour
That a boy counts so much when saved from work.
His sister stood beside them in her apron
To tell them "Supper." At the word, the saw,
15 As if to prove saws knew what supper meant,
Leaped out at the boy's hand, or seemed to leap—
He must have given the hand. However it was,
Neither refused the meeting. But the hand! **E**
The boy's first outcry was a rueful[1] laugh,
20 As he swung toward them holding up the hand
Half in appeal, but half as if to keep
The life from spilling. Then the boy saw all—
Since he was old enough to know, big boy
Doing a man's work, though a child at heart—
25 He saw all spoiled. "Don't let him cut my hand off—
The doctor, when he comes. Don't let him, sister!"
So. But the hand was gone already.
The doctor put him in the dark of ether.[2]
He lay and puffed his lips out with his breath.
30 And then—the watcher at his pulse took fright.
No one believed. They listened at his heart.
Little—less—nothing!—and that ended it.
No more to build on there. And they, since they
Were not the one dead, turned to their affairs. **F**

---

1. **rueful:** expressing sorrow or regret.
2. **ether:** a liquid used as an anesthetic. Its fumes cause unconsciousness when deeply inhaled.

D FROST'S STYLE
Reread lines 1 and 7. What sound is imitated by the repetition of words in these lines? Consider Frost's style here; how does this **imagery** contribute to the overall **mood?**

E FROST'S STYLE
Reread lines 13–18. What does the **diction** in these lines suggest about the accidental meeting of the saw and the hand? Explain the **irony** in these lines.

F RECOGNIZE AMBIGUITY
Identify the ambiguity in the last two lines of the poem. What does their **understatement** and lack of sentiment suggest about the survivors and their attitude toward the boy's death?

Comprehension

1. **Clarify** What is the setting, including the time of day, of "'Out, Out—'"?

2. **Summarize** What happens to the boy?

Literary Analysis

3. **Identify Rhymes** Examine the pairs of rhyming words in "Nothing Gold Can Stay." What ideas do the rhymes help Frost convey about the nature of beauty?

4. **Examine Theme** "'Out, Out—'" provides a portrait of **solitude** even among family. Identify words and phrases in which Frost suggests the solitude of these characters in the face of tragedy. What theme emerges about human relationships?

5. **Interpret Allusion** The title of "'Out, Out—'" is an **allusion,** or indirect reference to a well-known person, place, or literary work—in this case, a famous speech in Shakespeare's *Macbeth* (Act Five, Scene 5). How does the following quotation from *Macbeth* color your sense of Frost's poem?

   . . . Out, out brief candle!
   Life's but a walking shadow, a poor player
   That struts and frets his hour upon the stage
   And then is heard no more.

6. **Analyze Frost's Style** Identify several lines in any one of the three poems where Frost's **diction,** his use of **imagery,** and/or **mood** is particularly striking. Explain why you find it noteworthy and how Frost's style helps deliver the poem's message.

7. **Evaluate Ambiguity** Consult the chart in which you recorded different interpretations as you read. Identify the ambiguity that you found the most puzzling, contradictory, or profound. In your opinion, what does the ambiguity add to each poem? Explain.

Literary Criticism

8. **Critical Interpretation** The literary critic and scholar Lionel Trilling hailed Frost for his "representation of the terrible actualities of life in a new way." Apply this comment to the three Frost poems you have just read. What are the "terrible actualities of life" in each poem? What might be considered "new" or unusual about Frost's portrayal of these realities? Explain.

The Death of the Hired Man

Poem by
Robert Frost

● LITERARY ANALYSIS: NARRATIVE POETRY

Though primarily a lyric poet, Robert Frost also wrote **narrative poetry.** In contrast to the shorter poems by Robinson and Masters on pages 882–886, "The Death of the Hired Man" tells a story with a more fully developed plot, setting, and characters.

- **Dialogue**—This poem consists almost entirely of a conversation between two people, so the dialogue plays a greater role than usual in developing the narrative elements.
- **Plot**—Although the "now-time" of the poem consists almost entirely of a single conversation, the dialogue itself indirectly relates events that have unfolded over years.
- **Characterization**—Frost uses very little direct description by the speaker; instead, he conveys the characters' traits through their own words and what others say about them.
- **Setting**—Again, Frost uses little direct description of time and place, conveying these things primarily through what the characters say about their work and their relationships.

Review: **Blank Verse**

● READING SKILL: UNDERSTAND FORM IN POETRY

In poetry, **form** generally refers to the shape of text on the page. In a larger sense, however, it can refer to any technique used to convey meaning. The dialogue in this poem can be hard to follow; you won't find many *he said*'s or *she said*'s. However, Frost uses other devices to show who's speaking.

- **Quotation marks**—Double quotation marks indicate the beginning and end of each speech. Single quotation marks indicate dialogue within a speech.
- **Line breaks**—Frost leaves a blank line when the speaker changes; he never changes speaker in the middle of a line.
- **Point of view**—The poem's speaker uses only the third person; in dialogue, the characters speak in the first person.

Use a chart to keep track of who is speaking in the poem.

Elements of Form Used to Show Speakers		
Line Numbers	Who Is Speaking	How I Know

Explore the Key Idea

How do you know you're HOME?

KEY IDEA It's the moment when you close the door behind you, drop your bag on the floor, take off your coat, and kick off your shoes. Or maybe it's the greeting you get from a family member or even a pet. Walking up the driveway, seeing a familiar face, smelling a familiar food: we recognize **home** in various ways.

QUICKWRITE Identify the place where you feel the most at home. Then write a brief description of some moment or event that captures the features that make home different from other places.

The DEATH of the HIRED MAN

Robert Frost

Mary sat musing on the lamp-flame[1] at the table,
Waiting for Warren. When she heard his step,
She ran on tiptoe down the darkened passage
To meet him in the doorway with the news
5 And put him on his guard. "Silas is back."
She pushed him outward with her through the door
And shut it after her. "Be kind," she said.
She took the market things from Warren's arms
And set them on the porch, then drew him down
10 To sit beside her on the wooden steps. **Ⓐ**

"When was I ever anything but kind to him?
But I'll not have the fellow back," he said.
"I told him so last haying,[2] didn't I?
If he left then, I said, that ended it.
15 What good is he? Who else will harbor him
At his age for the little he can do?
What help he is there's no depending on.
Off he goes always when I need him most.
He thinks he ought to earn a little pay,
20 Enough at least to buy tobacco with,
So he won't have to beg and be beholden.
'All right,' I say, 'I can't afford to pay
Any fixed wages, though I wish I could.'
'Someone else can.' 'Then someone else will have to.' **Ⓑ**
25 I shouldn't mind his bettering himself
If that was what it was. You can be certain,
When he begins like that, there's someone at him
Trying to coax him off with pocket money—
In haying time, when any help is scarce.
30 In winter he comes back to us. I'm done."

"Sh! not so loud: he'll hear you," Mary said.

---

1. **musing on the lamp-flame:** looking thoughtfully at the flame of an oil lamp.
2. **last haying:** the last time the hay was cut.

ANALYZE VISUALS
Notice the shapes of the landscape in this image. How do these shapes compare with the outlines of the human figures? What might this suggest about the relationship between humans and nature? Explain.

Ⓐ NARRATIVE POETRY
Reread lines 1–10. What clues do they contain about the poem's **setting?** Explain.

Ⓑ FORM IN POETRY
Reread lines 11–24. Summarize these lines. Who is speaking? What is happening in lines 22–24?

Detail of *Island Hay* (1945), Thomas Hart Benton. © T.H. Benton and R.P. Benton Testamentary Trusts/UMB Bank Trustee/Licensed by VAGA, New York, N.Y.

"I want him to: he'll have to soon or late."

"He's worn out. He's asleep beside the stove.
When I came up from Rowe's I found him here,
35 Huddled against the barn door fast asleep,
A miserable sight, and frightening, too—
You needn't smile—I didn't recognize him—
I wasn't looking for him—and he's changed.
Wait till you see." **C**

      "Where did you say he'd been?"

40 "He didn't say. I dragged him to the house,
And gave him tea and tried to make him smoke.
I tried to make him talk about his travels.
Nothing would do: he just kept nodding off."

"What did he say? Did he say anything?"

45 "But little."

      "Anything? Mary, confess
He said he'd come to ditch³ the meadow for me."

"Warren!"
      "But did he? I just want to know."

"Of course he did. What would you have him say? **D**
Surely you wouldn't grudge the poor old man
50 Some humble way to save his self-respect.
He added, if you really care to know,
He meant to clear the upper pasture, too.
That sounds like something you have heard before?
Warren, I wish you could have heard the way
55 He jumbled everything. I stopped to look
Two or three times—he made me feel so queer—
To see if he was talking in his sleep.
He ran on⁴ Harold Wilson—you remember—
The boy you had in haying four years since.
60 He's finished school, and teaching in his college.
Silas declares you'll have to get him back.
He says they two will make a team for work:
Between them they will lay this farm as smooth! **E**

---

3. **ditch:** plow.

4. **ran on:** talked about without stopping.

C NARRATIVE POETRY
Reread Mary's description of Silas in lines 31–39. What **character traits** are revealed about Silas in these lines? about Mary?

D FORM IN POETRY
Reread lines 38–48. Identify the speaker of each speech. What devices indicate this? Explain what the rapid change of speakers emphasizes about the tone of this discussion.

E BLANK VERSE
Poetry written in unrhymed **iambic pentameter,** or blank verse, is said to be the poetic form that most resembles English speech. Read aloud lines 58–63. Would you agree? Explain.

The way he mixed that in with other things.
65 He thinks young Wilson a likely lad, though daft
On[5] education—you know how they fought
All through July under the blazing sun,
Silas up on the cart to build the load,
Harold along beside to pitch it on."

70 "Yes, I took care to keep well out of earshot."

"Well, those days trouble Silas like a dream.
You wouldn't think they would. How some things linger!
Harold's young college-boy's assurance piqued[6] him.
After so many years he still keeps finding
75 Good arguments he sees he might have used.
I sympathize. I know just how it feels
To think of the right thing to say too late.
Harold's associated in his mind with Latin.
He asked me what I thought of Harold's saying
80 He studied Latin, like the violin,
Because he liked it—that an argument!
He said he couldn't make the boy believe
He could find water with a hazel prong[7]—
Which showed how much good school had ever done him.
85 He wanted to go over that. But most of all
He thinks if he could have another chance
To teach him how to build a load of hay—" **F**

"I know, that's Silas' one accomplishment.
He bundles every forkful in its place,
90 And tags and numbers it for future reference,
So he can find and easily dislodge it
In the unloading. Silas does that well.
He takes it out in bunches like big birds' nests.
You never see him standing on the hay
95 He's trying to lift, straining to lift himself."

"He thinks if he could teach him that, he'd be
Some good perhaps to someone in the world.
He hates to see a boy the fool of books.
Poor Silas, so concerned for other folk,
100 And nothing to look backward to with pride,

F **NARRATIVE POETRY**
Reread lines 79–87. How
are Silas and Harold
characterized in these
lines?

---

5. **daft on:** crazy about; obsessed with.

6. **piqued** (pēkt): aroused resentment in.

7. **find . . . prong:** a reference to the practice of dowsing, in which a person uses
a forked stick made of hazel wood to try to find underground water.

And nothing to look forward to with hope,
So now and never any different."

Part of a moon was falling down the west,
Dragging the whole sky with it to the hills.
105 Its light poured softly in her lap. She saw it
And spread her apron to it. She put out her hand
Among the harplike morning-glory strings,
Taut[8] with the dew from garden bed to eaves,
As if she played unheard some tenderness
110 That wrought on[9] him beside her in the night. **G**
"Warren," she said, "he has come home to die:
You needn't be afraid he'll leave you this time."

"Home," he mocked gently.
                              "Yes, what else but home?
It all depends on what you mean by home.
115 Of course he's nothing to us, any more
Than was the hound that came a stranger to us
Out of the woods, worn out upon the trail."

"Home is the place where, when you have to go there,
They have to take you in."
                              "I should have called it
120 Something you somehow haven't to deserve."

Warren leaned out and took a step or two,
Picked up a little stick, and brought it back
And broke it in his hand and tossed it by.
"Silas has better claim on us you think
125 Than on his brother? Thirteen little miles
As the road winds would bring him to his door.
Silas has walked that far no doubt today.
Why doesn't he go there? His brother's rich,
A somebody—director in the bank."

130 "He never told us that."
                              "We know it, though." **H**

"I think his brother ought to help, of course.
I'll see to that if there is need. He ought of right
To take him in, and might be willing to—

G FORM IN POETRY
Reread lines 103–110.
The poem's speaker has
interrupted the dialogue
between Mary and
Warren. How does this
shift in **point of view**
affect the poem's **mood?**

H NARRATIVE POETRY
Reread lines 124–130.
What do these lines add
to your understanding of
Silas?

---

8. **taut:** pulled tight; straight.
9. **wrought** (rôt) **on:** worked on.

He may be better than appearances.[10]
135 But have some pity on Silas. Do you think
If he had any pride in claiming kin
Or anything he looked for from his brother,
He'd keep so still about him all this time?"

"I wonder what's between them."
                                        "I can tell you.
140 Silas is what he is—we wouldn't mind him—
But just the kind that kinsfolk can't abide.[11]
He never did a thing so very bad.
He don't know why he isn't quite as good
As anybody. Worthless though he is,
145 He won't be made ashamed to please his brother."

"I can't think Si ever hurt anyone."

"No, but he hurt my heart the way he lay
And rolled his old head on that sharp-edged chair-back.
He wouldn't let me put him on the lounge.[12]
150 You must go in and see what you can do.
I made the bed up for him there tonight.
You'll be surprised at him—how much he's broken.
His working days are done; I'm sure of it."

"I'd not be in a hurry to say that."

155 "I haven't been. Go, look, see for yourself.
But, Warren, please remember how it is:
He's come to help you ditch the meadow.
He has a plan. You mustn't laugh at him.
He may not speak of it, and then he may.
160 I'll sit and see if that small sailing cloud
Will hit or miss the moon." ❶
                                  It hit the moon.
Then there were three there, making a dim row,
The moon, the little silver cloud, and she.

Warren returned—too soon, it seemed to her—
165 Slipped to her side, caught up her hand and waited.

"Warren?" she questioned.
                              "Dead," was all he answered.

---

❶ **NARRATIVE POETRY**
In lines 150–161, the dialogue between Mary and Warren is coming to a head. What turn in the **plot** do you foresee?

10. **better than appearances:** better than he looks.
11. **abide:** put up with.
12. **lounge:** couch.

Comprehension

1. **Recall** Who is Silas, and what is his relationship to Mary and Warren?

2. **Recall** How does Silas look and act when Mary finds him?

3. **Clarify** Why is Warren angry with Silas?

4. **Clarify** In Mary's mind, why has Silas returned to the farm?

Literary Analysis

5. **Analyze Characterization** What does the **dialogue** between Mary and Warren reveal about their differing attitudes toward the following subjects?

   - Silas's return (lines 5–30)
   - Silas's appearance and plans (lines 42–61)
   - Silas's skills (lines 88–102)
   - Silas's relationship to his brother (lines 124–145)

   Based on these attitudes, identify Mary's and Warren's chief personality traits.

6. **Draw Conclusions** Silas has a long history with Mary and Warren. Based on what they say about him and their past interactions with them, why do you think he has come to regard their farm as **home?**

7. **Examine Narrative Poetry** Compare the events that occur during the conversation between Mary and Warren with those events—revealed through **dialogue**—that have taken place over the entire time they have known Silas. How would the poem's **plot** be different if Mary and Warren had not talked at such length about these earlier events? Explain.

8. **Evaluate Form in Poetry** Review the chart in which you kept track of the changing speakers. In your opinion, what is gained or lost by Frost's style of writing dialogue in terms of the following elements? Overall, do you think his technique was effective? Explain.

   - clarity   • rhythm   • sense of drama

Literary Criticism

9. **Biographical Context** Robert Frost spent 11 years farming and drew tremendous inspiration from farm life. The poet Ezra Pound, reviewing Frost's second book of poetry, wrote, "I know more of farm life than I did before I had read his poems. That means I know more of 'Life.'" Think of the Frost poems you've read. In what ways can the themes of farm life as depicted by Frost be said to reflect life in general?

Reading-Writing Connection

GRAMMAR AND STYLE

USE LANGUAGE EFFECTIVELY Poets strive to use words and phrases that will give their poems a musical quality and convey emphasis. One kind of phrase Frost uses frequently is the **infinitive phrase,** consisting of an infinitive—a verb form that begins with *to*—plus its modifiers and complements. Infinitive phrases can function as nouns, adjectives, or adverbs. For instance, in the examples below, Frost uses parallel infinitive phrases, highlighted in yellow, as adverbs modifying the verbs highlighted in green.

> She ran on tiptoe down the darkened passage
> To meet him in the doorway with the news (lines 3–4)

> She took the market things from Warren's arms
> And set them on the porch, then drew him down
> To sit beside her on the wooden steps. (lines 8–10)

Notice that the infinitive phrases help to give the poem a predictable rhythm and to call attention to Mary's actions.

PRACTICE Fill in the blank lines in the following poem with infinitive phrases that modify the boldfaced words.

He **ran** out to the garage

_____

A pair of bargain-hunters
Were fighting over a toaster.
He **tried** his best

_____

Offering a waffle iron,
But neither was satisfied.

WRITING TOOLS

For prewriting, revision, and editing tools, visit the **Writing Center** at **ClassZone.com.**

Ezra Pound
1885–1972

In a Station of the Metro

Poetry by Ezra Pound

Ezra Pound may have been the most influential poet of the 20th century, promoting the careers of experimental writers and founding the literary movement known as imagism. Pound encouraged poets to use everyday language and to express emotions and ideas through precise, concrete images. In his own work, Pound drew upon the poetic traditions of numerous countries; his masterwork, *The Cantos,* features heroic figures from world history. In life, he was an inflammatory figure. During World War II, he made anti-American radio broadcasts from Rome. He was eventually arrested and confined to a mental hospital. Following his release, he lived a quiet, secluded life in Italy.

H. D. (Hilda Doolittle)
1886–1961

Helen

Poetry by H. D.

As a young woman, Hilda Doolittle coped with the pain of alienation by befriending other artists. At 15, she met the poet Ezra Pound, who became her close friend and, briefly, her fiancé. A few years later she met the poets Marianne Moore and William Carlos Williams, beginning lifelong nurturing friendships.

Although no longer romantically involved with Pound, Doolittle joined his circle of friends when she moved to London in 1911. Her first published poems appeared in *Poetry* magazine (1913) under the signature "H. D., *Imagiste,*" as suggested by Pound. That year she married Richard Aldington, another imagist, who shared her fascination with the classical world. H. D.'s best poems retell Greek myths from the perspective of women who have suffered injustice.

William Carlos Williams
1883–1963

Spring and All / This Is Just to Say

Poetry by William Carlos Williams

William Carlos Williams crammed two lives into one. He worked full time as a doctor in Rutherford, New Jersey, yet managed to publish more than 40 books of poetry, fiction, plays, and essays. Often, he found inspiration while caring for his patients.

Born to an English father and a Puerto Rican mother, Williams grew up in Rutherford and considered America his home. While his contemporaries fled to Europe, he decided to write poems about the world around him. Williams felt strongly that a poem should be rooted in everyday life and not abstract ideas.

Author Online

For more on these poets, visit the **Literature Center** at **ClassZone.com.**

LITERARY ANALYSIS: IMAGISM

Early in the 20th century, a number of American and British poets undertook a collective effort to rejuvenate poetry in English, freeing it from standard conventions of form and subject matter. The **imagists,** influenced by Japanese haiku as well as ancient Greek lyric and French symbolist poetry, wrote according to strict principles.

- to use the language of **common speech;** yet also to choose words with extreme precision and economy
- to create new **rhythms** as a way of expressing new moods; this generally meant writing in **free verse**
- to have complete freedom in choice of **subject matter**
- to present a clear and highly concentrated **image**

The images in these poems do not generally carry a specific meaning; rather, they suggest a certain feeling or idea.

Ezra Pound and H. D. were among the most important founding members of imagism; William Carlos Williams emerged a few years later, making his own distinctive mark on the style. As you read their work, consider the principles outlined above. Be attuned to the images in these poems and think about what ideas or feelings they might suggest.

READING SKILL: MAKE INFERENCES

Imagist poems are tightly compressed, leaving out details and explanations in favor of sharp, spare images. They can be seen as highly efficient, saying a lot with very few words. This economic use of language can occasionally leave room for confusion, often requiring you to **make inferences,** or logical guesses based on the text (or prior knowledge), about what is not directly stated. This is often referred to as "reading between the lines." As you read each poem, use a chart like the one shown to record your inferences and the evidence on which you base them.

"Helen"	
Inferences	Details from Text or Prior Knowledge
Helen is beautiful.	First stanza focuses on her white skin and its "lustre."

Explore the Key Idea

How do you capture a MOMENT?

KEY IDEA "I'll never forget the sight of that wet scarf hanging out the car door." Many experiences leave us with a lingering mental **image,** which then becomes our means of remembering the experience. The gleaming surface of an empty swimming pool, a towering pile of unwashed dishes—something about such an image communicates the meaning or feeling of a moment. What is that meaning or feeling? How might you capture it?

QUICKWRITE Choose an image that stands out in your mind, whether it's from an important experience (your first day of school) or an ordinary moment (a walk to the store on a hot day). Then write a brief list of the sensory details that make the image so compelling for you.

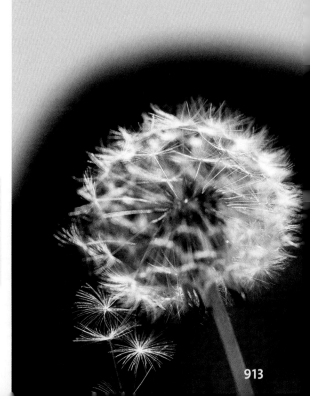

913

IN A STATION OF THE METRO[1]

Ezra Pound

The apparition of these faces in the crowd;
Petals on a wet, black bough. **A**

A MAKE INFERENCES
Note the use of the word *apparition* to describe the faces in the crowd. What does this suggest about the people?

HELEN

H. D.

All Greece hates
the still eyes in the white face,
the lustre as of olives
where she stands,
5 and the white hands. **B**

B IMAGISM
Reread the first stanza. What quality of Helen's is depicted in these lines? Identify the images that emphasize this quality.

All Greece reviles[2]
the wan face when she smiles,
hating it deeper still
when it grows wan and white,
10 remembering past enchantments
and past ills.

Greece sees unmoved,
God's daughter[3], born of love,
the beauty of cool feet
15 and slenderest knees,
could love indeed the maid,
only if she were laid,
white ash amid funereal cypresses.[4] **C**

C MAKE INFERENCES
Based on information you find in the text, why do you think the Greeks hate Helen?

---

1. **the Metro:** the subway in Paris.
2. **reviles:** to attack with hateful language.
3. **God's daughter:** Helen was a daughter of Zeus, the king of the gods; and Leda, a mortal.
4. **funereal cypresses:** The cypress, a type of evergreen tree, has been associated with death and funeral services since ancient times.

SPRING AND ALL

William Carlos Williams

By the road to the contagious hospital[1]
under the surge of the blue
mottled clouds driven from the
northeast—a cold wind. Beyond, the
5 waste of broad, muddy fields
brown with dried weeds, standing and fallen

patches of standing water
the scattering of tall trees

All along the road the reddish
10 purplish, forked, upstanding, twiggy
stuff of bushes and small trees
with dead, brown leaves under them
leafless vines— **D**

Lifeless in appearance, sluggish[2]
15 dazed spring approaches—

They enter the new world naked,
cold, uncertain of all
save that they enter. All about them
the cold, familiar wind— **E**

20 Now the grass, tomorrow
the stiff curl of wildcarrot leaf

One by one objects are defined—
It quickens:[3] clarity, outline of leaf

But now the stark dignity of
25 entrance—Still, the profound change
has come upon them: rooted, they
grip down and begin to awaken

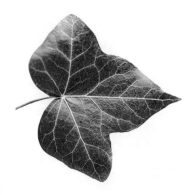

D **IMAGISM**
Identify the colors named
in lines 1–13. What aspect
of spring is emphasized
by these colors?

E **IMAGISM**
Reread lines 16–19. What
words and phrases
does Williams use to
characterize the newly
growing plants in these
lines? Then identify the
language in lines 20–27
that describes the change
that comes upon them.

---

1. **contagious hospital:** place where people with contagious
   diseases are hospitalized.

2. **sluggish:** slow to respond.

3. **quickens:** comes alive; revives.

THIS IS JUST TO SAY

William Carlos Williams

I have eaten
the plums
that were in
the icebox

5 and which
you were probably
saving
for breakfast

Forgive me
10 they were delicious
so sweet
and so cold **F**

F IMAGISM
Williams has chosen to
invoke only two senses
in this poem. What
are they? Explain how
this choice affects your
perception of those
sensory details.

Comprehension

1. **Clarify** In "Helen," what would it take for the Greeks to love Helen?

2. **Summarize** What signs of new life does the speaker of "Spring and All" notice by the road?

Literary Analysis

3. **Make Inferences** Reread the chart you created as you read "Helen." On the basis of these notes, what can you say about Helen's past and present relationship with the Greeks?

4. **Analyze Allusion** H. D. wrote many poems alluding to Greek mythology. The title "Helen" is an allusion to Helen of Troy, a great beauty whose abduction by Paris, a Trojan prince, prompted the Greeks to take up arms against Troy in a war that lasted for ten long years. How does this information change or deepen your understanding of the poem? Explain, citing evidence from the text.

5. **Examine Metaphor** The juxtaposition of the two images in "In a Station of the Metro" has the effect of a metaphor. What does the image in line 2 suggest about the faces in line 1?

6. **Interpret Imagist Poetry** Choose one of the poems in this lesson and identify its most prominent image or images. What feeling or idea are you left with at the end of the poem? Citing evidence from the text, explain what it is about the imagery that suggests this feeling.

7. **Compare Diction** William Carlos Williams favored the use of everyday language over highly formal poetic diction. Identify several examples of his ordinary diction in "Spring and All" and "This Is Just to Say." Compare Williams's language with the language H. D. uses in "Helen." Which, in your opinion, is more approachable? Which is more interesting? Cite details from the texts to support your opinion.

Literary Criticism

8. **Author's Style** Like other modernist poets, the Imagists eschewed the use of traditional rhyme schemes, meters, and other formal elements. Yet form was important to them; you may recall from page 893 that Williams once criticized Carl Sandburg's poetry as "formless." Choose one of the three poets featured in this lesson and examine his or her use of the following poetic devices, when relevant:

   • rhythm   • rhyme   • line breaks   • stanza breaks

   In your opinion, does the use of these elements seem deliberate or random? Cite evidence from the poem or poems to support your answer.

Reading-Writing Connection

WRITING PROMPT

WRITE AN IMAGIST POEM Think of a place that has inspired powerful emotions in you. What images come to mind when you think about that place? What feelings do your memories evoke in you? Use your responses to these questions as the starting point for an **eight-to-ten-line poem.** As you write, try to include concrete images that convey both emotions and meaning.

SELF-CHECK

A strong Imagist poem will . . .
- present a distinct image with sensory language
- contain concise, precisely chosen language
- be written in free verse
- display a sense of rhythm

GRAMMAR AND STYLE

CREATE IMAGERY Writers use fresh, **vivid adjectives** to create images that bring scenes to life. In the poem "Spring and All," for instance, Williams uses adjectives that lead readers to picture the way a landscape looks in the change from late winter to early spring. Carefully examine the adjectives Williams uses in the following lines. Notice how keenly they evoke the sight of a landscape in transition.

> *All along the road the reddish*
> *purplish, forked, upstanding, twiggy*
> *stuff of bushes and small trees* (lines 9–11)

> *Lifeless in appearance, sluggish*
> *dazed spring approaches—* (lines 14–15)

PRACTICE Write down each of the following sentences. Then try to enliven these sentences by inserting vivid adjectives. An example has been done for you.

EXAMPLE

The crowd stared at Helen's hands and face.

The angry crowd stared at Helen's delicate hands and ash-colored face.

---

1. She noticed fields and weeds by the side of the road.
2. I saw faces looking out from the windows of the train.
3. Slowly, the girl ate the peaches that we had plucked from the tree.

WRITING TOOLS

For prewriting, revision, and editing tools, visit the **Writing Center** at ClassZone.com.

E. E. Cummings
1894–1962

anyone lived in a pretty how town

Poetry by E. E. Cummings

E. E. Cummings believed deeply in two things: love and human individuality. He felt that both being an individual and being in a loving relationship led to joy and personal growth. His poems honor love in all its variety and pay tribute to people who resist group conformity and conventional thought.

Cummings's faith in love grew out of his tender relationship with his parents.

His father encouraged Cummings's literary ambitions and secured his release when he was imprisoned in France during World War I. After the war, Cummings lived in New York's Greenwich Village, a community of free-thinking artists and intellectuals, where he spent his days painting and writing. By the 1950s, Cummings's playful, innovative style had made him enormously popular.

Marianne Moore
1887–1972

Poetry

Poetry by Marianne Moore

Marianne Moore was a true original. Her interests ranged from baseball to Muhammad Ali to exotic animals, which she scrutinized during her frequent trips to the zoo. Gifted with an eye for detail, she wrote precise, witty descriptions of these and other subjects. Moore also affected an eccentric public appearance, often sporting a three-cornered hat and a black cape.

When she was 31, Moore moved to New York City, where she hobnobbed with other writers, served as editor of the prestigious literary journal *The Dial,* and wrote poetry. A highly innovative poet, she mixed direct observation with quoted material and experimented with stanza forms and line lengths. Her complex, meticulously crafted poems earned her the esteem of other poets, as well as a Pulitzer Prize.

Edna St. Vincent Millay
1892–1950

Recuerdo

Poetry by Edna St. Vincent Millay

In both her life and her art, Edna St. Vincent Millay expressed emotional extremes. This intensity, coupled with Millay's revolt against cultural expectations for women, made her a symbol of the "new woman" of the 1920s.

Although Millay endured childhood poverty and deprivation, she nevertheless managed to excel in school and to win poetry awards. After graduating from Vassar College, she became a central figure among the avant-garde set in New York's Greenwich Village. There, she led a bohemian lifestyle, juggling relationships and living in poverty so that she had ample time to write.

Author Online

For more on these authors, visit the **Literature Center** at ClassZone.com.

LITERARY ANALYSIS: FORM IN MODERN POETRY

Like other modernists, modern poets are known for challenging and experimenting with literary **form**. The term *form* refers primarily to the arrangement of words on the page and to the use of rhyme and meter, but also to the standard conventions of written language (spelling, punctuation, etc.). E. E. Cummings is widely noted for his playful sense of experimentation. In "anyone lived in a pretty how town," he abandons many rules of punctuation, spelling, grammar, and capitalization, creating striking (and sometimes puzzling) effects. Millay's "Recuerdo" is more traditional, with regular rhyme, stanzas, and meter.

Moore's poem "Poetry" is somewhere between these two. It observes the standard conventions of written language, yet it lacks regular rhyme, meter, and line length, giving it a more prose like feel than the other two poems. As you read, note how each poet responds to traditional form, whether by letting go of convention or adapting it. Remember that all good poets use form to help deliver or emphasize meaning.

READING STRATEGY: READING MODERN POETRY

Many readers enjoy the playful, unpredictable quality of modern poetry; others find it confusing or meaningless. There are a number of strategies that can help any reader enjoy these poems.

- **Paraphrase**—If a word, phrase, or sentence seems difficult, try restating it in your own words.

- **Read aloud**—Reading a poem aloud can sometimes help you hear the flow of a line or stanza and clarify its meaning, as well as emphasizing its musical qualities.

- **Observe mechanics**—Note the punctuation, spelling, capitalization, and grammar. How does this affect the sound or sense of the poem?

Using a chart like the one shown, record paraphrases for difficult lines in each poem, lines you would read aloud to help clarify meaning, and examples of unusual mechanics.

"anyone lived in a pretty how town"	"Poetry"	"Recuerdo"
Paraphrase: A character named "anyone" lived in some kind of town, year round, singing and dancing.		

Explore the Key Idea

Do poems have to follow the RULES?

KEY IDEA If it doesn't rhyme, is it still a poem? What if it's only two lines long? Do the lines have to break in a regular place? What if some of the words are upside-down on the page? The modernist poets asked questions like this, breaking **rules** right and left. Their work changed the accepted ideas about what poetry is.

DISCUSS With a small group, brainstorm a list of all the qualities you might find in a poem. From that list, come up with a set of rules that all poems follow.

Poetry Rules
- has to sound rhythmic
- must contain images

anyone
lived
in a
pretty
how
town

E. E. Cummings

anyone lived in a pretty how town
(with up so floating many bells down)
spring summer autumn winter
he sang his didn't he danced his did.

5 Women and men(both little and small)
cared for anyone not at all
they sowed their isn't they reaped their same
sun moon stars rain **Ⓐ**

children guessed(but only a few
10 and down they forgot as up they grew
autumn winter spring summer)
that noone loved him more by more

when by now and tree by leaf
she laughed his joy she cried his grief
15 bird by snow and stir by still
anyone's any was all to her **Ⓑ**

someones married their everyones
laughed their cryings and did their dance
(sleep wake hope and then)they
20 said their nevers they slept their dream

stars rain sun moon
(and only the snow can begin to explain
how children are apt to forget to remember
with up so floating many bells down)

25 one day anyone died i guess
(and noone stooped to kiss his face)
busy folk buried them side by side
little by little and was by was

all by all and deep by deep
30 and more by more they dream their sleep
noone and anyone earth by april
wish by spirit and if by yes. **Ⓒ**

Women and men(both dong and ding)
summer autumn winter spring
35 reaped their sowing and went their came
sun moon stars rain

ANALYZE VISUALS
Painter Marc Chagall is known for his whimsical and dream like images. Identify some unrealistic elements in the painting on page 923. What do they suggest about the couple depicted? Explain.

Ⓐ FORM IN MODERN POETRY
Many words in these stanzas are used in strange ways, but the verbs are still pretty straight forward. In lines 1–8, which actions are attributed to "anyone" and which to the women and men? What does this suggest about the differences between them?

Ⓑ READING MODERN POETRY
Paraphrase lines 13–16. How does "noone" feel about "anyone"?

Ⓒ FORM IN MODERN POETRY
Reread lines 25–32. Identify some ways in which Cummings breaks with the conventions of **mechanics.** How does this affect your sense of the poem? Explain.

Poetry

Marianne Moore

I, too, dislike it: there are things that are important beyond all this fiddle.
   Reading it, however, with a perfect contempt for it, one discovers in
   it, after all, a place for the genuine.
      Hands that can grasp, eyes
5   that can dilate,[1] hair that can rise
         if it must, these things are important not because a

high-sounding interpretation can be put upon them but because they are
   useful. When they become so derivative[2] as to become unintelligible,
   the same thing may be said for all of us, that we
10   do not admire what
      we cannot understand: the bat **D**
         holding on upside down or in quest of something to

eat, elephants pushing, a wild horse taking a roll, a tireless wolf under
   a tree, the immovable critic twitching his skin like a horse that feels a flea,
15   the base-
   ball fan, the statistician—
      nor is it valid
         to discriminate against "business documents and

school-books"; all these phenomena are important. One must make a
20   distinction
   however: when dragged into prominence by half poets, the result is not
                            poetry, **E**
   nor till the poets among us can be
      "literalists[3] of
25   the imagination"—above
         insolence and triviality and can present

D **READING MODERN POETRY**
Reread and **paraphrase** lines 1–11. What is important about "Hands that can grasp, eyes / that can dilate, hair that can rise"?

ANALYZE VISUALS
Consider what the speaker of this poem has to say about poetry. How do you think she might respond to this abstract painting?

E **FORM IN MODERN POETRY**
Note the extremely indented lines at lines 15, 20, and 22. What do these oddities of form contribute to the poem's meaning? Explain.

---

1. **dilate** (dī-lāt′): enlarge; open wide.
2. **derivative:** lacking originality.
3. **literalists:** people who interpret words in their usual or most basic sense.

Rising Moon (1965), Hans Hofmann. Private collection. © 2008 Estate of Hans Hofmann/Artists Rights Society (ARS), New York/Art Resource, New York.

for inspection, "imaginary gardens with real toads in them," shall we have
   it. In the meantime, if you demand on the one hand,
   the raw material of poetry in
30   all its rawness and
     that which is on the other hand
       genuine, you are interested in poetry. **F**

F READING MODERN
POETRY
Reread lines 28–32 aloud.
How, if at all, does this
change your sense of the
line breaks?

Recuerdo

Edna St. Vincent Millay

We were very tired, we were very merry—
We had gone back and forth all night on the ferry.
It was bare and bright, and smelled like a stable—
But we looked into a fire, we leaned across a table,
5 We lay on a hill-top underneath the moon;
And the whistles kept blowing, and the dawn came soon.

We were very tired, we were very merry—
We had gone back and forth all night on the ferry;
And you ate an apple, and I ate a pear,
10 From a dozen of each we had bought somewhere;
And the sky went wan,[1] and the wind came cold,
And the sun rose dripping, a bucketful of gold. **G**

We were very tired, we were very merry,
We had gone back and forth all night on the ferry.
15 We hailed, "Good morrow, mother!" to a shawl-covered head,
And bought a morning paper, which neither of us read;
And she wept, "God bless you!" for the apples and pears,
And we gave her all our money but our subway fares. **H**

---

1. **wan:** pale.

G READING MODERN POETRY
Read aloud lines 1–12. How does this poem sound different from the other two? What aspect of the subject matter is reflected by the poem's **rhyme** and **meter?**

H FORM IN MODERN POETRY
Identify the **repetition** that helps to shape each stanza. What meaning is emphasized by this device?

Port Scene, Paul Klee. Atheneum Museum, Helsinki, Finland. © Giraudon/Art Resource, New York. © 2007 Artists Rights Society (ARS), New York/VG Bild-Kunst, Bonn.

Comprehension

1. **Clarify** Who are the lovers described in "anyone lived in a pretty how town"?

2. **Clarify** What does the speaker of "Poetry" dislike about poetry? What does she value in it?

3. **Clarify** Where and when does "Recuerdo" take place?

Literary Analysis

4. **Analyze Modern Poetry** Review the chart you filled in as you read. In the Cummings poem, it is important not to try to read every line literally, but rather aim for the gist of these nonsense phrases. Choose one stanza from this poem and explain the general impression you get from the language in each line. Then paraphrase the entire stanza, making use of these impressions.

5. **Interpret Ideas** In "Poetry," what idea about poetry is represented by each of the following items? Explain.

   - "hands that can grasp" (line 4)
   - "elephants pushing" (line 13)
   - "business documents and school-books" (lines 18–19)
   - "imaginary gardens with real toads in them" (line 27)

6. **Evaluate Form in Modern Poetry** Each of these poems has a playful, irreverent quality, sometimes achieved by breaking **rules** of traditional poetry and sometimes by following them. Examine the poems in this lesson, identifying the most playful elements of each. In your opinion, which poem is the most radical? Cite evidence to support your answer.

Literary Criticism

7. **Critical Interpretations** In a review, the critic Edmund Wilson argued that "Behind [the] formidable barrier of punctuations for which Mr. Cummings seems unfortunately to have achieved most celebrity, his emotions are conventional and simple in the extreme." Do you agree or disagree with Wilson's argument? Whether or not you agree, do you view Wilson's statement as a positive or negative comment? Cite evidence to support your opinion.

The Love Song of J. Alfred Prufrock

Poem by T. S. Eliot

T. S. Eliot

1888–1965

When he was alive, T. S. Eliot was one of the most influential poets in the English-speaking world. His invention of new poetic rhythms, forms, and themes had an enormous impact on other writers and helped usher in a new era in poetry. Eliot, remarked the composer Igor Stravinsky, was "not only a great sorcerer of words, but the very key keeper of the language."

A Lover of Philosophy Eliot grew up in St. Louis, Missouri, in a household steeped in culture and tradition. His mother, Charlotte Champe Stearns, was an amateur poet, and his father, Henry Ware Eliot, was a successful businessman with New England roots. Eliot received a broad education, studying at Milton Academy and Harvard University. After earning both bachelor's and master's degrees from Harvard, Eliot continued his studies in philosophy at the Sorbonne in Paris and then back at Harvard. However, he never completed those

studies. While on a traveling fellowship in Europe, he met the poet Ezra Pound, who encouraged Eliot's poetic ambitions.

Literary Success Pound helped Eliot gain entry into London's avant-garde circle of writers, and he introduced Eliot's poetry to Harriet Monroe of *Poetry* magazine. In 1915, Eliot's masterpiece "The Love Song of J. Alfred Prufrock" appeared in *Poetry.* That same year, Eliot married Vivien Haigh-Wood, an Englishwoman. Struggling to make a living as a writer, Eliot worked as a teacher, a bank clerk, and finally as an editor.

Breakthroughs in Poetry The 1917 publication of Eliot's first book, *Prufrock and Other Observations,* signaled a distinct break with the past. Using colloquial speech laced with slang, Eliot created a new, highly original poetic diction. He also explored new poetic themes, such as the splendors and horrors of modern life and the effects of alienation. With the appearance of *The Waste Land* in 1922, Eliot's reputation was solidified. In this poem, Eliot articulated the disgust and disillusionment felt by his generation in the wake of World War I, as well as its longing for meaning in a chaotic, sometimes frightening, world.

Inspired by Religion Though a pioneer in poetry, Eliot became increasingly conservative in his personal views. Struggling with anxiety over his domestic troubles, he joined the Church of England in 1927 and embraced its traditional pieties. In his later collections, *Ash Wednesday* (1930) and *Four Quartets* (1943), he used poetry to stress the significance of accepting religious discipline.

● LITERARY ANALYSIS: STREAM OF CONSCIOUSNESS

Modern poets explored many ways of breaking free from the standard conventions of poetic form and even content, changing the nature of both narrative and lyric poetry. One of the most dramatic breaks from convention in the modern era was the development of **stream of consciousness.** Used by both poets and fiction writers, this technique presents a sometimes chaotic flow of images and ideas, meant to represent the unfiltered thoughts of the speaker or protagonist. "The Love Song of J. Alfred Prufrock" is a **dramatic monologue** in which Prufrock, the speaker, addresses a silent listener with a tumble of associative thoughts, allusions, and daydreams.

And indeed there will be time
For the yellow smoke that slides along the street
Rubbing its back upon the window-panes

As you read the poem, try not to be put off by the nonsensical nature of the verse, but be alert to any feelings or ideas that the images seem to suggest.

● READING SKILL: SUMMARIZE STANZAS

The difficult thing about reading stream of consciousness is figuring out how to connect seemingly unrelated ideas. A writer will often jump from one thought to the next without any clear transition. Fortunately, Eliot has done us the favor of grouping his thoughts in **stanzas.** If you read the stanzas closely, you will notice that each one expresses a fairly coherent idea. Once you **summarize** and identify the central idea or image of each stanza, you will have an easier time tracing the arc, and the sense, of the entire poem.

As you read, record your summary of each stanza in a chart like the one shown. Some stanzas have only two or three lines; in these cases, don't worry about providing a summary as much as a brief description of the central idea or image.

Stanza	Summary/Central Idea
1	Speaker suggests that listener join him on an evening trip through the lonely city streets.

What is ALIENATION?

KEY IDEA So many of us know the feeling of standing at the edge of a party, wanting to join but having no idea what to say or do. Everyone else is having more fun, making better jokes, or wearing nicer clothes. And it's all the worse if you are hoping to approach the object of your affections; do you even stand a chance? In this poem, J. Alfred Prufrock approaches a party with a similar sense of **alienation.** Full of dread and self-doubt and fearful of female rejection, he wonders whether he dares to step in and draw attention to himself.

QUICKWRITE Create a list of images that suggest alienation or isolation to you. They could be explicit, such as that of a person hesitating at the edge of a group, or implicit, such as the image of a lonely window lit in the darkness.

THE LOVE SONG OF
J. Alfred Prufrock

T. S. Eliot

S'io credessi che mia risposta fosse
a persona che mai tornasse al mondo,
questa fiamma staria senza più scosse.
Ma per ciò che giammai di questo fondo
non tornò vivo alcun, s'i'odo il vero,
senza tema d'infamia ti rispondo.

Let us go then, you and I,
When the evening is spread out against the sky
Like a patient etherised upon a table;
Let us go, through certain half-deserted streets,
5 The muttering retreats
Of restless nights in one-night cheap hotels
And sawdust restaurants with oyster-shells:
Streets that follow like a tedious argument
Of insidious intent
10 To lead you to an overwhelming question . . .
Oh, do not ask, "What is it?"
Let us go and make our visit.

In the room the women come and go
Talking of Michelangelo.

15 The yellow fog that rubs its back upon the window-panes,
The yellow smoke that rubs its muzzle on the window-panes,
Licked its tongue into the corners of the evening,
Lingered upon the pools that stand in drains,
Let fall upon its back the soot that falls from chimneys,

S'io credessi . . . ti rispondo: These lines are from the *Inferno*, written in the early 14th century by Italian poet Dante Alighieri. As Dante visits hell, one of the damned agrees to speak of his torment only because he believes that Dante cannot return to the living world to repeat the tale.

3 etherised: given ether, a liquid used as an anesthetic.

9 insidious (ĭn-sĭd'ē-əs): more dangerous than it seems.

20 Slipped by the terrace, made a sudden leap,
   And seeing that it was a soft October night,
   Curled once about the house, and fell asleep. **A**

   And indeed there will be time
   For the yellow smoke that slides along the street
25 Rubbing its back upon the window-panes;
   There will be time, there will be time
   To prepare a face to meet the faces that you meet;
   There will be time to murder and create,
   And time for all the works and days of hands
30 That lift and drop a question on your plate;
   Time for you and time for me,
   And time yet for a hundred indecisions,
   And for a hundred visions and revisions,
   Before the taking of a toast and tea.

35 In the room the women come and go
   Talking of Michelangelo.

   And indeed there will be time
   To wonder, "Do I dare?" and, "Do I dare?"
   Time to turn back and descend the stair,
40 With a bald spot in the middle of my hair—
   (They will say: "How his hair is growing thin!")
   My morning coat, my collar mounting firmly to the chin,
   My necktie rich and modest, but asserted by a simple pin—
   (They will say: "But how his arms and legs are thin!")
45 Do I dare
   Disturb the universe?
   In a minute there is time
   For decisions and revisions which a minute will reverse. **B**

   For I have known them all already, known them all—
50 Have known the evenings, mornings, afternoons,
   I have measured out my life with coffee spoons;
   I know the voices dying with a dying fall
   Beneath the music from a farther room.
        So how should I presume?

55 And I have known the eyes already, known them all—
   The eyes that fix you in a formulated phrase,
   And when I am formulated, sprawling on a pin,
   When I am pinned and wriggling on the wall,
   Then how should I begin

A STREAM OF CONSCIOUSNESS
Reread lines 1–22. Identify the figures of speech used to characterize the evening sky and the night fog. What **mood** or sensation do these images establish?

42 morning coat: a type of formal suit jacket with coattails.

B SUMMARIZE STANZAS
Summarize lines 37–48. What do Prufrock's repeated questioning and his preoccupation with his appearance indicate about his state of mind?

54 presume: act overconfidently; dare.
56 formulated: reduced to a formula.
55–58 And I have . . . on the wall: Prufrock recalls being scrutinized by women at other parties. He portrays himself as a live insect that has been classified, labeled, and mounted for display.

60 To spit out all the butt-ends of my days and ways?
    And how should I presume?

And I have known the arms already, known them all—
Arms that are braceleted and white and bare
(But in the lamplight, downed with light brown hair!)
65 Is it perfume from a dress
That makes me so digress?
Arms that lie along a table, or wrap about a shawl.
    And should I then presume?
    And how should I begin?
                    • • • • •

70 Shall I say, I have gone at dusk through narrow streets
And watched the smoke that rises from the pipes
Of lonely men in shirt-sleeves, leaning out of windows? . . .

I should have been a pair of ragged claws
Scuttling across the floors of silent seas.
                    • • • • •

75 And the afternoon, the evening, sleeps so peacefully!
Smoothed by long fingers,
Asleep . . . tired . . . or it malingers,
Stretched on the floor, here beside you and me.
Should I, after tea and cakes and ices,
80 Have the strength to force the moment to its crisis?
But though I have wept and fasted, wept and prayed,
Though I have seen my head (grown slightly bald) brought in
    upon a platter,
I am no prophet—and here's no great matter;
I have seen the moment of my greatness flicker,
85 And I have seen the eternal Footman hold my coat, and snicker,
And in short, I was afraid.

And would it have been worth it, after all,
After the cups, the marmalade, the tea,
Among the porcelain, among some talk of you and me,
90 Would it have been worth while,
To have bitten off the matter with a smile,
To have squeezed the universe into a ball
To roll it towards some overwhelming question,
To say: "I am Lazarus, come from the dead,
95 Come back to tell you all, I shall tell you all"—
If one, settling a pillow by her head,
    Should say: "That is not what I meant at all.
    That is not it, at all." C

66 **digress:** wander away from the main topic; ramble.

73–74 **I should . . . silent seas:** Here Prufrock presents an image of himself as a crayfish.

77 **malingers** (mə-lĭng'ərz): pretends illness in order to avoid duty or work.

81–83 **But though . . . prophet:** an allusion to the biblical story of John the Baptist, who is imprisoned by King Herod (Matthew 14; Mark 6). At the request of his wife, Herod had the Baptist's head cut off and brought to him on a platter.

94 **Lazarus:** In the biblical story (John 11:17–44) Lazarus lay dead in his tomb for four days before Jesus brought him back to life.

C **STREAM OF CONSCIOUSNESS**
Reread lines 75–98. Prufrock casts himself in three different **images** in this stanza, two of which are biblical allusions. Identify these images and explain what they have in common.

And would it have been worth it, after all,
100 Would it have been worth while,
    After the sunsets and the dooryards and the sprinkled streets,
    After the novels, after the teacups, after the skirts that trail along
        the floor—
    And this, and so much more?—
    It is impossible to say just what I mean!
105 But as if a magic lantern threw the nerves in patterns on a
        screen:
    Would it have been worth while
    If one, settling a pillow or throwing off a shawl,
    And turning toward the window, should say:
        "That is not it at all,
110   That is not what I meant, at all."
            • • • • •

    No! I am not Prince Hamlet, nor was meant to be;
    Am an attendant lord, one that will do
    To swell a progress, start a scene or two,
    Advise the prince; no doubt, an easy tool,
115 Deferential, glad to be of use,
    Politic, cautious, and meticulous;
    Full of high sentence, but a bit obtuse;
    At times, indeed, almost ridiculous—
    Almost, at times, the Fool.

120 I grow old . . . I grow old . . .
    I shall wear the bottoms of my trousers rolled. **D**

    Shall I part my hair behind? Do I dare to eat a peach?
    I shall wear white flannel trousers, and walk upon the beach.
    I have heard the mermaids singing, each to each.

125 I do not think that they will sing to me.

    I have seen them riding seaward on the waves
    Combing the white hair of the waves blown back
    When the wind blows the water white and black.

    We have lingered in the chambers of the sea
130 By sea-girls wreathed with seaweed red and brown
    Till human voices wake us, and we drown.

105 magic lantern: a forerunner of the slide projector.

115 deferential: yielding to someone else's opinion.

116 meticulous: extremely careful and precise about details.

117 obtuse: slow to understand; dull.

D STREAM OF CONSCIOUSNESS
What similarities can you detect between the "attendant lord" described in lines 112–119 and Prufrock's image of himself in lines 120–121? Explain.

124–125 mermaids . . . to me: In mythology, mermaids attract mortal men by their beauty and their singing, sometimes allowing men to live with them in the sea.

Comprehension

1. **Recall** What social situation does Prufrock reflect upon in this poem?

2. **Recall** How does he feel about this situation?

3. **Clarify** What is Prufrock's primary feeling about himself?

Literary Analysis

4. **Synthesize Summaries** Review the summaries and central ideas you recorded as you read. Now, viewing this series of ideas as a **narrative** with a conflict, a climax, and a resolution, write a summary of Prufrock's internal journey.

5. **Examine Poetic Devices** Review Eliot's use of **repetition** and **rhyme** in lines 23–34. Explain how these devices are used to convey Prufrock's sense of anxiety.

6. **Analyze Stream of Consciousness** In the final lines of the poem (lines 122–131), Prufrock offers his final reflection. For each of the following passages, offer an explication, or careful analysis. What does each group of lines suggest about Prufrock's sense of himself and his place in the world? What resonating idea are we left with at the poem's end?

   • lines 120–121 ("I grow old . . . trousers rolled.")

   • lines 122–123 ("Shall I part . . . walk upon the beach.")

   • lines 124–125 ("I have heard the mermaids . . . sing to me.")

   • lines 126–131 ("I have seen them riding seaward . . . and we drown.")

7. **Interpret Title** Some critics have contended that Prufrock's "overwhelming question" is actually a marriage proposal. True or not, it is clear that his relationships with women are a matter of concern to him. In what way can this poem be considered a love song? Consider the depictions of women and Prufrock's feelings of **alienation** from them. In your view, how does the poem's title color its meaning? Explain.

8. **Evaluate Form and Content** Consider the feelings and ideas that Eliot was trying to express; in what way can the stream of consciousness technique be said to reflect these ideas? Explain whether or not you think this technique is effective, citing evidence.

Literary Criticism

9. **Critical Interpretations** Literary critic Donald R. Fryxell wrote, "Prufrock is a trimmer . . . trimmers were those souls in Dante's *Inferno* who were condemned to the vestibule of hell because they had never really lived, although they were supposedly alive. . . . The Trimmers were lifeless, spiritless, mindless people." Do you agree or disagree with this statement? Give evidence from the text to support your answer.

Modernist Style

While there is no one thing that makes a poem "modern," most modernist literature does share some defining features.

Features of Modernism:

- nontraditional subject matter and themes
- a focus on alienated individuals rather than heroes
- use of understatement and irony to reveal emotions and ideas
- use of symbols and images to suggest meaning
- experimentation with style and language

Writing to Synthesize

Review the poems beginnning on page 882 to get a feel for how they incorporate the features of modernism. Then write your own poem in the modernist style.

Consider

- what your poem will be about (remember that traditional themes, such as love, were rejected or reinterpreted by the modernists)
- whether your poem will feature a speaker, and what he or she will be like
- how to use understatement or irony to bring out emotions
- what symbols or images might best convey your meaning
- whether you wish to experiment with language or style

Extension

SPEAKING & LISTENING
Choose a more traditional poem from Units 1–4, such as Poe's "The Raven," and modernize it. **Rewrite** two stanzas of the poem as a modernist poet might, using the features of modernism as a guideline. Then **recite** your stanzas for your classmates, and discuss the techniques you used to "update" the poem. You may need to write out your stanzas on poster board to show how you manipulated line length, stanza form, capitalization and punctuation, or other elements of style.

Winter Dreams

Short Story by F. Scott Fitzgerald

F. Scott Fitzgerald
1896–1940

F. Scott Fitzgerald experienced, and depicted in his fiction, both the material success and the crushing disillusionment that characterized the 1920s—a decade he dubbed the Jazz Age. He died young, famous for his flashy lifestyle, not his writing. But today, thanks to his dazzling prose style and piercing insight, Fitzgerald is heralded as the spokesperson of his era and as an American literary giant.

Midwest Boy Makes Good Born in St. Paul, Minnesota, Fitzgerald grew up in comfortable circumstances. His parents could afford to send him to prep school and then Princeton University, where he spent his time writing for the literary magazine and creating musical comedies. Low grades and the intervention of World War I kept him from graduating, but he left with a big dream. "I want to be one of the greatest writers who ever lived," he told a friend.

Jazz Age Romance In 1918, Fitzgerald fell madly in love with a flirtatious 18-year-old named Zelda Sayre. Zelda was as rich as she was beautiful and refused to marry him until he could support her financially. Two years later, Fitzgerald's first novel, *This Side of Paradise,* was finally published. Hailed as a daringly original story of the postwar generation's revolt against tradition, it more than doubled Fitzgerald's income, earned him widespread exposure as "the philosopher of the flapper," and won Zelda over. The two married and soon became the golden couple of the 1920s, partying at glamorous locations in the United States and Europe and living beyond the income Fitzgerald made from his writing.

Fall and Redemption Like the decade the Fitzgeralds epitomized, their high life came crashing down. In 1930, Zelda began the first of many hospital stays for mental illness, while Scott fell deeply into debt and alcoholism. *The Beautiful and Damned* (1922), a novel about the unraveling lives of a once-glamorous couple, was deemed "depressing" by reviewers, and Fitzgerald's masterpiece, *The Great Gatsby* (1925), was not the popular success he had hoped for. He died of a heart attack in 1940, at age 44, and it was years before he came to be regarded as anything more than a writer of showy period pieces. The reexamination of Fitzgerald's work was spurred not by critics, many of whom had always appreciated his talent, but by a new generation of readers who discovered the brilliance of his writing and told their friends. The year he died, his book sales—just 40 copies total—earned him $13.13 in royalties. Today, however, *The Great Gatsby* is a beloved American classic, and Fitzgerald's books sell about 500,000 copies annually.

● LITERARY ANALYSIS: CHARACTER MOTIVATION AND TRAITS

Some characters are so vividly portrayed, they seem like real people. The characters' traits and motivations are often familiar to us; we see them in ourselves or in others we know. **Character traits** are those qualities shown by a character, as implied by his or her physical appearance and expressions of personality, such as boldness or gentleness. By recognizing a character's traits, you are able to better understand the **character's motivation**—the stated or implied reason(s) behind the character's actions. As you read, note the words, actions, thoughts, and appearance of the **protagonist,** or main character, as well as of the **antagonist,** the person against which the protagonist struggles. What do these descriptions indicate about the characters' traits and motivations?

Review: **Theme**

● READING SKILL: PREDICT STORY DEVELOPMENT

Predicting is the process of using text clues to make a reasonable guess about what will happen in a story. Sometimes your predictions will hit the mark, and other times the characters' actions and the story's events may surprise you. As you come to know the characters in "Winter Dreams," see if you can predict what will happen to them next, or how they will react or feel toward other characters and events. Record your predictions and the text clues that led you to make them.

Predictions	Text Clues

▲ VOCABULARY IN CONTEXT

Fitzgerald uses the boldfaced words in his story of love and status. Determine the definition of each word from its context.

1. a girl whose mere presence could **precipitate** a sudden crush
2. due to her **patrimony,** would inherit a **surfeit** of money
3. attended parties surrounded by her **retinue**
4. flirted **blatantly,** without a trace of self-consciousness
5. pouting and **petulance** that seemed to attract men
6. unfriendly to women—no **camaraderie** with them
7. turned her nose up at **mundane,** ordinary things
8. enjoyed the **flux** of life, its **precarious** nature

KEY IDEA It's easy to get caught up in the pursuit of wealth and **status**—and to imagine that obtaining them would guarantee a perfect life. But would it? Can money buy love, and does high status guarantee happiness?

QUICKWRITE Envision the life you hope to lead ten years from now. Wealth and status top the list of many people's "must-haves," but what else holds a prominent place in your dreams? Jot down some of your aspirations on a graph like the one shown. Then fill in the graph, rating on a scale of 1 to 10 the importance you attach to each goal. Use your completed graph to write a short paragraph explaining which goal holds the top spot on your list, and why.

Aspiration	Rating
Wealth	
Social Status	
Exciting Career	
Happy Family	

0 1 2 3 4 5 6 7 8 9 10

Winter *Dreams*

F. Scott Fitzgerald

BACKGROUND Behind the glitz and glamour of the 1920s lay a profound loss of idealism. Though World War I gave rise to new opportunities and freedoms, especially for women, the shift to the modern age left a gap in values that the new generation struggled to fill. "Winter Dreams" mostly takes place before 1920, when a restless uncertainty was first being felt. The story appeared in the collection *All the Sad Young Men* (1926), a title that expresses Fitzgerald's deeper understanding of the decade.

ANALYZE VISUALS
How would you describe the subject of this portrait? Describe the **traits** you think he projects, citing details from the painting to support your answer.

I

Some of the caddies were poor as sin and lived in one-room houses with a neurasthenic[1] cow in the front yard, but Dexter Green's father owned the second best grocery-store in Black Bear—the best one was "The Hub," patronized by the wealthy people from Sherry Island—and Dexter caddied only for pocket-money. **Ⓐ**

In the fall when the days became crisp and gray, and the long Minnesota winter shut down like the white lid of a box, Dexter's skis moved over the snow that hid the fairways of the golf course. At these times the country gave him a feeling of profound melancholy—it offended him that the links should lie in enforced fallowness, haunted by ragged sparrows for the long season. It was dreary, too,
10 that on the tees where the gay colors fluttered in summer there were now only the desolate sand-boxes knee-deep in crusted ice. When he crossed the hills the wind blew cold as misery, and if the sun was out he tramped with his eyes squinted up against the hard dimensionless glare.

Ⓐ MOTIVATION AND TRAITS
Consider the kind of information you receive in the story's very first paragraph. What do you learn about Dexter's family and social position?

---

1. **neurasthenic** (nŏŏr'əs-thĕn'ĭk): weak and lacking in vigor.

Homme au Chapeau (1900s), Jean Berque. Waterhouse and Dodd, London. © Bridgeman Art Library.

In April the winter ceased abruptly. The snow ran down into Black Bear Lake scarcely tarrying for the early golfers to brave the season with red and black balls. Without elation, without an interval of moist glory, the cold was gone.

Dexter knew that there was something dismal about this Northern spring, just as he knew there was something gorgeous about the fall. Fall made him clinch his hands and tremble and repeat idiotic sentences to himself, and make brisk abrupt
20 gestures of command to imaginary audiences and armies. October filled him with hope which November raised to a sort of ecstatic triumph, and in this mood the fleeting brilliant impressions of the summer at Sherry Island were ready grist to his mill.² He became a golf champion and defeated Mr. T. A. Hedrick in a marvelous match played a hundred times over the fairways of his imagination, a match each detail of which he changed about untiringly—sometimes he won with almost laughable ease, sometimes he came up magnificently from behind. Again, stepping from a Pierce-Arrow automobile,³ like Mr. Mortimer Jones, he strolled frigidly into the lounge of the Sherry Island Golf Club—or perhaps, surrounded by an admiring crowd, he gave an exhibition of fancy diving from the spring-board of
30 the club raft. . . . Among those who watched him in open-mouthed wonder was Mr. Mortimer Jones. **B**

And one day it came to pass that Mr. Jones—himself and not his ghost—came up to Dexter with tears in his eyes and said that Dexter was the — — best caddy in the club, and wouldn't he decide not to quit if Mr. Jones made it worth his while, because every other — — caddy in the club lost one ball a hole for him—regularly—

"No, sir," said Dexter decisively, "I don't want to caddy any more." Then, after a pause: "I'm too old."

"You're not more than fourteen. Why the devil did you decide just this
40 morning that you wanted to quit? You promised that next week you'd go over to the State tournament with me."

"I decided I was too old."

Dexter handed in his "A Class" badge, collected what money was due him from the caddy-master, and walked home to Black Bear Village.

"The best — — caddy I ever saw," shouted Mr. Mortimer Jones over a drink that afternoon. "Never lost a ball! Willing! Intelligent! Quiet! Honest! Grateful!"

The little girl who had done this was eleven—beautifully ugly as little girls are apt to be who are destined after a few years to be inexpressibly lovely and bring no end of misery to a great number of men. The spark, however, was perceptible.
50 There was a general ungodliness in the way her lips twisted down at the corners when she smiled, and in the—Heaven help us!—in the almost passionate quality of her eyes. Vitality is born early in such women. It was utterly in evidence now, shining through her thin frame in a sort of glow. **C**

B MOTIVATION AND TRAITS
Reread lines 17–31. What can you tell about Dexter's aspirations based on this glimpse into his thoughts?

C PREDICT
Consider what you've learned about both Dexter and the "beautifully ugly" girl. How might she cause him to quit his job? Give reasons for your prediction.

---

2. **grist to his mill:** something that he could make good use of.

3. **Pierce-Arrow automobile:** a luxury car of the day.

She had come eagerly out onto the course at nine o'clock with a white linen nurse and five small new golf-clubs in a white canvas bag which the nurse was carrying. When Dexter first saw her she was standing by the caddy house, rather ill at ease and trying to conceal the fact by engaging her nurse in an obviously unnatural conversation graced by startling and irrelevant grimaces from herself.

"Well, it's certainly a nice day, Hilda," Dexter heard her say. She drew down
60 the corners of her mouth, smiled, and glanced furtively around, her eyes in transit falling for an instant on Dexter.

Then to the nurse:

"Well, I guess there aren't very many people out here this morning, are there?"

The smile again—radiant, **blatantly** artificial—convincing.

"I don't know what we're supposed to do now," said the nurse, looking nowhere in particular.

"Oh, that's all right. I'll fix it up."

Dexter stood perfectly still, his mouth slightly ajar. He knew that if he moved forward a step his stare would be in her line of vision—if he moved backward he
70 would lose his full view of her face. For a moment he had not realized how young she was. Now he remembered having seen her several times the year before—in bloomers.[4]

Suddenly, involuntarily, he laughed, a short abrupt laugh—then, startled by himself, he turned and began to walk quickly away.

"Boy!"

Dexter stopped.

"Boy—"

Beyond question he was addressed. Not only that, but he was treated to that absurd smile, that preposterous smile—the memory of which at least a dozen men
80 were to carry into middle age.

"Boy, do you know where the golf teacher is?"

"He's giving a lesson."

"Well, do you know where the caddy-master is?"

"He isn't here yet this morning."

"Oh." For a moment this baffled her. She stood alternately on her right and left foot.

"We'd like to get a caddy," said the nurse. "Mrs. Mortimer Jones sent us out to play golf, and we don't know how without we get a caddy."

Here she was stopped by an ominous glance from Miss Jones, followed
90 immediately by the smile.

"There aren't any caddies here except me," said Dexter to the nurse, "and I got to stay here in charge until the caddy-master gets here."

"Oh."

Miss Jones and her **retinue** now withdrew, and at a proper distance from Dexter became involved in a heated conversation, which was concluded by Miss Jones taking one of the clubs and hitting it on the ground with violence. For

blatantly (blāt'n-tlē) *adv.* in an extremely obvious way; conspicuously

retinue (rĕt'n-ōō') *n.* a group of attendants or followers

---

4. **bloomers:** baggy pants that end just below the knee, formerly worn by girls.

further emphasis she raised it again and was about to bring it down smartly upon the nurse's bosom, when the nurse seized the club and twisted it from her hands.

"You little mean old *thing!*" cried Miss Jones wildly.

100   Another argument ensued. Realizing that the elements of comedy were implied in the scene, Dexter several times began to laugh, but each time restrained the laugh before it reached audibility. He could not resist the monstrous conviction that the little girl was justified in beating the nurse.

The situation was resolved by the fortuitous appearance of the caddy-master, who was appealed to immediately by the nurse.

"Miss Jones is to have a little caddy, and this one says he can't go."

"Mr. McKenna said I was to wait here till you came," said Dexter quickly.

"Well, he's here now." Miss Jones smiled cheerfully at the caddy-master. Then she dropped her bag and set off at a haughty mince[5] toward the first tee.

110   "Well?" The caddy-master turned to Dexter. "What you standing there like a dummy for? Go pick up the young lady's clubs."

"I don't think I'll go out today," said Dexter.

"You don't—"

"I think I'll quit."

The enormity of his decision frightened him. He was a favorite caddy, and the thirty dollars a month he earned through the summer were not to be made elsewhere around the lake. But he had received a strong emotional shock, and his perturbation required a violent and immediate outlet.

It is not so simple as that, either. As so frequently would be the case in the 120 future, Dexter was unconsciously dictated to by his winter dreams. ⓓ

ANALYZE VISUALS
How does this painting differ—in both content and style—from the portrait on page 939? How might these differences be said to echo the changes in Dexter Green?

ⓓ MOTIVATION AND TRAITS
Why does Dexter quit caddying? Explain what his decision adds to your understanding of him.

II

Now, of course, the quality and the seasonability of these winter dreams varied, but the stuff of them remained. They persuaded Dexter several years later to pass up a business course at the State university—his father, prospering now, would have paid his way—for the **precarious** advantage of attending an older and more famous university in the East, where he was bothered by his scanty funds. But do not get the impression, because his winter dreams happened to be concerned at first with musings on the rich, that there was anything merely snobbish in the boy. He wanted not association with glittering things and glittering people—he wanted the glittering things themselves. Often he reached out for the best without 130 knowing why he wanted it—and sometimes he ran up against the mysterious denials and prohibitions in which life indulges. It is with one of those denials and not with his career as a whole that this story deals.

He made money. It was rather amazing. After college he went to the city from which Black Bear Lake draws its wealthy patrons. When he was only twenty-three and had been there not quite two years, there were already people who liked to say: "Now *there's* a boy—" All about him rich men's sons were peddling bonds precariously, or investing **patrimonies** precariously, or plodding through the two dozen volumes of the "George Washington Commercial Course," but Dexter

precarious (prĭ-kâr′ē-əs) *adj.* risky; uncertain

patrimony (păt′rə-mō′nē) *n.* estate or money inherited from ancestors

---

5. **at a haughty mince:** taking short, dainty steps in an arrogant, snobbish way.

Portrait of Marquess Sommi (1925), Tamara De Lempicka. Oil on canvas, 100 cm × 73 cm. Albert and Victoria Benalloul.
© 2007 Artists Rights Society (ARS), New York/ADAGP, Paris.

borrowed a thousand dollars on his college degree and his confident mouth, and
140 bought a partnership in a laundry.

It was a small laundry when he went into it but Dexter made a specialty of learning how the English washed fine woolen golf-stockings without shrinking them, and within a year he was catering to the trade that wore knickerbockers.[6] Men were insisting that their Shetland hose and sweaters go to his laundry just as they had insisted on a caddy who could find golf-balls. A little later he was doing their wives' lingerie as well—and running five branches in different parts of the city. Before he was twenty-seven he owned the largest string of laundries in his section of the country. It was then that he sold out and went to New York. But the part of his story that concerns us goes back to the days when he was making his
150 first big success.

When he was twenty-three Mr. Hart—one of the gray-haired men who liked to say "Now there's a boy"—gave him a guest card to the Sherry Island Golf Club for a weekend. So he signed his name one day on the register, and that afternoon played golf in a foursome with Mr. Hart and Mr. Sandwood and Mr. T. A. Hedrick. He did not consider it necessary to remark that he had once carried Mr. Hart's bag over this same links, and that he knew every trap and gully with his eyes shut—but he found himself glancing at the four caddies who trailed them, trying to catch a gleam or gesture that would remind him of himself, that would lessen the gap which lay between his present and his past.

160 It was a curious day, slashed abruptly with fleeting, familiar impressions. One minute he had the sense of being a trespasser—in the next he was impressed by the tremendous superiority he felt toward Mr. T. A. Hedrick, who was a bore and not even a good golfer any more.

Then, because of a ball Mr. Hart lost near the fifteenth green, an enormous thing happened. While they were searching the stiff grasses of the rough there was a clear call of "Fore!" from behind a hill in their rear. And as they all turned abruptly from their search a bright new ball sliced abruptly over the hill and caught Mr. T. A. Hedrick in the abdomen.

"By Gad!" cried Mr. T. A. Hedrick, "they ought to put some of these crazy
170 women off the course. It's getting to be outrageous."

A head and a voice came up together over the hill:

"Do you mind if we go through?"

"You hit me in the stomach!" declared Mr. Hedrick wildly.

"Did I?" The girl approached the group of men. "I'm sorry. I yelled 'Fore!'"

Her glance fell casually on each of the men—then scanned the fairway for her ball.

"Did I bounce into the rough?"

It was impossible to determine whether this question was ingenuous or malicious. In a moment, however, she left no doubt, for as her partner came up
180 over the hill she called cheerfully:

"Here I am! I'd have gone on the green except that I hit something."

---

6. **knickerbockers:** loose pants that end in a gathering just below the knee and are worn with long socks. Formerly popular as golf wear.

As she took her stance for a short mashie[7] shot, Dexter looked at her closely. She wore a blue gingham dress, rimmed at throat and shoulders with a white edging that accentuated her tan. The quality of exaggeration, of thinness, which had made her passionate eyes and down-turning mouth absurd at eleven, was gone now. She was arrestingly beautiful. The color in her cheeks was centered like the color in a picture—it was not a "high" color, but a sort of fluctuating and feverish warmth, so shaded that it seemed at any moment it would recede and disappear. This color and the mobility of her mouth gave a continual impression of **flux,** of intense life, of passionate vitality—balanced only partially by the sad luxury of her eyes.

190

She swung her mashie impatiently and without interest, pitching the ball into a sand-pit on the other side of the green. With a quick, insincere smile and a careless "Thank you!" she went on after it. **E**

"That Judy Jones!" remarked Mr. Hedrick on the next tee, as they waited— some moments—for her to play on ahead. "All she needs is to be turned up and spanked for six months and then to be married off to an old-fashioned cavalry captain."

"My God, she's good-looking!" said Mr. Sandwood, who was just over thirty.

"Good-looking!" cried Mr. Hedrick contemptuously, "she always looks as if she wanted to be kissed! Turning those big cow-eyes on every calf in town!"

200

It was doubtful if Mr. Hedrick intended a reference to the maternal instinct.

"She'd play pretty good golf if she'd try," said Mr. Sandwood.

"She has no form," said Mr. Hedrick solemnly.

"She has a nice figure," said Mr. Sandwood.

"Better thank the Lord she doesn't drive a swifter ball," said Mr. Hart, winking at Dexter.

Later in the afternoon the sun went down with a riotous swirl of gold and varying blues and scarlets, and left the dry, rustling night of Western summer. Dexter watched from the veranda of the Golf Club, watched the even overlap of the waters in the little wind, silver molasses under the harvest-moon. Then the moon held a finger to her lips and the lake became a clear pool, pale and quiet. Dexter put on his bathing-suit and swam out to the farthest raft, where he stretched dripping on the wet canvas of the springboard.

210

There was a fish jumping and a star shining and the lights around the lake were gleaming. Over on a dark peninsula a piano was playing the songs of last summer and of summers before that—songs from "Chin-Chin" and "The Count of Luxemburg" and "The Chocolate Soldier"[8]—and because the sound of a piano over a stretch of water had always seemed beautiful to Dexter he lay perfectly quiet and listened.

220

The tune the piano was playing at that moment had been gay and new five years before when Dexter was a sophomore at college. They had played it at a prom once when he could not afford the luxury of proms, and he had stood

flux (flŭks): n. change

E MOTIVATION AND TRAITS
Reread lines 171–193. What character traits are revealed by the description of Judy and her actions?

---

7. **mashie:** an old name for the golf club now known as a five iron.

8. **"Chin-Chin" . . . "The Chocolate Soldier":** three popular Broadway musicals, first performed in 1914, 1912, and 1909, respectively.

outside the gymnasium and listened. The sound of the tune **precipitated** in him a sort of ecstasy and it was with that ecstasy he viewed what happened to him now. It was a mood of intense appreciation, a sense that, for once, he was magnificently attuned to life and that everything about him was radiating a brightness and a glamour he might never know again.

A low, pale oblong detached itself suddenly from the darkness of the Island, spitting forth the reverberated sound of a racing motor-boat. Two white streamers
230 of cleft water rolled themselves out behind it and almost immediately the boat was beside him, drowning out the hot tinkle of the piano in the drone of its spray. Dexter raising himself on his arms was aware of a figure standing at the wheel, of two dark eyes regarding him over the lengthening space of water—then the boat had gone by and was sweeping in an immense and purposeless circle of spray round and round in the middle of the lake. With equal eccentricity one of the circles flattened out and headed back toward the raft.

"Who's that?" she called, shutting off her motor. She was so near now that Dexter could see her bathing-suit, which consisted apparently of pink rompers.[9]

The nose of the boat bumped the raft, and as the latter tilted rakishly he was
240 precipitated toward her. With different degrees of interest they recognized each other.

"Aren't you one of those men we played through this afternoon?" she demanded.

He was.

"Well, do you know how to drive a motor-boat? Because if you do I wish you'd drive this one so I can ride on the surf-board behind. My name is Judy Jones"— she favored him with an absurd smirk—rather, what tried to be a smirk, for, twist her mouth as she might, it was not grotesque, it was merely beautiful—"and I live in a house over there on the Island, and in that house there is a man waiting for
250 me. When he drove up at the door I drove out of the dock because he says I'm his ideal." **F**

There was a fish jumping and a star shining and the lights around the lake were gleaming. Dexter sat beside Judy Jones and she explained how her boat was driven. Then she was in the water, swimming to the floating surf-board with a sinuous crawl. Watching her was without effort to the eye, watching a branch waving or a sea-gull flying. Her arms, burned to butternut, moved sinuously among the dull platinum ripples, elbow appearing first, casting the forearm back with a cadence of falling water, then reaching out and down, stabbing a path ahead.

They moved out into the lake; turning, Dexter saw that she was kneeling on
260 the low rear of the now uptilted surf-board.

"Go faster," she called, "fast as it'll go."

Obediently he jammed the level forward and the white spray mounted at the bow. When he looked around again the girl was standing up on the rushing board, her arms spread wide, her eyes lifted toward the moon.

"It's awful cold," she shouted. "What's your name?"

---

9. **rompers:** a loose-fitting one-piece garment with bloomer like pants.

precipitate
(prĭ-sĭp′ĭ-tāt′) *v.* to bring about, especially abruptly

F MOTIVATION AND TRAITS
Do you think Judy has changed since Dexter first encountered her on the golf course years before? Cite **details** and **dialogue** to support your conclusion.

He told her.

"Well, why don't you come to dinner tomorrow night?"

His heart turned over like the fly-wheel of the boat, and, for the second time, her casual whim gave a new direction to his life.

III

270 Next evening while he waited for her to come downstairs, Dexter peopled the soft deep summer room and the sun-porch that opened from it with the men who had already loved Judy Jones. He knew the sort of men they were—the men who when he first went to college had entered from the great prep schools with graceful clothes and the deep tan of healthy summers. He had seen that, in one sense, he was better than these men. He was newer and stronger. Yet in acknowledging to himself that he wished his children to be like them he was admitting that he was but the rough, strong stuff from which they eternally sprang.

When the time had come for him to wear good clothes, he had known who were the best tailors in America, and the best tailors in America had made him the 280 suit he wore this evening. He had acquired that particular reserve peculiar to his university, that set it off from other universities. He recognized the value to him of such a mannerism and he had adopted it; he knew that to be careless in dress and manner required more confidence than to be careful. But carelessness was for his children. His mother's name had been Krimslich. She was a Bohemian of the peasant class and she had talked broken English to the end of her days. Her son must keep to the set patterns.

At a little after seven Judy Jones came downstairs. She wore a blue silk afternoon dress, and he was disappointed at first that she had not put on something more elaborate. This feeling was accentuated when, after a brief 290 greeting, she went to the door of a butler's pantry and pushing it open called: "You can serve dinner, Martha." He had rather expected that a butler would announce dinner, that there would be a cocktail. Then he put these thoughts behind him as they sat down side by side on a lounge and looked at each other.

"Father and mother won't be here," she said thoughtfully.

He remembered the last time he had seen her father, and he was glad the parents were not to be here tonight—they might wonder who he was. He had been born in Keeble, a Minnesota village fifty miles farther north, and he always gave Keeble as his home instead of Black Bear Village. Country towns were well enough to come from if they weren't inconveniently in sight and used as footstools 300 by fashionable lakes. **G**

They talked of his university, which she had visited frequently during the past two years, and of the near-by city which supplied Sherry Island with its patrons, and whither Dexter would return next day to his prospering laundries.

During dinner she slipped into a moody depression which gave Dexter a feeling of uneasiness. Whatever **petulance** she uttered in her throaty voice worried him. Whatever she smiled at—at him, at a chicken liver, at nothing—it disturbed him

G **MOTIVATION AND TRAITS**
Reread lines 270–300.
Summarize Dexter's ideas about social class and the status it confers. How does Dexter see himself? To what does he aspire?

petulance (pĕch'ə-ləns) *n.* ill temper; annoyance

that her smile could have no root in mirth, or even in amusement. When the scarlet corners of her lips curved down, it was less a smile than an invitation to a kiss.

Then, after dinner, she led him out on the dark sun-porch and deliberately changed the atmosphere.

"Do you mind if I weep a little?" she said.

"I'm afraid I'm boring you," he responded quickly.

"You're not. I like you. But I've just had a terrible afternoon. There was a man I cared about, and this afternoon he told me out of a clear sky that he was poor as a church-mouse. He'd never even hinted it before. Does this sound horribly **mundane?**"

"Perhaps he was afraid to tell you."

"Suppose he was," she answered. "He didn't start right. You see, if I'd thought of him as poor—well, I've been mad about loads of poor men, and fully intended to marry them all. But in this case, I hadn't thought of him that way, and my interest in him wasn't strong enough to survive the shock. As if a girl calmly informed her fiancé that she was a widow. He might not object to widows, but—

"Let's start right," she interrupted herself suddenly. "Who are you, anyhow?"

For a moment Dexter hesitated. Then:

"I'm nobody," he announced. "My career is largely a matter of futures."

"Are you poor?"

"No," he said frankly, "I'm probably making more money than any man my age in the Northwest. I know that's an obnoxious remark, but you advised me to start right."

There was a pause. Then she smiled and the corners of her mouth drooped and an almost imperceptible sway brought her closer to him, looking up into his eyes. A lump rose in Dexter's throat, and he waited breathless for the experiment, facing the unpredictable compound that would form mysteriously from the elements of their lips. Then he saw—she communicated her excitement to him, lavishly, deeply, with kisses that were not a promise but a fulfillment. They aroused in him not hunger demanding renewal but **surfeit** that would demand more surfeit . . . kisses that were like charity, creating want by holding back nothing at all.

It did not take him many hours to decide that he had wanted Judy Jones ever since he was a proud, desirous little boy.

IV

It began like that—and continued, with varying shades of intensity, on such a note right up to the dénouement. Dexter surrendered a part of himself to the most direct and unprincipled personality with which he had ever come in contact. Whatever Judy wanted, she went after with the full pressure of her charm. There was no divergence of method, no jockeying for position or premeditation of effects—there was a very little mental side to any of her affairs. She simply made men conscious to the highest degree of her physical loveliness. Dexter had no desire to change her. Her deficiencies were knit up with a passionate energy that transcended and justified them.

mundane (mŭn-dān′) *adj.* characteristic of or concerned with the ordinary

surfeit (sûr′fĭt) *n.* a fullness beyond the point of satisfaction

When, as Judy's head lay against his shoulder that first night, she whispered, "I
350 don't know what's the matter with me. Last night I thought I was in love with a
man and tonight I think I'm in love with you—"—it seemed to him a beautiful
and romantic thing to say. It was the exquisite excitability that for the moment he
controlled and owned. But a week later he was compelled to view this same quality
in a different light. She took him in her roadster[10] to a picnic supper, and after
supper she disappeared, likewise in her roadster, with another man. Dexter became
enormously upset and was scarcely able to be decently civil to the other people
present. When she assured him that she had not kissed the other man, he knew she
was lying—yet he was glad that she had taken the trouble to lie to him. **H**

He was, as he found before the summer ended, one of a varying dozen who
360 circulated about her. Each of them had at one time been favored above all
others—about half of them still basked in the solace of occasional sentimental

---

10. **roadster:** a sporty, two-seat, open automobile.

H MOTIVATION AND
TRAITS
Reread lines 340–358.
Dexter's thoughts
convey information
about Judy, but they
also reveal much about
Dexter himself. Explain
what you learn about
him from these lines.

Young Woman in Green (1927), Tamara de Lempicka. Musée National d'Art Moderne, Centre
Georges Pompidou, Paris. © CNAC/MNAM/Dist. Réunion des Musées Nationaux/Art Resource,
New York. © Artists Rights Society (ARS), New York.

revivals. Whenever one showed signs of dropping out through long neglect, she granted him a brief honeyed hour, which encouraged him to tag along for a year or so longer. Judy made these forays upon the helpless and defeated without malice, indeed half unconscious that there was anything mischievous in what she did.

When a new man came to town every one dropped out—dates were automatically canceled.

The helpless part of trying to do anything about it was that she did it all herself. She was not a girl who could be "won" in the kinetic sense—she was proof against 370 cleverness, she was proof against charm; if any of these assailed her too strongly she would immediately resolve the affair to a physical basis, and under the magic of her physical splendor the strong as well as the brilliant played her game and not their own. She was entertained only by the gratification of her desires and by the direct exercise of her own charm. Perhaps from so much youthful love, so many youthful lovers, she had come, in self-defense, to nourish herself wholly from within. ❶

Succeeding Dexter's first exhilaration came restlessness and dissatisfaction. The helpless ecstasy of losing himself in her was opiate rather than tonic.[11] It was fortunate for his work during the winter that those moments of ecstasy came infrequently. Early in their acquaintance it had seemed for a while that there was 380 a deep and spontaneous mutual attraction—that first August, for example—three days of long evenings on her dusky veranda, of strange wan kisses through the late afternoon, in shadowy alcoves or behind the protecting trellises of the garden arbors, of mornings when she was fresh as a dream and almost shy at meeting him in the clarity of the rising day. There was all the ecstasy of an engagement about it, sharpened by his realization that there was no engagement. It was during those three days that, for the first time, he had asked her to marry him. She said "maybe some day," she said "kiss me," she said "I'd like to marry you," she said "I love you"—she said—nothing.

The three days were interrupted by the arrival of a New York man who visited 390 at her house for half September. To Dexter's agony, rumor engaged them. The man was the son of the president of a great trust company. But at the end of a month it was reported that Judy was yawning. At a dance one night she sat all evening in a motor-boat with a local beau, while the New Yorker searched the club for her frantically. She told the local beau that she was bored with her visitor, and two days later he left. She was seen with him at the station, and it was reported that he looked very mournful indeed.

On this note the summer ended. Dexter was twenty-four, and he found himself increasingly in a position to do as he wished. He joined two clubs in the city and lived at one of them. Though he was by no means an integral part of the stag-lines 400 at these clubs, he managed to be on hand at dances where Judy Jones was likely to appear. He could have gone out socially as much as he liked—he was an eligible young man, now, and popular with downtown fathers. His confessed devotion to Judy Jones had rather solidified his position. But he had no social aspirations and rather despised the dancing men who were always on tap for the Thursday

❶ **MOTIVATION AND TRAITS**
Consider characters or people you've encountered who are similar to Judy Jones. What might **motivate** Judy to act as she does? Cite details you used to draw this **conclusion**.

---

11. **opiate ... tonic:** deadening rather than stimulating.

or Saturday parties and who filled in at dinners with the younger married set. Already he was playing with the idea of going East to New York. He wanted to take Judy Jones with him. No disillusion as to the world in which she had grown up could cure his illusion as to her desirability.

Remember that—for only in the light of it can what he did for her be understood.

Eighteen months after he first met Judy Jones he became engaged to another girl. Her name was Irene Scheerer, and her father was one of the men who had always believed in Dexter. Irene was light-haired and sweet and honorable, and a little stout, and she had two suitors whom she pleasantly relinquished when Dexter formally asked her to marry him.

Summer, fall, winter, spring, another summer, another fall—so much he had given of his active life to the incorrigible lips of Judy Jones. She had treated him with interest, with encouragement, with malice, with indifference, with contempt. She had inflicted on him the innumerable little slights and indignities possible in such a case—as if in revenge for having ever cared for him at all. She had beckoned him and yawned at him and beckoned him again and he had responded often with bitterness and narrowed eyes. She had brought him ecstatic happiness and intolerable agony of spirit. She had caused him untold inconvenience and not a little trouble. She had insulted him, and she had ridden over him, and she had played his interest in her against his interest in his work—for fun. She had done everything to him except to criticize him—this she had not done—it seemed to him only because it might have sullied the utter indifference she manifested and sincerely felt toward him. **J**

When autumn had come and gone again it occurred to him that he could not have Judy Jones. He had to beat this into his mind but he convinced himself at last. He lay awake at night for a while and argued it over. He told himself the trouble and the pain she had caused him, he enumerated her glaring deficiencies as a wife. Then he said to himself that he loved her, and after a while he fell asleep. For a week, lest he imagine her husky voice over the telephone or her eyes opposite him at lunch, he worked hard and late, and at night he went to his office and plotted out his years.

At the end of a week he went to a dance and cut in on her once. For almost the first time since they had met he did not ask her to sit out with him or tell her that she was lovely. It hurt him that she did not miss these things—that was all. He was not jealous when he saw that there was a new man tonight. He had been hardened against jealousy long before. **K**

He stayed late at the dance. He sat for an hour with Irene Scheerer and talked about books and about music. He knew very little about either. But he was beginning to be master of his own time now, and he had a rather priggish notion that he—the young and already fabulously successful Dexter Green—should know more about such things.

That was in October, when he was twenty-five. In January, Dexter and Irene became engaged. It was to be announced in June, and they were to be married three months later.

J GRAMMAR AND STYLE
Reread lines 416–428. Fitzgerald's long sentences, held together by the **coordinating conjunction** *and* and broken up by **dashes**, convey Dexter's perplexed thoughts about Judy's behavior.

K THEME
How does Dexter's response to this autumn compare with his reactions to the season at the beginning of the story? What theme in the story is suggested by the change in Dexter?

450   The Minnesota winter prolonged itself interminably, and it was almost May
when the winds came soft and the snow ran down into Black Bear Lake at last.
For the first time in over a year Dexter was enjoying a certain tranquillity of spirit.
Judy Jones had been in Florida, and afterward in Hot Springs,[12] and somewhere
she had been engaged, and somewhere she had broken it off. At first, when Dexter
had definitely given her up, it had made him sad that people still linked them
together and asked for news of her, but when he began to be placed at dinner next
to Irene Scheerer people didn't ask him about her any more—they told him about
her. He ceased to be an authority on her.

        May at last. Dexter walked the streets at night when the darkness was damp
460 as rain, wondering that so soon, with so little done, so much of ecstasy had gone
from him. May one year back had been marked by Judy's poignant, unforgivable,
yet forgiven turbulence—it had been one of those rare times when he fancied she
had grown to care for him. That old penny's worth of happiness he had spent
for this bushel of content. He knew that Irene would be no more than a curtain
spread behind him, a hand moving among gleaming tea-cups, a voice calling to
children . . . fire and loveliness were gone, the magic of nights and the wonder of
the varying hours and seasons . . . slender lips, downturning, dropping to his lips
and bearing him up into a heaven of eyes. . . . The thing was deep in him. He was
too strong and alive for it to die lightly. 🅛

470   In the middle of May when the weather balanced for a few days on the thin
bridge that led to deep summer he turned in one night at Irene's house. Their
engagement was to be announced in a week now—no one would be surprised
at it. And tonight they would sit together on the lounge at the University Club
and look on for an hour at the dancers. It gave him a sense of solidity to go with
her—she was so sturdily popular, so intensely "great."

        He mounted the steps of the brownstone house and stepped inside.
        "Irene," he called.
        Mrs. Scheerer came out of the living-room to meet him.
        "Dexter," she said, "Irene's gone upstairs with a splitting headache. She wanted
480 to go with you but I made her go to bed."
        "Nothing serious, I—"
        "Oh, no. She's going to play golf with you in the morning. You can spare her
for just one night, can't you, Dexter?"
        Her smile was kind. She and Dexter liked each other. In the living-room he
talked for a moment before he said good night.
        Returning to the University Club, where he had rooms, he stood in the
doorway for a moment and watched the dancers. He leaned against the door-post,
nodded at a man or two—yawned.
        "Hello, darling."
490   The familiar voice at his elbow startled him. Judy Jones had left a man and
crossed the room to him—Judy Jones, a slender enameled doll in cloth of gold:
gold in a band at her head, gold in two slipper points at her dress's hem. The
fragile glow of her face seemed to blossom as she smiled at him. A breeze of

🅛 PREDICT
Identify the **metaphors**
that come to Dexter's
mind with regard to Irene.
What do they suggest
about his feelings toward
her? Predict how Dexter
will treat Irene in the
future. Cite text clues
that helped you make
this guess.

---

12. **Hot Springs:** a spa city in west-central Arkansas.

warmth and light blew through the room. His hands in the pockets of his dinner-jacket tightened spasmodically. He was filled with a sudden excitement.

"When did you get back?" he asked casually.

"Come here and I'll tell you about it."

She turned and he followed her. She had been away—he could have wept at the wonder of her return. She had passed through enchanted streets, doing things that were like provocative music. All mysterious happenings, all fresh and quickening hopes, had gone away with her, come back with her now.

She turned in the doorway.

"Have you a car here? If you haven't, I have."

"I have a coupé."

In then, with a rustle of golden cloth. He slammed the door. Into so many cars she had stepped—like this—like that—her back against the leather, so—her elbow resting on the door—waiting. She would have been soiled long since had there been anything to soil her—except herself—but this was her own self-outpouring.

Autoportrait (1925), Tamara De Lempicka. Oil on wood, 35 cm × 26 cm. Private collection. © 2007 Artists Rights Society (ARS), New York/ADAGP, Paris.

ANALYZE VISUALS
Tamara De Lempicka's poster like oil paintings are often desribed as dramatic and aggressive. How does this description fit this particular painting? Explain, citing details.

With an effort he forced himself to start the car and back into the street. This
510 was nothing, he must remember. She had done this before, and he had put her
behind him, as he would have crossed a bad account from his books.

He drove slowly downtown and, affecting abstraction,[13] traversed the deserted
streets of the business section, peopled here and there where a movie was giving
out its crowd or where consumptive or pugilistic[14] youth lounged in front of pool
halls. The clink of glasses and the slap of hands on the bars issued from saloons,
cloisters[15] of glazed glass and dirty yellow light.

She was watching him closely and the silence was embarrassing, yet in this crisis
he could find no casual word with which to profane the hour. At a convenient
turning he began to zigzag back toward the University Club.
520 "Have you missed me?" she asked suddenly.

"Everybody missed you."

He wondered if she knew of Irene Scheerer. She had been back only a day—her
absence had been almost contemporaneous with his engagement.

"What a remark!" Judy laughed sadly—without sadness. She looked at him
searchingly. He became absorbed in the dashboard.

"You're handsomer than you used to be," she said thoughtfully. "Dexter, you
have the most rememberable eyes."

He could have laughed at this, but he did not laugh. It was the sort of thing
that was said to sophomores. Yet it stabbed at him.
530 "I'm awfully tired of everything, darling." She called every one darling,
endowing the endearment with careless, individual **camaraderie.** "I wish you'd
marry me."

The directness of this confused him. He should have told her now that he was
going to marry another girl, but he could not tell her. He could as easily have
sworn that he had never loved her.

"I think we'd get along," she continued, on the same note, "unless probably
you've forgotten me and fallen in love with another girl."

Her confidence was obviously enormous. She had said, in effect, that she found
such a thing impossible to believe, that if it were true he had merely committed a
540 childish indiscretion—and probably to show off. She would forgive him, because
it was not a matter of any moment but rather something to be brushed aside
lightly.

"Of course you could never love anybody but me," she continued, "I like the
way you love me. Oh, Dexter, have you forgotten last year?"

"No, I haven't forgotten."

"Neither have I!"

Was she sincerely moved—or was she carried along by the wave of her own
acting?

"I wish we could be like that again," she said, and he forced himself to answer:
550 "I don't think we can."

---

13. **affecting abstraction:** pretending to be lost in thought.

14. **consumptive or pugilistic** (pyo͞o′jə-lĭs′-tĭc): sickly or aggressive.

15. **cloisters:** here, places to escape from life's problems.

camaraderie
(kä′mə-rä′də-rē) *n.* a
spirit of friendly good-
fellowship

"I suppose not. . . . I hear you're giving Irene Scheerer a violent rush."

There was not the faintest emphasis on the name, yet Dexter was suddenly ashamed.

"Oh, take me home," cried Judy suddenly; "I don't want to go back to that idiotic dance—with those children."

Then, as he turned up the street that led to the residence district, Judy began to cry quietly to herself. He had never seen her cry before.

The dark street lightened, the dwellings of the rich loomed up around them, he stopped his coupé in front of the great white bulk of the Mortimer Joneses'
560 house, somnolent, gorgeous, drenched with the splendor of the damp moonlight. Its solidity startled him. The strong walls, the steel of the girders, the breadth and beam and pomp of it were there only to bring out the contrast with the young beauty beside him. It was sturdy to accentuate her slightness—as if to show what a breeze could be generated by a butterfly's wing.

He sat perfectly quiet, his nerves in wild clamor, afraid that if he moved he would find her irresistibly in his arms. Two tears had rolled down her wet face and trembled on her upper lip.

"I'm more beautiful than anybody else," she said brokenly, "why can't I be happy?" Her moist eyes tore at his stability—her mouth turned slowly downward
570 with an exquisite sadness: "I'd like to marry you if you'll have me, Dexter. I suppose you think I'm not worth having, but I'll be so beautiful for you, Dexter."

A million phrases of anger, pride, passion, hatred, tenderness fought on his lips. Then a perfect wave of emotion washed over him, carrying off with it a sediment of wisdom, of convention, of doubt, of honor. This was his girl who was speaking, his own, his beautiful, his pride.

"Won't you come in?" He heard her draw in her breath sharply.

Waiting. Ⓜ

"All right," his voice was trembling, "I'll come in."

V

It was strange that neither when it was over nor a long time afterward did he
580 regret that night. Looking at it from the perspective of ten years, the fact that Judy's flare for him endured just one month seemed of little importance. Nor did it matter that by his yielding he subjected himself to a deeper agony in the end and gave serious hurt to Irene Scheerer and to Irene's parents, who had befriended him. There was nothing sufficiently pictorial about Irene's grief to stamp itself on his mind.

Dexter was at bottom hard-minded. The attitude of the city on his action was of no importance to him, not because he was going to leave the city, but because any outside attitude on the situation seemed superficial. He was completely indifferent to popular opinion. Nor, when he had seen that it was no use, that he
590 did not possess in himself the power to move fundamentally or to hold Judy Jones, did he bear any malice toward her. He loved her, and he would love her until the

Ⓜ **PREDICT**
Do you think Judy has really changed? Will she really marry Dexter? Give reasons for your predictions.

day he was too old for loving—but he could not have her. So he tasted the deep pain that is reserved only for the strong, just as he had tasted for a little while the deep happiness.

Even the ultimate falsity of the grounds upon which Judy terminated the engagement—that she did not want to "take him away" from Irene—Judy, who had wanted nothing else—did not revolt him. He was beyond any revulsion or any amusement.

He went East in February with the intention of selling out his laundries and settling in New York—but the war came to America in March and changed his plans. He returned to the West, handed over the management of the business to his partner, and went into the first officers' training-camp in late April. He was one of those young thousands who greeted the war with a certain amount of relief, welcoming the liberation from webs of tangled emotion.

VI

This story is not his biography, remember, although things creep into it which have nothing to do with those dreams he had when he was young. We are almost done with them and with him now. There is only one more incident to be related here, and it happens seven years farther on.

It took place in New York, where he had done well—so well that there were no barriers too high for him. He was thirty-two years old, and, except for one flying trip immediately after the war, he had not been West in seven years. A man named Devlin from Detroit came into his office to see him in a business way, and then and there this incident occurred, and closed out, so to speak, this particular side of his life.

"So you're from the Middle West," said the man Devlin with careless curiosity. "That's funny—I thought men like you were probably born and raised on Wall Street. You know—wife of one of my best friends in Detroit came from your city. I was an usher at the wedding."

Dexter waited with no apprehension of what was coming.

"Judy Simms," said Devlin with no particular interest; "Judy Jones she was once."

"Yes, I knew her." A dull impatience spread over him. He had heard, of course, that she was married—perhaps deliberately he had heard no more.

"Awfully nice girl," brooded Devlin meaninglessly, "I'm sort of sorry for her."

"Why?" Something in Dexter was alert, receptive, at once.

"Oh, Lud Simms has gone to pieces in a way. I don't mean he ill-uses her, but he drinks and runs around—"

"Doesn't she run around?"

"No. Stays at home with her kids."

"Oh."

"She's a little too old for him," said Devlin.

"Too old!" cried Dexter. "Why, man, she's only twenty-seven."

He was possessed with a wild notion of rushing out into the streets and taking a train to Detroit. He rose to his feet spasmodically.

"I guess you're busy," Devlin apologized quickly. "I didn't realize—"

"No, I'm not busy," said Dexter, steadying his voice. "I'm not busy at all. Not busy at all. Did you say she was—twenty-seven? No, I said she was twenty-seven."

"Yes, you did," agreed Devlin dryly.

"Go on, then. Go on."

640 "What do you mean?"

"About Judy Jones."

Devlin looked at him helplessly.

"Well, that's—I told you all there is to it. He treats her like the devil. Oh, they're not going to get divorced or anything. When he's particularly outrageous she forgives him. In fact, I'm inclined to think she loves him. She was a pretty girl when she first came to Detroit."

A pretty girl! The phrase struck Dexter as ludicrous.

"Isn't she—a pretty girl, any more?"

"Oh, she's all right."

650 "Look here," said Dexter, sitting down suddenly. "I don't understand. You say she was a 'pretty girl' and now you say she's 'all right.' I don't understand what you mean—Judy Jones wasn't a pretty girl, at all. She was a great beauty. Why, I knew her, I knew her. She was—"

Devlin laughed pleasantly.

"I'm not trying to start a row,"[16] he said. "I think Judy's a nice girl and I like her. I can't understand how a man like Lud Simms could fall madly in love with her, but he did." Then he added: "Most of the women like her."

Dexter looked closely at Devlin, thinking wildly that there must be a reason for this, some insensitivity in the man or some private malice.

660 "Lots of women fade just like *that*," Devlin snapped his fingers. "You must have seen it happen. Perhaps I've forgotten how pretty she was at her wedding. I've seen her so much since then, you see. She has nice eyes."

A sort of dullness settled down upon Dexter. For the first time in his life he felt like getting very drunk. He knew that he was laughing loudly at something Devlin had said, but he did not know what it was or why it was funny. When, in a few minutes, Devlin went he lay down on his lounge and looked out the window at the New York sky-line into which the sun was sinking in dull lovely shades of pink and gold.

He had thought that having nothing else to lose he was invulnerable at last—
670 but he knew that he had just lost something more, as surely as if he had married Judy Jones and seen her fade away before his eyes.

The dream was gone. Something had been taken from him. In a sort of panic he pushed the palms of his hands into his eyes and tried to bring up a picture of the waters lapping on Sherry Island and the moonlit veranda, and gingham on

N MOTIVATION AND TRAITS
Based on Devlin's description of Judy, how would you say she has changed since Dexter knew her? What might have caused these changes?

---

16. **row** (rou): a noisy argument or dispute.

The Shelton with Sunspots (1926), Georgia O'Keeffe. Oil on canvas, 123.1 cm × 76.8 cm. The Art Institute of Chicago, gift of Leigh B. Block (1985.206) © 2007 The Georgia O'Keeffe Museum/Artists Rights Society (ARS), New York. Photo © 1994 The Art Institute of Chicago, all rights reserved.

the golf-links and the dry sun and the gold color of her neck's soft down. And her mouth damp to his kisses and her eyes plaintive with melancholy and her freshness like new fine linen in the morning. Why, these things were no longer in the world! They had existed and they existed no longer.

For the first time in years the tears were streaming down his face. But they were for himself now. He did not care about mouth and eyes and moving hands. He wanted to care, and he could not care. For he had gone away and he could never go back any more. The gates were closed, the sun was gone down, and there was no beauty but the gray beauty of steel that withstands all time. Even the grief he could have borne was left behind in the country of illusion, of youth, of the richness of life, where his winter dreams had flourished.

"Long ago," he said, "long ago, there was something in me, but now that thing is gone. Now that thing is gone, that thing is gone. I cannot cry. I cannot care. That thing will come back no more." ∾

Comprehension

1. **Recall** How does Dexter's social **status** change in the story, and why?

2. **Clarify** Why doesn't Dexter marry either Judy Jones or Irene Scheerer?

3. **Summarize** What has happened to Judy Jones by the end of the story?

Literary Analysis

4. **Predict Story Development** Review your list of predictions and clues. Were you able to predict everything that happened? Or were you surprised by how some aspects of the story developed? Support your answer with evidence from the story.

5. **Analyze Character Motivation and Traits** What kind of man is Dexter Green? Consider his values and beliefs. Does he deserve sympathy, criticism, or both? Using examples from the text, describe Dexter's traits and the motivations for his actions and feelings.

6. **Examine Symbol** Reread lines 490–494. Consider how Dexter pursues and responds to Judy throughout "Winter Dreams," and think about the young man's feelings regarding **status.** What might Judy **symbolize** in this story? Explain, citing evidence to support your answer.

7. **Analyze Imagery** Fitzgerald is celebrated for his use of imagery, which infuses his fiction with the flush of highly tuned emotions. Locate four or five examples of imagery in "Winter Dreams" that successfully convey the emotional intensity of Dexter and Judy's entanglement. Then explain how each example achieves this purpose.

8. **Interpret Theme** Reread lines 669–688 and consider what exactly Dexter has lost. What theme, or message about the human condition, does Fitzgerald convey through this loss?

Literary Criticism

9. **Critical Interpretations** Critic Marius Bewley has argued that Fitzgerald's main subject is always "the American Dream, in which . . . his principal heroes are all trapped." How well does this statement apply to "Winter Dreams"? Use examples from the story to support your opinion.

Vocabulary in Context

VOCABULARY PRACTICE

Decide whether the words in each pair are synonyms or antonyms.

1. precipitate/prevent
2. flux/change
3. retinue/troupe
4. petulance/pleasure
5. mundane/extraordinary
6. patrimony/inheritance
7. surfeit/shortage
8. blatantly/secretly
9. camaraderie/friendship
10. precarious/secure

WORD LIST

blatantly
camaraderie
flux
mundane
patrimony
petulance
precarious
precipitate
retinue
surfeit

VOCABULARY IN WRITING

Do you think Dexter would have been as attracted to Judy if he had met her in less opulent surroundings, and if she herself had been less wealthy? Using three or more vocabulary words, write an explanation of your opinion. You might begin like this.

> **EXAMPLE SENTENCE**
>
> *If Judy had been less well-off, I think her egotism and **petulance** would have quickly disillusioned Dexter.*

VOCABULARY STRATEGY: WORDS FROM THE JAZZ AGE

A number of the terms in this story, such as *roadster,* came into English in the early decades of the 20th century. The 1920s and the years just prior to it gave the language a particularly large group of new words and expressions. Many of these phrases, such as *the cat's pajamas* to denote a remarkable person or thing, have diminished in usage. Others, however, are still commonly used. Most started out as slang but over time have gained acceptance as standard everyday English.

PRACTICE Identify the Jazz Age term or terms in each sentence. Use context clues to help understand and explain the meaning of each term. Refer to a dictionary if you need help.

1. Fred is no pushover; he sticks to what he believes in.
2. He drove an old jalopy and lived in a hovel.
3. A uniformed guard was placed at the entrance to head off gate-crashers.
4. Though not totally perfect, everything here is pretty copasetic.
5. She thinks the story is the gospel truth, but I know it is baloney.

VOCABULARY PRACTICE
For more practice, go to the **Vocabulary Center** at **ClassZone.com.**

Reading-Writing Connection

GRAMMAR AND STYLE

CRAFT EFFECTIVE SENTENCES Review the **Grammar and Style** note on page 951. Fitzgerald's rich, evocative style in "Winter Dreams" comes in part from long sentences held together by the **coordinating conjunction** *and*. He often breaks up those long descriptions with **dashes** and **phrases** in a series.

> *Early in their acquaintance it had seemed for a while that there was a deep and spontaneous mutual attraction—that first August, for example—three days of long evenings on her dusky veranda, of strange wan kisses through the late afternoon, in shadowy alcoves or behind the protecting trellises of the garden arbors, of mornings when she was fresh as a dream and almost shy at meeting him in the clarity of the rising day. There was all the ecstasy of an engagement about it, sharpened by his realization that there was no engagement.*
> (lines 379–385)

Notice that this description has no action verbs and consists almost entirely of prepositional phrases. In this way, Fitzgerald perfectly expresses Dexter's emotional surrender in both style and content.

PRACTICE Study the following paragraph from the story, noting

- coordinating conjunctions in the first sentence that connect multiple images
- participial phrases that add a sense of motion and emotional significance

Continue these stylistic elements by writing two or three additional sentences.

> *There was a fish jumping and a star shining and the lights around the lake were gleaming. Dexter sat beside Judy Jones and she explained how her boat was driven. Then she was in the water, swimming to the floating surf-board with a sinuous crawl. Watching her was without effort to the eye, watching a branch waving or a seagull flying. Her arms, burned to butternut, moved sinuously among the dull platinum ripples, elbow appearing first, casting the forearm back with a cadence of falling water, then reaching out and down, stabbing a path ahead.* (lines 252–258)

WRITING TOOLS

For prewriting, revision, and editing tools, visit the **Writing Center** at ClassZone.com.

The Great Gatsby

F. Scott Fitzgerald

F. Scott Fitzgerald
1896–1940

ABOUT THE AUTHOR F. Scott Fitzgerald's writing reflects the dreams and insecurities he experienced in his own life. Growing up comfortably among the country-club set of St. Paul, Minnesota, Fitzgerald was embarrassed by his father's career failures and his mother's immigrant background. At Princeton University, he excelled in writing but left without graduating. He joined the army and fell in love with Zelda Sayre, the pampered daughter of a distinguished judge. At first, Zelda would not marry Fitzgerald because he could not support her. They wed only after he sold his first novel, *This Side of Paradise,* in 1920, and for a time the handsome couple was the toast of New York and Paris. However, by 1930 their glittering lifestyle had burned itself out: Zelda suffered a mental collapse from which she never recovered, and her husband was drinking heavily. Fitzgerald was working in relative obscurity as a Hollywood screenwriter when he died of a heart attack at age 44.

ABOUT THE NOVEL Fitzgerald wrote *The Great Gatsby* in the early 1920s, when he and Zelda were living in Great Neck, Long Island. Fitzgerald modeled the setting of his novel (a neighborhood called West Egg) after his own fashionable New York suburb. The novel's narrator, a Midwesterner named Nick Carraway, moves to West Egg to a home that is next door to a rich, mysterious man who calls himself Jay Gatsby. Gatsby, who acquired his wealth in questionable ways, throws huge parties in the hope that his lost love, Daisy, will be one of the hundreds to attend. Daisy had spurned his attentions when he was young and poor, and she now lives just across the water in the even fancier suburb of East Egg with her rich husband, Tom Buchanan. When Nick helps Gatsby meet Daisy again, tragedy follows.

LEGACY OF A MASTERPIECE From the time it was published in 1925, *The Great Gatsby* was recognized as Fitzgerald's finest achievement. It "has interested and excited me more than any new novel I have seen," said poet T. S. Eliot; decades later, author Tobias Wolff said that Fitzgerald "saw our American world . . . with clearer eyes than any of his contemporaries." In the following excerpt, Nick gets a taste of the extravagant world Gatsby has created for himself.

   "This is an unusual party for me. I haven't even seen the host. I live over there—" I waved my hand at the invisible hedge in the distance, "and this man Gatsby sent over his chauffeur with an invitation."
   For a moment he looked at me as if he failed to understand.
   "I'm Gatsby," he said suddenly.
   "What!" I exclaimed. "Oh, I beg your pardon."

"I thought you knew, old sport. I'm afraid I'm not a very good host."

He smiled understandingly—much more than understandingly. It was one of those rare smiles with a quality of eternal reassurance in
10 it, that you may come across four or five times in life. It faced—or seemed to face—the whole external world for an instant, and then concentrated on *you* with an irresistible prejudice in your favor. It understood you just as far as you wanted to be understood, believed in you as you would like to believe in yourself, and assured you that it had precisely the impression of you that, at your best, you hoped to convey. Precisely at that point it vanished—and I was looking at an elegant young roughneck, a year or two over thirty, whose elaborate formality of speech just missed being absurd. Some time before he introduced himself I'd got a strong impression that he was picking his words with care.

20 Almost at the moment when Mr. Gatsby identified himself, a butler hurried toward him with the information that Chicago was calling him on the wire. He excused himself with a small bow that included each of us in turn.

"If you want anything just ask for it, old sport," he urged me. "Excuse me. I will rejoin you later."

When he was gone I turned immediately to Jordan—constrained to assure her of my surprise. I had expected that Mr. Gatsby would be a florid and corpulent person in his middle years.

"Who is he?" I demanded. "Do you know?"

"He's just a man named Gatsby."

30 "Where is he from, I mean? And what does he do?"

"Now *you're* started on the subject," she answered with a wan smile. "Well, he told me once he was an Oxford man."

A dim background started to take shape behind him, but at her next remark it faded away.

"However, I don't believe it."

"Why not?"

"I don't know," she insisted, "I just don't think he went there."

Something in her tone reminded me of the other girl's "I think he killed a man," and had the effect of stimulating my curiosity. I would have accepted without
40 question the information that Gatsby sprang from the swamps of Louisiana or from the lower East Side of New York. That was comprehensible. But young men didn't—at least in my provincial inexperience I believed they didn't—drift coolly out of nowhere and buy a palace on Long Island Sound.

"Anyhow, he gives large parties," said Jordan, changing the subject with an urban distaste for the concrete. "And I like large parties. They're so intimate. At small parties there isn't any privacy."

Advertising in the Jazz Age

Print Advertisements on **MediaSmart** DVD

Whose **DREAM** *are you buying?*

KEY IDEA As a struggling writer, F. Scott Fitzgerald worked briefly for an advertising firm and became leery of the industry's emerging practices. In his writing, Fitzgerald expressed his views about materialism and the impact of advertising on the contemporary culture of his day. For him, advertising was part of the glittering surface of the **American dream,** a dream of success, whose cost was often underestimated. In this lesson, you'll study magazine ads of the 1920s to uncover persuasive techniques that took root during the Jazz Age and flourish to this day.

Background

Spending Spree The first years of the 1920s were a time of "more." Because of mass production, such innovations as the automobile and the radio were more available and affordable. Electrical power spread beyond big cities, enabling more Americans to use new, time-saving appliances. As modern-day conveniences took hold and salaries steadily rose, ordinary people reaped the benefits of more leisure time and more money to spend. "Buy now, pay later" installment plans made expensive items appear more obtainable by allowing consumers to pay bills over an extended period of time.

Because merchandise was now flooding the marketplace, a fundamental shift had to occur in how Americans spent money. Before, thriftiness had been the rule. To fuel consumer spending, advertising agencies enlisted the expertise of psychologists to find ways to motivate buyers. The result was advertising designed to appeal to the public's desire for convenience, youth, beauty, and, particularly, wealth and luxury.

With an emphasis on the visual, Jazz Age ads portrayed the lavish lifestyles of the rich. Over time, the print ads in the newspapers, magazines, and billboards contributed to the impression that it was now somehow possible for ordinary Americans to live a lifestyle similar to that of the "beautiful people." Due in part to the persuasive power of such ads, the United States became a nation of shoppers and thus a consumer society.

Media Literacy: Persuasion in 1920s Ads

The Jazz Age marks the period when the advertising industry developed. Numerous agencies were established on Madison Avenue in New York City, and ads began to appear in the new medium of mass-circulation magazines. As *Time*, the *New Yorker*, and the *Saturday Evening Post* became popular, the ads within them exposed a nationwide audience to a vast array of products and services.

Advertisers also devised more deliberate ways to persuade. In earlier decades, ads contained straightforward details about product features and prices. Magazine ads of the 1920s shifted away from the product to appeal more directly to the potential buyer. To explore some persuasive techniques commonly used in the 1920s, examine this automobile ad.

STRATEGIES FOR RECOGNIZING PERSUASIVE TECHNIQUES

- Understand the overall message. Behind the 1920s ads was the implication that purchases could bring higher social status and self-fulfillment.

- Look for **purr words,** words with positive connotations. For example, in the National car ad, the words *steady, flow, power, smoothly,* and *swiftly* suggest the car's ease of operation.

- Try to spot the **slogan,** the short phrase that, used in most ads, expresses something about the quality of the product or the company that makes it. Beginning in the 1920s, a slogan helped to make a product's name and purpose memorable to potential buyers.

- Recognize the technique of **transfer,** which refers to an advertiser's attempt to connect a product with someone or something that's pleasing or admired. Ask yourself: What might images of the rich at leisure have conveyed to working-class Americans of the 1920s?

For the out-of-doors days

KODAK

And not merely the alluring picture story, but on every negative at least a date; and a title, too, if you like. Titling is the work of but an instant with an Autographic Kodak; is as simple as making the picture itself—and there is no extra charge for Autographic film.

If it isn't an Eastman, it isn't a Kodak.

Viewing Guide for

Jazz Age Advertisements

To carefully examine the two advertisements, use the DVD. As you study them, keep in mind the high spirits and optimism of the Roaring Twenties. Use these questions as you examine the image and words of each ad.

NOW VIEW

FIRST VIEWING: Comprehension

1. **Recall** What product is advertised by a woman holding a bright orange parasol?

2. **Clarify** What leisure activity is depicted in the Kodak camera ad?

CLOSE VIEWING: Media Literacy

3. **Interpret Visuals** *Glamorous* and *elegant* are two words that would describe the images in these ads. What other words would you use to describe them?

4. **Analyze the Message** Note that in the National car ad, an expensive sports car is the dominant part of the visual presentation. Explain what message you think the 1920s advertisers specifically wanted to convey to average Americans through this image.

5. **Compare Advertisements** In what ways is the Kodak camera ad shown here similar to the ad for National cars?

6. **Evaluate an Advertisement** Choose the ad that appeals to you more. Evaluate it in terms of the effectiveness of its persuasive techniques. Think about
   - the ad's appeal to status, luxury, and style
   - the design of the visual and the choice and placement of text
   - how favorably you think 1920s Americans might have viewed the ad

Write or Discuss

Evaluate the Print Ads F. Scott Fitzgerald once wrote about the advertising profession: "Advertising is a racket.... You cannot be honest without admitting that its constructive contribution to humanity is exactly minus zero." In Fitzgerald's day, the advertising industry was taking root. Today, advertising is an integral part of everyday life. Think about the print ads in this lesson and how similar they might be to ads for similar products today. What persuasive techniques are still effective? Write a short evaluation of each ad. Keep the following points in mind:

- the deliberate appeals you saw that were embedded within the advertisements' visuals and text
- how potential buyers of the 1920s ads compare to today's buyers
- your own views about today's consumer society

Produce Your Own Media

Create a Contemporary Ad Poster Using one of the 1920s ads in this lesson as a model, create an advertisement as a modern-day counterpart. Individually or with a partner, decide on the product, target an audience of working-class buyers for the product, and determine the persuasive techniques you'll apply. Represent the ad in the form of a billboard poster.

HERE'S HOW As you design the ad, consider these suggestions:

- Put as much thought into the ad's visual design as into its wording. You might want to concentrate on designing the image of the ad while a partner focuses on devising the copy.
- Be sure to include appeals to status, wealth, and luxury through both the visual design and the text. Think about the leisure activities of today's wealthy people and what working people might find desirable about them.

MEDIA TOOLS

For help with creating a poster, visit the **Media Center** at ClassZone.com.

Tech Tip

If you create the ad on a computer, choose font styles and sizes with care.

Further Exploration

Explore Ads Across the 20th Century On the DVD, access examples of ads that exhibit the persuasive techniques of the 1920s in product advertisements from ensuing decades. What cleverly designed image or turn of phrase turns objects into necessities? What evidence do you see of such techniques as appeals to youth, beauty, wealth, and luxury? Examining these ads can offer insights into the evolving consumer culture of the United States.

In Another Country

Short Story by Ernest Hemingway

Ernest Hemingway

1899–1961

The embodiment of rugged individualism, Ernest Hemingway's image looms large on the 20th-century American cultural landscape. Whether he was trout fishing in Michigan, skiing in Switzerland, cheering for bullfighters in Spain, big-game hunting in Africa, marlin fishing off the coast of Key West, or drinking wine in a Paris café, the world was his playground. But his world was also a battleground, ripped apart by wars and rife with violence, corruption, and despair. He experienced first hand the major events of his time—the Italian front in World War I, Paris in the 1920s, the Spanish Civil War, and D-day and the Battle of the Bulge during World War II. Behind the legendary persona, however, Hemingway was first and foremost a writer. His experiences provided the raw material for a distinguished body of work that captured the essence of modernity and left his indelible stamp on the century.

Irrepressible Energy and Drive
Hemingway grew up in Oak Park, Illinois, a suburb of Chicago. After high school he got a job as a reporter for the *Kansas City Star,* where he developed both his deceptively simple writing style and a devotion to the truth. During World War I, he volunteered as an ambulance driver for the American Red Cross and was severely wounded. After the war he made his way to Paris as a correspondent for the *Toronto Star.* Paris in the 1920s was a magnet for young artists and writers of the new modernist movement, and the vibrant, sociable Hemingway soon became a star. By the end of the decade, he had made his own contribution by publishing two collections of short stories, *In Our Time* (1925) and *Men Without Women* (1927), as well as two highly acclaimed novels, *The Sun Also Rises* (1926) and *A Farewell to Arms* (1929).

End of an Epic Life Hemingway was living in Cuba when he wrote what many consider his finest novel, *For Whom the Bell Tolls* (1940), based on his reporting of the Spanish Civil War. When World War II broke out, he served as a journalist, often putting himself in dangerous combat situations. His last major work published in his lifetime was the highly popular *The Old Man and the Sea* (1952). In his final years he suffered a variety of ills—including diabetes, liver problems, hypertension, and depression—that led to his suicide at age 62. He left behind five unpublished manuscripts and a towering literary legacy.

For more on Hemingway's days as a war correspondent, see the biography on page 1048.

LITERARY ANALYSIS: STYLE

The manner in which a writer chooses to tell a story can often be as arresting as the story itself. **Style** is the particular way a piece of literature is written; it is the writer's individual way of communicating ideas. Hemingway began his literary career as a reporter, and his spare, direct prose—even in his works of fiction—reflects those roots. Elements of Hemingway's journalistic prose style include

- short sentences
- an objective tone
- few adverbs or adjectives
- sharp, concrete images

As you read, consider how Hemingway's stylistic choices affect your response to the narrator—a young soldier—and your reactions to the events and people he describes.

READING SKILL: MAKE INFERENCES

One aspect of Hemingway's lean, journalistic style is that he is not explicit about the effect of important events on his characters. He relates the events and then leaves it up to his readers to **make inferences,** or logical assumptions. As you read, note revealing details about these events. Combine these clues with your own personal knowledge and experiences to infer how the characters are affected by their situation. Revise your inferences as you learn new information.

Details from the Text	How Characters Are Affected
"The people hated us because we were officers."	

VOCABULARY IN CONTEXT

Hemingway uses these words to write about soldiers in a wartime hospital. Choose the word that you associate with each type of patient.

> **WORD LIST**   citation   detached   lurch   resign

1. a patient who remains aloof and uninterested
2. a decorated soldier
3. one who stoically tries to make the best of his situation
4. a soldier who has trouble walking due to injury

What are the COSTS of war?

KEY IDEA Some costs of war can be counted. World War I, the setting of Hemingway's story, claimed the lives of about 9 million soldiers and 13 million civilians. But what about the millions who survived the **trauma** of the bloodiest and most destructive war in history up to that time? What price did they pay?

DISCUSS Consider all the things that make a war and have to be paid for, in one way or another, by both soldiers and civilians. With a small group, list both the tangible and the intangible costs of war. Then get together with another group to compare and discuss your lists. In your opinion, which cost of war is the hardest to bear?

In ANOTHER *Country*

Ernest Hemingway

> **BACKGROUND** World War I was called the Great War and the War to End All Wars. It was the first large-scale modern war with the killing power of new technological weapons. Among the 21 million wounded was 18-year-old Ernest Hemingway, who later wrote this story about soldiers recuperating in Milan, Italy. "In the first war I was hurt very badly," he explained, "in the body, mind, and spirit, and also morally."

In the fall the war was always there, but we did not go to it any more. It was cold in the fall in Milan[1] and the dark came very early. Then the electric lights came on, and it was pleasant along the streets looking in the windows. There was much game hanging outside the shops, and the snow powdered in the fur of the foxes and the wind blew their tails. The deer hung stiff and heavy and empty, and small birds blew in the wind and the wind turned their feathers. It was a cold fall and the wind came down from the mountains. **Ⓐ**

We were all at the hospital every afternoon, and there were different ways of walking across the town through the dusk to the hospital. Two of the ways were 10 alongside canals, but they were long. Always, though, you crossed a bridge across a canal to enter the hospital. There was a choice of three bridges. On one of them a woman sold roasted chestnuts. It was warm, standing in front of her charcoal fire, and the chestnuts were warm afterward in your pocket. The hospital was very old and very beautiful, and you entered through a gate and walked across a courtyard and out a gate on the other side. There were usually funerals starting from the courtyard. Beyond the old hospital were the new brick pavilions, and there we met every afternoon and were all very polite and interested in what was the matter, and sat in the machines that were to make so much difference.

The doctor came up to the machine where I was sitting and said: "What did 20 you like best to do before the war? Did you practise a sport?"

I said: "Yes, football."

"Good," he said. "You will be able to play football again better than ever."

My knee did not bend and the leg dropped straight from the knee to the ankle without a calf, and the machine was to bend the knee and make it move as in riding a tricycle. But it did not bend yet, and instead the machine **lurched** when it came to the bending part. The doctor said: "That will all pass. You are a fortunate young man. You will play football again like a champion."

In the next machine was a major who had a little hand like a baby's. He winked at me when the doctor examined his hand, which was between two leather straps 30 that bounced up and down and flapped the stiff fingers, and said: "And will I too

---

1. **Milan:** a city in northern Italy.

Ⓐ STYLE
Reread lines 1–7. What style elements give this story's opening paragraph a journalistic feel? Explain, citing specific examples.

ANALYZE VISUALS
The photo on page 971 shows a young Ernest Hemingway at a Red Cross hospital in Milan in 1918. How does this photo, depicting real people in a real place, affect the way you read this work of fiction? Explain.

lurch (lûrch) *v.* to lean or roll suddenly to one side; stagger

play football, captain-doctor?" He had been a very great fencer,[2] and before the war the greatest fencer in Italy.

The doctor went to his office in a back room and brought a photograph which showed a hand that had been withered almost as small as the major's, before it had taken a machine course, and after was a little larger. The major held the photograph with his good hand and looked at it very carefully. "A wound?" he asked.

"An industrial accident," the doctor said.

"Very interesting, very interesting," the major said, and handed it back to the doctor.

40   "You have confidence?"

"No," said the major. **B**

There were three boys who came each day who were about the same age I was. They were all three from Milan, and one of them was to be a lawyer, and one was to be a painter, and one had intended to be a soldier, and after we were finished with the machines, sometimes we walked back together to the Café Cova, which was next door to the Scala.[3] We walked the short way through the communist quarter because we were four together. The people hated us because we were officers, and from a wine-shop some one would call out, "A basso gli ufficiali!"[4] as we passed. Another boy who walked with us sometimes and made us five wore
50 a black silk handkerchief across his face because he had no nose then and his face was to be rebuilt. He had gone out to the front from the military academy and been wounded within an hour after he had gone into the front line for the first time. They rebuilt his face, but he came from a very old family and they could never get the nose exactly right. He went to South America and worked in a bank. But this was a long time ago, and then we did not any of us know how it was going to be afterward. We only knew then that there was always the war, but that we were not going to it any more.

We all had the same medals, except the boy with the black silk bandage across his face, and he had not been at the front long enough to get any medals. The tall
60 boy with a very pale face who was to be a lawyer had been a lieutenant of Arditi[5] and had three medals of the sort we each had only one of. He had lived a very long time with death and was a little **detached**. We were all a little detached, and there was nothing that held us together except that we met every afternoon at the hospital. Although, as we walked to the Cova through the tough part of town, walking in the dark, with light and singing coming out of the wine-shops, and sometimes having to walk into the street when the men and women would crowd together on the sidewalk so that we would have had to jostle them to get by, we felt held together by there being something that had happened that they, the people who disliked us, did not understand.

70   We ourselves all understood the Cova, where it was rich and warm and not too brightly lighted, and noisy and smoky at certain hours, and there were always girls

B MAKE INFERENCES
In lines 16–41, Hemingway doesn't directly state how the soldiers feel about the machines. What can you infer about their emotions from their statements and reactions? Explain, citing evidence.

detached (dĭ-tăcht′) *adj.* reserved; aloof **detach** *v.*

---

2. **fencer:** one who fences—that is, practices the art of attack and defense using blunted swords or sabers.

3. **the Scala:** La Scala, a famous opera house in Milan.

4. **"A basso gli ufficiali!"** (ä bä′sō lē ōō′fē-chä′lē) *Italian:* "Down with officers!"

5. **Arditi:** a carefully chosen group of volunteers who specialized in dangerous campaigns.

at the tables and the illustrated papers on a rack on the wall. The girls at the Cova were very patriotic, and I found that the most patriotic people in Italy were the café girls—and I believe they are still patriotic.

The boys at first were very polite about my medals and asked me what I had done to get them. I showed them the papers, which were written in very beautiful language and full of *fratellanza* and *abnegazione*,[6] but which really said, with the adjectives removed, that I had been given the medals because I was an American. After that their manner changed a little toward me, although I was their friend

80 against outsiders. I was a friend, but I was never really one of them after they had read the **citations,** because it had been different with them and they had done very different things to get their medals. I had been wounded, it was true; but we all knew that being wounded, after all, was really an accident. I was never ashamed of the ribbons, though, and sometimes, after the cocktail hour, I would imagine myself having done all the things they had done to get their medals; but walking home at night through the empty streets with the cold wind and all the shops closed, trying to keep near the street lights, I knew that I would never have done such things, and I was very much afraid to die, and often lay in bed at night by myself, afraid to die and wondering how I would be when I went back to the front again. **C**

90 The three with the medals were like hunting-hawks; and I was not a hawk, although I might seem a hawk to those who had never hunted; they, the three, knew better and so we drifted apart. But I stayed good friends with the boy who had been wounded his first day at the front, because he would never know now how he would have turned out; so he could never be accepted either, and I liked him because I thought perhaps he would not have turned out to be a hawk either. **D**

The major, who had been the great fencer, did not believe in bravery, and spent much time while we sat in the machines correcting my grammar. He had complimented me on how I spoke Italian, and we talked together very easily. One day I had said that Italian seemed such an easy language to me that I could not

100 take a great interest in it; everything was so easy to say. "Ah, yes," the major said. "Why, then, do you not take up the use of grammar?" So we took up the use of grammar, and soon Italian was such a difficult language that I was afraid to talk to him until I had the grammar straight in my mind.

The major came very regularly to the hospital. I do not think he ever missed a day, although I am sure he did not believe in the machines. There was a time when none of us believed in the machines, and one day the major said it was all nonsense. The machines were new then and it was we who were to prove them. It was an idiotic idea, he said, "a theory, like another." I had not learned my grammar, and he said I was a stupid impossible disgrace, and he was a fool to have

110 bothered with me. He was a small man and he sat straight up in his chair with his right hand thrust into the machine and looked straight ahead at the wall while the straps thumped up and down with his fingers in them.

"What will you do when the war is over if it is over?" he asked me. "Speak grammatically!"

---

6. *fratellanza* and *abnegazione* (frä′tĕ-län′zä; äb-nĕ-gä-zē-o′nĕ) *Italian*: brotherhood and self-denial.

citation (sī-tā′shən) *n.* a formal statement praising a soldier's achievements

C MAKE INFERENCES
Consider how the narrator describes his relationship with his fellow soldiers. How might such interactions affect him?

D MAKE INFERENCES
Reread lines 90–95. How does the **metaphor** about hawks further describe the difference between the narrator and the young Italian soldiers? What sense do you get of how the narrator feels about this difference?

"I will go to the States."

"Are you married?"

"No, but I hope to be."

"The more of a fool you are," he said. He seemed very angry. "A man must not marry."

120 "Why, Signor Maggiore?"[7]

"Don't call me 'Signor Maggiore.'"

"Why must not a man marry?"

"He cannot marry. He cannot marry," he said angrily. "If he is to lose everything, he should not place himself in a position to lose that. He should not place himself in a position to lose. He should find things he cannot lose."

He spoke very angrily and bitterly, and looked straight ahead while he talked.

"But why should he necessarily lose it?"

"He'll lose it," the major said. He was looking at the wall. Then he looked down at the machine and jerked his little hand out from between the straps and 130 slapped it hard against his thigh. "He'll lose it," he almost shouted. "Don't argue with me!" Then he called to the attendant who ran the machines. "Come and turn this thing off."

He went back into the other room for the light treatment and the massage. Then I heard him ask the doctor if he might use his telephone and he shut the door. When he came back into the room, I was sitting in another machine. He was wearing his cape and had his cap on, and he came directly toward my machine and put his arm on my shoulder.

"I am so sorry," he said, and patted me on the shoulder with his good hand. "I would not be rude. My wife has just died. You must forgive me."

140 "Oh—" I said, feeling sick for him. "I am *so* sorry."

He stood there biting his lower lip. "It is very difficult," he said. "I cannot **resign** myself."

He looked straight past me and out through the window. Then he began to cry. "I am utterly unable to resign myself," he said and choked. And then crying, his head up looking at nothing, carrying himself straight and soldierly, with tears on both his cheeks and biting his lips, he walked past the machines and out the door. **E**

The doctor told me that the major's wife, who was very young and whom he had not married until he was definitely invalided[8] out of the war, had died of pneumonia. She had been sick only a few days. No one expected her to die. The 150 major did not come to the hospital for three days. Then he came at the usual hour, wearing a black band on the sleeve of his uniform. When he came back, there were large framed photographs around the wall, of all sorts of wounds before and after they had been cured by the machines. In front of the machine the major used were three photographs of hands like his that were completely restored. I do not know where the doctor got them. I always understood we were the first to use the machines. The photographs did not make much difference to the major because he only looked out of the window. ❧ **F**

---

7. **Signor Maggiore** (sēn-yôr′ mäd-jō′rě) *Italian:* Mr. Major—a respectful way of addressing an officer.

8. **invalided:** removed from active service because of sickness or injury.

resign (rĭ-zīn′) *v.* to submit or yield without complaint

E STYLE
Which **image** in lines 104–146 gives you the most vivid mental picture of the major? Explain why you found this image so evocative.

F GRAMMAR AND STYLE
Reread lines 149–157. Note that though Hemingway describes a highly emotional situation, his short, **declarative sentences** and **plain diction** keep his **tone** detached and objective.

Comprehension

1. **Recall** Why is the narrator in Milan?

2. **Recall** What did the major do before the war?

3. **Summarize** How is the narrator different from the other young soldiers?

Literary Analysis

4. **Make Inferences** Review the inferences you made as you read. The narrator of this story is literally "in another country"—he is far from home, in a foreign, war-torn nation. What other aspects of his situation serve to further isolate or alienate him? Describe the text clues and prior knowledge that allowed you to infer how the narrator's situation affects him. Be sure to address each of the following:

   • how the narrator differs from the young Italian officers
   • the Italian civilians' response to the soldiers
   • how the narrator's circumstances differ from the major's at the story's end

5. **Analyze Character** Review the story for details about what the major has lost, including information regarding what he does and does not believe in. What can you conclude is the damage wrought by the **trauma** of war?

6. **Analyze Style** Hemingway explained that he chose to focus on "what really happened in action; what the actual things were that produced the emotion you experienced." Reexamine the text, recording examples of each stylistic element listed on page 969. Then explain how Hemingway's style causes this story to be so emotionally charged despite the lack of direct commentary on the characters' emotions.

Stylistic Element	Examples
short sentences	

Literary Criticism

7. **Historical Context** Influential author and patron Gertrude Stein formed a community with Fitzgerald, Hemingway, and other modernist writers living as expatriates in Paris in the 1920s. Their particular disillusionment prompted her to characterize them as a "lost generation." In what way do the characters in both "Winter Dreams" on page 938 and "In Another Country" remain "lost" at the end of each story? What might this say about the era in which these stories were written? Explain, citing evidence from both stories.

Vocabulary in Context

VOCABULARY PRACTICE

Choose the word from the word list that best completes each sentence.

1. Though only a few soldiers had received a(n) _____ for bravery, many of the others had also performed commendably.
2. Some of the soldiers sought companionship, while others remained aloof and _____.
3. It was painful to see young men _____ around on unsteady legs.
4. Was it better to struggle or to _____ oneself to one's fate?

VOCABULARY IN WRITING

Imagine yourself in the place of one of the soldiers in this story. What kind of attitude might you take toward your situation? Use one or two vocabulary words in a short description of your feelings. You might start like this.

> **EXAMPLE SENTENCE**
>
> *As a wounded soldier, I think remaining **detached** from others is the best way to keep my feelings under control.*

VOCABULARY STRATEGY: WORDS FROM ITALIAN

As the narrator of this story would surely have noticed in his study of Italian, there are many English words derived from that language, especially in the areas of music, food, and architecture. Some Italian words have kept their original spelling, while others have changed somewhat. Many of these words trace their ultimate origins back to Latin.

PRACTICE Match each boldfaced term with its definition, consulting a dictionary if necessary. Then research the origin of each word to see which ones retain their Italian spelling.

1. **farfalle**   a. a circular part of a building, usually with a dome
2. **alfresco**   b. a slow movement in a piece of music
3. **vendetta**   c. a cave or cavern
4. **parapet**   d. butterfly-shaped pasta
5. **adagio**   e. a low wall at the edge of a balcony or roof
6. **grotto**   f. taking place in the open air
7. **rotunda**   g. potato dumplings
8. **gnocchi**   h. a bitter blood feud

VOCABULARY PRACTICE
For more practice, go to the **Vocabulary Center** at **ClassZone.com**.

Reading-Writing Connection

GRAMMAR AND STYLE

ESTABLISH TONE Review the **Grammar and Style** note on page 974. **Tone** is the expression of a writer's attitude toward a subject. Hemingway's early training as a newspaper reporter heavily influenced the tone of his fiction, giving it the emotional detachment and objectivity of a news report. Such a tone is achieved partly through his use of short, **declarative sentences** and **plain diction,** a style he also picked up from newspapers. Notice the simple language and understated quality of the following sentences:

> It was cold in the fall in Milan and the dark came very early. Then the electric lights came on, and it was pleasant along the streets looking in the windows. There was much game hanging outside the shops, and the snow powdered in the fur of the foxes and the wind blew their tails. The deer hung stiff and heavy and empty, and small birds blew in the wind and the wind turned their feathers. It was a cold fall and the wind came down from the mountains. (lines 1–7)

PRACTICE Rewrite the following paragraph, adapting the language and sentence types to mimic Hemingway's objectivity.

The horrible, fiery inferno had completely annihilated everything, like an angry, vengeful God. Only the charred foundation of the Harlington Hotel remained, with its lone chimney of chipped and blackened stone standing forlornly amid the devastation like a victim of survivor guilt. Never again would we see the thick forest in its green majestic splendor! Ugly black stumps studded the land like tombstones. It was the landscape of damnation! Gone were the songs of birds, the chirps of chipmunks, and the laughter of children! A deafening silence enveloped the area for miles around. Only black grasshoppers flitted about the soot, sending up tiny clouds of ash.

WRITING TOOLS

For prewriting, revision, and editing tools, visit the **Writing Center** at ClassZone.com.

The Grapes of Wrath

John Steinbeck

John Steinbeck
1902–1968

ABOUT THE AUTHOR John Steinbeck firmly followed the principle "Write about what you know." Much of his fiction is set in California's Salinas Valley, where he grew up, and other areas of California where he spent time. Often it deals with the problems of working men and women, which he knew first-hand from the string of odd jobs he held as a young man—fruit picker, ranch hand, and apprentice painter, to name just a few. Steinbeck published his first novel, *Cup of Gold,* just a few months before the stock market crash ushered in the Great Depression of the 1930s.

Many of his later works focus on the effects those hard times had on average Americans. Among those hit worst were farm families who left the drought-ravaged Dust Bowl for California, only to be packed into shantytowns and paid a pittance as farm laborers. In 1936, Steinbeck traveled from Oklahoma to California with a group of these migrants to report on their plight for the *San Francisco News;* it was this experience that inspired his greatest novel, *The Grapes of Wrath.*

ABOUT THE NOVEL The blockbuster novel of 1939, *The Grapes of Wrath* tells the story of the Joads, a family of Oklahoma migrant farmers, or "Okies," who leave their small farm in an old jalopy to make the long journey to California in search of work. Ma Joad holds the family together as they face untold hardships and disappointments. Despite their difficulties, the family never gives up their basic humanity and spirit of endurance. Interspersed between the chapters of their story are poetic chapters describing the situation in broader terms. The extract here, from one of those chapters, is a description of the temporary camps that the traveling farmers set up each night.

And the worlds were built in the evening. The people, moving in from the highways, made them with their tents and their hearts and their brains.

In the morning the tents came down, the canvas was folded, the tent poles tied along the running board, the beds put in place on the cars, the pots in their places. And as the families moved westward, the technique of building up a home in the evening and tearing it down with the morning light became fixed; so that the folded tent was packed in one place, the cooking pots counted in their box. And as the cars moved westward, each member of the family grew into his proper place, grew into

his duties; so that each member, old and young, had his place in the car;
10 so that in the weary, hot evenings, when the cars pulled into the camping
places, each member had his duty and went to it without instruction:
children to gather wood, to carry water; men to pitch the tents and
bring down the beds; women to cook the supper and to watch while the
family fed. And this was done without command. The families, which
had been units of which the boundaries were a house at night, a farm by
day, changed their boundaries. In the long hot light, they were silent in the cars moving
slowly westward; but at night they integrated with any group they found.

Thus they changed their social life—changed as in the whole universe only man
can change. They were not farm men any more, but migrant men. And the thought,
20 the planning, the long staring silence that had gone out to the fields, went now to the
roads, to the distance, to the West. That man whose mind had been bound with acres
lived with narrow concrete miles. And his thought and his worry were not any more
with rainfall, with wind and dust, with the thrust of the crops. Eyes watched the tires,
ears listened to the clattering motors, and minds struggled with oil, with gasoline,
with the thinning rubber between air and road. Then a broken gear was tragedy.
Then water in the evening was the yearning, and food over the fire. Then health to go
on was the need and strength to go on, and spirit to go on. The wills thrust westward
ahead of them, and fears that had once apprehended drought or flood now lingered
with anything that might stop the westward crawling.

30   The camps became fixed—each a short day's journey from the last.

And on the road the panic overcame some of the families, so that they drove night
and day, stopped to sleep in the cars, and drove on to the West, flying from the road,
flying from movement. And these lusted so greatly to be settled that they set their
faces into the West and drove toward it, forcing the clashing engines over the roads.

But most of the families changed and grew quickly into the new life. And when
the sun went down—

Time to look out for a place to stop.

And—there's some tents ahead.

The car pulled off the road and stopped, and because others were there first,
40 certain courtesies were necessary. And the man, the leader of the family, leaned from
the car.

Can we pull up here an' sleep?

Why, sure, be proud to have you.

Photo Essay: The Grapes of Wrath

Use with *The Grapes of Wrath,* page 978.

Before John Steinbeck wrote *The Grapes of Wrath,* he traveled through California's migrant labor camps with *Life* magazine photographer Horace Bristol. The following pictures were taken by Bristol at that time. The captions are Steinbeck's and the accompanying essay appeared along with the photos and captions. As you view "the worlds [that] were built in the evening" and the people who built and inhabited them, bear in mind that you will later be asked to decide which is more compelling, the photo essay or the excerpt from the novel.

Skill Focus: Analyze Photographs

The photographs on these next few pages can be analyzed and appreciated both as fine art and as a cultural record of how Depression-era migrant workers lived. Asking yourself the following questions as you view each photograph can help you do this:

- What shape or space is emphasized in the **composition?** What is the **focal point,** or spot that draws your attention? What else catches your eye?

- From what **vantage point,** or distance and position, did Bristol take the photograph? What impact does this have on your view of the subject?

- What **techniques** did Bristol use and why? For example, what sort of lighting did he choose, and what effect does it have?

- What is the **mood** created by the image?

- What information do you gather from the image and its **caption?**

For each image, note your observations on a chart like the one begun here.

Photograph #1: Ma Joad?	
Focal Point of Composition	Woman's face; I also notice her hands
Vantage Point and Its Impact	Next to woman at eye level; it makes me feel like I'm having a conversation with her, establishes a feeling of equality and intimacy
Techniques and Their Effects	Sunlight with shadow reveals wrinkles and dirt.
Mood	
Information from Image & Caption	

A

"I always kept 'em together and kept 'em fed. I planned for 'em. I can buy this house for ten dollars. I'll have a garden along there. Ducks can swim in the irrigation ditch. I got to get ten dollars."

The GRAPES of WRATH

Photographs by HORACE BRISTOL
Captions by JOHN STEINBECK

A ANALYZE PHOTOGRAPHS
What is emphasized in the photograph's **composition?** What does the **focal point** tell you about the woman? Explain.

In 1934, when the rest of the U.S. began to rise out of Depression, dust began to blow in Oklahoma and Montana, Arkansas and the Dakotas. Thousands of bewildered farmers and farm hands lost their holdings or their jobs and began to drift West. By the time the dust stopped blowing, the banks and the land companies found that mechanized farming over huge areas could make the land pay when individual farmers could not. The drift Westward continued and grew. Lured by assurances of green land and good money, the farmers sold their old tools and older houses, their livestock and furniture for anything they would bring. They used the money to buy shaky old cars, sawing off the bodies to
10 make sedans into flimsy trucks. Along Route 66, through the Texas Panhandle, New Mexico and Arizona, they squeaked and rattled by tens of thousands, a bedraggled leaderless horde, camping beside the creeks and prairie villages, headed for California as a promised land.

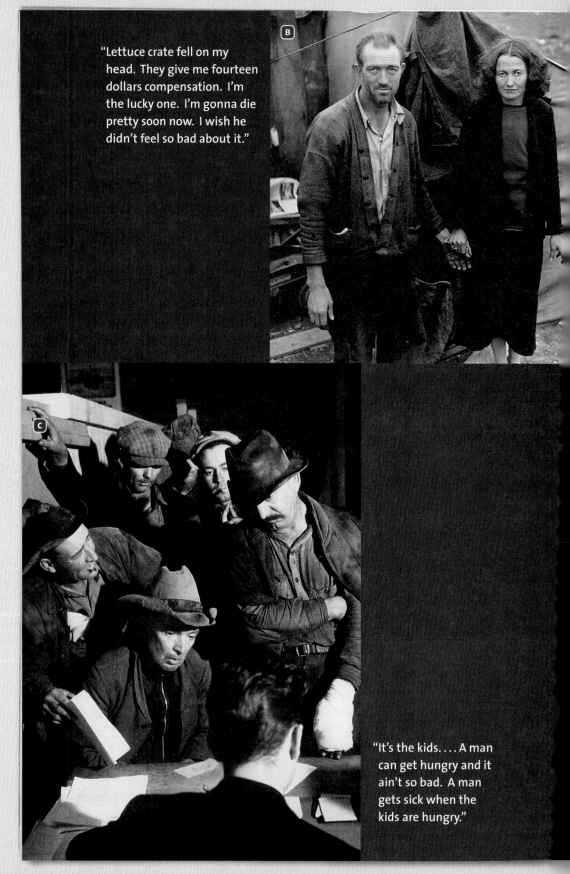

B ANALYZE PHOTOGRAPHS
Study the photograph and reread the **caption.** How does the text affect the impact of the photograph? Explain.

B

"Lettuce crate fell on my head. They give me fourteen dollars compensation. I'm the lucky one. I'm gonna die pretty soon now. I wish he didn't feel so bad about it."

C ANALYZE PHOTOGRAPHS
What is the **focal point** of this photograph? What **mood** is established? Explain.

C

"It's the kids.... A man can get hungry and it ain't so bad. A man gets sick when the kids are hungry."

In California the migrants found no promised land. Instead, they found that thousands of their own kind had already glutted the market for cheap itinerant labor. Furthermore, scrabbling about the State to look for work, fighting each other for jobs, they learned that California hated them because they were hungry and desperate. Because most of them came from Oklahoma, they were scornfully called "Okies," harried along between scarce jobs. Migrants are still in California,
20 squatting in hideous poverty and squalor on the thin margins of the world's richest land. Of the one-third of a nation which is ill-housed, ill-clad, ill-nourished these are the bitterest dregs.

The problem of the Okies, though grim, is not insoluble. Some hope of a solution is suggested by the fact that an American writer can not only write about the Okies but that the result can be hailed by U.S. critics as the book of the decade. In *The Grapes of Wrath* (The Viking Press, $2.75), John Steinbeck (*Of Mice and Men*) presents the Okies in all their stink and misery, their courage and confusion. His 600-page novel, which may become a 20th Century *Uncle Tom's Cabin,* is now a nationwide best-seller. Last week, Producer Darryl Zanuck paid
30 $75,000 for the right to make it into a movie.

"We just got in. Gonna work in the peas. Got a han'bill that says they's good wages pickin' peas."

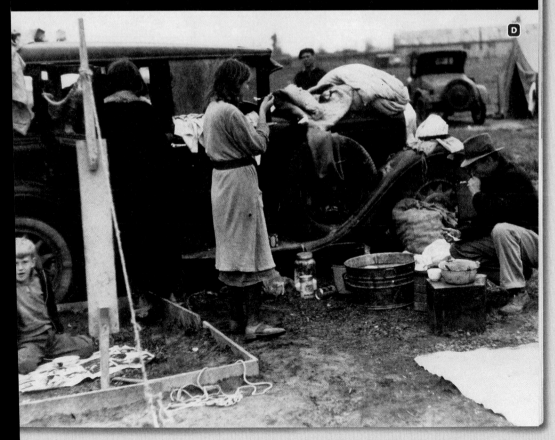

D ANALYZE PHOTOGRAPHS
What details of Depression-era migrant worker life are recorded

"The company lets us live in 'em when we're pickin' cotton. When we ain't workin', we pay rent. Water's comin' up in 'em now." **E**

E **ANALYZE PHOTOGRAPHS**
Reread the caption. What information do you get about the company from this caption? Based on this information, what can you infer about the company?

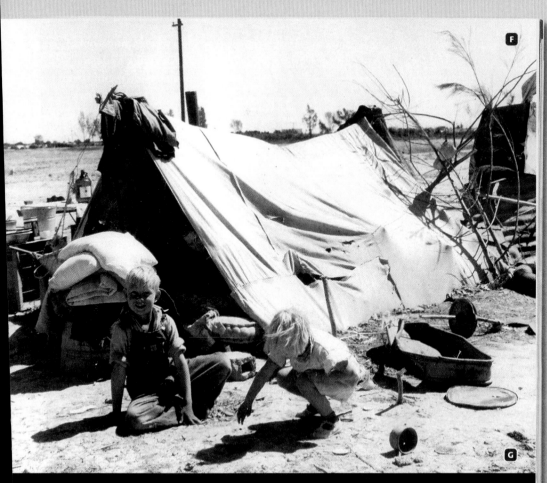

"We got to have a house when the rains come . . . jus' so's it's got a roof and a floor. Just to keep the little fellas off'n the groun'."

F ANALYZE PHOTOGRAPHS
How would you contrast the **mood** of the photographs on pages 984 and 985?

G ANALYZE PHOTOGRAPHS
What do the shadows in this photograph serve to emphasize? Explain.

The pictures on [these pages] are not simply types which resemble those described in *The Grapes of Wrath*. They are the people of whom Author Steinbeck wrote. Before starting his book, he lived in California's migratory labor camps. LIFE Photographer Horace Bristol accompanied him. The woman on [page 981] might well be Ma Joad, Author Steinbeck's heroine. The man with the double-edged ax [page 986] is a counterpart of his hero, Tom Joad. Captions for their pictures and all others on these pages were written by Steinbeck. Some are excerpts from his book. Others were written especially for LIFE's photographs.

H ANALYZE
PHOTOGRAPHS

ANALYZE PHOTOGRAPHS
Horace Bristol could have **cropped,** or cut, the background figure out of this image without losing any part of the man and ax in the foreground. Reread the caption. What is the impact of having the second man in the background?

"The whole thing's nuts. There's work to do and people to do it, but them two can't get together. There's food to eat and people to eat it, and them two can't get together neither."

"She's awful pretty. An' she been to high school. She could help a man with figuring and stuff like that."

ANALYZE PHOTOGRAPHS
From this last photograph and caption, what might you gather about people's attitudes toward their circumstances? How might the photographer's **vantage point** be said to contribute to this idea?

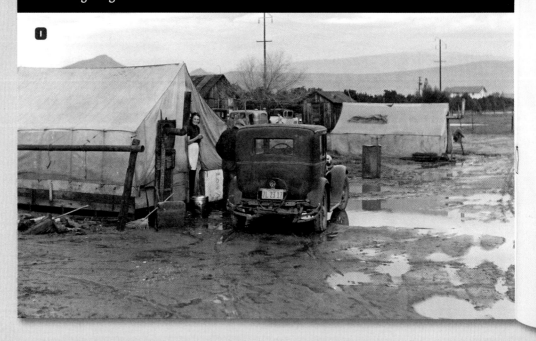

Comprehension

1. **Recall** In the late 1930s, what combination of events and promises prompted many farmers in the plains states to travel westward?

2. **Recall** Who wrote the captions for the photographs in this photo essay? Are they fiction, nonfiction, or a mixture of both?

3. **Summarize** What typically happened to the Midwestern farmers who migrated to California? How were they regarded by Californians?

Critical Analysis

4. **Analyze Tone** How would you describe the attitude of the speaker in the caption for the image on page 984? How does the information conveyed by the photograph and caption on page 985 help you understand this attitude?

5. **Analyze Photographs** Based on this photo essay, what have you gathered about the living conditions and attitudes of Depression-era migrant workers?

6. **Evaluate** Reread lines 23–30 of the essay text. Do you agree or disagree with the writer's assertion? Explain.

Read for Information: Compare and Evaluate

WRITING PROMPT

Reflect on the excerpt you read from *The Grapes of Wrath* and on the photo essay you just studied. In your opinion, which paints a more powerful portrait of the migrant farm workers? Why?

The following steps will help you answer the prompt:

1. Review the selections and decide based on your first reaction, which piece you find more powerful.

2. Now go back and analyze each piece, taking notes on the following elements:

   - the amount of information provided
   - the kinds of **details** and information conveyed
   - the ideas or **themes** emphasized
   - the **author's perspective** and the photographer's vantage point
   - the literary elements and the artistic techniques
   - the **mood** and thoughts evoked

3. Review your analysis. As you look at the relative strengths of each piece, do you still have the same opinion about which is more compelling? Why or why not?

4. Now state your opinion about which selection is more compelling, and give the reasons for your opinion, comparing the strengths and weaknesses of each piece.

The Jilting of Granny Weatherall

Short Story by Katherine Anne Porter

Katherine Anne Porter
1890–1980

Katherine Anne Porter has been called a "writer's writer"; in her lifetime she was more popular with critics and her fellow writers than with the public. She wrote mostly short fiction, a form with which it was difficult to build a popular reputation. What's more, all of her 27 short stories, including those technically classified as novellas (short novels), could fit into a single book. Still, Porter's work is celebrated for its nearly flawless consistency and style. Each one of her stories is a polished gem reflecting a hard truth about human experience.

Survival and Resiliency She was born Callie Russell Porter on a scrappy dirt farm in central Texas, where she dreamed of becoming an actress. She had the good looks, the drive, and the talent for performing but lacked the stamina. A two-year bout with tuberculosis permanently dashed her dreams of acting. However, while recuperating at a sanitorium, Porter

befriended a journalist who helped her start writing for newspapers. Living in Denver in 1918, Porter was again stricken by illness, this time by the deadly flu epidemic that swept the globe after World War I, killing 550,000 people in the United States and at least 25 million worldwide. This second brush with death inspired an idea that was later to become part of her novella *Pale Horse, Pale Rider* (1939). After her recovery, convinced of her true calling, Porter left Denver for the New York literary scene and the wider world.

Deep in the Heart of Texas Like many writers of her generation, Porter traveled widely, living in Mexico, Bermuda, Germany, Switzerland, and France, as well as New York for much of the 1920s and 1930s. Some of these places inspired her fiction: her time in Mexico enriched her first published story, "Maria Concepción" (1922), and several others, while pre–World War II Berlin informed "The Leaning Tower" (1944). But for the most part, foreign travel provided what Porter called a "constant exercise of memory" and brought her closer to her native land. Some of her best fiction—notably, "Noon Wine" (1937), "Old Mortality" (1939), and a series called "The Old Order" (1955)—takes place in Texas. Many of these stories, and "The Jilting of Granny Weatherall" (1929) in particular, include a dynamic grandmother based on Porter's own who raised her until age 11 and exerted a strong influence. Porter even took her grandmother's name after she divorced her first husband and began life on her own.

● LITERARY ANALYSIS: STREAM OF CONSCIOUSNESS

The very first paragraph of this story plunges readers directly into the thoughts of its protagonist. This literary technique, **stream of consciousness,** presents the flow of a character's seemingly unconnected thoughts, responses, and sensations. Rather than offering a logical account of events, it presents a series of associative connections, with one impression giving rise to another. This technique can be confusing to even the best readers; using these strategies will help:

- Remember that you are "inside" the main character's thoughts—the depictions of people and events you find there may not be completely reliable.

- Look for quotation marks to determine when Granny is speaking aloud and when she's not.

- Keep track of the twists and turns of Granny's thoughts to understand what she is reacting to.

■ READING SKILL: CLARIFY SEQUENCE

In this narrative, Porter shuffles together the past and the present to depict the distorted way Granny perceives the **sequence** of events. Porter achieves this effect in part through the use of **flashback,** in which she relates events that happened before the beginning of the story's "now" time. As you travel through Granny's memory, use a timeline to untangle the sequence of the main events in her life.

Jilting by George

Examination by
Dr. Harry

▲ VOCABULARY IN CONTEXT

Porter uses these words to take readers into the mind of a woman on her deathbed. Complete each phrase with a word from the list.

WORD LIST	amethyst	dwindle	plague
	assign	embroidered	

1. kept an elaborately _____ blanket on the sickbed
2. had a valuable _____ ring to pass on to her daughter
3. felt her time _____ as she got weaker and weaker

Explore the Key Idea

What makes a MEMORY *linger?*

KEY IDEA That perfect first date. The humiliating moment you realized you had failed your driving test. The elated, screaming crowd jumping to its feet as the last seconds of the big game ticked away. Whether pleasant or painful, there are some **memories** you just can't shake. In this story, as Granny Weatherall lies on her deathbed, she's haunted by an event that still affects her almost as powerfully as it did when she experienced it as a young woman.

QUICKWRITE Write a paragraph about a memory of your own that you can still recall in crisp detail. What images, feelings, sounds, or smells come to mind? Why do you think this moment lingers in your memory?

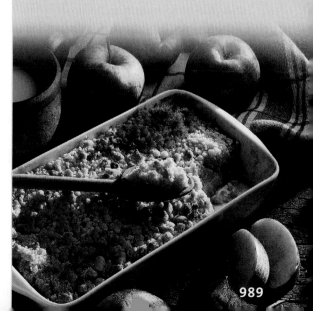

THE Jilting of GRANNY WEATHERALL

Katherine Anne Porter

She flicked her wrist neatly out of Doctor Harry's pudgy careful fingers and pulled the sheet up to her chin. The brat ought to be in knee breeches.[1] Doctoring around the country with spectacles on his nose! "Get along now, take your schoolbooks and go. There's nothing wrong with me." **A**

Doctor Harry spread a warm paw like a cushion on her forehead where the forked green vein danced and made her eyelids twitch. "Now, now, be a good girl, and we'll have you up in no time."

"That's no way to speak to a woman nearly eighty years old just because she's down. I'd have you respect your elders, young man."

10 "Well, Missy, excuse me." Doctor Harry patted her cheek. "But I've got to warn you, haven't I? You're a marvel, but you must be careful or you're going to be good and sorry."

"Don't tell me what I'm going to be. I'm on my feet now, morally speaking. It's Cornelia. I had to go to bed to get rid of her."

Her bones felt loose, and floated around in her skin, and Doctor Harry floated like a balloon around the foot of the bed. He floated and pulled down his waistcoat and swung his glasses on a cord. "Well, stay where you are, it certainly can't hurt you."

A STREAM OF CONSCIOUSNESS
In lines 1–4, how does Porter create the effect that you, the reader, are "inside" Granny's mind? Explain how your intimacy with this character affects your impression of her.

ANALYZE VISUALS
What does this unusual portrait suggest about its subject's thoughts or state of mind? Explain, citing details.

---

1. **knee breeches:** short pants formerly worn by young boys.

"Get along and doctor your sick," said Granny Weatherall. "Leave a well
20 woman alone. I'll call for you when I want you. . . . Where were you forty years
ago when I pulled through milk-leg[2] and double pneumonia? You weren't even
born. Don't let Cornelia lead you on," she shouted, because Doctor Harry
appeared to float up to the ceiling and out. "I pay my own bills, and I don't throw
my money away on nonsense!"

She meant to wave good-by, but it was too much trouble. Her eyes closed of
themselves, it was like a dark curtain drawn around the bed. The pillow rose and
floated under her, pleasant as a hammock in a light wind. She listened to the
leaves rustling outside the window. No, somebody was swishing newspapers: no,
Cornelia and Doctor Harry were whispering together. She leaped broad awake,
30 thinking they whispered in her ear. ⓑ

"She was never like this, *never* like this!" "Well, what can we expect?" "Yes,
eighty years old. . . ."

Well, and what if she was? She still had ears. It was like Cornelia to whisper
around doors. She always kept things secret in such a public way. She was always
being tactful and kind. Cornelia was dutiful; that was the trouble with her.
Dutiful and good: "So good and dutiful," said Granny, "that I'd like to spank her."
She saw herself spanking Cornelia and making a fine job of it.

"What'd you say, Mother?"

Granny felt her face tying up in hard knots.

40 "Can't a body think, I'd like to know?"

"I thought you might want something."

"I do. I want a lot of things. First off, go away and don't whisper."

She lay and drowsed, hoping in her sleep that the children would keep out and
let her rest a minute. It had been a long day. Not that she was tired. It was always
pleasant to snatch a minute now and then. There was always so much to be done,
let me see: tomorrow.

Tomorrow was far away and there was nothing to trouble about. Things were
finished somehow when the time came; thank God there was always a little
margin over for peace: then a person could spread out the plan of life and tuck in
50 the edges orderly. It was good to have everything clean and folded away, with the
hair brushes and tonic bottles sitting straight on the white **embroidered** linen: the
day started without fuss and the pantry shelves laid out with rows of jelly glasses
and brown jugs and white stone-china jars with blue whirligigs[3] and words painted
on them: coffee, tea, sugar, ginger, cinnamon, allspice: and the bronze clock with
the lion on top nicely dusted off. The dust that lion could collect in twenty-four
hours! The box in the attic with all those letters tied up, well, she'd have to go
through that tomorrow. All those letters—George's letters and John's letters and
her letters to them both—lying around for the children to find afterwards made
her uneasy. Yes, that would be tomorrow's business. No use to let them know how
60 silly she had been once.

ⓑ **STREAM OF CONSCIOUSNESS**
How does the description in lines 25–30 reinforce the idea that you are listening in on Granny's thoughts?

embroidered
(ĕm'broi'dərd) *adj.*
decorated with stitched designs **embroider** *v.*

---

2. **milk-leg:** a painful swelling of the leg experienced by some women after giving birth.

3. **stone-china . . . whirligigs** (hwûr'lĭ-gĭgz'): jars made of thick pottery with blue spiral designs.

While she was rummaging around she found death in her mind and it felt clammy and unfamiliar. She had spent so much time preparing for death there was no need for bringing it up again. Let it take care of itself now. When she was sixty she had felt very old, finished, and went around making farewell trips to see her children and grandchildren, with a secret in her mind: This is the very last of your mother, children! Then she made her will and came down with a long fever. That was all just a notion like a lot of other things, but it was lucky too, for she had once for all got over the idea of dying for a long time. Now she couldn't be worried. She hoped she had better sense now. Her father had lived to be one

70 hundred and two years old and had drunk a noggin of strong hot toddy[4] on his last birthday. He told the reporters it was his daily habit, and he owed his long life to that. He had made quite a scandal and was very pleased about it. She believed she'd just **plague** Cornelia a little. **C**

"Cornelia! Cornelia!" No footsteps, but a sudden hand on her cheek. "Bless you, where have you been?"

"Here, Mother."

"Well, Cornelia, I want a noggin of hot toddy." **D**

"Are you cold, darling?"

"I'm chilly, Cornelia. Lying in bed stops the circulation. I must have told you

80 that a thousand times."

Well, she could just hear Cornelia telling her husband that Mother was getting a little childish and they'd have to humor her. The thing that most annoyed her was that Cornelia thought she was deaf, dumb, and blind. Little hasty glances and tiny gestures tossed around her and over her head saying, "Don't cross her, let her have her way, she's eighty years old," and she sitting there as if she lived in a thin glass cage. Sometimes Granny almost made up her mind to pack up and move back to her own house where nobody could remind her every minute that she was old. Wait, wait, Cornelia, till your own children whisper behind your back!

In her day she had kept a better house and had got more work done. She

90 wasn't too old yet for Lydia to be driving eighty miles for advice when one of the children jumped the track, and Jimmy still dropped in and talked things over: "Now, Mammy, you've a good business head, I want to know what you think of this? . . ." Old. Cornelia couldn't change the furniture around without asking. Little things, little things! They had been so sweet when they were little. Granny wished the old days were back again with the children young and everything to be done over. It had been a hard pull, but not too much for her. When she thought of all the food she had cooked, and all the clothes she had cut and sewed, and all the gardens she had made—well, the children showed it. There they were, made out of her, and they couldn't get away from that. Sometimes she wanted to see

100 John again and point to them and say, Well, I didn't do so badly, did I? But that would have to wait. That was for tomorrow. She used to think of him as a man, but now all the children were older than their father, and he would be a child beside her if she saw him now. It seemed strange and there was something wrong in the idea. Why, he couldn't possibly recognize her. She had fenced in a hundred

plague (plāg) v. to annoy; harass

C STREAM OF CONSCIOUSNESS
Reread lines 47–73 and consider how Porter conveys the flow of Granny's thoughts. What idea triggers Granny's thoughts of death?

D CLARIFY SEQUENCE
Reread lines 61–77. Identify clues about the timing of Granny's father's "scandal" and subsequent death. What connection do you see between this memory and Granny's desire to "plague" Cornelia?

---

4. **noggin . . . toddy:** mug of a strong alcoholic drink.

acres once, digging the post holes herself and clamping the wires with just a negro boy to help. That changed a woman. John would be looking for a young woman with the peaked Spanish comb in her hair and the painted fan. Digging post holes changed a woman. Riding country roads in the winter when women had their babies was another thing: sitting up nights with sick horses and sick negroes and sick children and hardly ever losing one. John, I hardly ever lost one of them! John would see that in a minute, that would be something he could understand, she wouldn't have to explain anything! **E**

It made her feel like rolling up her sleeves and putting the whole place to rights again. No matter if Cornelia was determined to be everywhere at once, there were a great many things left undone on this place. She would start tomorrow and do them. It was good to be strong enough for everything, even if all you made melted and changed and slipped under your hands, so that by the time you finished you almost forgot what you were working for. What was it I set out to do? she asked herself intently, but she could not remember. A fog rose over the valley, she saw it marching across the creek swallowing the trees and moving up the hill like an army of ghosts. Soon it would be at the near edge of the orchard, and then it was time to go in and light the lamps. Come in, children, don't stay out in the night air.

Lighting the lamps had been beautiful. The children huddled up to her and breathed like little calves waiting at the bars in the twilight. Their eyes followed the match and watched the flame rise and settle in a blue curve, then they moved away from her. The lamp was lit, they didn't have to be scared and hang on to mother any more. Never, never, never more. God, for all my life I thank Thee. Without Thee, my God, I could never have done it. Hail, Mary, full of grace.[5]

I want you to pick all the fruit this year and see that nothing is wasted. There's always someone who can use it. Don't let good things rot for want of using. You waste life when you waste good food. Don't let things get lost. It's bitter to lose things. Now, don't let me get to thinking, not when I am tired and taking a little nap before supper. . . .

The pillow rose about her shoulders and pressed against her heart and the memory was being squeezed out of it: oh, push down the pillow, somebody: it would smother her if she tried to hold it. Such a fresh breeze blowing and such a green day with no threats in it. But he had not come, just the same. What does a woman do when she has put on the white veil and set out the white cake for a man and he doesn't come? She tried to remember. No, I swear he never harmed me but in that. He never harmed me but in that . . . and what if he did? There was the day, the day, but a whirl of dark smoke rose and covered it, crept up and over into the bright field where everything was planted so carefully in orderly rows. That was hell, she knew hell when she saw it. For sixty years she had prayed against remembering him and against losing her soul in the deep pit of hell, and now the two things were mingled in one and the thought of him was a smoky cloud from hell that moved and crept in her head when she had just got rid of Doctor Harry and was trying to rest a minute. Wounded vanity, Ellen, said a **F** sharp voice in the top of her mind. Don't let your wounded vanity get the upper

---

E CLARIFY SEQUENCE
Why does Granny say that today, John would be a child compared to her? Record on your timeline the information you learn in this paragraph.

F GRAMMAR AND STYLE
Reread lines 143–147. Porter uses **repetition** as well as short clauses joined by the **coordinating conjunction** *and* to present the circular nature of Granny's thoughts.

hand of you. Plenty of girls get jilted. You were jilted, weren't you? Then stand up
150 to it. Her eyelids wavered and let in streamers of blue-gray light like tissue paper
over her eyes. She must get up and pull the shades down or she'd never sleep. She
was in bed again and the shades were not down. How could that happen? Better
turn over, hide from the light, sleeping in the light gave you nightmares. "Mother,
how do you feel now?" and a stinging wetness on her forehead. But I don't like
having my face washed in cold water! **G**

Hapsy? George? Lydia? Jimmy? No, Cornelia, and her features were swollen
and full of little puddles. "They're coming, darling, they'll all be here soon." Go
wash your face, child, you look funny.

Instead of obeying, Cornelia knelt down and put her head on the pillow. She
160 seemed to be talking but there was no sound. "Well, are you tongue-tied? Whose
birthday is it? Are you going to give a party?"

Cornelia's mouth moved urgently in strange shapes. "Don't do that, you bother
me, daughter."

"Oh, no, Mother. Oh, no. . . ."

Nonsense. It was strange about children. They disputed your every word. "No
what, Cornelia?"

"Here's Doctor Harry."

"I won't see that boy again. He just left five minutes ago."

"That was this morning, Mother. It's night now. Here's the nurse." **H**

170 "This is Doctor Harry, Mrs. Weatherall. I never saw you look so young and
happy!"

"Ah, I'll never be young again—but I'd be happy if they'd let me lie in peace
and get rested."

She thought she spoke up loudly, but no one answered. A warm weight on her
forehead, a warm bracelet on her wrist, and a breeze went on whispering, trying to
tell her something. A shuffle of leaves in the everlasting hand of God, He blew on
them and they danced and rattled. "Mother, don't mind, we're going to give you a
little hypodermic."[6] "Look here, daughter, how do ants get in this bed? I saw sugar
ants yesterday." Did you send for Hapsy too?

180 It was Hapsy she really wanted. She had to go a long way back through a great
many rooms to find Hapsy standing with a baby on her arm. She seemed to
herself to be Hapsy also, and the baby on Hapsy's arm was Hapsy and himself and
herself, all at once, and there was no surprise in the meeting. Then Hapsy melted
from within and turned flimsy as gray gauze and the baby was a gauzy shadow,
and Hapsy came up close and said, "I thought you'd never come," and looked at
her very searchingly and said, "You haven't changed a bit!" They leaned forward to
kiss, when Cornelia began whispering from a long way off, "Oh, is there anything
you want to tell me? Is there anything I can do for you?"

Yes, she had changed her mind after sixty years and she would like to see
190 George. I want you to find George. Find him and be sure to tell him I forgot
him. I want him to know I had my husband just the same and my children and
my house like any other woman. A good house too and a good husband that I

---

6. **hypodermic:** injection.

G STREAM OF
CONSCIOUSNESS
Describe the major event
revealed by Granny's
thoughts in lines 134–155.
What is the significance
of the dark smoke Granny
sees covering the green,
orderly fields when she
recalls this event?

H STREAM OF
CONSCIOUSNESS
What clues in lines 156–
169 reveal to readers how
much Granny's condition
is deteriorating?

loved and fine children out of him. Better than I hoped for even. Tell him I was given back everything he took away and more. Oh, no, oh, God, no, there was something else besides the house and the man and the children. Oh, surely they were not all? What was it? Something not given back. . . . Her breath crowded down under her ribs and grew into a monstrous frightening shape with cutting edges; it bored up into her head, and the agony was unbelievable: Yes, John, get the Doctor now, no more talk, my time has come.

200   When this one was born it should be the last. The last. It should have been born first, for it was the one she had truly wanted. Everything came in good time. Nothing left out, left over. She was strong, in three days she would be as well as ever. Better. A woman needed milk in her to have her full health. ❶

"Mother, do you hear me?"

"I've been telling you—"

"Mother, Father Connolly's here."

"I went to Holy Communion only last week. Tell him I'm not so sinful as all that."

"Father just wants to speak to you."

He could speak as much as he pleased. It was like him to drop in and inquire
210 about her soul as if it were a teething baby, and then stay on for a cup of tea and a round of cards and gossip. He always had a funny story of some sort, usually about an Irishman who made his little mistakes and confessed them, and the point lay in some absurd thing he would blurt out in the confessional showing his struggles between native piety and original sin. Granny felt easy about her soul. Cornelia, where are your manners? Give Father Connolly a chair. She had her secret comfortable understanding with a few favorite saints who cleared a straight road to God for her. All as surely signed and sealed as the papers for the new Forty Acres. Forever . . . heirs and **assigns** forever. Since the day the wedding cake was not cut, but thrown out and wasted. The whole bottom dropped out of the world,
220 and there she was blind and sweating with nothing under her feet and the walls falling away. His hand had caught her under the breast, she had not fallen, there was the freshly polished floor with the green rug on it, just as before. He had cursed like a sailor's parrot and said, "I'll kill him for you." Don't lay a hand on him, for my sake leave something to God. "Now, Ellen, you must believe what I tell you. . . ."

So there was nothing, nothing to worry about any more, except sometimes in the night one of the children screamed in a nightmare, and they both hustled out shaking and hunting for the matches and calling, "There, wait a minute, here we are!" John, get the doctor now, Hapsy's time has come. But there was Hapsy
230 standing by the bed in a white cap. "Cornelia, tell Hapsy to take off her cap. I can't see her plain."

Her eyes opened very wide and the room stood out like a picture she had seen somewhere. Dark colors with the shadows rising towards the ceiling in long angles. The tall black dresser gleamed with nothing on it but John's picture, enlarged from a little one, with John's eyes very black when they should have been blue. You never saw him, so how do you know how he looked? But the man insisted the copy was perfect, it was very rich and handsome. For a picture, yes, but it's not my husband. The table by the bed had a linen cover and a candle and

❶ **STREAM OF CONSCIOUSNESS**
Reread lines 189–203. What has Granny decided about George? Trace the path of her thoughts from this decision to the memory of the birth of her child.

assign (ə-sīn') *n.* a person to whom property is transferred in a will or other legal document

a crucifix.[7] The light was blue from Cornelia's silk lampshades. No sort of light
at all, just frippery. You had to live forty years with kerosene lamps to appreciate
honest electricity. She felt very strong and she saw Doctor Harry with a rosy
nimbus[8] around him.

"You look like a saint, Doctor Harry, and I vow that's as near as you'll ever
come to it."

"She's saying something."

"I heard you, Cornelia. What's all this carrying-on?"

"Father Connolly's saying—"

Cornelia's voice staggered and bumped like a cart in a bad road. It rounded
corners and turned back again and arrived nowhere. Granny stepped up in the cart
very lightly and reached for the reins, but a man sat beside her and she knew him
by his hands, driving the cart. She did not look in his face, for she knew without
seeing, but looked instead down the road where the trees leaned over and bowed
to each other and a thousand birds were singing a Mass. She felt like singing too,
but she put her hand in the bosom of her dress and pulled out a rosary,[9] and
Father Connolly murmured Latin in a very solemn voice and tickled her feet. My
God, will you stop that nonsense? I'm a married woman. What if he did run away
and leave me to face the priest by myself? I found another a whole world better. I
wouldn't have exchanged my husband for anybody except St. Michael himself, and
you may tell him that for me with a thank you in the bargain.

Light flashed on her closed eyelids, and a deep roaring shook her. Cornelia, is
that lightning? I hear thunder. There's going to be a storm. Close all the windows.
Call the children in. . . . "Mother, here we are, all of us." "Is that you, Hapsy?"
"Oh, no, I'm Lydia. We drove as fast as we could." Their faces drifted above her,
drifted away. The rosary fell out of her hands and Lydia put it back. Jimmy tried
to help, their hands fumbled together, and Granny closed two fingers around
Jimmy's thumb. Beads wouldn't do, it must be something alive. She was so amazed
her thoughts ran round and round. So, my dear Lord, this is my death and I
wasn't even thinking about it. My children have come to see me die. But I can't,
it's not time. Oh, I always hated surprises. I wanted to give Cornelia the **amethyst**
set—Cornelia, you're to have the amethyst set, but Hapsy's to wear it when
she wants, and, Doctor Harry, do shut up. Nobody sent for you. Oh, my dear
Lord, do wait a minute. I meant to do something about the Forty Acres, Jimmy
doesn't need it and Lydia will later on, with that worthless husband of hers. I
meant to finish the altar cloth and send six bottles of wine to Sister Borgia for her
dyspepsia.[10] I want to send six bottles of wine to Sister Borgia, Father Connolly,
now don't let me forget.

Cornelia's voice made short turns and tilted over and crashed. "Oh, Mother, oh,
Mother, oh, Mother. . . ."

amethyst (ăm′ə-thĭst) *n.*
a purple form of quartz
used as a gemstone

---

7. **crucifix** (krōō′sə-fĭks′): a cross bearing a sculptured representation of the crucified Christ.

8. **nimbus** (nĭm′bəs): halo of light.

9. **rosary** (rō′zə-rē): a string of beads used by Roman Catholics to count their prayers.

10. **dyspepsia** (dĭs-pĕp′shə): indigestion.

Blue House (2004), Philip Hershberger. Encaustic on panel, 78″ × 48″. © Philip Hersheberger

"I'm not going, Cornelia. I'm taken by surprise. I can't go." **J**

280   You'll see Hapsy again. What about her? "I thought you'd never come." Granny
made a long journey outward, looking for Hapsy. What if I don't find her? What
then? Her heart sank down and down, there was no bottom to death, she couldn't
come to the end of it. The blue light from Cornelia's lampshade drew into a
tiny point in the center of her brain, it flickered and winked like an eye, quietly
it fluttered and **dwindled.** Granny lay curled down within herself, amazed and
watchful, staring at the point of light that was herself; her body was now only a
deeper mass of shadow in an endless darkness and this darkness would curl around
the light and swallow it up. God, give a sign!

        For the second time there was no sign. Again no bridegroom and the priest
290   in the house. She could not remember any other sorrow because this grief wiped
them all away. Oh, no, there's nothing more cruel than this—I'll never forgive it.
She stretched herself with a deep breath and blew out the light. ◖◗

J STREAM OF
CONSCIOUSNESS
Reread lines 266–279.
What is **ironic** about
Granny's response to the
imminence of her death?

dwindle (dwĭn'dl) *v.* to
become steadily less; to
shrink

Comprehension

1. **Recall** Which characters mentioned in the story belong exclusively to Granny Weatherall's past?

2. **Recall** Who is with Granny when she dies?

3. **Clarify** Who is Hapsy?

Literary Analysis

4. **Clarify Sequence** Using your timeline, retell the key events of Granny's life in chronological order. Which events mark the best and worst of Granny's life? Explain, citing Granny's own thoughts and feelings about each event.

5. **Make Inferences About Character** Go back through the story, noting thoughts and **memories** that linger in Granny's mind. What do they reveal about the kind of person she is? Record your answers in a chart like this one.

Granny's Thoughts	Character Traits Revealed
"It was good to have everything clean and put away . . . nicely dusted off." (lines 50–55)	She likes putting things in order and having control in life.

6. **Analyze Stream of Consciousness** Porter uses stream of consciousness to dramatize Granny's interior life. What effect does this approach have on her readers? For example, how might your reaction to the story have been different if Porter had presented the same events in a more traditional narrative? Cite specific examples from the story in your response.

7. **Interpret Symbolism** Consider Granny's final act of blowing out the light. What might this symbolize? Given what you know about her character, do you see it as an act of resignation or one of defiance? Support your answer.

8. **Analyze Theme** Which of the following statements best expresses the theme Porter conveys in this story? Support your choice with evidence from the text.

   - There is no deed so wrong it can't be forgiven.
   - In youth we are all foolish; with age comes true wisdom.
   - Life does not provide the answers or reassurances that people want, even at the moment of death.

Literary Criticism

9. **Critical Interpretations** Novelist Reynolds Price asserts that Porter's stories are "lethal to the most widely cherished illusions of the species"—in other words, they destroy our sentimental notions about things like romance, self-regard, and parenthood. What "cherished illusions" does Porter destroy here? What truths does she portray instead? Support your answer.

Vocabulary in Context

WORD LIST
amethyst
assign
dwindle
embroidered
plague

VOCABULARY PRACTICE

Decide whether each statement is true or false.

1. If your supplies have begun to **dwindle,** you probably need to find a way to get more.
2. An **amethyst** is a special shawl worn for good luck.
3. A tablecloth that is **embroidered** has beautiful designs painted on it.
4. If I am an **assign** in your will, I should expect to inherit at least a portion of what you have.
5. People who **plague** others are transmitting symptoms of a serious disease.

VOCABULARY IN WRITING

Why do you think that Granny Weatherall remembered George for so many years? Write a paragraph or two stating your opinion, using two or more vocabulary words. You could start this way.

> **EXAMPLE SENTENCE**
>
> I think that thoughts of George continued to **plague** Granny because of how he treated her.

VOCABULARY STRATEGY: NOUNS AND FIGURATIVE VERBS

Many English words start out as nouns. Over time, however, they also take on meaning as verbs. For example, the noun form of the vocabulary word *plague* refers to an affliction or disaster. What connection can you see between this meaning and the meaning of the verb form of *plague,* as in the phrase "plagued by doubts"?

PRACTICE Use context clues to determine the meaning of each underlined verb. Then write a definition for each word and explain how the definition relates to the meaning of the original noun form.

1. Ben **peppered** his explanation with "Unbelievable!" and other expressions of surprise.
2. Despite their refusal to help her, Pauline **harbored** no ill will toward her brothers.
3. Through hard work and clever planning, they **engineered** an election victory for the underdog candidate.
4. These conclusions are **anchored** in several months of experimentation and solid research.
5. Adam is an excellent goalie who doesn't need to **grandstand** for the fans.

VOCABULARY PRACTICE
For more practice, go to the **Vocabulary Center** at **ClassZone.com.**

Reading-Writing Connection

WRITING PROMPT

USE STREAM OF CONSCIOUSNESS Katherine Anne Porter wasn't the only modernist to experiment with stream of consciousness; T. S. Eliot, James Joyce, and William Faulkner all used it to explore the intricacies of the human mind. Some writers use it today. Now you'll get a chance to try it for yourself. Write a **three- or four-paragraph narrative** in stream of consciousness, depicting the thoughts and impressions of a character having a particular experience. You can either write about yourself or create a fictional character.

SELF-CHECK

A compelling narrative will . . .

- give readers a clear sense of the character's traits
- indicate the situation that sparks the character's thoughts
- show meaningful connections among thoughts and emotions
- have a point—an overall reason for revealing the connections

GRAMMAR AND STYLE

CRAFT EFFECTIVE SENTENCES Review the **Grammar and Style** note on page 994. Porter skillfully crafts her prose in "The Jilting of Granny Weatherall" to depict Granny's interior life—her secret longings, wishes, and memories. Through her use of **repetition** and the **coordinating conjunction** *and,* Porter reveals Granny's circular thoughts and hazy memories.

> *Then Hapsy melted from within and turned flimsy as gray gauze and the baby was a gauzy shadow, and Hapsy came up close and said, "I thought you'd never come," and looked at her very searchingly and said, "You haven't changed a bit!"* (lines 183–186)

Notice the dreamlike quality of the sentence, with its many *and*'s linking the images as well as its repetition of *gauze* and *gauzy* and related terms *flimsy* and *shadow.*

PRACTICE The following passage presents a character's thoughts as they might appear in a traditional third-person narrative. Rewrite the paragraph as a third-person stream of consciousness.

> Ron walked down the street whistling, his hands shoved deep into his pockets. He squinted up at the weak rays fighting to break through the winter cloud cover. When his gaze returned to street level, he almost tripped over his own feet. Abby was walking toward him.
> "I wonder if she'll even recognize me," Ron thought to himself, quickening his pace and trying to clear his face of emotion.

WRITING TOOLS

For prewriting, revision, and editing tools, visit the **Writing Center** at ClassZone.com.

A Worn Path

Short Story by Eudora Welty

Author Online

For more on Eudora Welty, visit the **Literature Center** at **ClassZone.com**.

One of Welty's WPA photographs from the 1930s

Eudora Welty

1909–2001

Mississippi born and bred, Eudora Welty wrote about her fellow Southerners at a crucial time in U.S. history. When she first began publishing her stories in the late 1930s, vestiges of the Old South still colored daily life. But Welty lived long enough to see the changes wrought by the civil rights movement in the 1960s and the rise of the New South on the eve of the new millennium. All the while, she recorded the lives of ordinary people, depicting the family life that sustained them and the small acts of heroism that dignified them. She was a modernist who believed in love, a Southerner who had faith in tolerance and change, and a successful, unmarried woman at a time when single women in Mississippi were not allowed to buy a house. At first dismissed as a regionalist and even a "feminine" writer, Welty lived long enough to see her fiction recognized for its artistic vision and universal appeal. Through it all, she accepted the changes with her characteristic sense of humor, modesty, and grace.

A Photographer's Eye Nourished by books and a close-knit community of family and friends, Welty lived most of her life in the house her father built in Jackson, Mississippi. Although she wrote stories even in childhood and attended college, her education as a writer didn't seriously begin until 1933, when she landed a job as a publicity agent with the federal government's Works Progress Administration (WPA). Interviewing and photographing all kinds of people throughout Mississippi during the Great Depression—one of the most impoverished regions during the poorest time in the nation's history—was an eye opener for Welty and gave her the first "real germ" of her writing. Her early stories, such as "Why I Live at the P.O." and "A Worn Path," are like photographs, capturing a specific moment that reveals something significant about a person and at the same time a greater truth about the human condition.

A Long, Productive Life Welty received numerous awards and honors for her works, including a Pulitzer Prize for her novel *The Optimist's Daughter* (1972) and an O. Henry Award for "A Worn Path." Her award-winning memoir, *One Writer's Beginnings* (1984), was a runaway bestseller. Despite being very articulate about her writing, sitting graciously through countless interviews, and receiving large numbers of young fans at her home, Welty remained a very private person who always maintained that "a fiction writer should let writing speak for itself."

● LITERARY ANALYSIS: UNIVERSAL THEME

You know that theme is the underlying message a writer wants readers to understand. A **universal theme** is a message that can be found throughout literature of all times and places. Works that convey a universal theme often contain **archetypes**—basic patterns found in a variety of works from different cultures throughout history. The perilous journey is one such archetype; the main character in this story travels a long and uncertain path in search of something.

As you read, consider what this journey might symbolize. Think about the main character's traits and how she deals with obstacles on the path, as well as the story's title and its setting. Taken together, what universal theme do these elements suggest?

● READING STRATEGY: MONITOR

This story has a dreamlike quality that can make it challenging to follow. **Monitoring** is the strategy of checking your comprehension as you are reading and using techniques such as **questioning** and **clarifying** to aid your understanding. As you read, stop every once in a while to consider how well you are comprehending the story. Jot down any questions that come to mind. Review what you do understand and use context clues and analysis of key words and details to clarify the meaning of anything you don't.

> Question:
> If Phoenix is alone on her journey, why does she keep speaking aloud?
> Clarification:

▲ VOCABULARY IN CONTEXT

Welty uses the boldfaced words in her story of one woman's pilgrimage. Replace each boldfaced word with a new word or phrase.

1. **Limber** branches swayed back and forth in the breeze.
2. She gazed at the **radiation** of ripples each raindrop created on the pond's surface.
3. He could not shake his **obstinate** cough.
4. The **meditative** hiker gazed at the sky.

What keeps us GOING?

KEY IDEA **Endurance** is crucial in any long-distance sport, and it's a necessity for surviving harsh conditions or extreme adventures. But what kind of endurance is required for daily life? And where does this type of endurance come from?

DISCUSS With a small group of classmates, discuss the preceding questions. Begin by talking about what you think motivates champion athletes or people facing extreme conditions. Then consider what motivates ordinary people to endure—to keep attending night school while working two day jobs, for example, or to sacrifice a favorite after school activity in order to drive younger siblings to theirs. In your opinion, is the motivation the same in both the extreme and the ordinary cases? If not, what's the difference?

A Worn Path

Eudora Welty

ANALYZE VISUALS
What thematic ideas might you ascribe to this painting? Identify the elements of the painting that suggest these ideas.

It was December—a bright frozen day in the early morning. Far out in the country there was an old Negro woman with her head tied in a red rag, coming along a path through the pinewoods. Her name was Phoenix Jackson. She was very old and small and she walked slowly in the dark pine shadows, moving a little from side to side in her steps, with the balanced heaviness and lightness of a pendulum in a grandfather clock. She carried a thin, small cane made from an umbrella, and with this she kept tapping the frozen earth in front of her. This made a grave and persistent noise in the still air, that seemed **meditative** like the chirping of a solitary little bird. ⓐ

meditative (mĕd′ĭ-tā′tĭv) *adj.* engaged in serious thought or reflection

ⓐ **UNIVERSAL THEME**
What details in lines 1–9 suggest that Phoenix is in for a long journey? As you read, keep in mind other **archetypal** journeys you know of.

Brooding Silence (date unknown), John Fabian Carlson. Smithsonian American Art Museum, Washington, D.C. © Smithsonian American Art Museum, Washington, D.C./Art Resource, New York.

10　　She wore a dark striped dress reaching down to her shoe tops, and an equally long apron of bleached sugar sacks, with a full pocket: all neat and tidy, but every time she took a step she might have fallen over her shoelaces, which dragged from her unlaced shoes. She looked straight ahead. Her eyes were blue with age. Her skin had a pattern all its own of numberless branching wrinkles and as though a whole little tree stood in the middle of her forehead, but a golden color ran underneath, and the two knobs of her cheeks were illumined by a yellow burning under the dark. Under the red rag her hair came down on her neck in the frailest of ringlets, still black, and with an odor like copper.

　　Now and then there was a quivering in the thicket. Old Phoenix said, "Out
20　of my way, all you foxes, owls, beetles, jack rabbits, coons and wild animals! . . . Keep out from under these feet, little bob-whites.[1] . . . Keep the big wild hogs out of my path. Don't let none of those come running my direction. I got a long way." Under her small black-freckled hand her cane, **limber** as a buggy whip, would switch at the brush as if to rouse up any hiding things.

　　On she went. The woods were deep and still. The sun made the pine needles almost too bright to look at, up where the wind rocked. The cones dropped as light as feathers. Down in the hollow was the mourning dove—it was not too late for him.

　　The path ran up a hill. "Seem like there is chains about my feet, time I get this
30　far," she said, in the voice of argument old people keep to use with themselves. "Something always take a hold of me on this hill—pleads I should stay."

　　After she got to the top she turned and gave a full, severe look behind her where she had come. "Up through pines," she said at length. "Now down through oaks."

　　Her eyes opened their widest, and she started down gently. But before she got to the bottom of the hill a bush caught her dress.

　　Her fingers were busy and intent, but her skirts were full and long, so that before she could pull them free in one place they were caught in another. It was not possible to allow the dress to tear. "I in the thorny bush," she said. "Thorns, you doing your appointed work. Never want to let folks pass, no sir. Old eyes
40　thought you was a pretty little *green* bush."

　　Finally, trembling all over, she stood free, and after a moment dared to stoop for her cane.

　　"Sun so high!" she cried, leaning back and looking, while the thick tears went over her eyes. "The time getting all gone here." **B**

　　At the foot of this hill was a place where a log was laid across the creek.

　　"Now comes the trial," said Phoenix.

　　Putting her right foot out, she mounted the log and shut her eyes. Lifting her skirt, leveling her cane fiercely before her, like a festival figure in some parade, she began to march across. Then she opened her eyes and she was safe on the other side.
50　　"I wasn't as old as I thought," she said.

limber (lĭm′bər) *adj.* bending or moving easily; supple

B UNIVERSAL THEME
Reread lines 34–44, and explain what you think the thorny bush might **symbolize**. What does Phoenix's way of dealing with this obstacle suggest about her character?

---

1. **bob-whites:** game birds that are a type of quail.

But she sat down to rest. She spread her skirts on the bank around her and folded her hands over her knees. Up above her was a tree in a pearly cloud of mistletoe. She did not dare to close her eyes, and when a little boy brought her a plate with a slice of marble-cake on it she spoke to him. "That would be acceptable," she said. But when she went to take it there was just her own hand in the air. **C**

So she left that tree, and had to go through a barbed-wire fence. There she had to creep and crawl, spreading her knees and stretching her fingers like a baby trying to climb the steps. But she talked loudly to herself: she could not let her dress be torn now, so late in the day, and she could not pay for having her arm or her leg sawed off if she got caught fast where she was.

At last she was safe through the fence and risen up out in the clearing. Big dead trees, like black men with one arm, were standing in the purple stalks of the withered cotton field. There sat a buzzard. **D**

"Who you watching?"

In the furrow she made her way along.

"Glad this not the season for bulls," she said, looking sideways, "and the good Lord made his snakes to curl up and sleep in the winter. A pleasure I don't see no two-headed snake coming around that tree, where it come once. It took a while to get by him, back in the summer."

She passed through the old cotton and went into a field of dead corn. It whispered and shook and was taller than her head. "Through the maze now," she said, for there was no path. **E**

Then there was something tall, black, and skinny there, moving before her.

At first she took it for a man. It could have been a man dancing in the field. But she stood still and listened, and it did not make a sound. It was as silent as a ghost.

"Ghost," she said sharply, "who be you the ghost of? For I have heard of nary[2] death close by."

But there was no answer—only the ragged dancing in the wind.

She shut her eyes, reached out her hand, and touched a sleeve. She found a coat and inside that an emptiness, cold as ice.

"You scarecrow," she said. Her face lighted. "I ought to be shut up for good," she said with laughter. "My senses is gone. I too old. I the oldest people I ever know. Dance, old scarecrow," she said, "while I dancing with you."

She kicked her foot over the furrow, and with mouth drawn down, shook her head once or twice in a little strutting way. Some husks blew down and whirled in streamers about her skirts.

Then she went on, parting her way from side to side with the cane, through the whispering field. At last she came to the end, to a wagon track where the silver grass blew between the red ruts. The quail were walking around like pullets,[3] seeming all dainty and unseen.

C **MONITOR**
Reread lines 51–56. What is happening in these lines? **Clarify** the meaning by considering the trials Phoenix has faced thus far, as well as how she feels at this point in her journey.

D **UNIVERSAL THEME**
Examine the images in lines 62–64. What **mood** do they help create? Explain.

E **GRAMMAR AND STYLE**
Welty uses a variety of sensory **details** to make Phoenix's journey riveting for readers. Reread lines 71–73, noting how the **verbs** *whispered* and *shook* conjure sights and sounds in your mind.

Snowy Woods at Dusk (date unknown), Dennis Sheehan. Oil, 20″ × 16″. Courtesy of Susan Powell Fine Art, Madison, Connecticut.

"Walk pretty," she said. "This the easy place. This the easy going." **F**

She followed the track, swaying through the quiet bare fields, through the little strings of trees silver in their dead leaves, past cabins silver from weather, with the doors and windows boarded shut, all like old women under a spell sitting there. "I walking in their sleep," she said, nodding her head vigorously.

In a ravine she went where a spring was silently flowing through a hollow log. Old Phoenix bent and drank. "Sweet-gum⁴ makes the water sweet," she said, and

100 drank more. "Nobody know who made this well, for it was here when I was born."

The track crossed a swampy part where the moss hung as white as lace from every limb. "Sleep on, alligators, and blow your bubbles." Then the track went into the road.

Deep, deep the road went down between the high green-colored banks. Overhead the live-oaks⁵ met, and it was as dark as a cave.

A black dog with a lolling tongue came up out of the weeds by the ditch. She was meditating, and not ready, and when he came at her she only hit him a little with her cane. Over she went in the ditch, like a little puff of milkweed.

F UNIVERSAL THEME
Consider Phoenix's statement in line 93. What does her familiarity with each leg of this trek, in addition to the story's **title,** suggest about her journey?

---

4. **sweet-gum:** a tree of the witch hazel family.

5. **live-oaks:** oak trees of a type that has evergreen foliage.

Down there, her senses drifted away. A dream visited her, and she reached her
110 hand up, but nothing reached down and gave her a pull. So she lay there and
presently went to talking. "Old woman," she said to herself, "that black dog come
up out of the weeds to stall you off, and now there he sitting on his fine tail,
smiling at you."

A white man finally came along and found her—a hunter, a young man, with
his dog on a chain. G

"Well, Granny!" he laughed. "What are you doing there?"

"Lying on my back like a June-bug waiting to be turned over, mister," she said,
reaching up her hand.

He lifted her up, gave her a swing in the air, and set her down. "Anything
120 broken, Granny?"

"No sir, them old dead weeds is springy enough," said Phoenix, when she had
got her breath. "I thank you for your trouble."

"Where do you live, Granny?" he asked, while the two dogs were growling at
each other.

"Away back yonder, sir, behind the ridge. You can't even see it from here."

"On your way home?"

"No sir, I going to town."

"Why, that's too far! That's as far as I walk when I come out myself, and I get
something for my trouble." He patted the stuffed bag he carried, and there hung
130 down a little closed claw. It was one of the bob-whites, with its beak hooked
bitterly to show it was dead. "Now you go on home, Granny!"

"I bound to go to town, mister," said Phoenix. "The time come around."

He gave another laugh, filling the whole landscape. "I know you old colored
people! Wouldn't miss going to town to see Santa Claus!"

But something held old Phoenix very still. The deep lines in her face went into
a fierce and different **radiation.** Without warning, she had seen with her own eyes
a flashing nickel fall out of the man's pocket onto the ground.

"How old are you, Granny?" he was saying.

"There is no telling, mister," she said, "no telling."

140 Then she gave a little cry and clapped her hands and said, "Git on away from
here, dog! Look! Look at that dog!" She laughed as if in admiration. "He ain't
scared of nobody. He a big black dog." She whispered, "Sic him!"

"Watch me get rid of that cur," said the man. "Sic him, Pete! Sic him!"

Phoenix heard the dogs fighting, and heard the man running and throwing
sticks. She even heard a gunshot. But she was slowly bending forward by that
time, further and further forward, the lids stretched down over her eyes, as if she
were doing this in her sleep. Her chin was lowered almost to her knees. The yellow
palm of her hand came out from the fold of her apron. Her fingers slid down and
along the ground under the piece of money with the grace and care they would
150 have in lifting an egg from under a setting hen. Then she slowly straightened up,

G MONITOR
Reread lines 106–115. How
can you tell when Phoenix
is experiencing actual
events or interacting with
real people and when she
has "drifted away" into
her own imagination?
Write two **questions** that
help you understand
what is real and what
is not.

radiation (rā′dē-ā′shən) n.
the movement of lines or
rays from a center point

she stood erect, and the nickel was in her apron pocket. A bird flew by. Her lips moved. "God watching me the whole time. I come to stealing."

The man came back, and his own dog panted about them. "Well, I scared him off that time," he said, and then he laughed and lifted his gun and pointed it at Phoenix.

She stood straight and faced him.

"Doesn't the gun scare you?" he said, still pointing it.

"No, sir, I seen plenty go off closer by, in my day, and for less than what I done," she said, holding utterly still.

160   He smiled, and shouldered the gun. "Well, Granny," he said, "you must be a hundred years old, and scared of nothing. I'd give you a dime if I had any money with me. But you take my advice and stay home, and nothing will happen to you." **H**

"I bound to go on my way, mister," said Phoenix. She inclined her head in the red rag. Then they went in different directions, but she could hear the gun shooting again and again over the hill. **I**

She walked on. The shadows hung from the oak trees to the road like curtains. Then she smelled wood-smoke, and smelled the river, and she saw a steeple and the cabins on their steep steps. Dozens of little black children whirled around her.

170 There ahead was Natchez shining. Bells were ringing. She walked on.

In the paved city it was Christmas time. There were red and green electric lights strung and criss-crossed everywhere, and all turned on in the daytime. Old Phoenix would have been lost if she had not distrusted her eyesight and depended on her feet to know where to take her.

She paused quietly on the sidewalk where people were passing by. A lady came along in the crowd, carrying an armful of red-, green- and silver-wrapped presents; she gave off perfume like the red roses in hot summer, and Phoenix stopped her.

"Please, missy, will you lace up my shoe?" She held up her foot.

"What do you want, Grandma?"

180 "See my shoe," said Phoenix. "Do all right for out in the country, but wouldn't look right to go in a big building."

"Stand still then, Grandma," said the lady. She put her packages down on the sidewalk beside her and laced and tied both shoes tightly.

"Can't lace 'em with a cane," said Phoenix. "Thank you, missy. I doesn't mind asking a nice lady to tie up my shoe, when I gets out on the street."

Moving slowly and from side to side, she went into the big building, and into a tower of steps, where she walked up and around and around until her feet knew to stop.

She entered a door, and there she saw nailed up on the wall the document

190 that had been stamped with the gold seal and framed in the gold frame, which matched the dream that was hung up in her head.

H MONITOR
Keep the story's **setting** in mind as you contemplate the way the hunter treats Phoenix. What does their interaction tell you about this time and place in history?

I UNIVERSAL THEME
Reread lines 114–166, and describe the **character traits** Phoenix exhibits during this episode with the hunter. How do her traits help her overcome this particular obstacle in her journey?

ANALYZE VISUALS
What elements of this portrait give the woman a look of inner strength and determination? Be specific.

Woman Peeling Apples (1924), Archibald J. Motley, Jr. Oil on canvas, 32¼″ × 28″. Art and Artifacts Division, Schomberg Center for Research in Black Culture, The New York Public Library, Astor, Lenox and Tilden Foundations.

"Here I be," she said. There was a fixed and ceremonial stiffness over her body.

"A charity case, I suppose," said an attendant who sat at the desk before her.

But Phoenix only looked above her head. There was sweat on her face, the wrinkles in her skin shone like a bright net.

"Speak up, Grandma," the woman said. "What's your name? We must have your history, you know. Have you been here before? What seems to be the trouble with you?"

Old Phoenix only gave a twitch to her face as if a fly were bothering her.

200 "Are you deaf?" cried the attendant.

But then the nurse came in.

"Oh, that's just old Aunt Phoenix," she said. "She doesn't come for herself—she has a little grandson. She makes these trips just as regular as clockwork. She lives away back off the Old Natchez Trace."[6] She bent down. "Well, Aunt Phoenix, why don't you just take a seat? We won't keep you standing after your long trip." She pointed.

The old woman sat down, bolt upright in the chair.

"Now, how is the boy?" asked the nurse.

Old Phoenix did not speak.

210 "I said, how is the boy?"

But Phoenix only waited and stared straight ahead, her face very solemn and withdrawn into rigidity.

"Is his throat any better?" asked the nurse. "Aunt Phoenix, don't you hear me? Is your grandson's throat any better since the last time you came for the medicine?"

With her hands on her knees, the old woman waited, silent, erect and motionless, just as if she were in armor.

"You mustn't take up our time this way, Aunt Phoenix," the nurse said. "Tell us quickly about your grandson, and get it over. He isn't dead, is he?"

At last there came a flicker and then a flame of comprehension across her face,
220 and she spoke.

"My grandson. It was my memory had left me. There I sat and forgot why I made my long trip."

"Forgot?" The nurse frowned. "After you came so far?"

Then Phoenix was like an old woman begging a dignified forgiveness for waking up frightened in the night. "I never did go to school, I was too old at the Surrender,"[7] she said in a soft voice. "I'm an old woman without an education. It was my memory fail me. My little grandson, he is just the same, and I forgot it in the coming."

"Throat never heals, does it?" said the nurse, speaking in a loud, sure voice to
230 old Phoenix. By now she had a card with something written on it, a little list. "Yes. Swallowed lye.[8] When was it?—January—two-three years ago—"

---

6. **Old Natchez Trace:** The Natchez Trace was an important wilderness road during the 18th and early 19th centuries, extending from Natchez, Mississippi, to Nashville, Tennessee.

7. **the Surrender:** the end of the Civil War, after which time slaves were free.

8. **lye:** a strong alkaline liquid used especially in making soap.

Phoenix spoke unasked now. "No, missy, he not dead, he just the same. Every little while his throat begin to close up again, and he not able to swallow. He not get his breath. He not able to help himself. So the time come around, and I go on another trip for the soothing medicine." **J**

"All right. The doctor said as long as you came to get it, you could have it," said the nurse. "But it's an **obstinate** case."

"My little grandson, he sit up there in the house all wrapped up, waiting by himself," Phoenix went on. "We is the only two left in the world. He suffer and it
240 don't seem to put him back at all. He got a sweet look. He going to last. He wear a little patch quilt and peep out holding his mouth open like a little bird. I remembers so plain now. I not going to forget him again, no, the whole enduring time. I could tell him from all the others in creation."

"All right." The nurse was trying to hush her now. She brought her a bottle of medicine. "Charity," she said, making a check mark in a book.

Old Phoenix held the bottle close to her eyes, and then carefully put it into her pocket.

"I thank you," she said.

"It's Christmas time, Grandma," said the attendant. "Could I give you a few
250 pennies out of my purse?"

"Five pennies is a nickel," said Phoenix stiffly.

"Here's a nickel," said the attendant.

Phoenix rose carefully and held out her hand. She received the nickel and then fished the other nickel out of her pocket and laid it beside the new one. She stared at her palm closely, with her head on one side.

Then she gave a tap with her cane on the floor.

"This is what come to me to do," she said. "I going to the store and buy my child a little windmill they sells, made out of paper. He going to find it hard to believe there such a thing in the world. I'll march myself back where he waiting, holding it straight
260 up in this hand."

She lifted her free hand, gave a little nod, turned around, and walked out of the doctor's office. Then her slow step began on the stairs, going down. ⟟

J UNIVERSAL THEME
What have you learned about Phoenix's **motivation** for making her perilous journey, and what can you **infer** about how often she makes it? Explain why Welty might have delayed revealing this information until the story's end.

obstinate (ŏb′stə-nĭt) *adj.* hard to control or treat

MEMOIR Always shy of biographers, Eudora Welty published her own memoir at the age of 74. This account of growing up in the South pays special attention to her development as a writer.

One Writer's Beginnings

Eudora Welty

The characters who go to make up my stories and novels are not portraits. Characters I invent along with the story that carries them. Attached to them are what I've borrowed, perhaps unconsciously, bit by bit, of persons I have seen or noticed or remembered in the flesh—a cast of countenance here, a manner of walking there, that jump to the visualizing mind when a story is underway. (Elizabeth
10 Bowen said, "Physical detail cannot be invented." It can only be chosen.) I don't write by invasion into the life of a real person: my own sense of privacy is too strong for that; and I also know instinctively that living people to whom you are close—those known to you in ways too deep, too overflowing, ever to be plumbed outside love—do not yield to, could never fit into, the demands of a story. On the other hand, what I do make my stories out of
20 is the *whole* fund of my feelings, my responses to the real experiences of my own life, to the relationships that formed and changed it, that I have given most of myself to, and so learned my way toward a dramatic counterpart. Characters take on life sometimes by luck, but I suspect it is when you can write most entirely out of yourself, inside the skin, heart, mind, and soul of a person who is not yourself, that a character becomes in his own right another human being
30 on the page.

Eudora Welty, early in her career

Comprehension

1. **Recall** Why does Phoenix Jackson travel to the city of Natchez?

2. **Recall** What does she intend to do with the ten cents she collects?

3. **Summarize** What physical problems does Phoenix seem to have, and how do they affect her on her journey?

Literary Analysis

4. **Monitor Reading** Look over the chart you filled in as you read. Identify at least one passage in the story that was challenging to understand. What clues in the text helped you **clarify** its meaning? Explain how they helped.

5. **Analyze Figurative Language** "A Worn Path" is rich with figurative language, especially **similes.** Skim the story, identifying examples of figurative language used to accomplish the following purposes. For each purpose, cite at least two examples.

   • give readers a clear mental picture of Phoenix's appearance
   • highlight Phoenix's main character traits
   • reveal the perilous nature of this journey
   • convey Phoenix's feelings about her grandson

6. **Understand Symbolism** In mythology, a phoenix is an immortal bird that represents renewal. It sets its nest on fire every 500 years; from the ashes, the phoenix is reborn. Why might Welty have bestowed this name upon her main character? In what way does the name fit the person who bears it?

7. **Interpret Universal Theme** Consider the trials and triumphs Phoenix faces on her journey, and think about what motivates her to **endure** her arduous trek. In what way does this **archetypal** journey mirror life itself? Use your answer to this question to formulate a sentence that states the theme of the story. Then explain what makes this theme universal.

Literary Criticism

8. **Critical Interpretations** This story's ambiguity has fascinated readers for over 65 years. Countless students have written Welty to ask if Phoenix's grandson is really alive at the story's end, or if Phoenix keeps making this journey though the boy is already gone. The author has replied, "It is the journey, the going of the errand, that is the story.... *Phoenix* is alive." In your opinion, does Welty bring this story to a satisfying conclusion? Explain why or why not, citing details from the text as well as your reaction to Welty's explanation.

Vocabulary in Context

WORD LIST

limber

meditative

obstinate

radiation

VOCABULARY PRACTICE

Demonstrate your understanding of the vocabulary words by answering these questions.

1. Would an **obstinate** cold go away in a few days or drag on for weeks?
2. If your leg muscles are **limber,** would you be more likely to excel at stretching exercises or to cramp up while swimming?
3. Would you expect someone to be **meditative** in a pep rally or in a quiet garden?
4. Does **radiation** from the sun provide or absorb heat and light?

VOCABULARY IN WRITING

What are Phoenix's most important qualities? Using at least two vocabulary words, write a brief character sketch about her. Here is a sample opening sentence.

> **EXAMPLE SENTENCE**
>
> *Phoenix is old and not particularly **limber**, but she has a single-mindedness that keeps her moving.*

VOCABULARY STRATEGY: THE ROOT *med* AND ITS MEANINGS

Sometimes roots can have several different meanings. The vocabulary word *meditative,* for example, is derived from the Latin root *med,* which can mean "think" or "ponder." In other words developed from this same root, however, *med* means "heal." There is another unrelated root, also spelled *med,* that means "middle." In dealing with words containing these roots, you will often have to rely on the context, and sometimes on affixes, to determine their correct meaning.

PRACTICE Using context clues and your knowledge of the root *med,* write a definition of each boldfaced word. Then check your definition against the one provided in a dictionary.

1. The two disputing groups had to call in an **intermediary** to resolve their differences.
2. The only **remedy** that the doctor could suggest was to get plenty of sleep.
3. Only a **premeditated** crime could be as carefully executed as this robbery was.
4. The **median** income in that city is considerably lower than the national average.
5. After considerable discussion, the workers on the case decided that her condition was **immedicable.**

VOCABULARY PRACTICE

For more practice, go to the **Vocabulary Center** at **ClassZone.com.**

Reading-Writing Connection

WRITING PROMPT

SELF-CHECK

WRITE A STORY Eudora Welty wrote "A Worn Path" in the late 1930s, a time when being elderly, poor, and black in the South made life extremely difficult. Think of a similarly extreme situation today in which a contemporary "Phoenix" would have to make a perilous journey. What hazards might he or she face along the way? What values and strengths would he or she need in order to **endure**? Write a **one-to-three-page story** updating Welty's tale.

A successful story will . . .

- feature a well-developed main character
- show how the time and place affect his or her journey
- give a compelling reason for the journey

GRAMMAR AND STYLE

ADD DESCRIPTIVE DETAILS Review the **Grammar and Style** note on page 1007. Welty's descriptions in the story give a wealth of sensory details that help readers get a clear picture of Phoenix and her actions. Welty makes particularly good use of **action verbs** (in yellow) and **participial phrases** (in green), as in this description of Phoenix crossing the precarious log bridge:

> *Putting her right foot out,* she *mounted* the log and shut her eyes. *Lifting her skirt, leveling her cane fiercely before her,* like a festival figure in some parade, she began to *march* across. (lines 47–49)

The highlighted participial phrases add key details to help readers visualize Phoenix. The first highlighted action verb, *mounted,* shows the physical exertion required for her to get on top of the log, while the third verb, *march,* works with the simile to suggest her regal bearing and sense of purpose.

PRACTICE The following sentences were written in response to the writing prompt above. Rewrite each sentence, adding more action verbs and participial phrases that help describe how things look, sound, smell, touch, or taste.

EXAMPLE

The sun was low on the horizon and made shadows between the bushes.

The sun crouched low on the horizon, casting long shadows between the scrubby bushes.

---

1. Tashi, a refugee fleeing her war-torn village, was on the high bank above the river.

2. She knew she had to cross in the shallows where the sand bar was.

3. The baby was still asleep in her arms but would wake soon and be hungry.

4. Suddenly, a dog barked in the distance.

WRITING TOOLS For prewriting, revision, and editing tools, visit the **Writing Center** at ClassZone.com.

A Rose for Emily

Short Story by William Faulkner

William Faulkner

1897–1962

Today, William Faulkner is considered one of the literary giants of the 20th century. This distinction didn't come easily, however. Faulkner took a while to find himself and his subject. Only after he decided to focus on his home state of Mississippi and his colorful family history was the full force of his creativity unleashed. Over an astonishing 13-year span, Faulkner churned out one masterpiece after another—among them, *The Sound and the Fury* (1929), *As I Lay Dying* (1930), *Sanctuary* (1931), *Absalom, Absalom!* (1936), and *Go Down, Moses* (1942). Of these artistic achievements, only *Sanctuary* was a bestseller—partly due to its scandalous subject matter—and none of the books earned Faulkner enough money to support his growing family. Although some critics raved about him, many others agreed with the *New York Times* that his South was "too often vicious, depraved, decadent, corrupt." By 1945, most of his books were out of print.

Yoknapa . . . What? Faulkner's initial unpopularity was directly related to his originality. Staking out new literary territory, he essentially broke all the rules—of chronology, of narrative structure, even of punctuation. Many of his short stories and 15 of his 19 novels take place in his imaginary world of Yoknapatawpha (yŏk'nə-pə-tô'fə) County, modeled on his own county in Mississippi and populated with an assortment of characters ranging from the bland to the bizarre. "I discovered," Faulkner explained, "that my own little postage stamp of native soil was worth writing about and that I would never live long enough to exhaust it." His themes often resonate with the thunder of the Old Testament, and his stream-of-consciousness narratives wander around the dark labyrinths of the heart and mind. To many readers, Faulkner's world was just too hard to understand and too weird to accept.

Resurgence In 1946, an enterprising editor named Malcolm Cowley published *The Portable Faulkner,* a collection of stories and novel excerpts that untangled Faulkner's elaborate saga. Cowley's blueprint plus a helpful introduction sparked new interest in Faulkner. With the anxieties of the Great Depression and World War II behind them, more readers were ready to accept Faulkner's challenge to revisit the crimes and passions of the South—and America itself—through a modern consciousness.

● LITERARY ANALYSIS: MOOD

A story's power to captivate us comes in part from its **mood**—the feeling or atmosphere that the writer creates for the reader. To analyze the mood Faulkner creates in "A Rose for Emily," pay close attention to his **diction,** or word choice and arrangement, as well as his use of **imagery** and **figurative language.** Think about how these elements work together to create a specific atmosphere in this description of Emily:

She looked bloated, like a body long submerged in motionless water, and of that pallid hue.

As you read, note passages that evoke a strong response from you. What part does the story's mood play in your reaction?

● READING SKILL: ANALYZE SEQUENCE

Faulkner had an unorthodox way of treating a story's chronology. He often rearranged the **sequence** of events, using **flashbacks** to offer a window into a character's past or dropping hints that ominously **foreshadow** what is yet to come. As you read, use a chart like the one shown to analyze this story's sequence. In the left column, record the story's major events in the order in which you learn about them. In the right column, write the order in which these events actually happened.

Order in Which Narrator Reveals Events	Order in Which Events Occur
1. Miss Emily dies.	8
2. The aldermen visit about taxes.	7

▲ VOCABULARY IN CONTEXT

Faulkner uses these words to create a story rich with atmosphere. Try to define each, based on its context.

1. The sleepy little town faced an **inextricable** problem.
2. The **cabal** executed their shady plans in secret.
3. A conniving con artist, he **circumvented** the city's laws.
4. The swaggering boy approached him with **temerity.**
5. **Virulent** fumes wafted out of the polluted swamp.
6. The vines **encroached** on the garden, killing the flowers.
7. Moonlight made the rickety house into a terrifying **tableau.**
8. Her **imperviousness** made her impossible to frighten.

Explore the Key Idea

What makes your SKIN CRAWL?

KEY IDEA *As the girl steps outside into the alley, the overpowering smell of rotting garbage assaults her nostrils. Her stomach turns as she tries not to stare at a mass of maggots eating a discarded hamburger, and she shies away from the dumpster, with its squeaking and squirming inhabitants.* Certain scenes from books or movies are so evocative that they leave you shaky and nauseated. Part of what you're responding to is the creepy **atmosphere** the writers or directors have created to mesmerize and repulse you.

DISCUSS In a small group, talk about the one thing that really gives you the creeps. Spiders, rats, the sight of blood—do any of these make your skin crawl? What movies or books have used these things to create an atmosphere that makes you shudder? Which works top your "creepiness scale"? Record the responses of your group to share with others.

1019

A Rose for Emily

William Faulkner

BACKGROUND "A Rose for Emily," like the majority of Faulkner's stories, takes place in the fictional Yoknapatawpha County, Mississippi. Published in 1930, the story portrays social customs of the small-town South at the turn of the 20th century. Be warned that the narrator refers to African Americans with a term that is offensive to contemporary readers.

I

When Miss Emily Grierson died, our whole town went to her funeral: the men through a sort of respectful affection for a fallen monument, the women mostly out of curiosity to see the inside of her house, which no one save an old manservant—a combined gardener and cook—had seen in at least ten years.

It was a big, squarish frame house that had once been white, decorated with cupolas and spires and scrolled balconies in the heavily lightsome style of the seventies,[1] set on what had once been our most select street. But garages and cotton gins had **encroached** and obliterated even the august names of that neighborhood; only Miss Emily's house was left, lifting its stubborn and coquettish decay above the cotton wagons and the gasoline pumps—an eyesore among eyesores. And now Miss Emily had gone to join the representatives of those august names where they lay in the cedar-bemused[2] cemetery among the ranked and anonymous graves of Union and Confederate soldiers who fell at the battle of Jefferson. **A**

---

1. **the seventies:** the 1870s.
2. **cedar-bemused:** almost lost in cedar trees.

encroach (ĕn-krōch') *v.* to take over the possessions or rights of another

A MOOD
Reread lines 5–11. What mood does Faulkner establish with his initial description of the Grierson house? Identify the striking **phrases** and vivid **images** he uses to create this mood.

Alive, Miss Emily had been a tradition, a duty, and a care; a sort of hereditary obligation upon the town, dating from that day in 1894 when Colonel Sartoris, the mayor—he who fathered the edict that no Negro woman should appear on the streets without an apron—remitted her taxes, the dispensation dating from the death of her father on into perpetuity.[3] Not that Miss Emily would have accepted
20 charity. Colonel Sartoris invented an involved tale to the effect that Miss Emily's father had loaned money to the town, which the town, as a matter of business, preferred this way of repaying. Only a man of Colonel Sartoris' generation and thought could have invented it, and only a woman could have believed it.

When the next generation, with its more modern ideas, became mayors and aldermen, this arrangement created some little dissatisfaction. On the first of the year they mailed her a tax notice. February came, and there was no reply. They wrote her a formal letter, asking her to call at the sheriff's office at her convenience. A week later the mayor wrote her himself, offering to call or to send his car for her, and received in reply a note on paper of an archaic shape, in a thin,
30 flowing calligraphy in faded ink, to the effect that she no longer went out at all. The tax notice was also enclosed, without comment. **B**

They called a special meeting of the Board of Aldermen. A deputation waited upon her, knocked at the door through which no visitor had passed since she ceased giving china-painting lessons eight or ten years earlier. They were admitted by the old Negro into a dim hall from which a stairway mounted into still more shadow. It smelled of dust and disuse—a close, dank smell. The Negro led them into the parlor. It was furnished in heavy, leather-covered furniture. When the Negro opened the blinds of one window, they could see that the leather was cracked; and when they sat down, a faint dust rose sluggishly about their thighs,
40 spinning with slow motes in the single sun-ray. On a tarnished gilt easel before the fireplace stood a crayon portrait of Miss Emily's father.

They rose when she entered—a small, fat woman in black, with a thin gold chain descending to her waist and vanishing into her belt, leaning on an ebony cane with a tarnished gold head. Her skeleton was small and spare; perhaps that was why what would have been merely plumpness in another was obesity in her. She looked bloated, like a body long submerged in motionless water, and of that pallid hue. Her eyes, lost in the fatty ridges of her face, looked like two small pieces of coal pressed into a lump of dough as they moved from one face to another while the visitors stated their errand. **C**
50 She did not ask them to sit. She just stood in the door and listened quietly until the spokesman came to a stumbling halt. Then they could hear the invisible watch ticking at the end of the gold chain.

Her voice was dry and cold. "I have no taxes in Jefferson. Colonel Sartoris explained it to me. Perhaps one of you can gain access to the city records and satisfy yourselves."

"But we have. We are the city authorities, Miss Emily. Didn't you get a notice from the sheriff, signed by him?"

B ANALYZE SEQUENCE
Explain when the events of the story's first paragraph happen in relation to those described in lines 15–31. Why might Faulkner have chosen to immediately announce Emily's death before revealing more about her life? Explain.

C MOOD
What is your initial reaction to Emily? Cite two examples of **figurative language** in lines 42–49 and explain what feeling they create.

---

3. **remitted . . . perpetuity:** released her from paying taxes forever from the time of her father's death.

"I received a paper, yes," Miss Emily said. "Perhaps he considers himself the sheriff . . . I have no taxes in Jefferson."

60   "But there is nothing on the books to show that, you see. We must go by the—"

"See Colonel Sartoris. I have no taxes in Jefferson."

"But, Miss Emily—"

"See Colonel Sartoris." (Colonel Sartoris had been dead almost ten years.) "I have no taxes in Jefferson. Tobe!" The Negro appeared. "Show these gentlemen out."

II

So she vanquished them, horse and foot, just as she had vanquished their fathers thirty years before about the smell. That was two years after her father's death and a short time after her sweetheart—the one we believed would marry her—had deserted her. After her father's death she went out very little; after her sweetheart went away, people hardly saw her at all. A few of the ladies had the **temerity** to
70   call, but were not received, and the only sign of life about the place was the Negro man—a young man then—going in and out with a market basket.

"Just as if a man—any man—could keep a kitchen properly," the ladies said; so they were not surprised when the smell developed. It was another link between the gross, teeming world and the high and mighty Griersons.

A neighbor, a woman, complained to the mayor, Judge Stevens, eighty years old.

"But what will you have me do about it, madam?" he said.

"Why, send her word to stop it," the woman said. "Isn't there a law?"

"I'm sure that won't be necessary," Judge Stevens said. "It's probably just a snake or a rat that nigger of hers killed in the yard. I'll speak to him about it."

80   The next day he received two more complaints, one from a man who came in diffident deprecation.[4] "We really must do something about it, Judge. I'd be the last one in the world to bother Miss Emily, but we've got to do something." That night the Board of Aldermen met—three graybeards and one younger man, a member of the rising generation.

"It's simple enough," he said. "Send her word to have her place cleaned up. Give her a certain time to do it in, and if she don't . . ."

"Dammit, sir," Judge Stevens said, "will you accuse a lady to her face of smelling bad?"

So the next night, after midnight, four men crossed Miss Emily's lawn and
90   slunk about the house like burglars, sniffing along the base of the brickwork and at the cellar openings while one of them performed a regular sowing motion with his hand out of a sack slung from his shoulder. They broke open the cellar door and sprinkled lime there, and in all the outbuildings. As they recrossed the lawn, a window that had been dark was lighted and Miss Emily sat in it, the light behind her, and her upright torso motionless as that of an idol. They crept quietly across the lawn and into the shadow of the locusts that lined the street. After a week or two the smell went away. **D**

temerity (tə-mĕr′ĭ-tē) *n.* foolish boldness

D MOOD
What words and **images** help create an ominous mood in lines 89–97?

---

4. **diffident deprecation:** timid disapproval.

That was when people had begun to feel really sorry for her. People in our town, remembering how old lady Wyatt, her great-aunt, had gone completely
100 crazy at last, believed that the Griersons held themselves a little too high for what they really were. None of the young men were quite good enough for Miss Emily and such. We had long thought of them as a **tableau,** Miss Emily a slender figure in white in the background, her father a spraddled silhouette in the foreground, his back to her and clutching a horsewhip, the two of them framed by the back-flung front door. So when she got to be thirty and was still single, we were not pleased exactly, but vindicated; even with insanity in the family she wouldn't have turned down all of her chances if they had really materialized. **E**

When her father died, it got about that the house was all that was left to her; and in a way, people were glad. At last they could pity Miss Emily. Being left
110 alone, and a pauper, she had become humanized. Now she too would know the old thrill and the old despair of a penny more or less.

The day after his death all the ladies prepared to call at the house and offer condolence and aid, as is our custom. Miss Emily met them at the door, dressed as usual and with no trace of grief on her face. She told them that her father was not dead. She did that for three days, with the ministers calling on her, and the doctors, trying to persuade her to let them dispose of the body. Just as they were about to resort to law and force, she broke down, and they buried her father quickly.

We did not say she was crazy then. We believed she had to do that. We
120 remembered all the young men her father had driven away, and we knew that with nothing left, she would have to cling to that which had robbed her, as people will. **F**

III

She was sick for a long time. When we saw her again, her hair was cut short, making her look like a girl, with a vague resemblance to those angels in colored church windows—sort of tragic and serene.

The town had just let the contracts for paving the sidewalks, and in the summer after her father's death they began the work. The construction company came with niggers and mules and machinery, and a foreman named Homer Barron, a Yankee—a big, dark, ready man, with a big voice and eyes lighter than his face. The little boys would follow in groups to hear him cuss the niggers,
130 and the niggers singing in time to the rise and fall of picks. Pretty soon he knew everybody in town. Whenever you heard a lot of laughing anywhere about the square, Homer Barron would be in the center of the group. Presently we began to see him and Miss Emily on Sunday afternoons driving in the yellow-wheeled buggy and the matched team of bays from the livery stable.

At first we were glad that Miss Emily would have an interest, because the ladies all said, "Of course a Grierson would not think seriously of a Northerner, a day laborer." But there were still others, older people, who said that even grief could not cause a real lady to forget *noblesse oblige*[5]—without calling it *noblesse oblige*.

tableau (tăb′lō′) *n.* a dramatic scene or picture

E **GRAMMAR AND STYLE** Reread lines 98–107. The **pronouns** *we* and *our* indicate that this story is told from the **first-person plural point of view.** The narrator is not a single character, but the collective voice of the townspeople.

F **ANALYZE SEQUENCE** Reread lines 108–121. Note Emily's reaction to her father's death, as well as the narrator's comments about her sanity. What might this **foreshadow?**

---

5. *noblesse oblige* (nō-blĕs′ ō-blēzh′): the responsibility of people in a high social position to behave in a noble fashion.

They just said, "Poor Emily. Her kinsfolk should come to her." She had some kin
140 in Alabama; but years ago her father had fallen out with them over the estate of
old lady Wyatt, the crazy woman, and there was no communication between the
two families. They had not even been represented at the funeral.

And as soon as the old people said, "Poor Emily," the whispering began. "Do
you suppose it's really so?" they said to one another. "Of course it is. What else
could . . ." This behind their hands; rustling of craned silk and satin behind
jalousies[6] closed upon the sun of Sunday afternoon as the thin, swift clop-clop-
clop of the matched team passed: "Poor Emily."

She carried her head high enough—even when we believed that she was
fallen. It was as if she demanded more than ever the recognition of her dignity
150 as the last Grierson; as if it had wanted that touch of earthiness to reaffirm her
imperviousness. Like when she bought the rat poison, the arsenic. That was over
a year after they had begun to say "Poor Emily," and while the two female cousins
were visiting her.

"I want some poison," she said to the druggist. She was over thirty then, still a
slight woman, though thinner than usual, with cold, haughty black eyes in a face
the flesh of which was strained across the temples and about the eye-sockets as you
imagine a lighthouse-keeper's face ought to look. "I want some poison," she said.

imperviousness
(ĭm-pûr′vē-əs-nəs) *n.* an
inability to be affected
or disturbed

---

6. **jalousies** (jăl′ə-sēz): blinds or shutters containing overlapping slats that can be opened or closed.

"Yes, Miss Emily. What kind? For rats and such? I'd recom—"

"I want the best you have. I don't care what kind."

160 The druggist named several. "They'll kill anything up to an elephant. But what you want is—"

"Arsenic," Miss Emily said. "Is that a good one?"

"Is . . . arsenic? Yes, ma'am. But what you want—"

"I want arsenic."

The druggist looked down at her. She looked back at him, erect, her face like a strained flag. "Why, of course," the druggist said. "If that's what you want. But the law requires you to tell what you are going to use it for."

Miss Emily just stared at him, her head tilted back in order to look him eye for eye, until he looked away and went and got the arsenic and wrapped it up. The
170 Negro delivery boy brought her the package; the druggist didn't come back. When she opened the package at home there was written on the box, under the skull and bones: "For rats." **G**

G ANALYZE SEQUENCE
Reread lines 154–172. What does this exchange indicate about Emily's character? What **foreshadowing** do you sense in her refusal to comply with the law?

IV

So the next day we all said, "She will kill herself"; and we said it would be the best thing. When she had first begun to be seen with Homer Barron, we had said, "She will marry him." Then we said, "She will persuade him yet," because Homer himself had remarked—he liked men, and it was known that he drank with the younger men in the Elks' Club—that he was not a marrying man. Later we said, "Poor Emily" behind the jalousies as they passed on Sunday afternoon in the glittering buggy, Miss Emily with her head high and Homer Barron with his hat
180 cocked and a cigar in his teeth, reins and whip in a yellow glove.

Then some of the ladies began to say that it was a disgrace to the town and a bad example to the young people. The men did not want to interfere, but at last the ladies forced the Baptist minister—Miss Emily's people were Episcopal—to call upon her. He would never divulge what happened during that interview, but he refused to go back again. The next Sunday they again drove about the streets, and the following day the minister's wife wrote to Miss Emily's relations in Alabama.

So she had blood-kin under her roof again and we sat back to watch developments. At first nothing happened. Then we were sure that they were to be married. We learned that Miss Emily had been to the jeweler's and ordered a man's
190 toilet set in silver, with the letters H. B. on each piece. Two days later we learned that she had bought a complete outfit of men's clothing, including a nightshirt, and we said, "They are married." We were really glad. We were glad because the two female cousins were even more Grierson than Miss Emily had ever been.

So we were not surprised when Homer Barron—the streets had been finished some time since—was gone. We were a little disappointed that there was not a public blowing-off,[7] but we believed that he had gone on to prepare for Miss Emily's coming, or to give her a chance to get rid of the cousins. (By that time it was a **cabal,** and we were all Miss Emily's allies to help **circumvent** the cousins.)

cabal (kə-băl´) *n.* a group united in a secret plot

circumvent (sûr'kəm-vĕnt´) *v.* to avoid or get around by clever maneuvering

---

7. **blowing-off:** here, a celebration.

Sure enough, after another week they departed. And, as we had expected all along, within three days Homer Barron was back in town. A neighbor saw the Negro man admit him at the kitchen door at dusk one evening.

And that was the last we saw of Homer Barron. And of Miss Emily for some time. The Negro man went in and out with the market basket, but the front door remained closed. Now and then we would see her at a window for a moment, as the men did that night when they sprinkled the lime, but for almost six months she did not appear on the streets. Then we knew that this was to be expected too; as if that quality of her father which had thwarted her woman's life so many times had been too **virulent** and too furious to die.

When we next saw Miss Emily, she had grown fat and her hair was turning gray. During the next few years it grew grayer and grayer until it attained an even pepper-and-salt iron-gray, when it ceased turning. Up to the day of her death at seventy-four it was still that vigorous iron-gray, like the hair of an active man.

From that time on her front door remained closed, save for a period of six or seven years, when she was about forty, during which she gave lessons in china-painting. She fitted up a studio in one of the downstairs rooms, where the daughters and granddaughters of Colonel Sartoris' contemporaries were sent to her with the same regularity and in the same spirit that they were sent to church on Sundays with a twenty-five-cent piece for the collection plate. Meanwhile her taxes had been remitted.

Then the newer generation became the backbone and the spirit of the town, and the painting pupils grew up and fell away and did not send their children to her with boxes of color and tedious brushes and pictures cut from the ladies' magazines. The front door closed upon the last one and remained closed for good. When the town got free postal delivery, Miss Emily alone refused to let them fasten the metal numbers above her door and attach a mailbox to it. She would not listen to them.

Daily, monthly, yearly we watched the Negro grow grayer and more stooped, going in and out with the market basket. Each December we sent her a tax notice, which would be returned by the post office a week later, unclaimed. Now and then we would see her in one of the downstairs windows—she had evidently shut up the top floor of the house—like the carven torso of an idol in a niche, looking or not looking at us, we could never tell which. Thus she passed from generation to generation—dear, inescapable, impervious, tranquil, and perverse.

And so she died. Fell ill in the house filled with dust and shadows, with only a doddering Negro man to wait on her. We did not even know she was sick; we had long since given up trying to get any information from the Negro. He talked to no one, probably not even to her, for his voice had grown harsh and rusty, as if from disuse.

She died in one of the downstairs rooms, in a heavy walnut bed with a curtain, her gray head propped on a pillow yellow and moldy with age and lack of sunlight.

virulent (vĭr′yə-lənt) *adj.* extremely poisonous or harmful

V

The Negro met the first of the ladies at the front door and let them in, with their hushed, sibilant voices and their quick, curious glances, and then he disappeared. He walked right through the house and out the back and was not seen again.

The two female cousins came at once. They held the funeral on the second day, with the town coming to look at Miss Emily beneath a mass of bought flowers, with the crayon face of her father musing profoundly above the bier[8] and the ladies sibilant and macabre; and the very old men—some in their brushed Confederate uniforms—on the porch and the lawn, talking of Miss Emily as if she had been a contemporary of theirs, believing that they had danced with her and
250 courted her perhaps, confusing time with its mathematical progression, as the old do, to whom all the past is not a diminishing road but, instead, a huge meadow which no winter ever quite touches, divided from them now by the narrow bottle-neck of the most recent decade of years.

Already we knew that there was one room in that region above stairs which no one had seen in forty years, and which would have to be forced. They waited until Miss Emily was decently in the ground before they opened it.

The violence of breaking down the door seemed to fill this room with pervading dust. A thin, acrid pall[9] as of the tomb seemed to lie everywhere upon this room decked and furnished as for a bridal: upon the valance curtains of faded
260 rose color, upon the rose-shaded lights, upon the dressing table, upon the delicate array of crystal and the man's toilet things backed with tarnished silver, silver so tarnished that the monogram was obscured. Among them lay a collar and tie, as if they had just been removed, which, lifted, left upon the surface a pale crescent in the dust. Upon a chair hung the suit, carefully folded; beneath it the two mute shoes and the discarded socks.

The man himself lay in the bed.

For a long while we just stood there, looking down at the profound and fleshless grin. The body had apparently once lain in the attitude of an embrace, but now the long sleep that outlasts love, that conquers even the grimace of love, had cuckolded
270 him.[10] What was left of him, rotted beneath what was left of the nightshirt, had become **inextricable** from the bed in which he lay; and upon him and upon the pillow beside him lay that even coating of the patient and biding dust.

Then we noticed that in the second pillow was the indentation of a head. One of us lifted something from it, and leaning forward, that faint and invisible dust dry and acrid in the nostrils, we saw a long strand of iron-gray hair. ᴄᴡ

inextricable
(ĭn-ĕk′strĭ-kə-bəl) *adj.*
incapable of being disentangled or untied

---

8. **bier:** coffin along with its stand.
9. **acrid pall:** bitter-smelling gloom.
10. **cuckolded him:** made his wife or lover unfaithful to him.

Comprehension

1. **Recall** Why was it difficult for Emily to meet suitable men in her youth?

2. **Clarify** What happened to Homer Barron?

3. **Clarify** What does the appearance of the upstairs room in the Grierson house and the iron-gray hair on the pillow indicate?

Literary Analysis

4. **Make Inferences** Use clues in the story to infer Emily's **motivation** for murdering Homer. Why was the relationship considered a "disgrace" and a "bad example to the young people"? What were Homer's intentions?

5. **Examine Methods of Characterization** Emily is a character who leaves quite an impression. How does Faulkner characterize her so effectively? Citing evidence, explain what each of the following reveals about her character:
   - her conflict with the aldermen over her taxes
   - her gifts for Homer
   - her physical appearance at various stages in her life
   - what the townspeople say about the Griersons

6. **Analyze Mood** How would you describe the overall mood of "A Rose for Emily"? Skim the story, identifying at least three passages that create an especially strong **atmosphere** for the reader. Explain which literary elements contribute to each passage's mood.

7. **Interpret Point of View** This story is told in the first-person plural point of view, giving the impression that it is narrated collectively by the entire town. What is the town's attitude toward Emily? Why do they generally let her do whatever she wants but allow "the ladies" to interfere after she starts seeing Homer? Explain what you think Faulkner is saying about small-town life in the South with this story.

8. **Evaluate Sequence** Examine the chart you filled in as you read. How does the order in which the story's major events occur differ from the order in which the narrator presents them? Consider the effect created by Faulkner's manipulation of the story's sequence. What would the story lose if it were told in strict chronological order?

Literary Criticism

9. **Historical Context** Faulkner lived, as one critic put it, "with one foot deep in the traditions of the Old South and the other poised for the possibilities of a modern era." What are some of the indications that this story was written in another time? Citing evidence, describe how Faulkner's story reflects an American society different from our own.

Vocabulary in Context

VOCABULARY PRACTICE

Chose the word that is not related in meaning to the other words.

1. (a) elude, (b) control, (c) circumvent, (d) sidestep
2. (a) overconfidence, (b) temerity, (c) dismay, (d) brashness
3. (a) enlist, (b) intrude, (c) infringe, (d) encroach
4. (a) contempt, (b) cabal, (c) disdain, (d) scorn
5. (a) endurance, (b) imperviousness, (c) decency, (d) resistance
6. (a) embroiled, (b) tangled, (c) inextricable, (d) reduced
7. (a) lethal, (b) virulent, (c) unwilling, (d) malignant
8. (a) tableau, (b) mesa, (c) plateau, (d) upland

WORD LIST

cabal

circumvent

encroach

imperviousness

inextricable

tableau

temerity

virulent

VOCABULARY IN WRITING

How did the Grierson family's position in the town affect the way Emily was treated? Write an explanation of your ideas, using three or more vocabulary words. You could start like this.

> **EXAMPLE SENTENCE**
>
> The family's position in the town made it almost unthinkable that anyone would **encroach** on Miss Emily's privacy.

VOCABULARY STRATEGY: ETYMOLOGIES

Many English words have intriguing **etymologies,** or word histories. The vocabulary word *cabal*, for instance, can be traced back to *kabbala*, the name of an ancient Jewish mystical belief system that at one time was followed by only an elite few. The sense of "secret group or society" came from this connotation. Other words also take their meaning from a reinterpretation of an older term. Though the etymologies of these words do not necessarily help in understanding their current meanings, they provide interesting examples of historical influence on English word meanings.

PRACTICE Using an etymological dictionary or the Internet, explain the origins of the following words.

1. trivial
2. decimate
3. abacus
4. aardvark
5. quarantine
6. malaria
7. ketchup
8. dexterity

VOCABULARY PRACTICE
For more practice, go to the **Vocabulary Center** at **ClassZone.com.**

Reading-Writing Connection

WRITING PROMPT

CONSTRUCT A PERSUASIVE ARGUMENT Do you think the townspeople in "A Rose for Emily" bear any responsibility for what becomes of Emily? Why did they initially think she would use the arsenic to kill herself—and what did they think of this decision? What if they had stopped the minister's wife from writing to her cousins? Why didn't they think to investigate Homer Barron's disappearance?

    Review the story, especially sections III and IV, to clarify your opinion and gather evidence. Then write a **three-to-five-paragraph argument** to try to convince someone else.

SELF-CHECK

A successful persuasive argument will . . .

- clearly state your opinion in the first paragraph
- support your position with evidence from the story
- show logical reasoning
- address possible objections to your position

GRAMMAR AND STYLE

CHOOSE EFFECTIVE POINT OF VIEW Review the **Grammar and Style** note on page 1024. Part of what makes "A Rose for Emily" so interesting is the first-person plural point of view—using *we* and related **pronouns** to tell the story. Usually, the first-person point of view is singular, an *I* who acts as both narrator and character. Faulkner's use of the plural creates a curious mixture of intimacy and anonymity. That is, the voice behind the *we* sounds personal, but readers don't know exactly who the voice is:

> *We learned that Miss Emily had been to the jeweler's and ordered a man's toilet set in silver, with the letters H. B. on each piece. Two days later we learned that she had bought a complete outfit of men's clothing, including a nightshirt, and we said, "They are married." We were really glad.* (lines 189–192)

This kind of narrator has the effect of making the town appear as a complete entity with a personality and opinions all its own.

PRACTICE Try using the first-person plural point of view to create a narrative of your own. Choose a group—a family, for example, or a sports team—and describe, in a paragraph, an event or experience from their point of view. Be sure to use the correct pronouns—*we, us, our, ours*—in your narrative.

WRITING TOOLS

For prewriting, revision, and editing tools, visit the **Writing Center** at ClassZone.com.

The Life You Save May Be Your Own

Short Story by Flannery O'Connor

Flannery O'Connor

1925–1964

As a child, Flannery O'Connor had a pet chicken that could walk backwards as well as forwards. News reporters—including a photographer all the way from New York City—were dispatched to her home in Savannah, Georgia, to take pictures of the unusual chicken. This experience, O'Connor later said, marked her for life. It began her preoccupation with the grotesque, a fascination she shares with other writers belonging to the literary tradition known as Southern Gothic. "Whenever I am asked why Southern writers particularly have a penchant for writing about freaks," O'Connor once commented, "I say it is because we are still able to recognize one."

Born to Write Always a bit shy but self-confident and spirited, O'Connor seemed born to be a writer. She wrote stories from an early age and described herself as a "pigeon-toed only child with a receding chin and a you-leave-me-alone-or-I'll-bite-you complex." In high school, she listed her hobby as "collecting rejection slips," as she was already sending out her stories to major literary journals. After graduating from college, she received a scholarship to attend the famed Writers' Workshop at the University of Iowa. In the late 1940s, she was twice invited to Yaddo, an exclusive artists' colony in upstate New York. In both places, she made lasting friends and developed the contacts she needed to succeed in the literary world.

A Life Cut Short At the age of 25, while writing her first novel, *Wise Blood* (1952), O'Connor was stricken with lupus, an autoimmune disease that had killed her father 9 years earlier. She moved with her mother to a farm outside of Milledgeville, Georgia, where she used her remaining 14 years to produce two highly acclaimed volumes of stories and another novel, *The Violent Bear It Away* (1960).

Defined by Region and Religion Being a Catholic in largely Protestant Georgia gave O'Connor a unique perspective. The South offered rich subject matter—sometimes violent, often humorous—and her Catholicism provided a unifying vision of the divine in everyday life. Her works, often difficult to categorize and to fully understand, weren't bestsellers and took some time to gain a following. Today, critics consider O'Connor one of the greatest short story writers of her time. Her novels and stories are more popular now than they've ever been.

● LITERARY ANALYSIS: IRONY

Irony is a contrast between appearance and actuality. You'll notice two kinds of irony at work in the story you're about to read.

- **Dramatic irony** occurs when readers know more about a situation than the characters themselves know —as though the writer is letting you in on a secret the characters aren't privy to.
- **Situational irony** is a contrast between what a character or reader expects to happen and what actually does happen. This kind of irony often takes the reader by surprise.

Irony is often indirect and subtle, making it difficult to detect. Recognizing it, however, can make a work infinitely more striking and memorable. As you read "The Life You Save May Be Your Own," look for examples of both situational and dramatic irony.

● READING SKILL: ANALYZE DESCRIPTIVE DETAILS

O'Connor asserted that "distortion is the only way to make people see." To that end, she employed a wealth of **descriptive details** to flesh out her grotesque characters and their often perverse situations. As you read, use a chart like the one shown to note examples of these details. Record your personal reactions as well as your analysis of what these details reveal or highlight about the characters and their bizarre behavior.

Striking Details from the Story	My Reactions	Analysis
"He offered the old woman a piece [of gum] but she only raised her upper lip to indicate she had no teeth."	This old woman gives me the creeps. I can picture her hostile stance and her toothless gums.	The woman lives in a poor, isolated area and probably doesn't have access to dental or medical care. But she's not ashamed of her circumstances, and she doesn't waste words explaining herself.

Could you spot a CON ARTIST?

KEY IDEA We've all seen—or heard of or read about—an instance in which someone was duped by a con artist. If you've ever watched a schemer in action, you may have thought to yourself, "I never would have fallen for that one." But literature, movies, and even newspapers are full of stories of people being conned. Why? What makes a con artist's **deception** so hard to spot?

QUICKWRITE Write a quick description of a con you've seen—on the big screen or in real life—or read about. Why do you think the victim fell for the con artist's antics? What traits did the con artist possess? If you'd been in the victim's shoes, do you honestly think you could have seen through the con artist's scheme, or would you too have been duped?

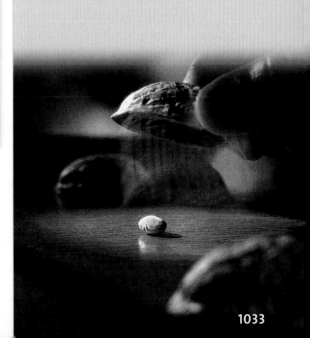

The Life You Save May Be Your Own

Flannery O'Connor

The old woman and her daughter were sitting on their porch when Mr. Shiftlet came up their road for the first time. The old woman slid to the edge of her chair and leaned forward, shading her eyes from the piercing sunset with her hand. The daughter could not see far in front of her and continued to play with her fingers. Although the old woman lived in this desolate spot with only her daughter and she had never seen Mr. Shiftlet before, she could tell, even from a distance, that he was a tramp and no one to be afraid of. His left coat sleeve was folded up to show there was only half an arm in it, and his gaunt figure listed slightly to the side as if the breeze were pushing him. He had on a black town suit and a brown felt hat that was turned up in the front and down in the back and he carried a tin tool box
10 by a handle. He came on, at an amble, up her road, his face turned toward the sun which appeared to be balancing itself on the peak of a small mountain.

The old woman didn't change her position until he was almost into her yard; then she rose with one hand fisted on her hip. The daughter, a large girl in a short blue organdy dress, saw him all at once and jumped up and began to stamp and point and make excited speechless sounds. **A**

Mr. Shiftlet stopped just inside the yard and set his box on the ground and tipped his hat at her as if she were not in the least afflicted; then he turned toward the old woman and swung the hat all the way off. He had long black slick hair
20 that hung flat from a part in the middle to beyond the tips of his ears on either side. His face descended in forehead for more than half its length and ended suddenly with his features just balanced over a jutting steel-trap jaw. He seemed to be a young man but he had a look of composed[1] dissatisfaction as if he understood life thoroughly.

"Good evening," the old woman said. She was about the size of a cedar fence post and she had a man's gray hat pulled down low over her head.

---

1. **composed:** calm; cool and collected.

Light of Lagrange (1997), Billy Morrow Jackson. Watercolor, 22″ × 29″. © Billy Morrow Jackson.

ANALYZE VISUALS
What compositional elements lend this scene a sense of isolation? Cite specific examples in your answer.

A **ANALYZE DETAILS**
Reread lines 1–16, recording in your chart the descriptive details O'Connor includes about each character. What does the old woman's body language suggest about her character? What does the girl's behavior indicate?

The tramp stood looking at her and didn't answer. He turned his back and faced the sunset. He swung both his whole and his short arm up slowly so that they indicated an expanse of sky and his figure formed a crooked cross. The old woman watched him with her arms folded across her chest as if she were the owner of the sun, and the daughter watched, her head thrust forward and her fat helpless hands hanging at the wrists. She had long pink-gold hair and eyes as blue as a peacock's neck.

He held the pose for almost fifty seconds and then he picked up his box and came on to the porch and dropped down on the bottom step. "Lady," he said in a firm nasal voice, "I'd give a fortune to live where I could see me a sun do that every evening."

"Does it every evening," the old woman said and sat back down. The daughter sat down too and watched him with a cautious sly look as if he were a bird that had come up very close. He leaned to one side, rooting in his pants pocket, and in a second he brought out a package of chewing gum and offered her a piece. She took it and unpeeled it and began to chew without taking her eyes off him. He offered the old woman a piece but she only raised her upper lip to indicate she had no teeth.

Mr. Shiftlet's pale, sharp glance had already passed over everything in the yard—the pump near the corner of the house and the big fig tree that three or four chickens were preparing to roost in—and had moved to a shed where he saw the square rusted back of an automobile. "You ladies drive?" he asked.

"That car ain't run in fifteen year," the old woman said. "The day my husband died, it quit running."

"Nothing is like it used to be, lady," he said. "The world is almost rotten."

"That's right," the old woman said. "You from around here?"

"Name Tom T. Shiftlet," he murmured, looking at the tires.

"I'm pleased to meet you," the old woman said. "Name Lucynell Crater and daughter Lucynell Crater. What you doing around here, Mr. Shiftlet?"

He judged the car to be about a 1928 or '29 Ford. "Lady," he said, and turned and gave her his full attention, "lemme tell you something. There's one of these doctors in Atlanta that's taken a knife and cut the human heart—the human heart," he repeated, leaning forward, "out of a man's chest and held it in his hand," and he held his hand out, palm up, as if it were slightly weighted with the human heart, "and studied it like it was a day-old chicken, and lady," he said, allowing a long significant pause in which his head slid forward and his clay-colored eyes brightened, "he don't know no more about it than you or me."

"That's right," the old woman said.

"Why, if he was to take that knife and cut into every corner of it, he still wouldn't know no more than you or me. What you want to bet?"

"Nothing," the old woman said wisely. "Where you come from, Mr. Shiftlet?"

He didn't answer. He reached into his pocket and brought out a sack of tobacco and a package of cigarette papers and rolled himself a cigarette, expertly with one hand, and attached it in a hanging position to his upper lip. Then he took a box of wooden matches from his pocket and struck one on his shoe. He held the burning match as if he were studying the mystery of flame while it traveled dangerously toward his skin. The daughter began to make loud noises and to point to his hand and shake her finger at him, but when the flame was just before touching him, he leaned down with his hand cupped over it as if he were going to set fire to his nose and lit the cigarette. **B**

He flipped away the dead match and blew a stream of gray into the evening. A sly look came over his face. "Lady," he said, "nowadays, people'll do anything anyways. I can tell you my name is Tom T. Shiftlet and I come from Tarwater, Tennessee, but
80 you never have seen me before: how you know I ain't lying? How you know my name ain't Aaron Sparks, lady, and I come from Singleberry, Georgia, or how you know it's not George Speeds and I come from Lucy, Alabama, or how you know I ain't Thompson Bright from Toolafalls, Mississippi?"

"I don't know nothing about you," the old woman muttered, irked.

"Lady," he said, "people don't care how they lie. Maybe the best I can tell you is, I'm a man; but listen lady," he said and paused and made his tone more ominous still, "what is a man?"

The old woman began to gum a seed. "What you carry in that tin box, Mr. Shiftlet?" she asked.
90 "Tools," he said, put back. "I'm a carpenter."

"Well, if you come out here to work, I'll be able to feed you and give you a place to sleep but I can't pay. I'll tell you that before you begin," she said.

There was no answer at once and no particular expression on his face. He leaned back against the two-by-four that helped support the porch roof. "Lady," he said slowly, "there's some men that some things mean more to them than money." The old woman rocked without comment and the daughter watched the trigger that moved up and down in his neck. He told the old woman then that all most people were interested in was money, but he asked what a man was made for. He asked her if a man was made for money, or what. He asked her
100 what she thought she was made for but she didn't answer, she only sat rocking and wondered if a one-armed man could put a new roof on her garden house. He asked a lot of questions that she didn't answer. He told her that he was twenty-eight years old and had lived a varied life. He had been a gospel singer, a foreman on the railroad, an assistant in an undertaking parlor, and he come over the radio for three months with Uncle Roy and his Red Creek Wranglers. He said he had fought and bled in the Arm Service of his country and visited every foreign land and that everywhere he had seen people that didn't care if they did a thing one way or another. He said he hadn't been raised thataway. **C**

A fat yellow moon appeared in the branches of the fig tree as if it were going to
110 roost there with the chickens. He said that a man had to escape to the country to see the world whole and that he wished he lived in a desolate place like this where he could see the sun go down every evening like God made it to do.

"Are you married or are you single?" the old woman asked.

There was a long silence. "Lady," he asked finally, "where would you find you an innocent woman today? I wouldn't have any of this trash I could just pick up."

The daughter was leaning very far down, hanging her head almost between her knees watching him through a triangular door she had made in her overturned

B ANALYZE DETAILS
Consider the wealth of details O'Connor offers about Tom Shiftlet in lines 45–76. Which details serve to reveal his important **traits?**

C IRONY
Reread lines 105–108. Explain the irony of Shiftlet's statement that he served in the "Arm Service."

hair; and she suddenly fell in a heap on the floor and began to whimper. Mr. Shiftlet straightened her out and helped her get back in the chair.

120   "Is she your baby girl?" he asked.

"My only," the old woman said, "and she's the sweetest girl in the world. I would give her up for nothing on earth. She's smart too. She can sweep the floor, cook, wash, feed the chickens, and hoe. I wouldn't give her up for a casket of jewels." **D**

"No," he said kindly, "don't ever let any man take her away from you."

"Any man come after her," the old woman said, " 'll have to stay around the place."

Mr. Shiftlet's eye in the darkness was focused on a part of the automobile bumper that glittered in the distance. "Lady," he said, jerking his short arm up as

130   if he could point with it to her house and yard and pump, "there ain't a broken thing on this plantation that I couldn't fix for you, one-arm jackleg[2] or not. I'm a man," he said with a sullen dignity, "even if I ain't a whole one. I got," he said, tapping his knuckles on the floor to emphasize the immensity of what he was going to say, "a moral intelligence!" and his face pierced out of the darkness into a shaft of doorlight and he stared at her as if he were astonished himself at this impossible truth.

The old woman was not impressed with the phrase. "I told you you could hang around and work for food," she said, "if you don't mind sleeping in that car yonder."

"Why listen, Lady," he said with a grin of delight, "the monks of old slept in

140   their coffins!"

"They wasn't as advanced as we are," the old woman said.

The next morning he began on the roof of the garden house while Lucynell, the daughter, sat on a rock and watched him work. He had not been around a week before the change he had made in the place was apparent. He had patched the front and back steps, built a new hog pen, restored a fence, and taught Lucynell, who was completely deaf and had never said a word in her life, to say the word "bird." The big rosy-faced girl followed him everywhere, saying "Burrttddt ddbirrrttdt," and clapping her hands. The old woman watched from a distance, secretly pleased. She was ravenous for a son-in-law.

150   Mr. Shiftlet slept on the hard narrow back seat of the car with his feet out the side window. He had his razor and a can of water on a crate that served him as a bedside table and he put up a piece of mirror against the back glass and kept his coat neatly on a hanger that he hung over one of the windows.

In the evenings he sat on the steps and talked while the old woman and Lucynell rocked violently in their chairs on either side of him. The old woman's three mountains were black against the dark blue sky and were visited off and on by various planets and by the moon after it had left the chickens. Mr. Shiftlet pointed out that the reason he had improved this plantation was because he had taken a personal interest in it. He said he was even going to make the automobile run.

2. **jackleg:** someone who does work he or she has not been trained to do.

D **IRONY**
O'Connor employs irony not just in her descriptions of her characters, but in their dialogue, as well. Reread lines 120–124. What double meaning might be suggested by the phrase "I would give her up for nothing on earth"?

ANALYZE VISUALS
Note that the painting on page 1039 is titled *The Interloper*. An interloper is an intruder. What does this title suggest about the man and the farmhouse depicted? How does the title work with the elements of the painting to establish a mood? Explain.

The Interloper (1958), Billy Morrow Jackson. Collection of Mrs. Virginia Penofsky.

160　　He had raised the hood and studied the mechanism and he said he could tell that the car had been built in the days when cars were really built. You take now, he said, one man puts in one bolt and another man puts in another bolt and another man puts in another bolt so that it's a man for a bolt. That's why you have to pay so much for a car: you're paying all those men. Now if you didn't have to pay but one man, you could get you a cheaper car and one that had had a personal interest taken in it, and it would be a better car. The old woman agreed with him that this was so.

　　Mr. Shiftlet said that the trouble with the world was that nobody cared, or stopped and took any trouble. He said he never would have been able to teach
170　Lucynell to say a word if he hadn't cared and stopped long enough. **E**

　　"Teach her to say something else," the old woman said.

　　"What you want her to say next?" Mr. Shiftlet asked.

　　The old woman's smile was broad and toothless and suggestive. "Teach her to say 'sugarpie,'" she said.

　　Mr. Shiftlet already knew what was on her mind. **F**

　　The next day he began to tinker with the automobile, and that evening he told her that if she would buy a fan belt, he would be able to make the car run.

　　The old woman said she would give him the money. "You see that girl yonder?" she asked, pointing to Lucynell who was sitting on the floor a foot away, watching

E IRONY
A "1928 or '29 Ford" like this one would, in fact, have been made on an assembly line, a feature that greatly reduced the cost of automobiles. What does this knowledge, combined with Shiftlet's statements in lines 160–170, tell you about his character? Explain which type of irony O'Connor is using here.

F ANALYZE DETAILS
What are Mrs. Crater's **motives** for wanting Lucynell to learn to say "sugarpie"? What details in line 173 suggest this?

180   him, her eyes blue even in the dark. "If it was ever a man wanted to take her away, I would say, 'No man on earth is going to take that sweet girl of mine away from me!' but if he was to say, 'Lady, I don't want to take her away, I want her right here,' I would say, 'Mister, I don't blame you none. I wouldn't pass up a chance to live in a permanent place and get the sweetest girl in the world myself. You ain't no fool,' I would say."

    "How old is she?" Mr. Shiftlet asked casually.

    "Fifteen, sixteen," the old woman said. The girl was nearly thirty but because of her innocence it was impossible to guess.

    "It would be a good idea to paint it too," Mr. Shiftlet remarked. "You don't
190 want it to rust out."

    "We'll see about that later," the old woman said.

    The next day he walked into town and returned with the parts he needed and a can of gasoline. Late in the afternoon, terrible noises issued from the shed and the old woman rushed out of the house, thinking Lucynell was somewhere having a fit. Lucynell was sitting on a chicken crate, stamping her feet and screaming, "Burrddttt! bddurrddttt!" but her fuss was drowned out by the car. With a volley of blasts it emerged from the shed, moving in a fierce and stately way. Mr. Shiftlet was in the driver's seat, sitting very erect. He had an expression of serious modesty on his face as if he had just raised the dead.

200   That night, rocking on the porch, the old woman began her business at once. "You want you an innocent woman, don't you?" she asked sympathetically. "You don't want none of this trash."

    "No'm, I don't," Mr. Shiftlet said.

    "One that can't talk," she continued, "can't sass you back or use foul language. That's the kind for you to have. Right there," and she pointed to Lucynell sitting cross-legged in her chair, holding both feet in her hands.

    "That's right," he admitted. "She wouldn't give me any trouble."

    "Saturday," the old woman said, "you and her and me can drive into town and get married."

210   Mr. Shiftlet eased his position on the steps.

    "I can't get married right now," he said. "Everything you want to do takes money and I ain't got any."

    "What you need with money?" she asked.

    "It takes money," he said. "Some people'll do anything anyhow these days, but the way I think, I wouldn't marry no woman that I couldn't take on a trip like she was somebody. I mean take her to a hotel and treat her. I wouldn't marry the Duchesser Windsor,"[3] he said firmly, "unless I could take her to a hotel and give her something good to eat.

    "I was raised thataway and there ain't a thing I can do about it. My old mother
220 taught me how to do."

    "Lucynell don't even know what a hotel is," the old woman muttered. "Listen here, Mr. Shiftlet," she said, sliding forward in her chair, "you'd be getting a

---

3. **Duchesser Windsor:** Duchess of Windsor. The title was given to the American divorcée Wallace Simpson upon her marriage to the former Edward VIII of England in 1937.

permanent house and a deep well and the most innocent girl in the world. You don't need no money. Lemme tell you something: there ain't any place in the world for a poor disabled friendless drifting man."

The ugly words settled in Mr. Shiftlet's head like a group of buzzards in the top of a tree. He didn't answer at once. He rolled himself a cigarette and lit it and then he said in an even voice, "Lady, a man is divided into two parts, body and spirit."

The old woman clamped her gums together.

230   "A body and a spirit," he repeated. "The body, lady, is like a house: it don't go anywhere; but the spirit, lady, is like a automobile: always on the move, always . . ."

"Listen, Mr. Shiftlet," she said, "my well never goes dry and my house is always warm in the winter and there's no mortgage on a thing about this place. You can go to the courthouse and see for yourself. And yonder under that shed is a fine automobile." She laid the bait carefully. "You can have it painted by Saturday. I'll pay for the paint."

In the darkness, Mr. Shiftlet's smile stretched like a weary snake waking up by a fire. After a second he recalled himself and said, "I'm only saying a man's spirit means more to him than anything else. I would have to take my wife off for the week end

240   without no regards at all for cost. I got to follow where my spirit says to go."

"I'll give you fifteen dollars for a week end trip," the old woman said in a crabbed voice. "That's the best I can do."

"That wouldn't hardly pay for more than the gas and the hotel," he said. "It wouldn't feed her."

"Seventeen-fifty," the old woman said. "That's all I got so it isn't any use you trying to milk me. You can take a lunch."

Mr. Shiftlet was deeply hurt by the word "milk." He didn't doubt that she had more money sewed up in her mattress but he had already told her he was not interested in her money. "I'll make that do," he said and rose and walked off

250   without treating[4] with her further. **G**

On Saturday the three of them drove into town in the car that the paint had barely dried on and Mr. Shiftlet and Lucynell were married in the Ordinary's[5] office while the old woman witnessed. As they came out of the courthouse, Mr. Shiftlet began twisting his neck in his collar. He looked morose and bitter as if he had been insulted while someone held him. "That didn't satisfy me none," he said. "That was just something a woman in an office did, nothing but paper work and blood tests. What do they know about my blood? If they was to take my heart and cut it out," he said, "they wouldn't know a thing about me. It didn't satisfy me at all."

"It satisfied the law," the old woman said sharply.

260   "The law," Mr. Shiftlet said and spit. "It's the law that don't satisfy me."

He had painted the car dark green with a yellow band around it just under the windows. The three of them climbed in the front seat and the old woman said, "Don't Lucynell look pretty? Looks like a baby doll." Lucynell was dressed up in a white dress that her mother had uprooted from a trunk and there was a Panama

G ANALYZE DETAILS
At this point in the story, what **conclusions** can you draw about each character? Cite details in lines 178–250 that influenced your judgments.

---

4. **treating:** discussing terms; negotiating.

5. **Ordinary's:** judge's.

hat on her head with a bunch of red wooden cherries on the brim. Every now and then her placid expression was changed by a sly isolated little thought like a shoot of green in the desert. "You got a prize!" the old woman said.

Mr. Shiftlet didn't even look at her.

They drove back to the house to let the old woman off and pick up the lunch. When they were ready to leave, she stood staring in the window of the car, with her fingers clenched around the glass. Tears began to seep sideways out of her eyes and run along the dirty creases in her face. "I ain't ever been parted with her for two days before," she said.

Mr. Shiftlet started the motor.

"And I wouldn't let no man have her but you because I seen you would do right. Good bye, Sugarbaby," she said, clutching at the sleeve of the white dress. Lucynell looked straight at her and didn't seem to see her there at all. Mr. Shiftlet eased the car forward so that she had to move her hands.

The early afternoon was clear and open and surrounded by pale blue sky. Although the car would go only thirty miles an hour, Mr. Shiftlet imagined a terrific climb and dip and swerve that went entirely to his head so that he forgot his morning bitterness. He had always wanted an automobile but he had never been able to afford one before. He drove very fast because he wanted to make Mobile[6] by nightfall.

Occasionally he stopped his thoughts long enough to look at Lucynell in the seat beside him. She had eaten the lunch as soon as they were out of the yard and now she was pulling the cherries off the hat one by one and throwing them out the window. He became depressed in spite of the car. He had driven about a hundred miles when he decided that she must be hungry again and at the next small town they came to, he stopped in front of an aluminum-painted eating place called The Hot Spot and took her in and ordered her a plate of ham and grits. The ride had made her sleepy and as soon as she got up on the stool, she rested her head on the counter and shut her eyes. There was no one in The Hot Spot but Mr. Shiftlet and the boy behind the counter, a pale youth with a greasy rag hung over his shoulder. Before he could dish up the food, she was snoring gently. **H**

"Give it to her when she wakes up," Mr. Shiftlet said. "I'll pay for it now."

The boy bent over her and stared at the long pink-gold hair and the half-shut sleeping eyes. Then he looked up and stared at Mr. Shiftlet. "She looks like an angel of Gawd," he murmured.

"Hitch-hiker," Mr. Shiftlet explained. "I can't wait. I got to make Tuscaloosa.[7]"

The boy bent over again and very carefully touched his finger to a strand of the golden hair, and Mr. Shiftlet left.

He was more depressed than ever as he drove on by himself. The late afternoon had grown hot and sultry and the country had flattened out. Deep in the sky a storm was preparing very slowly and without thunder as if it meant to drain every drop of air from the earth before it broke. There were times when Mr. Shiftlet

H **IRONY**
Consider what most people would expect from an establishment called The Hot Spot. What is ironic about this restaurant's name?

---

6. **Mobile:** a city in southwestern Alabama, along the Gulf Coast.

7. **Tuscaloosa:** a city in west-central Alabama.

preferred not to be alone. He felt too that a man with a car had a responsibility to others, and he kept his eye out for a hitch-hiker. Occasionally he saw a sign that warned: "Drive carefully. The life you save may be your own." **❶**

310   The narrow road dropped off on either side into dry fields and here and there a shack or a filling station stood in a clearing. The sun began to set directly in front of the automobile. It was a reddening ball that through his windshield was slightly flat on the bottom and top. He saw a boy in overalls and a gray hat standing on the edge of the road and he slowed the car down and stopped in front of him. The boy didn't have his hand raised to thumb the ride, he was only standing there, but he had a small cardboard suitcase and his hat was set on his head in a way to indicate that he had left somewhere for good. "Son," Mr. Shiftlet said, "I see you want a ride."

The boy didn't say he did or he didn't but he opened the door of the car and
320   got in, and Mr. Shiftlet started driving again. The child held the suitcase on his lap and folded his arms on top of it. He turned his head and looked out the window away from Mr. Shiftlet. Mr. Shiftlet felt oppressed. "Son," he said after a minute, "I got the best old mother in the world so I reckon you only got the second best."

The boy gave him a quick dark glance and then turned his face back out the window.

"It's nothing so sweet," Mr. Shiftlet continued, "as a boy's mother. She taught him his first prayers at her knee, she give him love when no other would, she told him what was right and what wasn't, and she seen that he done the right thing. Son," he said, "I never rued a day in my life like the one I rued when I left that
330   old mother of mine."

The boy shifted in his seat but he didn't look at Mr. Shiftlet. He unfolded his arms and put one hand on the door handle.

"My mother was a angel of Gawd," Mr. Shiftlet said in a very strained voice. "He took her from heaven and giver to me and I left her." His eyes were instantly clouded over with a mist of tears. The car was barely moving.

The boy turned angrily in the seat. "You go to the devil!" he cried. "My old woman is a flea bag and yours is a stinking pole cat!" and with that he flung the door open and jumped out with his suitcase into the ditch.

Mr. Shiftlet was so shocked that for about a hundred feet he drove along slowly
340   with the door still open. A cloud, the exact color of the boy's hat and shaped like a turnip, had descended over the sun, and another, worse looking, crouched behind the car. Mr. Shiftlet felt that the rottenness of the world was about to engulf him. He raised his arm and let it fall again to his breast. "Oh Lord!" he prayed. "Break forth and wash the slime from this earth!"

The turnip continued slowly to descend. After a few minutes there was a guffawing peal of thunder from behind and fantastic raindrops, like tin-can tops, crashed over the rear of Mr. Shiftlet's car. Very quickly he stepped on the gas, and with his stump sticking out the window he raced the galloping shower into Mobile. ❧

❶ IRONY
What is the irony in Shiftlet's reasons for looking for a hitchhiker?

Comprehension

1. **Recall** What are Lucynell's disabilities?

2. **Recall** When they first meet, what do Mr. Shiftlet and Mrs. Crater want from each other?

3. **Summarize** What is the bargain struck between Mr. Shiftlet and Mrs. Crater over her daughter, Lucynell?

4. **Clarify** What does Mr. Shiftlet's treatment of Lucynell at the end reveal about his intentions all along?

Literary Analysis

5. **Analyze Character** Explain why Mr. Shiftlet is able to get what he wants from Mrs. Crater. What traits make him a good con artist? What makes Mrs. Crater the perfect victim for this kind of **deception?** Cite evidence to support your response.

6. **Analyze Descriptive Details** Review the chart you created as you read. Because Mr. Shiftlet and Mrs. Crater are both hiding something during much of the story, readers must mine the details given about each character for clues to their true selves. Since Mr. Shiftlet's words and thoughts can't be trusted, what can you learn about him from the descriptions of his physical appearance? What details reveal the flaws in Mrs. Crater's character and give her motives away? Support your analysis with evidence from the text.

7. **Interpret Irony** In this story, much of O'Connor's wry humor comes from **situational** and **dramatic irony.** Review the story to find at least two examples of each kind of irony. Also, see whether you can find one example that reveals both kinds at once. What do these multiple ironies suggest about O'Connor's view of her fellow human beings?

8. **Make Judgments** What is the significance of the story's title, taken from a road sign? Explain how you think O'Connor judges Tom T. Shiftlet, as well as how you yourself do. Be sure to address the following:

   • the way in which Mr. Shiftlet is a potential savior of his own life and the lives of others

   • how and why he fails in this role

   • whether you think he has any redeeming features or see him as hopelessly lost

Literary Criticism

9. **Author's Style** For Flannery O'Connor, a devout Catholic, evidence of divine grace was everywhere, and her stories are full of religious **imagery.** Find at least two examples of religious imagery in this story and explain what they contribute to its meaning and its message.

The Essence of a Short Story

Stories by modernist writers, such as Fitzgerald, Hemingway, and Faulkner, are often complex or ambiguous. These works demand much of readers, who must pay attention to details of character, setting, plot, dialogue, and language in order to decipher meaning.

Writing to Evaluate

After reflecting on each of the short stories you have just read, choose one and evaluate it in order to distill its essence—that which is utterly indispensable—in no more than 300 of the author's own words. You may use portions of sentences and combine them, if appropriate and necessary. In addition, you may create your own paragraphing structure in order to give your distillation a desirable "flow."

Consider

- introductions or important descriptions of characters
- plot events essential to the story, especially the climax
- descriptions of setting that reveal important information
- dialogue that reveals character, motivation, or theme
- particularly meaningful language

Extension

VIEWING & REPRESENTING
Working with a partner, **choose or create an image** that you feel captures the essence of the story you evaluated. You may look for an image from a magazine, Web site, book of art, or other source, or you may create your own. Share your image with the class, and explain why you feel it represents or illustrates the story's essence.

Ernest Hemingway, working as a war correspondent, 1944

Journalism as Literature

Some journalists are writers of literature in disguise. They put together a news story or an opinion piece that is so well written and riveting that the article is elevated to the realm of literature. Have you ever read a news report or editorial that seemed to stand out from anything else you'd read in the newspaper? If so, you may have read an emerging literary classic.

The Fine Art of Journalism

Traditionally, journalism and literature are considered to be very different forms. **Journalism** is known for being factual, informative, and written for the moment. **Literature,** on the other hand, is built from the imagination and meant to last. Its language is often figurative, its images are symbolic, and the setting and characters are representative of deeper meaning. When journalism

becomes literature, it's not the imaginative use of facts that makes it so; rather, it's the imaginative use of language that transforms it from a standard news story into a piece of art.

Journalistic writing includes news reports, essays, editorials, feature articles, and critical reviews and has a long history in the United States. Many of the big issues of the day, since pre-Revolutionary times, have been debated in newspapers, magazines, and pamphlets. In the early 20th century, a number of serious literary writers began their writing careers as journalists, including Ernest Hemingway, E. B. White, and Dorothy Parker. The tradition of journalism as literature continued with writers such as Truman Capote, Tom Wolfe, and Joan Didion. In the 1960s, Wolfe coined the term "New Journalism" to describe the work of a journalist who sets out to create journalistic writing that uses literary techniques.

Tools of the Trade

Journalism that transcends the mundane and becomes literature is usually characterized by the use of certain literary techniques.

- **Imagery**—Traditionally, news writing contains only essential details, without any embellishment of description. In literary writing, the writer includes words and phrases that express sensory experiences in order to create a vivid picture or strong impression for the reader.

- **Narrative elements**—In the world of journalism, an article is figuratively called "a story." At times, this might be literally true, especially when a journalist relates an incident with all the elements of a good tale, including a suspenseful plot, detailed characterization and setting, and a well-defined point of view.

- **Style and voice**—Style is a writer's unique way of communicating ideas, and voice is the expression of his or her personality. Most news writing is made up of spare, plain prose, written for a mass audience. In literary writing, the writer may use figurative language, coin new words, or interject descriptive phrases. Each of these elements can add up to an original style and voice.

- **Writer's perspective**—In an editorial or literary review, you expect to find the writer's opinion, but in news reporting, the writer usually remains invisible. Hemingway and Jack London, however, were two journalists who wrote personal narratives of news events, including war experiences and unusual adventures, in which they interjected their own observations and opinions.

In the following passage from "A New Kind of War" (page 1050), notice how Hemingway included his observations instead of merely reporting the facts.

> In the war that I had known, men often lied about the manner of their wounding. Not at first; but later. I'd lied a little myself in my time. Especially late in the evening.
>
> **—Ernest Hemingway, "A New Kind of War"**

Close Read

What does Hemingway reveal about himself in this passage? Why wouldn't this be typical of journalism, which is known for being factual?

Dorothy Parker was always known for her acerbic wit. In the following excerpt from a literary review, notice the imagery and figurative language she uses in exaggerating the critics' reactions to Hemingway's first novel.

> Promptly upon its publication, Ernest Hemingway was discovered, the Stars and Stripes were reverentially raised over him, eight hundred and forty-seven book reviewers formed themselves into the word "welcome," and the band played "Hail to the Chief" in three concurrent keys.
>
> **—Dorothy Parker, "A Book of Great Short Stories"**

Close Read

In each of these examples, the writer's voice is well developed. How would you describe the personality of the writer in each?

A New Kind of War
News Dispatch by Ernest Hemingway

FYI

Did you know that Ernest Hemingway . . .

- began a romance in Spain with fellow war reporter Martha Gellhorn, who became his third wife?

- hunted Nazi submarines off the coast of Cuba in his private fishing boat?

Hemingway, center, among other correspondents covering the Spanish Civil War

Ernest Hemingway
1899–1961

Ernest Hemingway never considered his journalism as important as his fiction, but his journalism was admired anyway, particularly his war correspondence. Before he published his first stories and novels in the 1920s, he reported on European affairs for the *Toronto Star*. He covered the Greco-Turkish War of 1922, describing 20 miles of Greek refugees trudging through the rain. He also interviewed the fascist Italian dictator Benito Mussolini, calling him the "biggest bluff in Europe."

Taking Sides in Spain By the 1930s, Hemingway had become a famous literary figure. He returned to war reporting in 1937 after civil war broke out in Spain, the country that he loved. Hemingway is perhaps most identified with this conflict, in which the right-wing army of General Francisco Franco (the Nationalists) fought against supporters of the left-wing elected government of Spain (the Loyalists or Republicans). This war was widely seen as a struggle against fascism, or dictatorial government. Many world writers, including Hemingway, were sympathetic to the Loyalist side. These writers were greatly disheartened by Franco's eventual victory in 1939.

Celebrity Journalist Hemingway covered the war for the North American Newspaper Alliance (NANA), receiving the highest fee ever paid a war correspondent. His NANA dispatches have been called "a new style of reporting that told the public about every facet of the war, especially . . . its effects on the common man, woman, and child." One of these dispatches, "A New Kind of War," is considered classic.

Writer or Fighter? After World War II broke out, Hemingway once again became a war reporter, this time for *Collier's* magazine. He memorably described the D-day landing at Normandy, the liberation of Paris, and the Allied movement into Germany in 1944. His command of a French guerrilla band and his storage of weapons in his hotel room led him to be investigated for violating the Geneva Convention, which forbids journalists to take up arms. He was cleared of misconduct and later awarded a Bronze Star for his service as a war correspondent.

See also the biography on page 968, which covers Hemingway's entire career.

● LITERARY ANALYSIS: SUBJECTIVITY IN REPORTING

News reporters are trained to be **objective,** presenting facts without the intrusion of their own personal feelings or opinions. You will notice, however, that Hemingway does not strive for this ideal in his reporting on the Spanish Civil War. His writing is quite **subjective,** expressing his personal reactions to what he sees. He wants his readers to be in Madrid with him, experiencing exactly what he does. Toward this end he uses both the **second-person point of view** ("as you lie in bed, you hear the firing in the front line") and the **first-person point of view** ("I did not believe a word of it").

As you read, notice ways in which Hemingway reveals his feelings and opinions. Consider what his subjectivity offers that an objective news report could not.

Review: **Dialogue**

● READING SKILL: ANALYZE DESCRIPTIVE DETAILS

Hemingway makes powerful use of descriptive details. Many of these are **sensory details,** which appeal to the senses of sight, hearing, touch, smell, and taste. Notice the visual details in the following passage. What can you conclude from them?

On the corner, twenty yards away, is a heap of rubble, smashed cement and thrown up dirt, a single dead man, his torn clothes dusty, and a great hole in the sidewalk from which the gas from a broken main is rising....

Other descriptive details are not sensory, but they still convey important ideas. What might it mean, for example, that the large rooms at the front of Hemingway's hotel only cost a dollar a day? As you read, jot down descriptive details about

• Madrid and the hotel

• Raven, the wounded soldier Hemingway meets

• Raven's commander, Jock Cunningham

React to these details and make inferences from them.

Explore the Key Idea

What can we learn from WAR?

KEY IDEA The Spanish Civil War did not have immediate consequences for most Americans, yet American newspapers thought it was important enough to cover. Consider our own times. Why do newspapers and broadcast networks send reporters to cover fighting in foreign countries? What do these reports usually show or tell an audience about **war?**

DISCUSS Think about war coverage you have read, seen on television, or heard on the radio. Working in a small group, list types of information you would expect to be included in such reporting—the number of people killed in an attack, for example. After completing your list, discuss insights about war that you have gained from journalists.

1049

A New Kind of War

ERNEST HEMINGWAY

> **BACKGROUND** Hemingway and other journalists covering the Spanish Civil War stayed at the Hotel Florida in Madrid, the Spanish capital, which was under siege by General Franco's Nationalist forces. Franco was aided by the fascist governments of Italy and Nazi Germany, which sent troops and weapons. The Loyalist forces of the Spanish government were aided by the Soviet Union and volunteer International Brigades from across Europe and the United States. The soldiers that Hemingway profiles in this article were part of the International Brigades.

NANA Dispatch · APRIL 14, 1937

MADRID—The window of the hotel is open and, as you lie in bed, you hear the firing in the front line seventeen blocks away. There is a rifle fire all night long. The rifles go tacrong, capong, craang, tacrong, and then a machine gun opens up. It has a bigger calibre and is much louder, rong, cararong, rong, rong. Then there is the incoming boom of a trench mortar shell and a burst of machine gun fire. You lie and listen to it and it is a great thing to be in bed with your feet stretched out gradually warming the cold foot of the bed and not out there in University City or Carabanchel.[1] A man is singing hard-voiced in the street below and three drunks are arguing when you fall asleep. **Ⓐ**

10   In the morning, before your call comes from the desk, the roaring burst of a high explosive shell wakes you and you go to the window and look out to see a man, his head down, his coat collar up, sprinting desperately across the paved

ANALYZE VISUALS
Examine the composition, or arrangement, of shapes in the photograph on page 1051. What does the angle of the photo contribute to its impact? Explain.

Ⓐ SUBJECTIVITY IN REPORTING
What are Hemingway's thoughts and sensations in the first paragraph?

---

1. **University City or Carabanchel** (kär'-ə-bän-chel'): scenes of bloody battles in or on the outskirts of Madrid.

square. There is the acrid smell of high explosive you hoped you'd never smell again, and, in a bathrobe and bedroom slippers, you hurry down the marble stairs and almost into a middle-aged woman, wounded in the abdomen, who is being helped into the hotel entrance by two men in blue workmen's smocks. She has her two hands crossed below her big, old-style Spanish bosom and from between her fingers the blood is spurting in a thin stream. On the corner, twenty yards away, is a heap of rubble, smashed cement and thrown up dirt, a single dead man, his torn

20 clothes dusty, and a great hole in the sidewalk from which the gas from a broken main is rising, looking like a heat mirage in the cold morning air. **B**

"How many dead?" you ask a policeman.

"Only one," he says. "It went through the sidewalk and burst below. If it would have burst on the solid stone of the road there might have been fifty."

A policeman covers the top of the trunk, from which the head is missing; they send for someone to repair the gas main and you go in to breakfast. A charwoman,[2] her eyes red, is scrubbing the blood off the marble floor of the corridor. The dead man wasn't you nor anyone you know and everyone is very hungry in the morning after a cold night and a long day the day before up at the

30 Guadalajara[3] front. **C**

"Did you see him?" asked someone else at breakfast.

"Sure," you say.

"That's where we pass a dozen times a day. Right on that corner." Someone makes a joke about missing teeth and someone else says not to make that joke. And everyone has the feeling that characterizes war. It wasn't me, see? It wasn't me. **D**

The Italian dead up on the Guadalajara front weren't you, although Italian dead, because of where you had spent your boyhood, always seemed, still, like our dead.[4] No. You went to the front early in the morning in a miserable little car with a more miserable little chauffeur who suffered visibly the closer he came to the

40 fighting. But at night, sometimes late, without lights, with the big trucks roaring past, you came on back to sleep in a bed with sheets in a good hotel, paying a dollar a day for the best rooms on the front. The smaller rooms in the back, on the side away from the shelling, were considerably more expensive. After the shell that lit on the sidewalk in front of the hotel you got a beautiful double corner room on that side, twice the size of the one you had had, for less than a dollar. It wasn't me they killed. See? No. Not me. It wasn't me anymore. **E**

Then, in a hospital given by the American Friends of Spanish Democracy, located out behind the Morata front along the road to Valencia,[5] they said, "Raven wants to see you."

50 "Do I know him?"

"I don't think so," they said, "but he wants to see you."

---

2. **charwoman:** a woman employed to clean houses or offices.

3. **Guadalajara:** a city in Spain to the northeast of Madrid, strategically important because of its nearness to the capital. Battle had raged there through most of March 1937, with the Loyalists finally winning.

4. **Italian dead . . . our dead:** Italian forces fought on the side of the Nationalists; however, Hemingway had spent a long time in an Italian hospital as a young man during World War I.

5. **Morata . . . Valencia:** Morata de Tejuña, a small town southeast of Madrid, was heavily damaged at this time. Valencia is on the eastern coast of Spain, about 240 miles southeast of Madrid.

B **DESCRIPTIVE DETAILS**
Identify **sensory details** in lines 10–21, and the senses they appeal to. What **mood** do they create?

C **GRAMMAR AND STYLE**
Reread lines 28–30. Notice how the use of the **second-person pronoun** *you* places the reader in Hemingway's shoes.

D **SUBJECTIVITY IN REPORTING**
Interpret what Hemingway means by "the feeling that characterizes war."

E **SUBJECTIVITY IN REPORTING**
Reread lines 36–46. What is Hemingway's attitude toward the Italian dead? his chauffeur? his hotel room?

"Where is he?"

"Upstairs."

In the room upstairs they are giving a blood transfusion to a man with a very gray face who lay on a cot with his arm out, looking away from the gurgling bottle and moaning in a very impersonal way. He moaned mechanically and at regular intervals and it did not seem to be him that made the sound. His lips did not move.

"Where's Raven?" I asked.

60 "I'm here," said Raven.

The voice came from a high mound covered by a shoddy gray blanket. There were two arms crossed on the top of the mound and at one end there was something that had been a face, but now was a yellow scabby area with a wide bandage cross where the eyes had been.

"Who is it?" asked Raven. He didn't have lips, but he talked pretty well without them and with a pleasant voice. **F**

"Hemingway," I said. "I came up to see how you were doing."

"My face was pretty bad," he said. "It got sort of burned from the grenade, but it's peeled a couple of times and it's doing better."

70 "It looks swell," I said. "It's doing fine."

I wasn't looking at it when I spoke.

"How are things in America?" he asked. "What do they think of us over there?"

"Sentiment's changed a lot," I said. "They're beginning to realize the government is going to win this war."

F DESCRIPTIVE DETAILS
What emotional reaction do you have to the description of Raven?

Members of the International Brigades near Madrid in late 1936

"Do you think so?"

"Sure," I said.

"I'm awfully glad," he said. "You know, I wouldn't mind any of this if I could just watch what was going on. I don't mind the pain, you know. It never seemed important really. But I was always awfully interested in things and I really wouldn't
80 mind the pain at all if I could just sort of follow things intelligently. I could even be some use. You know, I didn't mind the war at all. I did all right in the war. I got hit once before and I was back and rejoined the battalion in two weeks. I couldn't stand to be away. Then I got this." **G**

He had put his hand in mine. It was not a worker's hand. There were no callouses and the nails on the long, spatulate[6] fingers were smooth and rounded.

"How did you get it?" I asked.

"Well, there were some troops that were routed and we went over to sort of reform them and we did and then we had quite a fight with the fascists and we beat them. It was quite a bad fight, you know, but we beat them and then
90 someone threw this grenade at me."

Holding his hand and hearing him tell it, I did not believe a word of it. What was left of him did not sound like the wreckage of a soldier somehow. I did not know how he had been wounded, but the story did not sound right. It was the sort of way everyone would like to have been wounded. But I wanted him to think I believed it.

"Where did you come from?" I asked.

"From Pittsburgh. I went to the University there."

"What did you do before you joined up here?"

"I was a social worker," he said. Then I knew it couldn't be true and I wondered
100 how he had really been so frightfully wounded and I didn't care. In the war that I had known, men often lied about the manner of their wounding. Not at first; but later. I'd lied a little myself in my time. Especially late in the evening. But I was glad he thought I believed it, and we talked about books, he wanted to be a writer, and I told him about what happened north of Guadalajara and promised to bring some things from Madrid next time we got out that way. I hoped maybe I could get a radio. **H**

"They tell me Dos Passos and Sinclair Lewis[7] are coming over, too," he said.

"Yes," I said. "And when they come I'll bring them up to see you."

"Gee, that will be great," he said. "You don't know what that will mean to me."
110 "I'll bring them," I said.

"Will they be here pretty soon?"

"Just as soon as they come I'll bring them."

"Good boy, Ernest," he said. "You don't mind if I call you Ernest, do you?"

The voice came very clear and gentle from that face that looked like some hill that had been fought over in muddy weather and then baked in the sun.

"Hell, no," I said. "Please. Listen, old-timer, you're going to be fine. You'll be a lot of good, you know. You can talk on the radio."

G DIALOGUE
What do Raven's words reveal about his character?

H SUBJECTIVITY IN REPORTING
Why doesn't Hemingway believe Raven? Do you believe Raven? Explain why or why not.

---

6. **spatulate** (spăch'ə-lĭt): having a broad, rounded end.

7. **Dos Passos and Sinclair Lewis:** well-known American writers.

"Maybe," he said. "You'll be back?"

"Sure," I said. "Absolutely."

120 "Goodbye, Ernest," he said.

"Goodbye," I told him.

Downstairs they told me he'd lost both eyes as well as his face and was also badly wounded all through the legs and in the feet.

"He's lost some toes, too," the doctor said, "but he doesn't know that."

"I wonder if he'll ever know it."

"Oh, sure he will," the doctor said. "He's going to get well."

And it still isn't you that gets hit but it is your countryman now. Your countryman from Pennsylvania, where once we fought at Gettysburg.

Then, walking along the road, with his left arm in an airplane splint, walking
130 with the gamecock walk of the professional British soldier that neither ten years of militant party work nor the projecting metal wings of the splint could destroy, I met Raven's commanding officer, Jock Cunningham, who had three fresh rifle wounds through his upper left arm (I looked at them, one was septic[8]) and another rifle bullet under his shoulder blade that had entered his left chest, passed through, and lodged there. He told me, in military terms, the history of the attempt to rally retiring troops on his battalion's right flank, of his bombing raid down a trench which was held at one end by the fascists and at the other end by the government troops, of the taking of this trench and, with six men and a Lewis gun,[9] cutting off a group of some eighty fascists from their own lines, and of the
140 final desperate defense of their impossible position his six men put up until the government troops came up and, attacking, straightened out the line again. He told it clearly, completely convincingly, and with a strong Glasgow[10] accent. He had deep, piercing eyes sheltered like an eagle's, and, hearing him talk, you could tell the sort of soldier he was. For what he had done he would have had a V.C.[11] in the last war. In this war there are no decorations. Wounds are the only decorations and they do not award wound stripes. ❶

"Raven was in the same show," he said. "I didn't know he'd been hit. Ay, he's a good mon. He got his after I got mine. The fascists we'd cut off were very good troops. They never fired a useless shot when we were in that bad spot. They waited
150 in the dark there until they had us located and then opened with volley fire. That's how I got four in the same place."

We talked for a while and he told me many things. They were all important, but nothing was as important as what Jay Raven, the social worker from Pittsburgh with no military training, had told me was true. This is a strange new kind of war where you learn just as much as you are able to believe. ∿

❶ SUBJECTIVITY IN REPORTING
What is Hemingway's attitude toward Jock Cunningham? How can you tell?

---

8. **septic:** infected with bacteria.

9. **Lewis gun:** a lightweight machine gun.

10. **Glasgow:** a city in Scotland.

11. **V.C.:** the Victoria Cross, an award for valor "in the face of the enemy," given by Great Britain.

Comprehension

1. **Recall** What happens in front of Hemingway's hotel before breakfast?

2. **Recall** Who is Raven, and what are his injuries?

3. **Clarify** What is the truth about how Raven was wounded?

Literary Analysis

4. **Analyze Descriptive Details** Look back at the descriptive details you noted and circle the ones you found most vivid or affecting. What do you infer from any of these details that Hemingway doesn't tell you outright?

5. **Analyze Subjectivity in Reporting** Hemingway's article differs greatly from an objective news report. What is he able to convey about the war through each of the following?

   - his recurrent thought "It wasn't me" (lines 35 and 46)
   - his reaction to the sight of Raven and to the story Raven tells (lines 61–106)
   - his description of Jock Cunningham (lines 129–146)
   - his belief about the most important thing he was told (lines 152–155)

6. **Examine Dialogue** A written news report often contains quotations from sources, but rarely does it contain dialogue between two people. Why might Hemingway have chosen to include dialogue in his dispatch?

7. **Interpret Title** What makes this conflict "a new kind of war"? Note what seems to surprise Hemingway about it.

8. **Synthesize Themes** The Spanish Civil War ended more than 65 years ago. What value is there in reading Hemingway's article today? What insights about **war** does it provide?

9. **Compare Texts** What similarities in **style** and **theme** do you see in "A New Kind of War" and "In Another Country," the Hemingway short story on page 970?

Literary Criticism

10. **Critical Interpretations** When the New York University journalism department compiled its list of the 100 best works of 20th-century American journalism, Hemingway's Spanish Civil War reporting was ranked 33rd. Do you agree that it should be esteemed so highly? Support your answer.

Reading-Writing Connection

GRAMMAR AND STYLE

CHOOSE EFFECTIVE POINT OF VIEW Review the **Grammar and Style** note on page 1052. At the beginning of his dispatch, Hemingway uses the **second-person pronoun** *you* to report his own experiences, where you would normally expect him to write in the first person. This has the effect of placing the reader ("you") at the point of the action. It also temporarily removes the narrator himself, creating a sense of detachment.

> *After the shell that lit on the sidewalk in front of the hotel you got a beautiful double corner room on that side, twice the size of the one you had had, for less than a dollar.* (lines 43–45)

Hemingway does periodically revert to the first person, as in the continuation of the preceding passage:

> *It wasn't me they killed. See? No. Not me. It wasn't me anymore.* (lines 45–46)

With this shifting point of view, Hemingway seems to step in and out of the narrative. The resulting detachment allows the reader to encounter the experience of war without added comment or sentiment.

PRACTICE Rewrite the following passage, inserting either first- or second-person pronouns to change the sense of immediacy or detachment.

> Hundreds of runners and spectators gather in Jonquil Park at dawn on Mother's Day. The air is crisp and the grass damp. The predominant color in the crowd is pink: pink ribbons, pink caps, pink shirts. Many people wear signs reading "In memory of . . ." There is an electric air of expectancy until the horn blasts. The runners are off!

WRITING TOOLS
For prewriting, revision, and editing tools, visit the **Writing Center** at ClassZone.com.

A Book of Great Short Stories

Book Review by Dorothy Parker

Dorothy Parker
1893–1967

Dorothy Parker's sophisticated and witty voice made her one of the most quoted women of the 20th century. She belonged to the Algonquin Round Table, an informal group of writers who met daily at New York's Algonquin Hotel for lunch and clever conversation. Nicknamed the "Vicious Circle," they helped shape the literary tastes of the country.

Caustic Critic A well-read but smart-mouthed student, Parker left school at 14. When she was 19, her father died, and she was forced to find a job. After selling a poem to *Vanity Fair,* she was hired to write captions for its sister magazine, *Vogue.* She rose to become drama critic at *Vanity Fair* but was fired in 1920 for panning a play that starred the wife of one of the magazine's advertisers. She landed on her feet, becoming drama critic for another magazine, *Ainslee's.* She was also one of the founding editors of the *New Yorker* and served as its book reviewer for six years. Signing her reviews "Constant Reader," she championed writers she admired and demolished those she didn't. About one book she pronounced, "This is not a novel to be tossed aside lightly. It should be thrown with great force."

Popular Poet Parker's own books of poetry, *Enough Rope* and *Sunset Gun,* were bestsellers. They contained rueful verses, usually about failed love. One of her most quoted poems is "Résumé," which ends, "Guns aren't lawful; / Nooses give; / Gas smells awful; / You might as well live." Though often humorous, her poems grew out of great personal pain. She had an unhappy marriage to Edwin Parker, who returned from World War I with a drug addiction. Before divorcing him, she had disastrous love affairs that led her to several suicide attempts.

Screenwriter and Activist In 1933, Parker married Alan Campbell and moved with him to Hollywood, where they collaborated on screenplays. She also became more politically active, protesting racism, organizing the Screenwriters Guild, founding an anti-Nazi group, and going to Madrid to report on the Spanish Civil War. Her socialist sympathies caused her to be brought before the House Un-American Activities Committee in the 1950s. After she died of a heart attack in 1967, it was discovered that she had left her literary estate to Dr. Martin Luther King Jr. and the NAACP.

LITERARY ANALYSIS: VOICE

Voice is that quality in writing that enables a reader to "hear" a personality behind the words. Style, tone, and level of language are some of the factors contributing to a writer's voice. Consider the voice in this passage:

After all the high screaming about The Sun Also Rises, *I feared for Mr. Hemingway's next book. You know how it is—as soon as they all start acclaiming a writer, that writer is just about to slip downward.*

What kind of person do you imagine is speaking? Male or female? Friendly or distant? Serious or playful? As you read, notice what makes Dorothy Parker's voice distinctive and entertaining. Use her comments to form an impression of her personality and attitude toward the literary world.

READING STRATEGY: READING A BOOK REVIEW

Most book reviews are published in newspapers and magazines. They usually

- describe a new or newly republished book
- give an evaluation of its literary worth
- offer reasons for this evaluation

As you read Dorothy Parker's review, look for the lines that fulfill these functions. She discusses three of Ernest Hemingway's books, not just one, and she mentions others' opinions as well as her own, so it may help to take notes on a chart like the one shown.

	Description	Parker's Evaluation	Reasons
The Sun Also Rises			
In Our Time			
Men Without Women			

Explore the Key Idea

What makes a GREAT short story?

KEY IDEA During your school years, you've read many classic stories described as "great," such as "The Necklace" by Guy de Maupassant and "The Tell-Tale Heart" by Edgar Allan Poe. But how can you learn about new stories that might be just as great? Would you trust a book reviewer's **evaluation?**

QUICKWRITE Think about the best short story you ever read, in school or on your own. With its qualities in mind, jot down the recipe for a great short story. What must one contain, in your opinion? In a small group, share your recipes. Do you all have similar tastes, or are your standards unique?

A BOOK OF GREAT SHORT STORIES

Dorothy Parker

October 29, 1927

Ernest Hemingway wrote a novel called *The Sun Also Rises*. Promptly upon its publication, Ernest Hemingway was discovered, the Stars and Stripes were reverentially raised over him, eight hundred and forty-seven book reviewers formed themselves into the word "welcome," and the band played "Hail to the Chief" in three concurrent keys. All of which, I should think, might have made Ernest Hemingway pretty reasonably sick. Ⓐ

For, a year or so before *The Sun Also Rises*, he had published *In Our Time*, a collection of short pieces. The book caused about as much stir in literary circles as an incompleted dogfight on upper Riverside Drive. True, there were a few that

10 went about quick and stirred with admiration for this clean, exciting prose, but most of the reviewers dismissed the volume with a tolerant smile and the word "stark." It was Mr. Mencken[1] who slapped it down with "sketches in the bold, bad manner of the Café du Dôme," and the smaller boys, in their manner, took similar pokes at it. Well, you see, Ernest Hemingway was a young American living on the left bank of the Seine in Paris, France; he had been seen at the Dôme and the Rotonde and the Select and the Closerie des Lilas.[2] He knew Pound, Joyce, and Gertrude Stein. There is something a little—well, a little *you*-know—in all of those things. You wouldn't catch Bruce Barton or Mary Roberts Rinehart[3] doing them. No, sir.

1. **Mr. Mencken:** H. L. Mencken, an American journalist and literary critic.

2. **Dôme...des Lilas:** cafés in Paris that were frequented by young American writers.

3. **Pound...Rinehart:** Ezra Pound and Gertrude Stein were experimental American writers living in Paris; James Joyce was an experimental Irish writer. Bruce Barton and Mary Roberts Rinehart were more conventional American writers who lived in the United States.

ANALYZE VISUALS
What ideas are suggested by the cover designs of these books by Ernest Hemingway?

Ⓐ **VOICE**
Notice the **exaggeration** in the first paragraph. What voice does it help establish?

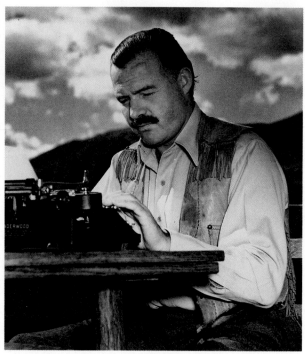

Dorothy Parker and Ernest Hemingway

20   And besides, *In Our Time* was a book of short stories. That's no way to start off. People don't like that; they feel cheated. Any bookseller will be glad to tell you, in his interesting *argot*,[4] that "short stories don't go." People take up a book of short stories and say, "Oh, what's this? Just a lot of those short things?" and put it right down again. Only yesterday afternoon at four o'clock sharp, I saw and heard a woman do that to Ernest Hemingway's new book, *Men Without Women*. She had been one of those most excited about his new novel. **B**

    Literature, it appears, is here measured by a yard-stick. As soon as *The Sun Also Rises* came out, Ernest Hemingway was the white-haired boy. He was praised, adored, analyzed, best-sold, argued about, and banned in Boston; all 30 the trimmings were accorded him. People got into feuds about whether or not his story was worth the telling. (You see this silver scar left by a bullet, right up here under my hair? I got that the night I said that any well-told story was worth the telling. An eighth of an inch nearer the temple, and I wouldn't be sitting here doing this sort of tripe.) They affirmed, and passionately, that the dissolute expatriates[5] in this novel of "a lost generation" were not worth bothering about; and then they devoted most of their time to discussing them. There was a time, and it went on for weeks, when you could go nowhere without hearing of *The Sun Also Rises*. Some thought it without excuse; and some, they of the cool, tall foreheads, called it the greatest American novel, tossing *Huckleberry Finn* and *The* 40 *Scarlet Letter*[6] lightly out the window. They hated it or they revered it. I may say, with due respect to Mr. Hemingway, that I was never so sick of a book in my life.

B VOICE
Reread lines 20–26, and describe the kind of person you imagine speaking to you. What is your reaction to this voice?

---

4. *argot* (är′gō) *French:* expressions and vocabulary that are used by a particular group.

5. **dissolute expatriates:** loose-living people—in this case, Americans—residing in a foreign land.

6. ***Huckleberry Finn*** **and** ***The Scarlet Letter:*** novels by Mark Twain and Nathaniel Hawthorne, respectively.

Now *The Sun Also Rises* was as "starkly" written as Mr. Hemingway's short stories; it dealt with subjects as "unpleasant." Why it should have been taken to the slightly damp bosom of the public while the (as it seems to me) superb *In Our Time* should have been disregarded will always be a puzzle to me. As I see it—I knew this conversation would get back to me sooner or later, preferably sooner—Mr. Hemingway's style, this prose stripped to its firm young bones, is far more effective, far more moving, in the short story than in the novel. He is, to me, the greatest living writer of short stories; he is, also to me, not the greatest living
50 novelist. **C**

After all the high screaming about *The Sun Also Rises,* I feared for Mr. Hemingway's next book. You know how it is—as soon as they all start acclaiming a writer, that writer is just about to slip downward. The littler critics circle like literary buzzards above only the sick lions. **D**

So it is a warm gratification to find the new Hemingway book, *Men Without Women,* a truly magnificent work. It is composed of thirteen short stories, most of which have been published before. They are sad and terrible stories; the author's enormous appetite for life seems to have been somehow appeased. You find here little of that peaceful ecstasy that marked the camping trip in *The Sun Also Rises*
60 and the lone fisherman's days in "Big Two-Hearted River" in *In Our Time*. The stories include "The Killers," which seems to me one of the four great American short stories. (All you have to do is drop the nearest hat, and I'll tell you what I think the others are. They are Wilbur Daniel Steele's "Blue Murder," Sherwood Anderson's "I'm a Fool," and Ring Lardner's "Some Like Them Cold," that story which seems to me as shrewd a picture of every woman at some time as is Chekhov's[7] "The Darling." Now what do *you* like best?) The book also includes "Fifty Grand," "In Another Country," and the delicate and tragic "Hills like White Elephants." I do not know where a greater collection of stories can be found.
70 Ford Madox Ford[8] has said of this author, "Hemingway writes like an angel." I take issue (there is nothing better for that morning headache than taking a little issue.) Hemingway writes like a human being. I think it is impossible for him to write of any event at which he has not been present; his is, then, a reportorial talent, just as Sinclair Lewis's[9] is. But, or so I think, Lewis remains a reporter and Hemingway stands a genius because Hemingway has an unerring sense of selection. He discards details with a magnificent lavishness; he keeps his words to their short path. His is, as any reader knows, a dangerous influence. The simple thing he does looks so easy to do. But look at the boys who try to do it. ❧ **E**

C BOOK REVIEW
Reread lines 42–50. Restate Parker's opinion of *In Our Time.* What does she say about Hemingway's **style?**

D GRAMMAR AND STYLE
In lines 51–54, notice how Parker uses the **first-person pronoun** *I* to refer to herself and addresses the reader with the **second-person pronoun** *you.* She also sets off her side remark with a **dash.** These choices establish an intimate conversational **voice.** Also notice her use of simile, comparing the critics to circling buzzards.

E BOOK REVIEW
Reread lines 70–78. How highly does Parker rate Hemingway, and why?

7. **Wilbur . . . Chekhov's:** Steele, Anderson, and Lardner were popular American writers of the era; Anton Chekhov was a 19th-century Russian short story writer and playwright.

8. **Ford Madox Ford:** an English writer, editor, and critic who lived for a time in Paris.

9. **Sinclair Lewis's:** Lewis was an American novelist and social critic who published articles in several popular magazines.

Comprehension

1. **Recall** What was Hemingway's latest book at the time Parker's review was written?

2. **Clarify** How did the reception of *In Our Time* compare to the reception of *The Sun Also Rises?*

3. **Paraphrase** What does Parker say is the difference between Hemingway and Sinclair Lewis?

Literary Analysis

4. **Reading a Book Review** Look back at the notes you took while reading, then summarize Parker's opinions of the three Hemingway books she discusses. With what evidence does she support her opinions?

5. **Analyze Voice** How would you describe Parker's voice in this book review? Discuss the effect of each of the following:

   - use of the first-person *I*
   - exaggeration
   - parenthetical asides
   - similes and metaphors
   - informal diction

6. **Interpret Tone** What is Parker's attitude toward book reviewers and the reading public? Support your answer with details.

7. **Evaluate Author's Work** Review Parker's statements about Hemingway's short stories (lines 42–50, 55–78). Then skim "In Another Country" (page 970). Do you agree with Parker's **evaluation** of Hemingway's short stories? Use a chart like the one shown to organize your thoughts.

"In Another Country"		
	Yes	No
Clean, Stripped-Down Prose		
Unpleasant Subject		
Sadness		
Reportorial Talent		
Effectiveness in Moving Readers		

Literary Criticism

8. **Critical Interpretations** One scholar wrote, "It is through Parker's refusal to claim authority . . . that her book reviews achieve it. She presents readers with an unpretentious, sometimes self-mocking voice that, while it expresses strong opinions, pretends no Olympian knowledge or status." Do you agree with this critic about the source of Parker's authority or trustworthiness? Explain your view.

Reading-Writing Connection

WRITING PROMPT

WRITE A BOOK REVIEW Dorothy Parker wrote book reviews for many years, and to one critic, they are the best expression of her literary sensibility. Choose a great book, or an "ungreat book," and write a **three-to-five-paragraph** review in your own personal voice. You might be as funny as Dorothy Parker, but in a different way. Or you might inspire readers to discover a book that could transform their lives. Think about what your own voice sounds like—perhaps tape-record yourself talking about the book. Then try to reproduce that voice in writing.

SELF-CHECK

A successful book review will . . .
- describe the book
- offer a positive or negative evaluation
- give reasons for your evaluation
- express a distinctive voice

GRAMMAR AND STYLE

ESTABLISH VOICE Review the **Grammar and Style** note on page 1063. Dorothy Parker's voice is intimate, enthusiastic, and humorously self-involved. Here is an example from her review:

> As I see it—I knew this conversation would get back to me sooner or later, preferably sooner—Mr. Hemingway's style, this prose stripped to its firm young bones, is far more effective, far more moving, in the short story than in the novel. (lines 45–48)

Notice Parker's use of the **first-person pronoun** *I* and her use of **dashes** to enclose a parenthetical comment about herself. It's as if Parker is having a conversation with the reader. Additionally, her use of **figurative language**—comparing Hemingway's prose to a fleshless body—creates a far more striking image than had she merely described it as "lean." You can use these and other elements to establish your own voice.

PRACTICE Rewrite each of the following sentences, using pronouns, figurative language, and punctuation, to achieve a voice that sounds like Dorothy Parker's. A sample answer has been done for you.

EXAMPLE

This book is not good.

This volume—in my view—is appallingly, criminally bad.

---

1. Other reviewers have disliked this book.
2. Sales have been high.
3. Reviewing books can seem useless.

WRITING TOOLS
For prewriting, revision, and editing tools, visit the **Writing Center** at ClassZone.com.

The Duty of Writers

Essay by E. B. White

E. B. White

1899–1985

Admired for his graceful style and gentle humor, E. B. White has been called the best essayist of the 20th century. For years readers looked forward to his columns in the *New Yorker* and *Harper's* magazines. Midcareer, he became a beloved children's author, writing the classics *Stuart Little* and *Charlotte's Web.* Later, he gained more fame with his update of *The Elements of Style,* a handbook used by millions of student writers.

New York Wit White enjoyed writing even as a child and won his first award when he was nine, for a poem about a mouse. In 1925, following unsuccessful stints in reporting and advertising, he was hired by a new magazine, the *New Yorker.* Its editor wanted it to be light, witty, and satirical. White did much to give it that voice. He wrote its opening "Notes and Comment" page and composed newsbreaks, fillers between articles with such headings as

"Letters We Never Finished Reading" and "Neatest Trick of the Week." He did captions for cartoons and even once illustrated the magazine's cover. The *New Yorker* provided White with an outlet for his talent—and a wife: he married the fiction editor, Katharine, living happily with her for 48 years.

Up on the Farm Eventually White felt constrained by the brief length and sheer number of the pieces he had to write for the *New Yorker.* He took a leave from the magazine and moved to a farmhouse in Maine in 1938. There he raised chickens, geese, sheep, and a milk cow. He also began a monthly column for *Harper's* called "One Man's Meat" (an allusion to the saying "One man's meat is another man's poison.") Some of his most memorable essays were published in this column, including "Once More to the Lake," about revisiting the place where he vacationed as a child.

"Unfit for Children" In Maine, White wrote his first children's book, *Stuart Little,* about a family that has a mouse for a son. The head children's librarian at the New York Public Library called his manuscript "unfit for children," but he published it anyway in 1945. Young people loved it, and in 1952 he followed it up with *Charlotte's Web,* about a literate spider who saves a pig from slaughter.

White lived quietly until his death at 86 from Alzheimer's disease. Among his many awards were the Presidential Medal of Freedom and a special Pulitzer Prize for his entire body of work.

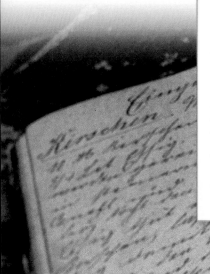

● LITERARY ANALYSIS: STYLE AND DICTION

Style is the particular way in which a piece of literature is written. It is not what is said, but how it is said. An essential element of style is **diction,** an author's choice of words and syntax. E. B. White's style is both casual and elegant. In the following passage, which particular words or phrases create casualness? elegance?

I was sorry to hear the other day that a certain writer, appalled by the cruel events of the world, had pledged himself never to write anything that wasn't constructive and significant and liberty-loving. I have an idea that this, in its own way, is bad news.

As you read this essay, notice what White's diction contributes to his style. Also, if an expression strikes you as humorous, think about what makes it so.

● READING SKILL: INTERPRET AUTHOR'S MESSAGE

An **author's message** is the main idea of a particular work, or the point it makes. White's essay presents his personal opinions on a topic, the duty of writers. These opinions are signaled by such words and phrases as

- "I have an idea that"
- "I don't think"
- "should"
- "shouldn't"
- "This seems to me"

As you read, use such clues to identify what kind of writing White favors and what he opposes. Make notes on a chart like the one shown.

Favors	Opposes
	writing only what is constructive, significant, and liberty-loving

What do writers OWE *us?*

KEY IDEA People often debate what writers should write. Should writers uplift the community or constantly denounce wrongs? Should they report every detail about a war or protect national security? Can they be blasphemous? frivolous? Decide what you believe is the duty of writers. Do they have a special **responsibility** in troubled times?

EVALUATE AND DISCUSS Explore your own ideas about a writer's obligations by completing this sentence: "I hate it when a writer ..." In a small group discuss your completed sentences. Is there any agreement about what writers should or should not do?

"Write about dogs!"

© The New Yorker Collection, George Booth (1976), from cartoonbank.com. All rights reserved.

The Duty of Writers

E. B. White

BACKGROUND This essay appeared in White's column for *Harper's* magazine in January 1939. It was a disturbing time, when it was clear that world war loomed. England and France had just appeased Hitler by allowing him to take over part of Czechoslovakia. The Nazis had looted and burned Jewish homes and businesses on a night that became known as Kristallnacht. Fascist forces were winning in the Spanish Civil War, and Japan had invaded China. In his State of the Union address, President Franklin D. Roosevelt warned that the freedoms Americans enjoyed were in danger.

I was sorry to hear the other day that a certain writer, appalled by the cruel events of the world, had pledged himself never to write anything that wasn't constructive and significant and liberty-loving. I have an idea that this, in its own way, is bad news.

All word-mongers,[1] at one time or another, have felt the divine necessity of using their talents, if any, on the side of right—but I didn't realize that they

---

1. **word-mongers:** those who deal in words for a living.

were making any resolutions to that effect, and I don't think they should. When liberty's position is challenged, artists and writers are the ones who first take up the sword. They do so without persuasion, for the battle is peculiarly their own. In the nature of things, a person engaged in the flimsy business of expressing

10 himself on paper is dependent on the large general privilege of being heard. Any intimation that this privilege may be revoked throws a writer into a panic. **Ⓐ** His is a double allegiance to freedom—an intellectual one springing from the conviction that pure thought has a right to function unimpeded, and a selfish one springing from his need, as a bread-winner, to be allowed to speak his piece. America is now liberty-conscious. In a single generation it has progressed from being toothbrush-conscious, to being air-minded, to being liberty-conscious. The transition has been disturbing, but it has been effected, and the last part has been accomplished largely by the good work of writers and artists, to whom liberty is a blessed condition that must be preserved on earth at all costs.

20   But to return to my man who has foresworn everything but what is good and significant. He worries me. I hope he isn't serious, but I'm afraid he is. Having resolved to be nothing but significant, he is in a fair way to lose his effectiveness. A writer must believe in something, obviously, but he shouldn't join a club. Letters flourish not when writers amalgamate,[2] but when they are contemptuous of one another. (Poets are the most contemptuous of all the writing breeds, and in the long run the most exalted and influential.) Even in evil times, a writer should cultivate only what naturally absorbs his fancy, whether it be freedom or cinch bugs, and should write in the way that comes easy. **Ⓑ**

    The movement is spreading. I know of one gifted crackpot who used to be

30 employed gainfully in the fields of humor and satire, who has taken a solemn pledge not to write anything funny or light-hearted or "insignificant" again till things get straightened around in the world. This seems to me distinctly deleterious[3] and a little silly. A literature composed of nothing but liberty-loving thoughts is little better than the propaganda which it seeks to defeat. **Ⓒ**

    In a free country it is the duty of writers to pay no attention to duty. Only under a dictatorship is literature expected to exhibit an harmonious design or an inspirational tone. A despot doesn't fear eloquent writers preaching freedom—he fears a drunken poet who may crack a joke that will take hold. His gravest concern is lest gaiety, or truth in sheep's clothing, somewhere gain a foothold, lest joy in

40 some unguarded moment be unconfined. I honestly don't believe that a humorist should take the veil[4] today; he should wear his bells night and day, and squeeze the uttermost jape,[5] even though he may feel more like writing a strong letter to the *Herald Tribune*. ☙ **Ⓓ**

Ⓐ **STYLE AND DICTION**
Paraphrase the passage beginning with "In the nature..." and ending with "...into a panic." How does changing the words affect the style?

Ⓑ **AUTHOR'S MESSAGE**
In lines 26–28, what does White state that a writer should do?

Ⓒ **STYLE AND DICTION**
What phrasings add humor to this paragraph?

Ⓓ **AUTHOR'S MESSAGE**
Reread lines 37–43. What value does White see in humor?

2. **Letters . . . amalgamate:** Writing and literature do not do well when writers form groups.

3. **deleterious:** harmful.

4. **take the veil:** become a nun or, here, a serious, religious person.

5. **wear his bells . . . jape:** consistently act like a jester (who wears a cap with bells) and see the humor in everything.

Comprehension

1. **Recall** At the beginning of the essay, what is White "sorry to hear"?

2. **Clarify** How has America changed in a generation, according to White?

3. **Paraphrase** What does White mean when he says, "Having resolved to be nothing but significant, he is in a fair way to lose his effectiveness"?

Literary Analysis

4. **Interpret Author's Message** Look back at the chart you created as you read. What kind of writing does White favor, and what does he oppose? Summarize his main message.

5. **Evaluate Opinions** Do you agree with White's opinions about the **responsibility** of writers? React to each of the following statements:

   - "A literature composed of liberty-loving thoughts is little better than the propaganda which it seeks to defeat." (lines 33–34)
   - "Even in evil times, a writer should cultivate only what naturally absorbs his fancy...." (lines 26–27)
   - "In a free country it is the duty of writers to pay no attention to duty." (line 35)
   - "A despot doesn't fear eloquent writers preaching freedom—he fears a drunken poet who may crack a joke that will take hold." (lines 37–38)

6. **Analyze Style and Diction** Choose a sentence from the essay that you find particularly thought provoking. Does it contain expressions that are casual, elegant, humorous, or a combination? Explain your answer.

7. **Compare Texts** Both White and Dorothy Parker (page 1058) wrote for the *New Yorker* magazine. How is White's **voice** different from Parker's? What do both essays suggest about the magazine's **tone?**

Literary Criticism

8. **Historical Context** White was writing at a time when fascism was on the rise overseas but America had not yet become involved in World War II. Do you think his message would have been the same if he were writing later, say, after the horrors of the Holocaust had become known? Would it have been the same if America had been turning toward fascism?

Journalism Beyond the Facts

Journalism is typically regarded as writing whose purpose is to convey to readers the facts as they are known—to answer the questions *who? what? when? where?* and *how?* Depending on their assignment and its purpose, journalists may strive for detached objectivity or may more subjectively shape the stories they report, the ideas they explore, and the claims they make.

Writing to Evaluate

Each of the selections beginning on page 1050 goes beyond "just the facts" and conveys the writer's perspective on a particular topic. This perspective largely determines the structure and flow of each piece. Skim each selection and look for words, phrases, or sentences that help you discern the writer's perspective. Then try your own hand at writing a news story that conveys more than just the facts. Choose an event, such as a school play, a varsity track meet, or even a typical lunch break in the cafeteria, and report it from your own perspective. Use the selections in this section as your inspiration.

Consider

- how the authors in this section revealed their personal perspectives and how their perspectives shaped their writing
- what basic facts you need to convey
- how best to reveal your thoughts about the event you witness

Extension

SPEAKING & LISTENING Much of journalism is distinguished by its tone. From factual, unemotional reporting to lurid mudslinging—today's journalism encompasses it all. Find three examples of current news stories that range widely in tone. You might search for stories in traditional newspapers, entertainment magazines, home decorating magazines, supermarket tabloids, or online news sources. Create a **poster** with copies of the stories and their headlines and **present** it to the class, explaining why you think—or do not think—the tone of each story is appropriate for its content.

Writing Workshop

Comparison-Contrast Essay

In this unit, you read about hope and despair, wealthy people and poor people, enormous cities and small rural towns. Noticing similarities and differences helps you to develop a fuller, richer understanding of whatever you are studying. To present comparisons and contrasts effectively, follow the **Writer's Road Map.**

WRITER'S ROAD MAP

Comparison-Contrast Essay

WRITING PROMPT 1

Writing from Literature Write an essay comparing and contrasting two poems. Your essay should concentrate on key aspects of the poems, such as theme, style, or word choice, and should give readers new insight into the works.

Poems to Compare

- "The Negro Speaks of Rivers" and "I, Too"
- "Any Human to Another" and "A Black Man Talks of Reaping"
- "Richard Cory" and "Lucinda Matlock"

WRITING PROMPT 2

Writing from the Real World Compare and contrast two creative works that strongly interest you. Choose key aspects of the works as the basis of your comparison. For instance, you might focus on visual style, characters, theme, or time period. Your essay should give new insight into the works.

Sources to Consider

- two detective shows on television
- two paintings or two pieces of sculpture
- two action-adventure movies

 WRITING TOOLS
For prewriting, revision, and editing tools, visit the **Writing Center at ClassZone.com.**

KEY TRAITS

1. IDEAS

- Clearly **identifies the works** being compared and contrasted
- Includes a **thesis statement** that identifies similarities and/or differences
- Uses **specific examples** to support key ideas

2. ORGANIZATION

- Includes an attention-getting **introduction** and a thoughtful **conclusion**
- Follows a consistent **organizational pattern**
- Links ideas with **transitions**

3. VOICE

- Maintains an appropriate **tone** for the audience and purpose

4. WORD CHOICE

- Uses **precise words** to explain similarities and differences

5. SENTENCE FLUENCY

- Varies **sentence beginnings**

6. CONVENTIONS

- Employs **correct grammar and usage**

Part 1: Analyze a Student Model

Dan Brantingham
Columbus Technical High School

Pride of Place

When you think of a city, do you picture crowds of people and beautiful, tall buildings? Or do you think of crime, poverty, and overcrowding? According to the speakers in "Chicago" by Carl Sandburg and "My City" by James Weldon Johnson, both of these views are accurate.
5 The poems share a dramatic tone and present the same theme: that despite its drawbacks, the city is a living, thrilling place that is worthy of admiration.

The dramatic tone of "Chicago" is clear from the first line. Proudly, the speaker shouts "Hog Butcher for the World" and then calls out other active,
10 living qualities of the "City of the Big Shoulders." The speaker celebrates a vibrant city that makes tools, stacks wheat, and is "Stormy, husky, brawling." The high energy of the city is clearest near the end of the poem, when the speaker can't seem to stop "bragging and laughing" about "this / my city."

15 Although both poems have a dramatic tone, Johnson's piece is quieter and more serious. "My City" also praises big-city life, but it celebrates Manhattan instead of Chicago. Statements such as "threshold of the unknown dark to cross" create a formal tone because they use some uncommon words in an unusual order. The speaker doesn't shout or brag
20 as the speaker in "Chicago" does. Even so, the first lines of "My City" are full of emotional power: "When I come down to sleep death's endless night, / . . . What to me then will be the keenest loss . . . ?" The drama builds throughout the poem as the speaker compares the beauties of nature with the sights, sounds, and smells of Manhattan. "My City" ends with a
25 startling exclamation: "O God! the stark, unutterable pity, / To be dead, and never again behold my city!"

KEY TRAITS IN ACTION

Introduction "hooks" the reader and **identifies the works** being compared and contrasted. **Thesis statement** identifies two similarities (tone and theme).

Has a sensible **organizational pattern,** discussing tone in both poems before moving on to a discussion of theme in both poems. The writer quotes and describes **specific examples** from the poems to support key points.

The dramatic tone of both poems matches their theme: that city life is wondrous and sometimes tragic. To the speaker of "Chicago," almost everything about that city is worth praising, from its smoke and dust to its pulse and "the heart of the people." The speaker admits that the city can be a harsh, violent place where "the gunman [can] kill and go free to kill again" and where there is "wanton hunger." However, the speaker offers this challenge: "Come and show me another city with lifted head singing so proud to be alive and coarse and strong and cunning." This is an assertion of Chicago's greatness despite its crime and hunger, a celebration of a city that is "alive" and "strong."

Similarly, "My City" praises "Manhattan's sights and sounds, her smells, / Her crowds, her throbbing force." The speaker is part of a living, breathing city that contains "shining towers." Like the speaker in "Chicago," the speaker in "My City" admits that the city can be a harsh place by mentioning "her slums," a jarring note in a poem that is otherwise full of admiration. Revealing a flaw in the city does not change the speaker's overall opinion, however. Instead, the slums are just one part of the speaker's beloved city.

"My City" and "Chicago" use a dramatic tone and a common theme to describe two dynamic cities. The bold speaker of "Chicago" laughs and brags, while the speaker of "My City" is more formal, even somber. Both poems are full of emotion and conviction. Each poet has written a love letter to his city.

The writer of the student model uses a formal, straightforward **tone** that makes sense for the audience (teacher and classmates) and purpose (to give new insight into two poems).

Highlighted **transitions** help show comparison and contrast. **Precise words** and varied **sentence beginnings** add polish.

Concludes effectively by summarizing the main ideas and adding an appropriate final thought.

2

Part 2: Apply the Writing Process

PREWRITING

What Should I Do?	**What Does It Look Like?**

1. Decide which works you will compare.
List pairs of works that you understand well or find appealing. Examine your list for pairs that have important similarities and distinct differences. Highlight the pair you choose.

▶ *Ideas for Prompt 1: Pairs of Poems*
- *"I, Too" and "Harlem" (both by Langston Hughes, both about social issues)*
- *"Chicago" and "My City" (both about cities)*
- *"Lucinda Matlock" and "Richard Cory" (one contented person, one discontented person)*

2. Analyze similarities and differences.
Use a Venn diagram to analyze your two subjects. List all the points you can think of—you do not have to use them all in your paper.

TIP If you can't list at least two or three major points in each section of the diagram, go back to your list and choose different works.

▶
"Chicago"
- *praises Chicago*
- *busy, active city*
- *brags, shouts, laughs*

Both
- *dramatic tone*
- *theme: great city*

"My City"
- *praises Manhattan*
- *contrasts nature and the city*
- *formal words and tone*

3. Write your thesis.
Your thesis statement can state similarities, differences, or both. Remember, your thesis is an overview of what your entire essay will explain.

TIP The order of the points in your paper should follow the order of your thesis.

▶ *Working Thesis:*
The poems both have a dramatic tone, and they have the same theme—that their city is a great place.

4. Collect evidence for each key point.
Use a chart or another graphic organizer to list evidence for each point you will make. Search for quotations and details in both works.

▶
Key Point: City Is a Great Place	
"Chicago"	*"My City"*
• *"lifted head"*	• *living, breathing city*
• *"so proud to be alive"*	• *"shining towers"*
• *"strong"*	• *mentions one flaw of Manhattan: "her slums"*
• *a great city despite corruption and hunger*	

What Should I Do?	What Does It Look Like?

1. Choose an organizational pattern.
Here are two ways to organize a comparison-contrast essay. The writer of the student model chose the point-by-point approach.

- **Point by Point**
  Compares and contrasts both subjects, one point at a time

- **Subject by Subject**
  Discusses all the points relating to the first subject, then moves on to the second subject

POINT BY POINT

Point 1: Dramatic tone

  Subject A ("Chicago"): includes laughing, bragging, and shouting

  Subject B ("My City"): quiet, somber, formal

Point 2: Theme (love of the city)

  Subject A ("Chicago"): speaker admires city but admits that tragedies occur there

  Subject B ("My City"): speaker loves the city, even its slums

SUBJECT BY SUBJECT

Subject A: "Chicago"

  Point 1: Tone (dramatic: shouts, brags, laughs)

  Point 2: Theme (love of the city, despite some problems)

Subject B: "My City"

  Point 1: Tone (dramatic, but more formal, with uncommon words)

  Point 2: Theme (love of the city, even its slums)

2. Provide evidence for each key point.
Whatever you claim, you must explain. Use details, examples, and quotations from both works. See page 1078 to learn how to punctuate quotations correctly.

TIP Be sure that each key point you make relates to your thesis.

See page 1078: Ask a Peer Reader

The dramatic tone of "Chicago" is clear from the first line.

Proudly, the speaker shouts "Hog Butcher for the World" and then calls out other active, living qualities of the "City of the Big Shoulders." The speaker celebrates a vibrant city that makes tools, stacks wheat, and is "Stormy, husky, brawling."

Point 1: dramatic tone

Supporting evidence for Point 1

3. Show how ideas are connected.
To show how things are alike, you could use a transitional word, such as *both, like, similarly,* or *also.* To show how things are different, you could use *in contrast, instead, on the other hand,* or *however.*

Similarly, "My City" praises "Manhattan's sights and sounds, her smells, / Her crowds, her throbbing force." The speaker is part of a living, breathing city that contains "shining towers." Like the speaker in "Chicago," the speaker in "My City" admits that the city can be a harsh place by mentioning "her slums," a jarring note in a poem that is otherwise full of admiration.

REVISING AND EDITING

What Should I Do?	*What Does It Look Like?*

1. Begin with a "hook."

- A hook makes your reader want to keep reading. It should also help to show the direction your paper will take. (Circle) the first sentence or two in your draft.

- If your first few lines seem dull, consider adding a question, a quotation, or some other kind of attention grabber.

▶

~~Some people don't like the city, but others think it's a great place to live.~~

When you think of a city, do you picture crowds of people and beautiful, tall buildings? Or do you think of crime, poverty, and overcrowding? According to the speakers in "Chicago" by Carl Sandburg and "My City" by James Weldon Johnson, both of these views are accurate.

2. Weave in supporting evidence.

- <u>Underline</u> supporting evidence—details, examples, and quotations.

- Ask yourself: Did I lead smoothly up to and out of the evidence? Or did I drop quotations and details into the essay without any context for them? Include explanations where they are needed.

▶

The speaker admits that the city can be a harsh, violent place where

~~The city is a place where~~ "the gunman [can] kill and go free to kill again" and where there is "wanton hunger."

However, the speaker offers this challenge:

~~The speaker says,~~ "Come and show me another city with lifted head singing so proud to be alive and coarse and strong and cunning." This is an assertion of Chicago's greatness despite its crime and hunger, a celebration of a city that is "alive" and "strong."

3. Double-check your transitions.

- Draw a [box] around each transition you used. Do you have enough transitions? Did you use the same one several times?

- Change or add transitions as necessary to make your essay clear and sophisticated.

▶

[Although both] poems have a dramatic tone, Johnson's piece is quieter and more serious. also ~~[Although]~~ "My City" praises big-city life, it but celebrates Manhattan [instead of] Chicago.

4. Improve your conclusion.

- Ask a peer reader to tell you whether your conclusion is clear and whether it gives your reader something to think about.

- Consider adding a summary, important details, or a new but related idea.

See page 1078: Ask a Peer Reader

▶

"My City" and "Chicago" use a dramatic tone and a common theme to describe two great cities. The bold speaker of "Chicago" laughs and brags, while the speaker of "My City" is more formal. Both poems are full of emotion and conviction. Each poet has written a love letter to his city.

Preparing to Publish

Comparison-Contrast Essay

Apply the Rubric

A strong comparison-contrast essay . . .

☑ begins with a "hook" and ends with a thoughtful summary

☑ includes a thesis that identifies the subjects being compared and contrasted

☑ is logically organized

☑ supports key ideas by using and explaining evidence from both works

☑ uses an appropriate tone

☑ varies sentence beginnings

☑ uses exact, specific words

☑ connects ideas with transitions

Ask a Peer Reader

• What does my thesis statement tell you about the content and organization of my essay?

• Does any part of the essay need more evidence? Does my evidence need a better lead-in or follow through? If so, where?

• What, if anything, should I do to make my conclusion clearer or more polished?

Check Your Grammar

• When quoting from a work, enclose the exact words in quotation marks. The period goes inside the quotation marks.

> The city is "alive" and "strong."

• Use an ellipsis [. . .] to show the omission of quoted words. Use a slash mark [/] to show a line break in a poem. If a question mark is part of the quoted material, place it inside the quotation marks.

> "When I come down to sleep death's endless night, / . . . What to me then will be the keenest loss . . . ?"

See pages R54: Quick Reference: Punctuation

• Use prepositional phrases to add important details.

> The dramatic tone of "Chicago" is clear from the first line.
>
> Each poet has written a love letter to his city.

See page R65: Prepositional Phrases

Writing Online

PUBLISHING OPTIONS
For publishing options, visit the **Writing Center** at ClassZone.com.

ASSESSMENT PREPARATION
For writing and grammar assessment practice, go to the **Assessment Center** at ClassZone.com.

Delivering an Oral Interpretation

When you perform the poems you wrote about, listeners are able to experience the comparisons and contrasts.

Planning the Interpretation

1. **Develop a plan for presenting the poems together.** Will you read each poem in its entirety, or will you compare and contrast line by line, stanza by stanza, or part by part?
2. **Vary your pacing and your tone.** Find the right speed and volume for the individual words and phrases.
3. **Mark up copies of the poems.** Decide how you will use your voice to show meaning. For example, you might underline what you will stress and draw a box around words you will play down. In places where you plan to pick up the pace, you might link words with hyphens. Consider adding slash marks to places where you plan to slow the poem down. If you wish, add gestures, such as a wave or a nod.

> But, _ah!_ / Manhattan's sights / and sounds, / her smells,
> Her crowds, her _throbbing force_, the _thrill_ that comes
> From being of her a part ...   [put fist on chest]

> _Building-breaking-rebuilding,_   [nod slightly on each emphasized syllable]

4. **Practice your presentation several times.** Adjust the notes on your copy of the poem as needed. Have a partner listen and give you advice.

Performing the Interpretation

1. **Be confident.** Speak up! Don't rush. Make eye contact with audience members.
2. **Ask for constructive criticism.** After your performance, invite a few listeners to comment on it. Could they hear aspects of the poems that were alike and different? Were the pace, volume, and gestures appropriate? Think about what you might do differently the next time.

See page R85: Evaluate an Oral Interpretation

Reading Comprehension

DIRECTIONS *Read these selections and answer the questions that follow.*

from Death in the Woods

Sherwood Anderson

The stock in the barn cried to her hungrily, the dogs followed her about. In the winter the hens laid few enough eggs. They huddled in the corners of the barn and she kept watching them. If a hen lays an egg in the barn in the winter and you do not find it, it freezes and breaks.

One day in winter the old woman went off to town with a few eggs and the dogs followed her. She did not get started until nearly three o'clock and the snow was heavy. She hadn't been feeling very well for several days and so she went muttering along, scantily clad, her shoulders stooped. She had an old grain bag in which she carried her eggs, tucked away down in the bottom. There weren't
10 many of them, but in winter the price of eggs is up. She would get a little meat in exchange for the eggs, some salt pork, a little sugar, and some coffee perhaps. It might be the butcher would give her a piece of liver.

When she had got to town and was trading in her eggs, the dogs lay by the door outside. She did pretty well, got the things she needed, more than she had hoped. Then she went to the butcher and he gave her some liver and some dog-meat.

It was the first time anyone had spoken to her in a friendly way for a long time. The butcher was alone in his shop when she came in and was annoyed by the thought of such a sick-looking old woman out on such a day. It was bitter cold and the snow, that had let up during the afternoon, was falling again. The
20 butcher said something about her husband and her son, swore at them, and the old woman stared at him, a look of mild surprise in her eyes as he talked. He said that if either the husband or the son were going to get any of the liver or the heavy bones with scraps of meat hanging to them that he had put into the grain bag, he'd see him starve first.

Starve, eh? Well, things had to be fed. Men had to be fed, and the horses that weren't any good but maybe could be traded off, and the poor thin cow that hadn't given any milk for three months.

Horses, cows, pigs, dogs, men.

To a Poor Old Woman

William Carlos Williams

munching a plum on
the street a paper bag
of them in her hand

They taste good to her
5 They taste good
to her. They taste
good to her

You can see it by
the way she gives herself
10 to the one half
sucked out in her hand

Comforted
a solace of ripe plums
seeming to fill the air
15 They taste good to her

World War II Poster

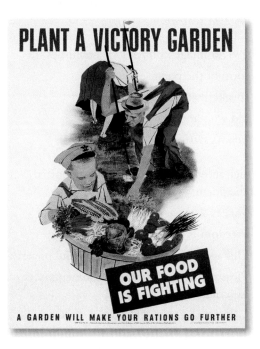

Public service poster from the United States Office of War Information, 1943

GO ON →

Comprehension

DIRECTIONS *Answer these questions about the excerpt from "Death in the Woods."*

1. Which word best describes the tone in this excerpt?
   A matter-of-fact
   B menacing
   C fanciful
   D witty

2. The tone is conveyed through language that is
   A understated
   B emotional
   C ambiguous
   D formal

3. The butcher's reaction to the woman in lines 17–18 suggests that he
   A would like to marry her
   B resents her begging
   C feels sorry for her
   D finds her repulsive

4. From the butcher's remarks in lines 20–24 you can infer that the woman's family
   A treats her badly
   B has many enemies
   C is related to the butcher
   D does not communicate with her

5. The images of winter in the excerpt emphasize that the woman's life is
   A peaceful and fulfilling
   B boring and idle
   C cold and bitter
   D pointless and tragic

6. The woman goes into town because she
   A wants to escape from her cruel husband and son
   B thinks it is her duty to feed the people and animals on the farm
   C is looking for someone friendly to talk to
   D needs to find a doctor to treat her illness

7. You can tell that line 28 is ironic because
   A the animals need to eat, but the woman resents their hunger
   B the author doesn't explain why the woman is the only person living on the farm who cares for the animals
   C the reader expects men and animals to be thought of differently, but the woman does not distinguish between them
   D the woman is hungry, too, but she does not admit it

DIRECTIONS *Answer these questions about the poem "To a Poor Old Woman."*

8. The vivid image in lines 1–3 establishes the
   A form of the poem
   B speaker's attitude
   C old woman's appearance
   D poem's setting and subject

9. Which inference is most clearly supported by the poem?
   A Variety is the essence of life.
   B Freedom is worth any sacrifice.
   C Old age often brings loneliness and poverty.
   D Pleasure can be found in a momentary experience.

10. Which statement explains the irony in the poem?

   A Images in the poem focus on an everyday activity.

   B The title suggests hardship, but the poem expresses enjoyment.

   C The reader never learns what the poet thinks of his subject.

   D The theme of the poem is implied, but it is never directly stated.

11. The image of "a solace of ripe plums / seeming to fill the air" (lines 13–14) appeals to the reader's sense of

   A sight

   B taste

   C smell

   D touch

DIRECTIONS *Answer this question about both selections.*

12. Which statement best describes the women?

   A The woman in the poem enjoys simple things; the woman in the story works hard.

   B The woman in the poem lives on the street; the woman in the story owns a farm.

   C The woman in the poem is a grandmother; the woman in the story is a beggar.

   D The woman in the poem is curious; the woman in the story is sensitive.

DIRECTIONS *Answer these questions about the poster.*

13. The words and images in the poster work together to

   A contrast each generation's wartime work

   B connect family gardens and military victory

   C illustrate the backbreaking nature of farming

   D emphasize the importance of financial prosperity

14. The slogan "Our Food Is Fighting" suggests that

   A fresh food builds a soldier's health and strength

   B in wartime, food is more important than fighting

   C those who don't fight will not have food to eat

   D people can help the war effort by growing food at home

Written Response

SHORT RESPONSE *Write three or four sentences to answer each question.*

15. In what way do the authors of "Death in the Woods" and "To a Poor Old Woman" use irony to help convey their ideas?

16. Describe the tone in "To a Poor Old Woman." Support your answer with details from the poem.

EXTENDED RESPONSE *Write two or three paragraphs to answer this question.*

17. What can you infer about the character of the woman in "Death in the Woods"? Cite two qualities that she exhibits and support your answer with details from the story.

GO ON ➤

Vocabulary

DIRECTIONS *Use the underlined etymology clues to help you choose the correct word that is missing from each of the following sentences.*

1. The ground was (<u>Middle English *skant*, "insufficient," from Old Norse *skammr*, "short"</u>) covered by thatches of parched grass.

   A barely   **C** scantily

   B scarcely   **D** starkly

2. The campers (<u>Middle English *hoderen*, "to crowd together," probably from Low German *hudeln*</u>) around the fire to warm themselves.

   A danced   **C** herded

   B huddled   **D** came

3. The (<u>Middle English, from Old French *boc*, "male goat"</u>) had a physically demanding job.

   A son   **C** husband

   B barber   **D** butcher

4. People turned up their collars against the (<u>Middle English, from Old English *biter*, "biting"</u>) north wind.

   A bitter   **C** blustery

   B heavy   **D** raw

5. The cold (<u>Middle English, from Old English, from Germanic *wintruz*, from Proto-Indo-European *wed*, "wet"</u>) kept people indoors for three months each year.

   A showers   **C** winter

   B snow   **D** weather

DIRECTIONS *Use context clues and your knowledge of Latin words and roots to answer the following questions.*

6. The word *victory* in the headline of the World War II poster comes from the Latin word *vincere*. What is the meaning of *vincere*?

   A conquer

   B avoid

   C vacate

   D fight

7. Which word from the selections most likely comes from the Latin word *papyrus*?

   A plums

   B poor

   C piece

   D paper

8. The Latin word *cambire* means "to barter." Which word in "Death in the Woods" most likely comes from the word *cambire*?

   A starve

   B carried

   C followed

   D exchange

9. The Latin word *pretium* means "reward, prize, or worth." Which word in "Death in the Woods" most likely comes from the word *pretium*?

   A grain

   B piece

   C price

   D eggs

Writing & Grammar

DIRECTIONS *Read this passage and answer the questions that follow.*

> (1) In second grade, my teacher took our class on a special "trip." (2) We decorated our room with posters and Japanese paper, and we ate sushi with chopsticks. (3) One poster showed <u>a garden soaked in rainwater</u>. (4) I remember thinking how beautiful it was. (5) There was something exotic in those garden trees that I just had to experience for myself. (6) Years later, I <u>finally did</u>.

1. Choose the correct way to rewrite sentence 1 by using an infinitive phrase.

A In second grade, my teacher took our class on a special "trip" for a day.

B In second grade, my teacher took our class on a special "trip" to visit the island country of Japan.

C In second grade, my teacher took our class on a special "trip" that I'll never forget.

D In second grade, my teacher took our class on a special "trip of a lifetime."

2. Choose the best way to rewrite sentence 2 by adding vivid adjectives.

A We eagerly decorated our room with posters and Japanese paper, and we ate cold sushi with chopsticks.

B We decorated our room with vibrant posters and silky Japanese paper, and we ate spicy sushi with chopsticks.

C We decorated our plain room with nice posters and Japanese paper, and we ate sushi with our chopsticks.

D We decorated our classroom with posters and Japanese paper, and we even ate great sushi with chopsticks.

3. Choose the best way to add vivid adjectives to the underlined part of sentence 3.

A a lush, sculpted garden soaked in glistening rainwater

B a large, green garden soaked in rainwater

C a pretty garden soaked in cold rainwater

D a tranquil garden soaked in some rainwater

4. Choose the revision of sentence 4 that contains an infinitive phrase.

A I remember thinking how beautiful the trees looked draping over the pond.

B I remember thinking how beautiful it was and how I'd never seen anything like it before.

C I remember thinking how beautiful and unusual it was.

D I remember thinking how beautiful it was and how much I'd like to visit it someday.

5. Choose the correct way to replace the underlined part of sentence 6 with an infinitive phrase.

A went to Japan

B saw them for myself

C got to see them in person

D visited Japan

Ideas for Independent Reading

Continue exploring the Questions of the Times on pages 822–823 by reading these additional works.

What is MODERN?

Prufrock and Other Observations
by T. S. Eliot

This volume contains 12 early poems by T.S. Eliot, including "The Love Song of J. Alfred Prufrock," regarded by some as the first modernist poem. The collection also includes "Portrait of a Lady," "Preludes," and "Rhapsody on a Windy Night," three other great poems about loneliness and alienation. Ezra Pound praised the book for "its fine tone, its humanity, and its realism."

Spoon River Anthology
by Edgar Lee Masters

This is Edgar Lee Masters's best-known work, a collection of free-verse monologues written in the voices of inhabitants of a small-town cemetery. The interconnected poems reveal the hidden loves, thwarted longings, and bitterness of people who lived and died in the confines of a small town.

The Autobiography of Alice B. Toklas
by Gertrude Stein

Gertrude Stein was at the center of a sparkling community of American writers who lived in Europe following World War I. She knew Picasso, Matisse, Joyce, Hemingway, and other important modernist figures. This book is her memoir of those heady days in Paris, playfully written in the voice of her lifelong companion, Alice B. Toklas.

Can ideals survive CATASTROPHE?

The Sun Also Rises
by Ernest Hemingway

After the end of World War I, a group of American expatriates in Europe try to wrest pleasure from a life that has lost meaning. They meet in Paris bistros, fish in the trout streams of Spain, and watch bullfights in Pamplona. Can such pleasures compensate them for their lost illusions? *The Sun Also Rises* leaves this question unanswered.

Blood on the Forge
by William Attaway

Following World War I, three African-American brothers—Big Mat, Chinatown, and Melody—flee the rural South for jobs in the steel mills of Pittsburgh. In search of a better life, they instead find dangerous work, terrible living conditions, and ethnic conflict. Each of the three brothers copes with his new life in a different way.

Waiting for Lefty
by Clifford Odets

During the time of reexamination that followed the Great Depression, the plays of Clifford Odets were a jolt of working-class lightning. Their affirmation of hope energized theatergoers from coast to coast. *Waiting for Lefty* dramatizes the courage and doubts of a group of cabdrivers who are debating whether to strike for a living wage.

How can people honor their HERITAGE?

The Souls of Black Folk
by W. E. B. Du Bois

This collection of essays, published in 1903, is unified by the idea of African-Americans' "double consciousness." As Americans, they are heirs to the nation's ideals of liberty and equality. But as a despised minority, they are barred from full participation in these ideals. W.E.B. Du Bois describes the struggles African Americans face and the gifts they offer the nation.

Their Eyes Were Watching God
by Zora Neale Hurston

Zora Neale Hurston brings an all-black Florida town to life in this moving love story. Janie Crawford has been taught by a fearful grandmother to value economic security over love. She marries an ambitious businessman who views her as a trophy rather than as a partner. When he dies, Janie finds fulfillment with the younger, free-spirited Tea Cake.

Cane
by Jean Toomer

Cane is a groundbreaking work of the Harlem Renaissance by a writer of mixed ancestry. It is composed of stories, poems, vignettes, and a short play. Part I, set in rural Georgia, presents the beauty of the land and the violence residents inflict on one another. Part II, set in the urban North, portrays a world of spiritual deadness. In Part III, a figure resembling Jean Toomer returns to the South to seek his identity.

What drives HUMAN BEHAVIOR?

As I Lay Dying
by William Faulkner

The dying wish of Addie Bundren, the wife of a Mississippi farmer, is to be buried in the county seat with the rest of her family. Her husband and children place her coffin in a wagon and undertake a dangerous odyssey. In a series of interior monologues, the characters—even the dead Addie—reveal the complex motivations that spur them forward.

Babbitt
by Sinclair Lewis

This satirical novel added a new word to American speech—*babbitt*, meaning "a smugly conventional person." When George Babbitt, a successful Midwestern businessman of the 1920s, rebels against his empty, conformist life, his friends reject him. Eventually he realizes that he is too old to rebel but that he can support his son's unconventional dreams.

Native Son
by Richard Wright

In this classic American novel, Wright questions whether people who are born poor, without any real opportunities, can ever be "free." Bigger Thomas is an impoverished African-American youth who resents the world of white power around him. Hired as a chauffeur by a white millionaire, he commits a shocking crime that seems oddly predestined. Who is responsible for Bigger's tragic life?

Preview Unit Goals

LITERARY ANALYSIS	• Understand and analyze historical and cultural context of contemporary literature • Identify and interpret allusions • Identify and interpret rhetorical devices, including paradox and repetition • Identify and analyze tone, imagery, voice, personification, and sound devices
READING	• Identify and evaluate key ideas • Identify main ideas and supporting details • Analyze and trace elements of an argument, including claim, reasons, evidence, and counterargument • Identify the general principle or assumption in an argument
WRITING AND GRAMMAR	• Write a problem-solution essay • Use word choice, sentence structure, and tone to establish voice • Use word choice, imagery, and tone to create mood
SPEAKING, LISTENING, AND VIEWING	• Create a Web site • Analyze the impact of media on audience perceptions • Compare and contrast perspectives in news reports
VOCABULARY	• Understand and use Greek prefixes to determine word meaning • Use context clues to determine the meaning of idioms
ACADEMIC VOCABULARY	• historical context • allusion • elements of an argument • cultural context • rhetorical devices • contemporary literature • general principle

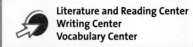

Literature and Reading Center
Writing Center
Vocabulary Center

Contemporary Literature

Sandra Cisneros

1940–PRESENT
NEW PERSPECTIVES

- Modern American Drama

- Responses to War

- Civil Rights and Protest Literature

- A Mosaic of American Voices

Questions of the Times

DISCUSS After reading these questions and talking about them with a partner, share with the class as a whole. Then read on to explore the ways in which writers of the contemporary era have dealt with the same issues.

Are we responsible for the WHOLE WORLD?

World War II brought the United States into a new role of increased power and involvement in the world, a role that expanded even further with the Cold War, Vietnam, and the "War on Terror." Do you believe America has a responsibility to intervene in other nations' conflicts? Does it have the right?

Can America achieve EQUAL RIGHTS?

In 1963, one hundred years after emancipation, African Americans still found themselves treated as second-class citizens, denied equal education, jobs, even the right to vote. The civil rights movement secured the legal right to equality, but in reality racism and injustice linger on. Do you believe America will ever achieve true equality?

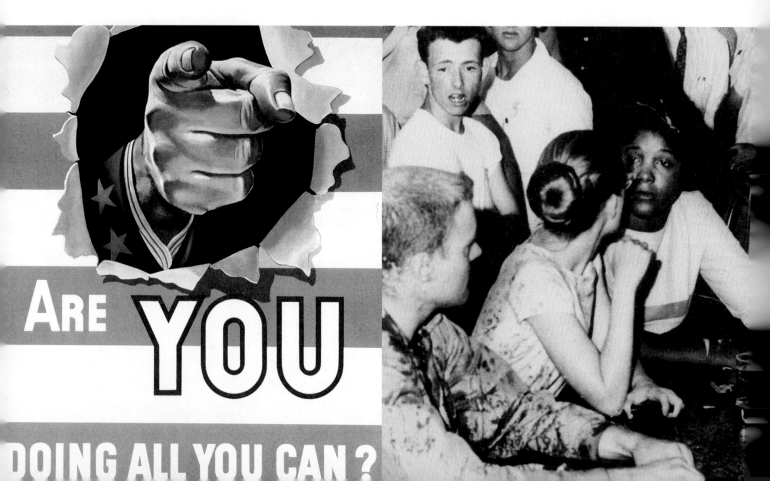

What makes an AMERICAN?

American writers of the 21st century reflect the diversity of the country itself. The United States has become a multicultural society whose citizens' experiences are endlessly varied. With no single "American experience" to bond citizens together, it seems logical to ask: What makes an American? Patriotism? Independence? Mere citizenship? Or something else?

What is the AMERICAN DREAM?

The Pilgrims and the Puritans dreamed of a new world where they would be free to practice their religion. Later immigrants dreamed of a country where any child could grow up to be the president. In the postwar era of the 1950s, the dream focused on consumer goods—"a car in every garage." How do you define the American dream?

Contemporary Literature
1940–PRESENT

New Perspectives

In the 1950s, America entered the Space Age—a beginning foray into our modern technological times. Looking down from space, the country's first astronauts marveled at the blue marble that was Earth floating in the blackness. From space, Earth looked peaceful and whole, with no divisions between nations, no conflict between races. It was a new way of looking at the world—just one of many new perspectives on modern life.

Contemporary Literature: Historical Context

KEY IDEAS Literature of the modern age reflects the uncertainty and anxiety brought on by the realities of war.

Modern Warfare

WORLD WAR II "Not a place on earth might be so happy as America," wrote Thomas Paine in the winter of 1776. "Her situation is remote from all the wrangling world." More than a century and a half later, as the Nazi army surged across Europe and Japan's expansionist government seized territories in Asia, many Americans still clung to the dream of isolationism—until **Pearl Harbor** woke them from their illusions.

On December 7, 1941, Japanese bombers struck the American naval base at Pearl Harbor, Hawaii, sinking ships, destroying planes, and killing over two thousand people. Though it lasted less than two hours, this surprise attack changed the course of history, bringing a reluctant United States into World War II.

The U.S. entry into the war turned the tide in favor of the Allies—England, France, and the Soviet Union—but it was a long, hard fight. By the time Germany and Japan surrendered to the Allied forces in 1945, more than 78 million people had been killed or wounded, including around six million Jews systematically murdered by the Nazis in what became known as the **Holocaust.** World War II was a catastrophe of epic dimensions, the first war in history in which more civilians than soldiers died. Never before had so many soldiers fought. Never before had such wholesale slaughter occurred. Writers such as **Randall Jarrell,** who had personal experience with the war, struggled to both document and examine the meaning of war on such a grand scale. Others, such as **Kurt Vonnegut** and **Bernard Malamud,** examined the rampant anti-Semitism that fueled the Holocaust. Malamud once remarked, "People say I write so much about misery, but you write about what you write best. As you are grooved, so you are grieved."

THE COLD WAR America came out of World War II a world power, wielding a new weapon of unparalleled destructive force: the atomic bomb. But along with strength and influence came deep uneasiness. The Soviet Union, once an ally, emerged as a rival superpower with equally large ambitions and a political system—communism—which many saw as a threat to the American way of life. Knowing any direct confrontation could end in nuclear annihilation, the two nations fought a "Cold War," each side racing to develop more and more devastating weapons while they jostled for strategic influence around the globe. As the arms race spiraled upward, ordinary citizens felt less and less secure. In literature, this pervasive fear of known and unknown dangers prompted a boom in **science fiction** writing, as writers pondered what might arise if the current trends continued.

▶ **TAKING NOTES**

Outlining As you read this introduction, use an outline to record the main ideas about the characteristics and literature of the period. You can use article headings, boldfaced terms, and the information in these boxes as starting points. (See page R49 in the **Research Handbook** for more help with outlining.)

I. *Historical Context*
 A. *World War II*
  1. *isolationism*
  2. *Pearl Harbor*
  3. *Holocaust*
 B. *Cold War*

ADDITIONAL BACKGROUND For more on the contemporary period, visit the **Literature Center** at ClassZone.com.

MODERN CONFLICTS Meanwhile, in an effort to contain the spread of communism, the U.S. military became deeply involved in civil wars first in Korea, then in Vietnam. The longest war in American history, the **Vietnam War** lasted over 20 years and bred a degree of domestic conflict unseen since the Civil War. As the death toll among U.S. soldiers rose—reaching about 58,000 in all—many Americans questioned the wisdom of our intervention and took to the streets in protest. The literature of the time reflects the conflicts within the country. Writer **Tim O'Brien** once remarked that "It's not really Vietnam that I was concerned about . . . ; rather, it was to have readers care about what's right and wrong and about the difficulty of doing right, the difficulty of saying no to a war."

The Cold War finally came to an end with the breakup of the Soviet Union in 1991, but America was not finished with warfare. That same year, U.S. troops were sent to counter the Iraqi invasion of Kuwait in the first Persian Gulf War. A longer struggle began on September 11, 2001, when hijackers flew commercial airplanes into the Pentagon and the World Trade Center, killing thousands and leading to U.S. invasions of Afghanistan and Iraq. At the same time, violence raged around the globe, and with nuclear weapons no longer limited to two superpowers, possibilities for worldwide disaster loomed. Writers of the last several generations have been profoundly affected by the sense of instability that has been brought on by near-constant war. "At all times," wrote novelist **John Updike,** "an old world is collapsing and a new world arising."

U. S. Marines training for Operation Desert Shield, 1990

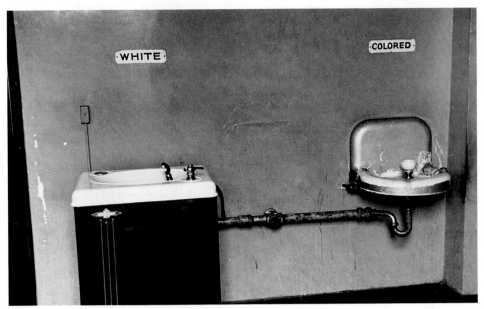

Segregated drinking fountains, North Carolina

Cultural Influences

KEY IDEAS Writers have both recorded and reflected upon the civil rights movement of the 1950s and 1960s—perhaps the most important social change in modern time.

The Civil Rights Movement

The civil rights movement had its roots in protests and legal actions of the 1950s. In 1954, the Supreme Court's ***Brown v. Board of Education*** ruling struck down school segregation as unconstitutional. Other civil rights advances followed, pushed along by black and white activists who organized protest marches, boycotts, voter registration drives, and sit-ins. **Dr. Martin Luther King Jr.** emerged as a leader during these times. King advocated nonviolent civil disobedience based on the philosophies of Henry David Thoreau and Indian social reformer Mohandas Gandhi.

Sadly, many of the peaceful demonstrations of the civil rights movement were met with mob violence and police brutality. While the nation watched on television, protestors were beaten, attacked by police dogs, and sprayed with fire hoses. King himself endured repeated imprisonment for his efforts. But the violence did not stop the movement.

During the famous March on Washington in 1963, which drew 200,000 participants, demonstrators demanded civil rights legislation at the national level, backed strongly by federal enforcement. Largely as a result of King's efforts, Congress passed the 1964 **Civil Rights Act** outlawing segregation in public places and guaranteeing legal equality to black citizens. In the years since, America has still not achieved true equality and opportunity for all, yet the civil rights movement has brought it much closer to King's dream of a land where people would "not be judged by the color of their skin, but by the content of their character."

> **A Voice from the Times**
>
> *I have a dream that one day this nation will rise up and live out the true meaning of its creed: "We hold these truths to be self-evident, that all men are created equal."*
>
> —Martin Luther King Jr.

Seattle-area neighborhood, 1955

Ideas of the Age

KEY IDEAS Modern writers have responded in a variety of ways to a peculiarly American philosophy: that of the American dream.

The American Dream

For earlier generations, the **American dream** had meant many things—political and religious freedom, economic opportunity, the chance to achieve a better life through talent, education, and hard work. After living through the Great Depression and two World Wars, however, many Americans in the 1950s whittled that dream down to something much simpler: the chance to own a home in a stable neighborhood.

For millions of mainly white Americans, life in the suburbs became the American dream. Families sought out communities with affordable single-family homes, good schools, shopping malls, and parking that was free and easy to find. People didn't care if their houses looked alike; they just wanted a safe place to raise their children.

As the years passed and the economy boomed, however, Americans began to add to their once-simple dream. *Things* became more important: a new television, car, or washing machine came to be seen as symbols of success. Soon the dream seemed to narrow to a vision of a consumer society in which conformity and "keeping up with the Joneses" was valued above all.

Writers from the mid-century to today have wrangled with the idea of the American dream. In the mid-'50s, **"beatniks"** such as **Jack Kerouac** and **Allen Ginsberg** protested the shallowness and conformity of American society. Dramatists such as **Arthur Miller** examined the strivings of ordinary Americans reaching for that American dream. Poets, novelists, short story writers—all have explored the many facets of the American dream.

Literature of the Times

KEY IDEAS The years between World War II and the present brought dramatic changes in the subjects and forms of literature, as well as a wider variety of authors represented.

Modern American Drama

In the years following World War II, some of the best and most influential writing was occurring within the community of American theater. Dramatists in the post-war years began to experiment stylistically and create works of social relevance that would prompt a revival in theater not only in America, but in Europe as well. Dramatists such as Arthur Miller and **Tennessee Williams** served as models of the liberated playwright—experimenting with stagecraft as well as modern themes often deemed provocative.

One of the most common themes explored by these playwrights was that of the American dream. "The American dream is the largely unacknowledged screen in front of which all American writing plays itself out," Arthur Miller once said. Indeed, Miller's Willy Loman, the main character in his *Death of a Salesman,* became the trademark figure of postwar American theater. A lowly salesman who has been discarded by the system to which he has mistakenly devoted his life, Willy Loman proved how the American dream could become twisted and broken.

A general disillusionment paired with an experimental style characterized many of the works of this period. While a play such as **Thornton Wilder's** *Our Town,* first produced in 1938, experimented with stagecraft by showing life literally "behind the scenes" on a stage bare of scenery, it still took a gentle view of small-town America. Works written in the 1940s and 1950s, however, were far less sympathetic. In *The Glass Menagerie* and *A Streetcar Named Desire,* for example, Southerner Tennessee Williams portrayed characters who, unsuited to modern life, retreat into the fantasy world of an earlier era. And Miller's critique of modern values in *Death of a Salesman* was found to be so threatening that Hollywood executives wanted to release the movie version along with a short film depicting the life of a salesman as blissful and carefree. Miller, however, protested.

Lorraine Hansberry's *A Raisin in the Sun,* written in 1957, looked at the American dream from the perspective of those who had been excluded. The first major Broadway play by an African-American writer, *A Raisin in the Sun* was hailed by critics as "universal," while also capturing unique aspects of the African-

▶ For Your Outline

MODERN AMERICAN DRAMA

- postwar revival in theater
- common theme was American dream
- characterized by disillusionment and experimental style
- broke boundaries and opened doors

Vivien Leigh and Marlon Brando in *A Streetcar Named Desire*

American experience. Writer **James Baldwin** said of the play, "[I]n order for a person to bear his life, he needs a valid re-creation of that life, which is why, as Ray Charles might put it, blacks chose to sing the blues. This is why *Raisin in the Sun* meant so much to black people . . . . In the theater, a current flowed back and forth between the audience and the actors, flesh and blood corroborating flesh and blood—as we say, testifying. . . ." In addition, the play opened the door to writers from outside the mainstream, who would revitalize American theater in the decades to follow.

Responses to War

War, with all its moral complexities and attendant brutality, has had a strong influence on writers throughout the 20th and 21st centuries. World War II brought with it previously unimaginable horrors: millions of casualties, the genocide of the Holocaust, the use of nuclear weapons. Struggling to come to terms with such destruction, some writers worked in the **modernist** style—giving detailed, realistic, and somewhat detached accounts of the war, as if told by an outside observer such as a journalist.

In fact, much of the most powerful literature of World War II was straight nonfiction, such as war correspondent **John Hersey's** *Hiroshima,* an unforgettable account of the first hours and days after the United States dropped atomic bombs on two Japanese cities, bringing massive destruction and an end to the war. **John Steinbeck,** better known for his Depression-era literature, worked as a war correspondent as well, spending time with troops in North Africa and England. His essay "Why Soldiers Won't Talk" explores how soldiers cope with the things they have witnessed.

Many writers of this period wrote of their own experiences—including the horrors of the Holocaust. **Elie Wiesel,** who was born in Europe and became an American citizen much later in life, was taken as a 15-year-old boy to a Nazi concentration camp in Poland. His memoir, *Night,* describes his nightmarish experiences in the camp, where he was beaten, starved, and nearly worked to death. Most members of his family did not survive.

In the 1960s, **Joseph Heller's** *Catch-22* and **Kurt Vonnegut's** *Slaughterhouse-Five* introduced a new style of war literature. Both writers had seen combat in World War II, and their novels shared a dark, ironic humor that focused on the absurdity of war. One such absurdity is the "catch" in Catch-22. It refers to a mysterious Air Force regulation which asserts that any person willing to go into battle should be considered insane, yet the very act of asking to be excused would prove one's sanity—and send a pilot back into battle. With their cynicism toward authority and sense of helplessness in the face of huge, inhuman forces, Heller and Vonnegut spoke to a younger generation caught up in a very different war: Vietnam.

Where World War II had united Americans in moral certainty against a common enemy, Vietnam drove them apart. Protesters—among them

▶ **For Your Outline**

RESPONSES TO WAR

- war influenced 20th- and 21st- century writers
- some worked in modernist style
- others wrote powerful nonfiction
- later focus is on absurdity of war
- postmodern style questioned conventions
- some blurred line between fiction and nonfiction

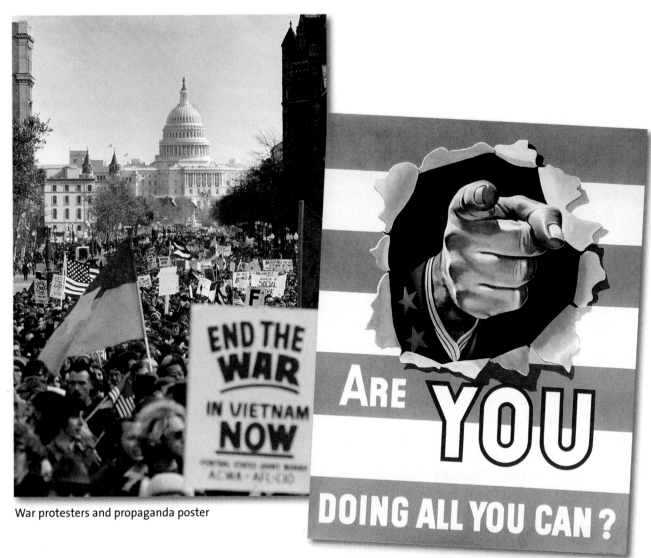

War protesters and propaganda poster

students, pacifists, and some returning veterans—marched in the streets, calling for an end to the war.

Writers of this time questioned authority, conventional values, and even the nature of reality. Some experimented with a "postmodern" style of fiction that drew attention to its own artificiality, pointing out the presence of the author by displaying its inner workings like a clock without a face. Others, like Vietnam veteran Tim O'Brien, wrote stories that blurred the lines between fiction and nonfiction. In *The Things They Carried*, O'Brien writes about telling his daughter how he killed a man in Vietnam—but this Tim O'Brien is a character, and the real O'Brien neither killed a man nor has a daughter. Can something that "didn't really happen" still be true? Postmodernism asks, What is fiction? What is truth?

ANALYZE VISUALS

The World War II propaganda poster shown here was meant to inspire support for the war. In your opinion, is it persuasive? How might the Vietnam War protesters shown in the other image have answered the question posed? How might they have responded to the intent of the poster?

Civil Rights and Protest Literature

The questioning of authority and conventional values applied not only to the writers of the Vietnam era but to those of the civil rights movement as well. To change laws, first it was necessary to change minds. The success of the civil rights movement depended on getting the message of justice out to the rest of America—telling people what was happening and making them care. One hundred years before, abolitionist writers had made a deep impact with novels and slave narratives that showed readers how it felt to live in bondage. In the 20th century, the written word still had a crucial role to play.

Even before the civil rights movement began in earnest, writers were examining issues of race and equality. Building upon the work of earlier Harlem Renaissance writers, black writers of the 1940s explored the dynamics of race relations and the injustice of discrimination in novels such as **Ann Petry's** *The Street,* which sold over a million copies, and **Richard Wright's** *Native Son.* As the civil rights movement gathered momentum in the early 1950s, African-American writers began to gain wider recognition, winning prestigious awards such as the Pulitzer Prize for poet **Gwendolyn Brooks** and the National Book Award for **Ralph Ellison's** *Invisible Man.*

The 1960s brought **James Baldwin's** influential essay collections as well as many important autobiographies, including *The Autobiography of Malcolm X* and **Anne Moody's** *Coming of Age in Mississippi.* By telling their own stories, these writers made a powerful statement about the harmful effects of racism and the need for change. Poets chimed in as well, reflecting upon the powerful events of the day. **Dudley Randall's** "Ballad of Birmingham," for example, was in response to the 1963 church bombing that killed four young girls.

▶ *For Your Outline*

CIVIL RIGHTS AND PROTEST LITERATURE

- questioned authority and tradition
- delivered message of justice
- examined race and equality
- reflected African-American experience
- showed varying viewpoints

A MOSAIC OF AMERICAN VOICES

- current outpouring from writers of various ethnicities
- new appreciation for diversity
- universal themes, yet rooted in culture

Martin Luther King Jr. and Malcolm X

A Voice from the Times

We are not fighting for integration, nor are we fighting for separation. We are fighting for recognition as human beings.

—Malcolm X

Malcolm X and **Martin Luther King Jr.,** two leaders of the civil rights movement, held opposing viewpoints on the use of violence as a means for change. Inspired by Thoreau and Gandhi, as well as the Bible, King's speeches and writings combined a steadfast belief in nonviolent resistance with a bold determination to bring an end to injustice. In his 1963 "I Have a Dream" speech, King argued, "Let us not seek to satisfy our thirst for freedom by drinking from the cup of bitterness and hatred. We must forever conduct our struggle on the high plane of dignity and discipline. We must not allow our creative protest to degenerate into physical violence." Malcolm X, on the other hand, advocated the use of militant armed resistance as a response to discrimination. "I *am* for violence," he said, "if nonviolence means we continue postponing a solution to the black man's problem—just to *avoid* violence." Their writings give readers insight into the various, and sometimes opposing, factions that made up the civil rights movement.

A Mosaic of American Voices

The last 30 years have seen an outpouring of talent from American writers of many different ethnic backgrounds, along with an increasingly widespread appreciation of diversity. Just a few decades ago, the literary scene was still dominated almost exclusively by men of European descent. Now, they have been joined by Native American writers such as **N. Scott Momaday** and **Louise Erdrich,** Asian-American writers such as **Maxine Hong Kingston** and **Amy Tan,** Hispanic writers such as **Rudolfo Anaya** and **Sandra Cisneros,** and African-American writers such as **Alice Walker, Rita Dove, Toni Morrison,** and **Maya Angelou,** to name just a few. Many of the most exciting contemporary writers are women; many, too, such as **Bharati Mukherjee** and **Edwidge Danticat,** were born outside the United States and bring a global perspective to American literature.

While earlier writers of color often focused on the experience of discrimination, writers today draw on different aspects of life in America, positive and negative, from family memories and relationships to contemporary politics. With such a broad array of published voices, no longer is any one author assumed to speak for all people of a given group. Instead, the most compelling work of today's literary marketplace is both expressive of the individual and rooted in culture and place, while still managing to speak to universal human concerns. American literature has changed, again, and will continue to evolve as long as writers continue to write.

Modern American Art

The power shift from Europe to the United States in the years after World War II had a parallel in the world of art. For the first time, international attention focused not on Paris's salon or London's Royal Academy but on the studios and galleries of New York City.

Abstract Expressionism During the 1940s and 1950s, a group of artists including **Mark Rothko** and **Jackson Pollock** dominated the New York art scene. Their style was abstract, intensely emotional, and focused as much on the process of painting as on the work itself. Jackson Pollock, who was famous for laying a giant canvas on the floor and throwing paint on it, described his art as "energy and motion made visible." Mark Rothko's signature style— floating rectangles of color aligned vertically against a colored background—is illustrated beautifully in his work *White Cloud Over Purple* (1957), shown here.

Pop Art In the early 1960s, a very different kind of art burst into public view. Pop art used familiar images from consumer culture to ask the question *What is art?* From **Andy Warhol,** with his silkscreened movie stars and soup cans, to **Roy Lichtenstein's** enormous blow-ups of comic strip panels, pop art celebrated modern methods of production while it subtly undermined the barrage of messages shaping Americans' attitudes and everyday lives.

Connecting Literature, History, and Culture

Use this timeline and the questions on the next page to gain insight about how American developments during this period reflected those in the world as a whole.

AMERICAN LITERARY MILESTONES

1940

1945 Richard Wright details coming of age in *Black Boy*; Randall Jarrell publishes World War II poem "The Death of the Ball Turret Gunner."

1947 Tennessee Williams's *A Streetcar Named Desire* is first produced.

1950

1951 J. D. Salinger's novel *The Catcher in the Rye* is published.

1952 Bernard Malamud publishes his baseball novel, *The Natural*.

1953 Arthur Miller's *The Crucible* reflects contemporary "witch hunt" of McCarthyism.

1960

1961 Joseph Heller's satirical war novel, *Catch-22*, is published.

1969 Kurt Vonnegut publishes *Slaughterhouse-Five*; N. Scott Momaday's *House Made of Dawn* wins Pulitzer Prize. ▶

HISTORICAL CONTEXT

1940

1941 Japanese bomb Pearl Harbor, ▲ bringing United States into World War II.

1945 United States drops two atomic bombs on Japan, ending the war in the Pacific.

1950

1954 In *Brown v. Board of Education*, the Supreme Court declares segregated schools unconstitutional. ▼

1959 Alaska and Hawaii join the Union as the 49th and 50th states.

1960

1963 Martin Luther King gives "I Have a Dream" speech in Washington, D.C.; President John F. Kennedy is assassinated in Dallas.

1965 Malcolm X is assassinated.

1967 Thurgood Marshall becomes the first African-American justice on the Supreme Court.

1968 Assassinations of Martin Luther King Jr., and Robert F. Kennedy shock the nation.

WORLD CULTURE AND EVENTS

1940

1940 German forces conquer much of Europe.

1945 Germany surrenders to Allies.

1948 State of Israel is founded; South African policy of apartheid begins.

1950

1953 Korean War ends.

1957 Soviet Union launches first space satellite, *Sputnik*.

1959 Fidel Castro takes control of Cuba after ouster of dictator.

1960

1965 First U.S. combat forces land in Vietnam.

1966 Mao Zedong launches Cultural Revolution in China (to 1976). ▶

1969 U.S. astronauts land on moon.

MAKING CONNECTIONS

- What important roles have new technologies played in this era?
- What evidence do you see that "American" and "world" events have become harder to separate?
- Which political and cultural trends have influenced American literature?

1970

1970 Maya Angelou publishes autobiographical *I Know Why the Caged Bird Sings.*

1983 Sandra Cisneros publishes *The House on Mango Street.* ▶

1985

1985 Anne Tyler publishes *The Accidental Tourist.*

1989 Amy Tan's *The Joy Luck Club* is published.

1993 Rita Dove becomes first African-American poet laureate; Toni Morrison wins Nobel Prize for literature. ▶

2000

2000 Lucille Clifton's poetry collection, *Blessing the Boats,* wins National Book Award.

2002 Diane McWhorter's history of Birmingham during the Civil Rights Movement, *Carry Me Home,* wins the Pulitzer Prize for Nonfiction.

2004 Ted Kooser is named U.S. poet laureate.

1970

1974 President Richard M. Nixon resigns to avoid impeachment over Watergate scandal.

1977 First practical home computer, Apple II, hits market.

1981 The space shuttle *Columbia* launches; Sandra Day O'Connor becomes the first woman to be appointed to the U.S. Supreme Court.

1985

1989 The oil tanker *Exxon Valdez* ▲ runs aground, creating a huge oil spill along Alaskan coast.

1991 The Persian Gulf War begins; the United States leads allied coalition against Iraq.

2000

2000 Fears of massive breakdown caused by "Y2K" computer problem prove unfounded.

2001 Hijackers fly commercial planes into World Trade Center and Pentagon, killing thousands.

2005 Hurricane Katrina hits New Orleans and surrounding area, causing massive destruction. ▼

1970

1975 South Vietnam surrenders as North Vietnamese troops occupy Saigon.

1979 Egypt's Anwar Sadat and Israel's Menachem Begin sign treaty ending war between Egypt and Israel.

1985

1989 The Berlin Wall comes down; ▶ student protesters in China are killed in Tiananmen Square.

1991 Soviet Union breaks up into 15 republics.

2000

2003 U.S. troops invade Iraq, deposing leader Saddam Hussein.

2004 Poland joins European Union; Indian Ocean earthquake causes deadly tsunamis, killing hundreds of thousands.

The Legacy of the Era

A New American Dream?

As rapid changes in society have given rise to fresh concerns about education, social mobility, family and community, the environment, and the hectic pace of modern life, it may be time to redefine the American dream for a new generation.

CREATE What might be the American dream for students and young adults today? For new immigrants? Working-class people? Others? As a class, share your thoughts. Then break into groups of four and create posters or collages that depict different aspects of today's American dream.

The Future of Literature

Technology has affected both the form and content of literature, offering new possibilities from hypertext to hand-held e-books to online publishing—though the predicted death of the printed book (and of narrative as we know it) has not come to pass. What do you think literature will be like in 20 years?

QUICKWRITE Taking the role of a future critic, write a "book review" discussing one new form of literature. Include your opinions about the limitations and possibilities this form presents.

Living in the Global Village

America's isolationism ended abruptly with the attack on Pearl Harbor in World War II. In the postwar years, international trade and travel greatly expanded. Today, huge improvements in communications and transportation have made globalism possible on many levels: political, economic, and cultural. Day by day, Americans are becoming more aware of their ties with the rest of the world.

DISCUSS How does globalization affect your everyday life? Brainstorm ideas with a small group, then report back to the class. If you're stuck, try thinking about what you wear, what you eat, and how you earn and spend money.

Our Town

Thornton Wilder

Thornton Wilder
1897–1975

ABOUT THE AUTHOR Thornton Wilder spent several years of his childhood in China, where his father was a high-ranking American diplomat. He attended Oberlin, Yale, and Princeton universities; studied archaeology in Rome; and taught literature at the University of Chicago. A world traveler, he hobnobbed with the most talented minds of his day—Sigmund Freud, Gertrude Stein, and T. S. Eliot, to name just a few. You might expect someone with this background to produce complex, sophisticated writings aimed at an intellectual elite—but you would be wrong. From his best-selling novel *The Bridge of San Luis Rey* to his charming comedy *The Matchmaker* (adapted into the hit musical *Hello Dolly!*), most of Wilder's writings have enjoyed broad popular appeal. *Our Town* is no exception. Since it first appeared on Broadway in 1938, not a day has gone by when it has not been staged somewhere in the world.

ABOUT THE PLAY Set in the small town of Grover's Corners, New Hampshire, *Our Town* traces the everyday experiences of two neighboring families, the Gibbses and the Webbs. In Act I, which depicts a single day in 1901, a friendship blooms between the Gibbses' son George and the Webbs' daughter Emily. Act II takes place three years later on their wedding day; and Act III opens with a funeral nine years after that. The play has several unusual touches: it is performed on a stage bare of all scenery; it depicts some characters from beyond the grave; and it employs a folksy but eerily omniscient narrator called the Stage Manager, who reveals characters' futures as well as their pasts and even fills us in on the geology of the region and the history and sociology of the town.

LEGACY OF A MASTERPIECE "*Our Town*," Thornton Wilder once explained, "is an attempt to find value above all price for the smallest events in our daily life." Most critics consider Wilder's attempt a successful one. The play's power, one critic observes, is in its duality: the events are "simple, modest, easy, plain," but the Stage Manager's commentary weights them with "birth and marriage and death, with aging and with change," so that "simultaneously we are made aware of what is momentary and what is eternal." The following scene is from Act II and is a flashback to the beginning of George and Emily's courtship.

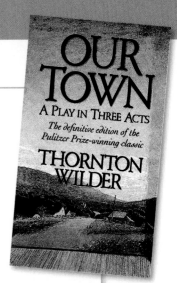

George. Emily, why are you mad at me?

Emily. I'm not mad at you.

George. You've been treating me so funny lately.

Emily. Well, since you ask me, I might as well say it right out, George,— (*She catches sight of a teacher passing.*) Good-by, Miss Corcoran.

George. Good-by, Miss Corcoran. —Wha—what is it?

Emily (*not scoldingly; finding it difficult to say*). I don't like the whole change that's come over you in the last year. I'm sorry if that hurts your feelings, but I've got to—tell the truth and shame the devil.

10 **George.** A *change?* —Wha—what do you mean?

Emily. Well, up to a year ago, I used to like you a lot. And I used to watch you as you did everything . . . because we'd been friends so long . . . and then you began spending all your time at *baseball* . . . and you never stopped to speak to anybody any more. Not even to your own family you didn't . . . and, George, it's a fact, you've got awful conceited and stuck-up, and all the girls say so. They may not say so to your face, but that's what they say about you behind your back, and it hurts me to hear them say it, but I've got to agree with them a little. I'm sorry if it hurts your feelings . . . but I can't be sorry I said it.

George. I . . . I'm glad you said it, Emily. I never thought that such a thing was hap-
20 pening to me. I guess it's hard for a fella not to have faults creep into his character.

(*They take a step or two in silence, then stand still in misery.*)

Emily. I always expect a man to be perfect and I think he should be.

George. Oh . . . I don't think it's possible to be perfect, Emily.

Emily. Well, my *father* is, and as far as I can see *your* father is. There's no reason on earth why you shouldn't be, too.

George. Well, I feel it's the other way round. That men aren't naturally good; but girls are.

Emily. Well, you might as well know right now that I'm not perfect. It's not as easy for a girl to be perfect as a man, because we girls are more—more—nervous.—Now
30 I'm sorry I said all that about you. I don't know what made me say it.

George. Emily,—.

Emily. Now I can see it's not the truth at all. And I suddenly feel that it isn't important, anyway.

George. Emily . . . would you like an ice-cream soda, or something, before you go home?

Emily. Well, thank you. . . . I would.

The Glass Menagerie

Tennessee Williams

Tennessee Williams
1911–1983

ABOUT THE AUTHOR The themes and characters in *The Glass Menagerie* were drawn from Tennessee Williams's own experiences. Williams suffered through a difficult childhood with an abusive, frequently absent father; a much-loved sister who suffered from mental illness; and a strong mother who desperately tried to hold the family together while longing for the happier days of her Southern girlhood. Williams showed early promise as a writer, but family problems often interrupted his education, and for a time his father forced him to work at the St. Louis shoe factory where he himself was employed. Eventually Williams returned to college and earned a degree from the University of Iowa, where his first full-length plays were performed. Moving to New York City, he began winning drama prizes. Financial success came in 1945, when *The Glass Menagerie* first appeared on Broadway.

ABOUT THE PLAY *The Glass Menagerie* tells the story of the Wingfield family, who live in a cramped apartment across the alley from the Paradise Dance Hall. The father is absent; Tom, the son, supports his mother and sister by working in a shoe factory—a job he hates. Laura, the sister, is lame from disease and painfully shy; she spends most of her time with her collection of old phonograph records and her "menagerie" of tiny glass animals—as fragile as she is. Amanda, the mother, is deeply concerned about her daughter's future. She wistfully recalls her youth as a Southern belle, when she once entertained 17 gentlemen callers at once, and wishes that Laura had a suitor who might offer the security of marriage. As the following scene opens, Amanda has been pressuring Tom to bring a friend home to meet Laura.

Tom. Mother, you mustn't expect too much of Laura.

Amanda. What do you mean?

Tom. Laura seems all those things to you and me because she's ours and we love her. We don't even notice she's crippled any more.

Amanda. Don't say crippled! You know that I never allow that word to be used!

Tom. But face facts, Mother. She is and—that's not all—

Amanda. What do you mean "not all"?

Tom. Laura is very different from other girls.

Amanda. I think the difference is all to her advantage.

10 **Tom.** Not quite all—in the eyes of others—strangers—she's terribly shy and lives in a world of her own and those things make her seem a little peculiar to people outside the house.

Amanda. Don't say peculiar.

Tom. Face the facts. She is.

(*The dance-hall music changes to a tango that has a minor and somewhat ominous tone.*)

Amanda. In what way is she peculiar—may I ask?

Tom (*gently*). She lives in a world of her own—a world of little glass ornaments, Mother. . . . (*He gets up.* Amanda *remains holding the brush, looking at him, troubled.*) She plays old phonograph records and—that's about all—

20 (*He glances at himself in the mirror and crosses to the door.*)

Amanda (*sharply*). Where are you going?

Tom. I'm going to the movies. (*He goes out the screen door.*)

Amanda. Not to the movies, every night to the movies! (*She follows quickly to the screen door.*) I don't believe you always go to the movies! (*He is gone.* Amanda *looks worriedly after him for a moment. Then vitality and optimism return and she turns from the door, crossing to portieres.*) Laura! Laura! (Laura *answers from kitchenette.*)

Laura. Yes, Mother.

Amanda. Let those dishes go and come in front! (Laura *appears with a dish towel.* Amanda *speaks to her gaily.*) Laura, come here and make a wish on the moon!

30 (*screen image: the moon*)

Laura (*entering*). Moon—moon?

Amanda. A little silver slipper of a moon. Look over your left shoulder, Laura, and make a wish! (Laura *looks faintly puzzled as if called out of sleep.* Amanda *seizes her shoulders and turns her at an angle by the door.*) Now! Now, darling, *wish!*

Laura. What shall I wish for, Mother?

Amanda (*her voice trembling and her eyes suddenly filling with tears*). Happiness! Good fortune!

(*The sound of the violin rises and the stage dims out.*)

Death of a Salesman

Arthur Miller

Arthur Miller
1915–2005

ABOUT THE AUTHOR "Success is the great man-eater," Arthur Miller once observed; "surviving it is as hard as attaining it." Miller knew a great deal about success and failure from his own experiences. As a young man during the Great Depression, he witnessed the collapse of his father's successful coat-manufacturing business. To scrape together the money for college, Miller put $13 of every $15 he earned into a college fund. After graduating from the University of Michigan, he returned to New York with dreams of Broadway glory but instead was forced into a variety of odd jobs— even living for a time on welfare. Then, after finally achieving success with plays such as *All My Sons, Death of a Salesman,* and *The Crucible,* Miller had the humiliating experience of being called to testify before the House Un-American Activities Committee during the "red scare" of the 1950s. He was found in contempt of Congress for refusing to name names and was blacklisted in Hollywood. Fortunately, he was able to continue working in New York, where producers and theater owners ignored the pressure to blacklist, and went on to have a long career in theater.

ABOUT THE PLAY Willy Loman, the lead character in Miller's *Death of a Salesman,* would like to see himself as successful in his business and family life. Yet in both areas, Willy seems headed for failure. In his longtime job as a traveling salesman for the Wagner Company, he has been reduced from a regular salary to a mere commission, and now his position is further threatened by his poor performance on the road. In his family life, his son Biff—once the star of the high-school football team—now cannot seem to find his footing in the world, and the pressures that Willy puts on Biff only widen the painful rift between the two men.

LEGACY OF A MASTERPIECE Miller's story of Willy Loman's shattered hopes and dreams won him the Pulitzer Prize in 1949 and is widely regarded as his finest work. Some critics see it as a brilliant dissection of the American dream; others commend its perceptive portrayal of family tensions and personal failings. A few debate whether a character as average and everyday as Willy Loman actually qualifies as a tragic hero. Yet most agree that the combination of realism and sympathy with which Miller traces Willy's downfall makes for an emotional theater experience.

In this excerpt, Willy meets with Howard Wagner, who has become head of the Wagner Company after his father's death. Howard is disappointed with Willy's sales performance and wants to let him go.

Willy (*angrily*). Business is definitely business, but just listen for a minute. You don't understand this. When I was a boy—eighteen, nineteen—I was already on the road. And there was a question in my mind as to whether selling had a future for me. Because in those days I had a yearning to go to Alaska. See, there were three gold strikes in one month in Alaska, and I felt like going out. Just for the ride, you might say.

Howard (*barely interested*) . Don't say.

Willy. Oh, yeah, my father lived many years in Alaska. He was an adventurous man. We've got quite a little streak of self-reliance in our family. I thought I'd go out
10 with my older brother and try to locate him, and maybe settle in the North with the old man. And I was almost decided to go, when I met a salesman in the Parker House. His name was Dave Singleman. And he was eighty-four years old, and he'd drummed merchandise in thirty-one states. And old Dave, he'd go up to his room, y'understand, put on his green velvet slippers—I'll never forget—and pick up his phone and call the buyers, and without ever leaving his room, at the age of eighty-four, he made his living. And when I saw that, I realized that selling was the greatest career a man could want. 'Cause what could be more satisfying than to be able to go, at the age of eighty-four, into twenty or thirty different cities, and pick up a phone, and be remembered and loved and helped by so many different people?
20 Do you know? when he died—and by the way he died the death of a salesman, in his green velvet slippers in the smoker of the New York, New Haven and Hartford, going into Boston—when he died, hundreds of salesmen and buyers were at his funeral. Things were sad on a lotta trains for months after that. (*He stands up.* Howard *has not looked at him.*) In those days there was personality in it, Howard. There was respect, and comradeship, and gratitude in it. Today, it's all cut and dried, and there's no chance for bringing friendship to bear—or personality. You see what I mean? They don't know me any more.

Howard (*moving away, to the right*). That's just the thing, Willy.

Willy. If I had forty dollars a week—that's all I'd need. Forty dollars, Howard.

30 **Howard.** Kid, I can't take blood from a stone, I—

Willy (*desperation is on him now*). Howard, the year Al Smith was nominated, your father came to me and—

Howard (*starting to go off*). I've got to see some people, kid.

Willy (*stopping him*). I'm talking about your father! There were promises made across this desk! You mustn't tell me you've got people to see—I put thirty-four years into this firm, Howard, and now I can't pay my insurance! You can't eat the orange and throw the peel away—a man is not a piece of fruit!

A Raisin in the Sun

Lorraine Hansberry

Lorraine Hansberry
1930–1965

ABOUT THE AUTHOR "I was born black and female," Lorraine Hansberry reflected, but she triumphed over the limits society placed on her race and gender. She was born in Chicago in 1930 and raised in a respected, middle-class family. Both her parents were political and social activists. African-American leaders, including Langston Hughes, W. E. B. DuBois, and Paul Robeson frequently visited Hansberry's home. When she was a young girl, her family bought a house in an all-white Chicago neighborhood. The racism they encountered would inspire *A Raisin in the Sun*. Hansberry developed an interest in writing at an early age and largely focused her talent on the theater. Tragically, her career was cut short when she died of cancer at 34.

ABOUT THE PLAY "What happens to a dream deferred? / Does it dry up / like a raisin in the sun?" These lines from Langston Hughes's poem "Harlem" provided Hansberry with both a theme and a title for *A Raisin in the Sun*. Written in 1957, the play tells the story of the Youngers, an African-American family whose long-cherished dreams are almost realized when Mama, the family's matriarch, comes into some money. But Mama's plans to buy a house in a white neighborhood nearly destroy the family.

Hansberry had difficulty finding backers to fund her play. With its all-black cast and racial themes, *A Raisin in the Sun* was very daring for its time. But once it finally opened, it received the New York Drama Critics' Circle Award for the best American play of 1959. Hansberry was the youngest person and the first African American to win the award.

LEGACY OF A MASTERPIECE The *New York Times* called *A Raisin in the Sun* the play that "changed American theater forever." It inspired a generation of young black writers and actors and brought a whole new audience to the theater. A glimpse into the private lives of African Americans was also a revelation for Broadway's white audiences. As Hansberry once observed, "The intimacy of knowledge which the Negro may culturally have of white Americans does not exist in the reverse." In the following scene, Mama teaches her daughter, Beneatha, about love and forgiveness after her son, Walter, loses their money and is in danger of losing his soul.

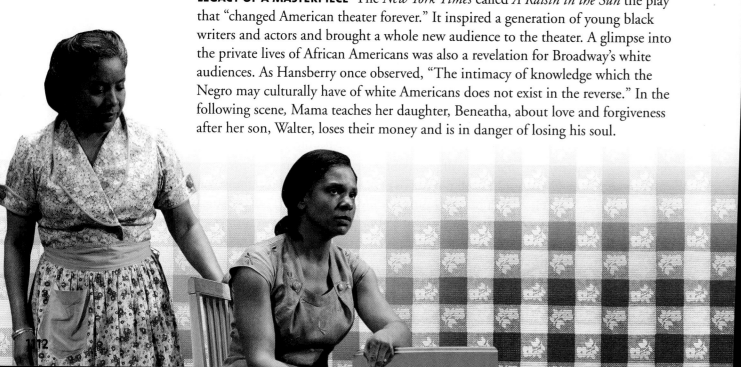

Beneatha. That is not a man. That is nothing but a toothless rat.

Mama. Yes—death done come in this here house. (*She is nodding, slowly, reflectively.*) Done come walking in my house on the lips of my children. You what supposed to be my beginning again. You—what supposed to be my harvest. (*to* Beneatha) You—you mourning your brother?

Beneatha. He's no brother of mine.

Mama. What you say?

Beneatha. I said that that individual in that room is no brother of mine.

Mama. That's what I thought you said. You feeling like you better than he is today? (Beneatha *does not answer.*) Yes? What you tell him a minute ago? That he wasn't a man? Yes? You give him up for me? You done wrote his epitaph too—like the rest of the world? Well, who give you the privilege?

Beneatha. Be on my side for once! You saw what he just did, Mama! You saw him—down on his knees. Wasn't it you who taught me to despise any man who would do that? Do what he's going to do?

Mama. Yes—I taught you that. Me and your daddy. But I thought I taught you something else too . . . I thought I taught you to love him.

Beneatha. Love him? There is nothing left to love.

Mama. There is *always* something left to love. And if you ain't learned that, you ain't learned nothing. (*looking at her*) Have you cried for that boy today? I don't mean for yourself and for the family 'cause we lost the money. I mean for him: what he been through and what it done to him. Child, when do you think is the time to love somebody the most? When they done good and made things easy for everybody? Well then, you ain't through learning—because that ain't the time at all. It's when he's at his lowest and can't believe in hisself 'cause the world done whipped him so! When you starts measuring somebody, measure him right, child, measure him right. Make sure you done taken into account what hills and valleys he come through before he got to wherever he is.

Why Soldiers Won't Talk

Essay by John Steinbeck

John Steinbeck
1902–1968

NOTABLE QUOTE

"[The writer] is charged with exposing our many grievous faults and failures, with dredging up to the light our dark and dangerous dreams for the purpose of improvement."

John Steinbeck created many memorable characters, from the downtrodden but dogged Joads in *The Grapes of Wrath* to George and Lennie in *Of Mice and Men.* Many of Steinbeck's characters convey his belief that people must fit into their surroundings—especially their natural surroundings—in order to find peace.

Childhood on the Land John Steinbeck grew up in the agricultural community of Salinas, California. The land profoundly influenced Steinbeck, who set many of his best works in these childhood scenes. He began to write early, encouraged by a high school teacher's praise.

Blending Life and Art While studying at Stanford University, Steinbeck worked in a factory and on road crews. Portraying people who lived by their hands became another key focus of Steinbeck's life and work. *The Grapes of Wrath* (1939) received a Pulitzer Prize for portraying down-and-out Oklahoma farmers during the Great Depression. Exhausted from writing the novel, Steinbeck moved in new directions. In 1943 he spent six months as a World War II correspondent, producing such writings as the following essay about the response of soldiers to combat. In 1962, he received the Nobel Prize in Literature "for his realistic as well as his imaginative writings."

The Death of the Ball Turret Gunner

Poem by Randall Jarrell

Randall Jarrell
1914–1965

NOTABLE QUOTE

"If we were in the habit of reading poets, their obscurity would not matter; and, once we are out of the habit, their clarity does not help."

Respected as a literary critic, Randall Jarrell is nonetheless best known for his searing poetry about World War II, notably a "stark five-line lyric . . . the ultimate poem of war." That poem is "The Death of the Ball Turret Gunner."

On the Road Again Born in Nashville, Tennessee, Jarrell moved often during his childhood. One important move took the family to a ranch in California. Later, Jarrell returned to California to live with his grandparents during his parents' divorce. Memories of this time filtered into one of Jarrell's best poems, "The Lost World," and childhood is a frequent, haunting topic throughout his work.

Making a Name With the help of a wealthy uncle, Jarrell went to college and began a lifelong career teaching literature in universities. At the same time, he worked at his own poetry. In 1942, he enlisted in the service, where he trained pilots and wrote poems capturing the horror and dreariness of military life.

Author Online

For more on John Steinbeck and Randall Jarrell, visit the **Literature Center** at ClassZone.com.

● LITERARY ANALYSIS: TONE AND IMAGERY

A writer sometimes conveys **tone,** his or her attitude toward a subject, through imagery. **Imagery** consists of the descriptive words and phrases used to re-create sensory experiences. One of the interesting aspects of Steinbeck's essay is the contrast between his clinical, detached, almost scientific tone and his use of sensory-rich imagery. Jarrell's poem also uses vivid imagery to convey an attitude about its subject. As you read each selection, think about the relationship between tone and imagery. Decide what each of these elements adds to the experience of reading.

● READING STRATEGY: ADJUST READING STRATEGIES

When you read literary works from different genres, you need to make adjustments in your reading strategies. For example, when you read an essay, follow these strategies:

- Identify the essay's **main ideas.**
- Look for **facts** and possibly **imagery** that support or reinforce the main ideas.
- Determine your own position on the ideas conveyed.

When reading a poem, try these strategies:

- Read the poem two or three times.
- Gather as much information as you can about the **speaker.**
- Try to picture the poem's **images** and think about what they convey.

As you read the two selections, make use of these strategies and any others that work for you. Take notes about the essay's main ideas and the poem's imagery and meaning.

Explore the Key Idea

When is SILENCE louder than words?

KEY IDEA People who have suffered greatly—fighting in a war, losing a loved one, witnessing tragedy—sometimes find it hard to communicate with others. Perhaps they cannot put their experiences and emotions into words. Perhaps they believe no one will understand. Others find silence and watchfulness more comfortable than talk and social engagement. Consider what **silence** can signify in a person's behavior, especially a soldier's in wartime.

QUICKWRITE Think of friends, family, peers, or even a character in a film or book. Identify someone you think of as more silent than talkative. Write a brief character description of this person. Read your description aloud, then share your ideas about why your subject is silent.

Why Soldiers Won't Talk

JOHN STEINBECK

> **BACKGROUND** Randall Jarrell's experience training pilots for the U.S. Army Air Force gained him firsthand knowledge of planes and gunners, including the view from the ball turret of a bomber. From this plexiglas bubble on the underside of the plane, gunners— totally exposed from below—fired at the enemy. During Steinbeck's time as a war correspondent, he too learned about bomber crews, as well as soldiers in the infantry.

During the years between the last war and this one, I was always puzzled by the reticence of ex-soldiers about their experiences in battle. If they had been reticent men it would have been different, but some of them were talkers and some were even boasters. They would discuss their experiences right up to the time of battle and then suddenly they wouldn't talk any more. This was considered heroic in them. It was thought that what they had seen or done was so horrible that they didn't want to bring it back to haunt them or their listeners. But many of these men had no such consideration in any other field.

Only recently have I found what seems to be a reasonable explanation, and the
10 answer is simple. They did not and do not remember—and the worse the battle was, the less they remember. **A**

In all kinds of combat the whole body is battered by emotion. The ductless glands[1] pour their fluids into the system to make it able to stand up to the great demand on it. Fear and ferocity are products of the same fluid. Fatigue toxins[2] poison the system. Hunger followed by wolfed food distorts the metabolic pattern already distorted by the adrenaline[3] and fatigue. The body and the mind so disturbed are really ill and fevered. But in addition to these ills, which come from the inside of a man and are given him so that he can temporarily withstand pressures beyond his ordinary ability, there is the further stress of explosion.

20 Under extended bombardment or bombing the nerve ends are literally beaten. The eardrums are tortured by blast and the eyes ache from the constant hammering.

This is how you feel after a few days of constant firing. Your skin feels thick and insensitive. There is a salty taste in your mouth. A hard, painful knot is in your stomach where the food is undigested. Your eyes do not pick up much detail and the sharp outlines of objects are slightly blurred. Everything looks a little unreal. When

A ADJUST READING STRATEGIES
Reread lines 1–11. What puzzles Steinbeck about soldiers, and what **main idea** provides the solution to his puzzlement?

ANALYZE VISUALS
How would you describe the look on this soldier's face? Explain what features convey this look.

---

1. **ductless glands:** glands, such as the thyroid or the pituitary gland, that secrete directly into the bloodstream.
2. **toxins:** poisons produced by the body that are capable of causing disease.
3. **adrenaline** (ə-drĕn′ə-lĭn): a substance secreted by the adrenal gland in response to stress.

you walk, your feet hardly seem to touch the ground and there is a floaty feeling all over your body. Even the time sense seems to be changed. Men who are really moving at a normal pace seem to take forever to pass a given point. And when you move it seems to you that you are very much slowed down, although actually you are probably moving more quickly than you normally do. **B**

Under the blast your eyeballs are so beaten that the earth and the air seem to shudder. At first your ears hurt, but then they become dull and all your other senses become dull, too. There are exceptions, of course. Some men cannot protect themselves this way and they break, and they are probably the ones we call shell-shock cases.[4]

In the dullness all kinds of emphases change. Even the instinct for self-preservation is dulled so that a man may do things which are called heroic when actually his whole fabric of reaction is changed. The whole world becomes unreal. You laugh at things which are not ordinarily funny and you become enraged at trifles. During this time a kind man is capable of great cruelties and a timid man of great bravery, and nearly all men have resistance to stresses beyond their ordinary ability.

Then sleep can come without warning and like a drug. Gradually your whole body seems to be packed in cotton. All the main nerve trunks are deadened, and out of the battered cortex[5] curious dreamlike thoughts emerge. It is at this time that many men see visions. The eyes fasten on a cloud and the tired brain makes a face of it, or an angel or a demon. And out of the hammered brain strange memories are jolted loose, scenes and words and people forgotten, but stored in the back of the brain. These may not be important things, but they come back with startling clarity into the awareness that is turning away from reality. And these memories are almost visions. **C**

And then it is over. You can't hear, but there is a rushing sound in your ears. And you want sleep more than anything, but when you do sleep you are dream-ridden, your mind is uneasy and crowded with figures. The anesthesia your body has given you to protect you is beginning to wear off, and, as with most anesthesia, it is a little painful.

And when you wake up and think back to the things that happened they are already becoming dreamlike. Then it is not unusual that you are frightened and ill. You try to remember what it was like, and you can't quite manage it. The outlines in your memory are vague. The next day the memory slips farther, until very little is left at all. A woman is said to feel the same way when she tries to remember what childbirth was like. And fever leaves this same kind of vagueness on the mind. Perhaps all experience which is beyond bearing is that way. The system provides the shield and then removes the memory, so that a woman can have another child and a man can go into combat again. **D**

It slips away so fast. Unless you made notes on the spot you could not remember how you felt or the way things looked. Men in prolonged battle are not normal men. And when afterward they seem to be reticent—perhaps they don't remember very well. ❧

B **TONE AND IMAGERY**
Reread lines 22–30, and note Steinbeck's use of **sensory detail.** What does this scene reveal about the soldier's mental state?

C **GRAMMAR AND STYLE** Reread lines 42–47. Notice how Steinbeck establishes his voice partly by using descriptions that contain realistic sensory **adjectives** and **verbs,** such as *battered, hammered,* and *jolted.*

D **ADJUST READING STRATEGIES**
Reread lines 55–63. What analogies does Steinbeck use to convey the **main idea** of this paragraph? What insight into experience does this suggest?

---

4. **shell-shock cases:** soldiers with a psychological disturbance as a result of prolonged exposure to active warfare.

5. **cortex:** part of the brain that plays an active role in consciousness.

The Death of the Ball Turret Gunner

RANDALL JARRELL

From my mother's sleep I fell into the State,
And I hunched in its belly till my wet fur froze.
Six miles from earth, loosed from its dream of life,
I woke to black flak[1] and the nightmare fighters.
5 When I died they washed me out of the turret with a hose. **E**

---

1. **flak:** the fire of anti-aircraft guns.

E TONE AND IMAGERY
What does the imagery of the last line suggest about the speaker's attitude toward death?

Comprehension

1. **Recall** According to Steinbeck, why don't soldiers talk about combat?

2. **Summarize** What physical changes does Steinbeck say happen during combat?

3. **Summarize** In Jarrell's poem, what happens to the speaker?

Literary Analysis

4. **Examine Author's Purpose** Steinbeck uses the second-person *you* in his recounting of the physical effects of combat. Why do you think he chose this **stylistic device?**

5. **Interpret the Poem** In reference to his poem, Jarrell wrote that the gunner, who sat hunched up and revolved with the turret, looked like a fetus in the womb. Based on this information, how would you interpret the first four lines of the poem?

6. **Analyze Tone and Imagery** Skim the two selections, and make a list of notable images found in each work. Based on these images, what would you say is Jarrell's attitude toward the ball turret gunner and his predicament? What is Steinbeck's attitude toward combat and its effect on soldiers? Decribe the overall tone of each work.

7. **Compare Texts** Jarrell and Steinbeck address the topic of war from different angles and through different genres. Do you think the two authors offer consistent or conflicting accounts of what combat feels like? Support your opinion with details.

8. **Evaluate Reading Strategies** Look back at the notes you took as you read the essay and poem. For each work, which strategy was most useful in helping you understand the ideas and images presented?

Literary Criticism

9. **Critical Interpretations** In discussing "The Death of the Ball Turret Gunner," one critic stated, "In the combination of death and consciousness is the awakening and final recognition on the part of the gunner that he exists only to be a victim." Based on your own reading of the poem, do you agree with this interpretation? Support your response.

Reading-Writing Connection

WRITING PROMPT

PERSUASIVE ESSAY Think about the adjustments veterans must make when they return from combat. What does society do to help ease their transition back into civilian life? What else do you think could be done? Write a **three-to-five-paragraph essay** on the importance of supporting veterans during this time of transition. Include specific suggestions of ways this might be effectively achieved.

SELF-CHECK

A convincing essay will...

- include information about current practices for helping veterans
- give reasons why your suggestions will make a difference
- establish a tone that helps persuade your readers

GRAMMAR AND STYLE

ESTABLISH VOICE Review the **Grammar and Style** note on page 1118. Voice is the unique way a writer uses **word choice, sentence structure,** and **tone** to express his or her personality or vision. John Steinbeck's voice reflects his personal experience with war. It flows from his short sentences, straightforward tone, and sensory language suited to the somber nature of his subject.

> *The eardrums are tortured by blast and the eyes ache from the constant hammering.* (line 21)

> *This is how you feel after a few days of constant firing. Your skin feels thick and insensitive. There is a salty taste in your mouth. A hard, painful knot is in your stomach where the food is undigested.* (lines 22–24)

Notice that the examples include percussive-sounding words that reflect the pain of combat. The short sentences give the impression that all information provided is essential and honest.

PRACTICE In the following sentences, revise the sentence structure and word choice to match Steinbeck's voice. Note how the revisions made to the example help to capture Steinbeck's voice.

EXAMPLE

Like a jackhammer pounding at solid concrete, the TV announcer gabs on and on, creating perpetual background noise that pollutes our homes.

The TV announcer talks on, creating a persistent, polluting noise.

---

1. The announcer chooses a topic, pushing it and pushing it as if it were bread dough, then kneading it into yet a new shape.

2. Must we sit there like zombies and put up with this endless chatter as though there were no alternative?

WRITING TOOLS
For prewriting, revision, and editing tools, visit the **Writing Center** at ClassZone.com.

Adam

Short Story by Kurt Vonnegut Jr.

Kurt Vonnegut Jr.
born 1922

The writing of Kurt Vonnegut Jr. defies simple classification. When his stories examine the moral implications of technology, they are called science fiction. When they make comedy out of the horrors and absurdities of the human condition, they are called black humor. With his deceptively simple style, he entertains yet at the same time forces his readers to think deeply about society and the world at large.

A Scientific Bent The son and grandson of architects, Vonnegut was born in Indianapolis, Indiana, the youngest of three children. He has said that he owes his scientific bent to his father, a true believer in technology who insisted that his sons study "something useful." As a result, after high school, where he edited the daily paper, Vonnegut went to Cornell University to study biochemistry. But war interceded, and during his third year Vonnegut decided to quit college and join the army.

Art from Life As an infantry combat scout in World War II, Vonnegut was captured by German soldiers during the Battle of the Bulge in 1944. Held as a prisoner of war in Dresden, Germany, he survived the 1945 Allied bombing of Dresden because the American prisoners took shelter in a meat locker three stories below the ground. Protected from the firestorm that destroyed much of the city, the prisoners emerged to discover that thousands had been killed. Years later, Vonnegut came to terms with that experience in his novel *Slaughterhouse-Five*.

Writer on Contemporary Issues Despite the somewhat pessimistic philosophy conveyed in many of his works, in which human beings are victims of circumstance in an indifferent universe, Vonnegut believes strongly in the value of kindness and is preoccupied with moral issues. Throughout his writing career, this man of contrasts has maintained a reputation as a bit of an outsider while at the same time enjoying a wide public following.

In addition to *Slaughterhouse-Five*, Vonnegut's novels include *The Sirens of Titan* (1959), *Mother Night* (1961), *Cat's Cradle* (1963), *God Bless You, Mr. Rosewater* (1965), and *Breakfast of Champions* (1973).

LITERARY ANALYSIS: CHARACTERIZATION

In fiction, a writer sometimes describes a character's personality directly, leaving little to the reader's imagination. However, it is more often the case—especially in modern fiction—that a writer develops his or her characters in an indirect manner, revealing personality traits quite subtly and allowing the reader to interpret characters' motivations more thoroughly. Kurt Vonnegut and many other writers achieve this through the use of the following four basic methods of **characterization:**

- description of the character's physical appearance
- presentation of the character's own speech, thoughts, or feelings
- the speech, thoughts, or feelings of other characters in response to the character
- the narrator's own comments about the character

As you read this story, record what you learn about the main character, Heinz Knechtmann, through these methods of characterization.

Physical Appearance	Character's Speech, Thoughts, Feelings	Other Characters' Speech, Thoughts, Feelings	Narrator's Comments

READING SKILL: ANALYZE HISTORICAL CONTEXT

When you read a literary work set at a particular time and place in history, it is important to focus on the **historical context**—the conditions and events that inspired or influenced its creation. In the case of this story, that context is the aftermath of the Holocaust. During World War II, millions of people died from executions, beatings, disease, and malnutrition in the Nazi concentration camps. As you read "Adam," use this information and the background information on page 1124, in addition to other facts you might know about World War II and the concentration camps, to help you gain a better understanding of Vonnegut's purpose in writing "Adam."

How do you AFFIRM LIFE?

KEY IDEA In the aftermath of tragedy or heartbreak, people are often counseled that "time heals all wounds." Some are able to bounce back, whether from grave illness, a traumatic car accident, or even the horrors of war and genocide. Others cannot find this **resilience** and instead struggle to carry on.

DISCUSS Work with a small group to brainstorm the characteristics people need to affirm life after surviving a horrible experience. Share examples from history, literature, or personal knowledge of people who have found the strength and will to start again. As a group, list the characteristics common to these people. Then compare your group's list with that of other groups and create a final class list.

What you need to affirm life:
- forgiveness

Adam

KURT VONNEGUT JR.

> **BACKGROUND** In the short story "Adam," set during the early 1950s, the main character, Heinz Knechtmann (knĕкнт'män), has survived the atrocities of the Holocaust and, like many Jewish survivors, has come to the United States seeking a better life. As the story begins, he and another expectant father, Mr. Sousa, are in the waiting room of a maternity hospital.

It was midnight in a Chicago lying-in hospital.

"Mr. Sousa," said the nurse, "your wife had a girl. You can see the baby in about twenty minutes."

"I know, I know, I know," said Mr. Sousa, a sullen gorilla, plainly impatient with having a tiresome and familiar routine explained to him. He snapped his fingers. "Girl! Seven, now. Seven girls I got now. A houseful of women. I can beat the stuffings out of ten men my own size. But, what do I get? Girls."

"Mr. Knechtmann," said the nurse to the other man in the room. She pronounced the name, as almost all Americans did, a colorless Netman. "I'm

10 sorry. Still no word on your wife. She is keeping us waiting, isn't she?" She grinned glassily and left.

Sousa turned on Knechtmann. "Some little son of a gun like you, Netman, you want a boy, bing! You got one. Want a football team, bing, bing, bing, eleven, you got it." He stomped out of the room.

The man he left behind, all alone now, was Heinz Knechtmann, a presser in a dry-cleaning plant, a small man with thin wrists and a bad spine that kept him slightly hunched, as though forever weary. His face was long and big-nosed and thin-lipped, but was so overcast with good-humored humility as to be beautiful. **A** His eyes were large and brown, and deep-set and longlashed. He was only twenty-

20 two, but seemed and felt much older. He had died a little as each member of his family had been led away and killed by the Nazis, until only in him, at the age of ten, had life and the name of Knechtmann shared a soul. He and his wife, Avchen, had grown up behind barbed wire.

ANALYZING VISUALS
What ideas are suggested by the images in the collage on page 1125? What is the cumulative impact of these images taken together? Explain.

A **CHARACTERIZATION**
Reread lines 15–18. Here Vonnegut combines his physical description of Heinz Knechtmann with a reflection on his personality. What might it look like to see a person "so overcast with good-humored humility as to be beautiful"?

Fatherhood (1990s). Ed Roskowski.
© Ed Roskowski/Corbis.

He had been staring at the walls of the waiting room for twelve hours now, since noon, when his wife's labor pains had become regular, the surges of slow rollers coming in from the sea a mile apart, from far, far away. This would be his second child. The last time he had waited, he had waited on a straw tick in a displaced-persons camp in Germany. The child, Karl Knechtmann, named after Heinz's father, had died, and with it, once more, had died the name of one of the
30 finest cellists ever to have lived. **B**

When the numbness of weary wishing lifted momentarily during this second vigil, Heinz's mind was a medley of proud family names, gone, all gone, that could be brought to life again in this new being—if it lived. Peter Knechtmann, the surgeon; Kroll Knechtmann, the botanist; Friederich Knechtmann, the playwright. Dimly recalled uncles. Or if it was a girl, and if it lived, it would be Helga Knechtmann, Heinz's mother, and she would learn to play the harp as Heinz's mother had, and for all Heinz's ugliness, she would be beautiful. The Knechtmann men were all ugly, the Knechtmann women were all lovely as angels, though not all angels. It had always been so—for hundreds and hundreds of years.

40 "Mr. Netman," said the nurse, "it's a boy, and your wife is fine. She's resting now. You can see her in the morning. You can see the baby in twenty minutes."

Heinz looked up dumbly.

"It weighs five pounds nine ounces." She was gone again, with the same prim smile and officious, squeaking footsteps.

"Knechtmann," murmured Heinz, standing and bowing slightly to the wall. "The name is Knechtmann." He bowed again and gave a smile that was courtly and triumphant. He spoke the name with an exaggerated Old World pronunciation, like a foppish footman announcing the arrival of nobility, a guttural drum roll, unsoftened for American ears. "KhhhhhhhhhhhhhhNECHT!
50 mannnnnnnnnnnnn." **C**

"Mr. Netman?" A very young doctor with a pink face and close cropped red hair stood in the waiting-room door. There were circles under his eyes, and he spoke through a yawn.

"Dr. Powers!" cried Heinz, clasping the man's right hand between both of his. "Thank God, thank God, thank God, and thank you."

"Um," said Dr. Powers, and he managed to smile wanly.

"There isn't anything wrong, is there?"

"Wrong?" said Powers. "No, no. Everything's fine. If I look down in the mouth, it's because I've been up for thirty-six hours straight." He closed his eyes,
60 and leaned against the doorframe. "No, no trouble with your wife," he said in a faraway voice. "She's made for having babies. Regular pop-up toaster. Like rolling off a log. Schnip-schnap."

"She is?" said Heinz incredulously.

Dr. Powers shook his head, bringing himself back to consciousness. "My mind—conked out completely. Sousa—I got your wife confused with Mrs. Sousa. They finished in a dead heat. Netman, you're Netman. Sorry. Your wife's the one with pelvis trouble."

B HISTORICAL CONTEXT
Reread lines 19–30. With the help of the historical information on page 1123 and the Background on page 1124, explain the various events that happened to Heinz and his family.

C CHARACTERIZATION
Reread lines 45–50. How does Heinz's pride in the birth of his son express itself in his words and actions?

"Malnutrition as a child," said Heinz. **D**

"Yeah. Well, the baby came normally, but, if you're going to have another one,
70 it'd better be a Caesarean. Just to be on the safe side."

"I can't thank you enough," said Heinz passionately.

Dr. Powers licked his lips, and fought to keep his eyes open. "Uh huh. 'S
O.K.," he said thickly. "'Night. Luck." He shambled out into the corridor.

The nurse stuck her head into the waiting room. "You can see your baby,
Mr. Netman."

"Doctor—" said Heinz, hurrying out into the corridor, wanting to shake
Powers' hand again so that Powers would know what a magnificent thing he'd
done. "It's the most wonderful thing that ever happened." The elevator doors
slithered shut between them before Dr. Powers could show a glimmer of response.

80 "This way," said the nurse. "Turn left at the end of the hall, and you'll find the
nursery window there. Write your name on a piece of paper and hold
it against the glass."

Heinz made the trip by himself, without seeing another human being until he
reached the end. There, on the other side of a large glass panel, he saw a hundred
of them cupped in shallow canvas buckets and arranged in a square block of
straight ranks and files.

Heinz wrote his name on the back of a laundry slip and pressed it to the
window. A fat and placid nurse looked at the paper, not at Heinz's face, and
missed seeing his wide smile, missed an urgent invitation to share for a moment
90 his ecstasy.

She grasped one of the buckets and wheeled it before the window. She turned
away again, once more missing the smile.

"Hello, hello, hello, little Knechtmann," said Heinz to the red prune on the
other side of the glass. His voice echoed down the hard, bare corridor, and came
back to him with embarrassing loudness. He blushed and lowered his voice.
"Little Peter, little Kroll," he said softly, "little Friederich—and there's Helga in
you, too. Little spark of Knechtmann, you little treasure house. Everything is
saved in you."

"I'm afraid you'll have to be more quiet," said a nurse, sticking her head out
100 from one of the rooms.

"Sorry," said Heinz. "I'm very sorry." He fell silent, and contented himself with
tapping lightly on the window with a fingernail, trying to get the child to look at
him. Young Knechtmann would not look, wouldn't share the moment, and after
a few minutes the nurse took him away again.

Heinz beamed as he rode on the elevator and as he crossed the hospital lobby,
but no one gave him more than a cursory glance. He passed a row of telephone
booths and there, in one of the booths with the door open, he saw a soldier with
whom he'd shared the waiting room an hour before.

"Yeah, Ma—seven pounds six ounces. Got hair like Buffalo Bill. No, we
110 haven't had time to make up a name for her yet . . . That you, Pa? Yup, mother
and daughter doin' fine, just fine. Seven pounds six ounces. Nope, no name. . . ."

D HISTORICAL CONTEXT
Consider why Heinz's wife might have suffered malnutrition as a child. What does this suggest about the impact of history on the present?

That you, Sis? Pretty late for you to be up, ain't it? Doesn't look like anybody yet.
Let me talk to Ma again. . . . That you, Ma? Well, I guess that's all the news from
Chicago. Now, Mom, Mom, take it easy—don't worry. It's a swell-looking baby,
Mom. Just the hair looks like Buffalo Bill, and I said it as a joke, Mom. That's
right, seven pounds six ounces. . . ."

There were five other booths, all empty, all open for calls to anyplace on earth.
Heinz longed to hurry into one of them breathlessly, and tell the marveolus news.
But there was no one to call, no one waiting for the news. **E**

120   But Heinz still beamed, and he strode across the street and into a quiet tavern
there. In the dank twilight there were only two men, tête-à-tête, the bartender
and Mr. Sousa.

"Yes sir, what'll it be?"

"I'd like to buy you and Mr. Sousa a drink," said Heinz with a heartiness
strange to him. "I'd like the best brandy you've got. My wife just had a baby!"

"That so?" said the bartender with polite interest.

"Five pounds nine ounces," said Heinz.

"Huh," said the bartender. "What do you know."

"Netman," said Sousa, "Wha'dja get?"

130   "Boy," said Heinz proudly.

"Never knew it to fail," said Sousa bitterly. "It's the little guys, all the time the
little guys."

"Boy, girl," said Heinz, "it's all the same, just as long as it lives. Over there in
the hospital, they're too close to it to see the wonder of it. A miracle over and over
again—the world made new."

"Wait'll you've racked up seven, Netman," said Sousa. "Then you come back
and tell me about the miracle."

"You got seven?" said the bartender. "I'm one up on you. I got eight." He
poured three drinks.

140   "Far as I'm concerned," said Sousa, "you can have the championship."

Heinz lifted his glass. "Here's long life and great skill and much happiness to—
to Peter Karl Knechtmann." He breathed quickly, excited by the decision.

"There's a handle to take ahold of," said Sousa. "You'd think the kid weighed
two hundred pounds."

"Peter is the name of a famous surgeon," said Heinz, "the boy's great-uncle,
dead now. Karl was my father's name." **F**

"Here's to Pete K. Netman," said Sousa, with a cursory salute.

"Pete," said the bartender, drinking.

"And here's to your little girl—the new one," said Heinz.

150   Sousa sighed and smiled wearily. "Here's to her. God bless her."

"And now, I'll propose a toast," said the bartender, hammering on the bar with
his fist. "On your feet, gentlemen. Up, up, everybody up."

Heinz stood, and held his glass high, ready for the next step in camaraderie,
a toast to the whole human race, of which the Knechtmanns were still a part.

"Here's to the White Sox!" roared the bartender.

"Minoso, Fox, Mele," said Sousa.

E CHARACTERIZATION
Reread lines 105–119.
What main method of
characterization does
Vonnegut employ to
emphasize Heinz's
isolation?

F HISTORICAL CONTEXT
Reread lines 141–146. Why
do you think Vonnegut
focuses so much
attention on the naming
of the baby?

"Fain, Lollar, Rivera!" said the bartender. He turned to Heinz. "Drink up, boy! The White Sox! Don't tell me you're a Cub fan."

"No," said Heinz, disappointed. "No—I don't follow baseball, I'm afraid." The other two men seemed to be sinking away from him. "I haven't been able to think about much but the baby."

The bartender at once turned his full attention to Sousa. "Look," he said intensely, "they take Fain off of first, and put him at third, and give Pierce first. Then move Minoso in from left field to shortstop. See what I'm doing?"

"Yep, yep," said Sousa eagerly.

"And then we take that no-good Carrasquel and . . ."

Heinz was all alone again, with twenty feet of bar between him and the other two men. It might as well have been a continent.

He finished his drink without pleasure, and left quietly.

At the railroad station, where he waited for a local train to take him home to the South Side, Heinz's glow returned again as he saw a co-worker at the dry-cleaning plant walk in with a girl. They were laughing and had their arms around each other's waist.

"Harry," said Heinz, hurrying toward them. "Guess what, Harry. Guess what just happened." He grinned broadly.

Harry, a tall, dapper, snub-nosed young man, looked down at Heinz with mild surprise. "Oh—hello, Heinz. What's up, boy?"

The girl looked on in perplexity, as though asking why they should be accosted at such an odd hour by such an odd person. Heinz avoided her slightly derisive eyes. **G**

"A baby, Harry. My wife just had a boy."

"Oh," said Harry. He extended his hand. "Well, congratulations." The hand was limp. "I think that's swell, Heinz, perfectly swell." He withdrew his hand and waited for Heinz to say something else.

"Yes, yes—just about an hour ago," said Heinz. "Five pounds nine ounces. I've never been happier in my life."

"Well, I think it's perfectly swell, Heinz. You should be happy."

"Yes, indeed," said the girl.

There was a long silence, with all three shifting from one foot to the other.

"Really good news," said Harry at last.

"Yes, well," said Heinz quickly, "Well, that's all I had to tell you."

"Thanks," said Harry. "Glad to hear about it."

There was another uneasy silence.

"See you at work," said Heinz, and strode jauntily back to his bench, but with his reddened neck betraying how foolish he felt.

The girl giggled.

Back home in his small apartment, at two in the morning, Heinz talked to himself, to the empty bassinet, and to the bed. He talked in German, a language he had sworn never to use again. **H**

"They don't care," said Heinz. "They're all too busy, busy, busy to notice life, to feel anything about it. A baby is born." He shrugged. "What could be duller?

G CHARACTERIZATION
What character trait of Heinz's does Vonnegut reveal through the sentence "Heinz avoided her slightly derisive eyes"?

H HISTORICAL CONTEXT
Reread lines 197–199. What is Vonnegut's purpose in including this description of Heinz's use of and feelings about speaking German? Explain.

Who would be so stupid as to talk about it, to think there was anything important or interesting about it?"

He opened a window on the summer night, and looked out at the moonlit canyon of gray wooden porches and garbage cans. "There are too many of us, and we are all too far apart," said Heinz. "Another Knechtmann is born, another O'Leary, another Sousa. Who cares? Why should anyone care? What difference does it make? None."

He lay down in his clothes on the unmade bed, and, with a rattling sigh, went
210 to sleep.

He awoke at six, as always. He drank a cup of coffee, and with a wry sense of anonymity, he jostled and was jostled aboard the downtown train. His face showed no emotion. It was like all the other faces, seemingly incapable of surprise or wonder, joy or anger.

He walked across town to the hospital with the same detachment, a gray, uninteresting man, a part of the city.

In the hospital, he was as purposeful and calm as the doctors and nurses bustling about him.
220 When he was led into the ward where Avchen slept behind white screens, he felt only what he had always felt in her presence—love and aching awe and gratitude for her.

"You go ahead and wake her gently, Mr. Netman," said the nurse.

"Avchen—" He touched her on her white-gowned shoulder. "Avchen. Are you all right, Avchen?"

"Mmmmmmmmmm?" murmured Avchen.
230 Her eyes opened to narrow slits. "Heinz. Hello, Heinz."

"Sweetheart, are you all right?"

"Yes, yes," she whispered. "I'm fine. How is the baby, Heinz?"

"Perfect. Perfect, Avchen."

"They couldn't kill us, could they, Heinz?"
"No."

"And here we are, alive as we can be."
"Yes."

240 "The baby, Heinz—" She opened her dark eyes wide. "It's the most wonderful thing that ever happened, isn't it?"

"Yes," said Heinz. ∿

ANALYZING VISUALS
Look at the collage after you have finished reading the story. What **theme** from the story is expressed in the collage? Explain.

Life Decisions (1995), Ed Roskowski. © Ed Roskowski/Corbis.

Comprehension

1. **Recall** From what country and historical events is Heinz Knechtmann a refugee?

2. **Recall** Why is he at the hospital?

3. **Summarize** Why is he so amazed that he and his wife have had a child?

Literary Analysis

4. **Make Inferences** In Jewish families, it is customary to name babies after family members who have died. Given this knowledge, what can you infer about Heinz from the following quotation: "Heinz's mind was a medley of proud family names, gone, all gone, that could be brought to life again in this new being—if it lived." (lines 32–33)

5. **Draw Conclusions** In your opinion, what gives Heinz and his wife the **resilience** to move forward with their lives after losing so much and seeing so much horror? Use evidence from the story and your own experience to support your answer.

6. **Examine Characterization** Look back at the chart you created as you read. Which method of characterization does Vonnegut depend on most heavily in his development of Heinz Knechtmann? Cite evidence.

7. **Analyze Historical Context** Vonnegut did not experience the Holocaust firsthand, yet this event in history inspired the creation of this story. In your opinion, what was Vonnegut's purpose in writing the story? Do you think that his purpose might have been better achieved in a historical essay, or was there an advantage in depicting historical events through a fictional lens? Support your opinions.

8. **Interpret Imagery** Each of the following images helps support an important **theme** in this story. Interpret each one.

   • "Heinz was all alone again, with twenty feet of bar between him and the other two men. It might as well have been a continent." (lines 167–168)

   • "They couldn't kill us, could they, Heinz?" (line 236)

9. **Evaluate the Title** Think about why Vonnegut might have chosen the title "Adam" for this story. In your opinion, is it an appropriate title? Explain.

Literary Criticism

10. **Social Context** Explain whether you agree with Heinz's conclusion that people in this country are "too busy," "too many," and "too far apart" to care about one another. Give reasons for your response.

from SURVIVAL
in Auschwitz

Primo Levi

> **BACKGROUND** Primo Levi (1919–1987) was an Italian chemist. In 1944, he was deported to Auschwitz, a Nazi concentration camp in Poland, where he remained for one year. Levi wrote about his nightmarish experiences in objective, scientific detail, believing that subjective commentary was unnecessary and that the events would speak for themselves. The following excerpt from his memoir describes the ritual in which prisoners were selected for condemnation.

Today is working Sunday, *Arbeitssonntag:* we work until 1 P.M., then we return to camp for the shower, shave and general control for skin diseases and lice. And in the yards, everyone knew mysteriously that the selection would be today.

The news arrived, as always, surrounded by a halo of contradictory or suspect details: the selection in the infirmary took place this morning; the percentage was seven per cent of the whole camp, thirty, fifty per cent of the patients. At Birkenau,[1] the crematorium chimney has been smoking for ten days. Room has to be made for an enormous convoy arriving from the Poznan ghetto.[2] The young tell the young that all the old ones will be chosen. The healthy tell the healthy that only the ill will
10 be chosen. Specialists will be excluded. German Jews will be excluded. Low Numbers[3] will be excluded. You will be chosen. I will be excluded.

At 1 P.M. exactly the yard empties in orderly fashion, and for two hours the gray unending army files past the two control stations where, as on every day, we are counted and recounted, and past the military band which for two hours without interruption plays, as on every day, those marches to which we must synchronize our steps at our entrance and our exit.

---

1. **Birkenau** (bûr′kən-ou): Also known as Auschwitz II, this camp stood about two miles from an older camp, called Auschwitz I. Between 1 million and 4 million people were murdered at Auschwitz-Birkenau during the years 1942–1945.

2. **Poznan** (pôz′năn′) **ghetto:** the area of the Polish city of Poznan in which Jews were forced to live.

3. **Low Numbers:** prisoners with low identification numbers.

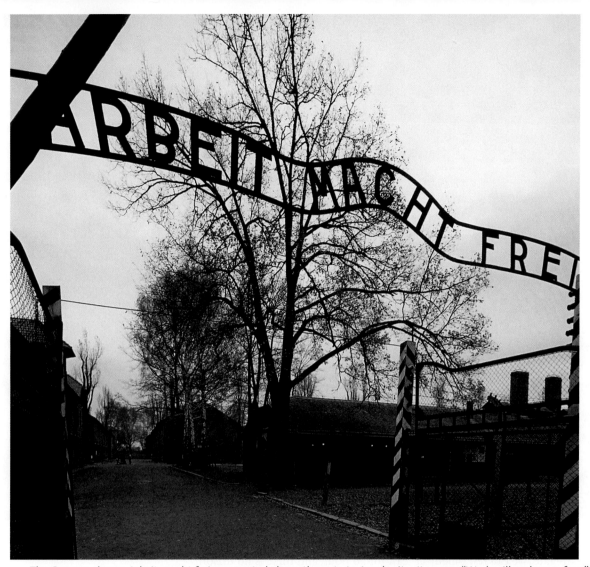

The German slogan *Arbeit macht frei* was posted above the gate to Auschwitz. It means "Work will make you free."

It seems like every day, the kitchen chimney smokes as usual, the distribution of the soup is already beginning. But then the bell is heard, and at that moment we realize that we have arrived.

20　　Because this bell always sounds at dawn, when it means the reveille;[4] but if it sounds during the day, it means "*Blocksperre*," enclosure in huts, and this happens when there is a selection to prevent anyone avoiding it, or when those selected leave for the gas, to prevent anyone seeing them leave.

Our *Blockältester*[5] knows his business. He has made sure that we have all entered, he has the door locked, he has given everyone his card with his number, name, profession, age and nationality and he has ordered everyone to undress completely, except for shoes. We wait like this, naked, with the card in our hands, for the commission to reach our hut. We are hut 48, but one can never tell if they are going to begin at hut 1

4.　**reveille** (rĕv′ə-lē): a signal used to awaken people.

5.　***Blockältester*** (blŏ′käl-tĕs′tər) *German*: block elder—a prisoner cooperating with the German guards by serving as the head of a block, or barracks.

The shoes of victims, on display at the Auschwitz Museum

or hut 60. At any rate, we can rest quietly at least for an hour, and there is no reason
30 why we should not get under the blankets on the bunk and keep warm.

Many are already drowsing when a barrage of orders, oaths and blows proclaims
the imminent arrival of the commission. The *Blockältester* and his helpers, starting
at the end of the dormitory, drive the crowd of frightened, naked people in front
of them and cram them in the *Tagesraum* which is the Quartermaster's office.[6] The
Tagesraum is a room seven yards by four: when the drive is over, a warm and compact
human mass is jammed into the *Tagesraum*, perfectly filling all the corners, exercising
such a pressure on the wooden walls as to make them creak. . . .

The *Blockältester* has closed the connecting-door and has opened the other two
which lead from the dormitory and the *Tagesraum* outside. Here, in front of the two
40 doors, stands the arbiter[7] of our fate, an SS subaltern.[8] On his right is the *Blockältester*,
on his left, the quartermaster of the hut. Each one of us, as he comes naked out of
the *Tagesraum* into the cold October air, has to run the few steps between the two

---

6. **Quartermaster's office:** the office of the person who distributes food and clothing to the prisoners.

7. **arbiter** (är′bĭ-tər): judge; decider.

8. **SS subaltern:** a low-ranking officer in the Nazi special security force.

doors, give the card to the SS man and enter the dormitory door. The SS man, in the fraction of a second between two successive crossings, with a glance at one's back and front, judges everyone's fate, and in turn gives the card to the man on his right or his left, and this is the life or death of each of us. In three or four minutes a hut of two hundred men is "done," as is the whole camp of twelve thousand men in the course of the afternoon.

50   Jammed in the charnel-house[9] of the *Tagesraum,* I gradually felt the human pressure around me slacken, and in a short time it was my turn. Like everyone, I passed by with a brisk and elastic step, trying to hold my head high, my chest forward and my muscles contracted and conspicuous. With the corner of my eye I tried to look behind my shoulders, and my card seemed to end on the right.

    As we gradually come back into the dormitory we are allowed to dress ourselves. Nobody yet knows with certainty his own fate, it has first of all to be established whether the condemned cards were those on the right or the left. By now there is no longer any point in sparing each other's feelings with superstitious scruples. Everybody crowds around the oldest, the most wasted-away, and most "muselmann";[10] if their cards went to the left, the left is certainly the side of the condemned.

60   Even before the selection is over, everybody knows that the left was effectively the "*schlechte Seite,*" the bad side. There have naturally been some irregularities: René, for example, so young and robust, ended on the left; perhaps it was because he has glasses, perhaps because he walks a little stooped like a myope,[11] but more probably because of a simple mistake. . . .

    There is nothing surprising about these mistakes: the examination is too quick and summary, and in any case, the important thing for the Lager[12] is not that the most useless prisoners be eliminated, but that free posts be quickly created, according to a certain percentage previously fixed. ๛

---

9. **charnel-house:** vault for the bones of the dead (used here figuratively).

10. **"muselmann"** (mōō'zəl-män): concentration-camp slang for a person near death from starvation.

11. **myope** (mī'ōp'): nearsighted person.

12. **Lager** (lä'gər) *German:* camp.

Literary Analysis

1. **Clarify** What was the purpose of the "selection" taking place?

2. **Examine Tone** Reread lines 60–64. What is **ironic** about Levi's reference to the "simple mistake" of René's selection?

3. **Compare Texts** Both Kurt Vonnegut's "Adam" and *Survival in Auschwitz* make a comment about the value of human life in the shadow of World War II. How would you compare or contrast the statement made by each piece? Explain, citing evidence from both texts to support your answer.

Ambush

Short Story by Tim O'Brien

Tim O'Brien
born 1946

Over and over again, Tim O'Brien has presented characters who are marked by the Vietnam War. From an infantryman on his first tour of duty, to a veteran struggling to readjust to his hometown, to an antiwar radical obsessed with death, his protagonists bring to life the complex issues raised by the war.

Opening New Doors O'Brien's writing career began at an early age. One day he fled from humiliation in the Little League to the Worthington, Minnesota, library. There he found the book *Larry of the Little League,* and soothed himself by writing an imitation of it. The library's other books became an escape from "loneliness and frustration" and an outlet for O'Brien's fertile imagination. O'Brien realized that fiction would let him experience "what could have been or should have been."

A Critical Choice As a young man, O'Brien faced another new door. He returned from four years at Macalaster College, where the Vietnam War was on students' minds, to find a draft notice waiting for him. O'Brien, who opposed the war, struggled mightily with his conscience and even considered fleeing the country to avoid service. In the end, he could not bring himself to run, and he reported for duty.

What Can You Teach? O'Brien was an army infantryman from 1968 to 1970, seeing combat in Vietnam's Quang Nai province and receiving a Purple Heart. After the war, he studied at Harvard University, worked as a reporter for the *Washington Post,* and began writing novels. He asked himself, "What can you teach people, just for having been in a war?" He concluded that he could offer insight into the "complexity and ambiguity of a set of moral issues—but without preaching a moral lesson." O'Brien's nine books have all been connected to Vietnam and have vividly explored "its aftermath and effect on the human heart and mind."

Higher Ambitions Even after great success—a National Book Award and a Pulitzer Prize nomination—O'Brien still hopes to achieve more. He'd like to write a bestseller, and he works at it every day, no matter what. "You shape your own universe," he has said. "You practice all the time, then practice some more."

LITERARY ANALYSIS: CONFLICT

A story's **conflict** is the struggle between opposing forces that is the basis of the story's plot. **External conflict**—a struggle between a character and some outside force—is usually easy to identify in a work of fiction. **Internal conflict**—a struggle within a character—may be more subtle and complex. For example, an internal conflict may revolve around a decision a character has to make, or it may be reflected in behavior that is contradictory. As you read this story, watch for the development of internal conflicts in the main character.

READING SKILL: ANALYZE STRUCTURE

The **structure** of a literary work is the way in which it is put together—the arrangement of its parts. Tim O'Brien's story "Ambush" includes a **frame story,** or a story within a story. The first paragraph provides a frame—the narrator recalls answering a question his daughter once asked him. In the second paragraph, he begins to recount in a **flashback** an experience he had earlier, during the war. As you read, use a chart to summarize what happens within the outer story and the inner story.

Beginning of Story 1:

> Beginning of Story 2:
>
> Middle of Story 2:
>
> End of Story 2:

End of Story 1:

How does the PAST affect the present?

KEY IDEA Perhaps more than any group in society, war veterans carry a difficult **past.** Some remember combat experiences vividly, some block them out entirely. The lucky ones find a way to reconcile their past with the present, to use the lessons of battle to inform their present perceptions and choices.

QUICKWRITE Think about war veterans you know or have heard about. They might have served in Vietnam, in the Persian Gulf, or in an international peacekeeping mission. Imagine one specific way in which a veteran's past experiences might affect his or her present life. How might they affect a father's relationship with his children, for example? Write down your thoughts and discuss them in a group.

Ambush

Tim O'Brien

BACKGROUND "Ambush" is a short story based upon the writer's combat experiences in Vietnam. The Vietnam War lasted nine years, left 58,000 Americans dead, and left another 365,000 Americans wounded. Although they were better equipped and trained than the enemy, American troops fought in an unfamiliar landscape for a cause that many of them did not support or understand. Vietnamese Communists were skilled guerilla fighters whose tactics created a climate of frustration, confusion, and fear. American soldiers never knew when an attack might come and were haunted by their memories long after the war.

ANALYZE VISUALS
What **tone** is conveyed by this image?

When she was nine, my daughter Kathleen asked if I had ever killed anyone. She knew about the war; she knew I'd been a soldier. "You keep writing these war stories," she said, "so I guess you must've killed somebody." It was a difficult moment, but I did what seemed right, which was to say, "Of course not," and then to take her onto my lap and hold her for a while. Someday, I hope, she'll ask again. But here I want to pretend she's a grown-up. I want to tell her exactly what happened, or what I remember happening, and then I want to say to her that as a little girl she was absolutely right. This is why I keep writing war stories: **Ⓐ**

He was a short, slender young man of about twenty. I was afraid of him—afraid
10 of something—and as he passed me on the trail I threw a grenade that exploded at his feet and killed him. **Ⓑ**

Ⓐ CONFLICT
Reread lines 1–8. What **internal conflict** does the narrator face in the first paragraph?

Ⓑ ANALYZE STRUCTURE
Reread lines 9–11. How does the **setting** of the story shift in the second paragraph?

The Green Machine (1977), Frank Dahmer. Screenprint on paper, 13½″ × 17¼″. © National Vietnam Veterans Art Museum.

Or to go back: **C**

Shortly after midnight we moved into the ambush site outside My Khe. The whole platoon was there, spread out in the dense brush along the trail, and for five hours nothing at all happened. We were working in two-man teams—one man on guard while the other slept, switching off every two hours—and I remember it was still dark when Kiowa shook me awake for the final watch. The night was foggy and hot. For the first few moments I felt lost, not sure about directions, groping for my helmet and weapon. I reached out and found three grenades and
20 lined them up in front of me; the pins had already been straightened for quick throwing. And then for maybe half an hour I kneeled there and waited. Very gradually, in tiny slivers, dawn began to break through the fog, and from my position in the brush I could see ten or fifteen meters up the trail. The mosquitoes were fierce. I remember slapping at them, wondering if I should wake up Kiowa and ask for some repellent, then thinking it was a bad idea, then looking up and seeing the young man come out of the fog. He wore black clothing and rubber sandals and a gray ammunition belt. His shoulders were slightly stooped, his head cocked to the side as if listening for something. He seemed at ease. He carried his weapon in one hand, muzzle down, moving without any hurry up the center
30 of the trail. There was no sound at all—none that I can remember. In a way, it seemed, he was part of the morning fog, or my own imagination, but there was also the reality of what was happening in my stomach. I had already pulled the pin on a grenade. I had come up to a crouch. It was entirely automatic. I did not hate the young man; I did not see him as the enemy; I did not ponder issues of morality or politics or military duty. I crouched and kept my head low. I tried to swallow whatever was rising from my stomach, which tasted like lemonade, something fruity and sour. I was terrified. There were no thoughts about killing. The grenade was to make him go away—just evaporate—and I leaned back and felt my mind go empty and then felt it fill up again. I had already thrown the
40 grenade before telling myself to throw it. The brush was thick and I had to lob it high, not aiming, and I remember the grenade seeming to freeze above me for an instant, as if a camera had clicked, and I remember ducking down and holding my breath and seeing little wisps of fog rise from the earth. The grenade bounced once and rolled across the trail. I did not hear it, but there must've been a sound, because the young man dropped his weapon and began to run, just two or three quick steps, then he hesitated, swiveling to his right, and he glanced down at the grenade and tried to cover his head but never did. It occurred to me then that he was about to die. I wanted to warn him. The grenade made a popping noise—not soft but not loud either—not what I'd expected—and there was a puff of dust
50 and smoke—a small white puff—and the young man seemed to jerk upward as if pulled by invisible wires. He fell on his back. His rubber sandals had been blown off. There was no wind. He lay at the center of the trail, his right leg bent beneath him, his one eye shut, his other eye a huge star-shaped hole. **D**

C ANALYZE STRUCTURE
In terms of the structure of this story, what does this line signal?

D ANALYZE STRUCTURE
Summarize what happens in lines 13–53. How do these lines relate to the first paragraph of the story?

Come a Little Closer (1997), Michael Brostowitz. Oil on board, 15¼″ × 19¾″. © National Vietnam Veterans Art Museum.

It was not a matter of live or die. There was no real peril. Almost certainly the young man would have passed by. And it will always be that way.

Later, I remember, Kiowa tried to tell me that the man would've died anyway. He told me that it was a good kill, that I was a soldier and this was a war, that I should shape up and stop staring and ask myself what the dead man would've done if things were reversed.

60   None of it mattered. The words seemed far too complicated. All I could do was gape at the fact of the young man's body. **E**

Even now I haven't finished sorting it out. Sometimes I forgive myself, other times I don't. In the ordinary hours of life I try not to dwell on it, but now and then, when I'm reading a newspaper or just sitting alone in a room, I'll look up and see the young man coming out of the morning fog. I'll watch him walk toward me, his shoulders slightly stooped, his head cocked to the side, and he'll pass within a few yards of me and suddenly smile at some secret thought and then continue up the trail to where it bends back into the fog. ❧ **F**

E CONFLICT
Reread lines 54–61. What **internal conflict** does the narrator express?

F CONFLICT
How does the vision the narrator imagines in lines 63–68 help resolve his conflict?

Comprehension

1. **Recall** What does the narrator tell his daughter when she asks if he ever killed someone?

2. **Summarize** What happened to the narrator outside My Khe?

3. **Clarify** What vision does the narrator sometimes see in his mind?

Literary Analysis

4. **Examine Conflicts** Identify the **internal conflicts** the narrator experiences in this story. How would you describe the way he resolves or tries to resolve them? Explain your answer.

5. **Analyze Structure** What does the **frame** contribute to the impact of this story? Consider what would be lost without the first and last paragraphs.

6. **Interpret Title** In what ways does the title "Ambush" relate to the events of the story? Think about the frame as well as the inner story.

7. **Evaluate a Character's Actions** Kiowa tells the narrator that this "was a good kill." Do you agree? In your opinion, can there be a "good kill"?

8. **Apply Theme** What does this story suggest about the effects of the **past** on the present?

9. **Compare Texts** Compare "Ambush" and "Why Soldiers Won't Talk" (page 1116) as portrayals of a soldier's experience. On a chart, note what each presents as the physical sensations and emotional aftereffects of war. Which piece—the story or the essay—had more impact on you? Why?

	Physical Sensations	Emotional Aftereffects
"Ambush"		
"Why Soldiers Won't Talk"		

Literary Criticism

10. **Author's Style** "Ambush" is a work of fiction, but the story reads like a nonfiction account of a true event. To readers who wonder how much of his work is actually true, O'Brien responds, "The literal truth is . . . irrelevant." Do you agree? Does it matter that O'Brien the writer does not have a daughter and does not know whether he ever killed anyone?

The Literary Legacy of War

Modernist writer Gertrude Stein once said, "War is never fatal but always lost. Always lost." One after another, the wars of the 20th century forced Americans to reconcile their sense of patriotism with the disillusionment that naturally comes from facing the realities of modern warfare. If it is an artist's job to find meaning, what meaning can be discerned from the act of war?

Writing to Synthesize

Each of the selections you have just read presents a variety of ideas and images in response to World War II and the Vietnam War. What do these pieces have in common? Reread the selections, pulling words or phrases from each that you find especially compelling—whether beautiful, ugly, moving, or surprising. When you have gathered 15–30 phrases, combine them artfully to create a poem that delivers a coherent impression about war. Your poem might tell a story, describe an image, or deliver a set of thoughts or pronouncements. It can take place on the battlefield or on the home front.

Consider

- what primary thought or feeling you were left with after reading all of the selections
- which parts of each selection had the strongest impact on you
- how to arrange the phrases in a way that communicates your own response to the literature

Extension

SPEAKING & LISTENING Give an **oral reading** of your poem, using your voice, posture, and gestures to emphasize its meaning. If you think it would be effective, consider performing a choral reading with some of your classmates or setting your poem to music.

American soldiers in Vietnam

from Letter from Birmingham Jail

Letter by Martin Luther King Jr.

FYI

Did you know that Martin Luther King Jr....

- enrolled in college when he was 15 years old?
- was the first African American to be named *Time* magazine's "Man of the Year"?
- won the Nobel Peace Prize in 1964?
- was arrested 30 times for his activism?

Author On|ine

For more on Martin Luther King Jr., visit the **Literature Center** at **ClassZone.com.**

Martin Luther King Jr.
1929–1968

An eloquent orator, a shrewd tactician, and a visionary leader, Martin Luther King Jr. became the catalyst for some of the most far-reaching social changes in U.S. history. Under his skillful leadership, the civil rights movement spurred passage of the Civil Rights Act of 1964 and the Voting Rights Act of 1965, laws that legally abolished racial segregation and voting discrimination. A tireless advocate for justice, King wrote five books, delivered about 2,500 speeches, and traveled more than 6 million miles in an effort to make his dream of equality a reality.

Boycott in Montgomery It was in Alabama that King first emerged as a civil rights leader to be reckoned with. In 1955, when Rosa Parks was arrested for breaking Montgomery's bus segregation laws, local civil rights advocates banded together to form a protest organization. They chose King, then pastor of the Dexter Avenue Baptist Church, to lead the new group. King mobilized African Americans to boycott city buses. The 381-day boycott tested the endurance of the entire black community, especially King, who was subjected to threats and bomb attacks. The steadfast boycotters ultimately triumphed, and the U.S. Supreme Court struck down the city's bus segregation laws. The success of the boycott launched the charismatic young leader onto the national stage, where he promoted his bold strategy: using nonviolent, direct action to achieve social change.

Expanding Influence King cautiously expanded the civil rights struggle throughout the South. He was particularly effective at organizing interracial coalitions to put pressure on lawmakers. One shining moment came at the 1963 March on Washington, a gathering of about 250,000 peaceful demonstrators supporting civil rights legislation. King's impassioned "I Have a Dream" speech, delivered on the steps of the Lincoln Memorial, is considered one of the greatest speeches in U.S. history.

Warrior for Peace King never wavered in his commitment to nonviolence and tried to extend his campaign to fight poverty and end the Vietnam War. Ultimately, he was unable to stem the surge of violence that overtook the country in the mid-1960s. In 1968, King was assassinated in Memphis, where he had gone to support a sanitation workers' strike. In the 12 years between the Montgomery boycott and his death, he had helped achieve the greatest advance in racial justice since the abolition of slavery.

LITERARY ANALYSIS: ALLUSION

An **allusion** is a reference within a work to historical, literary, or cultural details from outside the work. Writers choose allusions that are familiar to their target audience. In this case, because King is writing to fellow clergymen, he uses references to the Bible and to religious scholars to make his points.

I would agree with St. Augustine that "an unjust law is no law at all."

King's allusions help connect current events with respected historical and religious figures. As you read, use the footnotes to help you understand King's allusions.

READING SKILL: TRACE THE ELEMENTS OF AN ARGUMENT

King's letter is a beautifully written **argument** defending his activism. He organizes his letter as a series of counterarguments responding to public criticisms of his actions. He introduces each counterargument by partly restating these opposing positions. As you read, use King's restatements to infer what these positions are and record them in a chart like the one shown. Then, record King's own positions and the reasons and evidence he uses to support them.

Position of Opponents	King's Counterclaim	Reasons and Evidence
King doesn't belong in Birmingham.	"I am here because I have organizational ties here."	• leads the SCLC • invited by affiliated organization

VOCABULARY IN CONTEXT

King uses the following words to argue his views. Test yourself by replacing each boldfaced term with one vocabulary word.

WORD LIST		
affiliated	moratorium	scintillating
cognizant	paradoxical	substantive
estrangement	rabid	
latent	retaliating	

1. **aware** of the difficulties involved
2. **hidden** emotions called up by the encounter
3. **contradictory** views seemed to say two things at once
4. **temporary stoppage** on further discussions

When does ACTION speak louder than words?

KEY IDEA When you're trying to confront a difficult issue, words are your first option. But once you've explained your position, presented your demands, and tried unsuccessfully to convince others to make a change, you're at the point when words give way to **action**. Martin Luther King Jr. explains how civil rights activists in Birmingham, Alabama, faced their own decisive moment in 1963.

DISCUSS When do you respond with words and when do you turn to action? Working with a small group, brainstorm situations that call for each type of response. What guidelines did you use to classify your examples?

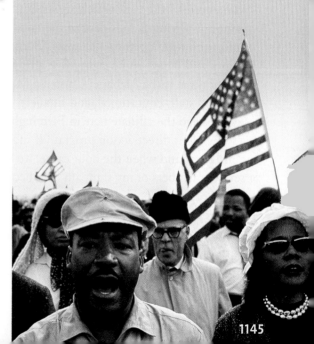

Letter from Birmingham Jail

Martin Luther King Jr.

BACKGROUND In the spring of 1963, Martin Luther King Jr. and his organization, the Southern Christian Leadership Conference (SCLC), targeted Birmingham, Alabama, with a series of peaceful demonstrations aimed at ending segregation. The police reacted violently with attack dogs and high-pressure fire hoses. Hundreds of protesters, including King, were jailed. At first, King was criticized for taking on Birmingham; eight white clergymen published a letter calling his actions "unwise and untimely." But he responded with his own letter citing philosophers, religious scholars, and biblical figures to justify his actions.

April 16, 1963

My Dear Fellow Clergymen:

While confined here in the Birmingham city jail, I came across your recent statement calling my present activities "unwise and untimely." Seldom do I pause to answer criticism of my work and ideas. If I sought to answer all the criticisms that cross my desk, my secretaries would have little time for anything other than such correspondence in the course of the day, and I would have no time for constructive work. But since I feel that you are men of genuine good will and that your criticisms are sincerely set forth, I want to try to answer your statement in what I hope will be patient and reasonable terms.

10   I think I should indicate why I am here in Birmingham, since you have been influenced by the view which argues against "outsiders coming in." I have the honor of serving as president of the Southern Christian Leadership Conference, an organization operating in every Southern state, with headquarters in Atlanta, Georgia. We have some eighty-five **affiliated** organizations across the South, and one of them is the Alabama Christian Movement for Human Rights. Frequently we share staff, educational, and financial resources with our affiliates. Several months ago the affiliate here in Birmingham asked us to be on call to engage in a nonviolent direct-action program if such were deemed necessary. We readily consented, and when the hour came, we lived up to our promise. So I, along with

20 several members of my staff, am here because I was invited here. I am here because I have organizational ties here. **A**

But more basically, I am in Birmingham because injustice is here. Just as the prophets of the eighth century B.C. left their villages and carried their "thus saith the Lord" far beyond the boundaries of their home towns, and just as the Apostle Paul left his village of Tarsus and carried the gospel of Jesus Christ to the

ANALYZE VISUALS
Look at this photograph of King in his jail cell in Birmingham. Based on the photo, what impressions do you have of his state of mind while in jail?

affiliated (ə-fĭl′ē-ā′tĭd) *adj.* joined in close association **affiliate** *v.*

A ELEMENTS OF AN ARGUMENT
Reread lines 10–21. Which sentence refers to the position that King is arguing against?

King in his jail cell in Birmingham

far corners of the Greco-Roman world, so am I compelled to carry the gospel of freedom beyond my own hometown. Like Paul, I must constantly respond to the Macedonian call for aid.[1] **B**

Moreover, I am **cognizant** of the interrelatedness of all communities and 30 states. I cannot sit idly by in Atlanta and not be concerned about what happens in Birmingham. Injustice anywhere is a threat to justice everywhere. We are caught in an inescapable network of mutuality, tied in a single garment of destiny. Whatever affects one directly, affects all indirectly. Never again can we afford to live with the narrow, provincial "outside agitator" idea. Anyone who lives inside the United States can never be considered an outsider anywhere within its bounds.

You deplore the demonstrations taking place in Birmingham. But your statement, I am sorry to say, fails to express a similar concern for the conditions that brought about the demonstrations. I am sure that none of you would want to rest content with the superficial kind of social analysis that deals merely 40 with effects and does not grapple with underlying causes. It is unfortunate that demonstrations are taking place in Birmingham, but it is even more unfortunate that the city's white power structure left the Negro community with no alternative.

In any nonviolent campaign there are four basic steps: collection of the facts to determine whether injustices exist; negotiation; self-purification; and direct action. We have gone through all these steps in Birmingham. There can be no gainsaying the fact that racial injustice engulfs this community. Birmingham is probably the most thoroughly segregated city in the United States. Its ugly record of brutality is widely known. Negroes have experienced grossly unjust treatment in the courts. 50 There have been more unsolved bombings of Negro homes and churches in Birmingham than in any other city in the nation. These are the hard, brutal facts of the case. On the basis of these conditions, Negro leaders sought to negotiate with the city fathers. But the latter consistently refused to engage in good-faith negotiations. **C**

Then, last September, came the opportunity to talk with leaders of Birmingham's economic community. In the course of the negotiations, certain promises were made by the merchants— for example, to remove the stores' humiliating racial signs.[2] On the basis of these promises, the Reverend Fred Shuttlesworth and the leaders of the Alabama Christian Movement for Human 60 Rights agreed to a **moratorium** on all demonstrations. As the weeks and months went by, we realized that we were the victims of a broken promise. A few signs, briefly removed, returned; the others remained.

As in so many past experiences, our hopes had been blasted, and the shadow of deep disappointment settled upon us. We had no alternative except to prepare for direct action, whereby we would present our very bodies as a means of laying our case before the conscience of the local and the national community. Mindful of the difficulties involved, we decided to undertake a process of self-purification.

B **ALLUSION**
Explain why King's allusions in lines 22–28 are appropriate for his audience. What shared beliefs does King appeal to?

cognizant (kŏg′nĭ-zənt) *adj.* aware

C **ELEMENTS OF AN ARGUMENT**
Reread lines 46–54. What **reasons** and **evidence** does King use to support his **claim** that there is racial injustice in Birmingham?

moratorium (môr′ə-tôr′ē-əm) *n.* a temporary stoppage or waiting period

---

1. **Macedonian** (măs′ĭ-dō′nē-ən) **call for aid:** According to the Bible (Acts 16), the apostle Paul received a vision calling him to preach in Macedonia, an area north of Greece.
2. **racial signs:** signs marking segregated buildings and other facilities.

We began a series of workshops on nonviolence, and we repeatedly asked ourselves: "Are you able to accept blows without **retaliating?**" "Are you able to
70 endure the ordeal of jail?" We decided to schedule our direct-action program for the Easter season, realizing that except for Christmas, this is the main shopping period of the year. Knowing that a strong economic-withdrawal program[3] would be the by-product of direct action, we felt that this would be the best time to bring pressure to bear on the merchants for the needed change.

retaliating (rĭ-tăl′ē-ā′tĭng) *n.* taking revenge **retaliate** *v.*

Then it occurred to us that Birmingham's mayoral election was coming up in March, and we speedily decided to postpone action until after election day. When we discovered that the Commissioner of Public Safety, Eugene "Bull" Connor, had piled up enough votes to be in the runoff, we decided again to postpone action until the day after the runoff so that the demonstrations could not be used to
80 cloud the issues. Like many others, we waited to see Mr. Connor defeated, and to this end we endured postponement after postponement. Having aided in this community need, we felt that our direct-action program could be delayed no longer.

You may well ask: "Why direct action? Why sit-ins, marches, and so forth? Isn't negotiation a better path?" You are quite right in calling for negotiation. Indeed, this is the very purpose of direct action. Nonviolent direct action seeks to create such a crisis and foster such a tension that a community which has constantly refused to negotiate is forced to confront the issue. It seeks so to dramatize the issue that it can no longer be ignored. My citing the creation of tension as part of
90 the work of the nonviolent-resister may sound rather shocking. But I must confess that I am not afraid of the word "tension." I have earnestly opposed violent tension, but there is a type of constructive, nonviolent tension which is necessary for growth. Just as Socrates[4] felt that it was necessary to create a tension in the mind so that individuals could rise from the bondage of myths and half-truths to the unfettered realm of creative analysis and objective appraisal, so must we see the need for nonviolent gadflies to create the kind of tension in society that will help men rise from the dark depths of prejudice and racism to the majestic heights of understanding and brotherhood.

The purpose of our direct-action program is to create a situation so crisis-
100 packed that it will inevitably open the door to negotiation. I therefore concur with you in your call for negotiation. Too long has our beloved Southland been bogged down in a tragic effort to live in monologue rather than dialogue.

One of the basic points in your statement is that the action that I and my associates have taken in Birmingham is untimely. Some have asked: "Why didn't you give the new city administration time to act?" The only answer that I can give to this query is that the new Birmingham administration must be prodded about as much as the outgoing one, before it will act. . . . My friends, I must say to you that we have not made a single gain in civil rights without determined legal and nonviolent pressure. Lamentably, it is a historical fact that privileged groups

---

3. **economic-withdrawal program:** boycott.

4. **Socrates** (sŏk′rə-tēz′): Greek philosopher (470–399 B.C.) who was a major influence in the development of Western thought.

110 seldom give up their privileges voluntarily. Individuals may see the moral light and voluntarily give up their unjust posture; but, as Reinhold Niebuhr[5] has reminded us, groups tend to be more immoral than individuals.

We know through painful experience that freedom is never voluntarily given by the oppressor; it must be demanded by the oppressed. Frankly, I have yet to engage in a direct-action campaign that was "well-timed" in the view of those who have not suffered unduly from the disease of segregation. For years now I have heard the word "Wait!" It rings in the ear of every Negro with piercing familiarity. This "Wait" has almost always meant "Never." We must come to see, with one of our distinguished jurists, that "justice too long delayed is justice denied."

120 We have waited for more than 340 years for our constitutional and God-given rights. The nations of Asia and Africa are moving with jetlike speed toward gaining political independence, but we still creep at horse-and-buggy pace toward gaining a cup of coffee at a lunch counter. Perhaps it is easy for those who have never felt the stinging darts of segregation to say, "Wait." But when you have seen vicious mobs lynch your mothers and fathers at will and drown your sisters and brothers at whim; when you have seen hate-filled policemen curse, kick, and even kill your black brothers and sisters; when you see the vast majority of your twenty million Negro brothers smothering in an airtight cage of poverty in the midst of an affluent society; when you suddenly find your tongue twisted and your speech
130 stammering as you seek to explain to your six-year-old daughter why she can't go to the public amusement park that has just been advertised on television, and see tears welling up in her eyes when she is told that Funtown is closed to colored children, and see ominous clouds of inferiority beginning to form in her little mental sky, and see her beginning to distort her personality by developing an unconscious bitterness toward white people; when you have to concoct an answer for a five-year-old son who is asking: "Daddy, why do white people treat colored people so mean?"; when you take a cross-country drive and find it necessary to sleep night after night in the uncomfortable corners of your automobile because no motel will accept you; when you are humiliated day in and day out by nagging
140 signs reading "white" and "colored"; when your first name becomes "nigger," your middle name becomes "boy" (however old you are) and your last name becomes "John," and your wife and mother are never given the respected title "Mrs."; when you are harried by day and haunted by night by the fact that you are a Negro, living constantly at tiptoe stance, never quite knowing what to expect next, and are plagued with inner fears and outer resentments; when you are forever fighting a degenerating sense of "nobodiness"—then you will understand why we find it difficult to wait. There comes a time when the cup of endurance runs over, and men are no longer willing to be plunged into the abyss of despair. I hope, sirs, you can understand our legitimate and unavoidable impatience. **D**

150 You express a great deal of anxiety over our willingness to break laws. This is certainly a legitimate concern. Since we so diligently urge people to obey the

D GRAMMAR AND STYLE
Reread lines 124–146. Note how King establishes **parallelism** by starting each subordinate clause with the words *when you.*

---

5. **Reinhold Niebuhr** (nē′bo͝or′): American theologian (1892–1971) whose writings deal mainly with moral and social problems.

Supreme Court's decision of 1954 outlawing segregation in the public schools,[6] at first glance it may seem rather **paradoxical** for us consciously to break laws. One may well ask: "How can you advocate breaking some laws and obeying others?" The answer lies in the fact that there are two types of laws: just and unjust. I would be the first to advocate obeying just laws. One has not only a legal but a moral responsibility to obey just laws. Conversely, one has a moral responsibility to disobey unjust laws. I would agree with St. Augustine[7] that "an unjust law is no law at all." **E**

160   Now, what is the difference between the two? How does one determine whether a law is just or unjust? A just law is a man-made code that squares with the moral law or the law of God. An unjust law is a code that is out of harmony with the moral law. To put it in the terms of St. Thomas Aquinas:[8] An unjust law is a human law that is not rooted in eternal law and natural law. Any law that uplifts human personality is just. Any law that degrades human personality is unjust. All segregation statutes are unjust because segregation distorts the soul and damages the personality. It gives the segregator a false sense of superiority and the segregated a false sense of inferiority. Segregation, to use the terminology of the Jewish philosopher Martin Buber,[9] substitutes an "I-it" relationship for an "I-
170 thou" relationship and ends up relegating persons to the status of things. Hence segregation is not only politically, economically, and sociologically unsound, it is morally wrong and sinful. Paul Tillich[10] has said that sin is separation. Is not segregation an existential expression of man's tragic separation, his awful **estrangement,** his terrible sinfulness? Thus it is that I can urge men to obey the 1954 decision of the Supreme Court, for it is morally right; and I can urge them to disobey segregation ordinances, for they are morally wrong.

Let us consider a more concrete example of just and unjust laws. An unjust law is a code that a numerical or power majority group compels a minority group to obey but does not make binding on itself. This is *difference* made legal. By the
180 same token, a just law is a code that a majority compels a minority to follow and that it is willing to follow itself. This is *sameness* made legal.

Let me give another explanation. A law is unjust if it is inflicted on a minority that, as a result of being denied the right to vote, had no part in enacting or devising the law. Who can say that the legislature of Alabama which set up that state's segregation laws was democratically elected? Throughout Alabama all sorts of devious methods are used to prevent Negroes from becoming registered voters, and there are some counties in which, even though Negroes constitute a majority of the population, not a single Negro is registered. Can any law enacted under such circumstances be considered democratically structured?

---

6. **Supreme Court decision . . . public schools:** the United States Supreme Court's decision in the case *Brown v. Board of Education of Topeka, Kansas.*

7. **St. Augustine** (ô'gə-stēn'): North African bishop (A.D. 354–430) regarded as a founding father of Christianity.

8. **St. Thomas Aquinas** (ə-kwī'nəs): noted philosopher and theologian (1225–1274).

9. **Martin Buber** (bōō'bər): influential philosopher (1878–1965) with great impact on Jewish and Christian theology.

10. **Paul Tillich** (tǐl'ǐk): German-born American theologian (1886–1965).

---

paradoxical
(păr'ə-dŏk'sǐ-kəl) *adj.* self-contradictory

E ELEMENTS OF AN ARGUMENT
Reread lines 150–159. How does King's distinction between just and unjust laws help support his claim that it is sometimes appropriate to break the law?

estrangement
(ǐ-strănj'mənt) *n.* separation; alienation

High school students jailed in Birmingham protests of 1963

190   Sometimes a law is just on its face and unjust in its application. For instance, I have been arrested on a charge of parading without a permit. Now, there is nothing wrong in having an ordinance which requires a permit for a parade. But such an ordinance becomes unjust when it is used to maintain segregation and to deny citizens the First Amendment privilege of peaceful assembly and protest.

    I hope you are able to see the distinction I am trying to point out. In no sense do I advocate evading or defying the law, as would the **rabid** segregationist. That would lead to anarchy. One who breaks an unjust law must do so openly, lovingly, and with a willingness to accept the penalty. I submit that an individual who breaks a law that conscience tells him is unjust, and who willingly accepts the

200 penalty of imprisonment in order to arouse the conscience of the community over its injustice, is in reality expressing the highest respect for law.

    Of course, there is nothing new about this kind of civil disobedience. It was evidenced sublimely in the refusal of Shadrach, Meshach, and Abednego to obey the laws of Nebuchadnezzar,[11] on the ground that a higher moral law was at stake. It was practiced superbly by the early Christians, who were willing to face hungry lions and the excruciating pain of chopping blocks rather than submit to certain unjust laws of the Roman Empire. To a degree, academic freedom is a reality today because Socrates practiced civil disobedience. In our own nation, the Boston Tea Party[12] represented a massive act of civil disobedience. **F**

rabid (răb′ĭd) *adj.* unreasonably extreme; fanatical

F ALLUSION
Reread lines 202–209. What message about civil disobedience does King send with his choice of allusions?

---

11. **the refusal . . . Nebuchadnezzar** (něb′ə-kəd-něz′ər): In the Bible (Daniel 3), Shadrach (shăd′răk), Meshach (mē′shăch), and Abednego (ə-běd′nĭ-gō′) are three Hebrews condemned to death for refusing to worship an idol set up by Nebuchadnezzar, king of Babylon. However, they were miraculously protected from the flames in the furnace into which they were thrown.

12. **Boston Tea Party:** In 1773, American rebels dumped 15,000 pounds of tea into Boston Harbor to protest the British Tea Act.

210   We should never forget that everything Adolf Hitler did in Germany was "legal" and everything the Hungarian freedom fighters[13] did in Hungary was "illegal." It was "illegal" to aid and comfort a Jew in Hitler's Germany. Even so, I am sure that, had I lived in Germany at the time, I would have aided and comforted my Jewish brothers. If today I lived in a Communist country where certain principles dear to the Christian faith are suppressed, I would openly advocate disobeying that country's antireligious laws.

    I must make two honest confessions to you, my Christian and Jewish brothers. First, I must confess that over the past few years I have been gravely disappointed with the white moderate. I have almost reached the regrettable conclusion that

220 the Negro's great stumbling block in his stride toward freedom is not the White Citizen's Counciler or the Ku Klux Klanner,[14] but the white moderate, who is more devoted to "order" than to justice; who prefers a negative peace which is the absence of tension to a positive peace which is the presence of justice; who constantly says: "I agree with you in the goal you seek, but I cannot agree with your methods of direct action"; who paternalistically believes he can set the timetable for another man's freedom; who lives by a mythical concept of time and who constantly advises the Negro to wait for a "more convenient season." Shallow understanding from people of goodwill is more frustrating than absolute misunderstanding from people of ill will. Lukewarm acceptance is much more

230 bewildering than outright rejection.

    I had hoped that the white moderate would understand that law and order exist for the purpose of establishing justice and that when they fail in this purpose, they become the dangerously structured dams that block the flow of social progress. I had hoped that the white moderate would understand that the present tension in the South is a necessary phase of the transition from an obnoxious negative peace, in which the Negro passively accepted his unjust plight, to a **substantive** and positive peace, in which all men will respect the dignity and worth of human personality. Actually, we who engage in nonviolent direct action are not the creators of tension. We merely bring to the surface the hidden tension that is

240 already alive. We bring it out in the open, where it can be seen and dealt with. Like a boil that can never be cured so long as it is covered up but must be opened with all its ugliness to the natural medicines of air and light, injustice must be exposed, with all the tension its exposure creates, to the light of human conscience and the air of national opinion before it can be cured.

    In your statement you assert that our actions, even though peaceful, must be condemned because they precipitate violence. But is this a logical assertion? Isn't this like condemning a robbed man because his possession of money precipitated the evil act of robbery? Isn't this like condemning Socrates because his unswerving commitment to truth and his philosophical inquiries precipitated the act by

250 the misguided populace in which they made him drink hemlock? Isn't this like

substantive (sŭb′stən-tĭv) *adj.* significant; with a strong basis

---

13. **Hungarian freedom fighters:** Hungarians who participated in an unsuccessful 1956 rebellion against the Communist government of their homeland. The rebellion was crushed by Soviet troops.

14. **the White . . . Klanner:** members of white supremacist groups.

condemning Jesus because his unique God-consciousness and never-ceasing devotion to God's will precipitated the evil act of crucifixion? We must come to see that, as the federal courts have consistently affirmed, it is wrong to urge an individual to cease his efforts to gain his basic constitutional rights because the quest may precipitate violence. Society must protect the robbed and punish the robber. . . .

Oppressed people cannot remain oppressed forever. The yearning for freedom eventually manifests itself, and that is what has happened to the American Negro. Something within has reminded him of his birthright of freedom, and something without has reminded him that it can be gained. Consciously or unconsciously,
260 he has been caught up by the *Zeitgeist*,[15] and with his black brothers of Africa and his brown and yellow brothers of Asia, South America, and the Caribbean, the United States Negro is moving with a sense of great urgency toward the promised land of racial justice. If one recognizes this vital urge that has engulfed the Negro community, one should readily understand why public demonstrations are taking place. The Negro has many pent-up resentments and **latent** frustrations, and he must release them. So let him march; let him make prayer pilgrimages to the city hall; let him go on freedom rides—and try to understand why he must do so. If his repressed emotions are not released in nonviolent ways, they will seek expression through violence; this is not a threat but a fact of history. So I have not
270 said to my people: "Get rid of your discontent." Rather, I have tried to say that this normal and healthy discontent can be channeled into the creative outlet of nonviolent direct action. And now this approach is being termed extremist.

But though I was initially disappointed at being categorized as an extremist, as I continued to think about the matter, I gradually gained a measure of satisfaction from the label. Was not Jesus an extremist for love: "Love your enemies, bless them that curse you, do good to them that hate you, and pray for them which despitefully use you, and persecute you." Was not Amos[16] an extremist for justice: "Let justice roll down like waters and righteousness like an ever-flowing stream." Was not Paul an extremist for the Christian gospel: "I bear in my body the marks
280 of the Lord Jesus." Was not Martin Luther[17] an extremist: "Here I stand; I cannot do otherwise, so help me God." And John Bunyan:[18] "I will stay in jail to the end of my days before I make a butchery of my conscience." And Abraham Lincoln: "This nation cannot survive half slave and half free." And Thomas Jefferson: "We hold these truths to be self-evident, that all men are created equal. . . ." So the question is not whether we will be extremists, but what kind of extremists we will be. Will we be extremists for hate or for love? Will we be extremists for the preservation of injustice or for the extension of justice? In that dramatic scene on Calvary's hill[19] three men were crucified. We must never forget that all

latent (lāt′nt) *adj.* existing in a hidden form

---

15. **Zeitgeist** (tsīt′gīst′) *German:* the spirit of the time; that is, the beliefs and attitudes shared by most people living in a particular period.

16. **Amos:** Hebrew prophet whose words are recorded in the Old Testament book bearing his name.

17. **Martin Luther:** German monk (1483–1546) who launched the Protestant Reformation.

18. **John Bunyan:** English preacher and author (1628–1688) who was twice imprisoned for unlicensed preaching.

19. **Calvary's hill:** the site of Jesus' crucifixion.

three were crucified for the same crime—the crime of extremism. Two were extremists for immorality, and thus fell below their environment. The other, Jesus Christ, was an extremist for love, truth, and goodness, and thereby rose above his environment. Perhaps the South, the nation and the world are in dire need of creative extremists. . . . **G**

I wish you had commended the Negro sit-inners and demonstrators of Birmingham for their sublime courage, their willingness to suffer, and their amazing discipline in the midst of great provocation. One day the South will recognize its real heroes. They will be the James Merediths,[20] with the noble sense of purpose that enables them to face jeering and hostile mobs, and with the agonizing loneliness that characterizes the life of the pioneer. They will be old, oppressed, battered Negro women, symbolized in a seventy-two-year-old woman in Montgomery, Alabama, who rose up with a sense of dignity and with her people decided not to ride segregated buses, and who responded with ungrammatical profundity to one who inquired about her weariness: "My feets is tired, but my soul is at rest." They will be the young high school and college students, the young ministers of the gospel and a host of their elders, courageously and nonviolently sitting in at lunch counters and willingly going to jail for conscience' sake. One day the South will know that when these disinherited children of God sat down at lunch counters, they were in reality standing up for what is best in the American dream and for the most sacred values in our Judaeo-Christian heritage, thereby bringing our nation back to those great wells of democracy which were dug deep by the founding fathers in their formulation of the Constitution and the Declaration of Independence.

Never before have I written so long a letter. I'm afraid it is much too long to take your precious time. I can assure you that it would have been much shorter if I had been writing from a comfortable desk, but what else can one do when he is alone in a narrow jail cell, other than write long letters, think long thoughts, and pray long prayers?

If I have said anything in this letter that overstates the truth and indicates an unreasonable impatience, I beg you to forgive me. If I have said anything that understates the truth and indicates my having a patience that allows me to settle for anything less than brotherhood, I beg God to forgive me.

I hope this letter finds you strong in the faith. I also hope that circumstances will soon make it possible for me to meet each of you, not as an integrationist or a civil-rights leader but as a fellow clergyman and a Christian brother. Let us all hope that the dark clouds of racial prejudice will soon pass away and the deep fog of misunderstanding will be lifted from our fear-drenched communities, and in some not too distant tomorrow the radiant stars of love and brotherhood will shine over our great nation with all their **scintillating** beauty.

Yours for the cause of Peace and Brotherhood,

Martin Luther King Jr.

G ALLUSION
Reread lines 275–293. Consider the usual connotations of the word *extremist*. How do King's allusions prompt the reader to think differently about this idea?

scintillating (sĭn'tl-ā'tĭng) *adj.* sparkling **scintillate** *v.*

---

20. **James Merediths:** people like James Meredith, who endured violent opposition from whites to become the first African American to attend the University of Mississippi.

Ballad
of Birmingham
Dudley Randall

"Mother dear, may I go downtown
instead of out to play,
and march the streets of Birmingham
in a freedom march today?"

5 "No, baby, no, you may not go,
for the dogs are fierce and wild,
and clubs and hoses, guns and jails
ain't good for a little child."

"But, mother, I won't be alone.
10 Other children will go with me,
and march the streets of Birmingham
to make our country free."

"No, baby, no, you may not go,
for I fear those guns will fire.
15 But you may go to church instead,
and sing in the children's choir."

She has combed and brushed her nightdark hair,
and bathed rose petal sweet,
and drawn white gloves on her small brown hands,
20 and white shoes on her feet.

The mother smiled to know her child
was in the sacred place,
but that smile was the last smile
to come upon her face.

25 For when she heard the explosion,
her eyes grew wet and wild.
She raced through the streets of Birmingham
calling for her child.

She clawed through bits of glass and brick,
30 then lifted out a shoe.
"O, here's the shoe my baby wore,
but, baby, where are you?"

Comprehension

1. **Summarize** What led to the decision to start the protests in Birmingham?

2. **Recall** What are the four steps involved in King's nonviolent campaigns?

3. **Clarify** What exactly does King mean by "nonviolent direct action"?

4. **Summarize** In King's view, what is the difference between defying the law and breaking an "unjust" law?

Literary Analysis

5. **Examine Elements of an Argument** Review the chart you created as you read. Which of King's **counterarguments** did you find most persuasive? Consider both his position, or claim, and his reasons and evidence in your answer.

6. **Understand Analogy** An analogy is an extended, point-by-point comparison of two different things, often using a familiar example to explain a difficult or abstract idea. In lines 241–244, King uses an analogy to explain his thoughts on injustice. Reread the analogy. What two things are compared, and in what ways are they similar?

7. **Interpret Allusions** Allusions can refer to people, places, events, or literary works. Choose at least four of King's allusions. Using the footnotes to help

Allusion	Possible Meaning	Why Included

you, interpret the meaning of King's references and tell why you think King included each allusion. Record your answers in a chart like the one shown.

8. **Analyze Persuasive Techniques** King's writings and speeches are filled with allusions that reveal his rhetorical mastery and breadth of knowledge. In what ways, if any, do his allusions also help him achieve the following possible purposes? Cite specific allusions that support your answers.

   - appealing to his readers' sense of right and wrong
   - establishing his credibility
   - invoking democratic ideals
   - making his ideas accessible to a wider audience

9. **Compare Texts** Compare the message of "Ballad of Birmingham" (page 1156) with that of King's letter. In what ways is Randall's poem also an argument for taking **action** against injustice?

Literary Criticism

10. **Author's Style** King is a master of the **aphorism,** a short, expressive statement of principle or truth. Here's a memorable one: "Injustice anywhere is a threat to justice everywhere" (line 31). Find two or three more aphorisms in King's letter and explain their effects.

Vocabulary in Context

VOCABULARY PRACTICE

Show your understanding of the vocabulary words by answering these questions.

1. If I am **cognizant** of your plans, do I know about them or have I forgotten them?
2. Would a **paradoxical** statement be easy or difficult to make sense of?
3. Would a **substantive** contribution be minimal or significant?
4. Would a **rabid** response involve shouting furiously or agreeing silently?
5. If my company is **affiliated** with yours, are they competitors or partners?
6. Which might cause a **moratorium** in road building, a bad storm or potholes?
7. Is a diamond or gold more accurately described as **scintillating?**
8. Which is a **latent** ailment, a toothache or a broken arm?
9. Would an argument cause **estrangement** or a meeting with a stranger?
10. Which might be a cause for **retaliating,** losing a game or taking a taxi?

WORD LIST

affiliated

cognizant

estrangement

latent

moratorium

paradoxical

rabid

retaliating

scintillating

substantive

VOCABULARY IN WRITING

What do you think of nonviolent protest? Explain your ideas in a short paragraph, using three or more vocabulary words. Here is a sample beginning.

> **EXAMPLE SENTENCE**
>
> By not **retaliating**, the protesters made their points effectively and powerfully.

VOCABULARY STRATEGY: ANALOGIES

An analogy compares two items that may have many points of similarity or may be alike in only one way. Analyzing an analogy is one way of determining the meaning of unfamiliar words in context, such as the word *boil* in this passage:

> *Like a boil that can never be cured so long as it is covered up but must be opened with all its ugliness to the natural medicines of air and light, injustice must be exposed, with all the tension its exposure creates, to the light of human conscience and the air of national opinion before it can be cured.* (lines 241–244)

Seeing that a boil is like an injustice to be cured only by exposure, we can infer that it is a sore that can be healed by exposure to air.

PRACTICE Use the comparison in each sentence as a context clue to help you define the boldfaced word. Then discuss the meaning of each analogy, including any inferences you draw based on the comparison and word choice.

1. Like birds migrating south, crocuses are a **harbinger** of seasonal change.
2. High cholesterol is thought to be as **deleterious** to health as smoking.
3. Our school considers cheating as much an **execration** as physical violence.

VOCABULARY PRACTICE

For more practice, go to the **Vocabulary Center** at ClassZone.com.

Reading-Writing Connection

WRITE A PERSUASIVE ARGUMENT Civil disobedience has been controversial ever since Henry David Thoreau first advocated it in 1847. Opposition to Martin Luther King's brand of nonviolent resistance came from some black activists as well as white segregationists. People still argue over the issue today.

Write a **four-to-six-paragraph persuasive argument** explaining your position on the issue of nonviolent civil disobedience. Model your argument on King's, using counterarguments to anticipate objections to your view.

An effective persuasive argument will . . .

- clearly state a position in the first paragraph
- support the position with facts, examples, quotations, or other forms of evidence
- address possible objections
- use logical reasoning
- conclude with a summary or a call to action

GRAMMAR AND STYLE

USE RHETORICAL DEVICES Review the **Grammar and Style** note on page 1150. In his letter, King uses **parallelism**—the repetition of grammatical structures—to create emphasis and to show comparisons, as in the following example:

> *Just as the prophets of the eighth century B.C. left their villages and carried their "thus saith the Lord" far beyond the boundaries of their hometowns, and just as the Apostle Paul left his village of Tarsus and carried the gospel of Jesus Christ to the far corners of the Greco-Roman world, so am I compelled to carry the gospel of freedom beyond my own hometown.* (lines 22–27)

Notice how King uses parallel adverb clauses beginning with "just as" to set up a comparison between himself and the biblical figures he cites. What is the impact of this comparison?

PRACTICE Identify the parallel adjective clauses in the following passage from King. Then write a paragraph of your own using similar parallel elements.

> [T]he Negro's great stumbling block in his stride toward freedom is not the White Citizen's Counciler or the Ku Klux Klanner, but the white moderate, who is more devoted to "order" than to justice; who prefers a negative peace which is the absence of tension to a positive peace which is the presence of justice; who constantly says: "I agree with you in the goal you seek, but I cannot agree with your methods of direct action"; who paternalistically believes he can set the timetable for another man's freedom; who lives by a mythical concept of time and who constantly advises the Negro to wait for a "more convenient season."

WRITING TOOLS
For prewriting, revision, and editing tools, visit the **Writing Center** at ClassZone.com.

from **Stride Toward Freedom**

Nonfiction by Martin Luther King Jr.

For a biography of Martin Luther King Jr., see page 1144.

Necessary to Protect Ourselves

Interview with Malcolm X by Les Crane

Malcolm X
1925–1965

NOTABLE QUOTE

"I see America through the eyes of the victim. I don't see any American dream; I see an American nightmare."

In 1944, while Martin Luther King Jr. was attending college classes in Atlanta, 19-year-old Malcolm Little was hustling on the streets of Harlem. By 1952, a jailhouse conversion transformed Little into the political firebrand we know as Malcolm X, whose separatist views posed a serious challenge to King's integrationist vision.

Bitter Legacy Where King grew up comfortably middle-class, Little's childhood was scarred by poverty and racial violence. His outspoken father, Earl Little, was an early advocate of black separatism who was murdered by white supremacists. His mother, left alone to raise eight children in dire poverty, suffered a mental breakdown. Her children, including Malcolm, were sent to separate foster homes.

By the time he was sent to prison in 1946, Little had been brutally disillusioned about his prospects in white-dominated society. While reading in the prison library, he discovered the teachings of a small religious sect called the Nation of Islam, or the Black Muslims, who called white people "a race of devils" and promoted a vision of black pride. They advocated a radical solution to the race problem: the establishment of a separate, self-reliant black nation.

Change of Heart Inspired by the Black Muslim vision, Malcolm Little converted to Islam and changed his last name to X, symbolizing his lost African name. Once released from prison, he became an influential spokesman for the Nation of Islam and was named their first national minister. Over time, however, he became critical of the organization. In 1964, Malcolm X experienced a second spiritual conversion while making a pilgrimage to Mecca. The sight of Muslims of many races worshipping together caused him to renounce all forms of racial hatred. On his return home, Malcolm X broke with the Nation of Islam and formed the Organization of Afro-American Unity, dedicated to promoting unity among black people all over the world.

Marked Man This new direction angered many Black Muslims, including the young Louis Farrakhan, who labeled Malcolm X a traitor. In February 1965, as Malcolm X was speaking to a crowd of 400 in Harlem, he was gunned down by three assassins, two of whom were Black Muslims.

Author Online

For more on the authors, visit the **Literature Center at ClassZone.com.**

● LITERARY ANALYSIS: HISTORICAL CONTEXT

When you look at a literary work in its **historical context,** you consider how events of the author's time influenced the creation of the text. Martin Luther King Jr. and Malcolm X were political leaders responding to unfolding events. Whereas the meaning of phrases like "the present crisis in race relations" would have been clear to audiences of that time, today's readers may need additional information to fully appreciate the authors' points. Before you read each selection, study the background information provided. Then, as you read each work, consider how the author's views were influenced by events of his time.

● READING SKILL: COMPARE AND CONTRAST AUTHORS' BELIEFS

King and Malcolm X had very different **beliefs** about how to confront racism. As you read each work, note how the author explains his beliefs. Use the authors' direct statements and your own inferences to determine their beliefs about

- the most effective response to injustice
- what justifies the actions they recommend
- winning the support of whites

Use a chart like the one shown to organize your notes.

Issues	King	Malcolm X
response to injustice		
justification of actions		
support from whites		

▲ VOCABULARY IN CONTEXT

King and Malcolm X use the boldfaced words to express their opposing views. Restate each phrase, using a different word or words for the boldfaced term.

1. need to **repudiate** those who oppress us
2. by not speaking out, **tacitly** accepting bad situations
3. cannot **succumb** to defeatist attitudes
4. must take **militant** stands against repression
5. refuse to accept **glib** promises that really mean nothing
6. realize that prejudice is applied **indiscriminately**
7. success through a **synthesis** of ideas and approaches
8. rioting and **anarchy** in the streets

How do we fight INJUSTICE?

KEY IDEA Most people would agree that it's important to stand up for your rights if you're being treated unfairly. However, there are many different opinions about the best way to fight back against **injustice.** In this lesson, Martin Luther King Jr. and Malcolm X argue two very different perspectives on this issue.

PRESENT What considerations do you think are important when choosing how to respond to injustice? Working in a small group, make a list of relevant concerns, such as obeying the law or achieving quick results. Then, rank them in order of importance. Share your opinions with the class.

STRIDE TOWARD FREEDOM

Martin Luther King Jr.

BACKGROUND In the 1950s, the civil rights movement focused its efforts on overturning the so-called Jim Crow laws, the segregation laws that kept African Americans from equal participation in public life. In 1954, the Supreme Court issued its decision in the landmark case *Brown v. Board of Education.* In this decision, the court declared that "separate but equal" education, a central provision of segregationist policy, was inherently discriminatory. Buoyed by this win, civil rights activists began to challenge Jim Crow through other forms of peaceful protest, such as the year-long mass boycott of segregated buses in Montgomery, Alabama, beginning in 1955. In *Stride Toward Freedom,* published in 1958, a confident and optimistic King describes the philosophy behind the successful boycott.

ANALYZE VISUALS
What does this photo reveal about the risks of nonviolent protest?

Oppressed people deal with their oppression in three characteristic ways. One way is acquiescence: the oppressed resign themselves to their doom. They **tacitly** adjust themselves to oppression, and thereby become conditioned to it. In every movement toward freedom some of the oppressed prefer to remain oppressed. Almost 2,800 years ago Moses set out to lead the children of Israel from the slavery of Egypt to the freedom of the promised land.[1] He soon discovered that slaves do not always welcome their deliverers. They become accustomed to being slaves. They would rather bear those ills they have, as Shakespeare pointed out, than flee to others that they know not of.[2] They prefer the "fleshpots of Egypt"[3]
10 to the ordeals of emancipation. **A**

tacitly (tăs'ĭt-lē) *adj.* silently

A AUTHOR'S BELIEFS
Consider King's **allusions** in lines 5–10. What do these allusions reveal about King's beliefs and the principles he uses to justify his actions?

---

1. **promised land:** the land of Canaan, promised by God in the Bible (Genesis 12:1–3, 7) to Abraham's descendants.

2. **bear those ills . . . know not of:** an allusion to a line in Act 3, Scene 1, of *Hamlet* by William Shakespeare.

3. **prefer the "fleshpots of Egypt":** an allusion to a line in the book of Exodus in the Bible. As Moses was leading the Israelites out of Egypt, some of them grumbled and wished they had stayed there.

Civil rights protestors being sprayed with high-pressure hoses

There is such a thing as the freedom of exhaustion. Some people are so worn down by the yoke of oppression that they give up. A few years ago in the slum areas of Atlanta, a Negro guitarist used to sing almost daily: "Been down so long that down don't bother me." This is the type of negative freedom and resignation that often engulfs the life of the oppressed.

But this is not the way out. To accept passively an unjust system is to cooperate with that system; thereby the oppressed become as evil as the oppressor. Noncooperation with evil is as much a moral obligation as is cooperation with good. The oppressed must never allow the conscience of the oppressor to slumber.
20 Religion reminds every man that he is his brother's keeper.[4] To accept injustice or segregation passively is to say to the oppressor that his actions are morally right. It is a way of allowing his conscience to fall asleep. At this moment the oppressed fails to be his brother's keeper. So acquiescence—while often the easier way—is not the moral way. It is the way of the coward. The Negro cannot win the respect of his oppressor by acquiescing; he merely increases the oppressor's arrogance and contempt. Acquiescence is interpreted as proof of the Negro's inferiority. The Negro cannot win the respect of the white people of the South or the peoples of the world if he is willing to sell the future of his children for his personal and immediate comfort and safety. **B**

A second way that oppressed people sometimes deal with oppression is to
30 resort to physical violence and corroding hatred. Violence often brings about momentary results. Nations have frequently won their independence in battle. But in spite of temporary victories, violence never brings permanent peace. It solves no social problem; it merely creates new and more complicated ones.

Violence as a way of achieving racial justice is both impractical and immoral. It is impractical because it is a descending spiral ending in destruction for all. The old law of an eye for an eye[5] leaves everybody blind. It is immoral because it seeks to humiliate the opponent rather than win his understanding; it seeks to annihilate rather than to convert. Violence is immoral because it thrives on hatred rather than love. It destroys community and makes brotherhood impossible. It
40 leaves society in monologue rather than dialogue. Violence ends by defeating itself. It creates bitterness in the survivors and brutality in the destroyers. A voice echoes through time saying to every potential Peter, "Put up your sword."[6] History is cluttered with the wreckage of nations that failed to follow this command. **C**

If the American Negro and other victims of oppression **succumb** to the temptation of using violence in the struggle for freedom, future generations will be the recipients of a desolate night of bitterness, and our chief legacy to them will be an endless reign of meaningless chaos. Violence is not the way.

B HISTORICAL CONTEXT
In lines 19–28, King states his position on how the oppressed should respond to oppression. What words and phrases reveal the specific historical example that has shaped his thinking?

C AUTHOR'S BELIEFS
Reread King's criticisms of violence in lines 34–43. In light of these criticisms, what does King believe an effective response to injustice should achieve?

succumb (sə-kŭm') v. to give in, especially to overpowering force or strength

---

4. **his brother's keeper:** In the book of Genesis, after Cain killed his brother Abel, he denied knowing Abel's whereabouts by asking, "Am I my brother's keeper?" In general, the saying refers to a reluctance to accept responsibility for others.

5. **an eye for an eye:** an allusion to Exodus 21:23–25: "You shall give life for life, eye for eye...."

6. **Peter ... sword":** When Jesus' disciple Peter drew his sword to try to protect Jesus, Jesus condemned his use of violence.

The third way open to oppressed people in their quest for freedom is the way of nonviolent resistance. Like the **synthesis** in Hegelian philosophy,[7] the
50 principle of nonviolent resistance seeks to reconcile the truths of two opposites—acquiescence and violence—while avoiding the extremes and immoralities of both. The nonviolent resister agrees with the person who acquiesces that one should not be physically aggressive toward his opponent but he balances the equation by agreeing with the person of violence that evil must be resisted. He avoids the nonresistance of the former and the violent resistance of the latter. With nonviolent resistance, no individual or group need submit to any wrong, nor need anyone resort to violence in order to right a wrong.

It seems to me that this is the method that must guide the actions of the Negro in the present crisis in race relations. Through nonviolent resistance the Negro will
60 be able to rise to the noble height of opposing the unjust system while loving the perpetrators of the system. The Negro must work passionately and unrelentingly for full stature as a citizen, but he must not use inferior methods to gain it. He must never come to terms with falsehood, malice, hate, or destruction.

Nonviolent resistance makes it possible for the Negro to remain in the South and struggle for his rights. The Negro's problem will not be solved by running away. He cannot listen to the **glib** suggestion of those who would urge him to migrate en masse to other sections of the country. By grasping his great opportunity in the South he can make a lasting contribution to the moral strength of the nation and set a sublime example of courage for generations yet unborn. **D**
70 By nonviolent resistance, the Negro can also enlist all men of good will in his struggle for equality. The problem is not a purely racial one, with Negroes set against whites. In the end, it is not a struggle between people at all, but a tension between justice and injustice. Nonviolent resistance is not aimed against oppressors but against oppression. Under its banner consciences, not racial groups, are enlisted. **E**

If the Negro is to achieve the goal of integration, he must organize himself into a **militant** and nonviolent mass movement. All three elements are indispensable. The movement for equality and justice can only be a success if it has both a mass and militant character; the barriers to be overcome require both. Nonviolence is
80 an imperative in order to bring about ultimate community.

A mass movement of a militant quality that is not at the same time committed to nonviolence tends to generate conflict, which in turn breeds anarchy. The support of the participants and the sympathy of the uncommitted are both inhibited by the threat that bloodshed will engulf the community. This reaction in turn encourages the opposition to threaten and resort to force. When, however, the mass movement **repudiates** violence while moving resolutely toward its goal, its opponents are revealed as the instigators and practitioners of violence if it occurs. Then public support is magnetically attracted to the advocates of nonviolence, while those who employ violence are literally disarmed by
90 overwhelming sentiment against their stand. ❧

---

7. **Hegelian** (hā-gā′lē-ən) **philosophy:** the philosophy of Georg Hegel (1770–1831), which proposed that each situation has an opposite and that both extremes will eventually be reconciled.

synthesis (sĭn′thĭ-sĭs) *n.* the union of parts or elements into a whole

glib (glĭb) *adj.* showing little thought, preparation, or concern

D HISTORICAL CONTEXT
Reread lines 65–69. What is the "great opportunity in the South" that King refers to?

E AUTHOR'S BELIEFS
Reread lines 70–75. What assumptions does King make about the value of gaining white support?

militant (mĭl′ĭ-tənt) *adj.* aggressively active, especially for a cause

repudiate (rĭ-pyōō′dē-āt′) *v.* to reject or renounce

NECESSARY *to* PROTECT OURSELVES

Interview with Malcolm X by Les Crane

BACKGROUND Malcolm X gave the following TV interview in 1964, at a time when violence against civil rights workers had escalated. Shocking images of protestors being beaten, clubbed, and tear-gassed had become staples of daily news coverage. Across the South, white supremacists tried to squelch the growing movement with murder, rifle attacks, bombings, and arson, crimes that frequently went unpunished. As attacks increased, many African Americans grew impatient with King's nonviolent tactics, expressing anger that chilled white listeners.

Events came to a head in 1964, with the Freedom Summer in Mississippi. Thousands of idealistic college students joined local civil rights activists in a massive voter registration drive, and violence exploded. Three young civil rights workers were murdered by local Klansmen with the help of the police. Despite increased FBI presence in the state, by summer's end 4 workers were dead, 80 had been beaten, and scores of black churches and businesses had been torched or bombed.

ANALYZE VISUALS
Based on this photo, what impressions do you have of Malcom X as a leader?

Crane: You've been a critic of some of the Negro leadership in this country—Martin Luther King, Roy Wilkins, Abernathy,[1] and others—have you changed in your feelings toward them of late? **F**

Malcolm X: I think all of us should be critics of each other. Whenever you can't stand criticism you can never grow. I don't think that it serves any purpose for the leaders of our people to waste their time fighting each other needlessly. I think that we accomplish more when we sit down in private and iron out

F HISTORICAL CONTEXT
What details in the interviewer's question help you identify the point in history when this interview occurred?

---

1. **Roy Wilkins, Abernathy:** Roy Wilkins (1901–1981) was executive secretary of the National Association for the Advancement of Colored People (NAACP) from 1955 to 1977. Ralph Abernathy (1926–1990) helped Martin Luther King Jr. found the Southern Christian Leadership Conference to combat racism.

Malcolm X at a Black Muslim rally

Nation of Islam members at a community event in Harlem

whatever differences that may exist and try and then do something constructive for the benefit of our people. But on the other hand, I don't think that we should
10 be above criticism. I don't think that anyone should be above criticism.

Crane: Violence or the threat of violence has always surrounded you. Speeches that you've made have been interpreted as being threats. You have made statements reported in the press about how the Negroes should go out and arm themselves, form militias of their own. I read a thing once, a statement I believe you made that every Negro should belong to the National Rifle Association—

Malcolm X: No, I said this: That in areas of this country where the government has proven its—either its inability or its unwillingness to protect the lives and property of our people, then it's only fair to expect us to do whatever is necessary to protect ourselves. And in situations like Mississippi, places like Mississippi where the **G**
20 government actually has proven its inability to protect us—and it has been proven that ofttimes the police officers and sheriffs themselves are involved in the murder that takes place against our people—then I feel, and I say that anywhere, that our people should start doing what is necessary to protect ourselves. This doesn't mean

G AUTHOR'S BELIEFS
Reread lines 16–19. What principles does Malcolm X invoke to justify his position? How do his justifications differ from King's?

that we should buy rifles and go out and initiate attacks **indiscriminately** against whites. But it does mean that we should get whatever is necessary to protect ourselves in a country or in an area where the governmental ability to protect us has broken down—

Crane: Therefore you do not agree with Dr. King's Gandhian philosophy[2]—

30 **Malcolm X:** My belief in brotherhood would never restrain me in any way from protecting myself in a society from a people whose disrespect for brotherhood makes them feel inclined to put my neck on a tree at the end of a rope.[3] [*Applause*] **H**

Crane: Well, it sounds as though you could be preaching a sort of an **anarchy**—

Malcolm X: No, no. I respect government and respect law. But does the government and the law respect us? If the FBI, which is what people depend upon on a national scale to protect the morale and the property and the lives of the people, can't do so when the property and lives of Negroes and whites who try and help Negroes are concerned, then I think that it's only fair to expect elements to do whatever is necessary to protect themselves. **I**

And this is no departure from normal procedure. Because right here in New 40 York City you have vigilante committees[4] that have been set up by groups who see where their neighborhood community is endangered and the law can't do anything about it. So—and even their lives aren't at stake. So—but the fear, Les, seems to come into existence only when someone says Negroes should form vigilante committees to protect their lives and their property.

I'm not advocating the breaking of any laws. But I say that our people will never be respected as human beings until we react as other normal, intelligent human beings do. And this country came into existence by people who were tired of tyranny and oppression and exploitation and the brutality that was being inflicted upon them by powers higher than they, and I think that it is only fair 50 to expect us, sooner or later, to do likewise. ∾

indiscriminately
(ĭn′dĭ-skrĭm′ə-nĭt-lē) *adv.*
randomly

H AUTHOR'S BELIEFS
Reread lines 29–31. On the basis of this comment, how important is winning white support to Malcolm X? Explain.

anarchy (ăn′ər-kē) *n.*
an absence of political authority

I HISTORICAL CONTEXT
Reread lines 34–38. To what events is Malcolm X alluding? Review the background information and the footnotes for details.

---

2. **Gandhian** (gän′dē-ən) **philosophy:** Mohandas Gandhi (1869–1948) was an Indian nationalist and spiritual leader. His use of nonviolent civil disobedience forced the British to grant India its independence in 1947.

3. **put my neck ... rope:** an allusion to lynching, the practice of putting someone to death without due process of law. Many African Americans were lynched, usually by hanging.

4. **vigilante** (vĭj′ə-lăn′tē) **committees:** volunteer citizen groups that unlawfully assume powers such as pursuing and punishing suspected criminals or offenders.

Comprehension

1. **Recall** What three ways of dealing with oppression does Martin Luther King identify?

2. **Clarify** In King's view, what three qualities must a movement have in order to achieve the goal of integration?

3. **Summarize** How does Malcolm X justify his criticisms of other civil rights leaders?

Literary Analysis

4. **Identify Allusion** Reread lines 47–50 of "Necessary to Protect Ourselves." Identify the historical event that Malcolm X is alluding to. What point does he make by invoking this event?

5. **Compare and Contrast Authors' Beliefs** Review the chart you created as you read both texts. Based on your reading, what are the main differences between the two leaders? What beliefs, if any, do they have in common? Be specific in your answers.

6. **Examine Historical Context** Reread the background information on pages 1162 and 1166. In what ways does each author respond directly to the events of his time? Identify at least two examples for each work.

7. **Analyze Structure** The structure of King's argument follows the formal logic of Hegelian philosophy, in which two opposing ideas are merged into a unified concept, or synthesis. To analyze this structure, complete a diagram like the one shown. In what way does the third response resolve the problems of the first two?

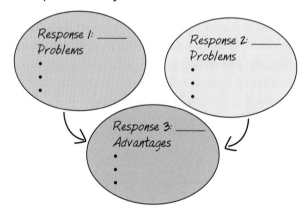

Response 1: _____
Problems
•
•
•

Response 2: _____
Problems
•
•
•

Response 3: _____
Advantages
•
•
•

8. **Make Judgments** Many commentators criticized Martin Luther King Jr. for using radical and provocative tactics. In what ways might perceptions of King's philosophy have changed after Malcolm X gained public prominence?

Literary Criticism

9. **Biographical Context** Reread the author biographies of King (page 1144) and Malcolm X (page 1160). What aspects of their personal histories may have influenced their different approaches to fighting racial **injustice**? Cite details in your answer.

Vocabulary in Context

VOCABULARY PRACTICE

Choose the letter of the phrase that defines or is related to the boldfaced word.

1. **succumb:** (a) a golfer practicing, (b) an army surrendering, (c) a teenager voting
2. **synthesis:** (a) a proposal combining several views, (b) a detailed analysis of a plan, (c) a group of protestors
3. **anarchy:** (a) an art auction, (b) an angry mob, (c) hereditary rule
4. **glib:** (a) a changing weather pattern, (b) a surprising viewpoint, (c) an insincere speaker
5. **indiscriminately:** (a) a decision based on evidence, (b) a choice made without thought, (c) unfair hiring practices
6. **militant:** (a) a pilot flying low, (b) a soldier asleep in the barracks, (c) a forceful march
7. **repudiate:** (a) retype a report, (b) vote someone out of office, (c) renew a promise
8. **tacitly:** (a) agree by nodding, (b) disagree by shouting, (c) celebrate by singing

WORD LIST

anarchy
glib
indiscriminately
militant
repudiate
succumb
synthesis
tacitly

VOCABULARY IN WRITING

Choose King or Malcolm X, and write a paragraph explaining that leader's philosophy. Use at least three vocabulary words. You could start this way.

> **EXAMPLE SENTENCE**
> Malcolm X was known for his **militant** stance on the right to use violence.

VOCABULARY STRATEGY: THE GREEK PREFIX *syn-*

The vocabulary word *synthesis* contains the Greek prefix *syn-*, which means "together" or "at the same time." This prefix, which may also be spelled *sym-* or in some cases *syl-*, is found in a number of English words, both scientific and nonscientific. To understand words with *syn-*, look for context clues and also use your knowledge of the meaning of the prefix. If these strategies do not work, consult a dictionary.

PRACTICE Choose the word from the word web that best completes each sentence. Use context clues to help you or, if necessary, check a dictionary.

1. They were able to _____ their watches and meet promptly at noon.
2. Though the halves of people's faces aren't exactly _____, they are fairly close.
3. Some animals have a _____ relationship and depend on each other for survival.
4. Groups or individuals in a _____ work together for some common interest.
5. A _____ can provide a quick overview of a story, play, or report.

VOCABULARY PRACTICE
For more practice, go to the **Vocabulary Center** at **ClassZone.com.**

Martin Luther King Jr.: He Showed Us the Way

Essay

Use with "Stride Toward Freedom" and "Necessary to Protect Ourselves," beginning on pages 1162 and 1166.

You have just read two civil rights leaders' positions on the use of force in political resistance. Now you will learn why César Chávez, a leader in the crusade for the fair treatment of migrant farm workers, advocated nonviolence to achieve his goals. As you read his argument, bear in mind that later you will be asked to support your own opinion on this weapon for social change.

Skill Focus: Analyze an Argument

Every day, political and social leaders, manufacturers and retailers, and even family and friends try to influence your beliefs and actions. You can begin to evaluate any argument by analyzing it, or breaking it down into its parts.

A well-formed argument typically contains

- a **claim,** or the writer or speaker's position on a problem or issue
- **support,** which consists of reasons and evidence that help to justify the claim
- **counterarguments,** or brief arguments that refute or answer objections to any claim that the opposition is likely to raise

A strong argument is usually based on a **general principle** or assumption that links the support to the claim. For example, someone arguing that a particular act is in violation of free speech is resting on the principle that free speech is a thing worth protecting. If you can't accept the general principle as a truth, then the entire argument falls apart.

To analyze the argument made by Chávez, as you read his speech complete a chart such as the one started here.

	Notes
Claim	Nonviolence is the "only weapon that Christians who struggle for social change can claim as their own."
General Principle	
Support	
Counterargument(s)	

MARTIN LUTHER KING JR.:

He Showed Us the Way

César Chávez

In honoring Martin Luther King Jr.'s memory we also acknowledge nonviolence as a truly powerful weapon to achieve equality and liberation—in fact, the only weapon that Christians who struggle for social change can claim as their own.

Dr. King's entire life was an example of power that nonviolence brings to bear in the real world. It is an example that inspired much of the philosophy and strategy of the farm workers' movement. This observance of Dr. King's death gives us the best possible opportunity to recall the principles with which our struggle has grown and matured. **A**

Our conviction is that human life is a very special possession given by God to man and that no one has the right to take it for any reason or for any cause, however just it
10 may be.

We are also convinced that nonviolence is more powerful than violence. Nonviolence supports you if you have a just and moral cause. Nonviolence provides the opportunity to stay on the offensive, and that is of crucial importance to win any contest.

If we resort to violence then one of two things will happen: either the violence will be escalated and there will be many injuries and perhaps deaths on both sides, or there will be total demoralization of the workers. **B**

Nonviolence has exactly the opposite effect. If, for every violent act committed against us, we respond with nonviolence, we attract people's support. We can gather the support of millions who have a conscience and would rather see a nonviolent
20 resolution to problems. We are convinced that when people are faced with a direct appeal from the poor struggling nonviolently against great odds, they will react positively. The American people and people everywhere still yearn for justice. It is to that yearning that we appeal.

A ANALYZE AN ARGUMENT
Notice that Chávez states his **claim** in his opening sentence. Now reread lines 4–7 to identify his first piece of **support** for this claim. Note this on your chart.

B ANALYZE AN ARGUMENT
Reread lines 11–16. What reasons does Chávez give to support his conviction that "nonviolence is more powerful than violence"? Note these reasons as "support" in your chart.

But if we are committed to nonviolence only as a strategy or tactic, then if it fails our only alternative is to turn to violence. So we must balance the strategy with a clear understanding of what we are doing. However important the struggle is and however much misery, poverty and exploitation exist, we know that it cannot be more important than one human life. We work on the theory that men and women who are truly concerned about people are nonviolent by nature. These people become violent when the deep concern they have for people is frustrated and when they are faced with seemingly insurmountable odds.

We advocate militant nonviolence as our means of achieving justice for our people, but we are not blind to the feelings of frustration, impatience and anger which seethe inside every farm worker. The burdens of generations of poverty and powerlessness lie heavy in the fields of America. If we fail, there are those who will see violence as the shortcut to change. **C**

It is precisely to overcome these frustrations that we have involved masses of people in their own struggle throughout the movement. Freedom is best experienced through participation and self-determination, and free men and women instinctively prefer democratic change to any other means. Thus, demonstrations and marches, strikes and boycotts are not only weapons against the growers, but our way of avoiding the senseless violence that brings no honor to any class or community. The boycott, as Gandhi taught, is the most nearly perfect instrument of nonviolent change, allowing masses of people to participate actively in a cause.

When victory comes through violence, it is a victory with strings attached. If we beat the growers at the expense of violence, victory would come at the expense of injury and perhaps death. Such a thing would have a tremendous impact on us. We would lose regard for human beings. Then the struggle would become a mechanical thing. When you lose your sense of life and justice, you lose your strength. **D**

The greater the oppression, the more leverage nonviolence holds. Violence does not work in the long run and if it is temporarily successful, it replaces one violent form of power with another just as violent. People suffer from violence. Examine history. Who gets killed in the case of violent revolution? The poor, the workers. The people of the land are the ones who give their bodies and don't really gain that much for it. We believe it is too big a price to pay for not getting anything. Those who espouse violence exploit people. To call men to arms with many promises, to ask them to give up their lives for a cause and then not produce for them afterwards, is the most vicious type of oppression. **E**

We know that most likely we are not going to do anything else the rest of our lives except build our union. For us there is nowhere else to go. Although we would like to see victory come soon, we are willing to wait. In this sense time is our ally. We learned many years ago that the rich may have money, but the poor have time.

It has been our experience that few men or women ever have the opportunity to know the true satisfaction that comes with giving one's life totally in the nonviolent struggle for justice. Martin Luther King Jr., was one of these unique servants and from him we learned many of the lessons that have guided us. For these lessons and for his sacrifice for the poor and oppressed, Dr. King's memory will be cherished in the hearts of the farm workers forever.

C ANALYZE AN ARGUMENT

In this paragraph, Chávez anticipates objection to his claim about the advantages of nonviolence. Identify these objections.

D ANALYZE AN ARGUMENT

What counterarguments does Chávez provide to refute the objections he just anticipated? Note these in your chart.

E ANALYZE AN ARGUMENT

What does Chávez say about those who espouse violence?

Comprehension

1. **Clarify** In addition to serving as weapons against growers, how do boycotts benefit the masses of people who participate in them?

Critical Analysis

2. **Examine General Principle** What is Chávez's basic assumption about social change and just people? Might someone disagree with him? Explain.

3. **Analyze Argument** Chávez acknowledges that nonviolent resistance has certain limitations. How does he answer each of the following objections?

   - People who have been oppressed may feel legitimately frustrated or impatient and turn to violence as a shortcut to change.
   - Violence does sometimes bring about victory.

Read for Information: Support an Opinion

WRITING PROMPT

What is your opinion of nonviolent resistance as a weapon of social change? State your position and support it with reasons and evidence from the three selections you have just read and, if you wish, with examples from history or your own experience.

The following steps will help you answer the prompt:

1. Carefully read the pieces by Chávez, King, and Malcolm X and determine your own opinion of nonviolent resistance. Write this opinion as a claim.

2. Gather support for your claim from the three selections, as well as from history or your own life experience.

3. Consider how an opponent might object to your claim. Insert one or more objections at the points in your essay where they would most naturally be raised. After anticipating each objection, write a counterargument to it.

4. Write a conclusion in which you restate your claim and summarize the most important elements of support.

Perspectives in the News

TV Newscast Clip / Magazine Article on *MediaSmart* DVD

Does the news SHAPE *history?*

KEY IDEA Recall the last time the news reported the death of someone who had played a pivotal role in history. Did the report provide new insights or change your opinion of the individual? Or did it reinforce your prior perceptions? In this lesson, you'll examine the way two different news forms covered a national figure and analyze the ways news reports can shape your **impressions** of that figure.

Background

Cultivating Activism As a teenager, César Chávez worked the fields of California with his family. After serving in the U.S. Navy in World War II, he returned to the fields but grew more politically active.

Inspired by the life and nonviolent teachings of Mohandas Gandhi and the activism of Martin Luther King Jr., Chávez helped found the National Farm Workers Association (NFWA) in 1962. "Nonviolence in action is a very potent force and it can't be stopped," said Chávez of the NFWA's founding principle. By staging peaceful strikes, marches, and boycotts, as well as fasting (as Gandhi had) in protest, Chávez garnered a wide swath of support for *La Causa* (the cause). Followers rallied to the call "*¡Si Se Puede!*" which, translated to English, means "Yes, we can!"

Another force contributing to Chávez's cause, as well as to the larger American civil rights movement of the 1950s and 60s, was mass media. Print and network TV news coverage of marches, boycotts, and other acts of protest helped to fuel a spirit of activism nationwide. Millions were stirred by coverage that spotlighted both extraordinary leaders like Chávez and ordinary people.

César Chávez died in 1993. In following the peaceful legacy of Gandhi and King, Chávez created one of his own.

Media Literacy: Historical Perspectives in the News

The news media uses images and words to depict the work of political figures who, in time, become history makers. Just as writers of literature present their perspectives through the use of tone and diction, journalists convey certain ideas, values, and beliefs through those elements and others that are unique to news reports. In addition, journalists can shape an audience's perceptions by reporting on the individual from a particular perspective.

News reports can appear in both electronic and print forms. To help you analyze the perspective of a news report, examine the images and statements to determine the overall purpose of the report. Then think about how the report affects your perceptions of the person depicted.

STRATEGIES FOR ANALYZING NEWS REPORTS

TV News Reports
A typical TV news report is quite brief. To convey a strong impression of the report's subject, journalists choose the visual and verbal elements carefully.

- Focus on the **footage**—the film, videotape, and photographs that are edited into a report. The footage compiled on a historical figure can an be edited to portray the individual in different ways.

- Notice what the **anchorperson** says in the **lead-in,** the introduction. The emphasis journalists put on certain words can suggest a figure's historical significance.

- Pay attention to descriptive words used in a reporter's **voice-over,** the narration that plays as images are shown. Also, listen for **sound bites,** statements excerpted from interviews or speeches that are edited into the report. Sound bites can be selected to create a certain impression of subject.

Magazine Article
The typical magazine feature article might cover a subject in more than one page, providing in-depth coverage.

- Consider how the **headline** and **subhead** frame the content of the article for a reader.

- Preview the **opening paragraph,** which often sets the tone for the article and is intended to draw in the reader.

- Make inferences about the **images.** Think about why certain photographs were chosen for an article.

- Scrutinize **quotes,** which might be made by the subject of the article or by others. Determine what the quotes reveal about the subject.

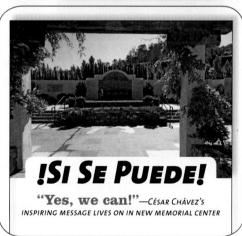

¡SI SE PUEDE!
"Yes, we can!"—*CÉSAR CHÁVEZ'S*
INSPIRING MESSAGE LIVES ON IN NEW MEMORIAL CENTER

MediaSmart DVD

- **Selection 1:** "Chávez" from the CBS Nightly News
- **Type:** Newscast clip
- **Anchor:** Dan Rather
- **Reporter:** John Blackstone
- **Running time:** 2.5 minutes
- **Selection 2:** "¡Si Se Puede!"
- **Type:** Magazine article

Viewing Guide for

News Perspectives

View the news clip and access the full text of the magazine article on the DVD. As you watch the TV news report, focus on the images that are used to tell César Chávez's story and listen for any descriptive words about Chávez's life and work. As you read the magazine article, look for the ways in which the writer describes Chávez and his legacy. To help you analyze these pieces, refer to these questions.

NOW VIEW

FIRST VIEWING: Comprehension

1. **Recall** In the TV news report, what does Chávez say he regards as his "biggest single accomplishment"?

2. **Summarize** Based on your review of the headline, subhead, and opening paragraph of the magazine article, summarize the ways Chávez has been honored since his death.

CLOSE VIEWING: Media Literacy

3. **Analyze Statements** What **descriptions** did you notice in the news anchor's **lead-in,** or introduction to the Chávez piece, or in the reporter's **voice-over** that reveal respect for the historical figure's accomplishments?

4. **Analyze Sound Bites** The clip includes a **sound bite** in which an individual states about Chávez, "His biggest legacy was to give his life for other people." Why do you think the news report includes this sound bite?

5. **Make Judgments** Briefly review the magazine article to choose a word or phrase that you think was carefully chosen to comment on the legacy of César Chávez. Describe what meaning this choice would have for viewers who had not been old enough to be aware of the leader in his lifetime.

6. **Compare Purposes** When and why do you think the TV news report was created? When and why was the magazine article published? Examine each news format and use a comparison chart to compare the purposes.

News Report	When First Reported	Purpose for Report
"Chávez"		
"¡Si Se Puede!"		

Write or Discuss

Determine Perspectives In two brief statements, describe the perspective of both the newscast clip and the magazine article. Review the reports closely, jotting down any descriptive words or phrases about César Chávez that give you a sense of him as a person and as a leader. In addition, refer to the chart you devised to compare the purposes of the news forms. Think about

- the overall tone each news report conveys
- the details each piece presents about Chávez's life and times
- the visual elements
- the use of sources who provide sound bites and quotes

Produce Your Own Media

Create a News Feature Celebrate the life of someone who has made a positive impact on your community by creating a news feature. The subject could be a friend, a family member, or anyone else you admire. The feature can be a visual piece, in the form of video, or a written piece with photographs that illustrate it in the style of a magazine.

HERE'S HOW Here are some suggestions for creating your news feature:

- Decide on your perspective for the feature. The basis for your perspective might be the subject's achievements or personal qualities.
- Research your subject: do interviews, gather facts and any visual images you may want to use. If possible, interview the people who know the subject.
- For a TV news story, write a script that plots out which visuals you will use with your voice-over narration. Allow plenty of time for actually putting your scrapbook, video, or presentation piece together.
- For a magazine article based on your research, write a first draft that covers as much of the material as you see fit. Then edit your article with an eye on where you might be able to use an image or two of the person in the layout.

Further Exploration

Analyze Words With a partner or in a small group, find two different types of media that cover the same subject or event. For example, the report could be a TV newscast and a weekly newsmagazine about a development in the U.S. space program, or a hometown newspaper and a national sports magazine reporting on steroid use in baseball, and so on. Look closely at each news source and jot down the adjectives and adverbs used to describe the event or people involved. What perspective do you think these words convey? Consider

- who created the news piece and what their opinion of the subject might be
- what audience the news piece is written for

Cite specific examples from the media sources to support your impressions.

MEDIA TOOLS

For help creating your news feature, visit the **Media Center** at **ClassZone.com.**

Tech Tip

You can use digital pictures with a presentation software program and provide the voice-over in real time.

from Coming of Age in Mississippi

Autobiography by Anne Moody

Anne Moody
born 1940

Anne Moody was one of many dedicated college students who were on the frontlines in the battle for civil rights. In her award-winning autobiography, she details the dangers she and other young activists faced as they challenged segregation laws across the South. Her unflinching descriptions of taunts, beatings, and intimidation reveal the violent realities of nonviolent protest. They also call to mind the words of Martin Luther King Jr., who commended these brave young men and women for "their sublime courage, their willingness to suffer, and their amazing discipline in the midst of great provocation."

Climate of Fear Moody was the oldest of nine children born to desperately poor African-American farmers in rural Mississippi. When she was just nine years old, Moody began working after school as a maid to help her family pay for food and clothing. Periodic acts of racist violence effectively intimidated the black community in Moody's hometown. When local white supremacists set fire to her neighbor's shack, killing the family inside, her mother advised her, "Just act like you don't know nothing." But Moody was part of a new generation that would no longer be silenced.

Dedicated Activist Moody first attended Natchez Junior College and later transferred to Tougaloo College, graduating in 1964. As a college student, she worked with major civil rights organizations such as the Congress for Racial Equality (CORE) and the National Association for the Advancement of Colored People (NAACP). Later, she became civil rights coordinator at Cornell University. Throughout her time in the movement, Moody faced constant threats to her life and worked to the point of exhaustion to integrate public facilities, extend voting rights, and promote literacy. Commenting on King's famous speech "I Have a Dream," she once quipped, "We never have time to sleep, much less dream." Often frustrated and discouraged at the slow pace of social change, Moody came to see the civil rights struggle as part of a larger fight for universal human rights. As she explained, "It's the fight of every ethnic and racial minority, every suppressed and exploited person, every one of the millions who daily suffer one or another of the indignities of the powerless and voiceless masses." Her autobiography is a moving testament to the dedication and courage that inspired hundreds of thousands of people to take action for social justice.

Negro Sitdowns Stir Fear Of Wider Unrest in South

LITERARY ANALYSIS: EYEWITNESS ACCOUNT

Anne Moody wrote this **eyewitness account** to document the violence she faced as a civil rights worker in Mississippi. Like a camera, Moody records events from her vantage point on the scene, using precise, factual descriptions to capture what she sees.

At exactly 11 A.M., Pearlena, Memphis, and I entered Woolworth's from the rear entrance.

Moody is not a journalist. The events she describes are part of her personal story. Her objective descriptions are interwoven with subjective details about her thoughts, feelings, and private life.

But something happened to me as I got more and more involved in the Movement. It no longer seemed important to prove anything.

As you read Moody's account, think about how her personal experiences influence the way she perceives events.

READING STRATEGY: READING A PRIMARY SOURCE

Because Anne Moody had firsthand knowledge of the events she describes, her account is considered a **primary source.** From her recollections, you can learn practical details about the workings of the civil rights movement that you won't find in philosophical works on nonviolence. Note what Moody's account reveals about

- individuals and groups involved in the movement
- types of activities movement workers organized
- risks and obstacles faced by activists

As you read, use a chart like the one shown to take notes.

Individuals and Groups	Types of Activities	Risks and Obstacles

Explore the Key Idea

Who makes HISTORY?

KEY IDEA Most people assume that **history** is made by great leaders, the ones who get their pictures in textbooks. But those leaders don't make history by themselves. Their achievements depend on the combined efforts of people like your parents, your teachers, and you.

DISCUSS Working in a small group, think of three or four historical events. In what ways did these events depend on the efforts of ordinary people? Make a list for each event.

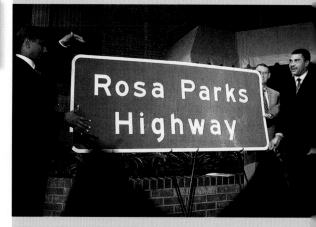

Coming of Age in Mississippi

ANNE MOODY

BACKGROUND On February 1, 1960, four African-American college freshmen seated themselves at a whites-only lunch counter in Greensboro, North Carolina, refusing to leave until they were served. Within a week, 300 people had joined the sit-in; within two months, sit-ins were being held in 54 cities across the South, most of them organized by college and high school students. By August 1961, more than 70,000 protesters, black and white, had participated in sit-ins. Students, impatient with the slow pace of change, had decided to confront segregation head-on. As you'll read in Anne Moody's account, those confrontations made the ugliness of racism impossible to ignore. Be warned that in relating the confrontations, Moody repeats certain offensive racial epithets.

I had counted on graduating in the spring of 1963, but as it turned out, I couldn't because some of my credits still had to be cleared with Natchez College. A year before, this would have seemed like a terrible disaster, but now I hardly even felt disappointed. I had a good excuse to stay on campus for the summer and work with the Movement, and this was what I really wanted to do. I couldn't go home again anyway, and I couldn't go to New Orleans—I didn't have money enough for bus fare.

During my senior year at Tougaloo,[1] my family hadn't sent me one penny. I had only the small amount of money I had earned at Maple Hill.[2] I couldn't
10 afford to eat at school or live in the dorms, so I had gotten permission to move off campus. I had to prove that I could finish school, even if I had to go hungry every

ANALYZE VISUALS
What details in the photo help convey the tension of the scene at the protest?

Left to right: John Salter, Joan Trumpauer, and Anne Moody, seated at the Woolworth's lunch counter

---

1. **Tougaloo:** Tougaloo College, a traditionally African-American college on the northern edge of Jackson, Mississippi.
2. **Maple Hill:** a restaurant in New Orleans where Moody had worked in the summer.

day. I knew Raymond and Miss Pearl[3] were just waiting to see me drop out. But something happened to me as I got more and more involved in the Movement. It no longer seemed important to prove anything. I had found something outside myself that gave meaning to my life. **Ⓐ**

I had become very friendly with my social science professor, John Salter, who was in charge of NAACP[4] activities on campus. All during the year, while the NAACP conducted a boycott of the downtown stores in Jackson, I had been one of Salter's most faithful canvassers[5] and church speakers. During the last week
20 of school, he told me that sit-in demonstrations were about to start in Jackson and that he wanted me to be the spokesman for a team that would sit-in at Woolworth's lunch counter. The two other demonstrators would be classmates of mine, Memphis and Pearlena. Pearlena was a dedicated NAACP worker, but Memphis had not been very involved in the Movement on campus. It seemed that the organization had had a rough time finding students who were in a position to go to jail. I had nothing to lose one way or the other. Around ten o'clock the morning of the demonstrations, NAACP headquarters alerted the news services. As a result, the police department was also informed, but neither the policemen nor the newsmen knew exactly where or when the demonstrations would start.
30 They stationed themselves along Capitol Street and waited.

To divert attention from the sit-in at Woolworth's, the picketing started at J. C. Penney's a good fifteen minutes before. The pickets were allowed to walk up and down in front of the store three or four times before they were arrested. At exactly 11 A.M., Pearlena, Memphis, and I entered Woolworth's from the rear entrance. We separated as soon as we stepped into the store, and made small purchases from various counters. Pearlena had given Memphis her watch. He was to let us know when it was 11:14. At 11:14 we were to join him near the lunch counter and at exactly 11:15 we were to take seats at it. **Ⓑ**

Seconds before 11:15 we were occupying three seats at the previously segregated
40 Woolworth's lunch counter. In the beginning the waitresses seemed to ignore us, as if they really didn't know what was going on. Our waitress walked past us a couple of times before she noticed we had started to write our own orders down and realized we wanted service. She asked us what we wanted. We began to read to her from our order slips. She told us that we would be served at the back counter, which was for Negroes.

"We would like to be served here," I said.

The waitress started to repeat what she had said, then stopped in the middle of the sentence. She turned the lights out behind the counter, and she and the other waitresses almost ran to the back of the store, deserting all their white customers.
50 I guess they thought that violence would start immediately after the whites at the counter realized what was going on. There were five or six other people at the counter. A couple of them just got up and walked away. A girl sitting next to me

Ⓐ EYEWITNESS ACCOUNT
Reread lines 1–15. In what ways do Moody's personal challenges motivate her to get involved in the civil rights movement?

Ⓑ PRIMARY SOURCE
Reread lines 26–38. Summarize the timeline of the sit-in. Why might this protest have been so carefully planned?

---

3. **Raymond and Miss Pearl:** Moody's stepfather and step-grandmother.

4. **NAACP:** National Association for the Advancement of Colored People, an organization that works to end discrimination against African Americans and other minorities.

5. **canvassers:** people who go from door to door to get support for a cause or gather opinions on an issue.

finished her banana split before leaving. A middle-aged white woman who had not yet been served rose from her seat and came over to us. "I'd like to stay here with you," she said, "but my husband is waiting."

The newsmen came in just as she was leaving. They must have discovered what was going on shortly after some of the people began to leave the store. One of the newsmen ran behind the woman who spoke to us and asked her to identify herself. She refused to give her name, but said she was a native of Vicksburg[6] and 60 a former resident of California. When asked why she had said what she had said to us, she replied, "I am in sympathy with the Negro movement." By this time a crowd of cameramen and reporters had gathered around us taking pictures and asking questions, such as Where were we from? Why did we sit-in? What organization sponsored it? Were we students? From what school? How were we classified?

I told them that we were all students at Tougaloo College, that we were represented by no particular organization, and that we planned to stay there even after the store closed. "All we want is service," was my reply to one of them. After they had finished probing for about twenty minutes, they were almost ready 70 to leave.

At noon, students from a nearby white high school started pouring in to Woolworth's. When they first saw us they were sort of surprised. They didn't know how to react. A few started to heckle and the newsmen became interested again. Then the white students started chanting all kinds of anti-Negro slogans. We were called a little bit of everything. The rest of the seats except the three we were occupying had been roped off to prevent others from sitting down. A couple of the boys took one end of the rope and made it into a hangman's noose. Several attempts were made to put it around our necks. The crowds grew as more students and adults came in for lunch.

80 We kept our eyes straight forward and did not look at the crowd except for occasional glances to see what was going on. All of a sudden I saw a face I remembered—the drunkard from the bus station sit-in. My eyes lingered on him just long enough for us to recognize each other. Today he was drunk too, so I don't think he remembered where he had seen me before. He took out a knife, opened it, put it in his pocket, and then began to pace the floor. At this point, I told Memphis and Pearlena what was going on. Memphis suggested that we pray. We bowed our heads, and all hell broke loose. A man rushed forward, threw Memphis from his seat, and slapped my face. Then another man who worked in the store threw me against an adjoining counter.

90 Down on my knees on the floor, I saw Memphis lying near the lunch counter with blood running out of the corners of his mouth. As he tried to protect his face, the man who'd thrown him down kept kicking him against the head. If he had worn hard-soled shoes instead of sneakers, the first kick probably would have

---

6. **Vicksburg:** a city in Mississippi, west of Jackson.

killed Memphis. Finally a man dressed in plain clothes identified himself as a police officer and arrested Memphis and his attacker. **C**

Pearlena had been thrown to the floor. She and I got back on our stools after Memphis was arrested. There were some white Tougaloo teachers in the crowd. They asked Pearlena and me if we wanted to leave. They said that things were getting too rough. We didn't know what to do. While we were trying to make up our minds, we were joined by Joan Trumpauer.[7] Now there were three of us and we were integrated. The crowd began to chant, "Communists, Communists, Communists." Some old man in the crowd ordered the students to take us off the stools.

"Which one should I get first?" a big husky boy said.

"That white nigger," the old man said.

The boy lifted Joan from the counter by her waist and carried her out of the store. Simultaneously, I was snatched from my stool by two high school students. I was dragged about thirty feet toward the door by my hair when someone made them turn me loose. As I was getting up off the floor, I saw Joan coming back inside. We started back to the center of the counter to join Pearlena. Lois Chaffee, a white Tougaloo faculty member, was now sitting next to her. So Joan and I just climbed across the rope at the front end of the counter and sat down. There were now four of us, two whites and two Negroes, all women. The mob started smearing us with ketchup, mustard, sugar, pies, and everything on the counter. Soon Joan and I were joined by John Salter, but the moment he sat down he was hit on the jaw with what appeared to be brass knuckles. Blood gushed from his face and someone threw salt into the open wound. Ed King, Tougaloo's chaplain, rushed to him. **D**

At the other end of the counter, Lois and Pearlena were joined by George Raymond, a CORE[8] field worker and a student from Jackson State College. Then a Negro high school boy sat down next to me. The mob took spray paint from the counter and sprayed it on the new demonstrators. The high school student had on a white shirt; the word "nigger" was written on his back with red spray paint.

We sat there for three hours taking a beating when the manager decided to close the store because the mob had begun to go wild with stuff from other counters. He begged and begged everyone to leave. But even after fifteen minutes of begging, no one budged. They would not leave until we did. Then Dr. Beittel, the president of Tougaloo College, came running in. He said he had just heard what was happening.

About ninety policemen were standing outside the store; they had been watching the whole thing through the windows, but had not come in to stop the mob or do anything. President Beittel went outside and asked Captain Ray to come and escort us out. The captain refused, stating the manager had to invite him in before he could enter the premises, so Dr. Beittel himself brought us out.

---

7. **Joan Trumpauer:** a white classmate of Moody's from Tougaloo College, who had been active in voter registration.

8. **CORE:** Congress of Racial Equality, a civil rights organization that coordinated marches and demonstrations in the 1960s.

C EYEWITNESS ACCOUNT
Reread lines 90–95. Identify details that convey the danger of the protesters' situation. What is surprising about Moody's **tone** in this passage?

D GRAMMAR AND STYLE
Reread lines 113–117. Note how Moody uses a serious tone and strong **verbs** and **verbals** like *smearing* and *gushed* to recreate the mood of the violent scene.

Anne Moody and other protesters leaving the sit-in

He had told the police that they had better protect us after we were outside the store. When we got outside, the policemen formed a single line that blocked the mob from us. However, they were allowed to throw at us everything they had collected. Within ten minutes, we were picked up by Reverend King in his station wagon and taken to the NAACP headquarters on Lynch Street.

140   After the sit-in, all I could think of was how sick Mississippi whites were. They believed so much in the segregated Southern way of life, they would kill to preserve it. I sat there in the NAACP office and thought of how many times they had killed when this way of life was threatened. I knew that the killing had just begun. "Many more will die before it is over with," I thought. Before the sit-in, I had always hated the whites in Mississippi. Now I knew it was impossible for me to hate sickness. The whites had a disease, an incurable disease in its final stage. What were our chances against such a disease? I thought of the students, the young Negroes who had just begun to protest, as young interns. When these young interns got older, I thought, they would be the best doctors in the world

150 for social problems. **E**

Before we were taken back to campus, I wanted to get my hair washed. It was stiff with dried mustard, ketchup and sugar. I stopped in at a beauty shop across the street from the NAACP office. I didn't have on any shoes because I had lost

E EYEWITNESS ACCOUNT
Reread lines 140–150. In what ways have Moody's attitudes and beliefs changed due to her experience at the sit-in?

them when I was dragged across the floor at Woolworth's. My stockings were sticking to my legs from the mustard that had dried on them. The hairdresser took one look at me and said, "My land, you were in the sit-in, huh?"

"Yes," I answered. "Do you have time to wash my hair and style it?"

"Right away," she said, and she meant right away. There were three other ladies already waiting, but they seemed glad to let me go ahead of them. The hairdresser
160 was real nice. She even took my stockings off and washed my legs while my hair was drying.

There was a mass rally that night at the Pearl Street Church in Jackson, and the place was packed. People were standing two abreast in the aisles. Before the speakers began, all the sit-inners walked out on the stage and were introduced by Medgar Evers.[9] People stood and applauded for what seemed like thirty minutes or more. Medgar told the audience that this was just the beginning of such demonstrations. He asked them to pledge themselves to unite in a massive offensive against segregation in Jackson, and throughout the state. The rally ended with "We Shall Overcome" and sent home hundreds of determined people. It
170 seemed as though Mississippi Negroes were about to get together at last. **F**

Before I demonstrated, I had written Mama. She wrote me back a letter, begging me not to take part in the sit-in. She even sent ten dollars for bus fare to New Orleans. I didn't have one penny, so I kept the money. Mama's letter made me mad. I had to live my life as I saw fit. I had made that decision when I left home. But it hurt to have my family prove to me how scared they were. It hurt me more than anything else—I knew the whites had already started the threats and intimidations. I was the first Negro from my hometown who had openly demonstrated, worked with the NAACP, or anything. When Negroes threatened to do anything in Centreville, they were either shot like Samuel O'Quinn or run
180 out of town, like Reverend Dupree.[10]

I didn't answer Mama's letter. Even if I had written one, she wouldn't have received it before she saw the news on TV or heard it on the radio. I waited to hear from her again. And I waited to hear in the news that someone in Centreville had been murdered. If so, I knew it would be a member of my family. ❧

F PRIMARY SOURCE
Reread lines 162–170. What does this paragraph tell you about the rally? Why would rallies like the one described be important to the success of the movement?

---

9. **Medgar Evers:** civil rights leader and organizer for the NAACP in Mississippi from 1954 until 1963, when he was killed by a sniper.

10. **Centreville . . . Samuel O'Quinn . . . Reverend Dupree:** In Centreville, the Mississippi town where Moody grew up, Samuel O'Quinn had been suspected of being associated with the NAACP. The Reverend Dupree had mentioned the NAACP in a sermon he preached.

Revolutionary Dreams

Nikki Giovanni

Love Letter I (1971), Charles Wilbert White. Color lithograph, 30" x 22½". Gift of June Wayne. Image © 2007 Board of Trustees, National Gallery of Art, Washington, D.C. 1974.99.158.(B-27792)/PR. © 1971 The Charles White Archives.

i used to dream militant
dreams of taking
over america to show
these white folks how it should be
5 done
i used to dream radical dreams
of blowing everyone away with my perceptive powers
of correct analysis
i even used to think i'd be the one
10 to stop the riot and negotiate the peace
then i awoke and dug
that if i dreamed natural
dreams of being a natural
woman doing what a woman
15 does when she's natural
i would have a revolution

Comprehension

1. **Recall** What kinds of abuses were directed at the protesters during the sit-in?

2. **Recall** What role did the police play in the sit-in?

3. **Clarify** Why didn't the protesters fight back?

Literary Analysis

4. **Make Inferences** After the sit-in, why was Anne Moody worried that a member of her family would be killed?

5. **Draw Conclusions from a Primary Source** Review the chart you created as you read. Identify three ways ordinary people contributed to the success of civil rights protest. Could the movement have succeeded without community support? Why or why not?

6. **Synthesize Details** In what ways were students critical to the success of the movement? Use details from the background and the selection in your answer.

7. **Analyze Author's Perspective** Consider what you learn about Moody's character and private life from the account. What factors contributed to her decision to take action and become part of **history?** Be specific in your answers.

8. **Evaluate an Eyewitness Account** In your opinion, is Moody a credible reporter of events? In your answer, consider each of the following aspects of her account:

   - presentation of facts (lines 31–38)
   - tone (lines 106–118)
   - opinions expressed (lines 140–147)
   - character traits (lines 171–180)

9. **Compare Texts** Reread the poem on page 1189. In what ways are Nikki Giovanni's thoughts about social change similar to Moody's? Cite details in your answer.

Literary Criticism

10. **Different Perspectives** Anne Moody and Martin Luther King Jr. provide different views of the struggle for civil rights: that of a rank-and-file activist and that of a movement leader. In what ways do their accounts reflect their different roles within the movement? Support your answer with details.

Reading-Writing Connection

WRITE AN EYEWITNESS REPORT An effective eyewitness report puts the reader in the midst of the action while providing the context needed to understand the events described. Write a **three-to-five-paragraph eyewitness report** on an event of your choosing, such as a sporting event or a community gathering. Use precise details and a clear, logical structure to make the event accessible to your audience.

A successful report will . . .

• answer the five *W*'s: *who, what, when, where,* and *why*

• use precise language and sensory images

• relate the event in a logical order

GRAMMAR AND STYLE

CREATE MOOD Review the **Grammar and Style** note on page 1186. Mood is the feeling that a writer creates for the reader through such elements as **word choice, imagery,** and **tone.** Moody's account has a tense, serious mood that is appropriate to the scene she describes. She uses plain but powerful language, avoiding sensationalism to let the mob's actions speak for themselves.

> *Simultaneously, I was snatched from my stool by two high school students. I was dragged about thirty feet toward the door by my hair when someone made them turn me loose.* (lines 107–109)

The author's choice of strong **verbs** like *snatched* and *dragged* allows her to convey the violence of the scene while maintaining a calm, controlled tone. Note that Moody uses straightforward **declarative sentences** to describe her experiences, without adding details about her own responses to what occurs.

PRACTICE The following paragraph is written to create a tense, dramatic mood. Rewrite the paragraph, adjusting word choice, imagery, and tone to create a lighter, more comic mood. A sample beginning is provided for you.

> We all sat quietly, waiting for news. My palms began to sweat and I had trouble swallowing. I looked over at my friend, seated two rows away, but I couldn't catch her eye. She looked like she was about to cry. I was hoping the news wouldn't be as bad as we feared, but everyone else seemed to have accepted the worst. Then, the door opened and he walked in, scanning the room with a frown. I couldn't believe it. All the rumors were true: we'd been assigned the toughest teacher in the entire school for homeroom. It was going to be a long, long year.

EXAMPLE

"Hi, everybody!" our new teacher said, holding a bunch of balloons. "Welcome to homeroom!"

WRITING TOOLS
For prewriting, revision, and editing tools, visit the **Writing Center** at ClassZone.com.

My Dungeon Shook: Letter to My Nephew

Open Letter by James Baldwin

Harlem in 1937

James Baldwin

1924–1987

In the turbulent 1960s, James Baldwin became one of the country's most sought-after commentators on racial politics. But Baldwin never considered himself a spokesperson. Rather, he saw his role as bearing witness "to whence I came, where I am . . . to what I've seen and the possibilities that I think I see." This autobiographical vantage point is the hallmark of Baldwin's greatest works, from his moving first novel, *Go Tell It on the Mountain* (1953), to the provocative essays collected in *Notes of a Native Son* (1955), *Nobody Knows My Name* (1961), and *The Fire Next Time* (1963).

Early Struggles Born and raised in Harlem, Baldwin never knew his biological father and had a strained relationship with his stepfather, a domineering, bitter man who preached at a storefront evangelical church on weekends. A star pupil and voracious reader, the young James also helped his overworked mother raise his eight brothers and sisters. After a dramatic religious conversion at age 14, he gained local acclaim as a "boy-preacher." Then, at 18, a crisis of faith drove Baldwin to break with the church and leave home.

Emerging Artist Working to establish his literary career, Baldwin supported himself by writing book reviews and waiting tables. Baldwin achieved some success but felt increasingly stifled by the racist climate of the United States. In a life-changing decision in 1948, he bought a one-way plane ticket to Paris. "Once I found myself on the other side of the ocean," he later explained, "I could see where I came from very clearly, and I could see that I carried myself, which is my home, with me. You can never escape that."

Long-Distance Outrage With their penetrating insight and apocalyptic tone, Baldwin's essay collections were bestsellers. By the mid-1960s, he was an international celebrity, popular on the lecture circuit and in public debates, interviews, and panel discussions in the United States and Europe. In writing about his perceptions and personal torments, Baldwin made white Americans deeply, painfully aware of the realities of African-American life. As black leaders in the 1950s and 1960s looked outward to break down barriers, Baldwin looked inward to examine the psychological damage of racism and the search for black identity and self-realization. In the words of playwright Amiri Baraka, "Jimmy's voice, as much as Dr. King's or Malcolm X's, helped shepherd and guide us toward black liberation."

● LITERARY ANALYSIS: RHETORICAL DEVICES

Baldwin is known for his passionate and poetic style, which is based on his skillful use of **rhetorical devices.** These techniques are used to drive home a writer's points and to create rhythmic effects that echo spoken language.

- A **paradox** is a statement that seems contradictory but really points to an important truth. Baldwin uses this device to push his readers to think more deeply about familiar ideas.

   It is the innocence which constitutes the crime.

- **Repetition** is the use of the same word, phrase, or sentence more than once for emphasis. Baldwin uses repetition expressively, to convey deep emotions.

   You must accept them and accept them with love....

As you read, note the rhetorical devices Baldwin uses, and consider their effects.

● READING STRATEGY: IDENTIFY IDEAS

Baldwin's sentences do more than simply explain his points; they stir powerful emotional responses in the reader. Often, the meaning of his statements becomes apparent only after careful thought and reflection. As you read this letter, use your own emotional responses to identify Baldwin's **ideas.** In a chart like the one shown, note five sentences that hit home for you. After you have finished the essay, review the sentences you chose and try to explain the key idea behind each one.

Baldwin's Sentence	Idea

▲ VOCABULARY IN CONTEXT

Baldwin uses the following words in his eloquent appeal. Complete each sentence with one of the words.

WORD LIST	constitute	mediocrity	unassailable
	impertinent	truculent	

1. You conceal your fears with a(n) _____ attitude.
2. Don't settle for _____; strive for excellence.
3. It is never _____ to speak honestly.
4. Know exactly what tasks and obligations _____ your duty.
5. Let your convictions be strong and your truth _____.

Explore the Key Idea

What protects your sense of SELF?

KEY IDEA Part of growing up is deciding who you want to be and how to make your vision a reality. But how do you keep your sense of self strong when others tell you who you can and cannot be? James Baldwin offers his nephew some advice on protecting his **self-worth** from the crushing forces of racism.

QUICKWRITE Think about the messages you get about yourself from family, friends, media, and other sources. Which ones support you and which ones seem to hold you back? List at least two examples in each category. Based on your list, what in your life most helps you protect your self-worth?

Support	Hold Back
1. With hard work you can achieve your dreams (my mom).	1. College is too expensive and not worth it (my friend George).
2.	2.

My Dungeon Shook

Letter to My Nephew on the One Hundredth Anniversary of the Emancipation

James Baldwin

BACKGROUND In 1963, as the nation's perspective on the race problem grew more pessimistic, James Baldwin published his essay collection *The Fire Next Time*. Expressing the pain and anger that African Americans had concealed for so long, Baldwin addressed his provocative essays to a sympathetic white audience that had failed to grasp the full magnitude of racial injustice. His searing attack fit the national mood, and the collection soared up the bestseller lists. Its success made Baldwin an icon of black rage and a widely televised commentator on racial issues throughout the 1960s. The following letter, taken from *The Fire Next Time*, captures the extremes of Baldwin's style: the righteous anger that made him famous and his fervent belief in the redeeming power of love.

ANALYZE VISUALS
Describe the story that this painting seems to tell. Which elements help the artist connect the two figures in the foreground with the main story of the painting?

Dear James:

I have begun this letter five times and torn it up five times. I keep seeing your face, which is also the face of your father and my brother. Like him, you are tough, dark, vulnerable, moody—with a very definite tendency to sound **truculent** because you want no one to think you are soft. You may be like your grandfather in this, I don't know, but certainly both you and your father resemble him very much physically. Well, he is dead, he never saw you, and he had a terrible life; he was defeated long before he died because, at the bottom of his heart, he really believed what white people said about him. This is one of the reasons that he

10 became so holy.[1] I am sure that your father has told you something about all that. Neither you nor your father exhibit any tendency towards holiness: you really *are*

truculent (trŭk′yə-lənt) *adj*. eager for a fight; fierce

---

1. **so holy:** Baldwin's stepfather was a minister who raised his children in a strict, conservative, religious environment.

Father, Charly Palmer. Mixed media collage on wood. 18″ × 12″. © Charly Palmer.

of another era, part of what happened when the Negro left the land and came into what the late E. Franklin Frazier[2] called "the cities of destruction." You can only be destroyed by believing that you really are what the white world calls a *nigger*. I tell you this because I love you, and please don't you ever forget it.

I have known both of you all your lives, have carried your Daddy in my arms and on my shoulders, kissed and spanked him and watched him learn to walk. I don't know if you've known anybody from that far back; if you've loved anybody that long, first as an infant, then as a child, then as a man, you gain a strange
20 perspective on time and human pain and effort. Other people cannot see what I see whenever I look into your father's face, for behind your father's face as it is today are all those other faces which were his. Let him laugh and I see a cellar your father does not remember and a house he does not remember and I hear in his present laughter his laughter as a child. Let him curse and I remember him falling down the cellar steps, and howling, and I remember, with pain, his tears, which my hand or your grandmother's so easily wiped away. But no one's hand can wipe away those tears he sheds invisibly today, which one hears in his laughter and in his speech and in his songs. I know what the world has done to my brother and how narrowly he has survived it. And I know, which is much worse, and this is
30 the crime of which I accuse my country and my countrymen, and for which neither I nor time nor history will ever forgive them, that they have destroyed and are destroying hundreds of thousands of lives and do not know it and do not want to know it. One can be, indeed one must strive to become, tough and philosophical concerning destruction and death, for this is what most of mankind has been best at since we have heard of man. (But remember: *most* of mankind is not all of mankind.) But it is not permissible that the authors of devastation should also be innocent. It is the innocence which **constitutes** the crime. 🅐

Now, my dear namesake, these innocent and well-meaning people, your countrymen, have caused you to be born under conditions not very far removed
40 from those described for us by Charles Dickens[3] in the London of more than a hundred years ago. (I hear the chorus of the innocents screaming, "No! This is not true! How *bitter* you are!"—but I am writing this letter to *you,* to try to tell you something about how to handle *them,* for most of them do not yet really know that you exist. I *know* the conditions under which you were born, for I was there. Your countrymen were *not* there, and haven't made it yet. Your grandmother was also there, and no one has ever accused her of being bitter. I suggest that the innocents check with her. She isn't hard to find. Your countrymen don't know that *she* exists, either, though she has been working for them all their lives.)

Well, you were born, here you came, something like fifteen years ago; and
50 though your father and mother and grandmother, looking about the streets through which they were carrying you, staring at the walls into which they brought you, had every reason to be heavyhearted, yet they were not. For here

constitute (kŏn′stĭ-tōōt′) *v.* to amount to; equal

🅐 **RHETORICAL DEVICES**
Consider the **paradox** in lines 36–37. What point is Baldwin making?

---

2. **E. Franklin Frazier:** African-American sociologist (1894–1962) who studied the structure of black communities.

3. **described . . . by Charles Dickens:** Dickens (1812–1870) was a British novelist whose works frequently described the hardships suffered by the poor in London.

you were, Big James, named for me—you were a big baby, I was not—here you were: to be loved. To be loved, baby, hard, at once, and forever, to strengthen you against the loveless world. Remember that: I know how black it looks today, for you. It looked bad that day, too, yes, we were trembling. We have not stopped trembling yet, but if we had not loved each other none of us would have survived. And now you must survive because we love you, and for the sake of your children and your children's children. **B**

60   This innocent country set you down in a ghetto in which, in fact, it intended that you should perish. Let me spell out precisely what I mean by that, for the heart of the matter is here, and the root of my dispute with my country. You were born where you were born and faced the future that you faced because you were black and *for no other reason.* The limits of your ambition were, thus, expected to be set forever. You were born into a society which spelled out with brutal clarity, and in as many ways as possible, that you were a worthless human being. You were not expected to aspire to excellence: you were expected to make peace with **mediocrity**. Wherever you have turned, James, in your short time on this earth, you have been told where you could go and what you could do (and *how* you could do it) and where you could live and whom you could marry. I know your countrymen do not agree with me about this, and I hear them saying, "You exaggerate." They do not know Harlem, and I do. So do you. Take no one's word for anything, including mine—but trust your experience. **C**

    Know whence you came. If you know whence you came, there is really no limit to where you can go. The details and symbols of your life have been deliberately constructed to make you believe what white people say about you. Please try to remember that what they believe, as well as what they do and cause you to endure, does not testify to your inferiority but to their inhumanity and fear. Please try to be clear, dear James, through the storm which rages about your youthful head today, about the reality which lies behind the words *acceptance* and *integration.* There is no reason for you to try to become like white people and there is no basis whatever for their **impertinent** assumption that *they* must accept *you.* The really terrible thing, old buddy, is that *you* must accept *them.* And I mean that very seriously. You must accept them and accept them with love. For these innocent people have no other hope. They are, in effect, still trapped in a history which they do not understand; and until they understand it, they cannot be released from it. They have had to believe for many years, and for innumerable reasons, that black men are inferior to white men. Many of them, indeed, know better, but, as you will discover, people find it very difficult to act on what they know. To act is to be committed, and to be committed is to be in danger. In this case, the danger, in the minds of most white Americans, is the loss of their identity. Try to imagine how you would feel if you woke up one morning to find the sun shining and all the stars aflame. You would be frightened because it is out of the order of nature. Any upheaval in the universe is terrifying because it so profoundly attacks one's sense of one's own reality. Well, the black man has functioned in the white man's world as a fixed star, as an immovable pillar: and as he moves out of his place, heaven and earth are shaken to their foundations. You, don't be afraid. I said that it was intended that you should perish in the ghetto, perish by never

B **RHETORICAL DEVICES**
Identify words and phrases that are repeated in lines 52–59. What does this **repetition** contribute to the paragraph's impact?

mediocrity
(mē′dē-ŏk′-rĭ-tē) *n.* lack of quality or excellence

C **IDENTIFY IDEAS**
Reread lines 60–73. In your opinion, which sentence best expresses the basis for Baldwin's anger? Explain your answer.

impertinent
(ĭm-pûr′tn-ənt) *adj.* rude; ill-mannered

Thinking (1990), Carlton Murrell. Oil on board. Private collection. © Bridgeman Art Library.

being allowed to go behind the white man's definitions, by never being allowed to
100 spell your proper name. You have, and many of us have, defeated this intention;
and, by a terrible law, a terrible paradox, those innocents who believed that your
imprisonment made them safe are losing their grasp of reality. But these men are
your brothers —your lost, younger brothers. And if the word *integration* means
anything, this is what it means: that we, with love, shall force our brothers to
see themselves as they are, to cease fleeing from reality and begin to change it.
For this is your home, my friend, do not be driven from it; great men have done
great things here, and will again, and we can make America what America must
become. It will be hard, James, but you come from sturdy, peasant stock, men
who picked cotton and dammed rivers and built railroads, and, in the teeth of[4]
110 the most terrifying odds, achieved an **unassailable** and monumental dignity. You
come from a long line of great poets, some of the greatest poets since Homer. One
of them said, *The very time I thought I was lost, My dungeon shook and my chains
fell off.*[5]

You know, and I know, that the country is celebrating one hundred years of
freedom one hundred years too soon. We cannot be free until they are free. God
bless you, James, and Godspeed.

Your uncle,

James

unassailable
(ŭn′ə-sā′lə-bəl) *adj.*
undeniable

D **IDENTIFY IDEAS**
Reread Baldwin's
definition of *integration*
in lines 103–105. In what
ways does his explanation
differ from the usual
meaning of this word?

---

4. **in the teeth of:** in spite of.

5. ***The very time . . . fell off:*** a quotation from the traditional spiritual "My Dungeon Shook." It alludes to the
Biblical story of Paul and Silas (Acts 16), who were freed from an unjust imprisonment by the action of an
earthquake.

Comprehension

1. **Recall** In Baldwin's view, why was the boy's grandfather defeated?

2. **Recall** What does Baldwin say *acceptance* means?

3. **Clarify** What crime does Baldwin accuse his country of committing?

Literary Analysis

4. **Identify Ideas** Review the five sentences that you selected and your interpretations of them. Which one best expresses the message of this letter? Explain your answer.

5. **Examine Rhetorical Devices** Baldwin sums up the themes of his letter with two concluding **paradoxes.** Reread lines 114–115. What insight about the problem of race in America do these two statements convey?

6. **Analyze Audience** Baldwin addressed this **open letter** to his 15-year-old nephew but published it in his book *The Fire Next Time.* In each of the following passages, identify details that seem directed to the nephew and those directed to a wider audience. Based on your analysis, who do you think is the primary audience of this work? Support your answer with details.

   • Baldwin's memories of his brother (lines 20–33)

   • criticisms of his readers (lines 38–44)

   • his advice to his nephew (lines 78–84)

   • his description of whites' fears (lines 90–97)

7. **Compare Style** Baldwin shared many of Martin Luther King's values, goals, and religious influences. What is similar and different about the authors' styles? In your answer, consider each author's tone as well as his use of logical arguments, allusions, and rhetorical devices.

8. **Make Judgments** Consider Baldwin's solution to the problem of racism. In your opinion, does Baldwin's letter contain useful advice for protecting his nephew's **self-worth?** Explain your opinions.

9. **Evaluate Impact** Reread the background information on page 1194. In your opinion, why did Baldwin's criticisms hit home for so many? In your answer, consider the author's style, themes, and the historical context of his work.

Literary Criticism

10. **Critical Interpretations** In *Soul on Ice* (1968), black activist Eldridge Cleaver criticized James Baldwin for his "grueling, agonizing, total hatred of the blacks, particularly of himself" and his "shameful, fanatical, fawning, sycophantic love of the whites." Do you see any evidence to support these accusations? Explain your answer, citing details from Baldwin's letter.

Vocabulary in Context

WORD LIST

constitute

impertinent

mediocrity

truculent

unassailable

VOCABULARY PRACTICE

Choose the word that is closest in meaning to the boldfaced vocabulary word.

1. **impertinent:** (a) insolent, (b) impossible, (c) unfriendly
2. **mediocrity:** (a) ordinariness, (b) indifference, (c) complexity
3. **unassailable:** (a) landlocked, (b) unknown, (c) indisputable
4. **truculent:** (a) uncivilized, (b) ferocious, (c) boorish
5. **constitute:** (a) connect, (b) compose, (c) conclude

VOCABULARY IN WRITING

What life advice might an older relative offer you? Write five sentences
of advice, using each of the vocabulary words. Here is a sample sentence.

> **EXAMPLE SENTENCE**
>
> *Only rarely will you need to be __impertinent__; choose those situations carefully.*

VOCABULARY STRATEGY: IDIOMS

An **idiom** is an expression whose overall meaning is different from the meaning
of the individual words that it includes. For example, in "My Dungeon Shook"
Baldwin uses the expression *in the teeth of* to describe overcoming difficult odds.
  If you encounter an unfamiliar idiom, use context clues to figure out its
meaning or consult a dictionary. In many dictionaries, idioms are listed under
the main word of the idiom, at the end of the entry. For example, *in the teeth
of* would likely be found under *tooth,* as part of a list like this:

> **fight tooth and nail** fight fiercely; **put teeth into** make effective or forceful

PRACTICE Use context clues to write a definition for each boldfaced idiom.
Use a dictionary if you need help.

1. Out of pity, he took the lost child **under his wing.**
2. No matter what trouble she's in, she always gets herself **off the hook.**
3. The puppy's playful antics **cracked us up.**
4. The meeting was a disaster, leaving us with **egg on our faces.**
5. You needn't **jump down my throat** for every little mistake.
6. Defiant to the end, he **thumbed his nose at** their offer of amnesty.
7. We don't have much time, so I'll **cut to the chase.**
8. Nervous and awkward, he always seemed to **put his foot in his mouth.**
9. She was a harsh critic who **pulled no punches.**
10. Once I discovered my mistake, all I could do was **eat crow.**

VOCABULARY PRACTICE
For more practice, go
to the **Vocabulary Center**
at **ClassZone.com.**

The March Toward Equality

In 1963, psychology professor Dr. Kenneth Clark conducted a series of interviews with Dr. Martin Luther King Jr., Malcolm X, and James Baldwin. Aired during a time of intense racial conflict, these interviews explored the differences in the ideals and world views of these three leading activists and thinkers. In his introduction to the interviews, Dr. Clark made this statement.

> "We have now come to the point where there are only two ways that America can avoid continued racial explosions. One would be total oppression. The other, total equality. There is no compromise. I believe, I hope, that we are on the threshold of a truly democratic America. It is not going to be easy to cross that threshold. But the achievement of the goals of justice, equality, and democracy for all American citizens involves the very destiny of our nation."

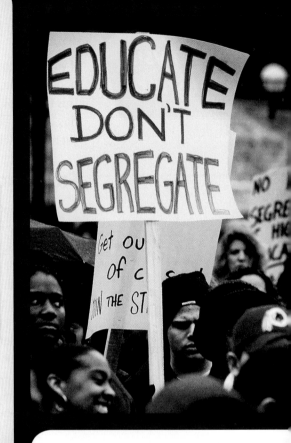

Writing to Persuade

Consider the state of civil rights in America today, in light of the goals and visions of the writers you have just read. In your opinion, have we reached total equality? Or would you say that we have arrived somewhere in between total equality and total oppression? Review the literature in this section and write a retrospective editorial in which you support a claim about whether or not the goals and visions of these writers have been realized.

Consider

- which ideas and details from the selections will help you articulate the vision of the civil rights leaders
- what stories, examples, or other details will help you support your view of civil rights in America today
- who your audience will be and what you want them to think or do
- how to express your viewpoint clearly and respectfully

Extension Online

INQUIRY & RESEARCH Use the Internet to **research** contemporary topics in civil rights. Look for news and commentary in mainstream and lesser-known publications, including private weblogs. Also look for Web sites of organizations devoted to advancing civil rights. Choose three issues that seem the most important or surprising to you and share them with your class.

Voice in Contemporary Literature

If you go into a bookstore and browse the "New Fiction" section, what types of books do you find? How are they different from literature of the past? Throughout this textbook, you have witnessed the evolution of American literature. Each period has been characterized by literary movements that determined the styles and themes in writing. What do you think the trends have been in your generation?

From Modern to Contemporary

The era of contemporary literature began around 1946, immediately after World War II. War has a way of changing a nation's literature because of its effects on an entire generation. Realism had risen from the ashes of the Civil War, while modernism had defined its vision through the ruins of World War I. After World War II, the development of the Cold War, the Vietnam War, and the civil violence of the 1960s, American literature changed again. Literature began to focus on personal experience as seen in the context of society. Writers began to address the emotional effects of wars, for example, as well as other issues of social, political, and cultural relevance.

Amy Tan

One of the most significant changes in American literature has been its increasing diversity—not only in forms and techniques, but in voices. With its history as the great "melting pot," the United States has been in a unique position to cultivate a literary community of authors from a wide variety of races, ethnicities, and religions. Increased publishing opportunities have given a public voice to more and more writers of African, Asian, Latino, and Native American descent, who often provide a new perspective on living in two cultures at once. Authors who have addressed such issues include Amy Tan, Sandra Cisneros, Rita Dove, Gwendolyn Brooks, Alice Walker, and N. Scott Momaday.

Rita Dove

N. Scott Momaday

Diverse Works, Common Ground

Several defining features set contemporary literature apart from the previous era of modernist literature.

Voice in literature is the expression of the writer's or narrator's personality. With its emphasis on personal experience, contemporary literature is often told from the first-person point of view, through a persona that represents the writer or main character. This persona has a distinctive personality that shapes a reader's experience with the text.

Tone is the attitude that a writer takes toward a subject. For the modernists, the numbing effects of the early 20th century led to a detached, unemotional tone. For example, Prufrock's failure at the end of T. S. Eliot's poem (page 930) is conveyed in a matter-of-fact tone that is sympathetic but distant. Compare this modernist aloofness to Tim O'Brien's Vietnam story "Ambush" (page 1138). The tone of this contemporary story is one of engagement rather than detachment.

> I did not hate the young man; I did not see him as the enemy; I did not ponder issues of morality or politics or military duty. I crouched and kept my head low. I tried to swallow whatever was rising from my stomach, which tasted like lemonade, something fruity and sour. I was terrified.
>
> **—Tim O'Brien, "Ambush"**

Close Read

How would you characterize the narrator of this passage? Do you think he would be personable? distant? intimidating?

As a rule, modernist writers did not view the irony of life as humorous; instead, they often expressed defeat in the face of life's irony. Contemporary writers, however, look at the absurdity of such situations as a cause for humor, which may then be expressed through an **ironic** presentation of characters and events.

Modernist writers typically viewed the individual in isolation, whereas contemporary writers present the individual in relation to the larger social context. Often contemporary writers hint at **social criticism.** They present a situation with only a suggestion of the social obstacles, and the reader must infer the writer's opinion. In her poem "Primer for Blacks" (page 1233), Gwendolyn Brooks encourages African Americans to appreciate their heritage. Note the unspoken message about social barriers for African Americans that Brooks conveys in this passage.

> Blackness
> is a title,
> is a preoccupation,
> is a commitment Blacks
> are to comprehend—
> and in which you are
> to perceive your Glory.
>
> **—Gwendolyn Brooks, "Primer for Blacks"**

Close Read

What is the social barrier for African Americans that Brooks wants her reader to infer?

Brooks is making an argument for self-respect and self-esteem among African Americans. However, she does not state what she is arguing against; she leaves it up to the reader to infer the social barriers she is addressing.

Mother Tongue

Essay by Amy Tan

Amy Tan
born 1952

In 1989, Amy Tan's first book, *The Joy Luck Club,* spent 40 weeks on the *New York Times* bestseller list. Praised for its authentic dialogue and its rich portrayal of Chinese history, the book established Tan as an insightful chronicler of the Chinese-American experience and of the fierce and conflicted love between mothers and daughters.

Troubled Times Born in Oakland, California in 1952, Tan spent her early childhood in the San Francisco Bay area. She enjoyed her first literary success at the age of eight, winning first prize in an elementary school contest for her essay "What My Library Means to Me." Six years later, Tan's life took a tragic turn when both her father and her brother died from brain tumors. Her grief-stricken mother moved teenaged Amy and her surviving brother to Europe, settling in Montreux, Switzerland, where Tan graduated from high school in 1969.

Although her mother had pushed her to become a neurosurgeon, the rebellious Tan defied her mother's wishes and studied literature and linguistics in college. In 1974, she enrolled in a doctoral program in linguistics, but she abandoned her studies after a close friend was murdered. Tan then put her expertise to work as a language development consultant for programs serving disabled children. Five years later, she adopted a new career as a freelance technical writer.

Confronting the Past Tan took up writing fiction as a form of therapy, hoping to curb her workaholic tendencies. Her first short story, "End Game," appeared in *Seventeen* magazine, bringing her to the attention of prominent literary agent Sandra Dijkstra. With Dijkstra's encouragement, Tan began writing a series of stories that evolved into *The Joy Luck Club.* For this tightly woven collection of short stories, Tan drew upon her personal story, exploring the generational and cultural gap between Chinese mothers and their American-born daughters.

Two years later, Tan published her second book, *The Kitchen God's Wife,* a novel inspired by her mother's life in China. Though she switched her focus from mother-daughter love to sisterhood in her third novel, *The Hundred Secret Senses,* she once again drew on her mother's life story in her fourth, *The Bonesetter's Daughter.* As Tan explains, "My books have amounted to taking her stories—a gift to me—and giving them back to her. To me, it was the ultimate thing I ever could have done for myself and my mother."

LITERARY ANALYSIS: PERSONAL ESSAY

Amy Tan could have written a research paper to get across her points about language and cultural identity. Instead, she chose to write a **personal essay,** where she combines her insights on the topic with details from her own life.

Just last week, as I was walking down the street with [my mother], I again found myself conscious of the English I was using, the English I do use with her.

Unlike a scholarly paper or a newspaper article, a personal essay gives you a snapshot of the writer's life or personality as well as his or her thoughts on a specific topic. As you read this essay, note how Tan connects her ideas about the power of language with her own experiences.

READING SKILL: IDENTIFY MAIN IDEAS

Amy Tan's essay is organized into a series of paragraphs, most of which develop one **main idea,** or central point. Facts, descriptions, or examples that are related to the main idea are called **supporting details.** When a main idea is not directly stated, you can figure it out by asking yourself how these supporting details fit together.

Amy Tan uses vivid supporting details to make her points. As you read, use a diagram like the one shown to record the main idea of each paragraph and list its supporting details.

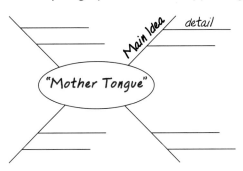

What LANGUAGES *do you speak?*

KEY IDEA Think about how you change the way you speak based on where you are and whom you're with. You might use slang when talking with friends but polite, formal language with adults. You might speak English at school and another language at home. In "Mother Tongue," you will read one writer's thoughts on her own different **languages.**

QUICKWRITE Make a list of places and situations where you use a different language or way of speaking. Then, for each situation, write a brief quotation that captures the sound of the language you use in that context.

1205

Mother Tongue

Amy Tan

I am not a scholar of English or literature. I cannot give you much more than personal opinions on the English language and its variations in this country or others.

I am a writer. And by that definition, I am someone who has always loved language. I am fascinated by language in daily life. I spend a great deal of my time thinking about the power of language—the way it can evoke an emotion, a visual image, a complex idea, or a simple truth. Language is the tool of my trade. And I use them all—all the Englishes I grew up with. **Ⓐ**

Recently, I was made keenly aware of the different Englishes I do use. I was giving a talk to a large group of people, the same talk I had already given to half a dozen other groups. The talk was about my writing, my life, and my book, *The Joy Luck Club,* and it was going along well enough, until I remembered one major difference that made the whole talk sound wrong. My mother was in the room. And it was perhaps the first time she had heard me give a lengthy speech, using the kind of English I have never used with her. I was saying things like "the intersection of memory and imagination" and "There is an aspect of my fiction that relates to thus-and-thus"—a speech filled with carefully wrought grammatical phrases, burdened, it suddenly seemed to me, with nominalized[1] forms, past perfect tenses, conditional phrases, forms of standard English that I had learned in school and through books, the forms of English I did not use at home with my mother.

---

1. **nominalized** (nŏm′ə-nəl-īz′d) **forms:** nouns formed from other parts of speech.

ANALYZE VISUALS
In this painting, the artist represents an apple in three different ways. What point about language might the artist be making?

Ⓐ PERSONAL ESSAY
Reread lines 1–8. What do you learn about the author in these opening lines?

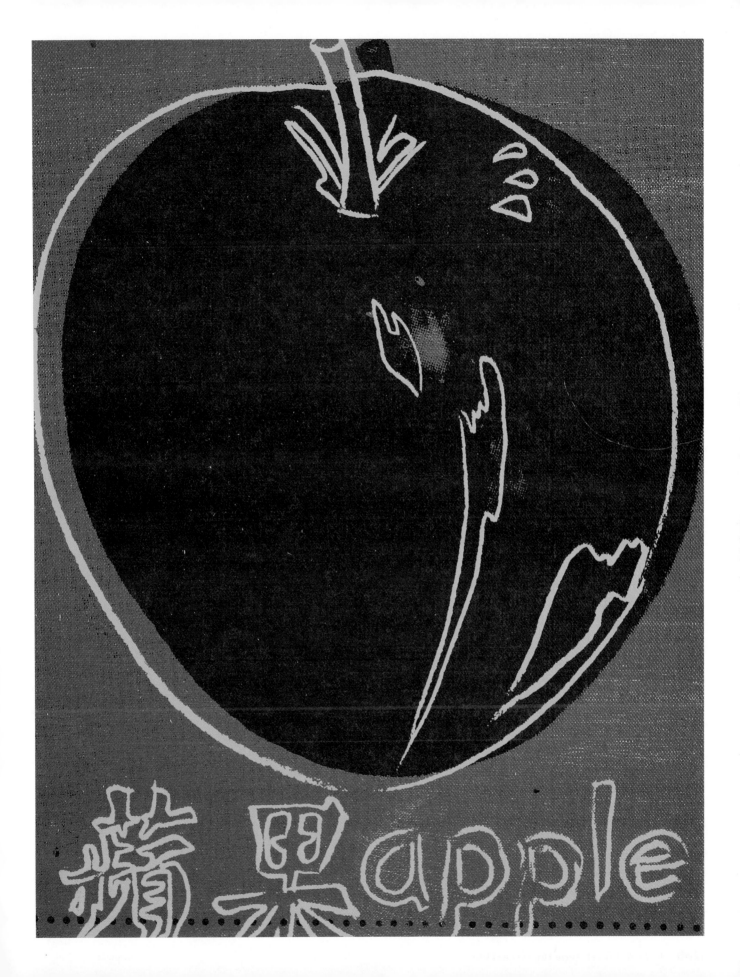

Just last week, as I was walking down the street with her, I again found myself conscious of the English I was using, the English I do use with her. We were talking about the price of new and used furniture, and I heard myself saying this: "Not waste money that way." My husband was with us as well, and he didn't notice any switch in my English. And then I realized why. It's because over the twenty years we've been together I've often used that same kind of English with him, and sometimes he even uses it with me. It has become our language of intimacy, a different sort of English that relates to family talk, the language I grew
30 up with.

So that you'll have some idea of what this family talk sounds like, I'll quote what my mother said during a conversation that I videotaped and then transcribed. During this conversation, she was talking about a political gangster in Shanghai who had the same last name as her family's, Du, and how in his early years the gangster wanted to be adopted by her family, who were rich by comparison. Later, the gangster became more powerful, far richer than my mother's family, and he showed up at my mother's wedding to pay his respects. Here's what she said in part: **B**

"Du Yusong having business like fruit stand. Like off-the-street kind. He is Du
40 like Du Zong—but not Tsung-ming Island[2] people. The local people call *putong*. The river east side, he belong to that side local people. That man want to ask Du Zong father take him in like become own family. Du Zong father wasn't look down on him, but didn't take seriously, until that man big like become a mafia. Now important person, very hard to inviting him. Chinese way, came only to show respect, don't stay for dinner. Respect for making big celebration, he shows up. Mean gives lots of respect. Chinese custom. Chinese social life that way. If too important won't have to stay too long. He come to my wedding. I didn't see, I heard it. I gone to boy's side, they have YMCA dinner. Chinese age I was nineteen."

You should know that my mother's expressive command of English belies how
50 much she actually understands. She reads the *Forbes*[3] report, listens to *Wall Street Week,* converses daily with her stockbroker, reads Shirley MacLaine's books[4] with ease—all kinds of things I can't begin to understand. Yet some of my friends tell me they understand fifty percent of what my mother says. Some say they understand eighty to ninety percent. Some say they understand none of it, as if she were speaking pure Chinese. But to me, my mother's English is perfectly clear, perfectly natural. It's my mother tongue. Her language, as I hear it, is vivid, direct, full of observation and imagery. That was the language that helped shape the way I saw things, expressed things, made sense of the world. **C**

Lately I've been giving more thought to the kind of English my mother speaks.
60 Like others, I have described it to people as "broken" or "fractured" English. But I wince when I say that. It has always bothered me that I can think of no way to describe it other than "broken," as if it were damaged and needed to be fixed, as if

---

B GRAMMAR AND STYLE
Reread lines 31–33. Note how Tan addresses her readers as *you,* as though in conversation. This use **of informal language** helps her create a warm, personal voice.

C MAIN IDEAS
Reread lines 49–58. What **supporting details** does Tan include to describe the way her mother uses English?

---

2. **Tsung-ming** (tsŏŏng-mĭng) **Island:** an island near the mouth of the Yangtze River, near Shanghai, in eastern China.

3. *Forbes:* a financial magazine.

4. **Shirley MacLaine's books:** works by the American actress Shirley MacLaine (born 1934), many of which deal with reincarnation.

it lacked a certain wholeness and soundness. I've heard other terms used, "limited English," for example. But they seem just as bad, as if everything is limited, including people's perceptions of the limited-English speaker.

I know this for a fact, because when I was growing up, my mother's "limited" English limited my perception of her. I was ashamed of her English. I believed that her English reflected the quality of what she had to say. That is, because she expressed them imperfectly, her thoughts were imperfect. And I had plenty of empirical evidence[5] to support me: the fact that people in department stores, at banks, and in restaurants did not take her seriously, did not give her good service, pretended not to understand her, or even acted as if they did not hear her. **D**

My mother has long realized the limitations of her English as well. When I was a teenager, she used to have me call people on the phone and pretend I was she. In this guise, I was forced to ask for information or even to complain and yell at people who had been rude to her. One time it was a call to her stockbroker in New York. She had cashed out her small portfolio, and it just so happened we were going to New York the next week, our first trip outside California. I had to get on the phone and say in an adolescent voice that was not very convincing, "This is Mrs. Tan."

My mother was standing in the back whispering loudly, "Why he don't send me check, already two weeks late. So mad he lie to me, losing me money."

And then I said in perfect English on the phone, "Yes, I'm getting rather concerned. You had agreed to send the check two weeks ago, but it hasn't arrived."

Then she began to talk more loudly. "What he want, I come to New York tell him front of his boss, you cheating me?" And I was trying to calm her down, make her be quiet, while telling the stockbroker, "I can't tolerate any more excuses. If I don't receive the check immediately, I am going to have to speak to your manager when I'm in New York next week." And sure enough, the following week, there we were in front of this astonished stockbroker, and I was sitting there red-faced and quiet, and my mother, the real Mrs. Tan, was shouting at his boss in her impeccable broken English.

We used a similar routine more recently, for a situation that was far less humorous. My mother had gone to the hospital for an appointment to find out about a CAT scan[6] she had had a month earlier. She said she had spoken very good English, her best English, no mistakes. Still, she said, the hospital did not apologize when they informed her they had lost the CAT scan and she had come for nothing. She said they did not seem to have any sympathy when she told them she was anxious to know the exact diagnosis, since her husband and her son had died of brain tumors. She said they would not give her any more information until the next time and she would have to make another appointment for that. So she said she would not leave until the doctor called her daughter. She wouldn't budge. And when the doctor finally called her daughter, me, who spoke in perfect English—lo and behold—we had assurances the CAT scan would be found, promises that a conference call on Monday would be held, and apologies for any suffering my mother had gone through for a most regrettable mistake.

D **PERSONAL ESSAY**
Reread lines 59–72. Explain Tan's point about the term "broken English." What personal experiences does she draw on to make her point?

---

5. **empirical evidence:** evidence derived from observation.

6. **CAT scan:** a three-dimensional image of structures inside the human body.

I think my mother's English almost had an effect on limiting my possibilities in life as well. Sociologists and linguists probably will tell you that a person's developing language skills are more influenced by peers than by family. But I do think that the language spoken in the family, especially in immigrant families

110 which are more insular,[7] plays a large role in shaping the language of the child. And I believe that it affected my results on achievement tests, IQ tests, and the SAT. While my English skills were never judged poor, compared with math, English could not be considered my strong suit. In grade school I did moderately well, getting perhaps B's, sometimes B-pluses, in English and scoring perhaps in the sixtieth or seventieth percentile on achievement tests. But those scores were not good enough to override the opinion that my true abilities lay in math and science, because in those areas I achieved A's and scored in the ninetieth percentile or higher.

This was understandable. Math is precise; there is only one correct answer. Whereas, for me at least, the answers on English tests were always a judgment call,

120 a matter of opinion and personal experience. Those tests were constructed around items like fill-in-the-blank sentence completion, such as, "Even though Tom was _____, Mary thought he was_____." And the correct answer always seemed to be the most bland combinations, for example, "Even though Tom was shy, Mary thought he was charming," with the grammatical structure "even though" limiting the correct answer to some sort of semantic opposites,[8] so you wouldn't get answers like, "Even though Tom was foolish, Mary thought he was ridiculous." Well, according to my mother, there were very few limitations as to what Tom could have been and what Mary might have thought of him. So I never did well on tests like that. **E**

130 The same was true with word analogies, pairs of words for which you were supposed to find some sort of logical semantic relationship, for instance, "Sunset is to nightfall as _____ is to_____." And here you would be presented with a list of four possible pairs, one of which showed the same kind of relationship: *red* is to *stoplight, bus* is to *arrival, chills* is to *fever, yawn* is to *boring*. Well, I could never think that way. I knew what the tests were asking, but I could not block out of my mind the images already created by the first pair, *sunset* is to *nightfall*—and I would see a burst of colors against a darkening sky, the moon rising, the lowering of a curtain of stars. And all the other pairs of words—*red, bus, stoplight, boring*— just threw up a mass of confusing images, making it impossible for me to see

140 that saying "A sunset precedes nightfall" was as logical as saying "A chill precedes a fever." The only way I would have gotten that answer right was to imagine an associative situation,[9] such as my being disobedient and staying out past sunset, catching a chill at night, which turned into feverish pneumonia as punishment— which indeed did happen to me.

I have been thinking about all this lately, about my mother's English, about achievement tests. Because lately I've been asked, as a writer, why there are not more Asian-Americans represented in American literature. Why are

E PERSONAL ESSAY
Reread lines 107–129. According to Tan, in what ways did her mother's use of English influence her own performance on standardized tests?

---

7. **insular:** isolated.

8. **semantic opposites:** words opposite in meaning.

9. **associative situation:** a circumstance or story based on mental connections.

there few Asian-Americans enrolled in creative writing programs? Why do so many Chinese students go into engineering? Well, these are broad sociological questions I can't begin to answer. But I have noticed in surveys—in fact, just last week—that Asian-American students, as a whole, do significantly better on math achievement tests than on English tests. And this makes me think that there are other Asian-American students whose English spoken in the home might also be described as "broken" or "limited." And perhaps they also have teachers who are steering them away from writing and into math and science, which is what happened to me.

Fortunately, I happen to be rebellious and enjoy the challenge of disproving assumptions made about me. I became an English major my first year in college, after being enrolled as pre-med. I started writing nonfiction as a freelancer the week after I was told by my boss at the time that writing was my worst skill and I should hone my talents toward account management. **F**

But it wasn't until 1985 that I began to write fiction. At first I wrote using what I thought to be wittily crafted sentences, sentences that would finally prove I had mastery over the English language. Here's an example from the first draft of a story that later made its way into *The Joy Luck Club,* but without this line: "That was my mental quandary in its nascent state."[10] A terrible line, which I can barely pronounce.

Fortunately, for reasons I won't get into here, I later decided I should envision a reader for the stories I would write. And the reader I decided on was my mother, because these were stories about mothers. So with this reader in mind—and in fact she did read my early drafts—I began to write stories using all the Englishes I grew up with: the English I spoke to my mother, which for lack of a better term might be described as "simple"; the English she used with me, which for lack of a better term might be described as "broken"; my translation of her Chinese, which could certainly be described as "watered down"; and what I imagined to be her translation of her Chinese if she could speak in perfect English, her internal language, and for that I sought to preserve the essence, but neither an English nor a Chinese structure. I wanted to capture what language ability tests can never reveal: her intent, her passion, her imagery, the rhythms of her speech and the nature of her thoughts.

Apart from what any critic had to say about my writing, I knew I had succeeded where it counted when my mother finished reading my book and gave me her verdict: "So easy to read." ◖◗

F MAIN IDEAS
Identify the main idea of lines 157–161. What details support this main idea?

---

10. **my mental quandary . . . state:** my mental predicament in its earliest form.

Comprehension

1. **Recall** What words does Tan typically use to describe her mother's English?

2. **Summarize** In general, how did people react to Mrs. Tan's use of English?

3. **Recall** According to Tan, what aspects of language do achievement tests fail to reveal?

Literary Analysis

4. **Identify the Main Idea** Review the diagram you created as you read. Based on your notes, what is the main idea of the entire essay? Explain your answer.

5. **Compare Roles** Tan describes situations in which she was forced to act as a go-between for her mother, as in the anecdote in lines 80–91. Describe the roles of Tan and her mother in these situations. In what ways do these interactions differ from the typical mother-daughter relationship? Be specific in your answer.

6. **Make Judgments** Tan describes her mother's English as "vivid, direct, full of observation and imagery." Reread the story Tan's mother tells in lines 39–48. Do you agree with Tan's opinion of her mother's speech? Why or why not?

7. **Analyze a Personal Essay** Describe Tan's changing perceptions of her mother's use of English. In what way did her changing views toward her mother influence her observations about the power of language? Include details from the essay in your answer.

8. **Interpret Title** Tan uses the expression "mother tongue" as the title of her essay. State the usual meaning of this expression. Then, use each of the following examples to develop a different or expanded meaning for this term:

   • the idea of family talk (lines 28–30)

   • Tan's description of her mother's speech (lines 55–58)

   • Tan's thoughts on language development (lines 107–110)

9. **Evaluate Author's Position** Tan claims that the **language** spoken within the family does more to shape the way a child speaks than the language spoken by his or her peers. Recall your answers to the opening activity on page 1205. Do you agree with Tan's opinion? Why or why not?

Literary Criticism

10. **Different Perspectives** Look at the essay again through the eyes of the following individuals. What important lessons about life and the uses of language might each draw from this essay?

    • an immigrant   • the child of an immigrant

    • a doctor   • a teacher

Reading-Writing Connection

WRITING PROMPT

WRITE AN ESSAY Choose a topic that lets you draw on your personal experiences—a longtime hobby, a trip you took, your family history. Write an **one-page essay** that communicates your unique perspective on this subject. Be sure to include relevant details from your own experiences in the essay.

SELF-CHECK

A successful essay will . . .

- open in a way that captures the reader's attention
- include appropriate and effective personal details
- create a compelling voice that conveys your personality

GRAMMAR AND STYLE

USE APPROPRIATE LANGUAGE Review the **Grammar and Style** note on page 1208. For this essay, Tan chooses a casual, conversational style that lets her establish a strong connection with her readers. One strategy that helps Tan create this distinctive style is her use of **informal language** that contains **contractions** and idiosyncratic terms like *Englishes*. She also addresses her readers in a personal voice, using the **pronoun** *you*, as in the following excerpt:

> *You should know that my mother's expressive command of English belies how much she actually understands. She reads the* Forbes *report, listens to* Wall Street Week, *converses daily with her stockbroker, reads Shirley MacLaine's books with ease—all kinds of things I can't begin to understand.* (lines 49–52)

Whenever you write, consider the audience you are addressing and choose the appropriate level of formality.

PRACTICE Rewrite each of the following sentences using the kind of informal language Tan might have used.

EXAMPLE

It is often difficult to make sense of the rules of effective language.

Sometimes it's hard to understand what makes language work well.

---

1. A lack of education caused my mother to speak a damaged, limited kind of English.

2. To demonstrate my use of these techniques, I have included some excerpts from my recent work.

3. A substantial portion of my fiction relates to my background and personal experiences.

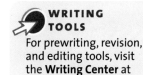

WRITING TOOLS
For prewriting, revision, and editing tools, visit the **Writing Center** at ClassZone.com.

from In Search of Our Mothers' Gardens

Essay by Alice Walker

Alice Walker

born 1944

Best known for her novels, author and activist Alice Walker also writes poems, short stories, and essays. Often inspired by her personal experiences, Walker portrays the struggles of African-American women to transcend the limits imposed on their lives by racism and sexism. Though her characters typically face violence and great hardships, Walker emphasizes the power of hope and the strength of the human will to survive.

Early Influences The daughter of a sharecropper, Walker grew up poor in Eatonton, Georgia. When she was eight, an accident left her permanently blind in her right eye. A shy and self-conscious Walker withdrew from the world and turned to poetry to soothe her feelings of isolation.

Although uneducated herself, Walker's mother supported her daughter's creative ambitions. Walker was an exceptional student who became class valedictorian and won a scholarship to Spelman College, a historically black women's college in Atlanta, Georgia. When she left for college, her mother gave her three gifts: a typewriter, a sewing machine, and a suitcase. For Walker, these gifts represented creativity, domesticity, and freedom—a legacy of hopes, dreams, and unfulfilled longings passed from mother to daughter.

Fighting for Equality In 1965, after graduating from college, Walker received a travel fellowship to Senegal. Instead, she went to Mississippi to help fight for racial justice. "That summer," explains Walker, "marked the beginning of a realization that I could never live happily in Africa—or anywhere else—until I could live freely in Mississippi." In 1967, she defied state law to marry white civil rights lawyer Melvyn Leventhal. In retaliation for their interracial marriage, the couple was subjected to constant harassment and even death threats.

Speaking for the Oppressed During the 1970s, Walker published two novels and volumes of poetry and short stories. Her breakthrough came with the publication of her third novel, *The Color Purple* (1982), which was later made into a successful film. Many critics attacked this novel for its unflattering portrayals of African-American men. In response, Walker insisted her work reflected the painful realities of many black women's lives: "The black woman," she explained, "is one of America's greatest heroes. . . . Not enough credit has been given to the black woman who has been oppressed beyond recognition."

● LITERARY ANALYSIS: AUTHOR'S MESSAGE

Authors write for a reason: they have a point to get across. In most nonfiction, you can find direct statements that reveal the **author's message,** as in this example:

And so our mothers and grandmothers have, more often than not anonymously, handed on the creative spark, the seed of the flower they themselves never hoped to see. . . .

Statements like these, and the examples used to support them, will help you identify the lesson Walker wants to teach.

Walker also includes one of her poems in the essay. In the poem, her message is expressed indirectly, through elements such as **mood, imagery,** and **figurative language.** As you read the essay, notice the different techniques Walker uses to reveal her message.

● READING SKILL: UNDERSTAND CULTURAL CONTEXT

When you analyze the **cultural context** of a literary work, you consider the social and cultural conditions that influenced how and why the work was written. Alice Walker's work reflects two key influences: her childhood experiences as a poor African-American female in the South and her adult commitment to feminist ideals. To fully appreciate Walker's points, use the following strategies:

• Before reading, study the details about cultural context provided in the background information on page 1216.

• Consult the footnotes as you read to clarify Walker's references to cultural details.

• Apply what you know about the social conditions that shaped the lives of African Americans in the South.

As you read, note details that reveal how Walker's social and cultural influences have shaped her views.

Explore the Key Idea

When does LIFE *become art?*

KEY IDEA Some people have an irresistible urge to create. Maybe they express it by sewing stylish clothes or cooking elaborate meals, by singing as they work, or by telling hilarious stories. For these people, even everyday chores can provide the **creative outlet** they need to release their artistic impulses.

DISCUSS In a small group, think of several ways that people express their creativity in everyday life. What do you think drives people to be creative? Record your responses and compare them with those of other groups.

In Search of Our Mothers' Gardens

Alice Walker

BACKGROUND Alice Walker wrote this essay in 1974, after decades of civil rights activism had broken down many barriers for African Americans. At the same time, the women's movement had begun to raise awareness of the social constraints imposed on women's lives. Women of Walker's generation were poised to claim personal and social freedoms that earlier generations of women could never have dreamed of. As these women looked back into history to find role models for their own lives, they began to appreciate the extraordinary sacrifices these earlier generations had made. In this essay, Walker examines her mother's life to uncover a hidden legacy of resilience, strength, and overlooked talent passed on to the women of her own time.

ANALYZE VISUALS
Describe the style of this painting. In what ways does the artist's use of color, line, and texture contrast with the activity depicted?

In the late 1920s my mother ran away from home to marry my father. Marriage, if not running away, was expected of seventeen-year-old girls. By the time she was twenty, she had two children and was pregnant with a third. Five children later, I was born. And this is how I came to know my mother: she seemed a large, soft, loving-eyed woman who was rarely impatient in our home. Her quick, violent temper was on view only a few times a year, when she battled with the white landlord who had the misfortune to suggest to her that her children did not need to go to school.

She made all the clothes we wore, even my brothers' overalls. She made all the
10 towels and sheets we used. She spent the summers canning vegetables and fruits. She spent the winter evenings making quilts enough to cover all our beds. **A**

During the "working" day, she labored beside—not behind—my father in the fields. Her day began before sunup, and did not end until late at night. There was never a moment for her to sit down, undisturbed, to unravel her own private thoughts; never a time free from interruption—by work or the noisy inquiries of her many children. And yet, it is to my mother—and all our mothers who were not famous—that I went in search of the secret of what has fed that muzzled and often mutilated,[1] but vibrant, creative spirit that the black woman has inherited, and that pops out in wild and unlikely places to this day.

A CULTURAL CONTEXT
What details in lines 1–11 convey the social conditions of African-American women in the early 20th century?

---

1. **mutilated** (myo͞ot′l-ā′tĭd): irreparably damaged.

Washerwoman, James Amos Porter. Oil on canvas, 18″ × 13″. Private collection. Reproduction rights given by the Dorothy Porter Wesley Research Center, Fort Lauderdale, Florida.

20　　But when, you will ask, did my overworked mother have time to know or care about feeding the creative spirit?

　　The answer is so simple that many of us have spent years discovering it. We have constantly looked high, when we should have looked high—and low.

　　For example: in the Smithsonian Institution in Washington, D.C., there hangs a quilt unlike any other in the world. In fanciful, inspired, and yet simple and identifiable figures, it portrays the story of the Crucifixion.[2] It is considered rare, beyond price. Though it follows no known pattern of quilt-making, and though it is made of bits and pieces of worthless rags, it is obviously the work of a person of powerful imagination and deep spiritual feeling. Below this quilt I saw a note that
30　says it was made by "an anonymous Black woman in Alabama, a hundred years ago."

　　If we could locate this "anonymous" black woman from Alabama, she would turn out to be one of our grandmothers—an artist who left her mark in the only materials she could afford, and in the only medium her position in society allowed her to use. **B**

　　As Virginia Woolf[3] wrote further, in *A Room of One's Own:*

Yet genius of a sort must have existed among women as it must have existed among the working class. [Change this to "slaves" and "the wives and daughters of sharecroppers."] Now and again an Emily Brontë or a Robert Burns [change this to "a Zora Hurston or a Richard Wright"[4]] blazes out and proves its presence. But
40　*certainly it never got itself on to paper. When, however, one reads of a witch being ducked, of a woman possessed by devils [or "Sainthood"[5]], of a wise woman selling herbs [our root workers], or even a very remarkable man who had a mother, then I think we are on the track of a lost novelist, a suppressed poet, of some mute and inglorious Jane Austen[6]. . . . Indeed, I would venture to guess that Anon, who wrote so many poems without signing them, was often a woman. . . .* **C**

　　And so our mothers and grandmothers have, more often than not anonymously, handed on the creative spark, the seed of the flower they themselves never hoped to see: or like a sealed letter they could not plainly read.

　　And so it is, certainly, with my own mother. Unlike "Ma" Rainey's songs,
50　which retained their creator's name even while blasting forth from Bessie Smith's[7] mouth, no song or poem will bear my mother's name. Yet so many of the stories that I write, that we all write, are my mother's stories. Only recently did I fully

---

2. **Crucifixion:** the death of Jesus Christ, who was nailed to a cross.

3. **Virginia Woolf:** English novelist, critic, and pioneering feminist (1882–1941). Her works frequently explore the inner lives of women living under severe social constraints.

4. **Emily Brontë . . . Richard Wright:** Brontë (1818–1848) was an English novelist and poet, and Burns (1759–1796) was a Scottish poet. Hurston (1891–1960) and Wright (1908–1960) were African-American writers.

5. **"Sainthood":** a reference to certain black women in the South called Saints. They were intensely spiritual women who were driven to madness by their unfulfilled creativity.

6. **Jane Austen:** British novelist (1775–1817), best known for *Pride and Prejudice*.

7. **"Ma" Rainey's . . . Bessie Smith's:** Ma Rainey was the nickname of Gertrude Malissa Nix Pridgett Rainey (1886–1939), a blues singer considered to be the mother of the blues. Bessie Smith (1894–1937), another blues singer, was mentored by Ma Rainey.

realize this: that through years of listening to my mother's stories of her life, I have absorbed not only the stories themselves, but something of the manner in which she spoke, something of the urgency that involves the knowledge that her stories—like her life—must be recorded. It is probably for this reason that so much of what I have written is about characters whose counterparts in real life are so much older than I am.

But the telling of these stories, which came from my mother's lips as naturally
60 as breathing, was not the only way my mother showed herself as an artist. For stories, too, were subject to being distracted, to dying without conclusion. Dinners must be started, and cotton must be gathered before the big rains. The artist that was and is my mother showed itself to me only after many years. This is what I finally noticed:

Like Mem, a character in *The Third Life of Grange Copeland*,[8] my mother adorned with flowers whatever shabby house we were forced to live in. And not just your typical straggly country stand of zinnias, either. She planted ambitious gardens—and still does—with over fifty different varieties of plants that bloom profusely from early March until late November. Before she left home for the
70 fields, she watered her flowers, chopped up the grass, and laid out new beds. When she returned from the fields she might divide clumps of bulbs, dig a cold pit,[9] uproot and replant roses, or prune branches from her taller bushes or trees—until night came and it was too dark to see.

Whatever she planted grew as if by magic, and her fame as a grower of flowers spread over three counties. Because of her creativity with her flowers, even my memories of poverty are seen through a screen of blooms—sunflowers, petunias, roses, dahlias, forsythia, spirea, delphiniums, verbena . . . and on and on.

And I remember people coming to my mother's yard to be given cuttings from her flowers; I hear again the praise showered on her because whatever rocky
80 soil she landed on, she turned into a garden. A garden so brilliant with colors, so original in its design, so magnificent with life and creativity, that to this day people drive by our house in Georgia—perfect strangers and imperfect strangers—and ask to stand or walk among my mother's art.

I notice that it is only when my mother is working in her flowers that she is radiant, almost to the point of being invisible—except as Creator: hand and eye. She is involved in work her soul must have. Ordering the universe in the image of her personal conception of Beauty.

Her face, as she prepares the Art that is her gift, is a legacy of respect she leaves to me, for all that illuminates and cherishes life. She has handed down respect for
90 the possibilities—and the will to grasp them.

For her, so hindered and intruded upon in so many ways, being an artist has still been a daily part of her life. This ability to hold on, even in very simple ways, is work black women have done for a very long time. **D**

D AUTHOR'S MESSAGE
Reread lines 88–93. What lessons does Walker take from her mother's life?

---

8. *The Third Life of Grange Copeland:* Alice Walker's first novel, published in 1970.

9. **cold pit:** shallow pit, usually covered with glass, used for rooting or sheltering young plants from temperature variations in the spring.

This poem is not enough, but it is something, for the woman who literally covered the holes in our walls with sunflowers:

> They were women then
> My mama's generation
> Husky of voice—Stout of
> Step
> 100 With fists as well as
> Hands
> How they battered down
> Doors
> And ironed
> Starched white
> Shirts
> How they led
> Armies
> Headragged Generals
> 110 Across mined
> Fields
> Booby-trapped
> Kitchens
> To discover books
> Desks
> A place for us
> How they knew what we
> *Must* know
> Without knowing a page
> 120 Of it
> Themselves. **E**

E AUTHOR'S MESSAGE
Reread the poem in lines 96–121. Identify images Walker uses to describe these women. What qualities are emphasized by these images?

Guided by my heritage of a love of beauty and a respect for strength—in search of my mother's garden, I found my own.

And perhaps in Africa over two hundred years ago, there was just such a mother; perhaps she painted vivid and daring decorations in oranges and yellows and greens on the walls of her hut; perhaps she sang—in a voice like Roberta Flack's[10]—*sweetly* over the compounds of her village; perhaps she wove the most stunning mats or told the most ingenious stories of all the village storytellers. Perhaps she was herself a poet—though only her daughter's name is signed to the 130 poems that we know.

Perhaps Phillis Wheatley's mother was also an artist.

Perhaps in more than Phillis Wheatley's[11] biological life is her mother's signature made clear. ❧

---

10. **Roberta Flack's:** Flack is a popular African-American singer-songwriter.

11. **Phillis Wheatley's:** American poet Phillis Wheatley (1753?–1783), was born in Africa and brought to America in slavery. She is often referred to as the first African-American poet.

Comprehension

1. **Recall** On what occasions did Walker's mother lose her temper?

2. **Summarize** What did Walker's mother do in a typical day?

3. **Recall** According to Walker, what change occurred in her mother as she worked in her garden?

Literary Analysis

4. **Make Inferences** Recall that a **paradox** is a statement that may appear contradictory but in fact communicates an important truth. Identify the paradox in Walker's poem in lines 117–121. What point is Walker making?

5. **Analyze Author's Message** Reread the conclusion of Walker's essay in lines 124–133. Explain what Walker means by her reference to Phillis Wheatley's mother. In what way does this passage express the message of Walker's essay?

6. **Examine Cultural Context** Consider the conditions that constrained Walker's mother's life. Within this context, what is so remarkable about what she achieved? Support your answer with details.

7. **Make Generalizations** Consider Walker's descriptions of the following works of art by African-American women. What does each of these examples tell you about this artistic tradition?

   - the description of the quilt (lines 24–34)
   - Walker's comments on her mother's stories (lines 49–56)
   - the garden Walker's mother plants (lines 65–77)

8. **Draw Conclusions** Think back to your discussion about the **creative outlets** people use to express their artistic impulses. Consider the creative outlets described in question 7. In your opinion, what inspires these women to make art despite the obstacles they face?

Literary Criticism

9. **Critical Interpretations** "Walker's optimism," writes critic Donna Haisty Winchell, "is ultimately born of her belief that something of the divine exists in every human and nonhuman participant in the universe. The inhabitants of her fictional world search . . . for that divine spark that makes them uniquely who they are." In what ways might this quote also apply to the women in this nonfiction essay? Cite evidence from the text to support your conclusions.

Straw into Gold: The Metamorphosis of the Everyday

Essay by Sandra Cisneros

Sandra Cisneros

born 1954

Author Online

For more on Sandra Cisneros, visit the **Literature Center** at ClassZone.com.

"I'm trying to write the stories that haven't been written," Sandra Cisneros has proclaimed. With her rich, intimate portraits of Mexicans and Mexican Americans, Cisneros hopes to make readers of all races aware of the complexities of straddling two cultures. As a female minority writer, she sees herself as a voice for the voiceless. "I'm determined," she explains, "to fill a literary void."

Fighting Tradition Born to a Mexican father and a Mexican-American mother, Cisneros grew up on Chicago's South Side. The only girl among seven children, she felt as if she had "seven fathers" because her brothers tried to control her behavior. Like their father, they thought Sandra should adopt a quiet, traditional lifestyle. Fortunately, she was blessed with a mother "brave enough to raise her daughter in a nontraditional way." "My mother didn't force me to learn how to cook," says Cisneros. "And she always told me, 'Make sure you can take care of yourself.'"

Growing Up Lonely Cisneros formed few lasting friendships in early childhood, because her family moved frequently between Chicago and Mexico. "The moving back and forth, the new school, were very upsetting to me as a child," she once said. Retreating into herself, Cisneros became a keen observer of others and a secret writer of poetry. After years of clandestine composition, she encountered a teacher in high school who appreciated her experiences and her writing. With the teacher's encouragement, Cisneros began to share her work with her classmates.

The Value of Heritage In 1976, Cisneros entered the University of Iowa's prestigious Writers' Workshop. Surrounded by people from more privileged backgrounds, Cisneros felt intimidated. Soon, however, she came to realize that she could write about something her classmates could not. "It was not until this moment," Cisneros recalls, "when I separated myself, when I considered myself truly distinct, that my writing acquired a voice." Cisneros's realization gave rise to the acclaimed *The House on Mango Street* (1984), a series of interlocking prose poems about a poor Mexican-American family. Her reputation was cemented with the publication in 1991 of *Woman Hollering Creek,* a collection of stories. "In everything I've done in my life," she maintains, "including all the choices I've made as a writer, I've followed my gut and my heart. It's taken me where I've needed to go so far."

● LITERARY ANALYSIS: VOICE

A writer's **voice** is his or her unique style of expression. This unique use of language is what allows you to "hear" a human personality behind the words you read. In "Straw into Gold," Sandra Cisneros writes:

> *I'd never seen anybody make corn tortillas. Ever.*

The informal tone, the use of a contraction, the everyday words, the short sentence followed by a fragment, and the pauses before and after the word *ever*—all help create Cisneros's voice in this essay—one that is personal, relaxed, and almost conversational in its natural sound. As you read, look for instances when you "hear" Cisneros behind her words. Note the stylistic elements that help create this unique effect.

● READING SKILL: ANALYZE STRUCTURE

The **structure** of a literary work, or how its different parts are organized, is directly tied to the author's purpose. Cisneros's purpose in this personal essay is twofold. She shares with readers some of her formative experiences—moments that helped shape her life as a writer. She also aims to convey a message about life.

Personal essays are often loosely structured, and "Straw into Gold" is no exception. Cisneros begins the essay with an **anecdote**—a brief story that makes a point. After you read it, summarize it in a chart like the one shown. As you continue to read, summarize Cisneros's other recollections.

Anecdote or Recollection	Summary
introductory anecdote (lines 1–30)	

Explore the Key Idea

Where do writers get their MATERIAL?

KEY IDEA Writers harvest **ideas** for their work in a variety of places. Some writers find inspiration in controversies ripped from the headlines. Others are intrigued by a particular moment in history. Literature can be inspired by a writer's travels around the world, but just as often, powerful stories start closer to home. In "Straw into Gold," you will meet a writer who has unearthed a wealth of ideas in her own experiences and heritage.

QUICKWRITE Think of a work of literature you're familiar with. Where do you think the writer came by his or her ideas? Whether it's a lyric poem about lost love or a novel about a historical event, try to imagine the writer's source of material. Explain your thoughts in a short paragraph.

Straw into Gold:

The Metamorphosis of the Everyday

Sandra Cisneros

> **BACKGROUND** Cisneros originally delivered the text of "Straw into Gold" as a speech. The essay still retains some characteristics of an oral work—for example, the voice has a distinctly conversational character. The phrase "Straw into Gold" refers to the challenge faced by the heroine in "Rumplestiltskin." In this fairy tale, as you may recall, a miller's daughter will be put to death unless she can do the seemingly impossible—namely, spin gold out of mere straw. The word *metamorphosis* in the subtitle means "transformation."

ANALYZE VISUALS
What does the image on page 1225 suggest about women's roles in traditional Mexican culture? Read the essay, then revisit your answer, citing details from the text.

When I was living in an artists' colony in the south of France, some fellow Latin-Americans who taught at the university in Aix-en-Provence[1] invited me to share a homecooked meal with them. I had been living abroad almost a year then on an NEA[2] grant, subsisting mainly on French bread and lentils so that my money could last longer. So when the invitation to dinner arrived, I accepted without hesitation. Especially since they had promised Mexican food.

What I didn't realize when they made this invitation was that I was supposed to be involved in preparing the meal. I guess they assumed I knew how to cook Mexican food because I am Mexican. They wanted specifically tortillas, though
10 I'd never made a tortilla in my life. **Ⓐ**

Ⓐ VOICE
Reread lines 1–10. What stylistic elements allow Cisneros's informal, conversational voice to emerge? Cite specific examples.

---

1. **Aix-en-Provence** (āk´sän-prō-väns´): French city about ten miles north of the Mediterranean Sea.

2. **NEA:** the National Endowment for the Arts, a federal agency that funds artistic projects of organizations and individuals.

Making Tortillas (1926), Diego Rivera. University of California, San Francisco. © Bridgeman Art Library.

It's true I had witnessed my mother rolling the little armies of dough into perfect circles, but my mother's family is from Guanajuato;[3] they are *provincianos*, country folk. They only know how to make flour tortillas. My father's family, on the other hand, is *chilango*[4] from Mexico City. We ate corn tortillas but we didn't make them. Someone was sent to the corner tortilleria to buy some. I'd never seen anybody make corn tortillas. Ever.

Somehow my Latino hosts had gotten a hold of a packet of corn flour, and this is what they tossed my way with orders to produce tortillas. *Así como sea.* Any ol' way, they said and went back to their cooking.

20 Why did I feel like the woman in the fairy tale who was locked in a room and ordered to spin straw into gold? I had the same sick feeling when I was required to write my critical essay for the MFA[5] exam—the only piece of noncreative writing necessary in order to get my graduate degree. How was I to start? There were rules involved here, unlike writing a poem or story, which I did intuitively. There was a step by step process needed and I had better know it. I felt as if making tortillas— or writing a critical paper, for that matter—were tasks so impossible I wanted to break down into tears.

Somehow though, I managed to make tortillas—crooked and burnt, but edible nonetheless. My hosts were absolutely ignorant when it came to Mexican 30 food; they thought my tortillas were delicious. (I'm glad my mama wasn't there.) Thinking back and looking at an old photograph documenting the three of us consuming those lopsided circles I am amazed. Just as I am amazed I could finish my MFA exam. I've managed to do a lot of things in my life I didn't think I was capable of and which many others didn't think I was capable of either. Especially because I am a woman, a Latina, an only daughter in a family of six men. My father would've liked to have seen me married long ago. In our culture men and women don't leave their father's house except by way of marriage. I crossed my father's threshold with nothing carrying me but my own two feet. A woman whom no one came for and no one chased away. **B**

40 To make matters worse, I left before any of my six brothers had ventured away from home. I broke a terrible taboo. Somehow, looking back at photos of myself as a child, I wonder if I was aware of having begun already my own quiet war.

I like to think that somehow my family, my Mexicanness, my poverty, all had something to do with shaping me into a writer. I like to think my parents were preparing me all along for my life as an artist even though they didn't know it. From my father I inherited a love of wandering. He was born in Mexico City but as a young man he traveled into the U.S. vagabonding. He eventually was drafted and thus became a citizen. Some of the stories he has told about his first months in the U.S. with little or no English surface in my stories in *The House on Mango* 50 *Street*[6] as well as others I have in mind to write in the future. From him I inherited

B ANALYZE STRUCTURE
What does Cisneros's completion of her MFA exam have in common with the experience recounted in the tortilla anecdote? Explain how these experiences make Cisneros feel like "the woman in the fairy tale" she alludes to in lines 20–21.

---

3. **Guanajuato** (gwä'nä-hwä'tō): state in central Mexico.

4. *chilango* (chē-läng'gō) *Mexican slang:* native to Mexico City.

5. **MFA:** Master of Fine Arts, an academic degree.

6. *The House on Mango Street:* Cisneros's first book of fiction, published in 1983.

a sappy heart. (He still cries when he watches Mexican soaps—especially if they deal with children who have forsaken their parents.)

My mother was born like me—in Chicago but of Mexican descent. It would be her tough streetwise voice that would haunt all my stories and poems. An amazing woman who loves to draw and read books and can sing an opera. A smart cookie. **C**

C VOICE
Reread Cisneros's description of her parents in lines 43–55. Identify the informal words, as well as the short sentences and fragments, that establish Cisneros's voice here.

When I was a little girl we traveled to Mexico City so much I thought my grandparents' house on La Fortuna, number 12, was home. It was the only constant in our nomadic ramblings from one Chicago flat to another. The house on Destiny Street, number 12, in the colonia Tepeyac would be perhaps the only
60 home I knew, and that nostalgia for a home would be a theme that would obsess me.

My brothers also figured greatly in my art. Especially the older two; I grew up in their shadows. Henry, the second oldest and my favorite, appears often in poems I have written and in stories which at times only borrow his nickname, Kiki. He played a major role in my childhood. We were bunk-bed mates. We were co-conspirators. We were pals. Until my oldest brother came back from studying in Mexico and left me odd woman out for always.

What would my teachers say if they knew I was a writer now? Who would've guessed it? I wasn't a very bright student. I didn't much like school because we
70 moved so much and I was always new and funny looking. In my fifth-grade report card I have nothing but an avalanche of C's and D's, but I don't remember being that stupid. I was good at art and I read plenty of library books and Kiki laughed at all my jokes. At home I was fine, but at school I never opened my mouth except when the teacher called on me.

When I think of how I see myself it would have to be at age eleven. I know I'm thirty-two on the outside, but inside I'm eleven. I'm the girl in the picture with skinny arms and a crumpled skirt and crooked hair. I didn't like school because all they saw was the outside me. School was lots of rules and sitting with your hands folded and being very afraid all the time. I liked looking out the window
80 and thinking. I liked staring at the girl across the way writing her name over and over again in red ink. I wondered why the boy with the dirty collar in front of me didn't have a mama who took better care of him.

I think my mama and papa did the best they could to keep us warm and clean and never hungry. We had birthday and graduation parties and things like that, but there was another hunger that had to be fed. There was a hunger I didn't even have a name for. Was this when I began writing? **D**

D ANALYZE STRUCTURE
Identify the six recollections Cisneros presents in lines 43–86. What do they have in common? Explain why Cisneros might have chosen to include these particular memories.

In 1966 we moved into a house, a real one, our first real home. This meant we didn't have to change schools and be the new kids on the block every couple of years. We could make friends and not be afraid we'd have to say goodbye to them
90 and start all over. My brothers and the flock of boys they brought home would become important characters eventually for my stories—Louie and his cousins, Meme Ortiz and his dog with two names, one in English and one in Spanish.

My mother flourished in her own home. She took books out of the library and taught herself to garden—to grow flowers so envied we had to put a lock on the gate to keep out the midnight flower thieves. My mother has never quit gardening.

This was the period in my life, that slippery age when you are both child and woman and neither, I was to record in *The House on Mango Street.* I was still shy. I was a girl who couldn't come out of her shell.

100   How was I to know I would be recording and documenting the women who sat their sadness on an elbow and stared out a window? It would be the city streets of Chicago I would later record, as seen through a child's eyes.

I've done all kinds of things I didn't think I could do since then. I've gone to a prestigious university, studied with famous writers, and taken an MFA degree. I've taught poetry in schools in Illinois and Texas. I've gotten an NEA grant and run away with it as far as my courage would take me. I've seen the bleached and bitter mountains of the Peloponnesus.[7] I've lived on an island. I've been to Venice twice. I've lived in Yugoslavia. I've been to the famous Nice[8] flower market behind the opera house. I've lived in a village in the pre-Alps and witnessed the daily parade

110   of promenaders. **E**

I've moved since Europe to the strange and wonderful country of Texas, land of polaroid-blue skies and big bugs. I met a mayor with my last name. I met famous Chicana and Chicano artists and writers and *políticos.*[9] **F**

Texas is another chapter in my life. It brought with it the Dobie-Paisano Fellowship,[10] a six-month residency on a 265-acre ranch. But most important, Texas brought Mexico back to me.

In the days when I would sit at my favorite people-watching spot, the snakey Woolworth's counter across the street from the Alamo[11] (the Woolworth's which has since been torn down to make way for progress), I couldn't think of anything

120   else I'd rather be than a writer. I've traveled and lectured from Cape Cod to San Francisco, to Spain, Yugoslavia, Greece, Mexico, France, Italy, and now today to Texas. Along the way there has been straw for the taking. With a little imagination, it can be spun into gold. ❧

E ANALYZE STRUCTURE
Reread lines 103–110. How does this list of accomplishments relate back to Cisneros's opening anecdote?

F VOICE
Cisneros's use of the word *políticos* in line 113 is one example of her technique of incorporating Spanish words and phrases in her writing. Find two other examples of this technique in the selection. What is her purpose for including these words?

---

7. **Peloponnesus** (pĕl'ə-pə-nē'-səs): peninsula forming the southern part of mainland Greece.

8. **Nice** (nēs): port city in southern France.

9. ***políticos*** (pō-lē'tē-kōs) *Spanish*: politicians.

10. **Dobie-Paisano** (dō'bē pī-zä'nō) **Fellowship:** a prestigious award offered to authors who are from or write about Texas. It includes cash as well as the use of living quarters.

11. **Alamo:** a mission chapel in San Antonio, Texas, site of a famous battle in Texas's war of independence from Mexico.

Comprehension

1. **Recall** What misunderstanding does Cisneros recount at the beginning of the essay?

2. **Recall** What traits do Cisneros and her father have in common?

3. **Summarize** As a child, how did Cisneros feel at school?

Literary Analysis

4. **Make Inferences** What childhood events and circumstances inspired Cisneros to become a writer? Cite evidence from the selection to support your inferences.

5. **Interpret Allusion** An allusion is an indirect reference to a person, a place, an event, or a literary work with which the writer believes the reader will be familiar. Reread lines 120–123 and consider the essay's title. By incorporating allusions to the fairy tale "Rumplestiltskin," what point is Cisneros making about ordinary experiences? What is she saying about the imagination?

6. **Draw Conclusions** From statements Cisneros makes in this essay, what can you conclude about her feelings regarding

   • traditional female roles in Latino culture (lines 33–42)?
   • home ownership (lines 56–61 and 87–90)?
   • racial or ethnic stereotypes (lines 7–16)?

7. **Analyze Structure** Review the chart you created. What idea does Cisneros return to throughout the essay? What is the function of this recurring idea in developing her message? Support your answer with evidence from the text.

8. **Compare Voice** In a chart, record examples of the stylistic elements that create Cisneros's unique voice. Then choose another prose selection from this unit, and analyze the voice of its author as well. Use your completed chart to explain how Cisneros's voice differs from that of the other writer's.

	Sentence Type/Length	Word Choice	Tone
Cisneros			
Other Writer			

Literary Criticism

9. **Critical Interpretations** Cisneros's candid recollections prompted one critic to say, "The memories that Cisneros offers . . . sometimes wrinkle the nose and scorch the palate." He went on to praise her talent for "evoking the sensations of the past in their full complexity." Why do you think Cisneros shares her insecurities and painful experiences as well as her triumphs? How might failing to do this have altered the essay's message? Explain, citing evidence.

Life for My Child Is Simple
Primer for Blacks

Poetry by Gwendolyn Brooks

Brooks at home on Chicago's South Side, 1960

Gwendolyn Brooks
1917–2000

Decades before urban musicians introduced Americans to rap and hip hop, Gwendolyn Brooks captured some of these same rhythms in her writing. In verse celebrated for its lyrical beauty, Brooks portrays the thoughts, feelings, and, often, extraordinary heroism of African Americans living amidst poverty and segregation.

An Early Start Though born in Topeka, Kansas, Brooks spent almost her entire life in Chicago. Even as a young girl, she loved to write. When she was 7, Brooks began filling composition books with "careful rhymes," prompting her mother to exclaim, "You are going to be the lady Paul Laurence Dunbar." By the age of 16, Brooks was a frequent contributor to *The Defender,* a prominent black newspaper in Chicago. During her teenage years, leading African-American poets James Weldon Johnson and Langston Hughes also recognized her immense talent.

Literary Triumph At 28, Brooks published *A Street in Bronzeville,* named for the bustling black enclave on Chicago's South Side. Written in a range of traditional forms, the poems explored the difficult lives of those around her. "I wrote about what I saw and heard in the street," Brooks said. "I lived in a small second-floor apartment at the corner, and I could look first on one side and then the other. There was my material." In 1949, Brooks published *Annie Allen,* a series of poems that trace the life of a Bronzeville girl. The book achieved literary acclaim and propelled its author into the spotlight. In 1950, Brooks became the first African-American writer to receive the Pulitzer Prize. The award brought her worldwide fame. "Sometimes," she quipped, "I feel that my name is Gwendolyn Pulitzer Brooks."

A Fateful Encounter Brooks experienced another turning point in 1967, when she attended a conference of black writers, meeting young African-American poets. Impressed by their commitment to a black aesthetic and issues of racial justice, Brooks became interested in writing a new kind of poetry. "If it hadn't been for these young people," she later remarked, "I wouldn't know what I know about this society. By associating with them I know who I am." Brooks began to experiment with free verse and to focus on the problems of color and justice. She started a poetry workshop for members of a Chicago street gang and became a lifelong advocate for the next generation. "My greatest interest," Brooks once said, "is being involved with young people."

LITERARY ANALYSIS: REPETITION

What keeps a song or a poem stuck in your mind long after you've heard it on the radio or read it in the classroom? Often, the answer lies in the writer's use of **repetition,** a technique in which a sound, word, phrase, or line is repeated for emphasis or to create rhythm. A related technique is **anaphora,** in which the same word or phrase is repeated at the beginning of two or more lines. Consider this example from "Primer for Blacks":

Blackness
is a title,
is a preoccupation,
is a commitment . . .

As you read, pay close attention to Brooks's use of repetition and especially of anaphora. Consider what these techniques emphasize in each poem, and note the rhythm they help build.

READING SKILL: COMPARE AND CONTRAST POEMS

Brooks's poetry career spanned six decades. She wrote "Life for My Child Is Simple" early in her career; it comes from *Annie Allen,* which traces the life of a fictional character but draws much of its inspiration from Brooks's own experiences. "Primer for Blacks" was written many years later, when Brooks was developing a deeper commitment to political and social issues. As you read, **compare and contrast** these two poems in a chart as shown. The following tips can help you:

- Ask yourself about the **subject** of each poem. Is it personal or political? Does it focus on a group or an individual?

- Describe the **tone.**

- Consider **stylistic elements** such as diction, punctuation, and capitalization.

- Identify the **theme** of each poem. What message does each suggest about life?

	"Life for My Child Is Simple"	"Primer for Blacks"
Subject		
Tone		
Speaker		
Style		
Theme		

What should we REACH for?

KEY IDEA Gwendolyn Brooks advised her readers to "exhaust the little moment"—to live richly and **strive** higher in each moment of their lives. What, in your opinion, is worth striving for?

QUICKWRITE Brainstorm a list of things that are worth reaching for. Start by listing personal goals. Then move on to more global issues: if you had unlimited resources, what would you fix or change? Come up with a top-ten list of the things most worth striving for.

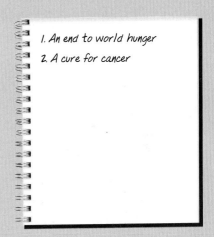

1. An end to world hunger
2. A cure for cancer

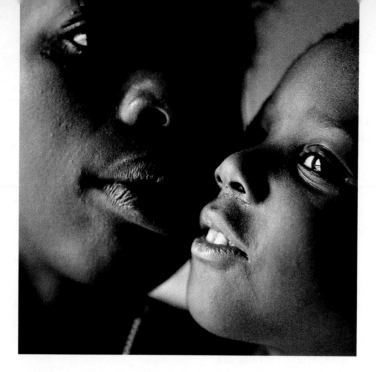

Life for My Child Is Simple

GWENDOLYN BROOKS

Life for my child is simple, and is good.
He knows his wish. Yes, but that is not all.
Because I know mine too.
And we both want joy of undeep and unabiding[1] things,
5 Like kicking over a chair or throwing blocks out of a window
Or tipping over an ice box pan[2]
Or snatching down curtains or fingering an electric outlet
Or a journey or a friend or an illegal kiss.
No. There is more to it than that. **Ⓐ**
10 It is that he has never been afraid.
Rather, he reaches out and lo the chair falls with a beautiful crash,
And the blocks fall, down on the people's heads,
And the water comes slooshing sloppily out across the floor.
And so forth.
15 Not that success, for him, is sure, infallible.[3]
But never has he been afraid to reach.
His lesions are legion.[4]
But reaching is his rule.

Ⓐ REPETITION
Reread lines 4–9
aloud. What happens
to the poem's pace as
the repetition builds?
Describe the feeling
created by the **rhythm**
in these lines.

---

1. **unabiding:** not lasting; continually changing.
2. **ice box pan:** a pan for collecting melted ice in an old-fashioned refrigerator.
3. **infallible:** foolproof.
4. **His lesions are legion:** His injuries are many.

Primer for Blacks

GWENDOLYN BROOKS

Blackness
is a title,
is a preoccupation,[1]
is a commitment Blacks
5 are to comprehend—
and in which you are
to perceive your Glory.

The conscious shout
of all that is white is
10 "It's Great to be white."
The conscious shout
of the slack[2] in Black is
"It's Great to be white."
Thus all that is white
15 has white strength and yours. **B**

The word Black
has geographic power,
pulls everybody in:
Blacks here—
20 Blacks there—
Blacks wherever they may be.
And remember, you Blacks, what they told you—
remember your Education:
"one Drop—one Drop[3]
25 maketh a brand new Black."

Oh mighty Drop.
And because they have given us kindly
so many more of our people

Everyman, Brenda Joysmith. 345″ × 58 1/4″. © Brenda Joysmith. Courtesy of Joysmith Gallery.

B COMPARE AND CONTRAST POEMS
So far, how does this poem differ from "Life for My Child Is Simple" in both **content** and **style?** Cite examples from both poems to support your answer.

---

1. **preoccupation:** something requiring full attention.
2. **slack:** lack of force.
3. **"one Drop":** At times in U.S. history, a person with only "one drop" of African blood has been considered black.

Blackness
30 stretches over the land.
Blackness—
the Black of it,
the rust-red of it,
the milk and cream of it,
35 the tan and yellow-tan of it,
the deep-brown middle-brown high-brown of it,
the "olive" and ochre[4] of it—
Blackness
marches on. **C**

40 The huge, the pungent[5] object of our prime out-ride
is to Comprehend,
to salute and to Love the fact that we are Black,
which *is* our "ultimate Reality,"[6]
which is the lone ground
45 from which our meaningful metamorphosis,
from which our prosperous staccato,[7]
group or individual, can rise.

Self-shriveled Blacks.
Begin with gaunt and marvelous concession:
50 YOU are our costume and our fundamental bone.

All of you—
you COLORED ones,
you NEGRO ones,
those of you who proudly cry
55 "I'm half INDian"—
those of you who proudly screech
"I'VE got the blood of George WASHington in MY veins"—
ALL of you—
you proper Blacks,
60 you half-Blacks,
you wish-I-weren't Blacks,
Niggeroes and Niggerenes.

You.

C **REPETITION**
Reread lines 31–39.
What does Brooks's use
of **anaphora** emphasize
about the many shades of
blackness she lists? What
point is she making here?

---

4. **ochre** (ō'kər): brownish orange-yellow.

5. **pungent** (pŭn'jənt): sharp and intense, like a powerful odor.

6. **the fact . . . "ultimate Reality":** a rewording of a quotation from black activist Ron Karenga.

7. **staccato** (stə-kä'tō): the playing of musical notes in a crisp, disconnected way.

Comprehension

1. **Recall** In "Life for My Child Is Simple," what things does the child enjoy doing?

2. **Clarify** How do the child's feelings differ from his mother's?

3. **Clarify** Reread lines 16–30 of "Primer for Blacks." Why does "the word Black" have "geographic power"?

4. **Clarify** What, according to Brooks, is the object of blacks' "prime out-ride," or most important undertaking?

Literary Analysis

5. **Interpret** Reread lines 10–18 of "Life for My Child Is Simple." Why has the speaker's son never been afraid of **striving** for what he wants? Why, in contrast, might the speaker have felt fearful?

6. **Examine Author's Purpose** Determine Brooks's intended audience for "Primer for Blacks." What do you think she wants her audience to feel? What action does she want her audience to take? Cite specific lines from the poem to support your answers.

7. **Analyze Style** Review "Primer for Blacks," noting Brooks's use of nonstandard capitalization. Why do you think she does this? How does this unorthodox capitalization affect the poem's meaning and contribute to the voice of the speaker?

8. **Analyze Repetition** Reconsider the annotated examples of repetition in Brooks's poems. Then find at least one other example in each work. Do your examples qualify as **anaphora?** In each case, what is the impact of repetition on the meaning?

9. **Compare and Contrast Poems** Using the chart you filled in as you read, summarize the similarities and the differences you found in the two poems. In your opinion, do the poems suggest similar or different ways of approaching life? Explain, citing evidence.

10. **Draw Conclusions About Theme** In these poems, what overall messages does Brooks communicate about

    • fulfilling one's potential?   • confidence and self-regard?

    • black identity?   • beauty?

Literary Criticism

11. **Author's Style** In the late 1960s, Brooks began experimenting with **free verse,** believing she was no longer living in "a sonnet kind of time." Why do you think Brooks chose free verse for these two poems? In your opinion, is free verse an appropriate poetic form for these works? Explain your opinions.

Adolescence—III
Testimonial

Poetry by Rita Dove

Rita Dove
born 1952

For Rita Dove, the personal and the historical are equally important. "I've been fascinated," she says, "by what I've called before 'the underside of history,' the dramas of ordinary people." In her poetry, Dove often interweaves historical events with personal narratives, producing lyric images of everyday life.

High Achiever The daughter of a research chemist who broke the color barrier in the tire industry, Dove was always encouraged, she says, "to go as far as [she] could." Her parents drove Dove to excel in school and counseled her to never give up. Their guidance served her well. As a teenager, she was one of only 100 high school seniors named Presidential Scholar. She also distinguished herself in college, graduating Phi Beta Kappa from Miami University in 1973.

A Passion for Words Dove first became aware of the power of storytelling as a young girl. Listening to local storytellers in her hometown of Akron, Ohio, Dove discovered "the delight of shaping life with words." She also began a lifelong love affair with poetry, sparked by her discovery of an anthology in the local library. Though Dove began writing as a child, she did not fully embrace literary pursuits until college. Determining then that she wanted to be a writer, she applied and was accepted to the prestigious Iowa Writers' Workshop.

National Acclaim Publication in magazines had already earned Dove widespread praise when her first poetry collection, *The Yellow House on the Corner*, came out in 1980. Over the next few years, she published several more books, including *Thomas and Beulah*, hailed as her masterpiece. The book, which drew its inspiration from the quiet heroism of Dove's grandparents' lives, won a Pulitzer Prize in 1987. Since then, Dove has gone on to collect numerous literary honors.

Illuminating the Everyday Though she touches on issues of race, her poems, Dove asserts, "are about humanity." They attempt to convey something about the gamut of human experiences, not just the positive moments. "All the moments that make up a human being," Dove says, "have to be written about, talked about, painted, danced, in order to really talk about life."

● LITERARY ANALYSIS: SOUND DEVICES

A musician as well as a poet, Rita Dove believes a poem's sound is paramount. "If a poem doesn't have a sense of music," she explains, "then that poem probably won't move me very much." To infuse her poems with this quality, Dove employs **sound devices**—patterns of word sounds that create musical or rhythmic effects. As you read Dove's poems, listen for the following sound devices:

- **alliteration**—the repetition of initial consonant sounds
- **assonance**—the repetition of vowel sounds within words
- **consonance**—the repetition of consonant sounds within and at the ends of words

Think about how these sound devices impart a musical quality to the poems. Also consider what words, images, and feelings these devices serve to highlight.

● READING SKILL: MAKE INFERENCES ABOUT SPEAKERS

The language in Dove's poems is often restrained and concise. She characterizes the **speaker** in each poem with a few well-chosen details but does not offer much explicit description or commentary. It is up to you to read between the lines, or **make inferences,** about each speaker's situation and state of mind. As you read, collect clues that tell you about each speaker's age, situation, and mindset. After you read, you'll use this information to **draw conclusions** about each speaker's experiences.

Clues from the Text	My Inferences and Reactions
"...Mom and I worked/ The dusky rows of tomatoes." (lines 1–2)	The speaker and her mother probably live in a rural area, not the city. They work hard in the fields.

Explore the Key Idea

How does your PERSPECTIVE *change?*

KEY IDEA As you get older, the way you think and feel about important events in your life changes. And your **perspective** on something that looms in your future—graduation, for instance—will probably change once that event has actually happened.

QUICKWRITE Think of a big event or an important moment from your recent past; write a paragraph describing your feelings about it. Then imagine how you will feel about this same event ten years from now. How might your perspective have changed? Pretending to be your future self, write a second paragraph describing the event from this later perspective.

Adolescence — III

Rita Dove

BACKGROUND Dove wrote "Adolescence—III" early in her career, for her first published collection of poems. She composed "Testimonial" many years later and read it in the spring of 2001 at Howard University's commencement. "Whenever you think back," Dove told the graduating seniors, "and wonder where the future is going to lead you, remember that others have stood at this position and wondered, too. What you should do is take a step, one step at a time."

ANALYZE VISUALS
What words would you use to describe the girl in the painting? What details support your impressions?

With Dad gone, Mom and I worked
The dusky rows of tomatoes.
As they glowed orange in sunlight
And rotted in shadow, I too
5 Grew orange and softer, swelling out
Starched cotton slips. **A**

The texture of twilight made me think of
Lengths of Dotted Swiss.[1] In my room
I wrapped scarred knees in dresses
10 That once went to big-band dances;
I baptized my earlobes with rosewater.
Along the window-sill, the lipstick stubs
Glittered in their steel shells. **B**

Looking out at the rows of clay
15 And chicken manure, I dreamed how it would happen:
He would meet me by the blue spruce,
A carnation over his heart, saying,
"I have come for you, Madam;
I have loved you in my dreams."
20 At his touch, the scabs would fall away.
Over his shoulder, I see my father coming toward us:
He carries his tears in a bowl,
And blood hangs in the pine-soaked air.

A MAKE INFERENCES
What inferences can you make about the **speaker's** age from lines 1–6 and the poem's title? Do you get a sense of her family's situation in life? Explain.

B SOUND DEVICES
Reread lines 7–13. Find one example of **alliteration** and one of **assonance** in these lines. What words or images are emphasized by these devices?

---

1. **Dotted Swiss:** crisp, sheer cotton fabric decorated with raised dots.

Evening Thoughts, Ernest Crichlow.
Lithograph, 25″ × 18″. Arisca Fine Art.

Testimonial
Rita Dove

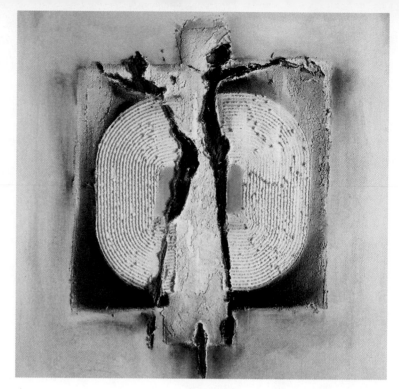

Discovery I, Alfred Gockel. 39¹/₄″ × 39¹/₄″. © Alfred Gockel.

Back when the earth was new
and heaven just a whisper,
back when the names of things
hadn't had time to stick;

5 back when the smallest breezes
melted summer into autumn,
when all the poplars quivered
sweetly in rank and file . . .

the world called, and I answered.
10 Each glance ignited to a gaze.
I caught my breath and called that life,
swooned between spoonfuls of lemon sorbet. **C**

I was pirouette¹ and flourish,
I was filigree² and flame.
15 How could I count my blessings
when I didn't know their names?

Back when everything was still to come,
luck leaked out everywhere. **D**
I gave my promise to the world,
20 and the world followed me here.

---

1. **pirouette** (pǐr'o͞o-ĕt'): in ballet, a full turn of the body on one
foot.

2. **filigree:** delicate ornamentation, often made of wire.

C **MAKE INFERENCES**
Reread the poem's first
three stanzas, noting
the verb tense and the
imagery. What can you
infer about the **speaker's**
age and state of mind?

D **SOUND DEVICES**
Identify the sound
device used in line 18.
What does this sense of
musicality contribute to
the poem's **tone?**

Comprehension

1. **Recall** In "Adolescence—III," what task occupies the speaker and her mother?

2. **Summarize** What does the adolescent speaker dream will happen to her?

3. **Summarize** In "Testimonial," how did the speaker respond to the world as a young person?

Literary Analysis

4. **Draw Conclusions About Speakers** Review the **inferences** you made as you read. Using this information, explain the conclusions you can draw about each speaker's situation and state of mind. How do the two speakers' **perspectives** differ? Explain, citing evidence from both poems.

5. **Compare Mood** How would you describe the mood of each poem? Citing specific words and phrases, explain how you think the moods of the two poems are similar or different.

6. **Interpret Imagery** Many critics admire Dove's use of imagery. Look back over the images listed below. What does each one tell you about Dove's thoughts on the nature of youth?

   - the description of the world in "Testimonial" (lines 1–9)
   - the kind of life the speaker of "Testimonial" leads (lines 11–14)
   - the changes the speaker of "Adolescence—III" undergoes (lines 4–11)
   - the final image of "Adolescence—III" (lines 21–23)

7. **Analyze Sound Devices** Reexamine the two poems, looking for examples of each sound device listed in the chart. Use your completed chart to explain what tone and sensibility is established by the sound devices in each poem.

Sound Device	"Adolescence—III"	"Testimonial"
alliteration		
assonance		
consonance		

Literary Criticism

8. **Cultural Context** Commenting on **themes** in her poetry, Dove has stated, "Obviously, as a black woman, I am concerned with race.... But certainly not every poem of mine mentions the fact of being black. They are poems about humanity, and sometimes humanity happens to be black." How does this view differ from the sensibility expressed by Gwendolyn Brooks in "Primer for Blacks" on page 1233? Explain your answer, citing evidence from each poet's work.

The Man in the Moon
Forgetfulness

Poetry by Billy Collins

Billy Collins
born 1941

Billy Collins is that rare thing—a celebrity poet. His books break poetry sales records, his readings pack concert halls, and his poems elicit rave reviews from writers and critics alike. Indeed, no American poet since Robert Frost has managed to acquire such a broad and devoted following.

New York Roots Born in a New York City hospital where poet William Carlos Williams once worked, Collins is a nearly lifelong New Yorker. Growing up in Queens, he displayed an early flair for writing and a deep passion for literature. After college, he earned a doctoral degree in Romantic poetry from the University of California. Today, however, Collins feels a certain aversion to this poetry. "The Romantics killed off humor," he once explained.

Grammar Teacher Makes It Big In 1971, Collins began teaching English at the City University of New York and writing poetry in his spare time. Absorbed by his teaching, Collins did not publish his first collection, *Pokerface* (1977), until he was 36. In the next 11 years, he published two additional collections. However, Collins did not achieve a widespread following until his fourth collection, *Questions About Angels* (1991), won the National Poetry Series competition. Since then his popularity has grown explosively, thanks in part to his charismatic poetry readings.

America's Poet In recognition of his poetic achievements, Collins was named U.S. poet laureate in 2001. During his two-year tenure, he encouraged the enjoyment of poetry in America's high schools, since "that's really where for most people poetry dies off and gets buried under other adolescent pursuits."

The Enigma of the Ordinary Though Collins has publicly expressed his political views, he is not a political poet. His poems are primarily concerned with the mystery of ordinary things and of everyday experiences. "Poetry is a home for ambiguity," he once noted. "It is one of the few places where ambiguity is honored." Often, a Collins poem begins with a humorous observation and then takes an unexpected turn, inviting readers to look afresh at the world around them.

● LITERARY ANALYSIS: IMAGERY

When you read a poem, you enter a world filled with sights, sounds, smells, and textures all its own. Poets draw you into this world using **imagery,** words and images that re-create sensory experiences for the reader. Billy Collins owes some of his enormous popularity to the world he creates for his readers—a world that is often intensely familiar. Collins writes about everyday topics, presenting images from the natural world and the domestic sphere that are as recognizable as they are memorable. Note the words that appeal to your senses of sight and touch in these lines from "The Man in the Moon":

He used to frighten me in the nights of childhood,
the wide adult face, enormous, stern, aloft.
I could not imagine such loneliness, such coldness.

As you read, look for language that appeals to your senses, especially your sense of sight. Consider whether the images seem familiar to you and what ideas they serve to emphasize in each poem.

● READING SKILL: TRACE THE DEVELOPMENT OF AN IDEA

Appreciating the sensory experience that a poem creates as you read it is one crucial aspect of analyzing poetry. Also important, however, is examining the **ideas** the poet presents. As you read, use the following strategies to trace the development of the ideas Collins puts forth in "The Man in the Moon" and "Forgetfulness." Use a chart like the one shown to organize your notes.

- Consider each poem's **title.** What idea does it suggest?

- Note the concept introduced or elaborated upon in each **stanza.** Consider how each stanza builds upon the one preceding it.

- Analyze Collins's **tone.** What attitude is expressed in each group of lines? Does the tone remain consistent throughout the poem, or does it change?

"The Man in the Moon"		
	Ideas Suggested	Tone
Title	The title makes me think of a children's story.	playful
Stanza 1		
Stanza 2		

What do the YEARS take with them?

KEY IDEA As we **age,** we gain some things, such as maturity and wisdom. Other things—energy, for example, or idealism—seem to slip from us. In your opinion, do the years take more than they give?

ROLE-PLAY With a partner, improvise a scene in which two characters talk about growing older. First, discuss what the characters might say to each other about the joys and ordeals of aging—maybe they miss letting their imaginations run wild, or perhaps they appreciate the wisdom they've developed over the years. Decide whether your scene will be a comic or a serious one. Then write a dialogue between the characters and act it out for the class.

The Man in the **Moon**
Billy Collins

He used to frighten me in the nights of childhood,
the wide adult face, enormous, stern, aloft.
I could not imagine such loneliness, such coldness.

But tonight as I drive home over these hilly roads
5 I see him sinking behind stands of winter trees
and rising again to show his familiar face. **A**

And when he comes into full view over open fields
he looks like a young man who has fallen in love
with the dark earth,

10 a pale bachelor, well-groomed and full of melancholy,
his round mouth open
as if he had just broken into song. **B**

A TRACE IDEAS
Reread lines 1–6. How do
you know what Collins is
referring to when he says
He? Explain how Collins's
description of his subject
changes from one stanza
to the next. Record your
answer in your chart.

B IMAGERY
Identify details that allow
you to **visualize** the sight
Collins describes. How
does this description
underscore the changing
attitude of the speaker?

Forgetfulness

Billy Collins

The name of the author is the first to go
followed obediently by the title, the plot,
the heartbreaking conclusion, the entire novel
which suddenly becomes one you have never read, never
5   even heard of,

as if, one by one, the memories you used to harbor
decided to retire to the southern hemisphere of the brain,
to a little fishing village where there are no phones. **C**

Long ago you kissed the names of the nine Muses[1] goodbye
10 and watched the quadratic equation[2] pack its bag,
and even now as you memorize the order of the planets,

something else is slipping away, a state flower perhaps,
the address of an uncle, the capital of Paraguay.

Whatever it is you are struggling to remember
15 it is not poised on the tip of your tongue,
not even lurking in some obscure corner of your spleen.

It has floated away down a dark mythological river
whose name begins with an L[3] as far as you can recall,
well on your own way to oblivion where you will join those
20 who have even forgotten how to swim and how to ride a
    bicycle.

No wonder you rise in the middle of the night
to look up the date of a famous battle in a book on war.
No wonder the moon in the window seems to have drifted
25 out of a love poem that you used to know by heart.

---

1. **nine Muses:** in Greek mythology, goddesses of various fine arts and sciences.
2. **quadratic equation:** equation involving squaring of an unknown quantity or quantities, such as x^2.
3. **dark . . . an L:** the river Lethe, located in Hades, according to Greek mythology. Drinking its water caused one to forget the past.

C **TRACE IDEAS**
Reread lines 1–8.
Describe Collins's **tone** as he introduces the idea of forgetfulness. What words and phrases help him achieve this tone? Note any changes in tone as you continue to read.

Comprehension

1. **Summarize** In "The Man in the Moon," how does the speaker's attitude toward the moon change as he gets older?

2. **Recall** List three things that the speaker of "Forgetfulness" has forgotten.

3. **Clarify** In "Forgetfulness," what troubles the speaker in the middle of the night?

Literary Analysis

4. **Interpret** What happens to the speaker of "The Man in The Moon" as the years pass? How does the speaker's outlook on life change? Citing evidence from the poem, describe what the years seem to take with them.

5. **Examine Allusions** In "Forgetfulness," what ideas are developed or underscored by each of the following allusions?

   • the Muses, the Greek goddesses who preside over the arts and sciences (line 9)

   • Lethe, the river of forgetfulness (lines 17–18)

6. **Analyze Personification** The giving of human qualities to an object, animal, or idea is called personification. Find at least two examples of personification in "Forgetfulness." What does Collins's use of this technique contribute to the poem's **tone?**

7. **Analyze Imagery** Reread lines 22–25 of "Forgetfulness." Compare the concrete image of the moon—the only real image that appears in the poem—with the fleeting, intangible nature of the things the speaker has forgotten. What does this contrast emphasize about the poem's meaning? Explain, citing lines that support your answer.

8. **Trace the Development of an Idea** Collins is known for writing poems that begin with humor and end in mystery and seriousness. Review the graphic organizer you filled in as you read. How, if at all, does the **tone** change over the course of each poem? Do the two poems present similar or different ideas about **aging?** Explain your answers, citing evidence from both poems.

Literary Criticism

9. **Critical Interpretations** Collins is beloved by readers for his fresh and often funny poems; he even won the Mark Twain Poetry Award, given for the "contribution of humor" to American verse. However, some critics argue that Collins's humor is hollow, weakened by clichés and lacking in originality and insight. On the basis of your reading of these poems, do you agree or disagree with this criticism? Explain your answer.

A New Diversity

Late in the 20th century, it grew increasingly apparent that there was no single "American experience" and therefore no typical American voice. Once primarily the province of white men, the American literary canon—the body of works considered representative—exploded into a diverse chorus of ethnic voices. The number and range of voices continues to grow today.

Writing to Reflect

Every writer of any significance brings something new to a literary tradition, whether in subject matter, style, or way of looking at the world. As you reflect on the selections you have just read, consider what unique contributions might be attributed to each writer. Choose one author and write an essay about how his or her writing, as shown in this unit, can be said to do something different from writers of previous generations.

Consider

- the author's choice of subject matter
- his or her use of language, including style and tone
- any cultural or philosophical lens through which the author views the subject matter

Extension

VIEWING & REPRESENTING

Gather clippings of articles and literary texts from print media, photographs and other images of writers, and quotations from the selections in this section. Use these items to create a **collage**—your own "Mosaic of American Voices" representing the vibrancy and diversity of contemporary American literature.

Increibles Las Cosas Q'se Ven, 2001. Mural at Ashland Avenue and 19th Street in Chicago. © Jeffrey Zimmermann.

Problem-Solution Essay

Much of the literature in this unit deals with life-changing problems, such as war, racial inequality, and cultural isolation. All of us face problems in our lives and in our communities. For help in sharing your thoughts about an important problem and its possible solutions, follow the **Writer's Road Map.**

WRITER'S ROAD MAP

Problem-Solution Essay

WRITING PROMPT 1

Writing for the Real World Problems at school, in your community, and in the wider world are inescapable. Choose a problem that deeply interests you and write an essay in which you define the problem, examine its causes, and explore possible solutions.

Problems to Explore

- social issues, such as homelessness or prejudice
- environmental issues, such as energy use or wetlands destruction
- school policies, such as locker searches or rules about athletic participation

WRITING PROMPT 2

Writing from Literature Perhaps something you read in this unit made you think about a problem in a new way. Choose a problem you found in a literary work. Write an essay in which you describe the problem and identify a possible solution.

Selections to Explore

- "My Dungeon Shook: Letter to My Nephew" (racial discrimination)
- "Mother Tongue" (cultural conflicts)
- "Adolescence—III" (growing up)

WRITING TOOLS
For prewriting, revision, and editing tools, visit the **Writing Center** at **ClassZone.com.**

KEY TRAITS

1. IDEAS

- States the **problem** in a clearly worded thesis statement
- Explores the **causes and effects** of the problem
- Uses relevant **details** to **support** the proposed solution
- Addresses **opposing viewpoints** and counterclaims

2. ORGANIZATION

- Shows the **significance** of the problem in the introduction
- Uses **transitions** to connect ideas
- Concludes by **summarizing** the proposed **solution**

3. VOICE

- **Tone** is suited to subject matter, audience, and purpose

4. WORD CHOICE

- Uses **precise words** to express the problem and solution

5. SENTENCE FLUENCY

- Uses a variety of **sentence types**

6. CONVENTIONS

- Employs **correct grammar and usage**

Part 1: Analyze a Student Model

Jordan Turner
Kingston Academy

Parking-Lot Lottery

It happened again yesterday morning. Two cars collided in the mad rush
to snag one of the few parking spaces in the school lot. Luckily, no one was
hurt, but who can say what might happen next time? Inadequate parking at
our school is a real—and dangerous—problem.

5   Since last fall, eight accidents have occurred in or at the entrance to the
student parking lot. Most of these involved two cars moving at relatively
slow speeds, so there were no injuries. Students walking or riding bikes in
the area are at risk, however, and something needs to be done about it now.
Because there are too many cars and not enough parking spaces, drivers
10   race to get into the lot, often ignoring the rules of the road and common
courtesy. Even when this early-morning derby doesn't result in dents,
scratched paint, or injuries, it leaves students stressed and jittery before
the school day has even begun.

    Should we extend the lot and create more parking spaces? That's what
15   the student council suggests. Our school is surrounded by privately owned
land, though, so this solution is just not possible right now. Also, it is
unreasonable to expect that fewer students will drive to school as time goes
on. Enrollment has increased with redistricting, and many students must
travel from areas where there is no public transportation. Based on these
20   realities, the problem can only get worse.

    A cheap, fair, and easy-to-implement solution to this problem is
just waiting to be set in motion—a parking-lot lottery run by the
administration. Each fall and spring, juniors and seniors who drive to
school would fill out a card and submit it to the principal. An administrator
25   would draw cards and assign each winner a numbered parking space. All
juniors and seniors, including those with parking assignments, would be
eligible to submit their names for the next lottery.

KEY TRAITS IN ACTION

Introductory paragraph shows the **significance** of the issue (students may be injured). Highlighted thesis statement clearly describes the **problem.**

Describes the **causes and effects** of the problem. Highlighted **transitions** help to show how ideas are related.

Examines an **opposing viewpoint** (in this case, another proposed solution) and explains why it is not workable. Varying **sentence types** by including a question keeps the essay fresh.

Proposes a **solution** and provides **details** about it.

This solution has several advantages. First, the only expense it would involve is paint and a few hours of labor to number the parking spaces.

30 Second, everyone would have an equal chance to get a space, since names would be drawn at random. Third, it would encourage students to carpool. This decrease in traffic would help protect student safety and the environment. Drivers who didn't abide by the system and parked in other students' spaces would be banned from the next lottery.

35 Students and administrators have responded positively to this idea. Almost everyone I asked agreed with the vice-principal that "It certainly would be worth a try." Although some students worried about having to carpool for months at a time, they said they preferred a lottery system to the current disorganized situation. A few students who didn't like the idea

40 said they wouldn't enter the lottery—which is fine, since participation would be voluntary. I'm confident that this system would work because a similar one has been running smoothly at my cousin's school for almost two years.

The student lot does not have to be a perpetual traffic jam. Let's agree

45 to make a U-turn and support a parking lottery. That way we can take this situation in a positive direction.

Straightforward, serious **tone** and highlighted **precise words** help to make the essay smooth and convincing.

Concludes with a summary of the proposed **solution.** By using words related to driving, the writer ends the essay in a clever and upbeat manner.

2

Part 2: Apply the Writing Process

PREWRITING

What Should I Do?	What Does It Look Like?

1. Analyze the prompt.
Choose one of the prompts on page 1248. Underline the part of the prompt that tells you the general topic and format of your writing. Note any questions or comments that come to mind.

▶ **WRITING PROMPT** Problems at school, in your community, and in the wider world are inescapable. <u>Choose a problem that deeply interests you and write an essay in which you define the problem, examine its causes, and explore possible solutions.</u>

What issues really matter to me? Can I think of a topic that affects my life?

2. List problems that concern you.
Think of problems that you might like to write about. Categorize them in a chart to help you sort out your ideas. (Circle) the idea that you think would make the best essay.

▶

Environment	Community	School
• Turtle Creek	• creating a skate park	• (student parking)
• Lyme disease		• phys ed cutbacks
• ozone layer	• ending curfews	

3. Brainstorm possible solutions.
Use a cluster diagram or other graphic organizer to help you explore possible solutions.

TIP Make sure the problem is solvable. If it isn't, go back to step 2, and choose a different problem to write about.

▶

bigger parking lot? — carpooling? — more bike racks? — Student Parking — lottery like at my cousin's school?

4. Compile evidence about each possible solution.
Look for facts, statistics, and expert opinions that support—or discredit—each solution. Also note what kinds of evidence you still need to research.

▶

I Already Know	I Need to Find Out
• There's no room for more parking.	• How would a lottery work?
• Lottery is working in cousin Ari's school.	• What are student/administrator reactions?
• Some kids already carpool.	• Are more students willing to bike or carpool?

What Should I Do?	What Does It Look Like?
1. State the problem clearly. In your introduction, explain exactly what problem you are writing about and why you feel strongly about it. **TIP** Include background information that will help your audience fully understand the problem.	▶ *The parking situation at our school is a real problem. There was an accident there just yesterday. Luckily, there were no injuries. Students walking or riding their bikes in the area are at risk, though, so something needs to be done now.*
2. Trace the causes and effects. Include details that give insight into the problem's origins and its possible consequences. Depending on your topic, you might include facts, statistics, examples, quotations, or expert opinions. **See page 1254:** Use Transitions	▶ *There are too many cars and not enough parking spaces. Drivers have to hurry to get into the lot, and they act rude.* ⎤ Cause *Even when this situation doesn't end in dents, scratched paint, or injuries, it leaves students angry and jittery before school has even begun.* ⎤ Effects
3. Address possible concerns or objections. Anticipate, describe, and answer objections others might have to your solution. Also, discuss other solutions and indicate why they are inferior.	▶ *Should we make the lot bigger and create more parking spaces? That's what the student council wants.* ⎤ Alternate solution *Our school is surrounded by homes, though, so this solution is just impossible.* ⎤ Why it won't work
4. Organize your ideas. Present your ideas in a logical sequence. Begin with the problem. Then either discuss other solutions and end with your solution (as the writer of the student model did), or state your solution first and then discuss other possibilities. **TIP** Before revising, consult the **key traits** on page 1248 and the **rubric** and **peer-reader questions** on page 1254.	▶ I. *Problem: lack of student parking* II. *Cause: too many cars/too little space; effects: accidents, jitters* III. *Some solutions: expand lot, have fewer students drive to school* IV. *Best solution: parking-lot lottery* V. *Conclusion*

REVISING AND EDITING

What Should I Do?	*What Does It Look Like?*

1. Strengthen supporting details.
- Have a peer reader draw a ⬚box⬚ around examples or explanations that are vague or unrelated.
- Replace these examples with specific support for your ideas.

See page 1254: Ask a Peer Reader

▶ ~~We could have two lotteries per year.~~ *Each fall and spring, juniors and seniors who drive to school would fill out a card and submit it to the principal. An administrator would draw cards and assign each winner a numbered parking space.*

This solution has several advantages. First, ~~it's cheap~~ *the only expense it would involve is paint and a few hours of labor to number the parking spaces.*

2. Vitalize your verbs.
- ⟳Circle⟲ weak verbs, such as forms of *be*, *have*, and *do*.
- Choose the best places to substitute stronger, more precise verbs.

▶ *Two cars collided in their mad rush to snag one of the few parking spaces*
~~There (was) an accident~~ *in the school lot.*

race
Drivers (have to) hurry to get into the lot.

3. Check that you have answered opposing viewpoints fully.
- <u>Underline</u> your answers to opposing viewpoints or alternate solutions.
- If the underlined statements seem vague or unconvincing, add details that show audience members why you disagree.

▶ *Also, it is unreasonable to expect that fewer students will drive to school as time goes on,* ~~since there are more and more cars on the road every day.~~ *Enrollment has increased with redistricting, and many students must travel from areas where there is no public transportation.*

4. Fine-tune your conclusion.
- Reread your conclusion. Does it summarize the problem and your proposed solution? If appropriate, include a direct call for action (such as "support a parking lottery").
- If necessary, add information or revise your writing to make your conclusion meaningful and memorable.

▶ *The student lot does not have to be a perpetual traffic jam. Let's agree to make a U-turn and support a parking lottery. That way we can take this situation in a positive direction.*

Problem-Solution Essay

Apply the Rubric

A strong problem-solution essay . . .

- ☑ introduces the problem and shows its significance
- ☑ includes an accurate thesis
- ☑ traces the causes and effects of the problem
- ☑ suggests a possible solution and gives relevant supporting details
- ☑ describes and rebuts opposing views and counterclaims
- ☑ links ideas with transitions
- ☑ maintains a tone suited to the audience, purpose, and subject matter
- ☑ uses precise words
- ☑ varies sentence types
- ☑ concludes with a summary of the proposed solution

Ask a Peer Reader

- Why do you think I chose to write about this problem?
- Are any supporting details weak or confusing? If so, which ones?
- How could I make my proposed solution more convincing?

Use Transitions

accordingly	first
after	for this reason
although	however
as a result	if . . . then
because	next
before	on the contrary
consequently	since
despite	so
finally	therefore

Check Your Grammar

Use the active voice rather than the passive voice whenever possible.

~~Cards would be drawn by an administrator.~~ An administrator would draw cards.

~~An equal chance to get a space would be had by everyone.~~ Everyone would have an equal chance to get a space.

See page R60: Active and Passive Voice

Writing On|ine

PUBLISHING OPTIONS
For publishing options, visit the **Writing Center** at ClassZone.com.

ASSESSMENT PREPARATION
For writing and grammar assessment practice, go to the **Assessment Center** at ClassZone.com.

Creating a Web Site

You can continue exploring the problem you wrote about by creating a Web site dedicated to the issue.

Planning the Web Site

1. **Think about your audience.** Are you trying to reach people who know a great deal on your topic, people who know little about it, or both?
2. **Brainstorm elements to include and make a flow chart to organize them.** You'll need a home page describing the problem, with hyperlinks to other pages for relevant research, your solution, and other possible solutions. Consider including an e-mail address so users can send feedback. (For safety reasons, do not post your name, address, or telephone number.)
3. **Decide on visuals.** Create your own or search the Internet, books, magazines, newspapers, or other sources. Your visuals should powerfully convey your main ideas.

    TIP If you did not create the visual, include a source line telling where it came from. Some materials require permission from their creators. Check online sources for terms-and-conditions statements that may specify whether students can use the media elements in school projects.

4. **Make a storyboard showing the design of each page.** Draw rough sketches showing the placement of titles, explanatory text, visuals, and navigation buttons.

Producing the Web Site

1. **Write the text.** Express ideas clearly and concisely. Use charts or bulleted lists whenever possible. Define unfamiliar terms.
2. **Build your site.** Ask your school's computer specialist which authoring program to use. An authoring program allows you to combine media elements into a Web document.
3. **Test the site and make necessary revisions.** Proofread the text, check the visuals for correct positioning, and try out all links and navigation buttons. Ask teachers or classmates to review your site. Create a short survey or questionnaire so you can analyze their responses. Make revisions as needed.
4. **Upload your site.** Ask the computer specialist for permission to make your site available on your school's internal server or on the Web.

Reading Comprehension

ASSESS

The practice test items on the next few pages match skills listed on the Unit Goals page (page 1088) and addressed throughout this unit. Taking this practice test will help you assess your knowledge of these skills and determine your readiness for the Unit Test.

REVIEW

After you take the practice test, your teacher can help you identify any skills you need to review.

- Main Ideas
- Historical Context
- Rhetorical Devices
  - Repetition
- Allusions
- Idioms
- Prefixes
- Create Mood
- Establish Voice

DIRECTIONS *Read these selections and answer the questions that follow.*

from Police Dogs in Alabama Spur North Carolina Unrest

Cliff MacKay

GREENSBORO, N.C., June 1, 1963—"When a police dog bites us in Birmingham, people of color bleed all over America."

That was the terse explanation given Saturday by Jesse Jackson, 21-year-old A. and T. College student president, for the social upheaval which is sweeping this state and the South.

There have been no biting police dogs used in North Carolina, but that memorable picture from Birmingham has served to launch a tidal wave of racial unrest that thus far has overwhelmed ten cities and still shows no signs of abating.

On one thing all of North Carolina's freedom fighters are in agreement: there
10 will be no turning back; the status quo is gone forever.

The state's largest city, Charlotte, under Mayor Stan Brookshire has already fallen in line with an announcement that "all public facilities will be integrated immediately." The Chamber of Commerce backed his statement.

Businessmen of Thomasville have assured NAACP[1] President, the Rev. W. E. Banks, that all downtown establishments will no longer discriminate.

A Durham bi-racial committee has launched a series of meetings designed to end discriminatory practices in all places licensed to serve the public.

Greensboro's Mayor David Schenk has appointed a special committee headed by Dr. G. W. Evans and empowered it to seek a solution "to our pressing racial
20 problems."

Fifteen hundred arrests afterward, it has finally dawned on Greensboro officials that fear of jail would not halt the protests.

A word from liberal Gov. Terry Sanford, and the Bennett and A. and T. College students were released from makeshift lockups here, sorely disappointing some 3,000 others who had been eagerly waiting to experience "the thrills" of going to jail.

The demonstrations only gained momentum. From Greensboro, they have spread to nearby High Point and Winston-Salem; to Raleigh and Durham, to Fayetteville, Thomasville, Edenton, Wilmington and Charlotte.

Their point proved by overflowing the jails, the youthful freedom fighters,
30 sponsored by CORE[2], immediately developed a new strategy—the silent march.

---

1. **NAACP:** National Association for the Advancement of Colored People.
2. **CORE:** Congress of Racial Equality, founded in 1942 as the Committee of Racial Equality.

ASSESSMENT ONLINE

For more assessment practice and test-taking tips, go to the **Assessment Center** at ClassZone.com.

A dignified, highly disciplined line of as high as 4,000 marchers nightly walks silently, almost prayerfully, through the downtown area. Grim faces show no smiles. There is no conversation, not a cigarette glows. Just the slap-slap-slap of hundreds of marching feet.

from Radio and Television Report to the American People on Civil Rights, June 11, 1963

John F. Kennedy

We are confronted primarily with a moral issue. It is as old as the scriptures and is as clear as the American Constitution.

The heart of the question is whether all Americans are to be afforded equal rights and equal opportunities, whether we are going to treat our fellow Americans as we want to be treated. If an American, because his skin is dark, cannot eat lunch in a restaurant open to the public, if he cannot send his children to the best public school available, if he cannot vote for the public officials who represent him, if, in short, he cannot enjoy the full and free life which all of us want, then who among us would be content to have the color of his skin changed and stand in his place?
10 Who among us would then be content with the counsels of patience and delay?

One hundred years of delay have passed since President Lincoln freed the slaves, yet their heirs, their grandsons, are not fully free. They are not yet freed from the bonds of injustice. They are not yet freed from social and economic oppression. And this nation, for all its hopes and all its boasts, will not be fully free until all its citizens are free.

We preach freedom around the world, and we mean it, and we cherish our freedom here at home, but are we to say to the world and, much more importantly, to each other that this is a land of the free except for the Negroes; that we have no second-class citizens except Negroes; that we have no class or
20 caste system, no ghettoes, no master race except with respect to Negroes?

Now the time has come for this nation to fulfill its promise. The events in Birmingham and elsewhere have so increased the cries for equality that no city or state or legislative body can prudently choose to ignore them.

The fires of frustration and discord are burning in every city, North and South, where legal remedies are not at hand. Redress is sought in the streets, in

GO ON ➡

demonstrations, parades, and protests which create tensions and threaten violence and threaten lives.

We face, therefore, a moral crisis as a country and as a people. It cannot be met by repressive police action. It cannot be left to increased demonstrations in the streets.
30 It cannot be quieted by token moves or talk. It is a time to act in the Congress, in your state and local legislative body and, above all, in all of our daily lives.

Comprehension

DIRECTIONS *Answer these questions about the excerpt from "Police Dogs in Alabama Spur North Carolina Unrest."*

1. To illustrate the idea in line 10 that "the status quo is gone forever," MacKay presents

   A an image of dogs attacking protesters

   B a description of the silent marches

   C a factual list of changes made in four North Carolina cities

   D an account of college students who participate in protests

2. Which statement conveys the main idea of lines 21–25?

   A Many people were jailed in Greensboro.

   B The local jails were too small to hold all of the arrested protesters.

   C The arrest of 1,500 people did not stop the protesters.

   D The governor released the protesters from jail.

3. What is the main idea of lines 29–34?

   A Many of the protesters were young people.

   B A civil rights group sponsored the freedom fighters.

   C Civil rights workers staged their demonstrations in large cities.

   D Thousands of people participated in silent nighttime marches for equality.

4. Which historical events most likely led African Americans to form the NAACP and CORE (lines 14 and 30)?

   A proposed civil rights legislation

   B Jim Crow laws and voting restrictions

   C the integration of public facilities

   D college students' civil rights activities

5. What is the main idea of this excerpt?

   A Police actions in Alabama fueled civil rights protests in North Carolina and across the South.

   B A. and T. College students took the lead in the struggle for racial equality.

   C Police in Birmingham used harsh tactics in their attempts to end protests.

   D People in North Carolina were willing to go to jail to protest racial injustice.

DIRECTIONS *Answer these questions about the excerpt from "Radio and Television Report to the American People on Civil Rights."*

6. Kennedy alludes to scriptures and the American Constitution in lines 1–2 to

   A educate citizens about U.S. history

   B point out that everyone has different ideas about equal rights

   C clarify the distinction between religious and secular ideas

   D remind his audience that there is moral and legal support for equality

7. The repetition of the phrase "if he cannot" in lines 5–9 highlights the

A restrictions that African Americans have lived with in the United States

B government's refusal to legally end racial inequality

C importance of patience and mutual understanding in resolving inequality

D lack of support for African-American small businesses at the local level

8. By alluding to President Lincoln in line 11, Kennedy calls particular attention to

A his and Lincoln's reputations as eloquent speakers and debaters

B the fact that African Americans were still denied freedoms guaranteed 100 years before

C his knowledge of the history of race relations in the North and the South

D the national discord that resulted from the Civil War

9. The phrase "land of the free" (line 18) appears in each stanza of "The Star Spangled Banner." Kennedy's allusion to the national anthem most likely invokes feelings of

A sympathy   **C** militarism

B patriotism   **D** indignity

10. What is the effect of Kennedy's repetition of "except" in lines 18–20?

A It reveals how Kennedy would like to change the world's perception of the United States.

B It shows that Americans are proud of their history of equality for all citizens.

C It emphasizes the exclusion of African Americans from the freedoms experienced by most Americans.

D It highlights Kennedy's view that the United States should spread freedom around the world.

11. In lines 28–30, the repetition of the phrase "it cannot be" emphasizes that

A demonstrations are spreading rapidly throughout the country

B social change can be brought about in many ways

C protesters must engage in a dialogue with public officials

D nothing less than a commitment to equality will end discrimination

DIRECTIONS *Answer this question about both selections.*

12. Which historical event of 1963 do MacKay and Kennedy both respond to in these excerpts?

A integration of public facilities in Durham

B repressive police action in Birmingham

C passage of equal pay laws by Congress

D silent marches in North Carolina

Written Response

SHORT RESPONSE *Write three or four sentences to answer this question.*

13. What historical change was occurring in North Carolina when "Police Dogs in Alabama Spur North Carolina Unrest" was written? Support your answer with two examples from the excerpt.

EXTENDED RESPONSE *Write two or three paragraphs to answer this question.*

14. What is Kennedy calling on people to do to end racial inequality? Identify two of his ideas and support your answer with quotations from the text.

GO ON ➡

Vocabulary

DIRECTIONS *Use context clues and your knowledge of idioms to answer the following questions.*

1. In line 12 of his news article, Cliff MacKay notes that the city of Charlotte has "fallen in line with an announcement" by the mayor. The idiom *fallen in line* means

    A retreated from

    B relied upon

    C enacted into law

    D conformed to

2. In line 21 of his news article, Cliff MacKay writes that it "dawned on Greensboro officials" that the threat of jail would not end the protests. The idiom *dawned on* means

    A brightened up

    B agreed with

    C became evident to

    D made an example of

3. In line 19 of his address, President Kennedy refers to "second-class citizens." This idiom describes people who

    A are treated as inferior to others

    B need help in finding a job

    C have not finished high school

    D play a minor role in government

4. In line 25 of his address, President Kennedy notes that discord is heightened "where legal remedies are not at hand." The idiom *at hand* means

    A accepted

    B available

    C trusted

    D practical

DIRECTIONS *Use context clues and your knowledge of prefixes to answer the following questions.*

5. The prefix *up-* means "upward," and the Old English word *hebban* means "to lift." What does the word *upheaval* mean in line 4 of the news story?

    A a command given to sailors

    B a raising of the earth's crust

    C the act of gagging

    D a sudden, violent disruption

6. The prefix *con-* means "with," and the Latin word *frons* means "front." What does the word *confronted* mean in line 1 of the president's address?

    A faced

    B attacked

    C defeated

    D bound

7. The prefix *dis-* means "apart," and the Latin stem *cor* means "heart." What does the word *discord* mean in line 24 of the president's address?

    A harsh or unpleasant sounds from the mingling of tones

    B tension or strife from the lack of agreement

    C emotional or cultural bonds formed from birth

    D lingering or chronic illness from damage to the aorta

8. The prefix *re-* means "again," and the Old French word *drecier* means "to arrange." What does the word *redress* mean in line 25 of the president's address?

    A correction of a wrong

    B correction of a factual error

    C payment of a financial debt

    D protection from enemies

Writing & Grammar

DIRECTIONS *Read each passage and answer the questions that follow.*

(1) They paddle the canoe swiftly through the darkness. (2) An owl hoots in the distance. (3) Mary gasps, not daring to speak. (4) Instead, she chomps down on a peanut butter sandwich. (5) The faint crackle of dry leaves comes from the shore. (6) Sam almost drops the paddle as a fish leaps from the water, startling both of them. (7) He stifles a warning as a large rock suddenly looms ahead. (8) The two strain to hear the sound of their pursuers, now closing in on them.

1. The verbs *gasps, stifles,* and *looms* help create a mood that is

  A sad   **C** suspenseful

  B humorous   **D** somber

2. Which sentence does not reflect the mood of the rest of the passage?

  A sentence 1   **C** sentence 5

  B sentence 4   **D** sentence 8

3. Which element does the writer use to help create mood in the passage?

  A a critical tone

  B figurative language

  C imperative sentences

  D sensory details

(1) Although we had seen the TV footage and read the newspapers, no one was prepared for the mud-caked debris we found when we returned. (2) Where had our pristine home gone? (3) Louise covered her face as if, by blocking this sight, she could erase the devastation before us. (4) Despondently, we joined our neighbors, who had found an heirloom that had somehow survived the ferocious winds, endless rains, and raging floods. (5) It reminded us that we had once lived happily in this now beleaguered city. (6) As I held the heirloom in my hand, I wondered: where would we go from here?

4. Which of the following are characteristics of the writer's voice?

  A a sad tone and complex vocabulary

  B simple sentence structures and basic vocabulary

  C a lighthearted tone and sensory details

  D figurative language and short sentences

5. Choose the best way to rewrite the following sentence, using the same voice as the passage.

> The storm was over, but it had been bad.

  A The unpleasant storm was finally over.

  B What a storm it had been!

  C Although the fury of the storm had subsided, it left misery in its wake.

  D Though now over, the storm caused a lot of damage.

UNIT 6 Great Reads

Ideas for Independent Reading

Continue exploring the Questions of the Times on pages 1090–1091 with these additional works.

Are we responsible for the WHOLE WORLD?

Catch-22
by Joseph Heller

This hilarious, heartbreaking novel brilliantly satirizes the "logic" of warfare. In the words of WWII airman Yossarian: "The enemy . . . is anybody who's going to get you killed, no matter which side he's on." Unfortunately for Yossarian, each time he completes the number of missions required for his discharge, that number is raised by his commanders.

Hiroshima
by John Hersey

In 1945, faced with a war that seemed as if it might never end, President Truman made the decision to drop an atomic bomb on the Japanese city of Hiroshima, killing between 70,000 and 80,000 people. John Hersey recorded the stories of Hiroshima survivors shortly after the explosion, bringing home for Americans the magnitude of the devastation and loss.

The Things They Carried
by Tim O'Brien

This collection of short stories focuses on a platoon of American soldiers in Vietnam. The things they carry—letters, photographs, Bibles, hand grenades—hint at the confused inner landscape of each young man. In this masterpiece of war literature, O'Brien makes clear that the burdens of war continue to weigh on the troops long after they lay down their arms.

Can America achieve EQUAL RIGHTS?

At Canaan's Edge: America in the King Years, 1965–68
by Taylor Branch

Third in a series on civil rights leader Martin Luther King Jr., *At Canaan's Edge* discusses the final years of King's life. The book begins with King's last great success: the marches in Selma, Alabama, that led to the passage of the Voting Rights Act. It then moves through the Vietnam years to the national tragedy of King's untimely death.

Vintage Baldwin
by James Baldwin

Author James Baldwin was extremely influential in exposing America's racial divide. Much of his writing focuses on the civil rights movement and the experience of African Americans living in white-controlled America. This collection includes short stories, essays, an excerpt from a novel, and a play.

A Gathering of Old Men
by Ernest Gaines

This quiet novel of race relations begins with the killing of a white bully by the only African-American man who has the courage to stand up for his rights. Eighteen elderly African-American men arrive at the scene of the crime, each carrying a shotgun with discharged shells. When the sheriff arrives, all 18 claim to be the murderer, forcing the community to reconsider how they treat one another.

What makes an
AMERICAN?

The Woman Warrior
by Maxine Hong Kingston

In this classic memoir, Maxine Hong Kingston encapsulates the confusion, anger, pleasure, and wonder of growing up Chinese American in California, the daughter of immigrants. Haunted by her mother's tales of the magical if sometimes brutal world she left behind, the young narrator is equally unsure about where she fits in among the "ghosts," her parents' term for the non-Chinese people they live among.

Arranged Marriage
by Chitra Banerjee Divakaruni

In this collection of short stories, Chitra Divakaruni focuses on the experiences of women living in India and of Indian women who have moved to America. The contrast between their two worlds, coupled with their inherent roles and expectations, is a common theme running throughout the stories.

Unsettling America
Edited by Maria Mazziotti Gillian and Jennifer Gillian

A diverse chorus of voices comment on ethnic pride and heritage, personal identity, and cultural stereotypes in this anthology of contemporary multicultural poetry. Pat Mora, Lucille Clifton, Li-Young Lee, Louise Erdrich, and Lawrence Ferlinghetti are among the notable poets included in this collection.

What is the
AMERICAN DREAM?

The Portable Arthur Miller
by Arthur Miller, edited by Christopher Bigsby

Playwright Arthur Miller once said, "Whoever is writing in the United States is using the American Dream as an ironical pole of his story. People elsewhere tend to accept, to a far greater degree anyway, that the conditions of life are hostile to man's pretensions." Miller's best work examines the average American's pursuit of the American dream and how that dream can become twisted or unattainable. This collection includes complete texts of his masterpieces *The Death of a Salesman* and *The Crucible,* as well as several later plays and excerpts from his memoir *Timebends.*

The Stories of John Cheever
by John Cheever

These stories describe a world that could be considered the epitome of the American dream—a place of leafy suburbs, summer homes, and cocktail parties. But beneath the surface lurks a darkness. Cheever's characters face a myriad of problems—aging, financial blunders, embarrassment, death. Cheever's graceful prose illuminates this world and makes readers care about the imperfect people who inhabit it.

UNIT **7**

Preview Unit Goals

DEVELOPING RESEARCH SKILLS

- Select and shape a topic
- Plan research
- Choose the best research tools, including primary and secondary sources and online resources
- Evaluate information and sources, including nonfiction books, newspapers, periodicals, and Web sites
- Make source cards and take notes
- Paraphrase and summarize information
- Avoid plagiarism by quoting directly and crediting sources
- Verify information, detect bias, and develop own perspective

WRITING

- Write a research paper
- Document sources
- Prepare Works Cited list
- Format your paper

SPEAKING, LISTENING, AND VIEWING

- Present results of investigation

ACADEMIC VOCABULARY

- research topic
- research paper
- documentation

- resources
- sources
- Works Cited

- source cards
- plagiarism

 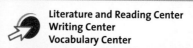

Online LITERATURE CLASSZONE.COM

Literature and Reading Center
Writing Center
Vocabulary Center

The Power of Research

RESEARCH WORKSHOPS

- Research Strategies
- Writing Research Papers

What Is the Power of Research?

Throughout this book, you have explored the "big questions" of literature, history, and life. You can take these questions to a new, more challenging level through formal research.

What is it like to be AT WAR?

You might investigate this question by writing a **historical research paper** that explores why some 18- and 19-year-olds enlisted to fight in Vietnam. Or you might create a **personal research paper** that describes how a particular war or conflict affected you or someone you know. How did that personal experience relate to the conflict as a whole?

How does SCIENCE *affect you?*

Is acid rain present in your community? Do high school students improve their academic performance if they eat breakfast each day? When and where was the last earthquake in your state? When you write a **scientific research paper,** you present data that you have collected yourself as well as the findings of others.

How does LIFE influence literature?

Novels, stories, and poems reflect how authors see the world. They can also shape our view of places and events. One way to explore a work of literature is to write a **literary research paper** that traces how history influenced a particular literary work or vice versa. For instance, you could learn more about the real people who inspired John Steinbeck to write *The Grapes of Wrath*.

Are we ready for the next natural DISASTER?

The question that captivates you may touch on several fields of study. A **multidisciplinary research paper** allows you to ask questions related to science, government, history, and many other subject areas and investigate how those subjects relate to each other.

Beginning Your Investigation

When you create a top-quality research paper, you go beyond merely finding and assembling information. Instead, you investigate, analyze, develop new perspectives, and perhaps do original research to reach your own conclusions.

Selecting and Shaping a Topic

In the past, your teacher probably assigned you a topic or had you choose from a list of topics. Now you may be asked to generate your own topic or put your own spin on an assigned topic. For instance, perhaps you need to write a paper for your American literature or American history class. Reading *The Grapes of Wrath* has heightened your interest in the historical events of that period, but you know that a topic like "the Dust Bowl" is too broad. Because you will spend hours researching and writing, you want to find a topic that will hold your interest over time. How can you shape a general idea into the right research topic for you?

TRY OUT DIFFERENT "LENSES"

To discover a unique approach to a particular topic, view it through different "lenses," or perspectives. A historian, an economist, a scientist, and an artist would look at the topic of the Dust Bowl in different ways. This cluster diagram illustrates questions you might develop when considering different aspects of a topic.

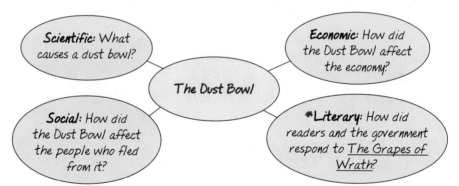

Choose the question that intrigues you the most and write a goal statement to focus your thinking and guide your research. You are likely to change or refine this statement as you do your research, but write the clearest, most focused statement that you can right now.

> **GOAL:** to write a research paper that investigates how <u>The Grapes of Wrath</u> affected government response to Dust Bowl evacuees

Your goal statement will develop into your thesis after you have read, interpreted, and drawn conclusions from a variety of sources.

Planning Your Research

To make your search efficient and effective, develop specific research questions and then choose the sources that are right for you.

FORMULATE RESEARCH QUESTIONS

List some questions that will help you investigate your topic. Highlight **keywords**—terms, names, and phrases that are specific to your topic. Later on, you might search for these keywords within a book's index, on a search engine, or in a database.

> How did the Dust Bowl affect the United States?
>
> Why did Steinbeck write _The Grapes of Wrath_? How did he do the research?
>
> What did the government do to help migrant workers like the Joad family?

IDENTIFY THE MOST RELEVANT SOURCES

The sources you choose depend on what your topic is and how much you already know about it. Take a few minutes to consider which sources make the most sense for the early stages of your research.

- **Encyclopedia articles** can provide a helpful overview of your topic as you begin researching.

- For the specific details you need, try **specialized reference works.** Visual dictionaries have diagrams and cross-sections, almanacs have facts and statistics, and biographical references have information on famous people. See page R44 to learn more about reference works.

- **Documentaries** often include valuable interviews , speeches, and "you are there" footage that help you understand historical, literary, and scientific topics.

- **Magazines and newspapers** can give insights into a topic's perceived importance. Has your topic ever been front-page news, or is it rarely covered? How has coverage of your topic changed over time? For topics related to economics, popular culture, or history, take a look at related **advertisements.**

- **Interviews and oral histories** are firsthand testimony about history and culture. Look for them on audio, on video, in books, or on Web sites.

- **Original research** is information you discover yourself. For example, you might interview an expert, listen to a speech or lecture, create a questionnaire, perform an experiment, or conduct field research. To learn more about original research, see page R47.

- Be creative as you search. You might find valuable information in song lyrics, illustrations, maps, photographs, obituaries, statistical data, government publications, or museum exhibits.

Share your research questions with a librarian. He or she can suggest print and electronic resources that you may not have considered.

RESEARCH TOOLS
For research tools and strategies, visit the **Research Center** at **ClassZone.com.**

Choosing the Right Research Tools

As you delve into your research, you will learn more about what types of sources are available and where you can find them.

Primary and Secondary Sources

Most research papers include both primary and secondary sources. As this chart shows, the two types have distinct differences, advantages, and disadvantages.

PRIMARY SOURCE	SECONDARY SOURCE
Definition: materials written or created by people who took part in events or observed them	**Definition:** records created after events occurred by people who were not directly involved
▼	▼
Examples: letters, diaries, speeches, photographs, autobiographies, e-mails, Weblogs, first-person newspaper and magazine articles, public documents such as birth certificates	**Examples:** biographies, textbooks, encyclopedias, third-person newspaper and magazine articles, most documentaries
▼	▼
Advantages: firsthand information; can give insight into attitudes and beliefs of the times; may contain very specific details	**Advantages:** sometimes include excerpts from many primary sources; often have a broad perspective and consider many viewpoints; useful for getting an overview of a topic
▼	▼
Disadvantages: limited perspective; may need interpretation; may be biased	**Disadvantages:** only as reliable as the sources on which they are based; may be biased

Online Resources

When you use online resources, can you locate exactly what you need? The next pages will show you how to improve your online search skills.

CONSULT SEARCH ENGINES

Many search engines are available to you, and each returns different results. For best results, click on the search engine's "advanced search" or "search tips" link. Follow these general rules for effective Internet searches.

- **Be specific.** Try combining two or three keywords. If you want to find out about labor camps in California, be sure *California* is one of your search terms.

- **Use search limiters.** Enclose phrases in quotation marks—for example, a search for *"The Grapes of Wrath"* will result in pages that have those words in that order. Some search engines allow you to add AND or a plus sign to be sure that certain results are included: *Depression AND California;* or *+Depression +California.* To exclude certain terms, use the word NOT or a minus sign: *evacuees NOT Katrina;* or *+evacuees -Katrina.* To learn more, see page R46.

- **Choose the most relevant pages.** Scan the first 10 to 15 descriptions the search engine provides. Which sites could help you answer your research questions? Consider adding, deleting, or changing keywords to improve your results.

TRY IT OUT! *Examine Search Engine Results*

Which of these results do you think would yield the most useful information?

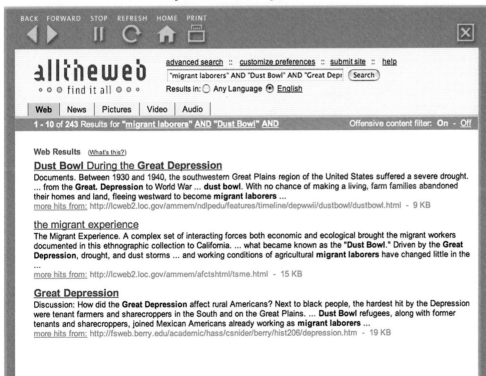

ACADEMIC VOCABULARY FOR THE INTERNET

Here are terms you will use when discussing the Internet:

- Web page
- Web site
- URL (uniform resource locator, also called Web address)
- search engine
- keyword search
- hyperlink
- menu

Close Read

1. This researcher did a search that combined three terms: "migrant laborers," "Dust Bowl," and "Great Depression." What are the advantages and disadvantages of doing such a specific search?

2. How might the search results change if the search was for "migrant laborers," "Dust Bowl," and "Oklahoma"?

3. What other search terms can you think of that might yield answers to the research questions on page 1269?

EXPLORE DATABASES

A **database** is any organized collection of data, whether print or electronic. Some of the databases in this chart are free to all; others may be available for free through your library or media center's Web site.

TYPES OF DATABASES	EXAMPLES
Internet search engines let you create customized databases of Web pages that include your keywords. Search engines examine literally billions of Web pages.	google.com altavista.com search.ask.com alltheweb.com dogpile.com Reproduced with permission of Yahoo! Inc. © 2007 by Yahoo! Inc. YAHOO! and the YAHOO! logo are trademarks of Yahoo! Inc.
Library catalogs let you create a customized database of materials related to your keywords—not only books but also magazine and journal articles, e-books, audio books, and DVDs.	www.imcpl.org suncat.co.sarasota.fl.us libweb.ci.albany.or.us
Newspaper databases contain articles from one newspaper or from many. You can access recent articles or ones that are decades old.	America's Newspapers The *New York Times Index* *Los Angeles Times Index*
Article databases allow you to access text from magazines and scholarly journals. Some are text only; others include photographs, diagrams, and other graphics.	*The Readers' Guide to Periodical Literature* InfoTrac (general-interest and business articles) Medline (medical information) PsycINFO (journal articles about psychology) Noticias or Informe (articles in Spanish)
Genealogy databases let you delve into family histories.	ancestry.com America's Obituaries and Death Notices HeritageQuest Online

ADVANTAGES OF SPECIALIZED DATABASES

"Why should I spend time figuring out how to use these databases?" you might ask. "I can just type my keywords into my favorite search engine." That's true—but when you're writing a research paper, specialized databases are often a better choice. Read on to find out why.

- **Specificity**—Some databases, such as the Internet Movie Database, cover only certain topics. Others cover only one type of material, such as articles from medical journals. Because these databases are targeted, you don't have to sift through pages of search results that have little or no relation to your topic.

- **No advertisements**—Unlike many search engines, most specialized databases do not have distracting pop-up windows or sidebar advertisements. No advertiser has paid to have a page show up first or in the top ten.

- **Access to the "invisible Web"**—Librarians call pages that are accessible through the Internet, but not through search engines, the "invisible Web." Many millions of Web pages are available through subscription-only databases—but if your library or media center subscribes to such databases, all you may need to access them is the bar code number on your library card.

- **Abstracts**—Many databases include an abstract—a short summary of an article's content—for each article. By reading abstracts, you can quickly decide whether the entire article is worth reading.

To find the most relevant results on a targeted database, read the article titles and notice the names of the publications the articles came from. Click on the most promising titles and read the abstracts or skim the first few paragraphs of each.

TRY IT OUT! *Examine Database Results*

These results are from a database called InfoTrac. Examine them and think about whether this search is effective.

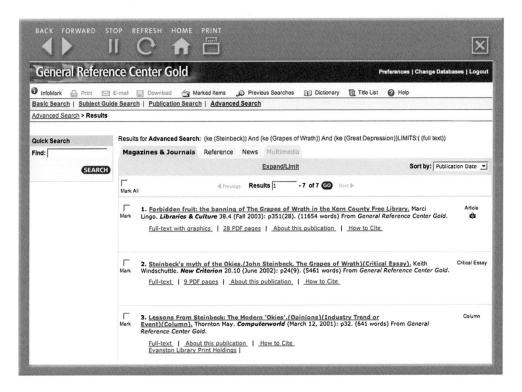

Close Read

1. Which three keyword phrases did this researcher use? On this database, the abbreviation "ke" means keyword.

2. Which result includes graphics? How do you know?

3. Of the three results shown here, which one is not likely to be useful? How do you know?

4. What other information does this database provide that the search engine on page 1271 does not? Give three examples.

Evaluating Sources

In this section, you will learn how to select the most trustworthy and reliable sources, whether in print or online.

GUIDELINES FOR EVALUATING SOURCES

Relevance	Is the source related to the goal statement and research questions you wrote on pages 1268–1269? Your goals and questions may change as you write; however, don't allow interesting but irrelevant sources to distract you.
Timeliness	Topics in science, medicine, and sports often require recently updated information. Older sources can be valuable for historical or literary topics. For a print source, check the copyright page. For a documentary, look for a copyright notice on the label. For online materials, look for a "last updated" notice.
Accuracy	Most encyclopedias, dictionaries, and almanacs are considered accurate because they are updated regularly and go through a rigorous review process. Online sources can have information that is even more accurate because of frequent updates. However, some online sources may not go through the same rigorous review process. Whenever possible, verify and clarify facts in more than one source.
Author's Credentials	Look for an author who has written on the same topic before or who has a position or job title that qualifies him or her as an expert.
Publisher's Credentials	A reputable publisher produces carefully researched materials. University presses tend to be reputable. Most publications and Web sites that focus on celebrities, fad diets, and gossip are not.
Author's Purpose	Why was the source created—to inform, entertain, persuade, or some combination of these? In general, informative pieces are researched more carefully than ones designed to entertain or to sell. For information on bias, see page 1282.
Breadth and Depth of Information	Match your needs to the source. Examine the table of contents, index, and appendix if this information is available. They will help you find an overview of a topic or just one detailed aspect of it. Also, think about whether the source is too basic or too dense and scholarly for your purposes.

Finding Trustworthy Web Sites

Anyone can create a Web site, so it is important to evaluate sites thoroughly.

QUESTIONS TO ASK ABOUT A WEB SITE

- **What does the address tell me?** Most sites with *.com* or *.net* in their addresses are personal or commercial sites. A personal site might be the work of just one person, so its information may not have been carefully checked. A commercial site exists to make a profit, so negative information about a product or service might be left out. Sites with the abbreviations *.edu* (educational), *.org* (nonprofit organization), or *.gov* (U.S. government) are more likely to be accurate because they are the work of many people.

- **Who created this site?** Look for sections labeled "About Us" or "Contact Us." How can you tell if an individual rather than an organization created a site? The lack of an institution name or logo is one clue. Other clues are the lack of an author biography, the absence of documentation for sources, or hyperlinks that lead nowhere or only to the author's own sites. You can also consult a domain lookup site, such as *easywhois.com*.

TIP Some *.org* and *.edu* sites are personal sites that are not reviewed by the sponsoring institution. A personal *.edu* address includes a forward slash and a tilde (/~) followed by a name or initials, as in *okies.utc.edu/~haylee.*

TRY IT OUT! *Evaluate a Web Site*

Would this site be useful for researching the goal statement from page 1268?

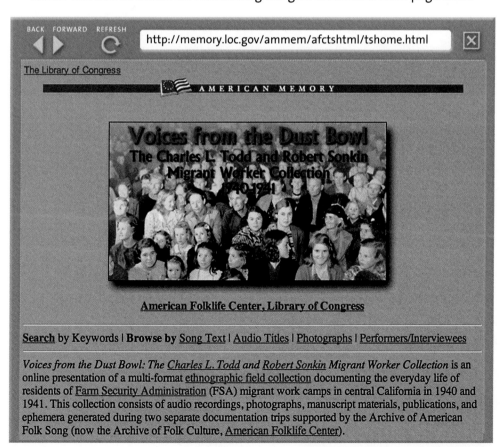

Close Read

1. What organization maintains this site? How do you know?

2. Why was the site created?

3. What clues do you have to the accuracy of the information on this site?

Evaluating Newspapers and Periodicals

Magazines, newspapers, and scholarly journals can be tricky to evaluate because you need to assess the publication itself, the author of the article, and the article's content.

QUESTIONS TO ASK ABOUT NEWSPAPERS AND PERIODICALS

- **Is the publication well-known and well-respected?** Most large-circulation newspapers and national magazines are reliable sources. Beware of supermarket tabloids and other sensationalist publications.

- **Who is the author?** Look for the writer's credentials. Generally, staff writers are as reliable as the publication in which they appear.

- **How old is the information?** Depending on your topic, you may need up-to-the-minute information, or you might look for information from a specific era.

- **Did the article originally appear in another source?** If so, make sure the original source is reliable. News services such as AP (Associated Press) and the New York Times News Service are the original sources of many reprinted articles.

- **Can the information be verified?** The best way to tell if a particular piece of information is accurate is to check it against other sources.

TRY IT OUT! *Evaluate a Newspaper Article*

Read and evaluate this newspaper article.

---

from the **Los Angeles Times, July 9, 1939**

Dust Bowl Book Brings Trouble

BY TOM CAMERON, TIMES STAFF REPRESENTATIVE

LOS GATOS, July 8. (Exclusive)— John Steinbeck, author of the best-selling novel, "Grapes of Wrath," has betaken himself to Moody Gulch, a secluded canyon three miles from here, and padlocked himself against the world.

For the first time in his career, Steinbeck is inaccessible to friend and enemy alike. . . .

There have been reports of threats against the author which induced him to retreat to an almost inaccessible citadel—a refuge from the very economic refugees he sought to befriend. . . .

"It isn't the refugees who have taken exception to what I wrote," he asserted. "It's the moneyed people back there in Oklahoma—the big oil men and outfits like the Oklahoma City Chamber of Commerce. If anybody's sore at me for the book it's that kind of people." . . .

Regarding the report that Ruth Comfort Mitchell planned to write a refutation of some of the statements in his book, Steinbeck laughed in scorn.

"I know what I was talking about. I lived, off and on, with those Okies for the last three years. Anyone who tries to refute me will just become ridiculous."

Close Read

1. Briefly summarize this article.

2. The *Los Angeles Times* is California's most widely read newspaper, so would you expect this article to be reliable? Give reasons for your answer.

3. Is this article useless because it is so old? Explain.

Choosing Reliable Books

Just as you write for different purposes and audiences, publishers put books on the market for different reasons. Some books are rushed to market and aimed at making money fast. Others are the result of years of work, including multiple edits and rewrites.

QUESTIONS TO ASK ABOUT NONFICTION BOOKS

- **Is the author an expert on this subject?** Check for information about the author on the book jacket, at the beginning of the book, and at the end.

- **Is the book based on research?** Check the back of the book for a bibliography. Look for footnotes, in which the author credits his or her sources and provides additional insights or information. Check for an appendix, which might add other information, such as maps, statistical tables, or family trees.

- **What is the author's or publisher's purpose?** This may be stated in a **preface,** a short introductory essay. The preface may also tell you more about the writer's background and research.

- **What is the copyright date?** A series of updates and printings is often a sign that the source has been highly regarded for years and is probably reliable.

TRY IT OUT! *Evaluate a Nonfiction Book*

Decide whether this book, *Dust Bowl Migration*, would be useful to someone focusing on government response to Dust Bowl evacuees.

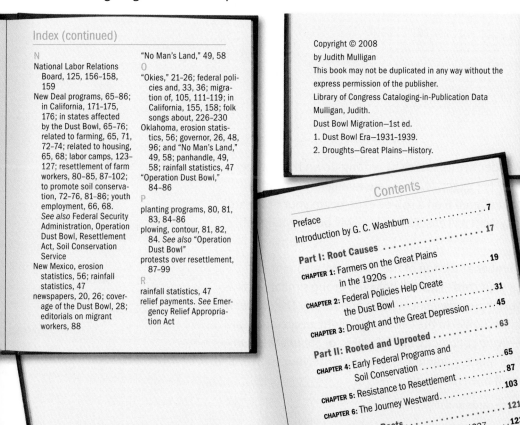

Index (continued)

N
National Labor Relations Board, 125, 156-158, 159
New Deal programs, 65–86; in California, 171-175, 176; in states affected by the Dust Bowl, 65–76; related to farming, 65, 71, 72-74; related to housing, 65, 68; labor camps, 123–127; resettlement of farm workers, 80-85, 87-102; to promote soil conservation, 72-76, 81-86; youth employment, 66, 68. *See also* Federal Security Administration, Operation Dust Bowl, Resettlement Act, Soil Conservation Service
New Mexico, erosion statistics, 56; rainfall statistics, 47
newspapers, 20, 26; coverage of the Dust Bowl, 28; editorials on migrant workers, 88

"No Man's Land," 49, 58
O
"Okies," 21-26; federal policies and, 33, 36; migration of, 105, 111-119; in California, 155, 158; folk songs about, 226-230
Oklahoma, erosion statistics, 56; governor, 26, 48, 96; and "No Man's Land," 49, 58; panhandle, 49, 58; rainfall statistics, 47
"Operation Dust Bowl," 84-86
P
planting programs, 80, 81, 83, 84-86
plowing, contour, 81, 82, 84. *See also* "Operation Dust Bowl"
protests over resettlement, 87-99
R
rainfall statistics, 47
relief payments. *See* Emergency Relief Appropriation Act

Copyright © 2008
by Judith Mulligan
This book may not be duplicated in any way without the express permission of the publisher.
Library of Congress Cataloging-in-Publication Data
Mulligan, Judith.
Dust Bowl Migration—1st ed.
1. Dust Bowl Era—1931-1939.
2. Droughts—Great Plains—History.

Contents

Close Read

1. Does this book contain information on federal policies that were related to the Dust Bowl? How do you know?

2. How useful might this book be to someone researching government response to Dust Bowl evacuees? Use page numbers and/or chapter numbers to support your answer.

Note Taking and Plagiarism

As you read and take notes from many sources, do not use the ideas of others without giving them credit. Plagiarism is dishonest and may result in your failing a class or being expelled.

TIP Cutting and pasting phrases, sentences, or paragraphs from a Web page or other electronic file into your research paper is plagiarism—unless you credit the source.

Recording Information

By taking careful notes, you will gather information and guard against plagiarism. One of the best ways of taking notes is by using index cards.

SOURCE CARDS

Begin by making one source card for every source. Assign each source a number, and write that number in the top right-hand corner. Then record the author and/or editor (if given), the title of the publication or Web page, and the date of publication. Also record the following for these sources:

- **Web source**—date created or posted, date accessed, Web address
- **Book**—publisher and publisher's location, library call number, relevant page numbers
- **Encyclopedia**—name and year of encyclopedia, publisher, publisher's location
- **Periodical article**—name of periodical, page numbers of article

Source Card: Encyclopedia Article

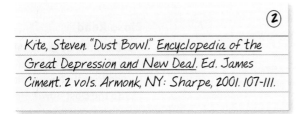

Kite, Steven. "Dust Bowl." *Encyclopedia of the Great Depression and New Deal*. Ed. James Ciment. 2 vols. Armonk, NY: Sharpe, 2001. 107-111.

NOTE CARDS

Before you take your first note, identify its source by writing down the number you assigned to the source card. For example, if you are taking notes from an encyclopedia article that you numbered 6 on a source card, begin your note card with that number. Using this system will ensure that you will be able to identify the source of the note.

In addition to putting a number at the top of the note card, also write a specific header or subtopic for your card. This will help you group similar ideas as you prepare more cards. For example, someone writing about how *The Grapes of Wrath* influenced government response to the Dust Bowl might create note card headings such as *Dust Bowl—living conditions, Bank failures,* or *Steinbeck—early writings about Dust Bowl.* Then quote, paraphrase, or summarize your source. End each card with a page number, if one is available.

See page R48 for examples of source cards and note cards.

PARAPHRASES AND SUMMARIES

A **paraphrase** is a restatement of an author's ideas in your own words. It includes all the ideas in the original statement and is about the same length as the original text. A **summary** is also a restatement, but it includes only key ideas and is therefore shorter than the original text. As these examples show, paraphrasing and summarizing carefully will help you avoid plagiarism.

Original Source

> With the introduction of the Soil Conservation Service (SCS) in 1935, the federal government began educating farmers in environmentally friendly farming techniques, such as shelterbelts, crop rotation, and introduction of soil-stabilizing grasses, terracing, and contour plowing.
>
> Kite, Steven. "Dust Bowl." *Encyclopedia of the Great Depression and New Deal*

Responsible Paraphrase

> **Government response to dust storms** ②
>
> The government also established the Soil Conservation Service in 1935. This program taught farmers to terrace their crops, plow along naturally occuring contours in the land, rotate crops, and practice other farming techniques that would protect the topsoil (110).

Carefully restates information; provides source number and page number

Responsible Summary

> **Government response to dust storms** ②
>
> The government also established the Soil Conservation Service in 1935, which taught farmers techniques to protect the topsoil (110).

Skillfully condenses original passage; includes source number and page number

The following examples show how sloppy paraphrasing and careless summarizing can lead to plagiarism.

Plagarized Paraphrase

> **Government response to dust storms**
>
> The government introduced the Soil Conservation Service in 1935 to educate farmers in environmentally friendly farming techniques, including crop rotation, terracing, and contour plowing.

Reproduces several phrases from the original without explaining where words and ideas came from

Plagarized Summary

> **Government response to dust storms**
>
> In 1935 the federal government introduced the Soil Conservation Service to teach farmers environmentally friendly farming techniques.

Takes a key phrase—"environmentally friendly farming techniques"—from the source without credit

Avoiding Plagiarism

By quoting and crediting information properly, you can include important ideas in your paper without plagiarizing them.

QUOTE INFORMATION ACCURATELY

Sometimes an idea is so significant or original that you want to reproduce it exactly as it was originally expressed. Place quotation marks around every word or phrase you take verbatim, or word for word, from a source. If you change the whole sentence except for one key phrase, that phrase still belongs to its author.

Original Source

> Life in what the newspapers call the Dust Bowl is becoming a gritty nightmare.
>
> Low, Ann Marie. _Dust Bowl Diary_. Qtd. in McElvaine, Robert S. _The Depression and New Deal: A History in Documents_

Plagiarized

Dust Bowl—Impact on farm families ⑦

In human terms, the Dust Bowl was a time of terrible suffering. Day by day, it was a gritty nightmare.

Does a good job of creating a new context, but the words "gritty nightmare" are not enclosed in quotation marks

Correctly Quoted

Dust Bowl—Impact on farm families ⑦

In human terms, the Dust Bowl was a time of terrible suffering. Day by day, it was "a gritty nightmare," a young North Dakotan named Ann Marie Low wrote in her diary (135).

Quotation marks and attribution show that the phrase "gritty nightmare" came from a source

CREDIT INFORMATION AND IDEAS FROM OTHERS

Sometimes it is difficult to know what needs to be credited and what does not. These tips can help you decide:

- **You must credit others' ideas.** Authors don't just compile facts and quotations; they give opinions and draw conclusions as well. If your paper includes a theory, explanation, or suggestion that you did not develop yourself, be sure to cite its source. For example, if one of your sources states that the Dust Bowl was more devastating than the stock-market crash, you must tell your reader where you found that assertion.

- **You do not need to credit facts that are considered common knowledge.** For instance, well-known historical information such as "Abraham Lincoln was president of the United States" does not need documentation. Neither do well-known sayings such as "Beauty is only skin deep" or general information such as "The sun rises in the east" and "Governments collect taxes from citizens and businesses." However, when in doubt, cite your source or sources.

Becoming a Critical Researcher

A critical researcher is one who carefully considers information from different sources and then uses that information to develop his or her own view of a topic.

Verifying Information

As you examine multiple sources, you may find information that appears to be incorrect. Here's how to review and evaluate sources that contradict each other.

RECONCILE DIFFERENCES

Even reliable experts can disagree. For example, historians disagree on exactly when the Dust Bowl started and on how many people abandoned their homes because of it. When you encounter varying sources, use the criteria listed on page 1274 to determine which sources are credible. If they all appear to be reliable, you could state in your paper that opinions vary and then describe the range that the different sources present.

Where can you check facts? Consult reputable print and online sources, such as encyclopedias, almanacs, and library databases. Here are some examples of reputable online sources.

FOR MORE INFORMATION . . .	TRY THIS ONLINE SOURCE
U.S. population statistics	www.census.gov (U.S. Bureau of the Census)
Primary sources, maps, audio, and video related to American history	www.loc.gov (Library of Congress)
Facts about the U.S. government	www.firstgov.gov (official U.S. government Web portal)
Facts about your state's history	your state's official Web site (visit www.firstgov.gov and click on "State Government")
International data	www.un.org (United Nations)
Information on technology	www.computerhistory.org (Computer History Museum) www.cnn.com/tech (CNN Technology News)
Data and resources on the environment	www.epa.gov (Environmental Protection Agency) www.webdirectory.com (The Environment Directory)
Information on space science	www.nasa.gov (NASA)

Detecting Bias

Bias is a preference or an attitude that can prevent a person from presenting information clearly and truthfully. Personal preferences and beliefs can sometimes be presented as facts. Sometimes bias is obvious; at other times it is very subtle.

QUESTIONS TO HELP YOU DETECT BIAS

- Who is the author, and what is his or her **background?** Does this person have ethical beliefs or personal experiences that might influence the writing?
- Why did the author write this piece? Did the **intent** influence his or her point of view? A person wishing to persuade readers may not fully present opposing viewpoints. For example, someone who contends that John Steinbeck single-handedly changed the government's response to migrant workers might leave out information about early government programs, private charities' efforts, and other artists' and writers' coverage of the problem.
- Are the writer's statements based on **verifiable evidence,** or are they speculation?
- Are **enough facts** presented to give a solid basis for the conclusions?
- Is the evidence **balanced,** or does one side get more support?
- How has the **time period** influenced the author's view of events or issues being discussed? For instance, a person writing during the Depression might be affected by the anxiety and despair of the time.
- Does the writer use **loaded language** that has extremely positive or extremely negative connotations, such as "Greedy bankers grew rich while despairing farmers starved"?

Developing Your Own Perspective

Each time you take notes, make connections by mentally attaching that note to something else you have read or discovered. As you synthesize more information, you will begin to develop your own viewpoint on your topic.

MAKE INFERENCES AND DRAW CONCLUSIONS

As you research, read between the lines of the author's words to find implied meanings and attitudes. An **inference** is a logical assumption that is based on observations or information in a text and one's own knowledge and experience. This chart shows the inference that one student made.

What the Source Says	What I Already Know	My Inference
Between 1929 and 1932, farm prices fell 55 percent.	The Great Depression started in 1929. The Dust Bowl started in the early 1930s.	Farmers were in serious trouble even before the Dust Bowl started.

If making an inference is "reading between the lines," then drawing a conclusion is "reading beyond the lines." A **conclusion** is a judgment or statement of belief based on evidence, experience, and reasoning. Making inferences is one of the necessary steps in drawing a conclusion, as you can see in this example.

What Sources Say	My Inferences	My Conclusion
John Steinbeck lived with migrant workers for about three years before he published <u>The Grapes of Wrath</u>.	Steinbeck's portrayal of the migrants was probably accurate.	<u>The Grapes of Wrath</u> was accurate, but not everyone wanted to believe its message.
Some growers in California got <u>The Grapes of Wrath</u> banned from several public libraries.	The book was controversial.	

DRAFT YOUR THESIS

As you read and take notes, think about what you are learning. Your thesis should be taking shape in your mind. That is, you will synthesize all that you have learned and thought about during your research. You will draw a larger conclusion about the topic you named in your goal statement.

This chart demonstrates the process of drafting a thesis based on your research.

Facts from My Research	My Conclusions	My Thesis
<u>The Grapes of Wrath</u> was published in 1939 and immediately became a best seller.	<u>The Grapes of Wrath</u> was one of the most important and influential novels of its era.	<u>The Grapes of Wrath</u> did not significantly affect the government's response to those who suffered from the effects of the Dust Bowl.
The President and the First Lady publicly discussed the book.		
As early as 1935, there were government programs to help Dust Bowl victims.	John Steinbeck was just one of many politicians, artists, and activists who were deeply concerned about the migrants.	
Many other writers and photographers chronicled the problems of the migrant laborers.		

Now it's time to put all your research and thinking to good use. In the next section, you will learn how to draft, revise, and perfect a research paper.—-

Writing Workshop

Research Paper

The true goal of most reading and research isn't repeating what you've read. Instead, it is putting together different sources of information to draw your own conclusions. The **Writer's Road Map** explains how to focus, synthesize, and interpret information in a carefully documented research paper.

WRITER'S ROAD MAP

Research Paper

WRITING PROMPT 1

Writing from Literature Develop a question about a piece of literature you have read. Write a research paper supporting a conclusion you reach about your topic. Present information from at least six sources as well as your own ideas and interpretations. Follow approved guidelines for format and documentation.

Literature to Consider

- *The Crucible*
- *The Scarlet Letter*
- *The Red Badge of Courage*
- *The Great Gatsby*

WRITING PROMPT 2

Historical Investigation Write a research paper that investigates an event or an idea from history. Your paper should present your own interpretations as well as information from at least six sources. Follow approved guidelines for format and documentation.

Questions to Investigate

- Was Reconstruction a success or a failure?
- Did propaganda lead the United States into World War I?
- Is my community typical of urban or suburban growth during the last 20 years?

 RESEARCH TOOLS
For research tools and citation guidelines, go to the **Research Center** at ClassZone.com.

KEY TRAITS

1. IDEAS
- Presents a **thesis statement** that identifies the controlling idea of the paper
- **Supports** the thesis with relevant and convincing evidence
- Synthesizes information from **multiple sources,** correctly **quoting** or **paraphrasing** those sources
- Includes the **writer's own ideas and interpretations**

2. ORGANIZATION
- Follows a clear **organizational pattern,** using transitions to connect ideas

3. VOICE
- Uses a **tone** that is suited to the audience, purpose, and subject
- Reflects the **writer's enthusiasm** for the topic

4. WORD CHOICE
- Uses **precise language** to convey ideas clearly

5. SENTENCE FLUENCY
- Varies **sentence lengths and structures**

6. CONVENTIONS
- Employs **correct grammar and usage**
- **Credits sources** properly
- Uses **correct formats and style**

Part 1: Analyze a Student Model

Chris Barron
Mrs. Machado
English III
29 April 2008

<u>The Grapes of Wrath</u>: A Reflection of Real Life

John Steinbeck's <u>The Grapes of Wrath</u>, now considered an American masterpiece, tells the gripping story of a family that abandons its Oklahoma farm during the Dust Bowl of the 1930s. Many people believe that the controversial novel raised public awareness about the suffering of "Okies"
5 who moved to California in search of a better life but found only poverty. Some experts also contend that Steinbeck's novel was the key factor in motivating the government to help these migrant workers. However, a close look at the evidence shows that although The Grapes of Wrath raised awareness of the Okies' plight, it did not significantly change how the
10 government responded to the crisis.

The Dust Bowl and Worsening Hard Times

To determine how much of an impact Steinbeck's novel had, it is important to have a clear understanding of what the Dust Bowl was and how it affected people. The Dust Bowl was a severe drought combined with
15 high heat and high winds. It occurred mainly in Oklahoma, Nebraska, Kansas, Texas, New Mexico, and Colorado, and it had its center at the Oklahoma panhandle. These conditions lasted about eight years, long enough to carry off tons of topsoil from the over-plowed fields in the region (Egan xi, 5). When Steinbeck wrote "the dawn came, but no day," he was
20 referring to the black clouds that swirled over the Great Plains during these desperate years (Steinbeck 5).

KEY TRAITS IN ACTION

A focused introduction leads up to a clear, original **thesis statement** (highlighted).

Has a clear **organizational pattern,** using headings to identify main parts.

Precise language makes the paper vivid and compelling.

Not all sources agree on when the Dust Bowl started, but some say that
the first devastating storms hit in 1931 and suggest that the full-blown
condition now called the Dust Bowl actually developed between 1933
25 and 1935 (Kite 107; "Timeline"). However, hard times were widespread
in the area before the drought occurred. The Great Depression began in
1929 when the stock market crashed. The following year, people all across
the country lost their jobs, and many banks could not pay their depositors
(Egan 95). Farm prices fell sharply, too: between 1929 and 1932, they
30 dove 55 percent (Himmelberg 9). By the time the Dust Bowl started,
Midwestern farm families had endured years of low prices and bank
failures, and high unemployment rates meant that family members could
not find work in nearby cities.

  In human terms, the Dust Bowl was a time of terrible suffering. Each
35 day was "a gritty nightmare," a young North Dakotan named Ann Marie
Low wrote in her diary. Sometimes dirt "lay inches deep on everything.
Every towel and curtain was just black" (McElvaine 134, 135). Homes
had to be shoveled out; nothing could be used before it was washed. The
dust also choked and killed cattle—and even some children (Egan 5-6).
40 Unable to grow anything on the land, many farm families had to leave the
Dust Bowl or die there. The estimate of just how many left varies widely.
Depending on how one defines the Dust Bowl area and its dates, the
number ranges from 16,000 to 315,000 (Windschuttle). Many families
traveled to California in search of work, as Steinbeck describes in his novel.

45 **Reactions to <u>The Grapes of Wrath</u>**

  Before Steinbeck began <u>The Grapes of Wrath</u>, he wrote newspaper
articles about living conditions in the California labor camps (Windschuttle).
He used this knowledge in his novel. "I know what I was talking about," he

Uses **transitions** to show the reader how ideas are related.

Synthesizes facts and details from **multiple sources, quoting** the most memorable and **paraphrasing** or **summarizing** the others.

Barron 3

told a reporter in July 1939. "I lived, on and off, with those Okies for

50 the last three years" (Cameron A2). The way the migrants were treated
angered and disturbed Steinbeck. In one of the most haunting passages
in The Grapes of Wrath, he wrote, "[I]n the eyes of the hungry there is a
growing wrath. In the souls of the people the grapes of wrath are filling and
growing heavy, growing heavy for the vintage" (Steinbeck 477). Because

55 Steinbeck knew his topic so well and presented it with such emotional
power, the novel was a huge success. Just two weeks after its publication, it
topped bestseller lists in New York, Philadelphia, Washington, Atlanta, San
Francisco, and Los Angeles ("Best Sellers").

   However, the book was not without controversy. Many people

60 disliked the novel; growers in California got it banned from several public
libraries there (Palos 22-23). When the Los Angeles Times reported that
some of the migrant workers had sent Steinbeck threatening letters, he
responded, "It isn't the refugees who have taken exception to what I wrote.
It's the moneyed people back there in Oklahoma—the big oil men and

65 outfits like the Oklahoma City Chamber of Commerce. If anybody's sore
at me for the book it's that kind of people" (Cameron A1-2). Steinbeck's
shocking novel brought him some influential enemies.

   Steinbeck did have important supporters, though. In December 1939,
First Lady Eleanor Roosevelt responded publicly to the book. She said that,

70 although she had read and heard others' criticisms about the novel, she
knew from her own travels and investigations that the living conditions
depicted in the book were at least "partly true" ("First Lady"). Then, in a
January 1940 radio address, President Franklin Roosevelt said, "I have read
a book recently; it is called Grapes of Wrath. There are 500,000 Americans

75 that live in the covers of that book" (McElvaine 148).

> **Serious tone** is appropriate to the subject matter, purpose, and audience.

> **Varied sentence lengths and structures** help to create a smooth flow of ideas.

Assessing the Novel's Impact

It is clear that Steinbeck's novel made a tremendous impression on some of the most powerful and influential people in the country. Yet it is not easy to establish any cause-and-effect relationship between <u>The Grapes</u>
80 <u>of Wrath</u> and improvements in the lives of Dust Bowl evacuees. The government had begun to respond to the problems of the Dust Bowl long before the book's publication. In 1935, four years before anyone read <u>The Grapes of Wrath</u>, the Emergency Relief Appropriation Act created jobs for unemployed farmers, set aside money for ranchers to feed their livestock
85 and farmers to buy seeds, and funded the construction of work camps for youths. In 1935, the Resettlement Administration began relocating farmers to better farming areas (Kite 107; "FSA Camp"). The government also established the Soil Conservation Service in 1935. This program taught farmers techniques to protect the topsoil (Kite 110). One of the most
90 important soil-saving programs was the Shelterbelt Project. This anti-erosion measure called for planting trees across the entire Great Plains. The program was already reducing blowing dirt by 1938, a year before <u>The Grapes of Wrath</u> appeared ("Timeline").

It is also a mistake to assume that Steinbeck's novel was the sole reason
95 that Americans focused their attention on victims of the Dust Bowl. For one thing, Steinbeck's wasn't the only voice crying out for justice. Woody Guthrie had long been writing social protest songs about the Okies. Bibliographies and library catalogs show several other books that could also be read as protests. For example, in 1939, Carey McWilliams
100 published <u>Factories in the Field</u>, an account of exploited migrants.

The **writer's own ideas and interpretations** appear throughout the paper.

Detailed evidence **supports** the thesis. The writer **credits sources** properly using **correct formats and style.**

Barron 5

It is also clear to anyone looking at Dorothea Lange's "Migrant Mother" and her other photographs that she was deeply concerned with the problems of poor people in California (McElvaine 105, 126, 175).

105 Steinbeck's novel and many other works raised awareness of the grim lives of the Okies. However, history makes it clear that what really changed Americans' lives in the years after the publication of The Grapes of Wrath was the buildup to World War II. By 1940, many new jobs had become available in factories—and in the military. The Great Depression ended; coincidentally, the drought in the Midwest also ended in 1939

110 ("Timeline"). These large forces are what truly put American workers back on the road to prosperity.

A Great Novel, but Only One Factor Among Many

The Grapes of Wrath is one of the most important novels of the 20th century. At the time of its publication it captivated thousands of readers,

115 including the president of the United States, and it helped to make the suffering of California migrant workers an issue of national importance. However, it is overstating the case to claim that the book motivated the government to help these workers. Many government programs were already in place at the time of the book's publication, and many other

120 writers and activists helped bring the problem to public attention. Other, larger factors—the end of the drought, an improved economy, and the looming possibility of another world war—also had important effects on the migrant workers' situation. Although Steinbeck's novel was factually accurate and artistically important, a thorough evaluation of the evidence

125 shows that it did not change the course of history.

Reflects the writer's interest in and **enthusiasm** for the subject matter.

Concludes with a summary and a statement of the **writer's own ideas.**

Works Cited

"Best Sellers of the Week." <u>New York Times</u> 1 May 1939: 19.

Cameron, Tom. "Dust Bowl Book Brings Trouble." <u>Los Angeles Times</u>
9 July 1939: A1+.

Egan, Timothy. <u>The Worst Hard Time.</u> Boston: Houghton, 2006.

"First Lady Stresses Community Interests." <u>New York Times</u> 8 Dec.
1939: 16.

"FSA Migratory Labor Camp." <u>Documenting America</u> Chapter 6. Lib.
of Congress. 9 Apr. 2008 <http://memory.loc.gov/ammem/fsahtml/
fachap06.html>.

Himmelberg, Robert F. <u>The Great Depression and the New Deal</u>.
Westport: Greenwood, 2001.

Kite, Steven. "Dust Bowl." <u>Encyclopedia of the Great Depression and the
New Deal</u>. Ed. James Ciment. 2 vols. Armonk, NY: Sharpe, 2001.
107-11.

McElvaine, Robert S. <u>The Depression and New Deal: A History in
Documents</u>. New York: Oxford UP, 2000. 132-7.

Palos, Elise. "'Grapes of Wrath' Banned in Kern County." <u>California
Historian</u> Mar. 1994: 22-23.

Steinbeck, John. <u>The Grapes of Wrath</u>. 1939. New York: Viking, 1964.

"Timeline." <u>American Experience: Surviving the Dust Bowl</u>. Pub.
Broadcasting Svc. 17 Apr. 2008 <http://www.pbs.org/wgbh/amex/
dustbowl/timeline/index.html>.

Windschuttle, Keith. "Steinbeck's Myth of the Okies." <u>New Criterion</u> June
2002: 24+.

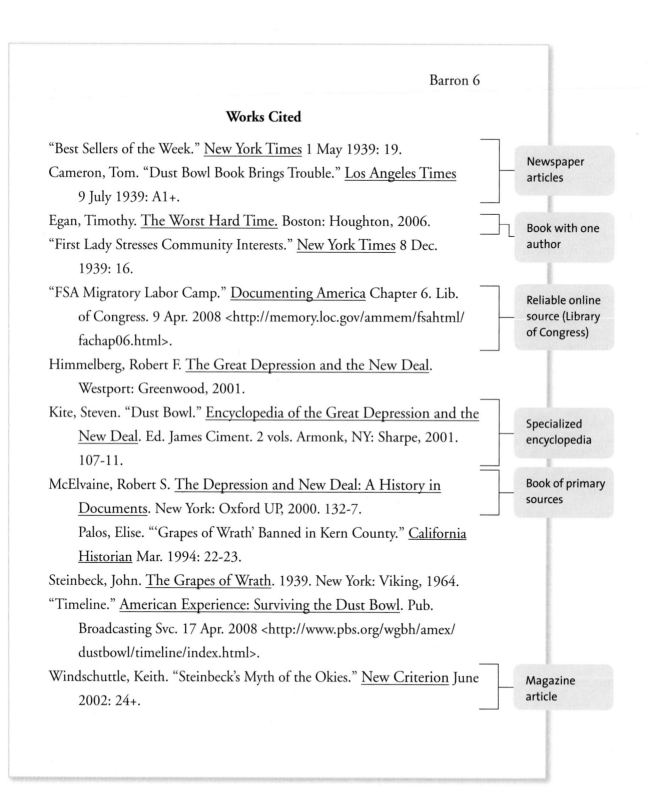

Newspaper articles

Book with one author

Reliable online source (Library of Congress)

Specialized encyclopedia

Book of primary sources

Magazine article

Part 2: Apply the Writing Process

PREWRITING

What Should I Do?	What Does It Look Like?

1. Analyze the prompt.

(Circle) words or phrases that tell you what you have to produce. <u>Underline</u> important details about the assignment. Take a few minutes to think about what you have to do and how you will do it. If you have questions about acceptable topics, format, paper length, or anything else, now is the time to ask your teacher.

▶ **WRITING PROMPT** <u>Develop a question about a piece of literature</u> you have read. Write a research (paper) (supporting) a conclusion you reach about your topic. Present <u>information from at least six sources</u> as well as <u>your own ideas and interpretations.</u> Follow approved guidelines for format and documentation.

> I have to ask my own question. I have to present and support my own ideas and conclusions. I have to use at least six sources. Also, I should try to find a subject that really interests me.

2. Find your topic.

Because you are going to be doing more than putting together other people's ideas, you need both a subject and an original approach to it. Explore a subject that interests you by looking at it through different "lenses" (see page 1268), by creating fresh new comparisons, by asking original questions, or by freewriting. One student's freewriting is shown here.

> ▶ The Grapes of Wrath is such a vivid picture of what one family went through, in Oklahoma, on the road, and in California. Maybe Steinbeck was just writing a good story, or maybe he was trying to be a political activist and cause change. I wonder what the state of California or the federal government did after this book was published. Did Steinbeck's novel really make a difference?

3. Develop an original focus and a working thesis.

Find some general encyclopedia articles, some Web sites, or a video about your topic. Don't take notes yet; just read or view to develop background knowledge. Then list questions you still have. Choose one of them as your focus and (circle) it. Develop this question into a working thesis statement.

See page 1269: Formulate Research Questions

> ▶ *My Remaining Questions*
> How true to life was <u>The Grapes of Wrath</u>?
> How did people at the time respond to the book? Was that different from readers' responses today?
> (Did the book cause a government response?)
>
> **Working thesis statement:** <u>The Grapes of Wrath</u> changed the government's response to migrant workers.

What Should I Do?	**What Does It Look Like?**

1. Investigate possible sources.

Once you narrow your topic, you can begin searching for sources. Places to look include the Internet, your school's media center, and your public library. As you search, make a list of sources that appear to have relevant information. Include the title, the author's name (if available), and where you found it. Then comment on what you think the source offers.

See page 1269: Identify the Most Relevant Sources

Sources	Comments
World Wide Web	
"Timeline," _American Experience: Surviving the Dust Bowl_	lists several government responses to Dust Bowl
"Grapes of Wrath Banned in Kern County" by Elise Palos	article won an award from the California Historical Association
"Dust Bowl Days," www.athens.edu/~johanna	great graphics: sights and sounds of Dust Bowl
Public Library	
The Worst Hard Time by Timothy Egan (978.032 Egan)	terrific source: lots of facts, illustrations, explanation
"On the Cause of the 1930s Dust Bowl," _Science_ magazine	all about the weather patterns that created the Dust Bowl; excellent graphics

2. Evaluate your sources.

Use the criteria on pages 1274–1277 to evaluate your sources. By choosing only relevant and reliable sources, you will save yourself time and frustration.

Reasons for Rejecting a Source

"Dust Bowl Days": This site doesn't name the author or list the author's credentials. It has no footnotes or bibliography.

"On the Cause . . .": This is a well-documented article, but it isn't really on my topic.

3. Make source cards.

When you have decided which sources to keep, create a numbered card for each source. Your source cards will provide the information for your Works Cited list—titles, authors, locations, publishers, and other important information. See page R48 to learn how to make source cards for different types of sources.

①

"Timeline." _American Experience: Surviving the Dust Bowl._ Pub. Broadcasting Svc. 17 Apr. 2008 <http://www.pbs.org/wgbh/amex/dustbowl/timeline/index.html>.

RESEARCHING

What Should I Do?	**What Does It Look Like?**

4. Start taking notes.

As you read your sources, look for information that supports or contradicts your working thesis statement. Record each piece of information on a separate index card. That way you can try different ways of organizing your ideas as you draft. On each card, include the main idea, the number of the source (from its source card), and a way of locating the information, such as a page number or section name.

TIP Record information honestly, giving credit where it is due. See pages 1278–1280 to learn about note taking and plagiarism.

▶ **Federal aid programs before Grapes of Wrath** ①

The Shelterbelt program started in 1937. The government paid farmers to plant trees so that less topsoil would blow away. By 1938, the tree planting and other methods had reduced blowing soil by 65 percent (4).

5. Create an outline.

Group your note cards by subtopic. Then put those groups in a logical order. For example, you might begin with background information. Use your note cards to write an outline of your paper. A partial example is shown here.

▶ **The Grapes of Wrath and the Dust Bowl**

I. Background information: The Dust Bowl
   A. What and where it was
   B. When it took place
   C. What people's lives were like
      1. "A gritty nightmare" (Low's diary)
      2. Dust killed children, animals
II. Background information: The Grapes of Wrath
   A. Based on Steinbeck's own research
   B. Reaction to the book

6. Revise your working thesis.

Now that your research paper is taking shape, it's time to revisit your working thesis statement. Think about what you have learned about your topic. Does your thesis need only minor revisions, or should you make significant changes?

▶ **Working thesis statement:** The Grapes of Wrath changed the government's response to migrant workers.

Revised thesis statement: Although The Grapes of Wrath raised awareness of the Okies' plight, it did not significantly change how the government responded to the crisis.

What Should I Do?	*What Does It Look Like?*
1. Draft your introduction. Many research papers begin by providing interesting background information that leads up to the thesis statement, which is often the final sentence of the introductory paragraph.	▶ John Steinbeck's <u>The Grapes of Wrath</u>, now considered an American masterpiece, tells the gripping story of a family that leaves Oklahoma because of the Dust Bowl. Many people believe that the controversial novel raised public awareness about the suffering of "Okies." However, a close look at the evidence shows that although <u>The Grapes of Wrath</u> raised awareness of the Okies' plight, it did not significantly change how the government responded to the crisis.
2. Incorporate information from your note cards. Using your outline as a guide, incorporate facts, ideas, and quotations from your note cards into your rough draft. Be sure to include the name of each source as you add it, plus a page number if one is available. To learn how to do this, see "Document your sources" on the next page.	▶ <u>Negative reaction to Grapes of Wrath</u>　⑤ Most of the novel takes place in Kern County, California. Steinbeck's version of events offended some landowners there. In August 1939 the county board of supervisors banned the novel from schools and libraries in the county (22-23). However, the book was not without controversy. Many people disliked the novel; growers in California got it banned from several public libraries there (Palos 22-23).
3. Blend material from multiple sources. If appropriate, compare and contrast ideas from different sources, or show how one source complements, enlarges, or expands on another. **TIP** Instead of dropping a quotation into the middle of your paper, weave it in with an introduction (*As Palos explains, . . .*) or by inserting phrases or words into a sentence (*Each day was "a gritty nightmare," . . .*).	▶ In human terms, the Dust Bowl was a time of terrible suffering. — Topic sentence Each day was "a gritty nightmare," a young North Dakotan named Ann Marie Low wrote in her diary (McElvaine 135). — Quoted source The dust also choked and killed cattle—and even some children (Egan 5-6). — Paraphrased source

DRAFTING

What Should I Do?	*What Does It Look Like?*

4. Share your own ideas and interpretations. Analyze others' ideas and make your own interpretations of them. Use facts, examples, and other evidence to support your ideas.

See pages 1282–1283: Developing Your Own Perspective

▶

> It is a mistake to assume that Steinbeck's novel was the sole reason that people focused their attention on victims of the Dust Bowl. For one thing, Steinbeck's wasn't the only voice crying out for justice. Woody Guthrie had long been writing social protest songs about the Okies. Bibliographies and library catalogs show several other books that could also be read as protests. For example, in 1939, Carey McWilliams published <u>Factories in the Field</u>, an account of exploited migrants. It is also clear to anyone looking at Dorothea Lange's "Migrant Mother" and her other photographs that she was deeply concerned with the problems of poor people in California (McElvaine 105, 126, 175).

5. Document your sources. Each time you quote, paraphrase, or summarize information from a source, include a parenthetical reference at the end of the sentence or sentences. In general, a parenthetical reference includes the author's **last name** and the **page number**: (Himmelberg 9). There are, however, many variations.

- **Author already mentioned in sentence**— give only the page number (110)
- **Author not known**—use a shortened form of the title of the work ("First Lady")
- **More than one author**—include last names for up to three authors (Lange and Taylor 409). For more than three authors, use the first author's last name and *et al.* (Zielonka et al. 138-145).
- **More than one source**—separate the information for each source with a semicolon (Kite 107; "Timeline")
- **More than one work by the same author**— include a shortened form of the work's title (Steinbeck, <u>Dubious</u> 61)

▶

> In 1935, the Resettlement Administration began relocating farmers to better farming areas (Kite 107).

⎤ Basic documentation: author and page number

> Not all sources agree on when the Dust Bowl started (Kite 107; "Timeline").

⎤ Evidence from two sources

> The Great Depression ended; coincidentally, the drought in the Midwest also ended in 1939 ("Timeline").

⎤ Author and page number unknown

What Should I Do?

What Does It Look Like?

6. Develop your concluding paragraph.
A thoughtful conclusion does more than just restate the facts you presented. It leaves your reader with something compelling to think about. The writer of the student model reflected on the overall significance of his topic. Other approaches include asking a thought-provoking question or including a compelling quotation.

▶ The Grapes of Wrath is one of the most important novels of the 20th century. At the time of its publication it captivated thousands of readers, including the president of the United States, and it helped to make the suffering of California migrant workers an issue of national importance. However, it is overstating the case to claim that the book motivated the government to help these workers. Many government programs were already in place at the time of the book's publication, and many other writers and activists helped bring the problem to public attention. Other, larger factors—the end of the drought, an improved economy, and the looming possibility of another world war—also had important effects on the migrant workers' situation.

7. Create a Works Cited list.
After you have written your draft, check that you have given proper credit in parentheses to each quotation or bit of information that you got from a source. Then go through your paper and find the source card for each parenthetical reference. Alphabetize the cards by the author's last name, if available, or by the title of the work. Then create a Works Cited list like the one shown.

TIP To make sure that you include all your sources in the Works Cited list, go through your rough draft and highlight each parenthetical reference.

See pages 1299–1300: MLA Citation Guidelines

▶
Works Cited

"Best Sellers of the Week." New York Times 1 May 1939: 19.

Cameron, Tom. "Dust Bowl Book Brings Trouble." Los Angeles Times 9 July 1939: A1+.

Egan, Timothy. The Worst Hard Time. Boston: Houghton, 2006.

"First Lady Stresses Community Interests." New York Times 8 Dec. 1939: 16.

REVISING AND EDITING

What Should I Do?	What Does It Look Like?

1. Improve your introduction.

- Reread your first paragraph. Does your first sentence surprise, challenge, or otherwise interest your reader? Did you explain terms your reader might not understand, such as *Okies?* Is your thesis clear?

- Add information or explanations to create a smooth flow of ideas leading up to your thesis.

▶ John Steinbeck's <u>The Grapes of Wrath</u>, now considered an American masterpiece, tells the gripping story of a family that ~~leaves Oklahoma because of the Dust Bowl~~ abandons its Oklahoma farm during the Dust Bowl of the 1930s.

Many people believe that the controversial novel raised public awareness about the suffering of "Okies," who moved to California in search of a better life but found only poverty. Some experts also contend that Steinbeck's novel was the key factor in motivating the government to help these migrant workers.

However, a close look at the evidence shows that...

2. Check the flow of your ideas.

- Ask a peer reader to draw a ☐ box around any places where ideas do not flow smoothly.

- Add transitional words and phrases where needed to link ideas.

See page 1301: Ask a Peer Reader

▶ It is clear that Steinbeck's novel made a tremendous impression on some of the most powerful and influential people in the country. It is not easy to establish a cause-and-effect relationship between <u>The Grapes of Wrath</u> and improvements in the lives of Dust Bowl evacuees.

Yet

3. Make sure that each idea has support.

- Examine each paragraph you wrote. Ask yourself, "Do I include enough explanation and evidence to support this point?"

- If needed, add more explanation, including correctly cited facts. Where **appropriate**, add your own insights and interpretations, **too**.

▶ The government had begun to respond to the problems of the Dust Bowl long before the book's publication. In 1935, four years before anyone read <u>The Grapes of Wrath</u>, the Emergency Relief Appropriation Act created jobs for unemployed farmers, set aside money for ranchers to feed their livestock and farmers to buy seeds, and funded the construction of work camps for youths (Kite 107). One of the most important soil-saving programs was the Shelterbelt Project. This anti-erosion measure called for planting trees across the entire Great Plains ("Timeline").

What Should I Do?	What Does It Look Like?
4. Eliminate unnecessary details. • Ask a peer reader to [bracket] any parts of your paper that are wordy or off topic. • Revise as needed until each paragraph is concise. **See page 1301: Ask a Peer Reader**	▶ Just two weeks after its publication, it topped bestseller lists in [the major American cities of] New York, Philadelphia, Washington, Atlanta, San Francisco, and Los Angeles. [That kind of success is very impressive!]
5. Refine your conclusion. • Reread your concluding paragraph. Be sure that you have used fresh, new phrasing for anything you have repeated for emphasis. • End with a final insight, a memorable phrase, or a question.	▶ It is overstating the case to claim that the book motivated the government to help these workers. Many government programs were already in place at the time of the book's publication, and many other writers and activists helped bring the problem to public attention. Other, larger factors—the end of the drought, an improved economy, and the looming possibility of another world war—also had important effects on the migrant workers' situation. Although Steinbeck's novel was factually accurate and artistically important, a thorough evaluation of the evidence shows that it did not change the course of history.
6. Proofread parenthetical documentation. • <u>Underline</u> any facts, key words, or other information that you haven't documented. • Add parenthetical references to show where you found the information. Check each citation throughout the paper for correct content, punctuation, and order.	▶ <u>When Steinbeck wrote "the dawn came, but no day," he was referring to the black clouds that swirled over the Great Plains during these desperate years</u>, (Steinbeck 5). <u>Depending on how one defines the Dust Bowl and its dates, the number ranges from 16,000 to 315,000</u>, (Windschuttle). <u>She said that, although she had read and heard others' criticisms about the novel, she knew from her own travels and investigations that the living conditions depicted in the book were at least "partly true</u>," ("First Lady").

MLA Citation Guidelines

The MLA (Modern Language Association) has developed guidelines for documenting research. Follow these examples to create the Works Cited list for your source cards and your research paper.

BOOKS

One author
Steinbeck, John. <u>The Grapes of Wrath</u>. 1939. New York: Viking, 1964.

Two authors or editors
Lange, Dorothea, and Paul Schuster Taylor. <u>An American Exodus: A Record of Human Erosion</u>.
New York: Reynal & Hitchcock, 1939.

Three authors or editors
Scheibel, Jeremy, Anne Chatsworth, and Ridley Davis, eds. <u>Stories from the Great Depression</u>.
Princeton: Princeton UP, 2008.

Four or more authors or editors
List the first author only. Then use the abbreviation et al., *which means "and others."*
Rutkowski, J., et al. <u>American Immigration and Migration in the 1930s</u>. Topeka: Sanders-Ellis, 2007.

No author given
<u>American Literature: 1865 to the Present</u>. Chicago: Omni, 2007.

PARTS OF BOOKS

An introduction, a preface, a foreword, or an afterword written by someone other than the author(s) of a work
Gorton, Terry. Foreword. <u>John Steinbeck: A Centennial Tribute</u>. Ed. Stephen K. George.
Westport: Praeger, 2002. xvii-xviii.

A poem, a short story, an essay, or a chapter in a collection of works
Steinbeck, John. "The Leader of the People." <u>The Portable Steinbeck</u>. Ed. Pascal Covici, Jr.
New York: Penguin, 1978. 397-415.

A poem, a short story, an essay, or a chapter in an anthology of works by several authors
Steinbeck, John. "The Red Pony." <u>The American Short Story: A Collection of the Best Known
and Most Memorable Short Stories by the Great American Authors</u>. Ed. Thomas K.
Parkes. New York: Galahad, 1994. 886-948.

A novel or a play in a collection
Steinbeck, John. <u>The Grapes of Wrath</u>. <u>The Grapes of Wrath and Other Writings, 1936–1941</u>.
New York: Library of America, 1996.

MAGAZINES, NEWSPAPERS, AND ENCYCLOPEDIAS

An article in a newspaper

Patel, Vikram. "Recalling the Days of Wrath." Los Angeles Times 8 Jan. 2008: 9.

An article in a magazine

Schubert, Siegfried D., et al. "On the Cause of the 1930s Dust Bowl." Science 19 Mar. 2004: 1855-60.

An article in an encyclopedia

Kite, Steven. "Dust Bowl." Encyclopedia of the Great Depression and New Deal. Ed. James Ciment. 2 vols. Armonk, NY: Sharpe, 2001. 107-11.

MISCELLANEOUS NONPRINT SOURCES

An interview

Sorenson, Elvina. Personal interview. 3 Feb. 2008.

A video recording or film

Our Daily Bread. Dir. King Vidor. Perf. Karen Morley, Tom Keene, Barbara Pepper, John Qualen. 1934. DVD. Film Preservation Assoc., 1999.

A sound recording

Guthrie, Woody. Library of Congress Recordings/Woody Guthrie. CD. Rounder, 1988.

ELECTRONIC PUBLICATIONS

A document from an Internet site

Include as much of the following information as available in the order given.

Author or compiler | Title or description of document | Title of Internet site

Neary, Walter. "Steinbeck & Salinas." About John Steinbeck.

Date of Internet site | Site sponsor | Date of access

5 June 1990. Rev. June 1995. National Steinbeck Center. 2 Apr. 2008

Complete URL enclosed in angle brackets. Break only after a slash.

<http://www.steinbeck.org/MainFrame.html>.

An online book or e-book

Wunder, John R., Frances Kaye, and Vernon Carstensen, eds. Americans View Their Dust Bowl Experience. Niwot: UP Colorado, 1999. NetLibrary. <http://library.minlib.net>.

A CD-ROM

"Dust Bowl." Britannica Student Encyclopedia. 2004 ed. CD-ROM. Chicago: Encyclopaedia Britannica, 2004.

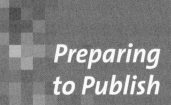

Preparing to Publish Research Paper

Apply the Rubric

A strong research paper . . .

☑ presents a clear, original thesis statement that is the governing idea of the entire paper

☑ supports the thesis with evidence from multiple sources

☑ includes the writer's own insights, interpretations, and conclusions

☑ correctly and honestly credits all sources

☑ maintains an appropriate tone

☑ reflects the writer's interest in the subject matter

☑ is logically organized

☑ has a focused introduction and an effective conclusion

☑ uses precise words

☑ varies the lengths and structures of sentences

Ask a Peer Reader

• What is my thesis? Where do I explain and support it most effectively?

• Do my ideas flow smoothly? If not, where should I add transitions?

• Did I include unnecessary details? If so, where?

Format Your Paper

Use these guidelines to prepare the final copy of your research paper:

• Double-space everything.

• Leave a one-inch margin at the left, right, top, and bottom of each page (except for page numbers).

• At the top left of the first page, type your name, your teacher's name, the class, and the date. Use a separate line for each item. On the rest of the pages, type your last name and the page number in the upper right corner, half an inch from the top.

• Indent all paragraphs one-half inch (or five spaces) and indent quotations of four or more lines one inch (or ten spaces) from the left margin.

• Start a new page for your Works Cited list. Begin each entry at the left margin, indenting any aditional lines one-half inch (or five spaces). End each entry with a period.

See the *MLA Handbook for Writers of Research Papers* for additional formatting guidelines.

Writing On|ine

PUBLISHING OPTIONS
For publishing options, visit the **Writing Center** at **ClassZone.com.**

ASSESSMENT PREPARATION
For writing and grammar assessment practice, go to the **Assessment Center** at **ClassZone.com.**

Presenting the Results of Your Investigation

You can create a presentation to showcase what you have learned.

Planning the Presentation

1. **Consider the sights and sounds of your subject matter.** Review your research paper with a focus on how to bring the subject matter to life for an audience. If your research paper is on the Dust Bowl, you might present any or all of these materials:
   - newsreel footage (now available on video)
   - excerpts from *The Grapes of Wrath*
   - maps showing the migrants' travels
   - folk songs about the Okies
   - photographs of migrant families

   Think about which primary and secondary sources would make your subject accessible and compelling. Use your research paper as a guide, but consider incorporating other sources as well.

2. **Make technology work for you.** Think about the best way to present the materials you want to share. Consider these options:

   - Create a power presentation—slides that you create and display on a computer.

   - Develop a Web site that has one or more pages for each major point you make in your paper. Your site might include databases, spreadsheets, or other graphics.

   - Design a series of posters and charts for display in your classroom, elsewhere at your school, or at a local community center.

   - Produce a video or audio documentary.

   Ask your teacher which presentation options might work best. See page 605 for information on producing a documentary. See page 811 for details on creating power presentations. Information on creating a Web site is on page 1255.

3. **Decide on your purpose.** Are you providing audience members with information? Are you trying to persuade them to hold a particular point of view? Do you want to describe a process or explain a complex historical event? You may have more than one purpose.

4. **Develop your script.** Find out how long you will speak and how many people will be present. Consider how much audience members are likely to know about your topic. Your script may be as simple as a stack of index cards or as complicated as a storyboard with notations for visuals, narration, music, and effects.

What Was the Dust Bowl?

- Severe drought combined with heat and winds
- Affected the Great Plains in the 1930s
- Center was the Oklahoma panhandle

Effects of the Dust Bowl

- Carried off tons of topsoil from over-plowed fields
- Caused choking, sometimes fatal dust clouds
- Displaced thousands, many of whom went to California

5. **Smoothly integrate materials from a variety of sources.** Visuals, audio or video clips, music, and other effects should all help audience members understand your topic. Avoid visuals and effects that are flashy but bring little new information.

6. **Get the details right.** Make sure that your information is accurate and properly credited. Any display text should be large enough to be read from the back of the room—and it should all be spelled correctly, too. If you are creating a Web site as part of your presentation, check that all links are working.

7. **Practice your presentation.** Practice will improve your delivery and soothe your nerves. Ideally, you should practice in the room where you will make your presentation and with the equipment you will use. Ask friends and family members to listen to your presentation. Invite them to give constructive criticism of your performance.

Making the Presentation

1. **Present, explain, elaborate.** Don't read to your audience. Discuss each point you make, providing details and examples from your sources. If certain sources disagree, point that out. Explain why some sources' perspectives may differ and what evidence you have for the sources' reliability.

2. **Invite audience members to ask questions.** Be sure to repeat any questions that audience members ask. That way you can confirm that you understand the question and make certain that the rest of the audience has heard it.

3. **Find out how you did.** Create a simple survey or questionnaire and ask audience members to complete it. Use what you learn to improve your next presentation's content and style.

Student Resource Bank

Reading any text—short story, poem, magazine article, newspaper, Web page—requires the use of special strategies. For example, you might plot events in a short story on a diagram, while you might use text features to spot main ideas in a magazine article. You also need to identify patterns of organization in the text. Using such strategies can help you read different texts with ease and also help you understand what you're reading.

1 Reading Literary Texts

Literary texts include short stories, novels, poems, and dramas. Literary texts can also be biographies, autobiographies, and essays. To appreciate and analyze literary texts, you will need to understand the characteristics of each type of text.

1.1 READING A SHORT STORY

Strategies for Reading

- Read the title. As you read the story, you may notice that the title has a special meaning.
- Keep track of events as they happen. Plot the events on a diagram like this one.

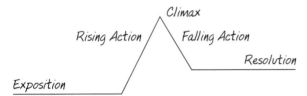

- Using the details the writer provides, **visualize** the characters. **Predict** what they might do next.
- Look for specific adjectives that help you visualize the **setting**—the time and place in which events occur.
- Note **cause-and-effect relationships** and how these affect the **conflict**.

1.2 READING A POEM

Strategies for Reading

- Notice the **form** of the poem, or the arrangement of its lines and stanzas on the page.
- Read the poem aloud a few times. Listen for and note the **rhymes** and **rhythms.**
- **Visualize** the images and comparisons.
- **Connect** with the poem by asking yourself what message the poet is trying to send.
- Create a word web or another **graphic organizer** to record your reactions and questions.

1.3 READING A PLAY

Strategies for Reading

- Read the stage directions to help you **visualize** the setting and characters.
- **Question** what the title means and why the playwright chose it.
- Identify the main conflict (struggle or problem) in the play. To **clarify** the conflict, make a chart that shows what the conflict is and how it is resolved.
- **Evaluate** the characters. What do they want? How do they change during the play? You may want to make a chart that lists each character's name, appearance, and traits.

1.4 READING LITERARY NONFICTION

Strategies for Reading

- If you are reading a biography, an autobiography, or another type of biographical writing, such as a diary or memoir, use a family tree to keep track of the people mentioned.
- When reading an essay, **analyze** and **evaluate** the writer's ideas and reasoning. Does the writer present a thesis statement? use sound logic? adequately support opinions with facts and other evidence?
- For all types of nonfiction, be aware of the **author's purpose,** and note any personal **bias** of the writer's that might influence the presentation of information.

❷ Reading Informational Texts: Text Features

An **informational text** is writing that provides factual information. Informational materials, such as chapters in textbooks and articles in magazines, encyclopedias, and newspapers, usually contain elements that help the reader recognize their purposes, organization, and key ideas. These elements are known as **text features.**

2.1 UNDERSTANDING TEXT FEATURES

Text features are design elements of a text that indicate its organizational structure or otherwise make its key ideas and information understandable. Text features include titles, headings, subheadings, boldface type, bulleted and numbered lists, and graphic aids, such as charts, graphs, illustrations, and photographs. Notice how the text features help you find key information on the textbook page shown.

Ⓐ The **title** identifies the topic.

Ⓑ A **subheading** indicates the start of a new topic or section and identifies the focus of that section.

Ⓒ **Boldface type** is used to make key terms obvious.

Ⓓ A **bulleted list** shows items of equal importance.

Ⓔ **Graphic aids,** such as illustrations, photographs, charts, graphs, diagrams, maps, and timelines, often clarify ideas in the text.

PRACTICE AND APPLY

1. What are the subheadings on the textbook page shown?

2. What are the key terms on the page? How do you know?

3. How do the bulleted list and the photograph help you understand the information on this page?

Ⓐ ## New Deal Programs: Helping the American People

While working on banking and financial matters, the Roosevelt administration also implemented programs to provide relief to farmers, perhaps the hardest hit by the depression. It also aided other workers and attempted to stimulate economic recovery.

Ⓑ **RURAL ASSISTANCE** The **Agricultural Adjustment Act (AAA)** sought to Ⓒ raise crop prices by lowering production, which the government achieved by paying farmers to leave a certain amount of every acre of land unseeded. The theory was that reduced supply would boost prices. In some cases, crops were too far advanced for the acreage reduction to take effect. As a result, the government paid cotton growers $200 million to plow under 10 million acres of their crop. It also paid hog farmers to slaughter 6 million pigs. This policy upset many Americans, who protested the destruction of food when many people were going hungry. It did, however, help raise farm prices and put more money in farmers' pockets.

An especially ambitious program of regional development was the Tennessee Valley Authority (TVA), established on May 18, 1933. (See Geography Spotlight on page 520.) Focusing on the badly depressed Tennessee River Valley, the TVA renovated five existing dams and constructed 20 new ones, created thousands of jobs, and provided flood control, hydroelectric power, and other benefits to an impoverished region.

PROVIDING WORK PROJECTS The administration also established programs to provide relief through work projects and cash payments. One important program, the **Civilian Conservation Corps (CCC),** put young men aged 18 to 25 to work building roads, developing parks, planting trees, and helping in soil-erosion and flood-control projects. By the time the program ended in 1942, almost 3 million young men had passed through the CCC. The CCC paid a small wage, $30 a month, of which $25 was automatically sent home to the worker's family. It also supplied free food and uniforms and lodging in work camps. Many of the camps were located on the Great Plains, where, within a period of eight years, the men of the CCC planted more than 200 million trees. This tremendous reforestation program was aimed at preventing another Dust Bowl.

The Public Works Administration (PWA), created in June 1933 as part of the **National Industrial Recovery Act (NIRA),** provided money to states to create jobs chiefly in the construction of schools and other community buildings. When these programs failed to make a sufficient dent in unemployment, President Roosevelt established the Civil Works Administration in November 1933. It provided 4 million immediate jobs during the winter of 1933–1934. Although some critics of the CWA claimed that the programs were "make-work" projects and a waste of money, the CWA built 40,000 schools and paid the salaries of more than 50,000 schoolteachers in America's rural areas. It also built more than half a million miles of roads. Ⓒ

Background
See *supply and demand* on page R46 in the Economics Handbook.

Ⓓ **Civilian Conservation Corps**

- The CCC provided almost 3 million men aged 18–25 with work and wages between 1933 and 1942.

- The men lived in work camps under a strict regime. The majority of the camps were racially segregated.

- By 1938, the CCC had an 11 percent African-American enrollment.

- Accomplishments of the CCC include planting over 3 billion trees, developing over 800 state parks, and building more than 46,000 bridges.

MAIN IDEA

Analyzing Effects
Ⓒ How did New Deal programs affect various regions of the United States?

Ⓔ *The New Deal* **491**

2.2 USING TEXT FEATURES

You can use text features to locate information, to help you understand it, and to categorize it. Just use the following strategies when you encounter informational text.

Strategies for Reading

- Scan the title, headings, and subheadings to get an idea of the main concepts and the way the text is organized.

- Before you begin reading the text more thoroughly, read any questions that appear at the end of a lesson or chapter. Doing this will help you set a purpose for your reading.

- Turn subheadings into questions. Then use the text below the subheadings to answer the questions. Your answers will be a summary of the text.

- Take notes by turning headings and subheadings into main ideas. You might enter them in a chart like the following.

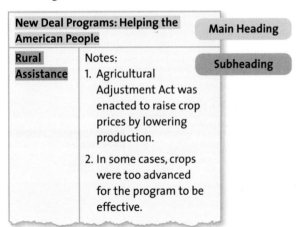

2.3 TURNING TEXT HEADINGS INTO OUTLINE ENTRIES

You can also use text features to take notes in outline form. The following outline shows how one student used text headings from the sample page on page R3. Study the outline and use the strategies that follow to create an outline based on text features.

Strategies for Using Text Headings

- Preview the headings and subheadings in the text to get an idea of what different kinds there are and what their positions might be in an outline.

- Be consistent. Note that subheadings that are the same size and color should be used consistently in Roman-numeral or capital-letter entries in the outline. If you decide that a chapter heading should appear with a Roman numeral, then that's the level at which all other chapter headings should appear.

- Write the headings and subheadings that you will use as your Roman-numeral and capital-letter entries first. As you read, fill in numbered details from the text under the headings and subheadings in your outline.

PRACTICE AND APPLY

Find a suitable chapter in one of your textbooks and, using its text features, take notes on the chapter in outline form.

Preview the subheadings in the text to get an idea of the different kinds. Write the headings and subheadings you are using as your Roman-numeral and capital-letter entries first. Then fill in the details.

2.4 GRAPHIC AIDS

Information is communicated not only with words but also with graphic aids. **Graphic aids** are visual representations of verbal statements. They can be charts, webs, diagrams, graphs, photographs, or other visual representations of information. Graphic aids usually make complex information easier to understand. For that reason, graphic aids are often used to organize, simplify, and summarize information for easy reference.

Graphs

Graphs are used to illustrate statistical information. A **graph** is a drawing that shows the relative values of numerical quantities. Different kinds of graphs are used to show different numerical relationships.

Strategies for Reading

A Read the title.

B Find out what is being represented or measured.

C In a circle graph, compare the sizes of the parts.

D In a line graph, study the slant of the line. The steeper the line, the faster the rate of change.

E In a bar graph, compare the lengths of the bars.

A **circle graph,** or **pie graph,** shows the relationships of parts to a whole. The entire circle equals 100 percent. The parts of the circle represent percentages of the whole.

MODEL: CIRCLE GRAPH

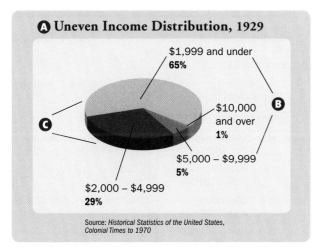

A Uneven Income Distribution, 1929

$1,999 and under
65%

$10,000 and over
1%

$5,000 – $9,999
5%

$2,000 – $4,999
29%

Source: *Historical Statistics of the United States, Colonial Times to 1970*

Line graphs show changes in numerical quantities over time and are effective in presenting trends, such as unemployment rates. A line graph is made on a grid. Here, the vertical axis indicates the percentage of the work force that is unemployed, and the horizontal axis shows years. Points on the graph indicate data. The lines that connect the points indicate the trends or patterns.

MODEL: LINE GRAPH

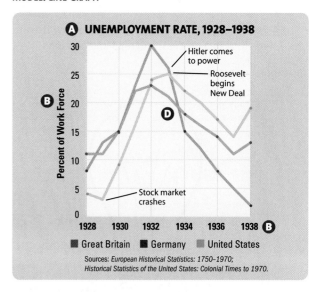

A UNEMPLOYMENT RATE, 1928–1938

Percent of Work Force

Hitler comes to power

Roosevelt begins New Deal

Stock market crashes

1928 1930 1932 1934 1936 1938

■ Great Britain ■ Germany ■ United States

Sources: *European Historical Statistics: 1750–1970;*
Historical Statistics of the United States: Colonial Times to 1970.

In a **bar graph,** vertical or horizontal bars are used to show or compare categories of information, such as average annual income during wartime. The lengths of the bars typically indicate quantities.

MODEL: BAR GRAPH

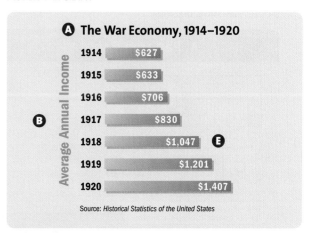

A The War Economy, 1914–1920

Average Annual Income

1914 $627
1915 $633
1916 $706
1917 $830
1918 $1,047
1919 $1,201
1920 $1,407

Source: *Historical Statistics of the United States*

WATCH OUT! Evaluate carefully the information presented in graphs. For example, circle graphs show major factors and differences well but tend to minimize smaller factors and differences.

Diagrams

A **diagram** is a drawing that shows how something works or how its parts relate to one another.

A **picture diagram** is a picture or drawing of the subject being discussed.

Strategies for Reading

Ⓐ Read the title.

Ⓑ Read each label and look at the part it identifies.

Ⓒ Follow any arrows or numbers that show the order of steps in a process, and read any captions.

MODEL: PICTURE DIAGRAM

In a **schematic diagram,** lines, symbols, and words are used to help readers visualize processes or objects they wouldn't normally be able to see.

MODEL: SCHEMATIC DIAGRAM

Charts and Tables

A **chart** presents information, shows a process, or makes comparisons, usually in rows or columns. A **table** is a specific type of chart that presents a collection of facts in rows and columns and shows how the facts relate to one another.

Strategies for Reading

Ⓐ Read the title to learn what information the chart or table covers.

Ⓑ Study column headings and row labels to determine the categories of information presented.

Ⓒ Look down columns and across rows to find specific information.

MODEL: CHART

Geographic Distribution of U.S. Population, 1930–1970 Ⓐ			
Year	Central Cities	Suburbs	Ⓑ Rural Areas and Small Towns
1930	31.8%	18.0%	50.2%
1940	31.6%	19.5%	48.9%
1950	32.3%	23.8%	43.9%
1960	32.6%	30.7%	36.7%
1970	31.4%	37.6%	31.0%

Source: Adapted from U.S. Bureau of the Census, *Decennial Censuses, 1930–1970*

MODEL: TABLE

New Deal Ⓐ

EMPLOYMENT PROJECTS		PURPOSE Ⓑ
1933	Civilian Conservation Corps	Provided jobs for single males on conservation projects
1933	Public Works Administration	Created jobs on government projects
1933	Civil Works Administration	Provided work in federal jobs
1935	Works Progress Administration	Quickly created as many jobs as possible—from construction jobs to positions in symphony orchestras
1935	National Youth Administration	Provided job training for unemployed young people and part-time jobs for needy students

Maps

A **map** visually represents a geographic region, such as a state or country. It provides information about areas through lines, colors, shapes, and symbols. There are different kinds of maps.

- **Political maps** show political features, such as national borders, states and capitols, and population demographics.
- **Physical maps** show the landforms in areas.
- **Road or travel maps** show streets, roads, and highways.
- **Thematic maps** show information on a specific topic, such as climate, weather, or natural resources.

Strategies for Reading

Ⓐ Read the title to find out what kind of map it is.

Ⓑ Read the labels to get an overall sense of what the map shows.

Ⓒ Look at the **key** or **legend** to find out what the symbols and colors on the map stand for.

MODEL: THEMATIC MAP

MODEL: ROAD MAP

PRACTICE AND APPLY

Use the graphic aids on pages R5–R7 to answer the following questions.

1. According to the circle graph, what percentage of the population in the 1920s earned $10,000 or over?

2. According to the line graph, which country had the highest unemployment rate in 1936?

3. According to the bar graph, by how much did the average annual income increase between 1914 and 1920?

4. What is used to contain the inert gases in a light bulb, according to the picture diagram?

5. Using the schematic diagram of the Panama Canal, describe the function of a sluice in the lock system.

6. According to the chart, in which type of area did the population steadily decrease between 1930 and 1970?

7. Use the table to determine the types of jobs found through the Public Works Administration.

8. On the thematic map, identify three ships that were sunk.

9. Use the 1920s map of Harlem to give directions from the Apollo Theatre to the Savoy Theatre.

3 Reading Informational Texts: Patterns of Organization

Reading any type of writing is easier once you recognize how it is organized. Writers usually arrange ideas and information in ways that best reveal how they are related. Here are the most common patterns of organization:

- order of importance
- chronological order
- cause-effect organization
- compare-and-contrast organization

3.1 ORDER OF IMPORTANCE

Order of importance is a pattern of organization in which information is arranged by its degree of importance. The information is often arranged in one of two ways: from **most important to least important** or from **least important to most important.** In the first way, the most important quality, characteristic, or fact is presented at the beginning of the text, and the remaining details are presented in an order ending with the least significant. The second pattern is the reverse: the text builds from the less important elements to the most important one. Order of importance is frequently used in persuasive writing.

Strategies for Reading

- To identify order of importance in a piece of writing, skim the text to see if it moves from items of greater importance to items of lesser importance, or the reverse.

- Next, read the text carefully. Look for words and phrases such as *first, second, mainly, more important, less important, least important* and *most important* to indicate the relative importance of the ideas and information.

- Identify the topic of the text and what aspect of the topic is being discussed—its complexity, size, effectiveness, varieties, or some other aspect. Note what the most important fact or idea seems to be.

- If you are having difficulty understanding the topic, try asking *who, what, when, where, why,* and *how* about the ideas or events.

Notice the degrees of importance of the ideas in the following model.

Subject	Words showing order of importance

MODEL

Why are some of us tempted to put off tasks when they could easily be done right away? In a word: procrastination. It affects all areas of life and can have some hefty consequences. By putting off tasks, we can cause unnecessary stress for ourselves and those around us. Many procrastinators say, "I work well under pressure," and this might be true. But better planning would lead to better grades, a more impressive report, and even career advancement. What can you do to curb your tendencies to delay the inevitable?

First, determine the cause of your procrastination. If you're honest with yourself, you might find that you set unrealistic goals, that you have a fear of failure or criticism, or that you feel guilty for delaying. Any of these reasons can paralyze your efforts to move forward.

The next important thing is to identify *the way in which* you procrastinate. Maybe you ignore the task as though it will go away. Maybe you underestimate the amount of time a task will take. Procrastinators sometimes misjudge the time it will take to prepare for a task, or they may even lower their standards to make the task seem easier. Think about what procrastination looks like for you.

Once you understand the *why* and *how* of procrastination, you can move on to the final and most important stage—turning "being" into "doing." First, keep a running list of priorities. Write down all the things that need to be done in order of urgency, and you will know where to begin. Second, break down projects into several tasks, or miniprojects. By creating small tasks out of larger ones, you won't feel overwhelmed by a single large task. Finally, set clear and reasonable goals for yourself. Be specific about how long each miniproject will take and what you can accomplish in an hour, a day, or a week.

Changing your ways is definitely possible, but it will take some honest evaluation. Hopefully, after the process of examining the *why* and *how* of procrastination, you will be ready to change your ways. Why not start right now?

PRACTICE AND APPLY

Read each paragraph, and then do the following:

1. Identify whether the order is from most important to least important or from least important to most important.

2. Identify key words and phrases that helped you figure out the order.

3. What is the order of importance indicated in the paragraph beginning, "Once you understand ... "? What are the key words?

3.2 CHRONOLOGICAL ORDER

Chronological order is the arrangement of events in their order of occurrence. This type of organization is used in fictional narratives, historical writing, biographies, and autobiographies. To indicate the order of events, writers use words such as *before, after, next,* and *later* and words and phrases that identify specific times of day, days of the week, and dates, such as *the next morning, Tuesday,* and *on July 4, 1776.*

Strategies for Reading

• Look in the text for headings and subheadings that may indicate a chronological pattern of organization.

• Look for words and phrases that identify times, such as *in a year, three hours earlier, in 1871,* and *the next day.*

• Look for words that signal order, such as *first, afterward, then, during,* and *finally,* to see how events or steps are related.

• Note that a paragraph or passage in which ideas and information are arranged chronologically will have several words or phrases that indicate time order, not just one.

• Ask yourself: Are the events in the paragraph or passage presented in time order?

Notice the words and phrases that signal time order in the first three paragraphs of the following model.

MODEL

History of the National Weather Service

Today, the U.S. National Weather Service is one of the best-known federal agencies. It was not always so popular, especially in its early years.

[Time words and phrases]

The first incarnation of the National Weather Service was founded in the wake of the Civil War, as an agency in the Army Signal Service Corps. Its mission was to "take observations at military stations and to warn of storms on the Great Lakes and on the Atlantic and Gulf Coasts." Very early in its existence the agency earned a reputation for the corruption of its personnel and the unreliability of its forecasting. In 1881, William Howgate, the chief financial manager of the agency, was arrested for embezzling a quarter million dollars. . . . During this time the U.S. military budget was about 40 million dollars. Howgate was tried and convicted, only to escape a year later. Other servicemen in stations around the country were investigated throughout the 1880s and fired in large numbers for reckless neglect. . . . Moreover, the agency's weather predictions were frequently and dangerously wrong. On March 12, 1888, the New York station's forecast called for "fair weather"; instead of fair weather, New York got the Blizzard of '88, which dumped 21 inches of snow on the city and killed 400 people throughout the Northeast. . . .

[Order words and phrases]

[Events]

In 1891, the Army Signal Service Corps's weather service was honorably discharged from the Department of War and given a new home in the civilian Department of Agriculture. It was named the Weather Bureau: it would not be called the National Weather Service until 1970. During the years leading up to 1900, the Weather Bureau's servicemen took regular measurement of such atmospheric conditions as temperature, wind speed, air pressure, rainfall, and cloud conditions. They transmitted their findings to one another via wireless telegraphy.

Refer to the preceding model to do the following:

1. List at least five words or phrases from the model that indicate time order. Do not use words that are already highlighted.

2. Draw a timeline beginning in 1881 and ending with "today." On the timeline chart major events in the formation of the National Weather Service as described in the model.

3. Sometimes more than one pattern of organization is used to help organize a text. Reread paragraph two, and find at least three causes for the Army Signal Service Corps's reputation as a corrupt and unreliable agency. Use the "multiple causes with a single effect" form shown on this page to chart this information.

3.3 CAUSE-EFFECT ORGANIZATION

Cause-effect organization is a pattern of organization that establishes causal relationships between events, ideas, and trends. Cause-effect relationships may be directly stated or merely implied by the order in which the information is presented. Writers often use the cause-effect pattern in historical and scientific writing. Cause-effect relationships may take several forms.

One cause with one effect

One cause with multiple effects

Multiple causes with a single effect

A chain of causes and effects

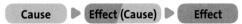

Strategies for Reading

- Look for headings and subheadings that indicate a cause-effect pattern of organization, such as "The Effects of Improved Weather Forecasting."
- To find the effect or effects, read to answer the question, What happened?
- To find the cause or causes, read to answer the question, Why did it happen?
- Look for words and phrases that help you identify specific relationships between events, such as *because, since, so, had the effect of, led to, as a result, resulted in, for that reason, due to, therefore, if ... then,* and *consequently.*
- Evaluate each cause-effect relationship. Do not assume that because one event happened before another, the first event caused the second event.
- Use graphic organizers like the diagrams shown to record cause-effect relationships as you read.

Notice the words that signal causes and effects in the following model.

MODEL

The Formation of a Hurricane: What Does It Take?

Hurricanes have waged war on U.S. cities like no other enemy. Each year, up to ten tropical storms may form in the Atlantic Ocean and make their way west. Typically, three to five have the potential to become a full-blown hurricane. These high-speed monsters are fueled by the simplest of natural elements: water, wind, and air. Given the right conditions, these essential elements for life can become lethal.

The first condition for the **Causes** formation of a hurricane involves warming ocean water in a relatively tranquil and tropical region of the Atlantic. By late summer, the surface water becomes thoroughly heated and begins to evaporate, or rise into the air. This process creates warm, moist air, which then **Effect that in** rises and eventually condenses to **turn becomes** form clouds and rain. During this **a cause** process, energy is released, warming the air further.

The second condition, ironically, is the lack of wind. In the tropical regions of the Atlantic, the air may be relatively stagnant in places, which causes the warm, moist air to remain in one spot. Because the air is continuing to warm and gain energy, it needs to move, and so it does: upward. This column of upward-moving warm air creates an area of low pressure over the water, which in turn draws even more air from the surrounding area toward the center of the column. In addition, the inward-moving air causes the warm air to rise even faster, which then draws even more air and increases its wind speed. Thus, the transfer of energy from ocean to air begins to fuel itself with ever-increasing speed.

Signal words and phrases

As the air moves toward the column's center, it does not move in a straight line, but moves in a circular motion as a result of the earth's rotation. As the air moves up the column, it continues swirling.

A storm that continues in this cycle may grow up to 500 miles in diameter. Its westward movement ensures that it will eventually hit land if it doesn't dissipate, and what began as a simple combination of water, wind, and air could turn into a catastrophic storm.

PRACTICE AND APPLY

Refer to the preceding model to do the following:

1. Use the pattern of multiple causes with a single effect illustrated on page R10 to make a graphic organizer showing the causes described in the text and the effect of those causes.

2. List any words and phrases the writer uses to signal cause and effect in the third paragraph.

3.4 COMPARE-AND-CONTRAST ORGANIZATION

Compare-and-contrast organization is a pattern of organization that serves as a framework for examining similarities and differences in two or more subjects. A writer may use this pattern of organization to analyze two or more subjects, such as characters or movies, in terms of their important points or characteristics. These points or characteristics are called points of comparison. The compare-and-contrast pattern of organization may be developed in either of two ways.

Point-by-point organization—The writer discusses one point of comparison for both subjects, then goes on to the next point.

Subject-by-subject organization—The writer covers all points of comparison for one subject and then all points of comparison for the next subject.

Strategies for Reading

- Look in the text for headings, subheadings, and sentences that may suggest a compare-and-contrast pattern of organization, such as "East Coast and West Coast Living: More than a Continent Apart." These will help you identify where similarities and differences are addressed.

- To find similarities, look for words and phrases such as *like, similarly, both, also,* and *in the same way.*

- To find differences, look for words and phrases such as *unlike, but, on the other hand, in contrast,* and *however.*

- Use a graphic organizer, such as a Venn diagram or a compare-and-contrast chart, to record points of comparison and similarities and differences.

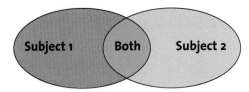

	Subject 1	Subject 2
Point 1		
Point 2		
Point 3		

Read the following models. As you read, use the signal words and phrases to identify the similarities and differences between the subjects and how the details are organized in each text.

MODEL 1

A Tale of Two Furies: Hurricane vs. Tornado

Two of the deadliest types of storms are hurricanes and tornadoes. **[Subjects]** While both are ferocious wind storms and require similar elements to form, each varies in speed and duration.

Hurricanes, like tornadoes, require the meeting of cool and warm air and begin as rain or thunderstorms. However, **[Contrast words and phrases]** one major difference between the two is that a hurricane forms at sea and moves toward land, while a tornado forms over, and remains on, land. Hurricanes require large amounts of warmth and moisture from ocean water to form, while tornadoes rely on the moisture already in the air. The duration of a hurricane is one week, on average. A few rare hurricanes have been known to last between 17 and 27 days. The average tornado, however, lasts 10 to 30 minutes, and may "touch down" on land for up to a minute.

Both tornadoes and hurricanes can be measured. The difference is in *how* and *when*. **[Comparison words]** The wind speed of a tornado is measured by the Fujita Scale, or F-Scale, which rates intensity from F0, with winds less than 73 miles per hour, through F5, with winds from 261–318 mph. Since tornados form very quickly and cannot be accurately predicted, the F-Scale can only measure the strength of a tornado *after* it has occurred. In contrast, the intensity of hurricanes can be measured *while* they are forming. This is because unlike tornados, hurricanes form slowly and can be photographed using satellite imagery. The satellite pictures are then studied, and the results applied to a scale of measure called the Saffir-Simpson Hurricane Scale. This scale rates intensity from Category One through the most intense Category 5 storm.

MODEL 2

Same Goal, Different Methods

Booker T. Washington and W. E. B. Du Bois were alike in many **[Subjects]** ways. Both were devoted to helping **[Comparison words]** their fellow African Americans attain equal rights. Both were educated black men with university teaching positions. Both also worked passionately toward their goal at the beginning of the 20th century. Nevertheless, they were not allies. Why? They had very different **[Contrast words and phrases]** ideas about how blacks should go about attaining equal rights.

Washington believed that for black people to achieve equal status and power as citizens they needed to focus on learning crafts, farming, and industrial skills. He argued that by gaining vocational skills and economic security, black people would naturally earn the respect and acceptance of the white community. To achieve these goals, however, Washington believed black people would need to let go temporarily of the fight for civil rights and political power.

In contrast to Washington, W. E. B. Du Bois believed that black people could not afford to stop fighting for civil rights and political power. In his opinion, only agitation and protest would achieve social change. According to Du Bois, in the climate of extreme racism that existed in America at the time, Washington's approach would merely cause blacks to suffer even more oppression.

So although these two African-American contemporaries had the same goal, their different approaches to achieving this goal made them adversaries rather than allies.

PRACTICE AND APPLY

Refer to the preceding models to do the following:

For each model, create a compare-and-contrast chart. In your chart, list the points of comparison in each model, and identify the similarities and differences between each model's subjects.

4 Reading Informational Texts: Forms

Magazines, newspapers, Web pages, and consumer, public, and workplace documents are all examples of informational materials. To understand and analyze informational texts, pay attention to text features and patterns of organization.

4.1 READING A MAGAZINE ARTICLE

Because people often skim magazines for topics of interest, magazine publishers use devices to attract attention to articles and to highlight key information.

Strategies for Reading

A Read the **title** and other **headings** to find out more about the article's topic and organization.

B Notice whether or not the article has a **byline,** a line naming the author, and make note of the date and source.

C Examine **illustrations, photos,** or other **graphic aids** that visually convey or illustrate additional information, or information from the text.

D Notice **pull quotes,** or quotations that a publisher has pulled out of the text and displayed to get your attention.

PRACTICE AND APPLY

Refer to the article to answer the following questions:

1. What does the title indicate the topic will be?

2. Why is this particular pull quote significant? What information does it convey?

3. Considering the information in the text and the visual image in the photo, what can you conclude about the severity of the hurricane mentioned in the article?

Katrina's South American Sister

A **Was Catarina an omen of things to come?**

For people along the Gulf Coast, Hurricane Katrina was an unimaginable disaster. In meteorological terms, however, she was not unusual—a major storm for sure, but not atypical of what comes across the North Atlantic at that time of year. The one thing experts did note was that ocean temperatures in the Gulf of Mexico are especially warm these days.

For hurricane watchers, however, the real shocker had come 18 months earlier. And her name was Catarina.

Catarina came ashore in Brazil on March 28, 2004—a category-one hurricane that damaged 30,000 homes. Scientists were baffled. Brazilian meteorologists didn't even use the term "hurricane" at first—not until they looked closely at the satellite images. Why? Very simply, no hurricanes had ever been recorded before in the South Atlantic. Conventional wisdom was that cool ocean temperatures and atmospheric differences made it impossible for hurricanes to form there.

But here was Hurricane Catarina, and, indeed, a couple of months earlier, on January 19th, a smaller tropical storm had also developed off the coast of Brazil.

D **"The real shocker had come 18 months earlier . . . And her name was Catarina."**

The entire phenomenon was unprecedented. . . . Is it another indicator of global warming? Researchers say that any such analysis is, at this stage, speculative. Regardless, it might make sense to plan for the worst, rather than continually hoping for the best.

4.2 READING A TEXTBOOK

Each textbook that you use has its own system of organization, based on the content in the book. Often an introductory unit will explain the book's organization and special features. If your textbook has such a unit, read it first.

Strategies for Reading

Ⓐ Before you begin reading the lesson or chapter, read any **questions** that appear at the end of it. Then use the questions to set your purpose for reading.

Ⓑ **Read slowly and carefully** to better understand and remember the ideas presented in the text. When you come to an unfamiliar word, first try to figure out its meaning from **context clues.** If necessary, find the meaning of the word in a **sidenote** on the page, in a **glossary** at the back of the book, or in a dictionary. Avoid interrupting your reading by constantly looking up words in a dictionary.

Ⓒ Use the book's **graphic aids,** such as illustrations, diagrams, and photos, to clarify your understanding of the text.

Ⓓ Take notes as you read. Use text features such as **subheadings** and **boldfaced terms** to help you organize your notes. Use graphic organizers, such as cause-effect charts, to help you clarify relationships among ideas.

PRACTICE AND APPLY

1. What is the definition of *nationalization*?

2. Where on the page do you find the combined private and public debt owed during this time? What was the total amount?

3. Use the text on this page and on R3 to answer the second question in the Section Review of the textbook page.

The New Deal Comes Under Attack

Ⓓ **THREE FIERY CRITICS** In 1934, some of the strongest conservative opponents of the New Deal banded together to form an organization called the American Liberty League. The American Liberty League opposed New Deal measures that it believed violated respect for the rights of individuals and property. Three of the toughest critics the president faced, however, were three men who expressed views that appealed to poor Americans: Charles Coughlin, Dr. Francis Townsend, and Huey Long.

Every Sunday, Father Charles Coughlin, a Roman Catholic priest from a suburb of Detroit, broadcast radio sermons that combined economic, political, and religious ideas. Initially a supporter of the New Deal, Coughlin soon turned against Roosevelt. He favored a guaranteed annual income and the **nationalization** of banks. At the height of his popularity, Father Coughlin claimed a radio audience of as many as 40–45 million people, but his increasingly anti-Semitic (anti-Jewish) views eventually cost him support.

Another critic of New Deal policies was Dr. Francis Townsend, a physician and health officer in Long Beach, California. He believed that Roosevelt wasn't doing enough to help the poor and elderly, so he devised a pension plan that would provide monthly benefits to the aged. The plan found strong backing among the elderly, thus undermining their support for Roosevelt.

Ⓓ Perhaps the most serious challenge to the New Deal came from Senator **Huey Long** of Louisiana. Like Coughlin, Long was an early supporter of the New Deal, but he, too, turned against Roosevelt. Eager to win the presidency for himself, Long proposed a nationwide social program called Share-Our-Wealth. Under the banner "Every Man a King," he promised something for everyone.

Ⓑ Vocabulary
nationalization: conversion from private to governmental ownership

Huey Long

A PERSONAL VOICE HUEY LONG

"We owe debts in America today, public and private, amounting to $252 billion. That means that every child is born with a $2,000 debt tied around his neck. . . . We propose that children shall be born in a land of opportunity, guaranteed a home, food, clothes, and the other things that make for living, including the right to education."
—*Record*, 74 Congress, Session 1

Long's program was so popular that by 1935 he boasted of having perhaps as many as 27,000 Share-Our-Wealth clubs and 7.5 million members. That same year, however, at the height of his popularity, Long was assassinated by a lone gunman.

As the initial impetus of the New Deal began to wane, President Roosevelt started to look ahead. He knew that much more needed to be done to help the people and to solve the nation's economic problems.

Ⓐ **① ASSESSMENT**

SECTION REVIEW

· Name the three outspoken critics of Roosevelt's New Deal.
· Describe one New Deal program, and explain one opponent's view of the New Deal.

· **Critical Thinking** Of the New Deal programs discussed, which do you consider the most important? Consider scope, impact, and type of assistance offered by each.

The New Deal **493**

4.3 READING A CONSUMER DOCUMENT

Consumer documents are materials that accompany products and services. They usually provide information about the use, care, operation, or assembly of the products they accompany. Some common consumer documents are contracts, warranties, manuals, instructions, schedules, and Web pages.

Strategies for Reading

Ⓐ Read the **title** to identify the purpose of the document.

Ⓑ Read the **general directions** to get started.

Ⓒ Look for **numbers** or **letters** that indicate the steps to be followed. Note whether the steps must be done in order and whether there are signal words such as *first, next, then,* and *finally* that indicate the order in which the steps should be followed. Follow the steps in order.

Ⓓ Refer to any **illustrations, diagrams,** or other **graphic aids** that accompany the numbered instructions. Use the graphic aids to help you understand each step.

Ⓔ Look for **verbs that describe actions you should take,** such as *press, use,* and *hold.*

PRACTICE AND APPLY

1. Explain the function of key number 10.

2. Identify the number of the key that allows you to engage the phone's locking function.

INSTRUCTIONS FOR USING A CELL PHONE

Ⓐ PHONE OVERVIEW

Ⓑ **Use this guide to get a quick overview of your phone's functions.**

Ⓒ 1. **Earpiece** Ⓔ

2. **Flip** Flip open the case to answer incoming calls and close to end calls.

3. **LCD Screen** Displays messages and icons.

4. **Left Soft Key** Use to display the function-setting menu.

5. **Headset Jack**

6. **END/POWER Key** Use to turn the power on or off and to end a call.

7. **Side Keys** Use to adjust the ringer volume in standby mode and the earpiece volume during a call.

8. **CLEAR Key** Press to delete a single space or character. Press and hold to delete entire words. Press this key once in a menu to go back one level.

9. **Navigation Key** Use for quick access to messages or Web.

10. **Speaker Key** Use to set Speaker on or off.

11. **Right Soft Key** Use to select an action in a menu.

12. **SEND Key** Use to place or answer calls.

13. **Message Key** Use to retrieve or send voice and text messages.

14. **Alphanumeric Keypad** Use the keys to enter numbers and characters and to select menu items.

15. **Lock Mode Key** Use in standby mode to set the lock function by pressing and holding the key for about 3 seconds.

4.4 READING A PUBLIC DOCUMENT

Public documents are documents that are written for the public to provide information that is of public interest or concern. These documents are often free. They can be federal, state, or local government documents. They can be speeches or historical documents. They may even be laws, posted warnings, signs, or rules and regulations. The following is a public document that has been posted on a U.S. government Web site and can be printed as a document.

Strategies for Reading

A Look at the **title** on the page to discover what the text is about.

B Note the **source** of the document.

C Carefully read **column headings** in the table. Items in a table are usually essential pieces of information.

D Be sure to read **parenthetical text** if there is any. This information may help clarify meaning, provide examples, or further explain an entry.

E Pay attention to **notes** and **asterisks** (*) and their accompanying footnotes. These will help clarify exceptions or exemptions to the rules, or add additional detail.

PRACTICE AND APPLY

Reread the TSA page and then answer the following questions:

1. Are knives allowed as a carry-on item? as a checked item?

2. Name the three types of scissors that are allowed as carry-on items.

3. Walking canes are allowed as a carry-on and as a checked item. Why do they need to be inspected?

4. Guidelines for acceptable carry-on and checked items on flights are revised periodically. Verify that the items listed here are up-to-date by checking the Transportation Security Administration Web site: www.tsa.gov. Search the site for a list of permitted and prohibited items. Key words to look for are *Travelers* and *Prohibited Items*.

RULES AND REGULATIONS FOR CARRY-ON ITEMS IN AIR TRAVEL

U.S. Department of Homeland Security
Transportation Security Administration
Arlington, VA 22202

A **Permitted and Prohibited Items**

Transportation Security Administration **B**

C

Can I take it?	Carry-on	Checked
Personal Items		
Cigar Cutters	Yes	Yes
Corkscrews	Yes	Yes
Cuticle Cutters	Yes	Yes
Eyeglass Repair Tools (including screwdrivers) **D**	Yes	Yes
Eyelash Curlers	Yes	Yes
Knitting and Crochet Needles	Yes	Yes
Knives - prohibited as carry-on except for plastic or round bladed butter knives.	**No**	Yes
Nail Clippers	Yes	Yes
Nail Files	Yes	Yes
Personal care or toiletries with aerosols, in limited quantities (such as hairsprays, deodorants)	Yes	Yes
Safety Razors (including disposable razors)	Yes	Yes
Scissors - plastic or metal with blunt tips	**Yes**	**Yes**
Scissors - metal with pointed tips and blades longer than four inches in length	**No**	Yes
Toy Transformer Robots	Yes	Yes
Toy Weapons (if not realistic replicas)	Yes	Yes
Tweezers	Yes	Yes
Umbrellas (allowed in carry-on baggage once they have been inspected to ensure that prohibited items are not concealed)	Yes	Yes
Walking Canes (allowed in carry-on baggage once they have been inspected to ensure that prohibited items are not concealed)	Yes	Yes

E Note Some personal care items containing aerosol are regulated as hazardous materials. The FAA regulates hazardous materials. This information is summarized at www.faa.gov, click on *Passengers*, then *Preparing to Fly*.

Medication and Special Needs Devices		
Braille Note-Taker, Slate and Stylus, Augmentation Devices	Yes	Yes
Diabetes-Related Supplies/Equipment, (once inspected to ensure prohibited items are not concealed) including: insulin and insulin loaded dispensing products; vials or box of individual vials; jet injectors; pens; infusers; and preloaded syringes; and an unlimited number of unused syringes, when accompanied by insulin; lancets; blood glucose meters; blood glucose meter test strips; insulin pumps; and insulin pump supplies. Insulin in any form or dispenser must be properly marked with a professionally printed label identifying the medication or manufacturer's name or pharmaceutical label.	Yes	Yes
Nitroglycerine pills or spray for medical use (if properly marked with a professionally printed label identifying the medication or manufacturer's name or pharmaceutical label)	Yes	Yes
Ostomy Scissors All scissors with blades four inches or less	Yes	Yes
Prosthetic Device Tools and Appliances, including drill, allen wrenches, pullsleeves used to put on or remove prosthetic devices, if carried by the individual with the prosthetic device or his or her companion	Yes	Yes

U.S. Department of Homeland Security
TSA- Rev. 12-1-2005   Page 3 of 5

4.5 READING A WORKPLACE DOCUMENT

Workplace documents are materials that are produced or used within a workplace, usually to aid in the functioning of a business. These documents include meeting minutes, sales reports, statements of company policy or organizational structure, and explanations of operating procedures. Workplace documents also include memos, business letters, job applications, and résumés.

Strategies for Reading

A Use **headings** and **subheadings** to help you locate information that is relevant or important to you.

B Read a workplace document slowly and carefully, as it may contain **details** that should not be overlooked.

C Notice how to contact the creator of the document. You will need this information to clear up anything that you don't understand.

PRACTICE AND APPLY

Refer to the company policy statement to answer the following questions:

1. How long does an employee need to work at HBA before he or she is eligible for three weeks of paid vacation?

2. Under which section(s) would you look if you traveled extensively for work and were interested in insurance that specifically covered accidents while traveling?

3. Does the company offer supplemental life insurance? Does the company or the employee pay for it?

4. How much short-term disability coverage does the company provide free of charge to an employee?

COMPANY POLICY STATEMENT

HBA Company
Employee Benefits Policy

A **B**

Medical Benefits

HBA offers four medical choices, which include two options that are at no cost to our employees. We also offer dental, vision, and an Employee Assistance Program at no cost to employees.

Retirement and Savings Plan

HBA's contributions to your retirement plan are guaranteed at 5% of your annual earnings, plus up to an additional 10% variable contribution (based on company performance).

Life Insurance

At no cost to the employee, life insurance is provided for three times his or her annual base salary, not to exceed $500,000. Employees may also elect to purchase supplemental life insurance for themselves, their spouse, and eligible dependent children.

Disability Programs

Accidental Death and Dismemberment Insurance—Eligible employees are covered for up to three times their annual base salary, not to exceed $500,000, depending on the extent of injury.

Short-Term Disability—Eligible employees receive a short-term disability benefit of 60% of their salary and may elect to "buy-up" additional coverage to a maximum 70% benefit.

Long-Term Disability—Eligible employees are provided coverage at a benefit amount of 50% of their salary and may elect to "buy-up" additional coverage to a total benefit level of 67%.

Travel Accident Insurance—Eligible employees are covered for $35,000 to $500,000, depending on their annual base salary.

Time Off Benefits

Vacation—Employees earn time off at the rate of two weeks per year for the first five years of employment, three weeks per year after five years of employment, and four weeks per year after ten years of employment.

Sick Leave—Employees earn at a rate of one week per year.

Holidays—Employees are paid for eight calendar holidays. Employees also receive three floating holidays per calendar year after six months of employment.

C If you have any questions, contact the HBA Human Resources Department.

4.6 READING ELECTRONIC TEXT

Electronic text is any text that is in a form that a computer can store and display on a screen. Electronic text can be part of Web pages, CD-ROMs, search engines, and documents that you create with your computer software. Like books, Web pages often provide aids to finding information. However, each Web page is designed differently, and information is not in the same location on each page. It is important to know the functions of different parts of a Web page so that you can easily find the information you want.

Strategies for Reading

A Look at the **title** of a page to determine what topics it covers.

B For an online source, such as a Web page or a search engine, note the **Web address,** known as a **URL** (uniform resource locator), in case you need to return to the page later or cite it as a source.

C Look for the **menu options,** or navigation options that allow you to navigate through the site's main categories and pages. These options are **links** to other pages providing more in-depth information on the topic listed.

D Read **introductory text** to get a sense of the site's subject matter and purpose.

E Use **hyperlinks** to get to other pages on the site. Hyperlinks may lead to pages listed in the menu options or to other Web sites related in subject matter.

F Look for **graphic aids,** such as photos, illustrations, or animation, that will provide you with more information about the site's topic(s).

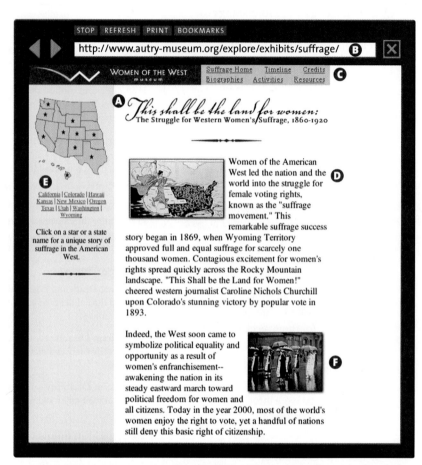

PRACTICE AND APPLY

1. What is the topic of this site?

2. If you were searching for information on suffrage in New Mexico, which links or hyperlinks would you use?

3. Who has produced this Web site?

4. Verify the information on women's suffrage in the Wyoming Territory presented on this Web page by consulting a reference source, such as an encyclopedia, or a government document.

5 Reading Persuasive Texts

5.1 ANALYZING AN ARGUMENT

An **argument** expresses a position on an issue or problem and supports it with reasons and evidence. Being able to analyze and evaluate arguments will help you distinguish between claims you should accept and those you should not. A sound argument should appeal strictly to reason. However, arguments are often used in texts that also contain other types of persuasive devices. An argument includes the following elements:

- A **claim** is the writer's position on an issue or problem.

- **Support** is any material that serves to prove a claim. In an argument, support usually consists of reasons and evidence.

- **Reasons** are declarations made to justify an action, a decision, or a belief—for example, "You should sleep on a good mattress *in order to avoid spinal problems.*"

- **Evidence** consists of the specific references, quotations, facts, examples, and opinions that support a claim. Evidence may also consist of statistics, reports of personal experience, or the views of experts.

- A **counterargument** is an argument made to oppose another argument. A good argument anticipates the opposition's objections and provides counterarguments to disprove or answer them.

Claim	Walt Whitman is one of the most important figures in American poetry.
Reason	He experimented with poetic form and content and created a quintessentially American voice in literature.
Evidence	His poetry influenced generations of poets. His poems celebrated the diversity and spirit of American culture.
Counterargument	No American poet before Whitman broke with tradition in the ways he did.

PRACTICE AND APPLY

In the early 1900s, Elinore Pruitt Stewart (formerly Rupert), was living in Burnt Fork, Wyoming, as a homesteader, a person who received public land free of charge under the Homestead Act of 1862. In the following letter to a friend, she makes an argument for homestead living over an impoverished city existence. Use a chart like the one shown to identify the claim, reason, evidence, and counterargument in her letter.

January 23, 1913

Dear Mrs. Coney,—

. . . When I read of the hard times among the Denver poor, I feel like urging them every one to get out and file on land. I am very enthusiastic about women homesteading. It really requires less strength and labor to raise plenty to satisfy a large family than it does to go out to wash, with the added satisfaction of knowing that their job will not be lost to them if they care to keep it. Even if improving the place does go slowly, it is that much done to stay done. Whatever is raised is the homesteader's own, and there is no house-rent to pay. This year Jerrine cut and dropped enough potatoes to raise a ton of fine potatoes. She wanted to try, so we let her, and you will remember that she is but six years old. We had a man to break the ground and cover the potatoes for her and the man irrigated them once. That was all that was done until digging time, when they were ploughed out and Jerrine picked them up. Any woman strong enough to go out by the day could have done every bit of the work and put in two or three times that much, and it would have been so much more pleasant than to work so hard in the city and then be on starvation rations in the winter.

To me, homesteading is the solution of all poverty's problems, but I realize that temperament has much to do with success in any undertaking, and persons afraid of coyotes and work and loneliness had better let ranching alone. At the same time, any woman who can stand her own company, can see the beauty of the sunset, loves growing things, and is willing to put in as much time at careful labor as she does over the washtub, will certainly succeed; will have independence, plenty to eat all the time, and a home of her own in the end.

5.2 RECOGNIZING PERSUASIVE TECHNIQUES

Persuasive texts typically rely on more than just the logical appeal of an argument to be convincing. They also rely on ethical and emotional appeals, as well as other **persuasive techniques**—devices that can sway you to adopt a position or take an action.

The chart shown here explains several of these techniques. Learn to recognize them, and you will be less likely to be influenced by them.

Persuasive Technique	Example
Appeals by Association	
Bandwagon appeal Suggests that a person should believe or do something because "everyone else" does	Join the millions who've contributed to The Cause: buy your 'Be Well' bracelet today.
Testimonial Relies on endorsements from well-known people or satisfied customers	DJ Super Dawg keeps songs spinning all day long with his new CompactM3 disc player. Give it a whirl!
Snob appeal Taps into people's desire to be special or part of an elite group	In Smart and Sassy cosmetics, you'll look and feel like the princess you are.
Transfer Connnects a product, candidate, or cause with a positive emotion or idea	Rediscover peace and tranquility with Back in Balance aromatherapy candles.
Appeal to loyalty Relies on people's affiliation with a particular group	Only Substantial Bank offers long-term customers better rates.
Emotional Appeals	
Appeals to pity, fear, or vanity Use strong feelings, rather than facts, to persuade	The cost of one candy bar can help buy a whole meal for a starving family.
Word Choice	
Glittering generality Makes a generalization that includes a word or phrase with positive connotations, such as *freedom* and *honor*, to promote a product or idea.	Improve your children's future: plant a tree on World Tree Day.

Identify the persuasive techniques used in the model.

The Real Scoop

On my last trip to the Splendid Dan's Ice Cream Shoppe to get a Swirling Fantasia Double Dip Delight, I was thrilled to find yet another reason that makes buying dessert at Dan's feel so splendid. During the next 30 days at the downtown location, a whopping 40 percent of Dan's proceeds will go toward helping the homeless in our city. Forty percent! No wonder so many local celebrities, like news anchor Tandy Marquez and Mayor Donald Townsend, have been spotted at Dan's. They know that with each purchase, they are also providing food, clothing, and shelter for those in need. If you join them, you'll have not only the most amazing ice cream on the planet, but also the added joy of providing life's basic necessities to the less fortunate. It's the least we can do to better our city, so stop by Splendid Dan's—he's got the "real scoop."

5.3 ANALYZING LOGIC AND REASONING

When you evaluate an argument, you need to look closely at the writer's logic and reasoning. In doing this, it is helpful to identify the type of reasoning the writer is using.

The Inductive Mode of Reasoning

When a writer leads from specific evidence to a general principle or generalization, that writer is using **inductive reasoning.** Here is an example of inductive reasoning.

SPECIFIC FACTS

Fact 1 Harriet Beecher Stowe's *Uncle Tom's Cabin* helped alert Americans to the horrors of slavery.

Fact 2 Rachel Carson's *Silent Spring* helped make the public aware of the dangers of overuse of pesticides.

Fact 3 Betty Friedan's *The Feminine Mystique* prompted women to seek equal rights.

GENERALIZATION

Literature can sometimes help to shape public opinion.

Strategies for Determining the Soundness of Inductive Arguments

Ask yourself the following questions to evaluate an inductive argument:

- **Is the evidence valid and sufficient support for the conclusion?** Inaccurate facts lead to inaccurate conclusions. Make sure all facts are accurate.

- **Does the conclusion follow logically from the evidence?** Make sure the writer has used sound reasons—those that can be proved—as the basis for the conclusion and has avoided logical fallacies, such as circular reasoning and oversimplification.

- **Is the evidence drawn from a large enough sample?** The three facts listed in the example are enough to support the claim. By qualifying the generalization with words such as *sometimes, some,* or *many,* the writer indicates the generalization is limited to a specific group.

The Deductive Mode of Reasoning

When a writer arrives at a conclusion by applying a general principle to a specific situation, the writer is using **deductive reasoning.** Here's an example.

| People have the right to revolt when oppressed. | General principle or premise |

| The American colonies are oppressed by British rule. | Specific situation |

| The American colonies are justified in fighting for freedom from British rule. | Specific conclusion |

Strategies for Determining the Soundness of Deductive Arguments

Ask yourself the following questions to evaluate a deductive argument:

- **Is the general principle stated, or is it implied?** Note that writers often use deductive reasoning in an argument without stating the general principle. They assume readers will understand the principle. You may want to identify the general principle for yourself.

- **Is the general principle sound?** Don't assume the general principle is sound. Determine whether it is proven.

- **Is the conclusion valid?** To be valid, a conclusion in a deductive argument must follow logically from the general principle and the specific situation.

The following chart shows two conclusions drawn from the same general principle.

General Principle: All government offices were closed last Monday.	
Accurate Deduction	**Inaccurate Deduction**
West Post Office is a government office; therefore, West Post Office was closed last Monday.	Soon-Lin's Spa was closed last Monday; therefore, Soon-Lin's Spa is a government office.

The conclusion that Soon-Lin's Spa is a government office does not make logical sense because other factors determine whether or not it is a government office.

PRACTICE AND APPLY

Identify the mode of reasoning used in the following:

Detailed research shows that using a cell phone while driving is a key cause of traffic accidents. Many states have already passed laws making "hands free" devices mandatory for cell phone users while driving. However, ear pieces or speaker phones provide very few true safety benefits. The problem is not the way in which a driver is distracted, but the distraction itself. Looking up a phone number, dialing, and concentrating on the conversation can all take a driver's focus, and eyes, off the road.

Betsie Edens, a 19-year-old college student, says she uses her cell phone to get in touch with family, old friends, and fellow college students while making the three-hour drive from her parent's house to Denton State University. "I talk on the phone or send text messages at least two and a half of the three hours it takes to get there," she says.

Betsie is one of millions of teenagers worldwide who do more talking on a cell phone than safe driving. It is time these unsafe drivers focus more on the road and less on their friends' gossip. For the sake of everybody's safety, cell phones must be turned off while on the road.

Identifying Faulty Reasoning

Sometimes an argument at first appears to make sense but isn't valid because it is based on a fallacy. A **fallacy** is an error in logic. Learn to recognize these common fallacies.

TYPE OF FALLACY	DEFINITION	EXAMPLE
Circular reasoning	Supporting a statement by simply repeating it in different words	Sport utility vehicles are popular **because more people buy them than any other category of new cars.**
Either/or fallacy	A statement that suggests that there are only two choices available in a situation that really offers more than two options	**Either** we raise the legal driving age **or** accidents caused by teenage drivers will continue to happen.
Oversimplification	An explanation of a complex situation or problem as if it were much more simple than it is	If we would only be more tolerant of people's differences, there would be **no more wars.**
Overgeneralization	A generalization that is too broad. You can often recognize overgeneralizations by the use of words such as *all, everyone, every time, anything, no one,* and *none.*	**Every time** I want to do something my way, my parents say no.
Stereotyping	A dangerous type of overgeneralization. Stereotypes are broad statements about people on the basis of their gender, ethnicity, race, or political, social, professional, or religious group.	**People who work for large corporations** are followers, not leaders.
Attacking the person or name-calling	An attempt to discredit an idea by attacking the person or group associated with it. Candidates often engage in name-calling during political campaigns.	The governor wants to eliminate candy machines in school cafeterias, but **he doesn't know what he's talking about.**
Evading the issue	Refuting an objection with arguments and evidence that do not address its central point	I know I wasn't supposed to use the car last night, **but I did fill up the tank and check the tire pressure.**
Non sequitur	A conclusion that does not follow logically from the "proof" offered to support it. A non sequitur is sometimes used to win an argument by diverting the reader's attention to proof that can't be challenged.	Mr. Crandall is my guidance counselor. **I will definitely get accepted to a private college.**
False cause	The mistake of assuming that because one event occurred after another event in time, the first event caused the second one to occur	The cheerleading squad did the Super Slam Dance, **and because of that, Donny slam-dunked the basketball, and we won the game.**
False analogy	A comparison that doesn't hold up because of a critical difference between the two subjects	Jenny didn't do well in Spanish, **so she'll probably fail German as well.**
Hasty generalization	A conclusion drawn from too little evidence or from evidence that is biased	Two jet planes crashed this year. **Air travel is extremely unsafe.**

PRACTICE AND APPLY

Look for examples of logical fallacies in the following argument. Identify each one and explain why you identified it as such.

> Elephants should be banned from circuses. Leaders of circus companies claim that healthy living environments are provided for the animals, but they, like most business owners, are liars. Sharp bullhooks are used for training, and the elephants are beaten severely everyday. Abuse makes animals more aggressive, everyone knows that. In the last 15 years, captive elephants have killed 65 people and injured 130, so it is clear the elephants are abused by their trainers. Legislation to stop this cruelty should be passed immediately!

5.4 EVALUATING PERSUASIVE TEXTS

Learning how to evaluate persuasive texts and identify bias will help you become more selective when doing research and also help you improve your own reasoning and arguing skills. **Bias** is an inclination for or against a particular opinion or viewpoint. A writer may reveal a strongly positive or negative opinion on an issue by presenting only one way of looking at it or by heavily weighting the evidence on one side of the argument. Additionally, the presence of either of the following is often a sign of bias:

Loaded language consists of words with strongly positive or negative connotations that are intended to influence a reader's attitude.

EXAMPLE: *The superior All-Star Road Warrior offers unparalleled excellence in all-wheel-drive capability and can outperform any car on the road.* (*Superior, unparalleled, excellence,* and *outperform* have positive connotations.)

Propaganda is any form of communication that is so distorted that it conveys false or misleading information. Many logical fallacies—such as name-calling, the either/or fallacy, and false causes—are often used in propaganda. The following example shows an oversimplification. The writer uses one fact to support a particular point of view but does not reveal another fact that does not support that viewpoint.

EXAMPLE: *Since the new administration took office, unemployment rates have been cut in half.* (The writer does not include information about legislation, passed by the previous administration, that created thousands of jobs.)

For more information, see **Identifying Faulty Reasoning,** *page R22.*

Strategies for Evaluating Evidence

It is important to have a set of standards by which you can evaluate persuasive texts. Use the questions below to help you critically assess facts and opinions that are presented as evidence.

- **Are the facts presented verifiable?** Facts can be proved by eyewitness accounts, authoritative sources such as encyclopedias and almanacs, experts, or research.

- **Are the opinions presented credible?** Any opinions offered should be supported by facts, research, eyewitness accounts, or the opinions of experts on the topic.

- **Is the evidence thorough?** Thorough evidence leaves no reasonable questions unanswered. If a choice is offered, background for making the choice should be provided. If taking a side is called for, all sides of the issue should be presented.

- **Is the evidence biased?** Be alert to evidence that contains loaded language or other signs of bias.

- **Is the evidence authoritative?** The people, groups, or organizations that provided the evidence should have credentials that verify their credibility.

- **Is it important that the evidence be current?** Where timeliness is crucial, as in the areas of medicine and technology, the evidence should reflect the latest developments in the areas.

Read the argument below. Identify the facts, opinions, and elements of bias.

In our city neighborhood, unnecessary speed bumps are being built on residential streets. Cars park bumper to bumper along both sides of the street, day and night. There is no place to pull over, causing cars to stop in the middle of the street to pick up and drop off passengers. My point is that it is impossible to drive fast on these streets anyway! Why do no-good politicians spend a lot of taxpayer money on a ridiculous irritation for drivers? They must figure wrongly that either they build speed bumps, or some little kid will get killed. That's never happened and it never will.

Strategies for Evaluating an Argument

Make sure that all or most of the following statements are true:

- The argument presents a claim or thesis.

- The claim is connected to its support by a general principle that most readers would readily agree with. Valid general principle: *It is the job of a corporation to provide adequate health benefits to full-time employees.* Invalid general principle: *It is the job of a corporation to ensure its employees are healthy and physically fit.*

- The reasons make sense.

- The reasons are presented in a logical and effective order.

- The claim and all reasons are adequately supported by sound evidence.

- The evidence is adequate, accurate, and appropriate.

- The logic is sound. There are no instances of faulty reasoning.

- The argument adequately anticipates and addresses reader concerns and counterclaims with counterarguments.

Use the preceding criteria to evaluate the strength of the following editorial:

This town needs an ice skating rink. Everybody knows that ice skating is the only real way to learn balance and coordination, while also exercising. It is, after all, an Olympic event. That is why I believe it is the responsibility of the town council to put aside funding for a year-round ice skating rink.

Our town has always believed that our children's future relies on good development. For intellectual stimulation, the council has provided the public library and the Nature Museum. For creativity, the council has funded the Community Art Center, where kids can learn to make pottery, paint, dance, and sing. But when it comes to a place where youth can go to develop physical skills of balance, rhythm, and strength, we have absolutely nothing.

We also need a rink because ice skating is fun! The town council members are themselves boring individuals and don't think kids should have fun. As one member put it, "There are many places in this town built especially with youth in mind. Ice skating is not a top priority on our list of community needs this year." They obviously feel this way because our football team came in fifth in the conference last year.

But the biggest reason we need an ice skating rink is so that kids can have a place to ice skate. And let's not forget, adults like ice skating, too. Most of the people who make it to the Olympics are over 18.

Either the town council will help our children develop by putting up the rink, or they prove themselves stingy politicians who do not have the town's best interest at heart.

6 Adjusting Reading Rate to Purpose

You may need to change the way you read certain texts in order to understand what you read. To properly adjust the way you read, you need to be aware of what you want to get out of the text you are reading. Once you know your purpose for reading, you can adjust the speed at which you read in response to your purpose and the difficulty of the material.

Determine Your Purpose for Reading

You read different types of materials for different purposes. You may read a novel for enjoyment. You may read a textbook unit to learn a new concept or to master the content for a test. When you read for enjoyment, you naturally read at a pace that is comfortable for you. When you read for information, you need to read material more slowly and thoroughly. When you are being tested on material, you may think you have to read fast, especially if the test is being timed. However, you can actually increase your understanding of the material if you slow down.

Determine Your Reading Rate

The rate at which you read most comfortably is called your **independent reading level.** It is the rate that you use to read materials that you enjoy. To learn to adjust your reading rate to read materials for other purposes, you need to be aware of your independent reading level. You can figure out your reading level by following these steps:

1. Select a passage from a book or story you enjoy.
2. Have a friend or classmate time you as you begin reading the passage silently.
3. Read at the rate that is most comfortable for you.
4. Stop when your friend or classmate tells you one minute has passed.
5. Determine the number of words you read in that minute and write down the number.
6. Repeat the process at least two more times, using different passages.
7. Add the numbers and divide the sum by the number of times your friend timed you. The number you end up with is the average number of words you read per minute—your independent reading rate.

Reading Techniques for Informational Material

Use the following techniques to adapt your reading for informational texts, to prepare for tests, and to better understand what you read:

- **Skimming** is reading quickly to get the general idea of a text. To skim, read only the title, headings, graphic aids, and highlighted words of the text, as well as the first sentence of each paragraph. In addition, read any introduction, conclusion, or summary. Skimming can be especially useful when taking a test. Before reading a passage, you can skim questions that follow it in order to find out what is expected and to better focus on the important ideas in the text.

  When researching a topic, skimming can help you determine whether a source has information that is pertinent to your topic.

- **Scanning** is reading quickly to find a specific piece of information, such as a fact or a definition. When you scan, your eyes sweep across a page, looking for key words that may lead you to the information you want. Use scanning to review for tests and to find answers to questions.

- **Changing pace** is speeding up or slowing down the rate at which you read parts of a particular text. When you come across familiar concepts, you might be able to speed up without misunderstanding them. When you encounter unfamiliar concepts or material presented in an unpredictable way, however, you may need to slow down to process and absorb the information better.

WATCH OUT! Reading too slowly can diminish your ability to comprehend what you read. Make sure you aren't just reading one word at a time.

PRACTICE AND APPLY

Find an article in a magazine or textbook. Skim the article. Then answer the following questions:

1. What did you notice about the organization of the article?
2. What is the main idea of the article?

Writing is a process, a journey of discovery in which you can explore your thoughts, experiment with ideas, and search for connections. Through writing, you can explore and record your thoughts, feelings, and ideas for yourself alone, or you can communicate them to an audience.

WRITING TOOLS
Go to the **Writing Center** at **ClassZone.com** for interactive models, publishing ideas, and other support.

1 The Writing Process

The writing process consists of the following stages: prewriting, drafting, revising and editing, proofreading, and publishing. These are not stages that you must complete in a set order. Rather, you may return to an earlier stage at any time to improve your writing.

1.1 PREWRITING

In the prewriting stage, you explore what you want to write about, what your purpose for writing is, whom you are writing for, and what form you will use to express your ideas. Ask yourself the following questions to get started.

Topic	• Is my topic assigned, or can I choose it? • What am I interested in writing about?
Purpose	• Am I writing to entertain, to inform, or to persuade—or some combination of these? • What effect do I want to have on my readers?
Audience	• Who is the audience? • What might the audience members already know about my topic? • What about the topic might interest them?
Format	• Which format will work best: essay, poem, speech, short story, article, or research paper?

Find Ideas for Writing

Here are some methods for generating topics:

• Browse through magazines, newspapers, and Web sites.

• Start a file of articles to save for future reference.

• With a group, brainstorm as many ideas as you can. Compile your ideas into a list.

• Interview an expert on a particular topic.

• Write down anything that comes into your head.

• Use a cluster map to explore subordinate ideas that relate to a general topic.

Organize Ideas

Once you've chosen a topic, you will need to compile and organize your ideas. If you are writing a description, you may need to gather sensory details. Or you may need to record information from different sources for an essay or a research paper. To record notes from sources you read or view, use any or all of these methods:

• **Summarize:** Briefly retell the main ideas of a piece of writing in your own words.

• **Paraphrase:** Restate all or almost all of the information in your own words.

• **Quote:** Record the author's exact words.

Depending on what form your writing takes, you may also need to arrange your ideas in a certain pattern.

*For more information, see the **Writing Handbook**, pages R32–R39.*

1.2 DRAFTING

In the drafting stage, you put your ideas on paper and allow them to develop and change as you write. You don't need to worry about correct grammar and spelling at this stage. There are two ways that you can write a draft:

Discovery drafting is a good approach when you are not quite sure what you think about your subject. You just start writing and let your feelings and ideas lead you in developing the topic.

Planned drafting may work better if you know that your ideas have to be arranged in a certain way, as in a research paper. Try making a writing plan or an informal outline before you begin drafting.

1.3 REVISING AND EDITING

The revising and editing stage allows you to polish your draft and make changes in its content, organization, and style. Use the questions that follow to assess problems and determine what changes would improve your work.

• Does my writing have a **main idea** or central focus? Is my thesis clear?

• Have I used **precise** nouns, verbs, and modifiers?

- Have I incorporated **adequate detail** and **evidence?** Where might I include a telling detail, a revealing statistic, or a vivid example?

- Is my writing **unified?** Do all ideas and supporting details pertain to my main idea or advance my thesis?

- Is my writing clear and **coherent?** Is the flow of sentences and paragraphs smooth and logical?

- Have I used a consistent **point of view?**

- Do I need to add **transitional words, phrases,** or **sentences** to clarify relationships among ideas?

- Have I used a **variety of sentence types?** Are they well constructed? What sentences might I combine to improve the rhythm of my writing?

- Have I used a **tone** appropriate for my audience and purpose?

1.4 PROOFREADING

When you are satisfied with your revision, proofread your paper for mistakes in grammar, usage, and mechanics. You may want to do this several times, looking for a different type of mistake each time. Use the following questions to help you correct errors:

- Have I corrected any errors in **subject-verb agreement** and **pronoun-antecedent agreement?**

- Have I double-checked for errors in **confusing word pairs,** such as *it's/its, than/then,* and *too/to?*

- Have I corrected any **run-on sentences** and **sentence fragments?**

- Have I followed rules for **correct capitalization?**

- Have I used **punctuation marks** correctly?

- Have I checked the **spellings of all unfamiliar words** in the dictionary?

TIP If possible, don't begin proofreading just after you've finished writing. Put your work away for at least a few hours. When you return to it, it will be easier for you to identify and correct mistakes.

*For more information, see the **Grammar Handbook** and the **Vocabulary and Spelling Handbook,** pages R50–R79.*

Use the proofreading symbols in the chart to mark changes on your draft.

Proofreading Symbols	
∧ Add letters or words.	/ Make a capital letter lowercase.
⊙ Add a period.	¶ Begin a new paragraph.
≡ Capitalize a letter.	⏟ Delete letters or words.
⊃ Close up space.	∿ Switch the positions of letters or words.
∧ Add a comma.	

1.5 PUBLISHING AND REFLECTING

Always consider sharing your finished writing with a wider audience. Reflecting on your writing is another good way to finish a project.

Publishing Ideas

- Post your writing on a Weblog.

- Create a multimedia presentation and share it with classmates.

- Publish your writing in a school newspaper, local newspaper, or literary magazine.

- Present your work orally in a report, speech, reading, or dramatic performance.

Reflecting on Your Writing

Think about your writing process and whether you would like to add what you have written to your writing portfolio. You might attach a note in which you answer questions like these:

- Which parts of the process did I find easiest? Which parts were more difficult?

- What was the biggest problem I faced during the writing process? How did I solve the problem?

- What changes have occurred in my writing style?

- Have I noticed any features in the writing of published authors or my peers that I can apply to my own work?

1.6 PEER RESPONSE

Peer response consists of the suggestions and comments you make about the writing of your peers and also the comments and suggestions they make about your writing. You can ask a peer reader for help at any time in the writing process.

Using Peer Response as a Writer

- Indicate whether you are more interested in feedback about your ideas or about your presentation of them.
- Ask open-ended questions that will help you get specific information about your writing. Avoid questions that require yes-or-no answers.
- Encourage your readers to be honest.

Being a Peer Reader

- Respect the writer's feelings.
- Offer positive reactions first.
- Make sure you understand what kind of feedback the writer is looking for, and then respond accordingly.

For more information on the writing process, see the **Introductory Unit**, *pages 11–13.*

2 Building Blocks of Good Writing

Whatever your purpose in writing, you need to capture your reader's interest and organize your thoughts clearly.

2.1 INTRODUCTIONS

An introduction should capture your reader's attention and present a thesis statement.

Kinds of Introductions

There are a number of ways to begin an introduction. The one you choose depends on who the audience is and on your purpose for writing.

Make a Surprising Statement Beginning with a startling statement or an interesting fact can arouse your reader's curiosity about a subject, as in the following model.

> **MODEL**
>
> Although she wrote nearly 1,800 poems, Emily Dickinson probably did not want to publish any of them. Most of her poems were first published almost 100 years after they were written.

Provide a Description A vivid description sets a mood and brings a scene to life for your reader. In the following model, details about a horse's actions set the tone for an essay about horse training.

> **MODEL**
>
> Dust flew as the horse stomped the ground. The puffs of moisture blowing from his nostrils and the laid-back ears let the spectators know the stomping was not some clever performance. As the trainer approached cautiously, she could see the wild look in the horse's eyes.

Pose a Question Beginning with a question can make your reader want to read on to find out the answer. The following introduction asks questions about the fate of a well-known and respected writer.

> **MODEL**
>
> Zora Neale Hurston was one of the most successful writers of the Harlem Renaissance period. She wrote plays, novels, and essays that were enthusiastically received. How did it happen that such a talented and popular author died in poverty?

Relate an Anecdote Beginning with an anecdote, or brief story, can hook your reader and help you make a point in a dramatic way. The following anecdote introduces an interview with a retired school teacher.

> **MODEL**
>
> "Down in the valley
> Where the green grass grows. . . ."
> The words and rhythm of the chanting children on the playground brought tears to Clara Jones's eyes. Though she could barely see the forms of the youngsters, she knew exactly the structure of the old jump-rope game they played.
> I began softly to ask her about her 45 years of teaching at Pleasant Hills Elementary School.

Address the Reader Speaking directly to your reader establishes a friendly, informal tone and involves the reader in your topic.

MODEL

> Do you know how many trees will be cut down for the new shopping mall to be built? Do you know how many families will have to give up their homes so that some shoppers can have yet another department store that sells the same things as five others in our area?

Begin with a Thesis Statement A thesis statement expressing a main idea may be woven into both the beginning and the end of a piece of nonfiction writing. The following is a thesis statement that introduces a literary analysis.

MODEL

> In "The Death of the Hired Man," Robert Frost uses the hushed conversation of a husband and wife to explore the meaning of a lonely person's life. The whole poem seems to take place in whispers, though the message is strong.

TIP To write a strong introduction, you may want to try more than one of the methods and then decide which is the most effective for your purpose and audience.

2.2 PARAGRAPHS

A paragraph is made up of sentences that work together to develop an idea or accomplish a purpose. Whether or not it contains a topic sentence stating the main idea, a good paragraph must have unity and coherence.

Unity

A paragraph has unity when all the sentences support and develop one stated or implied idea. Use the following techniques to create unity in your paragraphs:

Write a Topic Sentence A topic sentence states the main idea of the paragraph; all other sentences in the paragraph provide supporting details. A topic sentence is often the first sentence in a paragraph. However, it may also appear later in a paragraph or at the end, to summarize or reinforce the main idea, as shown in the model that follows.

MODEL

> Cats purr when they are being stroked by humans. Cats purr when they cuddle up with other cats. Many cats purr when they are in the veterinarian's office. Some cats purr when they are frightened. Since cats seem to purr in situations of both joy and stress, the cause of purring is still a mystery to humans.

Relate All Sentences to an Implied Main Idea A paragraph can be unified without a topic sentence as long as every sentence supports an implied, or unstated, main idea. In the example, all the sentences work together to create a unified impression of a frustrated writer trying to begin writing.

MODEL

> He picked up his pencil at 9:27 and set it down purposefully on the tablet. A minute or so passed. Well, maybe he should sharpen the pencil. That took 30 seconds—now 9:29. He set his pencil down again. He readjusted his chair. He raked his left hand through his thick hair. Was there a spot of thinning hair? He got up to go look in the mirror. No, not yet. At 9:31 he sat down again and took up the pencil. This time he moved the tablet a little to the right.

Coherence

A paragraph is coherent when all its sentences are related to one another and each flows logically to the next. The following techniques will help you achieve coherence in paragraphs:

- Present your ideas in the most logical order.
- Use pronouns, synonyms, and repeated words to connect ideas.
- Use transitional devices to show relationships among ideas.

In the model shown here, the writer used some of these techniques to create a unified paragraph.

MODEL

After you figure out how big to make the model ship for your film of a shipwreck, you will need to take some other factors into account as well. You will have to figure out how much to stir the water and what speed to set the film. Perhaps even more important is to be sure no real objects at full size can be seen by the camera. In other words, don't let your towels and soap dish sneak into the picture and be sure the cat is locked out of the bathroom.

2.3 TRANSITIONS

Transitions are words and phrases that show connections among details. Clear transitions help show how your ideas relate to one another.

Kinds of Transitions

The types of transitions you choose depend on the ideas you want to convey.

Time or Sequence Some transitions help to clarify the sequence of events over time. When you are telling a story or describing a process, you can connect ideas with such transitional words as *first, second, always, then, next, later, soon, before, finally, after, earlier, afterward,* and *tomorrow.*

MODEL

Before a blood donation can be used, it must be processed carefully. First, a sample is tested for infectious diseases and identified by blood type. Next, preservatives are added. Finally, a blood cell separator breaks up the blood into its parts, such as red blood cells, platelets, and plasma.

Spatial Relationships Transitional words and phrases such as *in front, behind, next to, along, nearest, lowest, above, below, underneath, on the left,* and *in the middle* can help your reader visualize a scene.

MODEL

Two rows of corn grew along the south side of the garden. In front of them stood the tomatoes climbing on wire enclosures and a couple of okra plants. In the middle rows were medium-height plants—bush beans, peas, potatoes, and a few peppers. Low-growing plants filled the front of the garden—radishes on the right, then rows of lettuce, spinach, and onions. On the left, squash and cucumber vines spread over the ground.

Degree of Importance Transitional words and phrases such as *mainly, strongest, weakest, first, second, most important, least important, worst,* and *best* may be used to rank ideas or to show degrees of importance.

MODEL

There are several reasons to eat plenty of fresh fruits and vegetables. The most important reason is that they help to fortify your immune system!

Compare and Contrast Words and phrases such as *similarly, likewise, also, like, as, neither . . . nor,* and *either . . . or* show similarity between details. *However, by contrast, yet, but, unlike, instead, whereas,* and *while* show difference. Note the use of both types of transitions in the model.

MODEL

Although I like to shop in the big stores in the mall, when I'm really serious about buying something I go to a small store. Like big stores, many small stores carry a good selection of merchandise. Whereas the big stores may have lower prices, the small stores have more personal service and clerks who know about the products they sell.

TIP Both *but* and *however* can be used to join two independent clauses. When *but* is used as a coordinating conjunction, it is preceded by a comma. When *however* is used as a conjunctive adverb, it is preceded by a semicolon and followed by a comma.

Cause and Effect When you are writing about a cause-effect relationship, use transitional words and phrases such as *since, because, thus, therefore, so, due to, for this reason,* and *as a result* to help clarify that relationship and make your writing coherent.

> **MODEL**
>
> Due to the unusual amount of rain this summer, the grass is still lush and green in August.

2.4 CONCLUSIONS

A conclusion should leave readers with a strong final impression.

Kinds of Conclusions

Good conclusions sum up ideas in a variety of ways. Here are some techniques you might try:

Restate Your Thesis A good way to conclude an essay is by restating your thesis, or main idea, in different words. The following conclusion restates the thesis introduced on page R29.

> **MODEL**
>
> In Robert Frost's "The Death of the Hired Man," a sad human life unfolds in the whispered conversations between Mary and Warren. Quiet compassion is also evident and is the point of the poem.

Ask a Question Try asking a question that sums up what you have said and gives your reader something new to think about. The following question concludes an appeal for preventing unwanted cats and dogs.

> **MODEL**
>
> Considering how many kittens, puppies, cats, and dogs are put to sleep or die on the streets, don't you think it makes sense that all household pets be spayed or neutered?

Make a Recommendation When you are persuading your audience to take a position on an issue, you can conclude by recommending a specific course of action.

> **MODEL**
>
> Help protect animals from careless humans. Volunteer at an animal shelter. Distribute literature around your neighborhood.

Make a Prediction Readers are concerned about matters that may affect them and therefore are moved by a conclusion that predicts the future.

> **MODEL**
>
> If the city council approves the new shopping mall, we will lose the woodlands that help make our neighborhood quiet and attractive. In their place, we will have traffic congestion, exhaust fumes, bright lights long into the night, and a source of danger to our children.

Summarize Your Information Summarizing reinforces your main idea, leaving a strong, lasting impression. The model concludes with a statement that summarizes a book review.

> **MODEL**
>
> Patricia McKissack's biography gives a strong picture of W. E. B. Du Bois, who was a link between Frederick Douglass, whom he knew early in life, and Martin Luther King Jr., whom he knew late in life.

2.5 ELABORATION

Elaboration is the process of developing an idea by providing specific supporting details that are relevant and appropriate to the purpose and form of your writing. In some cases, you may want to present support with a visual aid.

Facts and Statistics A fact is a statement that can be verified, and a statistic is a fact expressed as a number. Make sure the facts and statistics you supply are from reliable, up-to-date sources, and support your statements, as in the following model.

MODEL

A student who has an eye for beautiful gardens might consider a career in landscape architecture. The American Society of Landscape Architects has over 12,000 members, up 20 percent in the last five years. The average income of landscape architects is $74,644, which is higher than that of building architects.

Sensory Details Details that show how something looks, sounds, tastes, smells, or feels can enliven a description, making readers feel they are actually experiencing what you are describing.

MODEL

Sliding along on her cross-country skis, Sasha felt she was truly on top of the world. The action of the snow, skis, and sturdy boots massaged her feet. She opened her mouth to taste the sprinkles of snow. The view was a rainbow of color as snowflakes made tiny speckled prisms on her goggles.

Incidents From our earliest years, we are interested in "stories." One way to illustrate a point is to relate an incident or tell a story, as shown in the example.

MODEL

The East India Company had a monopoly on supplying tea to the American Colonies. Tea shipments took on the symbolism of the increasing tyranny of the English government. On December 16, 1773, a group of about 150 colonists put burnt cork on their faces, dressed as Mohawk warriors, boarded the tea-carrying ships, and proceeded to dump the entire tea cargoes into Boston Harbor.

Examples An example can help make an abstract idea concrete or can serve to clarify a complex point.

MODEL

Many of the stars and galaxies we see at night are showing us light from ancient times. Who knows where they really are today? For example, the light from the galaxy Andromeda has taken over 2 million years to get here.

Quotations Choose quotations that clearly support your points, and be sure that you copy each quotation word for word. Remember always to credit the source.

MODEL

Do you know anyone who says "you all" to mean "the group of you"? "Have you all seen this movie?" McCrum, Cran, and MacNeil explain in *The Story of English* that this famous Southern expression comes from a Scots-Irish translation of the plural for *you*. They say the expression "is typical both of Ulster and of the (largely southern) states of America." Did you all know that?

❸ Descriptive Writing

Descriptive writing allows you to paint word pictures about anything, from events of global importance to the most personal feelings. It is an essential part of almost every piece of writing.

RUBRIC: Standards for Writing

Successful descriptive writing should

- have a clear focus and sense of purpose
- use sensory details and precise words to create a vivid image, establish a mood, or express emotion
- present details in a logical order

3.1 KEY TECHNIQUES

Consider Your Goals What do you want to accomplish with your description? Do you want to show why something is important to you? Do you want to make a person or scene more memorable? Do you want to explain an event?

Identify Your Audience Who will read your description? How familiar are they with your subject? What background information will they need? Which details will they find most interesting?

Think Figuratively What figures of speech might help make your description vivid and interesting? What simile or metaphor comes to mind? What imaginative comparisons can you make? What living thing does an inanimate object remind you of?

Gather Sensory Details Which sights, smells, tastes, sounds, and textures make your subject come alive? Which details stick in your mind when you observe or recall your subject? Which senses does it most strongly affect?

You might want to use a chart like the one shown here to collect sensory details about your subject.

Sights	Sounds	Textures	Smells	Tastes

Create a Mood What feelings do you want to evoke in your readers? Do you want to soothe them with comforting images? Do you want to build tension with ominous details? Do you want to evoke sadness or joy?

3.2 OPTIONS FOR ORGANIZATION

Option 1: Spatial Order Choose one of these options to show the spatial order of elements in a scene you are describing.

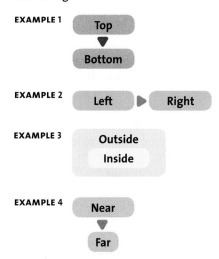

EXAMPLE 1 Top → Bottom

EXAMPLE 2 Left ▶ Right

EXAMPLE 3 Outside / Inside

EXAMPLE 4 Near → Far

MODEL

Peering through the goggles, the diver surveyed the reef. To the left, a school of silvery fish swam near the surface. Below them, the reef was a rainbow of color. In the middle of the scene, bright, tiny fish nosed along the reef. Below them on the sand, a crab looked for food. Further right, a cluster of fan coral waved its purple fronds in the gentle current. Beyond it lay the barnacle-encrusted shape of a ship's propeller.

Option 2: Order of Impression Order of impression is the order in which you notice details.

What first catches your attention
↓
What you notice next
↓
What you see after that
↓
What you focus on last

MODEL

Rain pelted against the windshield. Robbie narrowed his eyes to try to see the road in the brief clearing spasms between swipes of wiper blades. He could barely see that there was a little clearing far off in the horizon. Dark clouds made distinct shapes. Suddenly he noticed that against a small patch of lighter color was a swirling black cloud beginning to take the shape of a funnel.

TIP Use transitions that help readers understand the order of the impressions you are describing. Some useful transitions are *after, next, during, first, before, finally,* and *then.*

Option 3: Order of Importance You can use order of importance as the organizing structure for a description.

Least important
↓
More important
↓
Most important

MODEL

I checked my backpack for the comforting essentials. Book? Yes. Journal and pencil? Yes. Water bottle? Yes. Tissues? Yes. Then I checked for the required essentials. Passport? Yes. Airline ticket? Yes. Map? Yes. Last of all, I checked the most important possession for this trip—a light heart and a sense of adventure. I was beginning my first real vacation in two years!

*For more information, see **Transitions**, page R30.*

4 Narrative Writing

Narrative writing tells a story. If you write a story from your imagination, it is a fictional narrative. A true story about actual events is a nonfictional narrative. Narrative writing can be found in short stories, novels, news articles, personal narratives, and biographies.

RUBRIC: Standards for Writing

A successful narrative should

- hook the reader's attention with a strong introduction
- include descriptive details and dialogue to develop the characters, setting, and plot
- have a clear beginning, middle, and end
- have a logical organization, with clues and transitions that help the reader understand the order of events
- maintain a consistent tone and point of view
- use language that is appropriate to the audience
- demonstrate the significance of events or ideas

*For more information, see **Writing Workshop: Biographical Narrative**, pages 598–605.*

4.1 KEY TECHNIQUES

Identify the Main Events What are the most important events in your narrative? Is each event needed to tell the story?

Describe the Setting When do the events occur? Where do they take place? How can you use setting to create mood and to set the stage for the characters and their actions?

Depict Characters Vividly What do your characters look like? What do they think and say? How do they act? What details can show what they are like?

TIP Dialogue is an effective means of developing characters in a narrative. As you write dialogue, choose words that express your characters' personalities and that show how the characters feel about one another and about the events in the plot.

4.2 OPTIONS FOR ORGANIZATION

Option 1: Chronological Order One way to organize a piece of narrative writing is to arrange the events in chronological order, as shown in the following example.

EXAMPLE

A contemporary Navajo boy in New Mexico is nearing adulthood. His father wants him to learn the lore of his ancestors. His mother wants him to prepare for school instead.

> **Introduction**
> *Characters and setting*
>

The boy wants to please both his parents. He goes into the mountains to seek wisdom.

> **Event 1**

Animals visit the boy, representing both the old ways and the new.

> **Event 2**

The boy finds that he does not have to disappoint either parent. He finds that he must work hardest on learning what he himself is best suited for.

> **End**
> *Perhaps showing the significance of the events*

Option 2: Flashback In narrative writing, it is also possible to introduce events that happened before the beginning of the story. You can use a flashback to show how past events led up to the present situation or to provide background about a character or event. Use clue words such as *last summer, as a young girl, the previous school year,* and *his earliest memories* to let your reader know that you are interrupting the main action to describe earlier events. Notice how the flashback interrupts the action in the model.

MODEL

Mr. Robbins picked up the small, white ball that had just smashed his kitchen window and felt angry that the boys playing across the street could be so careless. Then he remembered a summer day over 50 years ago, when he himself had hit a home run – right into the Nelsons' living room. How frightened he had been when Mrs. Nelson walked out of her front door, holding the baseball! But she had simply laughed as she gave it back to him and said, "Boys will be boys." Mr. Robbins shook his head at the memory and looked back at his broken pane of glass.

Option 3: Focus on Conflict When a fictional narrative focuses on a central conflict, the story's plot may be organized as shown in the following example.

EXAMPLE

The day after their high school graduation, Angela and her twin brother, Alex, decided to take their canoe out on the river that ran past their family home. They had done it many times since childhood, and the river was familiar to both of them.

> **Describe main characters and setting.**

For two hours they traversed the river under a calm, clear sky, but by noon, rather ominous clouds had rolled in. Meanwhile, they had floated far downstream, and had taken a winding inlet off the river. Soon, they heard thunder in the distance, and Angela looked off to the southwest where she had noticed lightning. She alerted Alex and insisted they turn back immediately. Alex did not seem concerned, however, and refused to go back.

> **Present conflict.**

As the storm began to get nearer, Angela again insisted they turn around, but Alex, who was steering the boat, said the storm was too far away to hurt them. As the rain began to fall on them, Angela began to plead with her brother that they either pull over to the shore or turn back immediately. To prove her point, she stopped paddling.

> **Relate events that make conflict complex and cause characters to change.**

Alex ignored his sister and continued to paddle himself and steer them further downstream. Finally a bolt of lightning hit close by, and the rain started to pour. "Now do you believe me?!" shouted Angela through the driving rain. Alex turned the boat toward shore and didn't say a word.

> **Present resolution or outcome of conflict.**

5 Expository Writing

Expository writing informs and explains. You can use it to evaluate the effects of a new law, to compare two movies, to analyze a piece of literature, or to examine the problem of greenhouse gases in the atmosphere. There are many types of expository writing. Think about your topic and select the type that presents the information most clearly.

5.1 COMPARISON AND CONTRAST

Compare-and-contrast writing examines the similarities and differences between two or more subjects. You might, for example, compare and contrast two short stories, the main characters in a novel, or two movies.

> **RUBRIC: Standards for Writing**
>
> **Successful compare-and-contrast writing should**
> - hook the reader's attention with a strong introduction
> - clearly identify the subjects that are being compared and contrasted
> - include specific, relevant details
> - follow a clear plan of organization
> - use language and details appropriate to the audience
> - use transitional words and phrases to clarify similarities and differences

Options for Organization

Compare-and-contrast writing can be organized in different ways. The examples that follow demonstrate point-by-point organization and subject-by-subject organization.

Option 1: Point-by-Point Organization

EXAMPLE

I. Different beliefs about burial practices.   **Point 1**

> **Subject A.** Leon: traditional Laguna way.
>
> **Subject B.** Father Paul: last rites and a funeral mass.

II. Both want a proper burial.   **Point 2**

> **Subject A.** Leon: painted face, feather in hair, body to graveyard, cornmeal and pollen.
>
> **Subject B.** Father Paul: decide whether to sprinkle holy water without full Catholic rites.

Option 2: Subject-by-Subject Organization

> **EXAMPLE**
>
> I. Leon: **Subject A**
>
>   Point 1. Believes in traditional Laguna burial.
>
>   Point 2. Proper burial: painted face, feather in hair, body to graveyard, corn meal and pollen.
>
> II. Father Paul: **Subject B**
>
>   Point 1. Believes burial requires last rites and a funeral mass.
>
>   Point 2. Must decide whether to sprinkle holy water without full Catholic rites.

*For more information, see **Writing Workshop: Reflective Essay,** pages 474–481; **Writing Workshop: Literary Analysis,** pages 804–811; **Writing Workshop: Comparison-Contrast Essay,** pages 1072–1079; **Research Paper,** pages 1284–1299.*

5.2 CAUSE AND EFFECT

Cause-effect writing explains why something happened, why certain conditions exist, or what resulted from an action or a condition. You might use cause-effect writing to explain a character's actions, the progress of a disease, or the outcome of a war.

> **RUBRIC: Standards for Writing**
>
> **Successful cause-effect writing should**
>
> - hook the reader's attention with a strong introduction
> - clearly state the cause-and-effect relationship
> - show clear connections between causes and effects
> - present causes and effects in a logical order and use transitions effectively
> - use facts, examples, and other details to illustrate each cause and effect
> - use language and details appropriate to the audience

Options for Organization

Your organization will depend on your topic and your purpose for writing.

Option 1: Effect-to-Cause Organization If you want to explain the causes of an event, such as the closing of a factory, you might first state the effect and then examine its causes.

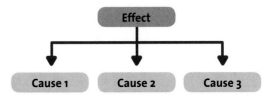

Option 2: Cause-to-Effect Organization If your focus is on explaining the effects of an event, such as the passage of a law, you might first state the cause and then explain the effects.

Option 3: Cause-Effect Chain Organization Sometimes you'll want to describe a chain of cause-effect relationships to explore a topic, such as the disappearance of tropical rain forests or the development of the Internet.

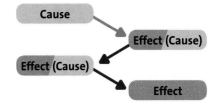

TIP Don't assume that a cause-effect relationship exists just because one event follows another. Look for evidence that the later event could not have happened if the first event had not caused it.

5.3 PROBLEM-SOLUTION

Problem-solution writing clearly states a problem, analyzes the problem, and proposes a solution to the problem. It can be used to identify and solve a conflict between characters, investigate global warming, or tell why the home team keeps losing.

RUBRIC: Standards for Writing

Successful problem-solution writing should

- hook the reader's attention with a strong introduction
- identify the problem and help the reader understand the issues involved
- analyze the causes and effects of the problem
- include quotations, facts, and statistics
- explore possible solutions to the problem and recommend the best one(s)
- use language, details, and a tone appropriate to the audience

Options for Organization

Your organization will depend on the goal of your problem-solution piece, your intended audience, and the specific problem you have chosen to address. The organizational methods that follow are effective for different kinds of problem-solution writing.

Option 1: Simple Problem-Solution

Option 2: Deciding Between Solutions

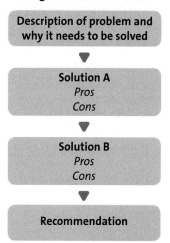

For more information, see **Writing Workshop: Problem and Solution,** *pages 1248–1255.*

5.4 ANALYSIS

In writing an analysis, you explain how something works, how it is defined, or what its parts are.

RUBRIC: Standards for Writing

A successful analysis should

- hook the reader's attention with a strong introduction
- clearly define the subject and its parts
- use a specific organizing structure to provide a logical flow of information
- show connections among facts and ideas through transitional words and phrases
- use language and details appropriate for the audience

Options for Organization

Organize your details in a logical order appropriate to the kind of analysis you're writing. Use one of the following options:

Option 1: Process Analysis A process analysis is usually organized chronologically, with steps or stages in the order in which they occur.

EXAMPLE

Navigating north from New Orleans

Mark Twain follows this process for his first trip as a cub pilot.

Step 1: Straighten out the boat.

Step 2: Stay close to the moored boats.

Step 3: Pass Six-Mile, Nine-Mile, and Twelve-Mile points.

Step 4: Cross the river when the calm water ends.

> Introduce process.
> Give background.
> Explain steps.

Option 2: Definition Analysis You can organize the details of a definition analysis in order of importance or impression.

EXAMPLE

A successful riverboat pilot must be a keen observer.

The riverboat pilot must observe the surface of the river, the landmarks along the shore, and signs of nature.

Quality 1: The surface can tell of rising water or hidden hazards.

Quality 2: Landmarks tell where the boat is; pilot must recall what dangers to avoid at that point.

Quality 3: The sky can give hints about what weather may be coming.

> Introduce term.
> General definition.
> Explain features or qualities.

Option 3: Parts Analysis A parts analysis is organized as a listing of the subject's parts, with each explained.

EXAMPLE

Piloting a riverboat requires several skills.

Part 1: recognize how weather might threaten the boat

Part 2: observe floating objects that could show a rising river; see ripples in the water surface that could indicate a hazard

Part 3: use landmarks to know where boat is and where dangers lie

> Introduce subject.
> Explain parts.

For more information, see **Writing Workshop: Literary Analysis,** *pages 804–811.*

6 Persuasive Writing

Persuasive writing allows you to use the power of language to inform and influence others. It includes speeches, persuasive essays, newspaper editorials, advertisements, and critical reviews.

RUBRIC: Standards for Writing

Successful persuasive writing should

- hook the reader's attention with a strong introduction
- state the issue and the writer's position
- give opinions and support them with facts or reasons
- have a reasonable and respectful tone
- answer opposing views
- use sound logic and effective language
- conclude by summing up reasons or calling for action

For more information, see **Writing Workshop: Persuasive Essay,** *pages 276–283.*

6.1 KEY TECHNIQUES

Clarify Your Position What do you believe about the issue? Determine how you can express your opinion most clearly.

Know Your Audience Who will read your writing? Think about what your audience already knows and believes about the issue. Imagine any objections to your position that your audience might have. Determine what additional information they will need. Decide on the tone and approach that would be most effective.

Support Your Opinion Why do you feel the way you do about the issue? Use facts, statistics, examples, quotations, anecdotes, or expert opinions to support your view. Think of reasons that will convince your readers and evidence that can answer their objections.

Ways to Support Your Argument	
Statistics	facts that are stated in numbers
Examples	specific instances that explain points
Observations	events or situations you yourself have seen
Anecdotes	brief stories that illustrate points
Quotations	direct statements from authorities

*For more information, see **Identifying Faulty Reasoning**, page R22.*

Begin and End with a Bang How can you hook your readers and make a lasting impression? Think of a quotation, an anecdote, or a statistic that will catch your reader's attention and remain memorable. Create a strong summary or call to action with which you can conclude.

MODEL

Beginning

Stop before you call your doctor for medicine to cure that cold or ease that sore throat. You might be doing your body more harm than good by taking an antibiotic.

Conclusion

Listen to doctors when they suggest that antibiotics should be reserved for serious illness. Take the doctor's advice to drink lots of liquids and get bed rest instead of taking drugs for a less serious illness. Maybe humanity can win the battle with microbes by slowing their evolution into supermicrobes that resist antibiotics.

6.2 OPTIONS FOR ORGANIZATION

In a two-sided persuasive essay, you want to show the weaknesses of other opinions as you explain the strengths of your own.

Option 1: Reasons for Your Opinion

Introduction states issue and your position on it.
▼
Reason 1 with evidence and support
▼
Reason 2 with evidence and support
▼
Reason 3 with evidence and support
▼
Objections to whole argument
▼
Response to objections
▼
Conclusion includes restatement of your position and recommended action.

Option 2: Point-by-Point Basis

Introduction states issue and your position on it.
▼
Reason 1 with evidence and support
▼
Objections and responses for reason 1
▼
Reason 2 with evidence and support
▼
Objections and responses for reason 2
▼
Reason 3 with evidence and support
▼
Objections and responses for reason 3
▼
Conclusion includes restatement of your position and recommended action.

7 Workplace and Technical Writing

Business writing is writing done in a workplace to support the work of a company or business. Several types of formats, such as memos, letters, e-mails, applications, and bylaws, have been developed to make communication easier.

RUBRIC: Standards for Writing

Successful business writing should

- be courteous
- use language that is geared to its audience
- state the purpose clearly in the opening sentences or paragraph
- have a formal tone and not contain slang, contractions, or sentence fragments
- use precise words
- present only essential information
- present details in a logical order
- conclude with a summary of important points

7.1 KEY TECHNIQUES

Think About Your Purpose Ask yourself why you are doing this writing. Do you want to promote yourself to a college admissions committee or a job interviewer? Do you want to order or complain about a product? Do you want to set up a meeting or respond to someone's ideas? Are you writing bylaws for an organization?

Identify Your Audience Determine who will read your writing. What background information will they need? What tone or language is appropriate?

Use a Pattern of Organization That Is Appropriate to the Content If you have to compare and contrast two products in a memo, for example, you can use the same compare-and-contrast organization that you would use in an essay.

Support Your Points What specific details might clarify your ideas? What reasons do you have for your statements?

Finish Strongly Determine the best way to sum up your statements. What is your main point? What action do you want the recipients to take?

Revise and Proofread Your Writing Just as you are graded on the quality of an essay you write for a class, you will be judged on the quality of your writing in the workplace.

7.2 MATCHING THE FORMAT TO THE OCCASION

E-mail messages, memos, and letters have similar purposes but are used in different situations. The chart shows how each format can be used.

Format	Occasion
Memo	Use to send correspondence **inside** the workplace only.
E-mail message	Use to send correspondence **inside or outside** the company.
Letter	Use to send correspondence **outside** the company.

TIP Memos are often sent as e-mail messages in the workplace. Remember that both require formal language and standard spelling, capitalization, and punctuation.

PRACTICE AND APPLY

Refer to the documents on page R41 to complete the following:

1. Draft a response to the letter. Then revise your letter as necessary according to the rubric at the beginning of this section. Make sure you have included the necessary information and have written in an appropriate tone. Proofread your letter for grammatical errors and spelling mistakes. Follow the format of the model and use appropriate spacing between elements.

2. Write a memo in response to the memo. Tell the recipient what actions you have taken. Follow the format of the model.

7.3 FORMATS

Business letters usually have a formal tone and a specific format as shown below. The key to writing a business letter is to get to the point as quickly as possible and to present your information clearly.

MODEL: BUSINESS LETTER

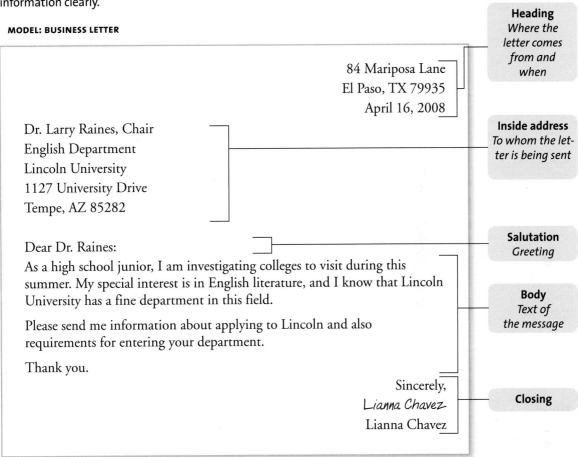

Heading
Where the letter comes from and when

84 Mariposa Lane
El Paso, TX 79935
April 16, 2008

Inside address
To whom the letter is being sent

Dr. Larry Raines, Chair
English Department
Lincoln University
1127 University Drive
Tempe, AZ 85282

Salutation
Greeting

Dear Dr. Raines:

Body
Text of the message

As a high school junior, I am investigating colleges to visit during this summer. My special interest is in English literature, and I know that Lincoln University has a fine department in this field.

Please send me information about applying to Lincoln and also requirements for entering your department.

Thank you.

Sincerely,
Lianna Chavez
Lianna Chavez

Closing

Memos are often used in workplaces as a way of conveying information in a direct and concise manner. They can be used to announce or summarize meetings and to request actions or specific information.

MODEL: MEMO

Heading
Receiver's name
Sender's name
Complete date
Topic of memo

To: Jane Bakerman
From: Larry Raines
Date: 4/20/08
Re: Prospective Student

Body

Jane, attached is a copy of a letter from a high school junior who is interested in our program. Will you please send her the English Department flyer and then forward to the dean's office the request for a catalog? Thanks.

TIP Don't forget to write the topic of your memo in the subject line. This will help the receiver determine the importance of your memo.

When you apply for a job, you may be asked to fill out an application form. Application forms vary, but most of them ask for similar kinds of information. If you are mailing your application, you may want to include a brief letter.

MODEL: JOB APPLICATION

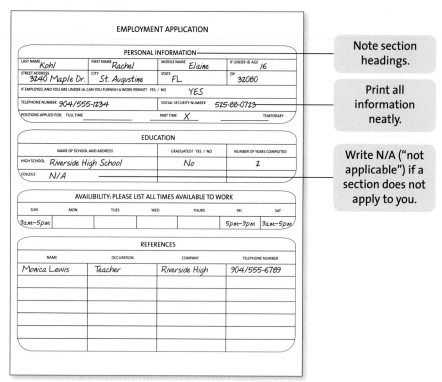

Note section headings.

Print all information neatly.

Write N/A ("not applicable") if a section does not apply to you.

MODEL: RÉSUMÉ

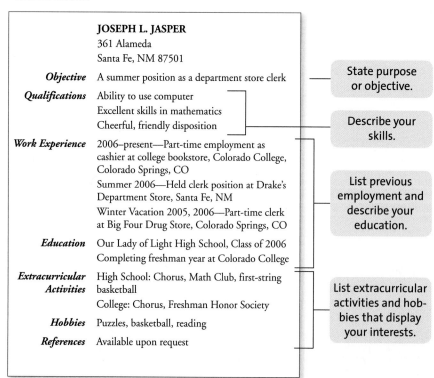

State purpose or objective.

Describe your skills.

List previous employment and describe your education.

List extracurricular activities and hobbies that display your interests.

Sometimes you may have to write technical documents, such as a list of procedures for conducting a meeting, a manual on rules of behavior, or the minutes of a meeting. These documents contain written descriptions of rules, regulations, and meetings and enable organizations and businesses to run smoothly. These bylaws for a poetry club include a description of the organization and information about how the club operates.

MODEL: BYLAWS DOCUMENT

Article I Name

SECTION 1. The name of this organization is the Free Verse Poets Society of North Shore High School.

Article II Purpose

SECTION 1. The purpose of this organization is to stimulate young developing poets, to create enthusiasm for poetry, to promote the scholarly study of poetry, and to inform the school and community about poetry.

Article III Membership Requirements

SECTION 1. To qualify for membership, a candidate must be a student at North Shore High School.

SECTION 2. Membership in Free Verse Poets Society is voluntary. However, all members are required to attend semimonthly meetings, participate in any club fundraisers, and assist in the quarterly publication of the club newsletter, *Plutonian Shore.*

Article IV Meetings

SECTION 1. Meetings will be held twice a month on a day designated by voting members. Meetings will be held in a classroom designated by the faculty advisor.

SECTION 2. A quorum shall consist of eight (8) members; at least two (2) student officers and the faculty advisor are required to be present at each meeting.

SECTION 3. All student officers are voting members of the Free Verse Poets Society; however, the faculty advisor may be called upon in the event of an evenly split vote.

Article V Officers

SECTION 1. This organization shall be governed by a faculty advisor and a panel of four (4) student officers: the president, vice-president, scribe, and treasurer. Each student officer will be elected at the start of the school year.

SECTION 2. For members to be eligible for election, they must have served one (1) year as a member in the Free Verse Poets Society. Freshmen are not eligible for election. Only seniors are eligible for the office of society president.

SECTION 3. The president will preside over regular and special meetings.

SECTION 4. The vice-president will guide activities of appointed committees.

SECTION 5. The scribe will record and distribute meeting minutes.

SECTION 6. The treasurer will be responsible for all money collected by the society.

PRACTICE AND APPLY

Refer to the documents on pages R42 and R43 to complete the following:

1. Visit a business and request an employment application for a job you would like to have. Make sure you understand what each question is asking before you begin to write. Fill out the application as neatly and completely as possible.

2. Write a set of bylaws for an organization that you already belong to or one that you would like to form. Follow the format of the document on page R43.

Good research involves using a variety of sources and materials. With an abundance of information at your fingertips, knowing where to go, how to access information, and how to record your findings are important skills and strategies.

WRITING TOOLS
For research tools and strategies, visit the **Research Center** at ClassZone.com.

1 Finding Sources

The **library** or **media center** and the **Internet** are the first places you will begin your research. Both the library and the Internet offer a wealth of resources, which include reference works, books, newspapers and periodicals, film, databases, catalogs, and other miscellaneous sources, such as music scores and maps.

1.1 REFERENCE WORKS

Reference works provide quick information that can help you refine or narrow your search. Reference works are roughly divided into two categories: general reference and specialized reference. Specialized reference works are focused on a particular field or area of study.

Reference Works	Examples
Encyclopedias—detailed information on nearly every subject, arranged alphabetically	*Encyclopaedia Britannica* *Encyclopedia.com* *Encyclopedia of Economics*
Dictionaries—word definitions, spellings, usage, pronunciations, and origins	*The American Heritage Dictionary* *Bartlett's Familiar Quotations*
Almanacs and Yearbooks—current facts and statistics	*World Almanac and Book of Facts*
Thesauri—lists of synonyms and antonyms	*Roget's International Thesaurus*
Biographical References—information on the lives of noteworthy people	*The Riverside Dictionary of Biography* *The International Who's Who*
Atlases—geographical and historical maps, charts, and graphics	*Rand McNally Atlas of the World*
Directories—names, addresses, and phone numbers of people and organizations	telephone books lists of business organizations, agencies, and publications
Indexes—alphabetical lists of newspaper and magazine articles	*Readers' Guide to Periodical Literature*

1.2 BOOKS

Nonfiction books provide in-depth information on specific topics. Your research may also require that you access fiction, poetry, or dramatic works. The following parts of a book will help you find information quickly and easily:

- **Title page**—a page that gives the book's name and the name of its author and publisher; usually the first full page of a book
- **Copyright page**—a page that gives the copyright date, or the date the book was published; usually located on the reverse side of the title page
- **Table of contents**—a list at the front of the book that gives the title of each chapter or section of the text and the page number on which it begins
- **Preface**—a short, preliminary section of a book in which the writer of the book briefly provides background information and, possibly, acknowledgments
- **Bibliography**—a list of related books and other materials used to write a text; usually placed at the end of the book
- **Glossary**—an alphabetized list of important and/or specialized words and their definitions; usually placed at the end of the book
- **Appendix**—a collection of additional materials that supply background or other related information on subject matter discussed in the main portion of the text; usually located at the end of the book
- **Index**—an alphabetized list of important topics, terms, and details covered in the book and the page numbers on which they can be found; located at the end of the book; useful for quickly finding specific information on a topic

*For more information, see **Choosing Reliable Books,** page 1277.*

Two basic systems are used to classify nonfiction books. Most high school and public libraries use the Dewey decimal system. University and research libraries generally use the Library of Congress system.

DEWEY DECIMAL SYSTEM

000–099	General works
100–199	Philosophy and psychology
200–299	Religion
300–399	Social science
400–499	Language
500–599	Natural sciences and mathematics
600–699	Technology (applied sciences)
700–799	Arts and recreation
800–899	Literature and rhetoric
900–999	Geography and history

LIBRARY OF CONGRESS SYSTEM

A	General works
B	Philosophy, psychology, religion
C	History
D	General history and history of Europe
E–F	American history
G	Geography, anthropology, recreation
H	Social sciences
J	Political science
K	Law
L	Education
M	Music
N	Fine arts
P	Language and literature
Q	Science
R	Medicine
S	Agriculture
T	Technology
U	Military science
V	Naval science
Z	Bibliography and library science

1.3 NEWSPAPERS AND PERIODICALS

Newspapers, magazines, and scholarly journals provide concise and current information on specific topics and the news of the day. Microforms are newspapers, periodicals, and reports stored on film (microfilm) or cards (microfiche) and viewable on special machines found at the library.

Types of Publications	Examples
Newspapers—published daily, weekly, or monthly; provide news reports, specialized features, and commentary; may be general or specialized	*New York Times Chicago Tribune Sacramento Bee*
Magazines—published monthly, quarterly, or at other intervals; provide news, articles on specific topics, and commentary; more in-depth than newspapers	*Newsweek Time Musician*
Journals—usually academic in scope; related to a specific field of study; highly specialized information	*Journal of Music Theory New England Journal of Medicine*

For more information, see **Evaluating Newspapers and Periodicals,** *page 1276.*

1.4 ELECTRONIC RESOURCES

Electronic resources include DVDs, videos, e-books, CD-ROMs, and audio resources. These resources may contain reference materials, movies, documentaries, television programs, books, music, speeches, textbooks, and various other content. While most documentaries, movies, and interviews are available on DVDs or CDs, you may want to directly access a film version. To quickly determine whether the piece is useful for your research, check the following:

- **Description or summary** of the piece—Does it contain the information you need, or is it otherwise relevant to your topic? Is it nonfiction or fiction?
- **Copyright date**—How current is the documentary or interview?
- **Producer** of the piece and its **participants**—Is the producer or creator reputable? Who is interviewed or featured?

1.5 DATABASES AND ONLINE CATALOGS

The library and Internet also offer large databases that allow you to search for articles on any number of topics. Often the library will subscribe to a database service, such as InfoTrac, Newsbank, or SIRS Researcher. The information on these databases is updated regularly.

Electronic catalogs have mostly replaced the card catalog system of book listings. Formerly filed in labeled drawers in libraries, listings can now be accessed from a library's Web site on the Internet.

1.6 OTHER RESOURCES

In addition to reference works found in the library or media center and on the Internet, you can get information from the following sources: corporate and nonprofit publications, lectures, correspondence, career guides, recordings, and television programming.

PRACTICE AND APPLY

1. If you were looking through a nonfiction book on penguins, which part of the book would you search in order to find information on emperor penguins, a specific type of penguin?

2. If you wanted the most current information on a given topic, which source(s) would you search first?

3. Describe a situation in which you might find it useful to search microfiche.

1.7 WEB SOURCES

Whole libraries are on the Internet, as are thousands of other reliable and comprehensive sources for research. To conduct a search efficiently and find the best information for your topic, familiarize yourself with the following terms and procedures.

The main search tools for finding information on the Web are search engines, metasearch tools, and directories. In addition, there are virtual libraries and a host of other sites, such as newspaper archives, news associations, encyclopedias, the Library of Congress, and specialized databases.

Search engines—A search engine is a Web site that allows you to look for information on the World Wide Web. Examples include Google, Alltheweb, AltaVista, HotBot, and Go.com.

Metasearch tools—A metasearch tool is similar to a search engine, except that it simultaneously searches multiple search engines for the keywords you request. Examples include Dogpile, SurfWax, and Metacrawler.

Directories—Directories arrange Internet resources into subject categories and are useful when you are researching a general topic. Examples include Lycos, Galaxy, Yahoo!, Web Directory, and About.com.

Keyword searches—In a keyword search, you access a search engine and type in a phrase or term related to your subject. This allows you to retrieve Web sites and documents that have those keywords in them. Here are some tips for doing a keyword search:

- In the search box, type in a specific word or two that clearly identify your subject.
- When you want to find an exact phrase, or words in a certain order, such as *recording studio* (and not just *recording* or just *studio*), use quotation marks around the entire phrase. For instance, "recording studio" will provide results using those words in that order.
- If necessary, replace the end of a word with an asterisk. For example, the keyword *music** leads to sites that contain *music, musician,* and *musicianship.*

Boolean searches—A Boolean search lets you specify how the keywords in your search are related. This type of search allows you to refine, narrow, or expand your search so that your results are more focused on your topic needs. Use the following tips to conduct a Boolean search:

- For a search containing two or more words that do not need to be in a specific order, use the word AND between the words to indicate that the site or document should contain all the words specified. For example, *internship* AND *radio* will produce results containing both those words, but not in any particular order. For some search engines, you can use a plus sign instead of AND.
- The word OR broadens the search to include all documents that contain either word (*job* OR *career*).
- The word NOT—or, for some search engines, a minus sign—excludes unwanted terms from the search (*songwriting* NOT *commercials*).

Each Web site you encounter in your search will have a **URL** (uniform resource locator), which is its Web address. The abbreviation usually located at the end of the URL indicates the type and purpose of the Web site.

URL ABBREVIATIONS AND MEANINGS

.COM commercial—product information and sales; personal sites; some combinations of products and information, such as World Book Online

.EDU education—information about schools, courses, campus life, and research projects; students' and teachers' personal sites

.GOV United States government—official sites of the White House and of NASA, the FBI, and other government agencies and offices

.MIL United States military—official sites of the army, navy, air force, and marines, as well as of the Department of Defense and related agencies

.NET network—product information and sales

.ORG organization—charities, libraries, and other nonprofits; political parties

*For more information, see **Online Resources,** pages 1271–1273.*

1.8 YOUR OWN ORIGINAL DATA

Sometimes you will need information that you just can't find in books or online. A good way to get in-depth, firsthand information is by interviewing experts, conducting surveys, and recording data from your own observations, fieldwork, or experiments.

Interviews with experts—Whatever the subject of your research, look for people who have knowledge or experience in that field. For example, if you were researching shipwrecks on the Great Lakes, you might interview someone from the Great Lakes Maritime Society or a captain of a ship on the Great Lakes. Use the following tips when conducting an interview:

1. Plan your questions and rehearse what you will say.

2. During the interview, listen carefully and take notes. Ask permission if you want to record the interview.

3. Request clarification and ask follow-up questions when necessary.

4. After the interview, review your notes and summarize the conversation. If you recorded the conversation, you might want to transcribe it.

5. Identify strong statements you might want to quote directly.

6. Send a thank-you note to the interviewee.

Oral histories—For some kinds of presentations and papers, you may want to include an **oral history,** or a story of a person's experiences told in his or her own words. For example, if you were writing a paper on Native Americans and reservation life, you might want to include an oral history of someone who is experiencing that life and who knows how his or her tribe came to live on the reservation. To conduct an oral history, follow all the tips for conducting an interview.

Surveys—Surveys allow you to gather information from a broad range of people through the use of a **questionnaire.** For example, you may want to gather and compare people's opinions, preferences, or beliefs about a current news topic. Use the following tips to conduct a survey or to distribute a questionnaire:

1. Plan the survey. Choose whether you want to ask multiple-choice questions, yes/no questions, open-ended questions, true/false questions, or questions that refer to a rating scale. Prepare your questionnaire.

2. Determine the sample population, or group of people, you want to survey.

3. Administer the survey the same way to each person. You may ask people to respond in person, on the phone, or by e-mail, but your method should be the same for each, with the questions asked in the same manner and order.

4. Once the questionnaires have been completed, compile and interpret the responses. Was there a clear preference or opinion from the entire group? Do certain groups of people think one way while others think another? What conclusions can you draw from the results?

5. Summarize your results in writing; use charts or other graphic aids to provide a visual representation of the data.

Independent observation and field research—Field research and independent observation include any purposeful observations you make at a site or an event related to your topic. For example, you might visit a movie set to learn more about how movies are made and then record the activity you observed. For some research projects you may want to set up a **field study,** which is a systematic series of observations or a planned course of data collection. For some topics you might conduct experiments, as for a report in a science class.

❷ Collecting Information

Once you have located your sources, you will need to sort through the information. To make it useful and manageable, you will want to take detailed notes, arrange your information in a logical and organized manner, and make sure your sources are reliable and credible.

2.1 TAKING NOTES

As you go through your sources, write down information that is relevant to your search.

Source cards—You will need to document the sources where you find your information or evidence so that you can credit the sources in your work. To create source cards, record on a separate index card all the information needed to identify each source you use in your research. Number each source card so that you can easily refer to it when you take notes and add documentation to your report, as in this example for a book.

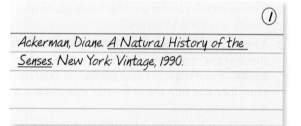

HERE'S HOW

MAKING SOURCE CARDS

Follow these guidelines when you make source cards:

- **Book** Write the author's or editor's complete name, the title, the location and name of the publisher, and the copyright date.
- **Magazine or Newspaper Article** Write the author's complete name (unless the article is unsigned), the title of the article, the name and date of the publication, and the page number(s) of the article.
- **Encyclopedia Article** Write the author's complete name (unless the article is unsigned), the title of the article, and the name and copyright date of the encyclopedia.
- **World Wide Web Site** Write the author's or editor's complete name (if available), the title of the document, publication information for any print version of it, the date of its electronic publication, the name of any institution or organization responsible for the site, the date when you accessed the site, and the document's address (in angle brackets).

Note cards—As you read your sources, write down all relevant facts, quotations, statistics, anecdotes, and examples on separate index cards, or **note cards.** When you're ready to draft your paper, you can arrange and organize the cards in different ways to present the information and then choose the best method of organization. Here is an example of a note card with an exact quotation from the Diane Ackerman book.

Insects and photoreception

"Bees can judge the angle at which light hits their photoreceptors, and therefore locate the position of the sun in the sky, even on a partly cloudy day" (265).

HERE'S HOW

TAKING NOTES

Follow these guidelines as you take your notes:

- **Use a separate index card** for each piece of information.
- **Write a heading** on each card, indicating the subject of the note.
- **Write the number of the corresponding source card** on each card.
- **Put direct quotations in quotation marks.**
- **Record the number of the page** where you found the material.

When recording information on note cards, you can use the following forms of **restatement** to avoid **plagiarism,** or presenting someone else's work as your own:

Paraphrase—When you paraphrase, you restate the writer's idea in your own words. Be sure to enclose in quotation marks any of the author's exact words that you include in a paraphrase.

Summary—When you summarize, you restate the main idea of the original, including key facts and statistics, but in a shorter version, usually about one-third the length of the original. A summary omits unnecessary details.

Quotation—When you use a writer's exact statement, you will need to place quotation marks around it. Be sure to copy the words exactly as the writer wrote them, including all punctuation. Use quotations for

- extremely important ideas that might be misrepresented by paraphrases
- clear and concise explanations
- ideas presented in unusually lively or vivid language

2.2 OUTLINING

Once you've arranged your note cards in a pattern of organization that is suitable for your topic, you can create a formal **outline** of how the information will be arranged in your report. An outline can be written in one of two ways: as a sentence outline or as a topic outline. The **sentence outline** contains entries written in sentence form; the **topic outline** contains only phrases or words that represent the ideas. With either choice, each main idea in the outline is designated by a Roman numeral. The subtopics that support the main ideas are designated with indented capital letters. The details that explain the subtopics are designated with numerals and lowercase letters.

MODEL: SENTENCE OUTLINE

> **Introduction:** The human senses are varied and differ from those in animals.
>
> I. Humans are believed to have five senses: sight, hearing, touch, taste, and smell.
>
>   A. Aristotle, a Greek philosopher, first categorized the senses.
>   B. Modern physics and physiology reclassified the senses.
>
> II. Photoreceptors are those sense organs in living organisms that react to light.
>
>   A. The human eye is a photoreceptor.
>   B. Animal photoreception can be superior to that of humans.
>   1. Insects have specialized eyes.
>   2. Nocturnal animals can see in the dark.
>   3. Some animals see the world in colors that are different from those perceived by humans.

MODEL: TOPIC OUTLINE

> **Introduction:** The human senses are varied and differ from those in animals.
>
> I. Five senses in humans
>
>   A. First categorization of senses
>   B. Modern reclassification of senses
>
> II. Photoreception
>
>   A. Human sight and photoreception
>   B. Animal sight and photoreception
>   1. Insects
>   2. Nocturnal animals
>   3. Animals vs. humans in perceiving colors

2.3 CHECKLIST FOR EVALUATING SOURCES

The information . . .

☑ is relevant to the topic you are researching

☑ is up-to-date (This point is especially important when researching time-sensitive topics in areas such as science, medicine, and sports.)

☑ is from an author who is qualified to write about the topic

☑ is from a trusted source that is updated or reviewed regularly

☑ makes the author's or institution's purpose for writing clear

☑ is written at the right level for your needs (For example, a children's book is probably too simplistic, while a scientific paper may be too complex.)

☑ has the level of detail you need—neither too general nor too specific

☑ can be verified in more than one source

3 Sharing Your Research

At last you have established your research goals, located sources of information, evaluated the materials, and taken notes on what you learned. Now you have a chance to share the results with people in your world—and even beyond. Here are some options you may choose to present your work:

- Give a speech to your classmates or to people in your community.
- Create a power presentation using desktop publishing software and share it with classmates, friends, or family members.
- Describe your research findings on your own Web site.
- Summarize the information in a newsletter or brochure.
- Share the results of your research in a formal research paper.

Writing that has a lot of mistakes can confuse or even annoy a reader. A business letter with a punctuation error might lead to a miscommunication and delay a reply. A sentence fragment might lower your grade on an essay. Paying attention to grammar, punctuation, and capitalization rules can make your writing clearer and easier to read.

Quick Reference: Parts of Speech

PART OF SPEECH	FUNCTION	EXAMPLES
Noun	names a person, a place, a thing, an idea, a quality, or an action	
Common	serves as a general name, or a name common to an entire group	coyote, hunter, spear, bonfire
Proper	names a specific, one-of-a-kind person, place, or thing	Rainy Mountain, Virginia, Puritans
Singular	refers to a single person, place, thing, or idea	field, pony, child, man
Plural	refers to more than one person, place, thing, or idea	fields, ponies, children, men
Concrete	names something that can be perceived by the senses	lemon, shores, wind, canoe
Abstract	names something that cannot be perceived by the senses	fear, intelligence, honesty
Compound	expresses a single idea through a combination of two or more words	birthright, folk tale, Sky-World
Collective	refers to a group of people or things	species, army, flock
Possessive	shows who or what owns something	America's, Douglass's, men's, slaves'
Pronoun	takes the place of a noun or another pronoun	
Personal	refers to the person(s) making a statement, the person(s) being addressed, or the person(s) or thing(s) the statement is about	I, me, my, mine, we, us, our, ours, you, your, yours, she, he, it, her, him, hers, his, its, they, them, their, theirs
Reflexive	follows a verb or preposition and refers to a preceding noun or pronoun	myself, yourself, herself, himself, itself, ourselves, yourselves, themselves
Intensive	emphasizes a noun or another pronoun	(same as reflexives)
Demonstrative	points to one or more specific persons or things	this, that, these, those
Interrogative	signals a question	who, whom, whose, which, what
Indefinite	refers to one or more persons or things not specifically mentioned	both, all, most, many, anyone, everybody, several, none, some
Relative	introduces an adjective clause by relating it to a word in the clause	who, whom, whose, which, that

PART OF SPEECH	FUNCTION	EXAMPLES
Verb	expresses an action, a condition, or a state of being	
Action	tells what the subject does or did, physically or mentally	run, reaches, listened, consider, decides, dreamed
Linking	connects the subject to something that identifies or describes it	am, is, are, was, were, sound, taste, appear, feel, become, remain, seem
Auxiliary	precedes the main verb in a verb phrase	be, have, do, can, could, will, would, may, might
Transitive	directs the action toward someone or something; always has an object	The wind **snapped** the young tree in half.
Intransitive	does not direct the action toward someone or something; does not have an object	The young tree **snapped.**
Adjective	modifies a noun or pronoun	**frightened** man, **two** epics, **enough** time
Adverb	modifies a verb, an adjective, or another adverb	walked **out**, **really** funny, **far** away
Preposition	relates one word to another word	at, by, for, from, in, of, on, to, with
Conjunction	joins words or word groups	
Coordinating	joins words or word groups used the same way	and, but, or, for, so, yet, nor
Correlative	used as a pair to join words or word groups used the same way	both ... and, either ... or, neither ... nor
Subordinating	introduces a clause that cannot stand by itself as a complete sentence	although, after, as, before, because, when, if, unless
Interjection	expresses emotion	whew, yikes, uh-oh

Quick Reference: The Sentence and Its Parts

The diagrams that follow will give you a brief review of the essentials of a sentence and some of its parts.

> Thoreau's original **cabin cost** less than 30 dollars.

The **complete subject** includes all the words that identify the person, place, thing, or idea that the sentence is about.

The **complete predicate** includes all the words that tell or ask something about the subject.

cabin

cost

The **simple subject** tells exactly whom or what the sentence is about. It may be one word or a group of words, but it does not include modifiers.

The **simple predicate**, or **verb**, tells what the subject does or is. It may be one word or several, but it does not include modifiers.

Every word in a sentence is part of a complete subject or a complete predicate.

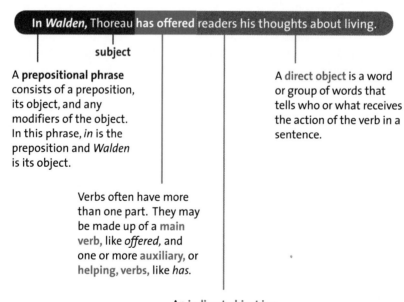

> In *Walden,* Thoreau **has offered** readers his thoughts about living.

subject

A **prepositional phrase** consists of a preposition, its object, and any modifiers of the object. In this phrase, *in* is the preposition and *Walden* is its object.

A **direct object** is a word or group of words that tells who or what receives the action of the verb in a sentence.

Verbs often have more than one part. They may be made up of a **main verb,** like *offered,* and one or more **auxiliary,** or **helping, verbs,** like *has.*

An **indirect object** is a word or group of words that tells *to whom* or *for whom* or *to what* or *for what* about the verb. A sentence can have an indirect object only if it has a direct object. The indirect object always comes before the direct object in a sentence.

Quick Reference: Punctuation

MARK	FUNCTION	EXAMPLES
End Marks period, question mark, exclamation point	end a sentence	The games begin today. Who is your favorite contestant? What a play Jamie made!
period	follows an initial or abbreviation **Exception:** postal abbreviations of states	Prof. Ted Bakerman, D. H. Lawrence, Houghton Mifflin Co., P.M., A.D., oz., ft., Blvd., St. NE (Nebraska), NV (Nevada)
period	follows a number or letter in an outline	I. Volcanoes A. Central-vent 1. Shield
Comma	separates parts of a compound sentence	I had never disliked poetry, but now I really love it.
	separates items in a series	She is brave, loyal, and kind.
	separates adjectives of equal rank that modify the same noun	The slow, easy route is best.
	sets off a term of address	America, I love you. Come to the front, children.
	sets off a parenthetical expression	Hard workers, as you know, don't quit. I'm not a quitter, believe me.
	sets off an introductory word, phrase, or dependent clause	Yes, I forgot my key. At the beginning of the day, I feel fresh. While she was out, I was here. Having finished my chores, I went out.
	sets off a nonessential phrase or clause	Ed Pawn, the captain of the chess team, won. Ed Pawn, who is the captain, won. The two leading runners, sprinting toward the finish line, finished in a tie.
	sets off parts of dates and addresses	Send it by August 18, 2010, to Cherry Jubilee, Inc., 21 Vernona St., Oakland, Minnesota.
	follows the salutation and closing of a letter	Dear Jim, Sincerely yours,
	separates words to avoid confusion	By noon, time had run out. What the minister does, does matter. While cooking, Jim burned his hand.
Semicolon	separates items in a series if one or more items contain commas	We invited my sister, Jan; her friend, Don; my uncle Jack; and Mary Dodd.
	separates parts of a compound sentence that are not joined by a coordinating conjunction	The small books are on the top shelves; the large books are below. I dusted the books; however, I didn't wipe the shelves.
	separates parts of a compound sentence when the parts contain commas	After I ran out of money, I called my parents; but only my sister was home, unfortunately.

MARK	FUNCTION	EXAMPLES
Colon	introduces a list	Those we wrote were the following: Dana, John, and Will.
	introduces a long quotation	Thomas Jefferson wrote: "We the people of the United States, in order to form a more perfect union...."
	follows the salutation of a business letter	Dear Ms. Williams: Dear Senator Wiley:
	separates certain numbers	1:28 P.M., Genesis 2:5
Dash	indicates an abrupt break in thought	I was thinking of my mother—who is arriving tomorrow—just as you walked in.
Parentheses	enclose less important material	Throughout her life (though some might think otherwise), she worked hard. The temperature on this July day (would you believe it?) is 65 degrees!
Hyphen	joins parts of a compound adjective before a noun	She lives in a first-floor apartment.
	joins parts of a compound with *all-, ex-, self-,* or *-elect*	The president-elect is a well-respected woman.
	joins parts of a compound number (to ninety-nine)	Today, I turn twenty-one.
	joins parts of a fraction	My cup is one-third full.
	joins a prefix to a word beginning with a capital letter	Life may have seemed simpler in pre-Civil War days. It's very chilly for mid-June.
	indicates that a word is divided at the end of a line	Did you know that school segregation has been illegal since 1954?
Apostrophe	used with *s* to form the possessive of a noun or an indefinite pronoun	my friend's book, my friends' books, anyone's guess, somebody else's problem
	replaces one or more omitted letters in a contraction or numbers in a date	don't (omitted *o*), he'd (omitted *woul*), the class of '99 (omitted *19*)
	used with *s* to form the plural of a letter	I had two A's on my report card.
Quotation Marks	set off a speaker's exact words	Sara said, "I'm finally ready." "I'm ready," Sara said, "finally." Did Sara say, "I'm ready"? Sara said, "I'm ready!"
	set off the title of a story, an article, a short poem, an essay, a song, or a chapter	I liked Oates's "Hostage," Steinem's "Sisterhood," and Plath's "Mirror." Chapter II is titled "Our Gang's Dark Oath."
Ellipses	replace material omitted from a quotation	"We the people ... in order to form a more perfect union ...."
Italics	indicate the title of a book, a play, a magazine, a long poem, an opera, a film, or a TV series, or the names of ships, trains, and spacecraft	*The Scarlet Letter, The Crucible, Time, The Death of the Hired Man, West Side Story, Citizen Kane, The Spirit of St. Louis, The Best of Frank Sinatra, Lusitania*

Quick Reference: Capitalization

CATEGORY	EXAMPLES
People and Titles	
Names and initials of people	Emily Dickinson, T. S. Eliot
Titles used before or in place of names	Professor Holmes, Senator Long
Deities and members of religious groups	Jesus, Allah, Buddha, Zeus, Baptists, Roman Catholics
Names of ethnic and national groups	Hispanics, Jews, African Americans
Geographical Names	
Cities, states, countries, continents	New York, Maine, Haiti, Africa
Regions, bodies of water, mountains	the South, Lake Erie, Mount Katahdin
Geographic features, parks	Continental Divide, Everglades, Yellowstone
Streets and roads, planets	55 East Ninety-fifth Street, Maple Lane, Venus, Jupiter
Organizations, Events, Etc.	
Companies, organizations, teams	General Motors, Lions Club, Utah Jazz
Buildings, bridges, monuments	the Alamo, Golden Gate Bridge, Lincoln Memorial
Documents, awards	the Constitution, World Cup
Special named events	Super Bowl, World Series
Government bodies, historical periods and events	the Supreme Court, U.S. Senate, Harlem Renaissance, World War II
Days and months, holidays	Friday, May, Easter, Memorial Day
Specific cars, boats, trains, planes	Mustang, *Titanic*, *California Zephyr*
Proper Adjectives	
Adjectives formed from proper nouns	American League, French cooking, Emersonian period, Arctic waters
First Words and the Pronoun I	
First word in a sentence or quotation	This is it. He said, "Let's go."
First word of sentence in parentheses that is not within another sentence	The spelling rules are covered in another section. (Consult that section for more information.)
First words in the salutation and closing of a letter	Dear Madam, Very truly yours,
First word in each line of most poetry Personal pronoun *I*	Then am I A happy fly If I live Or if I die.
First word, last word, and all important words in a title	"The Fall of the House of Usher," *Incidents in the Life of a Slave Girl*

1 Nouns

A **noun** is a word used to name a person, a place, a thing, an idea, a quality, or an action. Nouns can be classified in several ways.

For more information on different types of nouns, see **Quick Reference: Parts of Speech**, *page R50.*

1.1 COMMON NOUNS

Common nouns are general names, common to entire groups.

> EXAMPLES: *writer, song, bravery*

1.2 PROPER NOUNS

Proper nouns name specific, one-of-a-kind things.

Common	Proper
writer, song, bravery, hunter	Mourning Dove, Mississippi, Granny

For more information, see **Quick Reference: Capitalization**, *page R55.*

1.3 SINGULAR AND PLURAL NOUNS

A noun may take a singular or a plural form, depending on whether it names a single person, place, thing, or idea or more than one. Make sure you use appropriate spellings when forming plurals.

Singular	Plural
church, lily, wife	churches, lilies, wives

For more information, see **Forming Plural Nouns**, *page R78.*

1.4 COMPOUND AND COLLECTIVE NOUNS

Compound nouns are formed from two or more words but express a single idea. They are written as single words, as separate words, or with hyphens. Use a dictionary to check the correct spelling of a compound noun.

> EXAMPLES: *birthright, folk tale, Sky-World*

Collective nouns are singular nouns that refer to groups of people or things.

> EXAMPLES: *army, flock, class, species*

1.5 POSSESSIVE NOUNS

A **possessive noun** shows who or what owns something.

> EXAMPLES: *Welty's, jury's, children's*

For more information, see **Forming Possessives**, *page R78.*

2 Pronouns

A **pronoun** is a word that is used in place of a noun or another pronoun. The word or word group to which the pronoun refers is called its **antecedent**.

2.1 PERSONAL PRONOUNS

Personal pronouns change their form to express person, number, gender, and case. The forms of these pronouns are shown in the following chart.

	Nominative	Objective	Possessive
Singular			
First person	I	me	my, mine
Second person	you	you	your, yours
Third person	she, he, it	her, him, it	her, hers, his, its
Plural			
First person	we	us	our, ours
Second person	you	you	your, yours
Third person	they	them	their, theirs

2.2 AGREEMENT WITH ANTECEDENT

Pronouns should agree with their antecedents in number, gender, and person.

If an antecedent is singular, use a singular pronoun.

> EXAMPLE: *Sarah laughed as her dog splashed in the lake.*

If an antecedent is plural, use a plural pronoun.

> EXAMPLES:
>
> *Sarah and Barbara took turns holding the leash as they walked the dog home.*
>
> *Andrew and Ryan finished the race before the rest of their teammates.*

The gender of a pronoun must be the same as the gender of its antecedent.

> EXAMPLES:
>
> *The little girl ran outside without tying her shoelaces.*
>
> *Daniel waved to his friends before boarding the plane.*

The person of the pronoun must be the same as the person of its antecedent. As the chart in Section 2.1 shows, a pronoun can be in first-, second-, or third-person form.

> EXAMPLE:
>
> *Those of you who like animals should consider getting your degree in veterinary science.*

GRAMMAR PRACTICE

Rewrite each sentence so that the underlined pronoun agrees with its antecedent.

1. *The World on the Turtle's Back* is a myth that tells about a pregnant woman and how <u>it</u> helped create the earth.

2. Many of the sea creatures and birds tried to retrieve the dirt at the bottom of the ocean, but they could not reach <u>him</u>.

3. The woman circles the earth with <u>their</u> daughter, helping the plants to grow.

4. Both of the twins molded clay animals and gave <u>it</u> life.

2.3 PRONOUN CASE

Personal pronouns change form to show how they function in sentences. Different functions are shown by different **cases.** The three cases are **nominative, objective,** and **possessive.** For examples of these pronouns, see the chart in Section 2.1.

A **nominative pronoun** is used as a subject or a predicate nominative in a sentence.

An **objective pronoun** is used as a direct object, an indirect object, or the object of a preposition.

SUBJECT   OBJECT   OBJECT OF PREPOSITION

He explained it to me.

A **possessive pronoun** shows ownership. The pronouns *mine, yours, hers, his, its, ours,* and *theirs* can be used in place of nouns.

    EXAMPLE: *These letters are yours.*

The pronouns *my, your, her, his, its, our,* and *their* are used before nouns.

    EXAMPLE: *These are your letters.*

WATCH OUT! Many spelling errors can be avoided if you watch out for *its* and *their.* Don't confuse the possessive pronoun *its* with the contraction *it's,* meaning "it is" or "it has." The homonyms *they're* (a contraction of *they are*) and *there* ("in that place") are often mistakenly used for *their.*

TIP To decide which pronoun to use in a comparison, such as "He tells better tales than (I *or* me)," fill in the missing word(s): *He tells better tales than I **tell.***

GRAMMAR PRACTICE

Replace the underlined words in each sentence with an appropriate pronoun and identify the pronoun as a nominative, objective, or possessive pronoun.

1. <u>Arthur Miller</u> was a playwright from New York.

2. *The Crucible* is one of <u>Arthur Miller's</u> most well-known plays.

3. <u>John Proctor and Reverend Parris</u> are two of the main characters.

4. Reverend Hale tries to convince <u>Rebecca Nurse and John Proctor</u> to falsely confess to practicing witchcraft.

5. <u>The Salem witch hunt</u> illustrates how the town's strict Christian principles indirectly caused the deaths of innocent villagers.

2.4 REFLEXIVE AND INTENSIVE PRONOUNS

These pronouns are formed by adding *-self* or *-selves* to certain personal pronouns. Their forms are the same, and they differ only in how they are used.

A **reflexive pronoun** follows a verb or preposition and reflects back on an earlier noun or pronoun.

    EXAMPLES:

    He threw himself forward.

    Danielle mailed herself the package.

Intensive pronouns intensify or emphasize the nouns or pronouns to which they refer.

    EXAMPLES:

    The queen herself would have been amused.

    I saw it myself.

WATCH OUT! Avoid using *hisself* or *theirselves.* Standard English does not include these forms.

    NONSTANDARD: *He had painted hisself into a corner.*

    STANDARD: *He had painted himself into a corner.*

2.5 DEMONSTRATIVE PRONOUNS

Demonstrative pronouns point out things and persons near and far.

	Singular	Plural
Near	this	these
Far	that	those

2.6 INDEFINITE PRONOUNS

Indefinite pronouns do not refer to specific persons or things and usually have no antecedents. The chart shows some commonly used indefinite pronouns.

Singular	Plural	Singular or Plural	
another	both	all	none
anybody	few	any	some
no one	many	more	most
neither	several		

TIP Indefinite pronouns that end in *one*, *body*, or *thing* are always singular.

INCORRECT: *Does anybody think their hamburger is overcooked?*

CORRECT: *Does anybody think his or her hamburger is overcooked?*

If the indefinite pronoun might refer to either a male or a female, *his or her* may be used to refer to it, or the sentence may be rewritten.

EXAMPLES: *Everyone received his or her script.*
All the actors received their scripts.

2.7 INTERROGATIVE PRONOUNS

An **interrogative pronoun** is used to ask a question. The interrogative pronouns are *who, whom, whose, which,* and *what*.

EXAMPLES: *Whose backpack is on the kitchen table?*
Which dress do you prefer?

TIP *Who* is used as a subject, *whom* as an object. To find out which pronoun you need to use in a question, change the question to a statement.

QUESTION: *(Who/Whom) did you meet there?*

STATEMENT: *You met (?) there.*

Since the verb has a subject (*you*), the needed word must be the object form, *whom*.

EXAMPLE: *Whom did you meet there?*

WATCH OUT! A special problem arises when you use an interrupter, such as *do you think*, within a question.

EXAMPLE: *(Who/Whom) do you believe is the more influential musician?*

If you eliminate the interrupter, it is clear that the word you need is *who*.

2.8 RELATIVE PRONOUNS

Relative pronouns relate, or connect, dependent (or subordinate) clauses to the words they modify in sentences. The relative pronouns are *that, what, whatever, which, whichever, who, whoever, whom, whomever,* and *whose*.

Sometimes short sentences with related ideas can be combined by using a relative pronoun.

SHORT SENTENCE: *Mark Twain may be America's greatest humorist.*

RELATED SENTENCE: *Mark Twain wrote* Huckleberry Finn.

COMBINED SENTENCE: *Mark Twain, who wrote* Huckleberry Finn, *may be America's greatest humorist.*

GRAMMAR PRACTICE

Choose the appropriate interrogative or relative pronoun from the words in parentheses.

1. "The Notorious Jumping Frog" was written by Samuel Clemens, (who/whom) wrote under the pseudonym Mark Twain.

2. The story gained national fame for Mark Twain, (who/that) first published it in 1865.

3. (Who/Whom) do you think is funnier, Jim Smiley or the storyteller Simon Wheeler?

4. Smiley spent months educating his frog, (which/whose) fame as a jumper spread throughout the gold camps.

2.9 PRONOUN REFERENCE PROBLEMS

The referent of a pronoun should always be clear.

An **indefinite reference** occurs when the pronoun *it, you,* or *they* does not clearly refer to a specific antecedent.

UNCLEAR: *In the review, it claimed the movie is well done.*

CLEAR: *The review claimed the movie is well done.*

A **general reference** occurs when the pronoun *it, this, that, which,* or *such* is used to refer to a general idea rather than a specific antecedent.

UNCLEAR: *Stella tutors students every day after school. This lets her help kids who are struggling with their schoolwork.*

CLEAR: *Stella tutors students every day after school. Tutoring lets her help kids who are struggling with their schoolwork.*

Ambiguous means "having more than one possible meaning." An **ambiguous reference** occurs when a pronoun could refer to two or more antecedents.

UNCLEAR: *Stacey made Miranda a sandwich while she talked on the phone.*

CLEAR: *While Stacey talked on the phone, she made Miranda a sandwich.*

GRAMMAR PRACTICE

Rewrite the following sentences to correct indefinite, ambiguous, and general pronoun references.

1. In the poem "The Raven," it tells about a man who is grieving for his lover.

2. The raven refused to abandon its perch above the door. This frustrated the narrator.

3. The narrator told the raven that he thought he was a messenger from Lenore.

4. The raven always responded, "Nevermore." This frightened and confused the speaker.

❸ Verbs

A **verb** is a word that expresses an action, a condition, or a state of being.

*For more information, see **Quick Reference: Parts of Speech**, page R50.*

3.1 ACTION VERBS

Action verbs express mental or physical activity.

EXAMPLE: *I walked to the store.*

3.2 LINKING VERBS

Linking verbs join subjects with words or phrases that rename or describe them.

EXAMPLE: *You are my friend.*

3.3 PRINCIPAL PARTS

Action and linking verbs typically have four principal parts, which are used to form verb tenses. The principal parts are the **present,** the **present participle,** the **past,** and the **past participle.**

Action verbs and some linking verbs also fall into two categories: regular and irregular. A **regular verb** is a verb that forms its past and past participle by adding *-ed* or *-d* to the present form.

Present	Present Participle	Past	Past Participle
perform	(is) performing	performed	(has) performed
hope	(is) hoping	hoped	(has) hoped
stop	(is) stopping	stopped	(has) stopped
marry	(is) marrying	married	(has) married

An **irregular verb** is a verb that forms its past and past participle in some other way than by adding *-ed* or *-d* to the present form.

Present	Present Participle	Past	Past Participle
bring	(is) bringing	brought	(has) brought
swim	(is) swimming	swam	(has) swum
steal	(is) stealing	stole	(has) stolen
grow	(is) growing	grew	(has) grown

3.4 VERB TENSE

The **tense** of a verb indicates the time of the action or state of being. An action or state of being can occur in the present, the past, or the future. There are six tenses, each expressing a different range of time.

The **present tense** expresses an action or state that is happening at the present time, occurs regularly, or is constant or generally true. Use the present part.

NOW: *That poet reads well.*

REGULAR: *I swim every day.*

GENERAL: *Time flies.*

The **past tense** expresses an action that began and ended in the past. Use the past part.

EXAMPLE: *The storyteller finished his tale.*

The **future tense** expresses an action or state that will occur. Use *shall* or *will* with the present part.

EXAMPLE: *They will attend the next festival.*

The **present perfect tense** expresses an action or state that (1) was completed at an indefinite time in the past or (2) began in the past and continues into the present. Use *have* or *has* with the past participle.

EXAMPLE: *Poetry has inspired readers throughout the ages.*

The **past perfect tense** expresses an action in the past that came before another action in the past. Use *had* with the past participle.

> **EXAMPLE:** *The witness had testified before the defendant confessed.*

The future perfect tense expresses an action in the future that will be completed before another action in the future. Use *shall have* or *will have* with the past participle.

> **EXAMPLE:** *They will have finished the novel before seeing the movie version of the tale.*

TIP The past-tense form of an irregular verb is not paired with an auxiliary verb, but the past-perfect-tense form of an irregular verb is always paired with an auxiliary verb.

> **INCORRECT:** *I have went to that restaurant before.*
>
> **INCORRECT:** *I gone to that restaurant before.*
>
> **CORRECT:** *I have gone to that restaurant before.*

3.5 PROGRESSIVE FORMS

The progressive forms of the six tenses show ongoing actions. Use forms of *be* with the present participles of verbs.

> **PRESENT PROGRESSIVE:** *She is rehearsing her lines.*
>
> **PAST PROGRESSIVE:** *She was rehearsing her lines.*
>
> **FUTURE PROGRESSIVE:** *She will be rehearsing her lines.*
>
> **PRESENT PERFECT PROGRESSIVE:** *She has been rehearsing her lines.*
>
> **PAST PERFECT PROGRESSIVE:** *She had been rehearsing her lines.*
>
> **FUTURE PERFECT PROGRESSIVE:** *She will have been rehearsing her lines.*

WATCH OUT! Do not shift from tense to tense needlessly. Watch out for these special cases:

- In most compound sentences and in sentences with compound predicates, keep the tenses the same.

> **INCORRECT:** *Every morning they get up and went to work.*
>
> **CORRECT:** *Every morning they get up and go to work.*

- If one past action happened before another, indicate this with a shift in tense.

> **INCORRECT:** *She thought she forgot her toothbrush.*
>
> **CORRECT:** *She thought she had forgotten her toothbrush.*

GRAMMAR PRACTICE

Identify the tense of the verb(s) in each of the following sentences. If you find an unnecessary tense shift, correct it.

1. The setting of *The Crucible* is the late 17th century in Salem, Massachusetts.

2. Before the witch trials ended, people had lost their ability to make objective judgments.

3. Playwright Arthur Miller knew that the play pertains to his own time.

4. People will read it far into the future, and many will apply its message to their own time.

5. In the play some accuse others of being witches, even though they knew the accusation was false.

3.6 ACTIVE AND PASSIVE VOICE

The voice of a verb tells whether its subject performs or receives the action expressed by the verb. When the subject performs the action, the verb is in the **active voice.** When the subject is the receiver of the action, the verb is in the **passive voice.**

Compare these two sentences:

> **ACTIVE:** *The Puritans did not celebrate Christmas.*
>
> **PASSIVE:** *Christmas was not celebrated by the Puritans.*

To form the passive voice, use a form of *be* with the past participle of the verb.

WATCH OUT! Use the passive voice sparingly. It can make writing awkward and less direct.

> **AWKWARD:** *The stories of hysterical witnesses were believed by gullible and fearful jurors.*
>
> **BETTER:** *Gullible and fearful jurors believed the stories of hysterical witnesses.*

There are occasions when you will choose to use the passive voice because

- you want to emphasize the receiver: *The king was shot.*
- the doer is unknown: *My books were stolen.*
- the doer is unimportant: *French is spoken here.*

For the five items below, identify the boldfaced verb phrase as active or passive.

1. *The Crucible* **has played** in theaters throughout the world.

2. It **was written** by Arthur Miller, one of America's greatest dramatists.

3. Miller **did** not **approve** of Reverend Parris's greed for gold.

4. **Has** the reputation of the minister **been maligned?**

4 Modifiers

Modifiers are words or groups of words that change or limit the meanings of other words. Adjectives and adverbs are common modifiers.

4.1 ADJECTIVES

Adjectives modify nouns and pronouns by telling which one, what kind, how many, or how much.

WHICH ONE: *this, that, these, those*

EXAMPLE: *That couch needs to be reupholstered.*

WHAT KIND: *large, unique, anxious, moldy*

EXAMPLE: *The anxious speaker shuffled through her notes.*

HOW MANY: *ten, many, several, every, each*

EXAMPLE: *Each child grabbed several candies from the bowl.*

HOW MUCH: *more, less, little*

EXAMPLE: *There was more snow on the ground in the morning.*

4.2 PREDICATE ADJECTIVES

Most adjectives come before the nouns they modify, as in the previous examples. A **predicate adjective,** however, follows a linking verb and describes the subject.

EXAMPLE: *My friends are very intelligent.*

Be especially careful to use adjectives (not adverbs) after such linking verbs as *look, feel, grow, taste,* and *smell.*

EXAMPLE: *The weather grows cold.*

4.3 ADVERBS

Adverbs modify verbs, adjectives, and other adverbs by telling where, when, how, or to what extent.

WHERE: *The children played outside.*

WHEN: *The author spoke yesterday.*

HOW: *We walked slowly behind the leader.*

TO WHAT EXTENT: *He worked very hard.*

Adverbs may occur in many places in sentences, both before and after the words they modify.

EXAMPLES: *Suddenly the wind shifted.*

The wind suddenly shifted.

The wind shifted suddenly.

4.4 ADJECTIVE OR ADVERB?

Many adverbs are formed by adding *-ly* to adjectives.

EXAMPLES: *sweet, sweetly; gentle, gently*

However, *-ly* added to a noun will usually yield an adjective.

EXAMPLES: *friend, friendly; woman, womanly*

4.5 COMPARISON OF MODIFIERS

Modifiers can be used to compare two or more things. The form of a modifier shows the degree of comparison. Both adjectives and adverbs have three forms: the **positive,** the **comparative,** and the **superlative.**

The **positive form** is used to describe individual things, groups, or actions.

EXAMPLES:
Stephen Crane was a great writer.
His descriptions are vivid.

The **comparative form** is used to compare two things, groups, or actions.

EXAMPLES:
I think that Stephen Crane was a greater writer than Jack London.
Crane's descriptions are more vivid.

The **superlative form** is used to compare more than two things, groups, or actions.

EXAMPLES:
I think that Crane was the greatest writer of his era.
Crane's descriptions are the most vivid I have ever read.

4.6 REGULAR COMPARISONS

Most one-syllable and some two-syllable adjectives and adverbs have comparatives and superlatives formed by adding -er and -est. All three-syllable and most two-syllable modifiers have comparatives and superlatives formed with *more* and *most*.

Modifier	Comparative	Superlative
tall	taller	tallest
kind	kinder	kindest
droopy	droopier	droopiest
expensive	more expensive	most expensive
wasteful	more wasteful	most wasteful

WATCH OUT! Note that spelling changes must sometimes be made to form the comparatives and superlatives of modifiers.

EXAMPLES:

friendly, friendlier (Change *y* to *i* and add the ending.)
sad, sadder (Double the final consonant and add the ending.)

4.7 IRREGULAR COMPARISONS

Some commonly used modifiers have irregular comparative and superlative forms. They are listed in the following chart.

Modifier	Comparative	Superlative
good	better	best
bad	worse	worst
far	farther *or* further	farthest *or* furthest
little	less *or* lesser	least
many	more	most
well	better	best
much	more	most

4.8 PROBLEMS WITH MODIFIERS

Study the tips that follow to avoid common mistakes:

Farther and **Further** Use *farther* for distances; use *further* for everything else.

Double Comparisons Make a comparison by using *-er/-est* or by using *more/most*. Using *-er* with *more* or using *-est* with *most* is incorrect.

INCORRECT: *I like her more better than she likes me.*

CORRECT: *I like her better than she likes me.*

Illogical Comparisons An illogical or confusing comparison results when two unrelated things are compared or when something is compared with itself. The word *other* or the word *else* should be used in a comparison of an individual member to the rest of a group.

ILLOGICAL: *The narrator was more curious about the war than any student in his class.* (implies that the narrator isn't a student in the class)

LOGICAL: *The narrator was more curious about the war than any other student in his class.* (identifies that the narrator is a student)

Bad vs. **Badly** *Bad*, always an adjective, is used before a noun or after a linking verb. *Badly*, always an adverb, never modifies a noun. Be sure to use the right form after a linking verb.

INCORRECT: *Ed felt badly after his team lost.*

CORRECT: *Ed felt bad after his team lost.*

Good vs. **Well** *Good* is always an adjective. It is used before a noun or after a linking verb. *Well* is often an adverb meaning "expertly" or "properly." *Well* can also be used as an adjective after a linking verb when it means "in good health."

INCORRECT: *Helen writes very good.*

CORRECT: *Helen writes very well.*

CORRECT: *Yesterday I felt bad; today I feel well.*

Double Negatives If you add a negative word to a sentence that is already negative, the result will be an error known as a double negative. When using *not* or *-n't* with a verb, use *any-* words, such as *anybody* or *anything*, rather than *no-* words, such as *nobody* or *nothing*, later in the sentence.

INCORRECT: *I don't have no money.*

CORRECT: *I don't have any money.*

Using *hardly*, *barely*, or *scarcely* after a negative word is also incorrect.

INCORRECT: *They couldn't barely see two feet ahead.*

CORRECT: *They could barely see two feet ahead.*

Misplaced Modifiers Sometimes a modifier is placed so far away from the word it modifies that the intended meaning of the sentence is unclear. Prepositional phrases and participial phrases are often misplaced. Place modifiers as close as possible to the words they modify.

> **MISPLACED:** *The ranger explained how to find ducks in her office.* (The ducks were not in the ranger's office.)

> **CLEARER:** *In her office, the ranger explained how to find ducks.*

Dangling Modifiers Sometimes a modifier doesn't appear to modify any word in a sentence. Most dangling modifiers are participial phrases or infinitive phrases.

> **DANGLING:** *Coming home with groceries, our parrot said, "Hello!"*

> **CLEARER:** *Coming home with groceries, we heard our parrot say, "Hello!"*

GRAMMAR PRACTICE

Choose the correct word or words from each pair in parentheses.

1. Flannery O'Connor's story is (better/more better) than other stories I have read recently.

2. Mr. Shiftlet and Mrs. Crater (could/couldn't) hardly be less honest with each other.

3. Mr. Shiftlet says there isn't (any/no) broken thing on the farm that he can't fix.

4. He feels (good/well) about fixing the car.

5. Who do you think is the (stranger/strangest) person—Mr. Shiftlet or Mrs. Crater?

6. Mr. Shiftlet feels (bad/badly) about the rottenness of the world.

7. As Mr. Shiftlet drove on alone he felt (depresseder/more depressed) than ever.

8. Mr. Shiftlet didn't feel very (well/good) about being alone, so he picked up a hitchhiker.

9. One wonders how many other great stories Flannery O'Connor would have written had she lived (longer/more longer).

5 Prepositions, Conjunctions, and Interjections

5.1 PREPOSITIONS

A preposition is a word used to show the relationship between a noun or a pronoun and another word in the sentence.

Commonly Used Prepositions			
above	down	near	through
at	for	of	to
before	from	on	up
below	in	out	with
by	into	over	without

A preposition is always followed by a word or group of words that serves as its object. The preposition, its object, and modifiers of the object are called the **prepositional phrase.** In each example below, the prepositional phrase is highlighted and the object of the preposition is in boldface type.

> **EXAMPLES:**
> *The future of the entire **kingdom** is uncertain.*
> *We searched through the deepest **woods.***

Prepositional phrases may be used as adjectives or as adverbs. The phrase in the first example is used as an adjective modifying the noun *future.* In the second example, the phrase is used as an adverb modifying the verb *searched.*

WATCH OUT! Prepositional phrases must be as close as possible to the word they modify.

> **MISPLACED:** *We have clothes for leisurewear of many colors.*

> **CLEARER:** *We have clothes of many colors for leisurewear.*

5.2 CONJUNCTIONS

A conjunction is a word used to connect words, phrases, or sentences. There are three kinds of conjunctions: **coordinating conjunctions, correlative conjunctions,** and **subordinating conjunctions.**

Coordinating conjunctions connect words or word groups that have the same function in a sentence. They include *and, but, or, for, so, yet,* and *nor.*

Coordinating conjunctions can join nouns, pronouns, verbs, adjectives, adverbs, prepositional phrases, and clauses in a sentence.

These examples show coordinating conjunctions joining words of the same function:

EXAMPLES:

I have many friends but few enemies. (two noun objects)

We ran out the door and into the street. (two prepositional phrases)

They are pleasant yet seem aloof. (two predicates)

We have to go now, or we will be late. (two clauses)

Correlative conjunctions are similar to coordinating conjunctions. However, correlative conjunctions are always used in pairs.

Correlative Conjunctions		
both . . . and	neither . . . nor	whether . . . or
either . . . or	not only . . . but also	

Subordinating conjunctions introduce subordinate clauses—clauses that cannot stand by themselves as complete sentences. The subordinating conjunction shows how the subordinate clause relates to the rest of the sentence. The relationships include time, manner, place, cause, comparison, condition, and purpose.

Subordinating Conjunctions	
Time	*after, as, as long as, as soon as, before, since, until, when, whenever, while*
Manner	*as, as if*
Place	*where, wherever*
Cause	*because, since*
Comparison	*as, as much as, than*
Condition	*although, as long as, even if, even though, if, provided that, though, unless, while*
Purpose	*in order that, so that, that*

In the example below, the boldface word is the conjunction, and the highlighted words form a subordinate clause:

EXAMPLE: *Walt Whitman was a man of the people,* **although** *many did not appreciate his poems.*

Walt Whitman was a man of the people is an independent clause, because it can stand alone as a complete sentence. *Although many did not appreciate his poems* cannot stand alone as a complete sentence; it is thus a subordinate clause.

Conjunctive adverbs are used to connect clauses that can stand by themselves as sentences. Conjunctive adverbs include *also, besides, finally, however, moreover, nevertheless, otherwise,* and *then.*

EXAMPLE: *She loved the fall; however, she also enjoyed winter.*

5.3 INTERJECTIONS

Interjections are words used to show emotion, such as *wow* and *cool.* Interjections are usually set off from the rest of a sentence by a comma or by an exclamation mark.

EXAMPLE: *Thoreau lived in the woods by himself. Amazing!*

6 The Sentence and Its Parts

A **sentence** is a group of words used to express a complete thought. A complete sentence has a subject and a predicate.

For more information, see **Quick Reference: The Sentence and Its Parts,** *page R52.*

6.1 KINDS OF SENTENCES

There are four basic types of sentences.

Type	Definition	Example
Declarative	states a fact, a wish, an intent, or a feeling	I wrote an essay on "The Weary Blues" for class.
Interrogative	asks a question	Are you familiar with Langston Hughes?
Imperative	gives a command or direction	Read "The Weary Blues" aloud.
Exclamatory	expresses strong feeling or excitement	It sounds like a song!

6.2 COMPOUND SUBJECTS AND PREDICATES

A compound subject consists of two or more subjects that share the same verb. They are typically joined by the coordinating conjunction *and* or *or.*

EXAMPLE: *Courtney and Eric enjoy the theater.*

A compound predicate consists of two or more predicates that share the same subject. They too are typically joined by a coordinating conjunction, usually *and, but,* or *or.*

EXAMPLE: *The main character in "Winter Dreams" attended a prestigious university and became a successful businessman.*

6.3 COMPLEMENTS

A **complement** is a word or group of words that completes the meaning of the sentence. Some sentences contain only a subject and a verb. Most sentences, however, require additional words placed after the verb to complete the meaning of the sentence. There are three kinds of complements: direct objects, indirect objects, and subject complements.

Direct objects are words or word groups that receive the action of action verbs. A direct object answers the question *what* or *whom*.

> **EXAMPLES:**
>
> *The students asked many questions.* (Asked what?)
>
> *The teacher quickly answered the students.* (Answered whom?)

Indirect objects tell to whom or what or for whom or what the actions of verbs are performed. Indirect objects come before direct objects. In the examples that follow, the indirect objects are highlighted.

> **EXAMPLES:**
>
> My sister usually gave her *friends* good advice. (Gave to whom?)
>
> Her brother sent the store *a heavy package.* (Sent to what?)

Subject complements come after linking verbs and identify or describe the subjects. A subject complement that names or identifies a subject is called a **predicate nominative.** Predicate nominatives include **predicate nouns** and **predicate pronouns.**

> **EXAMPLES:**
>
> *My friends are very hard workers.*
>
> *The best writer in the class is she.*

A subject complement that describes a subject is called a **predicate adjective.**

> **EXAMPLE:** *The pianist appeared very energetic.*

7 Phrases

A **phrase** is a group of related words that does not contain a subject and a predicate but functions in a sentence as a single part of speech.

7.1 PREPOSITIONAL PHRASES

A **prepositional phrase** is a phrase that consists of a preposition, its object, and any modifiers of the object. Prepositional phrases that modify nouns or pronouns are called **adjective phrases.** Prepositional phrases that modify verbs, adjectives, or adverbs are **adverb phrases.**

> **ADJECTIVE PHRASE:** *The central character of the story is a villain.*
>
> **ADVERB PHRASE:** *He reveals his nature in the first scene.*

7.2 APPOSITIVES AND APPOSITIVE PHRASES

An **appositive** is a noun or pronoun that identifies or renames another noun or pronoun. An **appositive phrase** includes an appositive and modifiers of it.

An appositive can be either **essential** or **nonessential.** An **essential appositive** provides information that is needed to identify what is referred to by the preceding noun or pronoun.

> **EXAMPLE:** The Glass Menagerie *was written by playwright Tennessee Williams.*

A **nonessential appositive** adds extra information about a noun or pronoun whose meaning is already clear. Nonessential appositives and appositive phrases are set off with commas.

> **EXAMPLE:** *Williams uses Laura's glass menagerie, a collection of fragile animal figurines, to represent her relationship to reality.*

8 Verbals and Verbal Phrases

A **verbal** is a verb form that is used as a noun, an adjective, or an adverb. A **verbal phrase** consists of a verbal along with its modifiers and complements. There are three kinds of verbals: **infinitives, participles,** and **gerunds.**

8.1 INFINITIVES AND INFINITIVE PHRASES

An **infinitive** is a verb form that usually begins with *to* and functions as a noun, an adjective, or an adverb. An **infinitive phrase** consists of an infinitive plus its modifiers and complements. The examples that follow show several uses of infinitive phrases.

> **NOUN:** *To know her is my only desire.* (subject)
>
> *I'm planning to walk with you.* (direct object)
>
> *Her goal was to promote women's rights.* (predicate nominative)
>
> **ADJECTIVE:** *We saw his need to be loved.* (adjective modifying *need*)
>
> **ADVERB:** *She wrote to voice her opinions.* (adverb modifying *wrote*)

Because infinitives usually begin with *to,* it is usually easy to recognize them. However, sometimes *to* may be omitted.

> **EXAMPLE:** *Let no one dare [to] enter this shrine.*

8.2 PARTICIPLES AND PARTICIPIAL PHRASES

A **participle** is a verb form that functions as an adjective. Like adjectives, participles modify nouns and pronouns. Most participles are present-participle forms, ending in *-ing,* or past-participle forms ending in *-ed* or *-en.* In the examples that follow, the participles are highlighted:

> MODIFYING A NOUN: *The jogging woman completed another lap on the track.*

> MODIFYING A PRONOUN: *Bored, he began to doodle in the margins of his notebook.*

Participial phrases are participles with all their modifiers and complements.

> MODIFYING A NOUN: *Changing tactics, the attorney questioned the witness.*

> MODIFYING A PRONOUN: *Dismissed for the day, they filed out of the courtroom.*

8.3 DANGLING AND MISPLACED PARTICIPLES

A participle or participial phrase should be placed as close as possible to the word that it modifies. Otherwise the meaning of the sentence may not be clear.

> MISPLACED: *The boys were looking for squirrels searching the trees.*

> CLEARER: *The boys searching the trees were looking for squirrels.*

A participle or participial phrase that does not clearly modify anything in a sentence is called a **dangling participle.** A dangling participle causes confusion because it appears to modify a word that it cannot sensibly modify. Correct a dangling participle by providing a word for the participle to modify.

> DANGLING: *Running like the wind, my hat fell off.* (The hat wasn't running.)

> CLEARER: *Running like the wind, I lost my hat.*

8.4 GERUNDS AND GERUND PHRASES

A **gerund** is a verb form ending in *-ing* that functions as a noun. Gerunds may perform any function nouns perform.

> SUBJECT: *Running is my favorite pastime.*

> DIRECT OBJECT: *I truly love running.*

> INDIRECT OBJECT: *You should give running a try.*

> SUBJECT COMPLEMENT: *My deepest passion is running.*

> OBJECT OF PREPOSITION: *Her love of running keeps her strong.*

Gerund phrases are gerunds with all their modifiers and complements.

> SUBJECT: *Wishing on a star never got me far.*

> OBJECT OF PREPOSITION: *I will finish before leaving the office.*

> APPOSITIVE: *Her avocation, flying airplanes, finally led to full-time employment.*

GRAMMAR PRACTICE

Identify the underlined phrases as appositive phrases, infinitive phrases, participial phrases, or gerund phrases.

1. In "The Masque of the Red Death," Poe uses allegory, <u>a device representing abstract qualities.</u>

2. <u>To escape the plague,</u> Prince Prospero seals himself and his courtiers in a walled abbey.

3. <u>Feeling protected from the Red Death,</u> Prospero holds a lavish masquerade ball.

4. There suddenly appears in the last room a masked figure, <u>the Red Death in a ghastly shroud.</u>

5. <u>Killing the apparition</u> is impossible.

9 Clauses

A **clause** is a group of words that contains a subject and a verb. There are two kinds of clauses: independent clauses and subordinate clauses.

9.1 INDEPENDENT AND SUBORDINATE CLAUSES

An **independent clause** can stand alone as a sentence, as the word *independent* suggests.

> INDEPENDENT CLAUSE: *Frederick Douglass was an eloquent speaker.*

A sentence may contain more than one independent clause.

> EXAMPLE: *Frederick Douglass was an eloquent speaker, but he encountered a lot of opposition.*

In the preceding example, the coordinating conjunction *but* joins two independent clauses.

For more information, see **Conjunctions,** *page R63.*

A **subordinate clause** cannot stand alone as a sentence. It is subordinate to, or dependent on, an independent clause.

> **EXAMPLE:** *Although Frederick Douglass was a runaway slave, he frequently appeared in public to raise support for the abolitionist movement.*

The highlighted clause cannot stand by itself; it must be joined with an independent clause to form a complete sentence.

9.2 ADJECTIVE CLAUSES

An **adjective clause** is a subordinate clause used as an adjective. It usually follows the noun or pronoun it modifies. Adjective clauses are typically introduced by the relative pronoun *who, whom, whose, which,* or *that.*

> **EXAMPLES:** *Frederick Douglass wrote objectively about the whippings that Corey frequently gave him.*
>
> *The autobiographer whom I liked best was Frederick Douglass.*
>
> *He was a man who was determined to find freedom.*

*For more information, see **Relative Pronouns**, page R58.*

An adjective clause can be either essential or nonessential. An **essential adjective clause** provides information that is necessary to identify the preceding noun or pronoun.

> **EXAMPLE:** *The couch that we picked out will not be delivered for three weeks.*

A **nonessential adjective clause** adds additional information about a noun or pronoun whose meaning is already clear. Nonessential clauses are set off with commas.

> **EXAMPLE:** *Joel's grandmother, who was born in Italy, makes the best lasagna.*

TIP The relative pronouns *whom, which,* and *that* may sometimes be omitted when they are objects in adjective clauses.

> **EXAMPLE:** *The autobiographer [whom] I liked best was Frederick Douglass.*

9.3 ADVERB CLAUSES

An **adverb clause** is a subordinate clause that is used to modify a verb, an adjective, or an adverb. It is introduced by a subordinating conjunction.

*For more information, see **Conjunctions**, page R63.*

Adverb clauses typically occur at the beginning or end of sentences.

> **MODIFYING A VERB:** *When we need you, we will call.*
>
> **MODIFYING AN ADVERB:** *I'll stay here where there is shelter from the rain.*
>
> **MODIFYING AN ADJECTIVE:** *Roman felt as good as he had ever felt.*

9.4 NOUN CLAUSES

A **noun clause** is a subordinate clause that is used as a noun. A noun clause may be used as a subject, a direct object, an indirect object, a predicate nominative, or the object of a preposition. Noun clauses are introduced either by pronouns, such as *that, what, who, whoever, which,* and *whose,* or by subordinating conjunctions, such as *how, when, where, why,* and *whether.*

*For more information, see **Conjunctions**, page R63.*

TIP Because the same words may introduce adjective and noun clauses, you need to consider how a clause functions within its sentence. To determine if a clause is a noun clause, try substituting *something* or *someone* for the clause. If you can do it, it is probably a noun clause.

> **EXAMPLES:** *I know whose woods these are.*
>
> ("I know *something*." The clause is a noun clause, direct object of the verb *know*.)
>
> *Give a copy to whoever wants one.* ("Give a copy to *someone*." The clause is a noun clause, object of the preposition *to*.)

⑩ The Structure of Sentences

When classified by their structure, there are four kinds of sentences: simple, compound, complex, and compound-complex.

10.1 SIMPLE SENTENCES

A **simple sentence** is a sentence that has one independent clause and no subordinate clauses. Various parts of simple sentences may be compound, and simple sentences may contain grammatical structures such as appositive and verbal phrases.

> **EXAMPLES:**
>
> *Ambrose Bierce and Stephen Crane, two great American writers, both wrote during the latter half of the 19th century.* (compound subject and an appositive)
>
> *Crane, best known for writing fiction, also wrote great poetry.* (participial phrase containing a gerund phrase)

10.2 COMPOUND SENTENCES

A **compound sentence** consists of two or more independent clauses. The clauses in compound sentences are joined with commas and coordinating conjunctions (*and, but, or, nor, yet, for, so*) or with semicolons. Like simple sentences, compound sentences do not contain any subordinate clauses.

> **EXAMPLES:**
>
> *I enjoyed the free pottery class, and I would like to go again.*
>
> *Carl Sandburg's "Chicago" seems to celebrate the youthful energy of a booming industrial city; however, the poem dwells on the negative impacts of growth.*

WATCH OUT! Do not confuse compound sentences with simple sentences that have compound parts.

> **EXAMPLE:** *The center fielder caught the ball and immediately threw it toward second base.* (Here *and* joins parts of a compound predicate, not a compound sentence.)

10.3 COMPLEX SENTENCES

A **complex sentence** consists of one independent clause and one or more subordinate clauses. Each subordinate clause can be used as a noun or as a modifier. If it is used as a modifier, a subordinate clause usually modifies a word in the independent clause, and the independent clause can stand alone. However, when a subordinate clause is a noun clause, it is a part of the independent clause; the two cannot be separated.

> **MODIFIER:** *One should not complain unless one has a better solution.*
>
> **NOUN CLAUSE:** *We sketched pictures of whoever we wished.* (The noun clause is the object of the preposition *of* and cannot be separated from the rest of the sentence.)

10.4 COMPOUND-COMPLEX SENTENCES

A **compound-complex sentence** contains two or more independent clauses and one or more subordinate clauses. Compound-complex sentences are, simply, both compound and complex. If you start with a compound sentence, all you need to do to form a compound-complex sentence is add a subordinate clause.

> **COMPOUND:** *All the students knew the answer, yet they were too shy to volunteer.*
>
> **COMPOUND-COMPLEX:** *All the students knew the answer that their teacher expected, yet they were too shy to volunteer.*

10.5 PARALLEL STRUCTURE

When you write sentences, make sure that coordinate parts are equivalent, or **parallel,** in structure.

> **NOT PARALLEL:** *Erin loved basketball and to play hockey.* (*Basketball* is a noun; *to play hockey* is a phrase.)
>
> **PARALLEL:** *Erin loved basketball and hockey.* (*Basketball* and *hockey* are both nouns.)
>
> **NOT PARALLEL:** *He wanted to rent an apartment, a new car, and traveling around the country.* (*To rent* is an infinitive, *car* is a noun, and *traveling* is a gerund.)
>
> **PARALLEL:** *He wanted to rent an apartment, to drive a new car, and to travel around the country.* (*To rent, to drive,* and *to travel* are all infinitives.)

11 Writing Complete Sentences

Remember, a sentence is a group of words that expresses a complete thought. In formal writing, try to avoid both sentence fragments and run-on sentences.

11.1 CORRECTING FRAGMENTS

A **sentence fragment** is a group of words that is only part of a sentence. It does not express a complete thought and may be confusing to a reader or listener. A sentence fragment may be lacking a subject, a predicate, or both.

> **FRAGMENT:** *Waited for the boat to arrive.* (no subject)
>
> **CORRECTED:** *We waited for the boat to arrive.*
>
> **FRAGMENT:** *People of various races, ages, and creeds.* (no predicate)
>
> **CORRECTED:** *People of various races, ages, and creeds gathered together.*
>
> **FRAGMENT:** *Near the old cottage.* (neither subject nor predicate)
>
> **CORRECTED:** *The burial ground is near the old cottage.*

In your writing, fragments may be a result of haste or incorrect punctuation. Sometimes fixing a fragment will be a matter of attaching it to a preceding or following sentence.

> **FRAGMENT:** *We saw the two girls. Waiting for the bus to arrive.*
>
> **CORRECTED:** *We saw the two girls waiting for the bus to arrive.*

11.2 CORRECTING RUN-ON SENTENCES

A **run-on sentence** is made up of two or more sentences written as though they were one. Some run-ons have no punctuation within them. Others may have only commas where conjunctions or stronger punctuation marks are necessary. Use your judgment in correcting run-on sentences, as you have choices. You can make a run-on two sentences if the thoughts are not closely connected. If the thoughts are closely related, you can keep the run-on as one sentence by adding a semicolon or a conjunction.

RUN-ON: *We found a place for the picnic by a small pond it was three miles from the village.*

MAKE TWO SENTENCES: *We found a place for the picnic by a small pond. It was three miles from the village.*

RUN-ON: *We found a place for the picnic by a small pond it was perfect.*

USE A SEMICOLON: *We found a place for the picnic by a small pond; it was perfect.*

ADD A CONJUNCTION: *We found a place for the picnic by a small pond, and it was perfect.*

WATCH OUT! When you form compound sentences, make sure you use appropriate punctuation: a comma before a coordinating conjunction, a semicolon when there is no coordinating conjunction. A very common mistake is to use a comma alone instead of a comma and a conjunction. This error is called a **comma splice.**

INCORRECT: *He finished the apprenticeship, he left the village.*

CORRECT: *He finished the apprenticeship, and he left the village.*

GRAMMAR PRACTICE

Rewrite the following paragraph, correcting all fragments and run-ons.

The narrator in Charlotte Perkins Gilman's story "The Yellow Wallpaper" expects that her husband will laugh at her, that's an odd response, in my opinion. She could have lived more happily. If the relationship between her and her husband were an equal partnership. We can acknowledge that men and women may be different in some ways. Without believing that they are as different as this story suggests. The male character acts practical and "strong," the female character acts nervous and weak.

12 Subject-Verb Agreement

The subject and verb in a clause must agree in number. Agreement means that if the subject is singular, the verb is also singular, and if the subject is plural, the verb is also plural.

12.1 BASIC AGREEMENT

Fortunately, agreement between subjects and verbs in English is simple. Most verbs show the difference between singular and plural only in the third person of the present tense. In the present tense, the third-person singular form ends in -*s*.

Present-Tense Verb Forms	
Singular	**Plural**
I eat	we eat
you eat	you eat
she, he, it eats	they eat

12.2 AGREEMENT WITH *BE*

The verb *be* presents special problems in agreement, because this verb does not follow the usual verb patterns.

Forms of *Be*			
Present Tense		**Past Tense**	
Singular	**Plural**	**Singular**	**Plural**
I am	we are	I was	we were
you are	you are	you were	you were
she, he, it is	they are	she, he, it was	they were

12.3 WORDS BETWEEN SUBJECT AND VERB

A verb agrees only with its subject. When words come between a subject and a verb, ignore them when considering proper agreement. Identify the subject, and make sure the verb agrees with it.

EXAMPLES:

A story in the newspapers tells about the 1890s.

Dad as well as Mom reads the paper daily.

12.4 AGREEMENT WITH COMPOUND SUBJECTS

Use plural verbs with most compound subjects joined by the word *and*.

> **EXAMPLE:** *My mother and her sisters call each other every Sunday.*

To confirm that you need a plural verb, you could substitute the plural pronoun *they* for *my mother and her sisters.*

If a compound subject is thought of as a unit, use a singular verb. Test this by substituting the singular pronoun *it.*

> **EXAMPLE:** *Liver and onions [it] is Robert's least favorite dish.*

Use a singular verb with a compound subject that is preceded by *each, every,* or *many a.*

> **EXAMPLE:** *Not every dog and cat at the shelter makes a good pet.*

When the parts of a compound subject are joined by *or, nor,* or the correlative conjunctions *either . . . or* or *neither . . . nor,* make the verb agree with the noun or pronoun nearest the verb.

> **EXAMPLES:**
> *Baseball or football is my favorite sport.*
> *Either my rabbits or my turtle was loose in my room.*
> *Neither Mrs. Howard nor her two sons were home at the time of the accident.*

12.5 PERSONAL PRONOUNS AS SUBJECTS

When using a personal pronoun as a subject, make sure to match it with the correct form of the verb *be.* (See the chart in Section 12.2.) Note especially that the pronoun *you* takes the forms *are* and *were,* regardless of whether it is singular or plural.

WATCH OUT! *You is* and *you was* are nonstandard forms and should be avoided in writing and speaking. *We was* and *they was* are also forms to be avoided.

> **INCORRECT:** *You is facing the wrong direction.*
> **CORRECT:** *You are facing the wrong direction.*
> **INCORRECT:** *We was telling ghost stories.*
> **CORRECT:** *We were telling ghost stories.*

12.6 INDEFINITE PRONOUNS AS SUBJECTS

Some indefinite pronouns are always singular; some are always plural.

Singular Indefinite Pronouns			
another	either	neither	one
anybody	everybody	nobody	somebody
anyone	everyone	no one	someone
anything	everything	nothing	something
each	much		

> **EXAMPLES:**
> *Each of the writers was given an award.*
> *Somebody in the room upstairs is sleeping.*

Plural Indefinite Pronouns			
both	few	many	several

> **EXAMPLES:**
> *Many of the books in our library are not in circulation.*
> *Few have been returned recently.*

Still other indefinite pronouns may be either singular or plural.

Singular or Plural Indefinite Pronouns		
all	more	none
any	most	some

The number of the indefinite pronoun *any* or *none* often depends on the intended meaning.

> **EXAMPLES:**
> *Any of these topics has potential for a good article.* (any one topic)
> *Any of these topics have potential for good articles.* (all of the many topics)

The indefinite pronouns *all, some, more, most,* and *none* are singular when they refer to quantities or parts of things. They are plural when they refer to numbers of individual things. Context will usually give a clue.

> **EXAMPLES:**
> *All of the flour is gone.* (referring to a quantity)
> *All of the flowers are gone.* (referring to individual items)

12.7 INVERTED SENTENCES

Problems in agreement often occur in inverted sentences beginning with *here* or *there;* in questions beginning with *how, when, why, where,* or *what;* and in inverted sentences beginning with phrases. Identify the subject—wherever it is—before deciding on the verb.

EXAMPLES:

There clearly are far too many cooks in this kitchen.

What is the correct ingredient for this stew?

Far from the embroiled cooks stands the master chef.

GRAMMAR PRACTICE

Locate the subject of each clause in the sentences below. Then choose the correct verb.

1. Many poets have written great poetry, but few (is/are) as talented as Emily Dickinson.

2. There (is/are) many lines in her work that her readers (treasures/treasure).

3. Some of her readers (appreciates/appreciate) her use of dashes, while others (finds/find) it confusing.

4. Each of her poems (presents/present) an idea to think about.

5. What (is/are) the dominant vowel sound in the last four lines of "Much Madness is divinest Sense"?

6. The consonant that prevails in the same poem (seems/seem) to be *s.*

7. I can't decide whether the poem's sound or its ideas (is/are) more striking.

12.8 SENTENCES WITH PREDICATE NOMINATIVES

When a predicate nominative serves as a complement in a sentence, use a verb that agrees with the subject, not the complement.

EXAMPLES:

The hunting habits of the North American wolf are an example of how change in the environment affects animals. (The subject is the plural noun *habits*—not *wolf*—and it takes the plural verb *are.*)

An example of how change in the environment affects animals is seen in the hunting habits of the North American wolf. (The subject is the singular noun *example,* and it takes the singular verb *is seen.*)

12.9 *DON'T* AND *DOESN'T* AS AUXILIARY VERBS

The auxiliary verb *doesn't* is used with singular subjects and with the personal pronouns *she, he,* and *it.* The auxiliary verb *don't* is used with plural subjects and with the personal pronouns *I, we, you,* and *they.*

SINGULAR: *She doesn't have a costume for the rehearsal.*

Doesn't the doctor have an appointment Wednesday morning?

PLURAL: *They don't think they did very well on that math test.*

The cats don't need to be fed more than twice a day.

12.10 COLLECTIVE NOUNS AS SUBJECTS

Collective nouns are singular nouns that name groups of persons or things. *Team,* for example, is the collective name of a group of individuals. A collective noun takes a singular verb when the group acts as a single unit. It takes a plural verb when the members of the group act separately.

EXAMPLES:

Our team usually wins. (The team as a whole wins.)

Our team vote differently on most issues. (The individual members vote.)

12.11 RELATIVE PRONOUNS AS SUBJECTS

When the relative pronoun *who, which,* or *that* is used as a subject in an adjective clause, the verb in the clause must agree in number with the antecedent of the pronoun.

SINGULAR: *Have you selected one of the poems that is meaningful to you?*

The antecedent of the relative pronoun *that* is the singular *one;* therefore, *that* is singular and must take the singular verb *is.*

PLURAL: *The fairy tales, which have been collected from many different sources, are annotated.*

The antecedent of the relative pronoun *which* is the plural *fairy tales. Which* is plural, and it takes the plural verb *have been collected.*

The key to becoming an independent reader is to develop a toolkit of vocabulary strategies. By learning and practicing the strategies, you'll know what to do when you encounter unfamiliar words while reading. You'll also know how to refine the words you use for different situations—personal, school, and work.

Being a good speller is important when communicating your ideas in writing. Learning basic spelling rules and checking your spelling in a dictionary will help you spell words that you may not use frequently.

VOCABULARY PRACTICE

For more practice, go to the **Vocabulary Center** at **ClassZone.com.**

1 Using Context Clues

The context of a word is made up of the punctuation marks, words, sentences, and paragraphs that surround the word. A word's context can give you important clues about its meaning.

1.1 GENERAL CONTEXT

Sometimes you need to infer the meaning of an unfamiliar word by reading all the information in a passage.

> *I told my parents I wanted to quit playing the piano, but they told me to persevere anyway.*

You can figure out from the context that *persevere* means "continue."

1.2 SPECIFIC CONTEXT CLUES

Sometimes writers help you understand the meanings of words by providing specific clues such as those shown in the chart.

1.3 IDIOMS, SLANG, AND FIGURATIVE LANGUAGE

Use context clues to figure out the meanings of idioms, figurative language, and slang.

An **idiom** is an expression whose overall meaning is different from the meaning of the individual words.

> *If you're going to buy a house with a garden, you'd better have a green thumb. (Green thumb means "ability to grow plants.")*

Figurative language is language that communicates meaning beyond the literal meaning of the words. Note this example from "A Chip of Glass Ruby" by Nadine Gordimer:

> *There was the feeling, in the house, that he had wept and raged at her, that boulders of reproach had thundered down upon her absence, and yet he had said not one word. (Boulders of reproach had thundered down upon her absence means he was very angry that she was gone.)*

Slang is informal language composed of made-up words and ordinary words that are used to mean something different from their meanings in formal English.

> *My parents freaked out when I told them that I went to the concert without their permission. (Freaked out means "became greatly distressed.")*

Specific Context Clues		
Type of Clue	**Key Words/ Phrases**	**Example**
Definition or restatement of the meaning of the word	or, which is, that is, in other words, also known as, also called	*Perennials*—**plants that live for more than two years**—make up only one-third of the garden's exhibit.
Example following an unfamiliar word	such as, like, as if, for example, especially, including	Their new apartment was *arrayed* with many beautiful things, **such as a crystal lamp and a porcelain vase.**
Comparison with a more familiar word or concept	as, like, also, similar to, in the same way, likewise	The prairie grasses *undulated* in the wind **like the waves in the ocean.**
Contrast with a familiar word or experience	unlike, but, however, although, on the other hand, on the contrary	My dog is usually very **calm, unlike** our neighbor's dog, which is very *rowdy*.

*For more information, see **Vocabulary Strategy: Context Clues**, pages 210 and 1000, and **Vocabulary Strategy: Idioms**, page 1200.*

2 Analyzing Word Structure

Many words can be broken into smaller parts, such as base words, roots, prefixes, and suffixes.

2.1 BASE WORDS

A **base word** is a word part that by itself is also a word. Other words or word parts can be added to base words to form new words.

2.2 ROOTS

A **root** is a word part that contains the core meaning of the word. Many English words contain roots that come from older languages such as Greek, Latin, Old English (Anglo-Saxon), and Norse. Knowing the meaning of a word's root can help you determine the word's meaning.

Root	Meaning	Example
aster, astr (Greek)	star	asterisk
fic/ fac/ fec (Latin)	make, do	factory
spec/ spect/ spic (Latin)	look at, see, behold	spectator
ten (Latin)	stretch	tendon
derm/ derma (Greek)	skin	epidermis

For more information, see ***Vocabulary Strategy: Word Roots,*** *pages 86, 273, 326, 425, 472, 594, 686, 802, and 866.*

2.3 PREFIXES

A **prefix** is a word part attached to the beginning of a word. Most prefixes come from Greek, Latin, or Old English.

Prefix	Meaning	Example
un- (Old English)	not	unafraid
epi- (Greek)	upon, on, over	epicenter
syn- (Greek)	together, at the same time	synthesis
hexa- (Greek)	six	hexagram
geo- (Greek)	earth	geography
trans- (Latin)	across, beyond	transatlantic
dis- (Latin)	lack of, not	distrust
circum- (Latin)	around	circumvent
hemi- (Latin)	half	hemisphere

For more information, see ***Vocabulary Strategy: Prefixes,*** *pages 368, 390, 668, 736, and 1171.*

2.4 SUFFIXES

A **suffix** is a word part that appears at the end of a root or base word to form a new word. Some suffixes do not change word meaning. These suffixes are

- added to nouns to change the number of persons or objects
- added to verbs to change the tense
- added to modifiers to change the degree of comparison

Suffix	Meaning	Example
-s, -es	to change the number of a noun	trunk + s = trunks
-d, -ed, -ing	to change verb tense	sprinkle + d = sprinkled
-er, -est	to change the degree of comparison in modifiers	cold + er = colder icy + est = iciest

Other suffixes can be added to a root or base to change the word's meaning. These suffixes can also determine a word's part of speech.

Suffix	Meaning	Example
-ence	state or condition of	independence
-ous	full of	furious
-ate	to make	activate
-ly, -ily	manner	quickly

For more information, see ***Vocabulary Strategy: Suffixes,*** *pages 368 and 436.*

Strategies for Understanding Unfamiliar Words

- Look for any prefixes or suffixes. Remove them to isolate the base word or the root.
- See if you recognize any elements—prefix, suffix, root, or base—of the word. You may be able to guess its meaning by analyzing one or two elements.
- Consider the way the word is used in the sentence. Use the context and the word parts to make a logical guess about the word's meaning.
- Consult a dictionary to see whether you are correct.

Make inferences about the meanings of the following words from the fields of science and math. Consider what you have learned in this section about Greek, Latin, and Anglo-Saxon (Old English) word parts.

astronomy	efficacy	hexagonal
circumference	epidermis	spectrum
distend	geosciences	uncertainty

3 Understanding Word Origins

3.1 ETYMOLOGIES

Etymologies show the origin and historical development of a word. When you study a word's history and origin, you can find out when, where, and how the word came to be.

am•bas•sa•dor (ăm-băs′ə-dər, -dôr′) *n.* A diplomatic official of the highest rank appointed and accredited as representative in residence by one government or sovereign to another, usually for a specific length of time. [Middle English *ambassadour,* from Old French *ambassadeur,* from Medieval Latin *ambactia,* mission, from Latin *ambactus,* servant, ultimately of Celtic origin.]

com•mu•ni•ty (kə-myōō′nĭ-tē) *n., pl.* **-ties** A group of people living in the same locality and under the same government. [Middle English *communite,* citizenry, from Old French, from Latin *commūnitās,* fellowship, from *commūnis,* common.]

For more information, see **Vocabulary Strategy: Etymologies,** *pages 76, 253, and 1030.*

Trace the etymology of the words below, often used in the fields of history and political science.

diplomat	independence	legislature
government	justice	revolution
immigrant	laissez-faire	treaty

3.2 WORD FAMILIES

Words that have the same root make up a word family and have related meanings. The chart shows a common Greek and a common Latin root. Notice how the meanings of the example words are related to the meanings of their roots.

Latin Root	*med:* "middle"
English Words	**mediate** resolve or settle
	mediocre ordinary
	media² middle wall of a blood vessel
	medial toward the middle
	medium action midway between two extremes
Greek Root	*chron:* "time"
English Words	**chronicle** detailed narrative report
	chronic of long duration
	synchronize occur at same time
	anachronism out of proper order in time

For more information, see **Vocabulary Strategy: Word Family,** *page 1016.*

3.3 WORDS FROM CLASSICAL MYTHOLOGY

The English language includes many words from classical mythology. You can use your knowledge of these myths to understand the origins and meanings of these words. For example, *herculean task* refers to the strongman Hercules. Thus, *herculean task* probably means "a job that is large or difficult." The chart shows a few common words from mythology.

Greek	Roman	Norse
nemesis	insomnia	Thursday
atlas	fury	berserk
adonis	Saturday	rune
mentor	January	valkyrie

Look up the etymology of each word in the chart and locate the myth associated with it. Use the information from the myth to explain the origin and meaning of each word.

3.4 FOREIGN WORDS

The English language includes words from diverse languages, such as French, Dutch, Spanish, Italian, and Chinese. Many words stayed the way they were in their original language.

French	Dutch	Spanish	Italian
entree	maelstrom	rodeo	pasta
nouveau riche	trek	salsa	opera
potpourri	cookie	bronco	vendetta
tête-à-tête	snoop	tornado	grotto

*For more information, see **Vocabulary Strategy: Foreign Words,** pages 108 and 976.*

4 Synonyms and Antonyms

4.1 SYNONYMS

A **synonym** is a word with a meaning similar to that of another word. You can find synonyms in a thesaurus or a dictionary. In a dictionary, synonyms are often given as part of the definition of a word. The following word pairs are synonyms:

dry/arid   enthralled/fascinated   gaunt/thin

*For more information, see **Vocabulary Strategy: Synonyms,** page 119.*

4.2 ANTONYMS

An **antonym** is a word with a meaning opposite that of another word. The following word pairs are antonyms:

friend/enemy   absurd/logical
courteous/rude   languid/energetic

5 Denotation and Connotation

5.1 DENOTATION

A word's dictionary meaning is called its **denotation.** For example, the denotation of the word *rascal* is "an unethical, dishonest person."

5.2 CONNOTATION

The images or feelings you connect to a word add a finer shade of meaning, called **connotation.** The connation of a word goes beyond its basic dictionary definition. Writers use connotations of words to communicate positive or negative feelings.

Positive	Neutral	Negative
save	store	hoard
fragrance	smell	stench
display	show	flaunt

Make sure you understand the denotation and connotation of a word when you read it or use it in your writing.

*For more information, see **Vocabulary Strategy: Denotation and Connotation,** pages 127 and 754.*

6 Analogies

An **analogy** is a comparison between two things that are similar in some way but are otherwise dissimilar. Analogies are sometimes used in writing when unfamiliar subjects or ideas are explained in terms of familiar ones. Analogies often appear on tests as well, usually in a format like this:

TERRIER : DOG ::   A)   rat : fish
                      B)   kitten : cat
                      C)   trout : fish
                      D)   fish : trout
                      E)   poodle : collie

Follow these steps to determine the correct answer:

- Read the part in capital letters as "*bird* is to *fly* as ..."

- Read the answer choices as "*rat* is to *fish*," "*kitten* is to *cat*," and so on.

- Ask yourself how the words *terrier* and *dog* are related. (A terrier is a type of dog.)

- Ask yourself which of the choices shows the same relationship. (A kitten is a kind of cat, but not in the same way that a terrier is a kind of dog. A kitten is a baby cat. A trout however, is a type of fish in the sense that a terrier is a type of dog. Therefore, the answer is C.)

*For more information, see **Vocabulary Strategy: Analogy,** page 1158.*

7 Homonyms and Homophones

7.1 HOMONYMS

Homonyms are words that have the same spelling and sound but have different origins and meanings.

I don't want to bore you with a story about how I had to bore through the living room wall.

Bore can mean "cause a person to lose interest," but an identically spelled word means "to drill a hole."

My dog likes to bark while it scratches the bark on the tree in the backyard.

Bark can mean "the sound made by a dog." However, another identically spelled word means "the outer covering of a tree." Each word has a different meaning and its own dictionary entry.

Sometimes only one of the meanings of two homonyms may be familiar to you. Use context clues to help you figure out the meaning of an unfamiliar word.

7.2 HOMOPHONES

Homophones are words that sound alike but have different meanings and spellings. The following homophones are frequently misused:

it's/its	they're/their/there
to/too/two	stationary/stationery

Many misused homophones are pronouns and contractions. Whenever you are unsure whether to write *your* or *you're* and *who's* or *whose,* ask yourself if you mean *you are* or *who is/has.* If you do, write the contraction. For other homophones, such as *scent* and *sent,* use the meaning of the word to help you decide which one to use.

8 Words with Multiple Meanings

Some words have acquired additional meanings over time that are based on the original meaning.

> **EXAMPLES:** *I was in a hurry so I jammed my clothes into the suitcase. Unfortunately, I jammed my finger in the process.*

These two uses of *jam* have different meanings, but both of them have the same origin. You will find all the meanings of *jam* listed in one entry in the dictionary.

9 Specialized Vocabulary

Specialized vocabulary is special terms suited to a particular field of study or work. For example, science, mathematics, and history all have their own technical or specialized vocabularies. To figure out specialized terms, you can use context clues and reference sources, such as dictionaries on specific subjects, atlases, or manuals.

For more information, see **Vocabulary Strategy: Specialized Vocabulary,** *pages 60, 242, 704, 786, and 960.*

10 Using Reference Sources

10.1 DICTIONARIES

A **general dictionary** will tell you not only a word's definitions but also its pronunciation, its parts of speech, and its history and origin. A **specialized dictionary** focuses on terms related to a particular field of study or work. Use a dictionary to check the spelling of any word you are unsure of in your English class and other subjects as well.

10.2 THESAURI

A **thesaurus** (plural, thesauri) is a dictionary of synonyms. A thesaurus can be helpful when you find yourself using the same modifiers over and over again.

10.3 SYNONYM FINDERS

A **synonym finder** is often included in word-processing software. It enables you to highlight a word and be shown a display of its synonyms.

10.4 GLOSSARIES

A **glossary** is a list of specialized terms and their definitions. It is often found in the back of textbooks and sometimes includes pronunciations. In fact, this textbook has three glossaries: the **Glossary of Literary Terms,** the **Glossary of Reading & Informational Terms,** and the **Glossary of Vocabulary in English & Spanish.** Use these glossaries to help you understand how terms are used in this textbook.

11 Spelling Rules

11.1 WORDS ENDING IN A SILENT *E*

Before adding a suffix beginning with a vowel or *y* to a word ending in a silent *e,* drop the *e* (with some exceptions).

> **amaze + -ing = amazing**
> **love + -able = lovable**
> **create + -ed = created**
> **nerve + -ous = nervous**

Exceptions: *change + -able = changeable; courage + -ous = courageous.*

When adding a suffix beginning with a consonant to a word ending in a silent *e,* keep the *e* (with some exceptions).

 late + -ly = lately
 spite + -ful = spiteful
 noise + -less = noiseless
 state + -ment = statement

Exceptions: *truly, argument, ninth, wholly, awful,* and others.

When a suffix beginning with *a* or *o* is added to a word with a final silent *e,* the final *e* is usually retained if it is preceded by a soft *c* or a soft *g.*

 bridge + -able = bridgeable
 peace + -able = peaceable
 outrage + -ous = outrageous
 advantage + -ous = advantageous

When a suffix beginning with a vowel is added to words ending in *ee* or *oe,* the final silent *e* is retained.

 agree + -ing = agreeing **free + -ing = freeing**
 hoe + -ing = hoeing **see + -ing = seeing**

11.2 WORDS ENDING IN *Y*

Before adding most suffixes to a word that ends in *y* preceded by a consonant, change the *y* to *i.*

 easy + -est = easiest
 crazy + -est = craziest
 silly + -ness = silliness
 marry + -age = marriage

Exceptions: *dryness, shyness,* and *slyness.*

However, when you add *-ing,* the *y* does not change.

 empty + -ed = emptied but
 empty + -ing = emptying

When adding a suffix to a word that ends in *y* preceded by a vowel, the *y* usually does not change.

 play + -er = player
 employ + -ed = employed
 coy + -ness = coyness
 pay + -able = payable

11.3 WORDS ENDING IN A CONSONANT

In one-syllable words that end in one consonant preceded by one short vowel, double the final consonant before adding a suffix beginning with a vowel, such as *-ed* or *-ing.*

 dip + -ed = dipped **set + -ing = setting**
 slim + -est = slimmest **fit + -er = fitter**

The rule does not apply to words of one syllable that end in a consonant preceded by two vowels.

 feel + -ing = feeling **peel + -ed = peeled**
 reap + -ed = reaped **loot + -ed = looted**

In words of more than one syllable, double the final consonant when (**1**) the word ends with one consonant preceded by one vowel and (**2**) the word is accented on the last syllable.

 be•gin´ per•mit´ re•fer´

In the following examples, note that in the new words formed with suffixes, the accent remains on the same syllable:

 be•gin´ + -ing = be•gin´ning = beginning
 per•mit´ + -ed = per•mit´ted = permitted

In some words with more than one syllable, though the accent remains on the same syllable when a suffix is added, the final consonant is nevertheless not doubled, as in the following examples:

 tra´vel + -er = tra´vel•er = traveler
 mar´ket + -er = mar´ket•er = marketer

In the following examples, the accent does not remain on the same syllable; thus, the final consonant is not doubled:

 re•fer´ + -ence = ref´er•ence = reference
 con•fer´ + -ence = con´fer•ence = conference

11.4 PREFIXES AND SUFFIXES

When adding a prefix to a word, do not change the spelling of the base word. When a prefix creates a double letter, keep both letters.

 dis- + approve = disapprove
 re- + build = rebuild
 ir- + regular = irregular
 mis- + spell = misspell
 anti- + trust = antitrust
 il- + logical = illogical

When adding *-ly* to a word ending in *l,* keep both *l*'s, and when adding *-ness* to a word ending in *n,* keep both *n*'s.

 careful + -ly = carefully
 sudden + -ness = suddenness
 final + -ly = finally
 thin + -ness = thinness

11.5 FORMING PLURAL NOUNS

To form the plural of most nouns, just add -s.

prizes dreams circles stations

For most singular nouns ending in *o*, add -s.

solos halos studios photos pianos

For a few nouns ending in *o*, add -es.

heroes tomatoes potatoes echoes

When the singular noun ends in *s, sh, ch, x,* or *z,* add -es.

waitresses brushes ditches
axes buzzes

When a singular noun ends in *y* with a consonant before it, change the *y* to *i* and add -es.

army—armies candy—candies
baby—babies diary—diaries
ferry—ferries conspiracy—conspiracies

When a vowel (*a, e, i, o, u*) comes before the *y,* just add -s.

boy—boys way—ways
array—arrays alloy—alloys
weekday—weekdays jockey—jockeys

For most nouns ending in *f* or *fe,* change the *f* to *v* and add -es or -s.

life—lives calf—calves knife—knives
thief—thieves shelf—shelves loaf—loaves

For some nouns ending in *f,* add -s to make the plural.

roofs chiefs reefs beliefs

Some nouns have the same form for both singular and plural.

deer sheep moose salmon trout

For some nouns, the plural is formed in a special way.

man—men goose—geese
ox—oxen woman—women
mouse—mice child—children

For a compound noun written as one word, form the plural by changing the last word in the compound to its plural form.

stepchild—stepchildren firefly—fireflies

If a compound noun is written as a hyphenated word or as two separate words, change the most important word to the plural form.

brother-in-law—brothers-in-law
life jacket—life jackets

11.6 FORMING POSSESSIVES

If a noun is singular, add *'s.*

mother—my mother's car Ross—Ross's desk

Exception: The *s* after the apostrophe is dropped after *Jesus', Moses',* and certain names in classical mythology (*Zeus'*). These possessive forms can be pronounced easily.

If a noun is plural and ends with *s,* just add an apostrophe.

parents—my parents' car
the Santinis—the Santinis' house

If a noun is plural but does not end in *s,* add *'s.*

people—the people's choice
women—the women's coats

11.7 SPECIAL SPELLING PROBLEMS

Only one English word ends in -*sede: supersede.* Three words end in -*ceed: exceed, proceed,* and *succeed.* All other verbs ending in the sound "seed" are spelled with -*cede.*

concede precede recede secede

In words with *ie* or *ei,* when the sound is long *e* (as in *she*), the word is spelled *ie* except after *c* (with some exceptions).

| *i* before *e* | thief | relieve | field |
| | piece | grieve | pier |

| except after *c* | conceit | perceive | ceiling |
| | receive | receipt | |

Exceptions: *either, neither, weird, leisure, seize.*

12 Commonly Confused Words

WORDS	DEFINITIONS	EXAMPLES
accept/except	The verb *accept* means "to receive or believe"; *except* is usually a preposition meaning "excluding."	**Except** for some of the more extraordinary events, I can **accept** that the *Odyssey* recounts a real journey.
advice/advise	*Advise* is a verb; *advice* is a noun naming that which an *adviser* gives.	I **advise** you to take that job. Whom should I ask for **advice?**
affect/effect	As a verb, *affect* means "to influence." *Effect* as a verb means "to cause." If you want a noun, you will almost always want *effect*.	Did Circe's wine **affect** Odysseus' mind? It did **effect** a change in Odysseus' men. In fact, it had an **effect** on everyone else who drank it.
all ready/already	*All ready* is an adjective meaning "fully ready." *Already* is an adverb meaning "before or by this time."	He was **all ready** to go at noon. I have **already** seen that movie.
allusion/illusion	An *allusion* is an indirect reference to something. An *illusion* is a false picture or idea.	There are many **allusions** to the works of Homer in English literature. The world's apparent flatness is an **illusion.**
among/between	*Between* is used when you are speaking of only two things. *Among* is used for three or more.	**Between** *Hamlet* and *King Lear*, I prefer the latter. Emily Dickinson is **among** my favorite poets.
bring/take	*Bring* is used to denote motion toward a speaker or place. *Take* is used to denote motion away from such a person or place.	**Bring** the books over here, and I will **take** them to the library.
fewer/less	*Fewer* refers to the number of separate, countable units. *Less* refers to bulk quantity.	We have **less** literature and **fewer** selections in this year's curriculum.
leave/let	*Leave* means "to allow something to remain behind." *Let* means "to permit."	The librarian will **leave** some books on display but will not **let** us borrow any.
lie/lay	*Lie* means "to rest or recline." It does not take an object. *Lay* always takes an object.	Rover loves to **lie** in the sun. We always **lay** some bones next to him.
loose/lose	*Loose* (lo͞os) means "free, not restrained"; *lose* (lo͞oz) means "to misplace or fail to find."	Who turned the horses **loose?** I hope we won't **lose** any of them.
precede/proceed	*Precede* means "to go or come before." Use *proceed* for other meanings.	Emily Dickinson's poetry **precedes** that of Alice Walker. You may **proceed** to the next section of the test.
than/then	Use *than* in making comparisons; use *then* on all other occasions.	Who can say whether Amy Lowell is a better poet **than** Denise Levertov? I will read Lowell first, and **then** I will read Levertov.
their/there/they're	*Their* means "belonging to them." *There* means "in that place." *They're* is the contraction for "they are."	**There** is a movie playing at 9 P.M. **They're** going to see it with me. Sakara and Jessica drove away in **their** car after the movie.
two/too/to	*Two* is the number. *Too* is an adverb meaning "also" or "very." Use *to* before a verb or as a preposition.	Meg had **to** go **to** town, **too.** We had **too** much reading **to** do. **Two** chapters is **too** many.

Effective oral communication occurs when the audience understands a message the way the speaker intends it. Good speakers and listeners do more than just talk and hear. They use specific techniques to present their ideas effectively, and they are attentive and critical listeners.

1 Speech

In school, in business, and in community life, a speech is one of the most effective means of communicating.

1.1 AUDIENCE, PURPOSE, AND OCCASION

When developing and delivering a speech, your goal is to deliver a focused, coherent presentation that conveys your ideas clearly and relates to the background of your audience. By understanding your audience, you can tailor your speech to them appropriately and effectively.

- **Know Your Audience** What kind of group are you presenting to? Fellow classmates? A group of teachers? What are their interests and backgrounds? Understanding their different points of view can help you organize the information so that they understand and are interested in it.

- **Understand Your Purpose** Keep in mind your purpose for speaking. Are you trying to persuade the audience to do something? Perhaps you simply want to entertain them by sharing a story or experience. Your reason for giving the speech will guide you in organizing your thoughts and deciding on how to deliver it.

- **Know the Occasion** Are you speaking at a special event? Is it formal? Will others be giving speeches besides you? Knowing the type of occasion will help you tailor the language and length of your speech for the event.

1.2 PREPARING YOUR SPEECH

There are several approaches to preparing a speech. Your teacher may tell you which one to use.

- **Manuscript** Prepare a complete script of the speech in advance and use it to deliver the speech. Use for formal occasions, such as graduation speeches and political addresses, and to present technical or complicated information.

- **Memory** Prepare a written text in advance and then memorize it in order to deliver the speech word for word. Use for short speeches, as when introducing another speaker or accepting an award.

- **Extemporaneous** Prepare the speech and deliver it using an outline or notes. Use for informal situations, for persuasive messages, and to make a more personal connection with the audience.

1.3 DRAFTING YOUR SPEECH

If you are writing your speech beforehand, rather than working from notes, use the following guidelines to help you:

- **Create a Unified Speech** Do this first by organizing your speech into paragraphs, each of which develops a single main idea. All the sentences in a paragraph should support the main idea of the paragraph, and all the paragraphs should support the main idea of the speech. Be sure that your speech has an introduction and a conclusion. Just as in a written product, use a pattern of organization that is appropriate to your subject and purpose.

- **Use Appropriate Language** The subject of your speech—and the way you choose to present it—should match your audience, your purpose, and the occasion. You can use informal language, such as slang, to share a story with your classmates. For a persuasive speech in front of a school assembly, use formal, standard American English. If you are giving an informative presentation, be sure to explain any terms that the audience may not be familiar with.

- **Provide Evidence** Include relevant facts, statistics, and incidents; quote experts to support your ideas and opinions. Elaborate—provide specific details, perhaps with visual or media displays—to clarify what you are saying.

- **Emphasize Important Points** To help your audience follow the main ideas and concepts of your speech, be sure to draw attention to important points. You can use rhyme, repetition, parallelism, and other rhetorical devices. You can also use figurative language for effect.

- **Use Precise Language** Use precise language to convey your ideas, and vary the structure and length of your sentences. You can keep the audience's attention with a word that elicits strong emotion. You can use a question or an interjection to make a personal connection with the audience.

- **Start Strong, Finish Strong** As you begin your speech, consider using a "hook"—an interesting question or statement meant to capture your audience's attention. At the end of the speech, restate your main ideas simply and clearly. Perhaps conclude with a powerful example or anecdote to reinforce your message.

- **Revise Your Speech** After you write your speech, revise, edit, and proofread it as you would a written report. Use a variety of sentence structures to achieve a natural rhythm. Check for correct subject-verb agreement and consistent verb tense. Correct run-on sentences and sentence fragments. Use parallel structure to emphasize ideas. Make sure you use complete sentences and correct punctuation and capitalization, even if no one else will see it. Your written speech should be clear and error-free.

1.4 DELIVERING YOUR SPEECH

Confidence is the key to a successful presentation. Use these techniques to help you prepare and present your speech:

Prepare

- **Review Your Information** Reread your notes and review any background research. You'll feel more confident during your speech.

- **Organize Your Notes** Some people prefer to include only key points. Others prefer the entire script. Write each main point, or each paragraph, of your speech on a separate numbered index card. Be sure to include your most important evidence and examples.

- **Plan Your Visual Aids and Sound Effects** If you are planning on using visual aids, such as slides, posters, charts, graphs, video clips, transparencies, or computer projections, now is the time to design your visual and sound elements and work them into your speech.

Practice

- **Rehearse** Rehearse your speech several times, possibly in front of a practice audience. Maintain good posture by standing with your shoulders back and your head up. If you are using visual aids, practice handling them. Adapt your rate of speaking, pitch, and tone of voice to your audience and setting. Glance at your notes to refresh your memory, but avoid reading them word for word. Your style of performance should express the purpose of your speech. Use the following chart to help you.

Purpose	Pace	Pitch	Tone
to persuade	fast but clear	even	urgent
to inform	using plenty of pauses	even	authoritative
to entertain	usually building to a "punch"	varied to create characters or drama	funny or dramatic

- **Use Audience Feedback** If you had a practice audience, ask them specific questions about your delivery: Did I use enough eye contact? Was my voice at the right volume? Did I stand straight, or did I slouch? Use the audience's comments to evaluate the effectiveness of your delivery and to set goals for future rehearsals.

- **Evaluate Your Performance** When you have finished each rehearsal, evaluate your performance. Did you pause to let an important point sink in, or use gestures for emphasis? Make a list of the aspects of your presentation that you will try to improve for your next rehearsal.

Present

- **Begin Your Speech** Try to look relaxed and smile.

- **Make Eye Contact** Try to make eye contact with as many audience members as possible. This will establish personal contact and help you determine if the audience understands your speech.

- **Remember to Pause** A slight pause after important points will provide emphasis and give your audience time to think about what you're saying.

- **Speak Clearly** Speak loud enough to be heard clearly, but not so loud that your voice is overwhelming. Use a conversational tone.

- **Maintain Good Posture** Stand up straight and avoid nervous movements that may distract the audience's attention from what you are saying.

- **Use Expressive Body Language** Use facial expressions to show your feelings toward your topic. Lean forward when you make an important point; move your hands and arms for emphasis. Use your body language to show your own style and reflect your personality.

- **Watch the Audience for Responses** If they start fidgeting or yawning, speak a little louder or get to your conclusion a little sooner. Use what you learn to decide what areas need improvement for future presentations.
- **Close your speech** As part of your closing remarks, be sure to thank your audience.

Respond to Questions

Depending on the content of your speech, your audience may have questions. Follow these steps to make sure that you answer questions in an appropriate manner:

- Think about what your audience may ask and prepare answers before your speech.
- Tell your audience at the beginning of your speech that you will take questions at the end. This helps avoid audience interruptions that may make your speech hard to follow.
- Call on audience members in the order in which they raise their hands.
- Repeat each question before you answer it to ensure that everyone has heard it. This step also gives you time to prepare your answer.

2 Different Types of Oral Presentations

2.1 INFORMATIVE SPEECH

When you deliver an informative speech, you give the audience new information, provide a better understanding of information, or enable the audience to use the information in a new way.

Use the following questions to evaluate your own presentation or that of a peer or a public figure.

Evaluate an Informative Speech
- Did the speaker have a specific, clearly focused topic?
- Did the speaker take the audience's previous knowledge into consideration?
- Did the speaker cite sources for the information?
- Did the speaker communicate the information objectively?
- Did the speaker explain technical terms?
- Did the speaker use visual aids effectively?
- Did the speaker anticipate and address any audience concerns or misunderstandings?
- Is the speech informative and accurate?

2.2 PERSUASIVE SPEECH

When you deliver a persuasive speech, you offer a thesis or clear statement on a subject, you provide relevant evidence to support your position, and you attempt to convince the audience to accept your point of view.

Use the following questions to evaluate the presentation of a peer or a public figure, or your own presentation.

*For more information, see **Speaking and Listening: Presenting a Persuasive Speech**, page 283.*

Evaluate a Persuasive Speech
- Did the speaker present a clear thesis or argument?
- Did the speaker anticipate and address audience concerns, biases, and counterarguments?
- Did the speaker use sound logic and reasoning in developing the argument?
- Did the speaker support the argument with valid evidence, examples, facts, expert opinions, and quotations?
- Did the speaker use rhetorical devices, such as emotional appeals, to support assertions?
- Were the speaker's voice, facial expressions, and gestures effective?
- Is your reaction to the speech similar to that of other audience members?
- Did you believe the speaker to be truthful and ethical?

2.3 DEBATE

A debate is a balanced argument covering both sides of an issue. In a debate, two teams compete to win the support of the audience. In a formal debate, two teams, each with two members, present their arguments on a given proposition or policy statement. One team argues for the proposition or statement, and the other argues against it. Each debater must consider the proposition closely and must research both sides of it.

Preparing for the Debate

In preparing for a debate, the debaters prepare a **brief,** an outline of the debate, accounting for the evidence and arguments of both sides of the **proposition** (topic). Debaters also prepare a **rebuttal,** a follow-up speech to support their arguments and counter the opposition's. Propositions are usually one of four types:

- **Proposition of fact**—determines whether a statement is true or false. An example is "Deforestation is ruining the rain forest."

- **Proposition of value**—determines the value of a person, place, or thing. An example is "Free trade will help small countries develop."

- **Proposition of problem**—determines whether a problem exists and whether it requires action.

- **Proposition of policy**—determines the action that will be taken. An example is "Students will provide tutoring services."

The two groups of debaters who argue a topic are called the **affirmative side** and the **negative side.** The affirmative side tries to convince the audience that the proposition should be accepted. The negative side argues against the proposition.

Use the following steps to prepare a brief:

- **Gather Information** Consult a variety of primary and secondary sources to gather the most reliable, up-to-date information about the proposition.

- **Identify Key Ideas** Sort out the important points and arrange them in order of importance.

- **List Arguments for and Against Each Key Idea** Look for strong arguments that support your side of the proposition and also note those that support your opponents' side.

- **Support Your Arguments** Find facts, quotations, expert opinions, and examples that support your arguments and counter your opponents'.

- **Write the Brief** Begin your brief with a statement of the proposition. Then list the arguments and evidence that support both sides of the proposition.

Planning the Rebuttal

The rebuttal is the opportunity to rebuild your case. Use the following steps to build a strong rebuttal:

- Listen to your opponents respectfully. Note the points you wish to overturn.

- Defend what the opposition has challenged.

- Cite weaknesses in their arguments, such as points they overlooked.

- Present counterarguments and supporting evidence.

- Offer your summary arguments. Restate and solidify your stance.

Use the following questions to evaluate a debate.

Evaluate a Team in a Debate

- Did the team prove that a significant problem does or does not exist? How thorough was the team's analysis of the problem?

- How did the team convince you that the proposition is or is not the best solution to the problem?

- How effectively did the team present reasons and evidence supporting the case?

- How effectively did the team refute and rebut arguments made by the opposing team?

- Did the speakers maintain eye contact and speak at an appropriate rate and volume?

- Did the speakers observe proper debate etiquette?

PRACTICE AND APPLY

View a political debate for a local, state, or national election. Use the preceding criteria to evaluate it.

2.4 NARRATIVE SPEECH

When you deliver a narrative speech, you tell a story or present a subject using a story-type format. A good narrative keeps an audience informed and entertained. It also allows you to deliver a message in a creative way.

Use the following questions to evaluate a speaker or your own presentation.

Evaluate a Narrative Speech

- Did the speaker choose a context that makes sense and contributes to a believable narrative?

- Did the speaker locate scenes and incidents in specific places?

- Does the plot flow well?

- Did the speaker use words that convey the appropriate mood and tone?

- Did the speaker use sensory details that allow the audience to experience the sights, sounds, and smells of a scene and the specific actions, gestures, and thoughts of the characters?

- Did the speaker use a range of narrative devices to keep the audience interested?

- Is your reaction to the presentation similar to that of other audience members?

2.5 REFLECTIVE SPEECH

In a reflective speech, you describe a personal experience and explore its significance. Use vivid description, visuals, and sound effects to re-create the experience for your audience and convey meaning.

Use the following questions to evaluate a speaker or your own presentation.

Evaluate a Reflective Speech

- Did the speaker describe an important experience in his or her life?
- Did the speaker use figurative language, sensory details, or other techniques to re-create the event for the audience?
- Did the speaker explain the significance of the event to the audience?
- Does the experience relate to a broader theme or a more general abstract idea about life?
- Did the speaker convey the message through one specific event or several related incidents?
- Did the speaker encourage the audience to think about the significance of the experience and apply it to their own lives?
- Was your reaction to the presentation similar to that of other audience members?

2.6 DESCRIPTIVE SPEECH

In a descriptive speech, you describe a subject with which you are personally familiar. A good description will enable your listeners to tell how you feel toward your subject.

Use the following questions to evaluate a speaker or your own presentation.

Evaluate a Descriptive Speech

- Did the speaker make clear his or her point of view toward the subject being described?
- Did the speaker use sensory details, figurative language, and factual details?
- Did the speaker use tone and pitch to emphasize important details?
- Did the speaker use facial expressions to emphasize his or her feelings toward the subject?
- Did the speaker change vantage points to help the audience see the subject from another position?
- Did the speaker change perspectives to show how someone else might feel toward the subject?

2.7 ORAL INTERPRETATION

When you perform an oral interpretation, you use appropriate vocal intonations, facial expressions, and gestures to bring a literature selection to life.

In an **oral reading,** you will present or read a poem, monologue, or passage from a literary selection, in which you assume the voice of a character, the narrator, or the speaker. An oral reading can also be a presentation of a dialogue between two or more characters, in which you, as the sole performer, take on all the roles.

Use the following techniques when giving an oral reading:

- **Speak Clearly** As you speak, pronounce your words clearly.
- **Control Your Volume** Make sure that you are loud enough to be heard, but do not shout.
- **Pace Yourself** Read at a moderate rate, but vary your pace if it seems appropriate to the emotions of the character or to the action you perform.
- **Vary Your Voice** Use a different voice for each character. Stress important words and phrases. Use your voice to express different emotions.

In a **dramatic reading,** several speakers participate in the reading of a play or some other work. Use the following techniques in your dramatic reading:

- **Prepare** Rehearse your material several times. Become familiar with the humorous and serious parts of the script. Develop a special voice that fits the personality of the character you portray.
- **Project** As you read your lines, aim your voice toward the back of the room to allow everyone to hear you.
- **Perform** React to the other characters as if you were hearing their lines for the first time. Deliver your own lines with the appropriate emotion. Use not only hand gestures and facial expressions but also other body movements to express your emotions.

For more information, see **Speaking and Listening: Delivering an Oral Interpretation,** page 1079.

Use the following questions to evaluate an artistic performance by a peer or a public presenter, a media presentation, or your own performance.

Evaluate an Oral Interpretation

- Did the speaker speak clearly, enunciating each word carefully?
- Did the speaker maintain eye contact with the audience?
- Did the speaker control his or her volume, projecting without shouting?
- Did the speaker vary the rate of speech appropriately to express emotion, mood, and action?
- Did the speaker use a different voice for each character?
- Did the speaker stress important words or phrases?
- Did the speaker's presentation allow you to identify and appreciate elements of the text such as character development, rhyme, imagery, and language?

PRACTICE AND APPLY

Develop an oral reading and present it to your class; evaluate the oral readings of your classmates, using the preceding criteria.

2.8 ORAL RESPONSE TO LITERATURE

An oral response to literature is a personal, analytical interpretation of a writer's story, novel, poem, or drama.

Use the following questions to evaluate a speaker or your own presentation.

Evaluate an Oral Response to Literature

- Did the speaker choose an interesting piece that he or she understands and feels strongly about?
- Did the speaker make a judgment that shows an understanding of significant ideas from the text?
- Did the speaker direct the audience to specific parts of the piece that support his or her ideas?
- Did the speaker identify and analyze the use of artistic elements such as imagery, figurative language, and character development?
- Did the speaker demonstrate an appreciation of the author's style?
- Did the speaker discuss any ambiguous or difficult passages and the impact of those passages on the audience?

PRACTICE AND APPLY

Listen as a classmate delivers an oral response to a selection you have read. Use the preceding criteria to evaluate the presentation.

❸ Other Types of Communication

3.1 GROUP DISCUSSION

Successful groups assign a role to each member. These roles distribute responsibility among the members and help keep discussions focused.

Role	Responsibilities
Chairperson	• introduces topic • explains goal or purpose • participates in discussion and keeps it on track • helps resolve conflicts • helps group reach goal
Recorder	• takes notes on discussion • reports on suggestions and decisions • organizes and writes up notes • participates in discussion
Participants	• contribute relevant facts or ideas to discussion • respond constructively to one another's ideas • reach agreement or vote on final decision

3.2 INTERVIEWS

An **interview** is a formal type of conversation with a definite purpose and goal. To conduct a successful interview, use the following guidelines:

Prepare for the Interview

- Select your interviewee carefully. Identify who has the kind of knowledge and experience you are looking for.
- Set a time, a date, and a place. Ask permission to tape-record the interview.

- Learn all you can about the person you will interview or the topic you want information on.

- Prepare a list of questions. Create questions that encourage detailed responses instead of yes-or-no answers. Arrange your questions in order from most important to least important.

- Arrive on time with everything you need.

Conduct the Interview

- Ask your questions clearly and listen to the responses carefully. Give the person whom you are interviewing plenty of time to answer.

- Be flexible; follow up on any responses you find interesting.

- Avoid arguments; be tactful and polite.

- Even if you tape an interview, take notes on important points.

- Thank the person for the interview, and ask if you can call with any follow-up questions.

Follow Up on the Interview

- Summarize your notes or make a written copy of the tape recording as soon as possible.

- If any points are unclear or if information is missing, call and ask more questions while the person is still available.

- Select the most appropriate quotations to support your ideas.

- If possible, have the person you interviewed review your work to make sure you haven't misrepresented what he or she said.

- Send a thank-you note to the person in appreciation of his or her time and effort.

For more information, see **Speaking and Listening: Conducting an Interview**, *page 481.*

Evaluate an Interview
You can determine how effective your interview was by asking yourself these questions:

- Did you get the type of information you were looking for?

- Were your most important questions answered to your satisfaction?

- Were you able to keep the interviewee focused on the subject?

Responding to a Job Interview

In a job interview, you will be the person being interviewed. The person asking you questions will have several objectives in mind, and you will need to be prepared to respond in a professional manner. Keep these strategies in mind when you are being interviewed for employment:

- Prior to the interview, prepare a short list of questions relevant to the position.

- Respond honestly and effectively to each question, and use language that conveys sensitivity, maturity, and respect.

- Give responses that demonstrate knowledge of the subject or organization.

- Use active listening skills, as outlined in the next section.

4 Active Listening

Active listening is the process of receiving, interpreting, evaluating, and responding to a message. Whether you listen to a class discussion or a formal speech, use the following strategies to get as much as you can from the message.

Before Listening

- Learn what the topic is beforehand. You may need to read background information about the topic or learn technical terms in order to understand the speaker's message.

- Think about what you know or want to know about the topic.

- Have a pen and paper or a laptop computer to take notes.

- Establish a purpose for listening.

While Listening

- Focus your attention on the speaker.

- Listen for the speaker's purpose (usually stated at the beginning), which alerts you to main ideas.

- Listen for words or phrases that signal important points, such as *to begin with, in addition, most important, finally,* and *in conclusion.*

- Listen carefully for explanations of technical terms.

- Listen for ideas that are repeated for emphasis.

- Take notes. Write down only the most important points. Use an outline or list format to organize main ideas and supporting points.

- Note comparisons and contrasts, causes and effects, or problems and solutions.

- Note how the speaker uses word choice, voice pitch, posture, and gestures to convey meaning.

After Listening

- Ask relevant questions to clarify anything that was unclear or confusing.

- Review your notes to make sure you understand what was said.

- Summarize and paraphrase the speaker's ideas.

- You may also wish to compare your interpretation of the speech with the interpretations of others who listened to it.

4.1 CRITICAL LISTENING

Critical listening involves interpreting and analyzing a spoken message to judge its accuracy and reliability. Use these strategies as you listen to messages from advertisers, politicians, lecturers, and others:

- **Determine the Speaker's Purpose** Think about the background, viewpoint, and possible motives of the speaker. Separate facts from opinions. Listen carefully to details and evidence that a speaker uses to support the message.

- **Listen for the Main Idea** Figure out the speaker's main message before allowing yourself to be distracted by seemingly convincing facts and details.

- **Recognize the Use of Persuasive Techniques** Pay attention to a speaker's choice of words. Speakers may slant information to persuade you to buy a product or accept an idea. Persuasive devices such as inaccurate generalizations, either/or reasoning, and bandwagon or snob appeal may represent faulty reasoning and provide misleading information.

  *For more information, see **Persuasive Techniques,** page R20.*

- **Observe Verbal and Nonverbal Messages** A speaker's gestures, facial expressions, and tone of voice should reinforce the message. If they don't, you should question the speaker's sincerity and the reliability of his or her message.

- **Give Appropriate Feedback** An effective speaker looks for verbal and nonverbal cues from you, the listener, to gauge how the message is being received. For example, if you understand or agree with the message, you might nod your head. If possible, during or after a presentation, ask questions to clarify understanding.

4.2 VERBAL FEEDBACK

At times you will be asked to give direct feedback to a speaker. You may be asked to evaluate the way the speaker delivers the presentation as well as the content of the presentation.

Use the following questions to evaluate a speaker's delivery.

Evaluate Delivery

- Did the speaker articulate words clearly and distinctly?
- Did the speaker pronounce words correctly?
- Did the speaker vary his or her rate?
- Did the speaker's voice sound natural and not strained?
- Was the speaker's voice loud enough?

Use the following guidelines to give constructive suggestions for improvement on content.

Evaluate Content

Be Specific Don't make statements like "Your charts need work." Offer concrete suggestions, such as "Please make the type bigger so we can read the poster from the back of the room."

Discuss Only the Most Important Points Don't overload the speaker with too much feedback about too many details. Focus on important points, such as:

- Is the topic too advanced for the audience?
- Are the supporting details well organized?
- Is the conclusion weak?

Give Balanced Feedback Tell the speaker not only what didn't work but also what did work: "Consider dropping the last two slides, since you covered those points earlier. The first two slides got my attention."

Every day you are exposed to hundreds of images and messages from television, radio, movies, newspapers, and the Internet. What is the effect of all this media? What do you need to know to be a smart media consumer? Being media literate means that you have the ability to think critically about media messages. It means that you are able to analyze and evaluate media messages and how they influence you and your world. To become media literate, you'll need the tools to study media messages.

MEDIA TOOLS

For more information, visit the **Media Center** at **ClassZone.com.**

1 Five Core Concepts in Media Literacy

from The Center for Media Literacy

The five core concepts of media literacy provide you with the basic ideas you can consider when examining media messages.

All media messages are "constructed." All media messages are made by someone. In fact, they are carefully thought out and researched and have attitudes and values built into them. Much of the information that you use to make sense of the world comes from the media. Therefore, it is important to know how media are put together so you can better understand the message it conveys.

Media messages are constructed using a creative language with its own rules. Each means of communication—whether it is film, television, newspapers, magazines, radio, or the Internet—has its own language and design. Therefore, the content of a message must use the language and design of the medium that conveys the message. Thus, the medium actually shapes the message. For example, a horror film may use music to heighten suspense, or a newspaper may use a big headline to signal the significance of a story. Understanding the language of each medium can increase your enjoyment of it as well as alert you to obvious and subtle influences.

Different people experience the same media messages differently. Personal factors such as age, education, and experience will affect the way a person responds to a media message. How many times has your interpretation of a film or book differed from that of a friend? Everyone interprets media messages through their own personal lens.

Media have embedded values and points of view. Media messages carry underlying values, which are purposely built into them by the creators of the message. For example, a commercial's main purpose may be to persuade you to buy something, but it also conveys the value of a particular lifestyle. Understanding not only the core message but also the embedded points of view will help you decide whether to accept or reject the message.

Most media messages are organized to gain profit and/or power. The creators of media messages often provide a commodity, such as information or entertainment, in order to make money. The bigger the audience, the higher the cost of advertising. Consequently, media outlets want to build large audiences in order to bring in more revenue from advertising. For example, a television network creates programming that appeals to the largest audience possible, and then uses the viewer ratings to attract more advertising dollars.

2 Media Basics

2.1 MESSAGE

When a film or TV show is created, it becomes a media product. Each media product is created to send a **message,** or an expression of belief or opinion, that serves a specific purpose. In order to understand the message, you will need to deconstruct it.

Deconstruction is the process of analyzing a media presentation. To analyze a media presentation you will need to look at its content, its purpose, the audience it's aimed at, and the techniques and elements that are used to create certain effects.

2.2 AUDIENCE

A **target audience** is a specific group of people that a product or presentation is aimed at. The members of a target audience usually share certain characteristics, such as age, gender, ethnic background, values, or lifestyle. For example, a target audience may be adults ages 40 to 60 who want to exercise and eat healthful foods.

Demographics are the characteristics of a population, including age, gender, profession, income, education, ethnicity, and geographic location. Media decision makers use demographics to shape their content to suit the needs and tastes of a target audience.

Nielsen ratings are the system used to track TV audiences and their viewing preferences. Nielsen Media Research, the company that provides this system, monitors TV viewing in a random sample of 5,000 U.S. households selected to represent the population as a whole.

2.3 PURPOSE

The **purpose,** or intent, of a media presentation is the reason it was made. Most media messages have more than one purpose, but each has a **core purpose.** To discover that purpose, think about why its creator paid for and produced the message. For example, an ad might entertain you with humor, but its core purpose is to persuade you to buy something.

2.4 TYPES AND GENRES OF MEDIA

The term *media* refers to television, newspapers, magazines, radio, movies, and the Internet. Each is a **medium,** or means for carrying information, entertainment, and advertisements to a large audience.

Each type of media has different characteristics, strengths, and weaknesses. Understanding how different types of media work and the role they play will help you become more informed about the choices you make in response to the media.

2.5 PRODUCERS AND CREATORS

People who control the media are known as **gatekeepers.** Gatekeepers decide what information to share with the public and the ways it will be presented. The following diagram gives some examples.

Who Controls the Media?

Media Owners
TV networks
Recording companies
Publishing companies

Media Products
Television
Radio
Magazines
Movies
Newspapers
Internet

Media Creators
Actors
Writers
Directors
Webmasters

Media Sponsors
Clothing manufacturers
Fast-food restaurants
Department stores

Some forms of media are independently owned, while others are part of a corporate family. Some corporate families might own several different kinds of media. For example, a company may own three radio stations, five newspapers, a publishing company, and a small television station. Often a corporate "parent" decides the content for all of its holdings.

2.6 LAWS GOVERNING MEDIA

Four main laws and policies affect the content, delivery, and use of mass media.

The First Amendment to the Constitution forbids Congress to limit speech or the press.

Copyright law protects the rights of authors and other media creators against the unauthorized publishing, reproduction, and selling of their works.

Laws prohibit **censorship,** any attempt to suppress or control people's access to media messages.

Laws prohibit **libel,** the publication of false statements that damage a person's reputation.

2.7 INFLUENCE OF MEDIA

By sheer volume alone, media influences our very existence, values, opinions, and beliefs. Our environment is saturated with media messages from television, billboards, radio, newspapers, magazines, video games, and so on. Each of these media products is selling one message and conveying another—a message about values—in the subtext. For example, a car ad is meant to sell a car, but if you look closer, you will see that it is using a set of values, such as a luxurious lifestyle, to make the car attractive to the target audience. One message of the ad is that if you buy the car, you'll have the luxurious lifestyle. The other message is that the luxurious lifestyle is good and desirable. TV shows, movies, and news programs also convey subtexts of values and beliefs.

Media can also shape your opinions about the world. For example, news about crime shapes our understanding about how much and what type of crime is prevalent in the world around us. TV news items, talk show interviews, and commercials may shape our perception of a political candidate, a celebrity, an ethnic group, a country, or a region. As a consequence, our knowledge of someone or someplace may be completely based on the information we receive from the television or other media.

3 Film and TV

Films and television programs come in a variety of types. Films include comedies, dramas, documentaries, and animated features. Televison programs cover an even wider array, including dramas, sitcoms, talk shows, reality shows, newscasts, and so on. Producers of films and producers of television programs rely on many of the same elements to convey their messages. Among these elements are scripts, visual and sound elements, special effects, and editing.

3.1 SCRIPT AND WRITTEN ELEMENTS

The writer and editor craft a story for television or film using a script and storyboard. A **script** is the text or words of a film or television show. A **storyboard** is a device often used to plan the shooting of a film and to help the director envision and convey what the finished product will look like. It consists of a sequence of sketches showing what will appear in the film's shots, often with explanatory notes and dialogue written beside or underneath them as shown in the example.

For more information, see **Speaking and Listening: Producing a Video Documentary,** *page 605.*

Where is the cat?

I don't know. I haven't seen her.

Neither have I.

3.2 VISUAL ELEMENTS

Visual elements in film and television include camera shots, angles, and movements, as well as film components such as mise en scène, set design, props, and visual special effects.

A **camera shot** is a single, continuous view taken by a camera. **Camera angle** is the angle at which the camera is positioned during the recording of a shot or image. Each angle is carefully planned to create an effect. The following chart explains the different shots and angles.

Camera Shot/Angle	Effect
Establishing shot introduces viewers to the location of a scene, usually by presenting a wide view of an area	establishes the setting of a film
Close-up shot shows a detailed view of a person or an object	helps to create emotion and make viewers feel as if they know the character
Medium shot shows a view wider than a close-up but narrower than an establishing or long shot	shows part of an object or a character from the knees or waist up
Long shot is a wide view of a scene, showing the full figure(s) of a person or group and their surroundings	allows the viewer to see the "big picture" and shows the relationship between characters and the environment
Reaction shot shows someone reacting to something that occurred in a previous shot	allows the viewer to see how the subject feels in order to create empathy in the viewer
Low-angle shot looks up at an object or a person	makes a character, object, or scene appear more important or threatening
High-angle shot looks down on an object or a person	makes a character, object, or scene seem vulnerable or insignificant
Point-of-view (POV) shot shows a part of the story through a character's eyes	helps viewers identify with that character

Camera movement can create energy, reveal information, or establish a mood. The following chart shows some of the ways filmmakers move the camera to create an effect.

Camera Movement	Effect
Pan is a shot in which the camera scans a location from right to left or left to right	reveals information by showing a sweeping view of an area
Tracking shot is a shot in which the camera moves with the subject	establishes tension or creates a sense of drama
Zoom is the movement of the camera as it closes in on or moves farther away from the subject	captures action or draws the viewer's attention to detail

Mise en scène is a French term that refers to the arrangement of actors, props, and action on a film set. It is used to describe everything that can be seen in a frame, including the setting, lighting, visual composition, costumes, and action.

Framing is capturing people and objects within the "frame" of a screen or image. Framing is what the camera sees.

Composition is the arrangement of objects, characters, shapes, and colors within a frame and the relationship of the objects to one another.

3.3 SOUND ELEMENTS

Sound elements in film and television include music, voice-over, and sound effects.

Music may be used to set the mood and atmosphere in a scene. Music can have a powerful effect on the way viewers feel about a story. For example, fast-paced music helps viewers feel excited during an action scene.

Voice-over is the voice of the unseen commentator or narrator of a film, TV program, or commercial.

Sound effects are the sounds added to films, TV programs, and commercials during the editing process. Sound effects, such as laugh tracks or the sounds of punches in a fight scene, can create humor, emphasize a point, or contribute to the mood.

3.4 SPECIAL EFFECTS

Special effects include computer-generated animation, manipulated video images, and fast- or slow-motion sequences in films, TV programs, and commercials.

Animation on film involves the frame-by-frame photography of a series of drawings or objects. When these frames are projected—at a rate of 24 per second—the illusion of movement is achieved.

A **split screen** is a special-effects shot in which two or more separate images are shown in the same frame. One example is when two people, actually a distance apart, are shown talking to each other.

3.5 EDITING

Editing is the process of selecting and arranging shots in a sequence. The editor decides which scenes or shots to use, as well as the length of each shot, the number of shots, and their sequence. Editing establishes pace, mood, and a coherent story.

Cut is the transition from one shot to another. To create excitement, editors often use quick cuts, which are a series of short shots strung together.

Dissolve is a transitional device in which one scene fades into another.

Fade-in is a transitional device in which a white or black shot fades in to reveal the beginning of a new scene.

Fade-out is a transitional device in which a shot fades to darkness to end a scene.

Jump cut is an abrupt and jarring change from one shot to another. A jump cut shows a break in time or continuity.

Pace is the length of time each shot stays on the screen and the rhythm that is created by the transitions between shots. Short, quick cuts create a fast pace in a story. Long cuts slow down a story.

Parallel editing is a technique that cuts from one shot to another so as to suggest simultaneous action—often in different locations.

4 News

The **news** is information on events, people, and places in your community, your region, the nation, and the world. The news can be categorized by type, as shown in the chart.

Type	Description	Examples
Hard news	fact-based accounts of current events	local newspapers, newscasts, online wire services
Soft news	human-interest stories and other accounts that are less current or urgent than hard news	magazines and tabloid TV shows such as *Sports Illustrated, Access Hollywood*
News features	stories that elaborate on news reports	documentaries such as history reports on PBS
Commentary and opinion	essays and perspectives by experts, professionals, and media personalities	editorial pages, personal Web pages

4.1 CHOOSING THE NEWS

Newsworthiness is the significance of an event or action that makes it worthy of media reporting. Journalists and their editors usually weigh the following criteria in determining which stories should make the news:

Timeliness is the quality of being very current. Timely events usually take priority over previously reported events. For example, a car accident with fatalities will be timely on the day it occurs. Because of its timeliness it may be on the front page of a newspaper or the lead story on a newscast.

Widespread impact refers to the importance of an event and the number of people it could affect. The more widespread the impact of an event, the more likely it is to be newsworthy.

Proximity gauges the nearness of an event to a particular city, region, or country. People tend to be more interested in stories that take place locally and affect them directly.

Human interest is a quality of stories that cause readers or listeners to feel emotions such as happiness, anger, or sadness. People are interested in reading stories about other people.

Uniqueness refers to uncommon events or circumstances that are likely to be interesting to an audience.

Compelling video and **photographs** grab people's attention and stay in their minds.

4.2 REPORTING THE NEWS

While developing a news story, a journalist makes a variety of decisions about how to construct the story, such as what information to include and how to organize it. The following elements are commonly used in news stories:

5 *W*'s and *H* are the six questions reporters answer when writing news stories—*who, what, when, where, why,* and *how.* It is a journalist's job to answer these questions in any type of news report. These questions also serve as a structure for writing and editing a story.

Inverted pyramid is the means of organizing information according to importance. In the inverted pyramid diagram below, the most important information (the answers to the 5 *W*'s and *H*) appears at the top of the pyramid. The less important details appear at the bottom. Not all stories are reported using the inverted pyramid form. The style remains popular, however, because it enables a reader to get the essential information without reading the entire story. Notice the following example.

> About 2,000 people gathered at the Vietnam Veterans Memorial Wall on Friday in an antiwar demonstration.
>
> Demonstrators carried signs and sat peacefully as speakers from peace organizations around the world spoke on issues of ending the war.
>
> Speakers called for an immediate end to the war and urged citizens to voice their opinions to state officials and legislators.

Angle or slant is the point of view from which a story is written. Even an objective report must have an angle.

Consider these two headlines that describe a war demonstration.

The first headline suggests that the article following it will be focused on the sentiment or mood of the crowd gathered to demonstrate against a war. The second headline suggests the article will be focused on the event.

Standards for News Reporting

The ideal of journalism is to present news in a way that is objective, accurate, and thorough. The best news stories contain the following elements:

- **Objectivity** The story takes a balanced point of view toward the issues; it is not biased, nor does it reflect a specific attitude or opinion.

- **Accuracy** The story presents factual information that can be verified.

- **Thoroughness** The story presents all sides of an issue; it includes background information, telling *who, what, when, where, why,* and *how.*

Balanced Versus Biased Reporting

Objectivity in news reporting can be measured by how balanced or biased the story is.

Balanced reporting represents all sides of an issue equally and fairly.

A balanced news story

- represents people and subjects in a neutral light
- treats all sides of an issue equally
- does not include inappropriate questions
- does not show stereotypes or prejudice toward people of a particular race, gender, age, religion, or other group
- does not leave out important background information that is needed to establish a context or perspective

Biased reporting is reporting in which one side is favored over another or in which the subject is unfairly represented. Biased reporting may show an overly negative view of a subject, or it may encourage racial, gender, or other stereotypes and prejudices. Sometimes biased reporting is apparent in the journalist's choice of sources.

Sources are the people interviewed for the news report, and also any written materials and documents the journalist used for background information. From each source, the journalist gets a different point of view. To decide whether news reporting is balanced or biased, you will need to pay attention to the sources. For a news story on a new medicinal drug, for instance, if the journalist's only source is a representative from the company that made the drug, the report may be biased. But if the journalist also includes the perspective of someone neutral, such as a scientist who is objectively studying the effects of drugs, the report may be more balanced. It is important to evaluate the **credibility**, or believability and trustworthiness, of both a source and the report itself. The following chart shows which sources are credible.

Sources for News Stories	
Credible Sources	**Weak Sources**
• experts in a field • people directly affected by the reported event (eyewitnesses) • published reports that are specifically mentioned or shown	• unnamed or anonymous sources • people who are not involved in the reported event (for example, people who heard about a story from a friend) • research, data, or reports that are not specifically named or are referred to only in vague terms (for example, "Research shows that …")

5 Advertising

Advertising is a sponsor's paid use of various media to promote products, services, or ideas. Some common forms of advertising are shown in the chart.

Type of Ad	Characteristics
Billboard	large outdoor advertising sign
Print ad	typically appears in magazines and newspapers; uses eye-catching graphics and persuasive copy
Flyer	print ad that is circulated by hand or mail
Infomercial	an extended ad on TV that usually includes detailed product information, demonstrations, and testimonials
Public service announcement	a message aired on radio or TV to promote ideas that are considered to be in the public interest
Political ad	broadcast on radio or TV to promote political candidates
Trailer	a short film promoting an upcoming movie, TV show, or video game

Marketing is the process of transferring products and services from producer to consumer. It involves determining the packaging and pricing of a product, how it will be promoted and advertised, and where it will be sold. One way companies market their products is by becoming media sponsors.

Sponsors pay for their products to be advertised. These companies hire advertising agencies to create and produce specific campaigns for their products. They then buy television or radio airtime or magazine, newspaper, or billboard space to feature ads where the target audience is sure to see them. Because selling time and space to advertisers generates much of the income the media need to function, the media need advertisers just as much as advertisers need the media.

Product placement is the intentional and identifiable featuring of brand-name products in movies, television shows, video games, and other media. The intention is to have viewers feel positive about a product because they see a favorite character using it. Another purpose may be to promote product recognition.

5.1 PERSUASIVE TECHNIQUES

Persuasive techniques are the methods used to convince an audience to buy a product or adopt an idea. Advertisers use a combination of visuals, sound, special effects, and words to persuade their target audience. Recognizing the following techniques can help you evaluate persuasive media messages and identify misleading information:

Emotional appeals use strong feelings rather than factual evidence to persuade consumers. An example of an emotional appeal that targets people's fear is a statement such as this: "Is your identity safe? Protect yourself with ProTech software."

Bandwagon appeal uses the argument that a person should believe or do something because "everyone else" does. These appeals take advantage of people's desire to be socially accepted. Purchasing a popular product seems less risky when many others also find it worthy to buy. An example of a bandwagon appeal is "More and more people are switching to Bright 'n' Fresh laundry detergent."

Slogans are memorable phrases used in advertising campaigns. Slogans substitute catchy phrases for factual information.

Logical appeals rely on logic and facts, appealing to a consumer's reason and his or her respect for authority. Two examples of logical appeals are expert opinions and product comparison.

Celebrity ads use one of the following two categories of spokesperson:

- **Celebrity authorities** are experts in a particular field. Advertisers hope that audiences will transfer the respect or admiration they have for the person to the product. For example, a famous chef may endorse a particular brand of cookware. The manufacturers of the cookware want you to think that it is a good product because a cooking expert wouldn't endorse poor-quality pots and pans.

- **Celebrity spokespeople** are famous people who endorse a product. Advertisers hope that audiences will associate the product with the celebrity.

Product comparison involves comparing a product with its competition. The competing product is portrayed as inferior. The intended effect is for people to question the quality of the competing product and to believe the featured product is superior.

6 Elements of Design

The design of a media message is just as important as the words are in conveying the message. Like words, visuals are used to persuade, inform, and entertain.

Graphics and images, such as charts, diagrams, maps, timelines, photographs, illustrations, cartoons, book covers, and symbols, present information that can be quickly and easily understood. The following basic elements are used to give meaning to visuals:

Color can be used to highlight important elements such as headlines and subheads. It can also create mood, because many colors have a strong emotional or psychological impact on the reader or viewer. For example, warm colors more readily draw the eye and are often associated with happiness and comfort. Cool colors are often associated with feelings of peace and contentment or sometimes sadness.

Lines—strokes or marks—can be thick or thin, long or short, and smooth or jagged. They can focus attention and create a feeling of depth. They can frame an object. They can also direct a viewer's eye or create a sense of motion.

Texture is the surface quality or appearance of an object. For example, an object's texture can be glossy, rough, wet, or shiny. Texture can be used to create contrast. It can also be used to make an image look "real." For example, a pattern on wrapping paper can create a feeling of depth even though the texture is only visual and cannot be felt.

Shape is the external outline of an object. Shapes can be used to symbolize living things or geometric objects. They can emphasize visual elements and add interest. Shapes can also symbolize ideas.

Notice how this photograph uses these design elements to convey a message.

In "reading" this visual image for its message, take note of the following:

• The **foreground image** in this photo is of an unhappy young woman with a plume of smoke rising from her head, indicating she is angry or unhappy— presumably with the situation depicted behind her. The **background images** include smokestacks spewing smoke into the environment. This would suggest that the message concerns her feelings about the environment.

• The **colors** orange and black suggest danger, the need to be alert, or a threatening situation. The colors in this scene indicate that the situation is threatening or dangerous.

• The smokestacks in the background are in silhouette and can only be defined by their **shape.** This suggestion of the image lends an air of mystery and foreboding to the message.

• The **lines** in this picture are primarily vertical (the smokestacks, the young woman, and the white smoke plume). The vertical lines draw your focus toward the top of the photo, where it centers on the crossed smoke plumes.

Considering all the design elements in this photograph, what is its message?

7 Evaluating Media Messages

Being able to respond critically to media images and messages will help you evaluate the reliability of the content and make informed decisions. Here are six questions to ask about any media message:

Who made—and who sponsored—this message, and for what purpose? The source of the message is a clue to its purpose. If the source of the message is a private company, that company may be trying to sell you a product. If the source is a government agency, that agency may be trying to promote a program or philosophy. To discover the purpose, think about why its creator paid for and produced the message.

Who is the target audience and how is the message specifically tailored to it? Think about the age group, ethnic group, gender, and/or profession the message is targeting. Decide how it relates to you.

What are the different techniques used to inform, persuade, entertain, and attract attention? Analyze the elements, such as humor, music, special effects, and graphics, that have been used to create the message. Think about how visual and sound effects, such as symbols, color, photographs, words, and music, support the purpose behind the message.

What messages are communicated (and/or implied) about certain people, places, events, behaviors, lifestyles, and so forth? The media try to influence who we are, what we believe in, how we view things, and what values we hold. Look or listen closely to determine whether certain types of behavior are being depicted and if judgments or values are communicated through those behaviors. What are the biases in the message?

How current, accurate, and credible is the information in this message? Think about the reputation of the source. Note the broadcast or publication date of the message and whether the message might change quickly. If a report or account is not supported by facts, authoritative sources, or eyewitness accounts, you should question the credibility of the message.

What is left out of this message that might be important to know? Think about what the message is asking you to believe. Also think about what questions come to mind as you watch, read, or listen to the message.

Applying Strategies to the SAT* and ACT

The test items in this section are modeled after test formats that are used on the SAT and ACT. The strategies presented here will help you prepare for these tests and others. This section offers general test-taking strategies and tips for answering multiple-choice items in critical reading and writing, as well as samples for impromptu writing and essay writing. For each test, read the tips in the margin. Then apply the tips to the practice items. You can also apply the tips to Assessment Practice tests in this book.

1 General Test-Taking Strategies

- Arrive on time and be prepared. Be sure to bring either sharpened pencils with erasers or pens—whichever you are told to bring.
- If you have any questions, ask them before the test begins. Make sure you understand the test procedures, the timing, and the rules.
- Read the test directions carefully. Look at the passages and questions to get an overview of what is expected.
- Tackle the questions one at a time rather than thinking about the whole test.
- Refer back to the reading selections as needed. For example, if a question asks about an author's attitude, you might have to reread a passage for clues.
- If you are not sure of your answer, make a logical guess. You can often arrive at the correct answer by reasoning and eliminating wrong answers.
- As you fill in answers on your answer sheet, make sure you match the number of each test item to the numbered space on the answer sheet.
- Don't look for patterns in the positions of correct choices.
- Only change an answer if you are sure your original choice is incorrect. If you do change an answer, erase your original choice neatly and thoroughly.
- Look for main ideas as you read passages. They are often stated at the beginning or the end of a paragraph. Sometimes the main idea is implied.
- Check your answers and reread your essay.

* SAT® is a registered trademark of the College Board, which was not involved in the production of, and does not endorse, this product.

2 Critical Reading

Most tests contain a critical reading section that measures your ability to read, understand, and interpret passages. The passages may be either fiction or nonfiction, and they can be 100 words or 500 to 850 words. They are drawn from literature, the humanities, social studies, and the natural sciences.

Directions: Read the following passage. Base your answers to questions 1 and 2 on what is stated or implied in the passage.

PASSAGE

The chemical composition of diamond is extremely simple; like graphite it is composed of only one element: carbon. But the similarity ends there, for no two minerals could be more diverse. Diamond is hard, lustrous, and transparent; graphite is soft, dull, and opaque. Diamond has a specific gravity of 3.5, high for a nonmetallic mineral. Graphite's specific gravity is 2.2, extremely low for a metallic mineral. These strikingly different properties of the same element result from the way in which the carbon atoms are packed together. In diamond they are close together and held by strong electrical bonds, whereas in graphite they are far apart and have weak bonds.

Diamond is valued for its remarkable physical properties. It is harder and more resistant to abrasion than any other natural mineral; nothing can scratch it except another diamond. It is also insoluble in all acids and alkalis. Because of these resistant properties, the Greeks called the mineral *adamas,* meaning "invincible," and its present name derives from that.

—Cornelius Hurlbut, from *Minerals and Man*

❶ stem

1. The idea of the first paragraph is that **❷**

  (A) diamond and graphite consist of the same element but have different properties
  (B) the atoms in diamond and graphite are held together by electrical bonds
  ❸ choices
  (C) diamond is hard, lustrous, and transparent, while graphite is soft, dull, and opaque
  (D) diamond and graphite have a simple chemical composition consisting of one element
  (E) the specific gravity of diamond is high; graphite's specific gravity is low

2. The Greek word *adamas* is a fitting description of diamond's **❹**

  (A) international reputation
  (B) great value
  (C) jewelry applications **❺**
  (D) resistant properties
  (E) ancient lineage

Tips: Multiple Choice

A multiple-choice question consists of a stem and a set of choices. On some tests, there are four choices. On the SAT, there are five. The stem is usually in the form of a question or an incomplete sentence. One of the choices correctly answers the question or completes the sentence.

❶ Read the stem carefully and try to answer the question without looking at the choices.

❷ Pay attention to key words in the stem. They may direct you to the correct answer. Question 1 is looking for the *main* idea. Choices (B) through (E) focus on minor details.

❸ Read all the choices before deciding on the correct answer.

❹ Some questions ask you to interpret a word or a figure of speech. Question 2, for example, asks you to describe the character of a diamond based on the etymology of its name.

❺ After reading all of the choices, eliminate any that you know are incorrect. In question 2, you can safely eliminate choice (C) because this passage focuses on the scientific properties of diamond, not its uses.

Answers: 1. (A), **2.** (D)

Directions: Base your answers to questions 1 and 2 on the two passages below.

PASSAGE 1

❷

The president helps people make sense of politics. Congress is a tangle of committees, the bureaucracy is a maze of agencies. The president is one man ─❸ trying to do a job—a picture much more understandable to the mass of people who find themselves in the same boat. Furthermore, he is the top man. He ought to know what is going on and set it right. So when the economy goes sour, or war drags on, or domestic violence erupts, the president is available to take the blame. Then when things go right, it seems the president must have had a hand in it.

—James David Barber, "The Presidential Character"

PASSAGE 2

No man or group at either end of Pennsylvania Avenue shares his peculiar ─❷ status in our government and politics. That is why his services are in demand. By the same token, though, the obligations of all other men are different from his own. His Cabinet officers have departmental duties and constituents. His legislative leaders head Congressional parties, one in either House. His national party organization stands apart from his official family. His political allies in the states need not face Washington, or one another. The private groups that seek him out are not compelled to govern. And friends abroad are not compelled to run in our elections. Lacking his position and prerogatives, these ─❹ men cannot regard his obligations as his own. They have their jobs to do; none is the same as his.

—Richard E. Neustadt, "Presidential Power"

❶ 1. In Passage 1, what does the author mean when he says, "The president helps people make sense of politics"?

   (A) The government is sponsoring political education classes for voters.

   (B) People see the president in personal terms, as someone with a job to do.

   (C) The White House has valuable information about the legislative process.

   (D) Congress is an impenetrable maze of agencies and committees.

   (E) Citizens have to think about international issues before they vote.

2. The authors of both passages would probably agree with which one of these statements about government? ❺

   (A) It is difficult to penetrate the maze of government bureaucracies.

   (B) Many elected officials are only concerned with local issues.

   (C) Each president leaves an indelible imprint on the nation.

   (D) Not everyone supports the president or his policies.

   (E) The president holds a unique position in our political system.

Tips: Two Passages

Questions are sometimes based on a pair of related passages, which may have completely different views or may simply describe different aspects of the same subject. The two passages here discuss the role of the U.S. president.

❶ Before reading the passages, skim all the questions to see what information you will need.

❷ Find topic sentences and ask yourself whether the passages support or refute their topic sentences. In this case, both passages support their claims with examples and discussion.

❸ You can determine an author's attitude toward a subject by his or her choice of words. In passage 1, the words *tangle* and *maze* convey a subtle disapproval of government bureaucracies.

❹ Analyze supporting details. The author of passage 2 supports his claim that the president has unique responsibilities by contrasting his position with those of others.

❺ When working with two passages, look for related or contrasting ideas. To answer question 2, you have to find a common thread in the discussions of the presidency. Eliminate any answers that pertain to only one of the passages.

Answers: 1. (B), **2.** (E)

Directions: Read the following passage, taken from a novel published in 1900. Based on what is stated or implied in the passage, answer questions 1 through 5, which appear on the next page.

PASSAGE

When Caroline Meeber boarded the afternoon train for Chicago, her total outfit consisted of a small trunk, a cheap imitation alligator-skin satchel, a small lunch in a paper box, and a yellow leather snap purse containing her ticket, a scrap of paper with her sister's address in Van Buren Street, and four dollars in money. It was in August, 1889. She was eighteen years of age, bright, timid, and full of the illusions of ignorance and youth. Whatever touch of regret at parting characterized her thoughts, it was certainly not for advantages now being given up. A gush of tears at her mother's farewell kiss, a touch in her throat when the cars clacked by the flour mill where her father worked by the day, a pathetic sign as the familiar green environs of the village passed in review, and the threads which bound her so lightly to girlhood and home were irretrievably broken.

To be sure, there was always the next station, where one might descend and return. There was the great city, bound more closely by these very trains which came up daily. Columbia City was not so very far away, even once she was in Chicago. What, pray, is a few hours—a few hundred miles? She looked at the little slip bearing her sister's address and wondered. She gazed at the green landscape, now passing in swift review, until her swifter thoughts replaced its impression with vague conjectures of what Chicago might be.

When a girl leaves her home at eighteen, she does one of two things. Either she falls into saving hands and becomes better, or she rapidly assumes the cosmopolitan standard of virtue and becomes worse. Of an intermediate balance, under the circumstances, there is no possibility. The city has its cunning wiles, no less than the infinitely smaller and more human tempter. There are large forces which allure with all the soulfulness of expression possible in the most cultured human. The gleam of a thousand lights is often as effective as the persuasive light in a wooing and fascinating eye. Half of the undoing of the unsophisticated and natural mind is accomplished by forces wholly superhuman. A blare of sound, a roar of life, a vast array of human hives, appeal to the astonished senses in equivocal terms. Without a counselor at hand to whisper cautious interpretations, what falsehoods may not these things breathe into the unguarded ear! Unrecognized for what they are, their beauty, like music, too often relaxes, then weakens, then perverts the simpler human perceptions.

Tips: Reading Text

❶ Notice the characters who are presented in a passage. Be alert to details about their appearance, personality, or behavior.

❷ Identify the point of view from which the story is being told. In a first-person narrative, the narrator is a character in the story and uses the pronouns *I* and *me*. In a third-person narrative, the narrator is outside the story and uses the pronouns *he, she,* and *they.*

❸ Try to visualize the setting as you read, filling in details as they are presented. In this passage we see a young woman on a train headed for Chicago in 1889. She has left behind the "familiar green environs" of her home in the small town of Columbia City.

❹ Remember that a word can have several different meanings or subtle shades of meaning.

❺ Some test questions will ask you to interpret a figure of speech or an image. Try to understand why the author chose that particular image and what effect it achieves.

Answers: 1. (D), **2.** (B), **3.** (A), **4.** (C), **5.** (E)

1. The catalog of Caroline's belongings in lines 2–5 helps to
   (A) foreshadow her destiny
   (B) mock her appearance
   (C) create sympathy for her
   (D) convey her social status
   (E) portray her personality

2. What is implied about Caroline's life in the statement "Whatever touch of regret at parting characterized her thoughts, it was certainly not for advantages now being given up"?
   (A) It was hard for Caroline to leave behind the comforts of home.
   (B) Caroline's life at home offered few material benefits.
   (C) Caroline hated the life of poverty she led at home.
   (D) Moving to the city required a sacrifice on Caroline's part.
   (E) Once she left home, Caroline never looked back.

3. The description in lines 21–24 suggests that the city is a place that should be viewed with
   (A) distrust
   (B) respect
   (C) enthusiasm
   (D) contempt
   (E) nostalgia

4. The image of a tempter in lines 24–30 suggests the ❺
   (A) evils of human nature
   (B) simple beauty of music
   (C) corrupting influence of the city
   (D) vulnerable innocence of youth
   (E) pleasures of materialism

5. In line 29, "natural" most nearly means
   (A) normal
   (B) inborn
   (C) logical
   (D) real
   (E) naive

The critical reading section may feature sentence completion questions that test your knowledge of vocabulary. They may also measure your ability to figure out how different parts of a sentence logically fit together.

> **Directions:** Choose the word or set of words that, when inserted, best fits the meaning of the complete sentence.

1. The investigator constructed a _____ of events to _____ the cause of the accident. ❶
   - (A) chronology . . ascertain
   - (B) timeline . . predict ❷
   - (C) typology . . determine
   - (D) collation . . understand
   - (E) history . . prosecute

2. Russian author Alexander Solzhenitsyn tried to _____ government censorship by _____ some of his writings out of the country.
   - (A) encircle . . translating
   - (B) disrupt . . carrying
   - (C) circumvent . . smuggling ❸
   - (D) evade . . banishing
   - (E) prevent . . propelling

3. Automakers can _____ the effects of global warming by reducing carbon-dioxide and other _____ emissions from cars and trucks. ❹
   - (A) minimize . . natural
   - (B) misuse . . harmful
   - (C) correct . . excessive
   - (D) mitigate . . toxic
   - (E) relieve . . acute

4. Because they have a _____ appetite, bears will raid cabins, backpacks, and picnic areas in search of anything that smells of food. ❺ ❻
   - (A) vicious
   - (B) voracious
   - (C) refined
   - (D) notorious
   - (E) selective

Tips: Sentence Completion

❶ When you are completing sentences with two words missing, think about which pair of suggested words fits both blanks.

❷ If one word in the answer choice is wrong, eliminate that choice from consideration. In sentence 1, *timeline* makes sense, but *predict* does not, because the accident occurred in the past.

❸ A prefix can help to unlock the meaning of a word. The Latin prefix *circum-* means "around." The writer was trying to circumvent, or go around, government censorship.

❹ Look for key words or phrases that link the ideas in a sentence. The word *by* introduces a phrase that explains how to do something—in this case, how to reduce global warming.

❺ Look for words that link the ideas in a sentence. The word *because* in sentence 4 signals a cause-and-effect relationship between appetite and behavior.

❻ If you don't know a word's meaning, look for clues within the sentence. For sentence 4, ask yourself: What sort of appetite would lead a bear to eat almost anything? An animal with a *refined* (C) or *selective* (E) appetite, for example, would choose only certain foods.

Answers: 1. (A), **2.** (C), **3.** (D), **4.** (B)

3 Writing

The writing section of standardized tests measures your ability to express ideas clearly and correctly. You will be asked to identify errors in grammar and usage and to improve sentences and paragraphs.

Directions: The following sentence contains either a single error or no error. If it does contains an error, select the underlined part that must be changed to make the sentence correct. If the sentence is correct as written, select answer choice (E).

1. Neither the Supreme Court nor the president have the power to create laws,
   (A)   (B)   (C) ❷

   because the Constitution entrusts that responsibility to Congresss alone. No error
                           (D) ❸   (E) ❶

Directions: Determine if the underlined part of the following sentence needs improvement. If it does, select the best change presented. If the original phrasing is best, select answer (A).

2. Ancient Greeks believed in mythical creatures, they combined human and animal traits.
   ❹
   (A) creatures, they combined
   (B) creatures, and they combined
   (C) creatures that combined ❺
   (D) creatures, and which combined
   (E) creatures such as could combine

Directions: Following is an early draft of an essay. Read it and answer the question.

Controlling E-Waste

(1) It is estimated that Americans generate about 2 million tons of technology-related trash each year. (2) Computer circuit boards, monitors, and printers are piling up in landfills. (3) They decay. (4) They can leak mercury and other toxic substances as a result of the decay. (5) Some public health officials think the U.S. should develop a federal law that requires technology companies to take back their used products and reduce the amount of hazardous material they use in manufacturing.

---

3. Which one of the following sentences combines sentences 3 and 4? ❻
   (A) They can decay, also leaking mercury and other toxic substances.
   (B) When they decay, they can leak mercury and other toxic substances.
   (C) They decay; then they can leak mercury and other toxic substances.
   (D) They decay, and thus leak mercury and other toxic substances.
   (E) They can leak toxic substances such as mercury.

Tips: Grammar and Style

❶ Read the entire sentence or passage to grasp its overall meaning. Pay particular attention to any underlined portions.

❷ Watch for subject-verb agreement when using *neither...nor.* If both subjects are singular, the verb must be singular.

❸ Use prefixes to help you understand the meaning of words. The prefix *en-* in the word *entrust* means "in" or "within."

❹ Read through all of the choices before you decide which revision is best. In this case, answer (A) is *not* correct, because joining two independent clauses with only a comma creates a run-on sentence.

❺ Understand how to use *that* and *which. That* introduces an essential defining clause. *Which* introduces a nonessential clause. Use *which* if the clause can be omitted without changing the meaning of the sentence. Nonessential clauses are set off with commas.

❻ When combining sentences, think about how the ideas are related. Subordinating conjunctions such as *while, when, before, after,* and *until* express a relationship of time. *Because* and *since* indicate cause and effect.

Answers: 1. (C), **2.** (C), **3.** (B)

4 Essay

To determine how well you can develop and express ideas, many tests ask you to write an essay in response to an assignment, or prompt. The essay will represent a first draft and be scored based on the following criteria:

- **Focus** Establish a point of view in the opening paragraph.
- **Organization** Maintain a logical progression of ideas.
- **Support for Ideas** Use details and examples to develop an argument.
- **Style/Word Choice** Use words accurately and vary your sentences.
- **Grammar** Use Standard English and proofread for errors.

Think carefully about the issue presented in this quotation and the assignment below.

> Arts education and physical education both enjoy public support and help students grow and develop in many ways. In recent years, these programs have sometimes been marginalized or discontinued due to budget cuts or redirection of school resources. Sometimes schools have had to choose between these programs.

Assignment: If a school had to choose between funding its arts program and funding its physical education program, which option would you support? Plan and write an essay in which you develop your opinion on this issue. Support your position with specific reasons and examples taken from your studies and experience.

SAMPLE ESSAY

If I had to decide whether to cut arts or physical education programs from the curriculum, I would choose to save the arts. **❶**

It's hard to cut physical education programs when our nation is struggling with an obesity epidemic. We all know that Americans don't get enough exercise. We drive everywhere, and we spend hours in front of the TV. But physical fitness is a medical and lifestyle issue, not an academic pursuit. Exercise and good nutrition require a personal, lifelong commitment, and that goes beyond what can be taught in a gym class. **❷**

The arts, on the other hand, are as much an academic pursuit as science, history, or literature. Acting in a play requires reading and interpreting a work of literature. Composing even a simple tune requires knowledge of harmony, rhythm, and timing. Painting and drawing require some understanding of the principles of light, color, and perspective. Whereas high school athletes often struggle with academics because of the demands of their sport, students in music and performing arts don't seem to experience those conflicting demands in the same way. **❸**

Arts education encourages students to be creative and to take risks. There are no right or wrong answers in art, so students who might not excel in other areas of academic life can gain respect through their music or dancing.

Music, painting, literature, dance, and theater not only enrich our lives but also stimulate us and teach us life lessons that a gym class never could. **❹**

Tips: Writing an Essay

The SAT allows only 25 minutes for you to write an essay. Before you begin writing, take a few minutes to jot down the main points you want to make. Allow time to reread and proofread your essay before you hand it in.

❶ When you're writing a persuasive essay, state your point of view in the introduction. Be sure to keep your purpose in mind as you write.

❷ Take the opposing point of view into consideration and respond to it.

❸ Include concrete examples in the body of your essay to clarify your points and strengthen your arguments.

❹ Make sure your essay has a conclusion, even if it is just a single sentence. A conclusion pulls your ideas together and lets the reader know that you have finished.

❺ There will not be time to recopy your essay, so if you have to make a correction, do so neatly and legibly.

❻ You don't have to write a long essay. Length is less important than clarity of thought and correctness of expression. Your essay could range from 200 to 400 words.

Act An act is a major unit of action in a play, similar to a chapter in a book. Depending on their lengths, plays can have as many as five acts. Arthur Miller's play *The Crucible* has four acts.
See also **Drama; Scene.**

Allegory An allegory is a work with two levels of meaning, a literal one and a symbolic one. In such a work, most of the characters, objects, settings, and events represent abstract qualities. Personification is often used in traditional allegories. As in a fable or parable, the purpose of an allegory may be to convey truths about life, to teach religious or moral lessons, or to criticize social institutions.
Example: In Edgar Allan Poe's "The Masque of the Red Death," the main character Prospero, the sequence and the decorations of the rooms in the castle, and objects such as the ebony clock all have allegorical meaning.
See page 427.

Alliteration Alliteration is the repetition of consonant sounds at the beginnings of words. Poets use alliteration to impart a musical quality to their poems, to create mood, to reinforce meaning, to emphasize particular words, and to unify lines or stanzas. Note the examples of alliteration in the following line:

> Doubting, dreaming dreams no mortal ever dared to dream before.
> —Edgar Allan Poe, "The Raven"

See pages 437, 1237.

Allusion An allusion is an indirect reference to a person, place, event, or literary work with which the author believes the reader will be familiar.
Example: In "Speech in the Virginia Convention," Patrick Henry warns colonists not to be "betrayed with a kiss"—an allusion to the Apostle Judas, who betrayed Jesus by kissing him.
See pages 231, 902, 1145.

Ambiguity Ambiguity is a technique in which a word, phrase, or event has more than one meaning or can be interepreted in more than one way. Some writers deliberately create this effect to give richness and depth of meaning. T. S. Eliot and Robert Frost are two poets known for their use of ambiguity.
See pages 471, 897, 1015.

Analogy An analogy is a point-by-point comparison between two things for the purpose of clarifying the less familiar of the two subjects.
Example: In "My Dungeon Shook," James Baldwin draws an analogy between his nephew's probable reaction to seeing the stars shining while the sun is out and white people's reaction to black people moving out of their fixed places.
See pages 252, 272, 1157, 1197.

Anapest *See* **Meter.**

Anaphora Anaphora is a repetition of a word or words at the beginning of successive lines, clauses, or sentences.

> Blackness
> is a title,
> is a preoccupation,
> is a commitment . . .
> —Gwendolyn Brooks, "Primer for Blacks"

See pages 509, 1231.
See also **Repetition.**

Anecdote An anecdote is a brief story that focuses on a single episode or event in a person's life and that is used to illustrate a particular point.
Example: In "Straw into Gold," Sandra Cisneros provides an anecdote about the challenge she faced when ordered to make corn tortillas, a task she had never done before. This anecdote illustrates Cisneros's pluck in attempting the seemingly impossible.
See pages 371, 1223.

Antagonist An antagonist is usually the principal character in opposition to the **protagonist,** or hero of a narrative or drama. The antagonist can also be a force of nature.
Example: In "The Open Boat," the sea is the antagonist of the four shipwrecked men. Its powerful force is described in such detail that it seems like a character.
See pages 735, 937.
See also **Character; Protagonist.**

Antihero An antihero is a protagonist who has the qualities opposite to those of a hero; he or she may be insecure, ineffective, cowardly, sometimes dishonest or dishonorable, or—most often—a failure. A popular antihero in contemporary culture is the cartoon character Homer Simpson.

Aphorism An aphorism is a brief statement, usually one sentence long, that expresses a general principle or truth about life.

Example: Ralph Waldo Emerson's "Self-Reliance" is sprinkled with such memorable aphorisms as "A foolish consistency is the hobgoblin of little minds."
See pages 271, 361.

Archetype An archetype is a pattern in literature that is found in a variety of works from different cultures throughout the ages. An archetype can be a plot, a character, an image, or a setting. For example, the association of death and rebirth with winter and spring is an archetype common to many cultures.

Aside In drama, an aside is a short speech directed to the audience, or another character, that is not heard by the other characters on stage.
See also **Soliloquy.**

Assonance Assonance is the repetition of vowel sounds within words. Both poets and prose writers use assonance to impart a musical quality to their works, to create mood, to reinforce meaning, to emphasize particular words, and to unify lines, stanzas, or passages. Note examples of assonance in the following lines:

> Along the window-sill, the lipstick stubs
> Glittered in their steel shells.
> —Rita Dove, "Adolescence—III"

See also **Alliteration; Consonance; Rhyme.**

Atmosphere *See* **Mood.**

Audience Audience is the person or persons who are intended to read a piece of writing. The intended audience of a work determines its form, style, tone, and the details included. For example, Cabeza de Vaca's audience for *La Relación* was the king of Spain. Hence, *La Relación* took the form of a formal report with a patriotic tone that included details of the explorers' hardship and determination. Had the work been addressed to Cabeza de Vaca's wife, it would likely have been less formal and probably would have included details about his personal feelings.
See pages 69, 119, 1199.

Author's Purpose A writer usually writes for one or more of these purposes: to inform, to entertain, to express himself or herself, or to persuade readers to believe or do something. For example, the purpose of a news report is to inform; the purpose of an editorial is to persuade the readers or audience to do or believe something.
Examples: In *The Interesting Narrative of the Life of Olaudah Equiano,* the author's purpose is primarily to inform readers

about the horrors that captured Africans endured in the holds of slave ships during the Middle Passage. Thoreau's purpose in "Civil Disobedience," on the other hand, is to persuade his audience to use nonviolent resistance to oppose unjust laws.
See pages 79, 371.

Author's Perspective An author's perspective is a unique combination of ideas, values, feelings, and beliefs that influences the way the writer looks at a topic. **Tone,** or attitude, often reveals an author's perspective. For example, Jonathan Edwards was a Puritan minister whose father and grandfather were also Puritan ministers; he began his theological training at age 12. His family upbringing, his beliefs, and the time and place in which he lived all contributed to the perspective found in *Sinners in the Hands of an Angry God.*
See pages 118, 395, 745.
See also **Author's Purpose; Tone.**

Autobiographical Essay *See* **Essay.**

Autobiography An autobiography is the story of a person's life written by that person. Generally written from the first-person point of view, autobiographies can vary in style from straightforward chronological accounts to impressionistic narratives.
Example: Both *Narrative of the Life of Frederick Douglass, an American Slave* and *Coming of Age in Mississippi* are autobiographies.
See pages 262, 536, 634.

Ballad A ballad is a narrative poem that was originally meant to be sung. Ballads often contain dialogue and repetition and suggest more than they actually state. Traditional **folk ballads,** composed by unknown authors and handed down orally, are written in four-line stanzas with regular rhythm and rhyme. A **literary ballad** is one that is modeled on the folk ballads but written by a single author—for example, Dudley Randall's "Ballad of Birmingham."
See page 1156.
See also **Narrative Poem; Rhyme; Rhythm.**

Biography A biography is a type of nonfiction in which a writer gives a factual account of someone else's life. Written in the third person, a biography may cover a person's entire life or focus on only an important part of it. The poet Carl Sandburg wrote an acclaimed six-volume biography of Abraham Lincoln. Modern biography includes a popular form called **fictionalized biography,** in which writers use their imaginations to re-create past conversations and to elaborate on some incidents.

Blank Verse A poem written in blank verse consists of unrhymed lines of iambic pentameter. In other words, each line of blank verse has five pairs of syllables. In most pairs, an unstressed syllable is followed by a stressed syllable. The most versatile of poetic forms, blank verse imitates the natural rhythms of English speech, as in the following lines:

> She ran | on tip | toe down | the dark | ened passage
> To meet | him in | the door | way with | the news
> And put | him on | his guard. | "Silas | is back."
> She pushed | him out | ward with | her through |
>   the door
> And shut | it aft | er her. | "Be kind," | she said.
>   —Robert Frost, "The Death of the Hired Man"

See pages 329, 903.
See also **Iambic Pentameter; Meter; Rhythm.**

Caesura A caesura is a pause or a break in a line of poetry. Poets use a caesura to emphasize the word or phrase that precedes it or to vary the rhythmical effects. In the following line, a caesura follows the word *die*:

> If we must die, let it not be like hogs
>   —Claude McKay, "If We Must Die"

Cast of Characters The cast of characters is a list of all the characters in a play, usually in the order of appearance. This list is found at the beginning of a script.
See page 133.

Catalog A catalog is a list of people, things, or attributes. This technique, found in epics and in the Bible, also characterizes Whitman's style, as seen in the beginning of this line:

> Kanuck, Tuckahoe, Congressman, Cuff, I give them the same, I receive them the same.
>   —Walt Whitman, "Song of Myself"

See page 509.

Character Characters are the people, and sometimes animals or other beings, who take part in the action of a story or novel. Events center on the lives of one or more characters, referred to as **main characters.** The other characters, called **minor characters,** interact with the main characters and help move the story along. In Kurt Vonnegut's story "Adam," Heinz Knechtmann is the main character, while the other expectant father, Mr. Sousa, is a minor character.

Characters may also be classified as either static or dynamic. **Static characters** tend to stay in a fixed position over the course of the story. They do not experience life-altering moments and seem to act the same, even though their situations may change. In contrast, **dynamic characters** evolve as individuals, learning from their experiences and growing emotionally.
See pages 693, 903, 937, 1123.
See also **Antagonist; Characterization; Foil; Motivation; Protagonist.**

Characterization Characterization refers to the techniques a writer uses to develop characters. There are four basic methods of characterization:

1. A writer may use physical description. In F. Scott Fitzgerald's "Winter Dreams," Judy Jones is described as follows:

> She wore a blue gingham dress, rimmed at throat and shoulders with a white edging that accentuated her tan. . . . She was arrestingly beautiful. The color in her cheeks was centered like the color in a picture—it was not a "high" color, but a sort of fluctuating and feverish warmth. . . .

2. The character's own actions, words, thoughts, and feelings might be presented. In Fitzgerald's story, after Judy Jones tries to revive the romance between herself and Dexter, she cries and says, "I'm more beautiful than anybody else, . . . why can't I be happy?"

3. The actions, words, thoughts, and feelings of other characters provide another means of developing a character. Mr. Sandwood, in Fitzgerald's story, exclaims about Judy Jones: "My God, she's good-looking!" To which Mr. Hedrick replies: "Good-looking! She always looks as if she wanted to be kissed! Turning those big cow-eyes on every calf in town!"

4. The narrator's own direct comments also serve to develop a character. The narrator of "Winter Dreams" says of Judy Jones:

> Whatever Judy wanted, she went after with the full pressure of her charm. There was no divergence of method, no jockeying for position or premeditation of effects—there was very little mental side to any of her affairs. She simply made men conscious to the highest degree of her physical loveliness.

See pages 667, 881, 1123.
See also **Character; Narrator.**

Chorus *In the theater of ancient Greece, the chorus was a group of actors who commented on the action of the play. Between scenes, the chorus sang and danced to musical accompaniment, giving insights into the message of the play. The chorus is often considered a kind of ideal spectator, representing the response of ordinary citizens to the tragic events that unfold. Certain dramatists have continued to employ this classical convention as a way of representing the views of the society being depicted.*
See also **Drama.**

Cliché A cliché is an overused expression that has lost its freshness, force, and appeal. The phrase "happy as a lark" is an example of a cliché.

Climax In a plot structure, the climax, or turning point, is the moment when the reader's interest and emotional intensity reach a peak. The climax usually occurs toward the end of a story and often results in a change in the characters or a solution to the conflict.
Example: In Edgar Allan Poe's "The Masque of the Red Death," the climax occurs when the Red Death arrives at the masked ball and is confronted by Prince Prospero. Shortly afterward, Prospero and all of his guests die.
See also **Falling Action; Plot; Rising Action; Resolution.**

Comedy A comedy is a dramatic work that is light and often humorous in tone, usually ending happily with a peaceful resolution of the main conflict. A comedy differs from a **farce** by having a more believable plot, more realistic characters, and less boisterous behavior.
See also **Drama; Farce.**

Comic Relief Comic relief consists of humorous scenes, incidents, or speeches that are included in a serious drama to provide a reduction in emotional intensity. Because it breaks the tension, comic relief allows an audience to prepare emotionally for events to come.

Complication A complication is an additional factor or problem introduced into the rising action of a story to make the conflict more difficult. Often, a plot complication makes it seem as though the main character is getting farther away from the thing he or she wants.

Conceit *See* **Extended Metaphor.**

Conflict A conflict is a struggle between opposing forces that is the basis of a story's plot. An **external conflict** pits a character against nature, society, or another character. An **internal conflict** is a conflict between opposing forces within a character.
Example: In "Coyote and the Buffalo," Coyote's struggle to keep Buffalo Bull from killing him is an external conflict, whereas Coyote's struggle to decide whether to kill and eat the buffalo cow is an internal conflict.
See pages 44, 735, 759, 1137.
See also **Antagonist; Plot.**

Connotation Connotation is the emotional response evoked by a word, in contrast to its denotation, which is its literal meaning. *Kitten*, for example, is defined as "a young cat." However, the word also suggests, or connotes, images of softness, warmth, and playfulness.

Consonance Consonance is the repetition of consonant sounds within and at the ends of words.

> Some late visitor entreating entrance at my chamber door.
>
> —Edgar Allan Poe, "The Raven"

See also **Alliteration; Assonance.**

Couplet *See* **Sonnet.**

Creation Myth *See* **Myth.**

Critical Essay *See* **Essay.**

Cultural Hero A cultural hero is a larger-than-life figure who reflects the values of a people. Rather than being the creation of a single writer, this kind of hero evolves from the telling of folk tales from one generation to the next. The role of the cultural hero is to provide a noble image that will inspire and guide the actions of all who share that culture.

Dactyl *See* **Meter.**

Denotation *See* **Connotation.**

Dénouement *See* **Falling Action.**

Description Description is writing that helps a reader to picture scenes, events, and characters. Effective description usually relies on imagery, figurative language, and precise diction, as in the following passage:

> I saw again the naked house on the prairie, black and grim as a wooden fortress; the black pond where I had learned to swim, its margin pitted with sun-dried cattle tracks; the rain gullied clay banks about the naked house, the four dwarf ash seedlings where the dish-cloths were always hung to dry before the kitchen door.
> —Willa Cather, "A Wagner Matinee"

See pages 694, 711.
See also **Diction; Figurative Language; Imagery.**

Dialect A dialect is the distinct form of a language as it is spoken in one geographical area or by a particular social or ethnic group. A group's dialect is reflected in characteristic pronunciations, vocabulary, idioms, and grammatical constructions. When trying to reproduce a given dialect, writers often use unconventional spellings to suggest the way words actually sound. Writers use dialect to establish setting, to provide local color, and to develop characters. In the following passage, the use of dialect captures the sound and tang of frontier speech:

> And he had a little small bull-pup, that to look at him you'd think he warn't worth a cent but to set around and look ornery and lay for a chance to steal something.
> —Mark Twain,
> "The Notorious Jumping Frog of Calaveras County"

See pages 659, 1034.
See also **Local Color Realism.**

Dialogue Dialogue is conversation between two or more characters in either fiction or nonfiction. In drama, the story is told almost exclusively through dialogue, which moves the plot forward and reveals characters' motives.
See pages 650, 903, 1049.
See also **Drama.**

Diary A diary is a writer's personal day-to-day account of his or her experiences and impressions. Most diaries are private and not intended to be shared. Some, however, have been published because they are well written and provide useful perspectives on historical events or on the everyday life of particular eras. One important American diary found in this book is Mary Chesnut's diary of the Civil War.

Diction A writer's or speaker's choice of words is called diction. Diction includes both vocabulary (individual words) and syntax (the order or arrangement of words). Diction can be formal or informal, technical or common, abstract or concrete. In the following complex sentence, the diction is formal:

> When, however, the mass movement repudiates violence while moving resolutely toward its goal, its opponents are revealed as the instigators and practitioners of violence if it occurs.
> —Martin Luther King Jr., "Stride Toward Freedom"

See pages 255, 649, 1067.

Drama Drama is literature in which plot and character are developed through dialogue and action; in other words, drama is literature in play form. It is performed on stage and radio and in films and television. Most plays are divided into acts, with each act having an emotional peak, or climax, of its own. The acts sometimes are divided into scenes; each scene is limited to a single time and place. Most contemporary plays have two or three acts, although some have only one act.
See pages 128, 131, 1097.
See also **Act; Dialogue; Scene; Stage Directions.**

Dramatic Irony See **Irony.**

Dramatic Monologue A dramatic monologue is a lyric poem in which a speaker addresses a silent or absent listener in a moment of high intensity or deep emotion, as if engaged in private conversation. The speaker proceeds without interruption or argument, and the effect on the reader is that of hearing just one side of a conversation. This technique allows the poet to focus on the feelings, personality, and motivations of the speaker.
See also **Lyric Poetry; Soliloquy.**

Dynamic Character See **Character.**

Elegy An elegy is a poem written in tribute to a person, usually someone who has died recently. The tone of an elegy is usually formal and dignified.

Epic Poem An epic is a long narrative poem on a serious subject presented in an elevated or formal style. An epic traces the adventures of a hero whose actions consist of courageous, even superhuman, deeds, which often represent the ideals and values of a nation or race. Epics typically address universal issues, such as good and evil, life and death, and sin and redemption. Homer's *Iliad* and *Odyssey* are famous epics from western civilization. The *Ramayana* is an epic from India.

Epic Hero An epic hero is a larger-than-life figure who embodies the ideals of a nation or race. Epic heroes take part in dangerous adventures and accomplish great deeds. Many undertake long, difficult journeys and display great courage and superhuman strength.

Epithet An epithet is a brief descriptive phrase that points out traits associated with a particular person or thing.
Example: Carl Sandburg's "Chicago" begins with a series of epithets, such as "Hog Butcher for the World."

Essay An essay is a short work of nonfiction that deals with a single subject. Essays are often informal, loosely structured, and highly personal. They can be descriptive, informative, persuasive, narrative, or any combination of these. Amy Tan's personal essay "Mother Tongue" combines all of these qualities.

An **autobiographical essay** focuses on an aspect of a writer's life. Generally, writers of autobiographical essays use the first-person point of view, combining objective description with the expression of subjective feelings. Zora Neale Hurston's "How It Feels to Be Colored Me" is an example of an autobiographical essay.
See pages 371, 870, 1068, 1205.

Exaggeration *See* **Hyperbole.**

Experimental Poetry Poetry described as experimental is often full of surprises—unusual word order, invented forms, descriptions of ordinary objects, and other distinctive elements not found in traditional verse forms. William Carlos Williams belonged to a group of experimental poets known as the Imagists. Their poems contain sharp, clear images of striking beauty, similar to the ones found in haiku. E. E. Cummings's "anyone lived in a pretty how town" reflects his unique brand of poetic experimentation, such as altering the expected presentation of words.
See page 921.

Exposition Exposition is the part of a literary work that provides the background information necessary to understand characters and their actions. Typically found at the beginning of a work, the exposition introduces the characters, describes the setting, and summarizes significant events that took place before the action begins.
Example: In the exposition to "The Devil and Tom Walker," Washington Irving introduces the main characters—a miser and his wife—who dwell in a desolate house near a swamp and take wicked glee in hoarding things from each other.
See also **Plot; Rising Action.**

Expository Essay *See* **Essay.**

Extended Metaphor Like any metaphor, an extended metaphor is a comparison between two essentially unlike things that nevertheless have something in common. It does not contain the word *like* or *as*. An extended metaphor compares two things at some length and in various ways. Sometimes the comparison is carried throughout a paragraph, a stanza, or an entire selection. In the following stanza, notice the extended metaphor in which the speaker compares himself to a loom for God's use:

> Make me, O Lord, Thy spinning wheel complete.
> Thy holy word my distaff make for me.
> Make mine affections Thy swift flyers neat,
> And make my soul Thy holy spool to be.
> My conversation make to be Thy reel,
> And reel the yarn thereon spun of Thy wheel.
> —Edward Taylor, "Huswifery"

Like an extended metaphor, a **conceit** compares two apparently dissimilar things in several ways. The term usually implies a more elaborate, formal, and ingeniously clever comparison than the extended metaphor.
See pages 111, 857.

External Conflict *See* **Conflict.**

Eyewitness Account An eyewitness account is a firsthand report of an event written by someone who directly observed it or participated in it. As such, an eyewitness account is a primary source. Narrated from the first-person point of view, eyewitness accounts almost always include the following:

- objective facts about an event

- a chronological (time-order) pattern of organization

- vivid sensory details

- quotations from people who were present

- description of the writer's feelings and interpretations.

The excerpt from Anne Moody's autobiography, *Coming of Age in Mississippi,* is an eyewitness account of a sit-in in 1963.
See page 1181.
See also **Primary Source.**

Fable A fable is a brief tale that illustrates a clear, often directly stated, moral, or lesson. The characters in a fable are usually animals, but sometimes they are humans. The best-known fables—for example, "The Fox and the Crow" and "The Tortoise and the Hare" are those of Aesop, a Greek slave who lived about 600 B.C. Traditionally, fables are handed down from generation to generation as oral literature.
See also **Oral Literature.**

Falling Action In a plot structure, the falling action, or **resolution,** occurs after the climax to reveal the final outcome of events and to tie up any loose ends.
See also **Climax; Exposition; Plot; Rising Action.**

Farce A farce is a type of exaggerated comedy that features an absurd plot, ridiculous situations, and humorous dialogue. The main purpose of a farce is to keep an audience laughing. The characters are usually **stereotypes,** or simplified examples of different traits or qualities. Comic devices typically used in farces include mistaken identity, deception, wordplay—such as puns and double meanings—and exaggeration.
See also **Comedy; Stereotype.**

Fiction Fiction refers to works of prose that contain imaginary elements. Although fiction, like nonfiction, may be based on actual events and real people, it differs from nonfiction in that it is shaped primarily by the writer's imagination. For example, although Hemingway's "In Another Country" is based on autobiographical experiences, it cannot be classified as nonfiction because it is imbued with imaginary events and exaggeration in order to hold the reader's interest. The two major types of fiction are novels and short stories. The four basic elements of a work of fiction are **character, setting, plot,** and **theme.**
See also **Novel; Short Story.**

Figurative Language Figurative language is language that communicates ideas beyond the literal meaning of words. Figurative language can make descriptions and unfamiliar or difficult ideas easier to understand. Note the figurative language in this passage from "The Open Boat":

> A seat in this boat was not unlike a seat upon a bucking broncho, and, by the same token, a broncho is not much smaller. The craft pranced and reared, and plunged like an animal. As each wave came, and she rose for it, she seemed like a horse making at a fence outrageously high.
> —Stephen Crane, "The Open Boat"

The most common types of figurative language, called **figures of speech,** are **simile, metaphor, personification,** and **hyperbole.**
See pages 111, 525, 711, 853.
See also **Hyperbole; Metaphor; Personification; Simile.**

Figures of Speech *See* **Figurative Language.**

First-Person Point of View *See* **Point of View.**

Flashback A flashback is a scene that interrupts the action of a narrative to describe events that took place at an earlier time. It provides background helpful in understanding a character's present situation.
Example: William Faulkner's "A Rose for Emily" opens with Miss Emily's funeral, followed by a flashback that recounts how, when she was alive, Colonel Sartoris exempted her from paying taxes.

Foil A foil is a character whose traits contrast with those of another character. A writer might use a minor character as a foil to emphasize the positive traits of the main character.
Example: In Flannery O'Connor's "The Life You Save May Be Your Own," the innocent Lucynell Crater serves as a foil to the cunning, deceitful Mr. Shiftlet.
See page 1034.
See also **Character.**

Folk Tale A folk tale is a short, simple story that is handed down, usually by word of mouth, from generation to generation. Folk tales include legends, fairy tales, myths, and fables. Folk tales often teach family obligations or societal values. "Coyote and the Buffalo" is an Okanogan folk tale.
See also **Legend; Myth; Fable.**

Foot *See* **Meter.**

Foreshadowing Foreshadowing is a writer's use of hints or clues to indicate events that will occur in a story. Foreshadowing creates suspense and at the same time prepares the reader for what is to come.
Example: In Faulkner's "A Rose for Emily," the scene in which Miss Emily buys the rat poison foreshadows the death of Homer Barron.
See page 1020.

Form At its simplest, form refers to the physical arrangement of words in a poem—the length and placement of the lines and the grouping of lines into stanzas. The term can also be used to refer to other types of patterning in poetry—anything from rhythm and other sound patterns to the design of a traditional poetic type, such as a sonnet or dramatic monologue.

See also **Genre; Stanza.**

Frame Story A frame story exists when a story is told within a narrative setting, or "frame"; it creates a story within a story. This storytelling method has been used for over one thousand years and was employed in famous works such as *One Thousand and One Arabian Nights* and Geoffrey Chaucer's *The Canterbury Tales.* "The Notorious Jumping Frog of Calaveras County" by Mark Twain is also a frame story.

See page 667.

Free Verse Free verse is poetry that does not have regular patterns of rhyme and meter. The lines in free verse often flow more naturally than do rhymed, metrical lines and thus achieve a rhythm more like that of everyday human speech. Walt Whitman is generally credited with bringing free verse to American poetry.

> And you O my soul where you stand,
> Surrounded, detached, in measureless oceans of space,
> Ceaselessly musing, venturing, throwing, seeking
>   the spheres to connect them,
> Till the bridge you will need be form'd, till the
>   ductile anchor hold,
> Till the gossamer thread you fling catch
>   somewhere, O my soul.
>   —Walt Whitman, "The Noiseless Patient Spider"

See pages 509, 913.
See also **Meter; Rhyme.**

Genre Genre refers to the distinct types into which literary works can be grouped. The four main literary genres are fiction, poetry, nonfiction, and drama.

Gothic Literature Gothic literature is characterized by grotesque characters, bizarre situations, and violent events. Originating in Europe, gothic literature was a popular form of writing in the United States during the 19th century, especially in the hands of such notables as Edgar Allan Poe and Nathaniel Hawthorne. Interest in the gothic revived in the 20th century among southern writers such as William Faulkner and Flannery O'Connor.

See pages 403, 428, 1020.

Haiku Haiku is a form of Japanese poetry in which 17 syllables are arranged in three lines of 5, 7, and 5 syllables. The rules of haiku are strict. In addition to the syllabic count, the poet must create a clear picture that will evoke a strong emotional response in the reader. Nature is a particularly important source of inspiration for Japanese haiku poets, and details from nature are often the subjects of their poems.

Hero *See* **Cultural Hero; Tragic Hero.**

Historical Context The historical context of a literary work refers to the social conditions that inspired or influenced its creation. To understand and appreciate some works, the reader must relate them to particular events in history. For example, to understand fully Lincoln's "Gettysburg Address," the reader must imaginatively re-create the scene—Lincoln addressing a war-weary crowd on the very site where a horrific battle had recently been fought.

Example: Patrick Henry's "Speech in the Virginia Convention" was inspired by the British military buildup in the American colonies prior to the American Revolution; Martin Luther King's *Stride Toward Freedom* was inspired by the civil rights struggle of the 1950s to overturn segregation laws in the South.

See pages 69, 212, 226, 1161.

Historical Narratives Historical narratives are accounts of real-life historical experiences, given either by a person who experienced those events or by someone who has studied or observed them. Cabeza de Vaca's *La Relación*, William Bradford's *Of Plymouth Plantation*, and *The Interesting Narrative of the Life of Olaudah Equiano* all are historical narratives.

See pages 66, 70, 79, 89, 100.
See also **Primary Sources; Secondary Sources.**

Horror Fiction Horror fiction contains strange, mysterious, violent, and often supernatural events that create suspense and terror in the reader. Edgar Allan Poe is an author famous for his horror fiction.

Humor Humor is a term applied to a literary work whose purpose is to entertain and to evoke laughter—for example, Twain's "The Celebrated Jumping Frog of Calaveras County." In literature, there are three basic types of humor, all of which may involve exaggeration or irony. **Humor of situation,** which is derived from the plot of a work, usually involves exaggerated events or situational irony. **Humor of character** is often based on exaggerated personalities or on characters who fail to recognize their own flaws, a form of dramatic irony. **Humor of language** may include sarcasm, exaggeration, puns, or verbal irony, which occurs when what is said is not what is meant.

See pages 635, 1060, 1067.
See also **Comedy; Farce; Irony.**

Hyperbole Hyperbole is a figure of speech in which the truth is exaggerated for emphasis or for humorous effect. The expression "I'm so hungry I could eat a horse" is hyperbole. In the following passage, Dorothy Parker uses hyperbole to describe literary critics' love for a Hemingway novel:

> Ernest Hemingway wrote a novel called *The Sun Also Rises.* Promptly upon its publication, Ernest Hemingway was discovered, the Stars and Stripes were reverentially raised over him, eight hundred and forty-seven book reviewers formed themselves into the word "welcome," and the band played "Hail to the Chief" in three concurrent keys.
>
> —Dorothy Parker, "A Book of Great Short Stories"

See also **Understatement.**

Iamb See **Meter.**

Iambic Pentameter Iambic pentameter is a metrical pattern of five feet, or units, each of which is made up of two syllables, the first unstressed and the second stressed. Iambic pentameter is the most common meter used in English poetry; it is the meter used in blank verse and in the sonnet. The following lines are examples of iambic pentameter:

> So live, | that when | thy sum | mons comes | to join
> The innu | mera | ble car | avan, | which moves
> To that | myste | rious realm, | where each | shall take
> His cham | ber in | the si | lent halls | of death . . .
> —William Cullen Bryant, "Thanatopsis"

See pages 329, 903.
See also **Blank Verse; Meter; Sonnet.**

Idiom An idiom is a common figure of speech whose meaning is different from the literal meaning of its words. For example, the phrase "raining cats and dogs" does not literally mean that cats and dogs are falling from the sky; the expression means "raining heavily."

Imagery The descriptive words and phrases that a writer uses to re-create sensory experiences are called imagery. By appealing to the five senses, imagery helps a reader imagine exactly what the characters and experiences being described are like. In the following passage, the imagery lets the reader experience the miserliness of the main character and his wife:

> They lived in a forlorn-looking house that stood alone and had an air of starvation. A few straggling savin trees, emblems of sterility, grew near it; no smoke ever curled from its chimney. . . . A miserable horse, whose ribs were as articulate as the bars of a gridiron, stalked about a field, where a thin carpet of moss . . . tantalized and balked his hunger.
>
> —Washington Irving, "The Devil and Tom Walker"

The term *synesthesia* refers to imagery that appeals to one sense when another is being stimulated; for example, description of sounds in terms of colors, as in this passage:

> Music. The great blobs of purple and red emotion have not touched him.
>
> —Zora Neale Hurston,
> "How It Feels to Be Colored Me"

See page 860.
See also **Description; Kinesthetic Imagery.**

Imagists See **Experimental Poetry; Style.**

Interior Monologue See **Monologue; Stream of Consciousness.**

Internal Conflict See **Conflict.**

Inverted Syntax Inverted syntax is a reversal in the expected order of words.
Example: In the first line of "Upon the Burning of Our House," Anne Bradstreet writes "when rest I took" rather than "when I took rest."

Interview An interview is a conversation conducted by a writer or reporter in which facts or statements are elicited from another person, recorded, and then broadcast or published.

Irony Irony refers to a contrast between appearance and reality. **Situational irony** is a contrast between what is expected to happen and what actually does happen, as in the poem "Richard Cory," when a gentleman who is admired and envied commits suicide. **Dramatic irony** occurs when readers know more about a situation or a character in a story than the characters do. In Flannery O'Connor's "The Life You Save May Be Your Own," for example, readers find out that Mr. Shiftlet is a scoundrel before the other characters do. **Verbal irony** occurs when someone states one thing and means another, as in the following passage, when the narrator refers to honesty as an "incumbrance," or burden:

> Hicks was born honest, I without that incumbrance—so some people said.
> —Mark Twain, *The Autobiography of Mark Twain*

See pages 635, 882, 1033.

Kinesthetic Imagery Kinesthetic imagery re-creates the tension felt through muscles, tendons, or joints in the body. In the following passage, John Steinbeck uses kinesthetic imagery to describe a soldier's experience:

> This is how you feel after a few days of constant firing. Your skin feels thick and insensitive. There is a salty taste in your mouth. A hard, painful knot is in your stomach where the food is undigested. Your eyes do not pick up much detail and the sharp outlines of objects are slightly blurred. Everything looks a little unreal.
> —John Steinbeck, "Why Soldiers Don't Talk"

See page 1166.
See also **Imagery.**

Journal *See* **Diary.**

Legend A legend is a story passed down orally from generation to generation and popularly believed to have a historical basis. While some legends may be based on real people or situations, most of the events are either greatly exaggerated or fictitious. Like myths, legends may incorporate supernatural elements and magical deeds. But legends differ from myths in that they claim to be stories about real human beings and are often set in a particular time and place.

Limited Point of View *See* **Point of View.**

Line The line is the core unit of a poem. In poetry, line length is an essential element of the poem's meaning and rhythm. There are a variety of terms to describe the way a line of poetry ends or is connected to the next line. Line breaks, where a line of poetry ends, may coincide with grammatical units. However, a line break may also occur in the middle of a grammatical or syntactical unit, creating pauses or emphasis. Poets use a variety of line breaks to play with meaning, thus creating a wide range of effects.

Literary Criticism Literary criticism refers to writing that focuses on a literary work or a genre, describing some aspect of it, such as its origin, its characteristics, or its effects. Toni Morrison's "Thoughts on the African-American Novel" is an example of literary criticism.
See page 869.

Literary Letter A literary letter is a letter that has been published and read by a wider audience because it was written by a well-known public figure or provides information about the period in which it was written. Abigail Adams's "Letter to John Adams" is an example of a literary letter.
See pages 258, 1146, 1194.

Literary Nonfiction Literary nonfiction is nonfiction that is recognized as being of artistic value or that is about literature. Autobiographies, biographies, essays, and eloquent speeches typically fall into this category.

Local Color Realism Local color realism, especially popular in the late 18th century, is a style of writing that truthfully imitates ordinary life and brings a particular region alive by portraying the dialects, dress, mannerisms, customs, character types, and landscapes of that region. Mark Twain frequently uses local color realism in his writing for humorous effect.
See pages 660, 674.
See also **Dialect.**

Lyric Poem A lyric poem is a short poem in which a single speaker expresses thoughts and feelings. In a love lyric, a speaker expresses romantic love. In other lyrics, a speaker may meditate on nature or seek to resolve an emotional crisis. Anne Bradstreet's poem "To My Dear and Loving Husband" is a love lyric.

Magical Realism Magical realism is a style of writing that often includes exaggeration, unusual humor, magical and bizarre events, dreams that come true, and superstitions that prove warranted. Magical realism differs from pure fantasy in combining fantastic elements with realistic elements such as recognizable characters, believable dialogue, a true-to-life setting, a matter-of-fact tone, and a plot that sometimes contains historic events. This style characterizes some of the fiction of such influential South American writers as the late Jorge Luis Borges of Argentina and Gabriel García Márquez of Colombia.

Main Character *See* **Character.**

Memoir A memoir is a form of autobiographical writing in which a person recalls significant events and people in his or her life. Most memoirs share the following characteristics: (1) they usually are structured as narratives told by the writers themselves, using the first-person point of view; (2) although some names may be changed to protect privacy, memoirs are true accounts of actual events; (3) although basically personal, memoirs may deal with newsworthy events having a significance beyond the confines of the writer's life; (4) unlike strictly historical accounts, memoirs often include the writers' feelings and opinions about historical events, giving the reader insight into the impact of history on people's lives. N. Scott Momaday's *The Way to Rainy Mountain* is a memoir.

Metaphor A metaphor is a figure of speech that compares two things that have something in common. Unlike similes, metaphors do not use the words *like* or *as,* but make comparisons directly.
Example: Abigail Adams's statement "our country is . . . the first and greatest parent" is a metaphor.
See pages 111, 853, 918.
See also **Extended Metaphor; Figurative Language; Simile.**

Meter Meter is the repetition of a regular rhythmic unit in a line of poetry. Each unit, known as a **foot,** has one stressed syllable (indicated by a ´) and either one or two unstressed syllables (indicated by a ˇ). The four basic types of metrical feet are the **iamb,** an unstressed syllable followed by a stressed syllable; the **trochee,** a stressed syllable followed by an unstressed syllable; the **anapest,** two unstressed syllables followed by a stressed syllable; and the **dactyl,** a stressed syllable followed by two unstressed syllables.
Two words are typically used to describe the meter of a line. The first word identifies the type of metrical foot—iambic, trochaic, anapestic, or dactylic—and the second word indicates the number of feet in a line: monometer (one foot), **dimeter** (two feet), **trimeter** (three feet), **tetrameter** (four feet), **pentameter** (five feet), **hexameter** (six feet), and so forth.
Examples: In "To My Dear and Loving Husband," by Anne Bradstreet, the meter is iambic pentameter, the most common form of meter in English poetry.

> Ĭf év | ĕr mán | wĕre lóved | bў wífe | thĕn thée.

In the following lines from Henry Wadsworth Longfellow's "A Psalm of Life," the meter is trochaic tetrameter:

> Téll mĕ | nót, ĭn | móurnfŭl | númbĕrs,
> Lífe ĭs | bŭt án | émptў | dréam!—

See pages 335, 341, 847, 881.
See also **Rhythm; Scansion.**

Minor Character *See* **Character.**

Mise-en-Scène *Mise-en-scène* is a term from the French that refers to the various physical aspects of a dramatic presentation, such as lighting, costumes, scenery, makeup, and props.

Modernism Modernism was a literary movement that roughly spanned the time period between the two world wars, 1914–1945. Modernist works are characterized by a high degree of experimentation and spare, elliptical prose. Modernist characters are most often alienated people searching unsuccessfully for meaning and love in their lives. Katherine Ann Porter's "The Jilting of Granny Weatherall" is an example of modernist writing.
See page 894, 930, 990.

Monologue In a drama, the speech of a character who is alone on stage, voicing his or her thoughts, is known as a monologue. In a short story or a poem, the direct presentation of a character's unspoken thoughts is called an **interior monologue.** An interior monologue may jump back and forth between past and present, displaying thoughts, memories, and impressions just as they might occur in a person's mind.
See pages 111, 132.
See also **Stream of Consciousness.**

Mood Mood is the feeling or atmosphere that a writer creates for the reader. The writer's use of connotation, imagery, figurative language, sound and rhythm, and descriptive details all contribute to the mood. These elements help create a creepy, threatening mood in the following passage:

> The swamp was thickly grown with great gloomy pines and hemlocks, . . . It was full of pits and quagmires, partly covered with weeds and mosses, where the green surface often betrayed the traveler into a gulf of black, smothering mud; . . .
> —Washington Irving, "The Devil and Tom Walker"

See page 897.
See also **Connotation; Description; Diction; Figurative Language; Imagery; Style.**

Moral *See* **Fable.**

Motivation Motivation is the stated or implied reason behind a character's behavior. The grounds for a character's actions may not be obvious, but they should be comprehensible and consistent, in keeping with the character as developed by the writer.
See pages 403, 936, 1019.
See also **Character.**

Myth A myth is a traditional story, passed down through generations, that explains why the world is the way it is. Myths are essentially religious because they present supernatural events and beings and articulate the values and beliefs of a cultural group. A **creation myth** is a particular kind of myth that explains how the universe, the earth, and life on earth began. "The World on the Turtle's Back" is an Iroquois creation myth.
See page 33.

Narrative A narrative is any type of writing that is primarily concerned with relating an event or a series of events. A narrative can be imaginary, as is a short story or novel, or factual, as is a newspaper account or a work of history. The word *narration* can be used interchangeably with *narrative,* which comes from the Latin word meaning "tell."
See also **Fiction; Nonfiction; Novel; Plot; Short Story.**

Narrative Poem A narrative poem is a poem that tells a story using elements of character, setting, and plot to develop a theme. Edgar Allan Poe's "The Raven" is a narrative poem, as is Dudley Randall's "Ballad of Birmingham."
See pages 438, 903, 1156.
See also **Ballad.**

Narrator The narrator of a story is the character or voice that relates the story's events to the reader.
Example: The narrator of William Faulkner's "A Rose for Emily" is an unidentified citizen of Jefferson, Mississippi, Emily Grierson's hometown.
See pages 660, 1018.

Naturalism An offshoot of realism, naturalism was a literary movement that originated in France in the late 1800s. Like the realists, the naturalists sought to render common people and ordinary life accurately. However, the naturalists emphasized how instinct and environment affect human behavior. Strongly influenced by Charles Darwin's ideas, the naturalists believed that the fate of humans is determined by forces beyond individual control. Stephen Crane's story "The Open Boat" is an example of naturalism.
See pages 711, 745.

Nonfiction Nonfiction is writing about real people, places, and events. Unlike fiction, nonfiction is largely concerned with factual information, although the writer shapes the information according to his or her purpose and viewpoint. Biography, autobiography, and newspaper articles are examples of nonfiction.
See also **Autobiography; Biography; Essay.**

Novel A novel is an extended work of fiction. Like the short story, a novel is essentially the product of a writer's imagination. The most obvious difference between a novel and a short story is length. Because the novel is considerably longer, a novelist can develop a wider range of characters and a more complex plot.

Novella A novella is a work of fiction that is longer than a short story but shorter than a novel. A novella differs from a novel in that it concentrates on a limited cast of characters, a relatively short time span, and a single chain of events. The novella is an attempt to combine the compression of the short story with the development of a novel.

Octave *See* **Sonnet.**

Ode An ode is a complex lyric poem that develops a serious and dignified theme. Odes appeal to both the imagination and the intellect, and many commemorate events or praise people or elements of nature.

Off Rhyme *See* **Slant Rhyme.**

Omniscient Point of View *See* **Point of View.**

Onomatopoeia The word *onomatopoeia* literally means "name-making." It is the process of creating or using words that imitate sounds. The *buzz* of the bee, the *honk* of the car horn, the *peep* of the chick are all onomatopoetic, or echoic, words.
Onomatopoeia as a literary technique goes beyond the use of simple echoic words. Writers, particularly poets, choose words whose sounds suggest their denotative and connotative meanings: for example, *whisper, kick, gargle, gnash,* and *clatter.*

Open Letter An open letter is addressed to a specific person but published for a wider readership.
Example: James Baldwin's "My Dungeon Shook" is an open letter addressed to his nephew but intended for the general public, particularly white Americans.
See pages 1146, 1194.

Oral Literature Oral literature is literature that is passed from one generation to another by performance or word of mouth. Folk tales, fables, myths, chants, and legends are part of the oral tradition of cultures throughout the world.
See pages 34, 44.
See also **Fable; Folk Tale; Legend; Myth.**

Oxymoron An oxymoron is a special kind of concise paradox that brings together two contradictory terms, such as "venomous love" or "sweet bitterness."

Parable A parable is a brief story that is meant to teach a lesson or illustrate a moral truth. A parable is more than a simple story, however. Each detail of the parable corresponds to some aspect of the problem or moral dilemma to which it is directed. The story of the prodigal son in the Bible is a classic parable. In *Walden*, Thoreau's parable of the strong and beautiful bug that emerges from an old table is meant to show that, similarly, new life can awaken in human beings despite the deadness of society.

Paradox A paradox is a statement that seems to contradict itself but may nevertheless suggest an important truth.
Example: In *Walden*, Henry David Thoreau writes the paradox "I am not as wise as the day I was born." The statement suggests that civilization erases a child's innate wisdom and spiritual awareness.
   A special kind of paradox is the oxymoron, which brings together two contradictory terms, as in the phrases "wise fool" and "feather of lead."
See pages 372, 1192.

Parallel Plot A parallel plot is a particular type of plot in which two stories of equal importance are told simultaneously. The story moves back and forth between the two plots.

Parallelism Parallelism is the use of similar grammatical constructions to express ideas that are related or equal in importance. Note that in the following passage, Whitman begins the last three lines with the name of a type of tradesman, each followed by a gerund phrase beginning with *singing:*

> I hear America singing, the varied carols I hear,
> Those of mechanics, each one singing his as it should be blithe and strong,
> The carpenter singing his as he measures his plank or beam,
> The mason singing his as he makes ready for work, or leaves off work,
>   —Walt Whitman, "I Hear America Singing"

This parallel construction creates a rolling rhythm and emphasizes the different types of people that comprise America.
See page 509.

Parody Parody is writing that imitates either the style or the subject matter of a literary work for the purpose of criticism, humorous effect, or flattering tribute.
See page 445.

Persona *See* **Speaker.**

Personal Essay *See* **Essay.**

Personification Personification is a figure of speech in which an object, animal, or idea is given human characteristics.
Example: In Emily Dickinson's poem "Because I could not stop for Death," death is personified as a gentleman of kindness and civility.
See pages 525, 712.

Persuasive Writing Persuasive writing is intended to convince a reader to adopt a particular opinion or to perform a certain action. Effective persuasion usually appeals to both the reason and the emotions of an audience. Patrick Henry, Jonathan Edwards, Martin Luther King Jr., and Malcolm X all use persuasion in their writing.
See pages 226, 245, 1157, 1193.

Petrarchan Sonnet *See* **Sonnet.**

Plot The plot is the sequence of actions and events in a literary work. Generally, plots are built around a **conflict**—a problem or struggle between two or more opposing forces. Plots usually progress through stages: exposition, rising action, climax, and falling action.
   The **exposition** provides important background information and introduces the setting, characters, and conflict. During the **rising action,** the conflict becomes more intense and suspense builds as the main characters struggle to resolve their problem. The **climax** is the turning point in the plot when the outcome of the conflict becomes clear, usually resulting in a change in the characters or a solution to the conflict. After the climax, the **falling action** occurs and shows the effects of the climax. As the falling action begins, the suspense is over but the results of the decision or action that caused the climax are not yet fully worked out. The **resolution,** which often blends with the falling action, reveals the final outcome of events and ties up loose ends.
See pages 759, 1020.
See also **Climax; Conflict; Exposition; Falling Action; Rising Action.**

Poetry Poetry is language arranged in lines. Like other forms of literature, poetry attempts to re-create emotions and experiences. Poetry, however, is usually more condensed and suggestive than prose.

Poems often are divided into stanzas, or paragraph-like groups of lines. The stanzas in a poem may contain the same number of lines or may vary in length. Some poems have definite patterns of meter and rhyme. Others rely more on the sounds of words and less on fixed rhythms and rhyme schemes. The use of figurative language is also common in poetry.

The form and content of a poem combine to convey meaning. The way that a poem is arranged on the page, the impact of the images, the sounds of the words and phrases, and all the other details that make up a poem work together to help the reader grasp its central idea.

See pages 506, 839, 897, 1237.
See also **Experimental Poetry; Form; Free Verse; Meter; Rhyme; Rhythm; Stanza.**

Point of View Point of view refers to the narrative perspective from which events in a story or novel are told. In the **first-person point of view,** the narrator is a character in the work who tells everything in his or her own words and uses the pronouns *I, me,* and *my.* In the **third-person point of view,** events are related by a voice outside the action, not by one of the characters. A third-person narrator uses pronouns such as *he, she,* and *they.* In the **third-person omniscient point of view,** the narrator is an all-knowing, objective observer who stands outside the action and reports what different characters are thinking. Flannery O'Connor's "The Life You Save May Be Your Own" is told from the third-person omniscient point of view. In the **third-person limited point of view,** the narrator stands outside the action and focuses on one character's thoughts, observations, and feelings. Kate Chopin's "The Story of an Hour" is told from primarily the third-person limited point of view.

In the **second-person point of view,** rarely used, the narrator addresses the reader intimately as *you.* Much of John Steinbeck's essay "Why Soldiers Don't Talk" is narrated from the second-person point of view.

See pages 760, 1034, 1116.

Primary Sources Materials written or created by people who were present at events are called primary sources. Letters, diaries, speeches, autobiographies, and photographs are examples of primary sources, as are certain narrative accounts written by actual participants or observers.

See also **Secondary Sources.**

Prologue A prologue is an introductory scene in a drama.

Prop Prop, an abbreviation of *property,* refers to a physical object that is used in a stage production.

Example: In Arthur Miller's *The Crucible,* an important prop is the small rag doll that Mary Warren brings from the court and gives to Elizabeth Proctor.

Prose Generally, *prose* refers to all forms of written or spoken expression that are not in verse. The term, therefore, may be used to describe very different forms of writing—short stories as well as essays, for example.

Protagonist The protagonist is the main character in a work of literature, who is involved in the central conflict of the story. Usually, the protagonist changes after the central conflict reaches a climax. He or she may be a hero and is usually the one with whom the audience tends to identify. In Kurt Vonnegut's story "Adam," Heinz Knechtmann is the protagonist.

See page 1124.
See also **Antagonist; Character; Tragic Hero.**

Purpose *See* **Author's Purpose.**

Quatrain A quatrain is a four-line stanza, as in the following example:

> The snow had begun in the gloaming,
> And busily all the night
> Had been heaping field and highway
> With a silence deep and white.
> —James Russell Lowell, "The First Snowfall"

See page 348.
See also **Poetry; Stanza.**

Realism As a general term, *realism* refers to any effort to offer an accurate and detailed portrayal of actual life. Thus, critics talk about Shakespeare's realistic portrayals of his characters and praise the medieval poet Chaucer for his realistic descriptions of people from different social classes.

More specifically, realism refers to a literary method developed in the 19th century. The realists based their writing on careful observations of contemporary life, often focusing on the middle or lower classes. They attempted to present life objectively and honestly, without the sentimentality or idealism that had colored earlier literature. Typically, realists developed their settings in great detail in an effort to re-create a specific time and place for the reader. Willa Cather, Kate Chopin, and Mark Twain are all considered realists.

See pages 660, 692, 760.
See also **Local-Color Realism; Naturalism.**

Recurring Theme *See Theme.*

Reflective Essay *See Essay.*

Refrain In poetry, a refrain is part of a stanza, consisting of one or more lines that are repeated regularly, sometimes with changes, often at the ends of succeeding stanzas. For example, in "The Raven," the line "Quoth the Raven, 'Nevermore'" is a refrain. Refrains are often found in ballads.

Regionalism Regionalism is a literary movement that arose from an effort to accurately represent the speech, manners, habits, history, folklore, and beliefs of people in specific geographic areas. Bret Harte's "The Outcasts of Poker Flat" is a famous example of American regionalist writing.

Repetition Repetition is a technique in which a sound, word, phrase, or line is repeated for emphasis or unity. Repetition often helps to reinforce meaning and create an appealing rhythm. The term includes specific devices associated with both prose and poetry, such as **alliteration** and **parallelism.**

See pages 225, 509, 839, 1193.
See also **Alliteration; Parallelism; Sound Devices.**

Resolution *See Falling Action.*

Rhetorical Devices *See* **Analogy; Repetition; Rhetorical Questions,** *Glossary of Reading and Informational Terms,* page R123.

Rhyme Rhyme is the occurrence of similar or identical sounds at the end of two or more words, such as *suite, heat,* and *complete.* Rhyme that occurs within a single line of poetry, as in the following example, is called **internal rhyme.**

> Ah, distinctly I <u>remember</u> it was in the bleak <u>December</u>;
> —Edgar Allan Poe, "The Raven"

When rhyme comes at the end of a line of poetry, it is called **end rhyme.** The pattern of end rhyme in a poem is called the **rhyme scheme** and is charted by assigning a letter, beginning with the letter *a,* to each line. Lines that rhyme are given the same letter. The rhyme scheme of the following stanza is *aabbcc:*

In silent night when rest I took	*a*
For sorrow near I did not look	*a*
I wakened was with thund'ring noise	*b*
And piteous shrieks of dreadful voice.	*b*
That fearful sound of "Fire!" and "Fire!"	*c*
Let no man know is my desire.	*c*

—Anne Bradstreet, "Upon the Burning of Our House"

See pages 335, 438, 847.
See also **Slant Rhyme.**

Rhyme Scheme *See* **Rhyme.**

Rhythm Rhythm refers to the pattern or flow of sound created by the arrangement of stressed and unstressed syllables, particularly in poetry. Some poems follow a regular pattern, or **meter,** of accented and unaccented syllables. Poets use rhythm to bring out the musical quality of language, to emphasize ideas, to create mood, and to reinforce subject matter.

See pages 839, 509.
See also **Meter.**

Rising Action Rising action is the stage of a plot in which the conflict develops and story events build toward a climax. During this stage, complications arise that make the conflict more intense. Tension grows as the characters struggle to resolve the conflict.

See pages 712, 759, 768.
See also **Plot.**

Romanticism Romanticism was a movement in the arts that flourished in Europe and America throughout much of the 19th century. Romantic writers glorified nature and celebrated individuality. Their treatment of subject was emotional rather than rational, intuitive rather than analytic. Washington Irving and Henry Wadsworth Longfellow were popular American romantic writers.

See pages 292, 312, 334, 342.

Sarcasm Sarcasm, a type of verbal irony, refers to a critical remark expressed in a statement in which literal meaning is the opposite of actual meaning. Sarcasm is mocking, and its intention is to hurt.

See also **Irony.**

Satire Satire is a literary technique in which foolish ideas or customs are ridiculed for the purpose of improving society. Satire may be gently witty, mildly abrasive, or bitterly critical. Short stories, poems, novels, essays, and plays all may be vehicles for satire.

Example: In "The Devil and Tom Walker," Irving satirizes various aspects of 18th-century New England life, including religious hypocrisy and the institution of marriage.

Scansion The process of determining meter is known as scansion. When you scan a line of poetry, you mark its stressed (´) and unstressed syllables (ˇ) in order to identify the rhythm.

See also **Meter.**

Scene In drama, a scene is a subdivision of an act. Each scene usually establishes a different time or place.

See also **Act; Drama.**

Scenery Scenery is a painted backdrop or other structures used to create the setting for a play.

Science Fiction Science fiction is prose writing that presents the possibilities of the past or the future, using known scientific data and theories as well as the creative imagination of the writer. Most science fiction comments on present-day society through the writer's fictional conception of a past or future society. Ray Bradbury and Kurt Vonnegut Jr. are two popular writers of science fiction.

Screenplay A screenplay is a play written for film.

Script The text of a play, film, or broadcast is called a script.

Secondary Sources Accounts written by people were not directly involved in or witnesses to an event are called secondary sources. A history textbook is an example of a secondary source.

See also **Primary Sources.**

Sensory Details Sensory details are words and phrases that appeal to the reader's senses of sight, hearing, touch, taste, and smell. For example, the sensory detail "a fine film of rain" appeals to the senses of sight and touch. Sensory details stimulate the reader to create images in his or her mind.

See also **Imagery.**

Sermon A sermon is a form of religious persuasion in which a speaker exhorts the audience to behave in a more spiritual and moral fashion. "Sinners in the Hands of an Angry God" is a sermon.

Setting The setting of a literary work refers to the time and place in which the action occurs. A story can be set in an imaginary place, such as an enchanted castle, or a real place, such as New York City or Tombstone, Arizona. The time can be the past, the present, or the future. In addition to time and place, setting can include the larger historical and cultural contexts that form the background for a narrative. Setting is one of the main elements in fiction and often plays an important role in what happens and why.

Example: Willa Cather's story "A Wagner Matinee" is set in Boston around the turn of the 20th century.

See pages 131, 660, 693, 1034.

Sestet *See* **Sonnet.**

Short Story A short story is a work of fiction that centers on a single idea and can be read in one sitting. Generally, a short story has one main conflict that involves the characters, keeps the story moving, and stimulates readers' interest.

See also **Fiction.**

Simile A simile is a figure of speech that compares two things that have something in common, using a word such as *like* or *as.*

Examples: Abigail Adams's statement "power and liberty are like heat and moisture" and Thoreau's statement "we live meanly, like ants" contain similes.

See pages 258, 372, 525.
See also **Figurative Language; Metaphor.**

Situational Irony See Irony.

Slant Rhyme Rhyme that is not exact but only approximate is known as slant rhyme, or **off rhyme,** as in the second and fourth lines below:

> I heard a Fly buzz—when I died—
> The Stillness in the Room
> Was like the Stillness in the Air—
> Between the Heaves of Storm—
>
> —Emily Dickinson,
> "I heard a Fly buzz—when I died—"

See page 525.
See also **Rhyme.**

Slave Narrative A slave narrative is an autobiographical account written by someone who endured the miseries of slavery. Olaudah Equiano's and Frederick Douglass's autobiographies are examples of slave narratives. These writers often use sensory details to re-create their experiences. For example, to re-create the horror of confinement in the hold of a slave ship, Equiano gives the reader such details as "the galling of the chains" and "the groans of the dying."

See pages 79, 537, 552.
See also **Autobiography.**

Soliloquy *See* **Monologue.**

Sonnet A sonnet is a 14-line lyric poem, commonly written in iambic pentameter. The **Petrarchan sonnet** consists of two parts. The first eight lines, called the octave, usually have the rhyme scheme *abbaabba.* In the last six lines, called the sestet, the rhyme scheme may be *cdecde, cdcdcd,* or another variation. The **octave** generally presents a problem or raises a question, and the *sestet* resolves or comments on the problem. James Weldon Johnson's "My City" is a Petrarchan sonnet. A **Shakespearean sonnet** is divided into three **quatrains** (groups of four lines) and a **couplet** (two rhyming lines). Its rhyme scheme is *abab cdcd efef gg.* The couplet usually expresses a response to the important issue developed in the three quatrains. Claude McKay's "If We Must Die" is a Shakespearean sonnet.

See page 847.
See also **Meter; Quatrain; Rhyme.**

Sound Devices *See* **Alliteration; Assonance; Consonance; Meter; Onomatopoeia; Repetition; Rhyme; Rhyme Scheme; Rhythm.**

Speaker The speaker of a poem, like the narrator of a story, is the voice that talks to the reader. In some poems, the speaker can be identified with the poet. In other poems, the poet invents a fictional character, or a persona, to play the role of the speaker. *Persona* is a Latin word meaning "actor's mask."

See pages 881, 839, 930.

Speech A speech is a talk or public address. The purpose of a speech may be to entertain, to explain, to persuade, to inspire, or any combination of these aims.

Stage Directions Stage directions are the playwright's instructions for the director, performers, and stage crew. Usually set in italics, they are located at the beginning of and throughout a script. Stage directions usually tell the time and place of the action and explain how characters move and speak. They also describe scenery, props, lighting, costumes, music, or sound effects.

See pages 128, 132.
See also **Drama.**

Stanza A stanza is a group of lines that form a unit in a poem. A stanza is usually characterized by a common pattern of meter, rhyme, and number of lines. Longfellow's "A Psalm of Life" is written in four-line stanzas. During the 20th century, poets experimented more freely with stanza form than did earlier poets, sometimes writing poems without any stanza breaks.

See page 335.

Static Character *See* **Character.**

Stereotype A stereotype is an over simplified image of a person, group, or institution. Sweeping generalizations about "all Southerners" or "every used-car dealer" are stereotypes. Simplified or stock characters in literature are often called stereotypes. Such characters do not usually demonstrate the complexities of real people.

Example: In Washington Irving's "The Devil and Tom Walker," Tom Walker's wife is a stereotype of a greedy and shrewish wife.

Stream of Consciousness Stream of consciousness is a technique that was developed by modernist writers to present the flow of a character's seemingly unconnected thoughts, responses, and sensations. The term was coined by American psychologist William James to characterize the unbroken flow of thought that occurs in the waking mind.

Example: In "The Love Song of J. Alfred Prufrock," T. S. Eliot uses this technique to reveal the jumble of thoughts that flow through Prufrock's mind.

See pages 929, 989.
See also **Modernism.**

Structure The structure of a literary work is the way in which it is put together—the arrangement of its parts. In poetry, structure refers to the arrangement of words and lines to produce a desired effect. A common structural unit in poetry is the stanza, of which there are numerous types. In prose, structure is the arrangement of larger units or parts of a selection. Paragraphs, for example, are a basic unit in prose, as are chapters in novels and acts in plays. The structure of a poem, short story, novel, play, or nonfiction selection usually emphasizes certain important aspects of content.

See pages 235, 329, 581.
See also **Form; Stanza.**

Style Style is the distinctive way in which a work of literature is written. Style refers not so much to what is said but how it is said. Word choice, sentence length, tone, imagery, and use of dialogue all contribute to a writer's style. A group of writers might exemplify common stylistic characteristics; for example, the Imagists of the early 20th century wrote in a style that employs compression and rich sensory images.

Example: E. E. Cummings's style is decidedly unconventional, breaking rules of capitalization, punctuation, diction, and syntax.

See pages 525, 537, 897, 969.

Surprise Ending A surprise ending is an unexpected plot twist at the end of a story.

Example: "The Story of an Hour" ends with a surprise when Mrs. Mallard drops dead after her husband, presumed to be dead, reappears.

See page 759.
See also **Irony.**

Suspense Suspense is the excitement or tension that readers feel as they become involved in a story and eagerly await the outcome.

Example: In Ambrose Bierce's "An Occurrence at Owl Creek Bridge," the suspense builds as the reader awaits the outcome of Peyton Farquhar's attempted escape from hanging at the hands of Union troops.

See page 582.
See also **Rising Action.**

Symbol A symbol is a person, place, or object that has a concrete meaning in itself and also stands for something beyond itself, such as an idea or feeling.

Example: In Gilman's "The Yellow Wallpaper," the wallpaper in the narrator's bedroom comes to symbolize her growing madness.

See pages 457, 768.

Synesthesia *See* **Imagery.**

Tall Tale A tall tale is a distinctively American type of humorous story characterized by exaggeration. Tall tales and practical jokes have similar kinds of humor. In both, someone gets fooled, to the amusement of the person or persons who know the truth, as in Twain's "The Notorious Jumping Frog of Calaveras County."

See page 659.
See also **Humor; Hyperbole.**

Theme A theme is an underlying message that a writer wants the reader to understand. It is a perception about life or human nature that the writer shares with the reader. In most cases, themes are not stated directly but must be inferred.

Example: One theme of "The Masque of the Red Death" could be stated, "No one, not even the wealthiest person, has the power to escape death."

Recurring themes are themes found in a variety of works. For example, authors from varying backgrounds might convey similar themes having to do with the importance of family values. **Universal themes** are themes that are found throughout the literature of all time periods.

See pages 429, 745, 756, 1002.

Third-Person Point of View *See* **Point of View.**

Title The title of a literary work introduces readers to the piece and usually reveals something about its subject or theme. Often, a poet uses the title to provide information necessary for understanding a poem.

Example: "A Worn Path," the title of Eudora Welty's short story, suggests the main character, Phoenix, herself: the path of her life is worn with age and struggle, and her life has centered on a single routine motivated by love.

See pages 760, 1004, 1232.

Tone Tone is a writer's attitude toward his or her subject. A writer can communicate tone through diction, choice of details, and direct statements of his or her position. Unlike mood, which refers to the emotional response of the reader to a work, tone reflects the feelings of the writer. To identify the tone of a work of literature, you might find it helpful to read the work aloud, as if giving a dramatic reading before an audience. The emotions that you convey in an oral reading should give you hints as to the tone of the work.

Example: Claude McKay's tone in "If We Must Die" is proud, defiant, and urgent.

See pages 509, 791, 850, 1060.
See also **Connotation; Diction; Mood; Style.**

Tragedy A tragedy is a dramatic work that presents the downfall of a dignified character who is involved in historically, morally, or socially significant events. The main character, or **tragic hero,** has a **tragic flaw,** a quality that leads to his or her destruction. The events in a tragic plot are set in motion by a decision that is often an error in judgment caused by the tragic flaw. Succeeding events are linked in a cause-and-effect relationship and lead inevitably to a disastrous conclusion, usually death. Arthur Miller's *The Crucible* could be classified as a tragedy.

Tragic Flaw *See* **Tragedy.**

Tragic Hero The ancient Greek philosopher Aristotle defined a tragic hero as a character whose basic goodness and superiority are marred by a tragic flaw that brings about or contributes to his or her downfall. The flaw may be poor judgment, pride, weakness, or an excess of an admirable quality. The tragic hero recognizes his or her own flaw and its consequences, but only after it is too late to change the course of events.

See also **Character.**

Traits *See* **Character.**

Transcendentalism The philosophy of transcendentalism, an American offshoot of German romanticism, was based on a belief that "transcendent forms" of truth exist beyond reason and experience. Ralph Waldo Emerson, the leader of the movement, asserted that every individual is capable of discovering this higher truth through intuition. Henry David Thoreau is another well-known transcendentalist writer.

See pages 361, 372, 382.
See also **Romanticism.**

Trickster Tale A trickster tale is a folk tale about an animal or person who engages in trickery, violence, and magic. Neither all good nor all bad, a trickster may be foolish yet clever, greedy yet helpful, immoral yet moral. "Coyote and the Buffalo" is a trickster tale.

See page 43.
See also **Folk Tale.**

Trochee *See* **Meter.**

Turning Point *See* **Climax.**

Understatement Understatement is a technique of creating emphasis by saying less than is actually or literally true. It is the opposite of **hyperbole,** or exaggeration. One of the primary devices of **irony,** understatement can be used to develop a humorous effect, to create satire, or to achieve a restrained tone.

Example: In "Letter to John Adams," Abigail Adams points out the tyranny of male power by gently saying, "I cannot say that I think you very generous to the ladies."

See also **Hyperbole; Irony.**

Unity of Effect When all elements of a story—plot, character, setting, imagery, and other other literary devices—work together to create a single effect, it is known as unity of effect. Edgar Allan Poe's "The Fall of the House of Usher" demonstrates the unity of effect.

See page 403.

Universal Theme *See* **Theme.**

Verbal Irony *See* **Irony.**

Voice The term *voice* refers to a writer's unique use of language that allows a reader to "hear" a human personality in his or her writing. The elements of style that determine a writer's voice include sentence structure, diction, and tone. For example, some writers are noted for their reliance on short, simple sentences, while others make use of long, complicated ones. Certain writers use concrete words, such as *lake* or *cold*, which name things that you can see, hear, feel, taste, or smell. Others prefer abstract terms such as *memory*, which name things that cannot be perceived with the senses. A writer's tone also leaves its imprint on his or her personal voice. The term can be applied to the narrator of a selection, as well as the writer.

See pages 649, 1059.
See also **Diction; Tone.**

Word Choice *See* **Diction.**

Almanac *See* **Reference Works.**

Analogy *See Glossary of Literary Terms, page R104.*

Appeals by Association Appeals by association imply that one will gain acceptance or prestige by taking the writer's position.
See also **Recognizing Persuasive Techniques**—*Reading Handbook, page R20.*

Appeal to Authority An appeal to authority calls upon experts or others who warrant respect.
See also **Recognizing Persuasive Techniques**—*Reading Handbook, page R20.*

Appeal to Reason *See* **Logical Appeal.**

Argument An argument is speech or writing that expresses a position on an issue or problem and supports it with reasons and evidence. An argument often takes into account other points of view, anticipating and answering objections that opponents of the position might raise.
See also **Claim; Counterargument; Evidence; General Principle.**

Assumption An assumption is an opinion or belief that is taken for granted. It can be about a specific situation, a person, or the world in general. Assumptions are often unstated.
See also **General Principle.**

Author's Message An author's message is the main idea or theme of a particular work.
See also **Main Idea; Theme,** *Glossary of Literary Terms, page R121.*

Author's Perspective *See Glossary of Literary Terms, page R105.*

Author's Position An author's position is his or her opinion on an issue or topic.
See also **Claim.**

Author's Purpose *See Glossary of Literary Terms, page R105.*

Autobiography *See Glossary of Literary Terms, page R105.*

Bias Bias is an inclination toward a particular judgment on a topic or issue. A writer often reveals a strongly positive or strongly negative opinion by presenting only one way of looking at an issue or by heavily weighting the evidence. Words with intensely positive or negative connotations are often a signal of a writer's bias.

Bibliography A bibliography is a list of books and other materials related to the topic of a text. Bibliographies can be good sources of works for further study on a subject.
See also **Works Consulted.**

Biography *See Glossary of Literary Terms, page R105.*

Business Correspondence Business correspondence includes all written business communications, such as business letters, e-mails, and memos. In general, business correspondence is brief, to the point, clear, courteous, and professional.

Cause and Effect A **cause** is an event or action that directly results in another event or action. An **effect** is the direct or logical outcome of an event or action. Basic **cause-and-effect relationships** include a single cause with a single effect, one cause with multiple effects, multiple causes with a single effect, and a chain of causes and effects. The concept of cause and effect also provides a way of organizing a piece of writing. It helps a writer show the relationships between events or ideas.
See also **False Cause**—*Reading Handbook, page R22.*

Chronological Order Chronological order is the arrangement of events in their order of occurrence. This type of organization is used in both fictional narratives and in historical writing, biography, and autobiography.

Claim In an argument, a claim is the writer's position on an issue or problem. Although an argument focuses on supporting one claim, a writer may make more than one claim in a work.

Clarify Clarifying is a reading strategy that helps a reader to understand or make clear what he or she is reading. Readers usually clarify by rereading, reading aloud, or discussing.

Classification Classification is a pattern of organization in which objects, ideas, or information is presented in groups, or classes, based on common characteristics.

Cliché A cliché is an overused expression. "Better late than never" and "hard as nails" are common examples. Good writers generally avoid clichés unless they are using them in dialogue to indicate something about characters' personalities.

Compare and Contrast To compare and contrast is to identify similarities and differences in two or more subjects. Compare-and-contrast organization can be used to structure a piece of writing, serving as a framework for examining the similarities and differences in two or more subjects.

Conclusion A conclusion is a statement of belief based on evidence, experience, and reasoning. A **valid conclusion** is a conclusion that logically follows from the facts or statements upon which it is based. A **deductive conclusion** is one that follows from a particular generalization or premise. An **inductive conclusion** is a broad conclusion or generalization that is reached by arguing from specific facts and examples.

Connect Connecting is a reader's process of relating the content of a text to his or her own knowledge and experience.

Consumer Documents Consumer documents are printed materials that accompany products and services. They are intended for the buyers or users of the products or services and usually provide information about use, care, operation, or assembly. Some common consumer documents are applications, contracts, warranties, manuals, instructions, package inserts, labels, brochures, and schedules.

Context Clues When you encounter an unfamiliar word, you can often use context clues as aids for understanding. Context clues are the words and phrases surrounding the word that provide hints about the word's meaning.

Counterargument A counterargument is an argument made to oppose another argument. A good argument anticipates opposing viewpoints and provides counterarguments to refute (disprove) or answer them.

Credibility *Credibility* refers to the believability or trustworthiness of a source and the information it contains.

Critical Review A critical review is an evaluation or critique by a reviewer or critic. Different types of reviews include film reviews, book reviews, music reviews, and art-show reviews.

Database A database is a collection of information that can be quickly and easily accessed and searched and from which information can be easily retrieved. It is frequently presented in an electronic format.

Debate A debate is an organized exchange of opinions on an issue. In academic settings, *debate* usually refers to a formal contest in which two opposing teams defend and attack a proposition.
See also **Argument; Debate**—*Speaking and Listening Handbook, pages R82–R83.*

Deductive Reasoning Deductive reasoning is a way of thinking that begins with a generalization, presents a specific situation, and then advances with facts and evidence to a logical conclusion. The following passage has a deductive argument imbedded in it: "All students in the drama class must attend the play on Thursday. Since Ava is in the class, she had better show up." This deductive argument can be broken down as follows: generalization—all students in the drama class must attend the play on Thursday; specific situation—Ava is a student in the drama class; conclusion—Ava must attend the play.
See also **Analyzing Logic and Reasoning**—*Reading Handbook, pages R20–R21.*

Dictionary *See* **Reference Works.**

Draw Conclusions To draw a conclusion is to make a judgment or arrive at a belief based on evidence, experience, and reasoning.

Editorial An editorial is an opinion piece that usually appears on the editorial page of a newspaper or as part of a news broadcast. The editorial section of a newspaper presents opinions rather than objective news reports.
See also **Op-Ed Piece.**

Either/Or Fallacy An either/or fallacy is a statement that suggests that there are only two possible ways to view a situation or only two options to choose from. In other words, it is a statement that falsely frames a dilemma, giving the impression that no options exist but the two presented— for example, "Either we stop the construction of a new airport, or the surrounding suburbs will become ghost towns."
See also **Identifying Faulty Reasoning**—*Reading Handbook, page R22.*

Emotional Appeals Emotional appeals are messages that evoke strong feelings—such as fear, pity, or vanity—in order to persuade instead of using facts and evidence to make a point. An **appeal to fear** is a message that taps into people's fear of losing their safety or security. An **appeal to pity** is a message that taps into people's sympathy and compassion for others to build support for an idea, a cause, or a proposed action. An **appeal to vanity** is a message that attempts to persuade by tapping into people's desire to feel good about themselves.
See also **Recognizing Persuasive Techniques**—*Reading Handbook, page R20.*

Encyclopedia *See* **Reference Works.**

Essay *See Glossary of Literary Terms, page R109.*

Ethical Appeals Ethical appeals establish a writer's credibility and trustworthiness with an audience. When a writer links a claim to a widely accepted value, for example, the writer not only gains moral support for that claim but also establishes a connection with readers.
See also **Recognizing Persuasive Techniques**—*Reading Handbook, page R20.*

Evaluate To evaluate is to examine something carefully and judge its value or worth. Evaluating is an important skill for gaining insight into what you read. A reader can evaluate the actions of a particular character, for example, or can form an opinion about the value of an entire work.

Evidence Evidence is the specific pieces of information that support a claim. Evidence can take the form of facts, quotations, examples, statistics, or personal experiences, among others.

Expository Essay *See* **Essay**, *Glossary of Literary Terms, page R109.*

Fact versus Opinion A **fact** is a statement that can be proved or verified. An **opinion,** on the other hand, is a statement that cannot be proved because it expresses a person's beliefs, feelings, or thoughts.
See also **Inference; Generalization.**

Fallacy A fallacy is an error in reasoning. Typically, a fallacy is based on an incorrect inference or a misuse of evidence. Some common logical fallacies are **circular reasoning, either/or fallacy, oversimplification, overgeneralization,** and **stereotyping.**
See also **Either/Or Fallacy; Logical Appeal; Overgeneralization; Identifying Faulty Reasoning**—*Reading Handbook, page R22.*

Faulty Reasoning *See* **Fallacy.**

Feature Article A feature article is a main article in a newspaper or a cover story in a magazine. A feature article is focused more on entertaining than informing. Features are lighter or more general than hard news and tend to be about human interest or lifestyles.

Functional Documents *See* **Consumer Documents; Workplace Documents.**

Generalization A generalization is a broad statement about a class or category of people, ideas, or things, based on a study of only some of its members.
See also **Overgeneralization.**

General Principle In an argument, a general principle is an assumption that links the support to the claim. If one does not accept the general principle as a truth, then the support is inadequate because it is beside the point.

Government Publications Government publications are documents produced by government organizations. Pamphlets, brochures, and reports are just some of the many forms these publications may take. Government publications can be good resources for a wide variety of topics.

Graphic Aid A graphic aid is a visual tool that is printed, handwritten, or drawn. Charts, diagrams, graphs, photographs, and maps can all be graphic aids.
See also **Graphic Aids**—*Reading Handbook, pages R5–R7.*

Graphic Organizer A graphic organizer is a visual illustration of a verbal statement that helps a reader understand a text. Charts, tables, webs, and diagrams can all be graphic organizers. Graphic organizers and graphic aids can look the same. However, graphic organizers and graphic aids do differ in how they are used. Graphic aids are the visual representations that people encounter when they read informational texts. Graphic organizers are visuals that people construct to help them understand texts or organize information.

Historical Documents Historical documents are writings that have played a significant role in human events or are themselves records of such events. The Declaration of Independence, for example, is a historical document.

How-To Book A how-to book is a book that is written to explain how to do something—usually an activity, a sport, or a household project.

Implied Main Idea *See* **Main Idea.**

Index The index of a book is an alphabetized list of important topics and details covered in the book and the page numbers on which they can be found. An index can be used to quickly find specific information about a topic.

Inductive Reasoning Inductive reasoning is the process of logical reasoning from observations, examples, and facts to a general conclusion or principle.
See also **Analyzing Logic and Reasoning**—*Reading Handbook, pages R20–R21.*

Inference An inference is a logical assumption that is based on observed facts and one's own knowledge and experience.

Informational Nonfiction Informational nonfiction is writing that provides factual information. It often explains ideas or teaches processes. Examples include news reports, science textbooks, software instructions, and lab reports.

Internet The Internet is a global, interconnected system of computer networks that allows for communication through e-mail, listservers, and the World Wide Web. The Internet connects computers and computer users throughout the world.

Journal A journal is a periodical publication issued by a legal, medical, or other professional organization. Alternatively, the term may be used to refer to a diary or daily record.

Literary Criticism *See Glossary of Literary Terms, page R113.*

Loaded Language Loaded language consists of words with strongly positive or negative connotations intended to influence a reader's or listener's attitude.

Logical Appeal A logical appeal relies on logic and facts, appealing to people's reasoning or intellect rather than to their values or emotions. Flawed logical appeals—that is, errors in reasoning—are considered logical fallacies.
See also **Fallacy.**

Logical Argument A logical argument is an argument in which the logical relationship between the support and the claim is sound.

Main Idea A main idea is the central or most important idea about a topic that a writer or speaker conveys. It can be the central idea of an entire work or of just a paragraph. Often, the main idea of a paragraph is expressed in a topic sentence. However, a main idea may just be implied, or suggested, by details. A main idea and supporting details can serve as a basic pattern of organization in a piece of writing, with the central idea about a topic being supported by details.

Make Inferences *See* **Inference.**

Monitor Monitoring is the strategy of checking your comprehension as you are reading and modifying the strategies you are using to suit your needs. Monitoring may include some or all of the following strategies: **questioning, clarifying, visualizing, predicting, connecting,** and **rereading.**

Narrative Nonfiction *See Glossary of Literary Terms, page R115.*

News Article A news article is a piece of writing that reports on a recent event. In newspapers, news articles are usually written in a concise manner to report the latest news, presenting the most important facts first and then more detailed information. In magazines, news articles are usually more elaborate than those in newspapers because they are written to provide both information and analysis. Also, news articles in magazines do not necessarily present the most important facts first.

Nonfiction *See Glossary of Literary Terms, page R115.*

Op-Ed Piece An op-ed piece is an opinion piece that usually appears opposite ("op") the editorial page of a newspaper. Unlike editorials, op-ed pieces are written and submitted by named writers.

Organization *See* **Pattern of Organization.**

Overgeneralization An overgeneralization is a generalization that is too broad. You can often recognize overgeneralizations by the appearance of words and phrases such as *all, everyone, every time, any, anything, no one,* and *none.* Consider, for example, this statement: "None of the sanitation workers in our city really care about keeping the environment clean." In all probability, there are many exceptions. The writer can't possibly know the feelings of every sanitation worker in the city.
See also **Identifying Faulty Reasoning**—*Reading Handbook, page R22.*

Overview An overview is a short summary of a story, a speech, or an essay. It orients the reader by providing a preview of the text to come.

Paraphrase Paraphrasing is the restating of information in one's own words.
See also **Summarize.**

Pattern of Organization A pattern of organization is a particular arrangement of ideas and information. Such a pattern may be used to organize an entire composition or a single paragraph within a longer work. The following are the most common patterns of organization: **cause-and-effect, chronological order, compare-and-contrast, classification, deductive, inductive, order of importance, problem-solution, sequential,** and **spatial.**
See also **Cause and Effect; Chronological Order; Classification; Compare and Contrast; Problem-Solution Order; Sequential Order; Patterns of Organization**—*Reading Handbook, pages R8–R12.*

Periodical A periodical is a publication that is issued at regular intervals of more than one day. For example, a periodical may be a weekly, monthly, or quarterly journal or magazine. Newspapers and other daily publications generally are not classified as periodicals.

Personal Essay *See* **Essay,** *Glossary of Literary Terms, page R116.*

Persuasion Persuasion is the art of swaying others' feelings, beliefs, or actions. Persuasion normally appeals to both the intellect and the emotions of readers. **Persuasive techniques** are the methods used to influence others to adopt certain opinions or beliefs or to act in certain ways. Types of persuasive techniques include emotional appeals, ethical appeals, logical appeals, and loaded language. When used properly, persuasive techniques can add depth to writing that's meant to persuade. Persuasive techniques can, however, be misused to cloud factual information, disguise poor reasoning, or unfairly exploit people's emotions in order to shape their opinions.

See also **Appeals by Association; Appeal to Authority; Emotional Appeals; Ethical Appeals; Loaded Language; Logical Appeal; Recognizing Persuasive Techniques—** *Reading Handbook, page R20.*

Predict Predicting is a reading strategy that involves using text clues to make a reasonable guess about what will happen next in a story.

Primary Source *See* **Sources.**

Prior Knowledge Prior knowledge is the knowledge a reader already possesses about a topic. This information might come from personal experiences, expert accounts, books, films, or other sources.

Problem-Solution Order Problem-solution order is a pattern of organization in which a problem is stated and analyzed and then one or more solutions are proposed and examined. Writers use words and phrases such as *propose, conclude, reason for, problem, answer,* and *solution* to connect ideas and details when writing about problems and solutions.

Propaganda Propaganda is a form of communication that may use distorted, false, or misleading information. It usually refers to manipulative political discourse.

Public Documents Public documents are documents that were written for the public to provide information that is of public interest or concern. They include government documents, speeches, signs, and rules and regulations. *See also* **Government Publications.**

Reference Works General reference works are sources that contain facts and background information on a wide range of subjects. More specific reference works contain in-depth information on a single subject. Most reference works are good sources of reliable information because they have been reviewed by experts. The following are some common reference works: **encyclopedias, dictionaries, thesauri, almanacs, atlases, chronologies, biographical dictionaries,** and **directories.**

Review *See* **Critical Review.**

Rhetorical Devices *See Glossary of Literary Terms, page R118.*

Rhetorical Questions Rhetorical questions are those that do not require a reply. Writers use them to suggest that their arguments make the answer obvious or self-evident.

Scanning Scanning is the process of searching through writing for a particular fact or piece of information. When you scan, your eyes sweep across a page, looking for key words that may lead you to the information you want.

Secondary Source *See* **Sources.**

Sequential Order A pattern of organization that shows the order in which events or actions occur is called sequential order. Writers typically use this pattern of organization to explain steps or stages in a process.

Setting a Purpose The process of establishing specific reasons for reading a text is called setting a purpose.

Sidebar A sidebar is additional information set in a box alongside or within a news or feature article. Popular magazines often make use of sidebar information.

Signal Words Signal words are words and phrases that indicate what is to come in a text. Readers can use signal words to discover a text's pattern of organization and to analyze the relationships among the ideas in the text.

Sources A source is anything that supplies information. **Primary sources** are materials written or created by people who were present at events, either as participants or as observers. Letters, diaries, autobiographies, speeches, and photographs are primary sources. **Secondary sources** are records of events that were created sometime after the events occurred; the writers were not directly involved or were not present when the events took place. Encyclopedias, textbooks, biographies, most newspaper and magazine articles, and books and articles that interpret or review research are secondary sources.

Spatial Order Spatial order is a pattern of organization that highlights the physical positions or relationships of details or objects. This pattern of organization is typically found in descriptive writing. Writers use words and phrases such as *on the left, to the right, here, over there, above, below, beyond, nearby,* and *in the distance* to indicate the arrangement of details.

Speech *See Glossary of Literary Terms, page R120.*

Stereotyping Stereotyping is a dangerous type of overgeneralization. Stereotypes are broad statements made about people on the basis of their gender, ethnicity, race, or political, social, professional, or religious group.

Summarize To summarize is to briefly retell, or encapsulate, the main ideas of a piece of writing in one's own words.
See also **Paraphrase.**

Support Support is any material that serves to prove a claim. In an argument, support typically consists of reasons and evidence. In persuasive texts and speeches, however, support may include appeals to the needs and values of the audience.
See also **General Principle.**

Supporting Detail *See* **Main Idea.**

Synthesize To synthesize information is to take individual pieces of information and combine them with other pieces of information and with prior knowledge or experience to gain a better understanding of a subject or to create a new product or idea.

Text Features Text features are design elements that indicate the organizational structure of a text and help make the key ideas and the supporting information understandable. Text features include headings, boldface type, italic type, bulleted or numbered lists, sidebars, and graphic aids such as charts, tables, timelines, illustrations, and photographs.

Thesaurus *See* **Reference Works.**

Thesis Statement In an argument, a thesis statement is an expression of the claim that the writer or speaker is trying to support. In an essay, a thesis statement is an expression, in one or two sentences, of the main idea or purpose of the piece of writing.

Topic Sentence The topic sentence of a paragraph states the paragraph's main idea. All other sentences in the paragraph provide supporting details.

Transcript A transcript is a written record of words originally spoken aloud.

Visualize Visualizing is the process of forming a mental picture based on written or spoken information.

Web Site A Web site is a collection of "pages" on the World Wide Web that is usually devoted to one specific subject. Pages are linked together and are accessed by clicking hyperlinks or menus, which send the user from page to page within the site. Web sites are created by companies, organizations, educational institutions, branches of the government, the military, and individuals.

Workplace Documents Workplace documents are materials that are produced or used within a work setting, usually to aid in the functioning of the workplace. They include job applications, office memos, training manuals, job descriptions, and sales reports.

Works Cited A list of works cited lists names of all the works a writer has referred to in his or her text. This list often includes not only books and articles but also nonprint sources.

Works Consulted A list of works consulted names all the works a writer consulted in order to create his or her text. It is not limited just to those works cited in the text.
See also **Bibliography.**

abdicate (ăb'dĭ-kāt') *v.* to give up responsibility for
abdicar *v.* renunciar a una responsabilidad

aberration (ăb'ə-rā'shən) *n.* a disorder of the mind
aberración *s.* desorden mental

abhor (ăb-hôr') *v.* to regard with disgust
aborrecer *v.* detestar

abject (ăb'jěkt') *adj.* low; contemptible; wretched
abyecto *adj.* vil; despreciable; desgraciado

abominable (ə-bŏm'ə-nə-bəl) *adj.* thoroughly detestable
abominable *adj.* totalmente detestable

acquiesce (ăk'wē-ĕs') *v.* to comply or give in
consentir *v.* aceptar o ceder

adamant (ăd'ə-mənt) *adj.* immovable, especially in opposing something
inflexible *adj.* inquebrantable, especialmente en oposición a algo

admonitory (ăd-mŏn'ĭ-tôr'ē) *adj.* warning
admonitorio *adj.* que da una advertencia

affiliated (ə-fĭl'ē-āt-ĭd) *adj.* joined in close association affiliate *v.*
afiliado *adj.* asociado afiliar *v.*

affinity (ə-fĭn'ĭ-tē) *n.* a kinship or likeness
afinidad *s.* cercanía o semejanza

affluence (ăf'lōō-əns) *n.* wealth
opulencia *s.* riqueza

alleviation (ə-lē'vē-ā'shən) *n.* relief
alivio *s.* desahogo

ambiguity (ăm'bĭ-gyōō'ĭ-tē) *n.* unclearness; uncertainty
ambigüedad *s.* vaguedad; incertidumbre

ameliorate (əmēl'yə-rāt') *v.* to improve
mejorar *v.* aliviar

amethyst (ăm'ə-thĭst) *n.* purple or violet form of transparent quartz used as a gemstone
amatista *s.* cuarzo transparente púrpura o violeta usado como piedra preciosa

amicable (ăm'ĭ-kə-bəl) *adj.* characterized by friendly goodwill
amigable *adj.* caracterizado por buena voluntad

anarchy (ăn'ər-kē) *n.* condition of lawlessness and disorder, often due to lack of governmental authority
anarquía *s.* desorden y confusión por falta de gobierno

anathema (ə-năth'ə-mə) *n.* a strong denunciation; a curse
anatema *s.* fuerte rechazo; maldición

anomaly (ə-nŏm'ə-lē) *n.* departure from the normal rules
anomalía *s.* desviación de las reglas normales

apathy (ăp'ə-thē) *n.* lack of feeling or interest
apatía *s.* falta de sentimiento o de interés

appease (ə-pēz') *v.* to bring peace, quiet, or calm to; to soothe
aplacar *v.* apaciguar; calmar; aquietar

arbitrary (är'bĭ-trĕr'ē) *adj.* based on unpredictable decisions rather than law
arbitrario *adj.* que actúa basándose sólo en la voluntad o en el capricho y no sigue las leyes

ardor (är'dər) *n.* intense enthusiasm; passion
ardor *s.* fuerte entusiasmo; pasión

artifice (är'tə-fĭs) *n.* a clever means to an end
artificio *s.* estratagema; ardid

ascribe (ə-skrīb') *v.* to attribute to a specified cause or source
adscribir *v.* atribuir a una causa o a una fuente

assign (ə-sīn') *n.* person to whom property is transferred in a will or other legal document
beneficiario *s.* persona a la que transfiere propiedades un testamento u otro documento jurídico

attest (ə-tĕst') *v.* to affirm to be true; to be proof of
atestiguar *v.* dar testimonio; certificar

avarice (ăv'ə-rĭs) *n.* immoderate desire for wealth; greed
avaricia *s.* deseo desmedido de riqueza; codicia

aversion (ə-vûr'zhən) *n.* a strong dislike
aversión *s.* fuerte desagrado

blasphemous (blăs'fə-məs) *adj.* disrespectful or offensive
blasfemo *adj.* irrespetuoso u ofensivo

blatantly (blāt'nt-lē) *adv.* in an extremely obvious way; conspicuously
descaradamente *adv.* abiertamente; patentemente

cabal (kə-băl′) *n.* a group united in a secret plot
　cábala *s.* grupo unido en un complot secreto

callow (kăl′ō) *adj.* lacking adult experience; immature
　inmaduro *adj.* sin experiencia; inexperto

camaraderie (kä′mə-rä′də-rē) *n.* a spirit of friendly good-fellowship
　camaradería *s.* espíritu de amistad y compañerismo

cauterize (kô′tə-rīz′) *v.* to burn or sear to destroy diseased tissue
　cauterizar *v.* quemar o chamuscar para destruir tejido dañado

cavorting (kə-vôr′tĭng) *adj.* prancing about in a playful manner **cavort** *v.*
　retozón *adj.* que hace cabriolas de modo juguetón
　retozar *v.*

celestial (sə-lĕs′chəl) *adj.* heavenly
　celestial *adj.* del cielo

censurer (sĕn′shər-ər) *n.* one who expresses strong disapproval or harsh criticism
　censor *s.* persona que expresa una fuerte desaprobación o crítica

cessation (sĕ-sā′shən) *n.* a coming to an end; a stopping
　cesación *s.* fin; terminación

circumvent (sûr′kəm-vĕnt′) *v.* to avoid or get around by clever maneuvering
　circunvenir *v.* evitar o evadir con maniobras

citation (sī-tā′shən) *n.* formal statement of a soldier's achievements
　mención honorífica *s.* reconocimiento de los éxitos de un militar

coerce (kō-ûrs′) *v.* to force
　coaccionar *v.* obligar

cognizant (kŏg′nĭ-zənt) *adj.* aware
　enterado *adj.* informado

commiseration (kə-mĭz′ə-rā′shən) *n.* a feeling of sympathy or pity
　conmiseración *s.* sentimiento de compasión

comport (kəm-pôrt′) *v.* to agree
　concordar *v.* estar de acuerdo

conciliatory (kən-sĭl′ē-ə-tôr′ē) *adj.* showing goodwill to end an argument
　conciliador *adj.* que busca un acuerdo

congenial (kən-jēn′yəl) *adj.* suited to one's needs or nature; agreeable
　compatible *adj.* que concuerda con las necesidades o la naturaleza de uno; concorde

conjecture (kən-jĕk′chər) *v.* to guess
　conjeturar *v.* suponer

consternation (kŏn′stər-nā′shən) *n.* a state of paralyzing dismay; fear
　consternación *s.* estado de gran intranquilidad; temor

constitute (kŏn′stĭ-tōōt′) *v.* to amount to; equal
　constituir *v.* equivaler; formar

contentious (kən-tĕn′shəs) *adj.* quarrelsome
　discutidor *adj.* pendenciero

contrive (kən-trīv′) *v.* to plan skillfully; to design
　ingeniarse *v.* maquinar; inventar

convolution (kŏn′və-lōō′shən) *n.* a form or shape that is folded into curved, complicated windings
　circunvolución *s.* repliegue; enroscadura; enrollamiento

copious (kō′pē-əs) *adj.* in large amounts; abundant
　copioso *adj.* en gran cantidad; abundante

corroborate (kə-rŏb′ə-rāt′) *v.* to support with evidence
　corroborar *v.* comprobar con evidencia

cosmic (kŏz′mĭk) *adj.* of, or belonging to, the universe
　cósmico *adj.* relativo al universo

countenance (koun′tə-nəns) *n.* appearance, especially the expression of the face
　semblante *s.* apariencia, especialmente la expresión de la cara

credulity (krĭ-dōō′lĭ-tē) *n.* an inclination to believe too readily
　credulidad *s.* facilidad para creer

dastardly (dăs′tərd-lē) *adj.* characterized by underhandedness or treachery
　miserable *adj.* solapado o traidor

dearth (dûrth) *n.* lack
　escasez *s.* carencia

decorum (dǐ-kôr′əm) *n.* good taste in conduct or appearance
decoro *s.* buen gusto en la conducta y la apariencia

deference (děf′ər-əns) *n.* respect and honor due to a superior or elder
deferencia *s.* respeto y honor que se debe a un superior o mayor

deliberately (dǐ-lǐb′ər-ǐt-lē) *adv.* in an unhurried and thoughtful manner
deliberadamente *adv.* pausadamente

deliverance (dǐ-lǐv′ər-əns) *n.* rescue from danger
salvación *s.* rescate de un peligro

demeanor (dǐ-mē′nər) *n.* behavior
comportamiento *s.* conducta

depose (dǐ-pōz′) *v.* to remove from rule
deponer *v.* destituir del gobierno

deposition (děp′ə-zǐsh′ən) *n.* a written statement by a witness
deposición *s.* testimonio escrito de un testigo

derision (dǐ-rǐzh′ən) *n.* harsh ridicule or mockery; scorn
irrisión *s.* mofa o ridículo; escarnio

despotism (děs′pə-tǐz′əm) *n.* government by a ruler with unlimited power
despotismo *s.* gobierno de poder ilimitado

detached (dǐ-tăcht′) *adj.* reserved; aloof **detach** *v.*
alejado *adj.* reservado; distante **alejarse** *v.*

dilapidated (dǐ-lăp′ǐ-dā′tǐd) *adj.* in a state of disrepair; rundown **dilapidate** *v.*
dilapidado *adj.* en ruinas; desmantelado **dilapidar** *v.*

disapprobation (dǐs-ăp′rə-bā′shən) *n.* disapproval
desaprobación *s.* censura

discern (dǐ-sûrn′) *v.* to perceive or recognize something
discernir *v.* percibir o reconocer algo

dissembling (dǐ-sěm′blǐng) *n.* disguising the truth about something **dissemble** *v.*
disimulación *s.* encubrimiento de la verdad **disimular** *v.*

dominion (də-mǐn′yən) *n.* control; authority over
dominio *s.* control; soberanía

dwindle (dwǐn′dl) *v.* to become steadily less; to shrink
menguar *v.* disminuirse poco a poco; encogerse

effrontery (ǐ-frŭn′tə-rē) *n.* disrespectful and insulting boldness
insolencia *s.* desvergüenza y descaro

embody (ěm-bŏd′ē) *v.* to represent in human form
encarnar *v.* representar en forma humana

embroidered (ěm′broi′derd) *adj.* decorated with stitched designs **embroider** *v.*
bordado *adj.* decorado con cosidos en relieve **bordar** *v.*

encroach (ěn-krōch′) *v.* to take over the possessions or rights of another
invadir *v.* usurpar las posesiones o los derechos de otro

enmity (ěn′mǐ-tē) *n.* hostility; hatred
enemistad *s.* hostilidad; odio

enterprising (ěn′tər-prī′zǐng) *adj.* possessing imagination and initiative
emprendedor *adj.* que demuestra imaginación e iniciativa

entreaty (ěn-trē′tē) *n.* plea
súplica *s.* petición

epithet (ěp′ə-thět′) *n.* an abusive word or phrase
epíteto *s.* palabra o frase insultante

equanimity (ē′kwə-nǐm′ǐ-tē) *n.* evenness of temper, especially under stress
ecuanimidad *s.* serenidad y equilibrio, especialmente bajo presión

equivocal (ǐ-kwǐv′ə-kəl) *adj.* ambiguous
equívoco *adj.* ambiguo

eradicate (ǐ-răd′ǐ-kāt′) *v.* to destroy completely
erradicar *v.* destruir por completo

esteem (ǐ-stēm′) *v.* to set a high value on
estimar *v.* dar mucho valor

estrangement (ǐ-strānj′-mənt) *n.* separation; alienation
extrañamiento *s.* separación; desavenencia

excruciatingly (ǐk-skrōō′shē-ā′tǐng-lē) *adv.* in a way that causes great pain or distress
dolorosamente *adv.* de modo que causa mucho dolor o angustia

exhilaration (ǐg-zǐl′ə-rā′shən) *n.* a feeling of high spirits or lively joy
regocijo *s.* alborozo y gran alegría

expatriated (ĕk-spā′trē-ā′tĭd) *adj.* sent out of a country or area; banished **expatriate** *v.*
    expatriado *adj.* exiliado; desterrado **expatriar** *v.*

extenuate (ĭk-stĕn′yōō-āt′) *v.* to lessen the seriousness of, especially by providing partial excuses
    atenuar *v.* reducir la gravedad, especialmente dando excusas parciales

extenuating (ĭk-stĕn′yōō-āt′ĭng) *adj.* lessening the severity of **extenuate** *v.*
    atenuante *adj.* que reduce la gravedad **atenuar** *v.*

exultingly (ĭg-zult′ĭng-lē) *adv.* joyfully
    jubilosamente *adv.* con júbilo

fatuity (fə-tōō′ĭ-tē) *n.* something foolish or stupid
    fatuidad *s.* simpleza o estupidez

feigned (fānd) *adj.* not real; pretended **feign** *v.*
    fingido *adj.* irrea; ficticio **fingir** *v.*

felicity (fĭ-lĭs′ĭ-tē) *n.* great happiness
    felicidad *s.* dicha

flamboyant (flăm-boi′ənt) *adj.* marked by strikingly elaborate or colorful display
    flameante *adj.* llamativo; ostentoso; extravagante

flux (flŭks) *n.* change
    flujo *s.* fluctuación; cambio

garrulous (găr′ə-ləs) *adj.* extremely talkative
    locuaz *adj.* que habla mucho

glib (glĭb) *adj.* showing little thought, preparation, or concern
    simplista *adj.* que demuestra poca reflexión, preparación o interés

gullible (gŭl′ə-bəl) *adj.* easily deceived or tricked
    crédulo *adj.* que se deja engañar

harassing (hə-răs′ĭng) *adj.* persistently annoying **harass** *v.*
    molesto *adj.* que fastidia todo el tiempo **molestar** *v.*

harry (hăr′ē) *v.* to torment, often by constant attack
    hostilizar *v.* acosar con ataques constantes

imbued (ĭm-byōōd′) *adj.* deeply influenced by **imbue** *v.*
    imbuido *adj.* profundamente influenciado **imbuir** *v.*

immaculate (ĭ-măk′yə-lĭt) *adj.* without stain; pure
    inmaculado *adj.* sin mancha; puro

impede (ĭm-pēd′) *v.* to interfere with or slow the progress of
    impedir *v.* obstruir; dificultar

impel (ĭm-pĕl′) *v.* to drive forward; force
    impeler *v.* impulsar; obligar

impending (ĭm-pĕn′dĭng) *adj.* to be about to occur **impend** *v.*
    amenazante *adj.* a punto de ocurrir **amenazar** *v.*

imperceptible (ĭm′pər-sĕp′tə-bəl) *adj.* extremely slight; barely noticeable
    imperceptible *adj.* tenue; que casi no se nota

impertinent (ĭm-pûr′tn-ənt) *adj.* rude; ill-mannered
    impertinente *adj.* grosero; mal educado

imperviousness (ĭm-pûr′vē-əs-nəs) *n.* condition of not being able to be affected or disturbed
    imperturbabilidad *s.* imposibilidad de ser afectado o perturbado

impetuous (ĭm-pĕch′ōō-əs) *adj.* acting with sudden or rash energy; hasty
    impetuoso *adj.* que actúa de forma precipitada o irreflexiva; impulsivo

implacable (ĭm-plăk′ə-bəl) *adj.* impossible to satisfy
    implacable *adj.* que no se puede aplacar

importune (ĭm′pôr-tōōn′) *v.* to ask urgently or repeatedly; to annoy or trouble
    importunar *v.* preguntar con urgencia e insistencia; molestar

incense (ĭn-sĕns′) *v.* to cause to be extremely angry
    exasperar *v.* encolerizar; enfurecer

incorrigible (ĭn-kôr′ĭ-jə-bəl) *adj.* incapable of being reformed or corrected
    incorregible *adj.* que no se puede reformar o corregir

indifferent (ĭn-dĭf′ər-ənt) *adj.* having no particular interest
    indiferente *adj.* sin interés

induce (ĭn-dōōs′) *v.* to succeed in persuading someone to do something
    inducir *v.* persuadir; causar; producir

industry (ĭn′də-strē) *n.* hard work; diligence
    aplicación *s.* diligencia; laboriosidad

ineffable (ĭn-ĕf′ə-bəl) *adj.* beyond description; inexpressible
    inefable *adj.* que no se puede describir; inexpresable

inexorable (ĭn-ĕk′sər-ə-bəl) *adj.* relentless
inexorable *adj.* implacable

inextricable (ĭn-ĕk′strĭ-kə-bəl) *adj.* incapable of being disentangled or untied
inextricable *adj.* que no se puede descifrar o desenmarañar

infamous (ĭn′fə-məs) *adj.* having a very bad reputation; disgraceful
infame *adj.* de mala reputación; vergonzoso

infidel (ĭn′fĭ-dəl) *n.* a person with no religious beliefs
infiel *s.* el que no tiene creencias religiosas

ingenuously (ĭn-jĕn′yōō-əs-lē) *adv.* in a manner showing childlike innocence or simplicity
ingenuamente *adv.* con candidez infantil

ingratiate (ĭn-grā′shē-āt′) *v.* to gain another's favor by deliberate effort
congraciar *v.* conseguir aprobación o afecto con un esfuerzo deliberado

inherently (ĭn-hîr′ənt-lē′) *adv.* related to part of something's inmost nature
inherentemente *adv.* intrínsecamente

iniquity (ĭ-nĭk′wĭ-tē) *n.* wickedness
iniquidad *s.* maldad

inordinate (ĭn-ôr′dn-ĭt) *adj.* exceeding reasonable limits; excessive
excesivo *adj.* que sobrepasa los límites razonables; inmoderado

insidious (ĭn-sĭd′ē-əs) *adj.* treacherous
insidioso *adj.* traidor

insipid (ĭn-sĭp′ĭd) *adj.* lacking in flavor; bland
insípido *adj.* sin sabor; desabrido

interim (ĭn′tər-ĭm) *n.* period in between; interval
interin *s.* intermedio; intervalo

interminable (ĭn-tûr′mə-nə-bol) *adj.* endless
interminable *adj.* sin fin

interrogation (ĭn-tĕr′ə-gā′shən) *n.* a questioning
interrogación *s.* averiguación

inundate (ĭn′ŭn-dāt′) *v.* to cover with water; to overwhelm
inundar *v.* cubrir de agua; anegar

invincible (ĭn-vĭn′sə-bəl) *adj.* unbeatable
invencible *adj.* inconquistable

inviolate (ĭn-vī′ə-lĭt) *adj.* not violated; intact
inviolado *adj.* íntegro; intacto

jocular (jŏk′yə-lər) *adj.* humorous
jocoso *adj.* chistoso

latent (lāt′nt) *adj.* existing in a hidden form
latente *adj.* que existe en forma oculta

limber (lĭm′bər) *adj.* bending or moving easily; supple
flexible *adj.* que se dobla o se mueve con facilidad; ágil

locomotion (lō′kə-mō′shən) *n.* the power to move from place to place
locomoción *s.* movimiento de un lugar a otro

ludicrous (lōō′dĭ-krəs) *adj.* laughably absurd; ridiculous
absurdo *adj.* risible; ridículo

lurch (lûrch) *v.* to lean or roll suddenly to one side; to stagger
bambolearse *v.* dar banzados; tambalearse

lurid (lōōr′ĭd) *adj.* shocking; gruesome
escabroso *adj.* chocante; espeluznante

luxuriant (lŭg-zhōōr′ē-ənt) *adj.* characterized by abundant growth
frondoso *adj.* que tiene mucha vegetación

malign (mə-līn′) *adj.* evil; harmful
maligno *adj.* malo; dañino

martial (mär′shəl) *adj.* warlike
marcial *adj.* bélico

maudlin (môd′lĭn) *adj.* excessively sentimental
sensiblero *adj.* sentimental en exceso

mediocrity (mē′dē-ŏk′rĭ-tē) *n.* lack of quality or excellence
mediocridad *s.* poca calidad o mérito

meditative (mĕd′i-tā′tĭv) *adj.* engaged in serious thought or reflection
meditabundo *adj.* que medita o reflexiona en silencio

melancholy (mĕl′ən-kŏl′ē) *adj.* gloomy; sad
melancólico *adj.* triste; lúgubre

mercenary (mûr′sə-nĕr′ē) *n.* a professional soldier hired to fight in a foreign army
mercenario *s.* soldado profesional contratado para pelear en un ejército extranjero

militant (mĭl′i-tənt) *adj.* aggressively active, especially for a cause
    militante *adj.* que apoya enérgicamente una causa

minutest (mī-nōō′tĭst) *adj.* smallest; most precise
    el más diminuto adj. el más pequeño; minucioso

miscellany (mĭs′ə-lā′nē) *n.* a mixture of various things
    miscelánea *s.* mezcla de cosas

misconstrued (mĭs′kən-strōōd′) *adj.* misunderstood; misinterpreted **misconstrue** *v.*
    malinterpretado *adj.* mal entendido **malinterpretar** *v.*

misgiving (mĭs-gĭv′ĭng) *n.* a feeling of doubt, mistrust, or uncertainty
    recelo *s.* sentimiento de duda, desconfianza o temor

mitigation (mĭt-ĭ-gā′shən) *n.* lessening of something that causes suffering
    mitigación *s.* moderación de algo que causa sufrimiento

mollify (mŏl′ə-fī′) *v.* to soothe; to reduce in intensity
    aplacar *v.* calmar; apaciguar

moratorium (môr′a-tôr′ē-əm) *n.* temporary stoppage or waiting period
    moratoria *s.* aplazamiento; período de espera

motley (mŏt′lē) *adj.* composed of diverse, often mismatched elements
    abigarrado *adj.* formado por elementos diversos y dispares

multifariously (mŭl′tə-fâr′ē-əs-lē) *adv.* in many and various ways
    variadamente *adv.* de modos muy variados

mundane (mŭn-dān′) *adj.* characteristic of or concerned with the ordinary
    mundano *adj.* que se preocupa de lo ordinario

myriad (mîr′ē-əd) *adj.* exceedingly numerous
    innumerable *adj.* en excesiva cantidad

nettled (nĕt′əld) *adj.* irritated; annoyed **nettle** *v.*
    irritado *adj.* molesto; picado **irritar** *v.*

nocturnal (nŏk-tûr′nəl) *adj.* occurring at night
    nocturno *adj.* que ocurre por la noche

nominal (nŏm′ə-nəl) *adj.* in name but not in reality
    nominal *adj.* de palabra pero no de hecho

nonconformist (nŏn′kən-fôr′mĭst) *n.* one who does not follow generally accepted beliefs, customs, or practices
    inconformista *s.* el que no sigue las creencias, costumbres y prácticas acostumbradas

obstinate (ob′stə-nĭt) *adj.* hard to control or treat
    obstinado *adj.* terco; porfiado

obstreperous (ŏb-strĕp′ər-əs) *adj.* very noisy and unruly
    estrepitoso *adj.* ruidoso y revoltoso

occult (ə-kŭlt′) *adj.* secret or hidden from view
    oculto *adj.* secreto o escondido

opaque (ō-pāk′) *adj.* not allowing light to pass through
    opaco *adj.* que no deja pasar la luz

opprobrious (ə-prō′brē-əs) *adj.* scornful; derogatory
    oprobioso *adj.* despectivo; derogatorio

oscillation (ŏs′ə-lā′shən) *n.* the action of swinging back and forth
    oscilación *s.* movimiento alternativo de un lado hacia otro

ostentation (ŏs′tĕn-tā′shən) *n.* display meant to impress others; boastful showiness
    ostentación *s.* exhibición que se hace para impresionar; alarde

ostentatious (ŏs′tĕn-tā′shəs) *adj.* loud; overdone
    ostentoso *adj.* pretencioso; aparatoso

overture (ō′vər-chōōr′) *n.* the orchestral introduction to a musical dramatic work
    obertura *s.* pieza instrumental con que empieza una obra musical extensa

paradoxical (păr′ə-dŏks′-ĭ-kəl) *adj.* self-contradictory
    paradójico *adj.* que encierra una contradicción

pariah (pə-rī′ə) *n.* an outcast, someone or something looked down on by others
    paria *s.* persona a la que se considera inferior

patent (păt′nt) *adj.* obvious; apparent
    patente *adj.* obvio; aparente

patrimony (păt′rə-mō′nē) *n.* estate or money inherited from ancestors
    patrimonio *s.* propiedades o dinero heredados de los antepasados

perfidy (pûr′fĭ-dē) *n.* treachery
    perfidia *s.* traición

persecution (pûr'sĭ-kyōō'shən) *n.* the act or practice of oppressing or harassing with ill-treatment, especially because of race, religion, gender, or beliefs
  persecución *s.* acoso con malos tratos, castigos y penas, especialmente por motivo de raza, religión, género o creencias

pertinacity (pûr'tn-ăs'ĭ-tē) *n.* stubbornness; persistence
  pertinacia *s.* terquedad; persistencia

perturbation (pûr'tər-bā'shən) *n.* disturbance of the emotions; agitation; uneasiness
  perturbación *s.* alteración de las emociones; agitación; inquietud

pervade (pər-vād') *v.* to spread through every part of
  penetrar *v.* infiltrarse en todas las partes

pestilential (pĕs'tə-lĕn'shəl) *adj.* deadly; poisonous
  pestilente *adj.* mortal; venenoso

petulance (pĕch'ə-lənsĕ) *n.* ill temper; annoyance
  malhumor *s.* mal genio; disgusto

pigmentation (pĭg'mən-tā'shən) *n.* coloring
  pigmentación *s.* coloración

pillage (pĭl'ĭj) *n.* the act of looting or plundering by force
  pillaje *s.* saqueo o rapiña a la fuerza

plague (plāg) *v.* to annoy; harass
  fastidiar *v.* molestar; acosar

poignant (poin'yənt) *adj.* physically or mentally painful
  punzante *adj.* que causa dolor físico o mental

portend (pôr-tĕnd') *v.* to serve as an omen of; to signify
  augurar *v.* presagiar; significar

precarious (prĭ-kâr'ē-əs) *adj.* risky; uncertain
  precario *adj.* arriesgado; inseguro

precipitate (prĭ-sĭp'ĭ-tāt') *v.* to bring about, especially abruptly
  precipitar *v.* causar, especialmente de repente

predecessor (prĕd'ĭ-sĕs'ər) *n.* person who precedes or comes before
  predecesor *s.* persona que precede o viene antes

preeminently (prē-ĕm'ə-nənt-lē) *adv.* above all; most importantly
  preeminentemente *adv.* por encima de todo; sobre todo

presaging (prĕs'ĭj-ĭng) *adj.* predicting **presage** *v.*
  presagioso *adj.* que anuncia o presagia **presagiar** *v.*

prescience (prĕsh'əns) *n.* knowledge of events before they occur
  presciencia *s.* conocimiento de un suceso antes de que ocurra

preternatural (prē'tər-năch'ər-əl) *adj.* supernatural
  preternatural *adj.* sobrenatural

procure (prō-kyōōr') *v.* to get by special effort; to obtain
  adquirir *v.* conseguir con un esfuerzo especial; obtener

profusion (prə-fyōō'zhən) *n.* abundance; lavishness
  profusión *s.* abundancia; esplendidez

propitious (prə-pĭsh'əs) *adj.* helpful or advantageous; favorable
  propicio *adj.* benéfico; favorable

propriety (prə-prī'ĭ-tē) *n.* the quality of being proper; appropriateness
  corrección *s.* decoro; idoneidad

providence (prŏv'ĭ-dəns) *n.* an instance of divine care
  providencia *s.* ayuda divina

prudent (prōōd'nt) *adj.* showing caution or good judgment
  prudente *adj.* que actúa con moderación y cautela

querulous (kwĕr'ə-ləs) *adj.* complaining
  quejumbroso *adj.* quejicoso

rabid (răb'ĭd) *adj.* unreasonably extreme; fanatical
  rabioso *adj.* inmoderamente extremo; fanático

radiation (rā'dē-ā'shən) *n.* movement of lines or rays from a center point
  radiación *s.* movimiento de líneas o rayos desde un punto central

raiment (rā'ment) *n.* clothing; garments
  vestimenta *s.* ropa; indumentaria

rapt (răpt) *adj.* deeply moved, delighted, or absorbed
  arrebatado *adj.* profundamente conmovido, extasiado o absorto

rectitude (rĕk'tĭ-tōōd') *n.* morally correct behavior or thinking
  rectitud *s.* conducta o pensamiento justo en el sentido moral

recurrent (rǐ-kûr′ənt) *adj.* occurring time after time
   recurrente *adj.* que se repite una y otra vez

redress (rǐ-drěs′) *n.* the correction of a wrong; compensation
   remedio *s.* reparación de un daño; compensación

relinquish (rǐ-lǐng′kwǐsh) *v.* to withdraw from; to give up
   abandonar *v.* renunciar a; ceder

remonstrate (rǐ-mŏn′strāt′) *v.* to object; to protest strongly
   protestar *v.* reclamar; oponerse fuertemente

rendezvous (rän′dā-vōō) *n.* a gathering place
   lugar de reunión *s.* punto de encuentro

replenish (rǐ-plěn′ǐsh) *v.* to fill up again
   reabastecer *v.* volver a llenar

repudiate (rǐ-pyōō′dē-āt′) *v.* to reject or renounce
   repudiar *v.* rechazar o renunciar

repulse (rǐ-pǔls′) *v.* to drive back by force
   rechazar *v.* hacer retroceder a la fuerza

resign (rǐ-zīn′) *v.* to submit or adapt oneself quietly without complaint
   resignarse *v.* someterse o adaptarse sin queja

respite (rěs′pǐt) *n.* a period of rest or relief
   respiro *s.* período de descanso o de alivio

retaliating (rǐ-tǎl′ē-āt′ǐng) *n.* taking revenge **retaliate** *v.*
   vengador *s.* el que toma venganza **vengarse** *v.*

retinue (rět′n-ōō′) *n.* a group of attendants or followers
   séquito *s.* grupo de ayudantes o seguidores

retrospective (rět′rə-spěk′tǐv) *adj.* looking back into the past
   retrospectivo *adj.* que mira al pasado

reverie (rěv′ə-rē) *n.* daydream
   ensueño *s.* arrobamiento

scintillating (sǐn′tl-āt-ǐng) *adj.* sparkling **scintillate** *v.*
   centelleante *adj.* chispeante **centellear** *v.*

scruple (skrōō′pəl) *n.* feeling of uneasiness or guilt that keeps a person from doing something
   escrúpulo *s.* sentimiento de duda o de culpa que impide hacer algo

slovenly (slǔv′ən-lē) *adj.* untidy in personal appearance
   desaliñado *adj.* descuidado en la apariencia personal

solace (sŏl′ǐs) *n.* comfort in sorrow or distress
   solaz *s.* consuelo en el dolor o angustia

solstice (sŏl′stǐs) *n.* either of two days of the year when the sun is farthest from the celestial equator; the summer solstice is the longest day of the year, and the winter solstice is the shortest.
   solsticio *s.* uno de los dos días en que el Sol está más lejos del ecuador; el solsticio de verano es el día más largo del año y el solsticio de invierno es el más corto.

somnambulant (sŏm-nǎm′byə-lənt′) *adj.* sleepwalking
   sonámbulo *adj.* que camina dormido

sordid (sôr′dǐd) *adj.* wretched; dirty; morally degraded
   sórdido *adj.* vil; sucio; indecente

speculating (spěk′yə-lā′tǐng) *n.* engaging in risky business transactions on the chance of a quick or considerable profit
   especulación *s.* operaciones comerciales arriesgadas con la esperanza de obtener una ganancia rápida o considerable

subjugation (sǔb′jə-gā′shən) *n.* control by conquering
   subyugación *s.* sometimiento por la fuerza

subservient (səb-sûr′vē-ənt) *adj.* acting like a servant
   servil *adj.* que actúa como un sirviente

substantive (sǔb′stən-tǐv) *adj.* significant; with a strong basis
   sustantivo *adj.* importante, fundamental o esencial

succumb (sə-kǔm′) *v.* to give in, especially to overpowering force or strength
   sucumbir *v.* rendirse, especialmente a una fuerza mayor

summarily (sə-měr′ə-lē) *adv.* quickly and without ceremony
   sumariamente *adv.* rápidamente y sin ceremonia

supinely (sōō-pīn′lē) *adv.* in a manner with the face upward
   en posición supina *adv.* boca arriba

surfeit (sûr′fǐt) *n.* a fullness beyond the point of satisfaction
   hartura *s.* saciedad más allá del punto de satisfacción

synthesis (sǐn′thǐ-sǐs) *n.* union of parts or elements into a whole
   síntesis *s.* composición de un todo por la unión de sus partes

tableau (tăb′lo′) *n.* dramatic scene or picture
   cuadro *s.* escena dramática

tacitly (tăs′ĭt-lē) *adj.* silently
tácitamente *adv.* silenciosamente

tarry (tăr′ē) *v.* to delay
demorar *v.* tardar

temerity (tə-mĕr′ĭ-tē) *n.* foolish boldness
temeridad *s.* imprudencia

temperament (tĕm′prə-mənt) *n.* characteristic mode of emotional response
temperamento *s.* modo característico de respuesta emocional

tender (tĕn′dər) *v.* to offer formally
ofrecer *v.* presentar de modo formal

tentatively (tĕn′tə-tĭv-lē) *adv.* in a hesitant or uncertain manner
tentativamente *adv.* de modo provisional o cauteloso

tenuous (tĕn′yōō-əs) *adj.* having little substance or strength; flimsy
tenue *adj.* débil o delicado; endeble

tranquil (trăng′kwəl) *adj.* undisturbed; peaceful
tranquilo *adj.* quieto; sereno

transgress (trăns-grĕs′) *v.* to violate a command or law
transgredir *v.* quebrantar una orden o una ley

tremulous (trĕm′yə-ləs) *adj.* trembling; quivering
trémulo *adj.* tembloroso

trepidation (trĕp′ĭ-dā′shən) *n.* alarm or dread
inquietud *s.* alarma o miedo

truculent (trŭk′yə-lənt) *adj.* eager for a fight; fierce
belicoso *adj.* agresivo; feroz

tyranny (tĭr′ə-nē) *n.* cruel and oppressive government or rule
tiranía *s.* gobierno cruel y opresivo

unalienable (ŭn-āl′yə-nə-bəl) *adj.* not to be taken away (Today the usual form is *inalienable*.)
inalienable *adj.* que no se puede quitar

unassailable (ŭn′ə-sā′lə-bəl) *adj.* impossible to dispute or disprove
inexpugnable *adj.* que no se puede refutar

undulating (ŭn′jə-lā′tĭng) *adj.* appearing to move in waves undulate *v.*
ondulado *adj.* con movimiento de olas ondular *v.*

unremitting (ŭn′rĭ-mĭt′ĭng) *adj.* constant; never stopping
perseverante *adj.* constante; incansable

usurer (yōō′zhər-ər) *n.* one who lends money, at interest, especially at an unusually or unlawfully high rate of interest
usurero *s.* persona que presta dinero al interés, especialmente a una tasa muy alta o ilegal

usurpation (yōō′sər-pā′shən) *n.* the act of wrongfully taking over a right or power that belongs to someone else
usurpación *s.* apropiación indebida de un derecho o poder que pertenece a otro

vagary (vā′gə-rē) *n.* strange idea
capricho *s.* rareza

veritable (vĕr′ĭ-tə-bəl) *adj.* true; not unreal or imaginary
verdadero *adj.* real; auténtico

vigilant (vĭj′ə-lənt) *adj.* alert; watchful
vigilante *adj.* alerta; atento

virulent (vîr′yə-lənt) *adj.* extremely poisonous or harmful
virulento *adj.* sumamente venenoso o dañino

vituperative (vī-tōō′pər-ə-tĭv) *adj.* abusively critical
injurioso *adj.* que critica de modo ofensivo

whet (hwĕt) *adj.* sharpened whet *v.*
afilado *adj.* agudo afilar *v.*

wrangling (răng′glĭng) *adj.* arguing noisily wrangle *v.*
discutidor *adj.* que disputa en voz alta discutir *v.*

zealous (zĕl′əs) *adj.* eager and enthusiastic
fervoroso *adj.* dedicado y entusiasta

Pronunciation Key

Symbol	Examples	Symbol	Examples	Symbol	Examples
ă	**at**, **g**as	m	**m**an, see**m**	v	**v**an, sa**ve**
ā	**a**pe, **d**ay	n	**n**ight, mitte**n**	w	**w**eb, t**w**ice
ä	f**a**ther, b**a**rn	ng	si**ng**, ha**ng**er	y	**y**ard, law**y**er
âr	**fair**, **dare**	ŏ	**o**dd, n**o**t	z	**z**oo, rea**s**on
b	**b**ell, ta**b**le	ō	**o**pen, r**oa**d, gr**ow**	zh	trea**s**ure, gara**ge**
ch	**ch**in, lun**ch**	ô	**aw**ful, b**ough**t, h**o**rse	ə	**a**wake, ev**e**n, penc**i**l,
d	**d**ig, bor**ed**	oi	c**oi**n, b**oy**		pil**o**t, foc**u**s
ĕ	**e**gg, t**e**n	ŏŏ	l**oo**k, f**u**ll	ər	p**er**form, lett**er**
ē	**e**vil, s**ee**, m**ea**l	ōō	r**oo**t, gl**ue**, thr**ough**		
f	**f**all, lau**gh**, **ph**rase	ou	**ou**t, c**ow**	**Sounds in Foreign Words**	
g	**g**old, bi**g**	p	**p**ig, ca**p**	KH	*German* i**ch**, au**ch**;
h	**h**it, in**h**ale	r	**r**ose, sta**r**		*Scottish* lo**ch**
hw	**wh**ite, every**wh**ere	s	**s**it, fa**ce**	N	*French* e**n**tre, bo**n**, fi**n**
ĭ	**i**nch, f**i**t	sh	**sh**e, ma**sh**	œ	*French* f**eu**, c**œu**r;
ī	**i**dle, m**y**, tr**ie**d	t	**t**ap, hopp**ed**		*German* sch**ö**n
îr	d**ear**, h**ere**	th	**th**ing, wi**th**	ü	*French* **u**tile, r**ue**;
j	**j**ar, **g**em, ba**dge**	*th*	**th**en, o**th**er		*German* gr**ü**n
k	**k**eep, **c**at, lu**ck**	ŭ	**u**p, n**u**t		
l	**l**oad, ratt**le**	ûr	f**ur**, **ear**n, b**ir**d, w**or**m		

Stress Marks

′   This mark indicates that the preceding syllable receives the primary stress. For example, in the word *language*, the first syllable is stressed: lăng′gwĭj.

′   This mark is used only in words in which more than one syllable is stressed. It indicates that the preceding syllable is stressed, but somewhat more weakly than the syllable receiving the primary stress. In the word *literature*, for example, the first syllable receives the primary stress, and the last syllable receives a weaker stress: lĭt′ər-ə-chŏŏr′.

Adapted from *The American Heritage Dictionary of the English Language*, fourth edition. Copyright © 2000 by Houghton Mifflin Company. Used with the permission of Houghton Mifflin Company.

INDEX OF FINE ART

Index of Skills

tragedy, 128
types of characters, 131. *See also* Character types.
verbal irony, 635
Dramatic irony, 175, 635, 735, 759, 1033, 1044, R112–R113
Dramatic monologue, 929, R108
Drawing conclusions. *See* Conclusions.

E

Editing, of film and video, 605, 1177, R91. *See also* Camera shots
    in film and video; Media elements and techniques.
    cut, R91
    dissolve, R91
    fade-in, R91
    fade-out, R91
    jump cut, R91
    montage, 597
    pace, R91
    parallel editing, R91
Editing, of writing. *See* Revising and editing.
Effect. *See also* Cause-and-effect organization.
    unity of, 403–424
Either/or fallacy, R22, R124
Elaboration, R31
Electronic media. *See also* Multimedia presentations; References;
    Research.
    Internet, 1271–1275
Electronic sources. *See* References; Sources.
Electronic texts, strategies for reading, R18
Elements of design, R94
Ellipses, 1078, R54
Emotional appeals, 119–126, 223, 245, R20, R94, R124
Encyclopedia, 1269, R44, R124. *See also* References.
End marks, 480, R53
English sonnet. *See* Shakespearean sonnet.
Enjambment, 329, 330, 507
Essay questions in assessment. *See* Assessment; Writing for
    assessment.
Essays, literary, 244, 360, 365, 370, 382, 394, 450, 518, 784,
    858, 868, 1066, 1114, 1172, 1192, 1204, 1214, 1222,
    R109
    analysis of, 358–359, 371–380, 389
    personal, 1204, 1214, 1222
    persuasive, 244
    reflective, 360, 372, 1045
Essays, writing
    analytical, 109, 333, 535, 755, 804, 911, R37–R38
    autobiographical, 867, R109
    cause-effect, R36
    comparison-contrast, 65, 1072, R35–R36
    descriptive, 61, 595, 1213, R32–R33
    expository, 211, 217, 221, 473, 803, 875, 987, R35

interpretive, 755
persuasive, 275, 276–282, R38
problem-solution, 1248–1254, R37
reflective, 474–480
Etymologies, 76, 1030, 1080, R74. *See also* Word origins.
Evaluation
    of ideas, 371–380
Everyday texts. *See* Consumer documents; Workplace documents.
Evidence, 223, 235—241, 1145–1157, 1172–1175, R19, R23,
    R39. *See also* Arguments; Support.
    bias in, R23
    deductive reasoning and, R21
    evaluating, R23
    inductive reasoning and, R20
Exclamation points, R53
Exclamatory sentences, 233, R64
Experimental poetry, 921, R109
Explanatory writing. *See* Expository writing.
Exposition. *See* Plot.
Expository essay, 211, 221, 473, 803, 875, 987, R35
Expository texts. *See* Nonfiction.
Expository writing, 987, R35–R38
    analysis, 109, 211, 221, 473, 804–810, 875, R37–R38
    book review, 1065
    cause-effect, R36
    comparison-contrast, 65, 803, 987, 1072–1079, R35–R36
    eyewitness report, 1191
    options for organization, R35–R38
    problem-solution, 1248–1254, R37
    research papers, 1284–1301
Expressive writing. *See* Narrative writing.
Extended metaphors, 111, 857, R109
Eye contact, in speeches, 283, R81
Eyewitness account, 1181–1190, R109

F

Facial expression, in speeches, 283, R81
Facts, versus opinions, R125
Fallacies, 282, R22–R23, R125
    circular reasoning, 282, R22
    either/or fallacy, 282, R22, R124
    evading the issue, R22
    false analogy, R22
    false cause, 282, R22
    hasty generalization, R22
    name-calling, R22
    non-sequitur, R22
    overgeneralization, 282, R22
    oversimplification, R22
    stereotyping, 62–64, R22, R128
Falling action. *See* Plot.

H

Hasty generalizations, R22

Headlines, 738–743, 811, 1177–1178, R3–R4, R88, R92, R94

Hierarchical organization. *See* Order of importance.

Historical context of literature, R111

    analysis of, 69–75, 96, 284, 568, 1123–1131, 1161–1169, 1256

    influence of, 32, 44, 52, 70, 80, 90, 118, 120, 224, 226, 234, 244, 246, 254, 262, 312, 382, 392, 396, 564, 578, 650, 674, 694, 760, 846, 860, 888, 1050, 1138, 1144, 1216

    recognizing, 52, 894–895

    understanding, 68, 80, 90, 133, 212–217, 226, 246, 256, 566, 636, 670, 688, 712, 746, 792, 978, 1004, 1068, 1214

Historical documents, 234, 284, 566, R125

Historical narratives, 66–67, 68, 78, 88, 98, 100, 284, 536, 550, R111

Homographs, 648

Homonyms, R75–R76

Homophones, R76

Humor, 635, 1060, 1067, R111. *See also* Comedy; Parody; Understatement.

    analysis of, 658

Hyperbole, 111, 649, 659, R112

    analysis of, 667

Hyphens, R54

I

Iamb, 341. *See also* Blank verse; Iambic pentameter; Sonnet.

Iambic pentameter, 329, 903, R112. *See also* Blank verse; Sonnet.

Ideas. *See also* Main ideas.

    evaluating, 332, 356, 367, 371–380, 389, 927, 1256

    identifying, 859–865, 1193–1199, 1256

    tracing the development of, 1243–1246

    for writing, R26

Idioms, 1256, R72, R112

Illustrations

    analysis of, 447

Imagery, 860, R112

    analysis of, 311–325, 443, 711–735, 764, 857, 959, 1080, 1115–1121, 1131, 1166, 1241, 1243–1246

    kinesthetic, 1166

    in literary journalism, 1046

    in poetry, 347, 519, 525

Imagism, 913–918

Imperative sentences, 228, 233, 444

Indefinite pronouns, R58

Independent (main) clauses, R66

Independent observation, R47

Independent reading

    ideas for, 290–291, 488–489, 612–613, 818–819, 1086–1087, 1262–1263

Indexes, 1269, 1270, 1274, 1277, R44, R125. *See also* References.

Indirect objects, R65

Inductive reasoning, R20–R21, R125

Inferences, making, 195, 241, 380, 435, 534, 593, 703, 812, 840, 865, 910, 913–918, 1080, 1131, 1221, 1229, R125

    about authors, 263–272

    about characters, 667, 969–975

    about historical context, 96

    about poetry, 341–345, 356, 437–443

Infinitives and infinitive phrases, 911, 1080, R65

Informal language 859, 1208, 1213, R72, R80. *See also* Slang.

Informal speech, 221

Information. *See* Electronic media; Informational texts; Reading for information; References; Sources.

Informational texts, 212, 214, 274, 381, 738, 740, 741, 1256, R3–R18, R126. *See also* Nonfiction; Public documents; Reading for information.

    forms, R13–R18

    patterns of organization, R8–R12

    text features, R3–R7

Informative articles. *See* News articles; Reading for information.

Interjections, R51, R64

Internal conflict, 551, 759, 1137

Internal rhyme, 437, 482

Internet, 1271–1275, R46. *See also* Electronic media; References; Web sites.

Interrogative sentences, 228, 233, 391, R64

Interviews, R112

    conducting, 51, 481, R47, R86

    evaluating, R86

    following up on, R86

    oral histories, R47

    preparing for, 481

    as research source, 1269, R47

    responding to, R86

Intransitive verbs, R51

Introductions, R28

Inverted sentences, 211, R71

Inverted syntax, 111–117, R112

Irony, 175, 325, 471, 635–647, 882, 1033–1044, 1080, R112–R113

    dramatic, 175, 635, 735, 759, 1033, 1044, R112–R113

    situational, 635, 759, 1033, R112, R119

    verbal, 195, 471, 635, 719, R111, R113, R118

Issues

    evading, as logical fallacy, R22

Italics, R54.

M

O

Objective pronoun case, R56
Objects
  direct, R65
  indirect, R65
Observations, R47
Online catalogs, R46
Online information. *See* Internet; Web sites.
Onomatopoeia, 437, 482, R115
Open letter, 1146, 1194, R115
Opinions
  versus facts, R24, R87, R125
  support for, 1175, 1251, R2, R23, R38, R39, R80
Oral critique, 595
Oral histories, 1269, R47
Oral interpretation, 357, 1079, R84
Oral literature, 32, 42, R116
  creation myths, 33–41, 323, R115
  fables, 32, R104, R110
  folk tales, 32, 42, 43–49, R107, R110, R122
  myths, 33–41, R115
  tall tales, 659–667, R121
  trickster tales, 43–49, R122
Oral presentations. *See also* Speaking strategies.
  audience feedback, 1303, R82, R87
  critique, 595
  debate, 109, 673, R82
  delivery of, 1303, R81
  descriptive speech, R84
  dramatic reading, R84
  evaluating, R82, R83, R84, R85
  informal, 221
  informative, R82
  narrative speech, R83
  oral interpretations, 357, 1079, R84
  oral reading, 875
  oral response to literature, R85
  persuasive speech, 283, R82
  poetry, 935, 1079, 1143
  reflective speech, R84
Oral tradition. *See* Oral literature.
Order of importance, R8, R33
Organizational patterns. *See* Patterns of organization.
Organizing. *See* Graphic organizers; Patterns of organization.
Origin of words, 76, 1030, 1080, R74. *See also* Word roots.
Outlines
  for taking notes, 19, 297, 495, 619, R49
Overgeneralization, R22, R126
Oversimplification, R22

P

Pacing, in speech, 283, 1079, R84. *See also* Speaking strategies.
Paradox, 372, 1193, R116
  evaluating, 534
  interpreting, 389
Paragraphs, writing
  coherence of, R29
  conclusions in, R31
  descriptive, 426, 549, 705
  elaboration, R31
  reflective, 401
  transitions in, R29
  unity of, R29
Parallelism
  as a rhetorical device, 319, 327, 482, 509, 606, 1150, 1159, R116
Parallel structure, 223, 282, R68
Paraphrasing, 231, 339, 347–356, 427, 482, 519, 528, 530, 649–658, 851, 865
  main ideas, 395–400
Parentheses, R54
Parenthetical documentation, 1298. *See also* Works cited.
Parodies, 445, R116
Participles and participial phrases, 407, 426, 482, 1017, R66
  dangling, R66
  misplaced, R66
Parts of speech, R50, R56–R64. *See also* specific parts of speech.
Passive voice, 763, 765, 1255, R60
Patterns of organization, R8–R12, R126
  cause-effect chain, R10, R35
  cause-to-effect, R10–R11, R36, R123
  chronological order, R9, R34
  comparison-and-contrast, 1076, R11–R12, R35–R36
  deciding between solutions, R37
  deductive, R21, R124
  definition analysis, R38
  effect-to-cause, R10, R36
  flashback, R34
  focus on conflict, R35
  hierarchical, R8, R33
  inductive, R20–R21, R125
  main idea and details, R126
  order of importance, R8, R33
  order of impression, R33
  parts analysis, R38
  point-by-point, R35, R39
  problem-solution, 1248, R37
  process analysis, R38
  reasons for opinion, R39
  sequential, R127
  spatial order, R33
  subject-by-subject, R36

Title page, R44
Titles, R121
    analysis of, 332
    capitalization of, R55
    evaluating, 1131
    interpreting, 424, 934, 1142, 1212
    italics to set off, R54
Tone
    analysis of, 332, 345, 443, 509–519, 606, 711, 735, 791–802, 846, 857, 859–865, 889–893, 1058, 1064, 1080, 1115–1121, 1135, R121
    author's perspective and, 371, 395–400
    diction and, 559, 812, 889–893, 974, 977
    establishing, 559, 606, 974, 977, 1121
    repetition and, 812
Tragedy, 128, R121
Traits. *See* Character traits; Key traits of effective writing.
Transcendentalism, 370, R122
    analysis of, 361–367, 380
Transitions
    as clues to pattern of organization, R30–R31
    commas to set off introductory word, phrase, or clause, R53
Transitive verbs, R51
Trickster tales, 42, R122
    analysis, 43–49
Turning point. *See* Climax.

U

Understatement, 649, 659, R122
Unfamiliar words, understanding, R73
Unity of effect, 403–424, R122
Universal themes, 1003–1015
URLs, R18, R46–R47, R75
Usage. *See* Grammar handbook.

V

Validity of sources. *See* Sources, evaluating.
Venn diagrams, 41, 339, 753, 764
Verb agreement. *See* Subject-verb agreement.
Verbals and verbal phrases
    gerund, 727, 737, 812, R66
    infinitive, 911, R65
    participle, 407, 426, 482, 1017, R66
Verbs
    action, 1017, R51, R59
    auxiliary , R51
    direct objects, R65
    indirect objects, R65
    intransitive, R51
    irregular, R59
    linking, R51, R59

    principal parts, R59
    regular, R59
    tense, 480, 604, 771, 787, R59
    transitive, R51
    vivid, 541, 549, 606, 1007, 1017, 1186, 1191
    voice of, 762, 765, 812, 1255, R60
Verb tense
    future, R59
    future perfect, R60
    past, R59
    past perfect, R60
    present, 771, 787, R59
    present perfect, R59
    progressive forms, R60
Verse. *See* Poetic forms.
Video. *See also* Media.
    analyzing techniques, 63, 64
    images, examining, 62
    message, evaluating, 967, R95
    persuasive techniques, analyzing, 964
Viewpoint. *See* Author's perspective; Bias.
Visual aids. *See* Graphic aids.
Visual design, elements of, 447, R94–R95. *See also* Media elements and techniques.
    color, 447, R94
    lines, 447, R94
    shape, 447, R94
    texture, 447, R94
Visuals, analysis of, 22, 34, 52, 70, 80, 90, 100, 105, 112, 120, 226, 236, 264, 300, 312, 316, 337, 343, 344, 348, 362, 366, 372, 382, 396, 404, 410, 422, 438, 458, 467, 499, 515, 526, 538, 540, 544, 552, 582, 587, 591, 620, 636, 650, 674, 694, 712, 731, 746, 760, 768, 792, 840, 848, 856, 860, 891, 898, 904, 922, 924, 938, 942, 953, 970, 990, 1004, 1010, 1034, 1038, 1050, 1060, 1099, 1116, 1124, 1130, 1138, 1146, 1162, 1166, 1182, 1194, 1206, 1216, 1224, 1238. *See also* Visual elements.
Vocabulary. *See also* Vocabulary skills and strategies.
    assessment practice, 284, 482, 606, 812, 1080, 1256, 1080
    in context, 51, 60, 69, 76, 79, 86, 97, 99, 108, 119, 127, 131, 210, 225, 232, 235, 242, 245, 253, 263, 273, 311, 326, 361, 368, 371, 390, 403, 425, 427, 436, 457, 421, 581, 594, 635, 648, 659, 669, 673, 686, 693, 704, 711, 736, 745, 754, 767, 786, 791, 802, 859, 866, 937, 960, 969, 976, 989, 1000, 1003, 1016, 1019, 1030
    in writing, 60, 76, 86, 97, 108, 127, 210, 232, 242, 253, 273, 326, 368, 390, 425, 436, 472, 594, 648, 668, 686, 704, 736, 754, 786, 802, 866, 960, 976, 1000, 1016, 1030, 1158, 1200
Vocabulary skills and strategies, 60, 76, 86, 97, 108, 127, 210, 232, 242, 253, 273, 326, 368, 390, 425, 436, 472, 594,

INDEX OF TITLES & AUTHORS

Page numbers that appear in italics refer to biographical information.

ACKNOWLEDGMENTS

UNIT 1

American Anthropological Association: "The World on the Turtle's Back," from *The Great Tree and the Longhouse: The Culture of the Iroquois* (pp. 12–19) by Hazel W. Hertzberg. Copyright © 1966 American Anthropological Association. Reproduced by permission of the American Anthropological Association. Not for sale or further reproduction.

University of Nebraska Press: "Coyote and the Buffalo," from *Coyote Stories* by Mourning Dove. Collected in *Masterpieces of American Indian Literature.* Published by the University of Nebraska Press. Reprinted by permission.

N. Scott Momaday: Excerpt from *The Way to Rainy Mountain* by N. Scott Momaday. Copyright © N. Scott Momaday. Reprinted by permission of the author.

Scribner: From *Cabeza De Vaca's Adventures in the Unknown Interior of America,* translated and annotated by Cyclone Covey. Copyright © 1961 Macmillan Publishing Company. Reprinted with the permission of Scribner, an imprint of Simon & Schuster Adult Publishing Group.

University of North Carolina Press: From *The Complete Works of Captain John Smith, 1580–1631,* edited by Philip L. Barbour, with a foreword by Thad W. Tate. Published for the Omohundro Institute of Early American History and Culture. Copyright © 1986 by the University of North Carolina Press. Used by permission of the publisher.

Alfred A. Knopf: Excerpts from *Of Plymouth Plantation, 1620–1647* by William Bradford, edited by Samuel Eliot Morison. Copyright 1952 by Samuel Eliot Morison and renewed 1980 by Emily M. Beck. Used by permission of Alfred A. Knopf, a division of Random House, Inc. For on-line information about other Random House, Inc., books and authors, see the Internet Web site at http://www.randomhouse.com.

Viking Penguin: *The Crucible* by Arthur Miller. Copyright 1952, 1953, 1954, renewed © 1980, 1981, 1982 by Arthur Miller. Used by permission of Viking Penguin, a division of Penguin Group (USA) Inc.

Thirteen/WNET New York: "McCarthyism." Courtesy Thirteen/WNET New York.

New York Times: From "The Demons of Salem, With Us Still" by Victor Navasky, the *New York Times,* September 8, 1996. Copyright © 1996 by the New York Times Co. Reprinted with permission.

Grove/Atlantic: Excerpt from *Timebends* by Arthur Miller. Copyright © 1987 by Arthur Miller. Used by permission of Grove/Atlantic, Inc.

Rolling Stone: From "The Crucible (film review)" by Peter Travers, *Rolling Stone,* December 12, 1996. © Rolling Stone LLC 1996. All rights reserved. Reprinted by permission.

U.S. News & World Report: "50 Ways to Fix Your Life" by Carolyn Kleiner Butler, *U.S. News & World Report,* January 3, 2005. Copyright © 2005 U.S. News & World Report, L.P. Reprinted with permission.

UNIT 2

Cynthia G. La Ferle: From "Thoreau Still Beckons, if I Can Take My Laptop" by Cynthia G. La Ferle, the *Christian Science Monitor,* October 3, 1997. Copyright © 1997 by Cynthia G. La Ferle. Reprinted by permission of the author.

Navajivan Trust: Excerpt from "Readiness for Satyagraha" by Mahatma Gandhi, from *The Essential Writings of Mahatma Gandhi,* edited by Raghavan Iyer. Published by Oxford University Press. Reprinted by permission of the Navajivan Trust.

Stephen King: Excerpt from *Danse Macabre* by Stephen King. Copyright © Stephen King. All rights reserved. Reprinted with permission.

UNIT 3

Harvard University Press: Excerpt from "My life closed twice before its close—" by Emily Dickinson. Reprinted by permission of the publishers and the Trustees of Amherst College from *The Poems of Emily Dickinson,* Thomas H. Johnson, ed., Cambridge, Mass.: The Belknap Press of Harvard University Press, Copyright 1951, 1955, 1979, 1983 by the President and Fellows of Harvard College.

Agencia Literaria Carmen Balcells and Didier Tisdel Jaén: "Ode to Walt Whitman" by Pablo Neruda, translated by Didier Tisdel Jaén. Published in *Nuevas odas elementales* and *Homage to Walt Whitman: A Collection of Poems from the Spanish.* © Fundación Pablo Neruda, 1956. Translation copyright © Didier Tisdel Jaén. Used by permission of Agencia Literaria Carmen Balcells, S. A., and Didier Tisdel Jaén.

Harvard University Press: "Because I could not stop for Death—" by Emily Dickinson. Reprinted by permission of the publishers and the Trustees of Amherst College from *The Poems of Emily Dickinson,* Thomas H. Johnson, ed., Cambridge, Mass.: The Belknap Press of Harvard University Press, Copyright © 1951, 1955, 1979 by the President and Fellows of Harvard College.

"Success is counted sweetest" by Emily Dickinson. Reprinted by permission of the publishers and the Trustees of Amherst College from *The Poems of Emily Dickinson,* Thomas H. Johnson, ed., Cambridge, Mass.: The Belknap Press of Harvard University Press, Copyright © 1951, 1955, 1979, 1983 by the President and Fellows of Harvard College.

"Much Madness is divinest Sense—" by Emily Dickinson. Reprinted by permission of the publishers and the Trustees of Amherst College from *The Poems of Emily Dickinson,* Thomas H. Johnson, ed., Cambridge, Mass.: The Belknap Press of Harvard University Press, Copyright © 1951, 1955, 1979, 1983 by the President and Fellows of Harvard College.

"My life closed twice before its close—" by Emily Dickinson. Reprinted by permission of the publishers and the Trustees of Amherst College from *The Poems of Emily Dickinson,* Thomas H. Johnson, ed., Cambridge, Mass.: The Belknap Press of Harvard University Press, Copyright © 1951, 1955, 1979, 1983 by the President and Fellows of Harvard College.

CONSULTANTS

Title page © Brand X Pictures; Photo © Duane McCubrey; Photo © Mark Schmidt; Photo © Bruce Forrester; Photo © McDougal Littell; Photo © Howard Gollub; Photo © Tamra Stallings; Photo © Mark Schmidt; Photo © Robert J. Marzano; Photo © McDougal Littell; Photo © Dawson & Associates Photography; Photo © Gitchell's Studio; Photo © Michael Romeo; Photo © Monica Ani; Photo © William McBride; Photo © Bill Caldwell; Photo © Gabriel Pauluzzi; Photo © Steven Scheffler.

TABLE OF CONTENTS

Contents in Brief verso *top, Patrick Henry Before the Virginia House of Burgesses* (1851), Peter F. Rothermel. Red Hill, The Patrick Henry National Memorial, Brookneal, Virginia; *bottom* © Reza Estakhrian/ Getty Images; *recto top* © Burstein Collection/Corbis; *bottom* © Bob Adelman/Magnum Photos; **Unit 1 verso** *left, right* The Granger Collection, New York; *recto* © PunchStock; **Unit 2 verso** *left* © Gary Kelley, 1996; *right* © Gail Mooney/Masterfile; *recto* © PunchStock; **Unit 3 verso** *left* The Granger Collection, New York; *right* © Martin Rogers/ Getty Images; *recto* © PunchStock; **Unit 4 verso** *left* © Bettmann/ Corbis; *right* © Juniors Bildarchiv/Age Fotostock; *recto* © PunchStock; **Unit 5 verso** *left, Autoportrait* (1925), Tamara De Lempicka. Oil on wood, 35 cm × 26 cm. Private collection. © 2007 Artists Rights Society (ARS), New York/ADAGP, Paris; *right, The Cotton Club in Harlem, New York* (1930). Black and white photograph. Private collection. © Bridgeman Art Library; *recto* © PunchStock; **Unit 6 verso** *left, Thinking* (1990), Carlton Murrell. Oil on board. Private collection. © Bridgeman Art Library; *right* The Granger Collection, New York; *recto* © PunchStock; **Unit 7** *left* Cover of *The Grapes of Wrath* by John Steinbeck. © 1939 by John Steinbeck. Reprinted by permission of Penguin Books, a division of the Penguin Group (USA), Inc., 375 Hudson Street, New York, New York 10014. All rights reserved.; Cover photo: The Granger Collection, New York; *right* © Design Pics, Inc./Alamy Images; *inset right* © Bettmann/ Corbis.

INTRODUCTORY UNIT

xxxvi *top* The Granger Collection, New York; *center* © Images.com/ Corbis; *bottom* Library of Congress; **1** *top left, Kindred Spirits* (1849), Asher Brown Durand. © Francis G. Mayer/Corbis; *top right* © Bettmann/Corbis; *bottom* © 20th Century Fox Film Corp. All rights reserved/Courtesy The Everett Collection; **2** *left, The Mayflower in Plymouth Harbor* (1882), William Formby Halsall. © Pilgrim Hall Museum, Plymouth, Massachusetts; *right* Library of Congress; **3** *left* © Reza Estakhrian/Getty Images; *right* © James P. Blair/National Geographic Image Collection; **4** *left to right* © Bettmann/Corbis; © Richard T. Nowitz/Corbis; *The Bloody Massacre perpetrated in...Boston on March 5th, 1770* (1770), Paul Revere. Colored engraving. Private collection. © Art Resource, New York; © Gary Kelley, 1996; *Wanderer Above a Sea of Fog* (1817), Casper David Friedrich. Oil on canvas, 94.8 cm × 74.8 cm. Inv.: 5161. On permanent loan from the Foundation for the Promotion of the Hamburg Art Collections. Hamburger Kunsthalle, Hamburg, Germany. Photo by Elke Walford. © Bildarchiv Preussischer Kulturbesitz/Art Resource, New York; **5** *left to right* © New York Public Library, Schomburg Center; Library of Congress; © Hulton-Deutsch Collection/Corbis; *Street Shadows* (1959), Jacob Lawrence. Egg tempera on hardboard, 24″ × 30″. Private collection, New York. Photograph courtesy of Gwendolyn Knight Lawrence/Art Resource, New York. © 2007 The Jacob and Gwendolyn Lawrence Foundation, Seattle/Artists Rights Society (ARS), New York; *The Green Machine* (1977), Frank Dahmer. Screenprint on paper, 13½″ × 17¼″. © National Vietnam Veterans Art Museum; **6** *Top to bottom* Cover of *The Great Gatsby* by F. Scott Fitzgerald. © 1980 by Charles Scribner's Sons. Reprinted by permission of Simon & Schuster, New York, Cover photo: The Granger Collection, New York; © Historical Picture Archive/Corbis; © Culver Pictures/The Art Archive; *Autoportrait* (about 1925), Tamara de Lempicka. Oil on wood, 35 cm × 26 cm. Private collection. © 2007 Artists Rights Society (ARS), New York/ADAGP, Paris; **8** © Culver Pictures/The Art Archive; **10** *top left* © Time & Life Images/Getty Images; *top right* © Eve Arnold/Magnum Photos; *center* © Randy Faris/ Corbis; *bottom* © 20th Century Fox Film Corp. All rights reserved/ Courtesy The Everett Collection.

UNIT 1

15 *top* © Manuscripts, Archives and Special Collections, Washington State University Libraries, Neg No. 89–052; *bottom* The Granger Collection, New York; **16** *left, Mandan Offering the Buffalo Skull.* Edward S. Curtis Collection. © McCormick Library of Special Collections, Northwestern University Library; *right, Arrival of the English in Virginia* (1585–1588), Theodore de Bry. From *Admiranta Narratio*, page 47. Engraving. Service Historique de la Marine, Vincennes, France. Photo © Giraudon/Art Resource, New York; **17** *left, Fire, allegory* (1566), Giuseppe Arcimboldo. Painted for Emperor Maximilian II. Limewood, 66.5 cm × 51 cm. Inv 1585. Kunsthistorisches Museum, Vienna. Photo © Erich Lessing/Art Resource, New York; *right* Library of Congress; **20** *top, bottom* The Granger Collection, New York; **24** © Richard T. Nowitz/ Corbis; **25** The Granger Collection, New York; **27** *George Washington (Vaughn Portrait)* (1795), Gilbert Stuart. Oil on canvas, 28¾″ × 23¾″, Andrew W. Mellon Collection. © 2005 Board of Trustees, National Gallery of Art, Washington D.C.; **28** *top left* Library of Congress; *center left, Whaler off the Vineyard-Outward Bound* (1859), William Bradford. Oil on Fiberboard, 16″ × 24″. Smithsonian American Art Museum, Washington, D.C. © Smithsonian American Art Museum, Washington, D.C./Art Resource, New York; *bottom left* © Mary Evans Picture Library; *right* The Granger Collection, New York; **29** *top left* The Granger Collection, New York; *center left, bottom left* © North Wind/North Wind Picture Archives; **29** *top right* The Granger Collection, New York; *bottom right* Courtesy, American Antiquarian Society; **30** © Bruce Davidson/Magnum Photos, Courtesy of Toyota; **31** *top* © National Geographic/Getty Images; *bottom* AP/Wide World Photos; **32** *top* © North Wind/North Wind Picture Archives; *bottom* Fourteen foot Abnaki style birchbark canoe. © Henri Vaillancourt; **33** © ESA/PLI/Corbis; **t42** *top* © Manuscripts, Archives and Special Collections, Washington State University Libraries, Neg No. 89–052; *bottom* © Don Pitcher/Stock Boston; **43** © The Road Runner show, Wile E. Coyote, Road Runner, 1966–1973/The Everett Collection; **50** *top* © N. Scott Momaday/Royce Carlton, Inc.; *bottom* © Sharon Maritz/Age Fotostock America, Inc.; **51** © David Alan Harvey/Magnum Photos; **53** Library of Congress; **61** The Granger Collection, New York; **62** *background* © Nick Koudis/Photodisc

---

"The Soul selects her own Society" by Emily Dickinson. Reprinted by permission of the publishers and the Trustees of Amherst College from *The Poems of Emily Dickinson,* Thomas H. Johnson, ed., Cambridge, Mass.: The Belknap Press of Harvard University Press, Copyright 1951, 1955, 1979, 1983 by the President and Fellows of Harvard College.

"I heard a Fly buzz—when I died—" by Emily Dickinson. Reprinted by permission of the publishers and the Trustees of Amherst College from *The Poems of Emily Dickinson,* Thomas H. Johnson, ed., Cambridge, Mass.: The Belknap Press of Harvard University Press, Copyright © 1951, 1955, 1979 by the President and Fellows of Harvard College.

"My Life had stood—a Loaded Gun—" by Emily Dickinson. Reprinted by permission of the publishers and the Trustees of Amherst College from *The Poems of Emily Dickinson,* Thomas H. Johnson, ed., Cambridge, Mass.: The Belknap Press of Harvard University Press, Copyright © 1951, 1955, 1979, 1983 by the President and Fellows of Harvard College.

"Letter to Thomas Wentworth Higginson, April 16, 1862" by Emily Dickinson. Reprinted by permission of the publishers from *Letters of Emily Dickinson,* Thomas H. Johnson, ed., Cambridge, Mass.: The Belknap Press of Harvard University Press, Copyright © 1958, 1986, The President and Fellows of Harvard College; 1914, 1924, 1932, 1942 by Martha Dickinson Bianchi; 1952 by Alfred Leete Hampson; 1960 by Mary L. Hampson.

Scribner: "Letter to His Son, January 1861," by Robert E. Lee, from *R.E. Lee: A Biography* by Douglas Southall Freeman. Copyright © 1934, 1935 by Charles Scribner's Sons; copyright renewed © 1962, 1963 by Inez Goddin Freeman. Reprinted with the permission of Scribner, an imprint of Simon & Schuster Adult Publishing Group.

Thunder's Mouth Press: From "Letter, July 14, 1861, by Sullivan Ballou, from the book *For Love & Liberty: The Untold Civil War Story of Major Sullivan Ballou & His Famous Love Letter* by Robin Young. Copyright © 2003. Appears by permission of the publisher, Thunder's Mouth Press, A Division of Avalon Publishing Group.

UNIT 4

HarperCollins Publishers: From *The Autobiography of Mark Twain,* edited by Charles Neider. Copyright © 1917, 1940, 1958, 1959 by the Mark Twain Company, renewed 1987. Copyright 1924, 1945, 1952 by Clara Clemens Samossoud. Copyright © 1959 by Charles Neider, renewed 1987. Reprinted by permission of HarperCollins Publishers.

Viking Penguin: "Sumus Quod Sumus," from *Lake Wobegone Days* by Garrison Keillor. Copyright © 1985 by Garrison Keillor. Used by permission of Viking Penguin, a division of Penguin Group (USA) Inc.

UNIT 5

Alfred A. Knopf and Harold Ober Associates: "Harlem," from *The Collected Poems of Langston Hughes* by Langston Hughes. Copyright © 1994 by the Estate of Langston Hughes. Used by permission of Alfred A. Knopf, a division of Random House, Inc., and Harold Ober Associates Incorporated.

"The Negro Speaks of Rivers," from *The Collected Poems of Langston Hughes* by Langston Hughes. Copyright © 1994 by the Estate of Langston Hughes. Used by permission of Alfred A. Knopf, a division of Random House, Inc., and Harold Ober Associates Incorporated.

"I, Too," from *The Collected Poems of Langston Hughes* by Langston Hughes. Copyright © 1994 by the Estate of Langston Hughes. Used by permission of Alfred A. Knopf, a division of Random House, Inc., and Harold Ober Associates Incorporated.

"The Weary Blues," from *The Collected Poems of Langston Hughes* by Langston Hughes. Copyright © 1994 by the Estate of Langston Hughes. Used by permission of Alfred A. Knopf, a division of Random House, Inc., and Harold Ober Associates Incorporated.

Viking Penguin: "My City," from *Saint Peter Relates an Incident* by James Weldon Johnson. Copyright 1935 by James Weldon Johnson, © renewed 1963 by Grace Nail Johnson. Used by permission of Viking Penguin, a division of Penguin Group (USA) Inc.

Schomburg Center for Research in Black Culture: "If We Must Die" by Claude McKay. Courtesy of the Literary Representative for the Works of Claude McKay, Schomburg Center for Research in Black Culture, the New York Public Library, Astor, Lenox and Tilden Foundations.

GRM Associates: "Any Human to Another," from *The Medea and Some Poems* by Countee Cullen. Copyright 1936 by Harper and Brothers, copyright © renewed 1963 by Ida M. Cullen. Reprinted by permission of GRM Associates, Inc.

Liveright Publishing Corporation: "Storm Ending," from *Cane* by Jean Toomer. Copyright 1923 by Boni & Liveright, renewed 1951 by Jean Toomer. Used by permission of Liveright Publishing Corporation.

Harold Ober Associates: "A Black Man Talks of Reaping," from *Personals* by Arna Bontemps. Copyright © 1963 by Arna Bontemps. Reprinted by permission of Harold Ober Associates Incorporated.

Victoria Sanders & Associates: "How It Feels to Be Colored Me" by Zora Neale Hurston. Used with the permission of the Zora Neale Hurston Trust.

Doubleday: "Thoughts on the African-American Novel" by Toni Morrison, from *Black Women Writers,* edited by Mari Evans. Copyright © 1983 by Mari Evans. Used by permission of Doubleday, a division of Random House, Inc.

Harcourt: "Chicago," and "Grass," from *Chicago Poems* by Carl Sandburg. Copyright 1916 by Holt, Rinehart and Winston and renewed 1944 by Carl Sandburg. Reprinted by permission of Harcourt, Inc. This material may not be reproduced in any form or by any means without the prior written permission of the publisher.

Henry Holt and Company: "Acquainted with the Night" by Robert Frost, from *The Poetry of Robert Frost,* edited by Edward Connery Lathem. Copyright 1928, 1930, © 1969 by Henry Holt and , copyright 1944, 1951, 1956, 1958 by Robert Frost, copyright © 1967 by Lesley Frost Ballantine. Reprinted by permission of Henry Holt and Company, LLC.

"Nothing Gold Can Stay" by Robert Frost, from *The Poetry of Robert Frost,* edited by Edward Connery Lathem. Copyright 1928, 1930, 1969 by Henry Holt and , copyright 1944, 1951, 1956, 1958 by Robert Frost, copyright © 1967 by Lesley Frost Ballantine. Reprinted by permission of Henry Holt and Company, LLC.

"Out, Out—" by Robert Frost, from *The Poetry of Robert Frost*, edited by Edward Connery Lathem. Copyright 1928, 1930, 1969 by Henry Holt and , copyright 1944, 1951, 1956, 1958 by Robert Frost, copyright © 1967 by Lesley Frost Ballantine. Reprinted by permission of Henry Holt and Company, LLC.

"The Death of the Hired Man" by Robert Frost, from *The Poetry of Robert Frost,* edited by Edward Connery Lathem. Copyright 1928, 1930, 1969 by Henry Holt and , copyright 1944, 1951, 1956, 1958 by Robert Frost, copyright © 1967 by Lesley Frost Ballantine. Reprinted by permission of Henry Holt and Company, LLC.

New Directions Publishing Corporation: "Helen," from *Collected Poems, 1912–1944* by HD (Hilda Doolittle). Copyright © 1982 by the Estate of Hilda Doolittle. Reprinted by permission of New Directions Publishing Corp.

"In a Station of the Metro," from *Personae* by Ezra Pound. Copyright © 1926 by Ezra Pound. Reprinted by permission of New Directions Publishing Corp.

"Spring and All, Section I," and "This is Just to Say," from *Collected Poems, 1909–1939, Volume I* by William Carlos Williams. Copyright © 1938 by New Directions Publishing Corp. Reprinted by permission of New Directions Publishing Corp.

Liveright Publishing Corporation: "anyone lived in a pretty how town," from *Complete Poems: 1904–1962* by E. E. Cummings, edited by George J. Firmage. Copyright 1940, © 1968, 1991 by the Trustees for the E. E. Cummings Trust. Used by permission of Liveright Publishing Corporation. This selection may not be reproduced, stored in a retrieval system, or transmitted in any form or by any means without the prior written permission of the publisher. For more information about W. W. Norton/Liveright titles, please visit www.wwnorton.com.

Scribner: "Poetry," from *The Collected Poems of Marianne Moore* by Marianne Moore. Copyright © 1935 by Marianne Moore, copyright renewed © 1963 by Marianne Moore and T. S. Eliot. Reprinted with the permission of Scribner, an imprint of Simon & Schuster Adult Publishing Group.

Elizabeth Barnett, Literary Executor: "Recuerdo" by Edna St. Vincent Millay. From *Collected Poems,* HarperCollins. Copyright © 1922, 1950 by Edna St. Vincent Millay. All rights reserved. Used by permission of Elizabeth Barnett, Literary Executor.

Faber and Faber: "The Love Song of J. Alfred Prufrock," from *Collected Poems, 1909–1962* by T. S. Eliot. Reprinted by Faber and Faber Limited.

Scribner: From *The Great Gatsby* by F. Scott Fitzgerald. Copyright 1925 by Charles Scribner's Sons. Copyright renewed 1953 by Frances Scott Fitzgerald Lanahan. Reprinted with permission of Scribner, an imprint of Simon & Schuster Adult Publishing Group.

"In Another Country," from *Men Without Women* by Ernest Hemingway. Copyright 1927 Charles Scribner's Sons. Copyright renewed 1955 by Ernest Hemingway. Reprinted with permission of Scribner, an imprint of Simon & Schuster Adult Publishing Group.

Viking Penguin: From *The Grapes of Wrath* by John Steinbeck. Copyright 1939, renewed © 1967 by John Steinbeck. Used by permission of Viking Penguin, a division of Penguin Group (USA) Inc.

Time Inc.: "The Grapes of Wrath: Photo Essay," *Life,* 5 June 1939. Copyright 1939 Time Inc. Reprinted with permission.

Harcourt: "The Jilting of Granny Weatherall," from *Flowering Judas and Other Stories* by Katherine Anne Porter. Copyright 1930 and renewed 1958 by Katherine Anne Porter. Reprinted by permission of Harcourt, Inc. This material may not be reproduced in any form or by any means without prior written permission of the publisher.

"A Worn Path," from *A Curtain of Green and Other Stories* by Eudora Welty. Copyright 1941 and renewed 1969 by Eudora Welty. Reprinted by permission of Harcourt, Inc. This material may not be reproduced in any form or by any means without prior written permission of the publisher.

Harvard University Press: Reprinted by permission of the publisher from *One Writer's Beginnings* by Eudora Welty, pp. 99–100, Cambridge, Mass: Harvard Universiry Press, Copyright © 1983, 1984 by Eudora Welty.

Random House: "A Rose for Emily," from *Collected Stories of William Faulkner* by William Faulkner. Copyright 1930 and renewed 1958 by William Faulkner. Used by permission of Random House, Inc.

Harcourt: "The Life You Save May Be Your Own," from *A Good Man Is Hard to Find and Other Stories* by Flannery O'Connor. Copyright 1953 by Flannery O'Connor and renewed 1981 by Regina O'Connor. Reprinted by permission of Harcourt, Inc. This material may not be reproduced in any form or by any means without prior written permission of the publisher.

Scribner: "A New Kind of War" by Ernest Hemingway, from *By-Line: Ernest Hemingway,* edited by William White. Copyright 1937 by New York Times and North American Newspaper Alliance, Inc. Copyright © renewed 1965 by Mary Hemingway, By-Line Ernest Hemingway, Inc., and the New York Times Company.

Viking Penguin: "A Book of Great Short Stories," from *The Portable Dorothy Parker* by Dorothy Parker, edited by Brendan Gill. Copyright 1927, renewed © 1955 by Dorothy Parker. Used by permission of Viking Penguin, a division of Penguin Group (USA) Inc.

Allene White: "The Duty of Writers," from *One Man's Meat* by E. B. White. Copyright 1939 by E. B. White. Reprinted by permission of Allene White.

UNIT 6

Barbara Hogenson Agency: From *Our Town* by Thornton Wilder. Copyright © 1938 The Thornton Wilder Family, LLC. Reprinted by permission of the Barbara Hogenson Agency.

Georges Borchardt: From *The Glass Menagerie* by Tennessee Williams. Copyright © 1945 by the University of the South and Edwin D. Williams. Reprinted by permission of Georges Borchardt, Inc.

Viking Penguin: From *Death of a Salesman* by Arthur Miller. Copyright 1949, renewed © 1977 by Arthur Miller. Used by permission of Viking Penguin, a division of Penguin Group (USA) Inc.

Random House: From *A Raisin in the Sun* by Lorraine Hansberry. Copyright © 1958 by Robert Nemiroff, as an unpublished work. Copyright © 1959, 1966, 1984 by Robert Nemiroff. Copyright renewed 1986, 1987 by Robert Nemiroff. Used by permission of Random House, Inc.

Viking Penguin: "Symptoms," from *Once There Was a War* by John Steinbeck. Copyright 1943, 1958 by John Steinbeck. Renewed © 1971 by Elaine Steinbeck, John Steinbeck IV, and Thomas Steinbeck. Used by permission of Viking Penguin, a division of Penguin Group (USA) Inc.

Farrar, Straus and Giroux: "The Death of the Ball Turret Gunner," from *The Complete Poems* by Randall Jarrell. Copyright © 1969, renewed 1997 by Mary von S. Jarrell. Reprinted by permission of Farrar, Straus and Giroux, LLC. Caution: Users are warned that this work is protected under copyright laws and downloading is strictly prohibited. The right to reproduce or transfer the work via any medium must be secured with Farrar, Straus and Giroux, LLC.

Dell Publishing: "Adam," from *Welcome to the Monkey House* by Kurt Vonnegut Jr. Copyright 1954 by Kurt Vonnegut Jr. Used by permission of Dell Publishing, a division of Random House, Inc.

Viking Penguin: From *If This Is a Man (Survival in Auschwitz)* by Primo Levi, translated by Stuart Woolf. Translation copyright © 1959 by Orion Press Inc., © 1958 by Guilio Einaudi editore SpA. Used by permission of Viking Penguin, a division of Penguin Group (USA) Inc.

Houghton Mifflin Company/Seymour Lawrence: "Ambush," from *The Things They Carried* by Tim O'Brien. Copyright © 1990 by Tim O'Brien. Reprinted by permission of Houghton Mifflin Company/Seymour Lawrence. All rights reserved.

Writers House: "Letter from Birmingham Jail" by Martin Luther King Jr. Copyright 1963 Martin Luther King Jr., copyright renewed 1991 Coretta Scott King. Reprinted by arrangement with the Estate of Martin Luther King Jr., c/o Writers House as agent for the proprietor New York, NY.

Broadside Press: "Ballad of Birmingham," from *Cities Burning* by Dudley Randall. By permission of Broadside Press.

Writers House: From *Stride Toward Freedom* by Martin Luther King Jr. Copyright 1958 Martin Luther King Jr., copyright renewed 1986 Coretta Scott King. Reprinted by arrangement with the Estate of Martin Luther King Jr., c/o Writers House as agent for the proprietor New York, NY.

Pathfinder Press: "Necessary to Protect Ourselves" by Malcolm X, from *Malcolm X: The Last Speeches,* edited by Bruce Perry. Copyright © 1989 Betty Shabazz, Bruce Perry, Pathfinder Press. All rights reserved. Reprinted by permission of Pathfinder Press.

Doubleday: Excerpt from *Coming of Age in Mississippi* by Anne Moody. Copyright © 1968 by Anne Moody. Used by permission of Doubleday, a division of Random House, Inc. For online information about other Random House, Inc., books and authors, see the Internet Web site at http://www.randomhouse.com.

HarperCollins Publishers: "Revolutionary Dreams," from *The Women and the Men* by Nikki Giovanni. Copyright © 1971, 1974, 1975 by Nikki Giovanni. Reprinted by permission of HarperCollins Publishers.

James Baldwin Estate: "My Dungeon Shook: Letter to My Nephew on the One Hundredth Anniversary of the Emancipation" by James Baldwin. Copyright © 1962 by James Baldwin. Copyright renewed. Originally published in *The Progressive.* Collected in *The Fire Next Time,* published by Vintage Books. Reprinted by arrangement with the James Baldwin Estate.

Sandra Dijkstra Literary Agency: "Mother Tongue" by Amy Tan. Copyright © 1990 by Amy Tan. First appeared in *The Threepenny Review.* Reprinted by permission of the author and the Sandra Dijkstra Literary Agency.

Harcourt: Excerpt from "In Search of Our Mothers' Gardens," in *In Search of Our Mothers' Gardens: Womanist Prose* by Alice Walker. Copyright © 1974 by Alice Walker. Reprinted by permission of Harcourt, Inc.

"Women," from *Revolutionary Petunias & Other Poems* by Alice Walker. Copyright © 1970 and renewed 1998 by Alice Walker. Reprinted by permission of Harcourt, Inc. This material may not be reproduced in any form or by any means without prior written permission of the publisher.

Susan Bergholz Literary Services: "Straw Into Gold" by Sandra Cisneros. Copyright © 1987 by Sandra Cisneros. First published in the *Texas Observer,* September 1987. Reprinted by permission of Susan Bergholz Literary Services, New York. All rights reserved.

Brooks Permissions: "Life for My Child Is Simple," and "Primer for Blacks" by Gwendolyn Brooks. Reprinted by consent of Brooks Permissions.

Rita Dove: "Adolescence–III," from *The Yellow House on the Corner* by Rita Dove. Carnegie Mellon University Press. Copyright © 1980 by Rita Dove. Reprinted by permission of the author.

"Testimonial," from *On the Bus with Rosa Parks* by Rita Dove. W. W. Norton and Company. First published in *Poetry* magazine, January 1998. Copyright © 1999 by Rita Dove. Reprinted by permission of the author.

University of Pittsburgh Press: "Forgetfulness," and "The Man in the Moon," from *Questions About Angels* by Billy Collins. Copyright © 1991, Billy Collins. Reprinted by permission of the University of Pittsburgh Press.

UNIT 7

Los Angeles Times: From " 'Grapes of Wrath' Author Guards Self From Threats at Moody Gulch" by Tom Cameron, *Los Angeles Times,* July 9, 1939. Copyright ©, 1939, *Los Angeles Times.* Reprinted with permission.

STUDENT RESOURCE BANK

R5: Excerpt from "History of the National Weather Service," from the Random House Web site (http://www.randomhouse.com/features/isaacsstorm/science/history.html). Copyright © 1999 by Random House, Inc. Used by permission of Random House, Inc.

R13: Adapted from "Katrina's South American Sister," from *Best Friends Magazine,* November/December 2005. Copyright © 2005 by Best Friends Animal Society. Adapted with permission.

R74: word definition: ambasador. Copyright © 2006 by Houghton Mifflin Company. Reproduced by permission from *The American Heritage Dictionary of the English Language, Fourth Edition.*

R74: word definition: community. Copyright © 2006 by Houghton Mifflin Company. Reproduced by permission from *The American Heritage Dictionary of the English Language, Fourth Edition.*

UNIT 2

© Brooklyn Museum of Art/Bridgeman Art Library; **334** *top* © Stock Montage; *bottom* AP/Wide World Photos; **335** © Tommy Flynn/Getty Images; **340** *top* The Granger Collection, New York; *bottom* © Corbis; **341** © C Squared Studios/Getty Images; **343** © iconsight/Alamy Images; **344** © David Zimmerman/Corbis; **346** *top* The Granger Collection, New York; *center* Library of Congress; *bottom* © Joseph Sohm/Stock Connection; **349** © Reynolds Stock Photo; **355** © Swerve/Alamy Images; **357** © North Wind/North Wind Picture Archives; **358** © Judith Jango-Cohen; **360** *top* © Bettmann/Corbis; *bottom* © Michele Burgess/SuperStock; **361** Photograph by Jay Fechtman; **363** *Wanderer Above a Sea of Fog* (1817), Casper David Friedrich. Oil on canvas, 94.8 cm × 74.8 cm. Inv.: 5161 On permanent loan from the Foundation for the Promotion of the Hamburg Art Collections. Hamburger Kunsthalle, Hamburg, Germany. Photo by Elke Walford. © Bildarchiv Preussischer Kulturbesitz/Art Resource, New York; **370** *top* Detail of *Henry David Thoreau* (1856), Benjamin D. Maxham. Daguerreotype, 6.3 cm x 4.7 cm. National Portrait Gallery, Smithsonian Institution, Washington, DC. © National Portrait Gallery, Smithsonian Institution/Art Resource, New York; *bottom* © age fotostock/SuperStock; **371** © Duane Lofton/Painet Inc.; **373** © Gail Mooney/Masterfile; **376** *top* © Corbis; *bottom* © David Muench/Corbis; **377** *top* © RubberBall Productions/Getty Images; *bottom* © Arthur Morris/Corbis; **383** © Lynsey Addario/Corbis; **386** *left* © Underwood & Underwood/Corbis; *right* © Bettmann/Corbis; **386–387** *top on 2 pages* © Bettmann/Corbis; **387** *left* © Wally McNamee/Corbis; *right* © Reuters/Corbis; **393** Max Desfor/AP/Wide World Photos; **394** *top* © Brown Brothers, Sterling, PA; *bottom* © Corbis; **401** © Howard Kingsnorth/Getty Images; **402** *top* © Bettmann/Corbis; *bottom* © Lake County Museum/Corbis; **403** © Bertrand Demée/Getty Images; **429** Cloister (1370–1410), Gloucester Cathedral, Gloucestershire, United Kingdom © Bridgeman Art Library; **429** *top left* © Bill Ross/Corbis; **430** *background* © Roger Wright/Getty Images; *left* © PNC/Getty Images; **437** © Michael Llewellyn/Getty Images; **439** *Raven* (1996) © Keith Carter Photographs; **445** © Illustration Works; **446** Gargoyles. Notre Dame, Paris. Photo © Vanni/Art Resource, New York; **447** © Arthur Rackham/Mary Evans Picture Library; **448** *left* © Arthur Rackham/Mary Evans Picture Library; *bottom* © Tim Flach/Getty Images; **451** © David Elliott/Getty Images; **452–453** © PictureQuest; **452** *top* © Les Cunliffe/Age Fotostock America, Inc.; *bottom* The Granger Collection, New York; **453** © Mary Evans Picture Library/The Image Works, Inc.; **454** *top* © Les Cunliffe/Age Fotostock America, Inc.; *center* *Portrait of Nathaniel Hawthorne* (about 1862), Emanuel Gottlieb Leutze. National Portrait Gallery, Smithsonian Institution, Washington D.C. Photo © National Portrait Gallery, Smithsonian Institution/Art Resource, New York; *bottom* PBS/Courtesy of Photofest; **454–455** © PhotoDisc; **455** Cover illustration by Troy Thomas © McDougal Littell; **456** *top* National Archives; *bottom* © S. Solum/Photolink/Getty Images; **457** © Carlos Dominguez/Corbis; **462** *The Last Halt: Stop of Hooker's Band in East Hartford before Crossing River* (1939), Alton S. Tobey. Study for East Hartford, Connecticut Postal Office. Oil on fiberboard, 26″ × 44 1/8″ . Transfer from General Services Administration. © Smithsonian American Art Museum, Washington, D.C./Art Resource, New York www.altontobey.org; **473** © Gary Kelley, 1996; **474, 480** © Joseph Sohm; ChromoSohm Inc./Corbis; **481** *left* © David Young-Wolff/PhotoEdit; *right* © Getty Images; **488–489** © PunchStock.

UNIT 3

491 *top* © Getty Images; *bottom, Union Soldiers Fighting in the Field,* Albert Bierstadt. Photo © Geoffrey Clements/Corbis; **492** *left* © Corbis; *right* The Granger Collection, New York; **493** *left* The Granger Collection, New York; *right* © Mort Künstler, Inc.; **496** The Granger Collection, New York; **498** *top* © Mary Evans Picture Library/The Image Works, Inc.; *frame* © Image Farm, Inc.; *bottom, The Laughing Philosopher* (1887), George C. Cox. Photograph. © Museum of the City of New York/Bridgeman Art Library; *frame* © Image Farm, Inc.; **499** © Tom Gauld/Heart USA Inc.; **500** The Granger Collection, New York; **501** *Prisoners from the Front* (1866), Winslow Homer. Oil on canvas, 24″ × 38″. The Metropolitan Museum of Art, Gift of Mrs. Frank B. Porter, 1922 (22.207). Photo © 1995 The Metropolitan Museum of Art, New York/Art Resource, New York; **502** *top* Public Domain; *left* The Granger Collection, New York; *right* © Corbis; *bottom* The Granger Collection, New York; **503** *top left, The Gettysburg Address, 1863,* Jean Leon Jerome Ferris. Private collection. Photo © Bridgeman Art Library; *top right* © Bettmann/Corbis; *center left, center right* The Granger Collection, New York; *bottom* © Araldo de Luca/Corbis; **504** © Corbis Sygma; **505** *top left* © Blue Man Productions, Inc.; *top right* The Granger Collection, New York; *center left* © Reuters/Corbis; *center right* AP/Wide World Photos; *bottom left* © Mitchell Gerber/Corbis *bottom center* © Flip Schulke/Corbis; *bottom right* AP/Wide World Photos; **506** *Walt Whitman inciting the bird of freedom to soar* (1904), Max Beerbohm. Engraving. From *The Poets Corner* published by William Heinemann. © Central Saint Martins College of Art and Design, London/Bridgeman Art Library; **508** *top* National Archives; *bottom* © Fabio Cardoso/zefa/Corbis; **509** © Ken Fisher/Getty Images; **518** © PhotoDisc; **520** © Michael Powers/Veer; **521** © Alistair Forrester Shankie/istockphoto.com; **522** © Thomas Hoepker/Magnum Photos; **523** © Photodisc; **524** *top* The Granger Collection, New York; *bottom* © Gail Mooney/Masterfile; **525** © Photodisc/Veer; **527** © Carl Rosenstein/Getty Images; **528** © Martin Rogers/Getty Images; **529** © Nick Koudis/Getty Images; **530** © Todd Gipstein/Corbis; **531** © Dr. Dennis Kunkel/Getty Images; **532** © Jeremy Woodhouse/Getty Images; **533** *top* © ShutterStock; *center, bottom* © Artbeats; **535** © Mike Caplanis/Luminarygraphics.com; **536** *top* © Chester County Historical Society, West Chester, Pennsylvania; *bottom* © William Manning/Corbis; **540** *The Life of Harriet Tubman, #9* (1940), Jacob Lawrence. Casein tempera on hardboard, 12″ × 17 7/8″. Hampton University Museum. Photo courtesy of Gwendolyn Knight Lawrence/Art Resource, New York. © 2007 The Jacob and Gwendolyn Lawrence Foundation, Seattle/Artists Rights Society (ARS), New York; **550** *top, Harriet Jacobs,* 1894, Cabinet photograph by Gilbert Studios, Washington, D.C. Gold toned albumin print; *bottom* © Bettmann/Corbis; **553** © New York Public Library, Schomburg Center; **555** Photographic History Collection, National Museum of American History, Smithsonian Institution, Washington, D.C.; **560–561** © Map Division, New York Public Library, Astor, Lenox and Tilden Foundations; **562** *top* Library of Congress; *bottom* © Joseph Sohm; ChromoSohm Inc./Corbis; **566** National Archives; **570** © Reza Estakhrian/Getty Images; **571–580** *bottom* © Photodisc; **571** *center* © Artbeats; *bottom right* The Granger Collection, New York; *frame* © Image Farm, Inc.; **572** *top left* United States Army Military History Institute; *frame* © Image Farm, Inc.; *top right* © Getty Images; *center* © Artbeats; **573** *center* © Artbeats; *bottom left* © David Toase/Getty Images; *bottom right, Mary Boykin Chesnut* (1856), Samuel S. Osgood. Oil on canvas adhered to masonite, 48″ × 30″ with frame. © Private Collection/Art Resource, New York; **574** *top left* The Granger Collection, New York,

H. Alston. Oil on canvas, 481/4″ × 353/4″. Purchase with funds from the Artists and Students Assistance Fund. © 1997 Whitney Museum of American Art, New York © Estate of Charles Alston Courtesy of Michael Rosenfeld, LLC, New York; *right* © Bettmann/Corbis; **826** © Dorothea Lange/Corbis; **827** *left, right* The Granger Collection, New York; *bottom* © Bettmann/Corbis; **828** *top* Public Domain; *center* The Granger Collection, New York; *bottom* © Alfred Eisenstaedt/Pix Inc./Time & Life Pictures/Getty Images; **829** © Frank Jensen; **830** The Granger Collection, New York; **832** © Bettmann/Corbis; **833** The Granger Collection, New York; **834** *top* © The Poetry Foundation; *center left* © Hulton-Deutsch Collection/Corbis; *center right* © 2006, Mike Caplanis/www.luminarygraphics.com; *bottom left* The Granger Collection, New York; *bottom right* © Bettmann/Corbis; **835** *top* © Hulton Archive/Getty Images; *center left* © Bettmann/Corbis; *center* © Angelo Hornak/Corbis; *center right, The Wizard of Oz* (1939) MGM/Courtesy of Photofest; **836** © Alex McLean/Getty Images; **837** *top* © Najlah Feanny/Corbis; *bottom* Courtesy of the Federal Deposit Insurance Company; **838** *top* © Corbis; *bottom, The Cotton Club in Harlem, New York* (1930). Black and white photograph. Private collection. © Bridgeman Art Library; **839** © Frank Leather; Eye Ubiquitous/Corbis; **846** *top* © Time Life Pictures/Getty Images; *center* Courtesy of Yale Collection of American Literature, Beinecke Rare Book and Manuscript Library; *bottom* © K. Hackenberg/zefa/Corbis; **847** © Corbis/Jupiter Images; **849** © Bettmann/Corbis; **850** © Getty Images; **852** *top left* Courtesy of Yale Collection of American Literature, Beinecke Rare Book and Manuscript Library; *bottom left* AP/Wide World Photos; *bottom* © Charles E. Rotkin/Corbis; **853** © Ted Dayton/Index Stock Imagery, Inc.; **858** *top* © Bettmann/Corbis; *bottom* © Corbis; **868** *top* © Getty Images; *bottom* AP/Wide World Photos; **869** © Karl Grupe/Getty Images; **871** *Family* (1955), Charles H. Alston. Oil on canvas, 48 1/4″ × 35 3/4″. Whitney Museum of American Art, New York. Purchase, with funds from the Artists and Students Assistance Fund 55.47. © Estate of Charles H. Alston/Courtesy of Michael Rosenfeld Gallery, LLC, New York; **875** The Granger Collection, New York; **876** *front* Library of Congress, Prints and Photographs Division; *background* © Ian Cartwright/Getty Images; **877** *top, New York Times*, July 3, 1917 Public domain; *bottom, The Cotton Club in Harlem, New York* (1930). Black and white photograph. Private collection. © Bridgeman Art Library; **878** *top* Detail of *Church-goers, Eatonville* (1940), Jules André Smith. Oil on masonite. Courtesy The Maitland Art Center; *center* Courtesy Lucy Anne Hurston; *bottom* © John Springer Collection/Corbis; **880** *top* © Bettmann/Corbis; *center* © Brown Brothers, Sterling, PA; *bottom* © MedioImages/Getty Images; **881** © Russell Illig/Getty Images; **888** © Bettmann/Corbis; **889** *left* © A. Schein/zefa/Corbis; *right* © Craig Tuttle/Corbis; **891** *South of the Loop* (1936), Charles Turzak. Color woodcut, Image 10 2/3″ × 11 3/4″, Sheet 11 1/4″ × 15″. Mary and Leigh Block Museum of Art, Northwestern University, 1992.73. © Joan Turzak van Hess; **894** The Granger Collection, New York; **895** *The Red Room* (1908), Henri Matisse. Oil on canvas. State Hermitage Museum, St. Petersburg, Russia. © SuperStock, Inc./SuperStock. © 2007 Succession H. Matisse, Paris Artists Rights Society (ARS). New York; **896** *top* National Archives; *bottom* © Peter Miller/Getty Images; **897** © Brad Wilson/Getty Images; **903** © Bill Varie/Corbis; **904** Detail of *Island Hay* (1945), Thomas Hart Benton. Gift of John Nichols Estabrook and Dorothy Coogan Estabrook. 1987.41.5. © 2005 National Gallery of Art, Washington, D.C. © T. H. Benton and R. P. Benton Testamentary Trusts/UMB Bank Trustee/Licensed by VAGA, New York, N.Y.; **912** *top* © Time Life Pictures/Getty Images; *center* Courtesy of The Schnaffner Family Foundation and New Directions Publishing Corporation; *bottom* National Archives; *background* © P. Steeger/zefa/Corbis; **913** © Georgette Douwma/Getty Images; **915** © Hans Wolf/Getty Images; **916** © Corbis; **917** © Elizabeth Watt Photography/StockFoodAmerica; **920** *top, center, bottom* © Bettmann/Corbis; *background* © Elly Godfroy/Alamy Images; **928** *top* © Bettmann/Corbis; *bottom* © Corbis; **929** © Stephen Webster/Getty Images; **933** © Vernon Leach/Alamy Images; **936** *top* © Getty Images; *bottom* © Underwood & Underwood/Corbis; **949** *Young Woman in Green* (1927), Tamara de Lempicka. © 2007 Artists Rights Society (ARS), New York/ADAGP, Paris; **962** *top* © Les Cunliffe/Age Fotostock America, Inc.; *bottom* © Culver Pictures/The Art Archive; *bottom* © Bettmann/Corbis; **963** Cover of *The Great Gatsby* by F. Scott Fitzgerald. © 1980 by Charles Scribner's Sons. Reprinted by permission of Simon & Schuster, New York, Photo: The Granger Collection, New York; **964** The Granger Collection, New York; **965** © Bettmann/Corbis; **966** *top* Courtesy the Gaslight Collection; *bottom* © Bettmann/Corbis; **968** *top* © Getty Images; *bottom* © Suhaib Salem/Reuters/Corbis; **969** © Zigy Kaluzny/Getty Images; **971** © Corbis; **978** *top* © Les Cunliffe/Age Fotostock America, Inc.; *bottom* © Time Life Pictures/Getty Images; **978–979** © Bettmann/Corbis; **979** Cover of *The Grapes of Wrath* by John Steinbeck. © 1939 by John Steinbeck. Reprinted by permission of Penguin Books, a division of the Penguin Group (USA), Inc., 375 Hudson Street, New York, New York 10014. All rights reserved. Photo: The Granger Collection, New York; **980** *top left* © Les Cunliffe/Age Fotostock America, Inc.; *top right* Cover of *The Grapes of Wrath* by John Steinbeck. © 1939 by John Steinbeck. Reprinted by permission of Penguin Books, a division of the Penguin Group (USA), Inc., 375 Hudson Street, New York, New York 10014. All rights reserved. Photo:The Granger Collection, New York; *center left* © Time Life Pictures/Getty Images; *bottom* © Bettmann/Corbis; **981, 982, 983, 984, 985,986** © Horace Bristol/Corbis; **988** *top* The Granger Collection, New York; *bottom* © Corbis; **989** © photocuisine/Corbis; **991** © Images.com/Corbis; **1002** *top* © Getty Images; *bottom* © Eudora Welty/Corbis; **1003** © DiMaggio/Kalish/Corbis; **1014** © Mississippi Department of Archives Photo; **1018** *top* © Hulton Archive/Getty Images; *bottom* The Granger Collection, New York; **1019** © Saed Hindash/Star Ledger/Corbis; **1021** © Johner/Getty Images; **1025** © David Wasserman/Veer; **1032** *top* AP/Wide World Photos; *bottom* © Yuri Dojc/Getty Images; **1033** © Andy Sacks/Getty Images; **1045** © Hulton-Deutsch Collection/Corbis; **1046** © Archive Photos/Getty Images; **1048** *top* © Getty Images; *bottom* © Hulton-Deutsch Collection/Corbis; **1049** © Chris Hondros/Getty Images; **1051** © Hulton-Deutsch Collection/Corbis; **1053** © Robert Capa © 2001 by Cornell Capa/Magnum Photos; **1058** *top* The Granger Collection, New York; *bottom* © Getty Images; **1059** Photograph by Sharon Hoogstraten; **1061** *left* Image courtesy The Newberry Library; *right* The Granger Collection, New York; *bottom* © Herbert Orth/Time Life Pictures/Getty Images; **1062** *left* © Culver Pictures/The Art Archive; *right* © Getty Images; **1066** *top* © Bettmann/Corbis; *bottom* © PicturePress/Getty Images; **1067** *Write about dogs!*, George Booth. © The New Yorker Collection 1976 George Booth from cartoonbank.com. All Rights Reserved; **1068** © Corbis; **1071** © Ron Watts/Corbis; **1072, 1078** © Daryl Benson/Masterfile; **1079** © Junichi Kusaka/Getty Images; **1081** © Swim Ink 2, LLC/Corbis; **1086–1087** © PunchStock.

New York; *frame* © Image Farm, Inc.; *center* © Artbeats; **576** The Granger Collection, New York; **578–579** *Battle of Nashville,* Howard Pyle © Minnesota Historical Society/Corbis; **578** *top* © Les Cunliffe/ Age Fotostock America, Inc.; *bottom* © Alderman Library/University of Virginia; **579** Public Domain; **580** *top* © Bettmann/Corbis; *bottom* © Corbis; **581** © Nonstock/Jupiter Images; **583** © Stephen Graham/ Owl Creek Productions; **584** © Peter L. Chapman/Index Stock Imagery, Inc.; **587** © Ionpost/Owl Creek Productions; **589** © Stephen Frink/ Getty Images; **591** © Mike Zens/Corbis; **595** *Lincoln at Gettysburg II* (1939–1942), William H. Johnson. Gouache and pen and ink on paper, 19¾″ × 17¹⁄₁₆″. Gift of the Harmon Foundation. Smithsonian American Art Museum, Washington, D.C. © Smithsonian American Art Museum, Washington, D.C./Art Resource, New York; **596** *top* © Stephen Graham/ Owl Creek Productions; *bottom* Clip courtesy of Owl Creek Production, L.L.C. www.owlcreekproductions.com; **598, 604** © Daryl Benson/ Masterfile; **605** © Paul Edmondson/Corbis; **612–613** © PunchStock.

UNIT 4

615 *top, Willa Cather* (1923–1924), Nicholai Fechin. Oil on canvas. University of Nebraska Library. Gift of Dr. Philip L. and Helen Cather Southwick through University of Nebraska Foundation. Lincoln, Nebraska; *bottom, The Jolly Flatboatmen* (1877–1878), George Caleb Bingham. Oil on canvas, 26¹⁄₁₆″ × 36⅜″. Daniel J. Terra Acquisition Endowment Fund, 1992.15. Terra Foundation for American Art, Chicago. © Terra Foundation for American Art, Chicago/Art Resource, New York; **616** *left, Family and their Dugout* (1870s), Anonymous. Photo 11″ × 14″. Near McCook Nebraska. © Nebraska State Historical Society, Lincoln, Nebraska; *right* © Joel Sartore/National Geographic Image Collection; **617** *left, A Sketch of a Faraway Look,* Herman Jean Joseph Richir. Bonhams, London. © Bridgeman Art Library/SuperStock © 2007 Artists Rights Society (ARS), New York/ADAGP, Paris; *right* © Corbis; **620** *The Hatch Family* (1871), Eastman Johnson. Oil on canvas, 48″ × 73 3/8″. The Metropolitan Museum of Art, Gift of Frederic H. Hatch, 1926 (26.97). Photo © 1999 The Metropolitan Museum of Art/Art Resource, New York; **622** The Newberry Library, Chicago; **623** Photo Courtesy of the South Dakota State Historical Society, State Archives; **624–625** © 2006 John Hyde/AlaskaStock.com; **626** © Bettman/Corbis; **627** *In the Garden* (1904), Mary Stevenson Cassatt. Pastel on paper, 66 cm. × 81.3 cm. © The Detroit Institute of Arts/Bridgeman Art Library; **628** *top left* © Comstock/Superstock; *top center* © Harry Taylor/Dorling Kindersley; *top right* © Bettmann/Corbis; *center left* © Time & Life Pictures/Getty Images; *center right* © Corbis; *bottom* © Images.com/Corbis; **629** *top* © Bettmann/Corbis *center;* © Corbis; *bottom* Royal biscuit. Biscuit label by Carr & Co. (CT13673A). Victoria and Albert Museum, London. © Victoria and Albert Museum, London/Art Resource, New York; **630** © The Kobal Collection; **631** *top* © 2004 Getty Images; *bottom* © Layne Kennedy/Corbis; **632** © Bettmann/Corbis; **633** The Granger Collection, New York; **634** *top* Library of Congress; *bottom* © Stephen Alvarez/National Geographic Image Collection; **635** © Design Pics Inc./ Alamy; **637** Library of Congress; **639** *Levitation* © Scala/Art Resource, New York; **641** Library of Congress; **646** © Mike Caplains/www. luminarygraphics.com; **649** © Steve Bloom/Getty Images; **651** *background* Library of Congress; *inset* The Granger Collection, New York; *frame* © 1996 Image Farm, Inc. All rights reserved; **653** *left* © Mary Evans Picture Library/The Image Works, Inc.; *right* © The Mariners' Museum, Newport, Virginia; **659** © Rubberball/Age Fotostock America, Inc.; **661, 665, 666** The Granger Collection, New York; **670** *top* © Les Cunliffe/Age Fotostock America, Inc.; *bottom* © Corbis; **670–671** ©

Kevin Horan/Getty Images; **671** Cover of the original *The Adventures of Huckleberry Finn* by Mark Twain © 1885. Illustrated by E.W. Kemble/ The Granger Collection, New York; **672** *top* © Brown Brothers, Sterling, Pennsylvania; *bottom* © Thomas Morse/ PlaceStockPhoto.com; **673** © G. Brad Lewis/Getty Images; **678** © Bill Manns/The Art Archive; **682–683** Library of Congress; **684** Public Domain; **689** © Corbis; **692** *top* © Willa Cather Pioneer Memorial Collection/Nebraska State Historical Society; *bottom* © Age Fotostock/SuperStock; **693** © Terry Evans Photography; **695** *Old Souvenirs* (about 1881-1901), John F. Peto. Oil on canvas, 26 ¾″ × 22″. The Metropolitan Museum of Art, Bequest of Oliver Burr Jennings, 1968 (68.205.3) Photo © 1983 The Metropolitan Museum of Art, New York/Art Resource, New York; **705** Library of Congress; **706** © Hulton-Deutsch/Corbis; **707** *left* © Geoffrey Clements/Corbis; *right* © Corbis; **708** *top left, Castle Geyser and Firehole Basin (1871),* William Henry Jackson. Courtesy National Park Service, Yellowstone National Park, *YELL 36193;* (1871), William Henry Jackson. Courtesy Department of the Interior, Yellowstone National Park/ National Park Service; *bottom left, The Castle Geyser, Firehole Basin* (1872), Thomas Moran. 7¹⁄₂″ × 11″ The Gilcrease Musem, Tulsa, Oklahoma. 0226.1363. © The Gilcrease Museum; *background* © Bill Ross/Corbis; **710** *top* The Granger Collection, New York; *bottom* © Nicole Duplaix/ National Geographic Image Collection; **711** © Eric Nguyen/Jim Reed Photography/Corbis; **718-719** *The Much Resounding Sea* (1884), Thomas Moran. Oil on canvas, 25″ × 62″ unframed. Gift of the Avalon Foundation. 1967.9.1 © National Gallery of Art, Washington D.C; **738** Image manipulated German shipwreck survivors, Achille Beltrame. Engraving in Italian newspaper *La Domenica del Corriere,* February, 1941 Photo © Dagli Orti/The Art Archive; **739** Public Domain; **740** Library of Congress, Rare Book and Special Collections Division; **741** *top* Library of Congress, Rare Book and Special Collections Division; *bottom* © Bettmann/Corbis; **742** Library of Congress, Rare Book and Special Collections Division; **744** *top* © Underwood & Underwood/ Corbis; *bottom* © Allen Prier/Panoramic Images/NGSImages.com; **745** © David McLain/Aurora Photos; **747** © Werner Forman/akg-images; **751** © Alamy Images; **755** © Joel Sartore/National Geographic Image Collection; **756** © Hulton-Deutsch Collection/Corbis; **758** *top* The Granger Collection, New York; *bottom* © Lee Foster/Lonely Planet Images; **761** *A Sketch of a Faraway Look,* Herman Jean Joseph Richir. Bonhams, London. © 2007 Artists Rights Society (ARS), New York/ ADAGP, Paris ; **766** *top* © Brown Brothers, Sterling, PA; *bottom* © Getty Images; **767** © T. Kruesselmann/T.Hemmings/Espressokiss/zefa/Corbis; **784** Public Domain; **788** *top* © Les Cunliffe/Age Fotostock America, Inc.; *bottom* The Granger Collection, New York; **788–789** © John Churchman/Veer; **789** © McDougal Littell; **790** © Bettmann/Corbis; **791** © Gallery Stock Limited; **803** © 2005 Getty Images; **804, 810** © Richard Sisk/Jupiter Images; **811** *left* © Michael Newman/PhotoEdit; *right* © Lionel Isy-Schwart/Getty Images; **816–817** © PunchStock.

UNIT 5

821 *top* Photo by Robert W. Kelley. © Time & Life Pictures/Getty Images; *bottom, The Bicycle Race* (1912), Lyonel Feininger. Collection of Mr. and Mrs. Paul Mellon. © 2006 National Gallery of Art, Washington, D.C. © 2007 Artists Rights Society (ARS), New York/VG Bild-Kunst, Bonn; **822** *left, The Shelton with Sunspots* (1926), Georgia O'Keeffe. Oil on canvas, 123.1 cm × 76.8 cm. The Art Institute of Chicago, gift of Leigh B. Block (1985.206). © 1994 The Art Institute of Chicago, all rights reserved. © 2007 The Georgia O'Keeffe Museum/Artists Rights Society (ARS), New York; *right* © Corbis; **823** *left, Family* (1955), Charles

"The Soul selects her own Society" by Emily Dickinson. Reprinted by permission of the publishers and the Trustees of Amherst College from *The Poems of Emily Dickinson*, Thomas H. Johnson, ed., Cambridge, Mass.: The Belknap Press of Harvard University Press, Copyright 1951, 1955, 1979, 1983 by the President and Fellows of Harvard College.

"I heard a Fly buzz—when I died—" by Emily Dickinson. Reprinted by permission of the publishers and the Trustees of Amherst College from *The Poems of Emily Dickinson*, Thomas H. Johnson, ed., Cambridge, Mass.: The Belknap Press of Harvard University Press, Copyright © 1951, 1955, 1979 by the President and Fellows of Harvard College.

"My Life had stood—a Loaded Gun—" by Emily Dickinson. Reprinted by permission of the publishers and the Trustees of Amherst College from *The Poems of Emily Dickinson*, Thomas H. Johnson, ed., Cambridge, Mass.: The Belknap Press of Harvard University Press, Copyright © 1951, 1955, 1979, 1983 by the President and Fellows of Harvard College.

"Letter to Thomas Wentworth Higginson, April 16, 1862" by Emily Dickinson. Reprinted by permission of the publishers from *Letters of Emily Dickinson*, Thomas H. Johnson, ed., Cambridge, Mass.: The Belknap Press of Harvard University Press, Copyright © 1958, 1986, The President and Fellows of Harvard College; 1914, 1924, 1932, 1942 by Martha Dickinson Bianchi; 1952 by Alfred Leete Hampson; 1960 by Mary L. Hampson.

Scribner: "Letter to His Son, January 1861," by Robert E. Lee, from *R.E. Lee: A Biography* by Douglas Southall Freeman. Copyright © 1934, 1935 by Charles Scribner's Sons; copyright renewed © 1962, 1963 by Inez Goddin Freeman. Reprinted with the permission of Scribner, an imprint of Simon & Schuster Adult Publishing Group.

Thunder's Mouth Press: From "Letter, July 14, 1861, by Sullivan Ballou, from the book *For Love & Liberty: The Untold Civil War Story of Major Sullivan Ballou & His Famous Love Letter* by Robin Young. Copyright © 2003. Appears by permission of the publisher, Thunder's Mouth Press, A Division of Avalon Publishing Group.

UNIT 4

HarperCollins Publishers: From *The Autobiography of Mark Twain*, edited by Charles Neider. Copyright © 1917, 1940, 1958, 1959 by the Mark Twain Company, renewed 1987. Copyright 1924, 1945, 1952 by Clara Clemens Samossoud. Copyright © 1959 by Charles Neider, renewed 1987. Reprinted by permission of HarperCollins Publishers.

Viking Penguin: "Sumus Quod Sumus," from *Lake Wobegone Days* by Garrison Keillor. Copyright © 1985 by Garrison Keillor. Used by permission of Viking Penguin, a division of Penguin Group (USA) Inc.

UNIT 5

Alfred A. Knopf and Harold Ober Associates: "Harlem," from *The Collected Poems of Langston Hughes* by Langston Hughes. Copyright © 1994 by the Estate of Langston Hughes. Used by permission of Alfred A. Knopf, a division of Random House, Inc., and Harold Ober Associates Incorporated.

"The Negro Speaks of Rivers," from *The Collected Poems of Langston Hughes* by Langston Hughes. Copyright © 1994 by the Estate of Langston Hughes. Used by permission of Alfred A. Knopf, a division of Random House, Inc., and Harold Ober Associates Incorporated.

"I, Too," from *The Collected Poems of Langston Hughes* by Langston Hughes. Copyright © 1994 by the Estate of Langston Hughes. Used by permission of Alfred A. Knopf, a division of Random House, Inc., and Harold Ober Associates Incorporated.

"The Weary Blues," from *The Collected Poems of Langston Hughes* by Langston Hughes. Copyright © 1994 by the Estate of Langston Hughes. Used by permission of Alfred A. Knopf, a division of Random House, Inc., and Harold Ober Associates Incorporated.

Viking Penguin: "My City," from *Saint Peter Relates an Incident* by James Weldon Johnson. Copyright 1935 by James Weldon Johnson, © renewed 1963 by Grace Nail Johnson. Used by permission of Viking Penguin, a division of Penguin Group (USA) Inc.

Schomburg Center for Research in Black Culture: "If We Must Die" by Claude McKay. Courtesy of the Literary Representative for the Works of Claude McKay, Schomburg Center for Research in Black Culture, the New York Public Library, Astor, Lenox and Tilden Foundations.

GRM Associates: "Any Human to Another," from *The Medea and Some Poems* by Countee Cullen. Copyright 1936 by Harper and Brothers, copyright © renewed 1963 by Ida M. Cullen. Reprinted by permission of GRM Associates, Inc.

Liveright Publishing Corporation: "Storm Ending," from *Cane* by Jean Toomer. Copyright 1923 by Boni & Liveright, renewed 1951 by Jean Toomer. Used by permission of Liveright Publishing Corporation.

Harold Ober Associates: "A Black Man Talks of Reaping," from *Personals* by Arna Bontemps. Copyright © 1963 by Arna Bontemps. Reprinted by permission of Harold Ober Associates Incorporated.

Victoria Sanders & Associates: "How It Feels to Be Colored Me" by Zora Neale Hurston. Used with the permission of the Zora Neale Hurston Trust.

Doubleday: "Thoughts on the African-American Novel" by Toni Morrison, from *Black Women Writers*, edited by Mari Evans. Copyright © 1983 by Mari Evans. Used by permission of Doubleday, a division of Random House, Inc.

Harcourt: "Chicago," and "Grass," from *Chicago Poems* by Carl Sandburg. Copyright 1916 by Holt, Rinehart and Winston and renewed 1944 by Carl Sandburg. Reprinted by permission of Harcourt, Inc. This material may not be reproduced in any form or by any means without the prior written permission of the publisher.

Henry Holt and Company: "Acquainted with the Night" by Robert Frost, from *The Poetry of Robert Frost*, edited by Edward Connery Lathem. Copyright 1928, 1930, © 1969 by Henry Holt and , copyright 1944, 1951, 1956, 1958 by Robert Frost, copyright © 1967 by Lesley Frost Ballantine. Reprinted by permission of Henry Holt and Company, LLC.

"Nothing Gold Can Stay" by Robert Frost, from *The Poetry of Robert Frost*, edited by Edward Connery Lathem. Copyright 1928, 1930, 1969 by Henry Holt and , copyright 1944, 1951, 1956, 1958 by Robert Frost, copyright © 1967 by Lesley Frost Ballantine. Reprinted by permission of Henry Holt and Company, LLC.

"Out, Out—" by Robert Frost, from *The Poetry of Robert Frost,* edited by Edward Connery Lathem. Copyright 1928, 1930, 1969 by Henry Holt and , copyright 1944, 1951, 1956, 1958 by Robert Frost, copyright © 1967 by Lesley Frost Ballantine. Reprinted by permission of Henry Holt and Company, LLC.

"The Death of the Hired Man" by Robert Frost, from *The Poetry of Robert Frost,* edited by Edward Connery Lathem. Copyright 1928, 1930, 1969 by Henry Holt and , copyright 1944, 1951, 1956, 1958 by Robert Frost, copyright © 1967 by Lesley Frost Ballantine. Reprinted by permission of Henry Holt and Company, LLC.

New Directions Publishing Corporation: "Helen," from *Collected Poems, 1912–1944* by HD (Hilda Doolittle). Copyright © 1982 by the Estate of Hilda Doolittle. Reprinted by permission of New Directions Publishing Corp.

"In a Station of the Metro," from *Personae* by Ezra Pound. Copyright © 1926 by Ezra Pound. Reprinted by permission of New Directions Publishing Corp.

"Spring and All, Section I," and "This is Just to Say," from *Collected Poems, 1909–1939, Volume I* by William Carlos Williams. Copyright © 1938 by New Directions Publishing Corp. Reprinted by permission of New Directions Publishing Corp.

Liveright Publishing Corporation: "anyone lived in a pretty how town," from *Complete Poems: 1904–1962* by E. E. Cummings, edited by George J. Firmage. Copyright 1940, © 1968, 1991 by the Trustees for the E. E. Cummings Trust. Used by permission of Liveright Publishing Corporation. This selection may not be reproduced, stored in a retrieval system, or transmitted in any form or by any means without the prior written permission of the publisher. For more information about W. W. Norton/Liveright titles, please visit www.wwnorton.com.

Scribner: "Poetry," from *The Collected Poems of Marianne Moore* by Marianne Moore. Copyright © 1935 by Marianne Moore, copyright renewed © 1963 by Marianne Moore and T. S. Eliot. Reprinted with the permission of Scribner, an imprint of Simon & Schuster Adult Publishing Group.

Elizabeth Barnett, Literary Executor: "Recuerdo" by Edna St. Vincent Millay. From *Collected Poems,* HarperCollins. Copyright © 1922, 1950 by Edna St. Vincent Millay. All rights reserved. Used by permission of Elizabeth Barnett, Literary Executor.

Faber and Faber: "The Love Song of J. Alfred Prufrock," from *Collected Poems, 1909–1962* by T. S. Eliot. Reprinted by permission of Faber and Faber Limited.

Scribner: From *The Great Gatsby* by F. Scott Fitzgerald. Copyright 1925 by Charles Scribner's Sons. Copyright renewed 1953 by Frances Scott Fitzgerald Lanahan. Reprinted with permission of Scribner, an imprint of Simon & Schuster Adult Publishing Group.

"In Another Country," from *Men Without Women* by Ernest Hemingway. Copyright 1927 Charles Scribner's Sons. Copyright renewed 1955 by Ernest Hemingway. Reprinted with permission of Scribner, an imprint of Simon & Schuster Adult Publishing Group.

Viking Penguin: From *The Grapes of Wrath* by John Steinbeck. Copyright 1939, renewed © 1967 by John Steinbeck. Used by permission of Viking Penguin, a division of Penguin Group (USA) Inc.

Time Inc.: "The Grapes of Wrath: Photo Essay," *Life,* 5 June 1939. Copyright 1939 Time Inc. Reprinted with permission.

Harcourt: "The Jilting of Granny Weatherall," from *Flowering Judas and Other Stories* by Katherine Anne Porter. Copyright 1930 and renewed 1958 by Katherine Anne Porter. Reprinted by permission of Harcourt, Inc. This material may not be reproduced in any form or by any means without prior written permission of the publisher.

"A Worn Path," from *A Curtain of Green and Other Stories* by Eudora Welty. Copyright 1941 and renewed 1969 by Eudora Welty. Reprinted by permission of Harcourt, Inc. This material may not be reproduced in any form or by any means without prior written permission of the publisher.

Harvard University Press: Reprinted by permission of the publisher from *One Writer's Beginnings* by Eudora Welty, pp. 99–100, Cambridge, Mass: Harvard Universiry Press, Copyright © 1983, 1984 by Eudora Welty.

Random House: "A Rose for Emily," from *Collected Stories of William Faulkner* by William Faulkner. Copyright 1930 and renewed 1958 by William Faulkner. Used by permission of Random House, Inc.

Harcourt: "The Life You Save May Be Your Own," from *A Good Man Is Hard to Find and Other Stories* by Flannery O'Connor. Copyright 1953 by Flannery O'Connor and renewed 1981 by Regina O'Connor. Reprinted by permission of Harcourt, Inc. This material may not be reproduced in any form or by any means without prior written permission of the publisher.

Scribner: "A New Kind of War" by Ernest Hemingway, from *By-Line: Ernest Hemingway,* edited by William White. Copyright 1937 by New York Times and North American Newspaper Alliance, Inc. Copyright © renewed 1965 by Mary Hemingway, By-Line Ernest Hemingway, Inc., and the New York Times Company.

Viking Penguin: "A Book of Great Short Stories," from *The Portable Dorothy Parker* by Dorothy Parker, edited by Brendan Gill. Copyright 1927, renewed © 1955 by Dorothy Parker. Used by permission of Viking Penguin, a division of Penguin Group (USA) Inc.

Allene White: "The Duty of Writers," from *One Man's Meat* by E. B. White. Copyright 1939 by E. B. White. Reprinted by permission of Allene White.

UNIT 6

Barbara Hogenson Agency: From *Our Town* by Thornton Wilder. Copyright © 1938 The Thornton Wilder Family, LLC. Reprinted by permission of the Barbara Hogenson Agency.

Georges Borchardt: From *The Glass Menagerie* by Tennessee Williams. Copyright © 1945 by the University of the South and Edwin D. Williams. Reprinted by permission of Georges Borchardt, Inc.

Viking Penguin: From *Death of a Salesman* by Arthur Miller. Copyright 1949, renewed © 1977 by Arthur Miller. Used by permission of Viking Penguin, a division of Penguin Group (USA) Inc.

Random House: From *A Raisin in the Sun* by Lorraine Hansberry. Copyright © 1958 by Robert Nemiroff, as an unpublished work. Copyright © 1959, 1966, 1984 by Robert Nemiroff. Copyright renewed 1986, 1987 by Robert Nemiroff. Used by permission of Random House, Inc.

Viking Penguin: "Symptoms," from *Once There Was a War* by John Steinbeck. Copyright 1943, 1958 by John Steinbeck. Renewed © 1971 by Elaine Steinbeck, John Steinbeck IV, and Thomas Steinbeck. Used by permission of Viking Penguin, a division of Penguin Group (USA) Inc.

Farrar, Straus and Giroux: "The Death of the Ball Turret Gunner," from *The Complete Poems* by Randall Jarrell. Copyright © 1969, renewed 1997 by Mary von S. Jarrell. Reprinted by permission of Farrar, Straus and Giroux, LLC. Caution: Users are warned that this work is protected under copyright laws and downloading is strictly prohibited. The right to reproduce or transfer the work via any medium must be secured with Farrar, Straus and Giroux, LLC.

Dell Publishing: "Adam," from *Welcome to the Monkey House* by Kurt Vonnegut Jr. Copyright 1954 by Kurt Vonnegut Jr. Used by permission of Dell Publishing, a division of Random House, Inc.

Viking Penguin: From *If This Is a Man (Survival in Auschwitz)* by Primo Levi, translated by Stuart Woolf. Translation copyright © 1959 by Orion Press Inc., © 1958 by Guilio Einaudi editore SpA. Used by permission of Viking Penguin, a division of Penguin Group (USA) Inc.

Houghton Mifflin Company/Seymour Lawrence: "Ambush," from *The Things They Carried* by Tim O'Brien. Copyright © 1990 by Tim O'Brien. Reprinted by permission of Houghton Mifflin Company/ Seymour Lawrence. All rights reserved.

Writers House: "Letter from Birmingham Jail" by Martin Luther King Jr. Copyright 1963 Martin Luther King Jr., copyright renewed 1991 Coretta Scott King. Reprinted by arrangement with the Estate of Martin Luther King Jr., c/o Writers House as agent for the proprietor New York, NY.

Broadside Press: "Ballad of Birmingham," from *Cities Burning* by Dudley Randall. By permission of Broadside Press.

Writers House: From *Stride Toward Freedom* by Martin Luther King Jr. Copyright 1958 Martin Luther King Jr., copyright renewed 1986 Coretta Scott King. Reprinted by arrangement with the Estate of Martin Luther King Jr., c/o Writers House as agent for the proprietor New York, NY.

Pathfinder Press: "Necessary to Protect Ourselves" by Malcolm X, from *Malcolm X: The Last Speeches,* edited by Bruce Perry. Copyright © 1989 Betty Shabazz, Bruce Perry, Pathfinder Press. All rights reserved. Reprinted by permission of Pathfinder Press.

Doubleday: Excerpt from *Coming of Age in Mississippi* by Anne Moody. Copyright © 1968 by Anne Moody. Used by permission of Doubleday, a division of Random House, Inc. For online information about other Random House, Inc., books and authors, see the Internet Web site at http://www.randomhouse.com.

HarperCollins Publishers: "Revolutionary Dreams," from *The Women and the Men* by Nikki Giovanni. Copyright © 1971, 1974, 1975 by Nikki Giovanni. Reprinted by permission of HarperCollins Publishers.

James Baldwin Estate: "My Dungeon Shook: Letter to My Nephew on the One Hundredth Anniversary of the Emancipation" by James Baldwin. Copyright © 1962 by James Baldwin. Copyright renewed. Originally published in *The Progressive.* Collected in *The Fire Next Time,* published by Vintage Books. Reprinted by arrangement with the James Baldwin Estate.

Sandra Dijkstra Literary Agency: "Mother Tongue" by Amy Tan. Copyright © 1990 by Amy Tan. First appeared in *The Threepenny Review.* Reprinted by permission of the author and the Sandra Dijkstra Literary Agency.

Harcourt: Excerpt from "In Search of Our Mothers' Gardens," in *In Search of Our Mothers' Gardens: Womanist Prose* by Alice Walker. Copyright © 1974 by Alice Walker. Reprinted by permission of Harcourt, Inc.

"Women," from *Revolutionary Petunias & Other Poems* by Alice Walker. Copyright © 1970 and renewed 1998 by Alice Walker. Reprinted by permission of Harcourt, Inc. This material may not be reproduced in any form or by any means without prior written permission of the publisher.

Susan Bergholz Literary Services: "Straw Into Gold" by Sandra Cisneros. Copyright © 1987 by Sandra Cisneros. First published in the *Texas Observer,* September 1987. Reprinted by permission of Susan Bergholz Literary Services, New York. All rights reserved.

Brooks Permissions: "Life for My Child Is Simple," and "Primer for Blacks" by Gwendolyn Brooks. Reprinted by consent of Brooks Permissions.

Rita Dove: "Adolescence–III," from *The Yellow House on the Corner* by Rita Dove. Carnegie Mellon University Press. Copyright © 1980 by Rita Dove. Reprinted by permission of the author.

"Testimonial," from *On the Bus with Rosa Parks* by Rita Dove. W. W. Norton and Company. First published in *Poetry* magazine, January 1998. Copyright © 1999 by Rita Dove. Reprinted by permission of the author.

University of Pittsburgh Press: "Forgetfulness," and "The Man in the Moon," from *Questions About Angels* by Billy Collins. Copyright © 1991, Billy Collins. Reprinted by permission of the University of Pittsburgh Press.

UNIT 7

Los Angeles Times: From "'Grapes of Wrath' Author Guards Self From Threats at Moody Gulch" by Tom Cameron, *Los Angeles Times,* July 9, 1939. Copyright ©, 1939, *Los Angeles Times.* Reprinted with permission.

STUDENT RESOURCE BANK

R5: Excerpt from "History of the National Weather Service," from the Random House Web site (http://www.randomhouse.com/features/ isaacsstorm/science/history.html). Copyright © 1999 by Random House, Inc. Used by permission of Random House, Inc.

R13: Adapted from "Katrina's South American Sister," from *Best Friends Magazine,* November/December 2005. Copyright © 2005 by Best Friends Animal Society. Adapted with permission.

R74: word definition: ambasador. Copyright © 2006 by Houghton Mifflin Company. Reproduced by permission from *The American Heritage Dictionary of the English Language, Fourth Edition.*

R74: word definition: community. Copyright © 2006 by Houghton Mifflin Company. Reproduced by permission from *The American Heritage Dictionary of the English Language, Fourth Edition.*

CONSULTANTS

Title page © Brand X Pictures; Photo © Duane McCubrey; Photo © Mark Schmidt; Photo © Bruce Forrester; Photo © McDougal Littell; Photo © Howard Gollub; Photo © Tamra Stallings; Photo © Mark Schmidt; Photo © Robert J. Marzano; Photo © McDougal Littell; Photo © Dawson & Associates Photography; Photo © Gitchell's Studio; Photo © Michael Romeo; Photo © Monica Ani; Photo © William McBride; Photo © Bill Caldwell; Photo © Gabriel Pauluzzi; Photo © Steven Scheffler.

TABLE OF CONTENTS

Contents in Brief verso *top, Patrick Henry Before the Virginia House of Burgesses* (1851), Peter F. Rothermel. Red Hill, The Patrick Henry National Memorial, Brookneal, Virginia; *bottom* © Reza Estakhrian/ Getty Images; **recto** *top* © Burstein Collection/Corbis; *bottom* © Bob Adelman/Magnum Photos; **Unit 1 verso** *left, right* The Granger Collection, New York; **recto** © PunchStock; **Unit 2 verso** *left* © Gary Kelley, 1996; *right* © Gail Mooney/Masterfile; **recto** © PunchStock; **Unit 3 verso** *left* The Granger Collection, New York; *right* © Martin Rogers/ Getty Images; **recto** © PunchStock; **Unit 4 verso** *left* © Bettmann/ Corbis; *right* © Juniors Bildarchiv/Age Fotostock; **recto** © PunchStock; **Unit 5 verso** *left, Autoportrait* (1925), Tamara De Lempicka. Oil on wood, 35 cm × 26 cm. Private collection. © 2007 Artists Rights Society (ARS), New York/ADAGP, Paris; *right, The Cotton Club in Harlem, New York* (1930). Black and white photograph. Private collection. © Bridgeman Art Library; **recto** © PunchStock; **Unit 6 verso** *left, Thinking* (1990), Carlton Murrell. Oil on board. Private collection. © Bridgeman Art Library; *right* The Granger Collection, New York; **recto** © PunchStock; **Unit 7** *left* Cover of *The Grapes of Wrath* by John Steinbeck. © 1939 by John Steinbeck. Reprinted by permission of Penguin Books, a division of the Penguin Group (USA), Inc., 375 Hudson Street, New York, New York 10014. All rights reserved.; Cover photo: The Granger Collection, New York; *right* © Design Pics, Inc./Alamy Images; *inset right* © Bettmann/ Corbis.

INTRODUCTORY UNIT

xxxvi *top* The Granger Collection, New York; *center* © Images.com/ Corbis; *bottom* Library of Congress; **1** *top left, Kindred Spirits* (1849), Asher Brown Durand. © Francis G. Mayer/Corbis; *top right* © Bettmann/Corbis; *bottom* © 20th Century Fox Film Corp. All rights reserved/Courtesy The Everett Collection; **2** *left, The Mayflower in Plymouth Harbor* (1882), William Formby Halsall. © Pilgrim Hall Museum, Plymouth, Massachusetts; *right* Library of Congress; **3** *left* © Reza Estakhrian/Getty Images; *right* © James P. Blair/National Geographic Image Collection; **4** *left to right* © Bettmann/Corbis; © Richard T. Nowitz/Corbis; *The Bloody Massacre perpetrated in...Boston on March 5th, 1770* (1770), Paul Revere. Colored engraving. Private collection. © Art Resource, New York; © Gary Kelley, 1996; *Wanderer Above a Sea of Fog* (1817), Casper David Friedrich. Oil on canvas, 94.8 cm × 74.8 cm. Inv.: 5161. On permanent loan from the Foundation for the Promotion of the Hamburg Art Collections. Hamburger Kunsthalle, Hamburg, Germany. Photo by Elke Walford. © Bildarchiv Preussischer Kulturbesitz/Art Resource, New York; **5** *left to right* © New York Public Library, Schomburg Center; Library of Congress; © Hulton-Deutsch Collection/Corbis; *Street Shadows* (1959), Jacob Lawrence. Egg tempera on hardboard, 24″ × 30″. Private collection, New York. Photograph courtesy of Gwendolyn Knight Lawrence/Art Resource, New York. © 2007 The Jacob and Gwendolyn Lawrence Foundation, Seattle/Artists Rights Society (ARS), New York; *The Green Machine* (1977), Frank Dahmer. Screenprint on paper, 13½″ × 17¼″. © National Vietnam Veterans Art Museum; **6** *Top to bottom* Cover of *The Great Gatsby* by F. Scott Fitzgerald. © 1980 by Charles Scribner's Sons. Reprinted by permission of Simon & Schuster, New York, Cover photo: The Granger Collection, New York; © Historical Picture Archive/Corbis; © Culver Pictures/The Art Archive; *Autoportrait* (about 1925), Tamara de Lempicka. Oil on wood, 35 cm × 26 cm. Private collection. © 2007 Artists Rights Society (ARS), New York/ADAGP, Paris; **8** © Culver Pictures/The Art Archive; **10** *top left* © Time & Life Images/Getty Images; *top right* © Eve Arnold/Magnum Photos; *center* © Randy Faris/ Corbis; *bottom* © 20th Century Fox Film Corp. All rights reserved/ Courtesy The Everett Collection.

UNIT 1

15 *top* © Manuscripts, Archives and Special Collections, Washington State University Libraries, Neg No. 89–052; *bottom* The Granger Collection, New York; **16** *left, Mandan Offering the Buffalo Skull.* Edward S. Curtis Collection. © McCormick Library of Special Collections, Northwestern University Library; *right, Arrival of the English in Virginia* (1585–1588), Theodore de Bry. From *Admiranta Narratio*, page 47. Engraving. Service Historique de la Marine, Vincennes, France. Photo © Giraudon/Art Resource, New York; **17** *left, Fire, allegory* (1566), Giuseppe Arcimboldo. Painted for Emperor Maximilian II. Limewood, 66.5 cm × 51 cm. Inv 1585. Kunsthistorisches Museum, Vienna. Photo © Erich Lessing/Art Resource, New York; *right* Library of Congress; **20** *top, bottom* The Granger Collection, New York; **24** © Richard T. Nowitz/ Corbis; **25** The Granger Collection, New York; **27** *George Washington (Vaughn Portrait)* (1795), Gilbert Stuart. Oil on canvas, 28¾″ × 23¾″, Andrew W. Mellon Collection. © 2005 Board of Trustees, National Gallery of Art, Washington D.C.; **28** *top left* Library of Congress; *center left, Whaler off the Vineyard-Outward Bound* (1859), William Bradford. Oil on Fiberboard, 16″ × 24″. Smithsonian American Art Museum, Washington, D.C. © Smithsonian American Art Museum, Washington, D.C./Art Resource, New York; *bottom left* © Mary Evans Picture Library; *right* The Granger Collection, New York; **29** *top left* The Granger Collection, New York; *center left, bottom left* © North Wind/North Wind Picture Archives; **29** *top right* The Granger Collection, New York; *bottom right* Courtesy, American Antiquarian Society; **30** © Bruce Davidson/Magnum Photos, Courtesy of Toyota; **31** *top* © National Geographic/Getty Images; *bottom* AP/Wide World Photos; **32** *top* © North Wind/North Wind Picture Archives; *bottom* Fourteen foot Abnaki style birchbark canoe. © Henri Vaillancourt; **33** © ESA/PLI/Corbis; t**42** *top* © Manuscripts, Archives and Special Collections, Washington State University Libraries, Neg No. 89–052; *bottom* © Don Pitcher/Stock Boston; **43** © The Road Runner show, Wile E. Coyote, Road Runner, 1966–1973/The Everett Collection; **50** *top* © N. Scott Momaday/Royce Carlton, Inc.; *bottom* © Sharon Maritz/Age Fotostock America, Inc.; **51** © David Alan Harvey/Magnum Photos; **53** Library of Congress; **61** The Granger Collection, New York; **62** *background* © Nick Koudis/Photodisc

UNIT 6

1089 *left, Man in Red* (2003), Diana Ong. Computer graphics. © Purestock/SuperStock; *right* © Gene Blevins/Corbis; **1090** *left* © K.J. Historical/Corbis; *right* © Bettmann/Corbis; **1091** *left, Incredibles Las Cosas Q'Se Ven, 2001* Mural at Ashland Avenue and 19th Street in Chicago. © Jeffrey Zimmermann; *right* © Josef Scaylea/Corbis; **1092** Digital image © 1996 Corbis; Original image courtesy of NASA/Corbis; **1094** © Jacques Langevin/Corbis Sygma; **1095** © Elliott Erwitt/Magnum Photos; **1096** © Josef Scaylea/Corbis; **1097** © Warner Brothers/Getty Images; **1099** *left* © Wally McNamee/Corbis; *right* © K.J. Historical/Corbis; **1100** AP/Wide World Photos; **1101** *White Cloud Over Purple* (1957), Mark Rothko. Oil on canvas, 143 cm × 138 cm. © Private collection/Bridgeman Art Library. © 2007 Kate Rothko Prizel and Christopher Rothko/Artists Rights Society (ARS), New York.; **1102** *top* Associated Press; *center left* The Granger Collection, New York; *center right* © Bettmann/Corbis; *bottom* © Getty Images; **1103** *top left* Photograph by Carmine Fantasia/McDougall Littell; *top right* © Getty Images; *center left* © AFP/Getty Images; *center right* © NOAA/Corbis; *bottom* Central Intelligence Agency; **1104** © Corbis; **1105** *top* © Google; *bottom* © Steven Hunt/Getty Images; **1106** *top* © Les Cunliffe/Age Fotostock America, Inc.; *center* AP/Wide World Photos; *bottom* Showtime/Coutesy of Photofest; **1106–1107** © Corbis; **1107** Cover of *Our Town* by Thornton Wilder. © 1938, 1957 by Thornton Wilder. Cover illustration © William Low. Reprinted by permission of Harper Perennial, a Division of Harper Collins Publishers; **1108** *top* © Les Cunliffe/Age Fotostock America, Inc.; *center* © Bettmann/Corbis; *bottom* © ArenaPal/Topham/The Image Works, Inc.; **1109** © Playbill/Photofest; **1110** *top* © Les Cunliffe/Age Fotostock America, Inc.; *center* © Bettmann/Corbis; *bottom* Marilyn Kingwill/ArenaPAL © ArenaPAL/Topham/The Image Works, Inc.; **1110–1111** © Angela Cappetta/Getty Images; **1111** The Granger Collection, New York; **1112** *top* © Les Cunliffe/Age Fotostock America, Inc.; *center* © Bettmann/Corbis; *bottom* © Joan Marcus; **1112–1113** © PhotoDisc, Inc.; **1113** © McDougal Littell; **1114** *top* National Archives; *center* AP/Wide World Photos; *bottom* Courtesy of Franklin D. Roosevelt Presidential Library and Museum; **1115** © Todd Gipstein/Corbis; **1117** © Bettmann/Corbis; **1119** © Time Life Pictures/Getty Images; **1122** *top* © Marko Shark/Corbis; *bottom* © Bettmann/Corbis; **1133** © Michael St. Maur Sheil/Corbis; **1134** © Bruno Barbey/Magnum Photos; **1136** *top* © Marilyn Knapp Litt; *bottom* © Olivier Martel/Corbis; **1137** © Bernard Annebicque/Corbis; **1143** © Time & Life Pictures/Getty Images; **1144** *top* © Time & Life Images/Getty Images; *bottom* © Bob Adelman/Magnum Photos; **1145** © Bob Adelman/Magnum Photos; **1147** © Bettmann/Corbis; **1152** © Bob Adelman/Magnum Photos; **1156** Dave King © Dorling Kindersley; **1160** *top* © Bettmann/Corbis; *center* © Time & Life Images/Getty Images; *bottom* © Michael S. Yamashita/Corbis; **1161** AP/Wide World Photos; **1163** © Bob Adelman/Magnum Photos; **1167** © Eve Arnold/Magnum Photos; **1168** © James Nubile/The Image Works, Inc.; **1172** *top* © Bob Adelman/Magnum Photos; *bottom* © Eve Arnold/Magnum Photos; **1173** *left* © Bettmann/Corbis; *right* © Flip Schulke/Corbis; **1176** © Paul Fusco/Magnum Photos; **1177** *top* © Courtesy of CBS News Archives; *bottom* © Richard Thornton/ShutterStock; **1178** *top* © Courtesy of CBS News Archives; *bottom* © Owen Franken/Corbis; **1180** *top* Courtesy of Bantam Doubleday Dell; *bottom* © New York Times Agency; **1181** © Greenblatt Bill/Corbis Sygma; **1183** © Bettmann/Corbis; **1187** © Bettmann/Corbis; **1192** *top* © Bettmann/Corbis; *bottom* © Corbis; **1201** © Najlah Feanny/Corbis Saba; **1202** *top* AP/Wide World Photos; *center* © Christopher Felver/Corbis; *bottom* © Bassouls Sophie/Corbis; **1204** *top* © Getty Images; *bottom* © Alex Mares-Manton/Getty Images; **1205** © E. Streichan/zefa/Corbis; **1207** *Apple* (1983), Andy Warhol. Synthetic polymer paint and silkscreen ink on canvas, 14″ × 11″. © The Andy Warhol Foundation for the Visual Arts/Artists Rights Society (ARS), New York © The Andy Warhol Foundation, Inc./Art Resource, New York. Courtesy Ronald Feldman Fine Arts, New York; **1214** *top* © Getty Images; *bottom, Crazy Patchwork* Quilt (1875), unknown artist. Smithsonian Institution, Washington, D.C. © Bridgeman Art Library; **1215** © Botanica/Jupiter Images; **1222** *top* © Gene Blevins/Corbis; *bottom* © Randy Faris/Corbis; **1223** © Angelo Cavalli/Getty Images; **1225** *Making Tortillas* (1926), Diego Rivera. University of California, San Francisco. © Bridgeman Art Library © 2008 Banco de México Diego Rivera & Frida Kahlo Museums Trust. Av. Cinco de Mayo No. 2, Col. Centro, Del. Cuauhtémoc 06059, Mexico, D.F.; **1230** *top* Photo © Nancy E. Crampton; *bottom* © Getty Images; **1232** © Eli Reed/Magnum Photos; **1236** *top* © Photograph of Rita Dove by Fred Viebahn; *bottom left* Courtesy of Pulitzer.org; *bottom background* © Jean-Claude Marlaud/Getty Images; **1237** © Photodisc Photography/Veer; **1242** *top* © Christopher Felver/Corbis; *bottom* © Alan Schein Photography/Corbis; **1243** © Randy Faris/Corbis; **1244** © Arthur Morris/Corbis; **1248, 1254** © J. David Andrews/Masterfile; **1255** © Phil Boorman/Getty Images; **1262–1263** © PunchStock.

UNIT 7 RESEARCH UNIT

1265 *top* © Design Pics, Inc./Alamy Images; *top* inset © Bettmann/Corbis; *bottom* Photographer Dorothea Lange, 1935/Library of Congress; **1266** *left* © Bettmann/Corbis; *right* © Steven Hunt/Getty Images; **1267** *left* The Granger Collection, New York; *right* © NOAA/Corbis; **1270** *left* © Science Museum/SSPL/The Image Works, Inc.; *right inset* Public Domain; *right* © Jupiterimages; **1271** Reproduced with permission of Overture Inc. 2006 by Overture Inc. Alltheweb and the Alltheweb logo are trademarks of Overture Inc.; **1275** *Audience in recreation hall, Tulare Migrant Camp, Visalia, California* (1940). Photo by Arthur Rothstein. Voices From the Dust Bowl website. Courtesy of the American Folklife Center, Library of Congress; **1276** © Los Angeles Times. Reprinted with permission; **1281** *top* Library of Congress; *center* © United Nations; *bottom* NASA; **1284, 1301** © Jason Ernst/Age Fotostock America, Inc.; **1302** *left* © Bettmann/Corbis; *right* © Michael Newman/PhotoEdit; **1303** © Time Life Pictures/Getty Images.

STUDENT RESOURCE BANK

R03 National Archives; **R13** AP/Wide World Photos; **R14** ©
Bettmann/Corbis; **R16** Transportation Security Administration /U.S.
Department of Homeland Security; **R18** *top* Museum of the American
west, Autry National Center, Los Angeles; *bottom* © Denver Public
Library, Western History Collection. Photographer Underwood &
Underwood. Call number F46503. Denver, Colorado; **R95** *foreground,
top* © Photodisc; *background* © Alain Evrard/Getty Images.

BACK COVER

© Brand X Pictures.